14e

American Government

Institutions & Policies

American Government

14e

Institutions & Policies

James Q. Wilson
University of California, Los Angeles, emeritus
Pepperdine University
Boston College

John J. Dilulio, Jr.
University of Pennsylvania

Meena Bose
Hofstra University

CENGAGE
Learning·

Australia • Brazil • Japan • Korea • Mexico • Singapore • Spain • United Kingdom • United States

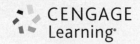
American Government: Institutions and Policies, AP® Edition
James Q. Wilson, John J. Dilulio, Jr., and Meena Bose

Product Director: Suzanne Jeans

Product Team Manager: Carolyn Merrill

Content Developer: Rebecca Green

Content Coordinator: Jessica Wang

Product Assistant: Abigail Hess

Senior Media Developer: Laura Hildebrand

Marketing Manager: Valerie Hartman

Senior Content Project Managers: Joshua Allen and Jessica Rasile

Senior Art Director: Linda May

Print Buyer: Fola Orekoya

Senior Rights Acquisitions Manager: Jennifer Meyer Dare

Vice President, Director of Advanced and Elective Products Program: Alison Zetterquist

Associate Content Developer, Advanced and Elective Products Program: Ashley Bargende

Senior Media Developer, Advanced and Elective Products Program: Philip Lanza

Production Service: Integra Software Services Pvt. Ltd.

Cover Image: ©Shutterstock

Compositor: Integra Software Services Pvt. Ltd.

For product information and technology assistance, contact us at
Cengage Learning Customer & Sales Support, 1-888-915-3276

For permission to use material from this text or product, submit all requests online at **www.cengage.com/permissions**
Further permissions questions can be emailed to
permissionrequest@cengage.com

Library of Congress Control Number: 2013952740

Student Edition:

ISBN-13: 978-1-285-19510-0

ISBN-10: 1-285-19510-8

Cengage Learning
200 First Stamford Place, 4th Floor
Stamford, CT 06902
USA

Cengage Learning is a leading provider of customized learning solutions with office locations around the globe, including Singapore, the United Kingdom, Australia, Mexico, Brazil, and Japan. Locate your local office at **www.cengage.com/global**

Cengage Learning products are represented in Canada by Nelson Education, Ltd.

To learn more about Cengage Learning, visit **www.cengage.com**

To find online supplements and other instructional support, please visit **www.cengagebrain.com**

Printed in the United States of America
2 3 4 5 6 7 18 17 16 15 14

Brief Contents

Contents

PART II   Opinions, Interests, and Organizations 151

Political Elites, Public Opinion, and
Public Policy 166

Chapter 12 The Media 276

PART III Institutions of Government 301

Chapter 13 Congress 302

Chapter 14 The Presidency 338

PART IV Public Policy and
American Democracy 437

Preface

We wrote *American Government: Institutions and Policies, AP Edition®* not only to explain to students how the federal government works, but also to clarify how its institutions have developed over time and describe their effects on public policy. Within this distinguishing framework, we explain the history of Congress, the presidency, the judiciary, and the bureaucracy because the politics we see today are different from those we would have seen a few decades ago. And, of course, change never stops: in another decade, federal politics may be very different from what they are today.

American Government: Institutions and Policies, AP Edition® is written around certain key ideas that help students understand, not simply American government, but the reasons why the government in this country is different from those in other democracies. These ideas are the U.S. Constitution, America's adversarial political culture, and a commitment to freedom and limited government. This book is an attempt to explain and give the historical and practical reasons for these differences.

And as always, the book is thoroughly revised to excite students' interest about the latest in American politics and encourage critical thinking.

Special Features

- **Learning Objectives** open and close each chapter, serving as a road map to the book's key concepts and helping students assess their understanding.

- **Now and Then** chapter-opening vignettes offer attention-grabbing looks at a particular topic in the past and in the present, reinforcing the historical emphasis of the text and applying these experiences to the students' lives. These will help sensitize students to the still-unfolding saga of continuity and change.

- New **Constitutional Connections** features raise analytical issues from the constitutional debates that remain relevant today.

- New **Policy Dynamics: Inside/Outside the Box** features present policy dynamics and encourage students to think about whether they are entrepreneurial, migrating from client to interest group, or safely majoritarian within *American Government*'s classic politics of policymaking framework, which is now being introduced in Chapter 1.

- New **What's Your Issue?** features pose contemporary issues, ask students how or whether the issues directly impact them, and encourage students to explore their views on the issues.

- **Landmark Cases** provide brief descriptions of important Supreme Court cases.

- **How We Compare** features show how other nations around the world structure their governments and policies in relation to the United States and ask students to think about the results of these differences.

- **How Things Work** boxes summarize key concepts and important facts that facilitate students' comprehension of the political process.

- **What Would You Do?** features place students in the role of a decision maker, presenting them with a realistic domestic or foreign policy issue that they can explore in a class discussion or assignment.

- **To Learn More** sections close each chapter with carefully selected Web resources and classic and contemporary suggested readings to further assist students in learning about American politics.

New to This Edition

Updates throughout the text reflect the latest scholarship and current events. The most current information available has been incorporated into the narrative, and the book's tables, figures, citations, and photographs have been thoroughly revised. The book has been streamlined and reorganized to introduce the politics of the policy process in Chapter 1, so that students can evaluate policy dynamics throughout the rest of the text within the narrative and new Policy Dynamics: Inside/Outside the Box features. The reorganization also consolidates the policy chapters down from five chapters to three to better fit the semester format and encourage reading.

Additionally, significant chapter-by-chapter changes have been made as follows:

- **Chapter 1**: *American Government's* classic politics of policymaking framework is now introduced in Chapter 1. New features include Constitutional Connections: Deciding What's Legitimate, What's Your Issue?: Medicare, and Policy Dynamics: Obamacare.

- **Chapter 2**: This chapter includes an expanded discussion of the views of John Locke and Thomas Hobbes and how their philosophies influenced the Framers. A new What's Your Issue? feature looks at income tax rates.

- **Chapter 3**: The opening vignette looks at the Antifederalists' opposition to the Constitution on the grounds that it gave too much power to the national government and how that has played out today. The chapter includes a new discussion on federalism and health care reform. New features include Constitutional Connections: States and Health Exchanges and What's Your Issue?: Marijuana Laws. The Landmark Cases: Federal-State Relations box has been greatly expanded.

- **Chapter 4**: The Civic Role of Religion discussion has been updated and includes a new table on American's Belief about Religion. The new What's Your Issue? feature looks at naturalized citizenship and a Constitutional Connections feature examines "A Religious People."

- **Chapter 5**: New features include Constitutional Connections: Selective Incorporation and What's Your Issue?: Gun Control and the Second Amendment.

- **Chapter 6**: The opening vignette explores how civil rights have changed over the years and a new section on Race and Civil Rights opens the chapter. The chapter includes updated coverage of affirmative action, same-sex marriage (including the Supreme Court's recent DOMA ruling), and other gay rights issues. New features look at suspect classifications, handguns and civil rights, and same-sex marriage policy. Rev. Dr. Martin Luther King, Jr.'s "I Have a Dream" speech now appears in the appendix.

- **Chapter 7**: Updated public opinion statistics are included throughout. A new discussion and table look at how religion factors into differences in opinion within different generations. Latino opinion is examined in more depth. The table on ideology typology has been largely revised. New features include Constitutional Connections: Majority Opinion and Public Policy and What's Your Issue?: The Electoral College.

- **Chapter 8**: A new Constitutional Connections feature looks at state voting laws and What's Your Issue? examines compulsory voting.

- **Chapter 9**: The chapter has been updated to cover the 2012 elections. A new figure looks at the fact that Americans are divided on the need for a third party, and a new table looks at historical convention bounces. New features include Constitutional Connections: The Spirit of Party, What's Your Issue?: Public Funding of Presidential Campaigns, and Policy Dynamics: The Auto Industry Bailout: Client Politics

- **Chapter 10**: 2012 election coverage is included throughout, including a special 2012 Election feature and the most recent statistics on campaign finance. New features include Constitutional Connections: "Natural Born" Presidents and What's Your Issue?: Super PACs.

- **Chapter 11**: A new section on lobbying closes the chapter and updated financial data are included throughout. New features include Constitutional Connections: "Factions" vs. Special Interests, What's Your Issue?: Lobbying, and Policy Dynamics: Immigration Reform: Client or Majoritarian.

- **Chapter 12**: This chapter includes expanded coverage of social media's role in politics and new figures on the state of news media. A new Constitutional Connections feature looks at the First Amendment and What's Your Issue? asks whether media news coverage is fair.

- **Chapter 13**: Updated coverage on the 113th Congress is included throughout. New features include Congressional Connections: From Convention to Congress, What's Your Issue?: A New Congress—and a New Constitution?, and Policy Dynamics: National Service: A Bridge to Entrepreneurial Politics.

- **Chapter 14**: This chapter includes updates throughout on the Obama administration, as well as the 2012 presidential election. New features include Constitutional Connections: Energy in the Executive, What's Your Issue?: Presidential Communication, and Policy Dynamics: Postal Service Reform: Client Politics.

- **Chapter 15**: New features include Constitutional Connections: Beyond Checks and Balances, What's Your Issue?: Fix the Sewers First, and Policy Dynamics: Postal Service Reform: Client Politics.

- **Chapter 16**: There is updated coverage on the increase in partisan wrangling over presidential judicial appointments and the confirmation process, including updated statistics about Obama's judicial appointments. The discussion of the public's approval of the Court's performance is expanded and updated. *National Federation of Independent Business v. Sebelius* and other recent Supreme Court cases are included. A new Constitutional Connections feature looks at the "exceptions" clause, What's Your Issue? explores the PRISM surveillance program, and Policy Dynamics examines telecommunications and "decency."

- **Chapter 17**: This new Domestic Policy chapter condenses material from the previous edition into new sections on Social Welfare Policy, Business Regulation Policy, and Environmental Policy for a more manageable policy unit.

- **Chapter 18**: This chapter includes updates on the U.S. economy and budget battles.

- **Chapter 19**: Updates include coverage of foreign-policy decisions on Afghanistan, the Middle East, and North Korea, as well as a new figure on the public's view of America's role as a world leader.

- **Chapter 20**: The closing chapter leaves readers with a portrait of the current political landscape and tasks them with future examination of their government using the tools they've acquired. A new How We Compare feature looks at deficit spending in America and Europe.

Student and Teacher Supplements

STUDENTS: Access the book's CourseMate resources via **www.cengagebrain.com/ and using the passcode on your Printed Access Card.**

CourseMate for *American Government: Institutions and Policies, 14e*

Cengage Learning's American Government CourseMate brings course concepts to life with interactive learning, study tools, and exam preparation tools that support the printed textbook. An eBook allows students to take notes, highlight, and search. Students can also take practice quizzes, review flashcards, watch videos, and increase their understanding of the book's concepts through animated learning modules, simulations, and timelines. American Government NewsWatch is a real-time news and information resource, updated daily, that includes interactive maps, videos, podcasts, and hundreds of articles from leading journals, magazines, and newspapers from the United States and the world. Also included is the KnowNow! American Government Blog, which highlights three current events stories per week and consists of a succinct analysis of the story, multimedia, and discussion-starter questions.

Teachers can use CourseMate's Engagement Tracker to assess student preparation and engagement in the course and watch student comprehension soar as their students work with the textbook-specific website.

Free Companion Website for *American Government: Institutions and Policies, 14e*

This free companion website accessible through **www.cengagebrain.com/shop/ISBN/9781285195094** allows access to chapter specific interactive learning tools including flashcards, quizzes, glossaries, and more.

Fast Track to a 5: Preparing for the AP® U.S. Government Examination

The Fast Track to a 5 is a test-preparation guide written by Eugene Chase of Edmond Public Schools. It includes information on the exam and strategies for answering each type of question, a diagnostic test, topic review chapters with practice questions, and two complete practice tests in AP® format. It is included in the back of the book.

TEACHERS: Access your course and teacher resources via **www.cengage.com/login** by logging on to or creating your faculty account and adding the resources for ISBN 9781285195100 to your Instructor Resource Center.

Online PowerLecture with ExamView for *American Government: Institutions and Policies, 14e*

This PowerLecture is an all-in-one multimedia online resource for class preparation, presentation, and testing. Accessible through **www.cengage.com/login** with your faculty account, you will find available for download: book-specific Microsoft® PowerPoint® presentations; a Test Bank in both Microsoft® Word® and ExamView formats; an AP® Teacher's Resource Guide; Microsoft® PowerPoint® Image Slides; and a JPEG Image Library.

- The Test Bank, offered in Microsoft® Word® and ExamView formats, contains Learning Objective-specific multiple-choice and essay questions for each chapter. This edition's Test Bank is authored by William Hatcher of Eastern Kentucky University.

- The Microsoft® PowerPoint® presentations are ready-to-use, visual outlines of each chapter. These presentations are easily customized for your lectures and offered along with chapter-specific Microsoft® PowerPoint® Image Slides and JPEG Image Libraries. Access your Online PowerLecture at **www.cengage.com/login**.

AP® Teacher's Resource Guide

The AP® Teacher's Resource Guide, written by Katherine Falconer of Reynolds Community College, is based on the college Instructor's Resource Guide.

It describes the AP® exam, offers recommendations to teachers, and suggests a pacing guide for the course. For each chapter of the text, it provides "AP® Focus" sections that offer suggestions for teaching particular topics and points out concepts that often appear on the exam.

CourseReader 0-30: American Government

CourseReader: American Government allows you to create your reader, your way, in just minutes. This affordable, fully customizable online reader provides instructors access to thousands of permissions-cleared readings, articles, primary sources, and audio and video selections from the regularly updated Gale research library database. This easy-to-use solution allows you to search for and select just the material you want for your courses. Each selection opens with a descriptive introduction to provide context, and concludes with critical-thinking and multiple-choice questions to reinforce key points. CourseReader is loaded with convenient tools like highlighting, printing, note-taking, and downloadable PDFs and MP3 audio files for each reading.

CourseReader is the perfect complement to any Political Science course. It can be bundled with your current textbook, sold alone, or integrated into your learning management system. CourseReader 0-30 allows access to up to 30 selections in the reader. Please contact your Cengage sales representative for details.

Custom Enrichment Module: Latino-American Politics Supplement

Authored by Fernando Pinon, this revised and updated supplement uses real examples to detail politics related to Latino Americans.

AP® and Advanced Placement Program® are trademarks registered and/or owned by the College Board, which was not involved in the production of, and does not endorse, this product.

Acknowledgments

Ryan Rodrick Beiler/Shutterstock.com

A number of scholars reviewed the book and made useful suggestions for the Fourteenth Edition. They include:

Dr. Robert Carroll, East West University

Albert Cover, Stony Brook University

Nicholas Damask, Scottsdale Community College

Virgil H. Davis, Pellissippi State Community College

Jenna P. Duke, Lehigh Carbon Community College

Ethan Fishman, University of South Alabama

Marvin Overb, University of Missouri

Erich Saphir, Pima Community College

Linda Trautman, Ohio University-Lancaster

A number of scholars reviewed the previous three editions. They include:

Philip Aka, Chicago State University

Lucas Allen, Michigan State University

Roger Ashby, Peace College

Michael Baranowski, Northern Kentucky University

Chuck Brownson, Stephen F. Austin High School

Jack Citrin, University of California, Berkeley

Zach Courser, Boston College

Stan Crippen, Riverside County Office of Education

Gregory Culver, University of Southern Indiana

Matthew Eshbaugh-Soha, University of North Texas

Terri Fine, University of Central Florida

Glenn David Garrison, Collin County Community College—Spring Creek Campus

Richard Grubbs, R.L. Paschal High School

Kipling Hagopian

Jeff Harmon, University of Texas at San Antonio

Kevin Hassett

Kathleen C. Hauger, Abington Senior High School

Stephen Kerbow, Southwest Texas Junior College

Halima Asghar Khan, Massasoit Community College

Young-Choul Kim, University of Evansville

Junius H. Koonce, Edgecombe Community College

William Lester, Jacksonville State University

Brad Lockerbie, University of Georgia

Randall McKeever, Forney ISD

Marvin Overby, University of Missouri

Anne F. Presley, McKinney High School

Gayle Randolph, Neosho County Community College

Donald Ranish, Antelope Valley College

Jonathan Roberts, Portland, OR, schools

P. S. Ruckman, Rock Valley College

Rebecca Small, Herndon High School

Randall Smith, Naperville Central High School

Greg Snoad, Mauldin High School

Jennifer Walsh, Azusa Pacific University

David Wigg, St. Louis Community College

Teresa Wright, California State University—Long Beach

Additional thanks go to Marc Siegal for his research assistance, William Hatcher of Eastern Kentucky University for his revision of the Test Bank, Katherine Falconer of Reynolds Community College for her revision of the Instructor's Manual, and Eugene Chase of Edmond Public Schools for creating the AP Edition's Fast Track to a Five.

About the Authors

John J. DiIulio, Jr.

John J. DiIulio, Jr., is a professor of political science at the University of Pennsylvania. From 1986 to 1999, he was a professor of politics and public affairs at Princeton University's Woodrow Wilson School of Public and International Affairs. He received B.A. and M.A. degrees from the University of Pennsylvania and M.A. and Ph.D. degrees from Harvard University. He is the author, coauthor, or editor of a dozen books, including *Godly Republic* (2007), *Medicaid and Devolution* (1998, with Frank Thompson), *Deregulating the Public Service* (1994), and *Governing Prisons* (1987). He has received many awards for excellence in teaching including Penn's two most prestigious, the Lindback Award and the Abrams Award.

DiIulio advised both Vice President Al Gore and Governor George W. Bush during the 2000 presidential campaign. While on leave in academic year 2000–2001, he served as assistant to the president of the United States. He served as the first Director of the White House Office on Faith-Based Initiatives and assisted the Obama administration in reconstituting it. He has advised officials at the National Performance Review, the Office of Management and Budget, the General Accounting Office, the US Department of Justice, and other federal agencies. He has served on the boards of Big Brothers Big Sisters of America and other nonprofit organizations.

In 1995, the Association of Public Policy Analysis and Management conferred on him the David N. Kershaw Award for outstanding research achievements, and in 1987 he received the American Political Science Association's Leonard D. White Award in public administration. In 1991–1994, he chaired the latter association's standing committee on professional ethics. Since 2005, he has had a leading role in nonprofit initiatives to assist post-Katrina New Orleans.

Meena Bose

Meena Bose is Director of the Peter S. Kalikow Center for the Study of the American Presidency at Hofstra University, as well as the Peter S. Kalikow Chair in Presidential Studies and Professor of Political Science. She is the author of *Shaping and Signaling Presidential Policy: The National Security Decision Making of Eisenhower and Kennedy* (1998) and editor of the reference volume *The New York Times on the Presidency* (2009), *Votes to Victory: Winning and Governing the White House in the Twenty-First Century* (2011), and *President or King? Evaluating the Expansion of Presidential Power from Abraham Lincoln to George W. Bush* (forthcoming). She also is coeditor (with Rosanna Perotti) of *From Cold War to New World Order: The Foreign Policy of George H. W. Bush* (2002), co-editor (with Mark Landis) of *The Uses and Abuses of Presidential Ratings* (2003), and co-editor (with John J. DiIulio, Jr.) of *Classic Ideas and Current Issues in American Government* (2007).

Bose was scholar-in-residence for a nonpartisan course sponsored by the Washington Center in connection with the 2008 Republican National Convention in Minneapolis, and she was active in both of the Center's convention courses in 2012. She also has designed and taught several courses for Elderhostel, including "The Wisdom of Our Fathers: The Mount Rushmore Presidents." *Long Island Business News* selected her as one of the "Top 40 Under 40" leaders on Long Island in 2009.

Bose taught for six years at the U.S. Military Academy at West Point, where she also served as Director of American Politics in 2006. She previously taught at Hofstra University from 1996 to 2000 and represented the American Political Science Association on the Department of State's Historical Advisory Committee from 2001 to 2004. She earned her B.A. degree in international politics from Penn State University (1990), and she received her M.A. (1992) and Ph.D. (1996) degrees in politics from Princeton University.

In Memoriam
James Q. Wilson
(May 27, 1931–March 2, 2012)

Cengage Learning

James Q. Wilson's death made news. There was a front-page story in *The New York Times*. There were stories in *The Wall Street Journal, The Washington Post*, and nearly every other major U.S. newspaper. There were also essays in *The Economist, The New Republic, The Weekly Standard*, and many other magazines; reflections by Ross Douthat, George Will, and many other leading syndicated columnists; postings by think tank leaders and big-time bloggers; and statements by present and former public officials in both parties.

In 1959, Wilson received his doctoral degree in political science from the University of Chicago. He held endowed chair professorships at Harvard, UCLA, and Pepperdine, and a final post as a Distinguished Scholar at Boston College. Harvard and a half-dozen other universities bestowed honorary degrees on him. He won numerous academic awards including ones from the American Political Science Association, the Academy of Criminal Justice Sciences, and the Policy Studies Organization. He held board chairmanships, memberships, directorships, or academic advisory group leadership positions with, among other institutions, the Joint Center for Urban Studies of Harvard and MIT, the American Academy of Arts and Sciences, the American Philosophical Society, the American Enterprise Institute, the National Academy of Sciences, the Robert A. Fox Leadership Program at the University of Pennsylvania, and the Pardee Rand Graduate School. He authored or co-authored 17 books, including 13 editions of *American Government* that, all told, sold more than a million copies. He also penned or co-penned several edited volumes and several hundred articles, plus scores of op-eds in leading newspapers.

Predictably, most of the public coverage that followed his passing, even the parts of it that included personal reminiscences or that quoted people who knew him, was mainly about Wilson the eminent and influential public intellectual. That is, it was about the Wilson who Senator Daniel Patrick Moynihan, his friend and former Harvard colleague, famously described to President Richard M. Nixon as "the smartest man in America." It was about the Wilson who served both Democratic and Republican officeholders, including six U.S. presidents, as an advisor. It was about the Wilson who was the chairperson of President Lyndon Johnson's White House Task Force on Crime, the chairperson of President Nixon's National Advisory Commission on Drug Abuse Prevention, and a member of many other public commissions or blue-ribbon bodies, including the President's Foreign Policy Intelligence Board, the President's Council on Bioethics, the Police Foundation's Board of Directors, and the International Council of the Human Rights Foundation. It was about the Wilson who received the Presidential Medal of Freedom in 2003 and was cited by President George W. Bush as "the most influential political scientist in America since the White House was home to Professor Woodrow Wilson."

Wilson, the eminent and influential public intellectual, was a real genius and a laudable giant, but that was not the whole of the man that I was blessed to know over the last 32 years. Even greater, in my view, were Wilson the deeply good family man and neighbor-citizen and Wilson the devoted teacher, dedicated mentor, and pure scholar.

A two-time national high school debate champion, Jim graduated from the University of Redlands and served in the U.S. Navy. He married his high school sweetheart, Roberta. They were happily married for nearly sixty years. Jim is survived by Roberta and their two children, Matthew and Annie, his children's spouses, a sister, and many grandchildren, nieces, and nephews. Somehow, for all his prolific public and professional pursuits, he spent several lifetimes of quality time with his children, time that included reading all of the Sunday comics to them when they were young, never missing an important event in their lives, and leading them on many trips abroad and other adventures. Jim loved to share the things that he loved. Those things included scuba diving and underwater photography. He and Roberta co-authored a book, *Watching Fishes: Life and Behavior on Coral Reefs* (1985). He also loved cars, fast ones, and was into racing. I once described him as "an open-highway patriot," and he smiled at the description. Jim was a model community member. He coached a local youth soccer team and he served on the board of his local library.

Jim was also an amazingly dedicated undergraduate and graduate student classroom teacher. He was an angel-on-the-shoulder thesis supervisor, dissertation advisor, colleague, co-author, editor, and co-editor. He loved to laugh at himself and with others, and his generosity was genuine and unfailing.

For all Jim's influence and diverse intellectual interests, at the core of his professional and civic being he was a proudly card-carrying political scientist who always pursued knowledge more for its intrinsic than for its instrumental value. Indeed, he was supremely skeptical about what policy-oriented public intellectuals (often offering himself as Exhibit A) had to offer real-world public policymakers and administrators.

In *The Politics of Regulation*, an edited volume featuring chapters by many of his former graduate students, Jim wrote:

> (M)uch, if not most, of politics consists of efforts to change wants by arguments, persuasion, threats, bluffs, and education. What people want—or believe they want—is the essence of politics ... Both economics and politics deal with problems of scarcity and conflicting preferences. Both deal with persons who ordinarily act rationally. But politics differs from economics in that it manages conflict by forming heterogeneous coalitions out of persons with changeable and incommensurable preferences in order to make binding decisions for everyone. Political science is an effort to make statements about the formation of preferences and nonmarket methods of managing conflict among those preferences; as a discipline, it will be as inelegant, disorderly, and changeable as its subject matter.

Requiescat in Pace: May he rest in peace.

John J. DiIulio, Jr.

A longer version of this essay appeared in PS: Political Science and Politics, 2012. *This excerpt is reprinted here by permission.*

PART 1

The American System

In framing a government which is to be administered by men over men, the great difficulty lies in this: You must first enable the government to control the governed; and in the next place oblige it to control itself.

— FEDERALIST NO.51

1

The Study of American Government

Orhan Cam/ShutterStock.com

LEARNING OBJECTIVES

1. What is meant by "politics"?

2. Can you give two definitions of "democracy"?

3. How is political power actually distributed in America?

4. What is the "political agenda" and why has it expanded?

5. How can you classify and explain the politics of different issues?

Today, Americans and their elected leaders are hotly debating the federal government's spending, taxing, and future finances.

Some things never change.

THEN

In 1786, a committee of Congress reported that since the Articles of Confederation were adopted in 1781, the state governments had paid only about one-seventh of the monies requisitioned by the federal government. The federal government was broke and sinking deeper into debt, including debt owed to foreign governments. Several states had financial crises, too.

In 1788, the proposed Constitution's chief architect, James Madison, argued that while the federal government needed its own "power of taxation" and "collectors of revenue," its overall powers would remain "few and defined" and its taxing power would be used sparingly.[1] In reply, critics of the proposed Constitution, including the famous patriot Patrick Henry, mocked Madison's view and predicted that if the Constitution were ratified, there would over time be "an immense increase of taxes" spent by an ever-growing federal government.[2]

NOW

In 2010, a bipartisan presidential commission warned that by 2015, the federal government would be paying well over $300 billion a year in interest on a roughly $20 trillion national debt, much of it borrowed from foreign nations. The federal budget initially proposed for 2014 called for spending about $3.8 trillion, roughly a fifth of it in deficit spending. Projected total state and local government spending for 2014 was about $3.2 trillion (including federal grants), and many states' and cities' finances were in shambles.[3]

So, in the 1780s, as in the 2010s, nearly everyone agreed that government's finances were a huge mess and that bold action was required, and soon; but in each case, then and now, there was no consensus about what action to take, or when.

Issues and Politics

This might seem odd. After all, it may appear that the government's financial problems, including big budget deficits and revenue shortfalls, could be solved by simple arithmetic: either spend and borrow less, or tax more, or both. But now ask: spend or borrow less for what, and raise taxes on whom, when, how, and by how much? For example, should we cut the defense budget but continue to fund health care programs, or the reverse? Or should we keep defense and health care funding at current levels but reduce spending on environmental protection or homeland security? Should we perhaps increase taxes on the wealthy (define *wealthy*) and cut taxes for the middle class (define *middle class*), or ... what?

issue A conflict, real or apparent, between the interests, ideas, or beliefs of different citizens.

Then, as now, the fundamental government finance problems were *political*, not mathematical. People disagreed not only over how much the federal government should tax and spend, but also over whether it should involve itself at all in various endeavors. For example, in 2011, the federal government nearly shut down, not mainly over disagreements between the two parties about how much needed to be cut from the federal budget (in the end, the agreed-to cuts totaled $38.5 billion), but primarily over whether any federal funding at all should go to certain relatively small-budget federal health, environmental, and other programs.

Fights over taxes and government finances; battles over abortion, school prayer, and gay rights; disputes about where to store nuclear waste; competing plans on immigration, international trade, welfare reform, environmental protection, or gun control; contention surrounding a new health care proposal. Some of these matters are mainly about money and economic interests; others are more about ideas and personal beliefs. Some people care a lot about at least some of these matters; others seem to care little or not at all.

Regardless, all such matters and countless others have this in common: each is an issue, defined as a conflict, real or apparent, between the interests, ideas, or beliefs of different citizens.[4]

An issue may be more apparent than real; for example, people might fight over two tax plans that, despite superficial differences, would actually distribute tax burdens on different groups in exactly the same way. Or an issue may be as real as it seems to the conflicting parties, as, for example, it is in matters that pose clear-cut choices (high tariffs or no tariffs; abortion legal in all cases or illegal in all cases).

And an issue might be more about conflicts over means than over ends. For example, on health care reform or other issues, legislators who are in the same party and have similar ideological leanings (like a group of liberal Democrats, or a group of conservative Republicans) might agree on objectives but still wrangle bitterly with each other over different means of achieving their goals. Or they might *politics* The activity by which an issue is agitated or settled.

power The ability of one person to get another person to act in accordance with the first person's intentions.

authority The right to use power.

agree on both ends and means but differ over priorities (which goals to pursue first), timing (when to proceed), or tactics (how to proceed).

Whatever form issues take, they are the raw materials of politics. By **politics** we mean "the activity— negotiation, argument, discussion, application of force, persuasion, etc.—by which an issue is agitated or settled."[5] There are many different ways that any given issue can be agitated (brought to attention, stimulate conflict) or settled (brought to an accommodation, stimulate consensus). And there are many different ways that government can agitate or settle, foster or frustrate political conflict.

This is a good time to ask yourself what, if any, issues matter to you. Generally speaking, do you care a lot, a little, or not at all about economic issues, social issues, or issues involving foreign policy or military affairs? Do you follow any particular, ongoing debates on issues like tightening gun control laws, expanding health care insurance, regulating immigration, or funding anti-poverty programs?

As you will learn in Part II of this textbook, some citizens are quite issue-oriented and politically active: they vote and try to influence others to vote likewise; they join political campaigns or give money to candidates; they keep informed about diverse issues, sign petitions, advocate for new laws, or communicate with elected leaders; and more.

But such politically attentive and engaged citizens are the exception to the rule, most especially among young adult citizens under age 30. According to many experts, ever more young Americans are closer to being "political dropouts" than they are to being "engaged citizens" (a fact that is made no less troubling by similar trends in the United Kingdom, Canada, Scandinavia, and elsewhere).[6] Many high school and college students believe getting "involved in our democracy" means volunteering for community service, but not voting.[7] Most young Americans do not regularly read newspapers (online or otherwise) or closely follow political news; and most know little about how government works, and exhibit no "regular interest in politics."[8] In response to such concerns, various analysts and study commissions have made proposals ranging from compulsory voting to enhanced "civic education" in high schools.[9]

The fact that you are reading this textbook tells us that you probably have some interest in American politics and government. To help enliven that interest as you learn more about the subject, each chapter in Parts I through III of this textbook contains a feature—**What's Your Issue?**—that encourages you to explore present-day debates over a particular issue.

Power, Authority, and Legitimacy

Politics, and the processes by which issues are normally agitated or settled, involves the exercise of power. By **power** we mean the ability of one person to get another person to act in accordance with the first person's intentions. Sometimes an exercise of power is obvious, as when the president tells the air force that it cannot build a new bomber or orders soldiers into combat in a foreign land. Other times an exercise of power is subtle, as when the president's junior speechwriters, reflecting their own evolving views, adopt a new tone when writing for their boss about controversial social issues like abortion. The speechwriters may not think they are using power—after all, they are the president's subordinates and may rarely see him face-to-face. But if the president lets their words exit his mouth in public, they have used power.

Power is found in all human relationships, but we shall be concerned here only with power as it is used to affect who will hold government office and how government will behave. We limit our view here to government, and chiefly to the American federal government. However, we shall repeatedly pay special attention to how things once thought to be "private" matters become "public"—that is, how they manage to become objects of governmental action. Indeed, as we will discuss more below, one of the most striking transformations of American politics has been the extent to which, in recent decades, almost every aspect of human life has found its way onto the political agenda.

People who exercise political power may or may not have the authority to do so. By **authority** we mean the right to use power. The exercise of rightful power—that is, of authority— is ordinarily easier than the exercise of power not supported by any persuasive claim of right. We accept decisions, often without question, if they are made by people who we believe have the right to make them; we may bow to naked power because we cannot resist it, but by our recalcitrance or our resentment we put the users of naked power to greater trouble than the wielders of authority. In this book, we will on occasion speak

WHAT'S YOUR ISSUE?

Medicare Reform

There are two basic questions to ask oneself about any given issue:

1. **What's my stake *in the issue?*** For instance, if you or people you care about are in college or headed for college, and if you or they rely on government-backed college loans to pay tuition bills, then you might perceive yourself as having a *stake* in the fate of proposals to cut or expand college loans. Perceiving your stake in the issue, you might pay attention to whether these proposals attract public support, gain legislative sponsors, and become laws. (*Do you* think you have a *stake* in this issue, and, if so, what is it?)

2. **What's my take *on the issue?*** But even if you perceive no economic, personal, or other stake in an issue, you might yet have a *take* on the issue. For example, you might believe that, in order to reduce socio-economic inequalities, or to ensure that America has a highly educated, globally competitive workforce, or for what you consider to be purely moral reasons, you would favor expanding (or oppose cutting) government-backed college loans. (*Do you* have a *take* on this issue, and, if so, what is it?)

Figuring out whether, or by what definition, you have a *stake*, direct or indirect, in any given issue, and deciding what, in any case, is your *take* on the same issue, can be illuminating, self-revealing, and (dare we political junkies add?) even fun.

For one thing, you will, we hope, not only think more, but learn more and think more deeply, about many different issues, including issues about which you already have opinions or know more than just a little. And, in more than a few cases, you may discover that you have both a stake in and a take on an issue about which you previously knew little and cared less.

For instance, take Medicare, the program that pays for part of the cost of medical care for retired or disabled people. The program is financed mainly by payroll taxes on employees and employers. So, *what's your issue* with Medicare? You might not be elderly, retired, disabled, an employee or an employer (not at present, anyway). But decisions about the program's future are likely to affect you and people you care about—plenty! And the issue involves many fundamental moral and value choices, including ones about government's present and future role in financing and administering health care.

To wit: Medicare cost nearly $600 billion in 2013, and it is projected to cost more than $1 trillion by 2022. The program's trustees announced in 2011 that it would become insolvent by 2017. Since then, no fewer than a dozen proposals have been made by various members of Congress, by the White House, and by various blue-ribbon commissions, to ensure the program's long-term solvency.

But some plans get there by raising taxes on all recipients (including young ones!) and cutting benefits (or just future benefits!); others get there mainly by raising taxes on the wealthiest recipients, or by raising the eligibility age (from 65 to 69 or 70), or by various other means. And some proposals would replace Medicare with a "premium-support" or voucher program. At present, no one Medicare reform plan has both wide and deep public support. Got a stake, a take, or a proposal on the issue? If you're using the full version of this book with separate policy chapters, hold on; you will revisit this issue in Chapter 17.

---

of "formal authority." By this we mean that the right to exercise power is vested in a governmental office. A president, a senator, and a federal judge have formal authority to take certain actions.

What makes power rightful varies from time to time and from country to country. In the United States, we usually say a person has political authority if his or her right to act in a certain way is conferred by a law or by a state or national constitution. But what makes a law or constitution a source of right? That is the question of **legitimacy**. In the United States, the Constitution today is widely, if not unanimously, accepted as a source of legitimate authority, but that was not always the case.

What Is Democracy?

On one matter, virtually all Americans seem to agree: no exercise of political power by government at any level is legitimate if it is not in some sense democratic. That wasn't always the prevailing view. In 1787, as the Constitution was being debated, Alexander Hamilton worried that the new government he helped create might be too democratic, while George Mason, who refused to sign the Constitution, worried that it was

> *legitimacy* Political authority conferred by law or by a state or national constitution.

democracy The rule of the many.

direct or participatory democracy A government in which all or most citizens participate directly.

representative democracy A government in which leaders make decisions by winning a competitive struggle for the popular vote.

not democratic enough. Today, however, almost everyone believes that democratic government is the only proper kind. Most people believe that American government is democratic; some believe that other institutions of public life—schools, universities, corporations, trade unions, churches—also should be run on democratic principles if they are to be legitimate; and some insist that promoting democracy abroad ought to be a primary purpose of U.S. foreign policy.

Democracy is a word with at least two different meanings. First, the term *democracy* is used to describe those regimes that come as close as possible to Aristotle's definition—the "rule of the many."[10] A government is democratic if all, or most, of its citizens participate directly in either holding office or making policy. This often is called **direct or participatory democracy**. In Aristotle's time—Greece in the 4th century B.C.—such a government was possible. The Greek city-state, or *polis,* was quite small, and within it citizenship was extended to all free adult male property holders. (Slaves, women, minors, and those without property were excluded from participation in government.) In more recent times, the New England town meeting approximates the Aristotelian ideal. In such a meeting, the adult citizens of a community gather once or twice a year to vote directly on all major issues and expenditures of the town. As towns have become larger and issues more complicated, many

town governments have abandoned the pure town meeting in favor of either the representative town meeting (in which a large number of elected representatives, perhaps 200–300, meet to vote on town affairs) or representative government (in which a small number of elected city councilors make decisions).

The second definition of *democracy* is the principle of governance of most nations that are called democratic. It was most concisely stated by the economist Joseph Schumpeter: "The democratic method is that institutional arrangement for arriving at political decisions in which individuals [that is, leaders] acquire the power to decide by means of a competitive struggle for the people's vote."[11] Sometimes this method is called, approvingly, **representative democracy**; at other times it is referred to, disapprovingly, as the elitist theory of democracy. It is justified by one or both of two arguments: first, it is impractical, owing to limits of time, information, energy, interest, and expertise, for the people to decide on public policy, but it is not impractical to expect them to make reasonable choices among competing leadership groups. Second, some people (including, as we shall see in the next chapter, many of the Framers of the Constitution) believe direct democracy is likely to lead to bad decisions, because people often decide large issues on the basis of fleeting passions and in response to popular demagogues. This concern about direct democracy persists today, as evidenced by the statements of leaders who disagree with voter decisions. For example, voters in many states have rejected referenda that would have increased public funding for private schools. Politicians who opposed the defeated referenda spoke approvingly of the "will of the people," but politicians who favored them spoke disdainfully of "mass misunderstanding."

Whenever we refer to that form of democracy involving the direct participation of all or most citizens, we shall use the term *direct* or *participatory* democracy. Whenever the word *democracy* is used alone in this book, it will have the meaning Schumpeter gave it. Schumpeter's definition usefully implies basic benchmarks that enable us to judge the extent to which any given political system is democratic.[12] A political system is *non*-democratic to the extent that it denies equal voting rights to part of its society and severely limits (or outright prohibits) "the civil and political freedoms to speak, publish, assemble, and organize,"[13] all of which are necessary to a truly "competitive struggle for the people's vote." A partial list of non-democratic political systems would include absolute monarchies, empires, military dictatorships, authoritarian systems, and totalitarian states.[14]

Scholars of comparative politics and government have much to teach about how different types of political systems, democratic and non-democratic,

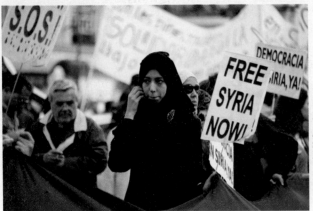

JAVIER SORIANO/AFP/Getty Images

As protestors around the world support democracy activists in Syria, the United States weighs how it should assist opposition groups in other countries that seek to establish democratic governments.

Comedians Jon Stewart (right) and Stephen Colbert (left) sing during the "Rally to Restore Sanity and/or Fear" on the Washington Mall, October 30, 2010.

arise, persist, and change. For our present purposes, however, it is most important to understand that America itself was once far less democratic than it is today and that it was so not by accident but by design. As we discuss in the next chapter, the men who wrote the Constitution did not use the word *democracy* in that document. They wrote instead of a "republican form of government," but by that they meant what we call "representative democracy." And, as we emphasize when discussing civil liberties and civil rights (see Chapter 5 and 6), and again when discussing political participation (see Chapter 8), America was not born as a full-fledged representative democracy; and, for all the progress of the past half-century or so, the nation's representative democratic character is still very much a work in progress.

For any representative democracy to work, there must, of course, be an opportunity for genuine leadership competition. This requires in turn that individuals and parties be able to run for office; that communications (through speeches or the press, in meetings, and on the internet) be free; and that the voters perceive that a meaningful choice exists. But what, exactly, constitutes a "meaningful choice"? How many offices should be elective and how many appointive? How many candidates or parties can exist before the choices become hopelessly confused? Where will the money come from to finance electoral campaigns? There are many answers to such questions. In some European democracies, for example, very few offices—often just those in the national or local legislature—are elective, and much of the money for campaigning for these offices comes from the government. In the United States, many offices—executive

and judicial as well as legislative—are elective, and most of the money the candidates use for campaigning comes from industry, labor unions, and private individuals.

Some people have argued that the virtues of direct or participatory democracy can and should be reclaimed even in a modern, complex society. This can be done either by allowing individual neighborhoods in big cities to govern themselves (community control) or by requiring those affected by some government program to participate in its formulation (citizen participation). In many states, a measure of direct democracy exists when voters can decide on referendum issues—that is, policy choices that appear on the ballot. The proponents of direct democracy defend it as the only way to ensure that the "will of the people" prevails.

As we discuss in the nearby **Constitutional Connections** feature, and as we explore more in Chapter 2, the Framers of the Constitution did not think that the "will of the people" was synonymous with the "common interest" or the "public good." They strongly favored representative democracy over direct democracy.

Political Power in America: Five Views

Scholars differ in their interpretations of the American political experience. Where some see a steady march of democracy, others see no such thing; where some emphasize how voting and other rights have been

CONSTITUTIONAL CONNECTIONS

Deciding What's Legitimate

Much of American political history has been a struggle over what constitutes legitimate authority. The Constitutional Convention in 1787 was an effort to see whether a new, more powerful federal government could be made legitimate; the succeeding administrations of George Washington, John Adams, and Thomas Jefferson were in large measure preoccupied with disputes over the kinds of decisions that were legitimate for the federal government to make. The Civil War was a bloody struggle over slavery and the legitimacy of the federal union; the New Deal of Franklin Roosevelt was hotly debated by those who disagreed over whether it

was legitimate for the federal government to intervene deeply in the economy. Not uncommonly, the federal judiciary functions as the ultimate arbiter of what is legitimate in the context of deciding what is or is not constitutional (see Chapter 16). For instance, in 2012, amidst a contentious debate over the legitimacy of the federal health care law that was enacted in 2010, the U.S. Supreme Court decided that the federal government could require individuals to purchase health insurance but could not require states to expand health care benefits for citizens participating in the federal-state program known as Medicaid.

---

elite Persons who possess a disproportionate share of some valued resource, like money, prestige, or expertise.

class view View that the government is dominated by capitalists.

power elite view View that the government is dominated by a few top leaders, most of whom are outside of government.

bureaucratic view View that the government is dominated by appointed officials.

steadily expanded, others stress how they were denied to so many for so long, and so forth. Short of attempting to reconcile these competing historical interpretations, let us step back now for a moment to our definition of representative democracy and five competing views about how political power has been distributed in America.

Representative democracy is defined as any system of government in which leaders are authorized to make decisions—and thereby to wield political power—by winning a competitive struggle for the popular vote. It is obvious then that very different sets of hands can control political power, depending on what kinds of people can become leaders, how the struggle for votes is carried on, how much freedom to act is given to those who win the struggle, and what other sorts of influence (besides the desire for popular approval) affect the leaders' actions.

The actual distribution of political power in a representative democracy will depend on the composition of the political elites who are involved in the struggles for power and over policy. By **elite** we mean an identifiable group of persons who possess a

disproportionate share of some valued resource—in this case, political power.

There are at least five views about how political power is distributed in America: (1) wealthy capitalists and other economic elites determine most policies; (2) a group of business, military, labor union, and elected officials controls most decisions; (3) appointed bureaucrats ultimately run everything; (4) representatives of a large number of interest groups are in charge; and (5) morally impassioned elites drive political change.

The first view began with the theories of Karl Marx, who, in the 19th century, argued that governments were dominated by business owners (the "bourgeoisie") until a revolution replaced them with rule by laborers (the "proletariat").[15] But strict Marxism has collapsed in most countries. Today, a **class view**, though it may derive inspiration from Marx, is less dogmatic and emphasizes the power of "the rich" or the leaders of multinational corporations.

The second view ties business leaders together with other elites whose perceived power is of concern to the view's adherents. These elites may include: top military officials, labor union leaders, mass media executives, and the heads of a few special-interest groups. Derived from the work of sociologist C. Wright Mills, this **power elite view** argues that American democracy is dominated by a few top leaders, many of them wealthy or privately powerful, who do not hold elective office.[16]

The third view is that appointed officials run everything despite the efforts of elected officials and the public to control them. The **bureaucratic view** was first set forth by the German scholar Max Weber (1864–1920). He argued that the modern state, in order to become successful, puts its affairs in the hands of appointed bureaucrats whose competence is essential to the management of complex affairs.[17] These officials, invisible to most people, have mastered the written records and legislative details of the government and do more than just implement democratic policies; they actually make those policies.

The fourth view holds that political resources—such as money, prestige, expertise, and access to the mass media—have become so widely distributed that no single elite, no social class, no bureaucratic arrangement, can control them. Many 20th-century political scientists, among them David B. Truman, adopted a **pluralist view**.[18] In the United States, they argued, political resources are broadly shared in part because there are so many governmental institutions (cities, states, school boards) and so many rival institutions (legislatures, executives, judges, bureaucrats) that no single group can dominate most, or even much, of the political process.

The fifth view maintains that while each of the other four views is correct with respect to how power is distributed on certain issues or during political "business as usual" periods, each also misses how the most important policy decisions and political changes are influenced by morally impassioned elites who are motivated less by economic self-interest than they are by an almost religious zeal to bring government institutions and policies into line with democratic ideals. Samuel P. Huntington articulated this **creedal passion view**, offering the examples of Patrick Henry and the revolutionaries of the 1770's, the advocates of Jackson-style democracy in the 1820's, the progressive reformers of the early 20th century, and the leaders of the civil rights and anti-war movements in the mid-20th century.[19]

Who Governs—and to What Ends?

So, which view is correct? At one level, all are correct, at least in part: economic class interests, powerful cadres of elites, entrenched bureaucrats, competing pressure groups, and morally impassioned individuals have all at one time or another wielded political power and played a part in shaping our government and its policies.

But, more fundamentally, understanding any political system means being able to give reasonable answers to each of two separate but related questions about it: who governs, and to what ends?

We want to know the answer to the first question because we believe that those who rule—their personalities and beliefs, their virtues and

vices—will affect what they do to and for us. Many people think they already know the answer to the question, and they are prepared to talk and vote on that basis. That is their right, and the opinions they express may be correct. But they also may be wrong. Indeed, many of these opinions must be wrong because they are in conflict. When asked, "Who governs?" some people will say "the unions" and some will say "big business"; others will say "the politicians," "the people," or "the special interests." Still others will say "Wall Street," "the military," "crackpot liberals," "the media," "the bureaucrats," or "white males." Not all these answers can be correct—at least not all of the time.

The answer to the second question is important because it tells us how government affects our lives. We want to know not only who governs, but what difference it makes who governs. In our day-to-day lives, we may not think government makes much difference at all. In one sense that is right, because our most pressing personal concerns—work, play, love, family, health—essentially are private matters on which government touches but slightly. But in a larger and longer perspective, government makes a substantial difference. Consider: in 1935, 96 percent of all American families paid no federal income tax, and for the 4 percent or so who did pay, the average rate was only about 4 percent of their incomes. Today almost all families pay federal payroll taxes, and the average rate is about 21 percent of their incomes. Or consider: in 1960, in many parts of the country, African Americans could ride only in the backs of buses, had to use washrooms and drinking fountains that were labeled "colored," and could not be served in most public restaurants. Such restrictions have almost all been eliminated, in large part because of decisions by the federal government.

It is important to bear in mind that we wish to answer two different questions, and not two versions of the same question. You cannot always predict what goals government will establish by knowing only who governs, nor can you always tell who governs by knowing what activities government undertakes. Most people holding national political office are middle-class, middle-aged, white, Protestant males, but we cannot then conclude that the government will adopt only policies that are to the narrow advantage of the middle class, the middle-aged, whites, Protestants, or men. If we thought that, we would be at a loss to explain why the rich

pluralist view View that competition among all affected interests shapes public policy.

creedal passion view View that morally impassioned elites drive important political changes.

political agenda
Issues that people believe require governmental action.

are taxed more heavily than the poor, why the War on Poverty was declared, why constitutional amendments giving rights to African Americans and women passed Congress by large majorities, or why Catholics and Jews have been appointed to so many important governmental posts.

This book is chiefly devoted to answering the question, who governs? It is written in the belief that this question cannot be answered without looking at how government makes—or fails to make—decisions about a large variety of concrete issues. Thus, in this book we shall inspect government policies to see

what individuals, groups, and institutions seem to exert the greatest power in the continuous struggle to define the purposes of government.

Expanding the Political Agenda

No matter who governs, the most important decision that affects policymaking is also the least noticed one: deciding what to make policy *about,* or in the language of political science, deciding what belongs on the **political agenda**. The political agenda consists of issues that people believe require governmental action. We take for granted that politics is about certain familiar issues such as taxes, energy, welfare, civil rights, and homeland security. We forget that there is nothing inevitable about having these issues—rather than some other ones—on the nation's political agenda.

For example, at one time, it was unconstitutional for the federal government to levy income taxes; energy was a nonissue because everyone (or at least everyone who could chop down trees for firewood) had enough; welfare was something for cities and towns to handle; civil rights were supposed to be a matter of private choice rather than government action; "homeland security" was not in the political lexicon, and a huge federal cabinet department by that name was nowhere on the horizon.

At any given time, what is on the political agenda is affected by at least four things:

- *Shared political values*—for example, if people believe that poverty is the result of social forces rather than individual choices, then there is a reason to enact or expand government programs to combat poverty.

- *The weight of custom and tradition*—people will usually accept what the government has customarily done, even if they are leery of what it proposes to do.

- *The impact of events* such as wars, terrorist attacks, and severe or sustained economic downturns alters our sense of the proper role of government.

- *Changes in the way political elites think and talk about politics.*

Because many people believe that whatever the government now does it ought to continue doing, and because changes in attitudes and the impact of events tend to increase the number of things that government does, the political agenda is always growing larger. Thus, today there are far fewer debates about the legitimacy of a proposed government policy than there were in the 1920s or the 1930s.

Iurii Konoval/Shutterstock.com

HOW WE COMPARE

Academic Freedom

You are reading a textbook on American government, but how is the freedom to study, teach, or do research protected from undue government interference? And how do European democracies protect academic freedom?

The U.S. Constitution does not mention academic freedom. Rather, in America, the federal and state courts have typically treated academic freedom, at least in tax-supported universities, as "free speech" strongly protected under the First Amendment.

In each of nine European nations, the constitution is silent on academic freedom, but various national laws protect it. In 13 other European nations, academic freedom is protected both by explicit constitutional language and by national legislation. But is academic freedom better protected in these nations than in either the United States or elsewhere in Europe?

Not necessarily. Germany's constitution states that "research and teaching are free" but subject to "loyalty to the constitution." Italy's constitution offers lavish protections for academic freedom, but its national laws severely restrict those same freedoms.

The United Kingdom has no written constitution, but its national laws regarding academic freedom (and university self-governance) are quite restrictive by American standards.

Source: Terence Karran, "Freedom in Europe: A Preliminary Analysis," *Higher Education Policy* 20 (2007):289–313.

For instance, in the 1930s, when what became the Social Security program was first proposed, the debate was largely about whether the federal government should have any role whatsoever in providing financial support for elderly or disabled citizens. In stark contrast, today, not a single member of Congress denies that the federal government should have a *major* role in providing financial support for elderly or disabled citizens or advocates ending Social Security. Instead, today's debates about the program are largely over competing plans to ensure its long-term financial solvency.

Popular views regarding what belongs on the political agenda are often changed by the impact of events. During wartime or after a terrorist attack on this country, many people expect the government to do whatever is necessary to win, whether or not such actions are clearly authorized by the Constitution. Economic depressions or deep recessions, such as the ones that began in 1929 and 2007, also lead many people to expect the government to take action. A coal mine disaster leads to an enlarged role for the government in promoting mine safety. A series of airplane hijackings leads to a change in public opinion so great that what once would have been unthinkable—requiring all passengers at airports to be searched before boarding their flights—becomes routine.

But sometimes the government enlarges the political agenda, often dramatically, without any crisis or widespread public demand. This may happen even at a time when the conditions at which a policy is directed are improving. For instance, there was no mass public demand for government action to make automobiles safer before 1966, when a law was passed imposing safety standards on cars. Though the number of auto fatalities (per 100 million miles driven) had gone up slightly just before the law was passed, in the long term, highway deaths had been more or less steadily trending downward.

It is not easy to explain why the government adds new issues to its agenda and adopts new programs when there is little public demand and when, in fact, there has been an improvement in the conditions to which the policies are addressed. In general, the explanation may be found in the behavior of groups, the workings of institutions, the media, and the action of state governments.

Groups

Many policies are the result of small groups of people enlarging the scope of government by their demands. Sometimes these are organized interests (for example, corporations or unions); sometimes they are intense but unorganized groups (such as urban minorities). The organized groups often work quietly, behind the scenes; the intense, unorganized ones may take their causes to the streets.

For example, organized labor favored a tough federal safety law governing factories and other workplaces, not because it was unaware that factory conditions had been improving, but because the standards by which union leaders and members judged working conditions had risen even faster. As people became better off, conditions that once were thought normal suddenly became intolerable.

On occasion, a group expresses in violent ways its dissatisfaction with what it judges to be intolerable conditions. The riots in American cities during the mid-1960s had a variety of causes, and people participated out of a variety of motives. For many, rioting was a way of expressing pent-up anger at what they regarded as an unresponsive and unfair society. A sense of relative deprivation—of being worse off than one thinks one *ought* to be—helps explain why so large a proportion of the rioters were not uneducated, unemployed recent migrants to the city, but rather young men and women born in the North, educated in its schools, and employed in its factories.[20] Life under these conditions turned out to

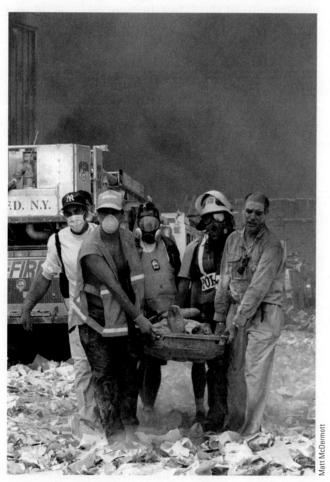

Americans felt powerfully connected to their fellow citizens in the immediate aftermath of 9/11.

Matt McDermott

be not what they had come to expect or what they were prepared to tolerate.

The new demands of such groups need not result in an enlarged political agenda, and they often do not produce such results when society and its governing institutions are confident of the rightness of the existing state of affairs. Unions could have been voted down on the occupational safety bill; rioters could have been jailed and ignored. At one time, this is exactly what would have happened. But society itself had changed: many people who were not workers sympathized with the plight of the injured worker and distrusted the good intentions of business in this matter. Many well-off citizens felt a constructive, not just a punitive, response to the urban riots was required and thus urged the formation of commissions to study—and the passage of laws to deal with—the problems of inner-city life. Such changes in the values and beliefs of people generally—or at least of people in key government positions—are an essential part of any explanation of why policies not demanded by public opinion nonetheless become part of the political agenda.

Government Institutions

Among the institutions whose influence on agenda-setting has become especially important are the courts, the bureaucracy, and the Senate.

The courts can make decisions that force the hand of the other branches of government. For example, when in 1954 the Supreme Court ordered schools desegregated, Congress and the White House could no longer ignore the issue. Local resistance to implementing the order led President Eisenhower to send troops to Little Rock, Arkansas, despite his dislike for using force against local governments. Similarly, when the Supreme Court ruled in 1973 that the states could not ban abortions during the first trimester of pregnancy, abortion suddenly became a national political issue. Right-to-life activists campaigned to reverse the Court's decision or, failing that, to prevent federal funds from being used to pay for abortions. Pro-choice activists fought to prevent the Court from reversing course and to get federal funding for abortions. In these and many other cases, the courts act like trip wires: when activated, they set off a chain reaction of events that alters the political agenda and creates a new constellation of political forces.

Indeed, the courts can sometimes be more than trip wires. As the political agenda has expanded, the courts have become the favorite method for effecting change for which there is no popular majority. There may be little electoral support for allowing abortion on demand, eliminating school prayer, ordering school busing, or attacking tobacco companies, but in the courts elections do not matter. The courts are the preferred vehicles for the advocates of unpopular causes.

The bureaucracy has acquired a new significance in American politics not simply because of its size or power but also because it is now a source of political innovation. At one time, the federal government *reacted* to events in society and to demands from segments of society; ordinarily it did not itself propose changes and new ideas. Today, the bureaucracy is so large and includes within it so great a variety of experts and advocates, that it has become a *source* of policy proposals as well as an implementer of those that become law. The late U.S. Senator Daniel Patrick Moynihan called this the "professionalization of reform," by which he meant, in part, that the government bureaucracy had begun to think up problems for government to solve rather than simply to respond to the problems identified by others.[21] In the 1930s, many of the key elements of the New Deal—Social Security, unemployment compensation, public housing, old-age benefits—were ideas devised by nongovernment experts and intellectuals here and abroad and then, as the crisis of the depression deepened, taken up by the federal government. In the 1960s, by contrast, most of the measures that became known as part of Lyndon Johnson's "Great Society"—federal aid to education, manpower development and training, Medicare and Medicaid, the War on Poverty, the "safe-streets" act providing federal aid to local law enforcement agencies—were developed, designed, and advocated by government officials, bureaucrats, and their political allies.

Chief among these political allies are U.S. senators and their staffs. Once the Senate was best described as a club that moved slowly, debated endlessly, and resisted, under the leadership of conservative southern Democrats, the plans of liberal presidents. With the collapse of the one-party South and the increase in the number of liberal activist senators, the Senate became in the 1960s an incubator for developing new policies and building national constituencies.[22]

Media

The national press can either help place new matters on the agenda or publicize those matters placed there by others. There was a close correlation between the political attention given in the Senate to proposals for new safety standards for industry, coal mines, and automobiles and the amount of space devoted to these questions in the pages of *The New York Times*. Newspaper interest in the matter, low before the issue was placed on the agenda, peaked at about the time the bill was passed.[23]

It is hard, of course, to decide which is the cause and which the effect. The press may have stimulated congressional interest in the matter or merely reported on what Congress had already decided to pursue. Nonetheless, the press must choose which of thousands of proposals it will cover. The beliefs of editors and reporters led it to select the safety issue.

Action by the States

National policy is increasingly being made by the actions of state governments. You may wonder how. After all, a state can only pass laws that affect its own people. Of course, the national government may later adopt ideas pioneered in the states, as it did when Congress passed a "Do Not Call" law to reduce how many phone calls you will get from salespeople while you are trying to eat dinner. The states had taken the lead on this issue.

But there is another way in which state governments can make national policy directly without Congress ever voting on the matter. The attorneys general of states may sue a business firm and settle the suit with an agreement that binds the industry throughout the country. The effect of one suit was to raise prices for consumers and create a new set of regulations. This is what happened in 1998 with the tobacco agreement negotiated between cigarette companies and some state attorneys general. The companies agreed to raise their prices, pay more than $240 billion to state governments (to use as they wished) and several billion dollars to private lawyers, and comply with a massive regulatory program. A decade later, the federal government passed laws that reinforced the states' regulations, culminating in the Family Smoking Prevention Tobacco Control Act of 2009.

The Politics of Different Issues

Once an issue is on the political agenda, its nature affects the kind of politicking that ensues. Some issues provoke intense interest group conflict; others allow one group to prevail almost unchallenged. Some issues involve ideological appeals to broad national constituencies; others involve quiet bargaining in congressional offices. We all know that private groups try to influence government policies; we often forget that the nature of the issues with which government is dealing influences the kinds of groups that become politically active.

One way to understand why government handles a given issue as it does is to examine what appear to be the costs and benefits of the proposed policy. The **cost** is any burden, monetary or nonmonetary, that some people must bear, or believe they must bear, if the policy is adopted. The costs of a government spending program are the taxes it entails; the cost of a foreign policy initiative may be the increased chance of having the nation drawn into war.

The **benefit** is any satisfaction, monetary or nonmonetary, that people believe they will enjoy if the policy is adopted. The benefits of a government spending program are the payments, subsidies, or contracts received by some people; the benefits of a foreign policy initiative may include the enhanced security of the nation, the protection of a valued ally, or the vindication of some important principle such as human rights.

> **cost** A burden that people believe they must bear if a policy is adopted.
>
> **benefit** A satisfaction that people believe they will enjoy if a policy is adopted.

Two aspects of these costs and benefits should be borne in mind. First, it is the *perception* of costs and benefits that affects politics. People may think the cost of an auto emissions control system is paid by the manufacturer, when it is actually passed on to the consumer in the form of higher prices and reduced performance. Political conflict over pollution control will take one form when people think that the polluting industries pay the costs and another form when they think that the consumers pay.

Second, people take into account not only who benefits but also whether it is legitimate for that group to benefit. When programs providing financial assistance to women with dependent children were first developed in the early part of the 20th century, they were relatively noncontroversial because people saw the money as going to widows and orphans who deserved such aid. Later on, giving aid to mothers with dependent children became controversial because some people now perceived the recipients not as deserving widows but as irresponsible women who had never married. Whatever the truth of the matter, the program had lost some of its legitimacy because the beneficiaries were no longer seen as "deserving." By the same token, groups once thought undeserving, such as men out of work, were later thought to be entitled to aid, and thus the unemployment compensation program acquired a legitimacy that it once lacked.

Politics is in large measure a process of raising and settling disputes over who *will* benefit or pay for a program and who *ought* to benefit or pay. Because beliefs about the results of a program and the rightness of those results are matters of opinion, it is evident that ideas are at least as important as interests in shaping politics. In recent years, ideas have become especially important with the rise of issues whose consequences are largely intangible, such as abortion, school prayer, and gay rights.

majoritarian politics
A policy in which almost everybody benefits and almost everybody pays.

Though perceptions about costs and benefits change, most people most of the time prefer government programs that provide substantial benefits to them at low cost. This rather obvious fact can have important implications for how politics is carried out. In a political system based on some measure of popular rule, public officials have a strong incentive to offer programs that confer—or appear to confer—benefits on people with costs either small in amount, remote in time, or borne by "somebody else." Policies that seem to impose high, immediate costs in return for small or remote benefits will be avoided, enacted with a minimum of publicity, or proposed only in response to a real or apparent crisis.

Ordinarily, no president would propose a policy that would immediately raise the cost of fuel, even if he were convinced that future supplies of oil and gasoline were likely to be exhausted unless higher prices reduced current consumption. But when a crisis occurs, such as the Arab oil cartel's price increases beginning in 1973, it becomes possible for the president to offer such proposals—as did Nixon, Ford, and Carter in varying ways. Even then, however, people are reluctant to bear increased costs, and thus many are led to dispute the president's claim that an emergency actually exists.

These entirely human responses to the perceived costs and benefits of proposed policies can be organized into a simple theory of politics.[24] It is based on the observation that the costs and benefits of a policy may be *widely distributed* (spread over many, most, or even all citizens) or *narrowly concentrated* (limited to a relatively small number of citizens or to some identifiable, organized group).

For instance, a widely distributed cost would include an income tax, a Social Security tax, or a high rate of crime; a widely distributed benefit might include retirement benefits for all citizens, clean air, national security, or low crime rates. Examples of narrowly concentrated costs include the expenditures by a factory to reduce its pollution, government regulations imposed on doctors and hospitals participating in the Medicare program, or restrictions on freedom of speech imposed on a dissident political group. Examples of narrowly concentrated benefits include subsidies to farmers or merchant ship companies, the enlarged freedom to speak and protest afforded a dissident group, or protection against competition given to an industry because of favorable government regulation.

The perceived distribution of costs and benefits shapes the *kinds of political coalitions that will form*—but it will not necessarily determine *who wins*. There are four types of politics, and a given popular majority, interest group, client, or entrepreneur may win or lose depending on its influence and the temper of the times.

Four Types of Politics

Majoritarian Politics: Distributed Benefits, Distributed Costs

Some policies promise benefits to large numbers of people at a cost that large numbers of people will have to bear (see Figure 1.1). For example, almost everyone will sooner or later receive Social Security benefits, and almost everyone who works has to pay Social Security taxes.

Such **majoritarian politics** are usually not dominated by pulling and hauling among rival

---

FIGURE 1.1 **A Way of Classifying and Explaining the Politics of Different Policy Issues**

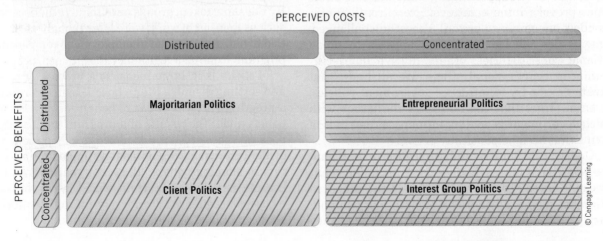

© Cengage Learning

interest groups; instead they involve making appeals to large segments of voters and their representatives in hopes of finding a majority. The reason why interest groups are not so important in majoritarian politics is that citizens rarely will have much incentive to join an interest group if the policy that such a group supports will benefit everybody, whether or not they are members of the group. This is the "free-rider" problem. Why join the Committee to Increase (or Decrease) the Defense Budget when what you personally contribute to that committee makes little difference in the outcome and when you will enjoy the benefits of more (or less) national defense even if you have stayed on the sidelines?

Majoritarian politics may be controversial, but the controversy is usually over matters of cost or ideology, not between rival interest groups. For example, there was intense controversy over the health care plan that President Obama signed into law, but the debate was not dominated by interest groups and many different types of politics were at play (see **Policy Dynamics: Inside/Outside the Box** on page 18). The military budget went up during the early 1980s, down in the late 1980s, up after 2001, and down again after 2010. These changes reflected different views on how much we need to spend on our military operations abroad.

Interest Group Politics: Concentrated Benefits, Concentrated Costs

In **interest group politics**, a proposed policy will confer benefits on some relatively small, identifiable group and impose costs on another small, equally identifiable group. For example, when Congress passed a bill requiring companies to give 60 days' notice of a plant closing or a large-scale layoff, labor unions (whose members would benefit) backed the bill, and many business firms (which would pay the costs) opposed it.

Issues of this kind tend to be fought out by organized interest groups. Each side will be so powerfully affected by the outcome that it has a strong incentive to mobilize: union members who worry about layoffs will have a personal stake in favoring the notice bill; business leaders who fear government control of investment decisions will have an economic stake in opposing it.

Interest group politics often produces decisions about which the public is uninformed. For instance, there have been bitter debates between television broadcasters and cable companies over who may send what kind of signals to which homes. But these debates hardly draw any public notice—until after a law is passed and people see their increased cable charges.

Though many issues of this type involve monetary costs and benefits, they can also involve intangible considerations. If the American Nazi party wants to march through a predominantly Jewish neighborhood carrying flags with swastikas on them, the community may organize itself to resist out of revulsion due to the horrific treatment of Jews by Nazi Germany. Each side may hire lawyers to debate the issue before the city council and in the courts.

Client Politics: Concentrated Benefits, Distributed Costs

With **client politics** some identifiable, often small group will benefit, but everybody—or at least a large part of society—will pay the costs. Because the benefits are concentrated, the group to receive those benefits has an incentive to organize and work to get them. But because the costs are widely distributed, affecting many people only slightly, those who pay the costs may be either unaware of any costs

During the Great Depression, depositors besiege a bank hoping to get their savings out.

Topham/The Image Works

pork-barrel legislation Legislation that gives tangible benefits to constituents in several districts or states in the hope of winning their votes in return.

log-rolling A legislator supports a proposal favored by another in return for support of his or hers.

entrepreneurial politics A policy in which almost everybody benefits and a small group pays.

policy entrepreneurs Activists in or out of government who pull together a political majority on behalf of unorganized interests.

or indifferent to them, because per capita they are so small.

This situation gives rise to client politics (sometimes called clientele politics); the beneficiary of the policy is the "client" of the government. For example, many farmers benefit substantially from agricultural price supports, but the far more numerous food consumers have no idea what these price supports cost them in taxes and higher food prices. Similarly, for some time airlines benefited from the higher prices they were able to charge on certain routes as a result of government regulations that restricted competition over prices. But the average passenger was either unaware that his or her costs were higher or did not think the higher prices were worth making a fuss about.

Not all clients have economic interests. Localities can also benefit as clients when, for example, a city or county obtains a new dam, a better harbor, or an improved irrigation system. Some of these projects may be worthwhile, others may not; by custom, however, they are referred to as *pork-barrel projects*. Usually several pieces of "pork" are put into one barrel—that is, several projects are approved in a single piece of **pork-barrel legislation**, such as the "rivers and harbors" bill that Congress passes almost every year. Trading votes in this way attracts the support of members of Congress from each affected area; with enough projects a majority coalition is formed. This process is called **log-rolling**.

Not every group that wants something from government at little cost to the average citizen will get it. Welfare recipients cost the typical taxpayer a small amount each year, yet there was great resistance to increasing these benefits. The homeless have not organized themselves to get benefits; indeed, most do not even vote. Yet benefits are being provided (albeit in modest amounts). These examples illustrate the importance of popular views concerning the legitimacy of client claims as a factor in determining the success of client demands.

By the same token, groups can lose legitimacy that they once had. People who grow tobacco once were supported simply because they were farmers, and were thus seen as both "deserving" and politically important. But when people began worrying about the health risks associated with using tobacco, farmers who produce tobacco lost some legitimacy compared to those who produce corn or cotton. As a result, it became harder to get votes for maintaining tobacco price supports and easier to slap higher taxes on cigarettes.

Entrepreneurial Politics: Distributed Benefits, Concentrated Costs

In **entrepreneurial politics**, society as a whole or some large part of it benefits from a policy that imposes substantial costs on some small, identifiable segment of society. The antipollution and safety requirements for automobiles were proposed as ways of improving the health and well-being of all people at the expense (at least initially) of automobile manufacturers.

It is remarkable that policies of this sort are ever adopted, and in fact many are not. After all, the American political system creates many opportunities for checking and blocking the actions of others. The Founders deliberately arranged things so that it would be difficult to pass a new law; a determined minority therefore has an excellent chance of blocking a new policy. And any organized group that fears the loss of some privilege or the imposition of some burden will become a very determined minority indeed. The opponent has every incentive to work hard; the large group of prospective beneficiaries may be unconvinced of the benefit or regard it as too small to be worth fighting for.

Nonetheless, policies with distributed benefits and concentrated costs are in fact adopted, and in recent decades they have been adopted with increasing frequency. A key element in the adoption of such policies has been the work of people who act on behalf of the unorganized or indifferent majority. Such people, called **policy entrepreneurs**, are those both in and out of government who find ways of pulling together a legislative majority on behalf of interests that are not well represented in the government. These policy entrepreneurs may or may not represent the interests and wishes of the public at large, but they do have the ability to dramatize an issue in a convincing manner. Ralph Nader is perhaps the best-known example of a policy entrepreneur, or as he might describe himself, a "consumer advocate." But there are other examples from both ends of the political spectrum, conservative as well as liberal.

Entrepreneurial politics can occur without the leadership of a policy entrepreneur if voters or legislators in large numbers suddenly become disgruntled by the high cost of some benefit that a group is receiving (or become convinced of the urgent need for a new policy to impose such costs). For example, voters may not care about government programs that benefit the oil industry when gasoline costs only one dollar a gallon, but they might care very much when the price rises to three dollars a gallon, even if the government benefits had nothing to do with the price increase. By the same token, legislators may not worry much about the effects of smog in the air until a lot of people develop burning eyes and runny noses during an especially severe smog attack.

In fact, most legislators did not worry very much about toxic or hazardous wastes until 1977, when the Love Canal dump site near Buffalo, New York, spilled some of its toxic waste into the backyards of an adjacent residential neighborhood and people were forced to leave their homes. Five years later, anyone who had forgotten about the Love Canal was reminded of it when the town of Times Beach, Missouri, had to be permanently evacuated because it had become contaminated with the chemical dioxin. Only then did it become widely known that there were more than 30,000 toxic waste sites nationwide that posed public safety risks. The Superfund program was born in 1980 of the political pressure that developed in the wake of these and other highly publicized tales of toxic waste dangers. Superfund was intended to force industries to clean up their own toxic waste sites. It also authorized the Environmental Protection Agency (EPA) to act speedily, with or without cooperation from industries, in identifying and cleaning up any sites that posed a large or imminent danger.

Superfund suffered a number of political and administrative problems, and only a few of the 1,300 sites initially targeted by the EPA had been cleaned up a dozen years after the program went into effect.[25] Regardless, Superfund is a good illustration of entrepreneurial politics in action. Special taxes on once largely unregulated oil and chemical companies funded the program. These companies once enjoyed special tax breaks, but as the politics of the issue changed, they were forced to shoulder special tax burdens. In effect, the politics of the issue changed from client politics to entrepreneurial politics.

Policy Dynamics: Inside/Outside the Box

Superfund also thereby illustrates how dynamic the politics of policymaking can be. Once an issue makes its way on to the political agenda, the politics of the issue can remain stable, change a little or a lot, and change very slowly or quite suddenly. And policy issues can "migrate" from one type of politics (and one of the four boxes) to another.

By the same token, the policy dynamics of some issues are simply harder to categorize and explain than the policy dynamics of others. For instance, in the mid-2000s, 13 states amended their state constitutions to prohibit or further restrict gay marriage. In 2008, California voters approved a ballot measure, Proposition 8, banning gay marriage. But virtually all of these policies were enacted at a time when popular support for gay rights including same-sex marriage was rising. In 2001, by a margin of 57 percent to 35 percent, Americans opposed gay marriage; but, by 2013, a 49 percent to 44 percent plurality favored gay marriage. In 2012, President Barack Obama, having previously ordered an end to the ban on gays in the U.S. military, publicly declared his support for legalizing same-sex marriage. Surveys indicated that the only groups still harboring wide majorities opposed to same-sex marriage were evangelical Christians and adults born in 1964 or earlier. In 2013, the U.S. Supreme Court struck down a 1996 federal law that allowed the federal government to discriminate against same-sex married couples but did not strike down the state laws banning same-sex marriage.

So, how best can we categorize or explain the politics of this issue? Which type of politics—majoritarian, client, interest group, or entrepreneurial—were most important to policymaking? Why did state laws become more restrictive at the very time that both mass public opinion and elite opinion were trending toward greater acceptance? Do the still-unfolding policy dynamics of this issue fit neatly (or fit at all) in any of our four boxes? Start thinking about these questions; we will revisit them in Chapter 6.

Finally, while the politics of some issues does fit neatly into one box or another, the politics of other issues reflects several different types of politics.

For example, most major pieces of social legislation reflect *majoritarian* politics—Social Security remains a prime example—but the politics of health care issues has often played out within all four boxes—majoritarian, client, interest group, and entrepreneurial—at once. This was certainly true of the politics of the Patient Protection and Affordable Care Act of 2010, better known as "Obamacare." As we illustrate nearby in our first **Policy Dynamics: Inside/Outside the Box** feature, the perceived costs and benefits of the Obama plan affected the political coalitions that formed around it and involved all four types of politics.

Understanding Politics

Whether pondering one's own positions on given issues, attempting to generalize about the politics of different policy issues, or tackling questions about

POLICY DYNAMICS: INSIDE/OUTSIDE THE BOX

Obamacare: All Four Boxes?

When Medicare was enacted in 1965, Democrats in the House and Senate voted for it by a wide margin, but roughly half of the Republicans in each chamber also supported it. But the 2010 health care bill was passed without any Republican support. In other words, the 1965 Medicare bill that President Johnson signed into law had broad bipartisan backing, but the 2010 health care bill that President Obama signed into law had none. Using the model of the policy process explained in this chapter, here is a summary of how the costs and benefits of the Obama plan affected the political coalitions that formed around health care.

Majoritarian Politics: The bill was opposed by a majority of Americans for a variety of easons. Many thought it too expensive ($940billion over 10 years) or worried about the government regulations the law contained.

Client Politics: Drug manufacturers looked forward to having many new customers as more people owned health insurance. To get this benefit, the pharmaceutical companies agreed to pay up to $85 billion in higher taxes. Many hospitals thought they would be helped by having more patients who could pay their bills with health insurance.

Interest Group Politics: Labor unions wanted health care coverage, but business firms were upset by the higher taxes and fees they would have to pay. Poorer people liked it, but those earning $200,000 a year or more would see their taxes escalate. Elderly people on Medicare and many doctors worried that the new law promised to cut payments to physicians, but the American Medical Association and the AARP (the largest organization representing senior citizens) endorsed the law.

Policy Entrepreneurs: In early 2010, the winners were President Obama and the Democratic leaders in the House who got a bill passed over popular and interest group opposition. In the latter half of 2010,

however, the winners were the Republicans who opposed "Obamacare" and used the issue on the way to sweeping GOP* victories in the November 2010 elections.

When the 112th Congress was seated in 2011, Republicans in the House made good on a pledge to vote for the outright repeal of the new law (the symbolic bill died in the Senate), and several state's attorneys general challenged the law's constitutionality in the federal courts (focusing mainly on the provision mandating that individuals purchase health insurance). In 2012, the U.S. Supreme Court upheld the constitutionality of the law's individual mandate, but ruled against certain other provisions of the law, including ones pertaining to changes in the federal-state program known as Medicaid, a program that was created in 1965 alongside Medicare (see Chapter 17 in full edition).

The Medicare law and the new health care law mobilized very different coalitions in part because, between 1965 and 2010, Congress became a far more polarized institution (see Chapter13). The "Obamacare" policy was based on a combination of majoritarian, client, interest group, and entrepreneurial politics. The politics of the issue was neither inside nor outside any one of the four boxes, but spread across all four.

*"GOP" refers to "Grand Old Party," a widely used synonym for the Republican party.

American government, institutions, and policies, an astute student will soon come to know what Aristotle meant when he wrote that it is "the mark of the educated person to look for precision in each class of things just so far as the nature of the subject admits."[26]

Ideally, political scientists ought to be able to give clear answers, amply supported by evidence, to the questions we have posed about American democracy, starting with "who governs?" In reality they

can (at best) give partial, contingent, and controversial answers. The reason is to be found in the nature of our subject. Unlike economists, who assume that people have more or less stable preferences and can compare ways of satisfying those preferences by looking at the relative prices of various goods and services, political scientists are interested in how preferences are formed, especially for those kinds of services, such as national defense or pollution

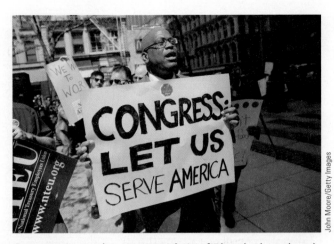

John Moore/Getty Images

Government employees protest being furloughed, or placed on unpaid leave, in response to the "sequester"—automatic budget cuts that began when Congress and the White House failed to reach a long-term budget agreement in early 2013.

control, that cannot be evaluated chiefly in terms of monetary costs.

Understanding preferences is vital to understanding power. Who did what in government is not hard to find out, but who wielded power—that is, who made a difference in the outcome and for what reason—is much harder to discover. *Power* is a word that conjures up images of deals, bribes, power plays, and arm-twisting. In fact, most power exists because of shared understanding, common friendships, communal or organizational loyalties, and different degrees of prestige. These are hard to identify and almost impossible to quantify.

Nor can the distribution of political power be inferred simply by knowing what laws are on the books or what administrative actions have been taken. The enactment of a consumer protection law does not mean that consumers are powerful, any more than the absence of such a law means that corporations are powerful. The passage of such a law could reflect an aroused public opinion, the lobbying of a small group claiming to speak for consumers, the ambitions of a senator, or the intrigues of one business firm seeking to gain a competitive advantage over another. A close analysis of what the law entails and how it was passed and administered is necessary before much of anything can be concluded.

This book will avoid sweeping claims that we have an "imperial" presidency (or an impotent one), an "obstructionist" Congress (or an innovative one), or "captured" regulatory agencies. Such labels do an injustice to the different roles that presidents, members of Congress, and administrators play in different kinds of issues and in different historical periods. The view taken in this book is that judgments about institutions and interests can be made only

after one has seen how they behave on a variety of important issues or potential issues, such as economic policy, the regulation of business, social welfare, civil rights and liberties, and foreign and military affairs. The policies adopted or blocked, the groups heeded or ignored, the values embraced or rejected—these constitute the raw material out of which one can fashion an answer to the central questions we have asked: Who governs—and to what ends?

The way in which our institutions of government handle social welfare, for example, differs from the way other democratic nations handle it, and it differs as well from the way our own institutions once treated it. The description of our institutions in Part III will therefore include not only an account of how they work today but also a brief historical background on their workings and a comparison with similar institutions in other countries. There is a tendency to assume that how we do things today is the only way they could possibly be done. In fact, there are other ways to operate a government based on some measure of popular rule. History, tradition, and belief weigh heavily on all that we do.

Although political change is not always accompanied by changes in public laws, the policy process is arguably one of the best barometers of changes in who governs. Our way of classifying and explaining the politics of different policy issues has been developed, refined, and tested over more than two decades (longer than most of our readers have been alive!). Our own students and others have valued it mainly because they have found it helps to answer such questions about who governs: How do political issues get on the public agenda in the first place? How, for example, did sexual harassment, which was hardly ever discussed or debated by Congress, burst onto the public agenda? Once on the agenda, how does the politics of issues like income security for older Americans—for example, the politics of Social Security, a program that has been on the federal books since 1935 (see Chapter 17 in full edition)—change over time? And if, today, one cares about expanding civil liberties (see Chapter 5) or protecting civil rights (see Chapter 6), what political obstacles and opportunities will one likely face, and what role will public opinion, organized interest groups, the media, the courts, political parties, and other institutions likely play in frustrating or fostering one's particular policy preferences, whatever they might be?

Peek ahead, if you wish, but understand that the place to begin a search for how power is distributed in national politics and what purposes that power serves is with the founding of the federal government in 1787: the Constitutional Convention and

WHAT WOULD YOU DO?

MEMORANDUM

To: *Governor Steven Finore*

From: *Edmund Heron, chief policy adviser*

Subject: *Initiative repeal*

You have supported several successful initiatives (life imprisonment for thrice-convicted violent felons, property tax limits), but you have never publicly stated a view on the initiative itself, and the repeal proposal will probably surface during tomorrow's press briefing.

Arguments for a ban:

1. Ours is a representative, not a direct, democracy in which voters elect leaders and elected leaders make policy decisions subject to review by the courts.

2. Voters often are neither rational nor respectful of constitutional rights. For example, many people demand both lower taxes and more government services, and polls find that most voters would prohibit people with certain views from speaking and deprive all persons accused of a violent crime from getting out on bail while awaiting trial.

3. Over the past 100 years, hundreds of state-wide ballot initiatives have been passed in 24 states. Rather than giving power to the people, special-interest groups have spent billions of dollars manipulating voters to pass initiatives that enrich or benefit them, not the public at large.

Arguments against a ban:

1. When elected officials fail to respond to persistent public majorities favoring tougher crime measures, lower property taxes, and other popular concerns, direct democracy via the initiative is legitimate, and the courts can still review the law.

News »

Legal and Policy Experts Call for a Ban on Ballot Initiatives

A report released yesterday and signed by more than 100 law and public policy professors statewide urges that the state's constitution be amended to ban legislation by initiative. The initiative allows state voters to place legislative measures directly on the ballot by getting enough signatures. The initiative "has led to disastrous policy decisions on taxes, crime, and other issues," the report declared.

2. More Americans than ever have college degrees and easy access to information about public affairs. Studies find that most average citizens are able to figure out which candidates, parties, or advocacy groups come closest to supporting their own economic interests and personal values.

3. All told, the 24 states that passed laws by initiative also passed thousands more laws by the regular legislative process (out of tens of thousands of bills they considered). Studies find that special-interest groups are severely limited in their ability to pass new laws by initiative, while citizens' groups with broad-based public support are behind most initiatives that pass.

Your decision:

Favor ban _____   Oppose ban _____

the events leading up to it. Though the decisions of that time were not made by philosophers or professors, the practical men who made them had a philosophic and professorial cast of mind, and thus they left behind a fairly explicit account of what values they sought to protect and what arrangements they thought ought to be made for the allocation of political power.

LEARNING OBJECTIVES

1. What is "politics"?

Politics is the activity by which an issue is agitated or settled. Politics occurs because people disagree and the disagreement must be managed. Disagreements over many political issues, including disputes over government budgets and finances, are often at their essence disagreements over what government should or should not do at all.

2. Can you give two definitions of "democracy"?

Democracy can mean either that everyone votes on all government issues (direct or participatory democracy) or that the people elect representatives to make most of these decisions (representative democracy).

3. How is political power actually distributed in America?

Some believe that political power in America is monopolized by wealthy business leaders, by other powerful elites, or by entrenched government bureaucrats. Others believe that political resources such as money, prestige, expertise, organizational position, and access to the mass media are so widely dispersed in American society, and the governmental institutions and offices in which power may be exercised so numerous and varied, that no single group truly has all or most political power. In this view, political power in America is distributed more or less widely. Still others suggest that morally impassioned leaders have at times been deeply influential in our politics. No one, however, argues that political resources are distributed equally in America.

4. What is the "political agenda" and why has it expanded?

The political agenda consist of those issues that people believe require government action. The behavior of groups, the workings of institutions, the media, and the actions of state governments have all figured in the expansion of America's political agenda. The great shifts in the character of American government—its size, scope, institutional arrangements, and the direction of its policies—have reflected complex and sometimes sudden changes in elite or mass beliefs about what government is supposed to do. The federal government now has policies on street crime, the environment, homeland security, and many other issues that were not on the federal agenda a half-century (or, in the case of homeland security, just 15 years) ago.

5. How can you classify and explain the politics of different issues?

One way to classify and explain the politics of different issues is in relation to the perceived costs and benefits of given policies and how narrowly concentrated (limited to a relatively small number of identifiable citizens) or widely distributed (spread over many, most, or all citizens) their perceived costs and benefits are. This approach gives us four types of politics: *majoritarian* (widely distributed costs and benefits), *interest group* (narrowly concentrated costs and benefits), *client* (widely distributed costs and narrowly concentrated benefits), and *entrepreneurial* (narrowly concentrated costs and widely distributed benefits). Different types of coalitions are associated with each type of politics. Issues can sometimes "migrate" from one type of politics to another. Some policy dynamics involve more than one type of politics. And the politics of some issues is harder to classify and explain than the politics of others.

TO LEARN MORE

Huntington, Samuel P. *American Politics: The Promise of Disharmony*. Cambridge, MA: Harvard University Press, 1981. A fascinating analysis of the American political experience as shaped by recurring "creedal passion" periods.

Marx, Karl, and Friedrich Engels. "The Manifesto of the Communist Party." In *The Marx-Engels Reader*, 2d ed., edited by Robert C. Tucker. New York: Norton, 1978, 469–500. The classic and historic statement suggesting that government is a mere instrument of the economic elite (wealthy capitalists in the modern world).

Meyerson, Martin, and Edward C. Banfield. *Politics, Planning, and the Public Interest*. New York: Free Press, 1955. An understanding of issues and politics comparable to the approach adopted in this book.

Schumpeter, Joseph A. *Capitalism, Socialism, and Democracy*. 3d ed. New York: Harper Torchbooks, 1950, chs. 20–23. A lucid statement of the theory of representative democracy and how it differs from participatory democracy.

Truman, David B. *The Governmental Process: Political Interests and Public Opinion*. New York: Knopf, 1951. A pluralist interpretation of American politics.

Weber, Max. *From Max Weber: Essays in Sociology*. Translated and edited by H. H. Gerth and C. Wright Mills. London: Routledge & Kegan Paul, 1948, ch. 8. A theory of bureaucracy and its power.

Wilson, James Q. *Political Organizations*. New York: Basic Books, 1973. It is from a theory originally developed in this treatise that the four-box model of how to classify and explain the politics of different issues that is presented in this chapter was derived.

Steve McAlister/Photographer's Choice/Getty Images

The Constitution

LEARNING OBJECTIVES

1. Why was a Bill of Rights adopted so soon after the ratification of the Constitution?

2. Why did so many authors of the Constitution fear factions?

3. Why did the Framers agree on the idea of a separation of powers?

4. What is the difference between a democracy and a republic?

5. How did Thomas Hobbes and John Locke differ about democracy, and which thinker did the Framers follow?

6. What branch of government has the greatest power?

7. Does the Constitution tell us what goals the government should serve?

8. Whose freedom does the Constitution protect?

THEN

When the Constitutional Convention was held in Philadelphia in 1787, its members were all white men. They were not chosen by popular election, and a few famous men, such as Patrick Henry of Virginia, refused to attend. One state, Rhode Island, sent no delegates at all. They met in secret and there was no press coverage. The delegates met to remedy the defects of the Articles of Confederation, under which the rebellious colonies had been governed, but instead of fixing the Articles, they wrote an entirely new constitution. They then publicized it and said that it would go into effect once it had been ratified, not by state legislatures, but by popular conventions in at least nine states.

NOW

Suppose you think we should have a new constitutional convention to remedy what you and others think are defects in the present document. As you will see later in this chapter, opinions about how our Constitution might be improved are quite diverse. Some critics want the Constitution to create an American version of the parliamentary system of government one finds in the United Kingdom; others would rather that it weaken the federal government by (for example) having a requirement that the budget be balanced or setting a limit on tax revenue each year. Now try to imagine your answers to these questions: How would delegates be picked? How many would there be? Is there any way to limit what the new convention does? Should the meeting be covered by live television, and should the delegates be free to send emails and Twitter messages to outsiders?

The Problem of Liberty

The goal of the American Revolution was liberty. It was not the first revolution with that object (nor was it the last), but it was perhaps the clearest case of a people altering the political order violently, simply in order to protect their liberties. Subsequent revolutions had more complicated or utterly different objectives. The French Revolution in 1789 sought not only liberty, but "equality and fraternity." The Russian Revolution (1917) and the Chinese Revolution (culminating in 1949) chiefly sought equality and were scarcely concerned with liberty as we understand it.

What the American colonists sought to protect when they signed the Declaration of Independence in 1776 were the traditional liberties to which they thought they were entitled as British subjects. These liberties included the right to bring their legal cases before truly independent judges, rather than ones subordinate to the king; to be free of the burden of having British troops quartered in their homes; to engage in trade without burdensome restrictions; and, of course, to pay no taxes levied by a British Parliament in which they had no direct representation. During the ten years or more of agitation and argument leading up to the War of Independence, most colonists believed their liberties could be protected while they remained a part of the British Empire.

Slowly but surely opinion shifted. By the time war broke out in 1775, a large number of colonists (though perhaps not a majority) had reached the conclusion that the colonies would have to become independent of Great Britain if their liberties were to be assured. The colonists had many reasons for regarding independence as the only solution, but one is especially important: they no longer had confidence in the English constitution. This constitution was not a single document, but rather a collection of laws, charters, and traditional understandings that proclaimed the liberties of British subjects. In the eyes of the colonists, these liberties were regularly violated, despite their constitutional protection. Clearly, then, the English constitution was an inadequate check on the abuses of political power. The revolutionary leaders sought an explanation of the insufficiency of the constitution and found it in human nature.

The Colonial Mind

"A lust for domination is more or less natural to all parties," one colonist wrote.[1] Men will seek power, many colonists believed, because they are ambitious, greedy, and easily corrupted. John Adams denounced the "luxury, effeminacy, and venality" of English politics; Patrick Henry spoke scathingly of the "corrupt House of Commons"; and Alexander Hamilton described England as "an old, wrinkled, withered, worn-out hag."[2] This was in part flamboyant rhetoric designed to whip up enthusiasm for the conflict, but it was also deeply revealing of the colonial mindset. Their belief that English politicians—and by implication, most politicians—tended to be corrupt was the colonists' explanation of why the English constitution was not an adequate guarantee of the liberty of the citizens. This opinion was to persist and, as we shall see, profoundly affect the way the Americans went about designing their own governments.

The liberties the colonists fought to protect were, they thought, widely understood. They were based not on the generosity of the king or the language of statutes but on a "higher law" embodying "natural rights" that were ordained by God, discoverable in nature and history, and essential to human progress.

These rights, John Dickinson wrote, "are born with us; exist with us; and cannot be taken away from us by any human power."[3] There was general agreement that the essential rights included life, liberty, and property long before Thomas Jefferson wrote them into the Declaration of Independence. (Jefferson changed "property" to "the pursuit of happiness," but almost everybody else went on talking about property.)

This emphasis on property did not mean the American Revolution was thought up by the rich and wellborn to protect their interests or that there was a struggle between property owners and the propertyless. In late-18th-century America, most people (except the black slaves) had property of some kind. The overwhelming majority of citizens were self-employed—as farmers or artisans—and rather few people benefited financially by gaining independence from England. Taxes were higher during and after the war than they were before it, trade was disrupted by the conflict, and debts mounted perilously as various expedients were invented to pay for the struggle. There were, of course, war profiteers and those who tried to manipulate the currency to their own advantage, but most Americans at the time of the war saw the conflict in terms of political rather than economic issues. It was a war of ideology.

We all recognize the glowing language with which Jefferson set out the case for independence in the second paragraph of the Declaration:

We hold these truths to be self-evident, that all men are created equal, that they are endowed by their Creator with certain unalienable Rights, that among these are Life, Liberty, and the pursuit of Happiness.— That to secure these rights, Governments are instituted among Men, deriving their just powers from the consent of the governed—that whenever any Form of Government becomes destructive of these ends, it is the Right of the People to alter or to abolish it, and to institute new Government, having its foundation on such principles, and organizing its powers in such form, as to them shall seem most likely to effect their Safety and Happiness.

unalienable A human right based on nature or God.

What almost no one recalls, but what is an essential part of the Declaration, are the next 27 paragraphs, in which Jefferson listed, item by item, the specific complaints the colonists had against George III and his ministers. None of these items spoke of social or economic conditions in the colonies; all spoke instead of specific violations of political liberties. The Declaration was in essence a lawyer's brief, prefaced by a stirring philosophical claim that the rights being violated were **unalienable**— that is, based on nature and Providence, and not on the whims or preferences of people. Jefferson, in his original draft, added another complaint—that the king had allowed the slave trade to continue *and* was inciting slaves to revolt against their masters. Congress, faced with so contradictory a charge, instead decided to include a muted reference to slave insurrections and omit all reference to the slave trade.

Signing the Declaration of Independence, painted by John Trumbull.

The Real Revolution

The Revolution was more than the War of Independence. It began before the war, continued after it, and involved more than driving out the British army by force of arms. The *real* Revolution, as John Adams afterward explained in a letter to a friend, was the "radical change in the principles, opinions, sentiments, and affections of the people."[4] This radical change had to do with a new vision of what could make political authority legitimate and personal liberties secure. Government by royal prerogative was rejected; instead, legitimate government would require the consent of the governed. Political power could not be exercised on the basis of tradition, but only as a result of a direct grant of power contained in a written constitution. Human liberty existed before government was organized, and government must respect that liberty. The legislative branch of government, in which the people were directly represented, should be superior to the executive branch.

These were indeed revolutionary ideas. No government at the time had been organized on the basis of these principles. To the colonists, such notions were not empty words, but rules to be put into immediate practice. In 1776, eight states adopted written constitutions. Within a few years, every former colony had adopted one except Connecticut and Rhode Island, two states that continued to rely on their colonial charters. Most state constitutions had detailed bills of rights defining personal liberties, and most placed the highest political power in the hands of elected representatives.

Written constitutions, representatives, and bills of rights are so familiar to us now that we don't realize how bold and unprecedented those innovations were in 1776. Indeed, many Americans did not think they would succeed: such arrangements would be either so strong that they would threaten liberty or so weak that they would permit chaos.

The 11 years that elapsed between the Declaration of Independence and the signing of the

FIGURE 2.1 North America in 1787

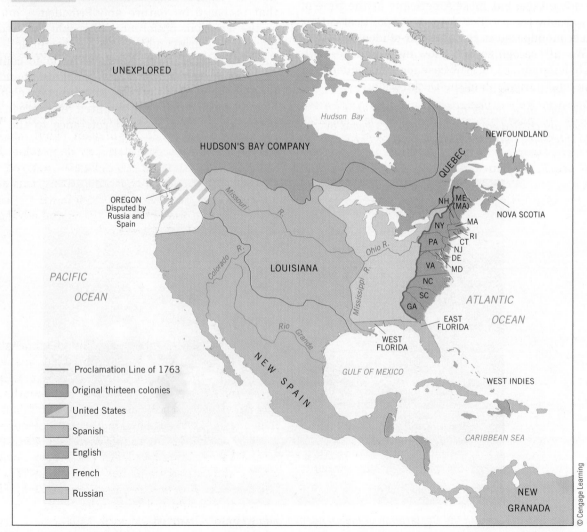

Proclamation Line of 1763

Original thirteen colonies

United States

Spanish

English

French

Russian

© Cengage Learning

Constitution in 1787 were years of turmoil, uncertainty, and fear. George Washington headed a bitter, protracted war effort without anything resembling a strong national government to support him. The supply and financing of his army were based on a series of hasty improvisations, most badly administered and few adequately supported by the fiercely independent states. When peace came, many parts of the nation were a shambles. At least a quarter of New York City was in ruins, and many other communities were nearly devastated. Though the British lost the war, they still were powerful on the North American continent, with an army available in Canada (where many Americans loyal to Britain had fled) and a large navy at sea. Spain claimed the Mississippi River Valley and occupied what are now Florida and California. Men who had left their farms to fight came back to discover themselves in debt with no money and heavy taxes. The paper money printed to finance the war was now virtually worthless.

Weaknesses of the Confederation

The 13 states had formed only a faint semblance of a national government with which to bring order to the nation. The **Articles of Confederation**, which went into effect in 1781, created little more than a "league of friendship" that could not levy taxes or regulate commerce. Each state retained its sovereignty and independence, each state (regardless of size) had one vote in Congress, nine (of 13) votes were required to pass any measure, and the delegates who cast these votes were picked and paid for by the state legislatures. Congress did have the power to make peace, and thus it was able to ratify the treaty with England in 1783. It could coin money, but there was precious little to coin; it could appoint the key

army officers, but the army was small and dependent for support on independent state militias; it was allowed to run the post office, then, as now, a thankless task that no one else wanted. In 1785, John Hancock was elected to the meaningless office of "president" under the Articles and never showed up to take the job. Several states claimed the unsettled lands in the West, and they occasionally pressed those claims with guns. Pennsylvania and Virginia went to war near Pittsburgh, and Vermont threatened to become part of Canada. There was no national judicial system to settle these or other claims among the states. To amend the Articles of Confederation, all 13 states had to agree.

Many of the leaders of the Revolution, such as George Washington and Alexander Hamilton, believed a stronger national government was essential. They lamented the disruption of commerce and travel caused by the quarrelsome states and deeply feared the possibility of foreign military intervention, with England or France playing one state off against another. A small group of men, conferring at Washington's home at Mount Vernon in 1785, decided to call a meeting to discuss trade regulation. That meeting, held at Annapolis, Maryland, in September 1786, was not well attended (no delegates arrived from New England), and so another meeting, this one in Philadelphia, was called for the following spring—in May 1787—to consider ways of remedying the defects of the Confederation.

Articles of Confederation A weak constitution that governed America during the Revolutionary War.

Constitutional Convention A meeting in Philadelphia in 1787 that produced a new constitution.

In 1775, British and American troops exchange fire in Lexington, Massachusetts, the first battle of the War of Independence.

Alonzo Chappel/Bettmann/Corbis

The Constitutional Convention

The delegates assembled at Philadelphia at the **Constitutional Convention**, for what was advertised (and authorized by Congress) as a meeting to revise the Articles; they adjourned four months later having written a wholly new constitution. When they met, they were keenly aware of the problems of the confederacy, but far from agreement as to what should be done about those problems. The protection of life, liberty, and property was their objective in 1787 as it had been in 1776, but they had no accepted political theory that would tell them what kind of national government, if any, would serve that goal.

Shays's Rebellion A 1787 rebellion in which ex–Revolutionary War soldiers attempted to prevent foreclosures of farms as a result of high interest rates and taxes.

The Lessons of Experience

They had read ancient and modern political history, only to learn that nothing seemed to work. James Madison spent a good part of 1786 studying books sent to him by Thomas Jefferson, then in Paris, in hopes of finding some model for a workable American republic. He took careful notes on various confederacies in ancient Greece and on the more modern confederacy of the United Netherlands. He reviewed the history of Switzerland and Poland and the ups and downs of the Roman republic. He concluded that there was no model; as he later put it in one of the *Federalist* papers, history consists only of beacon lights "which give warning of the course to be shunned, without pointing out that which ought to be pursued."[5] The problem seemed to be that confederacies were too weak to govern and tended to collapse from internal dissension, while all stronger forms of government were so powerful as to trample the liberties of the citizens.

State Constitutions

Madison and the others did not need to consult history, or even the defects of the Articles of Confederation, for illustrations of the problem. These could be found in the government of the American states at the time. Pennsylvania and Massachusetts exemplified two aspects of the problem. The Pennsylvania constitution, adopted in 1776, created the most radically democratic of the new state regimes. All power was given to a one-house (unicameral) legislature, the Assembly, the members of which were elected annually for one-year terms. No legislator could serve more than four years. There was no governor or president, only an Executive Council that had few powers. Thomas Paine, whose pamphlets had helped precipitate the break with England, thought the Pennsylvania constitution was the best in America, and in France philosophers hailed it as the very embodiment of the principle of rule by the people. Though popular in France, it was a good deal less popular in Philadelphia. The Assembly disfranchised the Quakers, persecuted conscientious objectors to the war, ignored the requirement of trial by juries, and manipulated the judiciary.[6] To Madison and his friends, the Pennsylvania constitution demonstrated how a government, though democratic, could be tyrannical as a result of concentrating all powers into one set of hands.

The Massachusetts constitution, adopted in 1780, was a good deal less democratic. There was a clear separation of powers among the various branches of government, the directly elected governor could veto acts of the legislature, and judges served for life. Both voters and elected officials had to be property owners; the governor, in fact, had to own at least £1,000 worth of property. The principal officeholders had to swear they were Christians.

Shays's Rebellion

But if the government of Pennsylvania was thought too strong, that of Massachusetts seemed too weak, despite its "conservative" features. In January 1787, a group of ex–Revolutionary War soldiers and officers, plagued by debts and high taxes and fearful of losing their property to creditors and tax collectors, forcibly prevented the courts in western Massachusetts from sitting. This became known as **Shays's Rebellion**, after one of the officers, Daniel Shays. The governor of Massachusetts asked the Continental Congress to send troops to suppress the rebellion, but it could not raise the money or the manpower. Then he turned to his own state militia, but discovered he did not have one. In desperation, private funds were collected to hire a volunteer army, which marched on Springfield and, with the firing of a few shots, dispersed the rebels, who fled into neighboring states.

Shays's Rebellion, occurring between the aborted Annapolis and the coming Philadelphia conventions, had a powerful effect on opinion. Delegates who might have been reluctant to attend the Philadelphia meeting, especially those from New England, were galvanized by the fear that state governments were about to collapse from internal dissension. George Washington wrote a friend despairingly: "For God's sake, if they [the rebels] have real grievances, redress them; if they have not, employ the force of government against them at once."[7] Thomas Jefferson, living in Paris, took a more detached view: "A little rebellion now and then is a good thing," he wrote. "The tree of liberty must be refreshed from time to time with the blood of patriots and tyrants."[8] Though Jefferson's detachment might be explained by the fact that he was in Paris and not in Springfield, there were others, like Governor George Clinton of New York, who shared the view that no strong central government was required. (Whether Clinton would have agreed about the virtues of spilled blood, especially his, is another matter.)

The Framers

The Philadelphia convention attracted 55 delegates, only about 30 of whom participated regularly in the proceedings. One state, Rhode Island, refused to send anyone. The convention met during a miserably hot Philadelphia summer, with the delegates pledged to keep their deliberations secret. The talkative and party-loving Benjamin Franklin was often accompanied by other delegates to make sure that neither wine nor his delight in telling stories would lead him to divulge delicate secrets.

Those who attended were for the most part young (Hamilton was 30; Madison 36) but experienced. Eight delegates had signed the Declaration of Independence, seven had been governors, 34 were lawyers and reasonably well-to-do, a few were wealthy. They were not "intellectuals," but men of practical affairs. Thirty-nine had served in the ineffectual Congress of the Confederation; a third of all delegates were veterans of the Continental Army.

Some names made famous by the Revolution were conspicuously absent. Thomas Jefferson and John Adams were serving as ministers abroad; Samuel Adams was ill; Patrick Henry was chosen to attend but refused, commenting that he "smelled a rat in Philadelphia, tending toward monarchy."

The key men at the convention were an odd lot. George Washington was a very tall, athletic man who was the best horseman in Virginia and who impressed everyone with his dignity, despite decaying teeth and big eyes. James Madison was the very opposite: quite short with a frail body, and not much of an orator, but possessed of one of the best minds in the country. Benjamin Franklin, though old and ill, was the most famous American in the world as a scientist and writer, and always displayed shrewd judgment, at least when sober. Alexander Hamilton, the illegitimate son of a French woman and a Scottish merchant, had so strong a mind and so powerful a desire that he succeeded in everything he did, from being Washington's aide during the Revolution to serving as a splendid secretary of the treasury during Washington's presidency.

The convention produced not a revision of the Articles of Confederation, as it had been authorized to do, but instead a wholly new written constitution creating a true national government unlike any that had existed before. That document is today the world's oldest written national constitution. Those who wrote it were neither saints nor schemers, and the deliberations were not always lofty or philosophical—much hard bargaining, more than a little confusion, and the accidents of personality and time helped shape the final product. The delegates were split on many issues—what powers should be given to a central government, how the states should be represented, what was to be done about slavery, the role of the people—each of which was resolved by a compromise. The speeches of the delegates (known to us from the detailed notes kept by Madison) did not explicitly draw on political philosophy or quote from the writings of philosophers. Everyone present was quite familiar with the traditional arguments and, on the whole, well read in history. Though the leading political philosophers were only rarely mentioned, the debate was profoundly influenced by philosophical beliefs, some

formed by the revolutionary experience and others by the 11-year attempt at self-government.

From the debates leading up to the Revolution, the delegates had drawn a commitment to liberty, which, despite the abuses sometimes committed in its name, they continued to share. Their defense of liberty as a natural right was derived from the writings of the 17th Century English philosopher John Locke. Unlike his English rival, Thomas Hobbes, Locke did not believe that it was necessary to have an all-powerful government or that democracy was impossible. Hobbes had argued that in any society without an absolute, supreme ruler there is bound to be ceaseless violent turmoil—a "war of all against all." Locke disagreed. In a "state of nature," Locke argued, all men cherish and seek to protect their life, liberty, and property. But in a state of nature—that is, a society without a government—the strong can use their liberty to deprive the weak of their own liberty. The instinct for self-preservation leads people to want a government that will prevent this exploitation. But if the government is not itself to deprive its subjects of their liberty, it must be limited. The chief limitation on it, he said, should derive from the fact that it is created, and governs, by the consent of the governed. People will not agree to be ruled by a government that threatens their liberty; therefore, the government to

Hulton Archive/Getty Images

Shays's Rebellion in western Massachusetts in 1786–1787 stirred deep fears of anarchy in America. The ruckus was put down by a hastily assembled militia, and the rebels were eventually pardoned.

Virginia Plan Proposal to create a strong national government.

New Jersey Plan Proposal to create a weak national government.

which they freely choose to submit themselves will be a limited government designed to protect liberty.[9]

The Pennsylvania experience as well as the history of British government led the Framers to doubt whether popular consent alone would be a sufficient guarantor of liberty. A popular government may prove too weak (as in Massachusetts) to prevent one faction from abusing another, or a popular majority can be tyrannical (as in Pennsylvania). In fact, the tyranny of the majority can be an even graver threat than rule by the few. In the former case, there may be no defenses for the individual—one lone person cannot count on the succor of public opinion or the possibility of popular revolt.

The problem, then, was a delicate one: how to devise a government strong enough to preserve order but not so strong that it would threaten liberty. The answer, the delegates believed, was not "democracy" as it was then understood. To many conservatives in the late 18th century, democracy meant mob rule—it meant, in short, Shays's Rebellion (or, if they had been candid about it, the Boston Tea Party). On the other hand, *aristocracy*—the rule of the few—was no solution, since the few were likely to be self-serving. Madison, writing later in the *Federalist* papers, put the problem this way:

> If men were angels, no government would be necessary. If angels were to govern men, neither external nor internal controls on government would be necessary. In framing a government which is to be administered by men over men, the great difficulty lies in this: you must first enable the government to control the governed; and in the next place oblige it to control itself.[10]

Striking this balance could not be done, Madison believed, simply by writing a constitution that set limits on what government could do. The example of British rule over the colonies proved that laws and customs were inadequate checks on political power. As he expressed it, "A mere demarcation on parchment of the constitutional limits [of government] is not a sufficient guard against those encroachments which lead to a tyrannical concentration of all the powers of government in the same hands."[11]

The Challenge

The resolution of political issues, great and small, often depends crucially on how the central question is phrased. The delegates came to Philadelphia in general agreement that there were defects in the Articles of Confederation that ought to be remedied. Had they, after convening, decided to make their business that of listing these defects and debating alternative remedies for them, the document that emerged would in all likelihood have been very different from what in fact was adopted. But immediately after the convention had organized itself and chosen Washington to be its presiding officer, the Virginia delegation, led by Governor Edmund Randolph but relying heavily on the draftsmanship of James Madison, presented to the convention a comprehensive plan for a wholly new national government. The plan quickly became the major item of business at the meeting; it, and little else, was debated for the next two weeks.

The Virginia Plan

When the convention decided to make the **Virginia Plan** its agenda, it had fundamentally altered the nature of its task. The business at hand was not to be the Articles and their defects, but rather how one should go about designing a true national government. The Virginia Plan called for a strong national union organized into three governmental branches—the legislative, executive, and judicial. The legislature was to be composed of two houses, the first elected directly by the people and the second chosen by the first house from among the candidates nominated by state legislatures. The executive was to be chosen by the national legislature, as were members of a national judiciary. The executive and some members of the judiciary were to constitute a "council of revision" that could veto acts of the legislature; that veto, in turn, could be overridden by the legislature. There were other interesting details, but the key features of the Virginia Plan were two: (1) a national legislature would have supreme powers on all matters on which the separate states were not competent to act, as well as the power to veto any and all state laws; and (2) at least one house of the legislature would be elected directly by the people.

The New Jersey Plan

As the debate continued, the representatives of New Jersey and other small states became increasingly worried that the convention was going to write a constitution in which the states would be represented in both houses of Congress on the basis of population. If this happened, the smaller states feared they would always be outvoted by the larger ones, and so, with William Paterson of New Jersey as their spokesman, they introduced a new plan. The **New Jersey Plan** proposed to amend, not replace, the old Articles of Confederation. It enhanced the power of the national government (though not as much as the Virginia Plan), but it did so in a way that left the states' representation in Congress unchanged from the Articles—each state would have one vote. Thus not only would the interests of the small states be protected, but Congress itself would remain to a substantial degree the creature of state governments.

If the New Jersey resolutions had been presented first and taken up as the major item of business, it is quite possible they would have become the framework for the document that finally emerged. But they were not. Offered after the convention had been discussing the Virginia Plan for two weeks, the resolutions encountered a reception very different from what they may have received if introduced earlier. The debate had the delegates already thinking in terms of a national government that was more independent of the states, and thus it had accustomed them to proposals that, under other circumstances, might have seemed quite radical. On June 19, the first decisive vote of the convention was taken: seven states preferred the Virginia Plan, three states the New Jersey Plan, and one state was split.

With the tide running in favor of a strong national government, the supporters of the small states had to shift their strategy. They now began to focus their efforts on ensuring that the small states could not be outvoted by the larger ones in Congress. One way was to have the members of the lower house elected by the state legislatures rather than the people, with each state getting the same number of seats rather than seats proportional to its population.

The debate was long and feelings ran high, so much so that Benjamin Franklin, the oldest delegate present (at 81 years of age), suggested that each day's meeting begin with a prayer. It turned out that the convention could not even agree on this:

Hamilton is supposed to have objected that the convention did not need "foreign aid," and others pointed out that the group had no funds with which to hire a minister. And so the argument continued.

> **Great Compromise**
> Plan to have a popularly elected House based on state population and a state-selected Senate, with two members for each state.

The Compromise

Finally, a committee was appointed to meet during the Fourth of July holidays to work out a compromise, and the convention adjourned to await its report. Little is known of what went on in that committee's session, though some were later to say that Franklin played a key role in hammering out the plan that finally emerged. That compromise, the most important reached at the convention, and later called the **Great Compromise** (or sometimes the Connecticut Compromise), was submitted to the full convention on July 5 and debated for another week and a half. The debate might have gone on even longer, but suddenly the hot weather moderated, and Monday, July 16, dawned cool and fresh after a month of misery. On that day, the plan was adopted: five states were in favor, four were opposed, and two did not vote.* Thus, by the narrowest of margins, the structure of the national legislature was set as follows:

- A House of Representatives consisting initially of 65 members apportioned among the states roughly on the basis of population and elected by the people.

- A Senate consisting of two senators from each state to be chosen by the state legislatures.

The Great Compromise reconciled the interests of small and large states by allowing the former to predominate in the Senate and the latter in the House. This reconciliation was necessary to ensure there would be support for a strong national government from small as well as large states. It represented major concessions on the part of several groups. Madison, for one, was deeply opposed to the idea of having the states equally represented in the Senate. He saw in that a way for the states to hamstring the national government and much preferred some measure of proportional representation in both houses. Delegates from other states worried that representation on the

Independence Hall in Philadelphia.

Andre Jenny / Alamy

*The states in favor were Connecticut, Delaware, Maryland, New Jersey, and North Carolina. Those opposed were Georgia, Pennsylvania, South Carolina, and Virginia. Massachusetts was split down the middle; the New York delegates had left the convention. New Hampshire and Rhode Island were absent.

republic A government in which elected representatives make the decisions.

basis of population in the House of Representatives would enable the large states to dominate legislative affairs. Although the margin by which the compromise was accepted was razor-thin, it held firm. In time, most of the delegates from the dissenting states accepted it.

After the Great Compromise, many more issues had to be resolved, but by now a spirit of accommodation had developed. When one delegate proposed having Congress choose the president, another, James Wilson, proposed that he be elected directly by the people. When neither side of that argument prevailed, a committee invented a plan for an "electoral college" that would choose the president. When some delegates wanted the president chosen for a life term, others proposed a seven-year term, and still others wanted the term limited to three years without eligibility for reelection. The convention settled on a four-year term with no bar to reelection. Some states wanted the Supreme Court picked by the Senate; others wanted it chosen by the president. They finally agreed to let the justices be nominated by the president and then confirmed by the Senate.

Finally, on July 26, the proposals that were already accepted, together with a bundle of unresolved issues, were handed over to the Committee of Detail, consisting of five delegates. This committee included Madison and Gouverneur Morris, who was to be the chief draftsman of the document that finally emerged. The committee hardly contented itself with mere "details," however. It inserted some new proposals and made changes in old ones, drawing for inspiration on existing state constitutions and the members' beliefs as to what the other delegates might accept. On August 6, the report—the first complete draft of the Constitution—was submitted to the convention. There it was debated item by item, revised, amended, and finally, on September 17, approved by all 12 states in attendance. (Not all *delegates* approved, however; three, including Edmund Randolph, who first submitted the Virginia Plan, refused to sign.)

The Constitution and Democracy

A debate continues to rage over whether the Constitution created, or was even intended to create, a democratic government. The answer is complex. The Framers did not intend to create a "pure democracy"— one in which the people rule directly. For one thing, the size of the country and the distances between

settlements would have made that physically impossible. But more importantly, the Framers worried that a government in which all citizens directly participate, as in the New England town meeting, would be a government excessively subject to temporary popular passions and one in which minority rights would be insecure. They intended instead to create a **republic**, by which they meant a government in which a system of representation operates.

The Framers favored a republic over a direct democracy because they believed that government should mediate, not mirror, popular views and that elected officials should represent, not register, majority sentiments. They supposed that most citizens did not have the time, information, interest, and expertise to make reasonable choices among competing policy positions. They suspected that even highly educated people could be manipulated by demagogic leaders who played on their fears and prejudices. They knew that representative democracy often proceeds slowly and prevents sweeping changes in policy, but they cautioned that a government capable of doing great good quickly can also do great harm quickly. They agreed that majority opinion should figure in the enactment of many or most government policies, but they insisted that protection of civil rights and civil liberties—the right to a fair trial; the freedom of speech, press, and religion; or the right to vote itself—ought never to hinge on a popular vote. Above all, they embraced representative democracy because they saw it as a way of minimizing the chances that power would be abused either by a tyrannical popular majority or by self-serving officeholders.

The Framers were influenced by philosophers who had discussed democracy. Aristotle, who lived four centuries before Christ, defined democracy as the rule of the many; that is, rule by ordinary people, most of whom would be poor. But democracy, he suggested, can easily decay into an oligarchy (rule of the rich) or a tyranny (the rule of a despot). To prevent this, a good political system will be a mixed regime, combining elements of democracy and oligarchy: most people will vote, but talented people will play a large role in managing affairs.

But, as we noted earlier in this chapter, the Framers were strongly influenced by John Locke, the 17th-century English writer who argued against powerful kings and in favor of popular dissent. In Locke's *Second Treatise of Civil Government* (1690), he argued that people can exist in a state of nature— that is, without any ruler—so long as they can find enough food to eat and a way to protect themselves. But food may not be plentiful and, as a result, life may be poor and difficult.

The human desire for self-preservation will lead people to want a government that will enable them to own property and thereby to increase their supply of food. But unlike his English rival, Thomas Hobbes, Locke did not think it necessary to have an all-powerful government. In *Leviathan* (1651), Hobbes had argued that people live in a "war of all against all" and so an absolute, supreme ruler was essential to prevent civil war. Locke disagreed: people can get along with one another if they can securely own their farms and live off what they produce. But for that to happen a decent government must exist with the consent of the governed and be managed by majority rule. To prevent a majority from hurting a minority, Locke wrote, the government should separate its powers, with different and competing legislative and executive branches.

Thus, what the Framers tried to do in 1787 was to create a republic that would protect freedom and private property, a moderate regime that would simultaneously safeguard people and leave them alone.

In designing that republic, the Framers chose, not without argument, to have the members of the House of Representatives elected directly by the people. Some delegates did not want to go even that far. Elbridge Gerry of Massachusetts, who refused to sign the Constitution, argued that though "the people do not want [that is, lack] virtue," they often are the "dupes of pretended patriots." Roger Sherman of Connecticut agreed. But George Mason of Virginia and James Wilson of Pennsylvania carried the day when they argued that "no government could long subsist without the confidence of the people," and this required "drawing the most numerous branch of the legislature directly from the people." Popular elections for the House were approved: six states were in favor, two opposed.

But though popular rule was to be one element of the new government, it was not to be the only one. State legislatures, not the people, would choose the senators; electors, not the people directly, would choose the president. As we have seen, without these arrangements, there would have been no Constitution at all, for the small states adamantly opposed any proposal that would have given undue power to the large ones. And direct popular election of the president would clearly have made the populous states the dominant ones. In short, the Framers wished to observe the principle of majority rule, but they felt that, on the most important questions, two kinds of majorities were essential—a majority of the voters and a majority of the states.

The power of the Supreme Court to declare an act of Congress unconstitutional—**judicial review**—is also a way of limiting the power of popular majorities. It is not clear whether the Framers intended that there be judicial review, but there is little doubt that in the Framers' minds the fundamental law, the Constitution, had to be safeguarded against popular passions. They made the process for amending

the Constitution easier than it had been under the Articles but still relatively difficult.

An amendment can be proposed either by a two-thirds vote of both houses of Congress *or* by a national convention called by Congress at the request of two-thirds of the states.[†] Once proposed, an amendment must be ratified by three-fourths of the states, either through their legislatures or through special ratifying conventions in each state. Twenty-seven amendments have survived this process, all of them proposed by Congress and all but one (the Twenty-first Amendment) ratified by state legislatures rather than state conventions.

judicial review The power of the courts to declare laws unconstitutional.

federalism Government authority shared by national and local governments.

In short, the answer to the question of whether the Constitution brought into being a democratic government is yes, if by *democracy* one means a system of representative government based on popular consent. The degree of that consent has changed since 1787, and the institutions embodying that consent can take different forms. One form, rejected in 1787, gives all political authority to one set of representatives, directly elected by the people. (That is the case, for example, in most parliamentary regimes, such as the United Kingdom, and in some city governments in the United States.) The other form of democracy is one in which different sets of officials, chosen directly or indirectly by different groups of people, share political power. (That is the case with the United States and a few other nations where the separation of powers is intended to operate.)

Key Principles

The American version of representative democracy was based on two major principles: the separation of powers and federalism. In America, political power was to be shared by three separate branches of government; in parliamentary democracies, that power was concentrated in a single, supreme legislature. In America, political authority was divided between a national government and several state governments—**federalism**—whereas in most European systems authority was centralized in the national government. Neither of these principles was especially controversial at Philadelphia.

[†]There have been many attempts to assemble a new constitutional convention. In the 1960s, 33 states, one short of the required number, requested a convention to consider the reapportionment of state legislatures. In the 1980s, efforts were made to call a convention to consider amendments to ban abortions and to require a balanced federal budget.

enumerated powers
Powers given to the national government alone.

reserved powers
Powers given to the state government alone.

concurrent powers
Powers shared by the national and state governments.

checks and balances
Authority shared by three branches of government.

The delegates began their work in broad agreement that separated powers and some measure of federalism were necessary, and both the Virginia and New Jersey plans contained a version of each. How much federalism should be written into the Constitution was quite controversial, however.

Under these two principles, governmental powers in this country can be divided into three categories. The powers given to the national government exclusively are the delegated or **enumerated powers**. They include the authority to print money, declare war, make treaties, conduct foreign affairs, and regulate commerce among the states and with foreign nations. Those given exclusively to the states are the **reserved powers** and include the power to issue licenses and to regulate commerce wholly within a state. Those shared by both the national and the state governments are called **concurrent powers** and include collecting taxes, building roads, borrowing money, and maintaining courts.

Government and Human Nature

The desirability of separating powers and leaving the states equipped with a broad array of rights and responsibilities was not controversial at the Philadelphia convention because the Framers' experiences with British rule and state government under the Articles had shaped their view of human nature. These experiences had taught most of the Framers that people would seek their own advantage in and out of politics; this pursuit of self-interest, unchecked, would lead some people to exploit others. Human

HOW THINGS WORK

Checks and Balances

The Constitution creates a system of *separate* institutions that *share* powers. Because the three branches of government share powers, each can (partially) check the powers of the others. This is the system of **checks and balances**. The major checks possessed by each branch are listed below.

Congress

1. Can check the president in these ways:

   a. By refusing to pass a bill the president wants

   b. By passing a law over the president's veto

   c. By using the impeachment powers to remove the president from office

   d. By refusing to approve a presidential appointment (Senate only)

   e. By refusing to ratify a treaty the president has signed (Senate only)

2. Can check the federal courts in these ways:

   a. By changing the number and jurisdiction of the lower courts

   b. By using the impeachment powers to remove a judge from office

   c. By refusing to approve a person nominated to be a judge (Senate only)

The President

1. Can check Congress by vetoing a bill it has passed

2. Can check the federal courts by nominating judges

The Courts

1. Can check Congress by declaring a law unconstitutional

2. Can check the president by declaring actions by him or his subordinates unconstitutional or not authorized by law

In addition to these checks specifically provided for in the Constitution, each branch has informal ways of checking the others. For example, the president can try to withhold information from Congress (on the grounds of "executive privilege"), and Congress can try to get information by mounting an investigation.

The exact meaning of the various checks is explained in Chapter 13 on Congress, Chapter 14 on the presidency, and Chapter 16 on the courts.

nature was good enough to make it possible to have a decent government based on popular consent, but it was not good enough to make it inevitable.

One solution to this problem would be to improve human nature. Ancient political philosophers such as Aristotle believed that the first task of any government was to cultivate virtue among the governed. Many Americans were of the same mind. To them, Americans would first have to become good people before they could have a good government. Samuel Adams, a leader of the Boston Tea Party, said that the new nation must become a "Christian Sparta." Others spoke of the need to cultivate frugality, industry, temperance, and simplicity.

But to James Madison and the other architects of the Constitution, the deliberate cultivation of virtue would require a government too strong and thus too dangerous to liberty, at least at the national level. Self-interest, freely pursued within reasonable limits, was a more practical and durable solution to the problem of government than any effort to improve the virtue of the citizenry. He wanted, he said, to make republican government possible "even in the absence of political virtue."

Madison argued that the very self-interest that leads people toward factionalism and tyranny might, if properly harnessed by appropriate constitutional arrangements, provide a source of unity and a guarantee of liberty. This harnessing was to be accomplished by dividing the offices of the new government among many people and giving to the holder of each office the "necessary means and personal motives to resist encroachments of the others." In this way, "ambition must be made to counteract ambition" so that "the private interest of every individual may be a sentinel over the public rights."[12]

If men were angels, all this would be unnecessary. But Madison and the other delegates pragmatically insisted on taking human nature pretty much as it was, and therefore they adopted "this policy of supplying, by opposite and rival interests, the defect of better motives."[13] The **separation of powers** would work, not in spite of the imperfections of human nature, but because of them.

So it also is with federalism. By dividing power between the states and the national government, one level of government can serve as a check on the other. This should provide a "double security" to the rights of the people: "The different governments will control each other, at the same time that each will be controlled by itself."[14] This was especially likely to happen in America, Madison thought, because it was a large country filled with diverse interests—rich and poor, Protestant and Catholic, northerner and southerner, farmer and merchant, creditor and debtor. Each of these interests would constitute a **faction** that would seek its own advantage. One

faction might come to dominate government, or a part of government, in one place, and a different and rival faction might dominate it in another. The pulling and hauling among these factions would prevent any single government—say, that of New York—from dominating all of government. The division of powers among several governments would provide virtually every faction an opportunity to gain some—but not full—power.

separation of powers Constitutional authority is shared by three different branches of government.

faction A group with a distinct political interest.

Federalists Those who favor a stronger national government.

Antifederalists Those who favor a weaker national government.

The Constitution and Liberty

A more difficult question is whether the Constitution created a system of government that would respect personal liberties. In fact, that is the question that was debated in the states when the document was presented for ratification. The proponents of the Constitution called themselves the **Federalists** (though they might more accurately have been called "nationalists"). The opponents came to be known as the **Antifederalists** (though they might more accurately have been called "states' rights advocates").[‡] To be put into effect, the Constitution had to be approved at ratifying conventions in at least nine states. This was perhaps the most democratic feature of the Constitution: it had to be accepted, not by the existing Congress (still limping along under the Articles of Confederation), nor by the state legislatures, but by special conventions elected by the people.

Though democratic, the process established by the Framers for ratifying the Constitution was technically illegal. The Articles of Confederation, which still governed, could be amended only with the approval of all 13 state legislatures. The Framers wanted to bypass these legislatures because they feared that, for reasons of ideology or out of a desire to retain their powers, the legislators would oppose the Constitution. The Framers wanted ratification

[‡]To the delegates a truly "federal" system was one, like the New Jersey Plan, that allowed for very strong states and a weak national government. When the New Jersey Plan lost, the delegates who defeated it began using the word *federal* to describe their plan even though it called for a stronger national government. Thus men who began as "Federalists" at the convention ultimately became known as "Antifederalists" during the struggle over ratification.

coalition An alliance of groups.

with less than the consent of all 13 states because they knew that such unanimity could not be attained. And indeed the conventions in North Carolina and Rhode Island did initially reject the Constitution.

The Antifederalist View

The great issue before the state conventions was liberty, not democracy. The opponents of the new Constitution, the Antifederalists, had a variety of objections but were in general united by the belief that liberty could be secure only in a small republic in which the rulers were physically close to—and closely checked by—the ruled. Their central objection was stated by a group of Antifederalists at the ratifying convention in an essay published just after they had lost: "a very extensive territory cannot be governed on the principles of freedom, otherwise than by a confederation of republics."[15]

These dissenters argued that a strong national government would be distant from the people and would use its powers to annihilate or absorb the functions that properly belonged to the states. Congress would

tax heavily, the Supreme Court would overrule state courts, and the president would come to head a large standing army. (Since all these things have occurred, we cannot dismiss the Antifederalists as cranky obstructionists who opposed without justification the plans of the Framers.) These critics argued that the nation needed, at best, a loose confederation of states, with most of the powers of government kept firmly in the hands of state legislatures and state courts.

But if a stronger national government was to be created, the Antifederalists argued, it should be hedged about with many more restrictions than those in the constitution then under consideration. They proposed several such limitations, including narrowing the jurisdiction of the Supreme Court, checking the president's power by creating a council that would review his actions, leaving military affairs in the hands of the state militias, increasing the size of the House of Representatives so that it would reflect a greater variety of popular interests, and reducing or eliminating the power of Congress to levy taxes. And some of them insisted that a *bill of rights* be added to the Constitution.

James Madison gave his answer to these criticisms in *Federalist* No. 10 and No. 51 (reprinted in the Appendix with a reading guide). It was a bold answer, for it flew squarely in the face of widespread popular sentiment and much philosophical writing. Following the great French political philosopher Montesquieu, many Americans believed liberty was safe only in small societies governed either by direct democracy or by large legislatures with small districts and frequent turnover among members.

Madison argued quite the opposite—that liberty is safest in *large* (or as he put it, "extended") republics. In a small community, he said, there will be relatively few differences in opinion or interest; people will tend to see the world in much the same way. If anyone dissents or pursues an individual interest, he or she will be confronted by a massive majority and will have few, if any, allies. But in a large republic there will be many opinions and interests; as a result, it will be hard for a tyrannical majority to form or organize, and anyone with an unpopular view will find it easier to acquire allies. If Madison's argument seems strange or abstract, ask yourself the following question: if I have an unpopular opinion, an exotic lifestyle, or an unconventional interest, will I find greater security living in a small town or a big city?

By favoring a large republic, Madison was not trying to stifle democracy. Rather, he was attempting to show how democratic government really works, and what can make it work better. To rule, different interests must come together and form a **coalition**—that is, an alliance. In *Federalist* No. 51, he argued that the coalitions that formed in a large republic would be more moderate than those that formed in a small

FIGURE 2.2 **Ratification of the Federal Constitution by State Constitutions, 1787–1790.**

MAINE (MA)

Lake Huron

Lake Ontario

Lake Erie

NEW YORK

NH

MA

CT

RI

PENNSYLVANIA

NJ

MD

DE

VIRGINIA

ATLANTIC OCEAN

NORTH CAROLINA

SOUTH CAROLINA

GEORGIA

- Strongly in favor, ratified early
- Initially opposed, later ratified
- Ratified initially after close struggle

© Cengage Learning

one because the bigger the republic, the greater the variety of interests, and thus the more a coalition of the majority would have to accommodate a diversity of interests and opinions if it hoped to succeed. He concluded that in a nation the size of the United States, with its enormous variety of interests, "a coalition of a majority of the whole society could seldom take place on any other principles than those of justice and the general good." Whether he was right in that prediction is a matter to which we shall return repeatedly.

The implication of Madison's arguments was daring, for he was suggesting that the national government should be at some distance from the people and insulated from their momentary passions, because the people did not always want to do the right thing. Liberty was threatened as much (or even more) by public passions and popularly based factions as by strong governments. Now the Antifederalists themselves had no very lofty view of human nature, as is evidenced by the deep suspicion with which they viewed "power-seeking" officeholders. What Madison did was take this view to its logical conclusion, arguing that if people could be corrupted by office, they could also be corrupted by factional self-interest. Thus the government had to be designed to prevent both the politicians and the people from using it for ill-considered or unjust purposes.

To argue in 1787 against the virtues of small democracies was like arguing against motherhood. Moreover, the Federalists' counterargument involved many steps: representative democracy over direct democracy; a large republic over a small republic; diversity of economic, religious, and other interests over homogeneity of such interests; and barriers, not boosts, to majority group formation and influence. Still, the Federalists prevailed, probably because many citizens were convinced that a reasonably strong national government was essential if the nation were to stand united against foreign enemies, facilitate commerce among the states, guard against domestic insurrections, and keep one faction from oppressing another. The political realities of the moment and the recent bitter experiences with the Articles probably counted for more in ratifying the Constitution than Madison's arguments. His cause was helped by the fact that, for all their legitimate concerns and their uncanny instinct for what the future might bring, the Antifederalists could offer no agreed-upon alternative to the new Constitution. In politics, then as now, you cannot beat something with nothing.

But this does not explain why the Framers failed to add a bill of rights to the Constitution. If they were so preoccupied with liberty, why didn't they take this most obvious step toward protecting liberty, especially since the Antifederalists were demanding it? Some historians have suggested that this omission was evidence that liberty was not as important to the Framers as they claimed. In fact, when one delegate suggested that a bill of rights be drawn up, the state delegations at the convention unanimously voted the idea down. There were several reasons for this.

First, the Constitution, as written, *did* contain a number of specific guarantees of individual liberty, including the right of trial by jury in criminal cases and the privilege of the writ of habeas corpus. The liberties guaranteed in the Constitution (before the **Bill of Rights** was added) are listed on the following (turn) page.

Bill of Rights First ten amendments to the Constitution.

habeas corpus An order to produce an arrested person before a judge.

bill of attainder A law that declares a person, without a trial, to be guilty of a crime.

ex post facto law A law that makes an act criminal although the act was legal when it was committed.

- Writ of **habeas corpus** may not be suspended (except during invasion or rebellion).

- No **bill of attainder** may be passed by Congress or the states.

- No **ex post facto law** may be passed by Congress or the states.

- Right of trial by jury in criminal cases is guaranteed.

- The citizens of each state are entitled to the privileges and immunities of the citizens of every other state.

- No religious test or qualification for holding federal office is imposed.

- No law impairing the obligation of contracts may be passed by the states.

Second, most states in 1787 had bills of rights. When Elbridge Gerry proposed to the convention that a federal bill of rights be drafted, Roger Sherman rose to observe that it was unnecessary because the state bills of rights were sufficient.[16]

But third, and perhaps most important, the Framers thought they were creating a government with specific, limited powers. It could do, they thought, only what the Constitution gave it the power to do, and nowhere in that document was there permission to infringe on freedom of speech or of the press or to impose cruel and unusual punishments. Some delegates probably feared that if any serious effort were made to list the rights that were guaranteed, later officials might assume that they had the power to do anything not explicitly forbidden.

Need for a Bill of Rights

Whatever their reasons, the Framers made at least a tactical and perhaps a fundamental mistake. It quickly became clear that without at least the promise of a bill of rights, the Constitution would not be ratified. Though the small states, pleased by their equal representation in the Senate, quickly ratified (in Delaware, New Jersey, and Georgia, the vote in the conventions was unanimous), the battle in the large states was intense and the outcome uncertain. In Pennsylvania, Federalist supporters dragged boycotting Antifederalists to the legislature in order to ensure a quorum was present so a convention could be called. There were rumors of other rough tactics.

In Massachusetts, the Constitution was approved by a narrow majority, but only after key leaders promised to obtain a bill of rights. In Virginia, James Madison fought against the fiery Patrick Henry, whose climactic speech against ratification was dramatically punctuated by a noisy thunderstorm outside. The Federalists won by 10 votes. In New York, Alexander Hamilton argued the case for six weeks against the determined opposition of most of the state's key political leaders; he carried the day, but only by three votes, and then only after New York City threatened to secede from the state if it did not ratify.

By June 21, 1788, the ninth state—New Hampshire—had ratified, and the Constitution was law.

Many people think that the first Congress moved quickly to adopt a Bill of Rights—that is, the first ten amendments to the Constitution—in order to satisfy demands made in state ratifying conventions that this be done. Unfortunately, that is not quite right. Of the many criticisms made of the proposed Constitution, hardly any referred to civil liberties. Take, for example, the Massachusetts convention. Several critics, including John Hancock, said they would vote to ratify the document if the new members of Congress did all they could to get nine amendments adopted. But these amendments had nothing to do with free speech or a free press. Instead, they involved the size of the House of Representatives, congressional influence on local elections, the power of Congress to impose taxes, and the need for grand juries in criminal cases.[17] Other speakers wanted an amendment that would have House members stand for election every year. Critics in other states made the same arguments.

Despite the bitterness of the ratification struggle, the new government that took office in 1789–1790, headed by President Washington, was greeted enthusiastically. By the spring of 1790, all 13 states had ratified. There remained, however, the task of fulfilling the promise of amending the document. To that end, James Madison introduced into the first session

HOW THINGS WORK

The Bill of Rights

The First Ten Amendments to the Constitution Grouped by Topic and Purpose

Protections Afforded Citizens to Participate in the Political Process

Amendment 1: Freedom of religion, speech, press, and assembly; the right to petition the government.

Protections Against Arbitrary Police and Court Action

Amendment 4: No unreasonable searches or seizures.

Amendment 5: Grand jury indictment required to prosecute a person for a serious crime.

No "double jeopardy" (being tried twice for the same offense).

Forcing a person to testify against himself or herself prohibited.

No loss of life, liberty, or property without due process.

Amendment 6: Right to speedy, public, impartial trial with defense counsel and right to cross-examine witnesses.

Amendment 7: Jury trials in civil suits where value exceeds $20.

Amendment 8: No excessive bail or fines, no cruel and unusual punishments.

Protections of States' Rights and Unnamed Rights of People

Amendment 9: Unlisted rights are not necessarily denied.

Amendment 10: Powers not delegated to the United States or denied to states are reserved to the states.

Other Amendments

Amendment 2: Right to bear arms.

Amendment 3: Troops may not be quartered in homes in peacetime.

of the First Congress a set of proposals, 12 of which were approved by Congress; 10 of these were ratified by the states and went into effect in 1791. But with only a few exceptions, these bore no relationship to the criticisms made in the state conventions. On what, then did Madison base them? Probably on the Virginia Declaration of Rights, written by George Mason and Madison, and unanimously approved by the Virginia legislature in 1776. These amendments, which no one called a Bill of Rights as late as 1792, did not limit the power of state governments over citizens, only the power of the federal government. Later, the Fourteenth Amendment, as interpreted by the Supreme Court, extended many of the guarantees of the Bill of Rights to cover state governmental action.

The Constitution and Slavery

Though slaves amounted to one-third of the population of the five southern states, nowhere in the Constitution can one find the word *slave* or *slavery*.

To some, the failure of the Constitution to address the question of slavery was a great betrayal of the promise of the Declaration of Independence that "all men are created equal." For the Constitution to be silent on the subject of slavery, and thereby to allow that odious practice to continue, was to convert, by implication, the wording of the Declaration to "all white men are created equal."

It is easy to accuse the signers of the Declaration and the Constitution of hypocrisy. They knew of slavery, many of them owned slaves, and yet they were silent. Indeed, British opponents of the independence movement took special delight in taunting the colonists about their complaints of being "enslaved" to the British Empire while ignoring the slavery in their very midst.

Increasingly, revolutionary leaders during this period spoke to this issue. Thomas Jefferson had tried to get a clause opposing the slave trade put into the Declaration of Independence. James Otis of Boston had attacked slavery and argued that black as well as white men should be free. As revolutionary fervor mounted, so did northern criticism of slavery. The Massachusetts legislature and then the Continental Congress voted to end the slave trade; Delaware prohibited the importation of slaves; Pennsylvania voted to tax slavery out of existence; and Connecticut and Rhode Island decided that all slaves brought into those states would automatically become free.

Slavery continued unabated in the South, defended by some whites because they thought it right, by others because they found it useful. But even in the South there were opponents, though rarely conspicuous ones. George Mason, a large Virginia slaveholder and a delegate to the convention, warned prophetically that "by an inevitable

Deck of a slave ship captured in 1860. Thousands of slaves died on such ships.

chain of causes and effects, providence punishes national sins [slavery] by national calamities."[18]

The blunt fact, however, was that any effort to use the Constitution to end slavery would have meant the end of the Constitution. The southern states would never have signed a document that seriously interfered with slavery. Without the southern states, there would have been a continuation of the Articles of Confederation, which would have left each state entirely sovereign and thus entirely free of any prospective challenge to slavery.

Thus the Framers compromised with slavery; political scientist Theodore Lowi calls this their Greatest Compromise.[19] Slavery is dealt with in three places in the Constitution, though never by name. In determining the representation each state was to have in the House, "three-fifths of all other persons" (that is, of slaves) are to be added to "the whole number of free persons."[20] The South originally wanted slaves to count fully even though, of course, none would be elected to the House; they settled for counting 60 percent of them. The Great (or Connecticut) Compromise favored smaller states, which were mostly northern, by giving each state two senators; but the three-fifths compromise even more strongly favored the South's slaveholding states. For example, apportioned according to its free population, the southern states would have had a combined total of 33 House seats rather than the 47

Does a Constitution Guarantee Freedom?

You may think that the best protection for individual freedom is for a nation to have a written constitution. After all, a constitution is supposed to limit governmental action. But if you look around the world, you will see that a constitution is not enough.

Here are three nations that do not have a written constitution and yet personal freedom is well established:

Israel   New Zealand   United Kingdom

And here are three nations with a written constitution where personal freedom is rare:

Iran   North Korea   Russia

What else must nations have in order to ensure personal freedom?

they claimed. The three-fifths compromise is the primary reason why southern-born presidents, House leaders, and Supreme Court justices generally dominated antebellum American national government.[21]

The convention also agreed not to allow the new government by law or even constitutional amendment to prohibit the importation of slaves until 1808.[22] The South thus had 20 years in which it could acquire more slaves from abroad; after that, Congress was free (but not required) to end the importation. Finally, the Constitution guaranteed that if a slave were to escape his or her master and flee to a free state, the slave would be returned by that state to "the party to whom … service or labour may be due."[23]

The unresolved issue of slavery was to prove the most explosive question of all. Allowing slavery to continue was a fateful decision, one that led to the worst social and political catastrophe in the nation's history—the Civil War. The Framers chose to sidestep the issue in order to create a union that, they hoped, would eventually be strong enough to deal with the problem when it could no longer be postponed. The legacy of that choice reverberates to this day.

The Motives of the Framers

The Framers were not saints or demigods. They were men with political opinions who also had economic interests and human failings. It would be a mistake to conclude that everything they did in 1787 was motivated by a disinterested commitment to the public good. But it would be an equally great mistake to think that what they did was nothing but an effort to line their pockets by producing a government that would serve their own narrow interests. As in almost all human endeavors, the Framers acted out of a mixture of motives. What is truly astonishing is that economic interests played only a modest role in their deliberations.

Economic Interests

Some of the Framers were wealthy; some were not. Some owned slaves; some had none. Some were creditors (having loaned money to the Continental Congress or to private parties); some were deeply in debt. For nearly a century, scholars have argued over just how important these personal interests were in shaping the provisions of the Constitution.

In 1913, Charles Beard, a historian, published a book—*An Economic Interpretation of the Constitution*—arguing that the better-off urban and commercial classes, especially those members who held the IOUs issued by the government to pay for the Revolutionary War, favored the new Constitution because they stood to benefit from it.[24] But in the 1950s, that view was challenged by historians who, after looking carefully at what the Framers owned or owed, concluded that one could not explain the Constitution exclusively or even largely in terms of the economic interests of those who wrote it.[25] Some of the richest delegates, such as Elbridge Gerry of Massachusetts and George Mason of Virginia, refused to sign the document, while many of its key backers—James Madison and James Wilson, for example—were men of modest means or heavy debts.

In the 1980s, a new group of scholars, primarily economists applying more advanced statistical techniques, found evidence that some economic considerations influenced how the Framers voted on some issues during the Philadelphia convention. Interestingly, however, the economic position of the *states* from which they came had a greater effect on their votes than did their *own* monetary condition.[26]

We have already seen how delegates from small states fought to reduce the power of large states and how those from slave-owning states made certain that the Constitution would contain no provision that would threaten slavery.

But contrary to what Beard asserted, the economic interests of the Framers themselves did not dominate the convention. Some delegates owned a lot of public debt they had purchased for low prices. A strong national government of the sort envisaged by the Constitution was more likely than the weak

Continental Congress to pay off this debt at face value, thus making the delegates who owned it much richer. Despite this, the ownership of public debt had no significant effect on how the Framers voted in Philadelphia. Nor did the big land speculators vote their interests. Some, such as George Washington and Robert Morris, favored the Constitution, while others, such as George Mason and William Blount, opposed it.[27]

In sum, the Framers tended to represent their states' interests on important matters. Since they were picked by the states to do so, this is exactly what one would expect. If they had not met in secret, perhaps they would have voted even more often as their constituents wanted.

With the grave and enormous exception of slavery, the Framers usually did not vote their own respective economic interests.

At the popularly elected state ratifying conventions, economic factors played a larger role. Delegates who were merchants, who lived in cities, who owned large amounts of western land, who held government IOUs, and who did not own slaves were more likely to vote to ratify the new Constitution than delegates who were farmers, who did not own public debt, and who did own slaves.[28] There were plenty of exceptions, however. Small farmers dominated the conventions in some states where the vote to ratify was unanimous.

Though interests made a difference, they were not simply elite interests. In most states, the great majority of adult white males could vote for delegates to the ratifying conventions. This means that women and blacks were excluded from the debates, but by the standards of the time—standards that did not change for over a century—the ratification process was remarkably democratic.

The Constitution and Equality

Ideas counted for as much as interests. At stake were two views of the public good. One, espoused by the Federalists, was that a reasonable balance of liberty, order, and progress required a strong national government. The other, defended by the Antifederalists, was that liberty would not be secure in the hands of a powerful, distant government; freedom required decentralization.

Today that debate has a new focus. The defect of the Constitution, to some contemporary critics, is not that the government it created is too strong but that it is too weak. In particular, the national government is too weak to resist the pressures of special interests that reflect and perpetuate social inequality.

This criticism reveals how our understanding of the relationship between liberty and equality

has changed since the Founding. To Jefferson and Madison, citizens naturally differed in their talents and qualities. What had to be guarded against was the use of governmental power to create unnatural and undesirable inequalities. This might happen, for example, if political power was concentrated in the hands of a few people (who could use that power to give themselves special privileges) or if it was used in ways that allowed some private parties to acquire exclusive charters and monopolies. To prevent the inequality that might result from having too strong a government, its powers must be kept strictly limited.

Today, some people think of inequality quite differently. To them, it is the natural social order—the marketplace and the acquisitive talents of people operating in that marketplace—that leads to undesirable inequalities, especially in economic power. The government should be powerful enough to restrain these natural tendencies and produce, by law, a greater degree of equality than society allows when left alone.

To the Framers, liberty and (political) equality were not in conflict; to some people today, these two principles are deeply in conflict. To the Framers, the task was to keep government so limited as to prevent it from creating the worst inequality—political privilege. To some modern observers, the task is to make government strong enough to reduce what they believe is the worst inequality—differences in wealth.

Constitutional Reform: Modern Views

Almost from the day it was ratified, the Constitution has been the object of debate over ways in which it might be improved. These debates have rarely involved the average citizen, who tends to revere the document even if he or she cannot recall all its details. Because of this deep and broad popular support, scholars and politicians have been wary of attacking the Constitution or suggesting many wholesale changes. But such attacks have occurred. During the 1980s—the decade in which we celebrated the bicentennial of its adoption—we heard a variety of suggestions for improving the Constitution, ranging from particular amendments to wholesale revisions. In general there are today, as in the 18th century, two kinds of critics: those who think the federal government is too weak and those who think it is too strong.

Reducing the Separation of Powers

To the first kind of critic, the chief difficulty with the Constitution is the separation of powers. By making every decision the uncertain outcome of the pulling

WHAT'S YOUR ISSUE?

Income Tax Rates

As we noted in Chapter 1, in 1788, the proposed Constitution's chief architect, James Madison, argued that the federal government needed its own "power of taxation," while critics of the proposed Constitution, including Patrick Henry, opposed giving the federal government this power. Madison's view prevailed, but it was not until 1913, with the passage of the Sixteenth Amendment to the Constitution, that the federal government acquired "the power to lay and collect taxes on incomes."

The federal income tax system is progressive, meaning that tax rates rise with income levels. In 2013, there were seven federal "tax brackets": 10, 15, 25, 28, 33, 35, and 39.6 percent. A single person would pay 10 percent in federal income taxes on the first $8,925 he or she earned that year, all the way up to 39.6 percent on every dollar above $400,000 that he or she earned that year. Thus, in 2013, 39.6 percent was the "top marginal income tax rate."

Every year there are proposals in Congress to make the federal income tax system even more steeply progressive, as well as proposals to lower income tax rates across the board. The debates over income tax rates can get quite technical and hard to follow, but you do not need to be an expert to hold an informed opinion on the issue; besides, how this issue gets decided affects just about everyone.

- Have you ever had to pay federal income taxes, and, if so, at what rate did you pay them?

- What, if any, stake do you have in relation to income tax reform proposals, and what is your take on the issue?

- Do you think federal income tax rates should be steeper for everyone, lower for everyone, steeper just for the highest earners, or what?

Today's top marginal federal income rate is low by historical standards. During World War I, the rate peaked at 77 percent. During World War II, it peaked at 91 percent. For most of the period from 1945 to 1985, it was above 50 percent. Students sometimes find this hard to believe: "You mean that more than 70 cents of every dollar in income a high-income person earned was owed to the federal government?"

Yes, but given the tax system's progressivity (the "first dollars" earned are taxed at lower rates than the "last dollars earned"), and accounting for allowable tax deductions for various things (like mortgage interest payments, charitable contributions, and tax-sheltered investments), the actual or "effective tax rate" paid by top earners (what they paid in taxes after all deductions) is lower than the stated top marginal tax rate.

For example, according to the U.S. Internal Revenue Service, in 2009, the top 1 percent of all earners had incomes that averaged about $344,000; this 1 percent of all taxpayers paid 36.7 percent of all federal income taxes and had an effective federal income tax rate of 24 percent. The top 10 percent of all earners had incomes that averaged $112,000; this 10 percent of all taxpayers paid 70 percent of all federal income taxes and had an effective federal income tax rate of 18 percent. And the top quarter of all earners had incomes that averaged $66,000; this top 25 percent of all taxpayers paid 87.3 percent of all federal income taxes and had an effective tax rate of 14.6 percent.

and hauling between the president and Congress, the Constitution precludes the emergence—except perhaps in times of crisis—of the kind of effective national leadership the country needs. In this view, our nation today faces a number of challenges that require prompt, decisive, and comprehensive action. Our problem is gridlock. Our position of international leadership, the dangerous and unprecedented proliferation of nuclear weapons among the nations of the globe, and the need to find ways of stimulating economic growth while reducing our deficit and conserving our environment—all these situations require the president be able to formulate and carry out policies free of some of the pressures and delays from interest groups and members of Congress tied to local interests.

Not only would this increase in presidential authority make for better policies, these critics argue, it would also help the voters hold the president and his party accountable for their actions. As matters now stand, nobody in government can be held responsible for policies: everyone takes the credit for successes and no one is willing to take the blame for failures. Typically, the president, who tends to be the major source of new programs, cannot get his policies adopted by Congress without long delays and much bargaining, the result of which often is some watered-down compromise that neither the president nor Congress really likes but that each must settle for if anything is to be done at all.

Finally, critics of the separation of powers complain that the government agencies responsible for implementing a program are exposed to undue interference from legislators and special interests. In this view, the president is supposed to be in charge of the bureaucracy but in fact must share this authority with countless members of Congress and congressional committees.

Not all critics of the separation of powers agree with all these points, nor do they all agree on what should be done about the problems. But they all have in common a fear that the separation of powers makes the president too weak and insufficiently accountable. Their proposals for reducing the separation of powers include the following:

- Allow the president to appoint members of Congress to serve in the cabinet (the Constitution forbids members of Congress from holding any federal appointive office while in Congress).

- Allow the president to dissolve Congress and call for a special election (elections now can be held only on the schedule determined by the calendar).

- Allow Congress to require a president who has lost its confidence to face the country in a special election before his term would normally end.

- Require the presidential and congressional candidates to run as a team in each congressional district; thus a presidential candidate who carries a given district could be sure the congressional candidate of his party would also win in that district.

- Have the president serve a single six-year term instead of being eligible for up to two four-year terms; this would presumably free the president to lead without having to worry about reelection.

- Lengthen the terms of members of the House of Representatives from two to four years so that the entire House would stand for reelection at the same time as the president.[29]

Some of these proposals are offered by critics out of a desire to make the American system of government work more like the British parliamentary system, in which, as we shall see in Chapters 13 and 14, the prime minister is the undisputed leader of the majority in the British Parliament. The parliamentary system is the major alternative in the world today to the American separation-of-powers system.

Both the diagnoses and the remedies proposed by these critics of the separation of powers have been challenged. Many defenders of our present constitutional system believe that nations, such as the United Kingdom, with a different, more unified political system have done no better than the United States in dealing with the problems of economic growth, national security, and environmental protection. Moreover, they argue, close congressional scrutiny of presidential proposals has improved these policies more often than it has weakened them. Finally, congressional "interference" in the work of government agencies is a good way of ensuring that the average citizen can fight back against the bureaucracy; without that so-called interference, citizens and interest groups might be helpless before big and powerful agencies.

Each of the specific proposals, defenders of the present constitutional system argue, would either make matters worse or have, at best, uncertain effects. Adding a few members of Congress to the president's cabinet would not provide much help in getting his program through Congress; there are 535 senators and representatives, and probably only about half a dozen would be in the cabinet. Giving either the president or Congress the power to call a special election in between the regular elections (every two or four years) would cause needless confusion and great expense; the country would live under the threat of being in a perpetual political campaign with even weaker political parties. Linking the fate of the president and congressional candidates by having them run as a team in each district would reduce the stabilizing and moderating effect of having them elected separately. A Republican presidential candidate who wins in the new system would have a Republican majority in the House; a Democratic candidate winner would have a Democratic majority. We might as a result expect dramatic changes in policy as the political pendulum swung back and forth. Giving presidents a single six-year term would indeed free them from the need to worry about reelection, but it is precisely that worry that keeps presidents reasonably concerned about what the American people want.

Making the System Less Democratic

The second kind of critic of the Constitution thinks the government does too much, not too little. Though the separation of powers at one time may have slowed the growth of government and moderated the policies it adopted, in the last few decades government has grown helter-skelter. The problem, these critics argue, is not that democracy is a bad idea but that democracy can produce bad—or at least unintended—results if the government caters to the special-interest claims of the citizens rather than to their long-term values.

To see how these unintended results might occur, imagine a situation in which every citizen thinks the government grows too big, taxes too heavily, and spends too much. Each citizen wants the government made smaller by reducing the benefits other

CONSTITUTIONAL CONNECTIONS

Women and the Constitution

Women were mentioned nowhere in the Constitution when it was written in 1787. Moreover, Article I, which set forth the provisions for electing members of the House of Representatives, granted the vote to those people who were allowed to vote for members of the lower house of the legislature in the states in which they resided. In no state at the time could women participate in those elections. In no state could they vote in any elections or hold any offices. Furthermore, wherever the Constitution uses a pronoun, it uses the masculine form—*he* or *him*.

In another sense, no: Wherever the Constitution or the Bill of Rights defines a right that people are to have, it either grants that right to "persons" or "citizens," not to "men," or it makes no mention at all of people or gender. For example:

- "The *citizens* of each State shall be entitled to all privileges and immunities of citizens of the several States."

[Art. I, sec. 9]

- "No *person* shall be convicted of treason unless on the testimony of two witnesses to the same overt act, or on confession in open court."

[Art. III, sec. 3]

- "No bill of attainder or ex post facto law shall be passed."

[Art. I, sec. 9]

- "The right of the *people* to be secure in their persons, houses, papers, and effects, against unreasonable searches and seizures, shall not be violated."

[Amend. IV]

- "No *person* shall be held to answer for a capital, or otherwise infamous crime, unless on presentment or indictment of a grand jury ... nor shall any *person* be subject for the same offense to be twice put in jeopardy of life or limb; ... nor be deprived of life, liberty, or property, without due process of law."

[Amend. V]

- "In all criminal prosecutions the *accused* shall enjoy the right to a speedy and public trial, by an impartial jury."

[Amend. VI]

Moreover, when the qualifications for elective office are stated, the word *person,* not *man,* is used.

- "No *person* shall be a Representative who shall not have attained to the age of twenty-five years."

[Art. I, sec. 2]

- "No *person* shall be a Senator who shall not have attained to the age of thirty years."

[Art. I, sec. 3]

- "No *person* except a natural born citizen ... shall be eligible to the office of President; neither shall any *person* be eligible to that office who shall not have attained to the age of thirty-five years."

[Art. II, sec. 1]

In places, the Constitution and the Bill of Rights used the pronoun *he,* but always in the context of referring back to a *person* or *citizen.* At the time, and until quite recently, the male pronoun was often used in legal documents to refer generically to both men and women.

Thus, though the Constitution did not give women the right to vote until the Nineteenth Amendment was ratified in 1920, it did use language that extended fundamental rights, and access to office, to women and men equally.

Of course, what the Constitution permitted did not necessarily occur. State and local laws denied women rights that in principle they ought to have enjoyed. Except for a brief period in New Jersey, no women voted in statewide elections until, in 1869, they were given the right to cast ballots in territorial elections in Wyoming.

When women were first elected to Congress, there was no need to change the Constitution; nothing in it restricted office-holding to men.

When women were given the right to vote by constitutional amendment, it was not necessary to amend any existing language in the Constitution, because nothing in the Constitution itself denied women the right to vote; the amendment simply added a new right:

- "The right of citizens of the United States to vote shall not be denied or abridged by the United States or any state on account of sex."

[Amend. XIX]

Source: Adapted from Robert Goldwin, "*Why Blacks, Women and Jews Are Not Mentioned in the Constitution,*" Commentary (May 1987): 28–33.

people get—but not by reducing the benefits he or she gets. In fact, such citizens may even be willing to see their own benefits cut, provided everyone else's benefits are cut as well, and by a like amount.

But the political system attends to individual wants, not general preferences. It gives aid to farmers, contracts to industry, grants to professors, pensions to the elderly, and loans to students. As someone once said, the government is like an adding machine: during elections candidates campaign by promising to do more for whatever group is dissatisfied with what the incumbents are doing for it. As a result, most elections bring to office men and women committed to doing more for somebody. The grand total of all these additions is more for everybody. Few politicians have an incentive to do less for anybody.

To remedy this state of affairs, these critics suggest various mechanisms, but principally a constitutional amendment that would either set a limit on the amount of money the government could collect in taxes each year or require that each year the government have a balanced budget (that is, not spend more than it takes in in taxes), or both. In some versions of these plans, an extraordinary majority (say, 60 percent) of Congress could override these limits, and the limits would not apply in wartime.

The effect of such amendments, the proponents claim, would be to force Congress and the president to look at the big picture—the grand total of what they are spending—rather than just to operate the adding machine by pushing the "add" button over and over again. If they could spend only so much during a given year, they would have to allocate what they spend among all rival claimants. For example, if more money were to be spent on the poor, less could then be spent on the military, or vice versa.

amendments A new provision in the Constitution that has been ratified by the states.

line-item veto An executive's ability to block a particular provision in a bill passed by the legislature.

Some critics of an overly powerful federal government think these amendments will not be passed or may prove unworkable; instead, they favor enhancing the president's power to block spending by giving him a **line-item veto**. Most state governors can veto a particular part of a bill and approve the rest using a line-item veto. The theory is that such a veto would better equip the president to stop unwarranted spending without vetoing the other provisions of a bill. In 1996, President Clinton signed the Line Item Veto Act, passed by the 104th Congress. But despite its name, the new law did not give the president full line-item veto power (only a change in the Constitution could confer that power). Instead the law gave the president authority to selectively eliminate individual items in large appropriations bills, expansions in certain

HOW THINGS WORK

Ways of Amending the Constitution

Under Article V, there are two ways to *propose* **amendments** to the Constitution and two ways to *ratify* them.

To Propose an Amendment

1. Two-thirds of both houses of Congress vote to propose an amendment, *or*

2. Two-thirds of the state legislatures ask Congress to call a national convention to propose amendments.

To Ratify an Amendment

1. Three-fourths of the state legislatures approve it, *or*

2. Ratifying conventions in three-fourths of the states approve it.

Some Key Facts

- Only the first method of proposing an amendment has been used.

- The second method of ratification has been used only once, to ratify the Twenty-first Amendment (repealing Prohibition).

- Congress may limit the time within which a proposed amendment must be ratified. The usual limitation has been seven years.

- Thousands of proposals have been made, but only 33 have obtained the necessary two-thirds vote in Congress.

- Twenty-seven amendments have been ratified.

- The first 10 amendments, ratified on December 15, 1791, are known as the Bill of Rights.

income-transfer programs, and tax breaks (giving the president what budget experts call *enhanced rescission authority*). But it also left Congress free to craft bills in ways that would give the president few opportunities to veto (or *rescind*) favored items. For example, Congress could still force the president to accept or reject an entire appropriations bill simply by tagging on this sentence: "Appropriations provided under this act (or title or section) shall not be subject to the provisions of the Line Item Veto Act." In *Clinton et al. v. New York et al.* (1998), the Supreme Court struck down the 1996 law, holding 6 to 3 that the Constitution does not allow the president to cancel specific items in tax and spending legislation. Clinton's successor, President George W. Bush, championed the line-item veto, but to no avail; and, when asked about the line-item veto in February 2009, President Barack Obama's press secretary, Robert Gibbs, quipped that the new president would "love to take that for a test drive."

Finally, some critics of a powerful government feel that the real problem arises not from an excess of "adding-machine" democracy but from the growth in the power of the federal courts, as described in Chapter 16. These critics would like to devise a set of laws or constitutional amendments that would narrow the authority of federal courts.

The opponents of these suggestions argue that constitutional amendments to restrict the level of taxes or to require a balanced budget are unworkable, even assuming—which they do not—that a smaller government is desirable. There is no precise, agreed-upon way to measure how much the government spends or to predict in advance how much it will receive in taxes during the year; thus defining and enforcing a "balanced budget" is no easy matter. Since the government can always borrow money, it might easily evade any spending limits. It has also shown great ingenuity in spending money in ways that never appear as part of the regular budget.

The line-item veto may or may not be a good idea. Unless the Constitution is amended to permit it, future presidents will have to do without it. The states, where some governors have long had the veto, are quite different from the federal government in power and responsibilities. Whether a line-item veto would work as well in Washington, D.C. as it does in many state capitals is something that we may simply never know.

Finally, proposals to curtail judicial power are thinly veiled attacks, the opponents argue, on the ability of the courts to protect essential citizen's rights. If Congress and the people do not like the way the Supreme Court has interpreted the Constitution, they can always amend the Constitution to change a specific ruling; there is no need to adopt some across-the-board limitation on court powers.

Who Is Right?

Some of the arguments of these two sets of critics of the Constitution may strike you as plausible or even entirely convincing. Whatever you may ultimately decide, decide nothing for now. One cannot make or remake a constitution based entirely on abstract reasoning or unproven factual arguments. Even when the Constitution was first written in

People write on a large copy of the U.S. Constitution in Washington, D.C., bringing their perspective on the relevance of the 18th-century document today.

Brendan Hoffman/Getty Images

WHAT WOULD YOU DO?

MEMORANDUM

To: *Elizabeth Anthony, Arkansas state senate majority leader*

From: *George Morris, chief of staff*

Subject: *Proposal for a new constitutional convention*

In the 1990s, Arkansas and several other states approved term limits for their members of Congress, but the Supreme Court ruled in 1995 that states do not have this authority. Now term-limit advocates are pursuing a broader strategy, calling for states to approve legislation that would require Congress to consider several amendment proposals, including term limits and abolishing the Electoral College to permit the direct popular election of the president. The Arkansas General Assembly passed such a bill last week, and several senators in your party have declared their support.

Arguments for:

1. The Twenty-second Amendment restricts presidents to two terms, so members of Congress should face similar limits.

2. Term limits will ensure that national leaders do not become career politicians.

3. The public favors the direct popular election of the president; this constitutional convention would make possible abolishing the Electoral College.

Arguments against:

1. Limiting members of Congress to two terms would increase the power of lobbyists, congressional staffers, and administrative officials.

News »

Twenty-Eight States Back Proposal for Constitutional Convention

Yesterday Pennsylvania's legislature approved a proposal for a constitutional convention, becoming the twenty-eighth state to do so. The Constitution states that Congress shall hold a convention for proposing amendments at the request of two-thirds of the state legislatures, but it has never happened in U.S. history. Six more states must approve for Congress to take action, and two announced yesterday that they plan to review similar proposals this week.

2. The Electoral College encourages a two-party system; a direct popular vote for the president would require runoff elections if no candidate won a majority.

3. The Constitutional Convention of 1787 was held in secret and involved only a few dozen people; today it would be heavily covered by the press and involve hundreds, perhaps thousands of people. No one knows what changes it might make.

Your decision:

Favor legislation _____   Oppose legislation _____

1787, it was not an exercise in abstract philosophy but rather an effort to solve pressing, practical problems in the light of a theory of human nature, the lessons of past experience, and a close consideration of how governments in other countries and at other times had worked.

Just because the Constitution is more than 200 years old does not mean it is out of date. The crucial questions are these: How well has it worked over the long sweep of American history? How well has it worked compared to the constitutions of other democratic nations?

The only way to answer those questions is to study American government closely—with special attention to its historical evolution and to the practices of other nations. That is what this book is about. Of course, even after close study, people will still disagree about whether our system should be changed. People want different things and evaluate human experience according to different beliefs. But if we first understand how, in fact, the government works and why it has produced the policies it has, we can then argue more intelligently about how best to achieve our wants and give expression to our beliefs.

LEARNING OBJECTIVES

1. Why was a Bill of Rights adopted so soon after the ratification of the Constitution?

A Bill of Rights was adopted by the First Congress because so many states had asked for amendments in exchange for their votes to ratify the Constitution. But what they got was quite different from what they requested. James Madison, in writing the amendments, used much of the language of the Virginia Declaration of Rights.

2. Why did so many authors of the Constitution fear factions?

Many Framers, but especially Madison, feared factions because human nature divides people, and when they are divided they are likely to oppose one another and so threaten the chances of arriving at the common good.

3. Why did the Framers agree on the idea of a separation of powers?

Almost all of the Framers agreed that our government should be based on the separation of powers among its three branches because such a system would provide better checks on power than what they had experienced with England.

4. What is the difference between a democracy and a republic?

A democracy means rule by the people; direct democracy means letting every important issue be decided by popular vote. A republic is a government in which authority has been given to elected representatives. The United States is a republic in which members of the House of Representatives are selected in democratic elections, members of the Senate (at least initially) were selected by state legislatures, and the courts are staffed by appointed judges.

5. How did Thomas Hobbes and John Locke differ about democracy, and which thinker did the Framers follow?

Hobbes thought democracy was impossible because the self-interest of people required an all-powerful government to prevent a "war of all against all;" Locke, by contrast, believed that people, though self-interested, can get along with one another if they consent to the government and it is ruled by the majority. The Framers followed Locke.

6. What branch of government has the greatest power?

Initially, Congress had the most authority. As we shall see in later chapters, the president and the federal courts grew in power, but even so Congress remains the most important institution.

7. Does the Constitution tell us what goals the government should serve?

Not really. The preface tells us what the Founders hoped the federal government would do, but that preface has no legal authority. By and large, the government has to set its own goals.

8. Whose freedom does the Constitution protect?

It was intended to protect everybody's freedom, except that of slaves. To create a national government, it was necessary that the Constitution ignore slavery, but without the Constitution, there would have been no national government to challenge slavery during the Civil War. Though women are not mentioned, in fact there is nothing in the Constitution to prevent them from holding national office or from voting in federal elections. Voting rights were to be decided by each state until the passage of a constitutional amendment (the Nineteenth, ratified in 1920) that prohibited the states from denying the vote to women.

TO LEARN MORE

To find historical and legal documents:
TeachingAmericanHistory.org

National Constitution Center: **www.constitutioncenter.org**

Congress: **thomas.loc.gov/** (choose Historical Documents)

To look at court cases about the Constitution: Cornell University, **www.law.cornell.edu/supct**

Bailyn, Bernard. *The Ideological Origins of the American Revolution*. Cambridge: Harvard University Press, 1967. A brilliant account of how the American colonists formed and justified the idea of independence.

Becker, Carl L. *The Declaration of Independence*. New York: Vintage, 1942. The classic account of the meaning of the Declaration.

Federalist papers. By Alexander Hamilton, James Madison, and John Jay. The definitive edition, edited by Jacob E. Cooke, was published in Middletown, CT, in 1961, by the Wesleyan University Press.

Maier, Pauline. *Ratification: The People Debate the Constitution, 1787–1788*. New York: Simon and Schuster, 2010. Not only is this a marvelous study of ratification, but it also is virtually the only one in existence. A splendid, comprehensive account.

McDonald, Forrest. *Novus Ordo Seclorum*. Lawrence: University of Kansas Press, 1985. A careful study of the intellectual origins of the Constitution. The Latin title means "New World Order," which is what the Framers hoped they were creating.

Sheldon, Garrett W. *The Political Philosophy of James Madison*. Baltimore: Johns Hopkins University Press, 2001. Masterful account of Madison's political thought and its roots in classical republicanism and Christianity.

Storing, Herbert J. *What the Anti-Federalists Were For*. Chicago: University of Chicago Press, 1981. Close analysis of the political views of those opposed to the ratification of the Constitution.

Wood, Gordon S. *The Creation of the American Republic*. Chapel Hill: University of North Carolina Press, 1969. A detailed study of American political thought before the Philadelphia convention.

___. *The Radicalism of the American Revolution*. New York: Knopf, 1992. Magisterial study of the nature and effects of the American Revolution and the relationship between the socially radical Revolution and the Constitution.

3

Vision of America/Joe Sohm/Getty Images

Federalism

LEARNING OBJECTIVES

1. Why does the United States have federalism?

2. How has American Federalism evolved from the Founding to the present?

3. Which level of government does federalism favor, the national government or the states?

4. Where is sovereignty located in the American political system?

5. How is power divided between the national government and the states under the Constitution?

6. What competing values are at stake in federalism?

7. Who should decide which matters ought to be governed mainly or solely by national laws?

When the Framers drafted the Constitution, the Antifederalists opposed it primarily on the grounds that it gave too much power to national government. The Antifederalists recognized the limitations of the Articles of Confederation, but they feared that the Constitution sacrificed liberty and civic responsibility with its expansion of the power of the national government.

The Federalists prevailed over the Antifederalists with the ratification of the Constitution. Amended only 27 times in more than 225 years, the Constitution is still the law of the land today. But, much as the Antifederalists predicted, the federal government has taken on responsibilities that traditionally were the province of state governments, such as social welfare policy, education, health care, and a minimum wage. States have some flexibility in implementing policies, but the national government sets the direction in many more policy areas today than it did originally; and, as the Antifederalists feared, we now have a large standing army and powerful federal courts.

These changes between then and now do not mean that the Constitution was wrong (if we were forced to take sides, we would have sided with the Federalists—would you?) But there is no denying that the federal government has grown far beyond anything that even the most ardent Federalists had envisioned. Much of that growth has occurred in just the last half-century or so. In 2010, the federal government spent roughly $4 trillion. Adjusted for inflation, that was more than five times what it spent in 1960.

But that is only about half of the story. Over the last half-century, state and local government spending has risen steeply, too. In 2010, state and local governments spent a combined total of nearly $2.5 trillion. Adjusted for inflation, that was nearly six times what they spent in 1960.

No less telling, virtually all of the post-1960 growth in government employees has been concentrated not in Washington, but in state capitals and city halls: the federal government's full-time civilian (nonmilitary) workforce numbers about 2 million (about the same number as in 1960), whereas state and local governments employ a combined total of about 12 million full-time workers (more than double the number they employed in 1960).

Back when the Federalists and the Antifederalists debated the Constitution, neither side anticipated that what today we call "big government" would encompass all three levels of government: federal, state, and local. Then: they fussed and fought over how vast the federal government might someday become. Now: the reality is that, apart from military affairs and international diplomacy, most "national" laws, policies, and programs are shaped, administered, or funded in whole or in part through a complex, and often contentious, system of federal–state relations.

> *Federalism*
> Government authority shared by national and local governments.

Why Federalism Matters

For example, the heated controversies that surrounded the enactment of the federal health reform law in 2010, and the ensuing legal challenge to that law brought by officials representing 26 states, were in large part battles over how the federal government should relate to the states. The fight over what some critics called "Obamacare" was not all about federal–state conflict. The most divisive issue was the law's "individual mandate," which required most Americans to purchase "minimum essential" health insurance or face a monetary "penalty." But federal–state politics also figured in the intense struggle over the law. Specifically, the law required that states greatly expand the scope of their support for Medicaid or risk losing all federal funding for the program. Medicaid assists low-income women, children, families, the blind, the elderly, and the disabled in obtaining medical care.

Many federal–state conflicts have ended up before the U.S. Supreme Court (for a short list, see the **Landmark Cases** feature on page 59), and this one did, too. In *National Federation of Business v. Sebelius* (2012), the Court, by a 5-to-4 majority led by Chief Justice John Roberts, held that the individual mandate was constitutional because it could be construed as a "tax" that was clearly within the power of Congress to levy, rather than as a "penalty" to be exacted pursuant to the more limited power of Congress to regulate interstate commerce. But the Court also held that the law's "Medicaid expansion violates the Constitution by threatening the states with the loss of their existing (federal) Medicaid funding," and by overstepping the federal government's authority to "alter" or "amend" the program in ways that states "could hardly anticipate" or be reasonably expected to approve. This was just the latest in a series of cases stretching back to the start of the republic in which the Court, in effect, refereed disputes relating to "federalism."

Federalism can be defined as a political system in which the national government shares power with local governments (state governments in the case of the United States, but other subnational governments in the case of federal systems including Australia, India, and Switzerland). Constitutionally, in America's federal system, state governments have a specially protected existence and the authority to make final decisions over many governmental activities. Even today, after more than a century during which the government headquartered in Washington, D.C., has grown, state and local governments are not mere junior partners in deciding important public policy matters. The national government can pass, and the federal courts can uphold, laws to protect the environment, store nuclear waste, expand low-income housing, guarantee the right to an abortion, provide special services for the handicapped, or toughen public-school graduation standards. But whether and how such federal laws are followed or funded often involves decisions by diverse state and local government officials, both elected and appointed.

Federalism or federal–state relations may seem like an arcane or boring subject until you realize that it is behind many things that matter to many people: how much you pay in certain taxes, whether you can drive above 55 miles per hour on certain roadways, whether or where you can buy liquor, how much money gets spent on schools, whether all or most children have health insurance coverage, and much more. For instance, as summarized in the **Constitutional Connections** feature on page 53, the Supreme Court's 2012 ruling on the new federal health care law's "federalism" provisions matters greatly to how Americans shop for health insurance. By the same token, federalism affects almost every aspect of

crime and punishment in America: persons convicted of murder are subject to the death penalty in some states but not in others; penalties for illegal drug sales vary widely from state to state; and, as you can explore in **What's Your Issue?** on page 70, there is an unresolved conflict between national law and certain states' laws regarding the use of marijuana. Perhaps most importantly, federalism is critical to how certain civil liberties (Chapter 5) and civil rights (Chapter 6) are defined and protected (for instance, some state constitutions mention God, and some state laws specifically prohibit funding for religious schools).

Federalism matters, but how it matters has changed over time. In 1908, Woodrow Wilson observed that the relationship between the national government and the states "is the cardinal question of our constitutional system," a question that cannot be settled by "one generation, because it is a question of growth, and every successive stage of our political and economic development gives it a new aspect, makes it a new question."[1]

Since the adoption of the Constitution in 1787, the single most persistent source of political conflict has been the relations between the national and state governments. The political conflict over slavery, for example, was intensified because some state governments condoned or supported slavery, while others took action to discourage it. The proponents and opponents of slavery were thus given territorial power centers from which to carry on the dispute. Other issues, such as the regulation of business and the provision of social welfare

After the passage of the 2010 health care law, critics declared that it would require thousands of pages of rules and regulations for implementation.

Bill Clark/CQ Roll Call/Getty Images

CONSTITUTIONAL CONNECTIONS

States and "Health Exchanges"

In *National Federation of Business v. Sebelius* (2012), the U.S. Supreme Court upheld the constitutionality of the "individual mandate" (effective January 1, 2014, individual citizens must carry health insurance or pay a "tax"), but it struck down provisions of the law that required the states to spend substantially more on Medicaid (the means-tested federal-state program that pays medical expenses for low-income and elderly people receiving certain other federal welfare benefits). At the same time, however, the Court let stand provisions of the law requiring the District of Columbia and the states to establish (by January 1, 2014) online "health exchanges" for people that are not enrolled in Medicare (the non-means-tested federal program that pays for part of the cost of medical care for retired or disabled people covered by Social Security). The "health exchanges" are supposed to enable consumers to compare different private insurance plans, find out if they are eligible for Medicaid, and choose among four levels of coverage designated as "bronze," "silver," "gold," and "platinum." But the Court's decision left each state free to choose whether to operate the exchange itself ("state-run exchange"), utilize an exchange established by the federal government ("federal exchange"), or set up a federal-state partnership under which the state chooses insurance options but the federal government runs the exchange ("planned partnership exchange"). According to tracking reports by the Kaiser Family Foundation, by mid-2013, the District of Columbia and 17 states had each opted to create its own exchange, 25 states had opted to utilize federal exchanges, and 8 states had selected the planned partnership exchange.

programs, were in large part fought out, for well over a century, in terms of "national interests" versus "states' rights." While other nations, such as Great Britain, were debating the question of whether the national government *ought* to provide old-age pensions or regulate the railroads, the United States debated a different question— whether the national government *had the right* to do these things.

The Founding

The goal of the Founders seems clear: federalism was one device whereby personal liberty was to be protected. (The separation of powers was another.) The Founders feared that placing final political authority in any one set of hands, even in the hands of persons popularly elected, would so concentrate power as to risk tyranny. But they had seen what happened when independent states tried to form a compact, as under the Articles of Confederation; what the states put together, they could also take apart. The alliance among the states that existed from 1776 to 1787 was a confederation, that is, a system of government in which the people create state governments which in turn create and operate a national government (see Figure 3.1). Since the national government in a confederation derives its powers from the states, it is dependent on their continued cooperation for its survival. By 1786, that cooperation was barely forthcoming.

A Bold, New Plan

A federation—or a "federal republic," as the Founders called it—derives its powers directly from the people, as do the state governments. As the Founders envisioned it, both levels of government, the national and the state, would have certain powers, but neither would have supreme authority over the other. Madison, writing in *Federalist* No. 46, said that both the state and federal governments "are in fact but different agents and trustees of the people, constituted with different powers." In *Federalist* No. 28, Hamilton explained how he thought the system would work: the people could shift their support between state and federal levels of government as needed to keep the two in balance. "If their rights are invaded by either, they can make use of the other as the instrument of redress."

It was an entirely new plan, for which no historical precedent existed. Nobody came to the Philadelphia convention with a clear idea of what a federal (as opposed to a unitary or a confederal) system would look like, and there was not much discussion at Philadelphia of how the system would work in practice. Few delegates then used the word *federalism* in the sense in which we now employ it (it was originally used as a synonym for *confederation* and only later came to stand for something different).[2] The Constitution does not spell out the powers that the states are to have, and until the Tenth Amendment was added at the insistence of various states, there was not even a clause in it saying (as did the amendment) that "the powers not delegated to the United States by the Constitution, nor

FIGURE 3.1 Lines of Power in Three Systems of Government

UNITARY SYSTEM

Power centralized.
State or regional governments derive authority from central government. Examples: United Kingdom, France.

FEDERAL SYSTEM

Power divided between central and state or local governments.
Both the government and constituent governments act directly upon the citizens.
Both must agree to constitutional change.
Examples: Canada, United States since adoption of Constitution.

**CONFEDERAL SYSTEM
(or CONFEDERATION)**

Power held by independent states.
Central government is a creature of the constituent governments.
Example: United States under the Articles of Confederation.

© Cengage Learning

prohibited by it to the states, are reserved to the states respectively, or to the people." The Founders assumed from the outset that the federal government would have only those powers given to it by the Constitution; the Tenth Amendment was an afterthought, added to make that assumption explicit and allay fears that something else was intended.[3]

The Tenth Amendment has rarely had much practical significance, however. From time to time, the Supreme Court has tried to interpret that amendment as putting certain state activities beyond the reach of the federal government, but usually the Court has later changed its mind and allowed Washington to regulate such matters as the hours that employees

of a city-owned mass-transit system may work. The Court did not find that running such a transportation system was one of the powers "reserved to the states."[4] But, as we explain later in this chapter, the Court has begun to give new life to the Tenth Amendment and the doctrine of state sovereignty.

Elastic Language

The need to reconcile the competing interests of large and small states and of northern and southern states, especially as they affected the organization of Congress, was sufficiently difficult without trying to spell out exactly what relationship ought to exist between the national and state systems. For example, Congress was given the power to regulate commerce "among the several states." The Philadelphia convention would have gone on for four years rather than four months if the Founders had decided that it was necessary to describe, in clear language, how one was to tell where commerce *among* the states ended and commerce wholly *within* a single state began. The Supreme Court, as we shall see, devoted more than a century to that task before giving up.

Though some clauses bearing on federal-state relations were reasonably clear (see the box on page 56), other clauses were quite vague. The Founders realized, correctly, that they could not make an exact and exhaustive list of everything the federal government was empowered to do—circumstances would change, and new exigencies would arise. Thus they added the following elastic language to Article I: Congress shall have the power to "make all laws which shall be necessary and proper for carrying into execution the foregoing powers."

The Founders themselves carried away from Philadelphia different views of what federalism meant. One view was championed by Hamilton. Since the people had created the national government, since the laws and treaties made pursuant to the Constitution were "the supreme law of the land" (Article VI), and since the most pressing needs were the development of a national economy and the conduct of foreign affairs, Hamilton thought that the national government was the superior and leading force in political affairs and that its powers ought to be broadly defined and liberally construed.

The other view, championed by Jefferson, was that the federal government, though important, was the product of an agreement among the states; and though "the people" were the ultimate sovereigns, the principal threat to their liberties was likely to come from the national government. (Madison, a strong supporter of national supremacy at the convention, later became a champion of states' rights.) Thus the powers of the federal government should be narrowly construed and strictly limited. As Madison

Benjamin Franklin, Thomas Jefferson, Livingston Adams, and Roger Sherman writing the Declaration of Independence.

put it in *Federalist* No. 45, in language that probably made Hamilton wince, "The powers delegated by the proposed Constitution to the federal government are few and defined. Those which are to remain in the State governments are numerous and indefinite."

Hamilton argued for national supremacy, Jefferson for states' rights. Though their differences were greater in theory than in practice (as we shall see in Chapter 14, Jefferson while president sometimes acted in a positively Hamiltonian manner), the differing interpretations they offered of the Constitution were to shape political debate in this country until well into the 1960s.

The Debate on the Meaning of Federalism

The Civil War was fought, in part, over the issue of national supremacy versus states' rights, but it settled only one part of that argument—namely, that the national government was supreme, its sovereignty derived directly from the people, and thus the states could not lawfully secede from the Union. Virtually every other aspect of the national-supremacy issue continued to animate political and legal debate for another century.

The Supreme Court Speaks

As arbiter of what the Constitution means, the Supreme Court became the focal point of that debate. In Chapter 16, we shall see in some detail how the Court made its decisions. For now it is enough to know that

> **"necessary and proper" clause** Section of the Constitution allowing Congress to pass all laws "necessary and proper" to its duties, and which has permitted Congress to exercise powers not specifically given to it (enumerated) by the Constitution.

during the formative years of the new Republic, the Supreme Court was led by a staunch and brilliant advocate of Hamilton's position, Chief Justice John Marshall. In a series of decisions, he and the Court powerfully defended the national-supremacy view of the newly formed federal government.

The box on page 59 lists some landmark cases in the history of federal-state relations. Perhaps the most important decision was in a case, seemingly trivial in its origins, which arose when James McCulloch, the cashier of the Baltimore branch of the Bank of the United States—which had been created by Congress—refused to pay a tax levied on that bank by the state of Maryland. He was hauled into state court and convicted of failing to pay the tax. In 1819, McCulloch appealed all the way to the Supreme Court in a case known as *McCulloch v. Maryland*. The Court, in a unanimous opinion, answered two questions in ways that expanded the powers of Congress and confirmed the supremacy of the federal government in the exercise of those powers.

The first question was whether Congress had the right to set up a bank, or any other corporation, since such a right is nowhere explicitly mentioned in the Constitution. Marshall said that, though the federal government possessed only those powers enumerated in the Constitution, the "extent"—that is, the meaning—of those powers required interpretation. Though the word *bank* is not in that document, one finds there the power to manage money: to lay and collect taxes, issue a currency, and borrow funds. To carry out these powers, Congress may reasonably decide that chartering a national bank is "necessary and proper." Marshall's words were carefully chosen to endow the **"necessary and proper" clause** with the widest possible sweep:

> *Let the end be legitimate, let it be within the scope of the Constitution, and all means which are appropriate, which are plainly adapted to that end, which are not prohibited, but consistent with the letter and spirit of the Constitution, are constitutional.*[5]

The second question was whether a federal bank could lawfully be taxed by a state. To answer it, Marshall went back to first principles. The government of the United States was not established by the states, but by the people, and thus the federal government was supreme in the exercise of those powers conferred upon it. Having already concluded that chartering a bank was within the powers of Congress, Marshall then argued that the only way for such powers to be supreme was for their use to be immune from state challenge and for the products of their use to be protected against state destruction. Since "the power to tax involves the power to destroy," and since the power to destroy a federal agency would confer upon the states supremacy over the federal government, the states may not tax any federal instrument. Hence the Maryland law was unconstitutional.

McCulloch won, and so did the federal government. Half a century later, the Court decided that what was sauce for the goose was sauce for the gander. It held that just as state governments could not tax federal bonds, the federal government could not tax the interest people earn on state and municipal bonds. In 1988, the Supreme Court reversed course and decided that Congress was now free, if it wished, to tax the interest on such state and local bonds.[6] Municipal bonds, which for nearly a century were a tax-exempt investment protected (so their holders thought) by the Constitution, were now protected only by politics. So far, Congress hasn't tried to tax them.

Nullification

The Supreme Court can decide a case without settling the issue. The struggle over states' rights versus

HOW THINGS WORK

The States and the Constitution

The Framers made some attempt to define the relations between the states and the federal government and how the states were to relate to one another. The following points were made in the original Constitution—before the Bill of Rights was added.

Restrictions on Powers of the States

States may not make treaties with foreign nations, coin money, issue paper currency, grant titles of nobility, pass a bill of attainder or an ex post facto law, or, without the consent of Congress, levy any taxes on imports or exports, keep troops and ships in time of peace, or enter into an agreement with another state or with a foreign power.

[Art. I, sec. 10]

Guarantees by the Federal Government to the States

The national government guarantees to every state a "republican form of government" and protection against foreign invasion and (provided the states request it) protection against domestic insurrection.

[Art. IV, sec. 4]

An existing state will not be broken up into two or more states or merged with all or part of another state without that state's consent.

[Art. IV, sec. 3]

Congress may admit new states into the Union.

[Art. IV, sec. 3]

Taxes levied by Congress must be uniform throughout the United States: they may not be levied on some states but not others.

[Art. I, sec. 8]

The Constitution may not be amended to give states unequal representation in the Senate.

[Art. V]

Rules Governing How States Deal with Each Other

"Full faith and credit" shall be given by each state to the laws, records, and court decisions of other states. (For example, a civil case settled in the courts of one state cannot be retried in the courts of another.)

[Art. IV, sec. 1]

The citizens of each state shall have the "privileges and immunities" of the citizens of every other state. (No one is quite sure what this is supposed to mean.)

[Art. IV, sec. 2]

If a person charged with a crime by one state flees to another, he or she is subjected to extradition—that is, the governor of the state that finds the fugitive is obliged to return the person to the governor of the state where he or she is wanted.

[Art. IV, sec. 2]

national supremacy continued to rage in Congress, during presidential elections, and ultimately on the battlefield. The issue came to center on the doctrine of **nullification**. When Congress passed laws (in 1798) to punish newspaper editors who published stories critical of the federal government, James Madison and Thomas Jefferson opposed the laws, suggesting (in statements known as the Virginia and Kentucky Resolutions) that the states had the right to "nullify" (that is, declare null and void) a federal law that, in the states' opinion, violated the Constitution. The laws expired before the claim of nullification could be settled in the courts.

Later the doctrine of nullification was revived by John C. Calhoun of South Carolina, first in opposition to a tariff enacted by the federal government and later in opposition to federal efforts to restrict slavery. Calhoun argued that if Washington attempted to ban slavery, the states had the right to declare such acts unconstitutional and thus null and void. This time the issue was settled—by war. The northern victory in the Civil War determined once and for all that the federal union is indissoluble and that states cannot declare acts of Congress unconstitutional, a view later confirmed by the Supreme Court.[7]

Dual Federalism

After the Civil War, the debate about the meaning of federalism focused on the interpretation of the commerce clause of the Constitution. Out of this debate emerged the doctrine of **dual federalism**, which held that though the national government was supreme in its sphere, the states were equally supreme in theirs, and that these two spheres of action should and could be kept separate. Applied to commerce, the concept of dual federalism implied that there were such things as *inter*state commerce, which Congress could regulate, and *intra*state commerce, which only the states could regulate, and that the Court could determine which was which.

For a long period the Court tried to decide what was interstate commerce based on the kind of business that was conducted. Transporting things between states was obviously interstate commerce, and so subject to federal regulation. Thus federal laws affecting the interstate shipment of lottery tickets,[8] prostitutes,[9] liquor,[10] and harmful foods and drugs[11] were upheld. On the other hand, manufacturing,[12] insurance,[13] and farming[14] were in the past considered *intra*state commerce, and so only the state governments were allowed to regulate them.

Such product-based distinctions turned out to be hard to sustain. For example, if you ship a case of whiskey from Kentucky to Kansas, how long is it in interstate commerce (and thus subject to federal law), and when does it enter intrastate commerce and become subject only to state law? For a while, the Court's answer was that the whiskey was in interstate commerce so long as it was in its "original package,"[15] but that only precipitated long quarrels as to what was the original package and how one is to treat things, like gas and grain, which may not be shipped in packages at all. And how could one distinguish between manufacturing and transportation when one company did both or when a single manufacturing corporation owned factories in different states? And if an insurance company sold policies to customers both inside and outside a given state, were there to be different laws regulating identical policies that happened to be purchased from the same company by persons in different states?

In time, the effort to find some clear principles that distinguished interstate from intrastate commerce was pretty much abandoned. Commerce was like a stream flowing through the country, drawing to itself contributions from thousands of scattered enterprises and depositing its products in millions of individual homes. The Court began to permit the federal government to regulate almost anything that affected this stream, so that by the 1940s not only had farming and manufacturing been redefined as part of interstate commerce,[16] but even the janitors and window washers in buildings that housed companies engaged in interstate commerce were now said to be part of that stream.[17]

Today lawyers are engaged in interstate commerce but professional baseball players are not. If your state has approved marijuana use for medical purposes, you can still be penalized under federal law even when the marijuana you consume was grown in a small pot in your backyard.[18]

State Sovereignty

It would be a mistake to think that the doctrine of dual federalism is entirely dead. Until recently, Congress, provided that it had a good reason, could pass a law regulating almost any kind of economic activity anywhere in the country, and the Supreme Court would call it constitutional. But in *United States v. Lopez* (1995), the Court held that Congress had exceeded its commerce clause power by prohibiting guns in a school zone.

nullification The doctrine that a state can declare null and void a federal law that, in the state's opinion, violates the Constitution.

dual federalism Doctrine holding that the national government is supreme in its sphere, the states are supreme in theirs, and the two spheres should be kept separate.

The Court reaffirmed the view that the commerce clause does not justify any federal action when, in May 2000, it overturned the Violence Against Women Act of 1994. This law allowed women who were the victims of a crime of violence motivated by gender to sue the guilty party in federal court. In *United States v. Morrison,* the Court, in a five-to-four decision, said that attacks against women are not, and do not substantially affect, interstate commerce, and hence Congress cannot constitutionally pass such a law. Chief Justice William Rehnquist said that "the Constitution requires a distinction between what is truly national and what is truly local." The states, of course, can pass such laws, and many have.

The Court has moved to strengthen states' rights on other grounds as well. In *Printz v. United States* (1997), the Court invalidated a federal law that required local police to conduct background checks on all gun purchasers. The Court ruled that the law violated the Tenth Amendment by commanding state governments to carry out a federal regulatory program. Writing for the five-to-four majority, Justice Antonin Scalia declared, "The Federal government may neither issue directives requiring the states to address particular problems, nor command the states' officers, or those of their political subdivisions, to administer or enforce a Federal regulatory program.... Such commands are fundamentally incompatible with our constitutional system of dual sovereignty."

The Court has also given new life to the Eleventh Amendment, which protects states from lawsuits by citizens of other states or foreign nations. In 1999, the Court shielded states from suits by copyright owners who claimed infringement of copyrights issued by state agencies and immunized states from lawsuits by people who argued that state regulations create unfair economic competition. In *Alden v. Maine* (1999), the Court held that state employees could not sue to force state compliance with federal fair-labor laws. In the Court's five-to-four majority opinion, Justice Anthony M. Kennedy stated, "Although the Constitution grants broad powers to Congress, our federalism requires that Congress treat the states in a manner consistent with their status as residuary sovereigns and joint participants in the governance of the nation." A few years later, in *Federal Maritime Commission v. South Carolina Ports Authority* (2002), the Court further expanded states' sovereign immunity from private lawsuits. Writing for the five-to-four majority, Justice Clarence Thomas declared that dual sovereignty "is a defining feature of our nation's constitutional blueprint," adding that the states "did not consent to become mere appendages of the federal government" when they ratified the Constitution.

HOW THINGS WORK

The Terms of Local Governance

Legally a **city** is a **municipal corporation** or **municipality** that has been chartered by a state to exercise certain defined powers and provide certain specific services. There are two kinds of charters: special-act charters and general-act charters.

A **special-act charter** applies to a certain city (for example, New York City) and lists what that city can and cannot do. A **general-act charter** applies to a number of cities that fall within a certain classification, usually based on city population. Thus in some states, all cities over 100,000 population will be governed on the basis of one charter, while all cities between 50,000 and 99,999 population will be governed on the basis of a different one.

Under **Dillon's rule,** the terms of these charters are to be interpreted very narrowly. This rule (named after a lawyer who wrote a book on the subject in 1911) authorizes a municipality to exercise only those powers expressly given, implied by, or essential to the accomplishment of its enumerated powers. This means, for example, that a city cannot so much as operate a peanut stand at the city zoo unless the state has specifically given the city that power by law or charter.

A **home-rule charter,** now in effect in many cities, reverses Dillon's rule and allows a city government to do anything not prohibited by the charter or state law. Even under a home-rule charter, however, city laws (called **ordinances**) cannot be in conflict with state laws, and the states can pass laws that preempt or interfere with what home-rule cities want to do.

In this country, there are more than 87,500 local governments, only about a fifth (19,500) of which are cities or municipalities. **Counties** (3,000) are the largest territorial units between a state and a city or town. Every state but Connecticut and Rhode Island has county governments. (In Louisiana, counties are called *parishes,* in Alaska *boroughs.*)

LANDMARK CASES

Federal-State Relations

- ***McCulloch v. Maryland* (1819):** The Constitution's "necessary and proper" clause permits Congress to take actions (in this case, to create a national bank) when it is essential to a power that Congress has (in this case, managing the currency).

- ***Gibbons v. Ogden* (1824):** The Constitution's commerce clause gives the national government exclusive power to regulate interstate commerce.

- ***Wabash, St. Louis and Pacific Railroad v. Illinois* (1886):** The states may not regulate interstate commerce.

- ***United States v. Lopez* (1995):** The national government's power under the commerce clause does not permit it to regulate matters not directly related to interstate commerce (in this case, banning firearms in a school zone).

- ***Printz v. United States* (1997):** The national government's authority to require state officials to administer or enforce a federal regulation is limited.

- ***Alden v. Maine* (1999):** Congress may not act to subject nonconsenting states to lawsuits in state courts.

- ***Reno v. Condon* (2000):** The national government's authority to regulate Interstate commerce extends to restrictions on how states gather, circulate, or sell certain information about citizens.

- ***U.S. v. Morrison* (2000):** The national government's power to regulate interstate commerce does not extend to giving female victims of violence the right to sue perpetrators in federal court.

- ***Federal Maritime Commission v. South Carolina Ports Authority* (2002):** Expanded states' sovereign immunity from private lawsuits and declared that the states "did not consent to become mere appendages of the federal government" when they ratified the Constitution.

- ***Kelo v. City of New London* (2005):** The Constitution allows a local government to seize property, not only for "public use" such as building highways, but also to "promote economic development" in a "distressed" community.

- ***National Federation of Independent Busness v. Sebelius* (2010):** The national government's authority to "alter" or "amend" programs that it jointly funds and administers with the states is limited.

Not all Court decisions, however, support greater state sovereignty. In 1999, for example, the Court ruled seven to two that state welfare programs may not restrict new residents to the welfare benefits they would have received in the states from which they moved. In addition, each of the Court's major prostate sovereignty decisions has been decided by a tenuous five-to-four margin. More generally, to empower states is not to disempower Congress, which, as it has done since the late 1930s, can still make federal laws regarding almost anything as long as it does not go too far in "commandeering" state resources or gutting states' rights.

New debates over state sovereignty call forth old truths about the constitutional basis of state and local government. In general, a state can do anything that is not prohibited by the Constitution or preempted by federal policy and that is consistent with its own constitution. One generally recognized state power is the **police power**, which refers to those laws and regulations, not otherwise unconstitutional, that promote health, safety, and morals. Thus the states can enact and enforce criminal codes, require children to attend school and citizens to be vaccinated, and restrict (subject to many limitations) the availability of pornographic materials or the activities of prostitutes and drug dealers.

> ***police power*** State power to enact laws promoting health, safety, and morals.

Governmental Structure

Federalism refers to a political system in which there are local (territorial, regional, provincial, state, or municipal) units of government, as well as a national government, that can make final decisions with respect to at least some governmental activities and whose existence is specially protected. Almost every nation in the world has local units of government of some kind, if for no other reason than to decentralize the administrative burdens of governing. But these governments are not federal unless the local units exist independent of the preferences of the national government and can make decisions on at least some matters without regard to those preferences.

The United States, Canada, Australia, India, Germany, and Switzerland are federal systems, as are a few other nations. France, Great Britain, Italy, and Sweden are not: they are unitary systems, because such local governments as they possess can be altered or even abolished by the national government and cannot plausibly claim to have final authority over any significant governmental activities.

HOW THINGS WORK

Sovereignty, Federalism, and the Constitution

Sovereignty means supreme or ultimate political authority: A sovereign government is one that is legally and politically independent of any other government.

A **unitary system** is one in which sovereignty is wholly in the hands of the national government, so that the states and localities are dependent on its will.

A **confederation or confederal system** is one in which the states are sovereign and the national government is allowed to do only that which the states permit.

A **federal system** is one in which sovereignty is shared, so that in some matters the national government is supreme and in other matters the states are supreme.

The Founding Fathers often took *confederal* and *federal* to mean much the same thing. Rather than establishing a government in which there was a clear division of sovereign authority between the national and state governments, they saw themselves as creating a government that combined some characteristics of a unitary regime with some of a confederal one. Or, as James Madison expressed the idea in *Federalist* No. 39, the Constitution "is, in strictness, neither a national nor a federal Constitution, but a composition of both." Where sovereignty is located in this system is a matter that the Founders did not clearly answer.

In this text, a **federal regime** is defined in the simplest possible terms—as one in which local units of government have a specially protected existence and can make some final decisions over some governmental activities.

The special protection that subnational governments enjoy in a federal system derives in part from the constitution of the country, but also from the habits, preferences, and dispositions of the citizens and the actual distribution of political power in society. The constitution of the former Soviet Union in theory created a federal system, as claimed by that country's full name—the Union of Soviet Socialist Republics—but for most of their history, none of these "socialist republics" were in the slightest degree independent of the central government. Were the American Constitution the only guarantee of the independence of the American states, they would long since have become mere administrative subunits of the government in Washington. Their independence results in large measure from the commitment of Americans to the idea of local self-government and from the fact that Congress consists of people who are selected by and responsive to local constituencies.

"The basic political fact of federalism," writes David B. Truman, "is that it creates separate, self sustaining centers of power, prestige, and profit."[19] Political power is locally acquired by people whose careers depend for the most part on satisfying local interests. As a result, though the national government has come to have vast powers, it exercises many of those powers through state governments. What many of us forget when we think about "the government in Washington" is that it spends much of its money and enforces most of its rules not directly on citizens, but on other, local units of government. A large part

of the welfare system, all of the interstate highway system, virtually every aspect of programs to improve cities, the largest part of the effort to supply jobs to the unemployed, the entire program to clean up our water, and even much of our military manpower (in the form of the National Guard) are enterprises in which the national government does not govern so much as it seeks, by regulation, grant, plan, argument, and cajolery, to get the states to govern in accordance with nationally (though often vaguely) defined goals.

In France, welfare, highways, education, the police, and the use of land are all matters that are directed nationally. In the United States, highways and some welfare programs are largely state functions (though they make use of federal money), while education, policing, and land-use controls are primarily local (city, county, or special-district) functions.

Sometimes, however, confusion or controversy about which government is responsible for which functions surfaces at the worst possible moment and lingers long after attempts have been made to sort it all out. Sadly, in our day, that is largely what "federalism" has meant in practice to citizens from New Orleans and the Gulf Coast region impacted by Hurricane Katrina in 2005.

Before, during, and after Hurricanes Katrina and Rita struck in 2005, federal, state, and local officials could be found fighting among themselves over everything from who was supposed to maintain and repair the levees to who should lead disaster relief initiatives. In the weeks after the hurricanes hit, it was widely reported that the main first-responders and

HOW WE COMPARE

American-Style Federalism

The United States has always had a federal form of government. By contrast, most of the nearly 200 nations in existence today have never had a federal form of government.

Depending on the stringency of the criteria used to delineate federal from unitary systems, the United States is one of a dozen to two dozen nations that now have federal forms of government: America, Australia, Belgium, Brazil, Canada, Ethiopia, Germany, India, Malaysia, Mexico, Nigeria, Pakistan, Russia, South Africa, Spain, and Switzerland are on nearly every expert's list of federal nations.

But some of these nations (for instance, Belgium, Spain, and South Africa) once had unitary systems, and many nations that have federal forms of government are multiparty parliamentary democracies. By contrast, American-style federalism has shaped and been shaped by the country's separation-of-powers system (see Chapter 2) and its two-party electoral system.

In some federal nations, public opinion favors the national government over subnational governments: people in these countries tend to trust their national governments as much or more than they trust other levels of government. In contrast, Americans tend to trust their state and local governments more than they trust Washington.

Sources: "Trust in Government Remains Low," Gallup Organization, September 2008; Richard Cole and John Kincaid, "Public Opinion on U.S. Federal and Intergovernmental Issues," *Publius* 36 (Summer 2006): pp. 443–459; John Kincaid and G. Alan Tarr, eds., *Constitutional Origins, Structure, and Change in Federal Countries* (Montreal: McGill-Queens Press, 2005); Pradeep Chhibber and Ken Kollman, *The Formation of National Party Systems: Federalism and Party Competition in Canada, Great Britain, India, and the United States* (Princeton: Princeton University Press, 2004).

disaster relief workers came not from government, but from myriad religious and other charitable organizations. Not only that, but government agencies, such as the Federal Emergency Management Agency (FEMA), often acted in ways that made it harder, not easier, for these volunteers and groups to deliver help when and where it was most badly needed.

Federalism needs to be viewed dispassionately through a historical lens wide enough to encompass both its worst legacies (for instance, state and

local laws that once legalized racial discrimination against blacks) and its best (for instance, blacks winning mayors' offices and seats in state legislatures when no blacks were in the U.S. Senate and not many blacks had been elected to the U.S. House).

Federalism, it is fair to say, has the virtues of its vices and the vices of its virtues. To some, federalism means allowing states to block action, prevent progress, upset national plans, protect powerful local interests, and cater to the self-interest of hack politicians. Harold Laski, a British observer, described American states as "parasitic and poisonous,"[20] and William H. Riker, an American political scientist, argued that "the main effect of federalism since the Civil War has been to perpetuate racism."[21] By contrast, another political scientist, Daniel J. Elazar, argued that the "virtue of the federal system lies in its ability to develop and maintain mechanisms vital to the perpetuation of the unique combination of governmental strength, political flexibility, and individual liberty, which has been the central concern of American politics."[22]

So diametrically opposed are the Riker and Elazar views that one wonders whether they are talking about the same subject. They are, of course, but they are stressing different aspects of the same phenomenon. Whenever the opportunity to exercise political power is widely available (as among the 50 states, 3,000 counties, and many thousands of municipalities in the United States), it is obvious that in different places different people will make use of that power for different purposes. There is no question that allowing states and cities to make autonomous, binding political decisions will allow some people in some places to make those decisions in ways that maintain racial segregation, protect vested interests, and facilitate corruption. It is equally true, however, that this arrangement also enables other people in other places to pass laws that attack segregation, regulate harmful economic practices, and purify politics, often long before these ideas gain national support or become national policy.

The existence of independent state and local governments means that different political groups pursuing different political purposes will come to power in different places. The smaller the political unit, the more likely it is to be dominated by a single political faction. James Madison understood this fact perfectly and used it to argue (in *Federalist* No. 10) that it would be in a large (or "extended") republic, such as the United States as a whole, that one would find the greatest opportunity for all relevant interests to be heard. When William Riker condemns federalism, he is thinking of the fact that in some places the ruling factions in cities and states have opposed granting equal rights to African Americans. When Daniel Elazar praises federalism, he is recalling that, in

initiative Process that permits voters to put legislative measures directly on the ballot.

referendum Procedure enabling voters to reject a measure passed by the legislature.

other states and cities, the ruling factions have taken the lead (long in advance of the federal government) in developing measures to protect the environment, extend civil rights, and improve social conditions. If you live in California, whether you like federalism depends in part on whether you like the fact that California has, independent of the federal government: cut property taxes, strictly controlled coastal land use, heavily regulated electric utilities, and increased (at one time) and decreased (at another time) its welfare rolls.

Increased Political Activity

Federalism has many effects, but its most obvious effect has been to facilitate the mobilization of political activity. Unlike Don Quixote, the average citizen does not tilt at windmills. He or she is more likely to become involved in organized political activity if he or she feels a reasonable chance exists of producing a practical effect. The chances of having such an effect are greater where there are many elected

Federalism has permitted experimentation. Women were able to vote in the Wyoming Territory in 1888, long before they could do so in most states.

officials and independent governmental bodies, each with a relatively small constituency, than where there are few elected officials, most of whom have the nation as a whole for a constituency. In short, a federal system, by virtue of the decentralization of authority, lowers the cost of organized political activity; a unitary system, because of the centralization of authority, raises the cost. We may disagree about the purposes of organized political activity, but the fact of widespread organized activity can scarcely be doubted—or if you do doubt it, that is only because you have not yet read Chapters 8 and 11.

It is impossible to say whether the Founders, when they wrote the Constitution, planned to produce such widespread opportunities for political participation. Unfortunately they were not very clear (at least in writing) about how the federal system was supposed to work, and thus most of the interesting questions about the jurisdiction and powers of our national and state governments had to be settled by a century and a half of protracted and often bitter conflict.

What the States Can Do

The states play a key role in social welfare, public education, law enforcement, criminal justice, health and hospitals, roads and highways, and managing water supplies. On these and many other matters, state constitutions are far more detailed and sometimes confer more rights than the federal one. For example, the California constitution includes an explicit right to privacy, says that noncitizens have the same property rights as citizens, and requires the state to use "all suitable means" to support public education.

Many state constitutions are now believed by some to be on the whole more progressive in their holdings on abortion rights (authorizing fewer restrictions on minors), welfare payments (permitting fewer limits on eligibility), employment discrimination (prohibiting discrimination based on sexual preference), and many other matters than federal courts generally are. As we saw in Chapter 2, the federal Constitution is based on a republican, not a democratic, principle: laws are to be made by the representatives of citizens, not by the citizens directly. But many state constitutions open one or more of three doors to direct democracy. About half of the states provide for some form of legislation by initiative. The **initiative** allows voters to place legislative measures (and sometimes constitutional amendments) directly on the ballot by getting enough signatures (usually between 5 and 15 percent of those who voted in the last election) on a petition. About half of the states permit the **referendum**, a procedure that enables voters to reject a measure adopted by the legislature. Sometimes the state constitution specifies that certain kinds of legislation (for example, tax increases) must be subject to a referendum whether the legislature wishes it or not. The **recall** is a procedure, in effect in more than 20 states, whereby voters can remove an elected official from office. If enough signatures are gathered on a petition, the official must go before voters, who can vote to leave the person in office, remove the person from office, or remove the person and replace him or her with someone else.

The existence of the states is guaranteed by the federal Constitution: no state can be divided without its consent, each state must have two representatives in the Senate (the only provision of the Constitution that may not be amended), every state is assured of a republican form of government, and the powers not granted to Congress are reserved for the states. By contrast, cities, towns, and counties enjoy no such protection; they exist at the pleasure of the states. Indeed, states have frequently abolished certain kinds of local governments, such as independent school districts.

This explains why there is no debate about city sovereignty comparable to the debate about state sovereignty. The constitutional division of power between them is settled: the state is supreme. But federal-state relations can be complicated, because the Constitution invites elected leaders to struggle over sovereignty. Which level of government has the ultimate power to decide where nuclear waste gets stored, how much welfare beneficiaries are paid, what rights prisoners enjoy, or whether supersonic jets can land at local airports? American federalism answers such questions, but on a case-by-case basis through intergovernmental politics and court decisions.

recall Procedure whereby voters can remove an elected official from office.

grants-in-aid Money given by the national government to the states.

Federal-State Relations

Though constitutionally the federal government may be supreme, politically it must take into account the fact that the laws it passes have to be approved by members of Congress selected from, and responsive to, state and local constituencies. Thus what Washington lawfully may do is not the same thing as what it politically may wish to do.

Grants-In-Aid

The best illustration of how political realities modify legal authority can be found in federal **grants-in-aid**. The first of these programs began even before the Constitution was adopted, in the form of land grants

HOW THINGS WORK

Government Powers: Federal, State, and Both

Federal Government Powers

- Subject to Article V of the Constitution, deciding on the process by which amendments to the Constitution are to be proposed and ratified

- Declaring war

- Maintaining and deploying military forces

- Making foreign policy, international treaties, and trade deals

- Printing money

- Regulating interstate commerce

- Maintaining postal offices and services

State Government Powers

- Ratifying amendments to the Constitution through state legislatures or ratifying conventions

- Conducting elections for public offices, initiatives, and referenda

- Establishing local governments

- Regulating intrastate commerce

- Licensing occupations and land uses

- Enacting laws to promote public safety, health, and morals (the "police power")

Powers Exercised by Both the Federal Government and State Governments

- Taxing citizens and businesses

- Chartering banks and corporations

- Building and maintaining roads

- Borrowing money and managing public debts

- Administering criminal justice institutions

- Regulating Native American gaming (casino) businesses

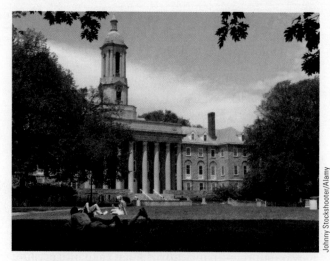

Some of the nation's top academic institutions, such as Penn State, began as land-grant colleges.

made by the national government to the states in order to finance education. (State universities all over the country were built with the proceeds from the sale of these land grants; hence the name *land-grant colleges.*) Land grants were also made to support the building of wagon roads, canals, railroads, and flood-control projects. These measures were hotly debated in Congress (President Madison thought some were unconstitutional), even though the use to which the grants were put was left almost entirely to the states.

Cash grants-in-aid began almost as early. In 1808, Congress gave $200,000 to the states to pay for their militias, with the states in charge of the size, deployment, and command of these troops. However, grant-in-aid programs remained few in number and small in price until the 20th century, when scores of new ones came into being. Today, federal grants go to hundreds of programs, including such giant federal-state programs as Medicaid (see Table 3.1).

The grants-in-aid system, once under way, grew rapidly because it helped state and local officials resolve a dilemma. On the one hand, they wanted

TABLE 3.1 Federal Grants to State and Local Governments (2011)

The federal government spent more than $625 billion on grants to states in 2011.	
Among the biggest items:	
Medicaid	$276.2 billion
Income Security	$116.4 billion
Education and training	$101.4 billion
Transportation	$61 billion
Community development	$18.6 billion

Source: U.S. Census Bureau, *Statistical Abstract of the United States: 2012*, Table 432, p. 269.

access to the superior taxing power of the federal government. On the other hand, prevailing constitutional interpretation, at least until the late 1930s, held that the federal government could not spend money for purposes not authorized by the Constitution. The solution was obviously to have federal money put into state hands: Washington would pay the bills; the states would run the programs.

To state officials, federal money seemed so attractive for four reasons. First, the money was there. Thanks to the high-tariff policies of the Republicans, Washington in the 1880s had huge budget surpluses. Second, in the 1920s, as those surpluses dwindled, Washington inaugurated the federal income tax. It automatically brought in more money as economic activity (and thus personal income) grew. Third, the federal government, unlike the states, managed the currency and could print more at will. (Technically, it borrowed this money, but it was under no obligation to pay it all back, because, as a practical matter, it had borrowed from itself.) States could not do this: if they borrowed money (and many could not), they had to pay it back, in full.

These three economic reasons for the appeal of federal grants were probably not as important as a fourth reason: politics. Federal money seemed to a state official to be "free" money. Governors did not have to propose, collect, or take responsibility for federal taxes. Instead, a governor could denounce the federal government for being profligate in its use of the people's money. Meanwhile, he or she could claim credit for a new public works or other project funded by Washington and, until recent decades, expect little or no federal supervision in the bargain.[23]

That every state had an incentive to ask for federal money to pay for local programs meant, of course, that it would be very difficult for one state to get money for a given program without every state getting it. The senator from Alabama who votes for the project to improve navigation on the Tombigbee will have to vote in favor of projects improving navigation on every other river in the country if the senator expects his or her Senate colleagues to support such a request. Federalism as practiced in the United States means that when Washington wants to send money to one state or congressional district, it must send money to many states and districts.

Shortly after September 11, 2001, for example, President George W. Bush and congressional leaders in both parties pledged new federal funds to increase public safety payrolls, purchase the latest equipment to detect bioterror attacks, and so on. Since then, New York City and other big cities have received tens of millions of federal dollars for such purposes, but so have scores of smaller cities and

An airline passenger goes through a scanner that searches electronically for any contraband.

towns. The grants allocated by the Department of Homeland Security were based on so-called fair-share formulas mandated by Congress, which are basically the same formulas the federal government uses to allocate certain highway and other funds among the states. These funding formulas not only spread money around but also generally skew funding toward states and cities with low populations. Thus, Wyoming received seven times as much federal homeland security funding per capita as New York State did, and Grand Forks County, North Dakota (population 70,000), received $1.5 million to purchase biochemical suits, a semi-armored van, decontamination tents, and other equipment to deal with weapons of mass destruction.[24]

Meeting National Needs

Until the 1960s, most federal grants-in-aid were conceived by or in cooperation with the states and were designed to serve essentially state purposes. Large blocs of voters and a variety of organized interests would press for grants to help farmers, build highways, or support vocational education. During the 1960s, however, an important change occurred: the federal government began devising grant programs based less on what states were demanding and more on what federal officials perceived to be important *national* needs (see Figure 3.2). Federal officials, not state and local ones, were the principal proponents of grant programs to aid the urban poor, combat crime, reduce pollution, and deal with drug abuse.

The rise in federal activism in setting goals and the occasional efforts, during some periods, to bypass state officials by providing money directly to cities or even local citizen groups, had at least two separate but related effects: one effect was to increase federal grants to state and local governments, and the other was to change the purposes to which those monies were put. Whereas federal aid amounted to less than 2 percent of state general revenue in 1927, by 2006 federal aid accounted for about 30 percent of state general revenue. In 1960, about 3 percent of federal grants to state and local governments were for health care. Today, however, one federal-state health care program alone, Medicaid, accounts for nearly half of all federal grants. And whereas in 1960 more than 40 percent of all federal grants to state and local governments went to transportation (including highways), today only about 10 percent is used for that purpose (see Figure 3.2). Even in the short term, the purposes to which federal grants are

FIGURE 3.2 **The Changing Purpose of Federal Grants to State and Local Governments**

1960

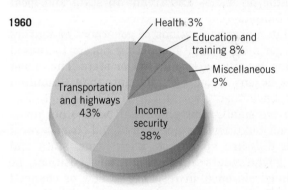

Health 3%
Education and training 8%
Miscellaneous 9%
Transportation and highways 43%
Income security 38%

2011

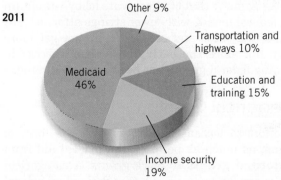

Other 9%
Transportation and highways 10%
Medicaid 46%
Education and training 15%
Income security 19%

Source: Congressional Budget Office, *Federal Grants to State and Local Governments*, March 2013, pp. 2–4.

categorical grants
Federal grants for specific purposes, such as building an airport.

put can shift; for example, after Hurricanes Katrina and Rita, federal grants for "community and regional development" spiked, but returned to pre-2005 levels by 2011.

The Intergovernmental Lobby

State and local officials, both elected and appointed, began to form an important new lobby—the "intergovernmental lobby," made up of mayors, governors, superintendents of schools, state directors of public health, county highway commissioners, local police chiefs, and others who had come to depend on federal funds.[25] Today, federal agencies responsible for health care, criminal justice, environmental protection, and other programs have people on staff who specialize in providing information, technical assistance, and financial support to state and local organizations, including the "Big 7": the U.S. Conference of Mayors; the National Governors Association; the National Association of Counties; the National League of Cities; the Council of State Governments; the International City/County Management Association; and the National Conference of State Legislatures. Reports by these groups and publications like *Governing* magazine are read routinely by many federal officials to keep a handle on issues and trends in state and local government.

National organizations of governors or mayors press for more federal money, but not for increased funding for any particular city or state. Thus most states, dozens of counties, and more than a hundred cities have their own offices in Washington, D.C. Some are small, some share staff with other jurisdictions, but a few are quite large and boast several dozen full-time employees. Back home, state and local governments have created new positions, or redefined old ones, in response to new or changed federal funding opportunities.

The purpose of the intergovernmental lobby has been the same as that of any private lobby—to obtain more federal money with fewer strings attached. For a while, the cities and states did in fact get more money, but since the early 1980s their success in obtaining federal grants has been more checkered.

Categorical Grants

The effort to loosen the strings took the form of shifting, as much as possible, the federal aid from **categorical grants** to block grants. A categorical grant is one for a specific purpose defined by federal law: to build an airport or a college dormitory, for

example, or to make welfare payments to low-income mothers. Such grants usually require that the state or locality put up money to "match" some part of the federal grant, though the amount of matching funds can be quite small (sometimes only 10 percent or less). Governors and mayors complained about these categorical grants because their purposes were often so narrow that it was impossible for a state to adapt federal grants to local needs. A mayor seeking federal money to build parks might have discovered that the city could get money only if it launched an urban-renewal program that entailed bulldozing several blocks of housing or small businesses.

One response to this problem was to consolidate several categorical or project grant programs into a single block grant devoted to some general purpose and with fewer restrictions on its use. Block grants began in the mid-1960s, when such a grant was created in the health field. Though many block grants were proposed between 1966 and 1980, only five were enacted. Of the three largest, one consolidated various categorical grant programs aimed at cities (Community Development Block Grants), another created a program to aid local law enforcement (Law Enforcement Assistance Act), and a third authorized new kinds of locally managed programs for the unemployed (CETA, or the Comprehensive Employment and Training Act).

In theory, block grants and revenue sharing were supposed to give the states and cities considerable freedom in deciding how to spend the money while helping to relieve their tax burdens. To some extent they did. However, for four reasons, neither the goal of "no strings" nor the one of fiscal relief was really attained. First, the amount of money available from block grants and revenue sharing did not grow as fast as the states had hoped nor as quickly as did the money available through categorical grants. Second, the federal government steadily increased the number of strings attached to the spending of this supposedly "unrestricted" money.

Third, block grants grew more slowly than categorical grants because of the different kinds of political coalitions supporting each. Congress and the federal bureaucracy liked categorical grants for the same reason the states disliked them—the specificity of these programs enhanced federal control over how the money was to be used. Federal officials, joined by liberal interest groups and organized labor, tended to distrust state governments. Whenever Congress wanted to address some national problem, its natural inclination was to create a categorical grant program so that it, and not the states, would decide how the money would be spent.

Fourth, even though governors and mayors like block grants, these programs cover such a broad

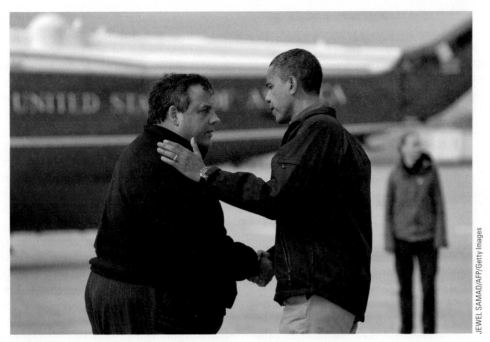

*New Jersey Governor Chris Christie greets President Barack Obama, who visits the state to
see the devastation caused by superstorm Sandy in October 2012.*

range of activities that no single interest group
has a vital stake in pressing for their enlargement.
Categorical grants, on the other hand, often are a
matter of life and death for many agencies—state
departments of welfare, of highways, and of health,
for example, are utterly dependent on federal aid.
Accordingly, the administrators in charge of these
programs will press strenuously for their expansion.
Moreover, categorical programs are supervised by
special committees of Congress, and as we shall see
in Chapter 13, many of these committees have an
interest in seeing their programs grow.

Rivalry among the States

The more important federal money becomes to
the states, the more likely the states are to compete among themselves for the largest share of it.
For a century or better, the growth of the United
States—in population, business, and income—was
concentrated in the industrial Northeast. In recent
decades, however, that growth—at least in population and employment, if not in income—has shifted
to the South, Southwest, and Far West. This change
has precipitated an intense debate over whether
the federal government, by the way it distributes
its funds and awards its contracts, is unfairly helping some regions and states at the expense of others. Journalists and politicians have dubbed the
struggle as one between Snowbelt (or Frostbelt) and
Sunbelt states.

Whether in fact there is anything worth arguing about is far from clear: the federal government

has had great difficulty in figuring out where it ultimately spends what funds for what purposes. For
example, a $1 billion defense contract may go to a
company with headquarters in California, but much
of the money may actually be spent in Connecticut
or New York, as the prime contractor in California
buys from subcontractors in the other states. It is
even less clear whether federal funds actually affect
the growth rate of the regions. The uncertainty about
the facts has not prevented a debate about the issue,
however. That debate focuses on the formulas written into federal laws by which block grants are allocated. These formulas take into account such factors
as a county's or city's population, personal income
in the area, and housing quality. A slight change in
a formula can shift millions of dollars in grants in
ways that favor either the older, declining cities of
the Northeast or the newer, still-growing cities of the
Southwest.

With the advent of grants based on distribu-
tional formulas (as opposed to grants for a particular project), the results of the census, taken every
10 years, assume monumental importance. A city or
state shown to be losing population may, as a result,
forfeit millions of dollars in federal aid. Senators
and representatives now have access to computers
that can tell them instantly the effect on their states
and districts of even minor changes in a formula
by which federal aid is distributed. These formulas
rely on objective measures, but the exact measure
is selected with an eye to its political consequences.
There is nothing wrong with this in principle, since
any political system must provide some benefits

conditions of aid
Terms set by the
national government
that states must meet
if they are to receive
certain federal funds.

mandates Terms set
by the national
government that states
must meet whether or
not they accept federal
grants.

waiver A decision by
an administrative
agency granting some
other part permission
to violate a law or rule
that would otherwise
apply to it.

for everybody if it is
to stay together. Given
the competition among
states in a federal
system, however, the
struggle over allocation
formulas becomes especially acute.

Federal Aid and Federal Control

So important has federal aid become for state and local governments that mayors and governors, along with others, began to fear that Washington was well on its way to controlling other levels of government. "He who pays the piper calls the tune," they muttered. In this view, the constitutional protection of state government to be found in the Tenth Amendment was in jeopardy as a result of the strings attached to the grants-in-aid on which the states were increasingly dependent.

Block grants were an effort to reverse this trend by allowing the states and localities freedom to spend money as they wished. But as we have seen, the new device did not in fact reverse the trend. Categorical grants—those with strings attached—continued to grow even faster.

There are two kinds of federal controls on state governmental activities. The traditional control tells the state government what it must do if it wants to get some grant money. These strings often are called **conditions of aid**. The newer form of control tells the state government what it must do, period. These rules are called **mandates**. Most mandates have little or nothing to do with federal aid—they apply to all state governments whether or not they accept grants.

Mandates

Most mandates concern civil rights and environmental protection. States may not discriminate in the operation of their programs, no matter who pays for them. Initially the antidiscrimination rules applied chiefly to distinctions based on race, sex, age, and ethnicity, but of late they have broadened to include physical and mental disabilities as well.

Various pollution control laws require the states to comply with federal standards for clean air, pure drinking water, and sewage treatment.[26]

Stated in general terms, these mandates seem reasonable enough. It is hard to imagine anyone arguing that state governments should be free to discriminate against people because of their race or national origin. In practice, however, some mandates create administrative and financial problems, especially when the mandates are written in vague language, thereby giving federal administrative agencies the power to decide for themselves what state and local governments are supposed to do.

But not all areas of public law and policy are equally affected by mandates. Federal-state disputes about who governs on such controversial matters as minors' access to abortion, same-sex marriage, and medical uses for banned narcotics make headlines. It is mandates that fuel everyday friction in federal-state relations, particularly those that Washington foists upon the states but funds inadequately or not at all. One study concluded that "the number of unfunded federal mandates is high in environmental policy, low in education policy, and moderate in health policy."[27] But why?

Some think that how much Washington spends in a given policy area is linked to how common federal mandates, funded or not, are in that same area. There is some evidence for that view. For instance, in recent years, annual federal grants to state and local governments for a policy area where unfunded mandates are pervasive—environmental protection—were about $4 billion, while federal grants for health care—an area where unfunded mandates have been less pervasive—amounted to about $200 billion. The implication is that when Washington itself spends less on something it wants done, it squeezes the states to spend more for that purpose. Washington is more likely to grant state and local governments waivers in some areas than in others. A **waiver** is a decision by an administrative agency granting some other party permission to violate a law or administrative rule that would otherwise apply to it. Generally, for instance, education waivers have been easy for state and local governments to get, but environmental protection waivers have proven almost impossible to acquire.[28]

However, caution is in order. Often, the more one knows about federal-state relations in any given area, the harder it becomes to generalize about present-day federalism's fiscal, administrative, and regulatory character, the conditions under which "permissive federalism" prevails, or whether new laws or court decisions will considerably tighten or further loosen Washington's control over the states.

Mandates are not the only way in which the federal government imposes costs on state and local governments. Certain federal tax and regulatory policies make it difficult or expensive for state and local governments to raise revenues, borrow funds, or privatize public functions. Other federal laws expose state and local governments to financial liability, and numerous federal court decisions and administrative regulations require state and local governments to do or not do various things, either by statute or through an implied constitutional obligation.[29]

It is clear that the federal courts have helped fuel the growth of mandates. As interpreted in this century by the U.S. Supreme Court, the Tenth Amendment provides state and local officials no protection against the march of mandates. Indeed, many of the more controversial mandates result not from congressional action but from court decisions. For example, many state prison systems have been, at one time or another, under the control of federal judges who required major changes in prison construction and management in order to meet standards the judges derived from their reading of the Constitution.

School-desegregation plans are the best-known example of federal mandates. Those involving busing—an unpopular policy—have typically been the result of court orders rather than of federal law or regulation.

Judges—usually, but not always, in federal courts—ordered Massachusetts to change the way it hires firefighters, required Philadelphia to institute new procedures to handle complaints of police brutality, and altered the location in which Chicago was planning to build housing projects. Note that in most of these cases nobody in Washington was placing a mandate on a local government; rather, a local citizen was using the federal courts to change a local practice.

The Supreme Court has made it much easier of late for citizens to control the behavior of local officials. A federal law, passed in the 1870s to protect newly freed slaves, makes it possible for a citizen to sue any state or local official who deprives that citizen of any "rights, privileges, or immunities secured by the Constitution and laws" of the United States. A century later, the Court decided that this law permitted a citizen to sue a local official if the official deprived the citizen of *anything* to which the citizen was entitled under federal law (and not just those federal laws protecting civil rights). For example, a citizen can now use the federal courts to obtain from a state welfare office a payment to which he or she may be entitled under federal law.

Conditions of Aid

By far the most important federal restrictions on state action are the conditions attached to the grants the states receive. In theory, accepting these conditions is voluntary—if you don't want the strings, don't take the money. But when the typical state depends for a quarter or more of its budget on federal grants, many of which it has received for years and on which many of its citizens depend for their livelihoods, it is not clear exactly how "voluntary" such acceptance is. During the 1960s, some strings were added, the most important of which had to do with civil rights. But beginning in the 1970s, the number of conditions began to proliferate and has expanded in each subsequent decade to the present.

Some conditions are specific to particular programs, but most are not. For instance, if a state builds something with federal money, it must first conduct an environmental impact study, it must pay construction workers the "prevailing wage" in the area, it often must provide an opportunity for citizen participation in some aspects of the design or location of the project, and it must ensure that the contractors who build the project have nondiscriminatory hiring policies. The states and the federal government, not surprisingly, disagree about the costs and benefits of such rules. Members of Congress and federal officials feel they have an obligation to develop uniform national policies with respect to important matters and to prevent states and cities from misspending federal tax dollars. State officials, on the other hand, feel these national rules fail to take into account diverse local conditions, require the states to do things that the states must then pay for, and create serious inefficiencies.

What state and local officials discovered, in short, was that "free" federal money was not quite free after all. In the 1960s, federal aid seemed entirely beneficial; what mayor or governor would not want such money? But just as local officials found it attractive to do things that another level of government then paid for, in time federal officials learned the same thing. Passing laws to meet the concerns of national constituencies—leaving the cities and states to pay the bills and manage the problems—began to seem attractive to Congress.

Because they face different demands, federal and local officials find themselves in a bargaining situation in which each side is trying to get some benefit (solving a problem, satisfying a pressure group) while passing on to the other side most of the costs (taxes, administrative problems). The bargains struck in this process used to favor the local officials, because members of Congress were essentially servants of

WHAT'S YOUR ISSUE?

Marijuana Laws: The Feds v. the States

In 1996, California citizens passed Proposition 215, a ballot measure permitting the "compassionate use" of marijuana for medicinal purposes. By early 2013, the District of Columbia and 17 states had passed laws variously permitting the possession, growth, or distribution of marijuana for medicinal purposes relating to treatment or pain management for diseases including cancer, glaucoma, and AIDS, among others. The federal government, however, under both Democratic and Republican presidents, has continued to ban all cultivation, production, sales, and uses of marijuana. Its power to do so has been upheld by the U.S. Supreme Court. Under the Controlled Substances Act of 1970, the federal government expressly forbids the cultivation, sale, or use of marijuana, including for medicinal purposes. The U.S. Department of Justice has threatened or taken severe action against both state officials

and "medical marijuana" distributors and users. In April 2013, Governor Jay Inslee of Washington State and Governor John Hickenlooper of Colorado petitioned the U.S. Department of Justice to stop opposing their states' respective laws decriminalizing multiple uses of marijuana. Public opinion on the issue has changed since that 1970 federal law was enacted. Today, in most surveys, majorities support legalizing "medical marijuana" and decriminalizing marijuana, period. So, there are two issues here: whether to legalize or decriminalize some or all uses of marijuana, and whether Washington should change its contrary laws or simply defer to states that have opted to legalize or decriminalize. Governors Inslee and Hickenlooper each oppose legalization, but each nonetheless believes that Washington should respect the wishes expressed by the citizens of their respective states.

local interests: they were elected by local political parties, they were part of local political organizations, and they supported local autonomy. Beginning in the 1960s, however, changes in American politics that will be described in later chapters—especially the weakening of political parties, the growth of public-interest lobbies in Washington, and the increased activism of the courts—shifted the orientation of many in Congress toward favoring Washington's needs over local needs.

A Devolution Revolution?

In 1981, President Ronald Reagan tried to reverse this trend. He asked Congress to consolidate scores of categorical grants into just six large block grants. Congress obliged. Soon state and local governments

The U.S. Border Patrol works with local ranchers on the U.S.-Mexico border to address issues such as drug smuggling and illegal immigration.

Federal, state, and local law enforcement officials work together to investigate the bombing of the 2013 Boston Marathon.

started getting less federal money, but with fewer strings attached to such grants. During the 1980s and into the early 1990s, however, many states also started spending more of their own money and replacing federal rules on programs with state ones.

With the election of Republican majorities in the House and Senate in 1994, a renewed effort was led by Congress to cut total government spending, roll back federal regulations, and shift important functions back to the states. The first key issue was welfare—that is, Aid to Families with Dependent Children (AFDC). Since 1935, there had been a federal guarantee of cash assistance to states that offered support to low-income, unmarried mothers and their children. In 1996, President Bill Clinton signed a new federal welfare law that ended any federal guarantee of support and, subject to certain rules, turned the management of the program entirely over to the states, aided by federal block grants.

These and other Republican initiatives were part of a new effort called devolution, which aimed to pass on to the states many federal functions. It is an old idea, but one that actually acquired new vitality because Congress, rather than the president, was leading the effort. Members of Congress traditionally liked voting for federal programs and categorical grants; that way they could take credit for what they were doing for particular constituencies. Under its new conservative leadership, Congress, especially the House, was looking for ways to scale back the size of the national government. President Clinton seemed to agree when, in his 1996 State of the Union address, he proclaimed that the era of big national government was over.

But was it over? No. By 2010, the federal government was spending about $30,000 per year per household, which, adjusted for inflation, was its highest annual per-household spending level since World War II.[30] Federal revenues represented almost 30 percent of gross domestic product, close to the late 1970s annual average, and inflation-adjusted federal debt totals hit new highs. Adjusted for inflation, total spending by state and local governments also increased every year after 1996, as did state and local government debt.[31]

Devolution did not become a revolution. AFDC was ended and replaced by a block grant program called Temporary Assistance for Needy Families (TANF). But far larger federal-state programs, most notably Medicaid, were not turned into block grant programs. Moreover, both federal and state spending on most programs, including the block-granted programs, increased after 1996. Although by no means the only new or significant block grant, TANF now looked like the big exception that proved the rule. The devolution revolution was curtailed by public opinion. Today, as in 1996 and 2006,

most Americans favor "shifting responsibility to the states," but not if that also means cuts in government programs that benefit most citizens (not just low-income families), uncertainty about who is eligible to receive benefits, or new hassles associated with receiving them.

Devolution seems to have resulted in more, not fewer, government rules and regulations. Research reveals that, in response to the federal effort to devolve responsibility to state and local governments, states have not only enacted new rules and regulations of their own, but also prompted Washington to issue new rules and regulations on environmental protection (especially greenhouse gas emissions) and other matters.[32]

Still, where devolution did occur, it has had some significant consequences. The devolution of welfare policy has been associated with dramatic decreases in welfare rolls. Scholars disagree about how much the drops were due to the changes in law and how much they were caused by economic conditions and other factors. Nor is it clear whether welfare-to-work programs have gotten most participants into decent jobs with adequate health benefits. But few now doubt that welfare devolution has made a measurable difference in how many people receive benefits and for how long.

Subject to state discretion, scores of local governments are now designing and administering welfare programs (job placement, child care, and others) through for-profit firms and a wide variety of nonprofit organizations, including local religious congregations. In some big cities, more than a quarter of welfare-to-work programs have been administered through public-private partnerships that have included various local community-based organizations as grantees.[33] By 2007, there was preliminary evidence that, at least in some states, such public-private partnerships were closer to the norm than they were only a half-decade or so earlier.[34]

A major challenge that states face in assuming more responsibilities for public programs is funding. By 2011, many states had lost the significant budget surpluses they had enjoyed just a few years ago and now faced enormous debt for the foreseeable future. While this was due in part to the national financial crisis, a longer-term factor was pension benefits for public employees, which are set by contract and can be changed only by mutual agreement between state governments and the unions that typically represent state and local officials. Consequently, several governors proposed restricting unions' collective-bargaining authority to balance budgets by reducing benefits. In Wisconsin, a gubernatorial proposal in 2011 to end some aspects of collective bargaining for public employees prompted huge protest rallies and led several state legislators who opposed the idea to flee the state for three weeks to avoid a vote (the bill passed anyway on a party-line vote). State legislators in Indiana did the same in response to a similar bill.

As states look to reduce costs, they need to consider which responsibilities are theirs to shoulder and which ones the federal government must bear. A 2011 study by the Government Accountability Office found extensive duplication of services both across federal government agencies and between the federal government and the states.[35] Areas of overlap include economic development, food regulation, and counterterrorism. But identifying bureaucratic overlap is easier than eliminating it (as we will see in Chapter 15), and federal public officials typically have very different views than their state counterparts about what qualifies as "wasteful" spending. Consequently, how states will address their long-term debt, and the implications for further devolution in policymaking, remains to be seen. And, as noted in a 2013 study by the Congressional Budget Office, intergovernmental programs involve administrative costs at multiple levels of government; any major cost-cutting efforts have to be coordinated between Washington and the states, and that never proves easy.

Congress and Federalism

Just as it remains to be seen whether the Supreme Court will continue to revive the doctrine of state sovereignty, so it is not yet clear whether the devolution movement will regain momentum, stall, or be reversed. But whatever the movement's fate, the United States will not become a wholly centralized nation. There remains more political and policy diversity in America than one is likely to find in any other large industrialized nation. The reason is not only that state and local governments have retained certain constitutional protections but also that members of Congress continue to think of themselves as the representatives of localities *to* Washington and not as the representatives *of* Washington to the localities. As we shall see in Chapter 13, American politics, even at the national level, remains local in its orientation.

But if this is true, why do these same members of Congress pass laws that create so many problems for, and stimulate so many complaints from, mayors and governors? One reason is that members of Congress represent different constituencies from the same localities. For example, one member of Congress from Los Angeles may think of the city as a collection of businesspeople, homeowners, and taxpayers, while another may think of it as a group of African Americans, Hispanics, and nature lovers. If Washington wants to simply send money to Los Angeles, these two representatives could be expected to vote together. But if Washington wants to impose mandates or restrictions on the city, these representatives might very well vote on opposite sides, each voting as his or her constituents would most likely prefer.

Another reason is that the organizations that once linked members of Congress to local groups have eroded. As we shall see in Chapter 9, the political parties, which once allowed many localities to speak with a single voice in Washington, have decayed to the point where most members of Congress now operate as free agents, judging local needs and national moods independently. In the 1960s, these needs and moods seemed to require creating new grant programs; in the 1970s, they seemed to require voting for new mandates; in the 1980s and 1990s, they seemed to require letting the cities and states alone experiment with new ways of meeting their needs; and today, some say they require rethinking devolution before it goes "too far."

There are exceptions. In some states, the parties continue to be strong, to dominate decision making in the state legislatures, and to significantly affect the way their congressional delegations behave. Democratic members of Congress from Chicago, for example, typically have a common background in party politics and share at least some allegiance to important party leaders.

But these exceptions are becoming fewer and fewer. As a result, when somebody tries to speak "for" a city or state in Washington, that person has little claim to any real authority. The mayor of Philadelphia may favor one program, the governor of Pennsylvania may favor another, and individual local and state officials—school superintendents, the insurance commissioner, public health administrators—may favor still others. In bidding for federal aid, those parts of the state or city that are best organized often do the best, and increasingly these groups are not the political parties but rather specialized occupational groups such as doctors or schoolteachers. If one is to ask, therefore, why a member of Congress does not listen to his or her state anymore, the answer is, "What do you mean by *the state?* Which official, which occupational group, which party leader speaks for the state?"

Finally, Americans differ in the extent to which we prefer federal as opposed to local decisions. When people are asked which level of government gives them the most for their money,

WHAT WOULD YOU DO?

MEMORANDUM

To: *Secretary of Education Julie Dew*

From: *White House Special Assistant Jack Patrick*

Subject: *National curriculum for elementary and secondary schools*

As promised in her campaign platform, the president would like to expand upon the No Child Left Behind Act to develop a national curriculum for all elementary and secondary schoolchildren, beginning with high school, to better prepare students for the 21st-century workforce. The major arguments for and against this proposal follow. Will you present the initiative and address states' concerns at the National Governors Association next week?

Arguments for:

1. American jobs in the 21st century will require advanced skills in literacy, mathematics, and information technology that all schools must teach.

2. Variations in state curriculum standards leave students ill-prepared for college, which increasingly is a necessary credential for long-term employment.

3. If the national government does not invest in creating a uniform school curriculum now, then increased funding will be needed for remedial instruction later.

Arguments against:

1. States are better able to determine educational standards that will prepare their diverse populations for the workforce than the federal government.

News »

Expanding No Child Left Behind?

The president seeks a national curriculum for all K-12 schoolchildren. Many state school boards argue that federally mandated standards will do more harm than good.

2. Imposing a national curriculum will stifle state and local creativity in education, and will be so basic that it will make little difference in college preparation.

3. The national government has a history of imposing educational mandates on states with insufficient funding, and governors are skeptical of receiving sufficient funding to successfully implement a national curriculum for students with varying needs.

4. Expressly preempting more state laws could come back to bite us when it comes to state laws that we favor over contrary federal ones.

Your decision:

Support bill _____   Oppose bill _____

---

relatively poor citizens are likely to mention the federal government first, whereas relatively well-to-do citizens are more likely to mention local government. If we add to income other measures of social diversity—race, religion, and region—there emerge even sharper differences of opinion about which level of government works best. It is this social diversity—and the fact that it is represented not only by state and local leaders but also by members of Congress—that keeps federalism alive and makes it so important. Americans simply do not agree on enough things, or even on which level of government ought to decide on those things, to make possible a unitary system.

LEARNING OBJECTIVES

1. Why does the United States have federalism?

The Framers of the Constitution created a federal system of government for the United States because they wanted to balance the power of the central government with states that would exercise independent influence over most areas of people's lives, outside of national concerns such as defense, coining money, and so forth. Liberty would be protected by requiring the federal government to share power and authority with the states.

2. How has American federalism evolved from the Founding to the present?

Since the Founding, the balance of power between the national government and the states has shifted over time. Overall, the federal government's power and responsibilities have increased, particularly with the expansion of programs in the 20th century. Still, states exercise broad latitude in implementing policies, and they frequently provide models for the federal government to consider in creating national policies.

3. Which level of government does federalism favor, the national government or the states?

The short answer is, "it depends." In some areas, such as national defense and homeland security, the federal government dominates. In other areas, such as crime control and driving regulations, states primarily decide policy. And in some areas, such as education and health care, states traditionally have made policy decisions, but the federal government has become increasingly involved as such issues are deemed national priorities.

4. Where is sovereignty located in the American political system?

Strictly speaking, the answer is "nowhere." Sovereignty means supreme or ultimate political authority. A sovereign government is one that is legally and politically independent of any other government. No government in America, including the national government headquartered in Washington, D.C., meets that definition. In the American political system, federal and state governments share sovereignty in complicated and ever-changing ways. Both constitutional tradition (the doctrine of dual sovereignty) and everyday politicking (fights over federal grants, mandates, and conditions of aid) render the national government supreme in some matters (national defense, for example) and the states supreme in others (education, for instance).

5. How is power divided between the national government and the states under the Constitution?

Early in American history, local governments and the states had most of it. In the 20th century, the national government gained power. In the last two decades, the states have won back some of their power because of Supreme Court decisions and legislative efforts to devolve certain federal programs to the states. But the distribution of power between the national government and the states is never as simple or as settled as it may appear.

6. What competing values are at stake in federalism?

Basically two: equality versus participation. Federalism means that citizens living in different parts of the country will be treated differently, not only in spending programs, such as welfare, but also in legal systems that assign in different places different penalties to similar offenses or that differentially enforce civil rights laws. But federalism also means that more opportunities exist for participation in making decisions—in influencing what is taught in the schools and in deciding where highways and government projects are to be built. Indeed, differences in public policy—that is, unequal treatment—are in large part the result of participation in decision making. It is difficult, perhaps impossible, to have more of one of these values without having less of the other.

7. Who should decide which matters ought to be governed mainly or solely by national laws?

In practice, the federal courts often have been the main or final arbiters of federalism. As we shall see in Chapter 6, it was the U.S. Supreme Court that decided to ban state and local laws that kept children in racially segregated public schools. Constitutional amendments initiated by members of Congress also have been used to apply legally enforceable national standards to matters once left to state or local governments. Examples would include the Twenty-sixth Amendment, which gave 18-year-old citizens the right to vote. Not surprisingly, when state and local officials have been permitted to decide, they usually have favored national laws or standards when that has served their political interests or desire for "free" money, but have decried them as "intrusive" or worse when that has not.

TO LEARN MORE

State news: **www.stateline.org**

Council of State Governments: **www.csg.org**

National Governors Association: **www.nga.org**

Supreme Court decisions: **www.findlaw.com/casecode/ supreme.html**

Beer, Samuel H. *To Make a Nation: The Rediscovery of American Federalism*. Cambridge: Harvard University Press, 1993. The definitive study of the philosophical bases of American federalism.

Conlan, Timothy. *From New Federalism to Devolution*. Washington, D.C.: Brookings Institution, 1998. A masterful overview of the politics of federalism from Richard Nixon to Bill Clinton.

Daniel, Ronald, Donald F. Kettl, and Howard Kureuther, eds. *On Risk and Disaster: Lessons from Hurricane Katrina*. Philadelphia: University of Pennsylvania Press, 2006. Several experts evaluate the government response.

Derthick, Martha N. *Keeping the Compound Republic*. Washington, D.C.: Brookings Institution, 2001. A masterful analysis of trends in American federalism from the Founding to the present.

Diamond, Martin. "The Federalist's View of Federalism." In *Essays in Federalism*, edited by George C.S. Benson.

Claremont, Calif.: Institute for Studies in Federalism of Claremont Men's College, 1961, pp. 21–64. A profound analysis of what the Founders meant by federalism.

Grodzins, Morton. *The American System*. Chicago: Rand McNally, 1966. Argues that American federalism has always involved extensive sharing of functions between national and state governments.

Melnick, R. Shep. *Between the Lines: Interpreting Welfare Rights*. Washington, D.C.: Brookings Institution, 1994. An examination of how trends in statutory interpretation have affected broader policy developments, including the expansion of the agenda of national government, the persistence of divided government, and the resurgence and decentralization of Congress.

Riker, William H. *Federalism: Origin, Operation, Significance*. Boston: Little, Brown, 1964. A classic explanation and critical analysis of federalism here and abroad.

Teske, Paul. *Regulation in the States*. Washington, D.C.: Brookings Institution, 2004. States have responded to devolution by adding new regulations of their own.

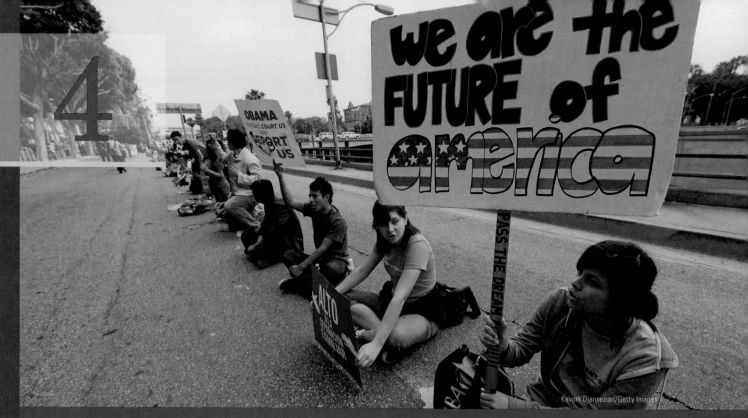

Kevork Djansezian/Getty Images

4

American Political Culture

LEARNING OBJECTIVES

1. What is American political culture?

2. How does political culture differ from political ideology?

3. Does the United States have a unique political culture compared to other advanced industrialized democracies?

4. Do Americans trust their government?

5. Why do Americans accept great differences in wealth and income?

6. Why does the American government behave differently than governments in countries with similar constitutions?

In 1835, a French political official, Alexis de Tocqueville, visited the United States to conduct research on its prison systems. Based on two years of travel across the country, de Tocqueville wrote a two-volume study titled *Democracy in America* that continues to be one of the defining texts of American political culture. De Tocqueville argued that democracy endured in the United States because of geography, laws, and "the manners and customs of the people."[1] He concluded that the attitude of Americans about the merits of democracy was fundamental to its success here.

In the 21st century, several issues divide Americans: how to address the rapidly growing national debt, how to battle terrorists, how to determine the appropriate scope of responsibility and power for the federal government, and so forth. But the political parties and interest groups (both of which we will discuss later in this textbook) that disagree about these issues share a common belief in preserving the principles of American constitutionalism— liberty, equality of opportunity, and so on—even if they differ over how to put those principles in to practice. The Tea Party movement that has developed in recent years, for example, derives its name from a historic event in American politics, and its adherents claim that they seek to return American democracy to its founding principles. People in the United States may have very different views today of what democracy means for policymaking, but they continue to display the same veneration for democracy that de Tocqueville identified more than 175 years ago.

The United States, the United Kingdom, and France are all western nations with well-established representative democracies. Millions of people in each country (maybe including you) have been tourists in one or both of the other two countries. Ask any American who has spent time in either country "what's it like?" and you probably will hear generalizations about the "culture"—"friendly" or "cold," "very different" or "surprisingly like home," and so on.

But "culture" also counts when it comes to politics and government. Politically speaking, there are at least three major differences among and between countries: constitutional, demographic, and cultural. Each difference is important, and the differences tend to feed each other. Arguably, however, the cultural differences are not only the most consequential, but also often the trickiest

to analyze. As we will see, that holds true not only for cross-national differences between America and other countries, but also when it comes to deciphering political divides within America itself. And the differences usually endure over time.

> *political culture* A patterned and sustained way of thinking about how political and economic life ought to be carried out.

Political Culture

Constitutional differences tend to be fairly obvious and easy to summarize. America and France each have a written constitution, while the United Kingdom does not. The United States separates powers between three equal branches of its national government. By contrast, the United Kingdom has a parliamentary system in which the legislature chooses a prime minister from within its own ranks. And France has a semi-presidential or quasi-parliamentary system divided into three branches: the president selects a prime minister from the majority party in the lower house of the parliament, and the prime minister exercises most executive powers.

Demographic differences are also straightforward. America is a large land with more than 300 million citizens. The dominant language is English, but millions of people also speak Spanish. About one-sixth of its population is Hispanic. More than 80 percent of its adults identify themselves as Christians, but they are divided between Catholics (about a quarter) and more than a dozen different Protestant denominations. By comparison, France and the United Kingdom are each home to about 60 million people and have small but growing immigrant and foreign-born subpopulations. Most French (more than 80 percent) are Catholic; most British belong to the Church of England (Anglican, the official state religion) or the Church of Scotland. But in neither country do many people go to church.

The differences among these three democracies go much deeper. Each country has a different **political culture**—a patterned and sustained way of thinking about how political and economic life ought to be carried out. Most Americans, British, and French think that democracy is good, favor majority rule, and believe in respecting minority rights. And few in each nation would say that a leader who loses office in an election has any right to retake office by force. Even so, their political cultures differ. Cross-national surveys consistently find that Americans are far more likely than the French or British to believe that everybody should be equal politically, but far less likely to think it important that everybody should be equal economically. For example, in one large survey, the French and British were more than twice as likely as Americans to agree that "it is government's responsibility to take care of the very poor," and less than a third as likely as Americans to agree that "government should *not* guarantee every citizen food and basic shelter."[2]

When it comes to ensuring political equality or equality before the law, Americans are more committed from an early age. For instance, a classic study compared how children aged 10 to 14 in the United States, Great Britain, and France responded to a series of questions about democracy and the law. They were asked to imagine the following:

> One day the President (substitute the Queen in England, President of the Republic in France) was driving his car to a meeting. Because he was late, he was driving very fast. The police stopped the car. Finish the story.[3]

The children from each country ended the story quite differently. French children declared that the president would not be reprimanded. British

Alexis de Tocqueville (1805–1859) was a young French aristocrat who came to the United States to study the American prison system. He wrote the brilliant Democracy in America (2 vols., 1835–1840), a profound analysis of our political culture.

children said the queen would not be punished. But American children were most likely to say that the president would be fined or ticketed, just like any other person should be.

Cross-national differences wrought by political culture seem to be even sharper between America and such countries as Argentina, Brazil, Mexico, and the Philippines. Why do these countries, whose constitutions are very much like the American one, have so much trouble with corruption, military takeovers, and the rise of demagogues? Each of these nations has had periods of democratic rule, but only for a short period of time, despite having an elected president, a separately elected congress, and an independent judiciary.

Some have argued that democracy took root in the United States but not in other countries that copied its constitution because America offered more abundant land and greater opportunities for people. No feudal aristocracy occupied the land, taxes remained low, and when one place after another filled up, people kept pushing west to find new opportunities. America became a nation of small, independent farmers with relatively few landless peasants or indentured servants.

However, as Alexis de Tocqueville, the perceptive French observer of American politics, noted in the 1830s, much of South America contains fertile land and rich resources, but democracy has not flourished there. The constitution and the physical advantages of the land cannot by themselves explain the persistence of any nation's democratic institutions. Nor can they account for the fact that American democracy survived a Civil War and thrived as wave after wave of immigrants became citizens and made the democracy more demographically diverse. What can begin to account for such differences are the customs of the people—what de Tocqueville called their "moral and intellectual characteristics,"[4] and what social scientists today call political culture.

Japan, like the United States, is a democracy. But while America is an immigrant nation that often has favored open immigration policies, Japan remains a Japanese nation in which immigration policies are highly restrictive and foreign-born citizens are few. America, like Saudi Arabia, is a country in which most people profess religious beliefs, and many people identify themselves as orthodox believers. But America's Christian majority favors religious pluralism and church-state separation, while Saudi Arabia's Muslim majority supports laws that maintain Islam as the state religion. In Germany, courts have held that non-Christian religious symbols and dress, but not Christian ones, may be banned from schools and other public places. In France, the government forbids wearing any religious garb in

At the height of immigration to this country, there was a striking emphasis on creating a shared political culture. Schoolchildren, whatever their national origin, were taught to salute this country's flag.

schools. In the United States, such rulings or restrictions would be unthinkable.

The Political System

There are at least five important elements in the American view of the political system:

- *Liberty:* Americans are preoccupied with their rights. They believe they should be free to do pretty much as they please, with some exceptions, as long as they don't hurt other people.

- *Equality:* Americans believe everybody should have an equal vote and an equal chance to participate and succeed.

- *Democracy:* Americans think government officials should be accountable to the people.

- *Civic duty:* Americans generally feel people ought to take community affairs seriously and help out when they can.[5]

- *Individual responsibility:* A characteristically American view is that, barring some disability, individuals are responsible for their own actions and well-being.

By vast majorities, Americans believe that every citizen should have an equal chance to influence government policy and to hold public office, and they oppose the idea of letting people have titles such as "Lord" or "Duke," as in England. By somewhat smaller majorities, they believe people should be allowed to vote even if they can't read or write or vote intelligently.[6] Though Americans recognize that people differ in their abilities, they overwhelmingly agree with the statement that "teaching children that all people are really equal recognizes that all people are equally worthy and deserve equal treatment."[7]

At least three questions can be raised about this political culture. First, how do we know that the American people share these beliefs? For most of our history there were no public opinion polls, and even after they became commonplace, they were rather crude tools for measuring the existence and meaning of complex, abstract ideas. There is in fact no way to prove that values such as those listed above are important to Americans. But neither is there good reason for dismissing the list out of hand. One can infer, as have many scholars, the existence of certain values by a close study of the kinds of books Americans read, the speeches they hear, the slogans to which they respond, and the political choices they make, as well as by noting the observations of insightful foreign visitors. Personality tests, as well as opinion polls—particularly those asking similar questions in different countries—also supply useful evidence, some of which will be reviewed in the following paragraphs.

Second, if these values are important to Americans, how can we explain the existence in our society of behavior that is obviously inconsistent with them? For example, if white Americans believe in equality of opportunity, why did so many of them for so long deny that equality to African Americans? That people act contrary to their professed beliefs is an everyday fact of life: people believe in honesty, yet they steal from their employers and sometimes underreport their taxable income. Besides values, self-interest and social circumstances also shape behavior. Gunnar Myrdal, a Swedish observer of American society, described race relations in this country as "an American dilemma" resulting from the conflict between the "American creed" (a belief in equality of opportunity) and American behavior (denying African Americans full citizenship).[8] But the creed remains important because it is a source of change: as more and more people become aware of the inconsistency between their values and their behavior, that behavior slowly changes.[9] Race relations in this country would take a very different course if instead of an abstract but widespread belief in equality there were an equally widespread belief that one race is inherently inferior to another.

The late political scientist, Samuel P. Huntington, put it this way: "Critics say that America is a lie because its reality falls so far short of its ideals. America is not a lie, it is a disappointment. And it can be a disappointment only because it is also a hope."[10]

Third, if there is agreement among Americans on certain political values, why has there been so much political conflict in our history? How could a people who agree on such fundamentals fight a bloody civil war, engage in violent labor-management disputes, take to the streets in riots and demonstrations, and sue each other in countless court battles? Conflict, even violent struggles, can occur over specific policies even among those who share, at some level of abstraction, common beliefs. Many political values may be irrelevant to specific controversies: there is no abstract value, for example, that would settle the question of whether steelworkers ought to organize unions. More important, much of our conflict has occurred precisely because we have strong beliefs that happen, as each of us interprets them, to be in conflict. Equality of opportunity seems an attractive idea, but sometimes it can be pursued only by curtailing another value that most people hold dear, personal liberty. The states went to war in 1861 over one aspect of that conflict—the rights of slaves versus the rights of slave-owners.

Indeed, the Civil War illustrates the way certain fundamental beliefs about how a democratic regime ought to be organized have persisted despite bitter conflict over the policies adopted by particular governments. When the southern states seceded from the Union, they formed not a wholly different government but one modeled, despite some important differences, on the U.S. Constitution. Even some of the language of the Constitution was duplicated, suggesting that the southern states believed not that a new form of government or a different political culture ought to be created, but rather that the South was the true repository of the existing constitutional and cultural order.[11]

Perhaps the most frequently encountered evidence that Americans believe themselves bound by common values and common hopes is the persistence of the word *Americanism* in our political vocabulary. Throughout the 19th and 20th centuries, *Americanism* and *the American dream* were familiar terms not only in Fourth of July speeches but also in everyday discourse. For many years, the House of Representatives had a committee called the House Un-American Activities Committee. There is hardly any example to be found abroad of such a way of thinking: There is no "Britishism" or "Frenchism," and when Britons and French people become worried about subversion, they call it a problem of internal security, not a manifestation of "un-British" or "un-French" activities.

We have ended slavery, endorsed civil rights, and expanded the scope of free discussion, but these gains have not ended political conflict. We argue about abortion, morality, religion, immigration, and affirmative action. Some people believe that core moral principles are absolute, while others feel they are relative to the situation. Some people believe all immigrants should become like every other American, while others argue that we should, in the name of diversity and multiculturalism, celebrate group differences.

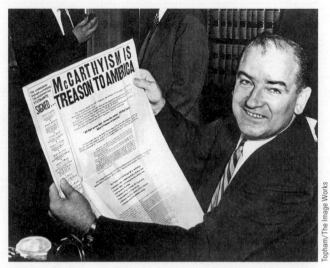

In the 1950s Senator Joseph McCarthy of Wisconsin was the inspiration for the word "McCarthyism" after his highly publicized attacks on alleged communists working in the federal government.

Much depends on how we define a good citizen. Some people define a good citizen as a person who votes, pays his or her taxes, obeys the law, and supports the military; others describe a good citizen as skeptical of government and ready to join protest movements and boycott products he or she does not like. These competing opinions reflect differences in age and education. Older people are more likely to take the first view, while younger people who have been to college are more likely to take the second.[12]

But these conflicts, though they affect every American, should not obscure the underlying level of agreement or the reality of a widely shared political culture.

The Economic System

Americans judge the economic system using many of the same standards by which they judge the political system, albeit with some very important differences. As it is in American politics, liberty is important in the U.S. economy. Thus Americans support the idea of a free-enterprise economic system, calling the nation's economy "generally fair and efficient" and denying that it "survives by keeping the poor down."[13] However, there are limits to how much freedom they think should exist in the marketplace. People support government regulation of business in order to keep some firms from becoming too powerful and to correct specific abuses.[14]

Americans are more willing to tolerate economic inequality than political inequality. They believe in maintaining "equality of opportunity" in the economy but not "equality of results." If everyone has an equal opportunity to get ahead, then it is all right for people with more ability to earn higher salaries and for wages to be set based on how hard people work rather than on their economic needs. Hardly anyone is upset by the fact that Bill Gates, Warren Buffett, and Donald Trump are rich men. Although Americans are quite willing to support education and training programs to help disadvantaged people get ahead, they are strongly opposed to anything that looks like preferential treatment (for example, hiring quotas) in the workplace.[15]

The leaders of very liberal political groups, such as civil rights and feminist organizations, are more willing than the average American to support preferential treatment in the hiring and promoting of minorities and women. They do so because, unlike most citizens, they believe that whatever disadvantages minorities and women face are the result of failures of the economic system rather than the fault of individuals. Even so, these leaders strongly support the idea that earnings should be based on ability and oppose the idea of having any top limit on what people can earn.[16]

This popular commitment to economic individualism and personal responsibility may help explain how Americans think about particular public policies, such as welfare and civil rights. Polls show

WHAT'S YOUR ISSUE?

Naturalized Citizenship Policies

Hispanics are the largest and fastest-growing minority group in America. The nation's 53 million Hispanics represent about 17 percent of the total U.S. population. They comprise more than a third of the population in several states, including California, New Mexico, and Texas. By 2050, about 1 in 4 U.S. residents will be Hispanic.

Some analysts have asserted that Hispanic immigrants to the United States, the vast majority of who come from Mexico, will remain strangers to American political culture. But all the evidence suggests that, if anything, Hispanic immigrants over time are far more likely to embrace and emulate, rather than to reject or refashion, American political culture.

- *Linguistic adaptation:* Regardless of age, educational level, or residential concentration, Hispanic immigrants from one generation to the next speak English as their first language (by the third generation, 71 percent are English-dominant).

- *Hyphenated-American identity:* Most Hispanics think of themselves as both American and Hispanic; and once Hispanic immigrants become citizens, they become far more likely to identify either as "just an American" or as "Hispanic-American."

- *Religiosity:* Measured by professed importance of religion and rates of church attendance, Hispanics are no more or less religious than non-Hispanic whites.

- *Patriotism:* 91 percent of Hispanic-Americans say they "love America," and 86 percent express "pride in the American flag."

- *Work ethic:* The higher the proportion of Hispanics living and working in a given state, the more likely it is that non-Hispanics will agree that Hispanics are especially hard-working.

In 2011, 15.5 million legal immigrants became naturalized U.S. citizens. U.S. citizenship confers benefits on recipients including the right to vote, eligibility to participate in federal programs, expanded job opportunities (including government employment), and others. The rate at which Hispanic immigrants become naturalized U.S. citizens continues to lag behind those of other immigrants. For instance, in 2011, the naturalization rate among all legal immigrants was 72 percent, but for Mexican legal immigrants the rate was only 36 percent. In surveys, among the main reasons given by Hispanic immigrants for not naturalizing are language barriers, financial barriers, confusion about the naturalization process, and, of course, ineligibility relating to length of stay requirements.

Many proposals have been made to change naturalized citizenship policies, overcome these problems, and expedite naturalization for Hispanics and all other legal immigrants. So far, however, no major reforms have been made. What do you suppose is behind the fact that the policies have remained largely unchanged, and what, if any, changes to naturalized citizenship policies might you favor (or oppose), and why?

Sources: Pew Hispanic Research Center, *An Awakened Giant: The Hispanic Electorate is Likely to Double by 2020*, November 14, 2012; Jack Citrin, et al., "Testing Huntington: Is Hispanic Immigration a Threat to American Identity?" *Perspectives on Politics* 5 (March 2007): pp. 31–48; Samuel P. Huntington, *Who Are We? The Challenges to America's National Identity* (Simon and Shuster, 2004); and U.S. Census Bureau, "Facts for Features," July 15, 2010.

that Americans are willing to help people "truly in need" (this includes the elderly and the disabled) but not those deemed "able to take care of themselves" (this includes, in the public's mind, people "on welfare"). Also, Americans dislike preferential hiring programs and the use of quotas to deal with racial inequality.

At the core of these policy attitudes is a widely (but not universally) shared commitment to economic individualism and personal responsibility. Some scholars, among them Donald Kinder and David Sears, interpret these individualistic values as "symbolic racism"—a kind of plausible camouflage for antiblack attitudes.[17] But other scholars, such as Paul M. Sniderman and Michael Gray Hagen, argue that these views are not a smoke screen for bigotry or insensitivity but a genuine commitment to the ethic of self-reliance.[18] Since there are many Americans on both sides of this issue, debates about welfare and civil rights tend to be especially intense. What is striking about the American political culture is that in this country the individualist view of social policy is by far the most popular.[19]

Views about specific economic policies change. Americans are now much more inclined than they once were to believe that the government should help the needy and regulate business. But the commitment to certain underlying principles has been remarkably enduring. In 1924, almost half of the high school students in Muncie, Indiana, said that "it is entirely the fault of the man himself if he cannot succeed" and disagreed with the view that differences in wealth showed that the system was unjust. More than half a century later, the students in this same high school were asked the same questions again, with the same results.[20]

How We Compare: Comparing America with Other Nations

Americans like their own country more than people in European democracies like theirs. In Table 4.1, we see that 71 percent of Americans are proud to be American compared to only 21 percent of Germans who are proud to be German. There are other differences as well: a majority of the French, Germans, and Italians think success in life is determined by forces outside an individual's own control; Americans deeply disagree. Most Americans think children should be taught the value of hard work and that a belief in God is necessary for morality; most western European countries have the opposite view.

America is not very popular abroad, but these data suggest that the reasons go well beyond the war in Iraq or the criticism of former president George W. Bush. Americans have very different views about important things than do Europeans. Following are some examples drawn from politics, the economy, and religion.

The Political System

Sweden has a well-developed democratic government, with a constitution, free speech, an elected legislature, competing political parties, and a reasonably honest and nonpartisan bureaucracy. But the Swedish political culture is significantly different from ours; it is more deferential than participatory. Though almost all adult Swedes vote in national elections, few participate in politics in any other way. They defer to the decisions of experts and specialists who work for the government, rarely challenge

TABLE 4.1   Attitudes in the USA and Other Democracies

	Pride	Outside Control	Teach Value of Work	God and Morality
USA	71%	32%	60%	58%
Canada	66	35	51	30
Britain	45	48	38	25
France	38	54	50	13
Germany	21	68	22	33
Italy	38	66	Na	27

Key to columns:

Pride: "I am very proud to be a member of [country]"

Outside Control: "Success in life is determined by forces outside our control"

Teach Value of Work: "Children should be taught the value of hard work"

God and Morality: "It is necessary to believe in God to be moral"

Source: © 2006 by Andrew Kohut and Bruce Stokes. Reprinted by permission of Henry Holt and Company, LLC and the Pew Research Center.

governmental decisions in court, believe leaders and legislators ought to decide issues on the basis of "what is best" more than on "what the people want," and value equality as much as (or more than) liberty.[21] Whereas Americans are contentious, Swedes value harmony; while Americans tend to assert their rights, Swedes tend to observe their obligations.

The contrast in political cultures is even greater when one looks at a nation, such as Japan, with a wholly different history and set of traditions. One study compared the values expressed by a small number of upper-status Japanese with those of some similarly situated Americans. Whereas the Americans emphasized the virtues of individualism, competition, and equality in their political, economic, and social relations, the Japanese attached greater value to maintaining good relations with colleagues, having decisions made by groups, preserving social harmony, and displaying respect for hierarchy. The Americans were more concerned than the Japanese with rules and with treating others fairly but impersonally, with due regard for their rights. The Japanese, on the other hand, stressed the importance of being sensitive to the personal needs of others, avoiding conflict, and reaching decisions through discussion rather than the application of rules.[22]

A classic study of political culture in five nations found that Americans, and to a lesser degree citizens of the United Kingdom, had a stronger sense of **civic duty** (a belief that one has an obligation to participate in civic and political affairs) and a stronger sense of **civic competence** (a belief that one can affect government policies) than the citizens of Germany, Italy, or Mexico. More than half of all Americans and a third of all Britons believed the average citizen ought to "be active in one's community," compared to only a tenth in Italy and a fifth in Germany. Moreover, many more Americans and Britons than Germans, Italians, or Mexicans believed they could "do something" about an unjust national law or local regulation.[23] A more recent study of citizen participation in politics found that while America lagged behind Austria, the Netherlands, Germany, and the United Kingdom in voter participation, when it came to campaigning, attending political meetings, becoming active in the local community, and contacting government officials, Americans were as active—or substantially more active—than citizens elsewhere.[24]

Today the American people have less trust in government than they once did. But even so, popular confidence in political institutions remains higher here than in many places abroad. In cross-national surveys conducted in the United States and 16 other democracies, Americans expressed more confidence in public institutions (the police, the armed forces, the legal system, and the civil service) than the citizens of all but four other countries (Denmark, Ireland,

Northern Ireland, and Norway), and greater confidence in private institutions (the church, major companies, the press, trade unions) than the citizens of any other nation.[25] In other cross-national surveys, Americans were more likely than the French or Germans to say they were "very patriotic" (see Figure 4.1). Of course, Americans know that their country has a lot of faults. But even the most disaffected voters believe the United States needs to change only certain policies, not its system of government.[26]

> **civic duty** A belief that one has an obligation to participate in civic and political affairs.
>
> **civic competence** A belief that one can affect government policies.

FIGURE 4.1 Political Culture in America and Other Democracies

Sources: World Values Survey Wave 4; International Social Survey Program National Identity Module II (2003–2004).

The Economic System

The political culture of Sweden is not only more deferential than ours but also more inclined to favor equality of results over equality of opportunity. Sidney Verba and Gary Orren compared the views of Swedish and American trade union and political party leaders on a variety of economic issues. In both countries, the leaders were chosen from either blue-collar unions or the major liberal political party (the Democrats in the United States, the Social Democrats in Sweden).

The results are quite striking. By margins of four or five to one, the Swedish leaders were more likely to believe in giving workers equal pay than their American counterparts. Moreover, by margins of at least three to one, the Swedes were more likely than the Americans to favor putting a top limit on incomes.[27]

Just what these differences in beliefs mean in dollars-and-cents terms was revealed by the answers to another question. Each group was asked what should be the ratio between the income of an executive and that of a menial worker (a dishwasher in Sweden, an elevator operator in the United States). The Swedish leaders said the ratio should be a little over two to one. That is, if the dishwasher earned $200 a week, the executive should earn no more than $440 to $480 a week. But the American leaders were ready to let the executive earn between $2,260 and $3,040 per week when the elevator operator was earning $200.

Americans, compared to people in many other countries, are more likely to think that freedom is more important than equality and less likely to think that hard work goes unrewarded or that the government should guarantee citizens a basic standard of living. These cultural differences make a difference in politics. In fact, there is less income inequality in Sweden than in the United States—the Swedish government sees to that.

The Civic Role of Religion

In the 1830s, de Tocqueville was amazed at how religious Americans were in comparison to his fellow Europeans. From the first days of the new Republic to the present, America has been among the most religious countries in the world. The average American is more likely than the average European to believe in God, to pray on a daily basis, and to acknowledge clear standards of right and wrong.[28]

Religious people donate more than three times as much money to charity as secular people, even when the incomes of the two groups are the same, and they volunteer their time twice as often. And this is true whether or not religious people go to church or synagogue regularly. Moreover, religious people are more likely to give money and donate time to nonreligious organizations, such as the Red Cross, than secular people.[29] It is clear that religion in America has a large effect on our culture.

Religion also affects our politics. The religious revivalist movement of the late 1730s and early 1740s (known as the First Great Awakening) transformed the political life of the American colonies. Religious ideas fueled the break with England, which, in the words of the Declaration of Independence, had violated "the laws of nature and nature's God." Religious leaders were central to the struggle over slavery in

The U.S. House of Representatives starts a new session of Congress with a prayer.

Chris Maddaloni/CQ Roll Call/Getty Images

the 19th century and the temperance movement of the early 20th century.

Both liberals and conservatives have used the pulpit to promote political change. The civil rights movement of the 1950s and 1960s was led mainly by black religious leaders, most prominently Martin Luther King, Jr. In the 1980s, a conservative religious group known as the Moral Majority advocated constitutional amendments that would allow prayer in public schools and ban abortion. In the 1990s, another conservative religious group, the Christian Coalition, attracted an enormous amount of media attention and became a prominent force in many national, state, and local elections.

Candidates for national office in most contemporary democracies mention religion rarely if they mention it at all. Not so in America. During the 2000 presidential campaign, for example, both Democratic candidate Al Gore and Republican candidate George W. Bush gave major speeches extolling the virtues of religion and advocating the right of religious organizations that deliver social services to receive government funding on the same basis as all other nonprofit organizations. President Barack Obama opted to keep the White House "faith-based" office that Bush had established, expanded the office to

cabinet centers at every federal cabinet department, and made frequent references to religion in public addresses throughout his first term.

The general American feeling about religion became apparent when a federal appeals court in 2002 tried to ban the Pledge of Allegiance because it contained the phrase "under God." There was an overwhelming and bipartisan condemnation of the ruling. To a degree that would be almost unthinkable in many other democracies, religious beliefs will probably continue to shape political culture in America for many generations to come. The Supreme Court, by deciding that the man who brought the case was not entitled to do so, left the Pledge intact without deciding whether it was constitutional.

Finally, even Americans who do not consider themselves "religious" or are unaffiliated with any organized religious group are not uniformly secular. For instance, while it is true that the fraction of Americans reporting no religious affiliation has risen in recent years to one-in-five adults, one-third of these religiously unaffiliated adults say that religion is important in their lives, 40 percent pray from time to time, half describe themselves as either "religious" or "spiritual," and two-thirds say they believe in God or a universal spirit (see Table 4.2).

TABLE 4.2 Americans' Beliefs about Religion, 2012

	U.S. General Public	Unaffiliated	Affiliated
How important is religion in your life?			
Very important	58	14	67
Somewhat	22	19	24
Not too/not at all	18	65	8
Don't know	1	1	-
	100	100	100
Believe in God or universal spirit			
Yes, absolutely certain	69	30	77
Yes, but less certain	23	38	20
No	7	27	2
Don't know	2	5	1
	100	100	100
Frequency of prayer			
Daily	58	21	66
Weekly/monthly	21	20	22
Seldom/never	19	58	11
Don't know	2	1	1
	100	100	100
Think of self as			
Religious person	65	18	75
Spiritual but not religious person	18	37	15
Neither religious nor spiritual	15	42	8
Don't know	2	2	1
	100	100	100

Source: Pew Research Center, "'Nones' on the Rise: One-in-Five Adults Have No Religious Affiliation," © 2012, http://www.pewforum.org/files/2012/10/ NonesOnTheRise-full.pdf. Figures may not add to 100% due to rounding.

CONSTITUTIONAL CONNECTIONS

"A Religious People"

Justice William O. Douglas was the U.S. Supreme Court's longest-serving member, beginning his term in 1939 and ending it in 1975. When Douglas died in 1980, he was widely remembered as the Court's most consistently liberal voice, a major force in legalizing abortion rights, and a proponent of the "wall-of-separation" doctrine regarding church-state relations (see Chapter 5). In *Zorach v. Clauson* (1952), however, Douglas held that a New York City policy permitting public school students to be released during the school day to receive religious instruction off school grounds was not only constitutional but consistent with Americans' best "traditions" as "a religious people:"

> *We are a religious people whose institutions presuppose a Supreme Being. We guarantee the freedom to worship ... We make room for a wide variety of beliefs ... When the state encourages religious instruction or cooperates with religious authorities, it follows the best of our traditions.*

Source: *Zorach v. Clauson*, 343 U.S. 306 (1952).

The Sources of Political Culture

That Americans bring a distinctive way of thinking to their political life is easier to demonstrate than to explain. But even a brief, and necessarily superficial, effort to understand the sources of our political culture can help make its significance clearer.

The American Revolution, as we discussed in Chapter 2, was essentially a war fought over liberty: an assertion by the colonists of what they took to be their rights. Though the Constitution, produced 11 years after the Revolution, had to deal with other issues as well, its animating spirit reflected the effort to reconcile personal liberty with the needs of social control. These founding experiences, and the political disputes that followed, have given to American political thought and culture a preoccupation with the assertion and maintenance of rights. This tradition has imbued the daily conduct of U.S. politics with a kind of adversarial spirit quite foreign to the political life of countries that did not undergo a libertarian revolution or that were formed out of an interest in other goals, such as social equality, national independence, or ethnic supremacy.

The adversarial spirit of the American political culture reflects not only our preoccupation with rights, but also our long-standing distrust of authority and of people wielding power. The colonies' experiences with British rule were one source of that distrust. But another, older source was the religious belief of many Americans, which saw human nature as fundamentally depraved. To the colonists, all of mankind suffered from original sin, symbolized by Adam and Eve eating the forbidden fruit in the Garden of Eden. Since no one was born innocent, no one could be trusted with power. Thus, the Constitution had to be designed in such a way as to curb the darker side of human nature. Otherwise, everyone's rights would be in jeopardy.

The contentiousness of a people animated by a suspicion of government and devoted to individualism could easily have made democratic politics so tumultuous as to be impossible. After all, one must be willing to trust others with power if there is to be any kind of democratic government, and sometimes those others will be people not of one's own choosing. The first great test case took place around 1800 in a battle between the Federalists, led by John Adams and Alexander Hamilton, and the Democratic-Republicans, led by Thomas Jefferson and James Madison. The two factions deeply distrusted each other: the Federalists had passed laws designed to suppress Jeffersonian journalists; Jefferson suspected the Federalists were out to subvert the Constitution; and the Federalists believed Jefferson intended to sell out the country to France. But as we shall see in Chapter 9, the threat of civil war never materialized, and the Jeffersonians came to power peacefully. Within a few years, the role of an opposition party became legitimate, and people abandoned the idea of making serious efforts to suppress their opponents. By happy circumstance, people came to accept that liberty and orderly political change could coexist.

The Constitution, by creating a federal system and dividing political authority among competing institutions, provided ample opportunity for widespread—though hardly universal—participation in politics. The election of Jefferson in 1800 produced no political catastrophe, and those who had predicted one were, to a degree, discredited. But other, more fundamental features of American life contributed to the same end. One of the most important of these was religious diversity.

The absence of an established or official religion for the nation as a whole, reinforced by a constitutional prohibition of such an establishment and by the migration to this country of people with different religious backgrounds, meant that religious diversity was inevitable. Since there could be no orthodox or official religion, it became difficult for a corresponding political orthodoxy to emerge. Moreover, the conflict between the Puritan tradition, with its emphasis on faith and hard work, and the Catholic Church, with its devotion to the sacraments and priestly authority, provided a recurrent source of cleavage in American public life. The differences in values between these two groups showed up not only in their religious practices but also in areas involving the regulation of manners and morals, and even in people's choice of political party. For more than a century, candidates for state and national office were deeply divided over whether the sale of liquor should be prohibited, a question that arose ultimately out of competing religious doctrines.

Even though there was no established church, there was certainly a dominant religious tradition—Protestantism, and especially Puritanism. The Protestant churches provided people with both a set of beliefs and an organizational experience that had profound effects on American political culture. Those beliefs encouraged, or even required, a life of personal achievement as well as religious conviction: a believer had an obligation to work, save money, obey the secular law, and do good works. Max Weber explained the rise of capitalism in part by what he called the Protestant ethic—what we now sometimes call the work ethic.[30] Such values had political consequences, as people holding them were motivated to engage in civic and communal action.

Churches offered ready opportunities for developing and practicing civic and political skills. Since most Protestant churches were organized along congregational lines—that is, the church was controlled by its members, who put up the building, hired the preacher, and supervised the finances—they were, in effect, miniature political systems with leaders and committees, conflict and consensus. Developing a participatory political culture was undoubtedly made easier by the existence of a participatory religious culture. Even some Catholic churches in early America were under a degree of lay control. Parishioners owned the church property, negotiated with priests, and conducted church business.

All aspects of culture, including the political, are preserved and transmitted to new generations primarily by the family. Though some believe that the weakening of the family unit has eroded the extent to which it transmits anything, particularly culture, and has enlarged the power of other sources of values—the mass media and the world of friends, fashion, leisure, and entertainment—there is still little doubt that the ways in which we think about the world are largely acquired within the family. In Chapter 7, we shall see that the family is the primary source of one kind of political attitude—identification with one or another political party. Even more important, the family shapes in subtle ways how we think and act on political matters. Erik Erikson, the psychologist, noted certain traits that are more characteristic of American than of European families—the greater freedom enjoyed by children, for example, and the larger measure of equality among family members. These familial characteristics promote a belief, carried through life, that every person has rights deserving protection and that a variety of interests have a legitimate claim to consideration when decisions are made.[31]

The combined effect of religious and ethnic diversity, an individualistic philosophy, fragmented political authority, and the relatively egalitarian American family can be seen in the absence of a high degree of **class-consciousness** among Americans. Class-consciousness means thinking of oneself as a worker whose interests are in opposition to those of management, or vice versa. In this country, most people, whatever their jobs, think of themselves as "middle class."

Though the writings of Horatio Alger are no longer popular, Americans still seem to believe in the message of those stories—that the opportunity for success is available to people who work hard. This may help explain why the United States is the only large industrial democracy without a significant socialist party and why the nation has been slow to adopt certain welfare programs.

The Culture War

Almost all Americans share some elements of a common political culture. Why, then, is there so much cultural conflict in American politics? For many years, the most explosive political issues have included abortion, gay rights, drug use, school prayer, and pornography. Viewed from a Marxist perspective, politics in the United States is utterly baffling: instead of two economic classes engaged in a bitter struggle over wealth, we have two cultural classes locked in a war over values.

> **class-consciousness** A belief that one is a member of an economic group whose interests are opposed to people in other such groups.

orthodox A belief that morality and religion ought to be of decisive importance.

progressive A belief that personal freedom and solving social problems are more important than religion.

As first formulated by sociologist James Davison Hunter, the idea is that there are, broadly defined, two cultural classes in the United States: the **orthodox** and the **progressive**. On the orthodox side are people who believe that morality is as important as, or more important than, self-expression and that moral rules derive from the commands of God or the laws of nature—commands and laws that are relatively clear, unchanging, and independent of individual preferences. On the progressive side are people who think that personal freedom is as important as, or more important than, certain traditional moral rules and that those rules must be evaluated in light of the circumstances of modern life—circumstances that are quite complex, changeable, and dependent on individual preferences.[32]

Most conspicuous among the orthodox are fundamentalist Protestants and evangelical Christians, and so critics who dislike orthodox views often dismiss them as the fanatical expressions of "the Religious Right." But many people who hold orthodox views are not fanatical or deeply religious or right-wing on most issues: they simply have strong views about drugs, pornography, and sexual morality. Similarly, the progressive side often includes members of liberal Protestant denominations (for example, Episcopalians and Unitarians) and people with no strong religious beliefs, and so their critics often denounce them as immoral, anti-Christian radicals who have embraced the ideology of secular humanism, the belief that moral standards do not require religious justification. But few progressives are immoral or anti-Christian, and most do not regard secular humanism as their defining ideology.

Groups supporting and opposing the right to abortion have had many angry confrontations in recent years. The latter have been arrested while attempting to block access to abortion clinics; some clinics have been fire-bombed and at least seven physicians have been killed. A controversy over what schoolchildren should be taught about homosexuals was responsible, in part, for the firing of the head of the New York City school system; in other states, there have been fierce arguments in state legislatures and before the courts over whether gay and lesbian couples should be allowed to marry or adopt children. Although most Americans want to keep heroin, cocaine, and other drugs illegal, a significant number of people want to legalize (or at least decriminalize) their use. The Supreme Court has ruled that there cannot be state-sponsored prayer in public schools, but this has not stopped many parents and school authorities from trying to reinstate school prayer, or at least prayer-like moments of silence. The discovery that a federal agency, the National Endowment for the Arts, had given money to support exhibitions and performances that many people thought were obscene led to a furious congressional struggle over the future of the agency.

The culture war differs from other political disputes (over such matters as taxes, business regulations, and foreign policy) in several ways: money is

Demonstrators from the Occupy Wall Street movement protested income inequality for several weeks in New York City in the fall of 2011, before New York City police cleared their camp area in lower Manhattan.

Paul Taggart/Bloomberg via Getty Images

not always at stake, compromises are almost impossible to arrange, and the conflict is more profound. It is animated by deep differences in people's beliefs about private and public morality—that is, about the standards that ought to govern individual behavior and social arrangements. It is about what kind of country we ought to live in, not just about what kinds of policies our government ought to adopt.

Two opposing views exist about the importance of the culture war. One view, developed by Morris Fiorina and others, holds that politically, the culture war is a myth. While political leaders are polarized, most Americans occupy a middle position. Journalists write about the split between "blue states" (those that vote Democratic) and "red states" (those that vote Republican), but in fact popular views across both kinds of states on many policy issues are similar.[33]

The rival view, developed by Alan Abramowitz and others, holds that more and more people are choosing their party affiliations on the basis of the party's position on moral issues. Moreover, a growing percentage of the public is politically engaged; that is, they do more to express their political views than simply vote.[34] Choosing between these two theories will take time, as we watch what happens in future elections.

Mistrust of Government

One aspect of public opinion worries many people. Since the late 1950s, there has been a more or less steady decline in the proportion of Americans who say they trust the government in Washington to do the right thing. In the past, polls showed that

about three-quarters of Americans said they trusted Washington most of the time or just about always. The percentage of people who say they trust the government has on occasion gone up (for example, when Ronald Reagan became president and again just after the 9/11 terrorist attacks), but by and large trust has been waning since at least the mid-1960s (see Figure 4.2).

Before we misinterpret this, we should remember that people are talking about government officials, not the system of government. Americans are much more supportive of the country and its institutions than Europeans are of theirs. Even so, the public decline in confidence in our officials is striking. There are all sorts of explanations for why it has happened. In the 1960s, there was our unpopular war in Vietnam; in the 1970s, President Nixon had to resign because of his involvement in the Watergate scandal; in the 1990s, President Clinton went through scandals that led to his impeachment by the House of Representatives (but was not convicted of that charge by the Senate); and in 2004 to 2007, President George W. Bush presided over a divisive war in Iraq.

But there is another way of looking at the matter. Maybe in the 1950s we had an abnormally *high* level of confidence in government, one that could never be expected to last no matter what any president did. After all, when President Eisenhower took office in 1952, we had won a war against fascism, overcome the Depression of the 1930s, possessed a near monopoly of the atom bomb, had a currency that was the envy of the world, and dominated international trade. Moreover, in those days not much

FIGURE 4.2 **Trust in the Federal Government, 1958–2013**

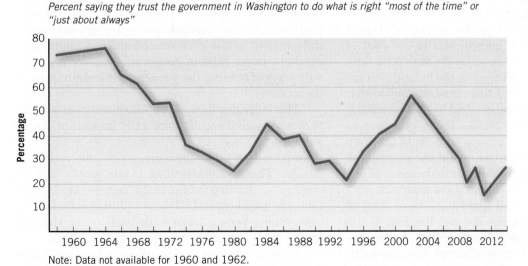

Percent saying they trust the government in Washington to do what is right "most of the time" or "just about always"

Note: Data not available for 1960 and 1962.

Source: Data for 1958-2008 compiled from the American National Election Studies (ANES);data for 2009-2011 compiled from the CNN/Opinion Research Corporation (ORC) Survey, September 2011; data for 2013 is from the Pew Research Center, February 2013

civil society Voluntary action that makes cooperation easier.

was expected out of Washington. Hardly anybody thought there should be important federal laws about civil rights, crime, illegal drugs, the environment, the role of women, highway safety, or almost anything else now on the national agenda. Since nobody expected much out of Washington, nobody was upset that they didn't get much out of it.

The 1960s and 1970s changed all of that. Domestic turmoil, urban riots, a civil rights revolution, the war in Vietnam, economic inflation, and a new concern for the environment dramatically increased what we expected Washington to do. And since these problems are very difficult ones to solve, a lot of people became convinced that our politicians couldn't do much.[35]

Those events also pushed the feelings Americans had about their country—that is, their patriotism—into the background. We liked the country, but there weren't many occasions when expressing that approval seemed to make much sense. But on September 11, 2001, when hijacked airliners were crashed by terrorists into the World Trade Center in New York City and the Pentagon in Washington, all of that changed. There was an extraordinary outburst of patriotic fervor; flags were displayed everywhere, fire and police heroes were widely celebrated, and there was strong national support for our going to war in Afghanistan to find the key terrorist, Osama bin Laden, and destroy the tyrannical Taliban regime that he supported. By November of that year, about half of all Americans of both political parties said they trusted Washington officials to do what is right most of the time, the highest level in many years.

Those who had hoped or predicted that this new level of support would last, not ebb and flow, have been disappointed. In October 2001, 57 percent of Americans (up from just 29 percent in July 2001) said they trusted the federal government to do what is right always or most of the time. But by May 2002, only 40 percent expressed such trust in the federal government, and 57 percent said they trusted Washington only some of the time or never. And by January 2013, the fraction that said they trusted the federal government to do what is right always or most of the time had fallen to about a quarter, while the percentage that said they trusted Washington only some of the time or never had risen to about three-quarters.

Only 13 percent of all Americans have a lot of confidence in Congress, but it—and the rest of the government—should not feel lonely. With few exceptions, Americans have lost confidence in many institutions. As Table 4.3 shows, newspapers, public schools, television news, and labor unions have all suffered a big drop in public confidence during the

TABLE 4.3 Confidence in American Institutions

Institution	1973	2013
Churches	66%	48%
Public schools	58	32
Newspapers	39	23
Labor unions	30	20
Big business	26	22
Congress	42	10
The military	58	76

Source: Gallup Poll, "Confidence in Institutions: Historical Trends," June 2013. Used with permission.

last three decades. Only the military has gained support (75 percent of us say we have "a great deal" or "a lot" of confidence in it).

Because Americans are less likely than they once were to hold their leaders in high esteem, to have confidence in government policies, and to believe the system will be responsive to popular wishes, some observers like to say that Americans today are more "alienated" from politics. Perhaps this is true, but careful studies of the subject have not yet been able, for example, to demonstrate any relationship between overall levels of public trust in government or confidence in leaders, on the one hand, and the rates at which people come out to vote, on the other. There is, however, some evidence that the less voters trust political institutions and leaders, the more likely they are to support candidates from the nonincumbent major party (in two-candidate races) and third-party candidates.[36]

Civil Society

Distrust of governmental and other institutions makes more important the role of **civil society**, that collection of private, voluntary groups that—independent of the government and the commercial market—make human cooperation easier and provide ways of holding the government accountable for its actions.

The individualism of the American political culture makes civil society especially important. As we shall see in Chapter 11, Americans are more likely than people in other democracies to join voluntary groups. These organizations teach people how to cooperate, develop community service skills, and increase social capital. This last phrase refers to the connections people have with each other through friendship, personal contact, and group efforts.

Several scholars, such as Robert Putnam, argue that the more social capital a community has, the greater the level of trust among its members. And the more trust that exists, the easier it is to achieve

FIGURE 4.3 The American Civic Health Index, 2009

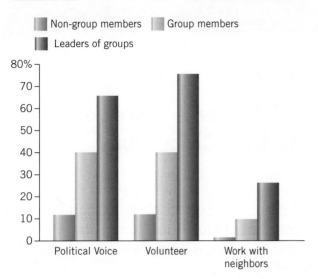

Non-group members   **Group members**

Leaders of groups

Source: 2010 Civic Health Assessment: Executive Summary, "Involvement by Group Membership," Washington, D.C.: National Conference on Citizenship. (September 2010), p. 3. Used by permission.

common goals such as improving a neighborhood, combating intolerance, and producing useful projects outside of government. Putnam worries that our social capital may be decreasing because people are less and less likely to join voluntary associations. In Putnam's famous phrase, we once bowled in leagues; now we bowl alone. We once joined the PTA, the NAACP, and the Veterans of Foreign Wars; now we stay home and watch television or spend time on our computer.[37]

There are three qualifications to this argument. First, Americans still join more groups than people in most other democracies. Second, a general measure of civic health (that examines group membership and informal human contact) shows high engagement by group leaders (see Figure 4.3). Third, in ethnically and racially diverse communities, we "hunker down"—that is, we don't trust our neighbors, contribute to charities, cooperate with others, or join voluntary groups.[38] Just where we most need social capital, we do not have as much as we would like.

Political Tolerance

Democratic politics depends crucially on citizens' reasonable tolerance of the opinions and actions of others. If unpopular speakers were always shouted down, if government efforts to censor newspapers were usually met with popular support or even public indifference, if peaceful demonstrations were regularly broken up by hostile mobs, if the losing candidates in an election refused to allow their victorious opponents to take office, then the essential elements of a democratic political culture would be missing, and democracy would fail. Democracy does not require perfect

tolerance; if it did, the passions of human nature would make democracy forever impossible. But at a minimum, citizens must have a political culture that allows the discussion of ideas and the selection of rulers in an atmosphere reasonably free of oppression.

Public opinion surveys show that the overwhelming majority of Americans agree with concepts such as freedom of speech, majority rule, and the right to circulate petitions—at least in the abstract.[39] But when we get down to concrete cases, a good many Americans are not very tolerant of groups they dislike. Suppose you must decide which groups will be permitted to espouse their causes at meetings held in your community's civic auditorium. Which of these groups would *you* allow to run such a meeting?

1. Protestants holding a revival meeting
2. Right-to-life groups opposing abortion
3. People protesting a nuclear power plant
4. Feminists organizing a march for the Equal Rights Amendment
5. Gays organizing for homosexual rights
6. Atheists preaching against God
7. Students organizing a sit-in to shut down city hall

In general, Americans have become a bit more tolerant and thus more willing to tolerate public speech by communists, atheists, and homosexuals.[40] People are today more likely than in the past to say they are willing to vote for a qualified person who runs for president even if the candidate is a Catholic, a Jew, a woman, a black, or a homosexual.[41]

One person's civic intolerance can be another person's heartfelt display of civic concern. Most Americans believe that serious civic problems are rooted in a breakdown of moral values.[42] Correctly or not, most citizens worry that the nation is becoming too tolerant of behaviors that harm society, and they favor defending common moral standards over protecting individual rights.

Nonetheless, this majority tolerance for many causes should not blind us to the fact that for most of us, there is some group or cause from which we are willing to withhold political liberties—even though we endorse those liberties in the abstract.

If most people dislike one or another group strongly enough to deny it certain political rights that we usually take for granted, how is it that such groups (and such rights) survive? The answer, in part, is that most of us don't act on our beliefs. We rarely take the trouble—or have the chance—to block another person from making a speech or teaching school. Some scholars have argued that among people who are in a position to deny other people rights—officeholders and political activists, for example—the level of political tolerance is somewhat greater than among the public at large, but that claim has been strongly disputed.[43]

WHAT WOULD YOU DO?

MEMORANDUM

To: *White House Chief of Staff Omar McField*

From: *Secretary of Education Alexandra Clark*

Subject: *Civics education in schools*

The decline in political knowledge that Americans have about our governmental system is alarming. We need to work in partnership with Congress and the states to promote civic education in secondary schools. In her upcoming State of the Union message, the President needs to make a case for high school civics education and endorse the creation of a bipartisan task force to develop guidelines for such classes.

Arguments for:

1. A recent survey finds that only about six of ten Americans can name the vice president, and more than half believe incorrectly that the Supreme Court prohibits public-school classes that compare world religions.

2. Schools have a responsibility to teach students the principles of American constitutionalism, such as federalism and separation of church and state.

3. If the federal government does not take the initiative in promoting civics education, then states will develop their own standards, which will weaken understanding of our shared political principles.

News »

U.S. Students Score Low Marks in Civics Study

A recent survey shows that only 24 percent of twelfth-graders scored proficient or higher in civics, a statistic that does not bode well for an informed and engaged U.S. citizenry.

Arguments against:

1. Civics education needs to be incorporated into existing courses, not taught separately.

2. Individuals need to take responsibility for understanding the political system in which they live.

3. Based on their individual historical experiences, states are better prepared than the federal government to determine how the underlying principles of American politics should be taught in their classrooms.

Your decision:

Support _____   Oppose _____

But another reason may be just as important. Most of us are ready to deny *some* group its rights, but we usually can't agree on which group that should be. Sometimes we can agree, and then the disliked group may be in for real trouble. There have been times (1919 to 1920, and again in the early 1950s) when socialists and communists were disliked by most people in the United States. The government on each occasion took strong actions against them. Today, fewer people agree that these left-wing groups are a major domestic threat, and so their rights are now more secure.

Finally, the courts are sufficiently insulated from public opinion that they can act against majority

sentiments and enforce constitutional protections (see Chapter 16). Most of us are not willing to give all rights to all groups, but most of us are not judges.

These facts should be a sober reminder that political liberty cannot be taken for granted. Men and women are not, it would seem, born with an inclination to live and let live, at least politically, and many—possibly most—never acquire that inclination. Liberty must be learned and protected. Happily, the United States during much of its recent history has not been consumed by revulsion for any one group, at least not revulsion strong enough to place the group's rights in jeopardy.

Nor should any part of society pretend that it is always more tolerant than another. In the 1950s, for example, ultraconservatives outside the universities were attacking the rights of professors to say and teach certain things. In the 1960s and 1970s, ultra-liberal students and professors inside the universities were attacking the rights of other students and professors to say certain things.

The American system of government is supported by a political culture that fosters a sense of civic duty, takes pride in the nation's constitutional arrangements, and provides support for the exercise of essential civil liberties. In recent decades, mistrust of government officials (though not of the system itself) has increased, and confidence in their responsiveness to popular feelings has declined.

Although Americans value liberty in both the political system and the economy, they believe equality is important in the political realm. In economic affairs, they wish to see equality of opportunity but accept inequality of results.

Not only is our culture generally supportive of democratic rule, it also has certain distinctive features that make our way of governing different from what one finds in other democracies. Americans are preoccupied with their rights, and this fact, combined with a political system that (as we shall see) encourages the vigorous exercise of rights and claims, gives to our political life an *adversarial* style. Unlike Swedes or Japanese, we do not generally reach political decisions by consensus, and we often do not defer to the authority of administrative agencies. American politics, more than that of many other nations, is shot through at every stage with protracted conflict.

But as we shall learn in the next chapter, that conflict is not easily described as, for example, always pitting liberals against conservatives. Not only do we have a lot of conflict, it is often messy conflict, a kind of political Tower of Babel. Foreign observers sometimes ask how we stand the confusion. The answer, of course, is that we have been doing it for more than 200 years. Maybe our Constitution is two centuries old, not in spite of this confusion, but because of it. We shall see.

LEARNING OBJECTIVES

1. What is American political culture?

American political culture refers to long-standing patterns in how people view government, politics, and the economy.

2. How does political culture differ from political ideology?

American political culture refers to views about how government should function and its guiding principles, whereas political ideology refers to specific views about which programs and policies government should pursue.

3. Does the United States have a unique political culture compared to other advanced industrialized democracies?

The question of whether the United States is "exceptional" among democracies sparks much debate among social scientists and historians. While characteristics of American exceptionalism are difficult to identify and measure, surveys discussed in this chapter do show that Americans view government, politics, religion, and economics differently than citizens of other advanced industrialized democracies.

4. Do Americans trust their government?

More than it sometimes appears. Compared to the 1950s, we are much less likely to think the government does the right thing or cares about what we think. But when we look at our system of government—the Constitution and our political culture—we are very pleased with it. Americans are much more patriotic than people in many other democracies. And we display a great deal of support for churches in large measure because we are more religious than most Europeans.

5. Why do Americans accept great differences in wealth and income?

Americans believe in equality of opportunity and not equality of results. Wealthy people may have more political influence than ordinary folks, but if Americans think they earned their money through their own efforts and if they follow legal rules, Americans have no complaint about their wealth.

6. Why does the American government behave differently than governments in countries with similar constitutions?

American political culture has imbued it with more tolerance and a greater respect for orderly procedures and personal rights than can be found in nations with constitutions like ours. Americans are willing to let whoever wins an election govern without putting up a fuss, and the U.S. military does not intervene.

TO LEARN MORE

Polling organizations that frequently measure aspects of political culture:

www.ropercenter.uconn.edu

www.gallup.com

U.S. Census Bureau: **www.census.gov**

Almond, Gabriel, and Sidney Verba. *The Civic Culture*. Princeton, NJ: Princeton University Press, 1963. Classic study of the political cultures of five nations—the United States, Germany, Great Britain, Italy, and Mexico—as they were in 1959.

Hartz, Louis. *The Liberal Tradition in America*. New York: Harcourt Brace Jovanovich, 1955. A stimulating interpretation of American political thought since the Founding, emphasizing the notion of a liberal consensus.

Lipset, Seymour Martin. *The First New Nation*. Rev. ed. New York: Norton, 1979. How the origins of American society gave rise to the partially competing values of equality and achievement and the ways in which these values shape political institutions.

McClosky, Herbert, and John Zaller. *The American Ethos: Public Attitudes toward Capitalism and Democracy*. Cambridge: Harvard University Press, 1984. Study of the ways in which Americans evaluate political and economic arrangements.

Nivola, Pietro S., and David W. Brady, eds. *Red and Blue Nation?* Washington, D.C.: Brookings Institution, 2006. Compares the arguments of those who do and do not believe that a culture war exists.

Putnam, Robert D. *Bowling Alone: The Collapse and Revival of American Community*. New York: Simon & Schuster, 2000. An important argument that American political culture has been harmed by the decline in membership in organizations that bring people together for communal activities.

Putnam, Robert D., and David E. Campbell. *American Grace: How Religion Unites and Divides Us*. New York: Simon and Shuster, 2010. State-of-the-art study of Americans' religious identities and how they matter to civic life.

Tocqueville, Alexis de. *Democracy in America*. Edited by Phillip Bradley. 2 vols. New York: Knopf, 1951. First published in 1835–1840, this was and remains the greatest single interpretation of American political culture.

Wilson, James Q., and Peter Schuck, eds. *Understanding America: Anatomy of an Exceptional Nation*. New York: Public Affairs, 2008. Topical essays on American political culture by leading experts.

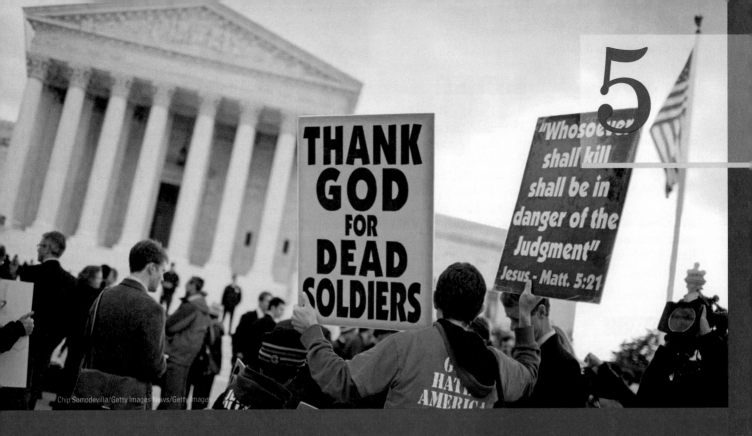

Chip Somodevilla/Getty Images News/Getty Images

Civil Liberties

LEARNING OBJECTIVES

1. Why do the courts play so large a role in deciding what our civil liberties should be?

2. Must the rights afforded to citizens by the Constitution be respected by not only the federal government but also by the states?

3. Are all forms of expression protected by the Constitution?

4. Is all political advertising constitutional?

5. Did America ever have state-supported churches, and do some modern democratic nations still have them?

6. How does the Constitution protect the liberties of persons accused of crimes or designated "enemy combatants"?

Civil liberties Rights—chiefly, rights to be free of government interference—accorded to an individual by the Constitution: free speech, free press, and so on.

THEN

In 1803, President Thomas Jefferson wrote to the governor of Pennsylvania complaining about the "licentiousness" of newspapers and urging him and other state leaders to bring about "a few prosecutions of the most prominent offenders." This would, Jefferson said, have a "wholesome effect in restoring the integrity of the presses."[1]

NOW

Today, a president writing such a letter to anyone, especially a governor, would be subject to intense criticism. Prosecuting publishers who had attacked the government would strike most people as outrageous.

There are two differences between then and now. First, as you will see later in this chapter, the Supreme Court decided in 1833 that the Bill of Rights only restricted the federal government. The only limits on state governments with regards to free speech, a free press, and religious freedom were those found in state constitutions. This law changed after the ratification of the Fourteenth Amendment in 1868 and was (slowly) interpreted by the Supreme Court to mean that the states must also honor freedom for speech, publications, and churches.

The second change occurred in the minds of the American people. Gradually, but especially in the 20th century, they acquired a libertarian view of personal freedom. According to this perspective, the government at every level ought to leave people alone with respect to what they say, write, read, or worship.

If you think that civil liberties are only an issue for people who make inflammatory speeches, think again. Imagine, for a moment, that you are a high school student. Dogs trained to sniff out drugs go down your high school corridors and detect marijuana in some lockers. The school authorities open and search your locker without permission or a court order. You are expelled from school without any hearing. Have your liberties been violated?

Angry at what you consider unfair treatment, you decide to wear a cloth American flag sewn to the seat of your pants, and your fellow students decide to wear black armbands to class to protest how you were treated. The police arrest you for wearing a flag on your seat, and the school punishes your classmates for wearing armbands contrary to school regulations. Have your liberties, or theirs, been violated?

You file suit in federal court to find out. We cannot be certain how the court would decide the issues in this particular case, but in similar cases in the past the courts have held that school authorities can use dogs to detect drugs in schools and that these officials can conduct a "reasonable" search of you and your effects if they have a "reasonable suspicion" that you are violating a school rule. But they cannot punish your classmates for wearing black armbands, they cannot expel you without a hearing, and the state cannot make it illegal to treat the flag "contemptuously" (by sewing it to the seat of your pants, for example). In 2007, however, the Supreme Court allowed a school principal to punish a student for displaying a flag saying "Bong Hits 4 Jesus" that the official felt endorsed drug use during a school-supervised event. So a student's free-speech rights (and a school's authority to enforce discipline) now lie somewhere between disgracing a flag (okay) and encouraging drug use (not okay).[2]

Your claim that these actions violated your constitutional rights would have astonished the Framers of the Constitution. They thought they had written a document that stated what the federal government *could* do, not one that specified what state governments (such as school systems) *could not* do. And they thought they had created a national government of such limited powers that it was not even necessary to add a list—a bill of rights—stating what that government was forbidden from doing. It would be enough, for example, that the Constitution did not authorize the federal government to censor newspapers; an amendment prohibiting censorship would be superfluous.

The people who gathered in the state ratifying conventions weren't so optimistic. They suspected—rightly, as it turned out—that the federal government might well try to do things it was not authorized to do, and so they insisted that the Bill of Rights be added to the Constitution. But even they never imagined that the Bill of Rights would affect what *state* governments could do. Each state would decide that for itself, in its own constitution. And if by chance the Bill of Rights did apply to the states, surely its guarantees of free speech and freedom from unreasonable search and seizure would apply to big issues—the freedom to attack the government in a newspaper editorial, for example, or to keep the police from breaking down the door of your home without a warrant. The courts would not be deciding who could wear what kinds of armbands or under what circumstances a school could expel a student.

Civil liberties are the rights—chiefly, rights to be free of government interference—accorded to an individual by the Constitution: free exercise of religion, free speech, and so on. Civil rights, to be discussed in the next chapter, usually refers to protecting certain groups—such as women, gays, and African Americans—from discrimination. In practice, however, there is no clear line between civil liberties and civil rights. For example, is the right to an abortion a civil liberty or a civil right? In this chapter, we take a look at free speech, free press, religious freedom, and the rights of the accused. In the next one, we look at discrimination and abortion.

Culture and Civil Liberties
Rights in Conflict

We often think of "civil liberties" as a set of principles that protect the freedoms of all of us all of the time. That is true—up to a point. But in fact, the Constitution and the Bill of Rights contain a list of *competing* rights and duties. That competition becomes obvious when one person asserts one constitutional right or duty and another person asserts a different one. For example:

- At the funeral of a Marine killed in Iraq, Phelps and others from a church picketed it with signs saying "Thank God for Dead Soldiers" and other outrageous remarks. (The opening photo for this chapter shows such picketers outside the Supreme Court.) The Marine's father sued the church, claiming the picketers caused him suffering. Free speech versus extreme emotional distress.

- The U.S. government has an obligation to "provide for the common defense" and, in pursuit of that duty, has claimed the right to keep secret certain military and diplomatic information. The *New York Times* claimed the right to publish such secrets as the "Pentagon Papers" without censorship, citing the Constitution's guarantee of freedom of the press. A duty and a right in conflict.

- Carl Jacob Kunz delivered inflammatory anti-Jewish speeches on the street corners of a Jewish neighborhood in New York City, suggesting, among other things, that Jews be "burnt in incinerators." The Jewish people living in that area were outraged. The New York police commissioner revoked Kunz's license to hold public meetings on the streets. When he continued to air his views on the public streets, Kunz was arrested for speaking without a permit. Freedom of speech versus the preservation of public order.

Even a disruptive high school student's right not to be a victim of arbitrary or unjustifiable expulsion is in partial conflict with the school's obligation to maintain an orderly environment in which learning can take place.

Political struggles over civil liberties follow much the same pattern as interest group politics involving economic issues, even though the claims in question are made by individuals. Indeed, there are formal, organized interest groups concerned with civil liberties. The Fraternal Order of the Police complains about restrictions on police powers, whereas the American Civil Liberties Union defends and seeks to enlarge those restrictions. Catholics have pressed for public support of parochial schools; Protestants and Jews have argued against it. Sometimes the opposing groups are entirely private; sometimes one or both are government agencies. Often their clashes end up in the courts. (When the Supreme Court decided the cases given earlier, Phelps, the *New York Times,* and Kunz all won.[3])

War has usually been the crisis that has restricted the liberty of some minority. For example:

- The Sedition Act was passed in 1798, making it a crime to write, utter, or publish "any false, scandalous, and malicious writing" with the intention of defaming the president, Congress, or the government or of exciting against the government "the hatred of the people." The occasion was a kind of half-war between the United States and France, stimulated by fear in this country of the violence following the French Revolution of 1789. The policy entrepreneurs were Federalist politicians who believed that Thomas Jefferson and his followers were supporters of the French Revolution and would, if they came to power, encourage here the kind of anarchy that seemed to be occurring in France.

- The Espionage and Sedition Acts were passed in 1917–1918, making it a crime to utter false statements that would interfere with the American military, to send through the mails material "advocating or urging treason, insurrection, or forcible resistance to any law of the United States," or to utter or write any disloyal, profane, scurrilous, or abusive language intended to incite resistance to the United States or to curtail war production. The occasion was World War I; the impetus was the fear that Germans in this country were spies and also that radicals were seeking to overthrow the government. Under these laws, more than 2,000 persons were prosecuted (about half were convicted), and thousands of aliens were rounded up and deported. The policy entrepreneur leading this massive crackdown (the so-called Red Scare) was Attorney General A. Mitchell Palmer.

- The Smith Act was passed in 1940, the Internal Security Act in 1950, and the Communist Control Act in 1954. These laws made it illegal to advocate the overthrow of the U.S. government by force or violence (Smith Act), required members of the Communist Party to register with the government (Internal Security Act), and declared the Communist Party to be part of a conspiracy to overthrow the government (Communist Control Act). The occasion was World War II and the Korean War,

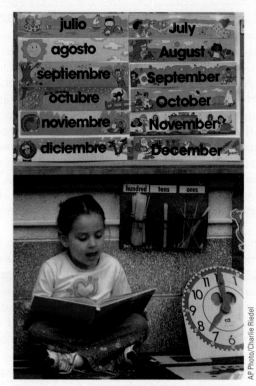

AP Photo/Charlie Riedel

A Hispanic girl studies both English and Spanish in a bilingual classroom.

which, like earlier wars, inspired fears that foreign agents (Nazi and Soviet) were trying to subvert the government. For the latter two laws, the policy entrepreneur was Senator Joseph McCarthy, who attracted a great deal of attention with his repeated (and sometimes inaccurate) claims that Soviet agents were working inside the U.S. government.

These laws had in common an effort to protect the nation from threats, real and imagined, posed by people who claimed to be exercising their freedom to speak, publish, organize, and assemble. In each case, a real threat (a war) led the government to narrow the limits of permissible speech and activity. Almost every time such restrictions were imposed, the Supreme Court was called upon to decide whether Congress (or sometimes state legislatures) had drawn those limits properly. In most instances, the Court tended to uphold the legislatures. But as time passed and the war or crisis ended, popular passions abated and many of the laws proved unimportant.

Though it is uncommon, some use is still made of the sedition laws. In the 1980s, various white supremacists and Puerto Rican nationalists were charged with sedition. In each case, the government alleged that the accused had not only spoken in favor of overthrowing the government but had actually engaged in violent actions such as bombings. Later in this chapter, we shall see how the Court has increasingly restricted the power of Congress and

state legislatures to outlaw political speech; to be found guilty of sedition now, it usually is necessary to do something more serious than just talk about it.

Cultural Conflicts

In the main, the United States was originally the creation of white European Protestants. Blacks were, in most cases, slaves, and American Indians were not citizens. Catholics and Jews in the colonies composed a small minority, and often a persecuted one. The early schools tended to be religious—that is, Protestant—ones, many of them receiving state aid. It is not surprising that under these circumstances a view of America arose that equated "Americanism" with the values and habits of white Anglo-Saxon Protestants.

But immigration to this country brought a flood of new settlers, many of them coming from very different backgrounds (see Figure 5.1). In the mid-19th century, the potato famine led millions of Irish Catholics to migrate here. At the turn of the century, religious persecution and economic disadvantage brought more millions of people, many Catholic or Jewish, from southern and eastern Europe.

In recent decades, political conflict and economic want have led Hispanics (mostly from Mexico but increasingly from all parts of Latin America), Caribbeans, Africans, Middle Easterners, Southeast Asians, and Asians to come to the United States,—most legally, but some illegally. Among them have been Buddhists, Catholics, Muslims, and members of many other religious and cultural groups.

Ethnic, religious, and cultural differences have given rise to different views as to the meaning and scope of certain constitutionally protected freedoms. For example:

- Many Jewish groups find it offensive for a crèche (that is, a scene depicting the birth of Christ in a manger) to be displayed in front of a government building such as city hall at Christmastime, while many Catholics and Protestants regard such displays as an important part of our cultural heritage. Does a religious display on public property violate the First Amendment requirement that the government pass no law "respecting an establishment of religion"?

- Many English-speaking people believe that the public schools ought to teach all students to speak and write English, because the language is part of our nation's cultural heritage. Some Hispanic groups argue that the schools should teach pupils in both English and Spanish, since Spanish is part of the Hispanic cultural heritage. Is bilingual education constitutionally required?

- The Boy Scouts of America refuses to allow homosexual men to become scout leaders even though

FIGURE 5.1 **Annual Legal Immigration, 1850–2012**

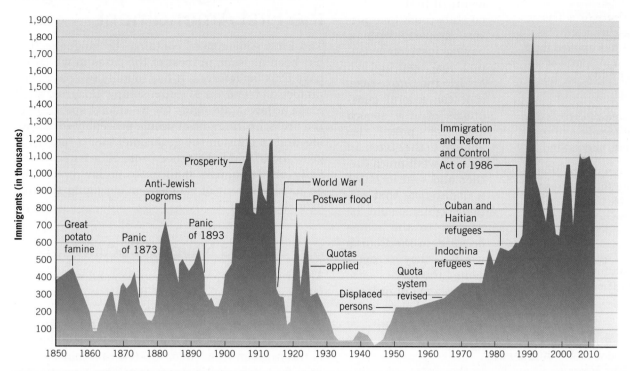

Note: Figures for 1989 and 1990 include persons granted permanent residence under the legalization program of the Immigration and Reform and Control Act of 1986.

Source: Data from Office of Immigration Statistics, *2010 Yearbook of Immigration Statistics* (Washington, D.C.: Department of Homeland Security, 2011), 1.

federal law says that homosexuals may not be the victims of discrimination. Many civil libertarians and homosexuals challenged this policy because it discriminated against gays, while the Boy Scouts defended it because their organization was a private association free to make its own rules. (The Supreme Court in 2000 upheld the Boy Scouts on the grounds of their right to associate freely.)

Even within a given cultural tradition there are important differences of opinion as to the balance between community sensitivities and personal self-expression. To some people, the sight of a store carrying pornographic books or a theater showing a pornographic movie is deeply offensive; to others, pornography is offensive but such establishments ought to be tolerated to ensure that laws restricting them do not also restrict politically or artistically important forms of speech; to still others, pornography itself is not especially offensive. What forms of expression are entitled to constitutional protection?

Applying the Bill of Rights to the States

For many years after the Constitution was signed and the Bill of Rights was added to it as amendments, the liberties these documents detailed

applied only to the federal government. The Supreme Court made this clear in a case decided in 1833.[4] Except for Article I which, among other things, banned ex post facto laws and guaranteed the right of habeas corpus, the Constitution was silent on what the states could not do to their residents.

This began to change after the Civil War, when new amendments were ratified in order to ban slavery and protect newly freed slaves. The Fourteenth Amendment, ratified in 1868, was the most important addition. It said that no state shall "deprive any person of life, liberty, or property without **due process of law**" (a phrase now known as the "due process clause") and that no state shall "deny to any person within its jurisdiction the **equal protection of the laws**" (a phrase now known as the "equal protection clause").

Beginning in 1897, the Supreme Court started to use these two phrases as a way of applying certain

due process of law Denies the government the right, without due process, to deprive people of life, liberty, and property.

equal protection of the laws A standard of equal treatment that must be observed by the government.

selective incorporation The process whereby the Court has applied most, but not all, parts of the Bill of Rights to the states.

freedom of expression Right of people to speak, publish, and assemble.

freedom of religion People shall be free to exercise their religion, and government may not establish a religion.

prior restraint Censorship of a publication.

rights to state governments. It first said that no state could take private property without paying just compensation, and then in 1925 held, in the *Gitlow* case, that the federal guarantees of free speech and free press also applied to the states. In 1937, it went much further and said in *Palko v. Connecticut* that certain rights should be applied to the states because, in the Court's words, they "represented the very essence of a scheme of ordered liberty" and were "principles of justice so rooted in the traditions and conscience of our people as to be ranked fundamental."[5]

The Supreme Court began the process of **selective incorporation** by which most, but not all, federal rights also applied to the states. But which rights are so "fundamental" that they ought to govern the states? There is no entirely clear answer to this question, but in general the entire Bill of Rights is now applied to the states except for the following:

- The right not to have soldiers forcibly quartered in private homes (Third Amendment)

- The right to be indicted by a grand jury before being tried for a serious crime (Fifth Amendment)

- The right to a jury trial in civil cases (Seventh Amendment)

- The ban on excessive bail and fines (Eighth Amendment)

The Second Amendment that protects "the right of the people to keep and bear arms" may or may not apply to the states. In 2008, the Supreme Court in *District of Columbia v. Heller* held for the first time that this amendment did not allow the federal government to ban the private possession of firearms. But the case arose in the District of Columbia, which is governed by federal law. The decision raised two questions: First, will this ruling be incorporated so that it also applies to state governments? In 2010, the Supreme Court said in *McDonald v. Chicago* that the decision in the *Heller* case also applied to the states.[6] Second, will it still be possible to regulate gun purchases and gun use even if the government cannot ban guns? Based on other court cases, the answer appears to be yes.

Interpreting and Applying the First Amendment

The First Amendment contains the language that has been at issue in most of the cases to which we have thus far referred. It has roughly two parts: one protecting **freedom of expression** ("Congress shall make no law ... abridging the freedom of speech, or of the press, or the right of people peaceably to assemble, and to petition the government for a redress of grievances") and the other protecting **freedom of religion** ("Congress shall make no law respecting an establishment of religion; or abridging the free exercise thereof").

Speech and National Security

The traditional view of free speech and a free press was expressed by William Blackstone, the great English jurist, in his *Commentaries,* published in 1765. A free press is essential to a free state, he wrote, but the freedom that the press should enjoy is the freedom from **prior restraint**—that is, freedom from censorship, or rules telling a newspaper in advance what it can publish. Once a newspaper has published an article or a person has delivered a speech, that paper or speaker has to take the consequences if what was written or said proves to be "improper, mischievous, or illegal."[7]

The U.S. Sedition Act of 1798 was in keeping with traditional English law. Like it, the act imposed no prior restraint on publishers; it did, however, make them liable to punishment after the fact. The act was an improvement over the English law, however, because unlike the British model, it entrusted the decision to a jury, not a judge, and allowed the defendant to be acquitted if he or she could prove the truth of what had been published. Although several newspaper publishers were convicted under the act, none of these cases reached the Supreme Court. When Jefferson became president in 1801, he pardoned the people who had been imprisoned under the Sedition Act. Though Jeffersonians objected vehemently to the law, their principal objection was not to the idea of holding newspapers accountable for what they published but to letting the *federal* government do this. Jefferson was perfectly prepared to have the *states* punish what he called the "overwhelming torrent of slander" by means of "a few prosecutions of the most prominent offenders."[8]

It would be another century before the federal government would attempt to define the limits of free speech and writing. Perhaps recalling the widespread opposition to the sweep of the 1798 act, Congress in 1917–1918 placed restrictions not on publications that were critical of the government but

CONSTITUTIONAL CONNECTIONS

Selective Incorporation

The selective incorporation process—the process by which the Supreme Court has applied most, but not all, parts of the Bill of Rights to the states—began in earnest in 1925 and has continued ever since, most recently with the Supreme Court's decision in the Second Amendment case of *McDonald v. Chicago*.

The selective incorporation process has never been straightforward or simple. For instance, in *Palko v. Connecticut* (1937), the Supreme Court held that states must observe all "fundamental" rights, but declared that the Fifth Amendment's protection against "double jeopardy" (being tried, found innocent, and then being tried again for the same crime), which was the issue at hand in the case, was *not* among those rights. It was only about three decades later, in its decision in *Benton v. Maryland* (1969), that the Court partially incorporated the double jeopardy provision of the Fifth Amendment. Still, to this day no provision of the Fifth Amendment has been fully incorporated, and the provision regarding the right to be indicted by a grand jury has not been incorporated at all.

Similarly, in *Powell v. Alabama* (1932), the Supreme Court incorporated the Sixth Amendment's right to counsel, but only in capital punishment cases. In *Gideon v. Wainwright* (1962), the Court extended that right to all felony defendants that might, if convicted, go to prison for years or for life. In the decade thereafter, the Court issued six more Sixth Amendment selective incorporation decisions. In the last of these, *Argersinger v. Hamlin* (1972), the Court extended the right to legal counsel to any defendant facing a sentence that might result in incarceration.

The Third Amendment, which establishes the right not to have soldiers forcibly "quartered in any home without the consent" of the homeowner, and the Seventh Amendment, which establishes the right to a trial in civil cases, each remains wholly unincorporated. The Eighth Amendment's prohibition against "cruel and unusual punishment" is partially incorporated, while its provision forbidding excessive bail or fines remains wholly unincorporated.

Year	Amendment	Provision	Case
1925	First	Free speech	*Gitlow v. New York*
1931	First	Free press	*Near v. Minnesota*
1932	Sixth	Legal counsel	*Powell v. Alabama*
1937	First	Free assembly	*De Jonge v. Oregon*
1937	Fifth	Double jeopardy	*Palko v. Connecticut*
1947	First	No religious establishment	*Everson v. Board of Education*
1948	Sixth	Public trial	*In re Oliver*
1949	Fourth	Unreasonable searches and seizures	*Wolf v. Colorado*
1958	First	Free association	*NAACP v. Alabama*
1961	Fourth	Warrantless searches and seizures	*Mapp v. Ohio*
1963	First	Free petition	*NAACP v. Button*
1963	Sixth	Legal counsel	*Gideon v. Wainwright*
1965	Sixth	Confront witnesses	*Pointer v. Texas*
1966	Sixth	Impartial jury	*Parker v. Gladden*
1967	Sixth	Speedy trial	*Klopfer v. North Carolina*
1967	Sixth	Compel witnesses	*Washington v. Texas*
1968	Sixth	Jury trial	*Duncan v. Louisiana*
1972	Sixth	Legal counsel	*Argersinger v. Hamlin*
2010	Second	Keep and bear arms	*McDonald v. Chicago*

only on those that advocated "treason, insurrection, or forcible resistance" to federal laws or attempted to foment disloyalty or mutiny in the armed services.

In 1919, this new law was examined by the Supreme Court when it heard the case of Charles T. Schenck, who had been convicted of violating the Espionage Act because he had mailed circulars to men eligible for the draft, urging them to resist. At issue was the constitutionality of the Espionage Act and, more broadly, the scope of Congress's power to

clear-and-present-danger test Law should not punish speech unless there was a clear and present danger of producing harmful actions.

control speech. One view held that the First Amendment prevented Congress from passing *any* law restricting speech; the other held that Congress could punish dangerous speech. For a unanimous Supreme Court, Justice Oliver Wendell Holmes announced a rule by which to settle the matter. It soon became known as the **clear-and-present-danger test**:

> *The question in every case is whether the words used are used in such circumstances and are of such a nature as to create a clear and present danger that they will bring about the substantive evils that Congress has a right to prevent.*[9]

The Court held that Schenck's leaflets did create such a danger, and so his conviction was upheld. In explaining why, Holmes said that not even the Constitution protects a person who has been "falsely shouting fire in a theatre and causing a panic." In this case, things that might safely be said in peacetime may be punished in wartime.

The clear-and-present-danger test may have clarified the law, but it kept no one out of jail. Schenck went, and so did the defendants in five other cases in the period 1919–1927, even though during this time Holmes, the author of the test, shifted his position and began writing dissenting opinions in which he urged that the test had not been met and so the defendant should go free.

In 1925, Benjamin Gitlow was convicted of violating New York's sedition law—a law similar to the federal Sedition Act of 1918—by passing out some leaflets, one of which advocated the violent overthrow of our government. The Supreme Court

Women picketed in front of the White House, urging President Warren Harding to release political radicals arrested during his administration.

upheld his conviction but added, as we have seen, a statement that changed constitutional history: freedom of speech and of the press were now among the "fundamental personal rights" protected by the due process clause of the Fourteenth Amendment from infringements by *state* action.[10] Thereafter, state laws involving speech, the press, and peaceful assembly were struck down by the Supreme Court for being in violation of the freedom-of-expression guarantees of the First Amendment, made applicable to the states by the Fourteenth Amendment.[11]

The clear-and-present-danger test was a way of balancing the competing demands of free expression and national security. As the memory of World War I and the ensuing Red Scare evaporated, the Court began to develop other tests, ones that shifted the balance more toward free expression. Some of these tests are listed in the box on page 105.

But when a crisis reappears, as it did in World War II and the Korean War, the Court has tended to defer, up to a point, to legislative judgments about the need to protect national security. For example, it upheld the conviction of 11 leaders of the Communist Party for having advocated the violent overthrow of the U.S. government, a violation of the Smith Act of 1940.

This conviction once again raised the hard question of the circumstances under which words can be punished. Hardly anybody would deny that actually *trying* to overthrow the government is a crime; the question is whether *advocating* its overthrow is a crime. In the case of the 11 communist leaders, the

LANDMARK CASES

Incorporation

- ***Gitlow v. New York* (1925):** Supreme Court says the First Amendment applies to states.

- ***Palko v. Connecticut* (1937):** Supreme Court says that states must observe all "fundamental" liberties.

- ***McDonald v. Chicago* (2010):** The Second Amendment that allows the people to keep and bear arms applies to state governments as well as the federal one.

Court said that the government did not have to wait to protect itself until "the *putsch* [rebellion] is about to be executed, the plans have been laid and the signal is awaited." Even if the communists were not likely to be successful in their effort, the Court held that specifically advocating violent overthrow could be punished. "In each case," the opinion read, the courts "must ask whether the gravity of the 'evil,' discounted by its improbability, justifies such invasion of free speech as is necessary to avoid the danger."[12]

But as the popular worries about communists began to subside and the membership of the Supreme Court changed, the Court began to tip the balance even farther toward free expression. By 1957, the Court made it clear that for advocacy to be punished, the government would have to show not just that a person believed in the overthrow of the government but also that he or she was using words "calculated to incite" that overthrow.[13]

By 1969, the pendulum had swung to the point where the speech would have to be judged likely to incite "imminent" unlawful action. When Clarence Brandenburg, a Ku Klux Klan leader in Ohio, made a speech before Klan members in which he called for "revengeance" [sic] against blacks and Jews (described with racial slurs) and called for a march on Washington, he was arrested and convicted for "advocating" violence. The U.S. Supreme Court reversed the conviction, holding that the First Amendment protects speech that abstractly advocates violence unless that speech will incite or produce "imminent lawless action."[14]

This means that no matter how offensive or provocative some forms of expression may be, this expression has powerful constitutional protections. In 1977, a group of American Nazis wanted to parade through the streets of Skokie, Illinois, a community with a large Jewish population. The residents, outraged, sought to ban the march. Many feared violence if it occurred. But the lower courts, under prodding from the Supreme Court, held that, noxious and provocative as the anti-Semitic slogans of the Nazis may be, the Nazi party had a constitutional right to speak and parade peacefully.[15]

Similar reasoning led the Supreme Court in 1992 to overturn a Minnesota statute that made it a crime to display symbols or objects, such as a Nazi swastika or a burning cross, that are likely to cause alarm or resentment among an ethnic or racial group, such as Jews or African Americans.[16] On the other hand, if you are convicted of actually hurting someone, you may be given a tougher sentence if it can be shown that you were motivated to assault them by racial or ethnic hatred.[17] To be punished for such a hate crime, your bigotry must result in some direct and physical harm and not just the display of an odious symbol.

What Is Speech?

> *libel* Writing that falsely injures another person.

If most political speaking or writing is permissible, save that which actually incites someone to take illegal actions, what *kinds* of speaking and writing qualify for this broad protection? Though the Constitution says that the legislature may make "no law" abridging freedom of speech or the press, and although some justices have argued that this means literally *no* law, the Court has held that there are at least four forms of speaking and writing that are not automatically granted full constitutional protection: libel, obscenity, symbolic speech, and false advertising.

Libel

A **libel** is a written statement that defames the character of another person. (If the statement is oral, it is called a *slander.*) The libel or slander must harm the person being attacked. In some countries, such as the United Kingdom, it is easy to sue another person for libel and to collect. In this country, it is much harder. For one thing, you must show that the libelous statement was false. If it was true, you cannot collect no matter how badly it harmed you.

A beauty contest winner was awarded $14 million (later reduced on appeal) when she proved that *Penthouse* magazine had libeled her. Actress Carol Burnett collected a large sum from a libel suit brought against a gossip newspaper. But when Theodore Roosevelt sued a newspaper for falsely claiming that he was a drunk, the jury awarded him damages of only six cents.[18]

A Ku Klux Klan member uses his constitutional right to free speech to utter "white power" chants in Skokie, Illinois.

Tim Boyle/Newsmakers/Getty Images News/Getty Images

If you are a public figure, it is much harder to win a libel suit. A public figure such as an elected official, a candidate for office, an army general, or a well-known celebrity must prove not only that the publication was false and damaging but also that the words were published with "actual malice"—that is, with reckless disregard for their truth or falsity or with knowledge that they were false.[19] Israeli General Ariel Sharon was able to prove that the statements made about him by *Time* magazine were false and damaging but not that they were the result of "actual malice."

For a while, people who felt they had been libeled would bring suit in the United Kingdom against an American author. One Saudi leader sued an American author who had accused him of financing terrorism even though she had not sold her book in the United Kingdom (but word about it had been on the internet). This strategy, called "libel tourism," was ended in 2010 when Congress unanimously passed and the president signed a bill that bars enforcement in U.S. courts of libel actions against Americans if what they published would not be libelous under American law.

Obscenity

Obscenity is not protected by the First Amendment. The Court has always held that obscene materials, because they have no redeeming social value and are calculated chiefly to appeal to one's sexual rather than political or literary interests, can be regulated by the state. The problem, of course, arises with the meaning of *obscene*. In the period from 1957 to 1968, the Court decided 13 major cases involving the definition of obscenity, which resulted in 55 separate opinions.[20] Some justices, such as Hugo Black, believed that the First Amendment protected all publications, even wholly obscene ones. Others believed that obscenity deserved no protection and struggled heroically to define the term. Still others shared the view of former Justice Potter Stewart, who objected to "hard-core pornography" but admitted that the best definition he could offer was "I know it when I see it."[21]

It is unnecessary to review in detail the many attempts by the Court at defining obscenity. The justices have made it clear that nudity and sex are not, by definition, obscene and that they will provide First Amendment protection to anything that has political, literary, or artistic merit, allowing the government to punish only the distribution of "hardcore pornography." Their most recent definition of this is as follows: to be obscene, the work, taken as a whole, must be judged by "the average person applying contemporary community standards" to appeal to the "prurient interest" or to depict "in a patently offensive way, sexual conduct specifically defined by applicable state law" and to lack "serious literary, artistic, political, or scientific value."[22]

After Albany, Georgia decided that the movie *Carnal Knowledge* was obscene by contemporary local standards, the Supreme Court overturned the distributor's conviction on the grounds that the authorities in Albany failed to show that the film depicted "patently offensive hard-core sexual conduct."[23]

It is easy to make sport of the problems the Court has faced in trying to decide obscenity cases (one conjures up images of black-robed justices leafing through the pages of *Hustler* magazine, taking notes), but these problems reveal, as do other civil liberties cases, the continuing problem of balancing competing claims. One part of the community wants to read or see whatever it wishes; another part wants to protect private acts from public degradation. The first part cherishes liberty above all; the second values decency above liberty. The former fears that *any* restriction on literature will lead to *pervasive* restrictions; the latter believes that reasonable people can distinguish (or reasonable laws can require them to distinguish) between patently offensive and artistically serious work.

Anyone strolling today through an "adult" bookstore must suppose that no restrictions at all exist on the distribution of pornographic works. This condition does not arise simply from the doctrines of the Court. Other factors operate as well, including the priorities of local law enforcement officials, the political climate of the community, the procedures that must be followed to bring a viable court case, the clarity and workability of state and local laws on the subject, and the difficulty of changing the behavior of many people by prosecuting one person. The current view of the Court is that localities can decide for themselves whether to tolerate hard-core pornography; but if they choose not to, they must meet some fairly strict constitutional tests.

The protections given by the Court to expressions of sexual or erotic interest have not been limited to books, magazines, and films. Almost any form of visual or auditory communication can be considered "speech" and thus protected by the First Amendment. In one case, even nude dancing was given protection as a form of "speech,"[24] although in 1991 the Court held that nude dancing was only "marginally" within the purview of First Amendment protections, and so it upheld an Indiana statute that banned *totally* nude dancing.[25]

Of late some feminist organizations have attacked pornography on the grounds that it exploits and degrades women. They persuaded Indianapolis, Indiana, to pass an ordinance that defined pornography as portrayals of the "graphic, sexually explicit subordination of women" and allowed people to sue the producers of such material. Sexually explicit portrayals of women in positions of equality were not defined as pornography. The Court disagreed. In 1986, it affirmed a lower-court ruling that such an ordinance was a violation of the First Amendment because it represented a legislative preference for one form of expression (women in positions of equality) over another (women in positions of subordination).[26]

One constitutionally permissible way to limit the spread of pornographic materials has been to establish rules governing where in a city they can be sold. When one city adopted a zoning ordinance prohibiting an "adult" movie theater from locating within 1,000 feet of any church, school, park, or residential area, the Court upheld the ordinance, noting that the purpose of the law was not to regulate speech but to regulate the use of land. And in any case, the adult theaters still had much of the city's land area in which to find a location.[27]

With the advent of the internet, it has become more difficult for the government to regulate obscenity. The internet spans the globe. It offers an amazing variety of materials—some educational, some entertaining, some sexually explicit. But it is difficult to apply the Supreme Court's standard for judging whether sexual material is obscene— the "average person" applying "contemporary community standards"—to the internet, because there is no easy way to tell what "the community" is. Is it the place where the recipient lives or the place where the material originates? And since no one is in charge of the internet, who can be held responsible for controlling offensive material? Since anybody can send anything to anybody else without knowing the age or location of the recipient, how can the internet protect children? When Congress tried to ban obscene, indecent, or "patently offensive" materials from the internet, the Supreme Court struck down the law as unconstitutional. The Court went even further with child pornography. Though it has long held that child pornography is illegal even if it is not obscene because of the government's interest in protecting children, it would not let Congress ban pornography involving computer-designed children. Under the 1996 law, it would be illegal to display computer simulations of children engaged in sex even if no real children were involved. The Court said "no." It held that Congress could not ban "virtual" child

HOW THINGS WORK

Testing Restrictions on Expression

The Supreme Court has employed various standards and tests to decide whether a restriction on freedom of expression is constitutionally permissible.

1. **Preferred position** The right of free expression, though not absolute, occupies a higher, or more preferred, position than many other constitutional rights, such as property rights. This is still a controversial rule; nonetheless, the Court always approaches a restriction on expression skeptically.

2. **Prior restraint** With scarcely any exceptions, the Court will not tolerate a prior restraint on expression, such as censorship, even when it will allow subsequent punishment of improper expressions (such as libel).

3. **Imminent danger** Punishment for uttering inflammatory sentiments will be allowed only if there is an imminent danger that the utterances will incite an unlawful act.

4. **Neutrality** Any restriction on speech, such as a requirement that parades or demonstrations not disrupt other people in the exercise of their rights,

must be neutral—that is, it must not favor one group more than another.

5. **Clarity** If you must obtain a permit to hold a parade, the law must set forth clear (as well as neutral) standards to guide administrators in issuing that permit. Similarly, a law punishing obscenity must contain a clear definition of obscenity.

6. **Least-restrictive means** If it is necessary to restrict the exercise of one right to protect the exercise of another, the restriction should employ the least-restrictive means to achieve its end. For example, if press coverage threatens a person's right to a fair trial, the judge may only do what is minimally necessary to achieve that end, such as transferring the case to another town rather than issuing a "gag order."

Cases cited, by item: (1) *United States v. Carolene Products,* 304 U.S. 144 (1938). (2) *Near v. Minnesota,* 283 U.S. 697 (1931). (3) *Brandenburg v. Ohio,* 395 U.S. 444 (1969). (4) *Kunz v. New York,* 340 U.S. 290 (1951). (5) *Hynes v. Mayor and Council of Oradell,* 425 U.S. 610 (1976). (6) *Nebraska Press Association v. Stuart,* 427 U.S. 539 (1976).

symbolic speech An act that conveys a political message.

pornography without violating the First Amendment because, in its view, the law might bar even harmless depictions of children and sex (for example, in a book on child psychology).[28]

Symbolic Speech

Ordinarily, you cannot claim that an illegal act should be protected because that action is meant to convey a political message. For example, if you burn your draft card in protest against the foreign policy of the United States, you can be punished for the illegal act (burning the card), even if your intent was to communicate your beliefs. The Court reasoned that giving such **symbolic speech** the same protection as real speech would open the door to permitting all manner of illegal actions—murder, arson, rape—if the perpetrator meant thereby to send a message.[29]

On the other hand, a statute that makes it illegal to burn the American flag is an unconstitutional infringement of free speech.[30] Why is there a difference between a draft card and the flag? The Court argues that the government has a right to run a military draft and so can protect draft cards, even if this incidentally restricts speech. But the only motive

that the government has in banning flag-burning is to restrict this form of speech, and that would make such a restriction improper.

The American people were outraged by the flag-burning decision, and in response the House and Senate passed by huge majorities (380 to 38 and 91 to 9) a law making it a federal crime to burn the flag. But the Court struck this law down as unconstitutional.[31] Now that it was clear that only a constitutional amendment could make flag-burning illegal, Congress was asked to propose one. But it would not. Earlier members of the House and Senate had supported a law banning flag-burning with more than 90 percent of their votes, but when asked to make that law a constitutional amendment they could not muster the necessary two-thirds majorities. The reason is that Congress is much more reluctant to amend the Constitution than to pass new laws. Several members decided that flag-burning was wrong, but not so wrong or so common as to justify an amendment.

Commercial and Youthful Speech

If people have a right to speak and publish, do corporations, interest groups, and children have the same right? By and large the answer is yes, though there are some exceptions.

Robert Pearce/The Sydney Morning Herald/Fairfax Media via Getty Images

"Symbolic speech:" When young men burned their draft cards during the 1960s to protest the Vietnam War, the Supreme Court ruled that it was an illegal act for which they could be punished.

When the attorney general of Massachusetts tried to prevent the First National Bank of Boston from spending money to influence votes in a local election, the Court stepped in and blocked him. The Court held that a corporation, like a person, has certain First Amendment rights. Similarly, when the federal government tried to limit the spending of a group called Massachusetts Citizens for Life (an antiabortion organization), the Court held that such organizations have First Amendment rights.[32] The Court has also told states that they cannot forbid liquor stores to advertise their prices and informed federal authorities that they cannot prohibit casinos from plugging gambling.[33]

When the California Public Utility Commission tried to compel one of the utilities it regulates, the Pacific Gas and Electric Company, to enclose in its monthly bills to customers statements written by groups attacking the utility, the Supreme Court blocked the agency, saying that forcing it to disseminate political statements violated the firm's free-speech rights. "The identity of the speaker is not decisive in determining whether speech is protected," the Court said. "Corporations and other associations, like individuals, contribute to the "discussion, debate, and the dissemination of information and ideas that the First Amendment seeks to foster." In this case, the right to speak includes the choice of what *not* to say.[34]

Even though corporations have some First Amendment rights, the government can place more limits on commercial than on noncommercial speech. The legislature can place restrictions on advertisements for cigarettes, liquor, and gambling; it can even regulate advertising for some less harmful products provided that the regulations are narrowly tailored and serve a substantial public interest.[35] If the regulations are too broad or do not serve a clear interest, then ads are entitled to some constitutional protection. For example, the states cannot bar lawyers from advertising or accountants from personally soliciting clients.[36]

A big exception to the free-speech rights of corporations and labor unions groups was imposed by the McCain-Feingold campaign finance reform law passed in 2002. Many groups, ranging from the American Civil Liberties Union and the AFL-CIO to the National Rifle Association and the Chamber of Commerce, felt that the law banned legitimate speech. Under its terms, organizations could not pay for "electioneering communications" on radio or television that "refer" to candidates for federal office within 60 days before the election. But the Supreme Court temporarily struck down these arguments, upholding the law in *McConnell v. Federal Election Commission.* The Court said ads that only mentioned but did not "expressly advocate" a candidate

were ways of influencing the election. Some dissenting opinion complained that a Court that had once given free-speech protection to nude dancing ought to give it to political speech.[37] But seven years later, the Court, in *Citizens United v. Federal Election Commission,* decided that the part of the McCain-Feingold law that denied corporations and labor unions the right to run ads (independently of a political party's or candidate's campaign) about the election violated their rights to free speech under the Constitution.

Under certain circumstances, young people may have less freedom of expression than adults. In 1988, the Supreme Court held that the principal of

LANDMARK CASES

Free Speech and Free Press

- *Schenck v. United States* (1919): Speech may be punished if it creates a clear-and-present-danger of illegal acts.

- *Chaplinsky v. New Hampshire* (1942): "Fighting words" are not protected by the First Amendment.

- *New York Times v. Sullivan* (1964): To libel a public figure, there must be "actual malice."

- *Tinker v. Des Moines* (1969): Public-school students may wear armbands to class protesting against America's war in Vietnam when such display does not disrupt classes.

- *Miller v. California* (1973): Obscenity defined as appealing to prurient interests of an average person with materials that lack literary, artistic, political, or scientific value.

- *Texas v. Johnson* (1989): There may not be a law to ban flag-burning.

- *Reno v. ACLU* (1997): A law that bans sending "indecent" material to minors over the internet is unconstitutional because "indecent" is too vague and broad a term.

- *FEC v. Wisconsin Right to Life* (2007): Prohibits campaign finance reform law from banning political advocacy.

- *Citizens United v. FEC* (2010): The part of the McCain-Feingold campaign finance reform law that prevents corporations and labor unions from spending money on advertisements (independent of political candidates or parties) in political campaigns is unconstitutional.

free-exercise clause
First Amendment requirement that law cannot prevent free exercise of religion.

establishment clause
First Amendment ban on laws "respecting an establishment of religion."

Hazelwood High School could censor articles appearing in the student-edited newspaper. The newspaper was published using school funds and was part of a journalism class. The principal ordered the deletion of stories dealing with student pregnancies and the impact of parental divorce on students. The student editors sued, claiming their First Amendment rights had been violated. The Court agreed that students do not "shed their constitutional rights to freedom of speech or expression at the schoolhouse gate" and that they cannot be punished for expressing on campus their personal views. But students do not have exactly the same rights as adults if the exercise of those rights impedes the educational mission of the school. Students may lawfully say things on campus, as individuals, that they cannot say if they are part of school-sponsored activities (such as plays or school-run newspapers) that are part of the curriculum. School-sponsored activities can be controlled so long as the controls are "reasonably related to legitimate pedagogical concerns."[38]

Church and State

Everybody knows, correctly, the language of the First Amendment that protects freedom of speech and the press, though most people are not aware of how complex the legal interpretations of these provisions have become. But many people also believe, wrongly, that the language of the First Amendment clearly requires the "separation of church and state." It does not.

What that amendment actually says is quite different and maddeningly unclear. It has two parts. The first, often referred to as the **free-exercise clause**, states that Congress shall make no law prohibiting the "free exercise" of religion. The second, which is called the **establishment clause**, states that Congress shall make no law "respecting an establishment of religion."

The Free-Exercise Clause

The free-exercise clause is the clearer of the two, though by no means is it lacking in ambiguity. It obviously means that Congress cannot pass a law prohibiting Catholics from celebrating Mass, requiring Baptists to become Episcopalians, or preventing Jews from holding a bar mitzvah. Since the First

Amendment has been applied to the states via the due process clause of the Fourteenth Amendment, it means that state governments cannot pass such laws either. In general, the courts have treated religion like speech: you can pretty much do or say what you want so long as it does not cause some serious harm to others.

Even some laws that do not appear on their face to apply to churches may be unconstitutional if their enforcement imposes particular burdens on churches or greater burdens on some churches than others. For example, a state cannot apply a license fee on door-to-door solicitors when the solicitor is a Jehovah's Witness selling religious tracts.[39] By the same token, the courts ruled that the city of Hialeah, Florida, cannot ban animal sacrifices by members of an Afro-Caribbean religion called Santeria. Since killing animals generally is not illegal (if it were, there could be no hamburgers or chicken sandwiches served in Hialeah's restaurants, and rat traps would be unlawful), the ban in this case was clearly directed against a specific religion and hence was unconstitutional.[40]

Having the right to exercise your religion freely does not mean, however, that you are exempt from laws binding other citizens, even when the law goes against your religious beliefs. A man cannot have more than one wife, even if (as once was the case with Mormons) polygamy is thought desirable on religious grounds.[41] For religious reasons, you may oppose being vaccinated or having blood transfusions, but if the state passes a compulsory vaccination law or orders that a blood transfusion be given to a sick child, the courts will not block it on grounds of religious liberty.[42] Similarly, if you belong to an Indian tribe that uses a drug, such as peyote, in religious ceremonies, you cannot claim that your freedom was abridged if the state decides to ban the use of that drug, provided the law applies equally to all.[43] Since airports have a legitimate need for tight security measures, begging can be outlawed in them even if some of the people doing the begging are part of a religious group (in this case, the Hare Krishnas).[44]

Unfortunately, some conflicts between religious belief and public policy are even more difficult to settle. What if you believe on religious grounds that war is immoral? The draft laws have always exempted a conscientious objector from military duty, and the Court has upheld such exemptions. But the Court has gone further: it has said that people cannot be drafted even if they do not believe in a Supreme Being or belong to any religious tradition, so long as their "consciences, spurred by deeply held moral, ethical, or religious beliefs, would give them no rest or peace if they allowed themselves to become part of an instrument of war."[45] Do exemptions on such

Public schools cannot organize prayers, but private ones can.

grounds create an opportunity for some people to evade the draft because of their political preferences? In trying to answer such questions, the courts often have had to try to define religion—no easy task.

And even when there is no question about your membership in a bona fide religion, the circumstances under which you may claim exemption from laws that apply to everybody else are unclear. What if you, a member of the Seventh-Day Adventists, are fired by your employer for refusing on religious grounds to work on Saturday, and then it turns out that you cannot collect unemployment insurance because you refuse to take an available job—one that also requires you to work on Saturday? Or what if you are a member of the Amish sect, which refuses, contrary to state law, to send its children to public schools past the eighth grade? The Court has ruled that the state must pay you unemployment compensation and cannot require you to send your children to public schools beyond the eighth grade.[46]

These last two decisions, and others like them, show that even the "simple" principle of freedom of religion gets complicated in practice and can lead to the courts' giving, in effect, preference to members of one church over members of another.

The Establishment Clause

What in the world did the members of the First Congress mean when they wrote into the First Amendment language prohibiting Congress from making a law "respecting" an "establishment" of religion? The Supreme Court has more or less consistently interpreted this vague phrase to mean that the Constitution erects a **"wall of separation"** between church and state.

That phrase, so often quoted, is not in the Bill of Rights nor in the debates in the First Congress that drafted the Bill of Rights; it comes from the pen of Thomas Jefferson, who was opposed to having the Church of England as the established church of his native Virginia. (At the time of the Revolutionary War, there were established churches—that is, official, state-supported churches—in at least eight of the 13 former colonies.) But it is not clear that Jefferson's view was the majority view.

During much of the debate in Congress, the wording of this part of the First Amendment was quite different and much plainer than what finally emerged. Up to the last minute, the clause was intended to read "no religion shall be established by law" or "no national religion shall be established." The meaning of those words seems quite clear: whatever the states may do, the federal government cannot create an official, national religion or give support to one religion in preference to another.[47]

But Congress instead adopted an ambiguous phrase, and so the Supreme Court had to decide what it meant. It has declared that these words do not simply mean "no national religion" but mean as well no government involvement with religion at all, even on a nonpreferential basis. They mean, in short, erecting a "wall of separation" between church and state.[48] Though the interpretation of the establishment clause remains a topic of great controversy among judges and scholars, the Supreme Court has more or less consistently adopted this wall-of-separation principle.

Its first statement of this interpretation was in 1947. The case involved a New Jersey town that reimbursed parents for the costs of transporting their children to school, including parochial (in this case Catholic) schools. The Court decided that this reimbursement was constitutional, but it made it clear that the establishment clause of the First Amendment applied (via the Fourteenth Amendment) to the states and that it meant, among other things, that the government cannot require a person to profess a belief or disbelief in any religion; it cannot aid one religion, some religions, or all religions; and it cannot spend any tax money, however small the amount might be, in support of any religious activities or institutions.[49] The reader may wonder, in view of the Court's reasoning, why it allowed the town to pay for busing children to Catholic schools. The answer it gave is that busing is a religiously neutral activity, akin to providing fire and police protection to Catholic schools. Busing, available to public- and private-school children alike, does not breach the wall of separation.

Since 1947, the Court has applied the wall-of-separation theory to strike down as unconstitutional most efforts to have any officially conducted or sponsored prayer in public schools, even if it is

wall of separation Court ruling that government cannot be involved with religion.

nonsectarian,[50] voluntary,[51] or limited to reading a passage of the Bible.[52] Since 1992, it has even been unconstitutional for a public school to ask a rabbi or minister to offer a prayer—an invocation or a benediction—at the school's graduation ceremony. Since 2000, it has been unconstitutional for a student to lead a prayer at a public high school football game because it was done "over the school's public address system, by a speaker representing the student body, under the supervision of the school faculty, and pursuant to school policy."[53] The Court made it clear, however, that public-school students could pray voluntarily during school provided that the school or the government did not sponsor that prayer. Moreover, the Court has held that laws prohibiting teaching the theory of evolution or requiring giving equal time to "creationism" (the biblical doctrine that God created mankind) are religiously inspired and thus unconstitutional.[54] A public school may not allow its pupils to take time out from their regular classes for religious instruction if this occurs within the schools, though "released-time" instruction is all right if it is done outside the public-school building.[55] The school prayer decisions in particular have provoked a storm of controversy, but efforts to get Congress to propose to the states a constitutional amendment authorizing such prayers have failed.

Almost as controversial have been Court-imposed restrictions on public aid to parochial schools, though here the wall-of-separation principle has not been used to forbid any and all forms of aid. For example, it is permissible for the federal government to provide aid for constructing buildings on denominational (as well as nondenominational) college campuses[56] and for state governments to loan free textbooks to parochial-school pupils,[57] grant tax-exempt status to parochial schools,[58] allow parents of parochial-school children to deduct their tuition payments on a state's income tax returns,[59] and pay for computers and deaf children's sign language interpreters at private and religious schools.[60] But the government cannot pay a salary supplement to teachers who teach secular subjects in parochial schools,[61] reimburse parents for the cost of parochial-school tuition,[62] supply parochial schools with services such as counseling,[63] give money with which to purchase instructional materials, require that "creationism" be taught in public schools, or create a special school district for Hasidic Jews.[64]

The Court sometimes changes its mind on these matters. In 1985, it said the states could not send teachers into parochial schools to teach remedial courses for needy children, but 12 years later it decided they could. "We no longer presume," the Court wrote, "that public employees will inculcate religion simply because they happen to be in a sectarian environment."[65]

Perhaps the most important establishment-clause decision in recent times was the Court ruling that vouchers can be used to pay for children being educated at religious and other private schools. The case began in Cleveland, Ohio, where the state offered money to any family (especially poor ones) whose children attended a school that had done so badly that it was under a federal court order requiring it to be managed directly by the state superintendent of schools. The money, a voucher, could be used to send a child to any other public or private school, including one run by a religious group. The Court held that this plan did not violate the establishment clause because the aid went, not to the school, but to the families who were to choose a school.[66]

If you find it confusing to follow the twists and turns of Court policy in this area, you are not alone. The wall-of-separation principle has not been easy to apply, and the Court has begun to alter its position on church-state matters. The Court has tried to sort out the confusion by developing a three-prong test to decide under what circumstances government involvement in religious activities is improper.[67] That involvement is constitutional if it meets these tests:

1. It has a strictly secular purpose.
2. Its primary effect neither advances nor inhibits religion.
3. It does not foster an excessive government entanglement with religion.

HOW WE COMPARE

Church and State

The American government cannot pay for or endorse any church. By contrast, the national governments in the United Kingdom, Greece, Germany, Norway, and Sweden can. Moreover, until recently there were state-supported churches in France, Italy, and Spain. Despite the absence of any governmental support for churches in this country, attendance in churches and synagogues is very high—by some estimates, as much as 40 percent of our population goes to these institutions every week. By contrast, in countries that have or have had state-supported churches, church attendance is sparse. Only 4 percent of the English and 5 percent of the French go to church at least once a week.

How would you explain high church attendance in a country where churches lack government backing and low attendance where they have that backing?

No sooner had the test been developed than the Court decided that it was all right for the government of Pawtucket, Rhode Island, to erect a Nativity scene as part of a Christmas display in a local park. But five years later, it said Pittsburgh could not put a Nativity scene in front of the courthouse, but could display a menorah (a Jewish symbol of Chanukah) next to a Christmas tree and a sign extolling liberty. The Court ruled that the crèche had to go (because, being too close to the courthouse, a government endorsement was implied) but the menorah could stay (because, being next to a Christmas tree, it would not lead people to think that Pittsburgh was endorsing Judaism).

When the Ten Commandments are displayed in or near a public building, a deeply divided Court has made some complicated distinctions. It held that it was unconstitutional for two Kentucky counties to put up the Ten Commandments in their courthouses because, the Court decided, the purpose was religious. It did no good for one Kentucky courthouse to surround the Ten Commandments with displays of the Declaration of Independence and the Star Spangled Banner so as to make the

Commandments part of America's political heritage. The Court said it was still a religious effort, even though it noted that there was a frieze containing Moses in the Supreme Court's own building. (This, the opinion held, was not religious.) But when the Ten Commandments were put up outside the Texas state capitol, this was upheld. Justice Stephen Breyer, who forbid the Kentucky display but allowed the Texas one, wrote that in Texas the Commandments now revealed a secular message and, besides, no one had sued to end this display until 40 years after it was erected.[68]

Though the Court has struck down prayer in public schools, it has upheld prayer in Congress (since 1789, the House and Senate open each session with a prayer).[69] A public school cannot have a chaplain, but the armed services can. The Court has said that the government cannot "advance" religion, but it has not objected to the printing of the phrase "In God We Trust" on the back of every dollar bill.

These distinctions reflect the fact that the Court tends to use the wall-of-separation test when it deals with public schools but that it tries to strike a reasonable balance when it deals with Congress or state office buildings, perhaps because schools have a young and captive population, whereas public forums have an adult and voluntary membership.

It is obvious that despite its efforts to set forth clear rules governing church-state relations, the Court's actual decisions are hard to summarize. It is deeply divided—some would say deeply confused—on these matters, and so the efforts to define the "wall of separation" will continue to prove to be as difficult as the Court's earlier efforts to decide what is interstate and what is local commerce (see Chapter 3).

Crime and Due Process

Whereas the central problem in interpreting the religion clauses of the First Amendment has been to decide what they mean, the central problem in interpreting those parts of the Bill of Rights that affect people accused of a crime has been to decide not only what they mean but also how to put them into effect. It is not obvious what constitutes an "unreasonable search," but even if we settle that question, we still must decide how best to protect people against such searches in ways that do not unduly hinder criminal investigations.

That protection can be provided in at least two ways. One is to let the police introduce in court evidence relevant to the guilt or innocence of a person, no matter how it was obtained, and then, after the case is settled, punish the police officer (or his or her superiors) if the evidence was gathered improperly (for example, by an unreasonable search). The other way is to exclude

LANDMARK CASES

Religious Freedom

- *Pierce v. Society of Sisters* (1925): Though states may require public education, they may not require that students attend only public schools.

- *Everson v. Board of Education* (1947): The wall-of-separation principle is announced.

- *Zorauch v. Clauson* (1952): States may allow students to be released from public schools to attend religious instruction.

- *Engel v. Vitale* (1962): There may not be a prayer, even a nondenominational one, in public schools.

- *Lemon v. Kurtzman* (1971): Three tests are described for deciding whether the government is improperly involved with religion.

- *Lee v. Weisman* (1992): Public schools may not have clergy lead prayers at graduation ceremonies.

- *Santa Fe Independent School District v. Doe* (2000): Students may not lead prayers before the start of a football game at a public school.

- *Zelman v. Simmons-Harris* (2002): Voucher plan to pay school bills is upheld.

WHAT'S YOUR ISSUE?

Gun Control and the Second Amendment

On December 14, 2012, a lone gunman killed twenty school children and six adults at Sandy Hook Elementary School in Newtown, Connecticut. The mass murder led to the latest round of intense national debates about gun control laws and the Second Amendment. On April 17, 2013, about four months after the mass murder, Congress failed to enact a proposed law that, among other provisions, would have expanded background checks on gun purchasers.

Gallup polls and other surveys indicate that in the months prior to the Sandy Hook incident, about 43 percent of the public supported some such gun control measures. In the weeks after the incident, support rose to nearly 60 percent; but, by the time Congress voted on the bill, public support had trended down to about 49 percent in favor versus about 43 percent opposed. Also, in many states, gun sales actually soared in the weeks and months following the Sandy Hook tragedy.

As discussed earlier in this chapter (see page 100), in 2008, the Supreme Court, citing the Second Amendment right to "keep and bear arms," ruled that the federal government did not have the right to ban the private possession of firearms; and, in 2010, the Court, once again citing the Second Amendment, forbade the states from banning the private possession of firearms.

Thus, while federal, state, and local laws regulating or restricting private gun purchases and gun use are constitutional, the Court has declared that outright bans by any level of government on private gun ownership are not. How would you describe your stake in gun control? What is your take on the issue, including the Court's decisions to ban governments from banning the private possession of firearms?

---

exclusionary rule
Improperly gathered evidence may not be introduced in a criminal trial.

improperly gathered evidence from the trial in the first place, even if it is relevant to determining the guilt or innocence of the accused.

Most democratic nations, including the United Kingdom, use the first method; the United States uses the second. Because of this, many of the landmark cases decided by the Supreme Court have been bitterly controversial. Opponents of these decisions have argued that a guilty person should not go free just because the police officer blundered, especially if the mistake was minor. Supporters rejoin that there is no way to punish errant police officers effectively other than by excluding tainted evidence; moreover, nobody should be convicted of a crime except by evidence that is above reproach.[70]

The Exclusionary Rule

The American method relies on what is called the **exclusionary rule**. That rule holds that evidence gathered in violation of the Constitution cannot be used in a trial. The rule has been used to implement two provisions of the Bill of Rights—the right to be free from unreasonable searches and seizures (Fourth Amendment) and the right not to be compelled to give evidence against oneself (Fifth Amendment).*

Not until 1949 did the Supreme Court consider whether to apply the exclusionary rule to the states. In a case decided that year, the Court made it clear that the Fourth Amendment prohibited the police from carrying out unreasonable searches and obtaining improper confessions, but held that it was not necessary to use the exclusionary rule to enforce those prohibitions. It noted that other nations did not require that evidence improperly gathered had to be excluded from a criminal trial. The Court said that the local police should not improperly gather and use evidence, but if they did, the remedy was to sue the police department or punish the officer.[71]

But in 1961, the Supreme Court changed its mind about the use of the exclusionary rule. It all began when the Cleveland police broke into the home of Dollree Mapp in search of a suspect in a bombing case. Not finding him, they instead arrested her for possessing some obscene pictures found there. The Court held that this was an unreasonable search and seizure because the police had not obtained a search warrant, though they had had ample time to do so. Furthermore, such illegally gathered evidence

---

*We shall consider here only two constitutional limits—those bearing on searches and confessions. Thus we will omit many other important constitutional provisions affecting criminal cases, such as rules governing wiretapping, prisoner rights, the right to bail and to a jury trial, the bar on ex post facto laws, the right to be represented by a lawyer in court, the ban on "cruel and unusual" punishment, and the rule against double jeopardy.

could not be used in the trial of Mapp.[72] Beginning with this case—*Mapp v. Ohio*—the Supreme Court required the use of the exclusionary rule as a way of enforcing a variety of constitutional guarantees.

Search and Seizure

After the Court decided to exclude improperly gathered evidence, the next problem was to decide what evidence was improperly gathered. What happened to Dollree Mapp was an easy case: hardly anybody argued that it was reasonable for the police to break into someone's home without a warrant, ransack their belongings, and take whatever they could find that might be incriminating. But that left a lot of hard choices still to be made.

When can the police search you without it being unreasonable? Under two circumstances—when they have a search warrant or when they have lawfully arrested you. A **search warrant** is an order from a judge authorizing the search of a place; the order must describe what is to be searched and seized, and the judge can issue it only if he or she is persuaded by the police that good reason (**probable cause**) exists to believe that a crime has been committed and that the evidence bearing on that crime will be found at a certain location. (The police can also search a building if the occupant gives them permission.)

> ***search warrant*** A judge's order authorizing a search.
>
> ***probable cause*** Reasonable cause for issuing a search warrant or making an arrest; more than mere suspicion.

WHAT WOULD YOU DO?

MEMORANDUM

To: *Rebecca Saikia, Supreme Court justice*

From: *David Wilson, law clerk*

Subject: *Patriot Act and libraries*

The Patriot Act allows the FBI to seek the records of possible terrorists from banks, businesses, and libraries. Many libraries claim this will harm the constitutional rights of Americans. You support these rights, but are also aware of the need to protect national security.

Arguments for:

1. The Patriot Act does not target individuals who have not violated a criminal law and who do not threaten human life.

2. For the FBI to collect information about borrowers, it must first obtain permission from a federal judge.

3. Terrorists may use libraries to study and plan activities that threaten national security.

Arguments against:

1. Freedom of speech and expression are fundamental constitutional guarantees that should not be infringed.

News »

High Court Hears from Libraries about War on Terror

Two public libraries have asked the Supreme Court to strike down provisions of the Patriot Act that allow the Federal Bureau of Investigation to see the borrowing records of persons who are under investigation.

2. The law might harm groups engaged in peaceful protests.

3. The law allows the government to delay notifying people that their borrowing habits are being investigated.

Your decision:

Uphold this provision _____   Overturn this provision _____

In addition, you can be searched if the search occurs when you are lawfully arrested. When can you be arrested? You can be arrested if a judge has issued an arrest warrant for you, if you commit a crime in the presence of a police officer, or if the officer has probable cause to believe you have committed a serious crime (usually a felony). If you are arrested and no search warrant has been issued, the police—not a judge—decide what they can search. What rules should they follow?

In trying to answer that question, the courts have elaborated a set of rules that are complex, subject to frequent change, and quite controversial. In general, the police, after arresting you, can search:

- You

- Things in plain view

- Things or places under your immediate control

As a practical matter, things "in plain view" or "under your immediate control" mean the room in which you are arrested but not other rooms of the house.[73] If the police want to search the rest of your house or a car parked in your driveway, they will first have to go to a judge to obtain a search warrant. But if the police arrest a college student on campus for underage drinking and then accompany that student back to his or her dormitory room so that the student can get proof that he or she was old enough to drink, the police can seize drugs in plain view in that room.[74] And if marijuana is growing in plain view in an open field, the police can enter and search that field even though it is fenced off with a locked gate and a "No Trespassing" sign.[75]

But what if you are arrested while driving your car—how much of it can the police search? The answer to that question has changed almost yearly. In 1979, the Court ruled that the police could not search a suitcase taken from a car of an arrested person, and in 1981 it extended this protection to any "closed, opaque container" found in the car.[76] But the following year, the Court decided that all parts of a car, closed or open, could be searched if the officers had probable cause to believe they contained contraband (that is, goods illegally possessed). And recently, the rules governing car searches have been relaxed even further. Officers who have probable cause to search a car can also search the things passengers are carrying in the car. And if the car is stopped for a traffic infraction, the car can be searched if the officer develops a "reasonable, articulable suspicion" that the car is involved in other illegal activity.[77]

In this confusing area of the law, the Court is attempting to protect those places in which a person has a "reasonable expectation of privacy." Your body is one such place, and so the Court has held that the police cannot compel you to undergo surgery to remove a bullet that might be evidence of your guilt or innocence in a crime.[78] But the police can require you to take a Breathalyzer test to see whether you have been drinking while driving.[79] Your home is another place where you have an expectation of privacy, but a barn next to your home is not, nor is your backyard viewed from an airplane, nor is your home if it is a motor home that can be driven away, and so the police need not have a warrant to look into these places.[80]

If you work for the government, you have an expectation that your desk and files will be private; nonetheless, your supervisor may search the desk and files without a warrant, provided that he or she is looking for something related to your work.[81] But bear in mind that the Constitution protects you only from *the government*; a private employer has a great deal of freedom to search your desk and files.

Confessions and Self-Incrimination

The constitutional ban on being forced to give evidence against oneself was originally intended to prevent the use of torture or "third-degree" police tactics to extract confessions. But it has since been extended to cover many kinds of statements uttered not out of fear of torture but from lack of awareness of one's rights, especially the right to remain silent, whether in the courtroom or in the police station.

For many decades, the Supreme Court had held that involuntary confessions could not be used in federal criminal trials but had not ruled that they were barred from state trials. But in the early 1960s, it changed its mind in two landmark cases—*Escobedo* and *Miranda*.[82] The story of the latter and of the controversy that it provoked is worth telling.

Ernesto A. Miranda was convicted in Arizona of the rape and kidnapping of a young woman. The conviction was based on a written confession that Miranda signed after two hours of police questioning. (The victim also identified him.) Two years earlier, the Court had decided that the rule against self-incrimination applied to state courts.[83] Now the question arose of what constitutes an "involuntary" confession. The Court decided that a confession should be presumed involuntary unless the person in custody had been fully and clearly informed of his or her right to be silent, to have an attorney present during any questioning, and to have an attorney provided free of charge if he or she could not afford one. The accused could waive these rights and offer to talk, but the waiver must have been truly voluntary. Since Miranda did not have a lawyer present when he was questioned and had not knowingly waived his right to a lawyer, the confession was excluded from evidence in the trial and his conviction was overturned.[84]

Miranda was tried and convicted again, this time on the basis of evidence supplied by his girlfriend, who testified that he had admitted to her that he was guilty. Nine years later, he was released from prison; four years after that, he was killed in a barroom fight. When the Phoenix police arrested the prime suspect in Ernesto Miranda's murder, they read him his rights from a "Miranda card."

Everyone who watches cops-and-robbers shows on television probably knows the "Miranda warning" by heart (see the box on page 116). The police now read it routinely to people whom they arrest. It is not clear whether it has much impact on who does or does not confess or what effect, if any, it may have on the crime rate.

In time, the Miranda rule was extended to mean that you have a right to a lawyer when you appear in a police lineup[85] and when you are questioned by a psychiatrist to determine whether you are competent to stand trial.[86] The Court threw out the conviction of a man who had killed a child, because the accused, without being given the right to have a lawyer present and having undergone harsh questioning, had led the police to the victim's body.[87] You do not have a right to a Miranda warning, however, if while in jail you confess a crime to another inmate who turns out to be an undercover police officer.[88]

Some police departments have tried to get around the need for a Miranda warning by training their officers to question suspects before giving them a Miranda warning and then, if the suspect confesses, giving the warning and asking the same questions over again. But the Supreme Court has not allowed this and has struck the practice down.[89]

Relaxing the Exclusionary Rule

Cases such as *Miranda* were highly controversial and led to efforts in Congress to modify or overrule the decisions by statute—without much coming of the attempts. But as the rules governing police conduct became increasingly more complex, pressure mounted to find an alternative. Some thought that any evidence should be admissible, with the question of police conduct left to lawsuits or other ways of punishing official misbehavior. Others felt that the exclusionary rule served a useful purpose but had simply become too technical to be an effective deterrent to police misconduct (the police cannot obey rules that they cannot understand). And still others felt that the exclusionary rule was a vital safeguard to essential liberties and should be kept intact. The Court has refused to let Congress abolish Miranda because it is a constitutional rule.[90]

The courts began to decide some cases in ways that modified—but retained—the exclusionary rule. The police were given greater freedom to question

juveniles.[91] If the police got a warrant they thought was valid but the judge had used the wrong form, they could use it under the **good faith exception**.[92] The Supreme Court has allowed the police to question a suspect without first issuing a Miranda warning if the questions were motivated by overriding considerations of public safety, referred to as a **public safety exception**.[93] And the Court changed its mind about the killer who led the police to the victim's body. Under the **inevitable discovery** rule, the Court decided that if a victim will be discovered anyway, the evidence will not be excluded.[94]

good faith exception An error in gathering evidence sufficiently minor that it may be used in a trial.

public safety exception The police can question an un-Mirandized suspect if there is an urgent concern for public safety.

inevitable discovery The police can use evidence if it would inevitably have been discovered.

Terrorism and Civil Liberties

The attacks of September 11, 2001, raised important questions about how far the government can go in investigating and prosecuting individuals.

A little more than one month after the attacks, Congress passed a new law, the USA Patriot Act, designed to increase federal powers to investigate terrorists.[†] Its main provisions are these:

- Telephone taps. The government may tap, if it has a court order, any telephone a suspect uses instead of having to get a separate order for each telephone.

- Internet taps. The government may tap, if it has a court order, internet communications.

- Voice mail. The government, with a court order, may seize voice mail.

- Grand jury information. Investigators can now share with other government officials things learned in secret grand jury hearings.

- Immigration. The attorney general may hold any noncitizen who is thought to be a national security risk for up to seven days. If the alien cannot be charged with a crime or deported within that time, he or she may still be detained if he or she is certified to be a security risk.

[†]The name of the law is an acronym derived from the official title of the bill, drawn from the first letters of the following capitalized words: Uniting and Strengthening America by Providing Appropriate Tools Required to Intercept and Obstruct Terrorism (USA Patriot).

- Money laundering. The government gets new powers to track the movement of money across U.S. borders and among banks.

- Crime. This provision eliminates the statute of limitation on terrorist crimes and increases the penalties.

About a month later, President Bush, by executive order, proclaimed a national emergency under which any noncitizen who is believed to be a terrorist or to have harbored a terrorist will be tried by a military, rather than a civilian, court. A military trial is carried on before a commission of military officers and not a civilian jury. The tribunal can operate in secret if classified information is used in evidence. Two-thirds of the commission must agree before the suspect can be convicted and sentenced. If convicted, the suspect can appeal to the secretary of defense and the president, but not to a civilian court. These commissions may eventually be used to try some of the men captured by the U.S. military during its campaign in Afghanistan against the Taliban regime and the al Qaeda terrorist network that was created by Osama bin Laden. The detainees held in a prison at our Guantanamo naval base in Cuba are not regarded by the Defense Department as ordinary prisoners of war.

The biggest legal issue created by this country's war on terrorism is whether the people we capture can be held by our government without giving them access to the courts. The traditional view, first announced during World War II, was that spies sent to this country by the Nazis could be tried by a military tribunal instead of by a civilian court. They were neither citizens nor soldiers, but "unlawful combatants."[95] The Bush administration relied on this view when it detained, in our military base in Guantanamo Bay, Cuba, men seized by American forces in Afghanistan. These men were mostly members of the al Qaeda terrorist movement or of the Taliban movement that governed Afghanistan before American armed forces, together with Afghan rebels, defeated them. These men, none of them American citizens, argued that they were neither terrorists nor combatants. They demanded access to American courts. By a vote of six to three, the Supreme Court held that American courts can consider challenges to the legality of the detention of these men. The Court's opinion did not spell out what the courts should do when it hears such petitions.[96]

In another decision given the same day, the Supreme Court ruled on the case of an American citizen who apparently was working with the Taliban

HOW THINGS WORK

The Miranda Rule

The Supreme Court has interpreted the due process clause to require that local police departments issue warnings of the sort shown below to people whom they are arresting.

```
        PHILADELPHIA POLICE DEPARTMENT
     STANDARD POLICE INTERROGATION CARD

        WARNINGS TO BE GIVEN ACCUSED

   We are questioning you concerning the
   crime of (state specific crime).

        We have a duty to explain to
        you and to warn you that you
        have the following legal rights:

   A.   You have a right to remain
        silent and do not have to say
        anything at all.

   B.   Anything you say can and will
        be used against you in Court.
```

```
   C.   You have a right to talk to a
        lawyer of your own choice
        before we ask you any questions,
        and also to have a lawyer here
        with you while we ask questions.

   D.   If you cannot afford to hire a
        lawyer, and you want one, we
        will see that you have one
        provided to you free of charge
        before we ask you any questions.

   E.   If you are willing to give us a
        statement, you have a right to
        stop any time you wish.

   75-Misc.-3              (Over)

   (6-24-70)
```

Philadelphia Police Department

Ernesto A. Miranda was convicted in Arizona of rape and kidnapping. When the Supreme Court overturned the conviction, it issued a set of rules—the "Miranda rule"—governing how police must conduct an arrest and interrogation.

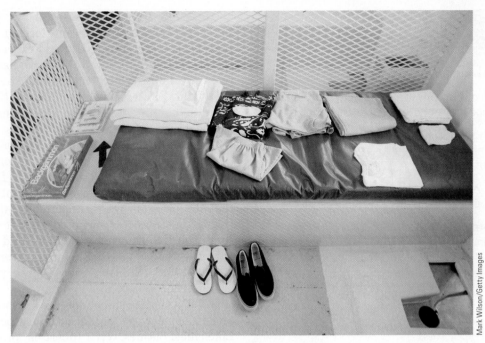

Mark Wilson/Getty Images

Inside a cell at the terrorist prison in Guantanamo, where Muslim inmates receive a copy of the Koran, a chess set, and an arrow pointing toward Mecca.

regime but was captured by our forces and imprisoned in South Carolina. The Court said that American citizens are entitled to a hearing before a neutral decision maker in order to challenge the basis for detention.[97]

That "neutral decision maker" was created in 2006 by a law authorizing military commissions to try alien enemy combatants. These are foreign fighters not in uniform, such as members of al Qaeda, who are captured by American forces. Each commission is to be composed of at least five military officers and is to allow the defendant certain fundamental rights (such as to see evidence and testify). Appeals from its decisions can be taken to the Court of Military Review, whose members are selected by the secretary of defense. The federal appeals court for the District of Columbia and, if it wishes, the Supreme Court may hear appeals from the Court of Military Review.[98]

Military commissions have conducted hearings about the inmates in the Guantanamo prison. Some were released, some were held, and for some no decision has been made. Right after he became president, Barack Obama issued an order to close the Guantanamo prison. But there is a problem: What do you do with the inmates? While George W. Bush was president, 420 of the more than 700 inmates were released, but another 50 or so, though declared eligible for release, could not find a country willing to accept them. Where will they go?

When it was first passed in 2001, the Patriot Act made certain provisions temporary, perhaps to allay the fears of civil libertarians. When the act was

renewed in March 2006, only a few changes were made and almost all of its provisions were made permanent.

In addition to the Patriot Act, Congress passed and the president signed in 2005 a law that required all states by 2008 to comply with federal standards when they issue driver licenses. States, not Washington, pass out these licenses, but by mid-2008 the Real ID Act says that no federal agency, including those that manage security at airports, may accept a license or state identification card that does not have the person's photograph, address, signature, and full legal name based on documents that prove he or she is legally in this country. Some people think this amounts to a required national ID card.[99]

Searches Without Warrants

For many decades, presidents of both parties authorized telephone taps without warrants when they believed the person being tapped was a foreign spy. Some did this to capture information about their political enemies. In 1978, Congress decided to bring this practice under legislative control. It passed the Foreign Intelligence Surveillance Act (FISA), which required the president to go before a special court, composed of seven judges selected by the Chief Justice, to obtain approval for electronic eavesdropping on persons who were thought to be foreign spies. The FISA court would impose a standard lower than that which governs the issuance of warrants against

LANDMARK CASES

Criminal Charges

- *Mapp v. Ohio* (1961): Evidence illegally gathered by the police may not be used in a criminal trial.

- *Gideon v. Wainwright* (1964): Persons charged with a crime have a right to an attorney even if they cannot afford one.

- *Miranda v. Arizona* (1966): Court describes warning that police must give to arrested persons.

- *United States v. Leon* (1984): Illegally obtained evidence may be used in a trial if it was gathered in good faith without violating the principles of the *Mapp* decision.

- *Dickerson v. United States* (2000): The *Mapp* decision is based on the Constitution and cannot be altered by Congress passing a law.

- *Rasul v. Bush* and *Hamdi v. Rumsfeld* (2004): Terrorist detainees must have access to a neutral court to decide if they are legally held.

criminals. For criminals, a warrant must be based on showing "probable cause" that the person is engaged in a crime; for FISA warrants, the government need only show that the person is likely to be working for a foreign government.

In late 2005, *The New York Times* and other newspapers revealed that the National Security Agency (NSA), this country's code-breaking and electronic surveillance organization, had a secret program to intercept telephone calls and email messages between certain people abroad and Americans. The Bush administration defended the program, arguing that the intercepts were designed not to identify criminals or foreign spies, but to alert the country to potential terrorist threats. It could not rely on FISA because its procedures took too long and its standards of proof were too high. Critics of the program said that it imperiled the civil liberties of Americans.

The Supreme Court has never spoken on this matter, but every lower federal court, including the court that hears appeals from the FISA court, has agreed that the president, as commander in chief, has the "inherent authority" to conduct warrantless searches to obtain foreign intelligence information.[100] The administration also argued that after 9/11, when Congress passed a law authorizing the president to exercise "all necessary and appropriate" uses of military force, it included warrantless intercepts of terrorist communications.

In 2008, Congress passed a bill that allowed the government to intercept foreign communications with people in the United States provided the FISA court had approved the surveillance methods. But the administration could begin the surveillance before the FISA ruling was made if it declared the need to be urgent. However, if Americans living overseas are made the target of this surveillance, then there must first be a FISA warrant. In addition, private telephone and internet companies that aided in the surveillance were exempt from lawsuits so long as they had received "substantial evidence" that the program was authorized by the president. In 2013, a controversy erupted when it was revealed that nine U.S. internet companies had collaborated with the NSA and British intelligence agencies on a secret and extensive surveillance program (see Chapter 16).

Civil liberties questions are in some ways like and in some ways unlike ordinary policy debates. Like most issues, civil liberties problems often involve competing interests—in this case, conflicting rights or conflicting rights and duties—and so we have groups mobilized on both sides of issues involving free speech and crime control. Like some other issues, civil liberties problems also can arise from the successful appeals of a policy entrepreneur, and so we have periodic reductions in liberty resulting from popular fears, usually aroused during or just after a war.

But civil liberties are unlike many other issues in at least one regard: more than struggles over welfare spending or defense or economic policy, debates about civil liberties reach down into our fundamental political beliefs and political culture, challenging us to define what we mean by religion, Americanism, and decency. The most important of these challenges focuses on the meaning of the First Amendment: What is "speech"? How much of it should be free? How far can the state go in aiding religion? How do we strike a balance between national security and personal expression? The zigzag course followed by the courts in judging these matters has, on balance, tended to enlarge freedom of expression.

Almost as important has been the struggle to strike a balance between the right of society to protect itself from criminals and the right of people (including criminals) to be free from unreasonable searches and coerced confessions. As with free-speech cases, the courts generally have broadened the rights of individuals at some expense to the power of the police. But in recent years, the Supreme Court has pulled back from some of its more sweeping applications of the exclusionary rule.

The resolution of these issues by the courts is political in the sense that differing opinions about what is right or desirable compete, with one side or another prevailing (often by a small majority). In this competition of ideas, federal judges, though not elected, often are sensitive to strong currents of popular opinion. When politics has produced new action against apparently threatening minorities, judges are inclined, at least for a while, to give serious consideration to popular fears and legislative majorities. And when no strong national mood is discernible, the opinions of elites influence judicial thinking (as described in Chapter 16).

At the same time, courts resolve political conflicts in a manner that differs in important respects from the resolution of conflicts by legislatures or executives. First, the very existence of the courts, and the relative ease with which one may enter them to advance a claim, facilitates challenges to accepted values. An unpopular political or religious group may have little or no access to a legislature, but it will have substantial access to the courts. Second, judges often settle controversies about rights not simply by deciding the case at hand, but rather by formulating a general rule to cover like cases elsewhere. This has

an advantage (the law tends to become more consistent and better known) but a disadvantage as well: a rule suitable for one case may be unworkable in another. Judges reason by analogy and sometimes assume two cases are similar when in fact important differences exist. For example, a definition of "obscenity" or "fighting words" may suit one situation but be inadequate in another. Third, judges interpret the Constitution, whereas legislatures often consult popular preferences or personal convictions. However much their own beliefs influence what judges read into the Constitution, almost all of them are constrained by its language.

Taken together, the desire to find and announce rules, the language of the Constitution, and the personal beliefs of judges have led to a general expansion of civil liberties. As a result, even allowing for temporary reversals and frequent redefinitions, any value thought to hinder freedom of expression and the rights of the accused has generally lost ground to the claims of the First, Fourth, Fifth, and Sixth Amendments.

LEARNING OBJECTIVES

1. Why do the courts play so large a role in deciding what our civil liberties should be?

The courts are independent of the executive and legislative branches, both of which will respond to public pressures. In wartime or in other crisis periods, people want "something done." The president and members of Congress know this. The courts usually are a brake on their demands. Of course, the courts can make mistakes or get things confused, as many people believe they have with the establishment clause and the rights of criminal defendants. Still, when it comes to government respecting civil liberties like the freedom to express unpopular beliefs, the courts are often citizens' last best hope.

2. Must the rights afforded to citizens by the Constitution be respected by not only the federal government but also by the states?

Yes, with only a few remaining exceptions. After the Fourteenth Amendment was adopted in 1868, the Supreme Court began the slow but steady process of "incorporation" by which federal rights deemed "fundamental" also applied to the states. Today, the entire Bill of Rights is now applied to the states except the Third Amendment right not to have

soldiers forcibly quartered in private homes, the Fifth Amendment right to be indicted by a grand jury before being tried for a serious crime, the Seventh Amendment right to a jury trial in civil cases, and the Eighth Amendment ban on excessive bail and fines. Although states can still regulate gun purchases and gun use, the latest incorporated right is the Second Amendment right to own and "bear arms," which the Court applied to the states in a 2010 decision.

3. Are all forms of expression protected by the Constitution?

No. Four forms of expression that are not protected are the following: libel (injurious written statements about another person); certain types of symbolic speech (actions that convey a political message); "fighting words" that incite others to commit illegal acts or that directly and immediately provoke another person to violent behavior; and obscenity (writing or pictures that the average person, applying the standards of his or her community, believes appeal to the prurient interest and lack literary, artistic, political, or scientific value).

4. Is all political advertising constitutional?

Since a Supreme Court decision in early 2010, corporations, unions, and nonprofit organizations can spend money for or against a candidate at any time. The Court upheld that decision in 2012.

5. Did America ever have state-supported churches, and do some modern democratic nations still have them?

Yes and yes. The First Amendment banned the federal government, but not the states, from having an "established," tax-supported church. Some states had tax-funded churches well into the 19th century. Today, the Supreme Court has long since outlawed state-sponsored churches, but the national governments of the United Kingdom, Greece, and several other modern democracies still either have "official" state religions, endorse certain religions, or give certain religions special privileges.

6. How does the Constitution protect the liberties of persons accused of crimes or designated as "enemy combatants"?

Mainly through a host of rules and procedures that government authorities are required to follow: the exclusionary rule (evidence gathered in violation of the Constitution cannot be used in a trial); the need for a search warrant (an order from a judge authorizing the search of a place); the Miranda rules (warnings that police must give to a person being arrested regarding the rights of the accused); and others. In 2004, the Supreme Court ruled that terrorist detainees and enemy combatants (persons who are neither citizens nor prisoners of war) must have access to a neutral court to decide if they are legally held.

TO LEARN MORE

Court cases: **www.law.cornell.edu**

Civil Rights Division of the Department of Justice: **www.usdoj.gov**

American Civil Liberties Union: **www.aclu.org**

American Center for Law and Justice: **www.aclj.org**

Americans United for Separation of Church and State: **www.au.org**

Institutional Religious Freedom Alliance: **www.irfalliance.org**

Abraham, Henry J., and Barbara A. Perry, *Freedom and the Court*, 7th ed. New York: Oxford University Press, 1998. Analysis of leading Supreme Court cases on civil liberties and civil rights.

Amar, Akhil Reed. *The Constitution and Criminal Procedure: First Principles*. New Haven, CT: Yale University Press, 1997. A brilliant critique of how the Supreme Court has interpreted those parts of the Constitution bearing on search warrants, the exclusionary rule, and self-incrimination.

Berns, Walter. *The First Amendment and the Future of American Democracy*. New York: Basic Books, 1976. A look at what the Founders intended by the First Amendment that takes issue with contemporary Supreme Court interpretations of it.

Clor, Harry M. *Obscenity and Public Morality*. Chicago: University of Chicago Press, 1969. Argues for the legitimacy of legal restrictions on obscenity.

Levy, Leonard W. *Legacy of Suppression: Freedom of Speech and Press in Early American History*. Rev. ed. New York: Oxford University Press, 1985. Careful study of what the Founders and the early leaders meant by freedom of speech and press.

Robert W. Kelley/Time Life Pictures/Getty Images

6

Civil Rights

LEARNING OBJECTIVES

1. If both African Americans and women benefit from civil rights, why do federal courts allow them to be treated somewhat differently?

2. What is the difference between "strict scrutiny" and "intermediate scrutiny"?

3. Legally, what is meant by "sexual harassment"?

4. Since Congress enacts our laws, why has it not made certain that all groups have the same rights?

5. After the Supreme Court ended racial segregation in the schools, what did the president and Congress do?

6. Under what circumstances can men and women be treated differently?

7. How has Court doctrine and public opinion on gay rights changed over the last decade or so?

civil rights The rights of people to be treated without unreasonable or unconstitutional differences.

THEN

In 1830, Congress passed a law requiring all Indians (they were so called in the law) east of the Mississippi River to move to the Indian Territory west of the river, and the army set about implementing it. In the 1850s, a major political fight broke out in Boston over whether the police department should be obliged to hire an Irish officer. Until 1920, women could not vote in most elections. In the 1930s, the Cornell University Medical School had a strict quota limiting the number of Jewish students who could enroll. In the 1940s, President Franklin D. Roosevelt ordered that all Japanese Americans be removed from their homes in California and placed them in relocation centers far from the coast. Until 1954, public schools in many states were required by law to be segregated by race. Until 1967, 16 states outlawed marriages between whites and nonwhites. Until 2003, 14 states outlawed consensual sexual relations between same-sex partners.

NOW

Now it would be inconceivable that the army would forcibly relocate American Indians. No one can be denied entry into a police department by reason of race, ethnicity, or religion. Women not only have long had the right to vote, but actually now vote at higher rates than men do. Unlike during World War II, today no group of people can be forcibly relocated or held against their will en masse, and even suspected terrorists and "enemy combatants" cannot be detained indefinitely without having their day in court. The quotas that once limited Jews' access to colleges and universities are history. State laws requiring segregated public schools and banning interracial marriage are history, too. And, within just the last decade, state laws forbidding consensual sexual relations between same-sex partners have been eliminated, and the constitutions or statutes that in dozens of states outlaw same-sex marriages or other same-sex unions have been challenged both in courts of law and in the court of public opinion.

Still, then as now, if the government passes a law that treats different groups of people differently, that law is not necessarily unconstitutional.

Civil rights is about cases in which some group, usually defined along racial or ethnic lines, is denied access to facilities, opportunities, or services that are available to other groups. The pertinent question regarding civil rights is not whether the government

has the authority to treat different people differently; it is whether such differences in treatment are reasonable. Many laws and policies make distinctions among people—for example, the tax laws require higher-income people to pay taxes at a higher rate than lower-income ones—but not all such distinctions are defensible. The courts have long held that classifying people on the basis of their income and taxing them at different rates is quite permissible because such classifications are not arbitrary or unreasonable and are related to a legitimate public need (that is, raising revenue). Increasingly, however, the courts have said that classifying people on the basis of their race or ethnicity is unreasonable.[1] The tests the courts use are summarized in the box on page 136.

To explain the victimization of certain groups and the methods by which they have begun to overcome it, we shall start with racial classifications and the case of African Americans. The strategies employed by or on behalf of African Americans have typically set the pattern for the strategies employed by other groups. At the end of this chapter, we shall look at the issues of women's rights and gay rights.

Race and Civil Rights

In July 2013, the National Urban League (NUL), led by its president, Marc H. Morial, the former mayor of New Orleans, came to Philadelphia for its annual conference. With the National Association for the Advancement of Colored People (NAACP), the NUL is among the nation's most historic and important civil rights organizations. Its 2013 conference theme was "Redeem the Dream." Fifty years earlier, in 1963, Reverend Dr. Martin Luther King, Jr. delivered his historic "I Have a Dream" speech in Washington, D.C. In its 2013 *State of Black America* report, the NUL credited civil rights laws (see the summary on page 124) for the progress made over the last half-century or so in closing white–black gaps in education and standards of living:

- The white–black high school completion rate gap has closed by 57 points; whereas only 25 percent of blacks graduated from high school in 1963, by 2013 the fraction had risen to 85 percent, and there had been a three-fold increase in the number of blacks enrolled in college.

- The white–black poverty rate gap fell by 23 points; whereas 48 percent of blacks lived in poverty in 1963, by 2013 the fraction had fallen to 28 percent.

- There was a 14 percent increase in the number of black homeowners.

Roger L. Wollenberg/Getty Images

National Urban League President Marc Morial speaks to reporters after meeting, along with other political leaders (including Rev. Al Sharpton, who is standing next to him), with President Obama following his re-election.

But the same report also documented numerous racial gaps and disparities in housing, education, health care, employment, and overall economic opportunity:

- In 2013, as in 1963, the black–white unemployment ratio was still 2-to-1, regardless of education, gender, region, or income level.

- In 2013, as in 1963, more than a third of all black children (38 percent) still lived in poverty.

- In 2013, as in 1963, blacks employed in the public sector earned less than whites in the same jobs, and a still-wider black–white wage disparity persisted in the private sector.

Citing the history surrounding Reverend Dr. King's "I Have a Dream" speech, Morial and other leaders called on all citizens to come together to eliminate these and other racial gaps and disparities in housing, education, employment, and other areas. As late as the mid-20th century, African Americans in many parts of the country could not vote, attend integrated schools, ride in the front seats of buses, or buy homes in white neighborhoods. Conditions were especially oppressive

in those parts of the country, notably the Deep South, where blacks were often in the majority. There, the politically dominant white minority felt keenly the potential competition for jobs, land, public services, and living space posed by large numbers of people of another race. But even in the North, black gains often appeared to be at the expense of lower-income whites who lived or worked near them, not at the expense of upper-status whites who lived in suburbs.

African Americans were not allowed to vote at all in many areas; they could vote only with great difficulty in others; and even in those places where voting was easy, they often lacked the material and institutional support for effective political organization. If your opponent feels deeply threatened by your demands and can deny you access to the political system that will decide the fate of those demands, you are, to put it mildly, at a disadvantage. Yet from the end of Reconstruction to the 1960s—for nearly a century—many blacks in the South found themselves in just such a position.

To the dismay of those who prefer to explain political action in terms of economic motives, people often attach greater importance to the intangible costs and benefits of policies than to the tangible ones. Thus, even though the average black represented no threat to the average white, antiblack attitudes—racism—produced some appalling actions. Between 1882 and 1946, 4,715 people, about three-fourths of them African Americans, were lynched in the United States.[2] Some of these brutalities were perpetrated by small groups of vigilantes acting with much ceremony, but others were the actions of frenzied mobs. In the summer of 1911, a black man charged with murdering a white man in Livermore, Kentucky, was dragged by a mob to the local theater, where he was hanged. The audience, which had been charged admission, was invited to shoot the swaying body (those in the orchestra seats could empty their revolvers; those in the balcony were limited to a single shot).[3]

Though the public in other parts of the country was shocked by such events, little was done: lynching was a local, not a federal, crime. It obviously would not require many killings to blacks African Americans in these localities that it would be foolhardy to try to vote or enroll in a white school. And even in those states where blacks did vote, popular attitudes were not conducive to blacks buying homes or taking jobs on an equal basis with whites. Even among those professing to support equal rights, a substantial portion opposed African Americans' efforts to obtain them and federal action to secure them. In 1942, a national poll showed that only 30 percent of whites thought black and white children should attend the same schools; in 1956, the proportion had risen, but only to 49 percent, still less than a majority. (In the South, white support for school

HOW THINGS WORK

Key Provisions of Major Civil Rights Laws

1957 **Voting** Made it a federal crime to try to prevent a person from voting in a federal election. Created the Civil Rights Commission.

1960 **Voting** Authorized the attorney general to appoint federal referees to gather evidence and make findings about allegations that African Americans were deprived of their right to vote. Made it a federal crime to use interstate commerce to threaten or carry out a bombing.

1964 **Voting** Made it more difficult to use devices such as literacy tests to bar African Americans from voting.

Public accommodations Barred discrimination on grounds of race, color, religion, or national origin in restaurants, hotels, lunch counters, gasoline stations, movie theaters, stadiums, arenas, and lodging houses with more than five rooms.

Schools Authorized the attorney general to bring suit to force the desegregation of public schools on behalf of citizens.

Employment Outlawed discrimination in hiring, firing, or paying employees on grounds of race, color, religion, national origin, or sex.

Federal funds Barred discrimination in any activity receiving federal assistance.

1965 **Voter registration** Authorized appointment by the Civil Service Commission of voting examiners who would require registration of all eligible voters in federal, state, and local elections, general or primary, in areas where discrimination was found to be practiced or where less than 50 percent of voting-age residents were registered to vote in the 1964 election.

Literacy tests Suspended use of literacy tests or other devices to prevent African Americans from voting.

1968 **Housing** Banned, by stages, discrimination in sale or rental of most housing (excluding private owners who sell or rent their homes without the services of a real-estate broker).

Riots Made it a federal crime to use interstate commerce to organize or incite a riot.

1972 **Education** Prohibited sex discrimination in education programs receiving federal aid.

Discrimination If any part of an organization receives federal aid, no part of that organization may discriminate on the basis of race, sex, age, or physical disability.

1991 **Discrimination** Made it easier to sue over job discrimination and collect damages; overturned certain Supreme Court decisions. Made it illegal for the government to adjust, or "norm," test scores by race.

---

integration was even lower—14 percent favored it in 1956, about 31 percent in 1963.) As late as 1956, a majority of southern whites were opposed to integrated public transportation facilities. Even among whites who generally favored integration, there was in 1963 (*before* the ghetto riots) considerable opposition to the black civil rights movement: nearly half of the whites classified in a survey as moderate integrationists thought demonstrations hurt the black cause; nearly two-thirds disapproved of actions taken by the civil rights movement; and more than a third felt civil rights should be left to the states.[4]

In short, the political position in which African Americans found themselves until the 1960s made it difficult for them to advance their interests through a feasible legislative strategy; their opponents were aroused, organized, and powerful. Thus, if black interests were to be championed in Congress or state legislatures, blacks would have to have white allies. Though some such allies could be found, they were too few to make a difference in a political system that gives a substantial advantage to strongly motivated opponents of any new policy. For that to change, one or both of two things would have to happen: additional allies would have to be recruited (a delicate problem, given that many white integrationists disapproved of aspects of the civil rights movement), or the struggle would have to be shifted to a policy-making arena in which the opposition enjoyed less of an advantage.

Partly by plan, and partly by accident, black leaders followed both of these strategies simultaneously. By publicizing their grievances and organizing a civil rights movement that (at least in its early stages) concentrated on dramatizing the denial to blacks

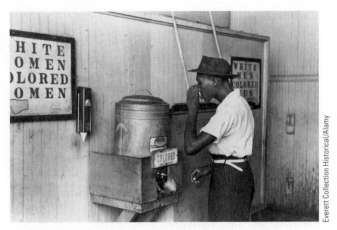

Segregated water fountain in Oklahoma City (1939).

of essential and widely accepted liberties, African Americans were able to broaden their base of support both among political elites and among the general public, thereby elevating the importance of civil rights issues on the political agenda. By waging a patient, prolonged, but carefully planned legal struggle, black leaders shifted decision-making power on key civil rights issues from Congress, where they had been stymied for generations, to the federal courts.

After this strategy had achieved some substantial successes—once blacks had become enfranchised and legal barriers to equal participation in political and economic affairs had been lowered—the politics of civil rights became more conventional. African Americans were able to assert their demands directly in the legislative and executive branches of government with reasonable (though scarcely certain) prospects of success. Civil rights became less a matter of gaining entry into the political system and more one of waging interest group politics within that system. At the same time, the goals of civil rights politics were broadened. The struggle to gain entry into the system had focused on the denial of fundamental rights (to vote, to organize, to obtain equal access to schools and public facilities); later the dominant issues were manpower development, economic progress, and the improvement of housing and neighborhoods.

The Campaign in the Courts

The Fourteenth Amendment was both an opportunity and a problem for black activists. Adopted in 1868, it seemed to guarantee equal rights for all: "No state shall make or enforce any law which shall abridge the privileges or immunities of citizens of the United States; nor shall any state deprive any person of life, liberty, or property, without due process of law; nor deny to any person within its jurisdiction the equal protection of the laws."

The key phrase was "equal protection of the laws." Read broadly, it might mean that the Constitution should be regarded as color-blind: no state law could have the effect of treating whites and blacks differently. Thus, a law segregating blacks and whites into separate schools or neighborhoods would be unconstitutional. Read narrowly, "equal protection" might mean only that blacks and whites had certain fundamental legal rights in common (such as the right to sign contracts, to serve on juries, or to buy and sell property), but otherwise they could be treated differently.

In a series of decisions beginning in the 1870s, the Supreme Court took the narrow view, albeit often by narrow majorities. Adopted in 1870, the Fourteenth Amendment had been proposed as a means to reinforce the Civil Rights Act of 1866. That Act was intended by Congress to ensure that former slaves' citizenship rights would be respected not only by the federal government but also by the state governments, both North and South. But in its 5-to-4 majority decision in the *Slaughter-House Cases* (1873), the Court ruled that the "privileges and immunities" clause of the Fourteenth Amendment did not protect citizens from discriminatory actions by state governments. Though in 1880 it declared unconstitutional a West Virginia law requiring juries to be composed only of white males,[5] the Court decided in 1883 that it was unconstitutional for Congress to prohibit racial discrimination in public accommodations such as hotels.[6] The difference between the two cases seemed, in the eyes of the Court, to be this: serving on a jury was an essential right of citizenship that the state could not deny to any person on racial grounds without violating the Fourteenth Amendment, but registering at a hotel was a convenience controlled by a private person (the hotel owner) who could treat blacks and whites differently if he or she wished.

The major decision that determined the legal status of the Fourteenth Amendment for more than half a century was *Plessy v. Ferguson*. Louisiana had passed a law requiring blacks and whites to occupy separate cars on railroad trains operating in that state. When Adolph Plessy, who was seven-eighths white and one-eighth black, refused to obey the law, he was arrested. He appealed his conviction to the Supreme Court, claiming that the law violated the Fourteenth Amendment. In 1896, the Court rejected his claim, holding that the law treated both races equally even though it required them to be separate. The equal protection clause guaranteed political and legal but not social equality. "Separate-but-equal" facilities were constitutional because if "one race be inferior to the other socially, the Constitution of the United States cannot put them on the same plane."[7]

separate-but-equal doctrine The doctrine established in *Plessy v. Ferguson* (1896) that African Americans could constitutionally be kept in separate but equal facilities.

"Separate But Equal"

Thus began the **separate-but-equal doctrine**. Three years later, the Court applied it to schools as well, declaring in *Cumming v. Richmond County Board of Education* that a decision in a Georgia community to close the black high school while keeping open the white high school was not a violation of the Fourteenth Amendment because blacks could always go to private schools. Here the Court seemed to be saying that not only could schools be separate, they could even be unequal.[8]

What the Court has made, the Court can unmake. But to get it to change its mind requires a long, costly, and uncertain legal battle. The National Association for the Advancement of Colored People (NAACP) was the main organization that waged that battle against the precedent of *Plessy v. Ferguson*. Formed in 1909 by a group of whites and blacks in the aftermath of a race riot, the NAACP did many things, including lobbying in Washington and publicizing black grievances (especially in the pages of *The Crisis,* a magazine edited by W. E. B. Du Bois). But its most influential role was played in the courtroom.

It was a rational strategy. Fighting legal battles does not require forming broad political alliances or changing public opinion, tasks that would have been very difficult for a small and unpopular organization. A court-based approach also enabled the organization to remain nonpartisan. But it was a slow and difficult strategy. The Court had adopted a narrow interpretation of the Fourteenth Amendment. To get the Court to change its mind would require the NAACP to bring before it cases involving the strongest possible claims that a black had been unfairly treated—and under circumstances sufficiently different from those of earlier cases, so that the Court could find some grounds for changing its mind.

The steps in that strategy were these: First, persuade the Court to declare unconstitutional laws creating schools that were separate but obviously unequal. Second, persuade it to declare unconstitutional laws supporting schools that were separate but unequal in not-so-obvious ways. Third, persuade it to rule that racially separate schools were inherently unequal and hence unconstitutional.

Can Separate Schools Be Equal?

The first step was accomplished in a series of court cases stretching from 1938 to 1948. In 1938, the Court held that Lloyd Gaines had to be admitted to an all-white law school in Missouri because no black law school of equal quality existed in that state.[9] In 1948, the Court ordered the all-white University of Oklahoma Law School to admit Ada Lois Sipuel, a black, even though the state planned to build a black law school later. For education to be equal, it had to be equally available.[10] It still could be separate, however: the university admitted Ms. Sipuel but required her to attend classes in a section of the state capitol, roped off from other students, where she could meet with her law professors.

The second step was taken in two cases decided in 1950. Heman Sweatt, an African American, was treated by the University of Texas Law School much as Ada Sipuel had been treated in Oklahoma: "admitted" to the all-white school but relegated to a separate building. Another African American, George McLaurin, was allowed to study for his Ph.D in a "colored section" of the all-white University of Oklahoma. The Supreme Court unanimously decided that these arrangements were unconstitutional because, by imposing racially based barriers on the black students' access to professors, libraries, and other students, they created unequal educational opportunities.[11]

The third step, the climax of the entire drama, began in Topeka, Kansas, where Linda Brown wanted to enroll in her neighborhood school but could not because she was black and the school was by law reserved exclusively for whites. When the NAACP took her case to the federal district court in Kansas, the judge decided the black school Linda could attend was substantially equal in quality to the white school she could not attend and, therefore, denying her access to the white school was constitutional. To change that, the lawyers would have to persuade the Supreme Court to overrule the district judge on the grounds that racially separate schools were unconstitutional even if they were equal. In other words, the separate-but-equal doctrine would have to be overturned by the Court.

It was a risky and controversial step to take. Many states, Kansas among them, were trying to make their all-black schools equal to those of whites by launching expensive building programs. If the NAACP succeeded in getting separate schools declared unconstitutional, the Court might well put a stop to the building of these new schools. Blacks could win a moral and legal victory but suffer a practical defeat—the loss of these new facilities. Despite these risks, the NAACP decided to go ahead with the appeal.

Brown v. Board of Education

On May 17, 1954, a unanimous Supreme Court, speaking through an opinion written and delivered by Chief Justice Earl Warren, found that "in the field of

AP Photo/Douglas Martin

Dorothy Counts, the first black student to attend Harding High School in Charlotte, NC, tries to maintain her poise as she is taunted by shouting, gesticulating white students in September 1957.

public education the doctrine of 'separate but equal' has no place" because "separate educational facilities are inherently unequal."[12] *Plessy v. Ferguson* was overruled, and "separate but equal" was dead.

The ruling was a landmark decision, but the reasons for it and the means chosen to implement it were as important and as controversial as the decision itself. There were at least three issues. First, how would the decision be implemented? Second, on what grounds were racially separate schools unconstitutional? Third, what test would a school system have to meet in order to be in conformity with the Constitution?

Implementation

The *Brown* case involved a class-action suit; that is, it applied not only to Linda Brown but to all others similarly situated. This meant that black children everywhere now had the right to attend formerly all-white schools. This change would be one of the most far-reaching and conflict-provoking events in modern American history. It could not be effected overnight or by the stroke of a pen. In 1955, the Supreme Court decided it would let local federal district courts oversee the end of segregation by giving them the power to approve or disapprove local desegregation plans. This was to be done "with all deliberate speed."[13]

In the South, "all deliberate speed" turned out to be a snail's pace. Massive resistance to desegregation broke out in many states. Some communities simply defied the Court; some sought to evade its edict by closing their public schools. In 1956, more than 100 southern members of Congress signed a "Southern Manifesto" that condemned the *Brown* decision as an "abuse of judicial power" and pledged to "use all lawful means to bring about a reversal of the decision."

In the late 1950s and early 1960s, the National Guard and regular army paratroopers were used to escort black students into formerly all-white schools and universities. It was not until the 1970s that resistance collapsed and most southern schools were integrated. The use of armed force convinced people that resistance was futile; the disruption of the politics and economy of the South convinced leaders that it was imprudent; and the voting power of blacks convinced politicians that it was suicidal. In addition, federal laws began providing financial aid to integrated schools and withholding it from segregated ones. By 1970, only 14 percent of southern black schoolchildren still attended all-black schools.[14]

The Rationale

As the struggle to implement the *Brown* decision continued, the importance of the rationale for that

WHAT WOULD YOU DO?

MEMORANDUM

To: *Justice Roberta Wilson*

From: *Robert Gilbert, law clerk*

Subject: *State support for predominantly black colleges*

Until school segregation ended, southern blacks could attend only all-black colleges. Now they are free to apply to previously all-white colleges, and these schools are integrated. But the traditional black colleges still exist, and very few whites apply to them. In 1992, the Supreme Court held that the state could not solve the problem by requiring a race-neutral admissions policy.* Now the Court must decide whether a predominantly black college can receive state support.

News »

Court to Rule on Black Colleges

The Supreme Court has announced that it will decide whether all-black colleges in the South can receive state support if there are too few whites attending them.

Arguments for:

1. These schools have a long tradition that ought to be preserved.

2. Many black students will learn better in an all-black environment.

3. African American organizations, in particular the United Negro College Fund, raise money for these schools.

Arguments against:

1. If the state once required single-race schools, it now has an obligation to dismantle them.

2. Race is a suspect classification, and no state program that chiefly serves one race can be allowed.

Your decision:

Allow all-black colleges _____

Ban all-black colleges _____

*United States v. Fordice, 505 U.S. 717 (1992).

In 1963, Governor George Wallace of Alabama stood in the doorway of the University of Alabama to block the entry of black students. Facing him is U.S. Deputy Attorney General Nicholas Katzenbach.

decision became apparent. The case was decided in a way that surprised many legal scholars.

The Court could have said that the equal protection clause of the Fourteenth Amendment makes the Constitution, and thus state laws, color-blind. Or it could have said that the authors of the Fourteenth Amendment meant to ban segregated schools. It did neither. Instead, it said segregated education is bad because it "has a detrimental effect upon the colored children" by generating "a feeling of inferiority as to their status in the community" that may "affect their hearts and minds in a way unlikely ever to be undone."[15] This conclusion was supported by a footnote reference to social science studies of the apparent impact of segregation on black children.

Why did the Court rely on social science as much as or more than the Constitution in supporting its decision? Apparently for two reasons. One was the

CONSTITUTIONAL CONNECTIONS

Suspect Classifications

Beginning with the *Brown* case, virtually every form of racial segregation imposed by law has been struck down as unconstitutional. Race has become a **suspect classification** such that any law making racial distinctions is now subject to **strict scrutiny.** To be upheld as constitutional, a suspect classification must be related to a "compelling government interest," be "narrowly tailored" to achieve that interest, and use the "least restrictive means" available. But the Court has also determined that though race is a suspect classification, the Constitution is not "color-blind," and so the government may make racial distinctions for the purpose of remedying past racial discrimination. Later in this chapter we discuss affirmative action, the laws or administrative regulations that require a business firm, government agency, labor union, school, college, or other organization to take positive steps to increase the number of African Americans, other minorities, or women in its membership.

---

justices' realization that the authors of the Fourteenth Amendment may *not* have intended to outlaw segregated schools. The schools in Washington, D.C., were segregated when the amendment was proposed, and when this fact was mentioned during the debate, it seems to have been made clear that the amendment was not designed to abolish this segregation. When Congress debated a civil rights act a few years later, it voted down provisions that would have ended segregation in schools.[16] The Court could not easily base its decision on a constitutional provision that had, at best, an uncertain application to schools. The other reason grew out of the first. On so important a matter the chief justice wanted to speak for a unanimous court. Some justices did not agree that the Fourteenth Amendment made the Constitution color-blind. In the interests of harmony, the Court found an ambiguous rationale for its decision.

Desegregation versus Integration

That ambiguity led to the third issue. If separate schools were inherently unequal, what would "unseparate" schools look like? Since the Court had not said race was irrelevant, an "unseparate" school could be either one that blacks and whites were free to attend if they chose or one that blacks and whites in fact attended whether they wanted to or not. The first might be called a desegregated school, and the latter an integrated school. Think of the Topeka case. Was it enough that there was now no barrier to Linda Brown's attending the white school in her neighborhood? Or was it necessary that there be black children (if not Linda, then some others) actually going to that school together with white children?

As long as the main impact of the *Brown* decision lay in the South, where laws had prevented blacks from attending white schools, this question did not seem important. Segregation by law (***de jure* segregation**) was now clearly unconstitutional. But in the North, laws had not kept blacks and whites apart; instead, all-black and all-white schools were the result of residential segregation, preferred living patterns, informal social forces, and administrative practices (such as drawing school district lines so as to produce single-race schools). This often was called segregation in fact (***de facto* segregation**).

In 1968, the Supreme Court settled the matter. In New Kent County, Virginia, the school board had created a "freedom-of-choice" plan under which every pupil would be allowed without legal restriction to attend the school of his or her choice. As it turned out, all the white children chose to remain in the all-white school, and 85 percent of the black children remained in the all-black school. The Court rejected this plan as unconstitutional because it did not produce the "ultimate end," which was a "unitary, nonracial system of education."[17] In the

suspect classification Classifications of people based on their race or ethnicity; laws so classifying people are subject to "strict scrutiny."

strict scrutiny The standard by which "suspect classifications" are judged. To be upheld, such a classification must be related to a "compelling government interest," be "narrowly tailored" to achieve that interest, and use the "least restrictive means" available.

de jure segregation Racial segregation that is required by law.

de facto segregation Racial segregation that occurs in schools, not as a result of the law, but as a result of patterns of residential settlement.

opinion written by Justice William Brennan, the Court seemed to be saying that the Constitution required actual racial mixing in the schools, not just the repeal of laws requiring racial separation.

This impression was confirmed three years later when the Court considered a plan in North Carolina under which pupils in Mecklenburg County (which includes Charlotte) were assigned to the nearest neighborhood school without regard to race. As a result, about half the black children now attended formerly all-white schools, with the other half attending all-black schools. The federal district court held that this was inadequate and ordered some children to be bused into more distant schools in order to achieve a greater degree of integration. The Supreme Court, now led by Chief Justice Warren Burger, upheld the district judge on the grounds that the court plan was necessary to achieve a "unitary school system."[18]

This case—*Swann v. Charlotte-Mecklenburg Board of Education*—pretty much set the guidelines for all subsequent cases involving school segregation. The essential features of those guidelines are as follows:

- To violate the Constitution, a school system, by law, practice, or regulation, must have engaged in discrimination. Put another way, a plaintiff must show intent to discriminate on the part of the public schools.

- The existence of all-white or all-black schools in a district with a history of segregation creates a presumption of intent to discriminate.

- The remedy for past discrimination will not be limited to freedom of choice, or what the Court called "the walk-in school." Remedies may include racial quotas in the assignment of teachers and pupils, redrawn district lines, and court-ordered busing.

- Not every school must reflect the social composition of the school system as a whole.

Relying on *Swann,* district courts have supervised redistricting and busing plans in localities all over the nation, often in the face of bitter opposition from the community. In Boston, the control of the city schools by a federal judge, W. Arthur Garrity, lasted for more than a decade and involved him in every aspect of school administration. One major issue not settled by *Swann* was whether busing and other remedies should cut across city and county lines. In some places, the central-city schools had become virtually all black. Racial integration could be achieved only by bringing black pupils to white suburban schools or moving white pupils into central-city schools. In a series of split-vote

Antibusing protesters buried a school bus (unoccupied) to dramatize their cause.

decisions, the Court ruled that court-ordered intercity busing could be authorized only if it could be demonstrated that the suburban areas as well as the central city had in fact practiced school segregation. Where that could not be shown, such intercity busing would not be required. The Court was not persuaded that intent had been proved in Atlanta, Detroit, Denver, Indianapolis, and Richmond, but it was persuaded that it had been proved in Louisville and Wilmington.[19]

The importance the Court attaches to intent means that if a school system that was once integrated becomes all black as a result of whites' moving to the suburbs, the Court will not require that district lines constantly be redrawn or new busing plans be adopted to adjust to the changing distribution of the population.[20] This in turn means that as long as blacks and whites live in different neighborhoods for whatever reason, there is a good chance that some schools in both areas will be heavily of one race. If mandatory busing or other integration measures cause whites to move out of a city at a faster rate than they otherwise would (a process often called "white flight"), then efforts to integrate the schools may in time create more single-race schools. Ultimately, integrated schools will exist only in integrated neighborhoods or where the quality of education is so high that both blacks and whites want to enroll in the school even at some cost in terms of travel and inconvenience.

Mandatory busing to achieve racial integration has been a deeply controversial program and has generated considerable public opposition. Surveys show that a majority of people oppose it.[21] As recently as 1992, a poll showed that 48 percent of whites in the Northeast and 53 percent of southern whites felt it was "not the business" of the federal government to ensure "that black and white children go to the same schools."[22] Presidents Nixon, Ford, and Reagan opposed busing; all three supported legislation to prevent or reduce it, and Reagan petitioned the courts to reconsider busing plans. The courts refused to reconsider, and Congress has passed only minor restrictions on busing.

The reason why Congress has not followed public opinion on this matter is complex. It has been torn between the desire to support civil rights and uphold the courts and the desire to represent the views of its constituents. Because it faces a dilemma, Congress has taken both sides of the issue simultaneously. By the late 1980s, busing was a dying issue in Congress, in part because no meaningful legislation seemed possible and in part because popular passion over busing had somewhat abated.

Then, in 1992, the Supreme Court made it easier for local school systems to reclaim control over their schools from the courts. In DeKalb County, Georgia (a suburb of Atlanta), the schools had been operating under court-ordered desegregation plans for many years. Despite this effort, full integration had not been achieved, largely because the county's neighborhoods had increasingly become either all black or all white. The Court held that local schools could not be held responsible for segregation caused solely by segregated living patterns and so the courts would have to relinquish their control over the schools. In 2007, the Court said race could not be the decisive factor in assigning students to schools that had either never been segregated (as in Seattle) or where legal segregation had long since ended (as in Jefferson County, Kentucky).[23]

The Campaign in Congress

The campaign in the courts for desegregated schools, though slow and costly, was a carefully managed effort to alter the interpretation of a constitutional

---

LANDMARK CASES

Civil Rights

- **Dred Scott case,** *Scott v. Sanford* **(1857):** Congress had no authority to ban slavery in a territory. A slave was considered a piece of property.

- *Plessy v. Ferguson* **(1896):** Upheld separate-but-equal facilities for white and black people on railroad cars.

- *Brown v. Board of Education* **(1954):** Said separate public schools are inherently unequal, thus starting racial desegregation.

- *Green v. County School Board of New Kent County* **(1968):** Banned a freedom-of-choice plan for integrating schools, suggesting blacks and whites must actually attend racially mixed schools.

- *Swann v. Charlotte-Mecklenburg Board of Education* **(1971):** Approved busing and redrawing district lines as ways of integrating public schools.

---

provision. But to get new civil rights laws out of Congress required a far more difficult and decentralized strategy, one that was aimed at mobilizing public opinion and overcoming the many congressional barriers to action.

The first problem was to get civil rights on the political agenda by convincing people that something had to be done. This could be achieved by dramatizing the problem in ways that tugged at the conscience of whites who were not racist but were ordinarily indifferent to black problems. Brutal lynching of blacks had shocked these whites, but the practice of lynching was on the wane in the 1950s.

Civil rights leaders could, however, arrange for dramatic confrontations between blacks claiming some obvious right and the whites who denied it to them. Beginning in the late 1950s, these confrontations began to occur in the form of sit-ins at segregated lunch counters and "freedom rides" on segregated bus lines. At about the same time, efforts were made to get blacks registered to vote in counties where whites had used intimidation and harassment to prevent it.

The best-known campaign occurred in 1955–1956 in Montgomery, Alabama, where blacks, led by a young minister named Martin Luther King, Jr., boycotted the local bus system after it had a black woman, Rosa Parks, arrested because she refused to surrender her seat on a bus to a white man.

civil disobedience
Opposing a law one considers unjust by peacefully disobeying it and accepting the resultant punishment.

These early demonstrations were based on the philosophy of **civil disobedience**—that is, peacefully violating a law, such as one requiring blacks to ride in a segregated section of a bus, and allowing oneself to be arrested as a result.

But the momentum of protest, once unleashed, could not be centrally directed or confined to nonviolent action. A rising tide of anger, especially among younger blacks, resulted in the formation of more militant organizations and the spontaneous eruption of violent demonstrations and riots in dozens of cities across the country. From 1964 to 1968, there were in the North as well as the South four "long, hot summers" of racial violence.

The demonstrations and rioting succeeded in getting civil rights on the national political agenda, but at a cost: many whites, opposed to the demonstrations or appalled by the riots, dug in their heels and fought against making any concessions to "lawbreakers," "troublemakers," and "rioters." In 1964 and again in 1968, more than two-thirds of the whites interviewed in opinion polls said the civil rights movement was pushing too fast, had hurt the black cause, and was too violent.[24]

In short, a conflict existed between the agenda-setting and coalition-building aspects of the civil rights movement. This was especially a problem since conservative southern legislators still controlled many key congressional committees that had for years been the graveyard of civil rights legislation. The Senate Judiciary Committee was dominated by a coalition of southern Democrats and conservative Republicans, and the House Rules Committee was under the control of a chairman hostile to civil rights

bills, Howard Smith of Virginia. Any bill that passed the House faced an almost certain filibuster in the Senate. Finally, President John F. Kennedy was reluctant to submit strong civil rights bills to Congress.

Four developments made it possible to break the deadlock. First, public opinion was changing. From the mid-1950s to the mid-1990s, surveys found that the proportion of whites who were willing to have their children attend a school that was half black increased sharply (though the proportion of whites willing to have their children attend a school that was predominantly black increased by much less). About the same change could be found in white attitudes toward allowing blacks equal access to hotels and buses.[25] Of course, support in principle for these civil rights measures was not necessarily the same as support in practice; nonetheless, clearly a major shift was occurring in popular approval of at least the principles of civil rights. At the leading edge of this change were young, college-educated people.[26]

Second, certain violent reactions by white segregationists to black demonstrators were vividly portrayed by the media (especially television) in ways that gave the civil rights cause a powerful moral force. In May 1963, the head of the Birmingham police, Eugene "Bull" Connor, ordered his men to use attack dogs and high-pressure fire hoses to repulse a peaceful march by African Americans demanding desegregated public facilities and increased job opportunities. The pictures of that confrontation (such as the one on page 133) created a national sensation and contributed greatly to the massive participation—by whites and blacks alike—in the "March on Washington" that summer. About a quarter of a million people gathered in front of the Lincoln Memorial to hear the Reverend Dr. Martin Luther King, Jr., deliver the aforementioned "I Have a Dream" speech, which is now widely regarded as one of the most significant public addresses in

Bettman/Corbis

AP Photo/Bob Jordan

In 1960, black students from North Carolina Agricultural and Technical College staged the first "sit-in" when they were refused service at a lunch counter in Greensboro (left). Twenty years later, graduates of the college returned to the same lunch counter (right). Though prices had risen, the service had improved.

American history, and which today is read, studied, or memorized in whole or in part by millions of school children each year (see Appendix). The following summer in Neshoba County, Mississippi, three young civil rights workers (two white and one black) were brutally murdered by Klansmen aided by the local sheriff. When the FBI identified the murderers, the effect on national public opinion was galvanic; no white southern leader could any longer offer persuasive opposition to federal laws protecting voting rights when white law enforcement officers had killed students working to protect those rights. And the next year, a white woman, Viola Liuzzo, was shot and killed while driving a car used to transport civil rights workers. Her death was the subject of a presidential address.

Third, President John F. Kennedy was assassinated in Dallas, Texas, in November 1963. Many people originally (and wrongly) thought he had been killed by a right-wing conspiracy. Even after the assassin had been caught and shown to have left-wing associations, the shock of the president's murder—in a southern city—helped build support for efforts by the new president, Lyndon B. Johnson (a Texan), to obtain passage of a strong civil rights bill as a memorial to the slain president.

Fourth, the 1964 elections not only returned Johnson to office with a landslide victory but also sent a huge Democratic majority to the House and retained the large Democratic margin in the Senate. This made it possible for northern Democrats to outvote or outmaneuver southerners in the House.

The cumulative effect of these forces led to the enactment of five civil rights laws between 1957 and 1968. Three (1957, 1960, and 1965) were chiefly directed at protecting the right to vote; one (1968) was aimed at preventing discrimination in housing; and one (1964), the most far-reaching of all, dealt with voting, employment, schooling, and public accommodations.

The passage of the 1964 act was the high point of the legislative struggle. Liberals in the House had drafted a bipartisan bill, but it was now in the House Rules Committee, where such proposals had often disappeared without a trace. In the wake of Kennedy's murder, a discharge petition was filed—with President Johnson's support—to take the bill out of committee and bring it to the floor of the House. But the Rules Committee, without waiting for a vote on the petition (which it probably realized it would lose), sent the bill to the floor, where it passed overwhelmingly. In the Senate, an agreement between Republican minority leader Everett Dirksen and President Johnson smoothed the way for passage in several important respects. The House bill was sent directly to the Senate floor, thereby bypassing the southern-dominated

This picture of a police dog lunging at a black man during a racial demonstration in Birmingham, Alabama, in May 1963 was one of the most influential photographs ever published. It was widely reprinted throughout the world and was frequently referred to in congressional debates on the civil rights bill of 1964.

Judiciary Committee. Nineteen southern senators began an eight-week filibuster against the bill. On June 10, 1964, by a vote of 71 to 29, cloture was invoked and the filibuster ended—the first time in history that a filibuster aimed at blocking civil rights legislation had been broken.

Since the 1960s, congressional support for civil rights legislation has grown—so much so, indeed, that labeling a bill a civil rights measure, once the kiss of death, now almost guarantees its passage. For example, in 1984 the Supreme Court decided the federal ban on discrimination in education applied only to the "program or activity" receiving federal aid and not to the entire school or university.[27] In 1988, Congress passed a bill to overturn this decision by making it clear that antidiscrimination rules applied to the entire educational institution and not just to that part (say, the physics lab) receiving federal money. When President Reagan vetoed the bill (because, in his view, it would diminish the freedom of church-affiliated schools), Congress overrode the veto. In the override vote, every southern Democrat in the Senate and almost 90 percent of those in the House voted for the bill. This was a dramatic change from 1964, when more than

Reverend Dr. Martin Luther King, Jr., delivers his "I Have a Dream" speech on the Washington, D.C., mall in 1963.

80 percent of the southern Democrats in Congress voted against the Civil Rights Act (see Figure 6.1). This change partly reflected the growing political strength of southern blacks. In 1960, less than one-third of voting-age blacks in the South were registered to vote; by 1971 more than half were, and by 1984 two-thirds were.

In 2008, Barack Obama was elected president and became the first African American to hold the nation's highest elected office. That monumental historic moment, which included Obama winning two southern states, was preceded by four decades of growth in the number of black elected officials at all levels of government. Between 1970 and 2010, the total number of black elected officials rose from

FIGURE 6.1 Increase in Support among Southern Democrats in Congress for Civil Rights Bills, 1957–1991

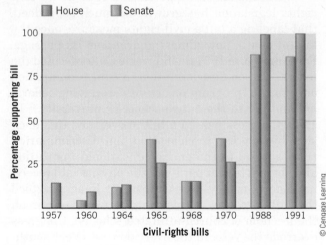

Source: Congressional Quarterly, *Congress and the Nation*, vols. 1, 2, 3, 7, 8.

fewer than 1,500 to more than 10,500 (see Table 6.1) In the presidential elections of 2008 and 2012, voter turnout rates among African Americans equaled or exceeded that of whites. Such parity in voter turnout rates and the aforementioned increase in the number of black elected officials could not have happened without civil rights laws like the Voting Rights Act (VRA) of 1965. In 2006, following more than 20 public hearings, and with support from then President George W. Bush, Congress reauthorized the VRA's key provisions for another quarter-century, including the section (Section 4) designating the "preclearance" formula used to determine which state or local jurisdictions must have any major changes to their voting laws or procedures approved in advance by the U.S. Department of Justice or by a federal court. Along with the need to remain vigilant in checking any recurrence of old methods of discrimination, the bill's bipartisan backers also cited concerns about "racial gerrymandering," the proliferation of "voter identification" laws, and other measures that could adversely and disproportionately affect minority participation in the electoral process.

But, in 2013, in the case of *Shelby County v. Holder*, the Supreme Court struck down the VRA's preclearance formula as unconstitutional. Writing for the Court's 5-to-4 majority, Chief Justice John Roberts declared that "things have changed dramatically" in the South since 1965; he also issued a statement from the bench indicating that Congress "may draft another formula based on current conditions." Writing for the four dissenting justices, Justice Ruth Bader Ginsburg declared that the majority had "failed to grasp why the VRA has proven effective;" she also issued a statement from the bench stressing that in 2006 Congress "found that 40 years has not been sufficient time to eliminate the vestiges of discrimination following 100 years of disregard for the 15th Amendment." President Obama issued a statement in which he observed that the decision "upsets decades of well-established practices that help to make sure voting is fair, especially in places where voting discrimination has been historically prevalent;" he also called on Congress to pass new voting rights legislation.

Women and Equal Rights

The political and legal efforts to secure civil rights for African Americans were accompanied by efforts to expand the rights of women. There was an important difference between the two movements, however: whereas African Americans

TABLE 6.1 Increase in Number of Black Elected Officials

	1970	2010
Federal Office	10	43
State Office	169	642
Local Office	1,290	9,800

Source: Statistical Abstract of the United States, 2003, table 417; Joint Center for Political and Economic Studies, *Roster of Black Elected Officials*, November 2011; "A Time to Reflect: Charting the Quality of Life for Black Americans: Politics," *USA Today*, February 21, 2011.

were arguing against a legal tradition that explicitly aimed to keep them in a subservient status, women had to argue against a tradition that claimed to be protecting them. For example, in 1908 the Supreme Court upheld an Oregon law that limited female laundry workers to a 10-hour workday against the claim that it violated the Fourteenth Amendment. The Court justified its decision with this language:

> The two sexes differ in structure of body, in the functions to be performed by each, in the amount of physical strength, in the capacity for long- continued labor, particularly when done standing ... the self-reliance which enables one to assert full rights, and in the capacity to maintain the struggle for subsistence. This difference justifies a difference in legislation and upholds that which is designed to compensate for some of the burdens which rest upon her.[28]

The origin of the movement to give more rights to women was probably the Seneca Falls Convention held in 1848. Its leaders began to demand the right to vote for women. Though this was slowly granted by several states, especially in the West, it was not until 1920 that the Nineteenth Amendment made

WHAT'S YOUR ISSUE?

Handguns and Civil Rights

David Kairys, a Temple University law professor, was a full-time civil rights lawyer across four decades. In his 2008 memoir, Kairys illustrates how intricately intertwined with other issues civil rights policies tend to be, how post-1980 civil rights laws on racial discrimination and other matters have often shifted without any legislative changes, and how novel applications of old legal theories can spark new debates about how to define or enforce civil rights.

For example, in the Anglo-American legal tradition, a noisy blacksmith shop teeming with hot objects and other dangers could be declared a "public nuisance" and forced by local government authorities to shut down or pay damages even if it was there before anybody lived nearby, and even if it had always operated legally. But today, new questions arise: should otherwise law-abiding handgun manufacturers be sued by city officials for creating a "public nuisance," and do citizens have a civil right to live free from violence perpetrated with handguns?

In the late 1990s, the mayors of New Orleans, Chicago, Philadelphia, and several dozen other cities, joined in some cases by civil rights groups, brought "public nuisance" lawsuits against handgun manufacturers. In response, many state legislatures passed new laws exempting the handgun industry from these lawsuits. In 2005, the U.S. Congress enacted and President George W. Bush signed a new federal law granting the handgun industry broad legal immunity and rejecting related civil rights claims. As discussed in Chapter 5, in 2010 the U.S. Supreme Court made it unconstitutional for states to ban gun ownership outright.

- Still, do you think that freedom from gun violence ought to be counted among "civil rights"?

- Do you think that permitting "public nuisance" or other lawsuits against otherwise law-abiding gun manufacturers might violate their "civil rights"?

- Do you think that a certain minimum standard of living, a certain minimum level of air quality, or a certain minimum degree of privacy ought to be considered a "civil right"?

- What, if any, contemporary issues do you think fall outside the domain of "civil rights," and why?

Source: David Kairys, *Philadelphia Freedom: Memoir of a Civil Rights Lawyer* (University of Michigan Press, 2008).

it clear that no state may deny the right to vote on the basis of sex. The great change in the status of women, however, took place during World War II when the demand for workers in our defense plants led to the employment of millions of women, such as "Rosie the Riveter," in jobs they had rarely held before. After the war, the feminist movement took flight with the publication in 1963 of *The Feminine Mystique* by Betty Friedan.

Congress responded by passing laws that required equal pay for equal work, prohibited discrimination on the basis of sex in employment and among students in any school or university receiving federal funds, and banned discrimination against pregnant women on the job.[29]

At the same time, the Supreme Court was altering the way it interpreted the Constitution. The key passage was the Fourteenth Amendment, which prohibits any state from denying to "any person" the "equal protection of the laws." For a long time the traditional standard, as we saw in the 1908 case, was a kind of protective paternalism. By the early 1970s, however, the Court had changed its mind. In deciding whether the Constitution bars all, some, or no sexual discrimination, the Court had a choice among three standards.

The first standard is the *reasonableness* standard. This says that when the government treats some classes of people differently from others—for example, applying statutory rape laws to men but not to women—the different treatment must be reasonable and not arbitrary.

The second standard is *intermediate scrutiny*. When women complained that some laws treated them unfairly, the Court adopted a standard somewhere between the reasonableness and strict scrutiny tests. Thus, a law that treats men and women differently must be more than merely reasonable, but the allowable differences need not meet the strict scrutiny test.

And so, in 1971, the Court held that an Idaho statute was unconstitutional because it required that males be preferred over females when choosing people to administer the estates of deceased children. To satisfy the Constitution, a law treating men and women differently "must be reasonable, not arbitrary, and must rest on some ground of difference having a fair and substantial relation to the object of legislation so that all persons similarly circumstanced shall be treated alike."[30] In later decisions, some members of the Court wanted to make classifications based on sex inherently suspect and subject to the strict scrutiny test, but no majority has yet embraced this position.[31]

The third standard is *strict scrutiny*. This says that some instances of drawing distinctions between different groups of people—for example, by treating whites and blacks differently—are inherently

HOW THINGS WORK

How the Court Decides If You Discriminate

The Supreme Court has produced three different tests to decide if a government policy produces unconstitutional discrimination. Don't be surprised if you find it a bit hard to tell them apart.

1. **Rational basis** If the policy uses reasonable means to achieve a legitimate government goal, it is constitutional.

   Examples: If the government says you can't buy a drink until you are 21, this meets the rational basis test: the government wants to prevent children from drinking, and age 21 is a reasonable means to define when a person is an adult. And a state can ban advertising on trucks unless the ad is about the truck owner's own business.

2. **Intermediate scrutiny** If the policy "serves an important government interest" and is "substantially related" to serving that interest, it is constitutional.

   Examples: Men can be punished for statutory rape even if women are not punished because men and women are not "similarly situated." And men can be barred from entering hospital delivery rooms even though (obviously) women are admitted.

3. **Strict scrutiny** To be constitutional, the discrimination must serve a "compelling government interest," it must be "narrowly tailored" to attain that interest, and it must use the "least restrictive means" to attain it.

   Examples: Distinctions based on race, ethnicity, religion, or voting must pass the strict scrutiny test. You cannot bar black children from a public school or black adults from voting, and you cannot prevent one religion from knocking on your door to promote its views.

suspect; thus, the Court will subject them to strict scrutiny to ensure they are clearly necessary to attain a legitimate state goal.

But sexual classifications can also be judged by a different standard. The Civil Rights Act of 1964 prohibits sex discrimination in the hiring, firing, and compensation of employees. The 1972 Civil Rights Act bans sex discrimination in local education programs receiving federal aid. These laws apply to *private,* and not just government, actions.

Over the years, the Court has decided many cases involving sexual classification. The following lists provide several examples of illegal sexual discrimination (violating either the Constitution or a civil rights act) and legal sexual distinctions (violating neither).

Illegal Discrimination

- A state cannot set different ages at which men and women legally become adults.[32]

- A state cannot set different ages at which men and women are allowed to buy beer.[33]

- Women cannot be barred from jobs by arbitrary height and weight requirements.[34]

- Employers cannot require women to take mandatory pregnancy leaves.[35]

- Girls cannot be barred from Little League baseball teams.[36]

- Business and service clubs, such as the Junior Chamber of Commerce and Rotary Club, cannot exclude women from membership.[37]

- Though women as a group live longer than men, an employer must pay them monthly retirement benefits equal to those received by men.[38]

- High schools must pay the coaches of girls' sports the same as they pay the coaches of boys' sports.[39]

Decisions Allowing Differences Based on Sex

- A law that punishes males but not females for statutory rape is permissible; men and women are not "similarly situated" with respect to sexual relations.[40]

- All-boy and all-girl public schools are permitted if enrollment is voluntary and quality is equal.[41]

- States can give widows a property-tax exemption not given to widowers.[42]

- The navy may allow women to remain officers longer than men without being promoted.[43]

LANDMARK CASES

Women's Rights

- *Reed v. Reed* (1971): Gender discrimination violates the equal protection clause of the Constitution.

- *Craig v. Boren* (1976): Gender discrimination can be justified only if it serves "important governmental objectives" and is "substantially related to those objectives."

- *Rostker v. Goldberg* (1981): Congress can draft men without drafting women.

- *United States v. Virginia* (1996): State may not finance an all-male military school.

The lower federal courts have been especially busy in the area of sexual distinctions. They have said that public taverns may not cater to men only and that girls may not be prevented from competing against boys in noncontact high school sports; on the other hand, hospitals may bar fathers from the delivery room. Women may continue to use their maiden names after marriage.[44]

In 1996, the Supreme Court ruled that women must be admitted to the Virginia Military Institute, until then an all-male state-supported college that had for many decades supplied what it called an "adversative method" of training to instill physical and mental discipline in cadets. In practical terms, this meant the school was very tough on students. The Court said that for a state to justify spending tax money on a single-sex school, it must supply an "exceedingly persuasive justification" for excluding the other gender. Virginia countered by offering to support an all-female training course at another college, but this was not enough.[45] This decision came close to imposing the strict scrutiny test, and so it has raised important questions about what could happen to all-female or traditionally black colleges that accept state money.

Perhaps the most far-reaching cases defining the rights of women have involved the draft and abortion. In 1981, the Court held in *Rostker v. Goldberg* that Congress may require men but not women to register for the draft without violating the due process clause of the Fifth Amendment.[46] In the area of national defense, the Court will give great deference to congressional policy (Congress had already decided to bar women from combat roles). For many *police powers* State power to effect laws promoting health, safety, and morals.

years, women could be pilots and sailors but not on combat aircraft or combat ships. In 1993, the secretary of defense opened air and sea combat positions to all persons regardless of gender; only ground-troop combat positions were still reserved for men. The issue played a role in preventing the ratification of the Equal Rights Amendment to the Constitution, because of fears that it would reverse *Rostker v. Goldberg*.

Sexual Harassment

When Paula Corbin Jones accused President Clinton of sexual harassment, the judge threw the case out of court because she had not submitted enough evidence such that, if the jury believed her story, she would have made a legally adequate argument that she had been sexually harassed.

What, then, is sexual harassment? Drawing on rulings by the Equal Employment Opportunities Commission, the Supreme Court has held that harassment can take one of two forms. First, it is illegal for someone to request sexual favors as a condition of employment or promotion. This is the "quid pro quo" rule. If a person does this, the employer is "strictly liable." Strict liability means the employer can be found at fault even if he or she did not know a subordinate was requesting sex in exchange for hiring or promotion.

Second, it is illegal for an employee to experience a work environment that has been made hostile or intimidating by a steady pattern of offensive sexual teasing, jokes, or obscenity. But employers are not strictly liable in this case; they can be found at fault only if they were "negligent"—that is, they knew about the hostile environment but did nothing about it.

In 1998, the Supreme Court decided three cases that made these rules either better or worse, depending on your point of view. In one, it determined that a school system was not liable for the conduct of a teacher who seduced a female student because the student never reported the actions. In a second, it held that a city was liable for a sexually hostile work environment confronting a female lifeguard even though she did not report this to her superiors. In the third, it decided that a female employee who was not promoted after having rejected the sexual advances of her boss could recover financial damages from the firm. But, it added, the firm could have avoided paying this bill if it had put in place an "affirmative defense" against sexual exploitation, although the Court never said what such a policy might be.[47]

Sexual harassment is a serious matter, but because there are almost no federal laws governing it, we are left with somewhat vague and often inconsistent court and bureaucratic rules to guide us.

Privacy and Sex

Regulating sexual matters has traditionally been left up to the states, which do so by exercising their **police powers**. These powers include more than the authority to create police departments; they include all laws designed to promote public order and secure the safety and morals of the citizens. Some have argued that the Tenth Amendment to the Constitution, by reserving to the states all powers not delegated to the federal government, meant that states could do anything not explicitly prohibited by the Constitution. But that changed when the Supreme Court began expanding the power of Congress over business and when it started to view sexual matters under the newly discovered right to privacy.

Until that point, it had been left up to the states to decide whether and under what circumstances a woman could obtain an abortion. For example, New York allowed abortions during the first 24 weeks of pregnancy, while Texas banned it except when the mother's life was threatened. That began to change in 1965 when the Supreme Court held that the states could not prevent the sale of contraceptives because by so doing it would invade a "zone of privacy." Privacy is nowhere mentioned in the Constitution, but the Court argued that it could be inferred from "penumbras" (literally, shadows) cast off by various provisions of the Bill of Rights.[48]

Eight years later the Court, in its famous *Roe v. Wade* decision, held that a "right to privacy" is "broad enough to encompass a woman's decision whether or not to terminate a pregnancy."[49] The case, which began in Texas, produced this view: during the first three months (or trimester) of pregnancy, a woman has an unfettered right to an abortion. During the second trimester, states may regulate abortions but only to protect the mother's health. In the third trimester, states might ban abortions.

In reaching this decision, the Court denied that it was trying to decide when human life began—at the moment of conception, at the moment of birth, or somewhere in between. But that is not how critics of the decision saw things. To them, life begins at conception, and so the human fetus is a "person" entitled to the equal protection of the laws guaranteed by the Fourteenth Amendment. People feeling this way began to use the slogans "right to life" and "pro-life." Supporters of the Court's action saw matters differently. In their view, no one can say for certain when human life begins; what one *can* say, however,

LANDMARK CASES

Privacy and Abortion

- *Griswold v. Connecticut* (1965): Found a "right to privacy" in the Constitution that would ban any state law against selling contraceptives.

- *Roe v. Wade* (1973): State laws prohibiting abortion were unconstitutional.

- *Webster v. Reproductive Health Services* (1989): Allowed states to ban abortions from public hospitals and permitted doctors to test to see if fetuses were viable.

- *Planned Parenthood v. Casey* (1992): Reaffirmed *Roe v. Wade* but upheld certain limits on its use.

- *Gonzales v. Carhart* (2007): Federal law may ban certain forms of partial-birth abortion.

is that a woman is entitled to choose whether or not to have a baby. These people took the slogans "right to choose" and "pro-choice."

Almost immediately, the congressional allies of pro-life groups introduced constitutional amendments to overturn *Roe v. Wade,* but none passed Congress. Nevertheless, abortion foes did persuade Congress, beginning in 1976, to bar the use of federal funds to pay for abortions except when the life of the mother is at stake. This provision is known as the Hyde Amendment, after its sponsor, Representative Henry Hyde. The chief effect of the amendment has been to deny the use of Medicaid funds to pay for abortions for low-income women.

Despite pro-life opposition, the Supreme Court for 16 years steadfastly reaffirmed and even broadened its decision in *Roe v. Wade*. It struck down laws requiring, before an abortion could be performed, a woman to have the consent of her husband, an "emancipated" but underage girl to have the consent of her parents, or a woman to be advised by her doctor as to the facts about abortion.[50]

But in 1989, under the influence of justices appointed by President Reagan, the Court began in the *Webster* case to uphold some state restrictions on abortions. When that happened, many people predicted that in time *Roe v. Wade* would be overturned, especially if President George H.W. Bush was able to appoint more justices. He appointed two (Souter and Thomas), but *Roe* survived. The key votes were cast by Justices O'Connor, Souter, and Kennedy. In 1992, in its *Casey* decision, the Court by a vote of five to four explicitly refused to overturn *Roe,* declaring

that there was a right to abortion. At the same time, however, it upheld a variety of restrictions imposed by the state of Pennsylvania on women seeking abortions. These included a mandatory 24-hour waiting period between the request for an abortion and the performance of it, the requirement that teenagers obtain the consent of one parent (or, in special circumstances, of a judge), and a requirement that women contemplating an abortion be given pamphlets about alternatives to it. Similar restrictions had been enacted in many other states, all of which looked to the Pennsylvania case for guidance as to whether they could be enforced. In allowing these restrictions, the Court overruled some of its own earlier decisions.[51] On the other hand, the Court did strike down a state law that would have required married women to obtain the consent of their husbands before having an abortion.

After a long political and legal struggle, the Court in 2007 upheld a federal law that bans certain kinds of partial-birth abortions. The law does not allow an abortion in which the fetus, still alive, is withdrawn until its head is outside the mother and then it is killed. But the law does not ban a late-term abortion if it is necessary to protect the physical health of the mother or if it is performed on an already dead fetus, even if the doctor has already killed it.[52]

There is one irony in all of this: "Roe," the pseudonym for the woman who started the suit that became *Roe v. Wade,* never had an abortion and many years later, using her real name, Norma McCorvey, became an evangelical Christian who published a book and started a ministry to denounce abortions.

equality of results Making certain that people achieve the same result.

Affirmative Action

A common thread running through the politics of civil rights is the argument between **equality of results** and equality of opportunity.

Equality of Results

One view, expressed by most civil rights and feminist organizations, is that the burdens of racism and sexism can be overcome only by taking race or sex into account in designing remedies. It is not enough that people be given rights; they also must be given benefits. If life is a race, everybody must be brought up to the same starting line (or possibly even to the same finish line). This means that the Constitution is not and should not be color-blind or sex-neutral. In education, this implies that the races must actually

affirmative action
Laws or administrative
regulations that
require a business firm,
government agency, labor
union, school, college,
or other organization
to take positive steps to
increase the number of
African Americans, other
minorities, or women in
its membership.

**reverse
discrimination** Using
race or sex to give
preferential treatment
to some people.

**equality of
opportunity** Giving
people an equal chance
to succeed.

be mixed in the schools, by busing if necessary. In hiring, it means that affirmative action must be used in the hiring process. **Affirmative action** refers to laws or administrative regulations that require a business firm, government agency, labor union, school, college, or other organization to take positive steps to increase the number of African Americans, other minorities, or women in its membership. It means that it is not enough that women should simply be free to enter the labor force; they should be given the material necessities (for example, free daycare) that will help them enter it. On payday, workers' checks should reflect not just the results of competition in the marketplace, but the results of plans designed to ensure that people earn comparable amounts for comparable jobs. Of late, affirmative action has been defended in the name of diversity or multiculturalism—the view that every institution (firm, school, or agency) and every college curriculum should reflect the cultural (that is, ethnic) diversity of the nation.

Equality of Opportunity

The second view holds that if it is wrong to discriminate *against* African Americans and women, it is equally wrong to give them preferential treatment over other groups. To do so constitutes **reverse discrimination**. The Constitution and laws should be color-blind and sex-neutral.[53] In this view, allowing children to attend the school of their choice is sufficient; busing them to attain a certain racial mixture is wrong. Eliminating barriers to job opportunities is right; using numerical "targets" and "goals" to place minorities and women in specific jobs is wrong. If people wish to compete in the market, they should be satisfied with the market verdict concerning the worth of their work.

Each of these views is intertwined with other deep philosophical differences. Supporters of **equality of opportunity** tend to have orthodox beliefs; they favor letting private groups behave the way that they want (and so may defend the right of a men's club to exclude women). Supporters of the opposite view are likely to

HOW THINGS WORK

Becoming a Citizen

For persons born in the United States, the rights of U.S. citizenship have been ensured, in constitutional theory if not in everyday practice, since the passage of the Fourteenth Amendment in 1868 and the civil rights laws of the 1960s. The Fourteenth Amendment conferred citizenship upon "all persons born in the United States . . . and subject to the jurisdiction thereof." Subsequent laws also gave citizenship to children born outside the United States to parents who are American citizens.

But immigrants, by definition, are not born with the rights of U.S. citizenship. Instead, those seeking to become U.S. citizens must, in effect, assume certain responsibilities in order to become citizens. The statutory requirements for naturalization, as they have been broadly construed by the courts, are as follows:

• Five years' residency, or three years if married to a citizen.

• Continuous residency since filing of the naturalization petition.

• Good moral character, which is loosely interpreted to mean no evidence of criminal activity.

• Attachment to constitutional principles. This means that potential citizens have to answer basic factual questions about American government (e.g., "Who was the first president of the United States?") and publicly denounce any and all allegiance to their native country and its leaders (e.g., Italy and the king of Italy), but devotion to constitutional principles is now regarded as implicit in the act of applying for naturalization.

• Being favorably disposed to "the good order and happiness of the United States."*

Today, about 97 percent of aliens who seek citizenship are successful in meeting these requirements and becoming naturalized citizens of the United States.

*8 U.S.C. 1423, 1427 (1970); *Girouard v. United States*, 328 U.S. 61 (1946).

be progressive in their beliefs and insist that private clubs meet the same standards as schools or business firms. Adherents to the equality-of-opportunity view often attach great importance to traditional models of the family and so are skeptical of subsidized daycare and federally funded abortions. Adherents to the equality-of-results view prefer greater freedom of choice in lifestyle questions and so take the opposite position on daycare and abortion.

Of course, the debate is more complex than this simple contrast suggests. Take, for example, the question of affirmative action. Both the advocates of equality of opportunity and those of equality of results might agree that there is something odd about a factory or university that hires no African Americans or women, and both might press it to prove that its hiring policy is fair. Affirmative action in this case can mean *either* looking hard for qualified women and minorities and giving them a fair shot at jobs *or* setting a numerical goal for the number of women and minorities that should be hired and insisting that that goal be met. Persons who defend the second course of action call these goals "targets"; persons who criticize that course call them "quotas."

The issue has largely been fought in the courts. Between 1978 and 1990, about a dozen

---

HOW THINGS WORK

The Rights of Aliens

America is a nation of immigrants. Some have arrived legally, others illegally. A person residing in this country who is not a citizen is referred to as an *alien*. An illegal, or undocumented, alien is subject to deportation. With the passage in 1986 of the Immigration Reform and Control Act, illegal aliens who have resided in this country continuously since before January 1, 1982, are entitled to amnesty—that is, they can become legal residents. However, the same legislation stipulated that employers (who once could hire undocumented aliens without fear of penalty) must now verify the legal status of all newly hired employees; if they knowingly hire an illegal alien, they face civil and criminal penalties.

Aliens cannot vote or run for office. Nevertheless, they must pay taxes just as if they were citizens. And they are entitled to many constitutional rights, even if they are in this country illegally. This is because most of the rights mentioned in the Constitution refer to "-people" or "persons," not to "citizens." For example, the Fourteenth Amendment bars a state from depriving "*any person* of life, liberty, or property, without due process of law" and from denying "to *any person* within its jurisdiction the equal protection of the laws" [italics added]. As a result, the courts have held that:

- The children of illegal aliens cannot be excluded from the public school system.[1]

- Legally admitted aliens are entitled to welfare benefits.[2]

- Illegal aliens cannot be the object of reprisals if they attempt to form a labor union where they work.[3]

- The First Amendment rights of free speech, religion, press, and assembly and the Fourth Amendment protections against arbitrary arrest and prosecution extend to aliens as well as to citizens.[4]

- Aliens are entitled to own property.

The government can make rules that apply to aliens only, but they must justify the reasonableness of the rules. For example:

- The Immigration and Naturalization Service has broader powers to arrest and search illegal aliens than police departments have to arrest and search citizens.[5]

- States can limit certain jobs, such as police officer and schoolteacher, to citizens.[6]

- The president or Congress can bar the employment of aliens by the federal government.[7]

- States can bar aliens from serving on a jury.[8]

- Illegal aliens are not entitled to obtain a Social Security card.

[1]*Plyler v.* Doe, 457 U.S. 202 (1982).

[2]*Graham v. Richardson*, 403 U.S. 365 (1971).

[3]*Sure-Tan v. National Labor Relations Board*, 467 U.S. 883 (1984).

[4]*Chew v. Colding*, 344 U.S. 590 (1953).

[5]*United States v. Brignoni-Ponce*, 422 U.S. 873 (1975); *INS v. Delgado*, 466 U.S. 210 (1984); *INS v. Lopez-Mendoza*, 486 U.S. 1032 (1984).

[6]*Cabell v. Chavez-Salido*, 454 U.S. 432 (1982); *Foley v. Connelie*, 435 U.S. 291 (1978); *Amblach v. Norwick*, 441 U.S. 68 (1979).

[7]*Hampton v. Mow Sun Wong*, 436 U.S. 67 (1976).

[8]*Schneider v. New Jersey*, 308 U.S. 147 (1939).

major cases involving affirmative action policies were decided by the Supreme Court; in about half the policies were upheld, and in the other half they were overturned. The different outcomes reflect two things—the differences in the facts of the cases and the arrival on the Court of three justices (Kennedy, O'Connor, and Scalia) appointed by a president, Ronald Reagan, who was opposed to (at least) the broader interpretation of affirmative action. As a result of these decisions, the law governing affirmative action is now complex and confusing.

Consider one issue: should the government be allowed to use a quota system to select workers, enroll students, award contracts, or grant licenses? In the *Bakke* decision in 1978, the Court said the medical school of the University of California at Davis could not use an explicit numerical quota in admitting minority students but could "take race into account."[54] So no numerical quotas, right?

Wrong. Two years later, the Court upheld a federal rule that set aside 10 percent of all federal construction contracts for minority-owned firms.[55] All right, maybe quotas can't be used in medical schools, but they can be used in the construction industry. Not exactly. In 1989, the Court overturned a Richmond, Virginia, law that set aside 30 percent of its construction contracts for minority-owned firms.[56] Well, maybe the Court just changed its mind between 1980 and 1989. No. One year later it upheld a federal rule that gave preference to minority-owned firms in the awarding of broadcast licenses.[57] Then in 1993, it upheld the right of white contractors to challenge minority set-aside laws in Jacksonville, Florida.[58]

It is too early to try to make sense of these twists and turns, especially since a deeply divided Court is still wrestling with these issues and Congress (as with the Civil Rights Act of 1991) is modifying or superseding some earlier Court decisions. But a few

HOW THINGS WORK

The Rights of the Disabled

In 1990, the federal government passed the Americans with Disabilities Act (ADA), a sweeping law that extended many of the protections enjoyed by women and racial minorities to disabled persons.

Who Is a Disabled Person?

Anyone who *has* a physical or mental impairment that substantially limits one or more major life activities (for example, holding a job), anyone who has a *record* of such impairment, or anyone who is *regarded* as having such an impairment is considered disabled.

What Rights Do Disabled Persons Have?

Employment

Disabled persons may not be denied employment or promotion if, with "reasonable accommodation," they can perform the duties of that job. (Excluded from this protection are people who currently use illegal drugs, gamble compulsively, or are homosexual or bisexual.) Reasonable accommodation need not be made if this would cause "undue hardship" on the employer.

Government Programs and Transportation

Disabled persons may not be denied access to government programs or benefits. New buses, taxis, and trains must be accessible to disabled persons, including those in wheelchairs.

Public Accommodations

Disabled persons must enjoy "full and equal" access to hotels, restaurants, stores, schools, parks, museums, auditoriums, and the like. To achieve equal access, owners of existing facilities must alter them "to the maximum extent feasible"; builders of new facilities must ensure they are readily accessible to disabled persons, unless this is structurally impossible.

Telephones

The ADA directs the Federal Communications Commission to issue regulations to ensure telecommunications devices for hearing- and speech-impaired people are available "to the extent possible and in the most efficient manner."

Congress

The rights under this law apply to employees of Congress.

Rights Compared

The ADA does not enforce the rights of disabled persons in the same way as the Civil Rights Act enforces the rights of African Americans and women. Racial or gender discrimination must end *regardless of cost*; denial of access to disabled persons must end unless "undue hardship" or excessive costs would result.

general standards seem to be emerging. In simplified form, they are as follows:

- The courts will subject any quota system created by state or local governments to "strict scrutiny" and will look for a "compelling" justification for it.

- Quotas or preference systems cannot be used by state or local governments without first showing that such rules are needed to correct an actual past or present pattern of discrimination.[59]

- In proving there has been discrimination, it is not enough to show that African Americans (or other minorities) are statistically underrepresented among employees, contractors, or union members; the actual practices that have had this discriminatory impact must be identified.[60]

- Quotas or preference systems created by *federal* law will be given greater deference, in part because Section 5 of the Fourteenth Amendment gives to Congress powers not given to the states to correct the effects of racial discrimination.[61]

- It may be easier to justify in court a voluntary preference system (for example, one agreed to in a labor-management contract) than one that is required by law.[62]

- Even when you can justify special preferences in *hiring* workers, the Supreme Court is not likely to allow racial preferences to govern who gets *laid off*. A worker laid off to make room for a minority worker loses more than a worker not hired in preference to a minority applicant.[63]

Complex as they are, these rulings still generate a great deal of passion. Supporters of the decisions barring certain affirmative action plans hail these decisions as steps back from an emerging pattern of reverse discrimination. In contrast, civil rights organizations have denounced those decisions that have overturned affirmative action programs.

In thinking about these matters, most Americans distinguish between compensatory action and preferential treatment. They define *compensatory action* as "helping disadvantaged people catch up, usually by giving them extra education, training, or services." A majority of the public supports this. They define preferential treatment as "giving minorities preference in hiring, promotions, college admissions, and contracts." Large majorities oppose this.[64] These views reflect an enduring element in American political culture—a strong commitment to individualism ("nobody should get something without deserving it") coupled with support for help for the disadvantaged ("somebody who is suffering through no fault of his or her own deserves a helping hand").

Where does affirmative action fit into this culture? Polls suggest that if affirmative action is defined as "helping," people will support it, but if it is defined as "using quotas," they will oppose it. On this matter, blacks and whites see things differently. Blacks think they should receive preferences in employment to create a more diverse workforce and to make up for past discrimination; whites oppose using goals to create diversity or to remedy past ills. In sum, the controversy over affirmative action depends on what you mean by it and on your racial identity.[65]

A small construction company named Adarand tried to get a contract to build guardrails along a highway in Colorado. Though it was the low bidder, it lost the contract because of a government policy that favors small businesses owned by "socially and economically disadvantaged individuals"—that is, by racial and ethnic minorities. In a five-to-four decision, the Court agreed with Adarand and sent the case back to Colorado for a new trial.

The essence of the Court's decision was that *any* discrimination based on race must be subject to strict scrutiny, even if its purpose is to help, not hurt, a racial minority. Strict scrutiny means two things:

- Any racial preference must serve a "compelling government interest."

- The preference must be "narrowly tailored" to serve that interest.[66]

To serve a compelling governmental interest, it is likely that any racial preference will have to remedy a clear pattern of past discrimination. No such pattern had been shown in Colorado.

This decision prompted a good deal of political debate about affirmative action. In California, an initiative was put on the 1996 ballot to prevent state authorities from using "race, sex, color, ethnicity, or national origin as a criterion for either discriminating against, or granting preferential treatment to, any individual or group" in public employment, public education, or public contracting. When the votes were counted, it passed. Michigan, Nebraska, and Washington have adopted similar measures, and other states may do so.

But the *Adarand* case and the passage of the California initiative did not mean affirmative action was dead. Though the federal Court of Appeals for the Fifth Circuit had rejected the affirmative action program of the University of Texas Law School,[67] the Supreme Court did not take up that case. It waited for several more years to rule on a similar matter arising from the University of Michigan. In 2003, the Supreme Court overturned the admissions policy of the University of Michigan that had given to every African American, Hispanic,

LANDMARK CASES

Affirmative Action

- ***Regents of the University of California v. Bakke (1978):*** In a confused set of rival opinions, the decisive vote was cast by Justice Powell, who said that a quota-like ban on Bakke's admission was unconstitutional but that "diversity" was a legitimate goal that could be pursued by taking race into account.

- ***United Steelworkers v. Weber (1979):*** Despite the ban on racial classifications in the 1964 Civil Rights Act, this case upheld the use of race in an employment agreement between the steelworkers union and steel plant.

- ***Richmond v. Croson (1989):*** Affirmative action plans must be judged by the strict scrutiny standard that requires any race-conscious plan to be narrowly tailored to serve a compelling interest.

- ***Grutter v. Bollinger* and *Gratz v. Bollinger (2003):*** Numerical benefits cannot be used to admit minorities into college, but race can be a "plus factor" in making those decisions.

- ***Parents v. Seattle School District (2007):*** Race cannot be used to decide which students may attend especially popular high schools because this was not "narrowly tailored" to achieve a "compelling" goal.

and Native American applicant a bonus of 20 points out of the 100 needed to guarantee admission to the University's undergraduate program.[68] This policy was not "narrowly tailored." In rejecting the bonus system, the Court reaffirmed its decision in the *Bakke* case made in 1978 in which it had rejected a university using a "fixed quota" or an exact numerical advantage to the exclusion of "individual" considerations.

But that same day, the Court upheld the policy of the University of Michigan Law School that used race as a "plus factor" but not as a numerical quota.[69] It did so even though using race as a plus factor increased by threefold the proportion of minority applicants who were admitted. In short, admitting more minorities serves a "compelling state interest," and doing so by using race as a plus factor is "narrowly tailored" to achieve that goal. But, in 2006, Michigan voters approved a ballot measure banning the use of race as a consideration in academic admissions, public employment, and government contracting. In 2012, a U.S. Circuit Court struck down the ban, but only

in relation to academic admissions. In 2013, the U.S. Supreme Court agreed to hear a challenge to the Circuit Court's ruling. And in *Fisher v. University of Texas* (2013), the Court, in a 7-to-1 decision, sent another affirmative action case involving college admissions back to the Fifth Circuit Court of Appeals for reconsideration. Invoking the *Bakke* (1978) and *Grutter* (2003) decisions (see **Landmark Cases** box on this page), the majority declared that the lower court had failed to apply the strict scrutiny test.

Gay Rights

At first, the Supreme Court was willing to let states decide how many rights homosexuals should have. Georgia, for example, passed a law banning sodomy (that is, any sexual contact involving the sex organs of one person and the mouth or anus of another). In *Bowers v. Hardwick* (1986), the Supreme Court decided, by a five-to-four majority, that there was no reason in the Constitution to prevent a state from having such a law. There was a right to privacy, but it was designed simply to protect "family, marriage, or procreation."[70]

But ten years later, the Court seemed to take a different position. The voters in Colorado had adopted a state constitutional amendment that made it illegal to pass any law to protect persons based on their "homosexual, lesbian, or bisexual orientation." The law did not penalize gays and lesbians; instead it said they could not become the object of specific legal protection of the sort that had traditionally been given to racial or ethnic minorities. (Ordinances to give specific protection to homosexuals had been adopted in some Colorado cities.) The Supreme Court struck down the Colorado constitutional amendment because it violated the equal protection clause of the federal Constitution.[71]

Now we faced a puzzle: a state can pass a law banning homosexual sex, as Georgia did, but a state cannot adopt a rule preventing cities from protecting homosexuals, as Colorado did. The matter was finally put to rest in 2003. In *Lawrence v. Texas,* the Court, again by a five-to-four vote, overturned a Texas law that banned sexual contact between persons of the same sex. The Court repeated the language it had used earlier in cases involving contraception and abortion. If "the right to privacy means anything, it is the right of the individual, married or single, to be free from unwanted governmental intrusion" into sexual matters. The right of privacy means the "right to define one's own concept of existence, of meaning, of the universe, and of the mystery of human life." It specifically overruled *Bowers v. Hardwick.*[72]

In 2003, the same year as the *Lawrence* decision, the Massachusetts Supreme Judicial Court decided,

LANDMARK CASES

Gay Rights

- *Boy Scouts of America v. Dale* (2000): A private organization may ban gays from its membership.

- *Lawrence v. Texas* (2003): State law may not ban sexual relations between same-sex partners.

- *United States v. Windsor* (2013): Gay couples married in states where same-sex marriage is legal must receive the same federal health, tax, and other benefits that heterosexual married couples receive.

by a four-to-three vote, that gays and lesbians must be allowed to be married in the state.[73] In response, the Massachusetts legislature passed a bill that would amend that state's constitution to ban gay marriage. But that amendment required another ratification vote, which took place in 2007, and the amendment was defeated. In the mid-2000s, while Massachusetts legalized same-sex marriage and officials in other states considered doing the same, 13 states amended their state constitutions to prohibit or further restrict it. State-by-state, a complicated set of political and legal actions and counter-actions had begun. For instance, in California, the mayor of San Francisco began issuing marriage licenses to hundreds of gay couples. In 2004, the California

Supreme Court overturned the mayor's decisions. The next year, the state legislature voted to make same-sex marriages legal, but Governor Arnold Schwarzenegger vetoed the bill. In 2008, the state's voters approved a ballot measure, Proposition 8, banning gay marriage. But, in 2010, a federal district judge overturned that vote. After a federal appeals court put the lower federal court's decision on hold, a case concerning Proposition 8 made its way before the U.S. Supreme Court.

In March 2013, the Court heard oral arguments in each of two same-sex marriage cases. In *Hollingsworth v. Perry*, the central issue was the constitutionality of California's Proposition 8: Does the Proposition 8 ban on same-sex marriage violate the Constitution's "equal protection" or other provisions? In *United States v. Windsor*, the central issue was the constitutionality of the Defense of Marriage Act (DOMA), a 1996 federal law that bars the federal government from recognizing same-sex marriage couples in relation to health, tax, and other benefits that it affords to heterosexual married couples: Does the DOMA violate the Constitution by depriving all persons that are legally married under the laws of their respective states the same recognition, benefits, and rights, and is same-sex marriage a fundamental right that all states must respect?

In June 2013, the Court issued opinions that in each case were widely understood as victories for same-sex marriage proponents, but that also in each case left the central constitutional questions for another day. In the Proposition 8 case, the Court, by a 5-to-4 majority, held that the private parties that

Proposition 8 opponents celebrate the ruling to overturn the proposition, which denied same-sex couples the right to marry in the state of California.

Justin Sullivan/Getty Images

brought the suit did not have standing to defend the law in federal court after California state officials had declined to do so. The practical effect was to let stand the lower federal court's decision striking down Proposition 8 as unconstitutional, and to thereby overturn the ban on same-sex marriage in California without, however, affecting laws in other states that prohibit same-sex marriage. In the more significant DOMA case, the Court, by a 5-to-4 majority, held that the 1996 law was unconstitutional because it deprived gay couples married in states where same-sex marriage is legal of the same federal health, tax, and other benefits that heterosexual married couples receive. But the Court stopped far short of declaring that same-sex marriage is a fundamental right that all states must respect. Still, in the months following the Court's decisions on Proposition 8 and the DOMA, new legal challenges to laws banning same-sex marriage were launched in a half-dozen states.

Thus far, the Court has continued to treat sexual orientation cases involving private groups differently from the way that it has treated such cases involving government agencies or benefits. The Court has maintained that private groups are free to exclude homosexuals from their membership. For example, in 2000, by a five-to-four vote, the Court decided that the Boy Scouts of America could exclude gay men and boys because that group had a right to determine its own membership.[74] In May 2013, following more than a decade of controversy over the decision and the policy, the Boy Scouts of America made public a plan that would have the organization admit openly gay boys but continue to exclude openly gay men from leadership and membership in the organization.

Looking Back—and Ahead

The civil rights movement in the courts and in Congress profoundly changed the nature of African American participation in politics by bringing southern blacks into the political system so they could become an effective interest group. The decisive move was to enlist northern opinion in this cause, a job made easier by the northern perception that civil rights involved simply an unfair contest between two minorities—southern whites and southern blacks. That perception changed when it became evident the court rulings and legislative decisions would apply to the North as well as the South, leading to the emergence of northern opposition to court-ordered busing and affirmative action programs.

By the time this reaction developed, the legal and political system had been changed sufficiently

HOW WE COMPARE

Same-Sex Marriages at Home and Abroad

During the first quarter of 2013, France, New Zealand, and Uruguay brought to 14 the number of nations that grant legal recognition to same-sex marriages.

Country (Year Legalized Gay Marriage)

The Netherlands (2000)

Belgium (2003)

Canada (2005)

Spain (2005)

South Africa (2006)

Norway (2009)

Sweden (2009)

Argentina (2010)

Iceland (2010)

Portugal (2012)

Denmark (2012)

France (2013)

New Zealand (2013)

Uruguay (2013)

As of mid-2013, in three other nations, same-sex marriage is legal in some, but not all, parts of the country:

United States (2003)

Mexico (2009)

Brazil (2011)

Source: Pew Forum on Religion and Public Life, *Gay Marriage around the World*, May 3, 2013.

to make it difficult—if not impossible—to limit the application of civil rights laws to the special circumstances of the South or to alter by legislative means the decisions of federal courts. Though the courts can accomplish little when they have no political allies (as revealed by the massive resistance to early school-desegregation decisions), they can accomplish a great deal, even in the face of adverse public opinion, when they have some organized allies. The feminist movement has paralleled in organization and tactics many

POLICY DYNAMICS: INSIDE/OUTSIDE THE BOX

Same-Sex Marriage: On the Way to Majoritarian?

Some ideas about public policy grab media attention, garner political support, and go on to become public laws; other ideas never even make it on to the "public agenda." Political scientists have many different theories, taxonomies, and models about the policy process. In Chapter 1, we outlined our way of classifying and explaining the politics of different issues: majoritarian politics, client politics, interest group politics, and entrepreneurial politics (see Chapter 1, pages 14-17).

First, take a moment now to reflect on what you have learned so far in the present chapter about the policy dynamics surrounding the civil rights laws that have affected all Americans, most especially African Americans, other minorities, and women. How might you begin to characterize the politics of the changes in law and policy that expanded civil rights for each group?

Next, how might you explain the still-unfolding politics of gay rights, including but not limited to the politics of same-sex marriage laws? This much seems clear: the politics of the issue have changed in recent years. For example, when President Clinton tried lifting the ban on gays in the military in 1993, the political reaction among both the public at large and leaders in both parties caused him in the first instance to back off the plan, and in the next instance to support not only the "Don't Ask, Don't Tell" (DADT) policy for the military, but also to support the Defense of Marriage Act (DOMA) of 1996. When he came to office in 2009, President Obama supported both DADT and DOMA. But, by 2013, he had lifted the ban on gays in the military and supported the repeal of the DOMA. In June 2013, the Supreme Court declared that the DOMA was unconstitutional (see pages 145-146).

Mass public support for same-sex marriage stood at 35 percent in 2001 (57 percent opposed), dropped a few points in 2004, but has been rising ever since then, reaching 47 percent in 2012 (43 percent opposed). By 2012, 61 percent of all 18-to-25 year-olds supported same-sex marriage, and the only groups harboring wide majorities opposed to same-sex marriage were evangelical Christians and adults born in 1964 or earlier. Also in 2012, Tammy Baldwin (D-WI), a seven-term congresswoman, became the first openly gay politician elected to the U.S. Senate.

Are the policy dynamics of gay rights in general and same-sex marriage in particular migrating quickly, as it were, to the majoritarian politics box? Politically, are these issues now becoming less like "culture war"

U.S. Senator Tammy Baldwin from Wisconsin is the first openly gay person to win election to Congress (in both chambers--she was elected to two terms in the U.S. House of Representatives before running successfully for the Senate in 2012).

issues featuring battles between diametrically opposed interest groups and more like majoritarian issues such as Social Security or Medicare? Would you suppose that policy entrepreneurs, some inside government and others outside it, played a major role in repealing the military's DADT policy? And what, if any, role would you expect the media, the two major parties, the courts, or other institutions to play in the still-unfolding political dramas surrounding same-sex marriage laws?.

Sources: Berkeley Center for Religion, Peace and World Affairs, Georgetown University, *Diverse, Disillusioned, and Divided: Millennial Values and Voter Engagement in the 2012 Election*, October 4, 2012; Pew Forum on Religion and Public Life, *Changing Attitudes on Gay Marriage*, June 2011; Emanuella Grinberg, "Wisconsin's Tammy Baldwin Is First Openly Gay Person Elected to Senate," CNN.com, November 7, 2012; Nathaniel Frank, *Unfriendly Fire: How the Gay Ban Undermines the Military and Weakens America* (New York: Thomas Dunne Books, 2009). Andrew Sullivan, ed., *Same-Sex Marriage: Pro and Con* (New York: Vintage, 2004).

aspects of the black civil rights movement, but with important differences. Women sought to repeal or reverse laws and court rulings that in many cases were ostensibly designed to protect rather than subjugate them. The conflict between protection and liberation was sufficiently intense to defeat the effort to ratify the Equal Rights Amendment.

Among the most divisive civil rights issues in American politics are abortion and affirmative action. From 1973 to 1989, the Supreme Court seemed committed to giving constitutional protection to all abortions within the first trimester; since 1989, it has approved various state restrictions on the circumstances under which abortions can be obtained.

There has been a similar shift in the Court's view of affirmative action. Though it will still approve some quota plans, it now insists they pass strict scrutiny to ensure they are used only to correct a proven history of discrimination, they place the burden of proof on the party alleging discrimination, and they are limited to hiring and not extended to layoffs. Congress has modified some of these rulings with new civil rights legislation.

Finally, while it remains uncertain whether both court doctrines and legislative initiatives on gay rights will follow patterns like those that expanded civil rights protections for African Americans, other minorities, and women, it is clear that the policy dynamics surrounding same-sex marriage are quite different from what they were only a dozen years ago (see **Policy Dynamics: Inside/Outside the Box**, page 147).

LEARNING OBJECTIVES

1. If both African Americans and women benefit from civil rights, why do federal courts allow them to be treated somewhat differently?

The Supreme Court allows blacks and women to be treated somewhat differently because race is a skin color (and thus laws affecting it are subjected to strict scrutiny) while gender is a different body type (and so laws affecting it are subjected to intermediate scrutiny).

2. What is the difference between "strict scrutiny" and "intermediate scrutiny"?

Strict scrutiny requires that a law be "narrowly tailored" and use "the least restrictive means" to serve a "compelling government interest." Intermediate scrutiny means that a law must be "substantially related" to serving "an important government interest."

3. Legally, what is meant by "sexual harassment"?

Sexual harassment exists when an employer requests sexual favors in order to obtain employment or promotions or when an employee experiences a hostile or intimidating work environment that exists because of sexual teasing, jokes, or obscenity.

4. Since Congress enacts our laws, why has it not made certain that all groups have the same rights?

Congress responds to public demands. During much of our history, people have expected women, African Americans, Native Americans, and many other groups to be treated differently than others. The Bill of Rights is a check on congressional and state authority; to be effective, it must be enforced by independent courts.

5. After the Supreme Court ended racial segregation in the schools, what did the president and Congress do?

For a while, not much. But in time, these institutions began spending federal money and using federal troops and law enforcement officials in ways that greatly increased the rate of integration.

6. Under what circumstances can men and women be treated differently?

A difference in treatment can be justified constitutionally if the difference is fair, reasonable, and not arbitrary. Sex differences need not meet the "strict scrutiny" test. It is permissible to punish men for statutory rape and to bar them from hospital delivery rooms; men are different from women in these respects. Congress may draft men without drafting women.

7. How has Court doctrine and public opinion on gay rights changed over the last decade or so?

As late as 1986, the Supreme Court upheld a state law forbidding certain homosexual acts. But, in 2003, the Court struck down state laws banning consensual sexual relations between same-sex partners. In the 2000s, while some states legalized same-sex marriage and other states outlawed it, public opinion shifted in favor of allowing gays and lesbians to marry, rising from 35 percent, a minority, in favor in 2001 to 47 percent, a plurality, in favor in 2012. And, in 2013, the Court struck down as unconstitutional the federal Defense of Marriage Act, declaring that the federal government must provide gay couples married in states where same-sex marriage is legal with the same health, tax, and other benefits that heterosexual married couples receive.

TO LEARN MORE

Court cases: **www.law.cornell.edu**

Department of Justice: **www.usdoj.gov**

Civil rights organizations: National Association for the Advancement of Colored People: **www.naacp.org**

National Organization for Women: **www.now.org**

National Gay and Lesbian Task Force: **www. thetaskforce.org**

National Council of La Raza: **www.nclr.org**

National Urban League: **http://nul.iamempowered.com**

American Arab Anti-Discrimination Committee: **www.adc.org**

Anti-Defamation League: **www.adl.org**

Branch, Taylor. *Parting the Waters: America in the King Years*. New York: Simon and Schuster, 1988. A vivid account of the civil rights struggle.

Flexner, Eleanor. *Century of Struggle: The Women's Rights Movement in the United States*. Rev. ed. Cambridge: Harvard University Press, 1975. A historical account of the feminist movement and its political strategies.

Foreman, Christopher A. *The African-American Predicament*. Washington, D.C.: Brookings Institution, 1999. Thoughtful essays on problems faced by African Americans today.

Franklin, John Hope. *From Slavery to Freedom*, 5th ed. New York: Knopf, 1980. A survey of black history in the United States.

Friedan, Betty. *The Feminine Mystique*. New York: Norton, 1963. Tenth anniversary edition, 1974. A well-known call for women to become socially and culturally independent.

Kluger, Richard. *Simple Justice*. New York: Random House/Vintage Books, 1977. Detailed and absorbing account of the school-desegregation issue, from the Fourteenth Amendment to the *Brown* case.

Kull, Andrew. *The Color-Blind Constitution*. Cambridge: Harvard University Press, 1992. A history of efforts, none yet successful, to make the Constitution color-blind.

Mansbridge, Jane J. *Why We Lost the ERA*. Chicago: University of Chicago Press, 1986. Explains why the Equal Rights Amendment did not become part of the Constitution.

Thernstrom, Stephan, and Abigail Thernstrom. *America in Black and White*. New York: Simon and Schuster, 1997. Detailed history and portrait of African Americans.

Wilhoit, Francis M. *The Politics of Massive Resistance*. New York: George Braziller, 1973. The methods—and ultimate collapse—of all-out southern resistance to school desegregation.

Woodward, C. Vann. *The Strange Career of Jim Crow*. New York: Oxford University Press, 1957. Brief, lucid account of the evolution of Jim Crow practices in the South.

The latent causes of faction are thus sown in the nature of man; and we see them everywhere brought into different degrees of activity, according to the different circumstances of civil society.

— FEDERALIST NO.10

7

Public Opinion

Sergieiev/Shutterstock.com

LEARNING OBJECTIVES

1. What is "public opinion" and how do we measure it?

2. What role did the Framers of the Constitution think public opinion should play in making public policy?

3. What is "political socialization" and how does it work?

4. What is "political ideology" and how does it matter for what elites and the mass public believe?

5. How much does public opinion in America vary by age and other characteristics?

6. People self-label as "liberal," "moderate," or "conservative," but are there more refined ways of describing and classifying citizens' political views?

Defined simply, **public opinion** refers to how people think or feel about particular things. In this chapter, we take a close look at what "public opinion" is, how it is formed, and how opinions differ. In later chapters, we examine the workings of political parties, interest groups, and government institutions and consider what impact they have on whether public opinion affects government policy. Let's begin this journey by recognizing how perspectives on the role public opinion is supposed to play in the country's representative democracy have changed since the nation was founded.

THEN

The Founding Fathers believed that most average citizens lacked the time, information, energy, interest, and experience to decide on public policy. The Constitution's chief architect, James Madison, argued that direct popular participation in the decisions of government was a recipe for disaster, and that "it is the reason, alone, of the public that ought to control and regulate the government."[1] Madison and the other Framers looked to "the representatives of the people," most particularly the U.S. Senators who, in their original plan and until the Seventeenth Amendment was ratified in 1913, were not popularly elected, "as a defense to the people against their own temporary errors and delusions."[2]

NOW

Try imagining any candidate for the U.S. Senate or, for that matter, for any federal, state, or local office, winning election or reelection, or maintaining high public approval ratings, after he or she had questioned "rule by the people" or doubted the majority's opinions the way that the Framers routinely, matter-of-factly, and publicly did.

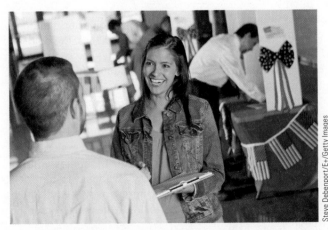

Exit polls are conducted on Election Day to collect data on what voters think about candidates, issues, and other related topics.

Ironically, today about the only circumstances under which elected leaders can get away with sounding the least bit that way is when public opinion polls get the public talking about how little most people know about government or civics. That happened briefly a few years ago when *Newsweek* magazine released the results of a twenty-five-item "U.S. Citizenship Test." Among other results, only 14 percent of the people knew that the U.S. House of Representatives has 435 voting members; only 39 percent knew that U.S. senators serve six-year terms; over a quarter did not know the name of the sitting vice president of the United States (at that time, Joe Biden); and only 12 percent could identify any one writer of *The Federalist Papers* (Madison, Alexander Hamilton, or John Jay).

> *public opinion* How people think or feel about particular things.

Public Opinion and Democracy

In the Gettysburg Address, Abraham Lincoln said the United States has a government "of the people, by the people, and for the people." That suggests the government should do what the people want. If that is the case, it is puzzling that:

- Today, the federal government is running budget deficits of over a trillion dollars a year, but most people want a balanced budget.

- In the 1970s, the Equal Rights Amendment to the Constitution was not ratified, but polls showed that most people supported it.

- Over the last several decades, most people have agreed that there should be a limit on the number of terms to which U.S. senators and members of the U.S. House of Representatives can be elected, but Congress has not approved term limits.

Some people, reflecting on the many gaps between what the government does and what the people want, may become cynical and think our system is democratic in name only. That would be a mistake. There are several very good reasons why government policy often appears to be at odds with public opinion.

First, it bears repeating that the Framers of the Constitution did not try to create a government that would do from day to day "what the people want." They created a government for the purpose of achieving certain substantive goals. The preamble to the Constitution lists six of these: "to form a more perfect Union, establish Justice, ensure domestic Tranquility, provide for the common defense, promote the general Welfare, and secure the Blessings of Liberty."

One means of achieving these goals was popular rule, as provided for by the right of the people to vote for members of the House of Representatives (and later for senators and presidential electors). But other means were provided as well: representative government, federalism, the separation of powers, a Bill of Rights, and an independent judiciary. These were all intended to be checks on public opinion. In addition, the Framers knew that in a nation as large and diverse as the United States there would rarely be any such thing as "public opinion"; rather there would be many "publics" (that is, factions) holding many opinions. The Framers hoped the struggle among these many publics would protect liberty (no one "public" would dominate) while at the same time permitting the adoption of reasonable policies that commanded the support of many factions.

Second, it is not easy to know what the public thinks. We are so inundated these days with public opinion polls that we may imagine that they tell us what the public believes. That may be true on a few rather simple, clear-cut, and widely discussed issues, but it is not true with respect to most matters on which the government must act. The best pollsters know the limits of their methods, and citizens should know them as well.

What Is Public Opinion?

Some years ago, researchers at the University of Cincinnati asked 1,200 local residents whether they favored passage of the Monetary Control Bill. About 21 percent said they favored the bill, 25 percent said they opposed it, and the rest said they hadn't thought much about the matter or didn't know. But there was no such thing as the Monetary Control Bill. The researchers made it up. About 26 percent of the people questioned in a national survey also expressed opinions on the same nonexistent piece of legislation.[3] In many surveys, wide majorities favor expanding most government programs *and* paying less in taxes. On some issues, the majority in favor one month gives way to the majority opposed the next, often with no obvious basis for the shift.

How much confidence should we place in surveys that presumably tell us "what the American people think" about legislation and other issues, and how should we assess "public opinion"? For businesses, understanding how people think or feel about particular things—for example, knowing whether consumers are likely to want a new product or be willing to pay more for an old one—can spell the difference between profit and loss. In the early 20th century, corporations and marketing firms pioneered attempts to systematically measure public views, and political scientists were not far behind them.

The first major academic studies of public opinion and voting, published in the 1940s, painted a distressing picture of American democracy. The studies found that, while a small group of citizens knew lots about government and had definite ideas on many issues, the vast majority knew next to nothing about government and had only vague notions even on much-publicized public policy matters that affected them directly.[4] In the ensuing

---

CONSTITUTIONAL CONNECTIONS

Majority Opinion and Public Policy

For the most part, the Framers of the Constitution thought that public opinion should play only a limited and indirect role in making public policy (see Chapters 1 and 2). They favored representative democracy over direct democracy. They doubted that most people would have the time, energy, interest, information, or expertise to deliberate and decide well on policy matters. They worried that majority opinion would often be fickle, factious, and overly influenced by short-term thinking. Thus, in *Federalist* No. 63, did James Madison reflect on the need to defend "the people against their own temporary errors and delusions" and the "tyranny of their own passions." On the other hand, however, the Framers believed that while the opinions held by a temporary or "transient" majority should carry little weight with elected policymakers, the opinions expressed by a persistent majority—for example, a majority that persists over the staggered terms of House and Senate and over more than a single presidential term—should be heard and, in many (though not in all) cases heeded. When it came to civil liberties and civil rights, Madison and the other Framers were not willing to empower even persistent majorities or subject fundamental freedoms to a popular vote. Still, they believed that, on most public policy issues, a truly representative democratic government would and should enact the policies persistently favored by most people.

decades, however, other studies painted a somewhat more reassuring picture. These studies suggested that, while most citizens are poorly informed about government and care little about most public policy issues, they are nonetheless pretty good at using limited information (or cues) to figure out what policies, parties, or candidates most nearly reflect their values or favor their interests, and then acting (or voting) accordingly.[5]

The more closely scholars have studied public opinion on particular issues, the less uniformed, indifferent, or fickle it has appeared to be. For example, a study by political scientist Terry M. Moe analyzed public opinion concerning whether the government should provide parents with publicly funded grants, or vouchers, that they can apply toward tuition at private schools. He found that although most people are unfamiliar with the voucher issue, "they do a much better job of formulating their opinions than skeptics would lead us to expect." When supplied with basic information, average citizens adopt "their positions for good substantive reasons, just as the informed do."[6]

How Polling Works

If properly conducted, a survey of public opinion—popularly called a **poll**—can capture the opinions of 300 million citizens by interviewing as few as 1,500 of them. There are many keys to good polling: posing comprehensible questions (asking people about things they have some basis for forming an opinion about), wording questions fairly (not using "loaded" or "emotional" words or indicating what the "right" answer is), and others.

However, no poll, whatever it asks and however it is worded, can provide us with a reasonably accurate measure of how people think or feel unless the persons polled are a **random sample** of the entire population, meaning that any given voter or adult has an equal chance of being interviewed. Through a process called stratified or multistage area sampling, the pollster makes a list of all the geographical units in the country—say all the counties—and groups (or "stratifies") them by size of their population. The pollster then selects at random units from each group or stratum in proportion to its total population. Within each selected county, smaller and smaller geographical units (down to particular blocks or streets) are chosen, and then, within the smallest unit, individuals are selected at random (by, for example, choosing the occupant of every fifth house).

If this process is repeated using equally randomized methods, the pollster might get slightly different results. The difference between the results of two surveys or samples is called **sampling error**.

For example, if one random sample shows that 70 percent of all Americans approve of the way the president is handling the job, and another random sample taken at the same time shows that 65 percent do, the sampling error is 5 percent.

Even if properly conducted, polls are hardly infallible. Since 1952, most major polls have in fact picked the winner of the presidential election. Likewise, **exit polls**, interviews with randomly selected voters conducted at polling places on election day in a representative sample of voting districts, have proven quite accurate. But as a result of sampling error and for other reasons, it is very hard for pollsters to predict the winner in a close election.

For any population over 500,000, pollsters need to make about 15,000 telephone calls to reach a number of respondents (technically, the number computes to 1,065) sufficient to ensure that the opinions of the sample differ only slightly (by a 3 percent plus or minus margin) from what the results would have been had they interviewed the entire population from which the sample was drawn. That can be very expensive to do. Polling firms can economize by using smaller-than-ideal samples or by under-sampling hard-to-contact people, but then they risk getting things wrong.

How Opinions Differ

Nobody fully understands how public opinion influences everything from who wins an election to what gets politicians' attention to whether given bills become law, but a few things are clear: some people care more about certain issues than other people do (*opinion saliency*); on some issues or choices, opinions are pretty steady, while on others they tend to be more volatile (*opinion stability*); and on some issues government seems to be largely in sync with popular views or majority sentiments, while on other issues it seems to be significantly out of sync (*opinion-policy congruence*). For example, most Americans had an opinion on U.S. involvement in Iraq, but some felt more strongly about it than others did, and opinions changed in response to news of positive or negative developments. In the mid-2000s, for example, many

---

poll A survey of public opinion.

random sample Method of selecting from a population in which each person has an equal probability of being selected.

sampling error The difference between the results of random samples taken at the same time.

exit polls Polls based on interviews conducted on election day with randomly selected voters.

political socialization
Process by which background traits influence one's political views.

elite People who have a disproportionate amount of some valued resource.

news reports on the situation in Iraq were negative, and mass public support for U.S. involvement fell.[7]

Studies also tell us that people with certain characteristics in common sometimes hold certain political beliefs in common. By no means do people with similar or even virtually identical family histories, religious affiliations, formal educations, or job experiences think or vote exactly the same way on all or most issues. But **political socialization**—the process by which personal and other background traits influence one's views about politics and government—matters. It is behind the fact, to be discussed in the next section, that children tend to share their parents' party affiliations; and it helps to explain why, as we shall see, opinions seem to vary in interesting ways associated with age, gender, religion, race, ethnicity, and other characteristics.

Research also has made clear that mass and elite opinions differ. By "elite" we do not mean people who are "better" than others. Rather, as discussed in Chapter 1, **elite** is a term used by social scientists to refer to people who have a disproportionate amount of some valued resource—money, schooling, prestige, political power, or whatever. Not only do political elites *know more* about politics than the rest of us, they *think differently* about it—they have different views and beliefs. As we explain later in this chapter, they are more likely than average citizens to hold a more or less consistent set of opinions about the policies government ought to pursue. The government attends more to the elite views than to popular views, at least on many matters.

Political Socialization

The Family

For a long time, scholars believed people acquired their political views from their families. There is a lot of truth in that argument. The great majority of high school students know the party affiliation of their parents, and only a tiny minority of children supports a party opposite that of their parents.[8]

But of late we have learned that genetic background also explains some of our political ideology, though rather little of our party affiliation. When we

HOW WE COMPARE

Opinions on Americans

It is not surprising that most Americans have a favorable view of Americans; but what opinions on Americans are held by people in other countries?

By the same token, a majority of Americans typically expresses confidence in the U.S. president; but do majorities in other nations share that confidence?

For several years now, the Pew Global Attitudes Project has conducted sophisticated, in-depth opinion polls in dozens of nations. Below are two sets of selected results from its 2009 survey.

Percent with "a favorable view of the American people," 2009	
Top Five	**Bottom Five**
1. United States 90%	1. Turkey 14%
2. Kenya 87%	2. Pakistan 20%
	2. Palestinian Territory 20%
3. South Korea 83%	3. Argentina 38%
4. Nigeria 76%	4. Jordan 39%
5. France 75%	5. Egypt 40%

Percent with "confidence in the U.S. president," 2009	
Top Five & U.S.	**Bottom Five**
1. Kenya 94%	1. Pakistan 13%
2. Germany 93%	2. Palestinian Territory 23%
3. Canada 88%	3. Jordan 31%
4. Nigeria 88%	4. Turkey 33%
5. Britain 86%	5. Russia 37%
11. United States 74%	

Source: Data from Pew Charitable Trusts.

Iraq War veteran Tammy Duckworth, who served as a U.S. Army helicopter pilot and lost both of her legs in combat, won election in 2012 to Illinois's eighth congressional district seat in the U.S. House of Representatives.

AP Photo/Paul Beaty

Bob Daemmrich/The Image Works

Children grow up learning, but not always following, their parents' political beliefs.

compare how identical twins (who are genetically the same) think about politics with how fraternal twins (who share only half of their genes) think about politics, we discover that identical twins are much more likely to have similar political views than fraternal twins. Some research has found that about one-third of the differences among people with regards to political beliefs comes from genetic makeup, but only one-tenth of these differences comes from family influences.[9]

These results should not surprise us. We know that children in the same family have different personalities even though they have the same parents. Genes play a big role in personality, as they also do in basic political beliefs. If you add together the big effect of genes and the smaller effect of parental influences, then half of our political views comes from our family backgrounds. The other half comes from our individual life experiences, such as the friends we acquire, the schools we attend, and what happens to us as adults.

But political beliefs are not necessarily the same as party affiliation. One can be a liberal or conservative Democrat, a liberal or conservative Republican. Studies that have shown that genes affect our political beliefs also suggest that they do not have much of an effect on our party affiliation. Whether we are Democrats, Republicans, or something else depends substantially on what we learn from our parents.

Still, the ability of the family to inculcate a strong sense of party identification has declined in recent years. The proportion of citizens who say they consider themselves Democrats or Republicans has become steadily smaller since the early 1950s. Accompanying this decline in partisanship has been a sharp rise in the proportion of citizens describing themselves as independents.[10]

Part of this change has resulted from the fact that young voters have always had a weaker sense of

partisanship than older ones. But the youthfulness of the population cannot explain all the changes, for the decline in partisanship has occurred at all age levels. Those who reached voting age in the 1960s were less apt than those who matured in the 1950s to keep the party identification of their parents.[11] Moreover, as personal policy preferences develop into adulthood, the effects of parental socialization on the partisanship of children decrease gradually over time.[12]

There are also sizable age-related differences in opinions on several issues. For example, in 2010 citizens under age 30 supported gay marriage by a margin of 24 percent more than those aged 65 and older.[13] In some ways, the opinions of younger citizens break old ideological molds. Compared to older Americans, for example, citizens aged 18 to 29 have been more likely to favor gay marriage and women's rights (generally labeled the liberal view), but also more likely to favor giving parents tax money in the form of vouchers for private or religious schools and letting people invest some of their Social Security contribution in the stock market (generally labeled the conservative view).[14] More generally, a majority of today's 18- to 24-year-olds thinks elected officials have priorities different from their own, but only one out of five thinks politics is not relevant to their lives at present (see Table 7.1).

Where do such views about politics come from? In most families, the dinner table is not a seminar in political philosophy but a place where people discuss school, jobs, dates, and chores. In some families, however, the dinner table is a political classroom. Studies of the participants in various radical student movements in the 1960s suggested that college radicals often were the sons and daughters of people who had themselves been young radicals; some commentators

TABLE 7.1 Young Adults on Politics and Politicians (2010)

Percent of 18- to 29-year-olds who agree that:	
politics has become too partisan	46%
elected officials don't have the same priorities I have	51%
getting involved in politics is an honorable thing to do	31%
people like me don't have any say about what government does	36%
it is difficult to find ways to be involved in politics	22%
politics is not relevant to my life right now	21%

Source: Institute of Politics, *The 17th Biannual Youth Survey on Politics and Public Service,* John F. Kennedy School of Government, Harvard University, Spring 2010.

dubbed them the "red-diaper babies." Presumably, deeply conservative people come disproportionately from families that were also deeply conservative. This transfer of political beliefs from one generation to the next reflects both heredity and family teaching.

But, again, this transfer of political beliefs leaves plenty of room for inter-generational differences in opinion. Whether and on what issues age-related opinion gaps are wider today than they were in the past is a subject on which more research is needed. But this much is clear: today, adults under age 30 differ markedly from senior citizens (persons age 65 or older) in their opinions on many issues pertaining to social change, religiosity, government, immigration, and civic engagement (see Table 7.2).

Religion

One way in which the family forms and transmits political beliefs is by its religious tradition. Religious differences make for political differences, but the differences generally are more complicated than first meet the eye.

Although most Americans remain somewhat or deeply religious, most seriously question religion's role in politics and government.[15] Religious influences on public opinion are pronounced with respect to social issues like abortion or gay marriage, but they matter less on most other issues; and when a war is perceived to be going badly or the economy is in trouble, most Americans of all faiths or of no faith agree that these are the issues that matter most.[16]

Opinions about politics and government vary not only across but also within given religious traditions. For instance, Table 7.3 shows four Christian religious groups' respective opinions on four issues. As the table illustrates, white Evangelicals and black Protestants hold similar views on environmental regulation, same-sex marriage, and faith-based initiatives, but differ over more aid to the poor. More generally, Table 7.4 shows that people of whatever religion who attend worship services regularly are considerably less likely to vote Democratic than otherwise comparable persons who attend worship services rarely or never.

TABLE 7.2 Opinion Gaps Between Young Adults and Senior Citizens in 2012

	Age 18 to 29 %	Age 65 and Older %	Gap
Social Change			
Favor allowing gay and lesbian couples to marry	65	31	+34
Believe one parent can bring up a child as well as two parents together	65	36	+29
It's all right for blacks and whites to date each other	95	68	+27
Religiosity			
Prayer is an important part of my daily life	61	85	−24
I never doubt the existence of God	67	87	−20
Government			
The Constitution should be interpreted in terms of what it means in modern times*	62	35	+27
A free market economy needs government regulation in order to best serve the public interest	74	57	+17
When something is run by the government it is usually inefficient and wasteful	47	69	−22
Immigrants			
Newcomers from other countries threaten traditional American customs and values	43	58	−15
It bothers me when I come in contact with immigrants who speak little or no English	30	44	−14
Civic Engagement			
I'm Interested in keeping up with national affairs (completely agree)	46	63	−17
I feel it's my duty as a citizen to always vote	84	98	−14

Source: Pew Research Center, "Partisan Polarization Surges in Bush, Obama Years: Trends in American Values, 1987–2012," June 2012, with one point (*) from Pew Research Center, "Ideological Chasm Over Interpreting Constitution," June 2011.

TABLE 7.3 Opinions by Four Christian Groups on Four Issues (2009–2010)

	Tougher Environmental Regulations	Same-Sex Marriage	More Aid to the Poor	Letting Faith-Based Groups Apply for Government Funding
	Percent in favor			
All Americans	81	41	63	69
White Evangelicals	73	22	54	77
Black Protestants	79	26	81	84
White Catholics	86	49	58	81
Hispanic Catholics	89	40	77	N/A

Source: Adapted from Pew Forum on Religion and Public Life, "American Views on Religion, Politics, & Public Policy, 2010," pp. 37, 41, and 46, and "Faith-Based Programs Still Popular, Less Visible," November 16, 2009, p. 2.

TABLE 7.4 Worship Service Attendance and the Probability of Voting Democratic (2000–2012)

Attendance at Worship Services	Probability of Voting for the Democratic Candidate			
	2000	2004	2008	2012
More than once a week	34%	30%	33%	36%
Once a week	44	39	43	41
A few times a month	54	49	54	55
A few times a year	64	59	65	56
Never	73	68	74	62

Source: Pew Forum on Religion and Public Life, "American Views on Religion, Politics & Public Policy, 2010," p. 85, and "How the Faithful Voted: 2012," November 7, 2012 p. 2.

Religion also figures in differences in opinion within each generation. For example, when asked in March 2012 whether they preferred Barack Obama or Mitt Romney, the opinions expressed by younger millennial citizens (ages 18 to 25) who were registered voters varied greatly by religious affiliation: like the cohort as a whole, younger millennial Catholics, minority Protestants, and those with no religious affiliation preferred Obama, while younger millennial white Evangelicals and white Mainline Protestants favored Romney (see Table 7.5). Additional opinion differences can be uncovered within each religious subgroup. For instance, the 2012 pre-election surveys as well as the 2012 presidential exit polls found that young Latino Catholic voters were even more likely to prefer and vote for Obama than young non-Latino Catholics were; and, with each religious subgroup, voters with higher annual household incomes were somewhat more likely to prefer and vote for Romney.

The Gender Gap

Journalists often point out that women have "deserted" Republican candidates to favor Democratic ones. In some cases, this is true. But it would be equally correct to say that men have "deserted"

Democratic candidates for Republican ones. The **gender gap** is the difference in political views between men and women. That gap has existed for a long time, and it is a problem for both political parties.

gender gap Difference in political views between men and women.

TABLE 7.5 Religious Affiliation and Younger Millennials (18–25) Registered to Vote

Religious Affiliation	Prefer Barack Obama	Prefer Mitt Romney
All	55	39
White Evangelicals	15	80
White Mainline Protestants	40	51
Catholics	55	38
Minority Protestants	70	26
Unaffiliated/No Religion	68	23

Source: Robert P. Jones et al, *Diverse, Disillusioned, and Divided: Millennial Values and Voter Engagement in the 2012 Election* (Washington, D.C.: Berkeley Center for Religion, Peace, and World Affairs, Georgetown University, surveys conducted in March 2012 and September 2012, report issued October 4, 2012).

TABLE 7.6	Gender Gaps in Presidential Voting, 1992–2012					
	Men			Women		
	Rep %	Dem %	D-R diff	Rep %	Dem %	D-R diff
2012	54	46	−8	44	56	+12
2008	50	50	0	43	57	+14
2004	44	56	−12	48	52	+4
2000	45	52	−7	45	53	+8
1996	45	44	+1	39	54	+15
1992	41	37	+4	38	46	+8

Source: Gallup Organization, *Gender Gap in 2012 is Largest in Gallup Survey's History*, November 9, 2012.

Women obtained the right to vote in 1920 when the Nineteenth Amendment to the Constitution was ratified. Until 1980, women voted at significantly lower rates than men. Since 1980, however, women have voted at somewhat higher rates than men, a difference amplified by the fact that women are also a larger proportion of the voting-age population. As Table 7.6 shows, in every presidential election from 1980 through 2012 women were more likely than men to favor the Democratic candidate. In the 2012 presidential election, women favored the Democrat by 12 points and men favored the Republican by 8 points, yielding a 20-point gender gap. Behind the gender gap in partisan self-identification and voting are differences between men and women over prominent political issues and which issues matter most. For example, as results from multiple national surveys have suggested, women are more likely than men to favor activist government, universal health care, environmental protection regulations, anti-poverty programs, and laws supporting same-sex marriage; less likely than men to favor cutting taxes at the expense of social services or to support military interventions; and more likely than men to consider social welfare issues important.

Cleavages in Public Opinion

The way in which political opinions are formed helps explain the cleavages that exist among these opinions and why these cleavages do not follow any single political principle but instead overlap and crosscut in bewildering complexity. If, for example, the United States lacked regional differences and was composed almost entirely of white Protestants who had never attended college, there would still be plenty of political conflict—the rich would have different views from the poor; workers would have

different views from farmers—but that conflict would be much simpler to describe and explain. It might even lead to political parties that were more clearly aligned with competing political philosophies than those we now have. In fact, some democratic nations in the world today have a population very much like the one just described, and the United States itself, during the first half of the 19th century, was overwhelmingly white, Protestant, and without much formal schooling.

Today, however, there are crosscutting cleavages based on race, ethnicity, religion, region, and education, in addition to those created by income and occupation. To the extent that politics is sensitive to public opinion, it is sensitive to a variety of different and even competing publics. Not all these publics have influence proportionate to their numbers or even to their numbers adjusted for the intensity of their feelings. As will be described later, a filtering process occurs that makes the opinions of some publics more influential than those of others.

Whatever this state of affairs may mean for democracy, it creates a messy situation for political scientists. It would be so much easier if everyone's opinion on political affairs reflected some single feature of his or her life, such as income, occupation, age, race, or sex. Of course, some writers have argued that political opinion is a reflection of one such feature, social class, usually defined in terms of income or occupation, but that view, though containing some truth, is beset with inconsistencies: poor blacks and poor whites disagree sharply on many issues involving race; well-to-do Jews and well-to-do Protestants often have opposing opinions on social welfare policy; and low-income elderly people are much more worried about crime than low-income graduate students. Plumbers and professors may have similar incomes, but they rarely have similar views, and businesspeople in New York City often take a very different view of government than businesspeople in Houston or Birmingham.

In some other democracies, a single factor such as class may explain more of the differences in political attitudes than it does in the more socially heterogeneous United States. Most blue-collar workers in America think of themselves as "middle-class," whereas most such workers in Britain and France describe themselves as "working-class."

Social Class

Americans speak of "social class" with embarrassment. The norm of equality tugs at our consciences, urging us to judge people as individuals, not as parts of some social group (such as "the lower class"). Social scientists speak of "class" with confusion. They know it exists but quarrel constantly about how to define it: by income? occupation? wealth? schooling? prestige? personality?

Let's face up to the embarrassment and skip over the confusion. Truck drivers and investment bankers look differently, talk differently, and vote differently. There is nothing wrong with saying that the first group consists of "working-class" (or "blue-collar") people and the latter of "upper-class" (or "management") people. Moreover, though different definitions of class produce slightly different groupings of people, most definitions overlap to such an extent that it does not matter too much which we use.

However defined, public opinion and voting have been less determined by class in the United States than in Europe, and the extent of class cleavage has declined in the last few decades in both the United States and Europe. In the 1950s, V. O. Key, Jr., found that differences in political opinion were closely associated with occupation. He noted that people holding managerial or professional jobs had distinctly more conservative views on social welfare policy and more internationalist views on foreign policy than manual workers.[17] During the next decade, this pattern changed greatly. Opinion surveys done in the late 1960s showed that business and professional people had views quite similar to those of manual workers on matters such as the poverty program, health insurance, American policy in Vietnam, and government efforts to create jobs.[18]

The voting patterns of different social classes also have become somewhat more similar. The differences in whether or not people vote, depending on their social class, have declined sharply since the late 1940s in the United States, France, Great Britain, and Germany and have declined moderately in Sweden.

Class differences remain, of course. Unskilled workers are more likely than affluent white-collar workers to be Democrats and to have liberal views on economic policy. And when economic issues pinch—for example, when farmers are hurting or steelworkers are being laid off—the importance of economic interests in differentiating the opinions of various groups rises sharply.

Still, many of the issues that now lead us to choose which party to support and that determine whether we think of ourselves as liberals or conservatives are noneconomic issues. In recent years, our political posture has been shaped by the positions we take on race relations, abortion, school prayer, environmentalism, and terrorism, issues that do not clearly affect the rich differently than the poor (or at least do not affect them as differently as do the union movement, the minimum wage, and unemployment). Moral, symbolic, and foreign policy matters do not divide rich and poor in the same way as economic ones. Thus, we have many well-off people who think of themselves as liberals because they take liberal positions on these noneconomic matters, and many not-so-well-off people who think of themselves as conservatives because that is the position they take on these issues.

Race and Ethnicity

African Americans are overwhelmingly Democratic, though younger ones are a bit more likely than older ones to identify with the Republican party.[19] Younger blacks are also much more likely to support the idea of using school vouchers to pay for education than older ones.

There are sharp differences between white and black attitudes on many public policy questions. For example, blacks are much more likely than whites to support affirmative action, to think that the criminal justice system is biased against blacks, to oppose the use of military force, to doubt that we all should be willing to fight for our country, and to think that believing in God is essential for a person to be moral.[20]

But there are also many areas of agreement. Both blacks and whites want our courts to be tougher in handling criminals, oppose the idea of making abortion legal in all cases, agree that people have become too dependent on government aid, and think that everyone has it in his or her own power to succeed.[21]

Latinos are the largest minority group in America, numbering more than 50 million people. Until recently, studies of Latino public opinion were "small, disproportionately oriented toward immigration, and relatively silent on the influence of gender" and other possible intragroup opinion cleavages.[22] An early survey of ethnic groups in California, a state where fully one-third of all recent immigrants to this country live, provided a hint—but only a hint—of how Latinos felt about political parties and issues, and how Latino opinion compared to that of other groups.[23]

Today, however, there is a growing body of survey and other data on Latino opinion, political behavior, and civic engagement. Among the many interesting findings that are emerging from this literature is how the gender gap in presidential voting is narrower among Latino voters than it is in the electorate as a whole; for example, in the 2012 presidential election, 77 percent of Latino women as well as 73 percent of Latino men voted for the Democrat. Table 7.7 offers a detailed snapshot of Latino opinion in the months prior to the 2012 presidential election.

Latinos are a diverse mix of Cuban Americans, Mexican Americans, Central Americans, and Puerto Ricans, each with distinct political views. Most studies of Latino voting show that people from Mexico vote heavily Democratic, those from Cuba mostly Republican, and those from Puerto Rico somewhere in between.[24] Local conditions also affect these views. Hispanics in Texas often vote for more conservative candidates than do those in California. Likewise, following the U.S. invasion of Iraq, most Latinos believed U.S. troops should have been withdrawn, but there were important differences between the views of native-born and foreign-born Latinos.[25]

Latinos have less money and are younger than non-Hispanic white Americans. In America, about

Marco Rubio, the Hispanic son of exiles from Cuba, is a Republican elected by Florida to the United States Senate in 2010.

four-fifths of all Latinos, but only half of all non-Hispanic whites, are younger than 45. It is possible that these differences affect their views.[26] Despite these differences, there are broad areas of agreement between Latinos and non-Hispanic whites. For instance, almost exactly the same percentage of both groups favor allowing people to invest some of their Social Security taxes into stock-market funds.[27]

TABLE 7.7 Latino Opinion, 2012

Most Important Issues Facing the Latino Community	
Immigration reform	58%
Create jobs/fix the economy	38
Education reform/schools	19
Health care	15
Immigration Policy	
Strongly/somewhat approve President Obama's handling of immigration policy	70%
Strongly/somewhat approve Democrats in Congress handling of immigration policy	61
Strongly/somewhat approve Republicans in Congress handling of immigration policy	25
Partisan Identification	
Think of myself as a "Strong Democrat"	32%
Think of myself as a "Strong Republican"	7
Think of myself as "Independent"	6
Voting History	
Ever voted for a Democrat for any federal, state, or local elective office	89
Ever voted for a Republican for any federal, state, or local elective office	52
Congress in 2014	
Will vote Democrat for Congress in 2014	56
Will vote Republican for Congress in 2014	14
Undecided/Don't Know how will vote for Congress in 2014	20

Source: Adapted from Latino Decisions, Immigration Poll, March 5, 2012; also see Latino Decisions, "The Untapped Potential of the Latino Electorate," January 15, 2013.

WHAT'S YOUR ISSUE?

The Electoral College

In November 2000, Al Gore received more than a half million more votes for president than George W. Bush did. A controversy erupted over the vote-count in Florida. The U.S. Supreme Court stepped in. When all the dust settled, Bush became the nation's 43rd president, and also the fourth president in American history to win the presidency while losing the popular vote (the other three were John Quincy Adams in 1824, Rutherford B. Hayes in 1876, and Benjamin Harrison in 1888).

With Florida counted in Bush's column, he won the Electoral College. Under Article II of the Constitution, Americans elect their presidents not by a direct popular vote, but by winning a majority of the "Electors" selected by each state in a number equal to the number of its House of Representatives plus two (for its two U.S. Senators). Most states (Maine and Nebraska are the two long-time exceptions) award all their Electors to whichever presidential ticket wins most (a majority or a plurality) of its popular votes.

In 2013, about two-thirds of Americans favored amending the Constitution to end the Electoral College system and having the candidate that wins the most popular votes nationally win the presidency.

In Chapter 14, we discuss the Electoral College system in more depth. Based on whatever you know and think about the issue now, would you support or oppose ending the system in favor of a direct popular election of the president? Why do you suppose a wide and persistent majority favors ending the Electoral College? What do you think might be gained or lost if it was abolished? For instance, what if the direct election system resulted in run-off elections among multiple candidates, none of whom won a majority of the popular vote? How do you suppose a direct popular election system would affect how presidential candidates campaign? Would candidates make fewer visits to "swing states" like Ohio and Florida? And how much attention would they pay to minority voters that are concentrated in what under the present system are "swing states"?

Source: Gallup Organization, "Americans Call for Term Limits, End to Electoral College," January 18, 2013; "Americans Would Swap Electoral College for Popular Vote," October 24, 2011; and "Public Flunks Electoral College System," November 2, 2004.

Region

It is widely believed that geographic region affects political attitudes and in particular that southerners and northerners disagree significantly on many policy questions. At one time, white southerners were conspicuously less liberal than easterners, midwesterners, and westerners on questions such as aid to minorities, legalizing marijuana, school busing, and enlarging the rights of those accused of crimes. Although more conservative on these issues, they held views on economic issues similar to those of whites in other regions of the country. This helps to explain why the South was for so long a part of the Democratic Party coalition: on national economic and social welfare policies, southerners expressed views not very different from those of northerners. That coalition was always threatened, however, by the divisiveness produced by issues of race and liberty.

The southern lifestyle is in fact different from that of other regions of the country. The South has, on the whole, been more accommodating to business enterprise and less so to organized labor than, for example, the Northeast; it gave greater support

to the third-party candidacy of George Wallace in 1968, which was a protest against big government and the growth of national political power as well as against civil rights; and it was in the South that the greatest opposition arose to income-redistribution plans such as the Family Assistance Plan of 1969. Moreover, there is some evidence that white southerners became by the 1970s more conservative than they had been in the 1950s, at least when compared to white northerners.[28] Finally, over the last several decades, white southerners have become decidedly less attached to the Democratic party: no Democratic candidate for president has won a majority of white southern votes since Lyndon Johnson did so in 1964, and most House seats in the South are now held by Republicans. In 2012, Barack Obama won the presidency with just 39 percent of the white vote *nationally* (the lowest share of the white vote received by any Democratic presidential candidate since Michael Dukakis got 40 percent in 1988), and with under a fifth of the white vote in several southern states.

Since 1980, southern states have gained seats in the House of Representatives, with Florida and Texas alone each gaining a dozen. The opposite *political ideology* A more or less consistent set of beliefs about what policies government ought to pursue.

shift has occurred in much of the Northeast, with voters becoming somewhat more reliably Democratic in states like New York, Ohio, and Pennsylvania where populations and hence congressional delegations have been shrinking.

Political Ideology

Up to now the words *liberal* and *conservative* have been used as though everyone agrees on what they mean and as if they accurately describe general sets of political beliefs held by large segments of the population. Neither of these assumptions is correct. Like many useful words—*love, justice, happiness*—they are as vague as they are indispensable.

When we refer to people as liberals, conservatives, socialists, or radicals, we are implying that they have a patterned set of beliefs about how government and other important institutions in fact operate and how they ought to operate, and in particular about what kinds of policies government ought to pursue. These groups are said to display to some degree a **political ideology**—that is, a more or less consistent set of beliefs about what policies government ought to pursue.

Political scientists measure the extent to which people have a political ideology in two ways. The first is by seeing how frequently people use broad political categories (such as "liberal," "conservative," "radical") to describe their own views or to justify their preferences for various candidates and policies, or, by seeing to what extent the policy preferences of a citizen are consistent over time or are based at any one time on consistent principles. This second method involves a simple mathematical procedure: measuring how accurately one can predict a person's view on a subject at one time based on his or her view on that subject at an earlier time, or measuring how accurately one can predict a person's view on one issue based on his or her view on a different issue. The higher the accuracy of such predictions (or correlations), the more we say a person's political opinions display "constraint" or ideology.

Despite annual fluctuations, ideological self-identification surveys show that over the last two decades, "conservative" and "moderate" have each been chosen by about 37 to 40 percent, while "liberal" has been chosen by about 20 percent.[29] For instance, from 2008 to 2011, 20 to 21 percent chose "liberal," 35 to 36 percent chose "moderate," and 38 to 39 percent chose "conservative." For three reasons,

however, these self-identification survey averages do not really tell us much at all about how or whether most people think about politics in an ideological manner. First, except when asked by pollsters, most Americans do not actually employ the words *liberal, conservative,* or *moderate* in explaining or justifying their preferences for parties, candidates, or policies, and not many more than half can give plausible definitions of these terms. The vast majority of Americans simply do not think about politics in an ideological or very coherent manner.

Second, over the last decade, survey research scholars have rediscovered old truths about the limitations of polling as a window into "the public mind."[30] Public opinion polls must of necessity ask rather simple questions. The apparent "inconsistency" in the answers people give at different times may mean only that the nature of the problem and the wording of the question have changed. Or it could simply mean that many people consistently want from politics or government things that, as a practical matter, they cannot have, or at least cannot have all at once or at a price they are willing to pay—for instance, a bigger military, more expansive public health insurance coverage for all, and greater funding for public schools, but no military draft, no new or increased taxes, and no government budget deficits. Ideological liberals might consistently covet everything on that list except the bigger military, and they might be willing to pay higher taxes to get it. Ideological conservatives might want only the bigger military, but only if getting it requires no tax increases. But most citizens are more inclined to pick and choose their positions without regard to conventional liberal or conservative views, and without feeling any need to be "consistent."

Third, when surveyed in person (including by telephone), some people will hide what they think are socially or morally unacceptable self-identifications or positions behind a "don't know" or "middle-ground" response.[31] This can happen not only when the questions concern specific labels like "liberal" or "conservative," or particular issues like racial integration or immigration restrictions, but also when the questions seem to ask about fundamental values, patriotism, or "Americanism." As we saw in Chapter 4, most Americans share a distinctive political culture—a belief in freedom, in equality of political condition and economic opportunity, and in civic duty. Trying to determine precisely where political culture ends and ideology begins often is difficult or impossible.

Mass Ideologies: A Typology

Partly in recognition of these and related limitations, pollsters have increasingly taken a fresh approach to documenting and analyzing average Americans' ideological cast and character. Essentially, rather than ask people to identify themselves as "liberal," "conservative," or "moderate," they ask people multiple questions about politics and government, and then use the answers to sort them into a half-dozen or more different groups.

The oldest political typology survey of this sort started in 1987 and has been updated four times since, with the latest survey completed in 2011. (To see where you fit, you can take the survey for yourself at http://typology.people-press.org/typology.) Americans, it finds, are divided into nine different groups, each defined by certain key characteristics (see Table 7.8). Measured by both their presence among registered voters and in the general population, "Solid Liberals" are the largest single political bloc. Together with "Hard-Pressed Democrats," they number nearly one in three registered voters and over a quarter of the general public.

But various types of Republican-identifying groups—"Staunch Conservatives," "Main Street Republicans," and "Libertarians"—together with Republican-leaning "Disaffecteds," comprise two-fifths of the adult population and nearly half (46 percent) of all registered voters. And one in ten Americans ("Bystanders") hold views that lead them to be cynical about politics or pay it no mind. Dig deeper into the data on these nine groups (also available via the same web site cited above), such as the related survey findings regarding each group's socioeconomic status and views on religion and other matters that affect politics, and you will see that the old three-way (liberal-conservative-moderate) self-identification surveys probably obscured more than they revealed regarding most Americans' opinions about many different political issues.

> *political elites* Persons with a disproportionate share of political power.

Liberal and Conservative Elites

Although the terms *liberal* and *conservative* do not adequately describe the political views held by most average Americans, they do capture the views held by many, perhaps most, people who are in the country's political elite. As we discussed in Chapter 1, every society has an elite, because in every society government officials have more power than ordinary folk, some persons make more money than others, and some people are more popular than others. The former Soviet Union even had an official name for the political elite—the *nomenklatura*.

In America, we often refer to **political elites** more casually as "activists"—people who hold

TABLE 7.8   Ideology Typology: Nine Types

Some Key Characteristics	Adult Population	Registered Voters	Partisan Identification/Leaning
Staunch Conservatives	9%	11%	Nearly 100% Republican/Lean Republican
• Extremely critical of the federal government; highly religious;90% non-Hispanic white			
Main Street Republicans	11%	14%	95% Republican/Lean Republican
• Fiscally and socially conservative; supportive of environmental protection laws; 88% non-Hispanic white			
Libertarians	9%	10%	77% Republican/Lean Republican
• Conservative on economic issues; liberal on social issues; highly pro-business; 85% non-Hispanic white			
Disaffecteds	11%	11%	60% Republican/Lean Republican
• Financially stressed; socially conservative; support welfare programs; 77% non-Hispanic white			
Post-Moderns	13%	14%	59% Democratic/Lean Democratic
• Well-educated; financially well off; very liberal on social issues; 70% non-Hispanic white; 32% under age 30			
New Coalition Democrats	10%	9%	81% Democratic/Lean Democratic
• Highly religious; financially stressed; divided on welfare and social issues; 34% white, 30% black, 26% Latino			
Hard-Pressed Democrats	13%	15%	Nearly 100% Democratic/Lean Democratic
• Struggling financially; very religious; critical of government and business; 53% non-Hispanic white, 35% black			
Solid Liberals	14%	16%	95% Democratic/Lean Democratic
• Very pro-government; highly secular; very supportive of environmental regulations; 72% white; 57% female			
Bystanders	10%	0%	49% Democratic/Lean Democratic
• Pay little attention to political news; high unemployment; 39% never vote; 44% white, 38% Latino, 9% black			

Source: Adapted from *Beyond Red v. Blue: The Political Typology*, Pew Research Center for the People and the Press, May 4, 2011.

norm A standard of right or proper conduct.

office, run for office, work in campaigns or on newspapers, lead interest groups and social movements, and speak out on public issues. Being an activist is not an all-or-nothing proposition: people display differing degrees of activism, from full-time politicians to persons who occasionally get involved in a campaign (see Chapter 8). But the more a person is an activist, the more likely it is that he or she will display ideological consistency on the conventional liberal-conservative spectrum.

The reasons for this greater consistency seem to be information and peers. First, we consider information. In general, the better informed people are about politics and the more interest they take in politics, the more likely they are to have consistently liberal or conservative views.[32] This higher level of information and interest may lead them to find relationships among issues that others don't see and to learn from the media and elsewhere what are the "right" things to believe. This does not mean there are no differences among liberal elites (or among conservative ones), only that the differences occur within a liberal (or conservative) consensus that is more well-defined, more consistent, and more important to those who share it than would be the case among ordinary citizens.

Second is the matter of peers. Politics does not make strange bedfellows. On the contrary, politics is a process of likes attracting likes. The more active you are in politics, the more you will associate with people who agree with you on some issues; the more time you spend with those people, the more your other views will shift to match theirs.

The greater ideological consistency of political elites can be seen in Congress. As we shall note in Chapter 13, Democratic members of Congress tend to be consistently liberal, and Republican members of Congress tend to be consistently conservative— *far more* consistently than Democratic voters and Republican voters. By the same token, we shall see in Chapter 9 that the delegates to presidential nominating conventions are far more ideological (liberal in the Democratic convention, conservative in the Republican one) than is true of voters who identify with the Democratic or Republican parties.

Still, on a large number of issues, the policy preferences of average Republican and Democratic voters do differ significantly from one another. Some political scientists argue that Republican and Democratic leaders in Congress are more polarized because voters are more polarized. Other political scientists, however, analyze the available polling and election data differently. They find

that ideological changes among voters have been small, while public opinion among Democrats voting in districts represented by Democrats and among Republicans voting in districts represented by Republicans has been remarkably stable. Which side is right? We have no data that allow us to compare in each district what voters think and how their representatives behave. To amass such data would require polls of perhaps 500 voters in each congressional district taken several years apart. Nobody thinks it is worth spending millions of dollars to interview more than 10,000 voters at different times just to answer this one academic puzzle.

Political Elites, Public Opinion, and Public Policy

Though the elites and the public see politics in very different ways, and though there often are intense antagonisms between the two groups, the elites influence public opinion in at least two important ways.

First, elites, especially those in or having access to the media (see Chapter 12), raise and frame political issues. At one time, environmentalism was not on the political agenda; at a later time, not only was it on the agenda, but it also was near the top of governmental concerns. At some times the government has had little interest in what it should do in South Africa or Central America; at other times the government has been preoccupied with these matters. Just as world events help shape the political agenda, so also do political elites.

Two decades ago, a pathbreaking study by John Zaller suggested that elite views shape mass views by influencing both what issues capture the public's attention and how those issues are debated and decided.[33] Subsequent studies in the 1990s hinted that, contrary to the myth of the pandering politician, what scholars of the subject call opinion-policy congruence (essentially the rate at which governments adopt crime, health, trade, and other policies supported by majorities in polls) had been declining, not rising, since 1980, a trend that could be interpreted to reflect greater elite influence over how policy options are presented to the public.[34] By the late 2000s, however, the rise of internet campaigning and the political blogosphere, among other developments, had scholars debating anew the extent and means of elite influence over mass views and policy agendas.

Second, elites state the norms by which issues should be settled. (A **norm** is a standard of right or proper conduct.) By doing this, they help

WHAT WOULD YOU DO?

MEMORANDUM

To: *Bill Byron, U.S. senator*

From: *Dan Joyce, legislative assistant*

Subject: *Vote on "path-to-citizenship" immigration bill*

Your state has only a small illegal immigration problem, but voters have concerns about both maintaining law and order, and providing economic opportunities and a "path to citizenship" for people who have resided in this country for many years. As you contemplate both your vote on the bill and your possible presidential bid as a Republican, note that public opinion on the subject is divided by party, race, ethnicity, and religion. For example, an August 2010 Pew poll asked about priorities in dealing with illegal immigration: 47 percent of Republicans, 34 percent of Independents, and 21 percent of Democrats cited "better border security"; and 41 percent of Hispanics versus 19 percent of white evangelicals cited "creating a path to citizenship."

Arguments for:

1. Your state contains a small but slowly growing proportion of first-generation Americans, who favor a "path to citizenship" for immigrants who have lived in this country for years, regardless of their legal status.

2. Illegal immigrants often take menial jobs that nobody else wants, and contribute to the U.S. economy by paying taxes and buying goods and services.

3. A "path to citizenship," with fines and other penalties for being in the country illegally, is the most realistic option for individuals who have family and other long-term ties in the United States.

Arguments against:

1. Your party leaders oppose comprehensive immigration reform, saying that enhanced border security must be a higher priority.

News »

U.S. House Considers Comprehensive Immigration Reform

The U.S. House of Representatives is weighing a bill that would result in the most comprehensive immigration reform in more than a decade. Proponents say it will both improve border security and provide opportunities for legal residency for more than 11 million illegal immigrants in the United States. The bill received a mixed reception, however, as critics denounced the provisions for illegal immigrants, saying they amount to "amnesty" for law breakers.

2. Illegal immigrants take jobs away from native-born Americans and cost more in public services, such as education and emergency health care, than they contribute to the economy.

3. People who entered the country illegally must not be rewarded for breaking the law, and enforcement can be effective with sufficient resources.

Your decision:

Vote for bill _____   Vote against bill _____

determine the range of acceptable and unacceptable policy options. For example, elites have for a long time emphasized that racism is wrong. Of late they have emphasized that sexism is wrong.

Over a long period, the steady repetition of views condemning racism and sexism will at least intimidate, and perhaps convince, those who are racist and sexist.

A recent example of this process has been the public discussion of AIDS and its relationship to homosexuality. The initial public reaction to AIDS was one of fear and loathing. But efforts to quarantine people infected with AIDS were met with firm resistance from the medical community and from other policy elites. The elites even managed to persuade some legislatures to bar insurance companies from testing insurance applicants for the disease.

There are limits to how much influence elites can have on the public. For instance, elites do not define economic problems—people can see for themselves the existence of unemployment, raging inflation, or high interest rates. Elite opinion may shape the policies, but it does not define the problem. Similarly, elite opinion has little influence on whether we think there is a crime or drug problem; it is, after all, *our* purses being snatched, cars being stolen, and children being drugged. On the other hand, elite opinion does define the problem as well as the policy options with respect to most aspects of foreign affairs; the public has little first-hand experience with which to judge the situation in Iraq.

Because elites affect how we see some issues and determine how other issues get resolved, it is important to study the differences between elite and public opinion. But it is wrong to suppose that there is just one elite group, unified in interests and opinions. Just as there are many publics, and hence many public opinions, there are many elites, and hence many different elite opinions. Whether there is enough variety of opinion and influence among elites to justify calling our politics "pluralist" is one of the central issues confronting any student of government.

LEARNING OBJECTIVES

1. What is "public opinion" and how do we measure it?

Public opinion refers to how people think or feel about particular things, including but not limited to politics and government. Today, it is commonly measured by means of scientific survey research or polls based on random samples of given populations.

2. What role did the Framers of the Constitution think public opinion should play in making public policy?

Basically, they believed that it should play a rather limited role. The Framers worried that majority opinion would often prove fickle, factious, or overly inclined toward short-term thinking. And they did not want fundamental rights and freedoms at the mercy of majority will. But, as explained in this chapter's **Constitutional Connections** feature, the Framers were sympathetic to the idea that a persistent majority—a majority, for example, that persisted over several national election cycles for Congress and the presidency— should often, though not always, be heeded by duly elected representatives and reflected in public policies. Of course, for good or ill, not all persistent majorities prevail. As this chapter's **What's Your Issue?** feature indicates, for more than a dozen years now more than six in ten Americans have favored amending the Constitution to end the Electoral College system and replace it with a system of direct popular election; it has not happened, and there is at present little chance that it will happen anytime soon.

3. What is "political socialization" and how does it work?

Political socialization refers to the process by which background traits influence one's political views. It works mainly through families, schools, and religious affiliations.

4. What is "political ideology" and how does it matter for what elites and the mass public believe?

Political ideology is defined as a more or less consistent set of beliefs about what policies government ought to pursue. Elites are more prone to think ideologically than average citizens are, but there are mass ideologies, and the relationship between what diverse elites believe and what the public at large believes admits of no easy generalizations. Political scientists measure the extent to which people have a political ideology by seeing how frequently people use broad political categories (such as "liberal" and "conservative") to describe their own views or to justify their preferences for candidates and policies. They also measure it by seeing to what extent the policy preferences of a citizen are consistent over time or are based at any one time on consistent principles. Many scholars believe that Americans are becoming more ideological. On many issues, for example, the policy preferences of average Republican and Democratic voters now differ significantly from one another. There is clear evidence that political elites are more ideological today than they were just a generation or two ago. The government attends more to the elite views than to popular views, at least on many matters.

5. How much does public opinion in America vary by age and other characteristics?

Lots. There are cleavages in American public opinion, but they change over time, and it is hard to generalize meaningfully about how they affect politics and government. For example, the opinions of voters under age 30 differ markedly from those of senior citizens (people age 65 and older) on numerous issues. Women are far more sympathetic to liberal causes and Democratic candidates than men, but these so-called gender gaps in opinion

and voting behavior are more pronounced in some elections than in others.

On some issues, the opinions of whites and blacks are similar or narrowing, but on other issues, wide opinion gaps remain between whites and blacks. People who attend worship services regularly are more conservative and far more likely to vote Republican in presidential elections than people who attend worship services rarely if ever.

6. People self-label as "liberal," "moderate," or "conservative," but are there more refined ways of describing and classifying citizens' political views?

Yes. One example is the political typology pioneered in 1987 by survey research experts with the Pew Research Center, and updated four times since then. The latest Pew political typology describes and classifies citizens' political views into nine different groups: go to the web site (www.people-press.org/typology/quiz) and see whether you are scored as a "Staunch Conservative," a "Solid Liberal," or one of the seven other categories in between.

TO LEARN MORE

CBS News/*New York Times* poll: **Topics.nytimes.com/top/reference/timestopics/ subjects/n/newyorktimes-poll-watch/**

Gallup opinion poll: **www.gallup.com**

The Pew Research Center for the People & the Press: **www.people-press.org**

Rasmussen Reports: **www.rasmussenreports.com**

Roper Center for Public Opinion Research: **www. ropercenter.uconn.edu**

Wall Street Journal/NBC News poll: **topics.wsj.com/ subject/W/wall-street-journal/nbc- news-polls/ 6052**

Berinsky, Adam J. *Silent Voices: Public Opinion and Political Participation in* America.Princeton, NJ: Princeton University Press, 2004. Shows how opinion polls can bias the results and induce people with unpopular views to say "don't know."

Erikson, Robert S., and Kent L. Tedin. *American Public Opinion*. 5th ed. Boston: Allyn and Bacon, 1995. An excellent (if dated) summary of how opinion is measured, what it shows, and how it affects politics.

Jennings, M. Kent, and Richard G. Niemi. *Generations and Politics*. Princeton, NJ: Princeton University Press, 1981. A study of persistence and change in the political views of young adults and their parents.

___. *The Political Character of Adolescence: The Influence of Families and Schools*. Princeton, NJ: Princeton University Press, 1974. A study of political attitudes among high school students.

Key, V. O., Jr. *The Responsible Electorate*. Cambridge: Harvard University Press, 1966. An argument, with evidence, that American voters are not fools.

Lewis-Beck, Michael S., et al. *The American Voter Revisited*. Ann Arbor, MI: University of Michigan Press, 2008. A careful comparison of how voters in the early 2000s compare to those in the mid-1950s.

Lipset, Seymour Martin. *Political Man: The Social Bases of Politics*. Garden City, NY: Doubleday, 1959. An exploration of the relationship between society, opinion, and democracy in America and abroad.

Moe, Terry M. *Schools, Vouchers, and the American Public*. Washington, D.C.: Brookings Institution Press, 2001. A masterful study of how public opinion matters to education policy, suggesting that most people, with only slight information, form reasonable views.

Nie, Norman H., Sidney Verba, and John R. Petrocik. *The Changing American Voter*. Cambridge: Harvard University Press, 1976. Traces shifts in American voter attitudes since 1960.

Weissberg, Robert. *Polling, Policy, and Public Opinion*. New York: Palgrave Macmillan, 2002. A critique of what we think we know from opinion polling, showing the many ways in which polls can give us misleading answers.

Zaller, John. *The Nature and Origins of Mass Opinion*. Cambridge, England: Cambridge University Press, 1992. A pathbreaking study of how the public forms an opinion, illustrating the ways in which elite views help shape mass views.

Edward Linsmier/Getty Images News/Getty Images

Political Participation

LEARNING OBJECTIVES

1. What is "political participation"?

2. How are voter turnout rates measured?

3. How, and how much, do most citizens participate?

4. Who votes, who doesn't?

5. Why do some people participate in politics at higher rates than others?

6. How did the Framers of the Constitution think average citizens should participate in America's representative democracy?

7. Should today's college-age citizens participate more in politics?

political participation The many different ways that people take part in politics and government.

voting-age population (VAP) Citizens who are eligible to vote after reaching the minimum age requirement.

voting-eligible population (VEP) Citizens who have reached the minimum age to be eligible to vote, excluding those who are not legally permitted to cast a ballot.

Defined simply, **political participation** refers to the many different ways that people take part in politics and government: voting or trying to influence others to vote, joining a political party or giving money to a candidate for office, keeping informed about government or debating political issues with others, signing a petition, protesting a policy, advocating for a new law, or just writing a letter to an elected leader. Some scholars of the subject profess that, in addition to these activities, almost any form of civic engagement, like helping out at a local homeless shelter or attending a school board meeting, should count as political participation. And some believe that the rise of the internet, political blogs, and social media make traditional ideas about what constitutes political participation obsolete.

But no matter how they define it, most academics who study political participation pay close attention to voting and begin with a puzzle: despite successive legal and other changes that might be expected to increase electoral participation, voter turnout rates in America today are lower than they were for previous generations, and scores of millions of Americans now sit out each presidential and midterm national election.

THEN

In most states, well into the 19th century, only property-owning white males could vote. After the Civil War and into the mid-20th century, many states used all manner of stratagems to keep blacks from voting. Women did not receive the right to vote until 1920 when the Nineteenth Amendment to the Constitution was ratified. Before 1961, residents of the District of Columbia could not vote in presidential elections; the Twenty-Third Amendment to the Constitution gave them the right. Into the 1960s, most whites had only limited formal education; women and many minority groups faced legal, social, and other barriers or disincentives to voting; and there was nothing resembling today's steady stream of political news via multiple media outlets.

NOW

National laws extend voter eligibility to all persons age 18 or older (courtesy of the Twenty-sixth Amendment to the Constitution ratified in 1971). No state may restrict voting based on discriminatory tests, taxes, or residency requirements. In areas where many non-English speakers live, election authorities must supply ballots written in their own language. People in all 50 states can register to vote when applying for a driver's license, and most states now allow voters to vote by absentee ballot prior to election day even if they are not residing outside their home state. Many states also now permit people to register on the same day that they vote. Over the last half-century, formal education levels have risen among all groups, and news, information, and opinion about politics and government are just about everywhere one turns (or clicks).

And yet, between 1860 and 1900, the percentage of eligible voters participating in presidential elections ranged between 65 percent and 80 percent. By comparison, over the last several decades, the percentage of eligible voters participating in presidential elections has dipped as low as half. Over the same period, voter turnout in midterm national elections has averaged below 50 percent. In 2006, the Democrats took majority-control of the U.S. House of Representatives, and then in 2010, the Republicans won the House majority back from the Democrats; but in each of these two recent, power-shifting midterm national elections, about 80 million U.S. residents age 18 or older did not vote. Young voters, despite averaging more years of formal education, facing fewer legal barriers, and enjoying more access to information than any previous generation could have imagined, are nonetheless mostly nonvoters; for example, in the four midterm national elections since 1998, barely one in five 18- to 24 year-olds cast a ballot.

What explains nonvoting? Are voter turnout rates in America today really as bad as they seem, either in historical terms or relative to rates in other modern democracies; and what about other forms of political participation in America today?

A Close Look at Nonvoting

Start with the fact that there are at least two different ways to measure voter turnout, and they give different answers about the prevalence of nonvoting.[1] All U.S. residents age 18 or older constitute the **voting-age population (VAP)**. But many residents of the United States who are of voting age (18 or older) are not, in fact, eligible to vote. Two such groups are noncitizens who reside in America and convicted felons who in most states are disenfranchised by state laws. Unlike the VAP, the **voting-eligible population (VEP)** measure excludes from the calculation U.S. residents age 18 or older who are not legally permitted to cast a ballot. For example, in 2008 the VAP numbered nearly 231 million, but that included about 18 million noncitizens and disenfranchised convicted felons. So, for example, measured by the VAP, the national voter turnout rate was 53.6 percent in 2012, but measured by the VEP it was 58.2 percent; and since 1948, as the percentage of the population age 18 and older that consists of noncitizens and disenfranchised convicted felons has grown, the gap between the VAP and the VEP measures of voter turnout has grown (see Table 8.1).

Another important nuance about nonvoting concerns registered versus unregistered voters. Take a look at Table 8.2. Column A compares democratic nations in terms of the average percentage of their VAP that went to the polls in dozens of post-1945 national legislative (congressional or parliamentary) elections. The United States ranks dead last with 47.7 percent voter turnout.

Now, however, look at Column B. It compares the same nations in terms of percentage of **registered voters** (those eligible voters who have completed a registration form by a set date) who went to the polls in the same legislative elections. The United States still ranks low but looks somewhat better, with 66.5 percent registered voter turnout; and the registered voter turnout in post-1968 U.S. presidential elections is about 70 percent.

registered voters
People who are registered to vote.

Nonvoting rates vary by age largely because voter registration rates vary by age. For example, in midterm and presidential elections alike, Americans ages 18 to 20 register at much lower rates and also fail to vote at much higher rates than do Americans age 65 and older (see Table 8.3). Yet the same data tell us that, without regard to age, citizens who register are highly likely to vote: for example, in the 2010 midterm congressional election, about half of all younger voters, and about four-fifths of all voters age 65 and older, who were registered to vote did cast a ballot.

TABLE 8.1 **Two Methods of Calculating Turnout in Presidential Elections, 1948–2012**

Year	Voting-Age Population (VAP)	Voting-Eligible Population (VEP)
1948	51.1%	52.2%
1952	61.6	62.3
1956	59.3	60.2
1960	62.8	63.8
1964	61.9	62.8
1968	60.9	61.5
1972	55.2	56.2
1976	53.5	54.8
1980	52.8	54.7
1984	53.3	57.2
1988	50.3	54.2
1992	55.0	60.6
1996	48.9	52.6
2000	51.2	55.6
2004	55.0	60.0
2008	56.8	61.7
2012	53.6	58.2

Source: Updated from Michael P. McDonald and Samuel L. Popkin, "The Myth of the Vanishing Voter," *American Political Science Review* 95 (December 2001): table 1, 966. Michael P. McDonald, "2008 General Election Turnout Rates," updated April 26, 2009, at http://elections.gmu.edu, accessed May 8, 2009; *Michael P. McDonald, George Mason University, United States Elections Project, 2012 General Elections Turnout Rate, March 25, 2013.*

TABLE 8.2 **Two Ways of Calculating Voting Turnout, Here and Abroad**

A		B	
	Turnout as Percentage of Voting-Age Population		Turnout as Percentage of Registered Voters
Italy	92.0%	Australia	94.5%
New Zealand	86.0	Belgium	92.5
Belgium	84.8	Austria	83.1
Austria	84.4	New Zealand	90.8
Australia	84.2	Italy	89.8
Sweden	84.1	Netherlands	87.5
Netherlands	83.8	Sweden	87.1
Denmark	83.6	Denmark	85.9
Canada	82.6	Germany	85.4
Germany	80.2	Norway	80.4
Norway	79.2	United Kingdom	75.2
United Kingdom	73.8	Canada	73.9
France	67.3	France	73.8
Switzerland	51.9	**United States**	**66.5**
United States	**47.7**	Switzerland	56.5

Source: Rafael Lopez Pintor, Maria Gratschew, and Kate Sullivan, "Voter Turnout Rates from a Comparative Perspective," in Voter Turnout Since 1945: A Global Report (Stockholm, Sweden: International Institute for Democracy and Electoral Assistance, 2002).

TABLE 8.3 Voter Registration and Turnout by Age

Age	Percent Registered/Voted, Midterm Elections				
	1994	1998	2002	2006	2010
18–20	37/17	32/14	33/15	37/17	34/16
21–24	46/22	35/19	43/19	45/22	47/22
25–34	52/32	52/28	50/27	50/28	50/27
65+	76/61	75/60	76/61	75/61	73/59
Age	Percent Registered/Voted, Presidential Elections				
	1996	2000	2004	2008	
18–20	46/31	41/28	51/41	53/44	
21–24	51/33	49/35	52/43	62/52	
25–34	57/43	55/44	56/47	66/57	
65+	77/67	76/68	77/69	77/70	

Source: Adapted from U.S. Bureau of the Census, *Current Population Reports*, June 2008, Table 400, and *Statistical Abstract of the United States: 2012*, Table 399, p. 246.

Still, simply getting more people registered to vote is not a cure-all for nonvoting, for in each national election since 2006, about half of all nonvoters were registered. When registered nonvoters were asked why they did not vote, three answers were most common: about a quarter of registered nonvoters said they were too busy or had scheduling conflicts (work or school mostly); about 12 percent cited family chores or obligations; and another 12 percent believed their vote would make no difference.[2]

In response to the number one reason why registered voters fail to vote (school, work, or other scheduling conflicts), some have proposed making election day a national holiday or holding national elections on weekends. Such proposals, though popular, remain only proposals; but all states now give voters the option to vote prior to election day via mail-in ballots, and by 2012, 27 states afforded voters the option of "no-fault" absentee voting, meaning that voters can vote absentee without having to demonstrate they are residing outside their home state or giving any other explanation. So far as most researchers have been able to determine, and with a few dramatic exceptions (for example, Oregon's 1996 all-mail-in election for the U.S. Senate), there is no definitive evidence that either the greater flexibility and convenience of these voting procedures, or the proliferation of less restrictive registration procedures, has increased voter turnout.[3]

If voter turnout rates are to rise substantially in the United States, then nonregistered voters must become registered to vote in ever greater numbers. In addition to the roughly 40 million registered nonvoters, another 40 million or so voting-age citizens were not registered to vote in each of several recent national elections.

In most European nations, registration is done for you—automatically—by the government. By contrast, in America, the entire burden of registering to vote falls on the individual voters: they must learn how and when and where to register; they must take the time and trouble to go somewhere and fill out a registration form; and they must register if they happen to move. It takes more effort to register to vote in this country than it does to register in other democracies; it should not be surprising that fewer people are registered here than abroad.

But would making it less burdensome to register necessarily result in higher percentages of Americans becoming registered voters *and* voting? In 1993, Congress passed a law designed to make it easier to register to vote. Known as the motor-voter law, the law allows people in all 50 states to register to vote when applying for driver's licenses and to provide registration through the mail and at some state offices that serve the disabled or provide public assistance (such as checks for eligible low-income families).

As with early, mail-in and absentee balloting (see the **Constitutional Connections** feature on page 176), the evidence regarding the motor-voter law's impact on voter participation remains hard to interpret definitively. In 2001, eight years after the law was enacted, millions of citizens had registered to vote via state motor vehicles bureaus or other state offices, but a study found "that those who register when the process is costless are less likely to vote."[4] By 2010, motor-voter law-related means of registration were the single most widely used (see Figure 8.1). But between 1993 and 2010, while voter registration rates had increased somewhat over pre-1993 levels, there still was no solid evidence that the law had substantially increased voter turnout.

FIGURE 8.1 **Method of Registration to Vote, 2010 Percent Distribution of Registered Voters**

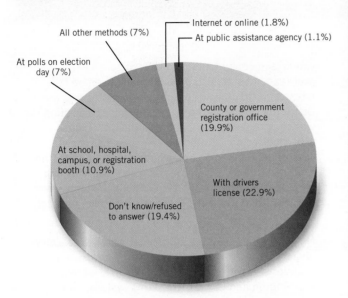

- Internet or online (1.8%)
- At public assistance agency (1.1%)
- All other methods (7%)
- At polls on election day (7%)
- County or government registration office (19.9%)
- At school, hospital, campus, or registration booth (10.9%)
- With drivers license (22.9%)
- Don't know/refused to answer (19.4%)

Source: U.S. Bureau of the Census, Current Population Survey, "Voting and Registration," November 2010.

Mounting a get-out-the-vote (GOTV) drive can make only a small difference depending on what tactic is used. In a 2008 study, political scientists Donald P. Green and Alan Gerber examined the findings from more than a hundred scientific studies of diverse GOTV tactics: door-to-door canvassing, leaflets, direct mail, email, phone calls, radio ads, television ads, and election-day festivals.[5] Door-to-door canvassing and phone calls were the only two tactics that demonstrated statistically significant results; but even most prospective voters touched by these tactics did not turn out. In a separate 2008 study, they found that "social pressure" exerted through mailings increased turnout, yet 62 percent of those pressured still did not vote.[6]

Of course, voting is only one way of participating in politics. It is important (we could hardly be considered a democracy if nobody voted), but it is not all-important. Joining civic associations, supporting social movements, writing to legislators, fighting city hall—all these and other activities are ways of participating in politics. It is possible that, by these measures, Americans participate in politics *more* than most Europeans—or anybody else, for that matter. Moreover, it is possible that low rates of registration indicate that people are reasonably well satisfied with how the country is governed. If 100 percent of all adult Americans registered and voted (especially under a system that makes registering relatively difficult), it could mean that people were deeply upset about how things were run. In short, it is not at all clear whether low voter turnout is a symptom of political disease or a sign of political good health.

HOW WE COMPARE

Laws on Voting

Ratified in 1971, the Twenty-sixth Amendment to the U.S. Constitution forbids states to deny "on account of age" the right to vote to citizens who are age 18 or older. But most states deny voting rights to voting-age citizens who have been convicted of felony crimes. Relevant state laws vary; for instance, Kentucky and Virginia have largely maintained laws that disenfranchise felons for life, while Maine and Vermont have permitted certain presently incarcerated felons to vote.

The legal voting age in almost all other nations is also 18. In about a dozen other countries, however, the legal voting age has been 16 (as in Brazil) or 17 (as in Indonesia); and in about twenty other nations the legal voting age is 19 (as in South Korea), 20 (as in Japan), or 21 (as in Lebanon).

Some democracies (for example, the United Kingdom) deny prisoners the right to vote, but it is far more common for democracies to permit all prisoners (save, in some nations, persons convicted of electoral fraud or related crimes) to vote. America is almost alone among democracies in the extent to which laws deny ex-prisoners the right to vote.

America is also in the international minority with respect to laws on voter registration. In most other nations it is legally compulsory for voters to register; a central, regional, or local government, or, most commonly, a specialized "Electoral Management Body," is expressly responsible for registering voters in national elections.

In America, voter registration is not legally required, and under a diverse array of state laws, individual voting-age citizens remain responsible for registering to vote.

Source: ACE Electoral Knowledge Network and United Nations Development Program, data on Voter Registration and Voting Age, http://www.aceproject.org, accessed May 2010; "Felony Disenfranchisement in the United States," The Sentencing Project, September 2008.

The important question about participation is not how much participation there is but how different kinds of participation affect the kind of government we get. This question cannot be answered just by looking at voter turnout, the subject of this chapter; it also requires us to look at the composition and activities of political parties, interest groups, and the media (the subjects of later chapters).

CONSTITUTIONAL CONNECTIONS

State Voting Laws and Procedures

"The Times, Places and Manner of holding Elections for Senators and Representatives, shall be prescribed in each State by the Legislature thereof..."

Thus begins Article I, Section 4, of the Constitution. As indicated in the nearby **How We Compare** feature, the United States is unique among modern democracies in the extent to which the laws and procedures under which its citizens vote vary according to where in the nation they reside. As discussed elsewhere in this chapter, the states are no longer free as they once were to decide who could vote for what office, but the shift to federal control has not eliminated differences in state voting laws and procedures. With few exceptions, the federal courts, including the U.S. Supreme Court, have let present-day differences in states' voting laws and procedures stand.

On the eve of the 2012 national election, in addition to the traditional Election Day trek to a polling place or "voting booth" in one's home voting district, there were three other ways for voting-age Americans to cast ballots.

- **Early Voting**: Thirty-two states and the District of Columbia permitted people to cast in-person ballots prior to Election Day, and without requiring that they furnish any excuse for doing so. The early voting periods ranged from the Friday before Election Day to 45 days before Election Day. The average early voting period was about 20 days.

- **Absentee Voting**: All states permitted absentee voting by mail for military personnel, their voting-age dependents, and U.S. citizens living overseas. All states also would mail absentee ballots to certain other voters; but in 27 states and the District of Columbia, no excuse for absentee voting was required, while in 21 other states, an excuse was required. In 7 states, certain citizens receive "permanent absentee ballot" privileges; in most, the citizens granted this status must give evidence of a chronic illness or disability; in Alaska, the status was also afforded to citizens that lived in remote parts of the state.

- **Mail Voting**: A ballot is automatically mailed to every eligible citizen, no request required. There are no traditional election day voting sites. Two states, Washington and Oregon, used this system.

It happens that the 15 states with the most restrictive voting laws and procedures—no early voting, and an excuse required for absentee voting—are all located in the eastern half of the country, with the highest concentration of them in the Northeast. Constitutionally, states have also been permitted to decide whether to deny voting rights to voting-age citizens who have been convicted of felony crimes. There continue to be wide state-by-state disparities in felon disenfranchisement laws and procedures. For instance, in 2012, a couple of states permitted convicted felons to vote; a dozen states permitted convicted felons on probation or parole, but not those in prison, to vote; and several states disenfranchised all convicted felons for life.

Nonetheless, voting is important. To understand why participation in American elections takes the form that it does, we must first understand how laws have determined who shall vote and under what circumstances.

The Rise of the American Electorate

It is ironic that relatively few citizens vote in American elections, since it was in this country that the mass of people first became eligible to vote. At the time the Constitution was ratified, the vote was limited to property owners or taxpayers, but by the administration of Andrew Jackson (1829–1837) it had been broadened to include virtually all white male adults. Only in a few states did property restrictions persist: they were not abolished in New Jersey until 1844 or in North Carolina until 1856. And, of course, African American males could not vote in many states, in the North as well as the South, even if they were not slaves. Women could not vote in most states until the 20th century; Chinese Americans were widely denied the vote; and being in prison is grounds for losing the franchise even today. Aliens, on the other hand, often were allowed to vote if they had at least begun the process of becoming citizens. By 1880, only an estimated 14 percent of all adult males in the United States could not vote; in England in the same period, about 40 percent of adult males were disfranchised.[7]

From State to Federal Control

Initially, it was left entirely to the states to decide who could vote and for what offices. The Constitution gave Congress the right to pick the day on which presidential electors would gather and to alter state regulations regarding congressional elections. The only provision of the Constitution requiring a popular election was the clause in Article I stating that members of the House of Representatives be chosen by the "people of the several states."

Because of this permissiveness, early federal elections varied greatly. Several states picked their members of the House at large (that is, statewide) rather than by district; others used districts but elected more than one representative from each. Some had their elections in odd-numbered years, and some even required that a congressional candidate win a majority, rather than simply a plurality, of votes to be elected (when that requirement was in effect, runoff elections—in one case, as many as 12—were necessary). Furthermore, presidential electors were at first picked by state legislatures rather than by the voters directly.

Congress, by law and constitutional amendment, has steadily reduced state prerogatives in these matters. In 1842, a federal law required that all members of the House be elected by districts; other laws over the years required that all federal elections be held in even-numbered years on the Tuesday following the first Monday in November.

The most important changes in elections have been those that extended the suffrage to women, African Americans, and 18-year-olds and made mandatory the direct popular election of U.S. senators. The Fifteenth Amendment, adopted in 1870, said that the "right of citizens of the United States to vote shall not be denied or abridged by the United States or by any state on account of race, color, or previous condition of servitude." Reading those words today, one would assume they gave African Americans the right to vote. That is not what the Supreme Court of the 1870s thought they meant. By a series of decisions, it held that the Fifteenth Amendment did not necessarily confer the right to vote on anybody; it merely asserted that if someone was denied that right, the denial could not be explicitly on the grounds of race. And the burden of proving that it was race that led to the denial fell on the black citizen who was turned away at the polls.[8]

This interpretation opened the door to three especially notorious but then-legal devices to keep blacks from voting. One was a **literacy test** (a large proportion of former slaves were illiterate); another was a requirement that a **poll tax** be paid (most former slaves were poor); and the third was the practice of keeping blacks from voting in primary elections (in the one-party South, the only meaningful election was the Democratic primary). To allow whites who were illiterate or poor to vote, a **grandfather clause** was added to the law, saying that a person could vote, even if he did not meet the legal requirements, if he or his ancestors voted before 1867 (blacks, of course, could not vote before 1867). When all else failed, blacks were

literacy test A requirement that citizens show that they can read before registering to vote.

poll tax A requirement that citizens pay a tax in order to register to vote.

grandfather clause A clause in registration laws allowing people who do not meet registration requirements to vote if they or their ancestors had voted before 1867.

WHITE SUPREMACY!

Attention, White Men!

Grand Torch-Light Procession

At JACKSON,

On the Night of the

Fourth of January, 1890.

The Final Settlement of Democratic Rule and White Supremacy in Mississippi.

GRAND PYROTECHNIC DISPLAY!
Transparencies and Torches Free for all.

All in Sympathy with the Grand Cause are Cordially and Earnestly Invited to be on hand, to aid in the Final Overthrow of Radical Rule in our State.

Come on foot or on horse-back; come any way, but be sure to get there.
Brass Bands, Cannon, Flambeau Torches, Transparencies, Sky-rockets, Etc.

A GRAND DISPLAY FOR A GRAND CAUSE.

After Reconstruction ended in 1876, black voting shrank under the attacks of white supremacists.

LANDMARK CASES

Right to Vote

Smith v. Allwright (1944): Because political parties select candidates for public office, they may not exclude blacks from voting in their primary elections.

white primary The practice of keeping blacks from voting in the southern states' primaries through arbitrary use of registration requirements and intimidation.

intimidated, threatened, or harassed if they showed up at the polls.

There began a long, slow legal process of challenging in court each of these restrictions in turn. One by one, the Supreme Court set most of them aside. The grandfather clause was declared unconstitutional in 1915,[9] and the **white primary** finally fell in 1944.[10] Some of the more blatantly discriminatory literacy tests also were overturned.[11] The practical result of these rulings was slight: only a small proportion of voting-age blacks were able to register and vote in the South, and they were found mostly in the larger cities. A dramatic change did not begin until 1965, with the passage of the Voting Rights Act. This act suspended the use of literacy tests and authorized the appointment of federal examiners who could order the registration of blacks in states and counties (mostly in the South) where fewer than 50 percent of the voting-age population were registered or had voted in the last presidential election. It also

provided criminal penalties for interfering with the right to vote.

Though implementation in some places was slow, the number of African Americans voting rose sharply throughout the South. For example, in Mississippi the proportion of voting-age blacks who registered rose from 5 percent to over 70 percent from 1960 to 1970. These changes had a profound effect on the behavior of many white southern politicians: Governor George Wallace stopped making pro-segregation speeches and began courting the black vote.

Women were kept from the polls by law more than by intimidation, and when the laws changed, women almost immediately began to vote in large numbers. By 1915, several states, mostly in the West, had begun to permit women to vote. But it was not until the Nineteenth Amendment to the Constitution was ratified in 1920, after a struggle lasting many decades, that women generally were allowed to vote. At one stroke, the size of the eligible voting population almost doubled. Contrary to the hopes of some and the fears of others, no dramatic changes occurred in the conduct of elections, the identity of the winners, or the substance of public policy. Initially, at least, women voted more or less in the same manner as men, though not quite as frequently.

The political impact of the youth vote was also less than expected. The Voting Rights Act of 1970 gave 18-year-olds the right to vote in federal elections beginning January 1, 1971. It also contained a provision lowering the voting age to 18 in state elections, but the Supreme Court declared this unconstitutional. As a result a constitutional amendment, the Twenty-sixth, was proposed by Congress and ratified by the states in 1971. The 1972 elections

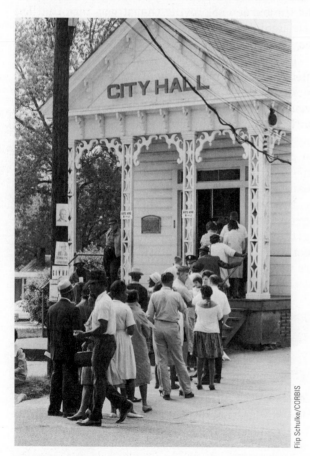

After the Civil Rights Act of 1964 was passed, blacks and whites voted together in a small Alabama town.

Flip Schulke/CORBIS

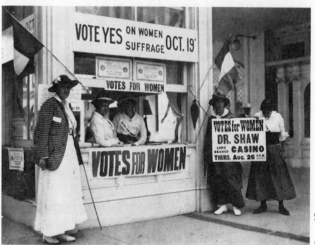

The campaign to win the vote for women nationwide succeeded with the adoption of the Nineteenth Amendment in 1920.

Library of Congress

became the first in which all people between the ages of 18 and 21 could cast ballots (before then, four states had allowed those under 21 to vote). About 25 million people suddenly became eligible to participate in elections, but their turnout (42 percent) was lower than for the population as a whole, and they did not flock to any particular party or candidate.

Every presidential election year since 1972 has been accompanied by predictions that the "youth vote" is likely to surge. Such predictions were especially prevalent in 2008. In 2008, 23 million citizens under age 30, representing 52 percent of the 18- to 29-year-old voting population, voted. That was a higher fraction than in 1996 (37 percent), 2000 (41 percent), and 2004 (48 percent), but lower than 1972 (55 percent) and the same as 1992 (52 percent). Moreover, in every presidential election from 1996 through 2004, the under-30 youth vote accounted for 17 percent of the total election-day electorate; in 2008 the fraction rose, but only to 18 percent.

Voter Turnout

The proportion of the voting-age population that has gone to the polls in presidential elections has remained about the same—between 50 and 63 percent of those eligible—at least since 1928, and appears today to be much smaller than it was in the latter part of the 19th century (see Figure 8.2). In every presidential election between 1860 and 1900, at least 70 percent of the eligible population apparently went to the polls, and in some years (1860 and 1876) almost 80 percent seem to have voted. Since 1900, in not a single presidential election has turnout reached 70 percent, and on two occasions (1920

and 1924), it did not even reach 50 percent.[12] Even outside the South, where efforts to disenfranchise African Americans make data on voter turnout especially hard to interpret, turnout seems to have declined: over 84 percent of the voting-age population participated in presidential elections in nonsouthern states between 1884 and 1900, but only 68 percent participated between 1936 and 1960, and even fewer have done so since 1960.[13]

Scholars have vigorously debated the meaning of these figures. One view is that this decline in turnout, even allowing for the shaky data on which the estimates are based, has been real and is the result of a decline of popular interest in elections and a weakening of the competitiveness of the two major parties. During the 19th century, according to this theory, the parties fought hard, worked strenuously to get as many voters as possible to the polls, afforded the mass of voters a chance to participate in party politics through caucuses and conventions, kept the legal barriers to participation (such as complex registration procedures) low, and looked forward to close, exciting elections. After 1896, by which time the South had become a one-party Democratic region and the North heavily Republican, both parties became more conservative, national elections usually resulted in lopsided victories for the Republicans, and citizens began to lose interest in politics because it no longer seemed relevant to their needs. The parties ceased functioning as organizations to mobilize the mass of voters and fell under the control of leaders, mostly conservative, who resisted mass participation.[14]

There is another view, however. It argues that the decline in voter turnout has been more apparent

FIGURE 8.2 **Voter Participation in Presidential Elections, 1860–2012**

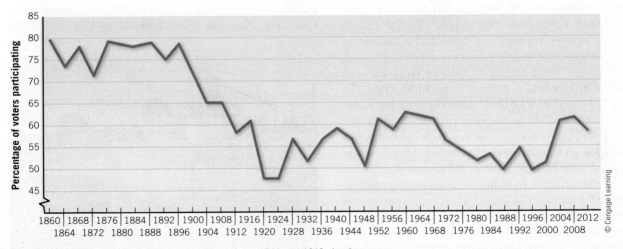

Note: Several southern states did not participate in the 1864 and 1868 elections.

Sources: For 1860–1928: Bureau of the Census, *Historical Statistics of the United States, Colonial Times to 1970*, part 2, p. 1071; 1932–1944: *Statistical Abstract of the United States*, 1992, p. 517; 1948–2000: Michael P. McDonald and Samuel L. Popkin, "The Myth of the Vanishing Voter," *American Political Science Review 95* (December 2001): table 1, p. 966; 2004–2012 elections, American National Election Studies (ANES).

Australian ballot A government-printed ballot of uniform dimensions to be cast in secret that many states adopted around 1890 to reduce voting fraud associated with party-printed ballots cast in public.

than real. Though elections were certainly more of a popular sport in the 19th century than they are today, the parties were no more democratic then than now, and voters then may have been more easily manipulated. Until around the beginning of the 20th century, voting fraud was commonplace, because it was easy to pull off. The political parties, not the government, printed the ballots; they often were cast in public, not private, voting booths; there were few serious efforts to decide who was eligible to vote, and the rules that did operate were easily evaded.

Under these circumstances, it was easy for a person to vote more than once, and the party machines made heavy use of these "floaters," or repeaters. "Vote early and often" was not a joke; it was a fact. The parties often controlled the counting of votes, padding the totals whenever they feared losing. As a result of these machinations, often the number of votes counted was larger than the number cast, and often the number cast was in turn larger than the number of individuals eligible to vote.

Around 1890, the states began adopting the **Australian ballot**. This was a government-printed ballot of uniform size and shape that was cast in secret, created to replace the old party-printed ballots cast in public. By 1910, only three states were without the Australian ballot. Its use cut back on (but certainly did not eliminate) vote buying and fraudulent vote counts.

In short, if votes had been legally cast and honestly counted in the 19th century, the statistics on election turnout might well be much lower than the inflated figures we now have.[15] To the extent that this is true, we may not have had a decline in voter participation as great as some have suggested. Nevertheless, most scholars believe that turnout probably did actually decline somewhat after the 1890s. One reason was that voter registration regulations became more burdensome: there were longer residency requirements; aliens who had begun but not completed the process of becoming citizens could no longer vote in most states; it became harder for African Americans to vote; educational qualifications for voting were adopted by several states; and voters had to register long in advance of the elections. These changes, designed to purify the electoral process, were aspects of the progressive reform impulse (described in Chapter 9) and served to cut back on the number of people who could participate in elections.

Strict voter registration procedures tended, like most reforms in American politics, to have unintended as well as intended consequences. These changes not only reduced fraudulent voting but also reduced voting generally, because they made it more difficult for certain groups of perfectly honest voters—those with little education, for example, or those who had recently moved—to register and vote. This was not the first time, and it will not be the last, that a reform designed to cure one problem created another.

Following the controversy over Florida's vote count in the 2000 presidential election, many proposals were made to overhaul the nation's voting system. In 2002, Congress passed a measure that for the first time requires each state to have in place a system for counting the disputed ballots of voters whose names were left off official registration lists. In addition, the law provides federal funds for upgrading voting equipment and procedures and for training election officials. But it stops short of creating a uniform national voting system. Paper ballots, lever machines, and punch-card voting systems will still be used in some places, while optical scan and direct recording electronic equipment will be used in others. Following the 2004 national elections, however, calls to overhaul the nation's voting system were more muted, partly because the popular vote for president was not terribly close (President Bush received 51 percent, John Kerry received 48 percent), and partly because in most states there were few reported problems.

Even after all the legal changes are taken into account, there seems to have been a decline in citizen participation in elections. Between 1960 and 1980, the proportion of voting-age people casting a ballot in presidential elections fell by about 10 percentage points, a drop that cannot be explained by how ballots were printed or how registration rules were rewritten. Nor can these factors explain why 1996

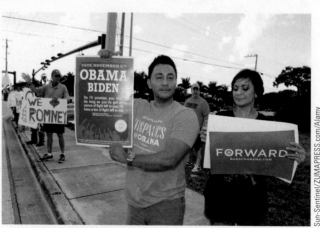

People show their support for the major-party presidential candidates in 2012.

WHAT'S YOUR ISSUE?

Compulsory Voting

Even though the latest and best scholarship suggests that election outcomes would change hardly at all if all eligible citizens voted, most Americans and most scholars of the subject believe that getting more citizens to vote is intrinsically worthwhile, expresses a sense of "civic duty," and has positive civic and social consequences that go well beyond what happens or who wins on election days. But, as discussed elsewhere in this chapter, efforts to make voting easier by making it easier to register and by affording citizens multiple ways and extended periods in which to cast ballots have not significantly increased voter turnout (not yet anyway). And while various "get out the vote" tactics have shown promise, none has yet demonstrated dramatic results, and among the most effective such tactics are ones that involve "social pressure."

Martin Wattenberg, a long-time scholar of voting behavior, argues that it is time to consider making voting compulsory. In *Is Voting for Young People?* (2012), he analyzes the data on how adult Americans under age 30 participate in politics, including how much attention they pay to political news, how much they engage in civic activities beyond volunteering or community service, and the rates at which they vote. To increase youth voting as well as overall voter turnout rates, he recommends that America follow the lead of several dozen other democracies and make voting compulsory.

Compulsory voting systems make it illegal not to vote in some or all elections. In these systems, nonvoters are fined or lose access to certain tax-funded social services. William Galston, a much-respected political scientist and former White House official, has also advocated compulsory voting, arguing that the system would serve "to even out disparities stemming from income, education and age," and enhance our democratic "system's inclusiveness." However, few other scholars favor the idea and polls stretching from the 1960s to the 2000s indicate that about 70 percent of Americans would oppose compulsory voting. What's your take? Given that jury duty is compulsory and you can be fined for overtime or illegal parking, what arguments favor the freedom to stay home on election days or to not bother casting an early, absentee, or mail-in ballot? Would you consider making voting compulsory for some elections (say, national elections) but not others? Do you think that making voting compulsory might backfire, and, if so, how? And, as an alternative to compulsory voting, what about a law that gives everyone the day off from work—and from high schools and colleges!—on election days?

Sources: Martin Wattenberg, *Is Voting for Yong People?*, 3ʳᵈ ed. (New York: Pearson, 2012); William Galston, "Telling Americans to Vote, or Else," *The New York Times*, November 6, 2011; and ABC News, "Poll: Americans Oppose Compulsory Voting," June 11, 2004.

witnessed not only the lowest level of turnout (49 percent) in a presidential election since 1924 but also the single steepest four-year decline (from 55 percent in 1992) since 1920.

Actual trends in turnout aside, what if they gave an election and everyone came? Would universal turnout change national election outcomes and the content of public policy? It has long been argued that because the poor, less educated, and minorities are overrepresented among nonvoters, universal turnout would strongly benefit Democratic candidates and liberal causes. But careful studies of this question have found that the "party of nonvoters" largely mirrors the demographically diverse and ideologically divided population that goes to the polls, and that "while nonvoters are more liberal and more Democratic than voters, the difference is so small that it would hardly change election outcomes if every American citizen voted.".[16]

Who Participates in Politics?

To understand better why voter turnout declined and what, if anything, that decline may mean, we must first look at who participates in politics.

Forms of Participation

Voting is by far the most common form of political participation, while giving money to a candidate and being a member of a political organization are the least common. Many Americans exaggerate how frequently they vote or how active they are in politics. In a study by Sidney Verba and Norman Nie, 72 percent of those interviewed said they voted "regularly" in presidential elections.[17] Yet we know that since 1960, on average under 60 percent of the voting-age population has actually cast presidential ballots. Obviously, many people claim to have voted when in fact they have not. If people misreport their voting behavior, it is likely *activists* People who tend to participate in all forms of politics

that they also misreport—that is, exaggerate—the extent to which they participate in other ways.

Indeed, most research shows that "politics is not at the heart of the day-to-day life of the American people."[18] Work, family, church, and other voluntary activities come first, both in terms of how Americans spend their time and in terms of the money they donate. For example, a study by Verba and others found that a higher proportion of citizens take part in nonpolitical than political activities: "More citizens reported giving time to church-related or charitable activities than indicated contacting a government official or working informally on a community problem, two of the most frequent forms of political participation beyond the vote."[19]

In an earlier study, Verba and Nie analyzed the ways in which people participate in politics and came up with six forms of participation that are characteristic of six different kinds of U.S. citizens. About one-fifth (22 percent) of the population is completely inactive: they rarely vote, they do not get involved in organizations, and they probably do not even talk about politics very much. These inactives typically have little education and low incomes and are relatively young. Many of them are African American. At the opposite extreme are the complete **activists,** constituting about one-ninth of the population (11 percent). These people are highly educated, have high incomes, and tend to be middle-aged rather than young or old. They tend to participate in all forms of politics.

Between these extremes are four categories of limited forms of participation. The *voting specialists* are people who vote but do little else; they tend not to have much schooling or income and to be substantially older than the average person. *Campaigners* not only vote but also like to get involved in campaign activities. They are better educated than the average voter, but what seems to distinguish them most is their interest in the conflicts, passions, and struggle of politics; their clear identification with a political party; and their willingness to take strong positions. *Communalists* are much like campaigners in social background but have a very different temperament: they do not like the conflict and tension of partisan campaigns. They tend to reserve their energy for community activities of a more nonpartisan nature—forming and joining organizations to deal with local problems and contacting local officials about these problems. Finally, there are some *parochial participants*, who do not vote and stay out of election

After Hurricane Sandy in 2012, volunteers help to rebuild homes destroyed in Far Rockaway, New York.

campaigns and civic associations but are willing to contact local officials about specific, often personal, problems.[20]

Participation: Causes and Meaning

Whether participation takes the form of voting or being a complete activist, it is higher among people who have gone to college than it is among those who have not, higher among people who are employed than among the unemployed, and higher among whites and blacks than among Hispanics. The differences in voting rates for these groups are shown in Figure 8.3.

It is, however, far easier to describe differences in voting rates by schooling, employment status, race, and other characteristics than it is to explain them. Not long ago, political scientists thought they had a pretty firm handle on how education, occupation, race, gender, religion, political ideology, and other factors mattered to who votes.

For instance, a rich, older, professional woman with a graduate degree who strongly identifies as liberal or conservative and has strong partisan attachments is far more likely to vote than a poor, young, unemployed male who dropped out of high school and has no interest in politics. And, other things being equal, the more schooling one has—independent of age, occupation, race, or income—the more likely one is to vote.

All true, but the more sophisticated research into voting behavior has become—and the more that this research has attempted to explain not just intergroup differences but intragroup differences in voting behavior (some rich, old, politically engaged professional women don't vote; some poor, young, politically disaffected men do vote)—the less confidence we can retain in broad generalizations about the causes of participation.

FIGURE 8.3 Voter Turnout in Presidential Elections, by Schooling, Employment, and Race, 1996–2008

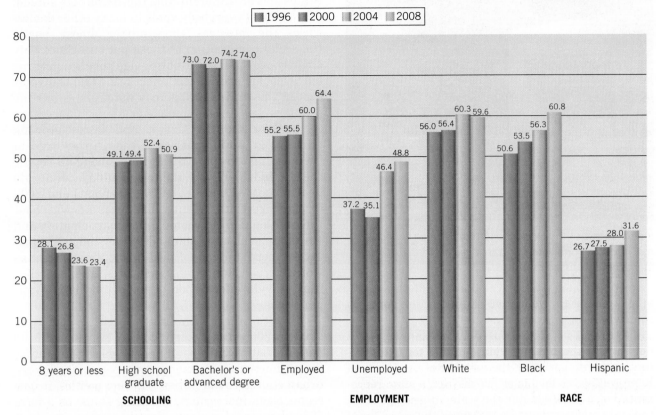

Source: Adapted from U.S. Bureau of the Census, *Current Population Reports*, June and November 2008.

One interesting explanation is religion. By at least some measures, religion does seem to boost participation in politics and in civic life more generally. Even with all the latest and best data at our disposal, however, it is wise to generalize with care: "religion increases participation" would be too sweeping, but "certain types of religious expression increase participation under some conditions" is about right.

The same caution applies when it comes to interpreting the meaning of participation. Although Americans are going to the polls less than earlier generations did, they are campaigning, contacting government officials, and (here the evidence is clearest, especially for younger Americans) volunteering and working on community issues no less and perhaps even more. And while the proportion of the population that votes is lower in the United States than in many other democracies, the percentage of Americans who engage in one or more political activities beyond voting is higher (see Table 8.4).

Although we vote at lower rates in the United States than people do abroad, the meaning of our voting is different. For one thing, we elect far more public officials than the citizens of any other nation do. There are more than a half million elective offices in the United States, and just about every

TABLE 8.4 Political Participation Here and Abroad

Percent of People Who ...	USA	Rank among 20 Democracies	Outranked by ...
Tried to persuade others to vote for a candidate	44%	2nd	Canada
Supported party by attending meeting, putting up poster	30%	2nd	Canada
Donated money to political group	21%	1st	None
Were contacted by party or candidate	47%	3rd	Canada, Ireland

Source: Professor Martin Wattenberg, University of California, Irvine, using data from the *Comparative Study of Electoral Systems*.

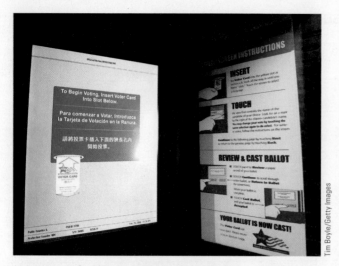

Tim Boyle/Getty Images

Instructions for the new electronic touch-screen voting machine for Illinois voters are displayed at the Cook County Clerk's office in Chicago, Illinois.

other week of the year there is an election going on somewhere in this country.

A citizen of Massachusetts, for example, votes not only for the U.S. president but also for two senators, the state governor, the member of the House of Representatives for his or her district, a state representative, a state senator, the state attorney general, the state auditor, the state treasurer, the secretary of state, a county commissioner, a sheriff, and clerks of various courts, as well as (in the cities) for the mayor, the city councilor, and school committee members and (in towns) for selectmen, town-meeting members, a town moderator, library trustees, health board members, assessors, water commissioners, the town clerk, housing authority members, the tree warden, and the commissioner of the public burial ground. (There are probably others whom we have forgotten.)

In many European nations, by contrast, the voters get to make just one choice once every four or five years: they can vote for or against a member of parliament. When there is only one election for one office every several years, that election is bound to assume more importance to voters than many elections for scores of offices. But one election for one office probably has less effect on how the nation is governed than many elections for thousands of offices. Americans may not vote at high rates, but voting affects a far greater part of the political system here than abroad.

The kinds of people who vote in the United States also are different from those who vote abroad. Since almost everybody votes in many other democracies, the votes cast there mirror almost exactly the social composition of those nations. Since only slightly over half of the voting-age population turns out even for presidential elections here, the votes cast in the United States may not truly reflect the country.

Latinos are the largest and fastest-growing minority group in America. Although they remain the most underrepresented group among all voters, the Latino share of the election-day electorate nearly doubled between 1996 (5 percent) and 2008 (9 percent). Until recently, little was known about the relationship between political participation and variables such as command of the language and involvement in nonpolitical institutions such as workplaces, voluntary associations, and churches that provide information or impart skills relevant to politics.

But together with other recent research, a detailed 2008 study examined how ever more of the nation's Latino citizens are participating in politics in conjunction with their participation in diverse urban church communities.[21] Latino politics, it now seems clear, increasingly is taking shape as a form of hyphenated-American identity politics in which many Latino voters, including the young and the poor, not only gain information and hone politically relevant skills via church membership but also attach quasi-religious meaning to many forms of civic engagement.

The popular view that Americans don't vote as a result of apathy is not quite right. It is nearer to the truth to say that we don't all register to vote and don't always vote even when registered. There are many factors having nothing to do with apathy that shape our participation rates—age, race, party organization, the barriers to registration, and popular views about the significance of elections.

Compared to other nations, Americans vote at lower rates but more frequently and for many more offices, so elections make a bigger difference in the conduct of public affairs here than abroad. We also engage somewhat more frequently than people abroad in various nonelectoral forms of participation.

WHAT WOULD YOU DO?

MEMORANDUM

To: *Senator Henry Gilbert*

From: *Peter Clark, legislative analyst*

Subject: *Voting reform legislation*

In the 2000s, barely half of the electorate voted for president, and only a third or so cast ballots for congressional elections. In a few recent presidential primaries and statewide special elections, turnout has run 10 percent or below. Studies show that often citizens miss the opportunity to vote because of complications with work or child care. To address this problem, legislators from both parties support celebrating Veterans Day on election day, which would create a national holiday for voting. Eligible voters who do not go to the polls would be fined.

Arguments for:

1. This proposal honors veterans by recognizing their service with the fundamental requirement of representative democracy, rule by the people through voting.

2. A voting holiday ensures that people who cannot take off time from work or other responsibilities to vote have the opportunity to exercise their democratic right.

3. Imposing a fine for nonvoting sends a moral message that voting is a civic duty in a democracy. More citizens will feel morally obliged to vote if all citizens are legally obliged to do so.

Arguments against:

1. Just as veterans volunteer their service, so, too, should citizens volunteer to exercise their democratic responsibilities.

News »

Congress Considers Voting Holiday to Honor Veterans and Nonvoting Fines to Increase Turnout

With bipartisan concern about maximizing voter turnout for the upcoming presidential election, both the House and the Senate are considering bills to combine Veterans Day with election day and/or impose fines on nonvoters. Members of Congress declare that increasing turnout is vital to the continued health of American democracy.

2. Voting is a right, but citizens have a civic duty to exercise that right, and the government should not, in effect, exercise that duty on their behalf. Moreover, people can vote by absentee ballot at their convenience.

3. Compulsory voting does not guarantee informed voting. It is both unwise and undemocratic to legally oblige people to vote.

Your decision:

Vote for bill _____   Vote against bill _____

LEARNING OBJECTIVES

1. What is "political participation"?

Political participation refers to the many different ways that people take part in politics and government. Voting is one of the most common and widely studied forms of political participation.

2. How are voter turnout rates measured?

There are at least two ways to measure voter turnout, by voting-age population (all residents age 18 and older) and voting-eligible population (all residents age 18 and older excluding noncitizens, disenfranchised convicted felons, and others who are not eligible to vote); voter turnout rates are higher when measured according to the voter-eligible population.

3. How, and how much, do most citizens participate?

Most citizens vote at least on occasion in national elections and engage in one or more other forms of political participation, but maybe only one citizen in ten both votes regularly and participates regularly and in many different ways in politics and government.

4. Who votes, who doesn't?

The most powerful determinants of voting are age (older people vote more than younger people) and education (college graduates vote more than high school graduates).

5. Why do some people participate in politics at higher rates than others?

Older people and college graduates have learned to have a greater interest in politics, in part because they see ways in which government policies will affect them, and in part because they may have acquired a political ideology that makes politics intrinsically interesting. As we have seen, Americans vote less than people in most other democratic nations. That gap is in part the result of the failure of many Americans to register to vote; efforts to increase registration, such as the motor-voter law, have gotten more names onto the voting rolls, but often these new additions do not vote as frequently as other registered voters. Most states now permit people to vote early, absentee, and by mail; but neither these measures, nor various "get out the vote" tactics, have yet been shown to increase voter turnout in ways that result in most eligible citizens voting in most elections.

6. How did the Framers of the Constitution think average citizens should participate in America's representative democracy?

The Framers believed citizens should play an important but not the decisive role in the American Republic. They elect the House, but until the Constitution was amended in 1913, they did not elect the Senate; the president and senators, not ordinary people, select federal judges; and the president is chosen by electors. Over time, the system has become much more responsive to public opinion. Voters now help pick party candidates through party primaries, and their views are regularly solicited by opinion polls.

7. Should today's college-age citizens participate more in politics?

We would say yes, but the fact is that many young adults seem less disposed to traditional forms of political activity, including voting, than they are toward other types of civic engagement, such as community service or volunteer work. One forecast to ponder: unless youth voting rates increase relative to those of senior citizens, then, on Election Day 2020, persons 65 and older (about 22 percent of the general population) will cast a quarter of all ballots, while persons 18 to 29 (about 21 percent of the general population) will account for less than an eighth of the voting electorate.

TO LEARN MORE

Information for voters:

Congress.org: **www.congress.org**

League of Women Voters: **www.lwv.org/**

Voter Information Services: **www.vis.org/**

Voting Guide: **www.vote411.org/**

National Mail Voter Registration Form: **www.fec.gov/votregis/vr.shtml**

Voter turnout statistics: **www.census.gov/compendia/statab/cats/elections/voting-age_population_and_voter_participation.html**

Burnham, Walter Dean. *Critical Elections and the Mainsprings of American Politics*. New York: Norton, 1970. A classic argument about the decline of voter participation, linking it to changes in the economic system.

Eisner, Jane. *Taking Back the Vote: Getting American Youth Involved in Our Democracy*. Boston: Beacon Press, 2004. Highly readable account of why millennium-generation college-age Americans volunteer lots but vote little, with recommendations for getting young people more interested in politics.

Green, Donald P., and Alan S. Gerber. *Get Out the Vote!: How to Increase Voter Turnout*. Washington, D.C. : Brookings Institution Press, 2nd edition, 2008. Excellent review of the evidence on what works—and what doesn't—to get more people to the polls.

Niemi, Richard, Herbert F. Weisberg, and David C. Kimball, eds. *Controversies in Voting Behavior*, 5th edition. Washington, D.C. : Congressional Quarterly Press, 2010. Essays on voting and related topics that summarize the most advanced empirical research and offer competing perspectives on what the data show.

Sniderman, Paul M., and Benjamin Highton, eds. *Facing the Challenge of Democracy: Explorations in the Analysis of Public Opinion and Political Participation*. Princeton, NJ: Princeton University Press, 2011. Essays on political participation and related topics that highlight new and unresolved research questions and, in many cases, update classic studies.

Verba, Sidney, Norman H. Nie, and Jae-on Kim. *Participation and Political Equality*. Cambridge: Cambridge University Press, 1978. Classic comparative study of political participation in seven nations.

Wattenberg, Martin P. *Is Voting for Young People?* New York: Pearson, 3rd edition, 2012. An account of why youth voter turnout in America has been so low and a case for compulsory voting.

Wilson, Catherine E. *The Politics of Latino Faith: Religion, Identity, and Urban Community*. New York: New York University Press, 2008. Richly detailed study of how Latino religious life intersects with politics in three cities.

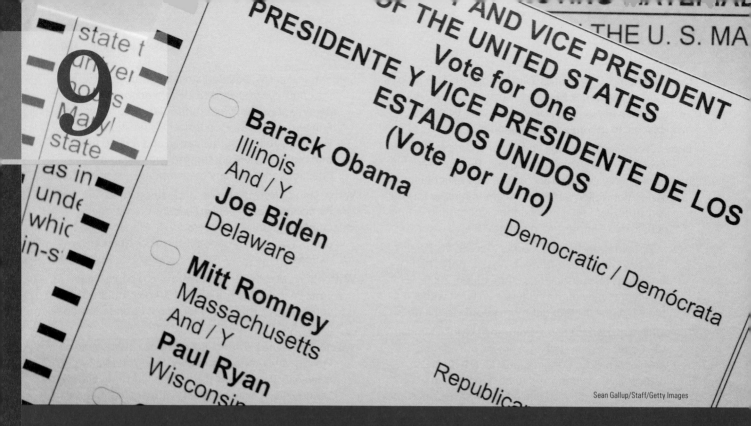

Sean Gallup/Staff/Getty Images

Political Parties

LEARNING OBJECTIVES

1. What is a political party, and why were the Framers of the Constitution concerned about the influence of political parties?

2. Why does the United States have a two-party system?

3. What are the prospects for a viable third party in the United States?

4. How has America's two-party system changed, and how does it differ from the party systems of other representative democracies?

5. How much do parties affect how Americans vote?

6. Did the Founding Fathers think political parties were a good idea?

7. How, if at all, should America's two-party system be reformed?

From 2006 through 2008, Democratic Party leaders had reason to smile. They won control of the House and the Senate in 2006, and then they achieved a unified government after Barack Obama won the 2008 presidential election. But in 2010, the Democrats lost a seat (and their filibuster-proof majority, which we will discuss in Chapter 13) in the Senate, after the Republican Party's upset victory in a special election in Massachusetts for the late Senator Ted Kennedy's seat. The Republican Party went on to regain control of the U.S. House of Representatives in the 2010 midterm elections, gaining more than 60 seats, and further reducing the Democratic majority in the Senate as well. Then, however, in 2012, President Obama won reelection, Republicans maintained control of the House, and Democrats kept control in the Senate.

What does the split in party control tell us about voter loyalties? Very little, actually. Party loyalty of voters remains about what it has been for many decades. For instance, at the time of the 2012 national elections, Gallup polls found that about 30 percent of voters self-identified as Republicans, a third as Independents, and 35 percent as Democrats; at the same time, 42 percent of voters self-identified as "Republican" or "lean Republican" while 45 percent chose "Democrat" or "lean Democrat." Even with occasional upticks in Independent self-identification (for example, as high as 40 percent in mid-2013), over the last many years the party affiliation numbers have changed relatively little. The central fact is that party attachment explains much but far from all of any election's results. Political parties must cope with economic conditions, personal popularity, crises in foreign policy, and various social issues. The attachment of voters to parties is weaker today than it was a century ago, but the very existence and endurance of political parties in the United States is significant, given how the Framers of the Constitution opposed them.

The Founders disliked parties, thinking of them as "factions" motivated by ambition and self-interest. George Washington, dismayed by the quarreling between Alexander Hamilton and Thomas Jefferson in his cabinet, devoted much of his Farewell Address to condemning parties. This hostility toward parties was understandable: the legitimacy and success of the newly created federal government were still very much in doubt. When Jefferson organized his followers to oppose Hamilton's policies, it seemed to Hamilton and *his* followers that Jefferson was opposing not just a policy or a leader but also the very concept of a national government. Jefferson, for his part, thought

Hamilton was not simply pursuing bad policies but was subverting the Constitution itself. Before political parties could become legitimate, it was necessary for people to separate in their minds quarrels over policies and elections from disputes over the legitimacy of the new government itself. The ability to make that distinction was slow in coming; thus, parties were objects of profound suspicion, at first defended only as temporary expedients.

> **political party** A group that seeks to elect candidates to public office.

American political parties are the oldest in the world, dating back to the first decade of the republic. They may be in decline, but they are not dead or dying. New parties (like the Green Party launched in 2000 by consumer advocate Ralph Nader, or the Tea Party movement that developed after the 2008 presidential election) may come and go, but two parties, the Democratic and Republican, still dominate the country's campaigns and elections. Nor have party leaders been wholly replaced by media consultants, pollsters, or others whose profession is raising money or devising strategies for whichever candidates bid highest for their services. What distinguishes political parties from other groups, and why are they a fundamental feature of American politics?

Parties—Here and Abroad

A **political party** is a group that seeks to elect candidates to public office by supplying them with a label—a "party identification"—by which they are known to the electorate.[1] This definition is purposefully broad so that it will include both familiar parties (Democratic, Republican) and unfamiliar ones (Whig, Libertarian, Socialist Workers) and will cover periods in which a party is very strong (having an elaborate and well-disciplined organization that provides money and workers to its candidates) as well as periods in which it is quite weak (supplying nothing but the label to candidates). The label by which a candidate is known may or may not actually be printed on the ballot opposite the candidate's name: in the United States, it does appear on the ballot in all national elections but in only a minority of municipal ones; in Australia and Israel (and in the United Kingdom before 1969), it never appears on the ballot at all.

America's political parties do not matter as much, or in the same ways, as they once did. For instance, one reason voter turnout is higher abroad than in this country is that political parties in other democratic nations are more effective at mobilizing voters. The sense of belonging to a party and the inclination to vote the party ticket are greater in France, Italy, and Sweden than in the United States.

It was not always thus. At one time, being a Democrat or a Republican was a serious commitment that people did not make lightly or abandon easily. In those days, it would have been hard to find anything in Europe that could match the vote-getting power of such party organizations as those in Chicago, New York, and Philadelphia.

Parties in the United States are relatively weak today mainly because the laws and rules under which they operate have taken away much of their power at the same time that many voters have lost their sense of commitment to party identification. This weakening has proceeded unevenly, however, because our constitutional system has produced a decentralized party system just as it has produced a decentralized governmental system, with the result that parties are strong in some places and almost nonexistent in other places.

There are three political arenas in which parties may be found and in which changes in their strength may be assessed. A party exists as a *label* in the minds of the voters, as an *organization* that recruits and campaigns for candidates, and as a *set of leaders* who try to organize and control the legislative and executive branches of government. A powerful party is one whose label has a strong appeal for voters, whose organization can decide who will be candidates and how their campaigns will be managed, and whose leaders can dominate one or all branches of government.

American parties have become weaker in all three arenas. As a *label* with which voters identify, the parties probably are much weaker than they were in the 19th century but only somewhat weaker than they were several decades ago (see Figure 9.1). In 1952, a total of 36 percent of the electorate identified strongly as Democrats (22 percent) or Republicans (14 percent), while a total of 23 percent of the electorate identified as independents. By 2012, total strong party identifiers had dropped to 34 percent of the electorate, while all independents had risen to 38 percent of the electorate. But the best evidence of weakening party identification is what voters *do*. As we shall see in the next chapter, in some elections many people vote split tickets—supporting a president from one party and members of Congress from the other.

As a *set of leaders* who organize government, especially Congress, political parties remain somewhat strong in ways that will be described in Chapter 13. As *organizations* that nominate and elect candidates, parties have become dramatically weaker since the 1960s. In most states, parties have very little control over who gets nominated to office. The causes and consequences of that change are the subject of this chapter.

In Europe, things are very different. Almost the only way a person can become a candidate for elective office is to be nominated by party leaders. Campaigns are run by the party, using party funds and workers, not by the candidate. Once in office, the elected officials are expected to vote and act together with other members of their party.

The principal criterion by which voters choose among candidates is their party identification or label. This has been changing somewhat of late:

FIGURE 9.1 Decline in Party Identification, 1952–2012

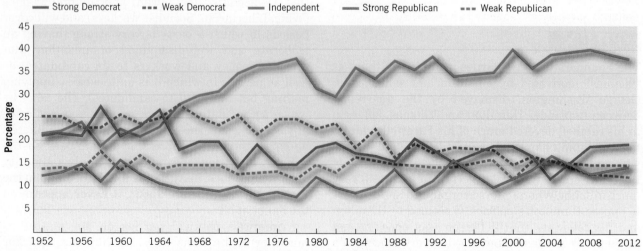

Source: American National Election Studies, Table 2A.1, "Party Identification, 1952–2012."

European parties, like American ones, have not been able to count as heavily as in the past on party loyalty among the voters.

Several factors explain the striking differences between American and European political parties. First, the federal system of government in the United States decentralizes political authority and thus decentralizes political party organizations. For nearly two centuries, most of the important governmental decisions were made at the state and local levels—decisions regarding education, land use, business regulation, and public welfare—and thus it was at the state and local levels that the important struggles over power and policy occurred. Moreover, most people with political jobs—either elective or appointive—worked for state and local government, and thus a party's interest in obtaining these jobs for its followers meant it had to focus attention on who controlled city hall, the county courthouse, and the state capitol. Federalism, in short, meant political parties would acquire jobs and money from local sources and fight local contests. This, in turn, meant the national political parties would be coalitions of local parties, and though these coalitions would have a keen interest in capturing the presidency (with it, after all, went control of large numbers of federal jobs), the national party leaders rarely had as much power as the local ones. The Republican leader of Cuyahoga County, Ohio, for example, could often ignore the decisions of the Republican national chair and even the Ohio state chair.

Political authority in the United States has recently become far more centralized: the federal government now makes decisions affecting almost all aspects of our lives, including those—such as schooling and welfare—once left entirely in local hands. Yet the political parties have not become more centralized as a result. If anything, they have become even weaker and more decentralized. One reason for this apparent paradox is that in the United States, unlike in most other democratic nations, political parties are closely regulated by state and federal laws, and these regulations have weakened the power of parties substantially. Perhaps the most important of these regulations are those that prescribe how a party's candidates are selected.

In the great majority of American states, the party leaders do not select people to run for office; by law, those people are chosen by the voters in primary elections. Though sometimes the party can influence who will win a primary contest, in general people running for state or national office in this country owe little to party leaders. In Europe, by contrast, there is no such thing as a primary election—the only way to become a candidate for office is to persuade party leaders to put your name on the ballot. In a later section of this chapter, the impact of the

Ten political parties competed in the French presidential elections in 2012.

direct primary will be discussed in more detail; for now, it is enough to note that its use removes from the hands of the party leadership its most important source of power over officeholders.

Furthermore, if an American political party wins control of Congress, it does not—as in most European nations with a parliamentary system of government—also win the right to select the chief executive of the government. The American president, as we have seen, is independently elected, and

HOW WE COMPARE

How Many Political Parties?

The United States has two political parties in Congress. Other countries have fewer or more parties in their national legislatures:

China 1

Canada 5

United Kingdom 8

Germany 6

Mexico 7

Russia 4

Israel 17

France 14

Brazil 22 (more or less)

India 43 (more or less)

Source: *Congressional Quarterly.* "Political Parties and Groups." *Political Handbook of the World*. Last Modified 2012. Accessed May 31, 2013.

this means that the president will choose his or her principal subordinates not from among members of Congress but from among persons out of Congress. Should the president pick a representative or senator for his or her cabinet, the Constitution requires that person to resign from Congress in order to accept the job. Thus, an opportunity to be a cabinet secretary is not an important reward for members of Congress, and so the president cannot use the prospect of that reward as a way of controlling congressional action. All this weakens the significance and power of parties in terms of organizing the government and conducting its business.

The Rise and Decline of the Political Party

Our nation began without parties, and today's parties, though far from extinct, are about as weak as at any time in our history. In between the Founding and the present, however, parties arose and became powerful. We can see this process in four broad periods of party history: when political parties were created (roughly from the Founding to the 1820s); when the more or less stable two-party system emerged (roughly from the time of President Jackson to the Civil War); when parties developed a comprehensive organizational form and appeal (roughly from the Civil War to the 1930s); and finally when party "reform" began to alter the party system (beginning in the early 1900s but taking effect chiefly since the New Deal).

The Founding

The first organized political party in American history was made up of the followers of Jefferson, who, beginning in the 1790s, called themselves *Republicans* (hoping to suggest thereby that their opponents were secret monarchists).[*] The followers of Hamilton kept the label *Federalist*, which once referred to all supporters of the new Constitution (hoping to imply that their opponents were "Antifederalists," or enemies of the Constitution).

These early parties were loose caucuses of political notables in various localities, with New England strongly Federalist and much of the South passionately Republican. Jefferson and ally James Madison thought their Republican party was a temporary arrangement designed to defeat John Adams, a Federalist, in his bid to succeed Washington in 1796. (Adams narrowly defeated Jefferson, who, under the

system then in effect, became vice president because he had the second most electoral votes.) In 1800, Adams's bid to succeed himself intensified party activity even more, but this time Jefferson won and the Republicans assumed office. The Federalists feared that Jefferson would dismantle the Constitution, but Jefferson adopted a conciliatory posture, saying in his inaugural address that "we are all Republicans, we are all Federalists."[2] It was not true, of course: the Federalists detested Jefferson, and some were planning to have New England secede from the Union. But it was good politics, expressive of the need that every president has to persuade the public that, despite partisan politics, the presidency exists to serve all the people.

So successful were the Republicans that the Federalists virtually ceased to exist as a party. Jefferson was reelected in 1804 with almost no opposition; Madison easily won two terms; James Monroe carried 16 out of 19 states in 1816 and was reelected without opposition in 1820. Political parties had seemingly disappeared, just as Jefferson had hoped. The parties that existed in these early years were essentially small groups of local notables. Political participation was limited, and nominations for most local offices were arranged rather casually.

The Jacksonians

What often is called the second party system emerged around 1824 with Andrew Jackson's first run for the presidency and lasted until the Civil War became inevitable. Its distinctive feature was that political participation became a mass phenomenon. For one thing, the number of voters to be reached had become quite large. Only about 365,000 popular votes were cast in 1824. But as a result of laws that enlarged the number of people eligible to vote and an increase in the population, by 1828 well over a million votes were tallied. By 1840, the figure was well over 2 million. (In England at this time, there were only 650,000 eligible voters.) In addition, by 1832 presidential electors were selected by popular vote in virtually every state. (As late as 1816, electors were chosen by the state legislatures, rather than by the people, in about half the states.) Presidential politics had become a truly national, genuinely popular activity; in many communities, election campaigns had become the principal public spectacle.

The party system of the Jacksonian era was built from the bottom up rather than—as during the period of the Founding—from the top down. No change better illustrates this transformation than the abandonment of the system of having caucuses composed of members of Congress nominate presidential candidates. The caucus system was an effort to unite the legislative and executive branches by

---

[*]The Jeffersonian Republicans were not the party that today we call Republican. In fact, present-day Democrats consider Jefferson to be the founder of their party.

CONSTITUTIONAL CONNECTIONS

"The Spirit of Party"

The noted historian Richard Hofstadter wrote about the Constitution as "A Constitution against Parties." That was the title Hofstadter gave to the second chapter of his 1969 book, *The Idea of a Party System: The Rise of Legitimate Opposition in the United States, 1780–1840.* For the republic's first half-century, most national leaders did not accept the idea that parties were a necessary and desirable feature of American government. For example, near the end of his second term as president, George Washington wrote a letter that later became known as his "Farewell Address." It reads in part:

...Let me now take a more comprehensive view, and warn you in the most solemn manner against the baneful effects of the spirit of party generally. This Spirit, unfortunately, is inseparable from our nature, having its root in the strongest passions of the human mind...The alternate domination of one faction over another, sharpened by the spirit of revenge natural to party dissension...is itself a frightful despotism...(The) common and continual mischiefs of the spirit of party are sufficient to make it the interest and the duty of a wise people to discourage and restrain it.

giving the former some degree of control over who would have a chance to capture the latter. The caucus system became unpopular when the caucus candidate for president in 1824 ran third in a field of four in the general election. It was completely discredited that same year when Congress denied the

" The man who has filled the measure of his Country's Glory. "
JEFFERSON.

Jackson,

DEMOCRACY,

And our Country.

" *The Union must be Preserved.*"
1. Samuel M'Kean.

When Andrew Jackson ran for president in 1828, more than a million votes were cast for the first time in American history. This poster, from the 1832 election, was part of the emergence of truly mass political participation.

presidency to Jackson, the candidate with the greatest share of the popular vote.

To replace the caucus, the party convention was invented. The first convention in American history was held by the Anti-Masonic party in 1831; the first convention of a major political party was held by the anti-Jackson Republicans later that year (it nominated Henry Clay for president). The Democrats held a convention in 1832 that ratified Jackson's nomination for reelection and picked Martin Van Buren as his running mate. The first convention to select a man who would be elected president and who was not already the incumbent president was held by the Democrats in 1836; they chose Van Buren.

The Civil War and Sectionalism

Though the party system created in the Jacksonian period was the first truly national system, with Democrats (followers of Jackson) and Whigs (opponents of Jackson) fairly evenly balanced in most regions, it could not withstand the deep split in opinion created by the agitation over slavery. Both parties tried, naturally, to straddle the issue, since neither wanted to divide its followers and thus lose the election to its rival. But slavery and sectionalism were issues that could not be straddled. The old parties divided and new ones emerged. The modern Republican Party (not the old Democratic-Republican party of Thomas Jefferson) began as a third party. As a result of the Civil War, it became a major party (the only third party ever to gain major-party status) and dominated national politics, with only occasional interruptions, for three-quarters of a century.

Republican control of the White House, and to a lesser extent Congress, was in large measure *mugwumps* or *progressives* Republican party faction of the 1890s to the 1910s, composed of reformers who opposed patronage.

the result of two events that gave to Republicans a marked advantage in the competition for the loyalties of voters. The first of these was the Civil War. This bitter, searing crisis deeply polarized popular attitudes. Those who supported the Union side became Republicans for generations; those who supported the Confederacy, or who had opposed the war, became Democrats.

As it turned out, this partisan division was nearly even for a while: though the Republicans usually won the presidency and the Senate, they often lost control of the House. There were many northern Democrats. In 1896, however, another event—the presidential candidacy of William Jennings Bryan—further strengthened the Republican party. Bryan, a Democrat, alienated many voters in the populous northeastern states while attracting voters in the South and Midwest. The result was to confirm and deepen the split in the country, especially North versus South, begun by the Civil War. From 1896 to the 1930s, with rare exceptions, northern states were solidly Republican, southern ones solidly Democratic.

This split had a profound effect on the organization of political parties, for it meant that most states were now one-party states. As a result, competition for office at the state level had to go on *within* a single dominant party (the Republican party in Massachusetts, New York, Pennsylvania, Wisconsin, and elsewhere; the Democratic party in Georgia, Mississippi, South Carolina, and elsewhere). Consequently, there emerged two major factions within each party, but especially within the Republican party. One was composed of the party regulars—the professional politicians, the "stalwarts," the Old Guard. They were preoccupied with building up the party machinery, developing party loyalty, and acquiring and dispensing patronage—jobs and other favors—for themselves and their faithful followers. Their great skills were in organization, negotiation, bargaining, and compromise; their great interest was in winning.

The other faction, variously called **mugwumps** or **progressives** (or "reformers"), was opposed to the heavy emphasis on patronage; disliked the party machinery because it permitted only bland candidates to rise to the top; was fearful of the heavy influx of immigrants into American cities and of the ability of the party regulars to organize them into "machines;" and wanted to see the party take unpopular positions on certain issues (such as free trade). Their great skills lay in the areas of advocacy and articulation; their great interest was in principle.

At first the mugwumps tried to play a balance-of-power role, sometimes siding with the Republican party of which they were members, at other times defecting to the Democrats (as when they bolted the Republican party to support Grover Cleveland, the Democratic nominee, in 1884). But later, as the Republican strength in the nation grew, progressives within that party became increasingly less able to play a balance-of-power role, especially at the state level. If the progressives were to have any power, they came to believe, it would require an attack on the very concept of partisanship itself.

The Era of Reform

Progressives began to espouse measures to curtail or even abolish political parties. They favored primary elections to replace nominating conventions because the latter were viewed as manipulated by party bosses; they favored nonpartisan elections at the city level and in some cases at the state level as well; they argued against corrupt alliances between parties and businesses. They wanted strict voter registration requirements that would reduce voting fraud (but would also, as it turned out, keep ordinary citizens who found the requirements cumbersome from voting); they pressed for civil service reform to eliminate patronage; and they made heavy use of the mass media as a way of attacking the abuses of partisanship and of promoting their own ideas and candidacies.

The progressives were more successful in some places than in others. In California, for example, progressives led by Governor Hiram Johnson in 1910–1911 were able to institute the direct primary and to adopt procedures—called the *initiative* and the *referendum*—so citizens could vote directly on proposed legislation, thereby bypassing the state legislature. Governor Robert La Follette brought about similar changes in Wisconsin.

The effect of these changes was to reduce substantially the worst forms of political corruption and ultimately to make boss rule in politics difficult if not impossible. But they also had the effect of making political parties, whether led by bosses or by statesmen, weaker, less able to hold officeholders accountable, and less able to assemble the power necessary for governing the fragmented political institutions created by the Constitution. In Congress, party lines began to grow fainter, as did the power of congressional leadership. Above all, the progressives did not have an answer to the problem first faced by Jefferson: If there is not a strong political party, by what other means will candidates for office be found, recruited, and supported?

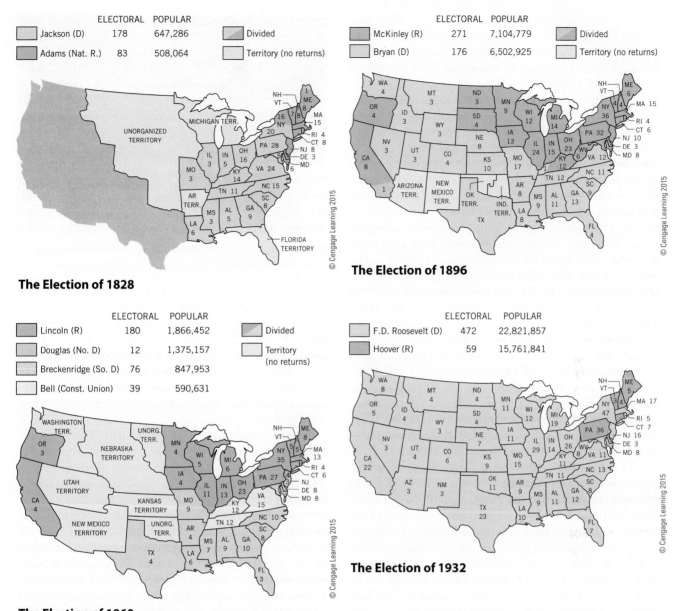

The Election of 1828

The Election of 1896

The Election of 1860

The Election of 1932

Party Realignments

There have clearly been important turning points in the strength of the major parties, especially in the 20th century, when for long periods we have not so much had close competition between two parties as we have had an alternation of dominance by one party and then the other. To help explain these major shifts in the tides of politics, scholars have developed the theory of **critical** or **realignment periods**. During such periods a sharp, lasting shift occurs in the popular coalition supporting one or both parties. The issues that separate the two parties change, and so the kinds of voters supporting each party change. This shift may occur at the time of the election or just after, as the new administration draws in new supporters.[3] There

seem to have been five realignments so far, during or just after these elections: 1800, when the Jeffersonian Republicans defeated the Federalists; 1828, when the Jacksonian Democrats came to power; 1860, when the Whig party collapsed and the Republicans under Lincoln came to power; 1896, when the Republicans defeated William Jennings Bryan; and 1932, when the Democrats under Roosevelt came into office.

critical or *realignment periods* A period when a major, lasting shift occurs in the popular coalition supporting one or both parties.

There are at least two kinds of realignments—one in which a major party is so badly defeated that it disappears and a new party emerges to take its place (this happened to the Federalists in 1800 and to the Whigs in 1856–1860), and another in which the two existing parties continue but voters shift their support from one to the other (this happened in 1896 and 1932).

The three clearest cases seem to be 1860, 1896, and 1932. By 1860, the existing parties could no longer straddle the fence on the slavery issue. The Republican party was formed in 1856 on the basis of clear-cut opposition to slavery; the Democratic party split in half in 1860, with one part (led by Stephen A. Douglas and based in the North) trying to waffle on the issue and the other (led by John C. Breckinridge and drawing its support from the South) categorically denying that any government had any right to outlaw slavery. The remnants of the Whig party, renamed the Constitutional Union party, tried to unite the nation by writing no platform at all, thus remaining silent on slavery. Lincoln and the anti-slavery Republicans won in 1860; Breckinridge and the pro-slavery Southern Democrats came in second. From that moment on, the two major political parties acquired different sources of support and stood (at least for a decade) for different principles. The parties that had tried to straddle the fence were eliminated. The Civil War fixed these new party loyalties deep in the popular mind, and the structure of party competition was set for nearly 40 years.

In 1896, a different kind of realignment occurred. Economics, rather than slavery, was at issue. A series of depressions during the 1880s and 1890s fell especially hard on farmers in the Midwest and parts of the South. The prices paid to farmers for their commodities had been falling more or less steadily since the Civil War, making it increasingly difficult for them to pay their bills. A bitter reaction against the two major parties, which were straddling this issue as they had straddled slavery, spread like a prairie fire, leading to the formation of parties of economic protest—the Greenbackers and the Populists. Reinforcing the economic cleavages were cultural ones: Populists tended to be fundamentalist Protestants; urban voters were increasingly Catholic.

Matters came to a head in 1896 when William Jennings Bryan captured the Democratic nomination for president and saw to it that the party adopted a Populist platform. The existing Populist party endorsed the Bryan candidacy. In the election, anti-Bryan Democrats deserted the party in droves to support the Republican candidate, William McKinley. Once again, a real issue divided the two parties: the Republicans stood for industry, business, hard money, protective tariffs, and urban interests; the Democrats for farmers, small towns, low tariffs, and rural interests. The Republicans won, carrying the cities, workers, and businesspeople; the Democrats lost, carrying most of the southern and midwestern farm states.

William Jennings Bryan giving a campaign speech during one of his three unsuccessful presidential campaigns.

The old split between North and South that resulted from the Civil War was now replaced in part by an East versus West, city versus farm split.[4] It was not, however, only an economic cleavage—the Republicans had been able to appeal to Catholics and Lutherans who disliked fundamentalism and its hostility toward liquor and immigrants.

This alignment persisted until 1932. Again, change was triggered by an economic depression; again, more than economic issues were involved. The New Deal coalition that emerged was based on bringing together into the Democratic party urban workers, northern blacks, southern whites, and Jewish voters. Unlike in 1860 and 1896, it was not preceded by any third-party movement; it occurred suddenly (though some groups had begun to shift their allegiance in 1928) and gathered momentum throughout the 1930s. The Democrats, isolated since 1896 as a southern and midwestern sectional party, had now become the majority party by finding a candidate and a cause that could lure urban workers, blacks, and Jews away from the Republican party, where they had been for decades. It was obviously a delicate coalition—blacks and southern whites disagreed on practically everything except their liking for Roosevelt; Jews and the Irish bosses of the big-city machines also had little in common. But the federal government under Roosevelt was able to supply enough benefits to each of these disparate groups to keep them loyal members of the coalition and to provide a new basis for party identification.

In short, an electoral realignment occurs when a new issue of utmost importance to the voters (slavery, the economy) cuts across existing party divisions and replaces old issues that formerly were the basis of party identification.

Some people wondered whether the election of 1980, since it brought into power the most conservative administration in half a century, signaled a new realignment. Many of President Reagan's supporters began talking of a "mandate" to adopt major new policies in keeping with the views of the "new majority." But Reagan won in 1980 less because of what he stood for than because he was not Jimmy Carter, and he was reelected in 1984 primarily because people were satisfied with how the country was doing, especially economically.[5]

Just because we have had periods of one-party dominance in the past does not mean we will have them in the future. Reagan's election could not have been a traditional realignment, because it left Congress in the hands of the Democratic Party. Moreover, some scholars are beginning to question the theory of critical elections, or at least the theory that they occur with some regularity.

Nevertheless, one major change has occurred of late—the shift in the presidential voting patterns of the South. From 1972 through 2008, the South was more Republican than the nation as a whole. The proportion of white southerners describing themselves to pollsters as "strongly Democratic" fell from more than one-third in 1952 to about one-seventh in 1984. There has been a corresponding increase in "independents." As it turns out, southern white independents have voted overwhelmingly Republican in recent presidential elections.[6] If you lump independents together with the parties for which they actually vote, the party alignment among white southerners has gone from 6 to 1 Democratic in 1952 to about 50/50 Democrats and Republicans. If this continues, it will constitute a major realignment in a region of the country that is growing rapidly in population and political clout.

In general, however, the kind of dramatic realignment that occurred in the 1860s or after 1932 may not occur again, because party labels have lost their meaning for a growing number of voters. For these people politics may *de*align rather than *re*align.

> *split ticket* Voting for candidates of different parties for various offices in the same election.
>
> *straight ticket* Voting for candidates of the same party.

Party Decline

The evidence that the parties are decaying, not realigning, is of several sorts. We have already noted that the proportion of people identifying with one or the other party declined between 1960 and 1980. Simultaneously, the proportion of those voting a **split ticket** (as opposed to a **straight ticket**) increased.

Split-ticket voting rose between 1952 and 1972 and hovered around 25 percent until it declined somewhat after 1992 (see Figure 9.2). For example, in 1988 more than *half* of all House Democrats were elected in districts that voted for Republican George Bush as president. This ticket splitting was greatest in the South, but it was common everywhere. If every district that voted for Bush had also elected a Republican to Congress, the Republican Party would have held a 2-to-1 majority in the House of Representatives. Ticket splitting creates divided government—the White House and Congress are controlled by different parties (see Chapter 14). Ticket splitting helped the Democrats keep control of the House of

FIGURE 9.2 **Split-Ticket Voting for President/House, 1952–2008**

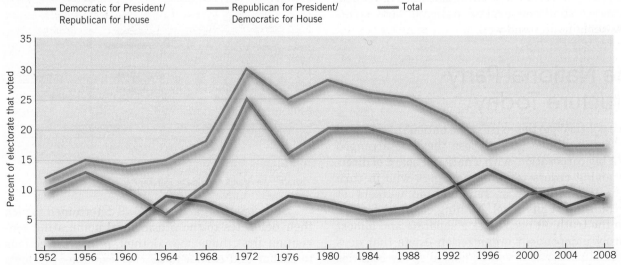

Source: American National Election Studies, Table 9B.2, "Split-Ticket Voting for President/Congress, 1952–2008."

office-bloc ballot A ballot listing all candidates of a given office under the name of that office; also called a "Massachusetts" ballot.

party-column ballot A ballot listing all candidates of a given party together under the name of that party; also called an "Indiana" ballot.

Representatives from 1954 to 1994.

Ticket splitting was almost unheard of in the 19th century, and for a very good reason. In those days, the voter was either given a ballot by the party of his choice and he dropped it, intact, into the ballot box (thereby voting for everybody listed on the ballot), or he was given a government-printed ballot that listed in columns all the candidates of each party. All the voter had to do was mark the top of one column in order to vote for every candidate in that column. (When voting machines came along, they provided a single lever that, when pulled, cast votes for all the candidates of a particular party.) Around the turn of the century progressives began to persuade states to adopt the **office-bloc** (or "Massachusetts") **ballot** in place of the **party-column** (or "Indiana") **ballot**. The office-bloc ballot lists all candidates by office; there is no way to vote a straight party ticket by making one mark. Not surprisingly, states using the office-bloc ballot show much more ticket splitting than those without it.[7]

It would be a mistake, however, to conclude that parties have declined simply because many voters now split tickets in national elections. Despite many changes and challenges (see Figure 9.3), America's two-party system remains strong. In most elections—national, state, and local—voters registered as Democrats still vote for Democratic candidates, and voters registered as Republicans still vote for Republican candidates. In Congress, state legislatures, and city councils, members still normally vote along party lines. Local political machines have died, but, as we shall now explain, national party structures remain alive and well.

The National Party Structure Today

Since political parties exist at the national, state, and local levels, you might suppose they are arranged like a big corporation, with a national board of directors giving orders to state managers who in turn direct the activities of rank-and-file workers at the county and city level. Nothing could be further from the truth. At each level, a separate and almost entirely independent organization exists that does pretty much what it wants, and in many counties and cities there is virtually no organization at all.

FIGURE 9.3   Cleavages and Continuity in the Two-Party System

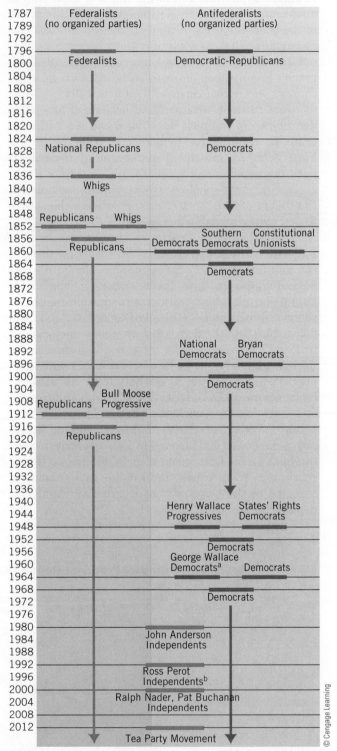

[a]American Independent party.

[b]United We Stand America or Reform Party.

© Cengage Learning

State party organizations, all determined to pick their delegates to the presidential nominating convention first, have moved their primary elections to earlier and earlier dates. For example, the Iowa caucus and the New Hampshire primary in the

1980s were held in March; in 2008, they were held in January. California moved its primary from June to February. This front-loaded set of primaries has made the campaign much longer and more expensive, but the national party organizations have been almost powerless to prevent it.

On paper, the national Democratic and Republican parties look quite similar. In both parties, ultimate authority is in the hands of the **national convention** that meets every four years to nominate a presidential candidate. Between these conventions, party affairs are managed by a **national committee** made up of delegates from each state and territory. In Congress, each party has a **congressional campaign committee** that helps members of Congress running for reelection or would-be members running for an open seat or challenging a candidate from the opposition party. The day-to-day work of the party is managed by a full-time, paid **national chair** elected by the committee.

For a long time, the two national parties were alike in behavior as well as description. The national chair, if his or her party held the White House, would help decide who among the party faithful would get federal jobs. Otherwise, the parties did very little.

But beginning in the late 1960s and early 1970s, the Republicans began to convert their national party into a well-financed, highly staffed organization devoted to finding and electing Republican candidates, especially to Congress. At about the same time, the Democrats began changing the rules governing how presidential candidates are nominated in ways that profoundly altered the distribution of power within the party. As a consequence, the Republicans became a bureaucratized party and the Democrats became a factionalized one. After the Republicans won four out of five presidential elections from 1968 to 1984 and briefly took control of the Senate, the Democrats began to suspect that maybe an efficient bureaucracy was better than a collection of warring factions, and so they made an effort to emulate the Republicans.

The Republicans had taken advantage of a new bit of technology—computerized mailings. They built up a huge file of names of people who had given or might give money to the party, usually in small amounts, and used that list to raise a big budget for the national party. The Republican National Committee (RNC) used this money to run, in effect, a national political consulting firm. Money went to recruit and train Republican candidates, give them legal and financial advice, study issues and analyze voting trends, and conduct national advertising campaigns on behalf of the party as a whole.

When the Democratic National Committee (DNC) decided to play catch-up, it followed the RNC strategy. Using the same computerized direct-mail techniques, the Democratic party committees—the National Committee, Senatorial Committee, and Congressional Committee—raised more money than ever before, though not as much as the Republicans. In 2004, the Democrats and their allies outspent the Republicans. The Democrats, like the Republicans, ship a lot of their national party money to state organizations to finance television ads supporting their parties.

Despite the recent enactment of campaign finance laws intended to check the influence of money on national elections, in 2004 both Democrats and Republicans redoubled efforts to raise *soft money*—that is, funds to aid parties (and their ads and polls). In the Democratic presidential primary, Howard Dean alone raised $30 million over the Internet with average contributions under $100. In 2010, new records were also set for spending on congressional races: the average cost for successful House candidates was more than $1.4 million, while the average cost for successful Senate candidates was close to $9 million. In contrast, the average numbers in 2002 were just under $1 million for successful House candidates and about $4.5 million for successful Senate candidates; and, by 2012, successful House candidates spent, on average, more than $1.5 million while successful Senate candidates spent, on average, more than $10 million (see Figure 9.4).

National Conventions

The national committee selects the time and place of the next national convention and issues a "call" for the convention that sets forth the number of delegates each state and territory is to have and the rules under which delegates must be chosen. The number of delegates and their manner of selection can significantly influence the chances of various presidential candidates, and considerable attention is thus devoted to these matters. In the Democratic Party, for example, a long struggle took place between those who wished to see southern states receive a large share of delegates to the convention, in recognition of their firm support of Democratic

national convention A meeting of party delegates held every four years.

national committee Delegates who run party affairs between national conventions.

congressional campaign committee A party committee in Congress that provides funds to members and would-be members.

national chair Day-to-day party manager elected by the national committee.

FIGURE 9.4 **Cost of Winning a Congressional Election, 2002–2012**

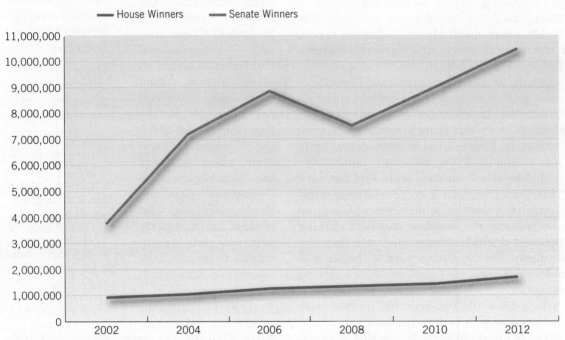

Source: Campaign Finance Institute, updated data from Vital Statistics on Congress, ed. Michael J. Malbin, Norman J. Ornstein, and Thomas E. Mann (Washington, D.C.: Brookings Institution Press, 2008); Jesse Crosson, reporting figures from the Federal Election through February 2013 as compiled by Jay Costa, "What's the Cost of a Seat in Congress?" MapLight.org (http://maplight.org/content/73190).

candidates in presidential elections, and those who preferred to see a larger share of delegates allotted to northern and western states, which, though less solidly Democratic, were larger or more liberal. A similar conflict within the Republican Party has pitted conservative Republican leaders in the Midwest against liberal ones in the East.

A compromise formula usually is chosen; nevertheless, over the years these formulas have gradually changed, shifting voting strength in the Democratic convention away from the South and toward the North and West and in the Republican convention away from the East and toward the South and Southwest. These delegate allocation formulas are but one sign (others will be mentioned later in this chapter) of the tendency of the two parties' conventions to move in opposite ideological directions—Democrats more to the left, Republicans more to the right.

The exact formula for apportioning delegates is extremely complex. For the Democrats, it takes into account the vote each state cast for Democratic candidates in past elections and the number of electoral votes of each state; for the Republicans, it takes into account the number of representatives in Congress and whether the state in past elections cast its electoral votes for the Republican presidential candidate and elected Republicans to the Senate, the House, and the governorship. Thus, the Democrats give extra delegates to large states, while the Republicans give extra ones to loyal states.

The way in which delegates are chosen can be even more important than their allocation. The Democrats, beginning in 1972, developed an elaborate set of rules designed to weaken the control over delegates by local party leaders and to increase the proportion of women, young people, African Americans, and Native Americans attending the convention. These rules were first drafted by a party commission chaired by Senator George McGovern (who later made skillful use of these new procedures in his successful bid for the Democratic presidential nomination). They were revised in 1974 by another commission, chaired by Barbara Mikulski, whose decisions were ratified by the 1974 midterm convention. After the 1976 election, a third commission, chaired by Morley Winograd, produced still another revision of the rules, which took effect in 1980. Then a fourth commission, chaired by North Carolina governor James B. Hunt, recommended in 1981 another set of rules, which became effective with the 1984 convention.

The general thrust of the work of the first three rules commissions was to broaden the antiparty changes started by the progressives at the beginning of the 20th century. Whereas the earlier reformers had tried to minimize the role of parties in the election process, those of the 1970s sought to weaken the influence of leaders within the party. In short, the newer reforms were aimed at creating *intra*party democracy as well as *inter*party

Digital communication is so widespread in American politics that during the 2011 debt ceiling crisis, President Barack Obama participated in a "Twitter Town Hall" from the White House, in which he addressed a question from House Speaker John Boehner.

democracy. Rules for the 1980 Democratic convention required:

- Equal division of delegates between men and women

- Establishment of "goals" for the representation of African Americans, Hispanics, and other groups in proportion to their presence in a state's Democratic electorate

- Open delegate selection procedures, with advance publicity and written rules

- Selection of 75 percent of the delegates at the level of the congressional district or lower

- No "unit rule" that would require all delegates to vote with the majority of their state delegation

- Restrictions on the number of party leaders and elected officials who could vote at the convention

- A requirement that all delegates pledged to a candidate vote for that candidate

In 1981, the Hunt Commission changed some of these rules—in particular, the last two—in order to increase the influence of elected officials and to make the convention a somewhat more deliberative body. The commission reserved about 14 percent of the delegate seats for party leaders and elected officials (the "**superdelegates**"), who would not have to commit themselves in advance to a presidential candidate, and it repealed the rule requiring that delegates pledged to a candidate vote for that candidate.

But the "reform" of the parties, especially the Democratic Party, has had far more profound consequences than merely helping one candidate or another. Before 1968, the Republican Party represented, essentially, white-collar voters and the Democratic Party represented blue-collar ones. After a decade of "reform," the Republican and the Democratic parties each represented two ideologically different sets of upper-middle-class voters. In the terminology of Chapter 7, the Republicans came to represent the more conservative wing of the traditional middle class and the Democrats the more leftist wing of the liberal middle class.

The DNC changed the rules for the 1992 campaign. Former DNC chair Ronald H. Brown (later President Clinton's secretary of commerce) won approval for three important requirements:

- The winner-reward systems of delegate distribution, which gave the winner of a primary or caucus extra delegates, were banned. (In 1988, fifteen states used winner-reward systems, including such vote-rich states as Florida, Illinois, New Jersey, and Pennsylvania.)

- The proportional representation system was put into use. This system divides a state's publicly elected delegates among candidates who receive at least 15 percent of the vote.

- States that violate the rules are now penalized with the loss of 25 percent of their national convention delegates.

Even though the Democrats have retreated a bit from the reforms of the 1960s and 1970s, the conventions of both parties have changed fundamentally, and probably permanently. Delegates once selected by party leaders are now chosen by primary elections and grassroots caucuses. As a result, the national party conventions are no longer places where party leaders meet to bargain over the selection of their presidential candidates; they are instead places where delegates come together to ratify choices already made by party activists and primary voters.

Most Americans dislike bosses, deals, and manipulation and prefer democracy, reform, and openness. These are commendable instincts. But such instincts, unless carefully tested against practice, may mislead us into supposing that anything carried out in the name of reform is a good idea. Rules must be judged by their practical results as well as by their conformity to some principle of fairness. Rules affect the distribution of power: they help some people win and others lose. Later in this chapter, we shall try to assess delegate selection rules by looking more closely at how they affect who attends conventions and which presidential candidates are selected there.

superdelegates Party leaders and elected officials who become delegates to the national convention without having to run in primaries or caucuses.

political machine A party organization that recruits members by dispensing patronage.

State and Local Parties

While the national party structures have changed, the grassroots organizations have withered. In between, state party systems have struggled to redefine their roles.

In every state, a Democratic and a Republican state party is organized under state law. Each typically consists of a state central committee, below which are county committees and sometimes city, town, or even precinct committees. The members of these committees are chosen in a variety of ways—sometimes in primary elections, sometimes by conventions, sometimes by a building-block process whereby people elected to serve on precinct or town committees choose the members of county committees, who in turn choose state committee members.

Knowing these formal arrangements is much less helpful than knowing the actual distribution of power in each state party. In a few places strong party bosses handpick the members of these committees; in other places, powerful elected officials—key state legislators, county sheriffs, or judges—control the committees. And in many places no one is in charge, so that either the party structure is largely meaningless or it is made up of the representatives of various local factions.

To understand how power is distributed in a party, we must first know what *incentives* motivate people in a particular state or locality to become active in a party organization. Different incentives lead to different ways of organizing parties.

The Machine

A **political machine** is a party organization that recruits its members by the use of tangible incentives—money, political jobs, an opportunity to get favors from government—and is characterized by a high degree of leadership control over member activity. At one time, many local party organizations were machines, and the struggle over political jobs—patronage—was the chief concern of their members. Though Tammany Hall in New York City began as a caucus of well-to-do notables in the local Democratic party, by the late 19th century, it had become a machine organized on the basis of political clubs in each assembly district. These clubs were composed of party workers whose job it was to get out the straight party vote in their election districts and who hoped for a tangible reward if they were successful.

And there were abundant rewards to hope for. During the 1870s, it was estimated that one out of

Ex-Senator George Washington Plunkitt of Tammany Hall explains machine politics from atop the bootblack stand in front of the New York County Courthouse around 1905.

Houghton Library

every eight voters in New York City had a federal, state, or city job.[8] The federal bureaucracy was one important source of those jobs. The New York Customhouse alone employed thousands of people, virtually all of whom were replaced if their party lost the presidential election. The postal system was another source, and it was frankly recognized as such. When James N. Tyner became postmaster general in 1876, he was "appointed not to see that the mails were carried, but to see that Indiana was carried."[9] Elections and conventions were so frequent and the intensity of party competition so great that being a party worker was for many a full-time paid occupation.

Well before the arrival of vast numbers of poor immigrants from Ireland, Italy, and elsewhere, old-stock Americans had perfected the machine, run up the cost of government, and systematized voting fraud. Kickbacks on contracts, payments extracted from officeholders, and funds raised from business-people made some politicians rich but also paid the huge bills of the elaborate party organization. When the immigrants began flooding the eastern cities, the party machines were there to provide them with all manner of services in exchange for their support at the polls: the machines were a vast welfare organization operating before the creation of the welfare state.

The abuses of the machine were well known and gradually curtailed. Stricter voter registration laws reduced fraud, civil service reforms cut down the number of patronage jobs, and competitive bidding laws made it harder to award overpriced contracts to favored businesses. The Hatch Act (passed by Congress in 1939) made it illegal for federal civil service employees to take an active part in political management or political campaigns by serving as party officers, soliciting campaign funds, running for partisan office, working in a partisan campaign, endorsing partisan candidates, taking voters to the polls, counting ballots, circulating nominating petitions, or being delegates to a party convention. (They may still vote and make campaign contributions.)

These restrictions gradually took federal employees out of machine politics, but they did not end the machines. In many cities—Chicago, Philadelphia, and Albany—ways were found to maintain the machines even though city employees were technically under the civil service. Far more important than the various progressive reforms that weakened the machines were changes among voters. As voters grew in education, income, and sophistication, they depended less and less on the advice and leadership of local party officials. And as the federal government created a bureaucratic welfare system, the parties' welfare systems declined in value.

It is easy either to scorn the political party machine as a venal and self-serving organization or to romanticize it as an informal welfare system. In truth, it was a little of both. Above all, it was a frank recognition of the fact that politics requires organization; the machine was the supreme expression of the value of organization. Even allowing for voting fraud, in elections where party machines were active, voter turnout was huge: more people participated in politics when mobilized by a party machine than when appealed to via television or good-government associations.[10] Moreover, because the party machines were interested in winning, they would subordinate any other consideration to that end. This has meant that the machines usually were willing to support the presidential candidate with the best chance of winning, regardless of his policy views (provided, of course, that he was not determined to wreck the machines once in office). Republican machines helped elect Abraham Lincoln as well as Warren G. Harding; Democratic machines were of crucial importance in electing Franklin D. Roosevelt and John F. Kennedy.

The old-style machine is almost extinct, though important examples still can be found in the Democratic organization in Cook County (Chicago) and the Republican organization in Nassau County (New York). But a new-style machine has emerged in a few places. It is a machine in the sense that it uses money to knit together many politicians, but it is new in that the money comes not from patronage and contracts but from campaign contributions supplied by wealthy individuals and the proceeds of direct-mail campaigns.

Ideological Parties

At the opposite extreme from the machine is the **ideological party**. Where the machine values winning above all else, the ideological party values principle above all else. Where the former depends on money incentives, the latter spurns them. Where the former is hierarchical and disciplined, the latter usually is contentious and factionalized.

> **ideological party** A party that values principled stands on issues above all else.

The most firmly ideological parties have been independent "third parties," such as the Socialist, Socialist Workers, Libertarian, and Right-to-Life parties. But there have been ideological factions within the Democratic and Republican parties as well, and in some places these ideological groups have taken over the regular parties.

In the 1950s and 1960s, these ideological groups were "reform clubs" within local Democratic and Republican parties. In Los Angeles, New York, and many parts of Wisconsin and Minnesota, issue-oriented activists fought to take over the party from election-oriented regulars. Democratic reform clubs managed to defeat the head of Tammany Hall in Manhattan; similar activist groups became the dominant force in California state politics.[11] Democratic club leaders were more liberal than rank-and-file Democrats, and Republican club leaders were often more conservative than rank-and-file Republicans.

The 1960s and 1970s saw these "reform" movements replaced by more focused social movements. The reform movement was based on a generalized sense of liberalism (among Democrats) or conservatism (among Republicans). With the advent of social movements concerned with civil rights, peace, feminism, environmentalism, libertarianism, and abortion, the generalized ideology of the clubs was replaced by the specific ideological demands of single-issue activists.

The result is that in many places, the party has become a collection of people drawn from various social movements. For a candidate to win the party's support, he or she often has to satisfy the "litmus test" demands of the ideological activists in the party. Democratic senator Barbara Mikulski put it this way: "The social movements are now our farm clubs."

With social movements as their farm clubs, the big-league teams—the Democrats and Republicans at the state level—behave very differently than they did when political machines were the farm clubs. Internal factionalism is more intense, and the freedom of action of the party leader (say, the chair of the state committee) has been greatly reduced. A leader who demands too little or gives up too much, or who says the wrong thing on a key issue, is quickly accused of having "sold out." Under these circumstances, many are "leaders" in name only.

solidary incentives The social rewards (sense of pleasure, status, or companionship) that lead people to join political organizations.

sponsored party A local or state political party largely supported by another organization in the community.

personal following The political support provided to a candidate on the basis of personal popularity and networks.

Solidary Groups

Many people who participate in state and local politics do so not in order to earn money or vindicate some cause, but simply because they find it fun. They enjoy the game, they meet interesting people, and they like the sense of being "in the know" and rubbing shoulders with the powerful. When people get together out of gregarious or game-loving instincts, they are responding to **solidary incentives**; if they form an organization, it is a solidary association.

Some of these associations were once machines. When a machine loses its patronage, some of its members—especially the older ones—may continue to serve in the organization out of a desire for camaraderie. In other cases precinct, ward, and district committees are built up on the basis of friendship networks. One study of political activists in Detroit found that most of them mentioned friendships and a liking for politics—rather than an interest in issues—as their reasons for joining the party organization.[12] Members of ward and town organizations in St. Louis County gave the same answers when asked why they joined.[13] Since patronage has declined in value and since the appeals of ideology are limited to a minority of citizens, the motivations for participating in politics have become very much like those for joining a bowling league or a bridge club.

The advantage of such groups is that they are neither corrupt nor inflexible; the disadvantage is that they often do not work very hard. Knocking on doors on a rainy November evening to try to talk people into voting for your candidate is a chore under the best of circumstances; it is especially unappealing if you joined the party primarily because you like to attend meetings or drink coffee with your friends.[14]

Sponsored Parties

Sometimes a relatively strong party organization can be created among volunteers without heavy reliance on money or ideology and without depending entirely on people's finding the work fun. This type of **sponsored party** occurs when another organization exists in the community that can create, or at least sponsor, a local party structure. The clearest example of this is the Democratic Party in and around Detroit, which has been developed, led, and to a degree financed by the political-action arm of the United Auto Workers (UAW) union. The UAW has had a long tradition of rank-and-file activism, stemming from its formative struggles in the 1930s, and since the city virtually is a one-industry town, it was not hard to transfer some of this activism from union organizing to voter organizing.

By the mid-1950s, union members and leaders made up over three-fourths of all the Democratic Party district leaders within the city.[15] On election day, union funds were available for paying workers to canvass voters; between elections, political work on an unpaid basis was expected of union leaders. Though the UAW–Democratic Party alliance in Detroit has not always been successful in city elections (the city is nonpartisan), it has been quite successful in carrying the city for the Democratic Party in state and national elections. Not many areas have organizations as effective or as dominant as the UAW that can bolster, sponsor, or even take over the weak formal party structure. Thus sponsored local parties are not common in the United States.

Personal Following

Because most candidates can no longer count on the backing of a machine, because sponsored parties are limited to a few unionized areas, and because solidary groups are not always productive, a person wanting to get elected often will try to form a **personal following** that will work for him or her during a campaign and then disband until the next election rolls around. Sometimes a candidate tries to meld a personal following with an ideological group, especially during the primary election campaign, when candidates need the kind of financial backing and hard work that only highly motivated activists are likely to supply.

To form a personal following, the candidate must have an appealing personality, a lot of friends, or a big bank account. The Kennedy family has all three, and the electoral success of the personal followings of John F. Kennedy, Edward M. Kennedy, Robert Kennedy, and Joseph P. Kennedy II are legendary. President George H. W. Bush also established such a following. After he left office, one son (Jeb) became governor of Florida and another one (George W.) became governor of Texas and the 43rd president of the United States.

Southern politicians who operate in one-party states with few, if any, machines have become grand masters at building personal followings, such as those of the Talmadge family in Georgia, the Long family in Louisiana, and the Byrd family in Virginia. But this strategy is increasingly followed wherever

The personal following of former President George H. W. Bush was passed on to his sons, George W. (left) and Jeb (right), both of whom became governors of large states, and the former of whom became president.

party organization is weak. The key asset is to have a known political name. This has helped the electoral victories of the son of Hubert Humphrey in Minnesota, the son and daughter of Pat Brown in California, the son of Birch Bayh in Indiana, the son of George Wallace in Alabama, and the son and grandson of Robert La Follette in Wisconsin.

By the mid-1980s, the traditional party organization—one that is hierarchical, lasting, based on material incentives, and capable of influencing who gets nominated for office—existed, according to political scientist David Mayhew, in only about eight states, mostly the older states of the Northeast. Another five states, he found, had faction-ridden versions of the traditional party organization.[16] The states in the rest of the country displayed the weak party system of solidary clubs, personal followings, ideological groups, and sponsored parties. What that meant could be seen in the composition of Democratic national conventions.

POLICY DYNAMICS: INSIDE/OUTSIDE THE BOX

The Auto Industry Bailout: Party-Based Client Politics?

Chrysler, Ford, and General Motors are known as the "Big Three" American auto companies. When the Big Three ran into big financial trouble in 2008, they asked the federal government for billions of dollars in loans. Most Americans opposed the bailout, but the majorities against helping the auto industry were not as wide as those against bailing out the "too big to fail" banks, insurance companies, and investment firms.

Reactions to various auto industry bailout bills broke down along party lines. Most Big Three blue-collar employees have been represented by the United Auto Workers (UAW), a labor union that has favored Democrats. Many Republican leaders, and most self-identified GOP voters, opposed any auto industry bailout by Washington. Instead, they favored having the Big Three enter bankruptcy proceedings. By contrast, many Democratic leaders, and most self-identified Democratic voters, favored the federal government loaning money to the Big Three to tide them over provided that executive bonuses were curtailed, and that taxpayers, functioning as shareholders, were paid back fully once the economy recovered and car sales improved.

But the pro-bailout policy had one supremely important Republican ally: namely, President George W. Bush. Several top Republicans in Congress insisted that any bailout would cost taxpayers billions of

dollars and benefit "the unions" without either saving the industry or benefitting most consumers. Rejecting such claims, in 2008 Bush directed that $17.4 billion from the anti-recession Troubled Asset Relief Program go to bailout Chrysler and General Motors; and, in December 2008, he supported various bills in Congress that succeeded his own initial bailout plan.

In 2009, President Barack Obama, a Democrat, made $60 billion more available to the companies. By 2012, the Big Three were doing much better, and Washington was on the way to recouping the bailout funds. Still, a February 2012 Gallup poll found that by a 51 percent to 44 percent majority, most Americans still disapproved of the federal government auto industry bailout, with opinions sharply divided by party: Democrats approved by 2 to 1, Republicans disapproved by 3 to 1, and Independents split 45 percent in favor to 50 percent against.

PERCEIVED COSTS		
	Distributed	Concentrated
Distributed	**Majoritarian Politics**	**Entrepreneurial Politics**
Concentrated	**Client Politics**	**Interest Group Politics**

PERCEIVED BENEFITS

two-party system An electoral system with two dominant parties that compete in national elections.

plurality system An electoral system in which the winner is the person who gets the most votes, even if he or she does not receive a majority; used in almost all American elections.

In 1984, over half of the delegates were drawn from the ranks of the AFL-CIO, the National Education Association, and the National Organization for Women.[17] By 2004, both national party organizations and their respective conventions had been dominated for at least two decades by ideological groups and the like.

The Two-Party System

With so many different varieties of local party organizations (or nonorganizations), and with such a great range of opinion found within each party, it is remarkable that we have had only two major political parties for most of our history. In the world at large a **two-party system** is a rarity; by one estimate only 18 nations have one.[18] Most European democracies are multiparty systems. We have only two parties with any chance of winning nationally, and these parties have been, over time, rather evenly balanced—between 1888 and 2012, the Republicans won 17 presidential elections and the Democrats 15. Furthermore, whenever one party has achieved a temporary ascendancy and its rival has been pronounced dead (as were the Democrats in the first third of the 20th century and the Republicans during the 1930s and the 1960s), the "dead" party has displayed remarkable powers of recuperation, coming back to win important victories.

At the state and congressional district levels, however, the parties are not evenly balanced. For a long time, the South was so heavily Democratic at all levels of government as to be a one-party area, while upper New England and the Dakotas were strongly Republican. All regions are more competitive today than once was the case. Parties are not as competitive in state elections as they are in presidential ones. States have rarely had, at least for any extended period, political parties other than the Democratic and Republican.

Scholars do not entirely agree on why the two-party system should be so permanent a feature of American political life, but two explanations are of major importance. The first has to do with the system of elections, the second with the distribution of public opinion.

Elections at every level of government are based on the plurality, winner-take-all method. The

plurality system means that in all elections for representative, senator, governor, or president, and in almost all elections for state legislator, mayor, or city councilor, the winner gets the *most* votes, even if he or she does not get a *majority* of all votes cast. We are so familiar with this system that we sometimes forget there are other ways of running an election. For example, one could require that the winner get a majority of the votes, thus producing runoff elections if nobody got a majority on the first try. France does this in choosing its national legislature. In the first election, candidates for parliament who win an absolute majority of the votes cast are declared elected. A week later, remaining candidates who received at least one-eighth, but less than one-half of the vote, go into a runoff election; those who then win an absolute majority are also declared elected.

The French method encourages many political parties to form, each hoping to win at least one-eighth of the vote in the first election and then to enter into an alliance with its ideologically nearest rival in order to win the runoff. In the United States, the plurality system means that a party must make all the alliances it can before the first election—there is no second chance. Hence, every party must be as broadly based as possible; a narrow, minor party has no hope of winning.

The winner-take-all feature of American elections has the same effect. Only one member of Congress is elected from each district. In many European countries, the elections are based on proportional representation. Each party submits a list of candidates for parliament, ranked in order of preference by the party leaders. The nation votes. A party winning 37 percent of the vote gets 37 percent of the seats in parliament; a party winning 2 percent of the vote gets 2 percent of the seats. Since even the smallest parties have a chance of winning something, minor parties have an incentive to organize.

The most dramatic example of the winner-take-all principle is the electoral college (see Chapter 14). In every state but Maine and Nebraska, the candidate who wins the most popular votes in a state wins *all* of that state's electoral votes. In 1992, for example, Bill Clinton won only 45 percent of the popular vote in Missouri, but he got all of Missouri's 11 electoral votes because his two rivals (George H. W. Bush and Ross Perot) each got fewer popular votes. Minor parties cannot compete under this system. Voters often are reluctant to "waste" their votes on a minor-party candidate who cannot win.

The United States has experimented with other electoral systems. Proportional representation was used for municipal elections in New York City at one time and still is in use in Cambridge, Massachusetts. Many states have elected more than one state legislator from each district. In Illinois, for example, three legislators have been elected from each district, with each voter allowed to cast two votes, thus virtually guaranteeing that the minority party will be able to win one of the three seats. But none of these experiments has altered the national two-party system, probably because of the existence of a directly elected president chosen by a winner-take-all electoral college.

The presidency is the great prize of American politics; to win it, you must form a party with as broad appeal as possible. As a practical matter, this means there will be, in most cases, only two serious parties—one made up of those who support the party already in power, and the other made up of everybody else. Only one third party ever won the presidency—the Republican party in 1860—and it had by then pretty much supplanted the Whig party. No third party is likely to win, or even come close to winning, the presidency anytime soon. Despite the decline in mass party attachment, among Americans who actually vote in presidential elections, party voting is almost as strong today as it was in the early 1950s. As Table 9.1 shows, in the presidential elections of 1992 through 2012, the vast majority of Democrats voted for the Democrat, and the vast majority of Republicans voted for the Republican. Meanwhile, most independents voted for the winning Republican in 1988 and 2000, and pluralities of independents voted for the winning Democrat in 1992 and 1996 and again in 2008; but, in 2012, the Democrat got 45 percent of the Independent vote, while the Republican got half of it.

The second explanation for the persistence of the two-party system is found in the opinions of the voters. National surveys have found that most Americans see "a difference in what Democratic and Republican parties stand for."[19] For the most part, the majority has deemed Democrats better at handling such issues as poverty, the environment, and health care and the Republicans better at handling such issues as national defense, foreign trade, and crime; but voters generally have split on which party is best at handling the economy and taxes.[20] And when it comes to which party is best able to handle whatever individuals see as the "most important problem" facing the nation, normally about 15 percent to a quarter each choose either Democrats or Republicans, while about 45 to 55 percent answer "not much difference."[21]

As we learned in Chapter 7, however, public opinion often is dynamic, not static. Mass perceptions concerning the parties are no exception. For instance, by 2004, a few years after President George W. Bush passed his No Child Left Behind education plan, Republicans cut into the Democrats' traditional slight edge in public school support concerning which party does better on public schools. After 2004, as the war in Iraq became unpopular, Republicans lost ground to Democrats on national defense. And on certain complicated or controversial issues, such as immigration policy, opinions can shift overnight in response to real or perceived changes in policy by those the public views as each party's respective leaders or spokespersons.

Though there have been periods of bitter dissent, most of the time most citizens have agreed enough to permit them to come together into two broad coalitions. There has not been a massive and persistent body of opinion that has rejected the prevailing economic system (and thus we have not had a Marxist party with mass appeal); there has not been in our history an aristocracy or monarchy (and thus there has been no party that has sought to restore aristocrats or monarchs to power). Churches and religion have almost always been regarded as matters of private choice that lie outside politics (and thus there has not been a party seeking to create or abolish special government privileges for one church or another). In some European nations, the organization of the economy, the prerogatives of the monarchy, and the role of the church have been major issues with long and bloody histories. So divisive have these issues been that they have helped prevent the formation of broad coalition parties.

But Americans have had other deep divisions—between white and black, for example, and between North and South—and yet the two-party system has endured. This suggests that our electoral procedures are of great importance—the winner-take-all, plurality election rules have made it useless for anyone

TABLE 9.1 Party Voting in Presidential Elections

Party Affiliation of Voter	1992			1996			2000			2004			2008			2012		
	Dem.	Rep.	Ind.	Dem.	Rep.	Ind.	Dem.	Rep.	Ind.	Dem.	Rep.	Ind.	Dem.	Rep.	Ind.	Dem.	Rep.	Ind.
Democrat	82%	8%	10%	84%	10%	5%	85%	10%	3%	89%	11%	0%	89%	10%	0%	92%	6%	1%
Republican	7	77	16	13	80	6	7	91	1	6	93	0	9	89	0	7	93	1
Independent	39	30	31	43	35	17	37	42	9	49	48	1	52	44	0	45	50	5

Source: Data from CNN exit polls for each year.

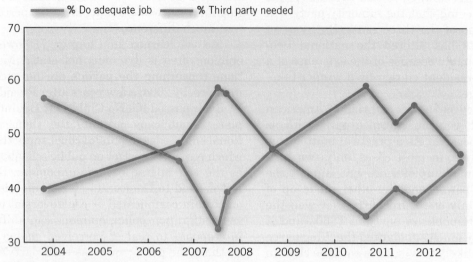

FIGURE 9.5 **Americans are Divided on the Need for a Third Party**

Source: Gallup Poll, *Americans Split on Need for Third Party*, September 12, 2012: http://www.gallup.com/poll/157427/americans-split-need-third-party.aspx

to attempt to create an all-white or an all-black national party except as an act of momentary defiance or in the hope of taking enough votes away from the two major parties to force the presidential election into the House of Representatives. (That may have been George Wallace's strategy in 1968.)

For many years, there was an additional reason for the two-party system: the laws of many states made it difficult, if not impossible, for third parties to get on the ballot. In 1968, for example, the American Independent party of George Wallace found that it would have to collect 433,000 signatures (15 percent of the votes cast in the last statewide election) in order to get on the presidential ballot in Ohio. Wallace took the issue to the Supreme Court, which ruled, 6 to 3, that such a restriction was an unconstitutional violation of the equal protection clause of the Fourteenth Amendment.[22] Wallace got on the ballot. In 1980, John Anderson, running as an independent, was able to get on the ballot in all 50 states; in 1992, Ross Perot did the same. But for the reasons already indicated, the two-party system will probably persist even without the aid of legal restrictions. Furthermore, the public appears ambivalent over whether a third party is needed in American politics, as a Gallup poll taken during the 2012 presidential campaign shows (see Figure 9.5).

Minor Parties

The electoral system may prevent minor parties from winning, but it does not prevent them from forming. Minor parties—usually called, erroneously,

"third parties"—have been a permanent feature of American political life. Four major kinds of minor parties, with examples of each, are described in the box on page 209.

The minor parties that have endured are the ideological ones. Their members feel outside the mainstream of American political life and sometimes, as in the case of various Marxist parties, look forward to a time when a revolution or some other dramatic change in the political system will vindicate them. They usually are not interested in immediate electoral success and thus persist despite their poor showing at the polls. One such party, however, the Socialist party of Eugene Debs, won nearly 6 percent of the popular vote in the 1912 presidential election. During its heyday, 1,200 candidates were elected to local offices, including 79 mayors. Part of the Socialist appeal arose from its opposition to municipal corruption, its opposition to American entry into World War I, and its critique of American society. No ideological party has ever carried a state in a presidential election.

Apart from the Republicans, who quickly became a major party, the only minor parties to carry states and thus win electoral votes were one party of economic protest (the Populists, who carried five states in 1892) and several factional parties (most recently, the States' Rights Democrats in 1948 and the American Independent party of George Wallace in 1968). Though factional parties may hope to cause the defeat of the party from which they split, they have not always been able to achieve this. Harry Truman was elected in 1948 despite the defections of both the leftist progressives, led by

Henry Wallace, and the right-wing Dixiecrats, led by J. Strom Thurmond. In 1968, it seems likely that Hubert Humphrey would have lost even if George Wallace had not been in the race (Wallace voters would probably have switched to Nixon rather than to Humphrey, though of course one cannot be certain). It is quite possible, on the other hand, that a Republican might have beaten Woodrow Wilson in 1912 if the Republican party had not split in two (the regulars supporting William Howard Taft, the progressives supporting Theodore Roosevelt).

What is striking is not that we have had so many minor parties but that we have not had more. There have been several major political movements that did not produce a significant third party: the civil rights movement of the 1960s, the antiwar movement of the same decade, and, most important, the labor movement of the 20th century. African Americans were part of the Republican party after the Civil War and part of the Democratic party after the New Deal (even though the southern wing of that party for a long time kept them from voting). The antiwar movement found candidates with whom it could identify within the Democratic party (Eugene McCarthy, Robert F. Kennedy, George McGovern), even though it was a Democratic president, Lyndon B. Johnson, who was chiefly responsible for the U.S. commitment in Vietnam. After Johnson only narrowly won the 1968 New Hampshire primary, he withdrew from the race. Unions have not tried to create a labor party—indeed, they were for a long time opposed to almost any kind of national political activity. Since labor became a major political force in the 1930s, the largest industrial unions have been content to operate as a part (a very large part) of the Democratic Party.

HOW THINGS WORK

Types of Minor Parties

1. **Ideological parties:** Parties professing a comprehensive view of American society and government radically different from the established parties. Most have been Marxist in outlook, but some are quite the opposite, such as the Libertarian party.

Examples:

Socialist party (1901 to 1960s)

Socialist Labor party (1888 to present)

Socialist Workers party (1938 to present)

Communist party (1920s to present)

Libertarian party (1972 to present)

Green party (1984 to present)

2. **One-issue parties:** Parties seeking a single policy, usually revealed by their names, and avoiding other issues.

Examples:

Free-Soil party—to prevent the spread of slavery (1848–1852)

American or "Know-Nothing" party—to oppose immigration and Catholics (1856)

Prohibition party—to ban the sale of liquor (1869 to present)

Woman's party—to obtain the right to vote for women (1913–1920)

3. **Economic-protest parties:** Parties, usually based in a particular region, especially involving farmers, that protest against depressed economic conditions. These tend to disappear as conditions improve.

Examples:

Greenback party (1876–1884)

Populist party (1892–1908)

4. **Factional parties:** Parties created by a split in a major party, usually over the identity and philosophy of the major party's presidential candidate.

Examples:

Split off from the Republican party:

"Bull Moose" Progressive party (1912)

La Follette Progressive party (1924)

Split off from the Democratic party:

States' Rights ("Dixiecrat") party (1948)

Henry Wallace Progressive party (1948)

American Independent (George Wallace) party (1968)

Split off from both Democrats and Republicans:

Reform party (Ross Perot)

Tea Party movement

One reason some potential sources of minor parties never formed such parties, in addition to the dim chance of success, is that the direct primary and the national convention made it possible for dissident elements of a major party—unless they become completely disaffected—to remain in the party and influence the choice of candidates and policies. The antiwar movement had a profound effect on the Democratic conventions of 1968 and 1972; African Americans have played a growing role in the Democratic Party, especially with the candidacy of Jesse Jackson in 1984 and 1988; only in 1972 did the unions feel that the Democrats nominated a presidential candidate (McGovern) unacceptable to them.

The impact of minor parties on American politics is hard to judge. One bit of conventional wisdom holds that minor parties develop ideas that the major parties later come to adopt. The Socialist party, for example, supposedly called for major social and economic policies that the Democrats under Roosevelt later embraced and termed the New Deal. It is possible the Democrats did steal the thunder of the Socialists, but it hardly seems likely that they did it because the Socialists had proposed these things or proved them popular. (In 1932, the Socialists received only 2 percent of the vote and in 1936 less than one-half of 1 percent.) Roosevelt probably adopted the policies

in part because he thought them correct and in part because dissident elements within his *own* party— leaders such as Huey Long of Louisiana—were threatening to bolt the Democratic party if it did not move to the left. Even Prohibition was adopted more as a result of the efforts of interest groups such as the Anti-Saloon League than as the consequence of its endorsement by the Prohibition party.

The minor parties that have probably had the greatest influence on public policy have been the factional parties. Mugwumps and liberal Republicans, by bolting the regular party, may have made that party more sensitive to the issue of civil service reform; the Bull Moose and La Follette Progressive parties probably helped encourage the major parties to pay more attention to issues of business regulation and party reform; the Dixiecrat and Wallace movements probably strengthened the hands of those who wished to go slow on desegregation. The threat of a factional split is a risk that both major parties must face, and it is in the efforts that each makes to avoid such splits that one finds the greatest impact of minor parties, or at least that was the case in the 20th century.

In 1992 and again in 1996, Ross Perot led the most successful recent third-party movement. It began as United We Stand America and was later renamed the Reform party. Perot's appeal seemed to

The Socialist party and the Progressive party were both minor parties, but their origins were different. The Socialist party was an ideological party; the "Bull Moose" Progressive party split off from the Republicans to support Theodore Roosevelt.

reflect a growing American dissatisfaction with the existing political parties and a heightened demand for bringing in a leader who would "run the government without politics." In 2000 and again in 2004, Ralph Nader led the Green party and rallied supporters by promising to remain above partisan politics and avoid making compromises if elected. Of course, it is no more possible to take politics out of governing than it is to take churches out of religion. Though unrealistic, some people seem to want policies without bargaining.

The Tea Party movement that has evolved in recent years is not a single national party, but it shares characteristics with minor parties: Tea Party supporters were active in the 2010 congressional midterm elections, and they seek to influence the national policy agenda. Although there are many groups within the movement with differing views, Tea Party activists seem to agree on the need to reduce taxes, government spending, budget deficits, and the national debt. They appear to have some influence within the Republican Party, where they have overturned a few establishment candidates for office whom they viewed as insufficiently dedicated to fiscal discipline. Whether the movement will turn into a cohesive minor party that shapes the major-party agenda remains to be seen.

Nominating a President

The major parties face, as we have seen, two contrary forces: one, generated by the desire to win the presidency, pushes them in the direction of nominating a candidate who can appeal to the majority of voters and who will thus have essentially middle-of-the-road views. The other, produced by the need to keep dissident elements in the party from bolting and forming a third party, leads them to compromise with dissidents or extremists in ways that may damage the party's standing with the voters.

The Democrats and Republicans have always faced these conflicting pressures, but of late they have become especially acute. When the presidential nomination was made by a party convention heavily influenced, if not controlled, by party leaders and elected officials, it was relatively easy to ignore dissident factions and pick candidates on the basis of who could win. The *electoral* objectives of the party were predominant. Often the result was that a faction left the party and ran a separate ticket—as in 1912, 1924, 1948, 1968, and 1980. Today the power of party leaders and elected officials within the parties is greatly diminished, with most delegates now selected by primary elections. A larger proportion of the delegates is likely to be more interested in issues and less amenable to compromise over those issues

than formerly. In these circumstances, the *policy* interests of the party activists are likely important.

Are the Delegates Representative of the Voters?

There would be no conflict between the electoral and policy interests of a political party if the delegates to its nominating convention had the same policy views as most voters, or at least as most party supporters. In fact, this is not the case: in parties, as in many organizations, the activists and leaders tend to have views different from those of the rank and file.[23] In American political parties in recent years, this difference has become very great.

In 1964, the Republican Party nominated the highly conservative Barry Goldwater for president. We have no opinion data for delegates to that convention as detailed and comprehensive as those available for subsequent conventions, but it seems clear that the Republican delegates selected as their nominee a person who was not the most popular candidate among voters at large and thus not the candidate most likely to win.

At every Democratic national convention since 1972, the delegates have had views on a variety of important issues vastly different from those of rank-and-file Democrats. On welfare, military policy, school desegregation, crime, and abortion, Democratic delegates expressed opinions almost diametrically opposed to those of most Democrats. The delegates to the 1980, 1984, and (to a lesser extent) 1988, 1992, 1996, 2000, and 2004 conventions were ideologically very different from the voters at large. The Democratic delegates were more liberal than the Democratic voters, and the Republican delegates were more conservative than the Republican voters.[24]

What accounts for the sharp disparity between delegate opinion (and often delegate candidate preference) and voter attitudes? Some blame the discrepancy on the rules, described earlier in this chapter, under which Democratic delegates are chosen, especially those that require increased representation for women, minorities, and the young. Close examination suggests this is not a complete explanation. For one thing, it does not explain why the Republicans nominated Goldwater in 1964 (and almost nominated Ronald Reagan instead of Gerald Ford in 1976). In addition, women, minorities, and youth have among them all shades of opinions: there are many middle-of-the-road women and young people, as well as very liberal or very conservative ones. (There are not many very conservative African Americans, at least on race issues, but there are certainly plenty who are moderate on race and conservative on other issues.) The question is why only *certain* elements of these groups are heavily represented at the conventions.

caucus A meeting of party members to select delegates backing one or another primary candidate.

Who Votes in Primaries?

Maybe delegates are unrepresentative of the party rank and file because they are chosen in caucuses and primary elections whose participants are unrepresentative. Before 1972, most delegates were picked by party leaders; primaries were relatively unimportant, and voter caucuses were almost unheard of. Adlai Stevenson in 1952 and Hubert Humphrey in 1968 won the Democratic presidential nominations without even entering a primary. Harry Truman once described primaries as "eyewash."[25] After 1972, the vast majority of delegates were selected in primaries and caucuses. In 1992, forty states and territories held primaries, and twenty held caucuses (some places had primaries and caucuses).

Only about half as many people vote in primaries as in general elections. If these primary voters have more extreme political views than rank-and-file party followers, then they might support presidential delegates who also have extreme views. However, little evidence suggests that such is the case. Studies comparing the ideological orientations of primary voters with those of rank-and-file party voters show few strong differences.[26]

When it comes to presidential primaries, a good fight draws a crowd. For example, in 12 of the first 18 Republican presidential primaries in 2000, voter turnout hit record highs as Governor George W. Bush battled state by state to stay ahead of Senator John McCain. But the "crowd" represented only 13.6 percent of the voting-age population, up 4.3 percent from the 1996 turnout, and the highest since Senator Barry Goldwater's campaign for the nomination divided Republicans in 1964.[27] In the states that voted after Bush had the nomination all but won, turnout was considerably lower. Likewise, the contest between Vice President Al Gore and Senator Bill Bradley resulted in the second-lowest Democratic presidential primary turnout since 1960.

Primaries differ from caucuses. A **caucus** is a meeting of party followers, often lasting for hours and held in the dead of winter in a schoolhouse sometimes miles from home, in which party delegates are picked. Only the most dedicated partisans attend. For the Democrats, these have been liberals; for the Republicans, conservatives. In 1988, the most liberal Democratic candidate, Jesse Jackson, got more delegates in the Alaska, Delaware, Michigan, and Vermont caucuses than Michael Dukakis, the eventual nominee. Republican evangelist Pat Robertson did not win any primary, but he won the caucuses in Alaska, Hawaii, and Washington. Barack Obama gained momentum in his presidential campaign with his upset victory in the 2008 Iowa caucuses; Hillary Rodham Clinton had been expected to secure the Democratic nomination early in the campaign, but after she narrowly came in third in Iowa, the race for the nomination became hotly competitive and was not resolved definitively until she conceded to Obama in June.

Who Are the New Delegates?

However delegates are chosen, they are a different breed today than they once were. Whether picked by caucuses or primaries, and whatever their sex and race, a far larger proportion of convention delegates, both Republican and Democratic, are issue-oriented activists—people with an "amateur" or "purist" view of politics. Far fewer delegates are in it for the money (there is no longer much patronage to pass around) or to help their own reelection prospects. For example, in 1980 only 14 percent of the Democratic senators and 15 percent of the Democratic members of the House were delegates to the national convention. In 1956, by contrast, 90 percent of the senators and 33 percent of the representatives were delegates.[28] Party activists, especially those who work without pay and who are in politics out of an interest in issues, are not likely to resemble the average citizen for whom politics is merely an object of observation, discussion, and occasional voting.

The changing incentives for participation in party work, in addition to the effects of the primary system, have contributed to the development of a national presidential nominating system different from that which once existed. The advantage of the new system is that it increases the opportunity for those with strong policy preferences to play a role in the party and thus reduces the chance that they will bolt the party and form a factional minor party. The disadvantage of the system is that it increases the chances that one or both parties may nominate presidential candidates who are not appealing to the average voter or even to a party's rank and file.

In sum, presidential nominating conventions are now heavily influenced by ideologically motivated activists. Democratic conventions have heavy representation from organized feminists, unionized schoolteachers, and abortion rights activists; Republican conventions have large numbers of antiabortion activists and Christian conservatives, and small numbers of government libertarians. As a result, the presidential nominating system is now fundamentally different from what it was as late as the mid-1960s. Furthermore, conventions have become the formal ratification of a party's presidential nominee, rather than a forum in which intra-party factions battle over nominee selection, as was typical from the 19th century through the 1960s. Consequently, the electoral benefit to presidential candidates of having a multi-day convention is unclear (though conventions

WHAT'S YOUR ISSUE?

Public Funding for Presidential Candidates

In 1907, President Theodore "Teddy" Roosevelt called for public funding of federal elections and a ban on private campaign contributions. Roosevelt's recommendation attracted little support. But, about seven decades later, in 1976, the Federal Election Commission (FEC) launched the first public funding program for presidential candidates. Over the last four decades, the terms and conditions under which candidates for president may qualify for public funding have changed many times, as have the amounts that eligible candidates may receive. In January 2013, the FEC issued a brochure, Public Funding of Presidential Elections. It indicated that the presidential nominee of each major party may become eligible for a public grant of $20 million (plus a cost-of-living adjustment) for campaigning in the general election. In addition, candidates who accept public funding may spend up to $50,000 from their own personal funds.

That might sound like a good deal, but the deal has been rejected for years by most presidential candidates

of both parties. For instance, in 2008, during the primary season, Barack Obama said he would accept federal public financing for the general election if his rival John McCain agreed to do the same. But Obama changed his mind and went on to shatter presidential general election fund-raising records.

Supreme Court decisions have made plain that while campaign expenditure limits are constitutional, outright bans on private contributions are not. And the most recent court decisions have only served to make it easier for large amounts of private money to flow into presidential and congressional campaigns. Still, would you favor requiring presidential candidates to accept public funding for the general election campaign, banning private contributions? Regardless, would you increase the public funding allotment, and, if so, by how much (to $50 million, $100 million, more?) If you reckoned that a publicly funded presidential election system would somehow strengthen political parties, would you be more or less inclined to support such a system, and why?

still are useful for rallying party activists and other reasons). The last time a winning presidential candidate experienced a post-convention "bounce," or increase in approval ratings, in the double-digits was

Bill Clinton in 1992. In 2012, President Obama had a post-convention "bounce" of just a few points, and Republican presidential candidate Mitt Romney had no "bounce" at all (see Table 9.2).

TABLE 9.2 **Historical Convention Bounces, 1964-2012 Gallup Polls, Registered Voters (in percentage points)**

	Democratic Candidate	Post-Dem. Convention bounce	Republican candidate	Post-Rep. convention bounce
2012	Obama	3	Romney	−1
2008	Obama	4	McCain	6
2004	Kerry	−1	G.W. Bush	2
2000	Gore	8	G.W. Bush	8
1996	Clinton	5	Dole	3
1992	Clinton	16	G.H.W. Bush	5
1988	Dukakis	7	G.H.W. Bush	6
1984	Mondale	9	Reagan	4
1980	Carter	10	Reagan	8
1976	Carter	9	Ford	5
1972	McGovern	0	Nixon	7
1968	Humphrey	2	Nixon	5
1964	Johnson	3	Goldwater	5

Source: Various Gallup Polls: *Candidate Support Typically Up Five Points After Convention*, August 23, 2012: http://www.gallup.com/poll/156845/candidate-support-typically-five-points-convention.aspx; Romney Gets No Bounce From Last Week's GOP Convention, September 4, 2012: http://www.gallup.com/poll/157262/romney-gets-no-bounce-last-week-gop-convention.aspx; and Obama Gets Three-Point Convention Bounce, September 11, 2012: http://www.gallup.com/poll/157406/obama-gets-three-point-convention-bounce.aspx

WHAT WOULD YOU DO?

MEMORANDUM

To: *Elizabeth Ramos, campaign manager*

From: *Isaac Marx, political consultant*

Subject: *Independent voters in the upcoming presidential election*

As you prepare for the upcoming presidential campaign, you need to consider how your candidate can build support among the growing number of independent voters. To do so, she must establish a centrist party platform that will appeal to voters beyond the party faithful.

Arguments for:

1. Independent and third-party voters can garner votes for president or tip an election result. In 1992, Ross Perot won nearly a fifth of the votes. In 2000, Green party candidate Ralph Nader got only 3 percent, but that included 100,000 votes in Florida where Republican Bush was credited with only 600 votes more than Democrat Gore.

2. Third-party voters can make a mark on American politics. Third parties have advocated policies later championed by the two main parties: abolishing slavery (Free-Soil party), women's right to vote (Woman's party), direct election of U.S. senators (Progressive party), and many others. The candidate can break out of the field of contenders by advocating far-reaching policy change that will appeal to independent voters.

3. In a tight presidential race, independent voters will be decisive.

Arguments against:

1. Independent and third-party voters do not direct the national agenda. It is virtually impossible for their candidates to win, thanks to the winner-take-all system of elections. Since the 1850s, more than a hundred third parties have come and gone. Better to be attentive to concerns within the major party

News »

Who Will Independent Voters Support in the Presidential Race?

A recent public opinion poll finds that independent voters are noncommital about which candidate they will support in the upcoming presidential race. A majority say issues, such as reducing the national debt, are more important than party labels. They have concerns about candidates who offer a stark choice between tax increases or spending cuts, saying a more moderate policy agenda is needed.

than to be distracted by issues that are not central to victory.

2. The two major parties have a long history of taking issues that are important to independent voters and making them more palatable to the larger electorate, which is more effective than appealing directly to independent voters. In the 1930s, for example, the Democrats plucked Social Security from the Socialist party's far-reaching plan. In the 1980s, the Republicans' position on taxes only faintly echoed the Libertarian party's.

3. In a close election, building support among likely and predictable voters is a more effective strategy than reaching out to possible but unpredictable voters.

Your decision:

Create a centrist platform _____ Keep the platform focused on core party issues _____

Parties versus Voters

The modern Democratic party has had no trouble winning congressional elections. For instance, the Democrats had a majority in the House of Representatives from 1954 to 1994, regained their House majority in 2006, and lost it again in 2010. Thus, from 1954 to 2014, the Democrats will have held the House majority 70 percent of the time (for all but 18 of 60 years).

But the Democratic party has done less well when it comes to winning presidential elections. In the sixteen presidential elections stretching from 1952 to 2012, the Democrat won seven, the Republican won nine. So, during virtually the same 60-year period that Democrats dominated the House, more Republicans than Democrats occupied the Oval Office.

There are many reasons for this odd state of affairs, most of which will be discussed later. But one requires attention here. The difficulty the Democrats have had in competing for the presidency is in part because their candidates for the presidency have had, on certain issues—chiefly social and taxation issues—views very different from those of the average voter. That disparity to a large degree mirrors (and may be caused by) the gulf that separates the opinions of delegates to Democratic nominating conventions from the opinions of most citizens.

The Republicans have not been immune to this problem. In 1964, they nominated Barry Goldwater, whose beliefs placed him well to the right of most voters. Not surprisingly, he lost. And the delegates to recent Republican conventions have held opinions on some matters that continue to be very different from most people's.

Either party can win if its delegates nominate a candidate whose views put him or her closer to the average citizen than to the average delegate or if the campaign is fought out over issues on which the delegates and the voters agree. For example, if the election turned on what to do about an economic recession, the delegates, the voters, and the candidate would probably all agree: do whatever is necessary to end the recession. Exactly that happened in 1992, and the Democrats won.

Of course, even without a scandal, recession, or some other unifying issue, the need to win an election will lead all candidates to move toward the middle of the road. That is where the votes are. But this creates a dilemma for a candidate of either party. The stance one takes to win support from party activists in the caucuses and primaries often will be quite different from the stance one should take to win votes from the general public. In the next chapter, we will look more closely at how politicians try to cope with that dilemma.

LEARNING OBJECTIVES

1. **What is a political party, and why were the Framers of the Constitution concerned about the influence of political parties?**

   A political party is an organization that works to elect candidates to public office and identifies candidates by a clear name or label. The Framers of the Constitution viewed political parties as "factions" that would promote the interests of a few over the public good. By the early 19th century, though, public parties were viewed as an inevitable feature of democratic politics.

2. **Why does the United States have a two-party system?**

   The United States has a two-party political system because of two structural features in American politics: single-member districts and winner-take-all elections. Both features encourage the existence of two major parties, as smaller parties face great difficulty in winning elective office.

3. **What are the prospects for a viable third party in the United States?**

   A third political party in the United States may build popular support and influence the two major parties, perhaps even ultimately replacing one of them, but the structural features of the American political system make establishment of a third party in electoral politics highly unlikely.

4. **How has America's two-party system changed, and how does it differ from the party systems of other representative democracies?**

   American parties during the 19th century and the first half of the 20th century were strong organizations that picked their candidates for office. Parties in European democracies still do that, but America has changed. Now, candidates usually are picked by direct primary elections, as the American voters' loyalty to parties has weakened.

5. How much do parties affect how Americans vote?

Registered Democrats are more likely to vote for Democratic candidates, and registered Republicans are more likely to vote for Republican candidates, but more voters now register as independents, the proportion of people identifying with one or the other party has declined, and split-ticket voting has been common in the American electorate. The declining attachment of voters to parties and their weaknesses as organizations have led many candidates for president and other offices to run more as individuals than as party members.

6. Did the Founding Fathers think political parties were a good idea?

No. For example, George Washington denounced parties as "factions." But as soon as it was time to select his replacement, the republic's first leaders realized they had to organize their followers to win the election, and parties were born. It was not, however, until well into the 19th century that the idea of a permanent two-party system was considered legitimate by virtually all of the country's political leaders.

7. How, if at all, should America's two-party system be reformed?

Any answer should depend, at least in part, on how one evaluates the many reforms already made. For instance, some argue that the parties should become more open to popular influences. To a large extent, however, that has already happened. Whereas once presidential candidates were selected by party leaders, today they are selected by primaries. Others maintain that there is little real difference between the two parties. That opinion, however, is at variance with the wide differences on many important issues one finds in party platforms, as well as with the fact that delegates to the Republican and Democratic national conventions differ widely on the issues. Still others contend that the plurality system in which the winner is the candidate with the most votes, even if he or she does not receive a majority, is unfair to minor or third-party candidates. Perhaps, but Bill Clinton was twice (1992 and 1996) a popular plurality president. Besides, America has had little experience with other voting or party systems, and democracies that have proportional voting or multiparty systems have other shortcomings (such as unduly empowering small parties with extreme views).

TO LEARN MORE

Democratic National Committee: **www.democrats.org**

Republican National Committee: **www.rnc.org**

Green party: **www.greens.org**

Libertarian party: **www.lp.org**

Reform party: **www.reformparty.org**

Aldrich, John H. *Why Parties?: The Origin and Transformation of Political Parties in America* (Chicago: University of Chicago Press, 1995). Explains why we have parties.

Goldwin, Robert A., ed. *Political Parties in the Eighties*. Washington, D.C.: American Enterprise Institute, 1980. Essays evaluating parties and efforts at reform.

Hofstadter, Richard. *The Idea of a Party System: The Rise of Legitimate Opposition in the United States, 1780–1840*. Berkeley: University of California Press, 1969. Brilliant history of how political parties came to be viewed by most leaders as necessary and desirable political institutions.

Key, V. O., Jr. *Southern Politics*. New York: Knopf, 1949. A classic account of the one-party South.

Mayhew, David R. *Placing Parties in American Politics*. Princeton, NJ: Princeton University Press, 1986.

A state-by-state description of state party organizations.

Nader, Ralph. *Crashing the Party: Taking on the Corporate Government in an Age of Surrender*. New York: St. Martin's Press, 2002. An impassioned attack on the two-party system by a well-known activist who ran for president as a minor-party candidate in 2000 and 2004.

Polsby, Nelson W. *Consequences of Party Reform*. New York: Oxford University Press, 1983. Fine analysis of how changed party rules have affected the parties and the government.

Ranney, Austin. *Curing the Mischiefs of Faction: Party Reform in America*. Berkeley: University of California Press, 1975. History and analysis of party "reforms," with special attention to the 1972 changes in the Democratic Party rules.

Riordan, William L. *Plunkitt of Tammany Hall*. New York: Knopf, 1948. (First published in 1905.) Insightful account of how an old-style party boss operated.

Schattschneider, E. E. *Party Government*. New York: Holt, Rinehart and Winston, 1942. An argument for a more disciplined and centralized two-party system.

Shafer, Byron E. *Quiet Revolution: The Struggle for the Democratic Party and the Shaping of Post-Reform Politics*. New York: Russell Sage Foundation, 1983. Detailed, insightful history of how the Democratic Party came to be reformed.

Sundquist, James L. *Dynamics of the Party System*, Rev. ed. Washington, D.C.: Brookings Institution, 1983. History of the party system, emphasizing the impact of issues on voting.

Wilson, James Q. *The Amateur Democrat*. Chicago: University of Chicago Press, 1962. Analysis of the issue-oriented political clubs that rose in the 1950s and 1960s.

Win McNamee/Getty Images

Elections and Campaigns

10

LEARNING OBJECTIVES

1. What is the difference between a primary election and a general election?

2. Does the federal government provide funding for political campaigns?

3. How do voters typically decide on a candidate?

4. How do American elections determine the kind of people who govern us?

5. What matters most in deciding who wins presidential and congressional elections?

6. Do elections make a real difference in what laws get passed?

National elections in the United States in the 21st century would be virtually unrecognizable to politicians in the early republic. As we saw in Chapter 9, political parties once determined, or powerfully influenced, who got nominated. In the 19th century, the members of Congress from a given caucus would meet to pick their presidential candidate. After the caucuses were replaced by the national nominating conventions, the real power was wielded by local party leaders, who came together (sometimes in the legendary "smoke-filled rooms") to choose the candidate, whom the rest of the delegates would then endorse. Congressional candidates were also often hand-picked by local party bosses. Most people voted a straight party ticket. This system endured until well into the 20th century.

THEN

In 1968, Vice President Hubert Humphrey won the Democratic presidential nomination without competing in a single state primary. His party's bosses pretty much delivered the nomination to him. He competed in a three-way race for president without having to raise nearly as much money as candidates routinely do today. (He lost in a close race to Republican Richard M. Nixon.)

NOW

Unlike in 2008, an incumbent, President Barack Obama, a Democrat, was running for president in 2012. But the Republican presidential primaries drew more than a half-dozen serious contenders. By the time that former Massachusetts Governor Mitt Romney won enough delegates to be assured of the nomination, both his campaign and the president's campaign were raising money at a furious pace. For example, by mid-2012, the president had held more than 100 fundraising events, which was nearly three times as many as his Republican predecessor, President George W. Bush, did when he sought reelection in 2004. By the time the election was over, the Obama campaign and the Romney campaigns, together with a dozen other contenders for the presidency, had raised and spent a combined total of more than $1.3 billion. And, as we shall see, that total was just a fraction of all the money raised from all sources for all candidates for federal office during the 2011–2012 federal election cycle.

Within the lifetimes of many a still-living national political leader, campaigns and elections have changed rather dramatically: parties have become less important; media or "media buys" have become more important; polling has become ubiquitous; and money—and the nonstop fundraising that keeps it coming—now matters more than ever.

Campaigns Today

With the parties' ability to control nominations weakened, candidates are now pretty much on their own. Most, however, do not go it alone. Rather, they hire people to perform several separate but related campaign tasks:[1]

- *Media consultants* who create advertisements and buy airtime from stations and networks.
- *Direct-mail firms* that design and produce mailings to promote the candidate or solicit money.
- *Polling firms* to survey voters on their attitudes toward issues and candidates and to run focus groups.
- *Political technology firms* to supply services such as web site design, online advertising, online fundraising, and voter-targeting.

To pay for all this help, today's candidates must raise and spend enormous sums of money. As Table 10.1 shows, in the 2010 midterm elections, all candidates for national office raised and spent more than $1.8 billion: more than $1 billion in House races, and about $765 million in Senate races. These campaign finance sums were unprecedented for a midterm congressional election. According to an April 2013 report by the Federal Election Commission, during the national election cycle that ended in 2012, presidential and congressional candidates combined total receipts (about $3.2 billion), plus those of party committees (about $1.6 billion) and PACs (about $2.2 billion), totaled about $7.1 billion.

Thus, we have entered the era of the $7 billion federal election cycle. The climb there has been steep but steady. For instance, in 1980, all presidential candidates raised about $162 million. In 2012, all presidential candidates raised about $1.3 billion. Adjusted for inflation, the 2012 total is about five times the 1980 total. As Table 10.2 shows, between 2000 and 2012, the amount of money received by all presidential candidates (including the two party nominees and all their respective primary challengers) more than doubled: in 2000, 17 presidential candidates had total receipts of about $578 million, while in 2012, 14 presidential candidates had receipts of roughly $1.3 billion. Adjusted for inflation, the 2012 total is about 1.7 times the 2000 total. Congressional fundraising tells much the same tale. Between 2002 and 2012, the total receipts of congressional candidates about doubled; adjusted for inflation, the 2012 total is about 1.5 times the 2002 total. Whether we will witness $8 billion (or $9 billion, or more) national election cycles before the decade is out remains to be seen, but there would appear to be no end in sight to increases in the amount of money that candidates, parties, and PACs collect.

TABLE 10.1 **The 2010 Midterm Elections: Money Raised and Spent**

	Total Raised	Total Spent
House Candidates	$1,102,340,257	$1,094,911,271
Senate Candidates	$766,716,134	$764,967,246
Total, All Candidates	$1,869,056,391	$1,859,878,517

Source: Federal Election Commission, 2010 House and Senate Campaign Finance Summary.

TABLE 10.2 **2004–2012 Campaign Receipts**

Presidential Candidates	Number of candidates/Total receipts
2012	14/$1.37 billion
2008	20/$1.67 billion
2004	12/$904 billion
2000	17/$578 million
Congressional Candidates	
2012	$1.87 billion
2010	$1.86 billion
2008	$1.41 billion
2006	$1.44 billion
2004	$1.29 billion
2002	$979 million

Source: Federal Election Commission, FEC Summary of the 2011–2012 Election Cycle, April 19, 2013.

Today's presidential candidates spend more on media consultants, television and radio ads, and diverse other forms of "media messages" than on any other category of campaign expenses. For example, 2008 presidential candidates spent about $569 million on media, representing about 31 percent of all their campaign expenditures. In 2012, campaigns spent more than $1 billion on advertising alone (see Figure 10.1). With so much money spent by candidates for media outlets and media consultants, you might think there is clear and convincing evidence that media exposure makes a critical difference in who wins elections, or that some types of televised appeals work better than others, or both.

But you would be wrong. About the only safe generalization one can presently make on the subject is not that "media buys" matter, but how common it is for today's candidates to purchase political ads embodying emotional appeals.

A comprehensive study carefully analyzed thousands of political ads.[2] A plurality, it found, were purposely designed (everything from the images used to the music playing in the background) to appeal mainly to voters' fears (impending war, losing a job, and so on). A smaller but significant

fraction was more focused on stirring positive emotions (patriotism and community pride). You might suppose that candidates favor ads that appeal to such emotions because they are particularly effective in reaching voters who know little and care less about politics.

Once again, you would be wrong. The political ads, televised and other, that appealed to emotion (fear or enthusiasm, mainly) wielded the greatest influence over voters with the greatest interest in politics and the most information about government.[3] Still, experts do not know how or whether televised political ads influence election outcomes.

Better or Worse?

There is less mystery in political polling than in trying to determine how campaign ads affect election results. Today, even many candidates running in relatively low-budget local races do extensive pre- and post-election voter polling, and often use the results to shape television ads, other campaign

FIGURE 10.1: **2012 Campaign Spending, Selected Items**

Includes spending by presidential candidates, parties, and political action committees

(rounded to nearest $1 million)

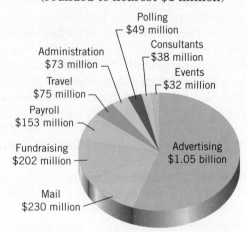

Source: Federal Election Commission Reports, December 2012, as compiled by *The Washington Post*, 2012 Campaign Finance Explorer, December 7, 2012.

communications, positions on the issues, and even what words candidates repeat (or eschew) and how they dress when in public.

It is, however, still only in the national political big leagues that many candidates do extensive polling designed not merely to test voters' existing attitudes, but also to discover how to change them. And it is still only in presidential races and especially well-funded contests for Congress (mostly for the Senate) that sophisticated surveys, much like those traditionally done by big corporations to identify markets where their goods or services are especially likely to sell, are used to mobilize voters.

In each of the last three presidential elections (2004 through 2012),these survey techniques "micro-targeted" people by using data about their consumer and recreational habits (small car or SUV, drink high-cost coffees or cheap brews, like watching professional sports or loathe it, and more). In 2008, micro-targeting software, databases, and techniques became highly refined and were used intensively by both the Obama and the McCain presidential campaigns.[4] By 2012, the techniques, together with ever more extensive campaign-related uses of social media, had become just a normal part of "campaign outreach." Of course, it is one thing to know where "your voters" are, but quite another thing to reach them through door-to-door drives like the ones that once were the political parties' chief stock-in-trade. In 2008 and again in 2012, both parties' national leaders stressed building or expanding grassroots get-out-the-vote organizations not dissimilar from those that, precinct by precinct, once dominated election days in most American cities. Such "high-tech canvassing," if it continues, may yet re-create something somewhat like the party organizations of old.

Patrick Caddell pioneered present-day political polling techniques when he served as Jimmy Carter's consultant in the mid-1970s. By the time Ronald Reagan followed Carter as president in 1980, pollsters like Caddell were the new political bosses, at least in presidential campaigns. As veteran political reporter Joe Klein has reflected, when they "endorsed" a candidate, "fund-raising, media buzz, and support from the party's special interests suddenly became easier."[5]

In 2006, Republican presidential hopeful Senator John McCain hired political consultants on to his campaign who had previously worked against him and developed harshly negative ads that he had in years past objected to as dishonest (and worse). But nobody who knows how the game is played today was really surprised. Today, candidates in both parties, whether ideologically liberal, conservative, or in between, routinely practice what the political professionals preach and purchase what they produce.

This is the main reason for the unceasing spiral in campaign spending, and hence for the fact that "campaigning" has become largely synonymous with "fundraising." Candidates for major offices have two top needs: money for television ads, followed by time for fundraising to generate the cash needed to pay for the ads.[6] Once elected, the permanent fundraising campaign continues for House members, and almost as much for senators and even for the president (who, especially when popular, also makes many trips to raise money for his party's candidates).

The American Association for Political Consultants (AAPC) is a trade association. In 1980, it had about 50 members. By 1990, it had around 700 members. Today, it has more than 1,100 members representing a campaign industry with more than 2,500 firms.[7] The industry's expansion coincided with decreased political participation, and—the only development that can definitely be laid at its door—a dramatic rise in negative, slick, and super-costly political ads. If that leads you to wonder whether, all told, campaigns were better for democracy when party bosses in smoke-filled rooms were more common than political consultants in high-tech firms, you are not alone.

Here and Abroad

Even the best American political consultants probably would have trouble exporting their wares. A campaign plan that will work here would be useless in almost any other democratic nation; one that would work abroad would be useless here.

Unlike in many other democratic nations, in America, elections have not one but two crucial phases—getting nominated and getting elected. Getting nominated means getting your name on the ballot. In the great majority of states, winning your party's nomination for either the presidency or Congress requires an *individual* effort—*you* decide

After working in the Obama administration to create the Consumer Financial Protection Bureau, Elizabeth Warren won election to the U.S. Senate from Massachusetts in 2012.

incumbent The person already holding an elective office.

coattails The alleged tendency of candidates to win more votes in an election because of the presence at the top of the ticket of a better-known candidate, such as the president.

to run, *you* raise money, *you* and your friends collect signatures to get your name on the ballot, and *you* appeal to voters in primary elections on the basis of your personality and your definition of the issues. In most European nations, winning your party's nomination for parliament involves an *organizational* decision—*the party* looks you over, *the party* decides whether to allow you to run, and *the party* puts your name on its list of candidates.

American political parties do play a role in determining the outcome of the final election, but even that role involves parties more as labels in the voters' minds than as organizations that get out the vote. By contrast, many other democratic nations conduct campaigns almost entirely as a contest between parties as organizations. In Israel and the Netherlands, the names of the candidates for the legislature do not even appear on the ballot; only the party names are listed there. And even where candidate names are listed, as in Great Britain, the voters tend to vote "Conservative" or "Labour" more than they vote for Smith or Jones. European nations (except France) do not have a directly elected president; instead, the head of the government—the prime minister—is selected by the party that has won the most seats in parliament.

Presidential versus Congressional Campaigns

Presidential and congressional races differ in important ways. The most obvious, of course, is size: more voters participate in the former than the latter contests, and so presidential candidates must work harder and spend more. But there are some less obvious differences that are equally important.

First, presidential races are more competitive than those for the House of Representatives. In the 41 elections from 1932 to 2012 the Republicans won control of the House ten times (about 25 percent of the time); in the 21 presidential elections during the same period the Republicans won the White House on nine occasions (about 43 percent of the time). In the typical presidential race, the winner gets less than 55 percent of the two-party vote; in the typical House race, the **incumbent** wins with over 60 percent of the vote.

Second, a much smaller proportion of people vote in congressional races during off years (that is,

when there is no presidential contest) than vote for president. This lower turnout (around 38 percent of the voting-age population in 2010) means that candidates in congressional races must be appealing to the more motivated and partisan voter.

Third, members of Congress can do things for their constituents that a president cannot. They take credit—sometimes deserved, sometimes not—for every grant, contract, bridge, canal, and highway that the federal government provides the district or state. They send letters (at the government's expense) to large factions of their constituents and visit their districts every weekend. Presidents get little credit for district improvements and must rely on the mass media to communicate with voters.

Fourth, a candidate for Congress can deny that he or she is responsible for "the mess in Washington," even when the candidate is an incumbent. Incumbents tend to run as individuals, even to the point of denouncing the very Congress of which they are a part. An incumbent president cannot get away with this; rightly or wrongly, he often is held responsible for whatever has gone wrong, not only in the government but in the nation as a whole.

These last three factors—low voter turnout, services to constituents, and the ability to duck responsibility—probably help explain why so high a percentage of congressional incumbents get reelected. But they do not enjoy a completely free ride. Members of Congress who belong to the same party as the president often feel voters' anger about national affairs, particularly economic conditions. When the economy turns sour and a Republican is in the White House, Republican congressional candidates lose votes; if a Democrat is in the White House, Democratic congressional candidates lose votes.

At one time the **coattails** of a popular presidential candidate could help congressional candidates in his or her own party. But there has been a sharp decline in the value of presidential coattails; indeed, some scholars doubt they still exist.

The net effect of all these factors is that, to a substantial degree, congressional elections have become independent of presidential ones. Though economic factors may still link the fate of a president and some members of his or her party, by and large the incumbent members of Congress enjoy enough of a cushion to protect them against whatever political storms engulf an unpopular president. This fact further reduces the meaning of party—members of Congress can get reelected even though their party's "leader" in the White House has lost popular support, and nonincumbent candidates for Congress may lose despite the fact that a very popular president from their party is in the White House.

Running for President

The first task facing anyone who wishes to be president is to get "mentioned" as someone who is of "presidential caliber." No one is quite sure why some people are mentioned and others are not. Journalist David Broder once suggested that somewhere there is "The Great Mentioner" who announces from time to time who is of presidential caliber (and only The Great Mentioner knows how big that caliber is).

But if The Great Mentioner turns out to be as unreal as the Easter Bunny, you have to figure out for yourself how to get mentioned. One way is to let it be known to reporters, "off the record," that you are thinking about running for president. Another is to travel around the country making speeches (Ronald Reagan, while working for General Electric, made a dozen or more speeches *a day* to audiences all over the country). Another way is to already have a famous name (John Glenn, the former astronaut, was in the public eye long before he declared for the presidency in 1984). Another way to get mentioned is to be identified with a major piece of legislation. Former Senator Bill Bradley of New Jersey was known as an architect of the Tax Reform Act of 1986; Representative Richard Gephardt of Missouri was known as an author of a bill designed to reduce foreign imports. Still another way is to be the governor of a big state. Former New York governors, such as Mario Cuomo, often are viewed as presidential prospects, partly because New York City is the headquarters of the television and publishing industries.

Once you are mentioned, it is wise to set aside a lot of time to run, especially if you are only "mentioned" as opposed to being really well known. Ronald Reagan devoted the better part of six years to running; Walter Mondale spent four years campaigning; Howard Baker resigned from the Senate in 1984 to prepare to run in 1988 (he finally dropped out of the race). However, many post-1988 candidates—senators Bob Dole, John Kerry, John McCain, and Barack Obama; governors Michael Dukakis, Bill Clinton, and George W. Bush; vice presidents George Bush and Al Gore; and House members Ron Paul and Dennis Kucinich—made the run while holding elective office.

Though presidential candidates come from various backgrounds, in general the voters tend to prefer those with experience as governors or military leaders rather than those who come immediately from Congress. Some candidates, such as John F. Kennedy and Barack Obama, have been elected president directly after being a senator, but most are either war heroes (Dwight Eisenhower), former governors (George W. Bush, Bill Clinton, Ronald Reagan, Jimmy Carter, and Franklin D. Roosevelt), or former members of Congress who have already had experience as vice presidents (Gerald Ford, Richard Nixon, Lyndon Johnson, and Harry Truman).

political action committee **(PAC)** A committee set up by a corporation, labor union, or interest group that raises and spends campaign money from voluntary donations.

Money

One reason why running takes so much time is that it takes so long to raise the necessary money and build up an organization of personal followers. As we shall see later in this chapter, federal law restricts the amount that any single individual can give a candidate to $2,000 in each election. (A **political action committee,** or **PAC**, which is a committee set up by and representing a corporation, labor union, or other special-interest group, can give up to $5,000.) Moreover, to be eligible for federal matching grants to pay for your primary campaign, you must first raise at least $5,000, in individual contributions of $250 or less, in each of 20 states.

Organization

Raising and accounting for money to campaign requires a staff of fundraisers, lawyers, and accountants. You also need a press secretary, a travel scheduler, an advertising specialist, a direct-mail company, and a pollster, all of whom must be paid, plus a large number of volunteers in at least those states that hold early primary elections or party caucuses. These volunteers will brief you on the facts of each state, try to line up endorsements from local politicians and celebrities, and put together a group of people who will knock on doors, make telephone calls, organize receptions and meetings, and try to keep you from mispronouncing the name of the town in which you are speaking. Finally, you have to assemble advisers on the issues. These advisers

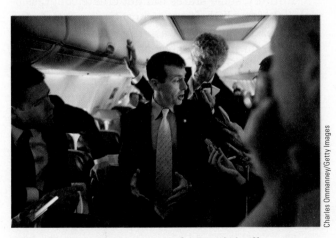

Charles Ommanney/Getty Images

Journalists have many questions for David Plouffe, campaign manager for Barack Obama in 2008 and 2012.

malapportionment
Drawing the boundaries of legislative districts so that they are unequal in population.

gerrymandering
Drawing the boundaries of legislative districts in bizarre or unusual shapes to favor one party.

will write "position papers" for you on all sorts of things you are supposed to know about (but probably don't). Because a campaign usually is waged around a few broad themes, these position papers rarely get used or even read. The papers exist so you can show important interest groups that you have taken "sound" positions, so you can be prepared to answer tough questions, and so journalists can look up your views on matters that may become topical.

Strategy and Themes

Every candidate picks a strategy for the campaign. In choosing one, much depends on whether you are the incumbent. Incumbents must defend their records, like it or not. (An incumbent ran for president in 1964, 1972, 1976, 1980, 1984, 1992, 1996, 2004, and 2012.) The challenger attacks the incumbent. When there is no incumbent (as in 1960, 1968, 1988, 2000, and 2008), both candidates can announce their own programs; however, the candidate from the party that holds the White House must take, whether or not the candidate thinks he deserves it, some of the blame for whatever has gone wrong in the preceding four years. Within these limits, a strategy consists of the answers to questions about tone, theme, timing, and targets:

- What *tone* should the campaign have? Should it be a positive (build-me-up) or negative (attack-the-opponent) campaign? In 1988, George H. W. Bush began with a negative campaign; Michael Dukakis followed suit.

- What *theme* can I develop? A theme is a simple, appealing idea that can be repeated over and over again. For Jimmy Carter in 1976, it was "trust"; for Ronald Reagan in 1980, it was "competence" and in 1984, it was "it's morning again in America"; for Bush in 1988, it was "stay the course"; for Clinton in 1992, it was "we need to change"; for George W. Bush in 2000, it was "compassionate conservatism"; for Barack Obama in 2008, it was "yes we can" and "change you can believe in."

- What should be the *timing* of the campaign? If you are relatively unknown, you will have to put everything into the early primaries and caucuses, try to emerge a frontrunner, and then hope for the best. If you are already the frontrunner, you may either go for broke early (and try to drive out all your opponents) or hold back some reserves for a long fight.

- Whom should you *target*? Only a small percentage of voters change their vote from one election to the next. Who is likely to change this time—unemployed steelworkers? Unhappy farmers? People upset by inflation?

Getting Elected to Congress

A president cannot serve more than two terms, so at least once every eight years you have a chance of running against a nonincumbent; members of Congress can serve for an unlimited number of terms, and so chances are you will run against an incumbent. If you decide to run for the House, the odds are very much against you. Since 1962, over 90 percent of the House incumbents who sought reelection won it.

But the incredible incumbency advantage enjoyed by modern-day House members is hardly the whole story of getting elected to Congress. Who serves in Congress, and what interests are represented there, is affected by how its members are elected. Each state is entitled to two senators who serve six-year terms and at least one representative who serves a two-year term. How many more representatives a state has depends on its population; what local groups these representatives speak for depends in part on how the district lines are drawn.

The Constitution says very little about how representatives will be selected except to require that they be inhabitants of the states from which they are chosen. It says nothing about districts and originally left it up to the states to decide who would be eligible to vote for representatives. The size of the first House was set by the Constitution at 65 members, and the apportionment of the seats among the states was spelled out in Article I, section 2. From that point on, it has been up to Congress to decide how many representatives each state would have (provided that each had at least one).

Initially, some states did not create congressional districts; all their representatives were elected at large. In other states, representatives were elected from multimember as well as single-member districts. In time, all states with more than one representative elected each from a single-member district. How those district boundaries were drawn, however, could profoundly affect the outcomes of elections. There were two problems. One was **malapportionment**, which results from having districts of very unequal size. If one district is twice as populous as another, twice as many votes are needed in the larger district to elect a representative. Thus, a citizen's vote in the smaller district is worth twice as much as a vote in the larger.

The other problem was **gerrymandering**, which means drawing a district boundary in some bizarre or unusual shape to make it easy for the candidate of one party to win election in that district. In a state entitled to ten representatives, where half the voters are Democrats and half are Republicans, district lines could be drawn so that eight districts would have a slight majority of citizens from one party and two districts would have lopsided majorities from the other. Thus, it can be made easy for one party to win eight of the ten seats.

Malapportionment and gerrymandering have been conspicuous features of American congressional politics. In 1962, for example, one district in Texas had nearly a million residents, while another had less than a quarter million. In California, Democrats in control of the state legislature drew district lines in the early 1960s so that two pockets of Republican strength in Los Angeles separated by many miles were connected by a thin strip of coastline. In this way, most Republican voters were thrown into one district, while Democratic voters were spread more evenly over several.

Hence, there are four problems to solve in deciding who gets represented in the House:

1. Establishing the total size of the House
2. Allocating seats in the House among the states
3. Determining the size of congressional districts within states
4. Determining the shape of those districts

By and large, Congress has decided the first two questions, and the states have decided the last two—but under some rather strict Supreme Court rules.

In 1911, Congress decided the House had become large enough and voted to fix its size at 435 members. There it has remained ever since (except for a brief period when it had 437 members owing to the admission of Alaska and Hawaii to the Union in 1959). Once the size was decided, it was necessary to find a formula for performing the painful task of apportioning seats among the states as they gained and lost population. The Constitution requires such reapportionment every ten years. A more or less automatic method was selected in 1929 based on a complex statistical system that has withstood decades of political and scientific testing. Since 1990, under this system 18 states have lost representation in the House and 11 have gained it. Florida and California posted the biggest gains, while New York and Pennsylvania suffered the largest losses (see Table 10.3).

The states did little about malapportionment and gerrymandering until ordered to do so by the Supreme Court. In 1964, the Court ruled that the Constitution requires districts be drawn so that, as nearly as possible, one person's vote would be worth as much as another's.[8] The Court rule, "one person, one vote,"

seems clear, but in fact leaves a host of questions unanswered. How much deviation from equal size is allowable? Should other factors be considered besides population? (For example, a state legislature might want to draw district lines to make it easier for African Americans, Italian Americans, farmers, or some other group with a distinct interest to elect a representative; the requirement of exactly equal districts might make this impossible.) And the gerrymandering problem remains: districts of the same size can be drawn to favor one party or another. The courts have struggled to find answers to these questions, but they remain far from settled.

sophomore surge An increase in the votes congressional candidates usually get when they first run for reelection.

Winning the Primary

However the district lines are drawn, getting elected to Congress first requires getting one's name on the ballot. At one time, the political parties nominated candidates and even printed ballots with the party slates listed on them. All the voter had to do was take the ballot of the preferred party and put it in the ballot box. Today, with rare exceptions, a candidate wins a party's nomination by gathering enough voter signatures to get on the ballot in a primary election, the outcome of which often is beyond the ability of political parties to influence. Candidates tend to form organizations of personal followings and win "their party's" nomination simply by getting more primary votes than the next candidate. It is quite unusual for an incumbent to lose a primary: from 1990 through 2008, only about 10 percent of incumbent senators and 5 percent of incumbent representatives seeking reelection failed to win renomination in primaries. These statistics suggest how little opportunity parties have to control or punish their congressional members.

Most newly elected members become strong in their districts very quickly; this is called the **sophomore surge**. It is the difference between the votes candidates get the first time they are elected (and thus become freshman members) and the votes they get when they run for reelection (in hopes of becoming sophomore members). Before the 1960s, House candidates did not do much better the second time they ran. Beginning then, however, the sophomore surge kicked in, so that today freshman candidates running for reelection will get 8 to 10 percent more votes than when they were first elected. Senate candidates also benefit now from a sophomore surge, though to a lesser degree.

The reason for this surge is that members of Congress have figured out how to use their offices to run *personal* rather than party campaigns. They

TABLE 10.3   Changes in State Representation in the House of Representatives

States	Number of Seats			
	After 1990 Census	After 2000 Census	After 2010 Census	Change
Gained/Maintained Seats				
Arizona	6	8	9	+3
California	52	53	53	+1
Florida	23	25	27	+4
Georgia	11	13	14	+3
North Carolina	12	13	13	+1
Texas	30	32	36	+6
Lost Seats				
Illinois	20	19	18	−2
Michigan	16	15	14	−2
New York	31	29	27	−4
Ohio	19	18	16	−3
Pennsylvania	21	19	18	−3

Source: U.S. Bureau of the Census

make use of free ("franked") mail, frequent trips home, radio and television broadcasts, and the distribution of services to their districts to develop among their constituents a good opinion of themselves, not their party. They also cater to their constituents' distrust of the federal government by promising to "clean things up" if reelected. They run *for* Congress by running *against* it.[9]

To the extent that they succeed, they enjoy great freedom in voting on particular issues and have less need to explain away votes that their constituents might not like. If, however, any single-issue groups are actively working in their districts for or against abortion, gun control, nuclear energy, or tax cuts, muting the candidates' voting record may not be possible.

Staying in Office

The way people get elected to Congress has two important effects. First, it produces legislators closely tied to local concerns (their districts, their states), and second, it ensures that party leaders will have relatively weak influence over them (because those leaders cannot determine who gets nominated for office).

The local orientation of legislators has some important effects on how policy is made. For example:

- Every member of Congress organizes his or her office to do as much as possible for people back home.

- If your representative serves on the House Transportation and Infrastructure Committee,

your state has a much better chance of getting a new bridge or canal than if you do not have a representative on this committee.[10]

- If your representative serves on the House Appropriations Committee, your district is more likely to get approval for a federal grant to improve your water and sewage-treatment programs than if your representative does not serve on that committee.[11]

Former House Speaker Thomas P. "Tip" O'Neill had this in mind when he said, "All politics is local." Some people think this localism is wrong; in their view members of Congress should do what is best for "the nation as a whole." This argument is about the role of legislators: Are they supposed to be *delegates* who do what their district wants or *trustees* who use their best judgment on issues without regard to the preferences of their district?

Naturally, most members are some combination of delegate and trustee, with the exact mix depending on the nature of the issue. But some, as we shall see, definitely lean one way or the other. All members want to be reelected, but "delegates" tend to value this over every other consideration and so seek out committee assignments and projects that will produce benefits for their districts. On the other hand, "trustees" will seek out committee assignments that give them a chance to address large questions, such as foreign affairs, that may have no implications at all for their districts.

Primary versus General Campaigns

When you run for federal office, you must run in two elections, not just one. The first consists of primary elections designed to choose each party's nominee, and the second is the general election that picks the winner who will hold office. If you are running for president, some states, such as Iowa, hold caucuses instead of primary elections. A caucus is a meeting of people, often in an auditorium or church basement, where they vote on who they would like for their party's nominee.

Each election or caucus attracts a different mix of voters. What may help you win a primary or a caucus may be very different from what will help you win the general election. To win a primary or a caucus, you must mobilize political activists who will give money, do volunteer work, and attend local caucuses. As we saw in Chapters 7 and 8, activists are more ideologically stringent than the voters at large. To motivate these activists, you must be more liberal (if you are a Democrat) in your tone and theme than rank-and-file Democrats, or more conservative (if you are a Republican) than rank-and-file Republicans.

Consider the caucuses held in Iowa in the winter preceding a presidential election year. This is the first real test of the candidates vying for the nomination. Anyone who does poorly here is at a disadvantage, in terms of media attention and contributor interest, for the rest of the campaign. The several thousand Iowans who participate in their parties' caucuses are not representative of the followers of their party in the state, much less nationally. In 1988, Senator Robert Dole came in first and evangelist Pat Robertson came in second in the Iowa Republican caucus, with Vice President George Bush finishing third. As it turned out, there was little support for Dole or Robertson in the rest of the country.

Democrats who participate in the Iowa caucus tend to be more liberal than Democrats generally. Moreover, the way the caucuses are run is a far cry from how most elections are held. To vote in the Republican caucus, you need not prove you are a Republican or even a voter. The Democratic caucus is not an election at all; instead, a person supporting a certain candidate stands in one corner of the room with people who also support that candidate, while those supporting other candidates stand in other corners with other groups. There is a lot of calling back and forth, intended to persuade people to leave one group and join another. No group with fewer than 15 percent of the people in attendance gets to choose any delegates, so people in these small groups then go to other, larger ones. It is a cross between musical chairs and fraternity pledge week.

Suppose you are a Democrat running for president and you do well in the Iowa caucus. Suppose you go on to win your party's nomination. Now you have to go back to Iowa to campaign for votes in the general election. Between 1940 and 2008, Iowa has voted Republican in every presidential election but eight (1948, 1964, 1988, 1992, 1996, 2000, 2008, and 2012). Your Republican opponent is not going to let you forget all of the liberal slogans you uttered nine months before. The Republican candidate faces the mirror image of this problem—sounding very conservative to get support from Republican activists in states such as Massachusetts and New York and then having to defend those speeches when running against his or her Democratic opponent in those states.

The problem is not limited to Iowa but exists in every state where activists are more ideologically polarized than the average voter. To get activist support for the nomination, candidates move to the ideological extremes; to win the general election, they try to move back to the ideological center. The typical voter looks at the results and often decides that neither candidate appeals to him or her very much, and so casts a **"clothespin vote."**

Early in the 2004 presidential caucuses and primaries, John Kerry claimed he was an opponent of the American invasion of Iraq in order to defeat Howard Dean, the Vermont governor who seemed to be capturing the antiwar vote among Democrats. But after he won his party's nomination, Kerry backed away from an antiwar stance in order to be more attractive to centrist voters. He had learned a lesson that George McGovern did not understand in 1972. McGovern maintained his liberal views on the war in Vietnam, decriminalizing marijuana, and providing amnesty for draft dodgers.[12] His opponent, Richard Nixon, defeated him easily by taking more centrist positions.

One last thing: if you decide to run for president as a Democrat, do not trust too much in the early polls indicating the frontrunner for the nomination. Edmund Muskie (1972), George Wallace (1976), Ted Kennedy (1980), Gary Hart (1988), Mario Cuomo (1992), and Joseph Lieberman (2004) were all early frontrunners among Democrats, but none got the party's nomination. Only frontrunners Walter Mondale (1984) and Al Gore (2000) prevailed (though neither went on to win the office). By contrast, since 1972, every early Republican frontrunner except one has won the nomination. In 2007, the Republican frontrunner was former

clothespin vote The vote cast by a person who does not like either candidate and so votes for the less objectionable of the two, putting a clothespin over his or her nose to keep out the unpleasant stench.

CONSTITUTIONAL CONNECTIONS

The "Natural Born" Presidents Clause

Article II, section 1, clause 5 of the Constitution states that "no person except a natural born Citizen, or a Citizen of the United States, at the time of the Adoption of this Constitution, shall be eligible to the Office of the President." During the Constitutional Convention, there was little debate on this clause. In *Federalist Paper* No. 3, John Jay wrote of possible "dangers from *foreign arms and influence*" (emphasis in the original), but he did not specifically mention the Constitution's "natural born" presidents clause.

Eight of the 55 delegates to the Constitutional Convention were themselves foreign-born. Among them was Alexander Hamilton, born in the West Indies. In *Federalist Paper* No. 67, the first of Hamilton's essays on the "constitution of the executive department," he answers critics that he says have depicted future presidents as "seated on a throne … giving audience to the envoys of foreign potentates," and have associated the office with "images of Asiatic despotism and voluptuousness." But, like Jay, he makes no specific mention of the clause requiring that all save those foreign-born citizens alive when the Constitution is ratified must be born on American soil to be eligible to serve as president. However, in the 19th century, persons associated with anti-immigrant, anti-Catholic "Nativist" groups sometimes invoked the "natural born" presidents clause.

In recent years, the clause has come to wide public attention twice. In 2003, Arnold Schwarzenegger, the Austrian-born action-movie star and former champion body-builder, was elected as California's governor. In 2004, persons supporting Schwarzenegger for a possible run for the presidency launched web sites and rallied to repeal the clause. But the "Amend for Arnold" movement (advocating repeal of the clause through a new constitutional amendment) was brief-lived. During his 2008 and 2012 campaigns, Barack Obama was subject to claims by various "birther" groups asserting that he was not born in Hawaii but in Kenya, or that he once held citizenship in Indonesia. Despite ample evidence that Obama is a native-born American, in an April 2011 CBS/New York Times poll, only 57 percent of respondents said they believed the president was born in the United States; a quarter said they believed he was not born in the United States; and 18 percent said they did not know. In 2011, Donald Trump, a real estate tycoon and television personality, announced that he might run for president, and questioned whether the president was a natural-born citizen. In 2012, Trump did not run, President Obama was re-elected, and both the controversy and the clause faded from public view.

---

position issue An issue about which the public is divided and rival candidates or political parties adopt different policy positions.

valence issue An issue about which the public is united and rival candidates or political parties adopt similar positions in hopes that each will be thought to best represent those widely shared beliefs.

New York City Mayor Rudolph Guiliani, and the Democratic front-runner was then New York State Senator Hillary Rodham Clinton. By early 2008, Guiliani faded, and Arizona Senator John McCain went on to win the Republican nomination. McCain lost the general election to Illinois Senator Barack Obama following Obama's protracted nomination battle with Clinton.

rival candidates have opposing views on a question that also divides the voters. For example, in the 2008 election, John McCain wanted to let people put some of their Social Security money into private savings accounts; Barack Obama opposed this.

Since 1860, many of the great party realignments have been based on differing position issues. After the Civil War, the question was whether African Americans should be slaves or free. In the 1890s, it was whether tariffs should be high or low and whether the dollar should be made cheaper. In the 1960s, it was whether broad new civil rights legislation was needed.

But sometimes voters are not divided on important issues. Instead, the question is whether a candidate fully supports the public's view on a matter about which nearly everyone agrees. A question such as this poses a **valence issue**. For example, everybody wants a strong economy and low crime rates, and so no candidate favors high unemployment or more crime. What voters look for on valence issues is which candidate seems most closely linked to a universally shared view.

Two Kinds of Campaign Issues

In election campaigns, there are two different kinds of issues.[13] A **position issue** is one in which the

HOW THINGS WORK

Qualifications for Entering Congress and Privileges of Serving in Congress

Representative

- Must be 25 years of age (when seated, not when elected)

- Must have been a citizen of the United States for seven years

- Must be an inhabitant of the state from which elected (*Note:* Custom, but *not* the Constitution, requires that a representative live in the district that he or she represents.)

Senator

- Must be 30 years of age (when seated, not when elected)

- Must have been a citizen of the United States for nine years

- Must be an inhabitant of the state from which elected

Judging Qualifications

Each house is the judge of the "elections, returns, and qualifications" of its members. Thus, Congress alone can decide disputed congressional elections. On occasion, it has excluded a person from taking a seat on the grounds that the election was improper. Either house can punish a member—by reprimand, for example—or, by a two-thirds vote, expel a member.

Privileges

Members of Congress have certain privileges, the most important of which, conferred by the Constitution, is that "for any speech or debate in either house they shall not be questioned in any other place." This doctrine of "privileged speech" has been interpreted by the Supreme Court to mean that members of Congress cannot be sued or prosecuted for anything that they say or write in connection with their legislative duties.

When Senator Mike Gravel read the Pentagon Papers—some then-secret government documents about the Vietnam War—into the *Congressional Record* in defiance of a court order restraining their publication, the Court held that this was "privileged speech" and beyond challenge (*Gravel v. United States*, 408 U.S. 606, 1972). But when Senator William Proxmire issued a press release critical of a scientist doing research on monkeys, the Court decided the scientist could sue him for libel because a press release was not part of the legislative process (*Hutchinson v. Proxmire*, 443 U.S. 111, 1979).

Valence issues are quite common. In 1968, Richard Nixon seemed more supportive of anticrime measures than his rival; in 1976, Jimmy Carter seemed more likely to favor honesty in government than his opponent; in 1984, Ronald Reagan seemed more closely identified with a strong economy than his opponent; in 1988, George H. W. Bush seemed more closely linked to patriotism than his opponent. Notice that we have said "seemed." This is how voters perceived the winners; it does not mean the opponents favored crime, corruption, unemployment, or anti-Americanism.

In 1992, Bill Clinton was beset with charges that he was guilty of dodging the draft, marital infidelity, and smoking pot. But his strategists decided to focus the campaign on the valence issue of the economy, and they went about rescuing Clinton from the other criticisms. One observer later reported, "Retooling the image of a couple who had already been in the public eye for five battering months required a campaign of behavior modification and media manipulation so elaborate that its outline ran to 14 single-spaced pages."[14] Bill and Hillary Clinton made joint appearances on television during which they demonstrated their affection for each other. The plan even called for staging an event where Bill Clinton and his daughter would surprise Hillary Clinton on Mother's Day.[15]

The 2008 campaign relied on both valence issues (Obama and McCain supported "reforming" the health care system to make it more "affordable," while differing on many details related to government-paid health insurance) and position issues (McCain supported tax cuts while Obama favored increasing taxes for people earning over $200,000 a year). The 2012 campaign also featured both valence issues (Mitt Romney depicting Obama as a profligate spender who loves "big government," and Obama depicting Romney as a corporate tycoon with little regard for average workers) and position issues (Obama defended the 2010 health care law while Romney promised to repeal it on his first day in office).

Campaigns usually combine both position and valence questions, but the latter have increased in importance over the last half-century. This has happened in part because post-1960 presidential *general election* An election held to choose which candidate will hold office.

primary election An election held to choose candidates for office.

closed primary A primary election in which voting is limited to already registered party members.

open primary A primary election in which voters may choose in which party to vote as they enter the polling place.

campaigns have been conducted largely on television, where it is important to project popular symbols and manipulate widely admired images. Candidates try to show they are likable, and they rely on televised portraits of their similarity to ordinary people.

Television, Debates, and Direct Mail

Once, campaigns mostly involved parades, big rallies, "whistle-stop" train tours, and shaking hands outside factory gates and near shopping centers. These types of activities still occur, but increasingly presidential and senatorial candidates (and those House candidates with television stations in their districts) use broadcasting to reach potential voters.

Television can be used in two ways—by running paid advertisements and by getting on the nightly news broadcasts. Short television ads are called *spots,* and a campaign activity that appears on a news broadcast is called a *visual.* Much has been written about the preparation of spots, usually under titles such as "the selling of the president" or "packaging the candidate" (and mostly by advertising executives, who are not especially known for underestimating their own influence). No doubt spots can have an important effect in some cases. A little-known candidate can increase his or her visibility by frequent use of spots (this is what Jimmy Carter did in the 1976 presidential primaries).

The effect of television advertising on general elections is probably a good deal less than its effect on primaries; indeed, as we shall see in Chapter 12, most scientific studies of television's influence on voting decisions have shown that either it has no effect or the effect is subtle and hard to detect. Nor is it surprising that this should be the case. In a general election, especially one for a high-visibility office (such as president or governor), the average voter has many sources of information—his or her own party or ideological preference, various kinds of advertising, the opinions of friends and family, and newspaper and magazine stories. Furthermore, both sides will use TV spots; if well done, they are likely to cancel each other out. In short, it is not yet clear that a gullible public is being sold a bill of goods by slick

Madison Avenue advertisers, whether the goods are automobiles or politicians.

Visuals are a vital part of any major campaign effort because, unlike spots, they cost the campaign little and, as "news," they may have greater credibility with the viewer. A visual is a brief, filmed episode showing the candidate doing something that a reporter thinks is newsworthy. Simply making a speech, unless the speech contains important new facts or charges, often is thought by TV editors to be uninteresting: television viewers are not attracted by pictures of "talking heads," and in the highly competitive world of TV, audience reactions are all-important determinants of what gets on the air. Knowing this, campaign managers will strive to have their candidates do something visually interesting every day, no later than 3:00 P.M. (if the visual is to be on the 6:00 P.M. news)—talk to elderly folks in a nursing home, shake hands with people waiting in an unemployment line, or sniff the waters of a polluted lake. Obviously, all these efforts are for naught if a TV camera crew is not around; great pains therefore are taken to schedule these visuals at times and in places that make it easy for photographers to be present.

Ironically, visuals—and television newscasts generally—may give the viewer less information than commercial spots. This, of course, is the exact opposite of what many people believe. It is commonplace to deplore political advertising, especially the short spot, on the grounds that it is either devoid of information or manipulative, and to praise television news programs, especially longer debates and interviews, because they are informative and balanced. In fact, the best research we have so far suggests that the reverse is true: news programs covering elections tend to convey very little information (they often show scenes of crowds cheering or candidates shouting slogans) and make little or no impression on viewers, if indeed they are watched at all. Paid commercials, on the other hand, especially the shorter spots, often contain a good deal of information that is seen, remembered, and evaluated by a public quite capable of distinguishing between fact and humbug.[16]

Although the Obama campaign and the Romney campaign each spent far less on online appeals than they did on television advertising, the Obama campaign made extensive use of voter information compiled through Facebook and other social media. With an email list of more than 12 million voters that supported Obama in 2008, in 2012, the Democrats were able to get ads, messages, and requests for donations out to likely supporters, including those in swing states. By comparison, the Romney campaign made relatively little such use of social media and email lists. Nonetheless, some Republican candidates did "go digital" in 2012; for example, Rafael Edward "Ted" Cruz, the 42-year-old Texas Tea Party conservative who won a U.S. Senate seat, made extensive use of Facebook ads both in his primary contest (which included a runoff) and in the general election. But precisely how, and how much, did online efforts actually affect 2012 national election outcomes (primaries and general elections)? It remains too soon to say.

A special kind of television campaigning is the campaign debate. Incumbents or well-known candidates have little incentive to debate their opponents; by so doing, they only give more publicity to lesser-known rivals. Despite the general rule among politicians never to help an opponent, Vice President Nixon debated the less-well-known John Kennedy in 1960, and President Gerald Ford debated the less-well-known Jimmy Carter in 1976. Nixon and Ford lost. Lyndon Johnson would not debate Barry Goldwater in 1964, nor would Nixon debate Humphrey in 1968 or McGovern in 1972. Johnson and Nixon won. Carter debated the equally well-known Reagan in 1980 (but refused to join in a three-way debate with Reagan and John Anderson). Carter lost.

It is hard to know what effect TV debates have on election outcomes, but poll data suggest that in 1980 voters who watched the debates were

blanket primary A primary election in which each voter may vote for candidates from both parties.

runoff primary A second primary election held when no candidate wins a majority of the votes in the first primary.

HOW THINGS WORK

Kinds of Elections

There are two kinds of elections in the United States: general and primary. A **general election** is used to fill an elective office. A **primary election** is used to select a party's candidates for an elective office, though in fact those who vote in a primary election may not consider themselves party members. Some primaries are closed. In a **closed primary**, you must declare in advance (sometimes several weeks in advance) that you are a registered member of the political party in whose primary you wish to vote. About 40 states have closed primaries.

Other primaries are open. In an **open primary**, you can decide when you enter the voting booth which party's primary you wish to participate in. You are given every party's ballot; you may vote on one. Idaho, Michigan, Minnesota, Montana, North Dakota, Utah, Vermont, and Wisconsin have open primaries. A variant on the open primary is the **blanket** (or "free love") **primary**—in the voting booth, you mark a ballot that lists the candidates of all the parties, and thus you can help select the Democratic candidate for one office and the Republican candidate for another. Alaska and Washington have blanket primaries.

The differences among these kinds of primaries should not be exaggerated, for even the closed primary does not create any great barrier for a voter who wishes to vote in the Democratic primary in one election and the Republican in another. Some states also have a **runoff primary**: if no candidate gets a majority of the votes, there is a runoff between the two with the most votes. Runoff primaries are common in the South.

A special kind of primary, a presidential primary, is used to pick delegates to the presidential nominating conventions of the major parties. Presidential primaries come in a bewildering variety. A simplified list looks like this:

- **Delegate selection only** Only the names of prospective delegates to the convention appear on the ballot. They may or may not indicate their presidential preferences.

- **Delegate selection with advisory presidential preference** Voters pick delegates and indicate their preferences among presidential candidates. The delegates are not legally bound to observe these preferences.

- **Binding presidential preference** Voters indicate their preferred presidential candidates. Delegates must observe these preferences, at least for a certain number of convention ballots. The delegates may be chosen in the primary or by a party convention.

In 1981, the Supreme Court ruled that political parties, not state legislatures, have the right to decide how delegates to national conventions are selected. Thus, Wisconsin could not retain an open primary if the national Democratic Party objected (*Democratic Party v. La Follette*, 101 S. Ct. 1010, 1981). Now the parties can insist that only voters who declare themselves Democrats or Republicans can vote in presidential primaries. The Supreme Court's ruling may have relatively little practical effect, however, since the "declaration" might occur only an hour or a day before the election.

reassured by Reagan's performance; after the second debate with Carter, he took a lead in the polls that he never relinquished.[17] In 1984, most people thought that Mondale did better than Reagan in the first debate, but there is little evidence that the debate affected the outcome of the election. In 1992 and 1996, Clinton was probably the better debater, but he most likely would have won even if he had stumbled. In 2008, Barack Obama and John McCain held three televised debates; in 2012, Barack Obama and Mitt Romney did the same. Opinions differ as to who did better, but there is little evidence that these encounters affected the election results.

Though TV visuals and debates are free for candidates, they are also risky. The risk is the slip of the tongue. You may have spent 30 years of your life in unblemished public service, you may have thought through your position on the issues with great care, you may have rehearsed your speeches until your dog started to howl, but just make one verbal blunder and suddenly the whole campaign focuses on your misstep. In 1976, President Ford erroneously implied that Poland was not part of the Soviet bloc. For days, the press dwelt on this slip. His opponent, Jimmy Carter, admitted in a *Playboy* interview that he sometimes had lust in his heart. It is hard to imagine anyone who has not, but apparently presidents are supposed to be above that sort of thing. In 1980, Ronald Reagan said trees cause pollution—oops, here we go again.

In the 1888 presidential campaign, supporters of Benjamin Harrison rolled a huge ball covered with campaign slogans across the country. The gimmick, first used in 1840, gave rise to the phrase "keep the ball rolling."

Because of the fear of a slip, because the voters do not want to hear long speeches about complex issues, and because general-election campaigns are fights to attract the centrist voter, the candidates will rely on a stock speech that sets out the campaign theme as well as on their ability to string together several proven applause-getting lines. For reporters covering the candidate every day, it can be a mind-numbing experience. Nelson Rockefeller spoke so often of the "brotherhood of man and the fatherhood of God" that the reporters started referring to it as his BOMFOG speech. Occasionally this pattern is interrupted by a "major" address—that is, a carefully composed talk on some critical issue, usually delivered before a live audience and designed to provide issue-related stories for the reporters to write.

If you dislike campaign oratory, put yourself in the candidate's shoes for a moment. Every word you say will be scrutinized, especially for slips of the tongue. Interest group leaders and party activists will react sharply to any phrase that departs from their preferred policies. Your opponent stands ready to pounce on any error of fact or judgment. You must give countless speeches every day. The rational reaction to this state of affairs is to avoid controversy, stick to prepared texts and tested phrases, and shun anything that sounds original (and hence untested). You therefore wind up trying to sell yourself as much as or more than your ideas. Voters may *say* they admire a blunt, outspoken person, but in a tough political campaign they would probably find such bluntness a little unnerving.

Television is the most visible example of modern technology's effect on campaigns. Since 1960, presidential elections have been contested largely through television. Without television, the campaign waged in 1992 by independent candidate Ross Perot might not have happened at all. Perot launched his candidacy with successive appearances on Cable News Network's call-in program "Larry King Live," and he bought several half-hour chunks of television time to air his views on the federal budget deficit. In early October, before the first of three televised debates featuring Perot, Republican incumbent George H. W. Bush, and Democratic challenger Bill Clinton, most national polls showed Perot with only 10 percent of the vote. But after the debates, Perot's support in the polls doubled, and he ended up with about 19 percent of the votes cast on election day.

In 1996, the big television networks agreed to make some free television time available to the major presidential candidates. The Federal Communications Commission approved the plan to limit the free TV to "major" candidates, thus denying it to minor third-party nominees.

Less visible than television but perhaps just as important is the internet. The computer allows for

Vice President Joe Biden and U.S. Representative Paul Ryan participate in the 2012 presidential campaign's vice-presidential debate.

sophisticated direct-mail campaigning, and this in turn makes it possible for a candidate to address specific appeals to particular voters easily and rapidly solicit campaign contributions. In the 2004 presidential campaign, Vermont Governor Howard Dean, at first largely unknown, raised a huge amount of money from internet appeals in which he emphasized his opposition to our war in Iraq. Other candidates will no doubt do the same. However, the internet lends itself to ideological appeals that motivate small contributions, and not every candidate will want to make such arguments.

Whereas television is heard by everybody—and thus leads the candidate using it to speak in generalities to avoid offending anyone—direct mail is aimed at particular groups (college students, Native Americans, bankers, autoworkers) to whom specific views can be expressed with much less risk of offending someone. So important are the lists of names of potential contributors to whom a computer may send appeals that a prized resource of any candidate, guarded as if it were a military secret, is "The List." Novices in politics must slowly develop their own lists or beg sympathetic incumbents for a peek at theirs.

The chief consequence of the new style of campaigning is not, as some think, that it is more manipulative than old-style campaigning (picnics with free beer and $5 bills handed to voters can be just as manipulative as TV ads); rather, it is that running campaigns has become divorced from the process of governing. Previously, the party leaders who ran the campaigns would take part in the government once it was elected, and since they were *party* leaders, they had to worry about getting their candidate *re*elected. Modern political consultants take no responsibility for governing, and by the time the next election rolls around, they may be working for someone else.

Money

As we outlined earlier in this chapter, all these consultants, TV ads, and computerized mailings cost money—lots of it. A powerful California politician once observed that "money is the mother's milk of politics," and many people think that our democracy is drowning in it. In Chapter 11, we will consider what, if anything, interest groups get for the money they give to politicians; in Chapter 12, we shall summarize what we know about the effects of television advertising on elections. Here let us try to answer four questions: Where does campaign money come from? What rules govern how it is raised and spent? What has been the effect of campaign finance reform? What does campaign spending buy?

The Sources of Campaign Money

Presidential candidates get part of their money from private donors and part from the federal government; congressional candidates get all of their money from private sources. In the presidential primaries, candidates raise money from private citizens and interest groups. The federal government will provide matching funds, dollar for dollar, for all monies raised from individual donors who contribute no more than $250. (To prove they are serious candidates, they must first raise $5,000 in each of 20 states from such small contributors.) The government also gives a lump-sum grant to each political party to help pay the costs of its nominating convention. In the general election, the government pays all the costs (up to a legal limit) of major-party candidates and part of the costs of minor-party candidates (those winning between 5 and 25 percent of the vote).

Candidates first made phonographic recordings of their speeches in 1908. Warren G. Harding is shown here recording a speech during the 1920 campaign.

John F. Kennedy and Richard Nixon debate during the 1960 presidential campaign.

Congressional candidates get no government funds; all their money must come out of their own pockets or be raised from individuals, interest groups (PACs), or the political parties. Contrary to what many people think, most of that money comes from—and has always come from—individual donors. Because the rules sharply limit how much any individual can give, these donors tend not to be fat cats, but people of modest means who contribute $100 or $200 per person.

Campaign Finance Rules

During the 1972 presidential election, men hired by President Nixon's campaign staff broke into the headquarters of the Democratic National Committee in the Watergate office building. They were caught by an alert security guard. The subsequent investigation disclosed that the Nixon people had engaged in dubious or illegal money-raising schemes, including taking large sums from wealthy contributors in exchange for appointing them to ambassadorships. Many individuals and corporations were indicted for making illegal donations (since 1925, it had been against the law for corporations or labor unions to contribute money to candidates, but the law had been unenforceable). Some of the accused had given money to Democratic candidates as well as to Nixon.

When the break-in was discovered, the Watergate scandal unfolded. It had two political results: President Nixon was forced to resign, and a new campaign finance law was passed.

Under the new law, individuals could not contribute more than $1,000 to a candidate during any single election. Corporations and labor unions had for many decades been prohibited from spending money on campaigns, but the new law created a substitute: political action committees. A PAC must have at least 50 members (all of whom enroll voluntarily), give to at least five federal candidates, and must not give more than $5,000 to any candidate in any election or more than $15,000 per year to any political party. In addition, the law made federal tax money available to help pay for presidential primary campaigns and for paying all of the campaign costs of a major-party candidate and a fraction of the costs of a minor-party candidate in a presidential general election.

The new law helped increase the amount of money spent on elections and, in time, changed the way money was spent. As Figure 10.2 shows, over the last several decades, different types of PACs have proliferated or dropped off. In each election since 2002, PACs have given over $250 million to congressional candidates. In its April 2013 report on the 2011–2012 federal election cycle, the Federal Election Commission reported that 7,311 PACs had total receipts of nearly $2.3 billion. The PACs that figured most prominently in that funding were the 1,851 corporate PACs (which had $361 million in receipts) and the 1,251 "non-connected" independent-expenditure only PACs (which had $824 million in receipts). These latter PACs, many organized around a particular political ideology or set of issues, included the so-called "super PACS" (see the nearby **What's Your Issue?** feature).

By contrast, when George McGovern ran against Richard Nixon in 1972, he was chiefly supported by the large contributions of one wealthy donor, and when Eugene McCarthy ran against Lyndon Johnson in 1968, he benefited from a few big donations and did not have to rely on massive fundraising appeals.

A candidate gets federal money to match, dollar for dollar, what he or she has raised in contributions of $250 or less. But a presidential candidate can decide to forgo federal primary funding and raise his or her own money. In 2000, George W. Bush relied entirely on his own fundraising, while his chief rival, John McCain, used federal matching funds. In 2004, Bush, Kerry, and Dean all declined federal matching funds in the primary elections. In 2008, John McCain declined public financing for the primaries but accepted it for the general election; Barack Obama relied entirely on his own fundraising for both the primaries and the general election. He did the same in 2012, as did his general election challenger, Mitt Romney.

If you are a minor-party candidate, you can get some support from the federal government provided you have won at least 5 percent of the vote in the last election. In 2000, both Pat Buchanan (Reform party) and Ralph Nader (Green party) got partial

WHAT'S YOUR ISSUE?

Super PACs

Their technical name is "independent expenditure-only committees," but they are more widely known as "super PACs," political action committees that raise and spend unlimited amounts of money from corporations, labor unions, individuals, and other groups. The traditional PAC can accept only so much money from individuals. But super PACs have no limits on who contributes or how much they give, with just this catch: the super PACs are not allowed to act "in concert or cooperation with" the candidate, his or her campaign organization, or a political party. So, for example, a super PAC television ad for a given candidate must be funded and fashioned without that candidate, his or her campaign managers, or the candidate's party leaders being involved in any way.

In 2010, the Supreme Court, in the case of *Citizens United v. Federal Elections Commission*, struck down the ban on corporate and labor union spending on campaign advertisements for and against candidates. This ruling, together with a few other court decisions and rule changes, was

behind the proliferation of super PACs in the 2012 national elections. According to an April 2013 report by the Federal Election Commission, in 2011–2012, the "independent-expenditure only" committees spent nearly $800 million, more than was spent by traditional corporate, union, and trade PACs combined. With super PACs, all PACs spent more than $2.1 billion, and PACS outspent the party committees, which spent "only" about $1.6 billion.

Do you think that super PACS are a plus or a minus for how campaigns and elections are conducted today in America? Would you reverse or uphold the 2010 Supreme Court ruling that made super PACs possible? More generally, when it comes to regulating campaigns and elections, how would you balance the right of individuals (including very wealthy ones) and private groups to spend their own money and express their political views, on the one side, with any possible negative consequences of having so much money flowing into the process from so many sources, on the other side?

support from Washington because their parties had won more than 5 percent of the vote in 1996. But no minor party won more than 5 percent in either 2004, 2008, or 2012, so none received partial support.

The 1973 campaign finance law produced two problems. The first was **independent expenditures**. A PAC, a corporation, or a labor union could spend whatever it wanted supporting or opposing a candidate, so long as this spending was "independent,"

that is, not coordinated with or made at the direction of the candidate's wishes. Simply put, independent expenditures are ordinary advertising directed at or against candidates.

independent expenditures Spending by political action committees, corporations, or labor unions to help a party or candidate but done independently of them.

FIGURE 10.2 **Growth of PACs 1979–2010**

Source: Federal Election Commission.

HOW THINGS WORK

Major Federal Campaign Finance Rules

General

- All federal election contributions and expenditures are reported to a Federal Election Commission.

- All contributions over $100 must be disclosed, with name, address, and occupation of contributor.

- No *cash* contributions over $100 or foreign contributions.

- No ceiling on how much candidates may spend out of their own money (unless they accept federal funding for a presidential race).

Individual Contributions

- An individual may not give more than $2,600 to any candidate in any election.

- An individual may not make federal political gifts exceeding $95,000 every two years, of which only $37,500 may go to candidates.

Political Action Committees (PACs)

- Each corporation, union, or association may establish one.

- A PAC must register six months in advance, have at least 50 contributors, and give to at least five candidates.

- PAC contributions may not exceed $5,000 per candidate per election or $15,000 to a national political party.

Ban on Soft Money

- No corporation or union may give money from its own treasury to any national political party.

Independent Expenditures

- Corporations, unions, and associations may use their own money to fund "electioneering communications." PACs may fund electioneering communications up to their expenditure limits.

Presidential Primaries

- Federal matching funds can be given to match individual contributions of $250 or less.

- To be eligible, a candidate must raise $5,000 in each of 20 states in contributions of $250 or less.

Presidential Election

- The federal government will pay all campaign costs (up to a legal limit) of major-party candidates and part of the costs of minor-party candidates (those winning between 5 and 25 percent of the vote).

---

soft money Funds obtained by political parties that are spent on party activities, such as get-out-the-vote drives, but not on behalf of a specific candidate.

The second was **soft money**. Under the law, individuals, corporations, labor unions, and other groups could give unlimited amounts of money to political parties provided the money was not used to back candidates by name. But the money could be used in ways that helped candidates by financing voter registration and get-out-the-vote drives. Over half a billion dollars in soft money was spent during each of the last four presidential campaigns (2000, 2004, 2008, 2012).

A Second Campaign Finance Law

Reform is a tricky word. We like to think it means fixing something gone wrong. But some reforms can make matters worse. For example, the campaign finance reforms enacted in the early 1970s helped matters in some ways by ensuring that all campaign contributors would be identified by name. But they made things worse in other ways by, for example, requiring candidates to raise small sums from many donors. This made it harder for challengers to run (incumbents are much better known and raise more money) and easier for wealthy candidates to run because, under the law as interpreted by the Supreme Court, candidates can spend as much of their own money as they want.

After the 2000 campaign, a strong movement developed in Congress to reform the reforms of the 1970s. The result was the Bipartisan Campaign Finance Reform Act of 2002, which passed easily in the House and Senate and was signed by President Bush. After the 1970s laws were passed, the Supreme Court, in *Buckley v. Valeo* (424 U.S. 1, 1976), upheld federal limits on campaign contributions even as it ruled that spending money to influence elections is a form of constitutionally

HOW THINGS WORK

2012 Election

Before the 2012 election, Democrats were in control of the White House and the Senate, and Republicans had a majority in the House. In the 2012 election, President Barack Obama was re-elected, defeating Republican challenger Governor Mitt Romney by about 51 percent to 48 percent in the popular vote and by 332 to 206 in the Electoral College vote. Democrats netted two Senate seats and increased their Senate majority to 55. Republicans retained control of the House, winning 234 seats to Democrats' 201seats.

Prior to the 2012 election, there was a great deal of speculation that polls showing President Obama ahead of Governor Romney were wrong because they supposedly oversampled Democrats. In fact, the polls were almost exactly on target regarding "likely voters'" preferences and the composition of the actual election day electorate. According to the first raft of exit polls, the voting electorate was 38 percent Democratic, 32 percent Republican, 55 percent female, 46 percent male, 72 percent white, 13 percent black, and 10 percent Latino.

Romney was widely regarded to have won the first presidential debate. His campaign spent big money on media, especially in ten states that the polls suggested could swing either way. But, by most accounts, Obama did better in the second two debates. His campaign also spent a lot on media and had a superior "ground game" when it came to identifying, registering, and getting likely supporters out to vote.

Obama won Florida and Ohio and every other "swing state" except North Carolina. As seen in Table 10.4, he won the support of most women as well as that of large majorities of black voters, voters under age 30, and Jewish voters (a small percentage of the electorate but important in swing states like Florida). The Catholic vote mirrored the national vote, the most loyal Democratic voters were black Protestants, and the most loyal Republican voters were white evangelicals. No Democratic presidential contender has won a majority of the white vote since Lyndon Johnson in 1964. Obama received about 40 percent of it in 2012. But in 2012 whites were a smaller percentage of the actual electorate than ever before. Latinos, though they constituted just 10 percent of the voting electorate, gave about 70 percent of their votes to Obama.

The polls were right, but numerous political science election forecasting models were wrong. These models predict election outcomes months in advance. Most of them feature algorithms weighted heavily by variables pertaining to the state of the economy (levels of disposable income, unemployment rates). Voters of every description put "the economy" at the top of their list of issues that affected their vote. The bad (if slowly recovering) economy hurt Obama. But long-term demographic trends, not least the declining fraction of the electorate that consists of GOP-leaning white males, plus a superior campaign strategy and get-out-the-vote organization, mattered more.

And while Republicans retained a majority in the House, Republicans received slightly less of the total national vote for the House than Democrats did. Between 1954 and 1994, Democrats often had a majority in the House that was significantly larger than their share of the national vote for the House. This "GOP vote-seat gap" in the House ended in 1992, and two years later Republicans gained control of the House for the first time in 40 years. Democrats regained the House in 2006 and lost it again in 2010. It is too soon to know whether the 2012 election is the start of a "Democratic vote-seat gap" in the House.

The 2012 elections also brought many firsts, including the election of Democrat Tammy Baldwin, now the first openly gay politician and the first Wisconsin woman to be elected to the Senate. Voters in four states also approved ballot measures favorable to same-sex marriage. This outcome is consistent with the recent trend in both court doctrine and public opinion shifting in favor of gay rights.

In a representative democracy, political demography is electoral destiny, and a political party that gets badly out of sync with any large subpopulations or with trends in public opinion usually suffers until it gets new leadership and forms new electoral coalitions. By mid-century, one in three citizens will be Latino. People under 30 were about 19 percent of the voting electorate in 2012, up from 17 percent in 2004 and 18 percent in 2008. Women vote at higher rates than men do. And blacks and other subpopulations that once held more conservative views on issues like gay rights have shifted their opinions in a progressive direction. In the wake of the GOP's losses among these groups, the party's leaders were grappling with how to compete in the future. What will they do, and what, if any, difference will it make to electoral outcomes? Nobody really knows, but stay tuned for Election Day 2014 and Election Day 2016.

TABLE 10.4   2012 Presidential Exit Poll Results

Candidate Receiving Largest Share of the Vote, % Received	
SEX	
Male	Romney, 52%
Female	Obama, 55%
MARITAL STATUS	
Married	Romney, 56%
Unmarried	Obama, 62%
PARTY	
Democrat	Obama, 92%
Republican	Romney, 93%
Independent/Other	Romney, 50%
RACE AND ETHNICITY	
White	Romney, 59%
Black	Obama, 93%
Hispanic	Obama, 71%
Asian	Obama, 73%
AGE	
Age 18-29	Obama, 60%
Age 30-44	Obama, 52%
Age 45-64	Romney, 51%
Age 65 and older	Romney, 56%
EDUCATION	
No college	Obama, 51%
Some college	Obama, 49%
College graduate	Romney, 51%
Postgraduate study	Obama, 55%
INCOME	
Under $30,000/year	Obama, 63%
$30,000-$49,999/year	Obama, 57%
$50,000 or more/year	Romney, 53%
$100,000 or more/year	Romney, 54%
LOCATION	
Big cities	Obama, 69%
Mid-sized cities	Obama, 58%
Small cities	Romney, 56%
Suburbs	Romney, 50%
IDEOLOGY	
Liberal	Obama, 86%
Conservative	Romney, 82%
Moderate	Obama, 56%
VIEW OF ECONOMY	
Excellent/good	Obama, 90%
Not so good/poor	Romney, 60%

Source: The New York Times 2012 Presidential Election Poll.

protected free speech (hence candidates were free to give unlimited amounts of money to their own campaigns). That precedent had pretty much held, but the new law made three important changes.

First, it banned soft money contributions to national political parties from corporations and unions. After the federal elections in 2002, no national party or party committee can accept soft money. Any money the national parties get must come from "hard money"—that is, individual donations or PAC contributions as limited by federal law.

Second, the limit on individual contributions was raised from $1,000 per candidate per election to $2,000.

Third, "independent expenditures" by corporations, labor unions, trade associations, and (under certain circumstances) nonprofit organizations are sharply restricted. Now none of these organizations can use their own money to refer to a clearly identified federal candidate in any advertisement during the 60 days preceding a general election or the 30 days preceding a primary contest. (PACs can still refer to candidates in their ads, but of course PACs are restricted to "hard money"—that is, the amount they can spend under federal law.)

Immediately after the law was signed, critics filed suit in federal court claiming it was unconstitutional. The suit brought together a number of organizations that rarely work together, such as the American Civil Liberties Union and the National Right to Life Committee. The suit claimed that the ban on independent spending that "refers to" clearly identified candidates 60 days before an election is unconstitutional because it is an abridgement of the right of free speech. Under the law, an organization need not even endorse or oppose a candidate; it is enough that it mention a politician. This means that 60 days before an election, an organization cannot say it "supports (or opposes) a bill proposed by Congresswoman Pelosi."

Newspapers, magazines, and radio and television stations are not affected by the law, so they can say whatever they want for or against a candidate. One way of evaluating the law is to observe that it shifts influence away from businesses and unions and toward the media.

In *McConnell v. Federal Election Commission* (2002), the Supreme Court decided to uphold almost all of the law. As we saw in Chapter 5, it rejected the argument of those who claimed that speech requires money and decided it was no violation of the free speech provisions of the First Amendment to eliminate the ability of corporations and labor unions (and the organizations that use their money) to even *mention* a candidate for federal office for 60 days before the national election. In 2007, however, the Court backed away from this view. An ad by a right-to-life group urged people to write to Senator Russell Feingold to convince him to vote for certain judicial nominees, but it did not tell people how to vote. The Court decided this was "issue advocacy" protected by the First Amendment and so could not be banned by the McCain-Feingold law. Three years later, the Court narrowly decided, in a 5 to 4 decision, to overturn the ban on corporate and union funding of campaign ads.

If the past is any guide, neither recent changes nor the existing legal maze will do much to keep individuals, PACs, party leaders, and others from funding the candidates they favor. Nor should we be surprised if groups continue to steer contributions much as one might expect.

For instance, PACs dedicated to a party, a policy position, or a cause (for example, pro-choice PACs that favor Democrats and pro-life PACs that favor Republicans) generally do not change how they give to candidates depending on who is in power. By contrast, trade and corporate PAC money tends to follow power: after the Democrats regained the House in 2006, scores of trade and corporate PACs started giving Democrats far more money and Republicans far less. The Wine and Spirits Wholesalers PAC gave 23 percent of its money to Democrats in 2005 and 65 percent of its money to Democrats in 2007; the Home Depot Inc. PAC gave 13 percent of its money to Democrats in 2005 and 46 percent of its money to Democrats in 2007—and so it went for numerous other trade or corporate PACs (see Table 10.5 for a list of the top 20 PAC contributors in 2009–2010). After the Republican Party won control of the House in 2010, shifts in PAC spending happened yet again.

New Sources of Money

If money is, indeed, the mother's milk of politics, efforts to make the money go away are not likely to work. The Bipartisan Campaign Reform Act, once enforced, immediately stimulated people to find other ways to spend political money.

The most common were **527 organizations**. These groups, named after a provision of the Internal Revenue Code, are designed to permit the kind of soft money expenditures once made by political parties. In 2004, the Democrats created the Media Fund, America Coming Together, America Votes, and many other groups. George Soros, the wealthy businessman, gave more than $23 million to organizations pledged to defeat George Bush. The Republicans responded by creating Progress for America, The Leadership Forum, America for Job Security, and other groups. Under the law, as it is now interpreted, 527 organizations can spend their money on politics so long as they do not coordinate with a candidate or lobby directly for that person. As early as the 2004 elections, 527 organizations raised and spent over one-third of a billion dollars. So far, the lesson seems to be this: campaign finance laws are not likely to take money out of politics.

527 organizations
Organizations under section 527 of the Internal Revenue Code that raise and spend money to advance political causes.

Money and Winning

In the general election for president, money does not make much difference, because both major-party candidates have the same amount, contributed by the federal government. During peacetime, presidential elections usually are decided by three things: political party affiliation, the state of the economy, and the character of the candidates.

For all the talk about voting for "the person, not the party," history teaches that at least 80 percent of the presidential vote will go to the candidates of the two main parties. This means that a presidential election will normally be decided by the 20 percent of voters who cannot be counted on to vote either Democratic or Republican.

In good economic times, the party holding the White House normally does well; in poor times, it does badly. This is sometimes called the "pocketbook vote." But it is not clear whose pocketbook determines how a person will vote. Many who are doing well financially will vote against the party in power if the country as a whole is not doing well. A person doing well may have friends or family members who are doing poorly. Or the well-off voter may think that if the country is doing poorly, he or she will soon feel the pinch by losing a job or losing customers.

Voters also care about character, and so some money from presidential campaign coffers goes to fund "character ads." *Character* here means several things: Is the candidate honest and reliable? Does the candidate think as the voter thinks about social issues such as crime, abortion, and school prayer? Does the candidate act presidential? Acting presidential seems to mean being an effective speaker, displaying dignity and compassion, sounding like someone who can take charge and get things done, and coming across consistently as a reasonable, likable person. Rash, disagreeable extremists need not apply.

Since both major candidates usually get the same amount of federal money for the general election campaign, money does not make much of a difference in determining the winner. Other factors

TABLE 10.5 **Top 20 PAC Contributors to Candidates, 2011– 2012**

PAC Name	Total Amount	Democratic Pct	Republican Pct
National Assn of Realtors	$3,960,282	44%	55%
National Beer Wholesalers Assn	$3,388,500	41%	59%
Honeywell International	$3,193,024	41%	59%
Operating Engineers Union	$3,186,387	84%	15%
National Auto Dealers Assn	$3,074,000	28%	72%
Intl Brotherhood of Electrical Workers	$2,853,000	97%	2%
American Bankers Assn	$2,736,150	20%	80%
AT&T Inc	$2,543,000	35%	65%
American Assn for Justice	$2,512,500	96%	3%
Credit Union National Assn	$2,487,600	47%	52%
Plumbers/Pipefitters Union	$2,395,150	94%	5%
Northrop Grumman	$2,353,900	41%	58%
American Fedn of St/Cnty/Munic Employees	$2,279,140	99%	1%
Lockheed Martin	$2,258,000	41%	59%
Blue Cross/Blue Shield	$2,177,898	33%	67%
Machinists/Aerospace Workers Union	$2,173,500	98%	1%
American Federation of Teachers	$2,171,644	99%	0%
MINT PAC	$2,138,229	0%	100%
Every Republican Is Crucial PAC	$2,086,000	0%	100%
Teamsters Union	$2,053,410	96%	4%

Source: Center for Responsive Politics. "PACs: Top PACs."*OpenSecrets.org*. Last modified March 2013. Accessed June 2, 2013. http://www.opensecrets.org/pacs/toppacs.php.

LANDMARK CASES

Financing Elections

- *Buckley v. Valeo* (1976): Held that a law limiting contributions to political campaigns was constitutional but that one restricting a candidate's expenditures of his or her own money was not.

- *McConnell v. Federal Election Commission* (2002): Upheld 2002 Bipartisan Campaign Reform Act (popularly known as "McCain-Feingold" law) prohibiting corporations and labor unions from running ads that mention candidates and their positions for 60 days before a federal general election.

- *Federal Election Commission v. Wisconsin Right to Life, Inc.* (2007): Held that issue ads may not be prohibited before a primary or general election.

- *Citizens United v. Federal Election Commission* (2010): Overturned part of 2002 law that had prohibited corporate and union funding of campaign ads.

that also do not make a difference include the following:

- *Vice-presidential nominee:* There has rarely been an election in which his or her identity has made a difference.

- *Political reporting:* It may make a difference in some elections, but not in presidential ones.

- *Religion:* Being a Catholic was once a barrier, but since John F. Kennedy was elected president in 1960, this is no longer true. Still, no president or vice president to date has had a non-Christian religious affiliation (though some have had no religious affiliation at all).

- *Abortion:* This probably affects who gets a party's nomination, but in the general election ardent supporters and ardent opponents are about evenly balanced.

In congressional races, however, in general it seems that money does make a decisive difference. Scholars are not entirely agreed on the facts, but strong evidence suggests that how much the challenger spends is most important, because the challenger usually must become known to the public. Buying name recognition is expensive. Gary Jacobson has shown that, other things being equal, in every congressional election from 1972 to the mid-1980s, challengers who spent more money did better than those who spent less.[18] Jacobson also suggested that how much the incumbents spent was not very important, presumably because they already had all the name recognition they needed (as well as the other benefits of holding office, such as free mail and travel). Other scholars, applying different statistical methods to the same facts, have come to different conclusions. It now seems that, other things being equal, high-spending incumbents do better than low-spending ones.[19] "Million-dollar challengers" are becoming more common in House races, but it remains to be seen if that will continue, and if so, whether it narrows the gap with incumbents.

Incumbents find it easier to raise money than challengers; incumbents provide services to their districts that challengers cannot; incumbents regularly send free ("franked") mail to their constituents, while challengers must pay for their mailings; incumbents can get free publicity by sponsoring legislation or conducting an investigation. Thus, it is hardly surprising that incumbents who run for re-election win in the overwhelming majority of races.

What Decides the Election?

To the voter, it all seems quite simple—he or she votes for "the best person" or maybe "the least-bad person." To scholars, it is all a bit mysterious. How do voters decide who the best person is? What does "best" mean, anyway?

Party

One answer to these questions is party identification. People may say they are voting for the "best person," but for many people the best person is always a Democrat or a Republican. Moreover, we have seen in Chapter 7 that many people know rather little about the details of political issues. They may not even know what position their favored candidate has taken on issues they care about. Given these facts, many scholars have argued that party identification is the principal determinant of how people vote.[20]

If it were only a matter of party identification, though, the Democrats would always win the presidency, since usually more people identify with the Democratic than the Republican party. But we know that the Democrats lost seven of the 12 presidential elections between 1968 and 2012. There are three reasons for this.

HOW WE COMPARE

Public Funding for National Political Campaigns

In the United States, national political campaigns are funded primarily through private donations by individuals, political parties, and interest groups. Only presidential campaigns are eligible to receive public funding, and even there, candidates may decide not to accept the funds so they are not restricted by a federal cap on spending. Despite efforts to regulate campaign contributions since the 1970s, American democracy has a longstanding tradition of applying the First Amendment protection of free speech to campaign spending, a position recently endorsed by the Supreme Court. Other advanced industrialized democracies take a different view.

Many democracies around the world rely much more heavily on public funding for elections than the United States, and have stricter regulations on campaign contributions and expenditures. Australia, Germany, France, and Israel all provide public funds for political campaigns, typically granting funds to parties that received a certain percentage of votes in the previous election. France and the United Kingdom ban paid political ads, and both countries as well as Israel provide free broadcasting time for candidates. All three countries also impose limits on campaign spending.

How do campaign finance rules affect elections? In many ways, campaigns in the United States run much longer than in other democracies—the countries listed above typically hold national elections in about six weeks, whereas the 2008 presidential race in the United States began two years earlier. This is because public funding typically strengthens political parties, whose leaders decide which candidates they will support. Unlimited campaign contributions may permit relatively unknown candidates to prevail in party nominating contests without initial support from the top leadership. But winning requires time and money in the United States, and the financial costs increase in every election cycle. Is money a form of free speech? Democracies disagree.

Sources: Law Library of Congress, "Campaign Finance: Comparative Summary;" Brennan Center for Justice, "Breaking Free with Fair Elections: A New Declaration of Independence," March 2007; Debate between Bradley Smith and Thomas E. Mann, "Campaign Finance Reloaded," *Los Angeles Times*, July 2007.

First, those people who consider themselves Democrats were less firmly wedded to their party than Republicans. Table 10.6 shows how people identifying themselves as Democrats, Republicans, or independents voted in presidential elections from 1960 to 2012. In every election except those of 1964, 1992, 1996, and 2012, Republicans were more likely to vote for the Republican candidate than Democrats were to vote for the Democratic candidate (with a tie in 2008). In every election except

1992, at least 80 percent of Republican voters supported the Republican candidate. By contrast, there have been a few dramatic defections among Democratic voters—in 1972, a third of Democrats supported Nixon, and in 1984, 26 percent supported Reagan.

The second reason, also clear from Table 10.6, is that the Republicans, from the election of 1960 through the election of 1988, did better than the Democrats among the self-described "independent"

TABLE 10.6 **Percentage of Popular Vote by Groups in Presidential Elections, 1960–2012**

		National	Republicans	Democrats	Independents
1960	Kennedy	50%	5%	84%	43%
	Nixon	50	95	16	57
1964	Johnson	61	20	87	56
	Goldwater	39	80	13	44
1968	Humphrey	43	9	74	31
	Nixon	43	86	12	44
	Wallace	14	5	14	25
1972	McGovern	38	5	67	31
	Nixon	62	95	33	69
1976	Carter	51	11	80	48
	Ford	49	89	20	52
1980ᵃ	Carter	41	11	66	30
	Reagan	51	84	26	54
	Anderson	7	4	6	12
1984	Mondale	41	7	73	35
	Reagan	59	92	26	63
1988	Dukakis	46	8	82	43
	Bush	54	91	17	55
1992	Clinton	43	10	77	38
	Bush	38	73	10	32
	Perot	19	17	13	30
1996	Clinton	49	13	84	43
	Dole	41	80	10	35
	Perot	8	6	5	17
2000	Gore	49	8	86	45
	Bush	48	91	11	47
2004	Kerry	49	6	89	49
	Bush	51	93	11	48
2008	Obama	52	9	89	52
	McCain	46	89	10	44
2012	Obama	51	6	92	45
	Romney	48	90	10	49

ᵃThe figures for 1980, 1984, 1988, 1996, and 2012 fail to add up to 100 percent because of missing data.

voters. In the fourteen presidential elections from 1960 to 2012, the Democratic candidate won a larger share of the independent vote six times (1964, 1992, 1996, 2000, 2004, and 2008) while the Republican candidate won it eight times (1960, 1968, 1972, 1976, 1980, 1984, 1988, and 2012). But in five of the last six elections (2012 being the one exception), the Democratic candidate won a larger share of the independent vote than the Republican candidate did.

Finally, a higher percentage of Republicans than Democrats voted in most post-1960 elections, and those describing themselves as "strongly Republican" were more likely to vote than those describing themselves as "strongly Democratic." But those Republican edges in partisan voter participation have ebbed in recent years just as minority voters that traditionally favor the Democratic presidential candidate have increased their participation. For instance, in 2012, Obama won 93 percent of the African American vote; and, at 66.2 percent, voter turnout among African Americans exceeded voter turnout for the electorate as a whole. In 2012, Latino voter turnout was higher than it was in 2008, and Obama won more than 70 percent of all Latino votes.

Issues, Especially the Economy

Even though voters may not know a lot about the issues, that does not mean issues play no role in elections or that voters respond irrationally to them. For example, V. O. Key, Jr., looked at those voters who switched from one party to another between elections and found that most of them switched in a direction consistent with their own interests. As Key put it, the voters are not fools.[21]

Moreover, voters may know a lot more than we suppose about issues that really matter to them. They may have hazy, even erroneous, views about monetary policy, business regulation, and the trade deficit, but they likely have a very good idea about whether unemployment is up or down, prices at the supermarket are stable or rising, or crime is a problem in their neighborhoods. And on some issues—such as abortion, school prayer, and race relations—they likely have some strong principles they want to see politicians obey.

Contrary to what we learn in our civics classes, representative government does not require voters to be well informed on the issues. If it were our duty as citizens to have accurate facts and sensible ideas about how best to negotiate with foreign adversaries, stabilize the value of the dollar, revitalize failing industries, and keep farmers prosperous, we might as well forget about citizenship and head for the beach. It would be a full-time job, and then some, to be a citizen. Politics would take on far more importance in our lives than most of us would want, given our need to earn a living and our belief in the virtues of limited government.

To see why our system can function without well-informed citizens, we must understand the differences between two ways in which issues can affect elections.

> **prospective voting**
> Voting for a candidate because you favor his or her ideas for handling issues.
>
> **retrospective voting**
> Voting for a candidate because you like his or her past actions in office.

Prospective Voting

Prospective means "forward-looking"—we vote prospectively when we examine the views the rival candidates have on the issues of the day and then cast our ballots for the person we think has the best ideas for handling these matters. **Prospective voting** requires a lot of information about issues and candidates. Some of us vote prospectively. Those who do tend to be political junkies. They are either willing to spend a lot of time learning about issues or are so concerned about some big issue (abortion, school busing, nuclear energy) that all they care about is how a candidate stands on that question.

Prospective voting is more common among people who are political activists, have a political ideology that governs their voting decision, or are involved in interest groups with a big stake in the election. They are a minority of all voters, but (as we saw in Chapters 7 and 8) they are more influential than their numbers would suggest. Some prospective voters (by no means all) are organized into single-issue groups, to be discussed in the next section.

Retrospective Voting

Retrospective means "backward-looking"—**retrospective voting** involves looking at how things have gone in the recent past and then voting for the party that controls the White House if we like what has happened and voting against that party if we do not like what has happened. Retrospective voting does not require us to have a lot of information—all we need to know is whether things have, in our view, gotten better or worse.

Elections are decided by retrospective voters.[22] In 1980, they decided to vote against Jimmy Carter because inflation was rampant, interest rates were high, and we seemed to be getting the worst of things overseas. The evidence suggests rather clearly that they did not vote *for* Ronald Reagan; they voted for *an alternative to* Jimmy Carter. (Some people did vote for Reagan and his philosophy; they were voting prospectively, but they were in the minority.)

In 1984, people voted for Ronald Reagan because unemployment, inflation, and interest rates were down and because we no longer seemed to be getting pushed around overseas. In 1980, retrospective voters wanted change; in 1984, they wanted continuity. In 1988, there was no incumbent running, but George H. W. Bush portrayed himself as the candidate who would continue the policies that had led to prosperity and depicted Michael Dukakis as a "closet liberal" who would change those policies. In 1992, the economy had once again turned sour, and so voters turned away from Bush and toward his rivals, Bill Clinton and Ross Perot.

Though most incumbent members of Congress get re-elected, those who lose do so, it appears, largely because they are the victims of retrospective voting. After Reagan was first elected, the economy went into a recession in 1981–1982. As a result, Republican members of Congress were penalized by the voters, and Democratic challengers were helped. But it is not just the economy that can hurt congressional candidates. In most midterm elections, the party holding the White House has lost seats in Congress. Just why this should be is not entirely clear, but it probably has something to do with the tendency of some voters to change their opinions of the presidential party once that party has had a chance to govern—which is to say, a chance to make some mistakes, disappoint some supporters, and irritate some interests.

Some scholars believe that retrospective voting is based largely on economic conditions. Figure 10.3 certainly provides support for this view. Each dot represents a presidential election (17 of them, from 1948 to 2012). The horizontal axis is the percentage increase or decrease in per capita disposable income (adjusted for inflation) during the election year. The vertical axis is the percentage of the two-party vote won by the party already occupying the White House. You can see that, as per capita income goes up (as you move to the right on the horizontal axis), the incumbent political party tends to win a bigger share of the vote.

Other scholars feel that matters are more complicated than this. As a result, a small industry has grown up consisting of people who use different techniques to forecast the outcome of elections. If you know how the president stands in the opinion polls several months before the election and how well the economy is performing, you can make a pretty good guess as to who is going to win the presidency. For congressional races, predicting the result is a lot tougher because so many local factors affect these contests. Election forecasting remains an inexact science. As one study of the performance of presidential election forecasting models concluded: "Models may be no improvement over pundits."[23]

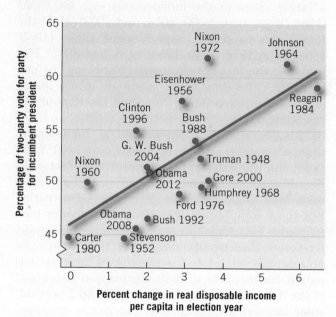

FIGURE 10.3 **The Economy and Vote for President 1948–2012**

Percentage of two-party vote for party for incumbent president (vertical axis)

Percent change in real disposable income per capita in election year (horizontal axis)

Notes: (1) Each dot represents a presidential election, showing the popular vote received by the incumbent president's party. (2) 1992 data do not include votes for independent candidate H. Ross Perot. (3) 2004 value on RDI is projection from data available in December 2004.

Source: From *American Public Opinion*, 5th ed., by Robert S. Erikson and Kent L. Tedin. Copyright © 1995 by Addison-Wesley Educational Publishers, Inc. Reprinted by permission of Pearson Education, Inc. 2008 update from Bureau of Economic Analysis, U.S. Department of Commerce. Federal Reserve of St. Louis. "FRED Economic Data: Real Disposable Personal Income Per Capita."Economic Research. Accessed June 2, 2013. http://research.stlouisfed.org/fred2/graph/?s[1][id]=A229RX0.

The Campaign

If party loyalty and national economic conditions play so large a role in elections, is the campaign just sound and fury, signifying nothing?

No. Campaigns can make a difference in three ways. First, they reawaken the partisan loyalties of voters. Right after a party's nominating convention selects a presidential candidate, that person's standing with voters of both parties goes way up in the polls. The reason is that the just-nominated candidate has received a lot of media attention during the summer months, when not much else is happening. When the campaign gets under way, however, both candidates get publicity, and voters return to their normal Democratic or Republican affiliations.

Second, campaigns give voters a chance to watch how the candidates handle pressure, and they give candidates a chance to apply that pressure. The two rivals, after promising to conduct a campaign "on the issues" without mudslinging, immediately start searching each other's personal histories and records

Union members were once heavily Democratic, but since Ronald Reagan began winning white union votes in 1980, these votes have been up for grabs.

to find acts, statements, or congressional votes that can be shown in the worst possible light in newspaper or television ads. Many voters don't like these "negative ads"—but they work. Careful statistical studies based on actual campaigns (as opposed to voter surveys or laboratory-like focus group studies) suggest that negative ads work by stimulating voter turnout.[24] As a result, every politician constantly worries about how an opponent might portray his or her record, a fact that helps explain why so many politicians never do or say anything that cannot be explained in a 30-second television spot.

Third, campaigns allow voters an opportunity to judge the character and core values of the candidates. Most voters don't study in detail a candidate's positions on issues; even if they had the time, they know you can't predict how politicians will behave just from knowing what a campaign manager has written in a position paper. The voters want some guidance as to how a candidate will behave once elected. They get that guidance by listening not to the details of what a candidate says but to the themes and tone of those statements. Is the candidate tough on crime and drugs? Are his or her statements about the environment sincere or perfunctory? Does the candidate favor having a strong military? Does the candidate care more about not raising taxes or more about helping the homeless?

The desire of voters to discern character, combined with the mechanics of modern campaigning—short radio and television ads and both online and printed direct mail—lend themselves to an emphasis on themes at the expense of details. This tendency is reinforced by the expectations of ideological party activists and single-issue groups.

Thematic campaigning, negative ads, and the demands of single-issue groups are not new; they are as old as the republic. In the 19th century, the theme was slavery and the single-issue groups were abolitionists and their opponents; their negative ads make the ones we have today sound like Sunday school sermons. At the turn of the century, the themes were temperance and the vote for women; both issues led to no-holds-barred, rough-and-tumble campaigning. In the 1970s and 1980s, new themes were advanced by fundamentalist Christians and by pro- and antiabortion groups.

What has changed is not the tone of campaigning but the advent of primary elections. Once, political parties picked candidates out of a desire to win elections. Today, activists and single-issue groups influence the selection of candidates, sometimes out of a belief that it is better to lose with the "right" candidate than to win with the wrong one. In a five-candidate primary, a minority of the voters can pick the winner. Single-issue groups can make a big difference under these conditions, even though they may not have much influence in the general election.

Finding a Winning Coalition

Putting together a winning electoral coalition means holding on to your base among committed partisans and attracting the swing voters who cast their ballots in response to issues (retrospectively or prospectively) and personalities.

There are two ways to examine the nature of the parties' voting coalitions. One is to ask what percentage of various identifiable groups in the population supported the Democratic or Republican candidate for president. The other is to ask what proportion of a party's total vote came from each of these groups. The answer to the first question tells us how *loyal* African Americans, farmers, union members, and others are to the Democratic or Republican party or candidate; the answer to the second question tells us how *important* each group is to a candidate or party.

Former Speaker of the U.S. House of Representatives Newt Gingrich campaigned for the Republican presidential nomination in 2012.

For the Democratic coalition, African Americans are the most loyal voters. In every election but one since 1952, two-thirds or more of all African Americans voted Democratic; since 1964, more than four-fifths have gone Democratic. Usually, Jewish voters are almost as solidly Democratic. Most Latinos have been Democrats, though there are differences among Cuban Americans (who often vote Republican) and Mexican Americans and Puerto Ricans (who are strongly Democratic). In recent elections, turnout rates among Latino voters have begun to rise. After losing the growing Latino vote by a lop-sided margin again in 2012, many Republican leaders vowed to make new and concerted efforts to win more Latino votes in time for the 2016 presidential campaign season; we shall see what happens.

The Democrats have lost their once strong hold on Catholics, southerners, and union members. In 1960, Catholics supported John F. Kennedy (a Democrat and fellow Catholic), but they also voted for Eisenhower, Nixon, and Reagan—all Republicans. Union members deserted the Democrats in 1968 and 1972, came back in 1980 and 1988, and divided about evenly between the two parties in 1952, 1956, and 1980. As Table 10.7 shows, in the 13 presidential

elections from 1964 through 2012, a majority of Catholics voted for the Democrat in five elections, for the Republican in six elections, and were split 50-50 in two elections (2000 and 2012). Thus, for any president and for either party, a winning coalition must be assembled anew in every election.

The Republican party often is described as the party of business and professional people. The loyalty of these groups to Republicans is strong: only in 1964 did they desert the Republican candidate to support Lyndon Johnson. Farmers usually have been Republican, but they are a volatile group, highly sensitive to the level of farm prices—and thus quick to change parties. In sum, the loyalty of most identifiable groups of voters to either party is not overwhelming. Only African Americans, businesspeople, and Jews usually give two-thirds or more of their votes to one party or the other; other groups display tendencies, but none that cannot be overcome.

The contribution that each of these groups makes to the party coalitions is a different matter. Though African Americans are overwhelmingly and persistently Democratic, they make up so small a portion of the total electorate that they have never accounted for more than a quarter of the total

TABLE 10.7 **Percentage of Various Groups Saying They Voted for the Democratic Presidential Candidate, 1964–2012**

		1964	1968[a]	1972	1976	1980[b]	1984	1988	1992[c]	1996	2000	2004	2008	2012
Sex	Men	60	41	37	53	37	37	41	41	43	42	45	49	45
	Women	62	45	38	48	45	42	49	46	54	54	52	56	55
Race	White	59	38	32	46	36	34	40	39	44	45	42	43	40
	Black	94	85	87	85	82	90	86	82	84	90	89	95	93
Education	College	52	37	37	42	35	40	43	44	44	45	47	49	47
	Grade school	66	52	49	58	43	49	56	55	59	52	51	63	63
Age	Under 30	64	47	48	53	43	41	47	44	53	48	54	66	60
	50 and over	59	41	36	52	41[d]	39	49	50	48	48	46	48	47
Religion	Protestant	55	35	30	46	na	na	33[e]	38	41	42	41	45	42
	Catholic	76	59	48	57	40	44	47	42	53	50	48	54	50
	Jewish[f]	89	85	66	68	45	66	64	68	78	79	76	78	69
Southerners		52	31	29	54	47	36	41	42	na	na	41	na	na

[a]1968 election had three major candidates (Humphrey, Nixon, and Wallace).
[b]1980 election had three major candidates (Carter, Reagan, and Anderson).
[c]1992 election had three major candidates (Clinton, George H. W. Bush, and Perot).
[d]For 1980–1992 and 2004, refers to age 60 and over.
[e]For 1988, white Protestants only.
[f]Jewish vote estimated from various sources; because the number of Jewish persons interviewed is often less than 100, the error in this figure, as well as that for nonwhites, may be large.
na, not available.

Source: Gallup poll data as tabulated in Jeane J. Kirkpatrick, "Changing Patterns of Electoral Competition," in Anthony King, ed.,*The New American Political System* (Washington, D.C.: American Enterprise Institute, 1978), pp. 264–265. 1980, 1984, 1988, 1992, 1996, 2000, 2004, and 2008 data from CBS News/New York Times survey and CNN poll. 2012 data on Protestant, Catholic, and Jewish, Prof. John Lapinski, University of Pennsylvania, other 2012 data from NEP exit poll data 2012 as reported in Wall Street Journal, November 8, 2012.

Democratic vote. The groups that make up the largest part of the Democratic vote—Catholics, union members, southerners—are also the least dependable parts of that coalition.[25]

When representatives of various segments of society make demands on party leaders and presidential candidates, they usually stress their numbers or their loyalty, but rarely both. African American leaders, for example, sometimes describe the black vote as of decisive importance to Democrats and thus deserving of special consideration from a Democratic president. But African Americans are so loyal that a Democratic candidate can almost take their votes for granted, and in any event they are not as numerous as other groups. Union leaders emphasize how many union voters there are, but a president will know that union leaders cannot "deliver" the union vote and that this vote may go to the president's opponent, whatever the leaders say. For any presidential candidate, a winning coalition must be put together anew for each election. Only a few voters can be taken for granted or written off as a lost cause.

The Effects of Elections on Policy

To the candidates, and perhaps to the voters, the only interesting outcome of an election is who won. To a political scientist, the interesting outcomes are the broad trends in winning and losing and what they imply about the attitudes of voters, the operation of the electoral system, the fate of political parties, and the direction of public policy.

Figure 10.4 shows the trend in the popular vote for president since before the Civil War. From 1876 to 1896, the Democrats and Republicans were hotly competitive. The Republicans won three times, the Democrats twice in close contests. Beginning in 1896, the Republicans became the dominant party, and except for 1912 and 1916, when Woodrow Wilson, a Democrat, was able to win owing to a split in the Republican party, the Republicans carried every presidential election until 1932. Then Franklin Roosevelt put together what has since become known as the "New Deal coalition," and the Democrats became the dominant party. They won every election until 1952, when Eisenhower, a Republican and a popular military hero, was elected for the first of his two terms. In the presidential elections since 1952, power has switched hands between the parties frequently.

Still, cynics complain that elections are meaningless: no matter who wins, crooks, incompetents, or self-serving politicians still hold office. The more charitable argue that elected officials usually are decent enough, but that public policy remains more or less the same no matter which official or party is in office.

There is no brief and simple response to this latter view. Much depends on which office or policy you examine. One reason it is so hard to generalize about

FIGURE 10.4 **Partisan Division of the Presidential Vote in the Nation, 1856–2012**

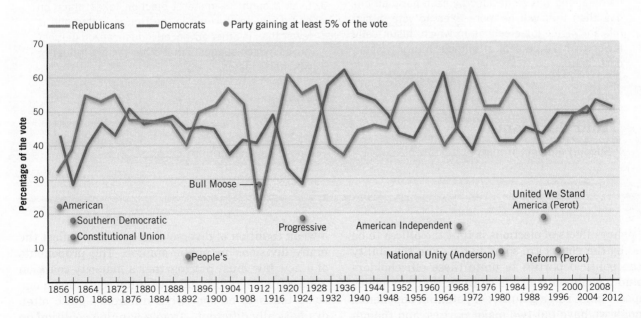

Sources: Information for 1856–1988, updated from Historical Data Archive, Inter-University Consortium for Political Research, as reported in William H. Flanigan and Nancy H. Zingale, *Political Behavior of the American Electorate*, 3rd ed., 32. For 1992: *World Almanac and Book of Facts 1994*, 73.

WHAT WOULD YOU DO?

MEMORANDUM

To: *Arjun Bruno, National party chairperson*

From: *Arlene Marcus, State party chairperson*

Subject: *Supporting a national primary*

In the past few election cycles, our state's role in the party nomination for president virtually has disappeared with a May primary date. Several states have leapfrogged ahead of us, and party leaders have indicated that they do not want any more states to move up their primary date. The national party needs to find a way to ensure that all states, large and small, have a real voice in nominating a presidential candidate.

Arguments for:

1. A single national primary permits equal participation by all states and presents a fair compromise with the increased number of delegates that larger states send to the national conventions, much like the compromises during the original constitutional debates.

2. The nominating process needs to be less costly, particularly when presidential candidates realistically need to raise $100 million a year before the general election to be competitive for the nomination. Holding all primaries and caucuses on a single day will reduce overall election expenses significantly.

3. If the American electorate knows presidential nominations will be decided by each party on one day, then they will be more likely to vote, a significant factor for elections in which, historically, fewer than 20 percent of eligible voters typically participate.

News »

Would a National Primary Date Give All States an Equal Voice?

With the increasing cost and length of presidential nominating contests, several political strategists favor creating a single national primary date. But party leaders are divided over the consequences for candidates and voters.

Arguments against:

1. Each state decides in conjunction with the national party when its primary or caucus will take place, and the federal system of government designed by the Framers did not guarantee that all states would be treated equally at all times.

2. A national primary would favor candidates with high name recognition and funding to further that recognition and would severely disadvantage lesser-known candidates within the party.

3. Even though the general election takes place on one day, voter turnout in the United States still is lower than in other advanced industrialized democracies, which suggests that other factors influence who participates.

Your decision:

Support national primary _____   Oppose national primary _____

---

the policy effects of elections is that the offices to be filled by the voters are so numerous and the ability of the political parties to unite these officeholders behind a common policy is so weak that any policy proposal must run a gauntlet of potential opponents. Though we have but two major parties, and though only one party can win the presidency, each party is a weak coalition of diverse elements that reflect the many divisions in public opinion. The proponents of a new law must put together a majority coalition almost from scratch, and a winning coalition on one issue tends to be somewhat different—quite often dramatically different—from a winning coalition on another issue.

In a parliamentary system with strong parties, such as that in the United Kingdom, an election often can have a major effect on public policy. When the Labour party won office in 1945, it put several major industries under public ownership and launched a comprehensive set of social services, including a nationalized health care plan. Its ambitious and controversial campaign platform was converted, almost item by item, into law. When the Conservative party returned to power in 1951, it accepted some of these changes but rejected others (for example, it denationalized the steel industry).

American elections, unless accompanied by a national crisis such as a war or a depression, rarely produce changes of the magnitude of those that occurred in Britain in 1945. The constitutional system within which our elections take place was designed to moderate the pace of change—to make it neither easy nor impossible to adopt radical proposals. But the fact that the system is intended to moderate the rate of change does not mean it will always work that way.

The election of 1860 brought to national power a party committed to opposing the extension of slavery and southern secession; it took a bloody war to vindicate that policy. The election of 1896 led to the dominance of a party committed to high tariffs, a strong currency, urban growth, and business prosperity—a commitment that was not significantly altered until 1932. The election of that year led to the New Deal, which produced the greatest single enlargement of federal authority since 1860. The election of 1964 gave the Democrats such a large majority in Congress (as well as control of the presidency) that there began to issue forth an extraordinary number of new policies of sweeping significance—Medicare and Medicaid, federal aid to education and to local law enforcement, two dozen environmental and consumer protection laws, the Voting Rights Act of 1965, a revision of the immigration laws, and a new cabinet-level Department of Housing and Urban Development.

The election of 1980 brought into office an administration determined to reverse the direction of policy over the preceding half century. Reagan's administration succeeded in obtaining large tax cuts, significant reductions in spending (or in the rate of increase of spending) on some domestic programs, and changes in the policies of some regulatory agencies. The election of 1982, in which the Democrats made gains in the House of Representatives, stiffened congressional resistance to further spending cuts and stimulated renewed interest in tax increases as a way of reducing the deficit. Following the election of 1984, a major tax

reform plan was passed. After the 1996 election, Clinton and Republican congressional leaders agreed on a plan to balance the budget.

In view of all these developments, it is hard to argue that the pace of change in our government is always slow or that elections never make a difference. Studies by scholars confirm that elections often are significant, despite the difficulty of getting laws passed. One analysis of about 1,400 promises made between 1944 and 1964 in the platforms of the two major parties revealed that 72 percent were put into effect.[26]

Another study examined the party platforms of the Democrats and Republicans from 1844 to 1968 and all the laws passed by Congress between 1789 and 1968. By a complex statistical method, the author of the study was able to show that during certain periods the differences between the platforms of the two parties were especially large (1856, 1880, 1896, 1932) and that there was at about the same time a high rate of change in the kinds of laws being passed.[27] This study supports the general impression conveyed by history that elections often can be central to important policy changes.

Why then do we so often think elections make little difference? It is because public opinion and the political parties enter a phase of consolidation and continuity between periods of rapid change. During this phase, the changes are digested, and party leaders adjust to the new popular consensus, which may (or may not) evolve around the merits of these changes. During the 1870s and 1880s, Democratic politicians had to come to terms with the failure of the southern secessionist movement and the abolition of slavery; during the 1900s, the Democrats had to adjust again, this time to the fact that national economic policy was going to support industrialization and urbanization, not farming; during the 1940s and 1950s, the Republicans had to learn to accept the popularity of the New Deal.

Elections in ordinary times are not "critical"—they do not produce any major party realignment, they are not fought out over a dominant issue, and they provide the winners with no clear mandate. In most cases, an election is little more than a retrospective judgment on the record of the incumbent president and the existing congressional majority. If times are good, incumbents win easily; if times are bad, incumbents may lose—even though their opponents may have no clear plans for change. But even a "normal" election can produce dramatic results if the winner is a person such as Ronald Reagan, who helped give his party a distinctive political philosophy, or Barack Obama, the nation's first African American president.

LEARNING OBJECTIVES

1. What is the difference between a primary election and a general election?

A primary election selects a political party's nominee for office, while a general election determines who will hold that office.

2. Does the federal government provide funding for political campaigns?

The federal government does not fund congressional elections, but it does provide public funding for presidential candidates (and their party conventions), though candidates may choose not to accept public funds and raise unlimited funding on their own, as happened in 2008 and 2012.

3. How do voters typically decide on a candidate?

Voters typically evaluate an incumbent's performance and vote for re-election if they are pleased; if not, then they cast a vote against the incumbent, but that may not necessarily mean they endorse the opponent's platform. Evaluating an incumbent's term is retrospective voting, while trying to determine how a candidate will act in office is prospective voting.

4. How do American elections determine the kind of people who govern us?

American democracy rewards candidates who have personal appeal rather than party endorsements. Politics here produces individualists who usually have a strong ideological orientation toward liberal or conservative causes, but only a weak sense of loyalty to the political parties who endorse those ideologies.

5. What matters most in deciding who wins presidential and congressional elections?

The party identification of the voters matters the most. Only 10 to 20 percent of the voters are available to have their votes changed. For them, the state of the economy, and in wartime the success or failures we have while fighting abroad, makes the most difference. Closely allied with those issues, at least for presidential candidates, is the voters' assessment of their character.

6. Do elections make a real difference in what laws get passed?

Yes. During campaigns parties may try to sound alike, in order to attract centrist voters, but when in office they differ greatly in the policies they put into law.

TO LEARN MORE

Federal Election Commission: **www.fec.gov**

Project Vote Smart: **www.vote-smart.org**

Election history: **clerk.house.gov**

Electoral college: **www.archives.gov/federal-register/electoral-college/**

Campaign finance: **www.opensecrets.org**

Bader, Ted. *Campaigning for Hearts and Minds: How Emotional Appeals in Political Ads Work*. Chicago: University of Chicago Press, 2006. Masterful analysis of how ads move voters and influence people who are most well-informed about politics.

Black, Earl, and Merle Black. *Divided America: The Ferocious Power Struggle in American Politics*. New York: Simon and Schuster, 2007. Detailed account of how evenly balanced the two parties are in all parts of the country.

Burnham, Walter Dean. *Critical Elections and the Mainsprings of American Politics*. New York: Norton, 1970. An argument about the decline in voting participation and the significance of the realigning election of 1896.

Klein, Joe. Politics Lost? *How American Democracy Was Trivialized by People Who Think You're Stupid*. New York: Doubleday, 2006. A veteran political reporter claims that political consultants are to blame for negative political developments.

Sundquist, James L. *Dynamics of the Party System: Alignment and Realignment of Political Parties in the United States*, Rev. ed. Washington, D.C.: Brookings Institution, 1983. Historical analysis of realigning elections from 1860 to the nonrealignment of 1980.

Interest Groups

LEARNING OBJECTIVES

1. What are interest groups and how did they arise in America?

2. What are the different kinds of interest groups and which types have been proliferating of late?

3. Why do people join interest groups?

4. How do interest groups attempt to influence public policy, and how does government regulate interest group activities?

5. Is the proliferation of political action committees (PACs) and other groups good or bad for America's representative democracy?

6. Should interest groups' political activities be restricted by law?

interest group An organization of people sharing a common interest or goal that seeks to influence public policy.

political action committee (PAC) A committee set up by a corporation, labor union, or interest group that raises and spends campaign money from voluntary donations.

lobbyist A person who tries to influence legislation on behalf of an interest group.

You probably do not think of yourself or of people you know as belonging to an "interest group." But are you or friends of yours part of an effort to improve the environment? Do you have family or friends who build houses, teach school, or practice law? If the answer to any of these questions is yes, then you likely know someone who belongs to the Sierra Club or the Audubon Society, a labor union, the American Federation of Teachers, or the American Bar Association. In short, if you examine your own activities and affiliations and those of at least some people you know well, chances are that you or they belong to one or more interest groups.

An **interest group** is an organization of people sharing a common interest or goal that seeks to influence public policy. The size and diversity of our country, the decentralizing effects of our Constitution, the vast number of nonprofit organizations, and the weakness of our political parties make it certain that interest groups will be an important way for people to have their voices heard. But while interest groups are as old as the republic itself, the number of interest groups has grown rapidly since 1960, and the number of interest groups that have lobbyists working full-time in Washington has reached new highs in just the last decade.

THEN

During the 1770s, many groups arose to agitate for American independence; during the 1830s and 1840s, the number of religious associations increased sharply, and the antislavery movement began. In the 1860s, craft-based trade unions emerged in significant numbers, farmers formed the Grange, and various fraternal organizations were born. In the 1880s and 1890s, business associations proliferated.

The great era of organization building, however, was in the first two decades of the 20th century. Within this 20-year period, many of the best-known and largest associations with an interest in national politics were formed: the Chamber of Commerce, the National Association of Manufacturers, the American Medical Association, the National Association for the Advancement of Colored People (NAACP), the Urban League, the American Farm Bureau Federation, the Farmers' Union, the National Catholic Welfare Conference, the American Jewish Committee, and the Anti-Defamation League.

NOW

The wave of interest group formation that occurred in the 1960s led to the emergence of environmental, consumer, and political reform organizations such as those sponsored by consumer activist Ralph Nader. In 1973, a new federal campaign finance law made it legal for interest groups to create political action committees. A **political action committee (PAC)** is an organization created by a business firm, labor union, trade association, or ideological group that recruits members from whom it obtains campaign contributions. By the mid-1990s, there were about six times as many PACs (more than 4,000) as there had been in the mid-1970s, about a quarter of them ideological in character.

The growth in ideological groups has been equaled and, of late, exceeded only by the growth in business groups. For instance, between 1981 and 2005, the number of full-time and part-time lobbyists—(a **lobbyist** tries to influence legislation on behalf of an interest group) in Washington representing just the S&P 500 corporations increased from 1,475 to 2,765.[1] Today about 14,000 lobbyists for business, union, and other groups are listed in the (over 2,000-page) *Washington Directory*, up from about 7,000 lobbyists (and 531 pages) three decades ago. Adjusted for inflation, the roughly $3.5 billion spent on lobbying in 2009 was nearly seven times the amount spent on lobbying a quarter-century earlier.[2]

Why are associations in general and political interest groups in particular created more rapidly in some periods than in others? After all, there have always been farmers in this country, but there were no national farm organizations until the latter part of the 19th century. Blacks were victimized by various white-supremacy policies from the end of the Civil War on, but the NAACP did not emerge until 1910. Men and women worked in factories for decades before industrial unions were formed. Every political era featured activists who believed strongly in liberal or conservative ideology, but only in recent decades have ideological groups become so pervasive. Organized business interests have battled organized labor interests over public policy for more than a hundred years, but only in recent decades has the big business lobbying presence in Washington expanded so dramatically both in absolute terms and relative to big labor.

Four factors have helped shape how and when given interest groups arose in America. We now turn to a consideration of them.

HOW WE COMPARE

Interest Groups in America, Great Britain, and Germany

Suppose we were a small country that had no state governments and operated under a parliamentary system that made the prime minister the only important official. Suppose further that strong parties dominated how policies were made and that our tax laws made it hard to support nonprofit organizations. If these things were true, then interest groups would be much less important. Most of the political decisions would be made by the ruling party. If you wanted to affect how those decisions were made, you would have to be a leader of that party or part of one or two very powerful interest groups.

But in America these things are not true. This country has a great variety of ethnic groups, scores of religious organizations, and a Constitution that requires power to be shared by three branches of government and that ensures independent authority for 50 state governments. In our diverse nation, political authority is so decentralized that it invites the creation of interest groups that try to affect some part of every decision. And the Constitution makes it clear that lobbyists are protected: they are exercising freedom of speech and petitioning the government for a redress of grievances, just as the First Amendment guarantees them the right to do.

Compare the United States with the United Kingdom. Both nations are democratic, but in the United Kingdom only a few big interest groups exist; here, there are thousands. In the United Kingdom, only one lobbying organization represents farmers; here, there are at least three major agribusiness lobbies, each of which contains numerous individual lobbies.

Or compare the United States and Germany. Both countries are democratic, but German environmentalists created an influential political party (the Green Party), which formed part of the federal government coalition from 1998–2005, and continues to have seats in the federal Parliament. In this country, the Green Party has won no seats in Congress; most environmentalists instead have worked through a score of interest groups.

The Rise of Interest Groups

At least four factors help explain the rise of interest groups. The first consists of broad economic developments that create new interests and redefine old ones. Farmers had little reason to become organized for political activity so long as most of them consumed what they produced. The importance of regular political activity became evident only after most farmers began to produce cash crops for sale in markets that were unstable or affected by forces (the weather, the railroads, foreign competition) that farmers could not control. Similarly, for many decades most workers were craftspeople working alone or in small groups. Such unions as existed were little more than craft guilds interested in protecting members' jobs and in training apprentices. The impetus for large, mass-membership unions did not exist until there arose mass-production industry operated by large corporations.

Second, government policy itself helps to create interest groups. Wars create veterans, who in turn demand pensions and other benefits. The first large veterans' organization, the Grand Army of the Republic, was made up of Union veterans of the Civil War. By the 1920s, these men were receiving about a quarter of a billion dollars a year from the government, and naturally they created organizations to watch over the distribution of this money. The federal government encouraged the formation of the American Farm Bureau Federation (AFBF) by paying for county agents who would serve the needs of farmers under the supervision of local farm organizations; these county bureaus eventually came together as the AFBF. The Chamber of Commerce was launched at a conference attended by President William Howard Taft. Professional societies, such as those made up of lawyers and doctors, became

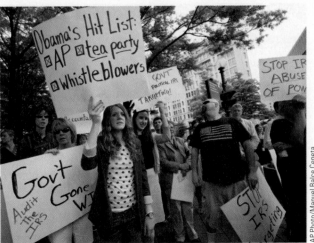

Tea Party activists protest in Washington, D.C., against the Internal Revenue Service's extra scrutiny of their organizations.

important in part because state governments gave to such groups the authority to decide who was qualified to become a lawyer or a doctor.

Workers had a difficult time organizing as long as the government, by the use of injunctions enforced by the police and the army, prevented strikes. Unions, especially those in mass-production industries, began to flourish after Congress passed laws in the 1930s that prohibited the use of injunctions in private labor disputes, that required employers to bargain with unions, and that allowed a union representing a majority of the workers in a plant to require all workers to join it.[3]

Third, political organizations do not emerge automatically, even when government policy permits them and social circumstances seem to require them. Somebody must exercise leadership, often at substantial personal cost. These organizational entrepreneurs are found in greater numbers at certain times than at others. Often they are young, caught up in a social movement, drawn to the need for change, and inspired by some political or religious doctrine.

Antislavery organizations were created in the 1830s and 1840s by enthusiastic young people influenced by a religious revival sweeping the country. The period from 1890 to 1920, when so many national organizations were created, was a time when the college-educated middle class was growing rapidly. (The number of men and women who received college degrees each year tripled between 1890 and 1920.)[4] During this era, natural science and fundamentalist Christianity were locked in a bitter contest, with the Gospels and Darwinism offering competing ideas about personal salvation and social progress. The 1960s, when many new organizations were born, was a decade in which young people were powerfully influenced by the civil rights and antiwar movements and when college enrollments more than doubled.

Finally, the more government does, the more interest groups will arise or expand and try to influence public policy. Most Washington offices representing corporations, labor unions, and trade and professional associations were established before 1960—in some cases many decades before—because it was during the 1930s or even earlier that the government began making policies important to business and labor. The great majority of "public-interest" lobbies (those concerned with the environment or consumer protection), social welfare associations, and organizations concerned with civil rights, the elderly, and the disabled established offices in Washington after major new federal laws in these respective areas were enacted.

The most recent and dramatic example is what happened in the post-9/11 years after the USA Patriot Act was enacted in 2001 and the Department of Homeland Security (DHS) was created in 2002. By 2010, with billions of dollars a year in federal funding for the purpose flowing, more than 500 new private companies specializing in work related to security and counterterrorism had come into being, and most of another 1,400 or so private companies that existed and did related work prior to 2001 had expanded.[5] New lobbies quickly formed to represent those firms and keep their homeland security grants and contracts coming; for example, the "full body scanner" lobby represents firms that sell body-scanning equipment used in airports to a DHS subunit, the Transportation Security Administration (TSA).[6] Moreover, many local governments, from big cities to small towns, have hired lobbyists to work on getting or sustaining their fair share of federal homeland security money.

CONSTITUTIONAL CONNECTIONS

A "Faction" or "Special Interest"?

While the Constitution does not discuss interest groups explicitly (though the First Amendment does guarantee their rights of assembly and speech), the Framers were very concerned about "factions" undermining the new republic. James Madison warned in *Federalist* 10 of the dangers of factions, and argued that republican (i.e., representative) democracy would control the effects of factions through elected officials and a large republic, in which groups would compete to influence policy, forcing compromise and preventing the domination of any single group. But what is a faction? Madison says any individual or group, whether a minority or majority of the whole, is a faction if it has interests that are opposed to the "permanent and aggregate interests of the community." Who defines those interests? The Framers thought our elected officials had the knowledge and expertise to do so, and those officials depend on interest groups for many resources, including information, campaign funds, and votes. A "faction" for one person may be a "special interest" for another. Madison's point about the need to limit the influence of factions remains true, but those groups also play an integral part in American democracy.

Kinds of Organizations

When we think of an organization, we usually think of something like the Boy Scouts or the League of Women Voters—a group consisting of individual members. In Washington, however, many organizations do not have individual members at all but are offices—corporations, law firms, public relations firms, or "letterhead" organizations that get most of their money from other organizations or from the government—out of which a staff operates. It is important to understand the differences between the two kinds of interest groups—institutional and membership interests.[7]

Institutional Interests

Institutional interests are individuals or organizations representing other organizations. For example, long before the government bailed it out in 2008, General Motors had representatives in Washington, and it is now not uncommon for even mid-sized corporations to have one or more full-time representatives plus part-time lawyers or public relations consultants working for them in Washington. Another kind of institutional interest is the trade or governmental association, such as the National Independent Retail Jewelers and the National Association of Counties.

Individuals or organizations that represent other organizations tend to be interested in bread-and-butter issues of vital concern to their clients. Some of the people who specialize in this work can earn very large fees. Top public relations experts and Washington lawyers can charge $500 an hour or more for their time. Since they earn a lot, they are expected to deliver a lot.

Just what they are expected to deliver, however, varies with the diversity of the groups making up the organization. The American Cotton Manufacturers Institute represents southern textile mills. Those mills are few enough in number and similar enough in outlook to allow the institute to carry out clear policies squarely based on the business interests of its clients. For example, the institute works hard to get the federal government to adopt laws and rules that will keep foreign-made textiles from competing too easily with American-made goods. Sometimes the institute is successful, sometimes not, but it is never hard to explain what it is doing.

By contrast, the U.S. Chamber of Commerce represents thousands of different businesses in hundreds of different communities. The Chamber has led all interest groups in annual lobbying expenditures. All told, from 1998 to 2012, it spent approximately $950 million on lobbying (see Figure 11.1),

FIGURE 11.1 **What the Top Lobby Spent, 1998–2012**

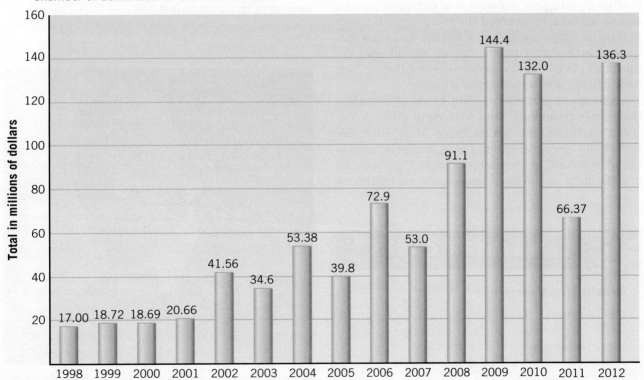

Annual lobbying expenditures by the Chamber of Commerce for the United States

Source: Center for Public Integrity, Georgetown University, Washington, D.C., 2011. Data for 2011 and 2012 from http://www.opensecrets.org/lobby/clientsum.php?id=D000019798&year=2011

a figure much larger than what was spent by any other organization over the same period, including corporate giants like Exxon Mobil and membership giants like AARP. Indeed, in 2012 alone, the Chamber spent $136 million on lobbying, more than the combined spending on lobbying by the next five largest spenders (the National Association of Realtors, Blue Cross/Blue Shield, General Electric, and the American Hospital Association, and the National Cable and Telecommunications Association, respectively).[8] Its membership is so large and diverse that the Chamber in Washington can speak out clearly and forcefully on only those relatively few matters in which all, or most, businesses take the same position. Since all businesses would like lower taxes, the Chamber favors that. On the other hand, since some businesses (those that import goods) want lower tariffs and other businesses (those that face competition from imported goods) want higher tariffs, the Chamber says little or nothing about tariffs.

Institutional interests do not just represent business firms; they also represent governments, foundations, and universities. For example, the American Council on Education speaks for most institutions of higher education, the American Public Transit Association represents local mass-transit systems, and the National Association of Counties argues on behalf of county governments.

Membership Interests

It often is said that America is a nation of joiners, and so we take for granted the many organizations around us supported by the activities and contributions of individual citizens. But we should not take this multiplicity of organizations for granted; in fact, their existence is something of a puzzle.

Americans join only certain kinds of organizations more frequently than citizens of other democratic countries. We are no more likely than the British, for example, to join social, business, professional, veterans', or charitable organizations, and we are *less* likely to join labor unions. Our reputation as

a nation of joiners arises chiefly out of our unusually high tendency to join religious and civic or political associations.

This proclivity of Americans to get together with other citizens to engage in civic or political action reflects, apparently, a greater sense of political efficacy and a stronger sense of civic duty than that found in some nations. In a classic study, Gabriel Almond and Sidney Verba asked citizens of five nations what they would do to protest an unjust local regulation; 56 percent of the Americans—but only 34 percent of the British and 13 percent of the Germans—said they would try to organize their neighbors to write letters, sign petitions, or otherwise act in concert.[9] Americans are also more likely than Europeans to think organized activity is an effective way to influence the national government, remote as that institution may seem. And even scholars who emphasize how this willingness to form civic or political groups seems to have declined in recent decades still generally agree that, compared to most other democratic peoples, Americans of every socioeconomic status and demographic description are joiners.[10]

But explaining the American willingness to join politically active groups by saying that Americans feel a "sense of political efficacy" is not much of an explanation; we might as well say people vote because they think their vote makes a difference. One vote clearly makes no difference at all in almost any election; similarly, one member, more or less, in the Sierra Club, the National Rifle Association, or the NAACP clearly will make no difference in the success of those organizations.

W.E.B. Du Bois, scholar and activist, was one of the founders of the NAACP.

C M Battey/Hulton Archive/Getty Images

LANDMARK CASES

Lobbying Congress

- *United States v. Harriss* (1954): The Constitution protects the lobbying of Congress, but the government may require information from groups that try to influence legislation.

And most people who are sympathetic to the aims of a mass-membership interest group do not join it. The NAACP, for example, enrolls as members only a tiny fraction of all African Americans. This is not because people are selfish or apathetic but because they are rational and numerous. A single African American, for example, knows that he or she can make no difference in the success of the NAACP, just as a single nature enthusiast knows that he or she cannot enhance the power of the Sierra Club. Moreover, if the NAACP or the Sierra Club succeeds, African Americans and nature lovers will benefit even if they are not members. Therefore, rational people who value their time and money would no more join such organizations than they would attempt to empty a lake with a cup—unless they got something out of joining.

Incentives to Join

Every interest group faces a free rider problem.[11] That is, many people who do not give it money or join as members are likely to benefit if the organization achieves its goal. They ride free on the organization's efforts. To overcome this, interest groups must offer people some **incentive** to join them. There are three kinds.

Solidary incentives are the sense of pleasure, status, or companionship that arises out of meeting together in small groups. Such rewards are extremely important, but because they tend to be available only from face-to-face contact, national interest groups offering them often have to organize themselves as coalitions of small local units. For example, the League of Women Voters, the Parent Teacher Association (PTA), the NAACP, the Rotary Club, and the American Legion all consist of small local chapters that support a national staff. It is the task of the local chapters to lure members and obtain funds from them; the state or national staff can then pursue political objectives by using these funds.

Forming organizations made up of small local chapters is probably easier in the United States than in Europe because of the great importance of local government in our federal system. There is plenty for a PTA, an NAACP, or a League of Women Voters to do in its own community, and so its members can be kept busy with local affairs while the national staff pursues larger goals.

A second kind of incentive consists of **material incentives**—that is, money, or things and services readily valued in monetary terms. Farm organizations have recruited many members by offering a wide range of services. The Illinois Farm Bureau, for example, offers to its members—and *only* to its members—a chance to buy farm supplies at discount prices, market their products through cooperatives, and purchase low-cost insurance. These material incentives help explain why the Illinois Farm Bureau has been able to enroll nearly every farmer in the state as well as many nonfarmers who also value these rewards.

Similarly, the American Association of Retired Persons (AARP) has recruited tens of millions of members by supplying them with everything from low-cost life insurance and mail-order discount drugs to tax advice and group travel plans. Almost half of the nation's population aged 50 and older—one out of every four registered voters—belongs to the AARP. With an annual operating budget of about $800 million and a yearly cash flow of several billion dollars, the AARP seeks to influence public policy in many areas, from health and housing to taxes and transportation. To gain additional benefits for members, interest groups like the AARP also seek to influence how public laws are administered and who gets government grants.

The third—and most difficult—kind of incentive is the *purpose* of the organization. Many associations rely chiefly on this **purposive incentive**—the appeal of their stated goals—to recruit members. If the attainment of those goals will also benefit people who do not join, individuals who do join will have to be those who feel passionately about the goal, who have a strong sense of duty (or who cannot say no to a friend who asks them to join), or for whom

incentive Something of value one cannot get without joining an organization.

solidary incentives The social rewards (sense of pleasure, status, or companionship) that lead people to join political organizations.

material incentives Money or things valued in monetary terms.

purposive incentive A benefit that comes from serving a cause or principle.

Union members hold a rally in Michigan to protest against right-to-work legislation.

HOW THINGS WORK

Public-Interest Law Firms

A special kind of public-interest lobby is an organization that advances its cause by bringing lawsuits to challenge existing practices or proposed regulations. A public-interest law firm will act in one of two ways: First, it will find someone who has been harmed by some public or private policy and bring suit on his

or her behalf. Second, it will file a brief with a court supporting somebody else's lawsuit (this is called an amicus curiae brief; it is explained in Chapter 16).

Here are some examples of liberal and conservative public-interest law firms:

Liberal

American Civil Liberties Union

Asian American Legal Defense Fund

Lawyers' Committee for Civil Rights

Mexican American Legal Defense Fund

NAACP Legal Defense and Education Fund

Natural Resources Defense Council

Women's Legal Defense Fund

Conservative

Atlantic Legal Foundation

The Center for Individual Rights

Center for Law and Justice

Institute for Justice

National Legal Center for the Public Interest

Pacific Legal Foundation

Washington Legal Foundation

---

ideological interest groups Political organizations that attract members by appealing to their political convictions or principles.

public-interest lobby A political organization whose goals will principally benefit nonmembers.

the cost of joining is so small that they are indifferent to joining or not. Organizations that attract members by appealing to their interest in a coherent set of (usually) controversial principles are sometimes called **ideological interest groups**.

When the purpose of the organization, if attained, will principally benefit nonmembers, it is customary to call the group a **public-interest lobby**. (Whether the public at large will really benefit, of course, is a matter of opinion, but at least the group members think they are working selflessly for the common good.)

Though some public-interest lobbies may pursue relatively noncontroversial goals (for example, persuading people to vote or raising money to house orphans), the most visible of these organizations are highly controversial. It is precisely the controversy that attracts the members, or at least those members who support one side of the issue. Many of these groups can be described as markedly liberal or decidedly conservative in outlook.

Perhaps the best known of the liberal public-interest groups are those founded by or associated with Ralph Nader. Nader became a popular figure in

the mid-1960s after General Motors made a clumsy attempt to investigate and discredit his background at a time when he was testifying in favor of an auto-safety bill. Nader won a large out-of-court settlement against General Motors, his books began to earn royalties, and he was able to command substantial lecture fees. Most of this money was turned over to various organizations he created that dealt with matters of interest to consumers. In addition, he founded a group called Public Citizen that raised money by direct-mail solicitation from thousands of small contributors and sought foundation grants. Finally, he helped create Public Interest Research Groups (PIRGs) in a number of states, supported by donations from college students (voluntary at some colleges, a compulsory assessment levied on all students at others) and concerned with organizing student activists to work on local projects.

Conservatives, though slow to get started, also have adopted the public-interest organizational strategy. As with such associations run by liberals, they are of two kinds: those that engage in research and lobbying and those that bring lawsuits designed to advance their cause. The boxes on this page and page 259 list some examples of public-interest organizations that support liberal or conservative causes.

Membership organizations that rely on purposive incentives, especially appeals to deeply controversial purposes, tend to be shaped by the mood of the times. When an issue is hot—in the media or with the public—such organizations can grow rapidly. When the spotlight fades, the organization

HOW THINGS WORK

Think Tanks in Washington

Think tanks are public-interest organizations that do research on policy questions and disseminate their findings in books, articles, conferences, op-ed essays for newspapers, and (occasionally) testimony before Congress. Some are nonpartisan and ideologically more or less neutral, but others—and many of the most important ones—are aligned with liberal or conservative causes. Here are some examples of each:

Liberal

Center for American Progress
Center on Budget and Policy Priorities
Center for Economic and Policy Research
Economic Policy Institute
Institute for Policy Studies
Progressive Policy Institute
Urban Institute

Conservative

American Enterprise Institute
Cato Institute
Foundation for Economic Education
Heritage Foundation
Hudson Institute
Media Research Center
Reason Foundation

Note that the labels "liberal" and "conservative," while generally accurate, conceal important differences among the think tanks in each list.

may lose support. Thus, such organizations have a powerful motive to stay in the public eye. To remain visible, public-interest lobbies devote a lot of attention to generating publicity by developing good contacts with the media and issuing dramatic press releases about crises and scandals.

Because of their need to take advantage of a crisis atmosphere, public-interest lobbies often do best when the government is in the hands of an administration that is *hostile,* not sympathetic, to their views. Environmentalist organizations could mobilize more resources when James Watt, an opponent of much of the environmental movement, was secretary of the interior than they could when Cecil D. Andrus, his pro-environment predecessor, was in office. By the same token, many conservative interest groups were able to raise more money with the liberal Jimmy Carter or Bill Clinton in the White House than with the conservative Ronald Reagan or George W. Bush there.

The Influence of the Staff

We often make the mistake of assuming that what an interest group does politically is simply to exert influence on behalf of its members. That is indeed the case when all the members have a clear and similar stake in an issue. But many issues affect different members differently. In fact, if the members joined to obtain solidary or material benefits, they may not care at all

about many of the issues with which the organization gets involved. In such cases, what the interest group does may reflect more what the staff wants than what the members believe.

For example, a survey of the white members of a large labor union showed that one-third of them believed the desegregation of schools, housing, and job opportunities had gone too fast; only one-fifth thought it had gone too slowly. But among the staff members of the union, *none* thought desegregation had gone too fast, and over two-thirds thought it had gone too slowly.[12] As a result, the union staff aggressively lobbied Congress for the passage of tougher civil rights laws, even though most of the union's members did not feel they were needed. The members stayed in the union for reasons unrelated to civil rights, giving the staff the freedom to pursue its own goals.

social movement A widely shared demand for change in some aspect of the social or political order.

Interest Groups and Social Movements

Because it is difficult to attract people with purposive incentives, interest groups employing them tend to arise out of social movements. A **social movement** is a widely shared demand for change in some aspect of the social or political order. The civil rights movement of the 1960s was such an event, as was the environmentalist movement of the 1970s.

A social movement need not have liberal goals. In the 19th century, for example, there were various nativist movements that sought to reduce immigration to this country or to keep Catholics or Masons out of public office. Broad-based religious revivals are social movements. In recent years, the conservative Tea Party movement, which has taken hold around issues like restraining government growth, has played a role in both local and national elections.[13]

No one is quite certain why social movements arise. At one moment, people are largely indifferent to some issue; at another moment, many of these same people care passionately about religion, civil rights, immigration, or conservation. A social movement may be triggered by a disaster (an oil spill on the Santa Barbara beaches helped launch the environmental movement), the dramatic and widely publicized activities of a few leaders (lunch counter sit-ins helped stimulate the civil rights movement), or the coming of age of a new generation that takes up a cause advocated by eloquent writers, teachers, or evangelists.

Whatever its origin, the effect of a social movement is to increase the value some people attach to purposive incentives. As a consequence, new interest groups are formed that rely on these incentives.

The Environmental Movement

The environmental movement provides a good example of how a social movement gives rise to interest groups formed from reliance on purposive incentives. In the 1890s, as a result of the emergence of conservation as a major issue, the Sierra Club was organized. In the 1930s, conservation once again became popular, and the Wilderness Society and the National Wildlife Federation took form. In the 1960s and 1970s, environmental issues again came to the fore, and we saw the emergence of the Environmental Defense Fund and Environmental Action.

The smallest of these organizations (Environmental Action and the Environmental Defense Fund) tend to have the most liberal members. This often is the case with organizations that arise from social movements. A movement will spawn many organizations. The most passionately aroused people will be the fewest in number, and they will gravitate toward the organizations that take the most extreme positions; as a result, these organizations are small but vociferous. The more numerous and less passionate people will gravitate toward more moderate, less vociferous organizations, which will tend to be larger.

As happens over the years to most politically successful movements, the environmental movement has become more fragmented than it was in the 1970s. Different leading voices and organizations within it have begun to advocate somewhat different policy approaches to achieving the same basic (in this case, environmental protection and sustainability) goals.[14]

The Feminist Movement

There have been several feminist social movements in this country's history—in the 1830s, in the 1890s, in the 1920s, and in the 1960s. Each period brought about new organizations, some of which have endured to the present. For example, the League of Women Voters was founded in 1920 to educate and organize women for the purpose of effectively using their newly won right to vote.

Though a strong sense of purpose may lead to the creation of organizations, each will strive to find some incentive that will sustain it over the long haul. These permanent incentives will affect how the organization participates in politics.

At least three kinds of feminist organizations exist. First, there are those that rely chiefly on solidary incentives, enroll middle-class women with relatively high levels of schooling, and tend to support those causes that command the widest support among women generally. The League of Women Voters and the Federation of Business and Professional Women are examples. Both supported the campaign to ratify the Equal Rights Amendment (ERA), but as Jane Mansbridge has observed in her history of the ERA, they were uneasy with the kind of intense, partisan fighting displayed by some other women's organizations and with the tendency of more militant groups to link the ERA to other issues, such as abortion. The reason for their uneasiness is clear: to the extent they relied on solidary incentives, they had a stake in avoiding issues and tactics that would divide their membership or reduce the extent to which membership provided camaraderie and professional contacts.[15]

Second, there are women's organizations that attract members with purposive incentives. The National Organization for Women (NOW) and the National Abortion Rights Action League (NARAL) are two of the largest such groups, though there are many smaller ones. Because they rely on purposes, these organizations must take strong positions, tackle divisive issues, and employ militant tactics. Anything less would turn off the committed feminists who make up the rank and file and contribute the funds. But because these groups take controversial stands, they are constantly embroiled in internal quarrels between those who think they have gone too far and those who think they have not gone far enough, between women who want NOW or NARAL to join with lesbian and socialist organizations and those who want them to steer clear. Moreover, as Jane Mansbridge showed, purposive organizations often

Zuma Press/Alamy

After the horrific school shooting in Newtown, Connecticut, in December 2012, thousands of people participated in the March on Washington for Gun Control.

cannot make their decisions stick on the local level (local chapters will do pretty much as they please).[16]

The third kind of women's organization is the caucus that takes on specific issues that have some material benefit to women. The Women's Equity Action League (WEAL) is one such group. Rather than relying on membership dues for financial support, it obtains grants from foundations and government agencies. Freed of the necessity of satisfying a large rank-and-file membership, WEAL has concentrated its efforts on bringing lawsuits aimed at enforcing or enlarging the legal rights of women in higher education and other institutions. In electoral politics, the National Women's Political Caucus (officially nonpartisan, but generally liberal and Democratic) and the National Federation of Republican Women (openly supportive of the Republican Party) work to get more women active in politics and more women elected or appointed to office.

The feminist movement has, of course, spawned an antifeminist movement, and thus feminist organizations have their antifeminist counterparts. The campaign by NOW for the ERA was attacked by a women's group called STOP ERA; the pro-choice position of NARAL has been challenged by the various organizations associated with the right-to-life movement. These opposition groups have their own tactical problems, which arise in large part from their reliance on different kinds of incentives. In the chapter on civil rights, we shall see how the conflict between these opposing groups shaped the debate over the ERA.

The Union Movement

When social movements run out of steam, they leave behind organizations that continue the fight. But with the movement dead or dormant, the organizations often must struggle to stay alive. This has happened to labor unions.

The major union movement in this country occurred in the 1930s when the Great Depression, popular support, and a sympathetic administration in Washington led to a rapid growth in union membership. In 1945, union membership peaked; at that time, nearly 36 percent of all nonfarm workers were union members.

Since then, union membership has fallen more or less steadily. Today, only about 12 percent of all workers are covered by unions. Between 1983 and 2010, the number of union members fell by about 3 million. This decline was caused by several factors. There has been a shift in the nation's economic life away from industrial production (where unions have traditionally been concentrated) and toward service delivery (where unions have usually been weak). But accompanying this decline, and perhaps contributing to it, has been a decline in popular approval of unions. Approval has moved down side by side with a decline in membership and declines in union victories in elections held to see whether workers in a plant want to join a union. The social movement that supported unionism has faded.

But unions will persist because most can rely on incentives other than purposive ones to keep them going. In many states, they can require workers to join unions if they wish to keep their jobs; in other places, workers believe they get sufficient benefits from the union to make even voluntary membership worthwhile. And in a few industries, such as teaching and government, there has been a growth in membership as some white-collar workers have turned to unions to advance their interests.

Unions composed of government workers are becoming the most important part of the union movement. Indeed, according to the U.S. Bureau of Labor Statistics, in 2010, 7.6 million public-sector employees belonged to a union, compared with 7.1 million union workers in the private sector; and the union membership rate for public-sector workers (36.2 percent) was more than five times that for private-sector workers (6.9 percent). In 2011, Wisconsin and several other states considered legislation that would restrict or eliminate certain bargaining rights and benefits enjoyed by public-employee unions including those representing public-school teachers.

Still, public-sector unions, led by groups like the American Federation of State County and Municipal Employees (AFSCME) and the American Federation of Teachers (AFT), remain robust, relatively well funded, and significant sources of campaign contributions. The Federal Election Commission (FEC) reported that, in 2009, AFSCME's PAC contributed over $1.2 million to candidates while AFT's PAC contributed over $800,000 to candidates, making them the ninth and twenty-sixth entries, respectively, on the FEC's list of the top 50 PAC contributors for that year.

Unions can more or less reliably raise at least a portion of the funds they need by charging their members dues, but many interest groups struggle with raising money; some cannot easily predict what their budget will be from one quarter to the next. This is especially true for membership organizations that rely on appeals to purpose—to accomplishing stated goals. As a result, the Washington office of a public-interest lobbying group is likely to be small, stark, and crowded, whereas that of an institutional lobby, such as the AFL-CIO or the American Council on Education, will be rather lavish.

To make ends meet and maintain such influence as they each may have, diverse interest groups attempt to fund themselves through some combination of private foundation grants, government grants, direct-mail solicitation, and online appeals and donations (some tied in to the group leaders' blogs or social media sites). After the 2007 recession began, each of those funding sources became more precarious, but at least through mid-2011 fundraising challenges had not led to any easily observable changes in the landscape of America's organized interest groups.

Upper-Class Bias?

Observers often believe that interest groups active in Washington reflect an upper-class bias. There are two reasons for this belief: first, well-off people are more likely than poor people to join and be active in interest groups; and second, interest groups representing business and the professions are much more numerous and better financed than organizations representing minorities, consumers, or the disadvantaged.

Many scholars have shown that people with higher incomes, those whose schooling went through college or beyond, and those in professional or technical jobs are much more likely to belong to a voluntary association than people with the opposite characteristics. Just as we would expect, higher-income people can afford more organizational memberships than lower-income ones; people in business and the professions find it easier to attend meetings (they have more control over their own work schedules) and more necessary to do so than people in blue-collar jobs; and people with college degrees often have a wider range of interests than those without.

One study found that between 1981 and 2006, the ratio of business lobbyists to union plus public-interest lobbyists prone to oppose business interests rose from about 12 to 1 to nearly 16 to 1.[17] Some now argue that the nation's 2007–2010 economic crises were due in part to the disproportionate political influence wielded during the preceding decade

Farmers once had great influence in Congress and could get their way with a few telephone calls. Today, they often must use mass-protest methods.

by rich Wall Street executives and related business interests. There is some truth to this view. In 1999, corporate lawyers and lobbyists won a long legislative battle to repeal the Banking Act of 1933, better known as the Glass-Steagall Act, which strictly separated investment from commercial banking and imposed many other restrictions on financial companies. The repeal permitted the home mortgage business to change in ways that made it easier to offer risky loans to people with poor credit histories, and it gave birth to new financial products and services that were weakly regulated by government and incomprehensible to most consumers.

But note that the 1933 law, albeit with certain changes made in subsequent decades, remained on the books for more than 60 years before it was repealed. And, strongly opposed though it was by myriad powerful business interests, today the Wall Street Reform and Consumer Protection Act of 2010 is law. Better known as Dodd-Frank, this law did not restore the Glass-Steagall Act's strict separation between depository banking and financial trading, but it did tighten regulations on virtually all financial companies and broaden consumer protections for all, including first-time mortgage-seekers and small investors.

As this example suggests, even if it is true that financial moguls, big business executives, and other wealthy people typically have more (and more high-priced) lobbyists looking out for their interests than other citizens do, the question of an upper-class bias is by no means entirely settled.

In the first place, lobbyists are only certain *inputs* into the political system; what matters are the *outputs*—that is, who wins and who loses on particular issues. For instance, even if scores and scores of groups inside the Washington beltway are pushing to protect the oil industry and those who benefit financially from it the most, this is important only if the oil industry in fact gets protected. Sometimes it does; sometimes it does not. At one time, when oil prices were low, oil companies were able to get Congress to pass a law that sharply restricted the importation of foreign oil. A few years later, after oil prices had risen and people were worried about energy issues, these restrictions were ended.

In the second place, business-oriented interest groups often are divided among themselves. Take one kind of business: farming. Once, farm organizations seemed so powerful in Washington that scholars spoke of an irresistible "farm bloc" in Congress that could get its way on almost anything. Today, dozens of agricultural organizations operate in the capital, with some (such as the Farm Bureau) attempting to speak for all farmers and others (such as the Tobacco Institute and Mid-America Dairymen) representing particular commodities and regions.

Whenever American politics is described as having an upper-class bias, it is important to ask exactly what this bias is. Most of the major conflicts in American politics—over foreign policy, economic affairs, environmental protection, and equal rights for women—are conflicts *within* the upper class; that is, they are conflicts among politically active elites. As we saw in Chapter 7, profound cleavages of opinion exist among these elites. Interest group activity reflects these cleavages.

It would be a mistake to ignore the overrepresentation of business in Washington. A student of politics should always take differences in the availability of political resources as an important clue to possible differences in the outcomes of political conflicts. Nonetheless, the differences are only clues, not conclusions.

The Activities of Interest Groups

Size and wealth are no longer entirely accurate measures of an interest group's influence—if indeed they ever were. Depending on the issue, the key to political influence may be the ability to generate a dramatic newspaper headline, mobilize a big letter-writing campaign, stage a protest demonstration, file a suit in federal court to block (or compel) some government action, or quietly supply information to key legislators. All of these things require organization, but only some of them require big or expensive organizations.

Information

Of all these tactics, the single most important one—in the eyes of virtually every lobbyist and every academic student of lobbying—is supplying credible information. The reason why information is so valuable is that, to busy legislators and bureaucrats, information is in short supply. Legislators in particular must take positions on a staggering number of issues about which they cannot possibly become experts.

> *political cue* A signal telling a legislator what values are at stake in a vote, and how that issue fits into his or her own political views on party agenda.

Nobody needs a lobbyist to access publicly available information via the internet, but politicians often covet information that is highly detailed, specific, up-to-date, and not publicly available in any easy-to-find form. This kind of information ordinarily will be gathered only by a group that has a strong interest in some issue. Lobbyists, for the most part, are not flamboyant, party-giving arm-twisters; they are specialists who gather information (favorable to their clients, naturally) and present it in as organized, persuasive, and factual a manner as possible. All lobbyists no doubt exaggerate, but few can afford to misrepresent the facts or mislead a legislator, and for a very simple reason: almost every lobbyist must develop and maintain the confidence of a legislator over the long term, with an eye on tomorrow's issues as well as today's.

Misrepresentation or bad advice can embarrass a legislator who accepts it or repel one who detects it, leading to distrust of the lobbyist. Maintaining contacts and channels of communication is vital; to that end, maintaining trust is essential.

The value of the information provided by a lobbyist often is greatest when the issue is fairly narrow, involving only a few interest groups or a complex economic or technical problem. The value of information, and thus the power of the lobbyist, is likely to be least when the issue is one of broad and highly visible national policy.

Sometimes the nature of an issue or the governmental process by which an issue is resolved gives a great advantage to the suppliers of certain information and imposes a great burden on would-be suppliers of contrary information. This is an example of "client politics." For example, the Civil Aeronautics Board (CAB) once set airline fares and decided what airlines would fly to what cities. Historically, the only organizations with any incentive to appear before the CAB and supply the necessary information were, naturally, the airlines. Until the CAB began to deregulate civil aviation, CAB decisions often tended to favor the established airlines.

Public officials not only want technical information, but they also want political cues. A **political cue** is a signal telling the official what values are *ratings* Assessments of a representative's voting record on issues important to an interest group.

earmark A provision in a law that provides a direct benefit to a client without the benefit having been reviewed on the merits by all of Congress.

at stake in an issue—who is for, who against a proposal—and how that issue fits into his or her own set of political beliefs. Some legislators feel comfortable when they are on the liberal side of an issue, and others feel comfortable when they are on the conservative side, especially when they are not familiar with the details of the issue. A liberal legislator will look to see whether the AFL-CIO, the NAACP, the Americans for Democratic Action, the Farmers' Union, and various consumer organizations favor a proposal; if so, that is often all he or she has to know. If these liberal groups are split, then the legislator will worry about the matter and try to look into it more closely. Similarly, a conservative legislator will feel comfortable taking a stand on an issue if the Chamber of Commerce, the National Rifle Association, the American Medical Association, various business associations, and Americans for Constitutional Action are in agreement about it; he or she will feel less comfortable if such conservative groups are divided. As a result of this process, lobbyists often work together in informal coalitions based on general political ideology.

One important way in which these cues are made known is by **ratings** that interest groups make of legislators. These are regularly compiled by the AFL-CIO (on who is pro-labor), by the Americans for Democratic Action (on who is liberal), by the Americans for Constitutional Action (on who is conservative), by the Consumer Federation of America (on who is pro-consumer), and by the League of Conservation Voters (on who is pro-environment). These ratings are designed to generate public support for (or opposition to) various legislators. They can be helpful sources of information, but they are sometimes biased by the arbitrary determination of what constitutes a liberal, pro-consumer, or conservative vote.

Both political information and political cues now arrive in the offices of politicians at a faster rate than ever before, thanks to fax machines and the internet. Many interest groups and political activists have banks of computer-operated fax machines that can get a short, snappy document into the hands of every legislator within minutes. William Kristol, a Republican activist, used this technique to good effect in 1993 when he bombarded Republican members of Congress with arguments concerning

why they should oppose President Clinton's health care plan. Many believe he played a major role in the defeat of that plan.

Earmarks

Information can be linked to influence. Lobbyists not only tell members of Congress facts, but they also learn from these members what Washington is doing and then look for ways to sell that information to their clients. What often results is an **earmark**, that is, a provision in a law that provides a direct benefit to a client without the benefit having been reviewed on the merits by all of Congress.

Earmarks have always existed, but they became much more common in the 1970s and later. There are two reasons for this. First, the federal government was doing much more and thus affecting more parts of the society. Second, lobbying organizations figured out that clients would pay for information about how to convert some bit of federal activity to their benefit.

One recent study showed how a new kind of lobbying firm was born. Cassidy and Associates prospered by helping clients get earmarks. The firm charged a flat fee ($10,000 or more per month) and devoted its energy to studying congressional laws in order to find opportunities for its clients.[18]

Its first big client was a university that wanted federal money to pay for a nutrition center it hoped to build. The Cassidy firm discovered that Congress had authorized a "national" nutrition center and then set about persuading key congressional leaders that such a center should be located at the university that was paying Cassidy a fee. Soon many more universities pushed for earmarks for their pet ideas (a foreign-service school, defense software institutes, and computer centers). Not long after that, business firms joined the hunt.

In 2008, the Office of Management and Budget estimated that more than 11,000 earmarks had been approved by Congress at a cost of more than $16 billion. Soon a movement started among some legislators to stop earmarks. But they have faced a problem. Many members of Congress think earmarks are good: Why should only the president or congressional committees decide on what things Congress should spend its money? Why not let individual legislators do good things for their constituents?

One way to attempt to balance these competing views is to try to tell the difference between a good and a bad earmark. Is a university nutrition center a good thing but a study on wood utilization a bad one? Is a computer center desirable but a bridge to a (largely) uninhabited island in Alaska undesirable? There is no easy way to make these judgments, and so earmarks continue to thrive in Washington.

Interest groups suggest ways legislators can help people who vote for them.

Public Support: The Rise of the New Politics

Once upon a time, when the government was small, Congress was less individualistic, and television was nonexistent, lobbyists mainly used an *insider strategy:* they worked closely with a few key members of Congress, meeting them privately to exchange information and (sometimes) favors. Matters of mutual interest could be discussed at a leisurely pace, over dinner or while playing golf. Public opinion was important on some highly visible issues, but there were not many of these.

Following an insider strategy is still valuable, but increasingly interest groups have turned to an *outsider strategy.* The newly individualistic nature of Congress has made this tactic useful, and modern technology has made it possible. Radio, fax machines, and the internet can now get news out almost immediately. Satellite television can be used to link interested citizens in various locations across the country. Toll-free phone numbers can be publicized, enabling voters to call the offices of their members of Congress without charge. Public opinion polls can be done by telephone, virtually overnight, to measure (and help generate) support for or opposition to proposed legislation. Mail can be directed by computers to people already known to have an interest in a particular matter.

This kind of *grassroots lobbying* is central to the outsider strategy. It is designed to generate public pressure directly on government officials. The "public" that exerts this pressure is not every voter or even most voters; it is that part of the public (sometimes called an *issue public*) directly affected by or deeply concerned with a government policy. What modern technology has made possible is the overnight mobilization of specific-issue publics.

Not every issue lends itself to an outsider strategy: it is hard to get many people excited about, for example, complex tax legislation affecting only a few firms. But as the government does more and more, and its policies affect more and more people, many more will join in grassroots lobbying efforts over matters such as abortion, Medicare, Social Security, environmental protection, and affirmative action.

Undoubtedly, the new politics creates new conflicts. Since conflict is the essence of politics, it may seem strange that politicians dislike controversy. But they do, and for perfectly human reasons: no one enjoys dealing with people who are upset or who find one's viewpoint objectionable or unworthy. Consequently, most legislators tend to hear what they want to hear and deal with interest groups that agree with them. Two senators from the same state may choose to listen to very different constituencies in that state and to take very different policy positions. Neither senator may feel "pressured" or "lobbied," because each has heard mostly from groups or persons who share his or her views. (Politicians define "pressure" as arguments and inducements supplied by somebody with whom they disagree.)

Members of interest groups also tend to work primarily with legislators with whom they agree; lobbyists do not like to argue with people who are suspicious of them or who are unlikely to change their minds no matter what is said. For the lobbyist, the key target is the undecided or wavering legislator or bureaucrat. Sometimes lobbyists make a major effort to persuade an undecided legislator that public opinion is strongly inclined in one direction. A lobbyist will do this by commissioning public opinion polls, stimulating local citizens to write letters or send telegrams, arranging for constituents to pay personal visits to the legislator, or getting newspapers to run editorials supporting the lobbyist's position.

Though most lobbying organizations cultivate the goodwill of government officials, there are important exceptions. Some groups, especially those that use an ideological appeal to attract supporters or that depend for their maintenance and influence on media publicity, will deliberately attack actual or potential allies in government in order to embarrass them.

Of late, interest groups have placed great emphasis on developing grassroots support. Sometimes it is impossible to develop such support, as when a complicated tax regulation of interest to only a few firms is changed. But sometimes a proposed bill touches a public nerve such that even businesses can help generate an outpouring of mail: a few decades ago, when the Food and Drug Administration announced it was going to ban saccharin on the grounds that it caused cancer in laboratory animals, the Calorie Control Council (closely tied to the Coca-Cola Company, a big user of saccharin in soft drinks such as Tab) ran newspaper ads denouncing the policy. The public, worried about losing access to an artificial sweetener important to dieters, responded with an avalanche of mail to Congress, which promptly passed a law reversing the ban.

Money and PACs

Contrary to popular suspicions, money is probably one of the less effective ways by which interest groups advance their causes. That was not always the case. Only a few decades ago, powerful interests used their bulging wallets to buy influence in Congress. The passage of campaign finance legislation in the early 1970s changed that. The laws had two effects. First, they sharply restricted the amount any interest could give to a candidate for federal office (see Chapter 10). Second, they made legal the creation by organizations of political action committees (PACs) that could make political contributions.

Once PACs became legal, they grew rapidly in numbers. Today there are more than 4,500 PACs. Over the last few years, so-called leadership PACs and super PACs have proliferated and received media attention. The former type of PAC is headed by a member of Congress who raises money for other candidates, while the latter type of PAC is an "independent expenditure-only committee" that is not allowed to coordinate with candidates or political party leaders. Among the best-known leadership PACs is the one formed by former House Speaker Nancy Pelosi to help fund Democratic candidates (Team Majority). Among the best-known super PACs is the one launched by former White House aide to President George W. Bush, Karl Rove, to assist Republican candidates (American Crossroads). The leadership PACs are a type of so-called non-Connected PACs that do not act on behalf of a particular corporation, labor union, or trade association, but are instead commonly organized around ideological views, particular issues, or leading political personalities. Still, the vast majority of PACs, including most of the 50 largest PAC contributors, are traditional so-called connected PACs, set up by and connected to business corporations, labor unions, or other interest groups that raise and spend campaign money from voluntary donations. The top ten PAC contributors alone combine to give millions of dollars a year to candidates of their choice (see Table 11.1). But there are strict limits on how much a member can contribute and

how much the PAC can give to candidates and parties. How they work is shown in Table 11.2.

Some people worry that the existence of all this political money has resulted in our having, as the late Senator Edward Kennedy put it, "the finest Congress that money can buy." More likely, the increase in the number of PACs has had just the opposite effect. The reason is simple: with PACs so numerous and so easy to form, it is now probable that money will be available on every side of almost every conceivable issue. As a result, members of Congress can take money and still decide for themselves how to vote. As we shall see, there is not much scholarly evidence that money buys votes in Congress.

Indeed, some members of Congress tell PACs what to do rather than take orders from them. Members will frequently inform PACs that they "expect" money from them; grumbling PAC officials feel they have no choice but to contribute for fear of alienating the members. Moreover, some members have created their *own* PACs—organizations set up to raise money from individual donors that is then given to favored political allies in and out of Congress or used to advance the members' own political ambitions. When Charles Rangel, congressman from New York, was hoping to be elected whip of the Democratic Party in the House, he set up a PAC that made campaign contributions to fellow representatives in hopes that they might vote for him as whip. There are many other examples from both sides of the aisle. An ironic consequence of this is that a conservative Republican may give money to a PAC set up by a moderate Democrat, who then gives the money to a liberal Democrat (or vice versa), with the result that the original donor winds up having his or her money go to somebody that he or she profoundly dislikes.

TABLE 11.1 Ten Largest PAC Contributors, 2011–2012

PAC Affiliation	Amount
American Federation of Teachers, AFL-CIO Committee on Political Education	$7,274,645
Senate Conservatives Fund	$6,488,757
Committee on Letter Carriers Political Education (Letter Carriers Political Action Fund)	$5,833,823
International Brotherhood of Electrical Workers Political Action Committee	$4,836,450
Honeywell International Political Action Committee	$4,809,325
National Association of Realtors Political Action Committee	$4,774,993
SEIU Cope (Service Employees International Union Committee on Political Education)	$4,618,455
D.R.I.V.E. (Democrat, Republican, Independent Voter Education—The PAC of the International Brotherhood)	$4,526,410
National Air Traffic Controllers Association PAC	$4,407,550
Engineers Political Education Committee (EPEC)/International Union of Operating Engineers	$4,241,689

Source: Federal Election Commission, "Top 50 PACs by Contributions to Candidates and Other Committees, January 1, 2011–December 31, 2012," 2013.

TABLE 11.2 **Political Action Committees (PACs)**

Can be formed by:

- Business firms
- Labor unions
- Trade associations
- Ideological organizations

Must have at least 50 individual members

- Each member can give up to $5,000 per election
- The sponsoring firm, union, association, or ideological group cannot contribute money

A PAC that contributes to at least five candidates may contribute the following:

- $5,000 to any federal candidate in any election
- $15,000 to any national political party
- $5,000 to any state or local party

(Non-multicandidate PACs have different contribution limits.)

Where the money goes:

- Business PACs give slightly more to Republicans than to Democrats
- Labor unions give more than 90 percent to Democrats
- Ideological PACs give to Democrats and Republicans in about equal amounts

Jack Abramoff, convicted of corruption in handling lobbying claims by certain Indian tribes, is sworn in before a congressional committee investigating this.

Almost any kind of organization—corporation, labor union, trade association, public-interest lobby, citizens group—can form a PAC. Over half of all PACs are sponsored by corporations or trade associations, about 6 percent by labor unions, and the rest by various groups, including independent and ideological ones. The rise of ideological PACs has been the most remarkable development in interest group activity in recent years. At various points over the last several decades, they have increased in number at a faster rate than business or labor PACs, and in several elections they raised more money than either business or labor.

In the 2011–2012 election cycle, PACs gave more than $437 million to candidates running for the House and Senate. The PACs that gave the most money to candidates included business organizations, labor unions, and groups that represented banks, realtors, and public employees. Incumbents received more PAC money than challengers. Labor PACs gave almost exclusively to Democrats. Business PACs favored Republicans.[19]

Both parties have become dependent on PAC money. Still, the popular image of rich PACs stuffing huge sums into political campaigns and thereby buying the attention and possibly the favors of the grateful candidates is a bit overdrawn. For one thing, the typical PAC contribution is rather small. The average PAC donation to a House candidate is only a few hundred dollars. Most PACs spread small sums of money over many candidates, and despite their great growth in numbers and expenditures, PACs still provide only about one-third of all the money spent by candidates for the House ($356 million of about $1.1 billion in 2011–2012). Moreover, scholars have yet to find systematic evidence that PAC contributions generally affect how members of Congress vote. On most issues, how legislators vote can be explained primarily by their general ideological outlooks and the characteristics of their constituents; how much PAC money they have received turns out to be a small factor. On the other hand, when an issue arises in which most of their constituents have no interest and ideology provides little guidance,

POLICY DYNAMICS: INSIDE/OUTSIDE THE BOX

Immigration Reform: Client or Majoritarian Politics?

One of President Obama's top domestic priorities at the start of his second term was immigration reform. Efforts to pass immigration legislation dated back to the George W. Bush administration, when a proposal to allow illegal immigrants residing in the United States an opportunity to earn citizenship after paying fines and back taxes, waiting for legal applicants to have their files processed, and meeting other requirements failed after vehement opposition from some interest groups. Since then, interest groups in support of a "path to citizenship" for illegal immigrants have mobilized, but major opposition continues to be active as well. Why is immigration reform such a politically charged issue?

Opponents of a "path to citizenship" (or what they call "amnesty") for illegal immigrants include the Federation for American Immigration Reform and the Center for Immigration Studies. These groups contend that people who have broken immigration laws should not be permitted to stay in the United States legally. They say the federal government should focus on border protection and law enforcement, not a reward for law-breakers. Immigration reform, in their view, is client politics – the American public at large pays for illegal immigrants through providing them education and emergency medical services (pursuant to Supreme Court decisions). Providing a path to citizenship additionally means that people lose confidence that the federal government will uphold the law, so the long-term health of American democracy suffers to benefit a few.

Supporters of immigration reform include the National Immigration Forum and the PICO (People Improving Communities Through Organizing) National Network.

They present a "path to citizenship" as majoritarian politics – everyone, including illegal immigrants, pays for this opportunity through hard work and taxes, and everyone benefits by ensuring an economically productive, just, and humane society. Advocates of the "DREAM Act" (Development, Relief, and Education for Alien Minors) make a client-politics case that the children of illegal immigrants should not suffer for their parents' mistakes and should have a path to citizenship; but these groups also make the majoritarian politics argument that the United States as a whole benefits from comprehensive immigration reform.

If an issue is perceived as client politics, then the group that benefits needs to be viewed as deserving of those benefits for legislation to pass. If an issue is viewed as majoritarian politics, then the legislation must be seen as in the general public interest. Is immigration reform an example of client or majoritarian politics? How is it perceived by different groups and why? What are the consequences for enacting legislation?

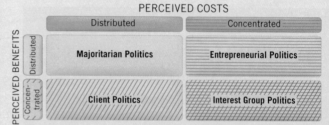

Sources: Ted Hesson, "Grassroots Activists and 5 Others Against Immigration Reform," ABCNews.com, 20 May 2013; "Evangelical Pastors Push Immigration Overhaul," LatinoTimes.com, 6 April 2013.

---

there is a slight statistical correlation between PAC contributions and votes. But even here the correlation may be misleading. The same groups that give money also wage intensive lobbying campaigns, flooding representatives with information, press releases, and letters from interested constituents.

In 2010, in *Citizens United v. Federal Election Commission*, the U.S. Supreme Court struck down as unconstitutional provisions of a 2002 federal campaign finance law that prohibited independent expenditures by business corporations, nonprofit organizations, and unions to fund "electioneering communications" within 30 days of a primary election or 60 days of a general election. This decision was the seedbed for the aforementioned super PACs,

but it is too soon to know whether, as many observers seem to fear, the decision will increase even more the vast amounts of money that interests groups of all sorts spend to influence lawmakers. But even if that fear is realized, it is not entirely certain that increased expenditures will result in increased influence over how lawmakers vote.

Of course, it is possible that money affects legislative behavior in ways that will never appear in studies of roll-call votes in Congress. Members of Congress may be more willing to set aside time in their busy schedules for a group that has given money than for a group that has not. In that case, what the money has bought is access: it has helped open the door. Or contributions might influence how legislators behave on the committees on which they serve, subtly shaping the way in which they respond to arguments and the facts on which they rely. No one knows, because the research has not been done.

In any event, if interest group money makes a difference at all, it probably makes it on certain kinds of issues more than others. In the chapter on policymaking, we define the kind of issues—we call them "client politics"—on which a given interest group is likely to be especially influential, whether by means of arguments, money, or both. After reading that chapter and considering the examples given there, it will be easier to put the present discussion of PAC money into context.

The "Revolving Door"

Every year, hundreds of people leave important jobs in the federal government to take more lucrative positions in private industry. Some go to work as lobbyists, others as consultants to business, still others as key executives in corporations, foundations, and universities. Many people worry that this "revolving door" may give private interests a way of improperly influencing government decisions. If a federal official uses his or her government position to do something for a corporation in exchange for a cushy

job after leaving government, or if a person who has left government uses his or her personal contacts in Washington to get favors for private parties, then the public interest may suffer.

From time to time, certain incidents stir these fears. For instance, as *The Washington Post* reported, following the attempted bombing of a U.S. airliner on Christmas Day 2009, Michael Chertoff, the former secretary of the Department of Homeland Security (DHS), "gave dozens of media interviews touting the need for the federal government to buy more full body-scanners for airports"; but in that media blitz Chertoff did not always make clear what his security consulting firm, the Chertoff Group, had disclosed in a statement issued before he made the media rounds, namely, that the former DHS chief represented a client that manufactured the machines and sold them to a DHS subunit, the Transportation Safety Administration.[20]

Over the years, more than a few scandals have emerged concerning corrupt dealings between federal department officials and industry executives. Many have involved contractors or their consultants bribing procurement officials. Far more common, however, have been major breakdowns in the procurement process itself. For example, in 2006, the Department of Homeland Security revealed the

---

HOW THINGS WORK

Conflict of Interest

In 1978, a new federal law, the Ethics in Government Act, codified and broadened the rules governing possible conflicts of interest among senior members of the executive branch. The key provisions were as follows.

The president, vice president, and top-ranking (GS-16 and above) executive branch employees must each year file a public financial disclosure report that lists:

- The source and amount of all earned income as well as income from stocks, bonds, and property; the worth of any investments or large debts; and the source of a spouse's income, if any

- Any position held in business, labor, or certain non-profit organizations

Employment after government service is restricted. Former executive branch employees may *not*:

- Represent anyone before their former agencies in connection with any matter that the former employees had been involved in before leaving the government

- Appear before an agency, for two years after leaving government service, on matters that came within the former employees' official sphere of responsibility, even if they were not personally involved in the matter

- Represent anyone on any matter before their former agencies, for one year after leaving them, even if the former employees had no connection with the matter while in the government

In addition, another law prohibits bribery. It is illegal to ask for, solicit, or receive anything of value in return for being influenced in the performance of one's duties.

Finally, an executive order forbids outside employment. An official may not hold a job or take a fee, even for lecturing or writing, if such employment or income might create a conflict of interest or an apparent conflict of interest.

Sources: *National Journal* (November 19, 1977): 1796–1803; *Congressional Quarterly Weekly Report* (October 28, 1978): 3121–3127.

results from an internal audit.[21] In the previous year, the department had spent $17.5 billion on contracts for airport security, radiation-monitor detectors, and other goods and services. But records for nearly three dozen contracts were completely missing, and records for many other contracts lacked evidence that the department had followed federal rules in negotiating best prices. (The internal audit itself was performed by private consultants, presumably in compliance with all relevant rules.)

Agencies differ in their vulnerability to outside influences. If the Food and Drug Administration is not vigilant, people in that agency who help decide whether a new drug should be placed on the market may have their judgment affected by the possibility that, if they approve the drug, the pharmaceutical company that makes it will later offer them a lucrative position. On the other hand, lawyers in the Federal Trade Commission who prosecute businesses that violate the antitrust laws may decide that their chances for getting a good job with a private law firm later on will increase if they are particularly vigorous and effective prosecutors. The firm, after all, wants to hire competent people, and winning a case is a good test of competence.[22]

Civil Disobedience

Public displays and disruptive tactics—protest marches, sit-ins, picketing, and violence—have always been a part of American politics. Indeed, they were among the favorite tactics of the American colonists seeking independence in 1776.

Both ends of the political spectrum have used display, disruption, and violence. On the left feminists, antislavery agitators, coal miners, autoworkers, welfare mothers, African Americans, antinuclear power groups, public housing tenants, the American Indian Movement, the Students for a Democratic Society, and the Weather Underground have created "trouble" ranging from peaceful sit-ins at segregated lunch counters to bombings and shootings. On the right, the Ku Klux Klan has used terror, intimidation, and murder; parents opposed to forced busing of schoolchildren have demonstrated; business firms have used strong-arm squads against workers; right-to-life groups have blockaded abortion clinics; and an endless array of "anti-" groups (anti-Catholics, anti-Masons, anti-Jews, anti-immigrants, anti-saloons, anti-blacks, anti-protesters, and probably even anti-antis) have taken their disruptive turns on stage. These various activities are not morally the same—a sit-in demonstration is quite different from a lynching—but politically they constitute a similar problem for a government official.

An explanation of why and under what circumstances disruption occurs is beyond the scope of this book. To understand interest group politics, however, it is important to remember that making trouble has, since the 1960s, become a quite conventional political resource and is no longer simply the last resort of extremist groups. Making trouble is now an accepted political tactic of ordinary middle-class citizens as well as the disadvantaged or disreputable.

There is of course a long history of the use of disruptive methods by "proper" people. For example, in a movement that began in England at the turn of the 20th century and then spread to America, feminists would chain themselves to lampposts or engage in what we now call "sit-ins" as part of a campaign to win the vote for women. The object then was much the same as the object of similar tactics today: to disrupt the working of some institution so that it is forced to negotiate with you, or, failing that, to enlist the sympathies of third parties (the media, other interest groups) who will come to your aid and press your target to negotiate with you, or, failing that, to goad the police into making attacks and arrests so that martyrs are created.

The civil rights and antiwar movements of the 1960s gave experience in these methods to thousands of young people and persuaded others of the

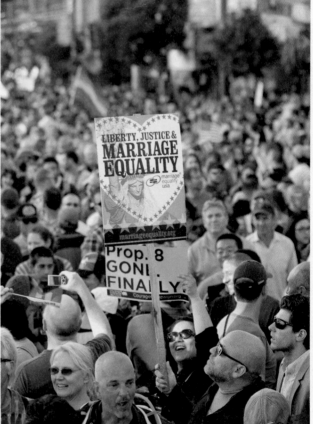

People celebrate after the Supreme Court overturns the Defense of Marriage Act and rules that supporters of California's Proposition 8 prohibiting same-sex marriage do not have standing in the case.

Josh Edelson/AFP/Getty Images

effectiveness of such methods under certain conditions. Though these movements have abated or disappeared, their veterans and emulators have put such tactics to new uses—trying to block the construction of a nuclear power plant, for example, or occupying the office of a cabinet secretary to obtain concessions for a particular group.

Government officials dread this kind of trouble. They usually find themselves in a no-win situation. If they ignore the disruption, they are accused of being "insensitive," "unresponsive," or "arrogant." If they give in to the demonstrators, they encourage more demonstrations by proving that this is a useful tactic. If they call the police, they run the risk of violence and injuries, followed not only by bad publicity but also by lawsuits.

Regulating Interest Groups

Interest group activity is a form of political speech protected by the First Amendment to the Constitution: it cannot lawfully be abolished or even much curtailed. In 1946, Congress passed the Federal Regulation of Lobbying Act, which requires groups and individuals seeking to influence legislation to register with the secretary of the Senate and the clerk of the House and to file quarterly financial reports. The Supreme Court upheld the law but restricted its application to lobbying efforts involving direct contacts with members of Congress.[23] More general "grassroots" interest group activity may not be restricted by the government. The 1946 law had little practical effect. Not all lobbyists took the trouble to register, and there was no guarantee that the financial statements were accurate. There was no staff in charge of enforcing the law.

After years of growing popular dissatisfaction with Congress, prompted in large measure by the (exaggerated) view that legislators were the pawns of powerful special interests, Congress in late 1995 unanimously passed a bill that tightened up the registration and disclosure requirements. Signed by the president, the law restated the obligation of lobbyists to register with the House and Senate, but it broadened the definition of a lobbyist to include the following:

- People who spend at least 20 percent of their time lobbying

- People who are paid at least $5,000 in any six-month period to lobby

- Corporations and other groups that spend more than $20,000 in any six-month period on their own lobbying staffs

The law covered people and groups who lobbied the executive branch and congressional staffers as well as elected members of Congress, and it included law firms that represent clients before the

government. Twice a year, all registered lobbyists were required to report the following:

- The names of their clients

- Their income and expenditures

- The issues on which they worked

The registration and reporting requirements did not, however, extend to so-called grassroots organizations—that is, campaigns (sometimes led by volunteers, sometimes by hired professionals) to mobilize citizens to write or call the government about some issue. Nor was any new enforcement organization created, although congressional officials could refer violations to the Justice Department for investigation. Fines for breaking the law could amount to $50,000. In addition, the law barred tax-exempt, nonprofit advocacy groups that lobby from getting federal grants.

Just as the Republicans moved expeditiously to pass new regulations on interest groups and lobbying when they regained majorities in Congress in the November 1994 elections, the Democrats' first order of business after retaking Congress in the November 2006 elections was to adopt sweeping reforms. Beginning March 1, 2007, many new regulations took effect, including the following:

- No gifts of any value from registered lobbyists or firms that employ lobbyists

- No reimbursement for travel costs from registered lobbyists or firms that employ lobbyists

- No reimbursement for travel costs, no matter the source, if the trip is in any part organized or requested by a registered lobbyist or firm that employs lobbyists

Strictly speaking, these and related new rules mean that a House member cannot go on a "fact-finding" trip to a local site or a foreign country and have anyone associated with lobbying arrange to pay for it. Even people who are not themselves registered lobbyists, but who work for a lobbying firm, are not permitted to take members of Congress to lunch or give them any other "thing of value," no matter how small.

But if past experience is any guide, "strictly speaking" is not how the rules will be followed or enforced. For instance, buried in the fine print of the new rules are provisions that permit members of Congress to accept reimbursement for travel from lobbyists if the travel is for "one-day trips," so long as the lobbyists themselves do not initiate the trip, make the reservations, or pick up incidental expenses unrelated to the visit. Moreover, these rules have not yet been adopted in precisely the same form by the Senate; and neither chamber has yet clarified language or closed loopholes related to lobbying registration and reporting.

WHAT WOULD YOU DO?

MEMORANDUM

To: *Dora Grace, Senate majority leader*

From: *Brian Luce, chief of staff*

Subject: *Full federal financing of presidential campaigns*

Every presidential election since 1976 has been financed in part by federal funds. Now presidential candidates say they will forego public funding for the general election, given the vastly greater resources available through private fundraising. Congress needs to decide whether elections are a public investment or a political free market for citizens and candidates.

Arguments for:

1. Legal precedents are promising. Federal matching funds already go to presidential primary candidates who have raised at least $5,000, in contributions of $250 or less, in each of 20 states. For the general election, each major party nominee already is eligible for federal funding if he or she agrees to spend no more than that amount.

2. The funding required would be small. Allocating $1 billion out of the public treasury for a presidential election every four years is hardly a fiscal drain on a nearly $2 trillion annual budget.

3. The effects would be pervasive. Candidates and party leaders would stop covertly courting big donors with phone calls, lunches, and personal visits, and would focus instead on the needs of average citizens.

Arguments against:

1. Constitutional precedent for requiring political candidates to accept public funds is weak. In *Buckley v. Valeo* (1976), the Supreme Court upheld limits on campaign contributions for candidates who accept public money, but it also defined spending money for political purposes as expression protected by

News »

Bipartisan Group in Senate Proposes Full Public Financing of Presidential Campaigns

With the upcoming presidential election expected to cost more than $1 billion, a bipartisan group of senators has proposed that Congress control those expenses by fully funding and setting an upper limit on financing for presidential campaigns. Presidential contenders so far have refrained from taking a position on the legislation.

the First Amendment, thereby giving individuals the right to raise and spend as much of their own money as they choose, if they forego federal funds.

2. Campaign spending would soon spiral once again. The federal government may not restrict spending by individuals or organizations working independently from the political parties, and federal funds would merely supplement, not supplant, private fundraising.

3. Less than 10 percent of taxpayers currently support public financing through voluntary federal income tax check-offs, and voters likely would view bankrolling elections as serving politicians, not the people.

Your decision:

Support legislation _____   Oppose legislation _____

Do not suppose, however, that such remaining gaps in lobbying laws render the system wide open to abuses or evasions. For one thing, loopholes and all, the lobbying laws are now tighter than ever.

For another, as we intimated earlier in this chapter, the most significant legal constraints on interest groups come not from the current federal lobbying law (though that may change) but from the tax code and the campaign finance laws. A nonprofit organization—which includes not only charitable groups but also almost all voluntary associations that have an interest in politics—need not pay income taxes, and financial contributions to it can be deducted on the donor's income tax return, provided that the organization does not devote a "substantial part" of its activities to "attempting to influence legislation."[24] Many tax-exempt organizations do take public positions on political questions and testify before congressional committees. If the organization does any serious lobbying, however, it will lose its tax-exempt status (and thus find it harder to solicit donations and more expensive to operate). Exactly this happened to the Sierra Club in 1968 when the Internal Revenue Service revoked its tax-exempt status because of its extensive lobbying activities. Some voluntary associations try to deal with this problem by setting up separate organizations to collect tax-exempt money—for example, the NAACP, which lobbies, must pay taxes, but the NAACP Legal Defense and Education Fund, which does not lobby, is tax-exempt.

Finally, the campaign finance laws, described in detail in Chapter 10, limit to $5,000 the amount any political action committee can spend on a given candidate in a given election. These laws have sharply curtailed the extent to which any *single* group can give money, though they have increased the *total* amount that different groups are providing.

Beyond making bribery or other manifestly corrupt forms of behavior illegal and restricting the sums that campaign contributors can donate, there is probably no system for controlling interest groups that would both make a useful difference and leave important constitutional and political rights unimpaired. Ultimately, the only remedy for imbalances or inadequacies in interest group representation is to devise and sustain a political system that gives all affected parties a reasonable chance to be heard on matters of public policy. That, of course, is exactly what the Founders thought they were doing. Whether they succeeded or not is a question to which we shall return at the end of this book.

Lobbying

In a representative democracy, elected officials make the laws, but we, the public, vote those officials into office and share our views on public policy, from taxes to education to U.S. responsibilities abroad. As we have seen in this chapter, we can share our views in many ways: communicating with elected officials in writing or in person; donating money to campaigns; organizing rallies or protests. We do not all have the same resources to exercise our lobbying rights, of course, but we have the opportunity to develop or find those resources, if we choose.

Sound about right? Not so fast. We all have the right to "lobby" elected officials, but lobbying has become a full-time occupation for political professionals, especially those representing large corporations. As Table 11.1 shows, the top contributions from Political Action Committees (PACs) in the 2011–2012 election cycle represented the defense and telecommunications industries, among others. This is not necessarily a problem—businesses have legitimate public interests, and those interests may well coincide with what many of us support as well—but it does mean that interest-group influence in American politics skews generally (though not always) toward larger, and typically well-funded, lobbying organizations.

Does the current American political system provide sufficient opportunity for anyone to lobby for change, if they have the time, inclination, and willingness to do the hard work necessary to be heard? Even if major lobbying firms have the ability to make large financial donations to campaigns, can we as individuals counter that potential influence through other resources, such as mobilizing grassroots organizations to convey their views to Washington? Or, has political influence tilted so far toward elite special interests that the general public has little, if any, say in what the government does? And if you lean toward the latter view, then how can the system be changed to promote greater diversity in lobbying while still protecting everyone's First Amendment right of free speech?

LEARNING OBJECTIVES

1. What are interest groups and how did they arise in America?

An interest group is an organization of people sharing a common interest or goal that seeks to influence public policy. Interest groups were present from the first days of the republic, but they proliferated thereafter in several different periods. The latest period of interest group expansion began in the 1960s and has accelerated over the last decade.

2. What are the different kinds of interest groups and which types have been proliferating of late?

There are two kinds of interest groups: institutional and membership. Institutional groups represent other organizations (like lobbying firms that represent corporations or trade groups in Washington), while membership groups represent their own members and their members' policy preferences and beliefs (like the National Association for the Advancement of Colored People, a historic civil rights membership organization). Membership groups organized around ideological beliefs and institutional groups representing corporate interests have proliferated in recent decades. Over just the last decade, there has been an especially large increase in the number of lobbyists representing business interests in Washington.

3. Why do people join interest groups?

Pretty much for the same basic reasons that people join any organization. There are three kinds of incentives: solidary, material, and purposive. Organizations, including interest groups, can attract members through one, two, or all three incentives. Some interest groups rely mainly on one incentive. For example, ideological political action committees (PACs) rely largely on purposive incentives, attracting members by appealing to their beliefs in a coherent set of principles or their passions on a particular set of issues. Even these groups, however, normally provide their members with certain tangible, members-only benefits (for example, magazines or special discounts on various products). Organizations that principally benefit nonmembers are sometimes called public-interest lobbies.

4. How do interest groups attempt to influence public policy, and how does government regulate interest group activities?

Among other things, interest groups use specialized information, political cues, ratings of legislators, and earmarks to sway politicians and influence policy. Government influences interest groups as much as interest groups influence government: detailed rules and regulations now govern most aspects of what lobbyists do.

5. Is the proliferation of political action committees (PACs) and other groups good or bad for America's representative democracy?

What would James Madison say? Go back to the Appendix and Federalist No. 10. Madison recognized that freedom begat factions, but he hoped that the government proposed under the Constitution would succeed in "regulating these various and interfering interests" in ways that secured the "public good." The mere proliferation of interest groups in our time does not justify a negative answer to that question. Rather, one would also have to believe the political process is dominated by groups that seek to serve their members with little or no regard for the well-being and rights of other citizens. To some pro-choice voters, certain pro-life groups may appear as factions, and to some pro-life citizens, certain pro-choice groups may appear as factions. Both these and other ideological groups have proliferated in recent decades. Whether this is good or bad for American's representative democracy is a question on which reasonable minds can and do differ. But this much is clear: in contemporary American politics, one citizen's special-interest group often is another citizen's public-interest lobby.

6. Should interest groups' political activities be restricted by law?

In fact, interest groups' activities are restricted by literally scores of laws that are already on the books. For example, Washington lobbyists must register with the House or Senate. All registered lobbyists must publicly divulge their client list and expenditures. There are legal limits on PAC contributions. Every new wave of campaign finance laws (see Chapter 10) has resulted in more rules regulating interest groups. The Internal Revenue Service (IRS) has tightly restricted political activity by religious groups, private schools, and other organizations as a condition for their exemption from federal income tax. The courts have consistently upheld such restrictions and ruled that they do not, under most circumstances, violate freedom of speech or other constitutional protections. On the other hand, the courts have effectively afforded even tax-exempt groups ways of legally, but indirectly, engaging in political activity. Finally, states and cities have their own laws regulating interest groups, and some places are more restrictive than others.

TO LEARN MORE

Conservative interest groups

American Conservative Union: **www.conservative.org**

Christian Coalition: **www.cc.org**

Liberal interest groups

American Civil Liberties Union: **www.aclu.org**

Americans for Democratic Action: **www.adaction.org**

Environmental groups

Environmental Defense: **www.environmentaldefense.org**

National Resources Defense Council: **www.nrdc.org**

Civil rights groups

NAACP: **www.naacp.org**

Center for Equal Opportunity: **www.ceousa.org**

Feminist group

National Organization for Women: **www.now.org**

Baumgartner, Frank R., Jeffrey M. Berry, Marie Hojnacki, David C. Kimball, and Beth L. Leech. *Lobbying and Policy Change: Who Wins, Who Loses, and Why*. Chicago: University of Chicago Press, 2009. Thorough empirical assessment of which interest groups exercise influence in Washington.

Cigler, Allan J., and Burdett A. Loomis, eds. *Interest Group Politics*, 8th ed. Washington, D.C.: Congressional Quarterly Press, 2011. Essays on interest groups active in American politics today.

Grossman, Matt. *The Not-So-Special Interests: Interest Groups, Public Representation, and American Governance*. Stanford: Stanford University Press, 2012. A comprehensive study of which interest groups become more influential in American politics and why.

Lowi, Theodore J. *The End of Liberalism*. New York: Norton, 1969. A critique of the role of interest groups in American government.

Mansbridge, Jane J. *Why We Lost the ERA*. Chicago: University of Chicago Press, 1986. Insightful analysis of the relationship between organizational incentives and tactics in the ERA campaign.

Olson, Mancur. *The Logic of Collective Action*. Cambridge: Harvard University Press, 1965. An economic analysis of interest groups, especially the "free-rider" problem.

Sabato, Larry. *PAC Power*. New York: Norton, 1985. A full discussion of the nature and activities of political action committees.

Schlozman, Kay Lehman, and John T. Tierney. *Organized Interests and American Democracy*. New York: Harper and Row, 1985. Comprehensive treatise on interest groups based on original research.

Truman, David B. *The Governmental Process*, 2d ed. New York: Knopf, 1971. First published in 1951, this was the classic analysis—and defense—of interest group pluralism.

Wilson, James Q. *Political Organizations*, Rev. ed. Princeton, NJ: Princeton University Press, 1995. A theory of interest groups emphasizing the incentives they use to attract members.

Kevin Dietsch/UPI/Newscom

12

The Media

LEARNING OBJECTIVES

1. What role do the media play in American politics?

2. Why are there so few restrictions on media coverage of politics and politicians in the United States?

3. How much power do the media have?

4. How has technology changed interactions between public officials and the media?

5. Can we trust the media to be fair?

Suppose you want to influence how other people think about health, politics, sports, or celebrities. What would you do? At one time, you might write a book or publish an essay in a newspaper or magazine. But unless you were very lucky, the book or article would only reach a few people. Today, you will have a much bigger impact if you can get on television or invent a controversial web log (or blog). Vastly more people watch *American Idol* than read newspaper editorials; many more get opinions from blogs—such as the Daily Kos on the left or Power Line on the right—than read essays in magazines.

Television and the internet are key parts of the New Media; newspapers and magazines are part of the Old Media. And when it comes to politics, the New Media are getting stronger and the Old Media weaker.

THEN

In 1972–1974, the Nixon administration's efforts to cover up the burglary of Democratic National Committee headquarters at the Watergate hotel in Washington, D.C., were revealed through a series of articles published in *The Washington Post*, which gained national fame for its riveting news coverage by journalists Bob Woodward and Carl Bernstein.[1] In the summer of 1987, Congress held live, televised hearings about the Iran-Contra scandal, which viewers watched at home as well as in stores and other public venues that broadcast the hearings on their televisions.[2]

NOW

In 2004, "*60 Minutes*," a CBS television news program, ran a story claiming that President Bush had performed poorly during his time in the Air National Guard. Within a few hours, bloggers produced evidence that the documents underlying this charge were forgeries, something CBS later conceded was true. Not long afterward, the producer and newscaster responsible for the charges left CBS. In 2008, then-presidential candidate Barack Obama stated at a private fundraiser that voters in economic distress "cling to guns or religion," and a freelance writer for *The Huffington Post* who attended the event decided to publish Obama's remarks, creating an uproar in his campaign.[3] In 2011, reports that the United States had captured and killed Osama bin Laden first appeared on the online site Twitter.

Social media are becoming a regular news source for people: a 2012 study found that almost one-fifth of Americans reported seeing news or headlines on a social networking site, almost twice as many as in 2010. Only 13 percent of adults under 30 read a newspaper, either in print or electronically, and the number of people getting news from

television or radio continued to decline, while use of online/mobile news sources increased (though more people still watch television news than view online).[4]

But not all of the users are convinced that the internet is entirely trustworthy. One-third of adults think it lets the loudest and most extreme voices prevail and feel that it is full of misinformation. And though newspapers are rapidly losing their audience, they remain vitally important: much of what is on the internet comes from newspaper reporters, and politicians devote at least as much time to getting good newspaper coverage as they devote to expanding their internet coverage.

The Media and Politics

The internet is an important new venue for politics, but it presents similar challenges for politicians as earlier technological advances in communication. From the beginning of the Republic, public officials have tried to get the media on their side while knowing that, because the media love controversy, they are as likely to attack as to praise. The internet may strike some politicians as the solution to this problem: they think that if they put their own web pages out there, they can reach the voters directly. They can, but so can rival politicians with their own web pages and with their allies attacking their competitors.

All of this takes place in a country so committed to a free press that there is little the government can do to control the process. As we shall see, there have been efforts to control radio and television as a result of the government's right to license broadcasters, but most of these attempts have evaporated.

Even strongly democratic nations restrict the press more than the United States. For example, the laws governing libel are much stricter in the United Kingdom than in the United States. As a result, it is easier in the United Kingdom for politicians to sue newspapers for publishing articles that defame or ridicule them. In this country, the libel laws make it almost impossible to prevent press criticisms of public figures. Moreover, England has an Official Secrets Act that can be used to punish any past or present public officials who leak information to the press.[5] In this country, leaking information occurs all the time, and our Freedom of Information Act makes it relatively easy for the press to extract documents from the government.

European governments can be much tougher on people who make controversial statements than the American political system. In 2006, an Austrian court sentenced a man to three years in prison for having denied that the Nazi death camp at Auschwitz killed its inmates. A French court convicted a distinguished American historian for telling a French newspaper that the slaughter of Armenians may not have been the result of planned effort. An Italian journalist stood trial for having written things "offensive to Islam." In this country, such statements would be protected by the Constitution even if, as with the man who denied the existence of the Holocaust, they were profoundly wrong.[6]

America has a long tradition of privately owned media. By contrast, private ownership of television has come only recently to France. And the internet is not owned by anybody: here and in many nations, people can say or read whatever they want on their computers. Newspapers in this country require no government permission to operate, but radio and television stations need licenses granted by the Federal Communications Commission (FCC). These licenses must be renewed periodically. On occasion, the White House has made efforts to use license renewals as a way of influencing station owners who were out of political favor, but of late the level of FCC control over what is broadcast has lessened.

There are two potential limits to the freedom of privately owned newspapers and broadcast stations. First, they must make a profit. Some critics believe the need for profit will lead media outlets to distort the news in order to satisfy advertisers or to build an audience. Though there is some truth to this argument, it is too simple. Every media outlet must satisfy a variety of people—advertisers, subscribers, listeners, reporters, and editors—and balancing those demands is complicated and will be done differently by different owners.

The second problem is media bias. If most of the reporters and editors have similar views about politics and if they act on those views, then the media will give us only one side of many stories. Later in this chapter, we shall take a close look at this possibility.

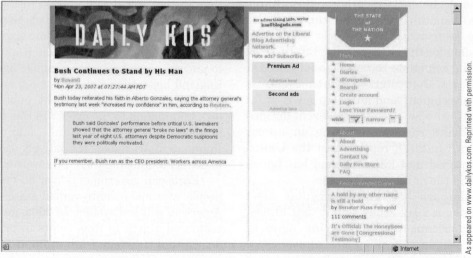

Blogs, both conservative and liberal, have become an important form of political communication.

Journalism in American Political History

Important changes in the nature of American politics have gone hand in hand with major changes in the organization and technology of the press. It is the nature of politics, essentially a form of communication, to respond to changes in how communications are carried on. This can be seen by considering five important periods in journalistic history.

The Party Press

In the early years of the Republic, politicians of various factions and parties created, sponsored, and controlled newspapers to further their interests. This was possible because circulation was of necessity small (newspapers could not easily be distributed to large audiences, owing to poor transportation) and newspapers were expensive (the type was set by hand and the presses printed copies slowly). Furthermore, there were few large advertisers to pay the bills. These newspapers circulated chiefly among the political and commercial elites who could afford the high subscription prices. Even with high prices, the newspapers often required subsidies that frequently came from the government or a political party.

During the Washington administration, the Federalists, led by Alexander Hamilton, created the *Gazette of the United States*. The Republicans, led by Thomas Jefferson, retaliated by creating the *National Gazette* and made its editor, Philip Freneau, "clerk for foreign languages" in the State Department at $250 a year to help support him. After Jefferson became president, he induced another publisher, Samuel Harrison Smith, to start the *National Intelligencer*, subsidizing him by giving him a contract to print government documents. Andrew Jackson, when he became president, aided in the creation of *The Washington Globe*. By some estimates, there were more than 50 journalists on the government payroll during this era. Naturally, these newspapers were relentlessly partisan in their views. Citizens could choose among different party papers, but only rarely could they find a paper that presented both sides of an issue.

The Popular Press

Changes in society and technology made possible the rise of a self-supporting, mass-readership daily newspaper. The development of the high-speed rotary press enabled publishers to print thousands of copies of a newspaper cheaply and quickly. The invention of the telegraph in the 1840s meant that news from Washington could be flashed almost immediately to New York, Boston, Philadelphia, and Charleston, thus providing local papers with access to information that once only the Washington papers enjoyed. The creation in 1848 of the Associated Press allowed telegraphic dissemination of information to newspaper editors on a systematic basis. Since the AP provided stories that had to be brief and that went to newspapers of every political hue, it could not afford to be partisan or biased; to attract as many subscribers as possible, it had to present the facts objectively.

Meanwhile, the nation was becoming more urbanized, with large numbers of people brought together in densely settled areas. These people could support a daily newspaper by paying only a penny per copy and by patronizing merchants who advertised in its pages. Newspapers no longer needed political patronage to prosper, and soon such subsidies began to dry up. In 1860, the Government Printing Office was established, thereby putting an end to most of the printing contracts that Washington newspapers had once enjoyed.

The mass-readership newspaper was scarcely nonpartisan, but the partisanship it displayed arose from the convictions of its publishers and editors rather than from the influence of its party sponsors. And these convictions blended political beliefs with economic interest. The way to attract a large readership was with sensationalism: violence, romance, and patriotism, coupled with exposés of government, politics, business, and society. As practiced by Joseph Pulitzer and William Randolph Hearst, founders of large newspaper empires, this editorial policy had great appeal for the average citizen and especially for the immigrants flooding into the large cities.

Strong-willed publishers could often become powerful political forces. Hearst used his papers to agitate for war with Spain when the Cubans rebelled against Spanish rule. Conservative Republican political leaders were opposed to the war, but a steady diet of newspaper stories about real and imagined Spanish brutalities whipped up public opinion in favor of intervention. At one point, Hearst sent the noted artist Frederic Remington to Cuba to supply paintings of the conflict. Remington cabled back: "Everything is quiet. ... There will be no war." Hearst supposedly replied: "Please remain. You furnish the pictures and I'll furnish the war."[7] When the battleship USS *Maine* blew up in Havana harbor, President William McKinley felt helpless to resist popular pressure, and war was declared in 1898.

For all their excesses, the mass-readership newspapers began to create a common national culture, to establish the feasibility of a press free of government control or subsidy, and to demonstrate how exciting (and profitable) the criticism of public policy and the revelation of public scandal could be.

Magazines of Opinion

The growing middle class often was repelled by what it called "yellow journalism" and was developing around the turn of the century a taste for political reform and a belief in the doctrines of the progressive movement. To satisfy this market, a variety of national magazines appeared that—unlike those devoted to manners and literature—discussed issues of public policy. Among the first of these were the *Nation,* the *Atlantic Monthly,* and *Harper's,* founded in the 1850s and 1860s; later came the more broadly based mass-circulation magazines such as *McClure's, Scribner's,* and *Cosmopolitan.* They provided the means for developing a national constituency for certain issues such as regulating business (or in the language of the times, "trust-busting"), purifying municipal politics, and reforming the civil service system. Lincoln Steffens and other so-called muckrakers were frequent contributors to the magazines, setting a pattern for what we now call "investigative reporting."

The national magazines of opinion provided an opportunity for individual writers to gain a nationwide following. The popular press, though initially under the heavy influence of founder-publishers, made the names of certain reporters and columnists household words. In time, the great circulation wars between the big-city daily newspapers started to wane, as the more successful papers bought up or otherwise eliminated their competition. This reduced the need for the more extreme forms of sensationalism, a change reinforced by the growing sophistication and education of America's readers. And the founding publishers gradually were replaced by less flamboyant managers. All of these changes—in circulation needs, audience interests, managerial style, and the emergence of nationally

known writers—helped increase the power of editors and reporters and make them a force to be reckoned with.

Although politics dominated the pages of most national magazines in the late 19th century, today national magazines that focus mainly on politics and government affairs account for only a small and declining portion of the national magazine market. Among all magazines in circulation today, only a fraction focus on politics—the majority of today's magazines focus on popular entertainment and leisure activities.

Electronic Journalism

Radio came on the national scene in the 1920s, television in the late 1940s. They represented a major change in the way news was gathered and disseminated, though few politicians at first understood the importance of this change. A broadcast permits public officials to speak directly to audiences without their remarks being filtered through editors and reporters. This was obviously an advantage to politicians, provided they were skilled enough to use it: they could in theory reach the voters directly on a national scale without the services of political parties, interest groups, or friendly editors.

But there was an offsetting disadvantage—people could easily ignore a speech broadcast on a radio or television station, either by not listening at all or by tuning to a different station. By contrast, the views of at least some public figures would receive prominent and often unavoidable display in newspapers, and in a growing number of cities there was only one daily paper. Moreover, space in a newspaper is cheap compared to time on a television broadcast.

Adding one more story, or one more name to an existing story, costs the newspaper little. By contrast,

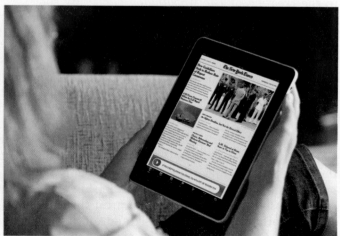

News used to come by radio, but today many people read news on iPads and other electronic devices.

less news can be carried on radio or television, and each news segment must be quite brief to avoid boring the audience. As a result, the number of political personalities that can be covered by radio and television news is much smaller than is the case with newspapers, and the cost (to the station) of making a news item or broadcast longer often is prohibitively large.

Thus, to obtain the advantages of electronic media coverage, public officials must do something sufficiently bold or colorful to gain free access to radio and television news—or they must find the money to purchase radio and television time. The president of the United States, of course, is routinely covered by radio and television and can ordinarily get free time to speak to the nation on matters of importance. All other officials must struggle for media attention by making controversial statements, acquiring a national reputation, or purchasing expensive time.

The rise of the talk show as a political forum has increased politicians' access to the electronic media, as has the televised "town meeting." But such developments need to be understood as part of a larger story.

Until the 1990s, the "big three" television networks (ABC, CBS, and NBC) together claimed 80 percent or more of all viewers. Their evening newscasts dominated electronic media coverage of politics and government affairs. When it came to presidential campaigns, for example, the three networks were the only television games in town— they reported on the primaries, broadcast the party conventions, and covered the general election campaigns, including any presidential debates. But over the last few decades, the networks' evening newscasts have changed in ways that have made it harder for candidates to use them

> **sound bite** A radio or video clip of someone speaking.

to get their messages across. For instance, the average **sound bite**—a video clip of a presidential contender speaking—dropped from about 42 seconds in 1968 to 7.3 seconds in 2000.[8] Furthermore, as Figure 12.1 shows, the audience for the evening news has been in decline since the 1980s.

Today, politicians have sources other than the network news for sustained and personalized television exposure. Cable television, early-morning news and entertainment programs, and prime-time "newsmagazine" shows have greatly increased and diversified politicians' access to the electronic media.

Naturally, many politicians favor the call-in format, town-meeting setups, lengthy human interest interviews, and casual appearances on entertainment shows to televised confrontations on policy issues with seasoned network journalists who push, probe, and criticize. And naturally, they favor being a part of visually interesting programs rather than traditional "talking heads" news shows. But what is preferable to candidates is not necessarily helpful to the selection process that voters must go through in choosing a candidate.

One thing is clear: most politicians crave the media spotlight, both on the campaign trail and in office. The efforts made by political candidates to get "-visuals"—filmed stories—on television continue

FIGURE 12.1   **Evening News Audience Continues a 30-Year Decline**

November-to-November Average Viewers per Night In Millions

Source: Nielsen Media Research, used under license. Pew Research Center's Project for Excellence in Journalism, 2013 State of the News Media.

blog A series, or log, of discussion items on a page of the World Wide Web.

after they are elected. Since the president is always news, a politician wishing to make news is well advised to attack the president.

The Internet

More than half of all Americans used the internet to get political news about the 2010 midterm elections.[9] The political news found there ranges from summaries of stories from newspapers and magazines to political rumors and hot gossip. For example, viewers may scan political ideas posted on a **blog**; many blogs specialize in offering liberal, conservative, or libertarian perspectives. The internet is the ultimate free market in political news: no one can ban, control, or regulate it, and no one can keep facts, opinions, or nonsense off of it.

The internet is beginning to play a big role in politics. When Howard Dean ran for the Democratic presidential nomination in 2004, he raised most of his money from internet appeals. When John Kerry, who won the nomination, was campaigning, the internet and the blogs on it were a major source of discussion of the criticisms made of him by former Vietnam War veterans. Now every candidate for important offices has a web site.

The rise of the internet has completed a remarkable transformation in American journalism. In the days of the party press, only a few people read newspapers. When mass-circulation newspapers arose, mass politics also arose. When magazines of opinion developed, interest groups also developed. When radio and television became dominant, politicians could build their own bridges to voters without party or interest group influence. And now, with the internet, voters and political activists can talk to each other. This is true in many dictatorships. When popular revolutions broke out against the autocratic leaders of Egypt and Libya, the activists used the internet (namely, Twitter) to inform their colleagues. It is becoming much harder for a powerful leader to control what other people can learn.

Most users think the internet is a wonderful innovation, but some worry that using email, YouTube, Facebook, text messaging, blogs, and Twitter to communicate will isolate people from one another and make public opinion more extreme. There have been several studies of this possibility, but they have not produced a clear answer. A Stanford study argued that the internet isolates people from ordinary human contact and makes them become anonymous. A study at Carnegie Mellon University came to much the same conclusion. By contrast, a study done at UCLA found that internet users are more likely to consult newspapers and magazines and that they spend just as much time on the telephone as people not on the internet. And a Pew survey suggested that email makes people feel more, not less, connected to others.[10]

But one thing is clear: the internet has profoundly affected politics by making it easier to (1) raise money in small donations, (2) organize people to attend meetings, (3) take instant (though probably unreliable) opinion polls, (4) disseminate instant criticism of your opponent, (5) mobilize local followers, and (6) provide campaigners with the names of people they should contact.

The Structure of the Media

The relationship between journalism and politics is a two-way street: though politicians take advantage as best they can of the communications media available to them, these media in turn attempt to use politics and politicians as a way of both entertaining and informing their audiences. The mass media, whatever their disclaimers, are not simply a mirror held up to reality or a messenger that carries the news. There is inevitably a process of selection, of editing, and of emphasis, and this process reflects, to some degree, the way in which the media are organized, the kinds of audiences they seek to serve, and the preferences and opinions of the members of the media.

Degree of Competition

There has been a large decline in the number of daily newspapers that serve large communities. There were competing papers in 60 percent of American cities in 1900 but in only 4 percent in 1972. Several large cities—Boston, Chicago, Detroit, Los Angeles, New York, Philadelphia, and Washington, D.C.— have more than one paper, but in some of these cities the same business owns both papers. And newspaper circulation has fallen in recent years, with more and more people getting their news from radio and television. Young people especially have turned away from political news. In the 1940s and 1950s, age did not make much difference; people under the age of 30 read about the same amount of news as people over the age of 50. But by the 1970s, that had changed dramatically: young people read less political news than older people, a trend that continues today. In Figure 12.2, we can see that today only half as many people between the ages of 18 and 34 read newspapers as did in 2000.

FIGURE 12.2 Newspaper Readership Falls for Most Age Groups

Percentage Nationally Who Read Any Daily Newspaper Yesterday

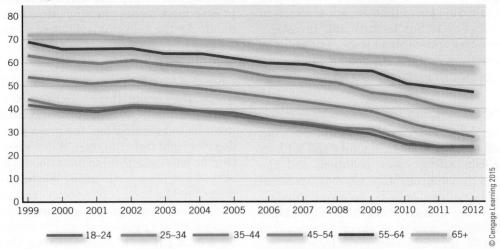

© Cengage Learning 2015

Source: Data adapted from Pew Research Center's Project for Excellence in Journalism, 2013 State of the News Media.

To a degree that would astonish most foreigners, the American press—radio, television, and newspapers—is made up of locally owned and managed enterprises. In the United Kingdom, France, Germany, Japan, Sweden, and elsewhere, the media are owned and operated with a national audience in mind. *The Times* of London may be published in that city, but it is read throughout the United Kingdom, as are *The Guardian, The Daily Telegraph,* and the *Daily Mirror.* Radio and television broadcasts are centrally planned and nationally aired.

The American newspaper, however, is primarily oriented to its local market and local audience, and there is typically more local than national news in it. Radio and television stations accept network programming, but the early- and late-evening news programs provide a heavy diet of local political, social, and sports news. Government regulations developed by the Federal Communications Commission (FCC) are in part responsible for this. Until the mid-1990s, no one could own and operate more than one newspaper, one AM radio station, one FM radio station, or one television station in a given market. The networks still today may not compel a local affiliate to accept any particular broadcast. (In fact, almost all network news programs are carried by the affiliates.) The result has been the development of a decentralized broadcast industry.

The National Media

The local orientation of much of the American communications media is partially offset, however, by the emergence of certain publications and broadcast services that constitute a kind of national press. The wire services—the Associated Press and United Press International—supply most of the national news that local papers publish. Certain newsmagazines, such as *Time* and *Newsweek*, have a national readership. The network evening news broadcasts produced by ABC, CBS, and NBC are carried by most television stations with a network affiliation. Both CNN (Cable News Network) and Fox News broadcast news around the clock and have large audiences, as does MSNBC. Though most newspapers have only local audiences, several have acquired national influence. *The New York Times* and *The Wall Street Journal* are printed in several locations and can be delivered to many homes early in the morning. *USA Today* was created as a national newspaper and is distributed everywhere, aimed especially at people who travel a lot.

These newspapers have national standing for several reasons. First, they distribute a lot of copies: more than 1 million each day for the *Times* and the *Journal,* and more than 2 million a day for *USA Today.* Second, these papers, as well as *The Washington Post,* are carefully followed by political elites. Unlike most people, the elites even read the editorials. By contrast, local newspapers and radio stations may be invisible to Washington politicians. Third, radio and television stations often decide what to broadcast by looking at the front pages of the *Times* and the *Post.* The front page of the *Times* is a model for each network's evening news broadcast.[11] Finally, the editors and reporters for the national press tend to be better educated and more generously paid than their counterparts in local outlets.

And as we shall see, the writers for the national press tend to have distinctly liberal political views. Above all they seek—and frequently obtain—the opportunity to write stories that are not accounts of a particular news event but "background," investigative, or interpretive stories about issues and policies.

The national press plays the role of gatekeeper, scorekeeper, and watchdog for the federal government.

Gatekeeper

As gatekeeper, the national media can influence what subjects become national political issues and for how long. Automobile safety, water pollution, and the quality of prescription drugs were not major political issues before the national press began giving substantial attention to these matters and thus helped place them on the political agenda. When crime rates rose in the early 1960s, the subject was given little political attention in Washington, in part because the media did not cover it extensively. Media attention to crime increased in the late 1960s and early 1970s, slackened in the late 1970s, and rose again in the 1980s and early 1990s. Throughout most of these years, crime went up. In short, *reality* did not change during this time; only the focus of media and political attention shifted. Elite opinion about the war in Vietnam also changed significantly as the attitude toward the war expressed by the national media changed.

Scorekeeper

As scorekeepers, the national media keep track of and help make political reputations, note who is "mentioned" as a presidential candidate, and help decide who is winning and losing in Washington politics. When Jimmy Carter, a virtually unknown former governor of Georgia, was planning his campaign to get the Democratic nomination for president, he understood clearly the importance of being "mentioned." So successful was he in cultivating members of the national press that, before the first primary election was held, he was the subject of more stories in *The New York Times, The Washington Post,* and *The Columbus Dispatch* than any other potential Democratic presidential candidate.

The scorekeeper role of the media often leads the press to cover presidential elections as if they were horse races rather than choices among policies. Consider the enormous attention the media give to the Iowa caucus and the New Hampshire primary election, despite the fact that these states produce only a tiny fraction of the delegates to either party's nominating convention and that neither state is representative of the nation as a whole. The results of the Iowa caucus, the first in the nation, are given great importance by the press. Consequently, the coverage received by a candidate who does well in Iowa constitutes a tremendous amount of free publicity that can help him or her in the New Hampshire primary election. Doing well in that primary results in even more media attention, thus boosting the candidate for the next primaries, and so on.

Watchdog

Once the scorekeepers decide you are the person to watch, they adopt their watchdog role. When Gary Hart was the front-runner for the 1988 Democratic presidential nomination, the press played its watchdog role right from the start. When rumors circulated that he was unfaithful to his wife, the *Miami Herald* staked out his apartment in Washington, D.C., and discovered he had spent several evening hours there with an attractive young woman, Donna Rice. Soon other stories appeared about his having taken Rice on a boat trip to Bimini. Not long thereafter, Hart dropped out of the presidential race, accusing the press of unfair treatment.

This close scrutiny is natural. The media have an instinctive—and profitable—desire to investigate personalities and expose scandals. To some degree, all reporters probably share the belief that the role of the press is to "comfort the afflicted and afflict the comfortable." They tend to be tolerant of underdogs, tough on front-runners. Though some reporters develop close relations with powerful personages, many—especially younger ones—find the discovery of wrongdoing both more absorbing and more lucrative. Bob Woodward and Carl Bernstein, who wrote most of the Watergate stories for *The Washington Post,* simultaneously performed an important public service, received the accolades of their colleagues, and earned a lot of money.

Newspapers and television stations play these three roles in somewhat different ways. A newspaper can cover more stories in greater depth than a TV station and faces less competition from other papers than TV stations face from other broadcasters. A TV station faces brutal competition, must select its programs in part for their visual impact, and must keep its stories short and punchy. As a result, newspaper reporters have more freedom to develop their own stories, but they earn less money than television news broadcasters. The latter have little freedom (the fear of losing their audience is keen), but they can make a lot of money (if they are attractive personalities who photograph well).

Rules Governing the Media

Ironically, the least competitive media outlets—the big-city newspapers—are almost entirely free from government regulation, while the most competitive ones—radio and television stations—must have a government license to operate and must adhere to a variety of government regulations.

Newspapers and magazines need no license to publish, their freedom to publish may not be restrained in advance, and they are liable for punishment for what they do publish only under certain highly restricted circumstances. The First Amendment has been interpreted as meaning that no government, federal or state, can place "prior restraints" (that is, censorship) on the press except under very narrowly defined circumstances.[12] When the federal government sought to prevent *The New York Times* from publishing the Pentagon Papers, a set of secret government documents stolen by an antiwar activist, the Supreme Court held that the paper was free to publish them.[13]

Once something is published, a newspaper or magazine may be sued or prosecuted if the material is libelous or obscene or if it incites someone to commit an illegal act. But these usually are not very serious restrictions, because the courts have defined *libelous, obscene,* and *incitement* so narrowly as to make it more difficult here than in any other nation to find the press guilty of such conduct. For example, for a paper to be found guilty of libeling a public official or other prominent person, the person must not only show that what was printed was wrong and damaging but must also show, with "clear and convincing evidence," that it was printed maliciously—that is, with "reckless disregard" for its truth or falsity.[14] When in 1984 Israeli General Ariel Sharon sued *Time* magazine for libel, the jury decided the story *Time* printed was false and defamatory but that *Time* had not published it as the result of malice, and so Sharon did not collect any damages.

There are also laws intended to protect the privacy of citizens, but they do not really inhibit newspapers. In general, your name and picture can be printed without your consent if they are part of a news story of some conceivable public interest. And if a paper attacks you in print, the paper has no legal obligation to give you space for a reply.[15]

It is illegal to use printed words to advocate the violent overthrow of the government if by your advocacy you incite others to action, but this rule has only rarely been applied to newspapers.[16]

Confidentiality of Sources

Reporters believe they should have the right to keep confidential the sources of their stories. Some states agree and have passed laws to that effect. Most states and the federal government do not agree, so the courts must decide in each case whether the need of a journalist to protect confidential sources does or does not outweigh the interest of the government in gathering evidence in a criminal investigation.

In general, the Supreme Court has upheld the right of the government to compel reporters to divulge information as part of a properly conducted criminal investigation, if it bears on the commission of a crime.[17]

This conflict arises not only between reporters and law enforcement agencies but also between reporters and persons accused of committing a crime. Myron Farber, a reporter for *The New York Times,* wrote a series of stories that led to the indictment and trial of a physician on charges he had murdered five patients. The judge ordered Farber to show him his notes to determine whether they should be given to the defense lawyers. Farber refused, arguing that revealing his notes would infringe upon the confidentiality he had promised to his sources. Farber was sent to jail for contempt of court. On appeal, the New Jersey Supreme Court and the U.S. Supreme Court decided against Farber, holding that the accused person's right to a fair trial includes the right to compel the production of evidence, even from reporters.

In 2005, two reporters were sentenced to jail when they refused to give prosecutors information about who in the Bush administration had told them that a woman was in fact a CIA officer. A federal court decided they were not entitled to any protection for their sources in a criminal trial. *The New York Times* reporter, Judith Miller, spent 85 days in jail; she was released after a government official authorized her to talk about their conversation. There is no federal shield law that will protect journalists, though such laws exist in 34 states.

In another case, the Supreme Court upheld the right of the police to search newspaper offices, so long as they have a warrant. But Congress then passed a law forbidding such searches (except in special cases), requiring instead that the police subpoena the desired documents.[18]

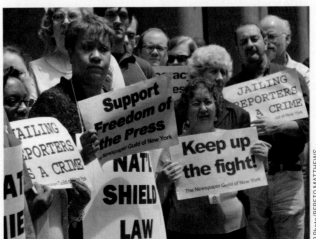

Activists urge Congress to pass a law shielding reporters from being required to testify about their sources.

equal time rule An FCC rule that if a broadcaster sells time to one candidate, it must sell equal time to other candidates.

Regulating Broadcasting

Although newspapers and magazines by and large are not regulated, broadcasting is regulated by the government. No one may operate a radio or television station without a license from the Federal Communications Commission, renewable every seven years for radio and every five for television stations. An application for renewal is rarely refused, but until recently the FCC required the broadcaster to submit detailed information about its programming and how it planned to serve "community needs" in order to get a renewal. Based on this information or on the complaints of some group, the FCC could use its powers of renewal to influence what the station put on the air. For example, it could induce stations to reduce the amount of violence shown, increase the proportion of "public service" programs on the air, or alter the way it portrayed various ethnic groups.

Of late a movement has arisen to deregulate broadcasting, on the grounds that so many stations are now on the air that competition should be allowed to determine how each station defines and serves community needs. In this view, citizens can choose what they want to hear or see without the government's shaping the content of each station's programming. For example, since the early 1980s, a station can simply submit a postcard requesting that its license be renewed, a request automatically granted unless some group formally opposes the renewal. In that case, the FCC holds a hearing. As a result, some of the old rules—for instance, that each hour on TV could contain only 16 minutes of commercials—are no longer rigidly enforced.

Radio broadcasting has been deregulated the most. Before 1992, one company could own one AM and one FM station in each market. In 1992, this number was doubled. And in 1996, the Telecommunications Act allowed one company to own as many as eight stations in large markets (five in smaller ones) and as many as it wished nationally. This trend has had two results. First, a few large companies now own most of the big-market radio stations. Second, the looser editorial restrictions that accompanied deregulation mean that a greater variety of opinions and shows can be found on radio. There are many more radio talk shows than would have been heard when content was more tightly controlled.

Deregulation has also lessened the extent to which the federal government shapes the content of

LANDMARK CASES

The Rights of the Media

- ***Near v. Minnesota* (1931):** Freedom of the press applies to state governments, so that they cannot impose prior restraint on newspapers.

- ***New York Times v. Sullivan* (1964):** Public officials may not win a libel suit unless they can prove that the statement was made knowing it to be false or with reckless disregard of its truth.

- ***Miami Herald v. Tornillo* (1974):** A newspaper cannot be required to give someone a right to reply to one of its stories.

broadcasting. At one time, for example, a "fairness doctrine" required broadcasters that air one side of a story to give time to opposing points of view. But there are now so many radio and television stations that the FCC relies on competition to manage differences of opinion. The abandonment of the fairness doctrine permitted the rise of controversial talk radio shows. If the doctrine had stayed in place, there would be no Rush Limbaugh or Al Franken. The FCC decided that competition among news outlets protected people by giving them many different sources of news.

There still exists an **equal time rule** that obliges stations that sell advertising time to one political candidate to sell equal time to that person's opponents. When candidates wish to campaign on radio or television, the equal time rule applies.

Campaigning

During campaigns, a broadcaster must provide equal access to candidates for office and charge them rates no higher than the cheapest rate applicable to commercial advertisers for comparable time. At one time, this rule meant that a station or network could not broadcast a debate between the Democratic and Republican candidates for an office without inviting all other candidates as well—Libertarian, Prohibitionist, or whatever. Thus, a presidential debate in 1980 could be limited to the major candidates, Reagan and Carter (or Reagan and Anderson), only by having the League of Women Voters sponsor it and then allowing radio and TV to cover it as a "news event." Now stations and networks can themselves sponsor debates limited to major candidates.

Though laws guarantee that candidates can buy time at favorable rates on television, not all candidates take advantage of this. The reason is that television is not always an efficient way to reach voters. A television message is literally "broad cast"—spread out to a mass audience without regard to the boundaries of the district in which a candidate is running. Presidential candidates, of course, always use television because their constituency is the whole nation. Candidates for senator or representative, however, may or may not use television, depending on whether the boundaries of their state or district conform well to the boundaries of a television market.

A *market* is an area easily reached by a television signal; there are about 200 such markets in the country. If you are a member of Congress from South Bend, Indiana, you come from a television market based there. You can buy ads on the TV stations in South Bend at a reasonable fee. But if you are a member of Congress from northern New Jersey, the only television stations are in nearby New York City. In that market, the costs of a TV ad are very high because they reach a lot of people, most of whom are not in your district and so cannot vote for you. Buying a TV ad is a waste of money. As a result, a much higher percentage of Senate than House candidates use television ads.

One aspect of campaigning that worries scholars is the media's reliance on **horse-race journalism**, that is, covering a campaign based on guesses about who is ahead rather than on candidates' positions on the issues. For example, in 2008 the journalists talked about how Barack Obama would win the New Hampshire primary because that is what the polls and political insiders told them. But then Hillary Clinton won. Nowhere in the press coverage was any attention given to the positions Clinton and Obama had on the issues. The public says they want more such coverage, though one suspects that they actually like horse-race journalism.

Are the National Media Biased?

Everyone believes the media have a profound effect, for better or for worse, on politics. Many think the political opinions of writers and editors influence that effect. To decide whether these statements are true, we must answer three questions:

1. Do members of the media have a distinctive political attitude?
2. Does that attitude affect what they write or say?
3. Does what they write or say affect what citizens believe?

The answers to these questions, to be discussed below, are yes, yes, and probably.

A Liberal Majority

Many studies, dating back to the early 1980s, have concluded that members of the national press are more liberal than the average citizen.[19] In 1992, 91 percent of the media members interviewed said they had voted for the Democratic candidate for president. By contrast, only 43 percent of the public voted that way.[20]

Not only are the media more liberal, they also tend to be secular. About 70 percent say they never or only a few times a year attend a religious service. And in recent years, the surveys suggest they have become even more liberal. For example, between 1980 and 1995, the proportion of media members who believe the government should guarantee jobs to people rose, and the proportion who think government should reduce the regulation of business fell. A 2004 study found that a majority of journalists identified themselves as liberal.[21]

The public certainly believes that members of the media are liberals. A Gallup Poll done in 2003 found that 45 percent of Americans believe the media are "too liberal" (15 percent thought they were "too conservative"). In another study, even Democrats agreed with this view. A survey taken just a few weeks before the 2008 presidential election found that more than two-thirds of voters believed that the media favored Barack Obama over John McCain.[22]

Conservative media outlets have become more visible in recent years. More radio talk shows, such as those hosted by Rush Limbaugh and Sean Hannity, are politically conservative, as is some of the TV reporting broadcast on Fox News, such as on the *O'Reilly Factor*. Limbaugh and Hannity have large audiences, and Fox News has grown in popularity.

> **horse-race journalism** News coverage that focuses on who is ahead rather than on the issues.

Political leaders no longer depend on traditional news media to reach voters, as President Obama demonstrates in appearing on Comedy Central's Daily Show with Jon Stewart.

BRENDAN SMIALOWSKI/AFP/Getty Images

routine stories Media stories about events regularly covered by reporters.

feature stories Media stories about events that, though public, are not regularly covered by reporters.

insider stories Media stories about events that are not usually made public.

trial balloon Information leaked to the media to test public reaction to a possible policy.

loaded language Words that imply a value judgment, used to persuade a reader without having made a serious argument.

One-fifth of all Americans listen to radio talk shows every day and another tenth listen several times a week. A puzzling fact is that talk radio, which has grown rapidly in importance, is predominately conservative. Almost half of the 28 largest talk shows have been hosted by outspoken conservatives.

None of this dominance is the result of radio station owners plotting to put conservatives on the air. Media owners are interested in ratings—that is, in measures of how big their audiences are. Liberal talk-show hosts have had big corporate sponsors that dropped away when the shows did not get good ratings. If Vladimir Putin got high ratings by playing the harmonica, then Putin likely would be on the air.

William G. Mayer, a political scientist, has speculated as to why conservative talk shows are so common. First, there are more self-described conservatives than liberals in this country. Second, conservative listeners do not think their views are reflected in what big-city newspapers, the major television networks, and the leading newsmagazines display. Liberals, by contrast, think their views are encouraged by newspapers and television stations. Third, much of the liberal audience is broken up into distinctive racial and ethnic groups that have their own radio outlets. Many Hispanics listen to stations that broadcast in Spanish; many African Americans prefer stations that have black hosts and focus on black community issues.[23]

Neutral and Objective?

In the United States, the journalistic philosophy in many media documents is that the press, when it reports the news (though not in editorial pages), should be neutral and objective. That view, of course, does not cover radio talk shows, but it is supposed to cover newspapers. A different view can be found in France or the United Kingdom where newspapers often clearly identify with one party or another.

But it is hard to measure whether the American commitment to objectivity is actually achieved. One would have to take into account not only how much space a politician or policy receives, but also the tone in which it is handled and the adjectives used to describe people who are part of those stories.

New stories differ significantly in the opportunity for bias. **Routine stories** cover major political events that will be covered by many reporters and that involve relatively simple matters. For example: the president takes a trip, Congress passes a major bill, or the Supreme Court issues a ruling. **Feature stories** cover events that, though public, a reporter has to seek out because they are not routinely covered by the press. The reporter has to find the story and persuade an editor to publish it. For example: an interest group works hard to get a bill passed, a government agency adopts a new ruling, or a member of Congress conducts an unusual investigation. **Insider stories** cover things that are often secret. Investigative reporters are often credited with uncovering these stories, though it is often the case that some government insider has leaked the story to the press. Which leak a reporter picks up on may be influenced by the reporter's view of what is important, that is, by what is important to the reporter.

Routine stories often are covered in much the same way by reporters. The space given to the story and the headline attached to it may reflect the political views of the editor, but the story itself often is written about the same way by every reporter. Feature and insider stories, by contrast, may more easily reflect the political views of reporters and editors. On these stories, journalists have to make choices.

Early in American history, newspapers had virtually no routine stories; almost everything they printed was an expression of opinion. By the 20th century, with the advent of telephone and telegraph lines that made it easy for news organizations such as the Associated Press to send the same story to almost every newspaper, routine stories became commonplace. But with the advent of radio and television and the rise of around-the-clock news broadcasting, feature and insider stories became much more important to newspapers. If people got their routine news from radio and television, newspapers had to sell something different; feature and insider stories were different.

A conservative newspaper might print feature or insider stories about crime, drug abuse, or welfare cheats, while a liberal newspaper might run ones on feminism, the environment, or civil rights. There are, however, very few conservative newspapers with a national audience.

HOW THINGS WORK

How to Read the News

News articles don't simply report the news; they report somebody's idea of what is news, written in language intended to persuade as well as inform. To read a news article intelligently, look for three things: what is covered, who are the sources, and how language is used.

Coverage

Every major national news media outlet will cover a big story, such as a flood, fire, or presidential trip, but different media can pick and choose among lesser stories. One television network will select stories about the environment, business fraud, and civil rights, while a digital media publication may choose to publish stories about crime, drug dealers, and "welfare cheats." What do these choices tell you about the beliefs of the editors and reporters working for these news organizations? What do these people want you to believe are the important issues?

Sources

For some stories, the source is obvious: "The Supreme Court decided...," "Congress voted...," or "The president said..." For others, the source is not so obvious. There are two kinds of sources you should beware of. The first is an anonymous source. When you read phrases such as "a high-ranking official said today..." or "White House sources revealed that...," always ask yourself this question: Why does the source want me to know this? The answer usually will be this: because if I believe what he or she said, it will advance his or her interests. This can happen in one of three ways. First, the source may support a policy or appointment and want to test public reaction to it. This is called floating a **trial balloon**. Second, the source may oppose a policy or appointment and hope that by leaking word of it, the idea will be killed. Third, the source may want to take credit for something good that happened or shift blame onto somebody else for something bad that happened. When you read a story based on anonymous sources, ask yourself these

questions: Judging from the tone of the story, is this leak designed to support or kill an idea? Is it designed to take credit or shift blame? In whose interest is it to accomplish these things? By asking these questions, you often can make a pretty good guess as to the identity of the anonymous source.

Some stories depend on the reader's believing a key fact, previously unknown. For example: "The world's climate is getting hotter because of manmade pollution," "drug abuse is soaring," "the death penalty will prevent murder," "husbands are more likely to beat up on their wives on Super Bowl Sunday." Each of these "facts" is wrong, grossly exaggerated, or stated with excessive confidence. But each comes from an advocate organization that wants you to believe it, because if you do, you will take that organization's solution more seriously. Be skeptical of key facts if they come from an advocacy source. Don't be misled by the tendency of many advocacy organizations to take neutral or scholarly names like "Center for the Public Interest" or "Institute for Policy Research." Some of these really are neutral or scholarly, but many aren't.

Language

Everybody uses words to persuade without actually making a clear argument. This is called using **loaded language**. For example: if you like a politician, call him "Senator Smith"; if you don't like him, refer to him as "right-wing (or left-wing) senators such as Smith." If you like an idea proposed by a professor, call her "respected"; if you don't like the idea, call her "controversial." If you favor abortion, call somebody who agrees with you "pro-choice" ("choice" is valued by most people); if you oppose abortion, call those who agree with you "pro-life" ("life," like "choice," is a good thing). Recognizing loaded language in a news article can give you important clues to the journalist's own point of view.

A key question is whether there are facts to back up these generalizations. There are no definitive answers; here we can take a look at a few of the better studies.

One study looked at 12 years' worth of political stories published in *The New York Times* and *The Washington Post*. It asked how these papers described the 10 most liberal and the 10 most conservative senators. The authors found that

conservative senators were about three times more likely to be called conservative than liberal senators were to be called liberal.[24] The difference in the use of adjectives may influence how readers feel about the story. Politically independent readers might (no one knows) take more seriously the views of senators who are given no ideological labels than they will of those to whom such labels have been attached.

> **selective attention**
> Paying attention only to those news stories with which one already agrees.

There have been efforts to see how newspapers and magazines cover specific issues. When *Time* and *Newsweek* ran stories about nuclear power, scholars found they tended to avoid quoting scientists and engineers working in this field because these specialists were in favor of nuclear power at a time when the magazines were opposed to it.[25]

Another study looked at how the top 10 newspapers and the Associated Press cover economic news when there is either a Democratic or Republican president in office. The news was based on government reports about sales, unemployment, and economic growth over a 13-year period. The authors decided whether a newspaper's headline covering that news (on the day it was released) was either positive, negative, or neutral. In general, these headlines gave a more positive spin when there was a Democrat in the White House and a more negative one when there was a Republican there.[26]

Newspapers are privately owned, so perhaps some of their bias comes from decisions made by the publishers. When scholars looked at 400 daily newspapers, they found that the "ideology of the owners doesn't correlate in any significant way with the political slant of their newspapers' coverage." Instead, a newspaper's bias tends to reflect the political views of its readers. If the same person owns several newspapers, each paper's style is tailored to its own market more than to the owner's beliefs.[27]

But perhaps the easiest evidence to understand comes from reporters themselves. *The New York Times* has a "public editor," that is, a person charged with receiving complaints from the public. When asked, "Is *The New York Times* a liberal newspaper?" he answered, in print, very simply: "Of course it is."

Public distrust of the media has grown. As shown in Figure 12.3, the percentage of people saying they believe news organizations has declined significantly in just the first decade of the 21st century.

Media's Influence

Some people will be influenced by what they read or hear, but others will not be. There is a well-known psychological process called **selective attention**. It means that people remember or believe only what they want to. If they see or hear statements inconsistent with their existing beliefs, they will tune out these messages.[28]

But after the 1964 presidential election, one study suggested that in the northern part of the United States a newspaper endorsement favoring Democratic candidate Lyndon Johnson added about five percentage points to the vote he received.[29]

Another study examined the vote in more than 60 contests for the U.S. Senate held over a five-year period. Newspaper stories about the rival candidates were scored as positive, negative, or neutral. Voters' feelings about the candidates were learned from public opinion polls. Obviously, many things other than newspaper stories will affect how voters feel, and so the authors of this study tried to control for these factors. They held constant the seniority of incumbent candidates, the level of political experience of challengers, the amount of campaign spending, how close each race was, and the political ideology and party identification of voters. After doing all of this, they discovered two things. First, newspapers that endorsed incumbents on their editorial pages gave more positive news coverage to them than newspapers that did not endorse them. Second, the voters had more positive feelings about endorsed incumbents than they did about nonendorsed ones. In short, editorial views affect news coverage, and news coverage affects public attitudes.[30]

A fascinating natural experiment occurred when Fox News, a network that generally favors Republicans, began to air in an increasing number of cities. When two scholars compared the effects on voting patterns in cities where Fox News was on the air with similar cities in which it was not, they found that there was a 3 to 8 percent increase in the vote for Republican candidates and about a half a percent increase in the Republican vote for president in the Fox towns.[31] Another study even manufactured an experiment: the authors gave, at no charge, *The Washington Post* (a liberal newspaper) or *The Washington Times* (a conservative newspaper) to people who subscribed to neither in a northern Virginia county. In the next election, those people receiving the *Post* were more likely to vote for the Democratic candidate for governor.[32]

What the press covers affects the policy issues that people think are important. Experiments conducted in New Haven, Connecticut, and a study done in North Carolina show that what citizens believe about some policy questions reflects what newspapers and television stations say about them.[33]

But there are limits to media influence. If people are unemployed, the victims of crime, or worried about high gasoline prices, they do not have to be told these things by the media.[34] But most people have no personal knowledge of highway fatalities, the condition of the environment, or American foreign policy in Europe. On these matters, the media are likely to have much more influence.

FIGURE 12.3 **Credibility Ratings for Many News Organizations Have Declined in the Twenty-First Century**

Newspapers

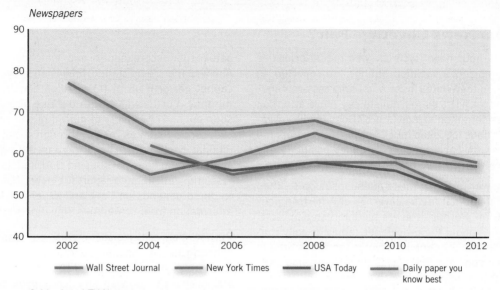

Wall Street Journal — New York Times — USA Today — Daily paper you know best

Cable, Local TV News

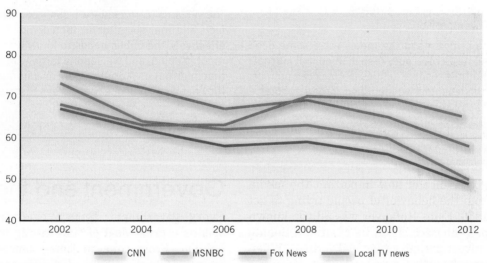

CNN — MSNBC — Fox News — Local TV news

Network News, 60 Minutes

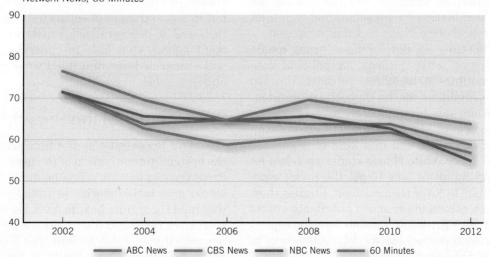

ABC News — CBS News — NBC News — 60 Minutes

Source: Pew Research Center for the People & the Press, "Further Decline in Credibility Ratings for Most News Organizations," August 16, 2012.

WHAT'S YOUR ISSUE

Is Media News Coverage Fair?

Has the 24-hour news cycle skewed media priorities when a president's vacation outings are reported as news? When the White House and Congress are negotiating budget bills, do journalists pay more attention to the president than to legislators? Does media coverage of elections focus too much on who's ahead/behind rather than on each candidate's policy positions and experience?

If your answer to any of these questions is "yes," then you likely think that media coverage of American politics is not fair. Perhaps you are not interested in "soft" news stories about the president's family or daily routine, or you think the media devotes too much time to reporting on one elected official, thereby missing critical moments or opportunities in American politics. You may find that campaign coverage overtakes the news cycle so often that actual governance receives scant attention in comparison.

While these criticisms of the media raise some good points about news coverage, keep in mind that journalists have multiple responsibilities in American politics. Earlier in this chapter, we identified three key roles –

gatekeeper, scorekeeper, and watchdog (page 284). A newspaper, radio station, television show, or web site cannot perform all of these roles equally well all of the time. Furthermore, with the rise of multiple news sources, and the ability of individuals to present their own commentary as "news" through social media, traditional news outlets face increased competition for audience and financial support. Journalists have a professional obligation to report the news, but their ability to do so depends on time and expertise to ferret out information from sometimes unwilling sources.

Rather than criticize the media, perhaps we should concentrate on becoming better consumers of news. Don't rely on just one newspaper, radio station, television channel, or web site for information – check multiple sources. Be aware of the difference between "news" and "commentary"; don't confuse opinion for facts and analysis. After all, for a democracy to function effectively, the public needs to know what the government is doing, and we depend largely on the media for that information. For the media to continue providing it, they need an audience that agrees that news matters.

The best evidence of how important the media are comes from the behavior of people trying to get elected. In 1950, Estes Kefauver was a little-known senator from Tennessee. Then he chaired a Senate committee investigating organized crime. When these dramatic hearings were televised, Kefauver became a household name. In 1952, he ran for the Democratic nomination for president and won a lot of primary votes before losing to Adlai Stevenson.

From that time on, developing a strong media presence became a top priority for political candidates. Sometimes it backfires. In 2004, Howard Dean, then a candidate for the Democratic presidential nomination, saw his campaign start to sputter after television carried a speech he gave to his supporters that seemed to end in a kind of anguished scream. And every White House staffer spends a lot of time worrying about how to get the press, especially television, to cover the president. Studies show that television commentary about presidents affects their popularity.[35] President Lyndon Johnson reportedly concluded that the war he was supporting in Vietnam was a hopeless cause after Walter Cronkite, then the star of the popular CBS News program, turned against the war.

Government and the News

Every government agency, every public official, spends a great deal of time trying to shape public opinion. From time to time, somebody publishes an exposé of the efforts of the Pentagon, the White House, or some bureau to "sell" itself to the people, but in a government of separated powers, weak parties, and a decentralized legislature, any government agency that fails to cultivate public opinion will sooner or later find itself weak, without allies, and in trouble.

Prominence of the President

Theodore Roosevelt was the first president to raise the systematic cultivation of the press to an art form. From the day he took office, he made it clear that he would give inside stories to friendly reporters and withhold them from hostile ones. He made sure that scarcely a day passed without his doing something newsworthy. In 1902, he built the West Wing of the White House and included in it, for the first time, a special room for reporters near his office, and he invited the press to become fascinated by the antics of his children. In return, the reporters adored him. Teddy's nephew Franklin Roosevelt institutionalized this system by making his press secretary (a job created by Herbert Hoover) a major instrument for cultivating and managing, as well as informing, the press.

Today, the press secretary heads a large staff that meets with reporters, briefs the president on questions he is likely to be asked, attempts to control the flow of news from cabinet departments to the press, and arranges briefings for out-of-town editors (to bypass what many presidents think are the biases of the White House press corps).

All this effort is directed primarily at the White House press corps, a group of men and women who have a lounge in the White House where they wait for a story to break, attend the daily press briefing, or take advantage of a "photo op"—an opportunity to photograph the president with some newsworthy person.

No other nation in the world has brought the press into such close physical proximity to the head of its government. The result is that the actions of our government are personalized to a degree not found in most other democracies. Whether the president rides a horse, comes down with a cold, greets a Boy Scout, or takes a trip, the press is there. The prime minister of the United Kingdom does not share his home with the press or expect to have his every sneeze recorded for posterity.

Coverage of Congress

Congress has watched all this with irritation and envy. It resents the attention given the president, but it is not certain how it can compete. The 435 members of the House are so numerous and play such specialized roles that they do not get much individualized press attention. In the past, the House was quite restrictive about television or radio coverage of its proceedings. Until 1978, it prohibited television cameras on the floor except on purely ceremonial occasions (such as the annual State of the Union message delivered by the president). From 1952 to 1970, the House would not even allow electronic coverage of its committee hearings (except for a few occasions during those periods when the Republicans were in the majority). Significant live coverage of committee hearings began in 1974 when the House Judiciary Committee was discussing the possible impeachment of President Nixon. Since 1979, cable TV (C-SPAN) has provided gavel-to-gavel coverage of speeches on the House floor.

The Senate has used television much more fully, heightening the already substantial advantage that senators have over representatives in getting the public eye. Although radio and television coverage of the Senate floor was not allowed until 1978 (when the debates on the Panama Canal treaties were broadcast live), Senate committee hearings have frequently been televised for either news films or live broadcasts ever since Estes Kefauver demonstrated the power of this medium in 1950. Since 1986, the Senate has allowed live C-SPAN coverage of its sessions.

Senatorial use of televised committee hearings has helped turn the Senate into the incubator for presidential candidates. At least in most states, if you are a governor, you are located far from network television news cameras; news cameras are most likely to focus on your leadership in times of crisis or major disaster, during a flood or a blizzard, for example. But senators all work in Washington, a city filled with cameras. No disaster is necessary to get on the air; only an investigation, a scandal, a major political conflict, or an articulate and telegenic personality is needed.

HOW THINGS WORK

The Maxims of Media Relations

The importance of the national media to politicians has given rise to some shared understandings among officeholders about how one deals with the media. Some of these are caught in the following maxims:

- All secrets become public knowledge. The more important the secret, the sooner it becomes known.

- All stories written about me are inaccurate; all stories written about you are entirely accurate.

- The rosier the news, the higher ranking the official who announces it.

- Always release bad news on Saturday night. Fewer people notice it.

- Never argue with a person who buys ink by the barrel.

adversarial press The tendency of the national media to be suspicious of officials and eager to reveal unflattering stories about them.

Why Do We Have So Many News Leaks?

American government is the leakiest in the world. The bureaucracy, members of Congress, and the White House staff regularly leak stories favorable to their interests. Of late, the leaks have become geysers, gushing forth torrents of insider stories. Many people in and out of government find it depressing that our government seems unable to keep anything secret for long. Others think the public has a right to know even more and that there are still too many secrets.

However you view leaks, you should understand why we have so many. The answer is found in the Constitution. Because we have separate institutions that must share power, each branch of government competes with the others to get power. One way to compete is to try to use the press to advance your pet projects and to make the other side look bad. There are far fewer leaks in other democratic nations in part because power is centralized in the hands of a prime minister, who does not need to leak in order to get the upper hand over the legislature, and because the legislature has too little information to be a good source of leaks. In addition, we have no Official Secrets Act of the kind that exists in the United Kingdom; except for a few matters, it is not against the law for the press to receive and print government secrets.

Even if the press and the politicians loved each other, the competition between the various branches of government would guarantee plenty of news leaks. But since the Vietnam War, the Watergate scandal, and the Iran-Contra affair, the press and the politicians have come to distrust one another. As a result, journalists today are far less willing to accept at face value the statements of elected officials and are far more likely to try to find somebody who will leak "the real story." We have come, in short, to have an **adversarial press**—that is, one that (at least at the national level) is suspicious of officialdom and eager to break an embarrassing story that will win for its author honor, prestige, and (in some cases) a lot of money.

This cynicism and distrust of government and elected officials have led to an era of attack journalism—seizing upon any bit of information or rumor that might call into question the qualifications or character of a public official. Media coverage of gaffes—misspoken words, misstated ideas, clumsy moves—has become a staple of political journalism. At one time, such "events" as President Ford

HOW WE COMPARE

Freedom of the Press

The Antifederalists insisted on adding a Bill of Rights to the Constitution because they feared government intrusion into citizens' lives. Their first concern, as reflected in the First Amendment, was to protect speech and expression, which includes freedom of the press. Although the protection is not absolute—the Supreme Court has ruled that there are times when that freedom may be restricted by the government for national security, for example—the burden of proof is on the government to demonstrate when imposing a restriction is constitutionally necessary.

Not all advanced industrialized democracies provide such broad protection for the media. In the United Kingdom, for example, libel laws are stricter than in the United States, which is why celebrities and business sometimes seek restitution in the former over the latter. Some European democracies have prohibitions on hate speech, which the United States does not (though the United States does impose restrictions on other types of speech that can appear in media outlets, such as obscenity or threats of violence). According to a recent report by Freedom House, an organization that tracks various measurements of freedom cross-nationally, access to free and independent media has declined worldwide to its lowest level in more than 10 years. Of 197 countries and territories for which Freedom House evaluated media coverage in 2012, 63 (32 percent) were rated Free, 70 (36 percent) were rated Partly Free, and 64 (32 percent) were rated Not Free.

Countries at Top of Global Press Freedom Rankings, Freedom House, 2012

1. Norway and Sweden (tied for first place)

2. Belgium, Finland, Netherlands (tied for next ranking)

(The United States is tied for 23rd place.)

Countries at Bottom of Global Press Freedom Rankings, Freedom House, 2012

1. Turkmenistan and North Korea (tied for first place)

2. Uzbekistan

3. Eritrea

4. Belarus

Source: Freedom House, "Freedom of the Press 2013."

When President Theodore Roosevelt cultivated the media, reporters usually were unknown and poorly paid.

election, 89 percent of respondents agreed that the media's "political views influence coverage" often (57 percent) or sometimes (32 percent); 47 percent believed that "most journalists" were "pulling for" Gore to win; and 23 percent believed that most journalists were partial to Bush.[36] Most Americans really dislike biased journalism (or journalism they perceive as biased): 53 percent say they would require a license to practice journalism, and 70 percent favor court-imposed fines for inaccurate or biased reporting.[37]

Given their experiences with Watergate and Irangate, given the highly competitive nature of national newsgathering, and given their political ideology (which tends to put them to the left of any administration in power), American editors and reporters, at least at the national level, are likely to have an adversarial relationship with government for a long time to come. Given our constitutional system, there will always be plenty of people in government eager to help them with leaks hostile to one faction or another.

Sensationalism in the Media

Back in the 1930s, newspaper reporters knew President Franklin Roosevelt had a romantic affair with a woman other than his wife. They did not report it. In the early 1960s, many reporters knew President John Kennedy had many sexual affairs outside his marriage. They did not report this. In 1964, the director of the Federal Bureau of Investigation played for reporters secret tape recordings of the Reverend Martin Luther King, Jr., having sex with women other than his wife. They did not report it.

By the 1980s, sex and politics were extensively covered. When presidential candidate Gary Hart was caught in adultery and when President Bill Clinton was accused of adultery by Gennifer Flowers, of asking for sexual favors by Paula Jones, and of having sex with Monica Lewinsky in the Oval Office, these were headline news stories.

What had changed? Not politics: all of the people whom the press protected or reported on were Democrats. The big change was in the economics of journalism and the ideas of reporters. Until the 1970s, Americans gathered their political news from one of three networks—ABC, CBS, or NBC. For a long time, these networks had only one half-hour news show a day. Today, however, viewers have the same three networks plus three cable news networks, two sports networks, 10 weekly newsmagazine shows, countless radio talk shows, and the internet. Many of the cable networks, such as CNN, carry news 24 hours a day. The result of this intense

slipping down some stairs, Governor Dukakis dropping the ball while playing catch with a Boston Red Sox player, or Vice President Quayle misspelling the word *potato* would have been ignored, but now they are hot news items. Attacking public figures has become a professional norm, where once it was a professional taboo.

During the 1992 election, most of the national press clearly supported Bill Clinton. The love affair between Clinton and reporters lasted for several months after his inauguration. But when stories began to appear about Whitewater (a questionable Arkansas real estate deal in which the Clintons were once involved), Clinton's alleged sexual escapades, and Hillary Rodham Clinton's profits in commodities trading, the press went into a feeding frenzy. The Clintons learned the hard way the truth of an old adage: if you want a friend in Washington, buy a dog.

Many people do not like this type of journalism, and the media's rising cynicism about the government is mirrored by the public's increasing cynicism about the media. In a national survey of registered voters conducted shortly before the 2000 presidential competition is that each radio or television network has a small share of the audience. Today, less than half the public watches the evening network news shows. Dozens of news programs are trying to reach a shrinking audience, with the result that the audience share of each program is small. To attract any audience at all, each program has a big incentive to rely on sensational news stories—ones filled with sex, violence, and intrigue. Reinforcing this desire to report sensationalism is the fact that covering such stories is cheaper than investigating foreign policy or analyzing the tax code. During its first month, the Lewinsky story consumed more than one-third of the on-air time of the news networks—more than the U.S. showdown with Iran, the Winter Olympics, the pope's visit to Cuba, and the El Niño weather pattern combined.

Since the days of Vietnam and Watergate, journalists have become adversaries of the government. They instinctively distrust people in government. But to that attitude change can be added an economic one: in their desperate effort to reclaim market share, journalists are much more likely to rely on unnamed sources than once was the case. When *The Washington Post* broke the Watergate story in the 1970s, it required the reporters to have at least two sources for their stories. Now many reporters break stories that have only one unnamed source, and often not a source at all but a rumor posted on the internet.

Before the terrorist attack on the United States on September 11, 2001, the big stories were the sexual conduct of President Clinton and the connection between California representative Gary Condit and a missing young woman. After September 11, the press focused on a more important matter—defeating terrorism at home and abroad. By early 2002, surveys indicated that the number of people who said they followed national news closely had increased slightly from 48 percent to 53 percent, and the number who said the media usually get the facts straight rose from 35 percent to 46 percent (the best public grade for accuracy in a decade). But within a year after the terrorist attacks, public confidence in the media had collapsed, with more people than before saying the press was often inaccurate.[38] The television networks did not seem to gain any viewers back as a result of the crisis: fully 53 percent cited cable as their primary source for news on terrorism, versus 18 percent for local television and 17 percent for national networks.[39]

Government Constraints on Journalists

An important factor works against the influence of ideology and antiofficial attitudes on reporters—the need every reporter has for access to key officials. A reporter is only as good as his or her sources, and it is difficult to cultivate good sources if you regularly antagonize them. Thus, Washington reporters must constantly strike a balance between expressing their own views (and risk losing a valuable source) and keeping a source (and risk becoming its mouthpiece).

The great increase in the number of congressional staff members has made striking this balance easier than it once was. Since it is almost impossible

In 1939, White House press conferences were informal affairs, as when reporters gathered around Franklin Roosevelt's desk in the Oval Office. Today, they are huge gatherings held in a special conference room, as shown on the right.

to keep anything secret from Congress, the existence of 15,000 to 20,000 congressional staffers means there is a potential source for every conceivable issue and cause. Congress has become a gold mine for reporters. If a story annoys one congressional source, another source can easily be found.

The government is not without means to fight back. The number of press officers on the payroll of the White House, Congress, and the executive agencies has grown sharply in recent decades. Obviously, these people have a stake in putting out news stories that reflect favorably on their elected superiors. They can try to do this with press releases, but adversarial journalists are suspicious of "canned news" (although they use it nonetheless). Or the press officers can try to win journalistic friends by offering leaks and supplying background stories to favored reporters.

There are four ways in which reporters and public officials, or their press officers, can communicate:

- On the record: The reporter can quote the official by name.

- Off the record: What the official says cannot be used.

- On **background**: What the official says can be used but may not be attributed to him or her by name. Reporters often call such an anonymous source "a high-ranking official" or "a knowledgeable member of Congress."

- On deep background: What the official says can be used but not attributed to anybody, even an anonymous source.

To get around the national press, public officials and their press officers can try to reach the local media directly by giving interviews or appearing on radio talk shows. The local media are a bit less likely than the national media to have an adversarial attitude toward the national government, and one can select talk-show hosts on the basis of their known ideology.

> ***background*** A public official's statement to a reporter given on condition that the official not be named.

The ultimate weapon in the government's effort to shape the press to its liking is the president's rewarding of reporters and editors who treat him well and his punishing of those who treat him badly. President Kennedy regularly called in offending reporters for brutal tongue-lashings and favored friendly reporters with tips and inside stories. Johnson did the same, with special attention to television reporters. Nixon made the mistake of attacking the press publicly, thereby allowing it to defend itself with appeals to the First Amendment. (Kennedy's and Johnson's manipulative skills were used privately.) Probably every president tries to use the press with whatever means are at his disposal, but in the long run it is the press, not the president, who wins. Johnson decided not to run again in 1968 in part because of press hostility to him; Nixon was exposed by the press; Carter and Bush came to be disliked by national reporters. The press and the president need, but do not trust, one another; it is inevitably a stormy relationship.

CONSTITUTIONAL CONNECTIONS

Journalism, Secrecy, and Politics

The role of media in American politics was not a high priority in drafting the Constitution. The First Amendment (added as part of the Bill of Rights in 1897) guaranteed freedom of the press, and the Framers appreciated the need for independent journalism in a democracy, but they did not pay significant attention to how journalists would affect governance. Yet the very ratification of the Constitution depended partly on cooperation from journalists, first in the secrecy surrounding the constitutional convention debates in Philadelphia in the summer of 1787, and second in the publication in New York newspapers of the *Federalist Papers* endorsing ratification of the Constitution (though newspapers at the time were party presses rather than independent organizations). With the 24-hour news cycle, politicians today have fewer opportunities to engage in policymaking without media scrutiny, and while media coverage provides an essential check on elected officials, it also can hinder prospects for decision making and compromise.

WHAT WOULD YOU DO?

MEMORANDUM

To: *Senator Brian Dillon*

From: *Political communication strategist Lucy Rae*

Subject: *Protecting journalists*

The Supreme Court has held that forcing a reporter to testify does not violate the First Amendment to the Constitution. But Congress could pass a law, similar to that in many states, banning such testimony if it reveals a confidential source.

Arguments for:

1. Thirty-four states now have shield laws similar to the one proposed by Congress.

2. Effective journalism requires protecting sources from being identified; without protection, a lot of important stories would not be written.

3. The government should be able to collect sufficient information to prosecute cases without relying on journalists to do this work for them.

Arguments against:

1. Every person accused in a criminal trial has a right to know all of the evidence against him or her and to confront witnesses. A shield law would deprive people of this right.

2. A shield law would allow any government official to leak secret information with no fear of being detected.

News »

Should a Shield Law Be Passed to Protect Journalists?

Efforts by the White House to find out who is the "high-ranking official" cited in recent news stories about possible ethics violations by some Cabinet secretaries have renewed calls by media groups for a "shield law" for journalists. Congress may hold hearings later this week.

3. The Supreme Court already has imposed a high barrier to forcing reporters to reveal confidential information, but that barrier should not be absolute, as situations can and do arise where a reporter is the only person who has the information necessary to investigate alleged criminal activity that threatens national security.

Your decision:

Support bill _____   Oppose bill _____

LEARNING OBJECTIVES

1. What role do the media play in American politics?

The media serve three major roles in American politics: gatekeeper, scorekeeper, and watchdog. They identify priorities for policymaking, keep track of which candidates are doing well and which are doing poorly in political campaigns, and oversee the workings of government to ensure that public officials are meeting their responsibilities.

2. Why are there so few restrictions on media coverage of politics and politicians in the United States?

The First Amendment to the Constitution explicitly guarantees that Congress may not pass a law abridging freedom of speech or of the press. While this protection is not absolute—journalists may be required by courts, for example, to divulge information about confidential sources in the interest of national security—the burden of proof is on the government to explain why violating this constitutional guarantee is necessary. Government officials have fewer protections from media coverage of their actions than private citizens because of their public responsibilities.

3. How much power do the media have?

A lot, but it is limited by selective attention and personal knowledge. Selective attention means that people tend to believe only those arguments consistent with their own beliefs. Personal knowledge means people know a lot based on their own experiences regardless of what the press says. Politicians in and out of office spend a great deal of time cultivating the media, but in many campaigns it is clear that the press is more likely to favor some people over others.

4. How has technology changed interactions between public officials and the media?

Changes in technology, particularly the advent of the internet, have fundamentally changed how politicians and the media interact. Elected officials now can reach constituents directly via email, web sites, instant messages, and so forth, whereas previously they were primarily dependent on the media for conveying their messages. Electronic media, in turn, are able to cover elected officials 24 hours a day, further narrowing the zone of privacy that politicians may realistically expect.

5. Can we trust the media to be fair?

The public does not believe we can trust the press, and that hostility has increased in recent years. Members of the national media are disproportionately liberal and secular, and there is evidence that these liberal views affect what they say or write. The extent of that political influence will differ, however, depending on whether a story is a routine feature or an insider account.

TO LEARN MORE

To search many news sources: **www.ipl.org**

To get analyses of the press

Nonpartisan view: **www.cmpa.com**

Liberal view: **www.fair.org**

Conservative view: **www.mrc.org**

Public opinion about the press

Pew Research Center: **www.people-press.org**

National media:

The New York Times: **www.nytimes.com**

The Wall Street Journal: **www.wsj.com**

The Washington Post: **www.washingtonpost.com**

Compilation of major daily news sources: **www. realclearpolitics.com**

Crouse, Timothy. *The Boys on the Bus*. New York: Random House, 1973. A lively, irreverent account by a participant of how reporters cover a presidential campaign.

Epstein, Edward J. *Between Fact and Fiction: The Problem of Journalism*. New York: Random House, 1975. Essays by a perceptive student of the press on media coverage of Watergate, the Pentagon Papers, the deaths of Black Panthers, and other major stories.

Epstein, Edward J. *News from Nowhere*. New York: Random House, 1973. Analysis of how television network news programs are produced and shaped.

Garment, Suzanne. *Scandal*. New York: Random House, 1991. A careful look at the role of the media (and others) in fostering the "culture of mistrust."

Graber, Doris A. *Mass Media and American Politics*, 8th ed. Washington, D.C.: Congressional Quarterly Press, 2009. A good summary of what we know about the press and politics.

Groseclose, Tim. *Left Turn: How Liberal Media Bias Distorts the American Mind*. New York: St. Martin's Press, 2011. Excellent study, written for the general reader, of new findings about media bias.

Iyengar, Shanto, and Donald R. Kinder. *News That Matters*. Chicago: University of Chicago Press, 1987. The report of experiments testing the effect of television news on public perceptions of politics.

Lichter, S. Robert, Stanley Rothman, and Linda S. Lichter. *The Media Elite*. Bethesda, MD: Adler and Adler, 1986. A study of the political beliefs of "elite" journalists and how those beliefs influence what we read and hear.

McGowan, William. *Coloring the News*. San Francisco: Encounter Books, 2001. An argument about the harmful effects of affirmative action and "identity politics" on news coverage.

Stroud, Natalie Jomini. *Niche News: The Politics of News Choice*. New York: Oxford University Press, 2011. Extensive empirical analysis of how political partisanship shapes the news sources that people use.

3

Institutions of Government

But the great security against a gradual concentration of the several powers in the same department consists in giving to those who administer each department the necessary constitutional means and personal motives to resist encroachments of the others.

—FEDERALIST NO. 51

Congress

LEARNING OBJECTIVES

1. In what respects is Congress "the first branch" of American national government?

2. Why do most Americans and many experts now view Congress as "the broken branch"?

3. What are the main differences between a congress and a parliament?

4. How has the legislative productivity of the U.S. Congress varied over time?

5. Are the American people as deeply divided in partisan and ideological terms as their representatives in Congress now appear to be?

6. How closely do members of Congress mirror the American people in terms of gender, race, and other demographic characteristics?

7. Does Congress normally do what most citizens want it to do?

8. Should Congress run under strong leadership?

9. Should Congress act more quickly?

If you are like most Americans, you trust the Supreme Court, respect the presidency (whether or not you like the president), and dislike Congress (even if you like your own representative and senators). Congress is the most unpopular branch of government. But it is also the most important one. You cannot understand the national government without first understanding Congress. Glance at the Constitution and you will see why Congress is so important: the first four and a half pages are about Congress, while the presidency gets only a page and a half and the Supreme Court about three-quarters of one page.

To the Framers of the Constitution, the bicameral (two-chamber) Congress was "the first branch." They expected Congress to wield most of the national government's powers, including its most important ones like the "power of the purse" (encompassing taxation and spending decisions) and the ultimate authority to declare war. They understood Congress as essential to sustaining federalism (guaranteeing two senators to each state without regard to state population) and maintaining the separation of powers (ensuring that no lawmaker would be allowed to serve in either of the other two branches while in Congress). They also viewed Congress as the linchpin of the system of checks and balances, constitutionally empowered as it was both to override presidential vetoes and to determine the structure and the appellate jurisdiction of the federal judiciary, including the Supreme Court.

Most contemporary Americans and many experts, however, think of Congress not as the first branch but as "the broken branch," unable to address the nation's most pressing domestic, economic, and international problems in an effective way; unduly responsive to powerful organized special interests; awash in nonstop campaign fundraising and other activities that many believe border on political corruption; and unlikely to fix itself through real reforms.[1]

Consistent with this broken branch view, in recent decades, public approval of Congress has rarely ranged much above a third. In the 2000s, ratings in the 20s or 30s were the norm. In recent years, several ratings in the teens have been recorded. In July 2008, the Gallup Organization, which has tracked public approval of Congress for decades, recorded an all-time low of 14 percent public approval. In March 2010, public approval of Congress stood at 16 percent. In November 2010, Republicans regained control of the House after four years of Democratic control; and in March 2011, public approval of Congress was at 18 percent. The 2012 elections also resulted in little change: Republicans retained control of the House, and by May 2013, Congress's approval stood at 16 percent.

Many academic analysts and veteran Washington journalists echo the popular discontent with Congress as the broken branch, but the experts focus more on two things, the first a paradox and the second a puzzle. The paradox is that most Americans consistently disapprove of Congress yet routinely reelect their own members to serve in it. In political scientist Richard F. Fenno's famous phrase, if "Congress is the broken branch then how come we love our congressmen so much more than our Congress?"[2] Despite public approval ratings that almost never reach as high as half, since 1980 over 90 percent of all congressional incumbents who have sought reelection have won it, most by comfortable margins. Even in elections in which "anti-incumbent" public sentiment seems rife and voters effect a change in party control of one or both chambers of Congress, incumbents prevail and dominate the institution. For example, in the 2010 midterm elections, Democrats suffered historic losses in the House, but most Democratic and Republican incumbents alike who sought reelection won it. In the 112th Congress that began in 2011, 80 percent of House members, and 70 percent of Senators, were incumbents. Likewise, in 2012, despite gains by Democrats in both chambers, about 90 percent of House incumbents and 91 percent of Senate incumbents that sought re-election won it. Even though they have been fussing over it for several decades now, political scientists are still not sure how to answer Fenno's question and resolve the paradox.

The puzzle is why the post-1970 Congress has become ever more polarized by partisanship and divided by ideology, and whether this development reflects ever-widening political cleavages among average Americans or instead constitutes a disconnect between the people and their representatives on Capitol Hill.

> **partisan polarization**
> A vote in which a majority of Democratic legislators oppose a majority of Republican legislators.

THEN

During 1890–1910, about two-thirds of all votes in Congress evoked a party split, and in several sessions more than half the roll calls found about 90 percent of each party's members opposing the other party.[3] But, during the 1970s, such **partisan polarization** in Congress was very much the exception to the rule. Well into the 1960s, Congress commonly passed major legislation on most issues on a bipartisan basis, and there were liberal members and conservative members in leadership positions in both parties and in both chambers. Such liberal and conservative voting blocs as existed typically crossed party lines, like the mid-20th-century conservative bloc featuring

The Powers of Congress

The powers of Congress are found in Article I, section 8, of the Constitution.

- To lay and collect taxes, duties, imposts, and excises

- To borrow money

- To regulate commerce with foreign nations and among the states

- To establish rules for naturalization (that is, becoming a citizen) and bankruptcy

- To coin money, set its value, and punish counterfeiting

- To fix the standard of weights and measures

- To establish a post office and post roads

- To issue patents and copyrights to inventors and authors

- To create courts inferior to (below) the Supreme Court

- To define and punish piracies, felonies on the high seas, and crimes against the law of nations

- To declare war

- To raise and support an army and navy and make rules for their governance

- To provide for a militia (reserving to the states the right to appoint militia officers and to train the militia under congressional rules)

- To exercise exclusive legislative powers over the seat of government (the District of Columbia) and other places purchased to be federal facilities (forts, arsenals, dockyards, and "other needful buildings")

- To "make all laws which shall be necessary and proper for carrying into execution the fore-going powers, and all other powers vested by this Constitution in the government of the United States." (*Note:* This "necessary and proper," or "elastic," clause has been generously interpreted by the Supreme Court, as explained in Chapter 16.)

Republicans and southern Democrats. Leaders in Congress in each party were usually veteran politicians interested mainly in winning elections, dispensing patronage, obtaining tangible benefits for their own districts or states and constituents, and keeping institutional power and perks. Even members with substantial seniority did not get the most coveted committee chairmanships unless they were disposed to practice legislative politics as the art of the possible and the art of the deal. This meant forging interparty coalitions and approaching interbranch (legislative-executive) relations in ways calculated to result ultimately in bipartisan bargains and compromises, and doing so even on controversial issues and even when congressional leaders and the president were not all in the same party.

NOW

When the 91st Congress ended in 1970, the more liberal half of the House had 29 Republicans and the more conservative half of the House had 59 Democrats.[4] By the time the 105th Congress ended in 1998, the more liberal half of the House had only ten Republicans while the more conservative half of the

House had zero Democrats.[5] (Zero!) In the 2000s, liberal Republicans and conservative Democrats became virtually extinct in both the House and the Senate. For example, in 2010, the major health care reform bill (the Patient Protection and Affordable Care Act) proposed by Democrats passed in the House without a single Republican member of the House voting for it. In 2011, the far-reaching Fiscal Year 2012 budget plan (cutting trillions of dollars in spending over the next decade) drafted by Republicans passed in the House without a single Democratic member of the House voting for it. The 112th Congress began in January 2011, and during its first quarter-year a post-1945 record high of about 80 percent of all roll-call votes in the House pitted a majority of Democrats against a majority of Republicans.[6] Or consider: In the 93rd Congress that began in 1973, the GOP's House "conservative caucus" (the Republican Study Committee) claimed just 4 of the chamber's 192 Republican House members (or about 2 percent); but, four decades later, in the 113th Congress that began in 2013, it claimed 171 of the 233 Republican members of the House (or about 74 percent).[7]

As we discuss in more detail later in this chapter, some scholars insist that the "disappearing center" in Congress reflects partisan and ideological divisions among average Americans,[8] while other scholars seem equally sure that we are instead witnessing a "disconnect" between a still nonideological and politically centrist mass public and its representatives on Capitol Hill.[9] Whichever side is more right, three things remain clear.

First, Congress has never perfectly embodied the Founders' fondest hopes for the first branch, not when the First Congress met in 1789–1791 (and wrangled endlessly over the Bill of Rights); not during the decades before, during, and just after the Civil War; not during the late 19th century through 1970; and certainly not since. James Madison envisioned members of Congress as "proper guardians of the public weal," public-spirited representatives of the people who would govern by intelligently mediating and dispassionately resolving conflicts among and between the large republic's diverse and competing financial, religious, and other interests.[10] Representatives or senators who might instead fan partisan passions, stir civic discord while refusing all compromises, or otherwise fuel rather than frustrate "factions" that trample citizens' rights or toy with the public's true needs, were disparaged by Madison as selfish, unenlightened, or "theoretic politicians" (what today we might call "extremists," "hyper-partisans," or "ideologues").[11] At least if judged by the Founders' highest aspirations for the first branch and its members, Congress has always been something of a broken branch.

Second, Congress is now home to ideologically distinct political parties that seem more unified than ever with respect to how their respective members vote, but the body still does not come close to matching the near-total party unity that has been typical in the national legislatures of the United Kingdom and other parliamentary democracies.

Third, Madison and the other Framers expressly rejected a parliamentary system like Great Britain's in favor of a system featuring both a separation of powers and checks and balances. They understood the fundamental differences between a "congress" and a "parliament," and so must every present-day student who hopes to really understand the U.S. Congress.

Congress versus Parliament

The United States (along with many Latin American nations) has a congress; the United Kingdom (along with most Western European nations) has a parliament. A hint as to the difference between the two kinds of legislatures can be found in the original meanings of the words. *Congress* derives from a Latin term that means "a coming together," a meeting, as of representatives from various places. *Parliament* comes from a French word, *parler,* that means "to talk."

There is of course plenty of talking—some critics say there is nothing *but* talking—in the U.S. Congress, and certainly members of a parliament represent to a degree their local districts. But the differences implied by the names of the lawmaking groups are real ones, with profound significance for how laws are made and how the government is run. These differences affect two important aspects of lawmaking bodies: how one becomes a member and what one does as a member.

Ordinarily, a person becomes a member of a parliament (such as the British House of Commons) by persuading a political party to put his or her name on the ballot. Though usually a local party committee selects a person to be its candidate, that committee often takes suggestions from national party headquarters. The local group selects as its candidate someone willing to support the national party program and leadership. In the election, voters in the district choose not between two or three personalities running for office, but between two or three national parties.

By contrast, a person becomes a candidate for representative or senator in the U.S. Congress by running in a primary election. Except in a very few places, political parties exercise little control over the choice of who is nominated to run for congressional office. (This is the case even though the person who wins the primary will describe himself or herself in the general election as a Democrat or a Republican.) Voters select candidates in the primaries because of their personalities, positions on issues, or overall reputation. Even in the general election, where the party label affects who votes for whom, many citizens vote "for the man" (or for the woman), not for the party.

As a result of these different systems, a parliament tends to be made up of people loyal to the national party leadership who meet to debate and vote on party issues. A congress, on the other hand, tends to be made up of people who think of themselves as independent representatives of their districts or states and who, while willing to support their party on many matters, expect to vote as their (or their constituents') beliefs and interests require.

Once they are in the legislature, members of a parliament discover they can make only one important decision—whether or not to support the government. The government in a parliamentary system such as that of the United Kingdom consists of a prime minister and various cabinet officers selected from the party that has the most seats in parliament. As long as the members of that party vote together, that government will remain in power (until the next election). Should members of a party in power in parliament decide to vote against their leaders, the leaders lose office, and a new government must be formed. With so much at stake, the leaders of a party in parliament have a powerful incentive to keep their followers in line. They insist that all members of the party vote together on almost all issues. If someone refuses, the penalty is often drastic: the party does not renominate the offending member in the next election.

Members of the U.S. Congress do not select the head of the executive branch of government—that is done by the voters when they choose a president. Far from making members of Congress less powerful, this makes them more powerful. Representatives and senators can vote on proposed laws without worrying that their votes will cause the government to collapse and without fearing that a failure to support their party will lead to their removal from the ballot in the next election. Congress has independent powers, defined by the Constitution, that it can exercise without regard to presidential preferences. Political parties do not control nominations for office, and thus they cannot discipline members of Congress who fail to support the party leadership. Because Congress is constitutionally independent of the president, and because its members are not tightly disciplined by a party leadership, individual members of Congress are free to express their views and vote as they wish.

They are also free to become involved in the most minute details of lawmaking, budget making, and supervision of the administration of laws. They do this through an elaborate set of committees and subcommittees.

A real parliament, such as that in Britain, is an assembly of party representatives who choose a government and discuss major national issues. The principal daily work of a parliament is debate. A congress, such as that in the United States, is a meeting place of the representatives of local constituencies—districts and states. Members of the U.S. Congress can initiate, modify, approve, or reject laws, and they share with the president supervision of the administrative agencies of the government. The principal work of a congress is representation and action, most of which takes place in committees.

What this means in practical terms to the typical legislator is easy to see. Since members of the British House of Commons have little independent power, they get rather little in return. They are poorly paid, may have no offices of their own and virtually no staff, are allowed only small sums to buy stationery, and can make a few free local telephone calls. Each is given a desk, a filing cabinet, and a telephone, but not always in the same place.

By contrast, a member of the U.S. House of Representatives, even a junior one, has power and is rewarded accordingly. For example, in 2013, each member earned a substantial base salary ($174,000) plus generous health care and

Three powerful Speakers of the House: Thomas B. Reed (1889–1891, 1895–1899) (left), Joseph G. Cannon (1903–1911) (center), and Sam Rayburn (1941–1947, 1949–1953, 1955–1961) (right). Reed put an end to a filibuster in the House by refusing to allow dilatory motions and by counting as "present"—for purposes of a quorum—members in the House even though they were not voting. Cannon further enlarged the Speaker's power by refusing to recognize members who wished to speak without Cannon's approval and by increasing the power of the Rules Committee, over which he presided. Cannon was stripped of much of his power in 1910. Rayburn's influence rested more on his ability to persuade than on his formal powers.

retirement benefits, and was entitled to a large office (or "clerk-hire") allowance, to pay for about two dozen staffers. (Each chamber's majority and minority leaders earned $193,400 a year, and the Speaker of the House earned $223,500.) Each member also received individual allowances for travel, computer services, and the like. In addition, each member could mail newsletters and certain other documents to constituents for free using the "franking privilege." Senators, and representatives with seniority, received even larger benefits. Each senator is entitled to a generous office budget and legislative assistance allowance and is free to hire as many staff members as he or she wishes with the money. These examples are not given to suggest that members of Congress are overrewarded, but only that their importance as individuals in our political system can be inferred from the resources they command.

Because the United States has a congress made up of people chosen to represent their states and districts, rather than a parliament made up to represent competing political parties, no one should be surprised to learn that members of the U.S. Congress are more concerned with their own constituencies and careers than with the interests of any organized party or program of action. And since Congress does not choose the president, members of Congress know that worrying about the voters they represent is much more important than worrying about whether the president succeeds with his programs. These two factors taken together mean that Congress tends to be a decentralized institution, with each member more interested in his or her own views and those of his or her voters than with the programs proposed by the president.

Indeed, Congress was designed by the Founders in ways that almost inevitably make it unpopular with voters. Americans want government to take action, follow a clear course of action, and respond to strong leaders. Americans dislike political arguments, the activities of special-interest groups, and the endless pulling and hauling that often precede any congressional decision. But the people who feel this way are deeply divided about what government should do: Be liberal? Be conservative? Spend money? Cut taxes? Support abortions? Stop abortions? Since they are divided, and since members of Congress must worry about how voters feel, it is inevitable that on controversial issues Congress will engage in endless arguments, worry about what interest groups (who represent different groups of voters) think, and work out compromise decisions. When it does those things, however, many people feel let down and say they have a low opinion of Congress.

Of course, a member of Congress might explain all these constitutional facts to the people, but not many members are eager to tell their voters that they do not really understand how Congress was created and organized. Instead they run for re-election by promising voters they will go back to Washington and "clean up that mess."

> **bicameral legislature**
> A lawmaking body made up of two chambers or parts.

The Evolution of Congress

The Framers chose to place legislative powers in the hands of a congress rather than a parliament for philosophical and practical reasons. They did not want to have all powers concentrated in a single governmental institution, even one that was popularly elected, because they feared such a concentration could lead to rule by an oppressive or impassioned majority. At the same time, they knew the states were jealous of their independence and would never consent to a national constitution if it did not protect their interests and strike a reasonable balance between large and small states. Hence, they created a **bicameral** (two-chamber) **legislature**—with a House of Representatives, elected directly by the people, and a Senate, consisting of two members from each state, chosen by the legislatures of each state. Though "all legislative powers" were vested in Congress, those powers would be shared with the president (who could veto acts of Congress), limited to powers explicitly conferred on the federal government, and, as it turned out, subject to the power of the Supreme Court to declare acts of Congress unconstitutional.

For decades, critics of Congress complained that the body cannot plan or act quickly. They are right, but two competing values are at stake: centralization versus decentralization. If Congress acted quickly and decisively as a body, then there would have to be strong central leadership, restrictions on debate, few opportunities for stalling tactics, and minimal committee interference. If, on the other hand, the interests of individual members— and the constituencies they represent—were protected or enhanced, then there would have to be weak leadership, rules allowing for delay and discussion, and many opportunities for committee activity.

Though there have been periods of strong central leadership in Congress, the general trend, especially since the mid-20th century, has been toward decentralizing decision making and enhancing the power of the individual member at the expense of the congressional leadership. This decentralization may not have been inevitable. Most American states have constitutional systems quite similar to the federal one, yet in many state legislatures, such as those in New York, Massachusetts, and Indiana, the leadership is quite powerful. In part, the position of these strong state legislative leaders may be the result of the greater strength of political parties in some states than in the nation as a whole. In large measure, however, it is a consequence of permitting state legislative leaders to decide who shall chair what committee and who shall receive what favors.

The House of Representatives, though always powerful, often has changed the way in which it is organized and led. In some periods, it has given its leader, the Speaker, a lot of power; in other periods, it has given much of that power to the chairs of the House committees; and in still other periods, it has allowed individual members to acquire great influence. To simplify a complicated story, the box starting on page 309 outlines six different periods in the history of the House.

The House faces fundamental problems: it wants to be big (it has 435 members) and powerful, and its members want to be powerful as individuals and as a group. But being big makes it hard for the House to be powerful unless some <u>small</u> group is given the authority to run it. If a group runs the place, however, the individual members lack much power. Individuals can gain power, but only at the price of making the House harder to run and thus reducing its collective power in government. There is no lasting solution to these dilemmas, and so the House will always be undergoing changes.

The Senate does not face any of these problems. It is small enough (100 members) that it can be run without giving much authority to any small group of leaders. In addition, it has escaped some of the problems the House once faced. During the period leading up to the Civil War, it was carefully balanced so that the number of senators from slave-owning states exactly equaled the number from free states. Hence, fights over slavery rarely arose in the Senate.

From the first, the Senate was small enough that no time limits had to be placed on how long a senator could speak. This meant there never was anything like a Rules Committee that controlled the amount of debate.

Finally, senators were not elected by the voters until the 20th century. Prior to that, they were picked instead by state legislatures. Thus senators often were the leaders of local party organizations, with an interest in funneling jobs back to their states.

The big changes in the Senate came not from any fight about how to run it (nobody ever really ran it), but from a dispute over how its members should be chosen. For more than a century after the Founding, members of the Senate were chosen by state legislatures. Though often these legislatures picked popular local figures to be senators, just as often there was intense political maneuvering among the leaders of various factions, each struggling to win (and sometimes buy) the votes necessary to become senator. By the end of the 19th century, the Senate was known as the Millionaires' Club because of the number of wealthy party leaders and businessmen in it.

CONSTITUTIONAL CONNECTIONS

From Convention to Congress

Article I of the Constitution (on Congress) is several times longer than Articles II (on the presidency and executive branch) and Article III (on the federal judiciary) combined. The Framers treated Congress as "the first branch" of American national government. As evidenced by the records of the debates among the 55 men that convened the Constitutional Convention, they had good philosophical reasons for treating the new republic's new legislature with special care. Besides, most of the delegates were themselves former legislators: 41 of the 55 had served, or at the time of the Convention, were still serving, as members of the Continental Congress. Moreover, 28 of the 55 delegates

would go on to serve in the new Congress created by Article I: 4 served in both the House and the Senate; 9 served in the House only; and 15 served in the Senate only. Among those that went on to serve in the House was the Constitution's chief intellectual architect, James Madison. Madison would also go on to serve as Secretary of State (under President Thomas Jefferson) and, of course, as the nation's fourth president (succeeding Jefferson).

Source: Adapted from The U.S. National Archives & Records Administration, "The Founding Fathers: A Brief Overview," 2013.

HOW THINGS WORK

House History: Six Phases

Phase One: The Powerful House

During the first three administrations—of George Washington, John Adams, and Thomas Jefferson—leadership in Congress often was supplied by the president or his cabinet officers. Rather quickly, however, Congress began to assert its independence. The House of Representatives was the preeminent institution, overshadowing the Senate.

Phase Two: The Divided House

In the late 1820s, the preeminence of the House began to wane. Andrew Jackson asserted the power of the presidency by vetoing legislation he did not like. The party unity necessary for a Speaker, or any leader, to control the House was shattered by the issue of slavery. Of course, representatives from the South did not attend during the Civil War, and their seats remained vacant for several years after it ended. A group called the Radical Republicans, led by men such as Thaddeus Stevens of Pennsylvania, produced strong majorities for measures aimed at punishing the defeated South. But as time passed, the hot passions the war had generated began to cool, and it became clear that the leadership of the House remained weak.

One of the most powerful Speakers of the House, Henry Clay, is shown here addressing the U.S. Senate around 1850.

Library of Congress Prints and Photographs Division (LC-DIG-ppmsca-09398)

Phase Three: The Speaker Rules

Toward the end of the 19th century, the Speaker of the House gained power. When Thomas B. Reed of Maine became Speaker in 1889, he obtained by vote of the Republican majority more authority than any of his predecessors, including the right to select the chairs and members of all committees. He chaired the Rules Committee and decided what business would come up for a vote, any limitations on debate, and who would be allowed to speak and who would not. In 1903, Joseph G. Cannon of Illinois became Speaker. He tried to maintain Reed's tradition, but he had many enemies within his Republican ranks.

Phase Four: The House Revolts

In 1910–1911, the House revolted against "Czar" Cannon, voting to strip the Speaker of his right to appoint committee chairs and to remove him from the Rules Committee.

The powers lost by the Speaker flowed to the party caucus, the Rules Committee, and the chairs of the standing committees. It was not, however, until the 1960s and 1970s that House members struck out against all forms of leadership.

Phase Five: The Members Rule

Newly elected Democrats could not get the House to vote on a meaningful civil rights bill until 1964 because powerful committee chairs, most of them from the South, kept such legislation bottled up. In response, Democrats changed the rules so that chairpersons lost much of their authority. Beginning in the 1970s, committee chairs would no longer be selected simply on the basis of seniority: they had to be elected by the members of the majority party. Chairpersons could no longer refuse to call committee meetings, and most meetings

(Continued)

had to be public. Committees without subcommittees had to create them and allow their members to choose subcommittee chairs. Individual members' staffs were greatly enlarged, and half of all majority-party members were chairs of at least one committee or subcommittee.

Phase Six: The Leadership Returns

Since every member had power, it was harder for the House to get anything done. By slow steps, culminating in some sweeping changes made in 1995, there were efforts to restore some of the power the Speaker had once had. The number of committees and subcommittees was reduced. Republican Speaker Newt Gingrich dominated the choice of committee chairs, often passing over more senior members for more agreeable junior ones. But Gingrich's demise was as quick as his rise. His decision not to pass some appropriations bills forced many government offices to close for a short period, he had to pay a fine for using tax-exempt funds for political purposes, and then the

Republicans lost a number of seats in the 1998 election. Gingrich resigned as Speaker and as a member of the House and was replaced by a more moderate Speaker, Republican Dennis Hastert of Illinois, with a penchant for accommodating his colleagues. When the 110th Congress began in 2007, Democrat Nancy Pelosi of California held the Speaker's gavel. Pelosi was the sixtieth Speaker in House history but the first woman to lead the House. She presided over many battles with the House's GOP leaders, but her most memorable role as Speaker occurred in 2010 when she struck assorted (and some critics claimed sordid) deals with members of her own party to garner their votes for the president's sweeping health care overhaul plan. Following heavy Democratic losses in the 2010 midterm elections, in January 2011 Pelosi was succeeded as Speaker by Republican John Boehner of Ohio. Even some liberal Democratic members of his state's congressional delegation (for example, Ohio Representative Dennis Kucinich) characterized Boehner as a committed but pragmatic conservative and professional legislator.

filibuster An attempt to defeat a bill in the Senate by talking indefinitely, thus preventing the Senate from taking action on the bill.

There arose a demand for the direct, popular election of senators.

Naturally the Senate resisted, and without its approval the necessary constitutional amendment could not pass Congress. When some states threatened to demand a new constitutional convention, the Senate feared that such a convention would change more than just the way in which senators were chosen. A protracted struggle ensued, during which many state legislatures devised ways to ensure that the senators they picked would already have won a popular election. The Senate finally agreed to a constitutional amendment that required the popular election of its members, and in 1913 the Seventeenth Amendment was approved by the necessary three-fourths of the states. Ironically, given the intensity of the struggle over this question, no great change in the composition of the Senate resulted; most of those members who had first been chosen by state legislatures managed to win re-election by popular vote.

The other major issue in the development of the Senate was the filibuster. A **filibuster** is a prolonged speech, or series of speeches, made to delay action in a legislative assembly. It had become a common—and unpopular—feature of Senate life

THE WAY WE BECOME SENATOR NOWADAYS.

The New York Public Library/Art Resource, NY

A cartoon from Puck *in 1890 expressed popular resentment over the "Millionaires' Club," as the Senate had become known.*

by the end of the 19th century. It was used by liberals and conservatives alike and for lofty as well as self-serving purposes. The first serious effort to restrict the filibuster came in 1917, after an important foreign policy measure submitted by President Wilson had been talked to death by, as Wilson put it, "eleven willful men." Rule 22 was adopted by a Senate fearful of tying a president's hands during a wartime crisis. The rule provided that debate could be cut off if two-thirds of the senators present and voting agreed to a "cloture" motion (it has since been revised to allow 60 senators to cut off debate). Two years later, it was first invoked successfully when the Senate voted cloture to end, after 55 days, the debate over the Treaty of Versailles. Despite the existence of Rule 22, the tradition of unlimited debate remains strong in the Senate.

Who Is in Congress?

With power so decentralized in Congress, the kind of person elected to it is especially important. Since each member exercises some influence, the beliefs and interests of each individual affect policy. Viewed simplistically, most members of Congress seem the same: the typical representative or senator is a middle-aged white Protestant male lawyer. If all such persons usually thought and voted alike, that would be an interesting fact, but they do not, and so it is necessary to explore the great diversity of views among seemingly similar people.

Gender and Race

Congress has gradually become less male and less white. Between 1950 and 2013, the number of women in the House increased from nine to 78 and the number of African Americans from two to 42. There are also 29 Latino members.

Until recently, the Senate changed much more slowly (see Table 13.1). Before the 1992 election, there were no African Americans and only two women in the Senate. But in 1992, four more women, including one black woman, Carol Mosely Braun of Illinois, were elected. Two more were elected in 1994, when a Native American, Ben Nighthorse Campbell of Colorado, also became a senator. Today there are 20 women in the Senate.

TABLE 13.1   **Blacks, Hispanics, and Women in Congress, 1971–2013**

Congress	Senate			House		
	Blacks	Latinos	Women	Blacks	Latinos	Women
113th (2013–2014)	2	3	20	42	29	82
112th	0	2	17	42	30	79
111th	1	3	17	42	25	77
110th	1	3	16	38	23	74
109th	1	0	14	37	23	59
108th	0	0	13	39	23	62
107th	0	0	13	36	19	59
106th	0	0	9	39	19	58
105th	1	1	9	37	18	51
104th	1	0	8	38	18	48
103rd	1	0	6	38	17	47
102nd	0	0	2	26	10	29
101st	0	0	2	24	11	25
100th	0	0	2	23	11	23
99th	0	0	2	20	11	22
98th	0	0	2	21	10	22
97th	0	0	2	17	6	19
96th	0	0	1	16	6	16
95th	1	0	2	16	5	18
94th	1	1	0	15	5	19
93rd	1	1	0	15	5	14
92nd (1971–1972)	1	1	2	12	5	13

Source: Congressional Quarterly, various years.

The relatively small number of African Americans and Latinos in the House understates their influence, at least when the Democrats are in the majority. In 1994, four House committees were chaired by blacks and three by Latinos. In the same year, however, no woman chaired a committee. The reason for this difference in power is that the former tend to come from districts in which incumbents have normally won re-election by comfortable margins and thus have more seniority than the latter. When the Democrats retook control of Congress in 2007, African Americans and Latinos became chairpersons of several important committees.

Similarly, the first woman to become Speaker (Nancy Pelosi in 2007) was a Democrat, and the post-1970 increase of women in Congress has been led by Democrats: in the 113th Congress that began in 2013, 16 of the 20 women in the Senate, and 62 of the 82 women in the House, were Democrats. Among the notable women in the 112th Congress was Gabrielle Dee "Gabby" Giffords, a 41-year-old Democrat of Arizona elected to her third House term in 2010, and only the third woman from Arizona to serve in Congress. Representative Giffords served on the House Armed Services Committee and was a member of the "Blue Dog" Caucus of moderately conservative House Democrats. In January 2011, she was shot in the head by a would-be assassin, but made such remarkable and rapid progress toward recovery that in spring 2011 she was able to attend the scheduled but aborted launch of a NASA shuttle co-commanded by her husband. In 2012, she retired from Congress to concentrate more fully on her recovery, received a public tribute from all members of the House, and vowed that she would return to public service in the future.

Middle-aged white males with law degrees are still prevalent in Congress, but as Table 13.2 shows, compared to the makeup of the 102nd Congress that

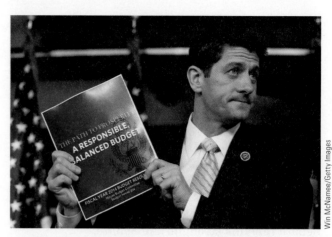

U.S. House Budget Chairman Paul Ryan, who was the Republican vice-presidential candidate in 2012, presents his party's budget plan.

began in 1991, the 113th Congress that began in 2013 had not only more women, blacks, and Latinos, but also fewer lawyers, fewer persons who had served in the armed forces, more businesspeople, more people over the age of 55, and more members (about 1 in 6 overall) serving their first term.

Incumbency

The recent spike in first-termers in Congress is interesting, but the most important change that has occurred in the composition of Congress has been so gradual that most people have not noticed it. In the 19th century, a large fraction—often a majority—of congressmen served only one term. In 1869, for example, more than half the members of the House were serving their first term in Congress. Being a

U.S. House Minority Leader Nancy Pelosi, who previously was the first female Speaker of the House, speaks at a weekly press conference.

TABLE 13.2   Who's in Congress, 1991–1992 versus 2013–2014

	102nd Congress (1991–1992)	113th Congress (2013–2014)
Average Age		
House	53	57
Senate	57	62
Occupation		
Law	244	211
Business	189	214
Military		
Had served	277	108
Incumbency		
In first term	44	89

Source: Adapted from chart based on Congressional Research Service and Military Officers Association data in John Harwood, "For New Congress, Data Shows Why Polarization Abounds," *The New York Times*, March 6, 2011. Updated from *Congressional Directory 2013*.

congressman in those days was not regarded as a career. This was in part because the federal government was not very important (most of the interesting political decisions were made by the states); in part because travel to Washington, D.C. was difficult and the city was not a pleasant place in which to live; and in part because being a congressman did not pay well. Furthermore, many congressional districts were highly competitive, with the two political parties fairly evenly balanced in each.

By the 1950s, however, serving in Congress had become a career. Between 1863 and 1969, the proportion of first-termers in the House fell from 58 percent to 8 percent.[12] As the public took note of this shift, people began to complain about "professional politicians" being "out of touch with the people." A movement to impose term limits was started. In 1995, the House approved a constitutional amendment to do just that, but it died in the Senate. Then the Supreme Court struck down an effort by a state to impose term limits on its own members of Congress.

As it turned out, natural political forces were already doing what the term limits amendment was supposed to do. The 1992 and 1994 elections brought scores of new members to the House, with the result that by 1995 the proportion of members who were serving their first or second terms had risen sharply. Three things were responsible for this change. First, when congressional district lines were redrawn after the 1990 census, a lot of incumbents found themselves running in new districts they couldn't carry. Second, voter disgust at a variety of Washington political scandals made them receptive to appeals from candidates who could describe themselves as "outsiders." And third, the Republican victory in 1994—made possible in part by the conversion of the South from a Democratic bastion to

a Republican stronghold—brought a lot of new faces to the Capitol. In the 2006 midterm elections, the Democrats regained control of the House from Republicans; they retained it in 2008, but then lost it again in the 2010 midterm elections. As in 1994, in 2006 and in 2010 there was an influx of freshmen members. The November 2012 elections brought 75 first-term members to the House.

But these periodic power-shifts accompanied by the arrival of scores of new faces in Congress should not obscure an important fact that was documented decades ago by political scientists[13] and is still true today: even in elections that result in the out party regaining power, most incumbent House members who seek re-election not only win but win big in their districts. And while Senators have been somewhat less secure than House members, most Senate incumbents who have sought re-election have won it by a comfortable margin.

Figure 13.1 shows the 1964–2010 re-election rates for incumbent House and Senate members who sought re-election. Over that span of two dozen elections, the average re-election rate for House incumbents was 93 percent and the average re-election rate for Senate incumbents was 82 percent. For the 16 elections from 1980 through 2012, the House and Senate incumbent re-election averages are 94 percent and 87 percent, respectively. In the 2010 midterm election, despite polls showing mass disaffection with Congress and a strongly "anti-incumbent" mood, 87 percent of House incumbents who sought re-election won it (53 House incumbents who sought re-election lost), and 84 percent of Senate incumbents who sought re-election won it (4 Senate incumbents who sought re-election lost, two in primary elections and two in the general election). In 2012, among re-election-seeking

FIGURE 13.1 **Re-election Rates for House and Senate Incumbents, 1964–2012**

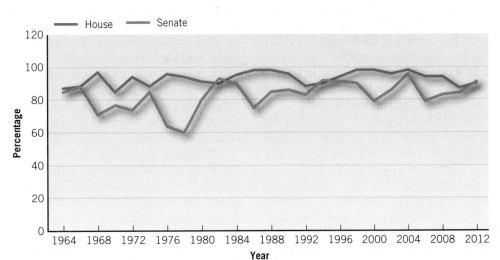

Sources: For 1964–2008 data, The Center for Responsive Politics; 2010 data compiled by author; and 2012 data drawn from The Center for Responsive Politics, OpenSecrets.org, accessed by Jesse Crosson, May 28, 2013.

marginal districts
Political districts in
which candidates
elected to the House of
Representatives win in
close elections, typically
by less than 55 percent
of the vote.

safe districts Districts
in which incumbents
win by margins of
55 percent or more.

incumbents, 90 per-
cent of House incum-
bents and 91 percent
of Senate incumbents
won re-election.

House incumbents
who seek re-election
normally beat their
opponents by 10 points
or more. Political scien-
tists call districts that
have close elections
(when the winner gets
less than 55 percent of
the vote) **marginal districts** and districts where
incumbents win by wide margins (55 percent or
more) **safe districts**. Even by a more exacting standard—winning with 60 percent or more of the vote—
in all but one of the two elections from 1964 to 2010
(the election of 1994), between 60 and 80 percent of
House incumbents who were re-elected won with
60 percent or more of the vote.[14] By contrast, over
the same period, well under half of all Senate incumbents who won re-election did so by such a wide margin. In 1998 and again in 2008, about two-thirds of
Senate incumbents won with 60 percent or more of
the vote, but "safe states" remain far less common
than safe districts.

Why congressional seats have become less marginal—that is, safer—is a matter on which scholars
do not agree. Some feel it is the result of television
and other media. But challengers can go on television, too, so why should this benefit incumbents?
Another possibility is that voters are becoming less
and less likely to automatically support whatever
candidate wins the nomination of their own party.
They are more likely, in short, to vote for the person
rather than the party. And they are more likely to
have heard of a person who is an incumbent: incumbents can deluge the voter with free mailings, they
can travel frequently (and at public expense) to meet
constituents, and they can get their names in the
headlines by sponsoring bills or conducting investigations. Simply having a familiar name is important in getting elected, and incumbents find it easier
than challengers to make their names known.

Finally, some scholars argue that incumbents
can use their power to get programs passed or funds
spent to benefit their districts—and thereby to benefit themselves.[15] They can help keep an army base
open, support the building of a new highway (or
block the building of an unpopular one), take credit
for federal grants to local schools and hospitals,
make certain a particular industry or labor union
is protected by tariffs against foreign competition,
and so on.

Probably all of these factors make some difference. Whatever the explanation, the tendency of
voters to return incumbents to office means that in
ordinary times no one should expect any dramatic
changes in the composition of Congress. Even when
elections effect a change in party control in one or
both chambers, even when new leaders are in charge
and new members abound, many old hands will still
be on hand in Congress.

Party

Forty-one Congresses convened between 1933 and
2013 (a new Congress convenes every two years).
The Democrats controlled both houses in 27 of
these Congresses and at least one house in 31 of
them. Scholars differ in their explanations of why
the Democrats have so often had the upper hand in
Congress. Most of the research on the subject has
focused on the reasons for Democratic control of the
House.

In every election from 1968 to 1992, the percentage of the popular vote for Republican candidates to
the House was higher than the percentage of House
seats that actually went to Republicans. For example, in 1976 the Republicans won 42.1 percent of
the vote but received only 32.9 percent of the seats.
Some argued that this gap between votes and seats
occurred because Democratic-controlled state legislatures redrew congressional district maps in ways
that make it hard for Republicans to win House seats.
Some striking anecdotal evidence supports this conclusion. For example, following the 1990 census,
the Democratic-controlled Texas legislature crafted
a new congressional district map clearly designed
to benefit Democrats. In 1992, Republicans won
48 percent of the House vote in Texas but received
only 30 percent of the seats. But after Republicans
won control of more state legislatures, matters
began to change. In Texas, a new districting plan
was adopted that ensured more House seats would
be won by Republicans. And when a court, rather
than the Democratic legislature, redrew California's
district lines, both parties won the same proportion
of seats as their share of the popular vote.[16] In 2006,
things had evened out nationally: both parties won
about the same share of House seats as their percentage of the vote.

Partisan tinkering with district maps and
other structural features of House elections is not
a sufficient explanation of why Democrats dominated the House in the four decades prior to 1994.
As one study concluded, "Virtually all the political
science evidence to date indicates that the electoral system has little or no partisan bias, and that
the net gains nationally from redistricting for one

party over another are very small."[17] To control the redistricting process, one party must control both houses of the legislature, the governor's office, and, where necessary, the state courts. These conditions simply do not exist in most states. For these and related reasons, the gains made by Republicans in the 2010 elections are unlikely to be expanded to any significant degree in the decade ahead purely by virtue of the redistricting required by the results of the 2010 Census.[18]

Congressional incumbents have come to enjoy certain built-in electoral advantages over challengers. Democrats were in the majority as the advantages of incumbency grew, but Republicans enjoyed the same or greater advantages from 1994 to 2006. Studies suggest the incumbency advantage was worth about 2 percentage points prior to the 1960s but has grown to 6 to 8 points today.

It is important to remember that from time to time major electoral convulsions do alter the membership of Congress. For example, in the election of 1938 the Democrats lost 70 seats in the House; in 1942, they lost 50; in 1950, they lost 29; and, in 1966, they lost 48. Despite these big losses, the Democrats retained a majority in the House in each of these years. Not so, however, in 1994, when the Democrats lost 52 House seats (the largest loss by either party since the Republicans had lost 75 seats in 1948), and Republicans gained majorities in both the House and the Senate. And not so in 2010, when Republicans gained more than 60 House seats and narrowly failed to take the Senate as well.

Just as it is not easy to explain why Democrats dominated Congress for half a century, so it is not easy to explain why that domination ended when and as it did in 1994, or why Democrats regained control in 2006 only to lose it again just four years later. Several reasons, however, stand out.

By the 1990s, certain advantages of incumbency had turned into disadvantages: voters increasingly came to dislike "professional politicians," whom they held responsible for "the mess in Washington." Just what "the mess" was varied according to which voter you asked, but it included chronic budget deficits, the congressional habit of exempting itself from laws that affected everybody else, constant bickering between Congress and the White House, and various congressional scandals. During the 1980s, about 40 members of Congress were charged with misconduct ranging from having sex with minors to accepting illegal gifts. When it was disclosed that the House had its own bank that would cash checks even for members who (temporarily) had no funds in their accounts, public indignation exploded, even though almost no taxpayer money was lost. Public

respect for Congress, as measured by the polls, plummeted. The Democrats had the misfortune of being the majority party in

conservative coalition
An alliance between Republican and conservative Democrats.

Congress when all of this happened. The anti-incumbent mood, coupled with the effects of redistricting after the 1990 census and the shift of the South to the Republican Party, brought the Republicans into power in the House and Senate in the 1994 elections.

By 2006, however, with an unpopular Republican president in the White House and most voters blaming congressional leaders for moving the country in the "wrong direction," Democrats regained control of both chambers. And, in 2010, with a Democrat in the White House and three years into a deep economic recession that had more people than ever feeling that the country was heading in the "wrong direction," Republicans reclaimed the House, nearly retook the Senate, and also made historic gains in races for governorships and state legislatures.

In the past, the Democratic party was more deeply divided than the Republicans because of the presence in Congress of conservative Democrats from the South. These southern Democrats often would vote with the Republicans in the House or Senate, thereby forming what came to be called the **conservative coalition**. During the 1960s and 1970s, that coalition came together in about one-fifth of all roll-call votes. When it did, it usually won, defeating northern Democrats. But since the 1980s, and especially since the watershed election of 1994, the conservative coalition has become much less important. The reason is simple: many southern Democrats in Congress have been replaced by southern Republicans, and the southern Democrats who remain (many of them African Americans) are as liberal as northern Democrats. The effect of this change is to make Congress, and especially the House, more ideologically partisan—Democrats are liberals, Republicans are conservatives—and this in turn helps explain why there is more party unity in voting—no matter which party is in charge.

Representation and Polarization

In a decentralized, individualistic institution such as Congress, it is not obvious how its members will behave. They could be devoted to doing whatever their constituents want or, since most voters are not aware of what their representatives do, act in accordance with their own beliefs, the demands of pressure groups, or the expectations of congressional leaders. You may think it would be easy to figure out whether members are devoted to their constituents by analyzing how they vote, but that is not quite right. Members can influence legislation in many ways other than by voting: they can conduct hearings, help mark up bills in committee meetings, and offer amendments to the bills proposed by others. A member's final vote on a bill may conceal as much as it reveals: some members may vote for a bill that contains many things they dislike because it also contains a few things they value.

There are at least three theories about how members of Congress behave: representational, organizational, and attitudinal. The *representational* explanation is based on the reasonable assumption that members want to get re-elected, and therefore they vote to please their constituents. The *organizational* explanation is based on the equally reasonable assumption that since most constituents do not know how their legislator has voted, it is not essential to please them. But it is important to please fellow members of Congress, whose goodwill is valuable in getting things done and in acquiring status and power in Congress. The *attitudinal* explanation is based on the assumption that there are so many conflicting pressures on members of Congress that they cancel one another out, leaving them virtually free to vote on the basis of their own beliefs. Political scientists have studied, tested, and argued about these (and other) explanations for decades, and nothing like a consensus has emerged. Some facts have been established, however, in regard to these three views.

Representational View

The representational view has some merit under certain circumstances—namely, when constituents have a clear view on some issue and a legislator's vote on that issue is likely to attract their attention. Such is often the case for civil rights laws: representatives with significant numbers of black voters in their districts are not likely to oppose civil rights bills; representatives with few African Americans in their districts are comparatively free to oppose such bills. Until the late 1960s, many southern representatives were able to oppose civil rights measures because the African Americans in their districts were prevented from voting. On the other hand, many representatives without black constituents have supported civil rights bills, partly out of personal belief and partly perhaps because certain white groups in their districts—organized liberals, for example—have insisted on such support.

From time to time, an issue arouses deep passions among the voters, and legislators cannot escape the need either to vote as their constituents want,

AP Photo/Marco Garcia

U.S. Representative Tulsi Gabbard is the first American Samoan, first Hindu, and one of the first female combat veterans to serve in Congress. She won election in 2012 from Hawaii.

whatever their personal views, or to anguish at length about which side of a divided constituency to support. Gun control has been one such question and the use of federal money to pay for abortions has been another. Some fortunate members of Congress get unambiguous cues from their constituents on these matters, and no hard decision is necessary. Others get conflicting views, and they know that whichever way they vote, it may cost them dearly in the next election. Occasionally, members of Congress in this fix will try to be out of town when the matter comes up for a vote.

You might think that members of Congress who won a close race in the last election—who come from a "marginal" district—would be especially eager to vote the way their constituents want. Research so far has shown that is not generally the case. There seem to be about as many independent-minded members of Congress from marginal as from safe districts. Perhaps it is because opinion is so divided in a marginal seat that one cannot please everybody; as a result, the representative votes on other grounds.

In general, the problem with the representational explanation is that public opinion is not strong and clear on most measures on which Congress must vote. Many representatives and senators face constituencies that are divided on key issues. Some constituents go to special pains to make their views known (these interest groups were discussed in Chapter 11). But as we indicated, the power of interest groups to affect congressional votes depends, among other things, on whether a legislator sees them as united and powerful or as disorganized and marginal.

This does not mean that constituents rarely have a direct influence on voting. The influence they have probably comes from the fact that legislators risk defeat should they steadfastly vote in ways that can be held against them by a rival in the next election. Though most congressional votes are not known to most citizens, blunders (real or alleged) quickly become known when an electoral opponent exploits them.

Still, any member of Congress can choose the positions he or she takes on most roll-call votes (and on all voice or standing votes, where names are not recorded). And even a series of recorded votes against constituency opinion need not be fatal: a member of Congress can win votes in other ways—for example, by doing services for constituents or by appealing to the party loyalty of the voters.

Organizational View

When voting on matters where constituency interests or opinions are not vitally at stake, members of Congress respond primarily to cues provided by their colleagues. This is the organizational explanation of their votes. The principal cue is party; as already noted, what party a member of Congress belongs to explains more about his or her voting record than any other single factor. Additional organizational cues come from the opinions of colleagues with whom the member of Congress feels a close ideological affinity: for liberals in the House, it is the Democratic Study Group; for conservatives, it often has been the Republican Study Committee or the Wednesday Club. But party and other organizations do not have clear positions on all matters. For the scores of votes that do not involve the "big questions," a representative or senator is especially likely to be influenced by the members of his or her party on the sponsoring committee.

It is easy to understand why. Suppose you are a Democratic representative from Michigan who is summoned to the floor of the House to vote on a bill to authorize a new weapons system. You haven't the faintest idea what issues might be at stake. There is no obvious liberal or conservative position on this matter. How do you vote? Simple. You take your cue from several Democrats on the House Armed Services Committee that handled the bill. Some are liberal; others are conservative. If both liberals and conservatives support the bill, you vote for it unhesitatingly. If they disagree, you vote with whichever Democrat is generally closest to your own political ideology. If the matter is one that affects your state, you can take your cue from members of your state's delegation to Congress.

Attitudinal View

There is evidence that the ideology of a member of Congress affects how he or she votes. This should not be entirely surprising. As we saw in Chapter 7,

political elites generally think more ideologically than the public. But, as we suggested at the start of this chapter, Congress has become an increasingly ideological organization, that is, its members are more sharply divided by political ideology than they once were. Today, all of Congress's most liberal members are Democrats, and all of its most conservative ones are Republicans.

Why attitudes have hardened along ideological and partisan lines in Congress is a topic of much scholarly debate. The representational view would suggest that members are simply behaving the way their constituents wish them to behave. The organizational view would suggest that members are responding to cues from their colleagues and party leaders. Of course, the representational and organizational influences on members' attitudes could be mutually reinforcing, and one important recent study explains the "disappearing center" in Congress based on certain evidence suggesting that they are.[19]

According to this theory, growing ideological and partisan splits among voters themselves have resulted in ever more partisan polarization among congressional leaders and senior members from safe districts where the only serious threats to an incumbent's re-election prospects are primary election challenges from the right (if a Republican) or the left (if a Democrat).[20] Only about 20 percent of Americans who harbor moderate views and favor bipartisanship are politically attentive, while the rest are largely "disengaged moderates."[21] By contrast, a majority of the growing number of citizens who identify themselves as "strongly liberal" or "strongly conservative" are engaged in obtaining political news (often from sources like talk radio or preferred internet blogs that mainly serve to reinforce their pre-existing views), debating controversial issues, and influencing others (either in person or via the internet and other means of communication) to think, join groups, *and* vote as they do.[22]

Most scholars agree that in recent decades, the parties in Congress have "sorted" themselves ever more clearly on ideological hot-button issues like abortion, and increasingly favored candidates and leaders, including relative political novices, with ideologically consistent profiles.[23] But many dispute the notion that the American electorate on the whole has become so highly partisan and ideological. Studies like the one summarized above claiming that it has, say their critics, generally rely too much on voters' ideological self-identifications and focus too narrowly on only the most ideologically loaded issues.[24] Measured across dozens of domestic, economic, and other issues, the policy differences and ideological distances between registered

majority leader The legislative leader elected by party members holding the majority of seats in the House or the Senate.

minority leader The legislative leader elected by party members holding a minority of seats in the House or the Senate.

whip A senator or representative who helps the party leader stay informed about what party members are thinking.

Republicans and registered Democrats have increased only a bit since the mid-1980s; and, depending on how the survey questions are worded, there is substantial overlap among voters even on a topic like abortion.[25] In short, this theory holds that we are witnessing, not a "disappearing center," but rather a breakdown of representation in American politics, an attitudinal "disconnect" between average voters and national lawmakers that has made the post-1970 Congress far less representative of the American people than the pre-1970 Congress was.[26]

By the same token, how much congresspersons' attitudes are influenced by committee chairpersons and other party leaders is also a matter of some scholarly dispute. The most sophisticated studies to date indicate that, while these organizational influences matter, individual members' ideological views probably matter more. "Members of Congress," one study concluded, "come to Washington with a staked-out position on the (liberal-conservative) continuum, and then, largely 'die with their ideological boots on.' "[27] Everything from which "ideological boots" a given member chooses to wear in the first place to how he or she votes on a particular issue "may result as much from external pressures of campaign donors and primary voters as from the internal pressures of the congressional party."[28]

The Organization of Congress: Parties and Interests

Congress is not a single organization; it is a vast and complex collection of organizations by which the business of Congress is carried on and through which members of Congress form alliances. Unlike the British Parliament, in which the political parties are the only important kind of organization, parties are only one of many important units in Congress. In fact, other organizations have grown in number as party influence has declined.

Party Organizations

The Democrats and Republicans in the House and the Senate are organized by party leaders, who in turn are elected by the full party membership within the House and Senate.

The Senate

The majority party chooses one of its members—usually the person with the greatest seniority—to be president pro tempore of the Senate. This is usually an honorific position, required by the Constitution so that the Senate will have a presiding officer when the vice president of the United States (according to the Constitution, the president of the Senate) is absent. In fact, both the president pro tem and the vice president usually assign the tedious chore of presiding to a junior senator.

The real leadership is in the hands of the majority and minority leaders. The principal task of the **majority leader** is to schedule the business of the Senate, usually in consultation with the **minority leader**. A majority leader who has a strong personality and is skilled at political bargaining (such as Lyndon Johnson, the Democrats' leader in the 1950s) may also acquire much influence over the substance of Senate business.

A **whip**, chosen by each party, helps party leaders stay informed about what the party members are thinking, rounds up members when important votes are taken, and attempts to keep a nose count of how voting on a controversial issue is likely to go. Several senators assist each party whip.

Each party also chooses a Policy Committee composed of a dozen or so senators who help the party leader schedule Senate business, choosing what bills will be given major attention and in what order.

For individual senators, however, the key party organization is the group that assigns senators to the Senate's standing committees: for the Democrats, a 22-member Steering Committee; for the Republicans, an 18-member Committee on Committees. For newly elected senators, their political careers, opportunities for favorable publicity, and chances for helping their states and constituents depend in great part on the committees to which they are assigned.

Achieving ideological and regional balance is a crucial—and delicate—aspect of selecting party leaders, making up important committees, and assigning freshmen senators to committees. Liberals and conservatives in each party fight over the choice of majority and minority leaders.

The House of Representatives

The party structure is essentially the same in the House as in the Senate, though the titles of various

U.S. House of Representatives Speaker John Boehner won re-election in his party in 2013 to lead the chamber for a second term.

SAUL LOEB/AFP/Getty Images

posts are different. But leadership carries more power in the House than in the Senate because of the House rules. Being so large (435 members), the House must restrict debate and schedule its business with great care; thus leaders who manage scheduling and determine how the rules shall be applied usually have substantial influence.

The **Speaker**, who presides over the House, is the most important person in that body and is elected by whichever party has a majority. Unlike the president pro tem of the Senate, this position is anything but honorific, for the Speaker is also the principal leader of the majority party. Though Speakers as presiders are expected to be fair, Speakers as party leaders are expected to use their powers to help pass legislation favored by their party.

In helping his or her party, the Speaker has some important formal powers. He or she decides who shall be recognized to speak on the floor of the House, rules whether a motion is relevant and germane to the business at hand, and decides (subject to certain rules) the committees to which new bills shall be assigned. He or she influences what bills are brought up for a vote and appoints the members of special and select committees. Since 1975, the Speaker has been able to select the majority-party members of the Rules Committee, which plays an important role in the consideration of bills.

The Speaker also has some informal powers. He or she controls some patronage jobs in the Capitol building and the assignment of extra office space. Though now far less powerful than some of his or

her predecessors, the Speaker is still an important person to have on one's side.

In the House, as in the Senate, the majority party elects a floor leader, called the majority leader. The other party chooses the minority leader. Traditionally, the majority leader becomes Speaker when the person in that position dies or retires— provided, of course, that his or her party is still in the majority. Each party also has a whip, with several assistant whips in charge of rounding up votes. For the Democrats, committee assignments are made and the scheduling of legislation is discussed in a Steering and Policy Committee chaired by the Speaker. The Republicans have divided responsibility for committee assignments and policy discussion between two committees. Each party also has a congressional campaign committee to provide funds and other assistance to party members running for election or re-election to the House.

Party Voting

The effect of this elaborate party machinery can be crudely measured by the extent to which party members vote together in the House and the Senate. A **party vote** can be defined in various ways; naturally, the more stringent the definition, the less party voting we will observe.

Figure 13.2 shows two measures of party voting in the House of Representatives during the last century. By the strictest measure, a party vote occurs when 90 percent or more of the Democrats vote together against 90 percent or more of the Republicans. A looser measure counts as a party vote one in which at least 50 percent of the Democrats vote together against 50 percent of the Republicans. By the 90 percent measure, the extent of party voting is low and has declined since the turn of the century. By the 50 percent measure, it is as high today as it was in 1920 and has risen sharply since 1970.

Given that political parties as organizations do not tightly control a legislator's ability to get elected, what is surprising is not that strict party votes are relatively rare, but that they occur at all. There are

Speaker The presiding officer of the House of Representatives and the leader of his or her party in the House.

party vote There are two measures of such voting. By the stricter measure, a party vote occurs when 90 percent or more of the Democrats in either house of Congress vote together against 90 percent or more of the Republicans. A looser measure counts as a party vote any case where at least 50 percent of the Democrats vote together against at least 50 percent of the Republicans.

HOW THINGS WORK

Key Facts About Congress

Qualifications

Representative

- Must be 25 years of age (when seated, not when elected).

- Must have been a citizen of the United States for seven years.

- Must be an inhabitant of the state from which elected. (*Note:* Custom, but *not* the Constitution, requires that a representative live in the district he or she represents.)

Senator

- Must be 30 years of age (when seated, not when elected).

- Must have been a citizen of the United States for nine years.

- Must be an inhabitant of the state from which elected.

Judging Qualifications

Each house is the judge of the "elections, returns, and qualifications" of its members. Thus, Congress alone decides disputed congressional elections. On occasion it has excluded a person from taking a seat on the grounds that the election was improper.

Privileges

Members of Congress have certain privileges, the most important of which, conferred by the Constitution, is that "for any speech or debate in either house they shall not be questioned in any other place." This doctrine of "privileged speech" has been interpreted by the Supreme Court to mean that members of Congress cannot be sued or prosecuted for anything they say or write in connection with their legislative duties.

When Senator Mike Gravel read the Pentagon Papers—some then-secret government documents about the Vietnam War—into the *Congressional Record* in defiance of a court order restraining their publication, the Court held this was "privileged speech" and beyond challenge (*Gravel* v. *United States*, 408 U.S. 606, 1972). But when Senator William Proxmire issued a press release critical of a scientist doing research on monkeys, the Court decided the scientist could sue him for libel because a press release was not part of the legislative process (*Hutchinson* v. *Proxmire*, 443 U.S. 111, 1979).

The Size of Congress

Congress decides the size of the House of Representatives. The House began with 65 members in 1790 and has had 435 members since 1912. Each state must have at least one representative. Regardless of its population, each state has two senators. Equal suffrage for states in the Senate is enshrined in Article I of the Constitution, the only provision that cannot be amended (see Article V).

---

several reasons that congressional members of one party sometimes do vote together against a majority of the other party. First, members of Congress do not randomly decide to be Democrats or Republicans; at least for most members, these choices reflect some broad policy agreements. By tabulating the ratings that several interest groups give members of Congress for voting on important issues, it is possible to rank each member of Congress from most to least liberal in three policy areas: economic affairs, social questions, and foreign and military affairs. Democrats in the House and Senate are much more liberal than Republicans, and this has been true for many years. The ideological differences between the parties are so pronounced that even the average southern Democrat in the House is more liberal than the average northern Republican.

In addition to their personal views, members of Congress have other reasons for supporting their party's position at least some of the time. On many matters that come up for vote, members of Congress often have little information and no opinions. It is only natural that they look to fellow party members for advice. Furthermore, supporting the party position can work to the long-term advantage of a member interested in gaining status and influence in Congress. Though party leaders are weaker today than in the past, they are hardly powerless. Sam Rayburn reputedly told freshman members of Congress that "if you want to get along, go along." That is less true today, but still good advice.

In short, party *does* make a difference—though not as much as it did 90 years ago and not nearly as

FIGURE 13.2 **Party Votes in the House, 1877–2010**

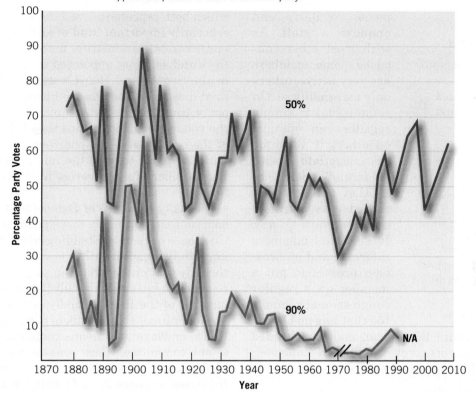

——— *Percentage of votes in which 50 percent or more of one party opposes 50 percent or more of the other party.*

——— *Percentage of votes in which 90 percent or more of one party opposes 90 percent or more of the other party.*

Note: A party vote occurs when the specified percentage (or more) of one party votes against the specified percentage (or more) of the other party.

Sources: Updated through 2008 by Zach Courser; NES data as reported in 2001–2002; Harold W. Stanley and Richard G. Niemi, *Vital Statistics on American Politics* (CQ Press, 2001), 211.

much as it does in a parliamentary system—party affiliation is still the single most important thing to know about a member of Congress. Because party affiliation in the House today embodies strong ideological preferences, the mood of the House is often testy and strident. Members no longer get along with each other as well as they did 40 years ago. Many liberals and conservatives dislike each other intensely, despite their routine use of complimentary phrases.

Although political parties may be less powerful in Congress than once was the case, ideology is more influential. In the last several Congresses, the 20 most liberal representatives were all Democrats and the 20 most conservative were all Republicans.

Caucuses

Congressional caucuses are a growing rival to the parties as a source of policy leadership. A **caucus** is an association of members of Congress created to advocate a political ideology or to advance a regional, ethnic, or economic interest. In 1959, only four such caucuses existed; by the early 1980s, there were more than 70. The more important among them have included the Democratic Study Group (uniting more than 200 liberal Democrats, though their names are not publicized to avoid embarrassing them with constituents), the Coalition (more popularly known as the Blue Dog Democrats), a group of moderate-to-conservative Democrats, and the Tuesday Lunch Bunch. Other caucuses include the delegations from certain large states who meet on matters of common interest, as well as the countless groups dedicated to racial, ethnic, regional, and policy interests. The

caucus An association of congressional members created to advance a political ideology or a regional, ethnic, or economic interest.

standing committees
Permanently established legislative committees that consider and are responsible for legislation within a certain subject area.

select committees
Congressional committees appointed for a limited time and purpose.

joint committees
Committees on which both senators and representatives serve.

conference committee
Joint committees appointed to resolve differences in the Senate and House versions of the same bill.

Congressional Black Caucus in the House is one of the best known of these and is probably typical of many in its operations. It meets regularly and employs a staff. As with most other caucuses, some members are very active, others only marginally so. On some issues it simply registers an opinion; on others it attempts to negotiate with leaders of other blocs so that votes can be traded in a mutually advantageous way. It keeps its members informed and on occasion presses to put a member on a regular congressional committee that has no blacks. In 1995, the House Republican majority decided to eliminate government funding of caucuses, forcing some to shrivel and others to seek outside support.

The Organization of Congress: Committees

The most important organizational feature of Congress is the set of legislative committees of the House and Senate. In the chairmanship of these committees, and their subcommittees, most of the power of Congress is found. The number and jurisdiction of these committees are of the greatest interest to members of Congress because decisions on these subjects determine what groups of legislators with what political views will pass on legislative proposals, oversee the workings of agencies in the executive branch, and conduct investigations. A typical Congress has, in each house, about two dozen committees and well over 100 subcommittees.

Periodically, efforts have been made to cut the number of committees to give each a broader jurisdiction and to reduce conflict between committees over a single bill. But as the number of committees declined, the number of subcommittees rose, leaving matters much as they had been.

There are three kinds of committees: **standing committees** (more or less permanent bodies with specific legislative responsibilities), **select committees** (groups appointed for a limited purpose, which do not introduce legislation and which exist for only a few years), and **joint committees** (on which both representatives and senators serve). An especially important kind of joint committee is the **conference committee**, made up of representatives and senators appointed to resolve differences in the Senate and House versions of a bill before final passage. Though members of the majority party could in theory occupy all the seats on all the committees, in practice they take the majority of the seats, name the chairperson, and allow the minority party to have the remainder of the seats. The number of seats varies from about 6 to more than 50.

Usually the ratio of Democrats to Republicans on a committee roughly corresponds to their ratio in the House or Senate. Standing committees are more important because, with a few exceptions, they are the only committees that can propose legislation by reporting a bill out to the full House or Senate. Each member of the House usually serves on two standing committees (but members of the Appropriations, Rules, or Ways and Means committees are limited to one committee). Each senator may serve on two major committees and one minor committee (see the boxes on pages 323 and 324), but this rule is not strictly enforced.

In the past, when party leaders were stronger, committee chairs were picked on the basis of loyalty to the leader. When this leadership weakened, seniority on the committee came to govern the selection of chairpersons. Of late, however, seniority has been under attack. In 1971, House Democrats decided in their caucus to elect committee chairs by secret ballot; four years later, they used that procedure to remove three committee chairs who held their positions by seniority. Between 1971 and 1992, the Democrats replaced a total of seven senior Democrats with more junior ones as committee chairs. When Republicans took control of the House in 1995, Speaker Newt Gingrich ignored seniority in selecting several committee chairs, picking instead members who he felt would do a better job. In this and other ways, Gingrich enhanced the Speaker's power to a degree not seen since 1910.

Throughout most of the 20th century, committee chairs dominated the work of Congress. In the early 1970s, their power came under attack, mostly from liberal Democrats upset at the opposition by conservative southern Democratic chairs to civil rights legislation. The liberals succeeded in getting the House

HOW THINGS WORK

Standing Committees of the Senate

Major Committees

*No senator is supposed to serve on more than two.**

Agriculture, Nutrition, and Forestry

Appropriations

Armed Services

Banking, Housing, and Urban Affairs

Budget Commerce, Science, and Transportation Energy and Natural Resources

Environment and Public Works

Finance

Foreign Relations

Health, Education, Labor, and Pensions

Homeland Security and Governmental Affairs

Judiciary

Minor Committees

No senator is supposed to serve on more than one.

Rules and Administration

Small Business and Entrepreneurship

Veterans' Affairs

Select Committees

Aging

Ethics

Indian Affairs

Intelligence

*Despite the rules, some senators serve on more than two major committees.

---

to adopt rules that weakened the chairs and empowered individual members. Among the changes were these:

- Committee chairs must be elected by the majority party, voting by secret ballot.

- The ability of committee chairs to block legislation by refusing to refer it to a subcommittee for a hearing is banned.

- All committees and subcommittees must hold public meetings unless the committee has voted to close them.

- Subcommittee chairs must be elected by committee members.

- Subcommittee chairs can hire their own staffs, independent of the committee chair.

The effect of these and other changes was to give individual members more power and committee chairs less. When the Republicans took control of the House in 1995, they made more changes, including the following:

- They reduced the number of committees and subcommittees.

- They authorized committee chairs to hire subcommittee staffs.

- They imposed term limits on committee and subcommittee chairs of three consecutive terms (or six years) and on the Speaker of four consecutive terms (or eight years).

- They prohibited chairs from casting an absent committee member's vote by proxy.

The House Republican rules gave back some power to chairpersons (for example, by letting them pick all staff members) but further reduced it in other ways (for example, by imposing term limits and banning proxy voting). The commitment to public meetings remained.

In the Senate there have been fewer changes, in part because individual members of the Senate have always had more power than their counterparts in the House. There were, however, three important changes made by the Republicans in 1995:

- A six-year term limit was set on all committee chairs (but not on the term of majority leader).

- Committee members were required to select their chairs by secret ballot

- Beginning in 1997, the chairs of Senate committees were limited to one six-year term.

Despite these new rules, the committees remain the place where the real work of Congress is done. These committees tend to attract different kinds of members. Some, such as the committees that draft tax legislation (the Senate Finance Committee and the House Ways and Means Committee) or that oversee foreign affairs (the Senate and House Foreign Relations Committees), have been attractive to members who want to shape public policy, become experts on important issues, and have influence with their colleagues. Others, such as the House and Senate committees dealing with public lands, small business, and veterans' affairs, are attractive to members who want to serve particular constituency groups.[29]

The Organization of Congress: Staffs and Specialized Offices

In 1900, representatives had no personal staff, and senators averaged fewer than one staff member each. By 1979, the average representative had 16 assistants and the average senator had 36. Since then the numbers have remained about the same. To the more than 10,000 people on the personal staffs of members of Congress must be added another 3,000 who work for congressional committees and yet another 3,000 employed by various congressional research agencies. Congress has produced the most rapidly growing bureaucracy in Washington: the personal staffs of legislators have increased more than fivefold since 1947.[30] Though many staffers perform routine chores, many others help draft legislation, handle constituents, and otherwise shape policy and politics.

Tasks of Staff Members

A major function of a legislator's staff is to help constituents solve problems and thereby help that member of Congress get re-elected. Indeed, over the last two decades, a growing portion of congressional staffs have worked in the local (district or state) offices of the legislator rather than in Washington. Almost all members of Congress have at least one such home office, and most have two or more. Some

HOW THINGS WORK

Standing Committees of the House

Exclusive Committees

Member may not serve on any other committee, except Budget.

Appropriations

Rules

Ways and Means

Major Committees

Member may serve on only one major committee.

Agriculture

Armed Services

Education and Labor

Energy and Commerce

Financial Services

Foreign Affairs

Homeland Security

Judiciary

Transportation and Infrastructure

Nonmajor Committees

Member may serve on one major and one nonmajor or two nonmajor committees.

Budget

House Administration

Natural Resources

Oversight and Government Reform

Science and Technology

Small Business

Standards of Official Conduct

Veterans' Affairs

Select Committees

Intelligence

Note: In 1995, the House Republican majority abolished three committees—District of Columbia, Post Office and Civil Service, and Merchant Marine and Fisheries—and gave their duties to other standing committees.

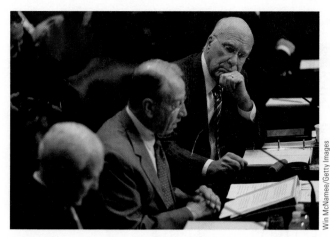

U.S. Senators Chuck Grassley (center) and Patrick Leahy (right) participate in a Judiciary Committee hearing on immigration reform.

scholars believe that this growth in constituency-serving staff helps explain why it is so difficult to defeat an incumbent.[31]

The legislative function of congressional staff members is also important. With each senator serving on an average of more than two committees and seven subcommittees, it is virtually impossible for members of Congress to become familiar with the details of all the proposals that come before them or to write all the bills that they feel ought to be introduced.[32] The role of staff members has expanded in proportion to the tremendous growth in Congress's workload.

The orientation of committee staff members differs. Some think of themselves as—and to a substantial degree they are—politically neutral professionals whose job it is to assist members of a committee, whether Democrats or Republicans, in holding hearings or revising bills. Others see themselves as partisan advocates, interested in promoting Democratic or Republican causes, depending on who hired them.

Those who work for individual members of Congress, as opposed to committees, see themselves entirely as advocates for their bosses. They often assume an entrepreneurial function, taking the initiative in finding and selling a policy to their boss—a representative or senator—who can take credit for it. Lobbyists and reporters understand this completely and therefore spend a lot of time cultivating congressional staffers.

The increased reliance on staff has changed Congress, mainly because the staff has altered the environment within which Congress does its work. In addition to their role as entrepreneurs promoting new policies, staffers act as negotiators: members of Congress today are more likely to deal with one another through staff intermediaries than through personal contact. Congress has thereby become less collegial, more individualistic, and less of a deliberative body.[33]

Staff Agencies

In addition to increasing the number of staff members, Congress also has created a set of staff agencies that work for Congress as a whole. These have come into being in large part to give Congress specialized knowledge equivalent to what the president has by virtue of his or her position as chief of the executive branch. One of these, the *Congressional Research Service (CRS)*, is part of the Library of Congress and employs almost 900 people; it is politically neutral, responding to requests by members of Congress for information and giving both sides of arguments. The *Government Accountability Office (GAO)*, once merely an auditing agency, now has about 5,000 employees and investigates policies and makes recommendations on almost every aspect of government; its head, though appointed by the president for a 15-year term, is very much the servant of Congress rather than the president. The *Congressional Budget Office (CBO)*, created in 1974, advises Congress on the likely impact of different spending programs and attempts to estimate future economic trends.

How a Bill Becomes Law

Some bills zip through Congress; others make their way painfully and slowly, sometimes emerging in a form very different from their original one. Congress is like a crowd, moving either sluggishly or, when excited, with great speed. While reading the following account of how a bill becomes law (see Figure 13.3), keep in mind that the complexity of congressional procedures ordinarily gives powerful advantages to the opponents of any new policy. There are many points at which action can be blocked. This does not mean that nothing gets done, but that to get something done, a member of Congress must *either* slowly and painstakingly assemble a majority coalition or take advantage of enthusiasm for some new cause that sweeps away the normal obstacles to change.

Introducing a Bill

Any member of Congress may introduce a bill—in the House by handing it to a clerk or dropping it in a box; in the Senate by being recognized by the presiding officer and announcing the bill's introduction. Bills are then numbered and printed. If a bill is not passed within one session of Congress, it is dead and must be reintroduced during the next Congress.

We often hear that legislation is initiated by the president and enacted by Congress. The reality

FIGURE 13.3 How a Bill Becomes Law

HOUSE

INTRODUCTION
HR1 Introduced in House

COMMITTEE ACTION
Referred to
House committee

Referred to subcommittee

Reported by full committee

Rules committee action

FLOOR ACTION
House debate,
vote on passage

SENATE

INTRODUCTION
S2 Introduced in Senate

COMMITTEE ACTION
Referred to
Senate committee

Referred to subcommittee

Reported by full committee

FLOOR ACTION
Senate debate,
vote on passage

HOUSE OF REPRESENTATIVES

CONFERENCE ACTION
Once both chambers have passed related bills, conference committee of members from both houses is formed to work out differences.

Compromise version from conference is sent to each chamber for final approval.

SENATE

PRESIDENT
Compromise version approved by both houses is sent to president, who can either sign it into law or veto it and return it to Congress. Congress may override a veto by two-thirds majority vote in both houses; bill then becomes law without president's signature.

HR1 VETO

S2 PASS

© Cengage Learning

---

simple resolution An expression of opinion either in the House or Senate to settle procedural matters in either body.

concurrent resolution An expression of opinion without the force of law that requires the approval of both the House and the Senate, but not the president.

joint resolution A formal expression of congressional opinion that must be approved by both houses of Congress and by the president; constitutional amendments need not be signed by the president.

is more complicated. Congress often initiates legislation (for example, most consumer and environmental laws passed since 1966 originated in Congress), and even laws formally proposed by the president have often been incubated in Congress. Even when he is the principal author of a bill, a president usually submits it (if he is prudent) only after careful consultation with key congressional leaders. In any case, he cannot himself introduce legislation; he must get a member of Congress to do it for him.

In addition to bills, Congress can also pass resolutions. Either house can use a **simple resolution** for such matters as establishing operating rules. A **concurrent resolution** is used to settle housekeeping and procedural matters that affect both houses. Simple and concurrent resolutions are not signed by the president and do not have the force of law. A **joint resolution** requires approval by both houses and a presidential signature; it is essentially the same as a law. A joint resolution is also used to propose a constitutional amendment, in which case it must be approved by a two-thirds vote in each house, but does not require the signature of the president.

Study by Committees

A bill is referred to a committee for consideration by either the Speaker of the House or the Senate's presiding officer. If a chairperson or committee is known to be hostile to a bill, assignment can be a crucial matter. Rules govern which committee will get which bill, but sometimes a choice is possible. In the House, the Speaker's right to make such a choice (subject to appeal to the full House) is an important source of his or her power.

The Constitution requires that "all bills for raising revenue shall originate in the House of Representatives." The Senate can and does amend such bills, but only after the House has acted first. Bills that are not for raising revenue—that is, that do not alter tax laws—can originate in either chamber. In practice, the House also originates *appropriations bills* (bills that direct the spending of money). Because of the House's special position on revenue legislation, the committee that handles tax bills— the Ways and Means Committee—is particularly powerful.

Most bills die in committee. They are often introduced only to get publicity for various members of Congress or to enable them to say to a constituent or pressure group that they "did something" on some matter. Bills of general interest—many of them drafted in the executive branch though introduced by members of Congress—are assigned to a subcommittee for a hearing where witnesses appear, evidence is taken, and questions are asked. These hearings are used to inform members of Congress, to permit interest groups to speak out (whether or not they have anything helpful to say), and to build public support for a measure favored by the majority on the committee.

Though committee hearings are necessary and valuable, they also fragment the process of considering bills dealing with complex matters. Both power and information are dispersed in Congress, and thus it is difficult to take a comprehensive view of matters cutting across committee boundaries. This has made it harder to pass complex legislation. For example, President George W. Bush's proposals to expand government support for religious groups that supply social services were dissected into small sections for the consideration of the various committees that had jurisdiction; after three years, no laws emerged. But strong White House leadership and supportive public opinion can push through controversial measures without great delay, as in the cases of Bush's tax cuts in 2001 and homeland security plans in 2002.

After the hearings, the committee or subcommittee makes revisions and additions (sometimes extensive) to the bill, but these changes do not become part of the bill unless they are approved by the entire house. If a majority of the committee votes to report a bill favorably to the House or Senate, it goes forward, accompanied by an explanation of why the committee favors it and why it wishes to see its amendments, if any, added; committee members who oppose the bill may include their dissenting opinions.

If the committee does not report the bill out to the house favorably, that ordinarily kills it, though there are complex procedures whereby the full House can get a bill that is stalled in committee out and onto the floor. The process involves getting a majority of all House members to sign a **discharge petition**. If 218 members sign, then the petition can be voted on; if it passes, then the stalled bill goes directly to the floor for a vote. These procedures are rarely attempted and even more rarely succeed.

For a bill to come before either house, it must first be placed on a calendar. There are five of these in the House and two in the Senate. Though the bill goes onto a calendar, it is not necessarily considered in chronological order or even considered at all. In the House, the powerful Rules Committee—an arm of the party leadership, especially of the Speaker— reviews most bills and sets the *rule*— that is, the procedures—under which they will be considered by the House. A **restrictive** or **closed rule** sets strict limits on debate and confines amendments to those proposed by the committee; an **open rule** permits amendments from the floor. The Rules Committee is no longer as mighty as it once was, but it can still block any House consideration of a measure and can bargain with the legislative committee by offering a helpful rule in exchange for alterations in the substance of a bill. In the 1980s, closed rules became more common.

The House needs the Rules Committee to serve as a traffic cop; without some limitations on debate and amendment, nothing would ever get done. The House can bypass the Rules Committee in a number of ways, but it rarely does so unless the committee departs too far from the sentiments of the House.

No such barriers to floor consideration exist in the Senate, where bills may be considered in any order at any time whenever a majority of the Senate chooses. In practice, bills are scheduled by

discharge petition A device by which any member of the House, after a committee has had the bill for 30 days, may petition to have it brought to the floor.

restrictive An order from the House Rules Committee that permits certain kinds of amendments but not others to be made into a bill on the floor.

closed rule An order from the House Rules Committee that sets a time limit on debate; forbids a bill from being amended on the floor.

open rule An order from the House Rules Committee that permits a bill to be amended on the floor.

quorum The minimum number of members who must be present for business to be conducted in Congress.

riders Amendments on matters unrelated to a bill that are added to an important bill so that they will "ride" to passage through the Congress. When a bill has many riders, it is called a Christmas-tree bill.

cloture rule A rule used by the Senate to end or limit debate.

double tracking A procedure to keep the Senate going during a filibuster in which the disputed bill is shelved temporarily so that the Senate can get on with other business.

the majority leader in consultation with the minority leader.

Floor Debate

Once on the floor, the bills are debated. In the House all revenue and most other bills are discussed by the *Committee of the Whole*—that is, whoever happens to be on the floor at the time, so long as at least 100 members are present. The Committee of the Whole can debate, amend, and generally decide the final shape of a bill but technically cannot pass it—that must be done by the House itself, for which the **quorum** is half the membership (218 representatives). The sponsoring committee guides the discussion, and normally its version of the bill is the version that the full House passes.

Procedures are a good deal more casual in the Senate. Measures that have already passed the House can be placed on the Senate calendar without a committee hearing. There is no Committee of the Whole and no rule (as in the House) limiting debate, so that filibusters (lengthy speeches given to prevent votes from being taken) and irrelevant amendments, called **riders**, are possible. Filibusters can be broken if three-fifths of all senators resolve to invoke the **cloture rule**. This is a difficult and rarely used procedure. (Both conservatives and liberals have found the filibuster useful, and therefore its abolition is unlikely.)

The sharp increase in Senate filibusters has been made easier by a new process called **double tracking**. When a senator filibusters against a bill, it is temporarily put aside so the Senate can move on to other business. Because of double tracking, senators no longer have to speak around the clock to block a bill. Once they talk long enough, the bill is shelved. So common has this become that, for all practical purposes, any controversial bill can pass the Senate only if it gets enough votes (60) to end a filibuster.

The Senate has made an effort to end filibusters aimed at blocking the nomination of federal judges. In 2005, seven Democrats and seven Republicans agreed not to filibuster a nomination except in "exceptional circumstances." A few nominees whose appointment had been blocked managed to get confirmed by this arrangement. Whether it holds for the

HOW THINGS WORK

House and Senate Differences: A Summary

House	Senate
435 members serving two-year terms	100 members serving six-year terms
House members have only one major committee assignment, and thus tend to be policy specialists	Senators have two or more major committee assignments, and thus tend to be policy generalists
Speaker referral of bills to committee is hard to challenge	Referral decisions easy to challenge
Committees almost always consider legislation first	Committee consideration easily bypassed
Scheduling and rules controlled by majority party	Scheduling and rules generally agreed to by majority and minority leaders
Rules Committee powerful; controls time of debate, admissibility of amendments	Rules Committee weak; few limits on debate or amendments
Debate usually limited to one hour	Unlimited debate unless shortened by unanimous consent or by invoking cloture
Nongermane amendments may not be introduced from floor	Nongermane amendments may be introduced

future depends on how senators define "exceptional circumstances."

One rule was once common to both houses: courtesy, often of the most exquisite nature, was required. Members always referred to each other as "distinguished" even if they were mortal political enemies.

Personal or ad hominem criticism was frowned upon, but of late it has become more common. In recent years, members of Congress—especially of the House—have become more personal in their criticisms of one another, and human relationships have deteriorated.

POLICY DYNAMICS: INSIDE/OUTSIDE THE BOX

National Service: A Bridge to Entrepreneurial Politics?

As you are learning in this chapter, the process by which a bill becomes law can be quite complicated. Most bills, in fact, never do become law. And even bills that are broadly popular often go nowhere unless there is at least one wise, well-positioned, and energetic policy entrepreneur, whether inside or outside the government, to get the idea on the policy agenda, sustain interest in it, and navigate the legislative process.

John M. Bridgeland, known widely in Washington, D.C. as "Bridge," has been the policy entrepreneur behind successive recent federal national service initiatives. Before serving in the early 2000s as a senior White House assistant, Bridgeland, a Harvard-educated, moderate Republican from Ohio with a law degree, had spent a half-decade as a top legislative aide on Capitol Hill.

Working both within the West Wing and inside the halls of Congress, in 2002, "Bridge" got President George W. Bush, congressional leaders in both parties, diverse business and nonprofit leaders, and others to support an effort to expand existing national service programs including AmeriCorps, Senior Corps, and Peace Corps, encourage each American to commit at least two years (4,000 hours) to volunteer service over his or her lifetime, and boost federal support for myriad other volunteer and community service projects. He created what became officially known as USA Freedom Corps, and served as its founding director. Although he functioned as a classic policy entrepreneur, his case for the plan was steadfastly majoritarian in character: everybody contributes, everybody benefits.

After leaving the White House, Bridgeland founded a policy research and development organization and continued to develop national service proposals. For instance, in 2008, he co-led the "Service Nation" summit that brought together then presidential candidates Barack Obama and John McCain. In 2009, with the summit's network behind it, a broadly bipartisan coalition of more than 100 organizations supported the Edward M. Kennedy Serve America Act. The bill passed with 79 votes in the Senate, and was signed into law by President Obama in April 2009.

John Bridgeland

The 2009 law authorized, and in some cases revitalized, many of the USA Freedom Corps initiatives that Bridgleand had crafted in 2002; and, in 2013, he was still at it. Through the Aspen Institute's "Franklin Project," he led in developing a proposal for a million, full-time, year-round national service slots for the nation's 18 – 28 year-olds, including recently returned military veterans.

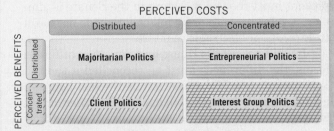

Source: John M. Bridgeland, *Heart of the Nation: Volunteering and America's Civic Spirit* (Rowman and Littlefield, 2013).

voice vote A congressional voting procedure in which members shout "yea" in approval or "nay" in disapproval, permitting members to vote quickly or anonymously on bills.

division vote A congressional voting procedure in which members stand and are counted.

roll-call vote A congressional voting procedure that consists of members answering "yea" or "nay" to their names.

teller vote A congressional voting procedure in which members pass between two tellers, the "yeas" first and the "nays" second.

veto Literally, "I forbid": it refers to the power of a president to disapprove a bill; it may be overridden by a two-thirds vote of each house of Congress.

Methods of Voting

There are several methods of voting in Congress, which can be applied to amendments to a bill as well as to the question of final passage. Some observers of Congress make the mistake of deciding who was for and who against a bill by the final vote. This can be misleading. Often, a member of Congress will vote for final passage of a bill after having supported amendments that, if they had passed, would have made the bill totally different. To keep track of someone's voting record, therefore, it is often more important to know how that person voted on key amendments than how he or she voted on the bill itself.

Finding that out is not always easy, though it has become simpler in recent years. The House has three procedures for voting. A **voice vote** consists of the members shouting "aye" or "no"; a **division** (or standing) **vote** involves the members standing and being counted. In neither case are the names recorded of who voted which way. This is done only with a **roll-call vote**. Since 1973, an electronic voting system has been in use that greatly speeds up roll-call votes, and the number of recorded votes has thus increased sharply. To ensure a roll-call vote, one-fifth of house members present must request it. Voting in the Senate is simpler: it votes by voice or by roll call; they do not use a **teller vote** or electronic counters.

If a bill passes the House and Senate in different forms, the differences must be reconciled if the bill is to become law. If they are minor, the last house to act may simply refer the bill back to the other house, which then accepts the alterations. Major differences must be ironed out in a conference committee, though only a minority of bills requires a conference. Each house must vote to form such a committee. The members are picked by the chairs of the standing committees that have been handling the legislation; the minority as well as the majority party is represented. No decision can be made unless approved by a majority of *each* delegation. Bargaining is long and hard; in the past it was also secret, but some sessions are now public. Often—as with Carter's energy bill—the legislation is substantially rewritten in conference. Theoretically nothing already agreed to by both the House and Senate is to be changed, but in the inevitable give-and-take, even those matters already approved may be modified.

Conference reports on spending bills usually split the difference between the House and Senate versions. Overall, the Senate tends to do slightly better than the House.[34] But whoever wins, conferees report their agreement back to their respective houses, which usually consider the report immediately. The report can be accepted or rejected; it cannot be amended. In the great majority of cases, it is accepted—the alternative is to have no bill at all, at least for that Congress.

The bill, now in final form, goes to the president for signature or **veto**. A vetoed bill returns to the house of origin, where an effort can be made to override the veto. Two-thirds of those present (provided there is a quorum) must vote, by roll call, to override. If both houses override, the bill becomes law without the president's approval.

Legislative Productivity

In recent years, political scientists have studied how productive Congress has been and whether the post-9/11 Congress has performed especially well or especially poorly. The first issue concerns how best to measure the body's major and minor "legislative productivity." It is clear that Congress passed and funded an enormous number of bills in response to the Great Depression in the 1930s and

An electronic board displays the present votes of members of the 113th U.S. House of Representatives during the opening session at the U.S. Capitol in Washington, D.C., on January 3, 2013.

in the mid-1960s, mainly in conjunction with that era's "war on poverty." And most scholars agree that in recent decades the body's legislative output has often slowed or declined.[35]

The second issue is how best to evaluate changes in the legislation Congress produces from one time period to the next. For instance, some scholars argue that the relatively low levels of legislative output of the late 1990s, together with decreases in the body's

HOW WE COMPARE

Number of Legislators

Writing in *Federalist* paper No. 55, James Madison insists that in any legislative body the number of legislators "ought at most to be kept within a certain limit, in order to avoid the confusion and intemperance of a multitude."

America has heeded Madison's advice. With 435 members of the House and 100 members of the Senate, the Congress has a total of 535 members representing more than 310 million citizens, or roughly one national legislator for every 590,000 citizens.

In most democracies, the ratio of national legislators to citizens is far higher than it is in the United States. For example, with a population of just over 60 million, the British Parliament's two houses total more than 1,300 members, or roughly one national legislator for every 48,000 citizens; and, with a population of about 10 million, Sweden's legislature has nearly 350 members, or roughly one national legislator for every 27,100 citizens.

At the same time, however, America has more numerous and more powerful subnational legislators (more than 7,300 in all) than most other nations do, including, in Madison's home state of Virginia, 140 state lawmakers representing about 8 million citizens, or roughly one state lawmaker for every 57,000 citizens.

Also, the U.S. Constitution would permit the U.S. House to expand enough to approximate the representation ratios of nations like the United Kingdom and Sweden and states like Virginia: Article 1, section 2 states that "the Number of Representatives shall not exceed one for every thirty Thousand."

Thus, given 300 million citizens, the Constitution would allow there to be as many as 10,000 members of the U.S. House (300 million divided by 30,000). But the mere thought heralds Madison's warning, harkening back to ancient Greece's large legislatures, that even if "every Athenian citizen had been a Socrates, every Athenian assembly would have been a mob."

oversight hearings and related activities, betokened an institutional decline of Congress; others, however, reject the view that Congress, by passing fewer laws and holding fewer hearings, had thereby become a "broken branch."[36]

The third issue is whether **divided government** (one party in control of the presidency and the other in charge of one or both chambers of Congress) decreases legislative productivity. Although there are some exceptions, most studies of the subject suggest that divided party government only reduces the passage of the most far-reaching and costly legislation.[37] As we shall discuss in Chapter 14, divided party government does not lead inevitably to "policy gridlock" any more than having **unified government** (a single party in power in the White House and in both chambers of Congress) makes enacting ever more sweeping laws easy or inevitable.

The fourth issue involves so-called **earmarks**—congressional provisions that direct the federal government to fund specific projects or exempt specific persons or groups from needing to pay specific federal taxes or fees. Earmarks have tripled since 1994; in 2006 alone, nearly 13,000 earmarks cost about $64 billion.[38] Earmarks are legally binding, but few appear in a bill's text; rather, most are "hidden" in conference reports not subject to amendment.

This form of "legislative productivity" is criticized by most scholars and, in principle at least, by most citizens. Earmarks figured in the scandals surrounding lobbyist Jack Abramoff and the convicted Congressman Randy "Duke" Cunningham; Barack Obama and John McCain argued against earmarks during the 2008 presidential campaign. Still, earmarks, in one form or another, have proliferated because individuals and institutions—including not just businesses but also private universities, hospitals, and other nonprofit organizations—persist in demanding them from constituency-oriented members of Congress.

The fifth issue is how the post-9/11 Congress has legislated on matters directly relevant to homeland security, especially its own. The Framers crafted Congress as an institution that favors deliberation over dispatch; to act boldly only when backed by a persistent popular majority, or a broad consensus

divided government
One party controls the White House and another party controls one or both houses of Congress.

unified government
The same party controls the White House and both houses of Congress.

earmarks "Hidden" congressional provisions that direct the federal government to fund specific projects or that exempt specific persons or groups from paying specific federal taxes or fees.

pork-barrel legislation Legislation that gives tangible benefits to constituents in several districts or states in the hope of winning their votes in return.

franking privilege The ability of members to mail letters to their constituents free of charge by substituting their facsimile signature for postage.

among its leaders, or both; and to be slow to change its time-honored procedures and structures.

But intelligence officials believe that a fourth plane involved in the 9/11 terrorist attacks was headed for the Capitol. In its June 2003 report, the bipartisan Continuity of Government Commission concluded that "the greatest hole in our constitutional system is the possibility of a terrorist attack that would kill or injure many members of Congress."[39]

This "hole" is relatively small with respect to the Senate. The Seventeenth Amendment allows the emergency replacement of senators by the governors of their states provided the state legislature allows it; otherwise, the governors must call for new elections. But the problem is greater for the House, where vacancies can only be filled by special elections, a process that can take many months.

Congress has enacted some, but by no means all, of the 9/11 Commission's recommendations.[40] But, as of 2013, more than a decade after the 9/11 attacks on the United States, it had failed to enact comprehensive legislation or proposals for constitutional amendments to ensure that "the first branch" can continue to function should a terrorist attack kill or incapacitate many or most of its members.

Reforming Congress

While most citizens are only vaguely familiar with the rules and procedures under which Congress operates, they do care whether Congress as an institution serves the public interest and fulfills its mission as a democratic body. Over the last several decades, many proposals have been made to reform and improve Congress—term limitations, new ethics and campaign finance laws, and organizational changes intended to reduce the power and perks of members while making it easier for Congress to pass needed legislation in a timely fashion. Some of these proposals—for example, campaign finance reforms (see Chapter 10)—have recently become law.

Many would-be reformers share the view that Congress is overstaffed and self-indulgent. It is, they complain, quick to impose new laws on states, cities, businesses, and average citizens but slow to apply those same laws to itself and its members. It is quick to pass **pork-barrel legislation**—bills that

give tangible benefits (highways, dams, post offices) to constituents in the hope of winning their votes in return—but slow to tackle complex and controversial questions of national policy. The reformers' image of Congress is unflattering, but is it wholly unwarranted?

No perk is more treasured by members of Congress than the frank. Members of Congress are allowed by law to send material through the mail free of charge by substituting their facsimile signature (*frank*) for postage. But rather than using this **franking privilege** to keep their constituents informed about the government, most members use franked newsletters and questionnaires as campaign literature. That is why use of the frank soars in the months before an election. Thus, the frank amounts to a taxpayer subsidy of members' campaigns, a perk that bolsters the electoral fortunes of incumbents. Some reformers do not believe it is possible to fence in congressional use of the frank for public education or other legitimate purposes, and so they propose abolishing it outright. Other reformers argue that the frank can be fenced in by prohibiting mailings just before primaries and general elections.

For years, Congress routinely exempted itself from many of the laws it passed. In defense of this practice, members said that if members of Congress were subject to, for example, the minimum wage laws, the executive branch, charged with enforcing these laws, would acquire excessive power over Congress. This would violate the separation of powers. But as public criticism of Congress grew and confidence in government declined, more and more people demanded that Congress subject itself to the laws that applied to everybody else. In 1995, the 104th Congress did this by passing a bill that obliges Congress to obey 11 important laws governing things such as civil rights, occupational safety, fair labor standards, and family leave.

The bipartisan Congressional Accountability Act of 1995 had to solve a key problem: under the constitutional doctrine of separated powers, it would have been unwise and perhaps unconstitutional for the executive branch to enforce congressional compliance with executive-branch regulations. So Congress created the independent Office of Compliance and an employee grievance procedure to deal with implementation. Now Congress, too, must obey laws such as the Civil Rights Act, the Equal Pay Act, the Age Discrimination Act, and the Family and Medical Care Leave Act.

As already mentioned, bills containing money for local dams, bridges, roads, and monuments are referred to disparagingly as pork-barrel legislation. Reformers complain that when members act to "bring home the bacon," Congress misallocates

WHAT'S YOUR ISSUE?

A New Congress—and a New Constitution?

In 1992, James L. Sundquist, a noted Brookings Institution Congress scholar, published *Constitutional Reform and Effective Government*. Whatever the Constitution's virtues, argued Sundquist, the separation of powers system had by the late 20th century saddled the nation with a Congress that could not plan, could not act quickly, and could not solve major problems of all sorts. He favored replacing the Congress and the Constitution with a parliamentary system like that in the United Kingdom, but he reckoned that no such radical reform was politically possible. Instead, he advocated a host of institutional and other reforms that he thought might foster more "effective government."

Twenty years later, in 2012, another noted Brookings Institution scholar, Thomas E. Mann, co-authored with Norman J. Ornstein, a scholar at the American Enterprise Institute, a book that became a bestseller: *It's Even Worse Than It Looks: How the American Constitutional System Collided with the New Politics of Extremism*. Echoing Sundquist, the two veteran Congress-watchers argued that a British-style parliamentary system would provide a "much cleaner form of democratic accountability," but they called instead for more minor reforms, as well as for "creating a shadow Congress of former lawmakers from across the political spectrum that would periodically gather and debate key issues facing the country."

Others, however, have gone further than either Sundquist or Mann and Ornstein. For example, the celebrated University of Texas political scientist, Sanford V. Levinson, in his 2012 book, *Framed: America's 51 Constitutions and the Crisis of Governance*,

calls for a new Constitutional Convention that would fashion a new Constitution; and, Louis Michael Seidman, a well-respected Georgetown University constitutional law scholar, in his 2013 bestseller, *On Constitutional Disobedience*, advocates that both elected leaders and the mass public begin "ignoring" the Constitution and move quickly (and without regard for the amendment process specified in Article V) to do away with it.

Still, both Congress and the Constitution have their defenders. For example, Andrew J. Taylor, a North Carolina State University political scientist, in his 2013 book, *Congress: A Performance Appraisal*, argues that "Congress's performance does not warrant the tremendous disdain in which it is currently held." Taylor teaches that "the principal causes of Congress's failings" is not the Constitution, but the unrealistic demands that people make of Congress. He suggests that "we should perhaps first look in the mirror" before criticizing Congress or pushing for far-reaching reforms.

Are you ready for a radically reformed or all-new Congress? Do you think a parliamentary or quasi-parliamentary system would yield more "effective government"? Would you vote for a new Constitutional Convention? Are "We the People" as much to blame as our elected leaders are for the problems that we face—or even maybe more to blame since it is we that elected (and, in the case of Congress, routinely re-elected) them? Do you think at least some problems with Congress or the Constitution itself can and should be fixed short of any far-reaching reforms?

---

tax dollars by supporting projects with trivial social benefits in order to bolster their re-election prospects.

No one can doubt the value of trimming unnecessary spending, but pork is not necessarily the villain it is made out to be. For example, the main cause of the budget deficit was the increase in spending on entitlement programs (like health care and interest on the national debt) without a corresponding increase in taxes. Spending on pork is a small fraction of total annual federal spending (about 2.5 percent, on average, from 1993 to 2005).[41] By 2013, what most observers would count as pork spending was below 1 percent of total federal

spending. But many categories of pork spending have increased in the last 10 or 15 years. Of course, one person's pork is another person's necessity. No doubt some congressional districts get an unnecessary bridge or highway, but others get bridges and highways that are long overdue. The notion that every bridge or road a member of Congress gets for his or her district is wasteful pork is tantamount to saying that no member attaches any importance to merit.

Even if all pork were bad, it would still be necessary. Congress is an independent branch of government, and each member is, by constitutional design, the advocate of his or her district or state.

HOW THINGS WORK

Rules on Congressional Ethics

Senate

Gifts: No gifts (in money, meals, or things) totalling $100 or more from anyone except a spouse or personal friend.

Lobbyists may not pay for gifts, official travel, legal defense funds, or charitable contributions to groups controlled by senators.

Fees: No fees for lectures or writing ("honoraria"), except that fees of up to $2,000 may go to a senator-designated charity.

Outside earned income may not exceed 15 percent of a senator's salary.

Ex-senators may not try to influence members of Congress for one year after leaving the Senate.

Mass mailings: No senator may receive more than $50,000 from the Senate to send out a mailing to constituents.

House

Gifts: No gifts (in money, meals, or things) totalling $100 or more from anyone except a spouse or personal friend.

Lobbyists may not offer gifts or pay for travel, even if a lobbyist is a spouse or personal friend.

Travel: House members may travel at the expense of others if travel is for officially connected meetings.

Fees: No honoraria for House members.

Ex–House members may not lobby Congress for one year after leaving office.

No member's vote can be won by coercion, and few can be had by mere appeals to party loyalty or presidential needs. Pork is a way of obtaining consent. The only alternative is bribery, but bribery, besides being wrong, would benefit only the member, whereas pork usually benefits voters in the member's district. If you want to eliminate pork, you must eliminate Congress, by converting it into a parliament under the control of a powerful party leader or prime minister. In a tightly controlled parliament, no votes need

HOW THINGS WORK

How Congress Raises Its Pay

For more than 200 years, Congress has tried to find a politically painless way to raise its own pay. It has managed to vote itself a pay increase 23 times in those two centuries, but usually at the price of a hostile public reaction. Twice during the 19th century, a pay raise led to a massacre of incumbents in the next election.

Knowing this, Congress has invented various ways to get a raise without actually appearing to vote for it. These have included the following:

- Voting for a tax deduction for expenses incurred as a result of living in Washington

- Creating a citizens' commission that could recommend a pay increase that would take effect automatically, provided Congress did not vote against it

- Linking increases in pay to decreases in honoraria (that is, speaking fees)

In 1989, a commission recommended a congressional pay raise of over 50 percent (from $89,500 to $135,000) and a ban on honoraria. The House planned to let it take effect automatically. But the public wouldn't have it, demanding that Congress vote on the raise—and vote it down. It did.

Embarrassed by its maneuvering, Congress retreated. At the end of 1989, it voted itself (as well as most top executive and judicial branch members) a small pay increase (7.9 percent for representatives, 9.9 percent for senators) that also provided for automatic cost-of-living adjustments (up to 5 percent a year) in the future. But the automatic adjustments in congressional pay have been rejected every year in recorded roll-call votes. Apparently nobody in Congress wants to be accused of "getting rich" at the taxpayers' expense.

be bought; they can be commanded. But members of such a parliament can do little to help their constituents cope with government or to defend them against bureaucratic abuses, nor can they investigate the conduct of the executive branch. The price of a citizen-oriented Congress is a pork-oriented Congress.

WHAT WOULD YOU DO?

MEMORANDUM

To: *Representative Peter Skerry*

From: *Martha Bayles, legislative aide*

Subject: *The size of the House of Representatives*

The House can decide how big it wishes to be. When it was created, there was one representative for every 30,000 people. Now there is one for every 600,000. In most other democracies, each member of parliament represents far fewer than 600,000 people. Doubling the size of the House may be a way of avoiding term limits.

Arguments for:

1. Doubling the size of the House would reduce the huge demand for constituent services each member now faces.

2. A bigger House would represent more shades of opinion more fairly.

3. Each member could raise less campaign money because his or her campaign would be smaller.

Arguments against:

1. A bigger House would be twice as hard to manage, and it would take even longer to pass legislation.

News »

Should We Have a Bigger Congress?

A powerful citizens' organization has demanded that the House of Representatives be made larger so that voters can feel closer to their members. Each representative now speaks for about 600,000 people—far too many, the group argues, to make it possible for all points of view to be heard.

2. Campaigns in districts of 300,000 people would cost as much as ones in districts with 600,000 people.

3. Interest groups do a better job of representing public opinion than would a House with more members.

Your decision:

Increase size of House:_____   Do not increase size of House:_____

LEARNING OBJECTIVES

1. In what respects is Congress "the first branch" of American national government?

Congress is one of three co-equal branches, but it is "the first branch" by virtue of the especially extensive and important powers bestowed on it by Article I of the Constitution, and with respect to the Framers' belief that Congress was pivotal to making federalism, the separation of powers, and checks and balances work.

2. Why do most Americans and many experts now view Congress as "the broken branch"?

Most Americans and many experts express disapproval of Congress and believe that it is ineffective at solving important problems, beholden to contributors and special interests, and unable to reform itself. Yet upward of 90 percent of the "broken branch's" incumbents who seek re-election win it, usually by wide margins. And the experts offer conflicting views regarding why Congress remains "broken" and how, if at all, it can be fixed.

3. What are the main differences between a congress and a parliament?

A congress differs from a parliament in two basic ways: how one becomes a member and what one does as a member. To run for a seat in a parliament like the United Kingdom's, you first need a political party to put your name on a ballot, but to become a candidate for representative or senator in Congress, you first need to enter a primary election (political parties exercise relatively little control over who runs). In a parliament, the head of the executive branch (the prime minister) is selected by the majority party from among its members, and once in office a member of parliament has only one important decision to make—whether or not to support the government. By contrast, the voters, not the congress, pick the president, and once elected a member of congress has powers that he or she can exercise without regard to presidential preferences.

4. How has the legislative productivity of the U.S. Congress varied over time?

In some periods, like the 1930s (the New Deal) and the 1960s (the Great Society), Congress has produced lots of major legislation. In other periods, however, its legislative output has been less robust. But scholars disagree about what explains these changes and also over how to measure "legislative productivity" in the first place.

5. Are the American people as deeply divided in partisan and ideological terms as their representatives in Congress now appear to be?

Nobody disputes that Congress in recent decades has become more polarized in partisan and ideological terms, but some leading scholars argue that the trend reflects the growing political polarization in the American electorate, while others argue instead that voters remain far less polarized than those elected political elites who now represent them.

6. How closely do members of Congress mirror the American people in terms of gender, race, and other demographic characteristics?

Demographically, not at all closely: most Americans, unlike most members of Congress, are not middle-aged white males with law degrees or past political careers. Some groups (for example, women, African Americans, and Latinos) are much less prevalent in Congress than they are in the nation as a whole, while other groups (for example, Catholics) constitute about the same fraction of Congress as they do of the American people. Ideologically, Republican members of Congress are more conservative than average Americans, and Democratic members of Congress are more liberal than average Americans.

7. Does Congress normally do what most citizens want it to do?

On most issues most of the time, Congress is in step with the public. But on some issues, most representatives' opinions generally are out of sync with mass public preferences. For example, most Americans have long favored protectionist trade policies, but most members of Congress have consistently voted for free-trade policies. Likewise, most citizens are less solicitous of laws that reinforce civil liberties than the Congress has traditionally been. This, however, is much as the Framers of the Constitution had hoped and expected. They believed that representatives should refine, not reflect, public wishes, and mediate, not mirror, public views.

8. Should Congress run under strong leadership?

Congress has tried it both ways. Sometimes the House has had a strong Speaker, sometimes a weak one; sometimes committee chairs were selected by seniority, sometimes by the Speaker, and sometimes by party vote. If we want a Congress that can act quickly and decisively as a body, then we should desire strong leadership, place restrictions on debate, provide few opportunities for stalling tactics, and brook only minimal committee interference. But if we want a Congress in which the interests of individual members and the people they represent are routinely protected or enhanced, then we must reject strong leadership, proliferate rules allowing for delay and discussion, and permit many opportunities for committee activity. Unfortunately, the public often wants both systems to operate, the first for some issues and the second for others.

9. Should Congress act more quickly?

The Framers of the Constitution knew that Congress would normally proceed slowly and err in favor of deliberative, not decisive, action. Congress was intended to check and balance strong leaders in the executive branch, not automatically cede its authority to them, not even during a war or other national crisis. Today, the increased ideological and partisan polarization among members has arguably made Congress even less capable than it traditionally has been of planning ahead or swiftly adopting coherent changes in national policies. There is, however, only conflicting evidence concerning whether so-called policy gridlock has become more common than in decades past. Since the September 11, 2001, terrorist attacks on the United States, Congress has passed a host of new laws intended to enhance America's homeland security. Still, Congress took its time with several major proposals to reorganize the government around homeland security priorities. Some cite this as but the latest, and potentially the gravest, example of what's wrong with Congress. But others cite it as a salutary reminder that a Congress that could move swiftly to enact wise homeland security or other policies could also move swiftly to adopt unwise ones.

TO LEARN MORE

House of Representatives: **www.house.gov**

Senate: **www.senate.gov**

Library of Congress: **www.loc.gov**

For news about Congress
Roll Call magazine: **www.rollcall.com**
C-SPAN: **www.c-span.org**

Abramowitz, Alan I. *The Disappearing Center: Engaged Citizens, Polarization, and American Democracy*. New Haven and London: Yale University Press, 2010. Claims that polarization in Congress reflects how politically attentive and active voters are polarized, while less informed but more moderate voters are disengaged.

Arnold, R. Douglas. *The Logic of Congressional Action*. New Haven and London: Yale University Press, 1990. Masterful analysis of how Congress sometimes passes bills that serve the general public, not just special interests.

Black, Amy E. *From Inspiration to Legislation: How an Idea Becomes a Bill*. Upper Saddle River, NJ: Pearson, 2007. An insider's account of the creation of the Safe Haven Act of 2001.

Fenno, Richard F., Jr. *Congressmen in Committees*. Boston: Little, Brown, 1973. Classic study of the styles of 12 standing committees.

Fiorina, Morris P. *Disconnect: The Breakdown of Representation in American Politics*. Oklahoma: University of Oklahoma Press, 2009. Offers evidence suggesting that the increasingly ideological and partisan Congress represents the still-centrist and moderate American people far less well than it did in the past.

Fiorina, Morris P. *Congress: Keystone of the Washington Establishment*, 2nd ed. New Haven, CT: Yale University Press, 1989. Argues that congressional behavior is aimed at guaranteeing the members' chances for re-election.

Jacobson, Gary. *The Politics of Congressional Elections*, 6th ed. New York: Longman, 2004. Authoritative study of how members of Congress are elected.

Maass, Arthur. *Congress and the Common Good*. New York: Basic Books, 1983. Insightful account of congressional operations, especially those involving legislative-executive relations. Disputes Fiorina's argument that re-election needs explain congressional behavior.

Mann, Thomas E., and Norman J. Ornstein, *Broken Branch: How Congress Is Failing America and How to Get It Back on Track*, 2nd ed. New York: Oxford University Press, 2008. Critically compares the post-1994 Congress to its predecessors and suggests several major reforms.

Poole, Keith T., and Howard Rosenthal. *Congress: A Political-Economic History of Roll Call Voting*. New York: Oxford University Press, 1997. Sophisticated study of why members of Congress vote as they do and how relatively stable congressional voting patterns have been throughout American history.

Sundquist, James L. *The Decline and Resurgence of Congress*. Washington, D.C.: Brookings Institution, 1981. A history of the fall and, after 1973, the rise of congressional power vis-à-vis the president.

Taylor, Andrew J. *Congress: A Performance Appraisal*. Boulder, CO: Westview Press, 2013. Offers evidence and arguments to suggest that the present-day Congress is not the dysfunctional body that the mass public and many scholars believe it to be.

White House Photo / Alamy

14

The Presidency

LEARNING OBJECTIVES

1. How do presidents differ from prime ministers?

2. Did the Founders expect the presidency to be the most important political institution?

3. How have the constitutional and political powers of the presidency evolved from the founding of the United States to the present?

4. How do presidents make policy?

5. Is it harder to govern when the presidency and the Congress are controlled by different political parties?

When the Framers wrote the Constitution in the summer of 1787, they did not have a ready consensus on how to select the chief executive or define the powers of the office. James Wilson of Pennsylvania wanted the president to be elected by the people, Roger Sherman of Connecticut wanted him elected by Congress. Wilson's view got almost no support because the size of the United States (in 1787 it was as large as England, Ireland, France, Germany, and Italy combined) made it unlikely that anybody save George Washington could obtain a popular majority. Sherman's view got a lot of support, but many delegates worried that the president would become nothing more than a tool of Congress. Ultimately, a small subset of the group, the Committee on Postponed Matters, came up with the idea of creating an electoral college to choose the president. The Framers approved the plan, but they expected that most elections would ultimately be decided by the House of Representatives, as they thought candidates would have difficulty winning a majority in the electoral college.

More than two hundred years later, the electoral college endures, and the House has not chosen a president since 1824. The stability of this institution is surprising, given that the Framers settled on it as a last-minute compromise, and yet it is the only part of the presidential campaign process that the Framers would recognize in the 21st century. The lengthy road to the nomination, extensive fundraising required (in the 2012 presidential race, the two major-party candidates and their parties raised approximately $2 billion for campaign spending),[1] and 24-hour media coverage are all standard features of modern presidential selection, and the weighty demands of winning the White House affect how the victorious candidate governs as president. As you read this chapter, think about which features of the American presidency make sense today and which might merit change, keeping in mind that the Framers were not necessarily wedded to all aspects of the institution they created, nor could they have anticipated how technology and other factors would change it.

Professor Jones speaks to his political science class:

> The president of the United States occupies one of the most powerful offices in the world. Presidents Kennedy and Johnson sent American troops to Vietnam, President Bush sent them to Saudi Arabia, and President Clinton sent them to Kosovo,

all without war being declared by Congress. In fact, Clinton ordered our air force to bomb parts of the old Yugoslavia despite the fact that the House of Representatives had rejected a resolution that would have authorized the bombing. President Nixon imposed wage and price controls on the country. Between them, Presidents Carter and Reagan selected most of the federal judges now on the bench; thus the political philosophies of these two men were stamped on the courts. President George W. Bush created military tribunals to try captured terrorists and persuaded Congress to toughen antiterrorist laws. President Barack Obama, within just months of taking office, got Congress to go along with his plans for giving the executive branch new and sweeping powers to regulate financial markets. No wonder people talk about our having an "imperial presidency."

A few doors down the hall, Professor Smith speaks to her class:

> The president, compared to the prime ministers of other democratic nations, is one of the weakest chief executives anywhere. President Carter signed an arms-limitation treaty with the Soviets, but the Senate wouldn't ratify it. President Reagan was not allowed even to test antisatellite weapons, and in 1986 Congress rejected his budget before the ink was dry. President Clinton's health care plan was ignored, and the House voted to impeach him. The federal courts struck down several parts of President Bush's antiterrorist policies. Even with his party in control of both houses of Congress, President Obama's first budget proposals were nixed on Capitol Hill, and his first health care reform plans were quickly recast by congressional committee chairpersons. Regularly, subordinates who are supposed to be loyal to the president leak his views to the press and undercut his programs before Congress. No wonder people call the U.S. president a "pitiful, helpless giant."

Can Professors Jones and Smith be talking about the same office? Who is right? In fact, they are both right. The American presidency is a unique office, with elements of great strength and profound weakness built into it by its constitutional origins.

Presidents and Prime Ministers

The popularly elected president is an American invention. Of the roughly five dozen countries in which there is some degree of party competition and thus, presumably, some measure of free choice for the voters, only 16 have a directly elected president, and 13 of these are nations of North and South America. The democratic alternative is for the chief executive to be a prime minister, chosen by and responsible to the parliament. This system prevails in most Western European countries as well as in Israel and Japan. There is no nation with a purely presidential political system in Europe; France combines a directly elected president with a prime minister and parliament.[2]

In a parliamentary system, the prime minister is the chief executive. The prime minister is chosen not by the voters but by the legislature, and he or she in turn selects the other ministers from the members of parliament. If the parliament has only two major parties, the ministers usually will be chosen from the majority party; if there are many parties (as in Israel), several parties may participate in a coalition cabinet. The prime minister remains in power as long as his or her party has a majority of the seats in the legislature or as long as the coalition he or she has assembled holds together. The voters choose who is to be a member of parliament—usually by voting for one or another party—but cannot choose who is to be the chief executive officer. Whether a nation has a presidential or a parliamentary system makes a big difference in the identity and powers of the chief executive.

Presidents Are Often Outsiders

People become president by winning elections, and sometimes winning is easier if you can show the voters that you are not part of "the mess in Washington." Prime ministers are selected from among people already in parliament, and so they are always insiders.

Jimmy Carter, Ronald Reagan, Bill Clinton, and George W. Bush did not hold national office before becoming president. Franklin Roosevelt had been assistant secretary of the navy, but his real political experience was as governor of New York. Dwight Eisenhower was a general, not a politician. John F. Kennedy, Lyndon Johnson, and Richard Nixon had been in Congress, but only Nixon had had top-level experience in the executive branch (he had been vice president). George H. W. Bush had had a great deal of executive experience in Washington—as vice president, director of the CIA, and representative to China, whereas Bill Clinton and George W. Bush both served as governors. Barack Obama is the third president to be elected directly from the U.S. Senate to the White House—the other two were Warren G. Harding and John F. Kennedy.

Thirty-two different people were elected president between 1828 and 2012. Of these, the great majority were governors, military leaders, or vice

The first cabinet: left to right, Secretary of War Henry Knox, Secretary of State Thomas Jefferson, Attorney General Edmund Randolph, Secretary of the Treasury Alexander Hamilton, and President George Washington.

presidents; just 13 percent were legislators immediately before becoming president.

Presidents Choose Cabinet Members from Outside Congress

Under the Constitution, no sitting member of Congress can hold office in the executive branch. The persons chosen by a prime minister to be in the cabinet are almost always members of parliament.

Of the 15 heads of cabinet-level departments in the first George W. Bush administration, only four had been members of Congress. The rest, as is customary with most presidents, were close personal friends or campaign aides, representatives of important constituencies (for example, farmers, blacks, or women), experts on various policy issues, or some combination of all three. The prime minister of the United Kingdom, by contrast, picks all of his or her cabinet ministers from among members of Parliament. This is one way by which the prime minister exercises control over the legislature. If you were an ambitious member of Parliament, eager to become prime minister yourself someday, and if you knew that your main chance of realizing that ambition was to be appointed to a series of ever-more-important cabinet posts, then you would not likely antagonize the person doing the appointing.

Presidents Have No Guaranteed Majority in the Legislature

A prime minister's party (or coalition) always has a majority in parliament; if it did not, somebody else would be prime minister. A president's party often does not have a congressional majority; instead, Congress often is controlled by the opposite party, creating a divided government. Divided government means that cooperation between the two branches, hard to achieve under the best of circumstances, is often further reduced by partisan bickering. Even when one party controls both the White House and Congress, the two branches often work at cross-purposes. The U.S. Constitution created a system of separate branches sharing powers. The authors of the document expected there would be conflict between the branches, and they have not been disappointed.

When Kennedy was president, his party, the Democrats, held a big majority in the House and the Senate. Yet Kennedy was frustrated by his inability to get Congress to approve proposals to enlarge civil rights, supply federal aid for school construction, create a Department of Urban Affairs and Housing, or establish a program of subsidized medical care for the elderly. During his last year in office, Congress passed only about one-fourth of his proposals. Carter did not fare much better; even though the Democrats controlled Congress, many of his most important proposals were defeated or greatly modified. Only Franklin Roosevelt (1933–1945) and Lyndon Johnson (1963–1969) had even brief success in leading Congress, and for Roosevelt most of that success was confined to his first term or to wartime.

Presidents and Prime Ministers at War

These differences in political position are illustrated by how George W. Bush and Tony Blair managed the war in Iraq.

- Once Bush decided to fight, he had to cajole Congress, even though it was controlled by his own party, to support him. Once Blair decided to fight, there could not be any meaningful political resistance in Parliament.

- When public opinion turned against Bush, he continued the fight because he could not be removed from office. When public opinion turned against

Blair, he announced he would resign from office and turn over the job of prime minister to another person in his party.

> **divided government**
> One party controls the White House and another party controls one or both houses of Congress.

> **unified government**
> The same party controls the White House and both houses of Congress.

Divided Government

In the 60 years from 1952 through 2012, there were 31 congressional elections and 16 presidential elections. Nineteen of the 31 produced **divided government**—a government in which one party controls the White House and a different party controls one or both houses of Congress. When Barack Obama became president in 2009, it was only the fourth time since 1969 that the same party controlled the White House and Congress, creating a **unified government**. Eight years earlier, the inauguration of President George W. Bush marked the first time since 1953 that the Republicans were fully in charge of both branches of government (they controlled the White House and the Senate from 1981 to 1987). But not long after the Senate convened, one Republican, James Jeffords of Vermont, announced that he was an independent and voted with the Democrats. Divided government returned until an additional Republican was elected to the Senate in 2002. But the Democrats retook control in 2007 and increased their majorities in both chambers two years later, even gaining the 60 votes necessary to halt filibusters in the Senate following a contested Minnesota race that ended with Democrat Al Franken being declared the winner and seated. They lost their filibuster-proof majority in 2010, when Republican Scott Brown won a surprise victory to fill the seat of recently deceased Senator Ted Kennedy of Massachusetts. And President Obama faced partially divided government after two years in office, with a Republican-led House and a narrowly Democratic Senate, a division of power that continued even after Obama won re-election in 2012.

Americans say they don't like divided government. They, or at least the pundits who claim to speak for them, think divided government produces partisan bickering, political paralysis, and policy gridlock. During the 1990 battle between President Bush and a Democratic Congress, one magazine compared it to a movie featuring the Keystone Kops, characters from the silent movies who wildly chased each other around while accomplishing nothing.[3] In the 1992 campaign, Bush, Clinton, and Ross Perot bemoaned the "stalemate" that had developed in Washington. When Clinton was sworn in as president, many

gridlock The inability of the government to act because rival parties control different parts of the government.

commentators spoke approvingly of the "end of gridlock."

There are two things wrong with these complaints. First, it is not clear that divided government produces a gridlock that is any worse than that which exists with unified government. Second, it is not clear that, even if **gridlock** does exist, it is always, or even usually, a bad thing for the country.

Does Gridlock Matter?

Despite the well-publicized stories about presidential budget proposals being ignored by Congress (Democrats used to describe Reagan's and Bush's budgets as being "dead on arrival"), it is not easy to tell whether divided governments produce fewer or worse policies than unified ones. The scholars who have looked closely at the matter have, in general, concluded that divided governments do about as well as unified ones in passing important laws, conducting important investigations, and ratifying significant treaties.[4] Political scientist David Mayhew studied 267 important laws that were enacted between 1946 and 1990. These laws were as likely to be passed when different parties controlled the White House and Congress as when the same party controlled both branches.[5] For example, divided governments produced the 1948 Marshall Plan to rebuild war-torn Europe and the 1986 Tax Reform Act. The box below lists six examples of divided government in action.

Why do divided governments produce about as much important legislation as unified ones? The main reason is that "unified government" is something of a myth. Just because the Republicans control both the presidency and Congress does not mean that the Republican president and the Republican senators and representatives will see things the same way. For one thing, Republicans are themselves divided between conservatives (mainly from the South) and liberals (mainly from the Northeast and Midwest). They disagree about policy almost as much as Republicans and Democrats disagree. For another thing, the Constitution ensures that the president and Congress will be rivals for power and thus rivals in policymaking. That's what the separation of powers and checks and balances are all about.

As a result, periods of unified government often turn out not to be so unified. Democratic president Lyndon Johnson could not get many Democratic members of Congress to support his war policy in Vietnam. Democratic president Jimmy Carter could not get the Democratic-controlled Senate to ratify his strategic arms-limitation treaty. Democratic president Bill Clinton could not get the Democratic Congress to go along with his policy on gays in the military or his health proposals; and when the heavily revised Clinton budget did pass in 1993, it was by just one vote.

The only time there really is a unified government is when not just the same party but the same *ideological wing* of that party is in effective control of both branches of government. This was true in 1933 when Franklin Roosevelt was president and change-oriented Democrats controlled Congress, and it was true again in 1965 when Lyndon Johnson

---

HOW THINGS WORK

Divided Government at Work: Six Examples

President George W. Bush and the partly Democratic-controlled Congress (Senate) passed legislation to institute assessment requirements in primary and secondary education. President Bill Clinton and the Republican-controlled Congress overhauled the nation's welfare system and balanced the federal budget.

President George H. W. Bush and the Democratic-controlled Congress enacted historic legislation to aid disabled persons.

President Ronald Reagan and the partly Democratic-controlled Congress (House) reformed the federal tax system.

President Richard Nixon and the Democratic-controlled Congress created many new federal environmental policies and programs.

President Dwight D. Eisenhower and the Democratic-controlled Congress established the interstate highway system.

Source: Eisenhower to Clinton examples adapted from Associated Press, "Major Laws Passed in Divided Government," November 9, 2006.

and liberal Democrats dominated Congress. Both were periods when many major policy initiatives became law: Social Security, business regulations, Medicare, and civil rights legislation. But these periods of ideologically unified government are very rare.

Is Policy Gridlock Bad?

An American president has less ability to decide what laws get passed than does a British prime minister. If you think the job of a president is to "lead the country," that weakness will worry you. The only cure for that weakness is either to change the Constitution so that our government resembles the parliamentary system in effect in the United Kingdom, or always to vote into office members of Congress who not only are of the same party as the president but also agree with him on policy issues.

We suspect that even Americans who hate gridlock and want more leadership aren't ready to make sweeping constitutional changes or to stop voting for presidents and members of Congress from different parties. This unwillingness suggests they like the idea of somebody being able to block a policy he or she doesn't like. Since all of us don't like something, we all have an interest in some degree of gridlock.

And we seem to protect that interest. In a typical presidential election, about one-fourth of all voters will vote for one party's candidate for president and the other party's candidate for Congress. As a result, about one-fourth of all congressional districts will be represented in the House by a person who does not belong to the party of the president who carried that district. Some scholars believe that voters split tickets deliberately in order to create divided government and thus magnify the effects of the checks and balances built into our system, but the evidence supporting this belief is not conclusive.

Gridlock, to the extent that it exists, is a necessary consequence of a system of representative democracy. Such a system causes delays, intensifies deliberations, forces compromises, and requires the creation of broad-based coalitions to support most new policies. This system is the opposite of direct democracy. If you believe in direct democracy, you believe that what the people want on some issue should become law with as little fuss and bother as possible. Political gridlocks are like traffic gridlocks—people get overheated, things boil over, nothing moves, and nobody wins except journalists who write about the mess and lobbyists who charge big fees to steer their clients around the tie-up. In a direct democracy, the president would be a traffic cop with broad powers to decide in what direction the traffic should move and to make sure that it moves that way.

HOW WE COMPARE

Presidential Systems

Most modern democracies feature one of three systems:

- Parliamentary systems (like the United Kingdom) in which prime ministers are selected by a legislative majority and can be removed by a legislative majority at virtually any time;

- Presidential systems (like the United States) in which the president and the legislators are separately elected and serve fixed terms, with the president subject to removal by the legislature only under extreme circumstances (for example, in the United States, impeachment by the House and removal from office by the Senate); or

- Semi-presidential systems (like France) in which there is a prime minister selected and subject to removal by a parliamentary majority, as well as a president who is separately elected.

Using a multidimensional definition of "democratic," in 1950, about 60 percent of democratic nations had parliamentary systems, 30 percent had semi-presidential systems, and 10 percent had presidential systems. Today, however, about two-thirds of all democratic nations have either semi-presidential (about 36 percent) or presidential (about 30 percent) systems.

Are elected officials and party leaders in presidential systems like that in the United States more or less likely to deliver on campaign promises than are their counterparts in the other two systems? The most in-depth studies to date say "less likely": The rate at which a party in power pursues the policies it offered to voters in its platform is generally lower in presidential systems; and the incidence of "policy-switching" (pursuing policies directly contrary to those promised during the campaign) is more than four times as common in presidential systems as it is in parliamentary systems, with semi-presidential systems being in the middle.

Source: David Samuels and Matthew Shugart, *Presidents, Parties, and Prime Ministers: How the Separation of Powers Affects Party Organization and Behavior* (Cambridge University Press, 2010); "Presidents, Prime Ministers, and Mandate Representation: A Global Test," paper prepared for presentation at the 2006 Annual Meeting of the American Political Science Association, Philadelphia, Pennsylvania.

But if unified governments are not really unified—if in fact they are split by ideological differences within each party and by the institutional rivalries between the president and Congress—then this change is less important than it may seem. What *is* important is the relative power of the president and Congress. That has changed greatly.

The Powers of the President

Though the president, unlike a prime minister, cannot command an automatic majority in the legislature, he does have some formidable, albeit vaguely defined, powers. These are mostly set forth in Article II of the Constitution and are of two sorts: those he can exercise in his own right without formal legislative approval, and those that require the consent of the Senate or of Congress as a whole.

Powers of the President Alone

- Serve as commander in chief of the armed forces

- Commission officers of the armed forces

- Grant reprieves and pardons for federal offenses (except impeachment)

- Convene Congress in special sessions

- Receive ambassadors

- Take care that the laws be faithfully executed

- Wield the "executive power"

- Appoint officials to lesser offices

Powers the President Shares with the Senate

- Make treaties

- Appoint ambassadors, judges, and high officials

Powers the President Shares with Congress as a Whole

- Approve legislation

Taken alone and interpreted narrowly, this list of powers is not very impressive. Obviously, the president's authority as commander in chief is important, but literally construed, most of the other constitutional grants seem to provide for little more than a president who is chief clerk of the country. A hundred years after the Founding, that is about how matters appeared to even the most astute observers. In 1884, Woodrow Wilson wrote a book about American politics titled *Congressional Government,* in which he described the business of the president as "usually not much above routine," mostly "*mere* administration." The president might as well be an officer of the civil service. To succeed, he need only obey Congress and stay alive.[6]

A military aide to the president carries a leather briefcase containing the classified nuclear war plan, popularly known as the "football," up the steps of Air Force One.

But even as Wilson wrote, he was overlooking some examples of enormously powerful presidents, such as Lincoln, and was not sufficiently attentive to the potential for presidential power to be found in the more ambiguous clauses of the Constitution as well as in the political realities of American life. The president's authority as commander in chief has grown—especially, but not only, in wartime—to encompass not simply the direction of the military forces, but also the management of the economy and the direction of foreign affairs as well. A quietly dramatic reminder of the awesome implications of the president's military powers occurs at the precise instant that a new president assumes office. A military officer carrying a locked briefcase moves from the side of the outgoing president to the side of the new one. In the briefcase are the secret codes and orders that permit the president to authorize the launching of American nuclear weapons.

The president's duty to "take care that the laws be faithfully executed" has become one of the most elastic phrases in the Constitution. By interpreting this broadly, Grover Cleveland was able to use federal troops to break a labor strike in the 1890s, and Dwight Eisenhower was able to send troops to help integrate a public school in Little Rock, Arkansas, in 1957.

The greatest source of presidential power, however, is not found in the Constitution at all but in politics and public opinion. Increasingly since the 1930s, Congress has passed laws that confer on the executive branch broad grants of authority to achieve some general goals, leaving it up to the president and his deputies to define the regulations and programs that will actually be put into effect. In Chapter 15, we shall see how this delegation of legislative power to the president has contributed to the growth of the bureaucracy. Moreover, the American people—always in times of crisis, but increasingly as an everyday matter—look to the president for leadership and hold him responsible for a large and growing portion of our national affairs. The public thinks, wrongly, that the presidency is the "first branch" of government.

The Evolution of the Presidency

Not surprisingly, given the preeminence of the presidency in American politics today, few issues inspired as much debate or concern among the Framers in 1787 as the problem of defining the chief executive. The delegates feared anarchy and monarchy in about equal measure. When the Constitutional Convention met, the existing state constitutions gave most, if not all, power to the legislatures. In eight states, the governor actually was chosen by the legislature, and in ten states, the governor could not serve more than one year. Only in New York, Massachusetts, and Connecticut did governors have much power or serve for any length of time.

Some of the Framers proposed a plural national executive (that is, several people would each hold the executive power in different areas, or they would exercise the power as a committee). Others wanted the executive power checked, as it

HOW THINGS WORK

The President: Qualifications and Benefits

Qualifications

- A natural-born citizen (can be born abroad of parents who are American citizens)
- 35 years of age
- A resident of the United States for at least 14 years (but not necessarily the 14 years just preceding the election)

Benefits

- A nice house
- A salary of $400,000 per year (taxable)

- An expense account of $50,000 per year (tax-free)
- Travel expenses of $100,000 per year (tax-free)
- A pension, on retirement, equal to the pay of a cabinet member (taxable)
- Staff support and Secret Service protection for 10 years on leaving the presidency
- A White House staff of 400 to 500
- A place in the country—Camp David
- A personal airplane—Air Force One
- A fine chef

electoral college The people chosen to cast each state's votes in a presidential election. Each state can cast one electoral vote for each senator and representative it has. The District of Columbia has three electoral votes, even though it cannot elect a representative or senator.

was in Massachusetts, by a council that would have to approve many of the chief executive's actions. Alexander Hamilton strongly urged the exact opposite: in a five-hour speech, he called for something very much like an elective monarchy, patterned in some respects after the British kind. No one paid much attention to this plan or even, at first, to the more modest (and ultimately successful) suggestion of James Wilson for a single, elected president.

In time, those who won out believed that the governing of a large nation, especially one threatened by foreign enemies, required a single president with significant powers. Their cause was aided, no doubt, by the fact that everybody assumed George Washington would be the first president, and confidence in him—and in his sense of self-restraint—was widely shared. Even so, several delegates feared the presidency would become, in the words of Edmund Randolph of Virginia, "the foetus of monarchy."

Concerns of the Founders

The delegates in Philadelphia, and later the critics of the new Constitution during the debate over its ratification, worried about aspects of the presidency that were quite different from those that concern us today. In 1787–1789, some Americans suspected that the president, by being able to command the state militia, would use the militia to overpower state governments. Others were worried that if the president were allowed to share treaty-making power with the Senate, he would be "directed by minions and favorites" and become a "tool of the Senate."

But the most frequent concern was over the possibility of presidential re-election: Americans in the late 18th century were sufficiently suspicious of human nature and sufficiently experienced in the arts of mischievous government to believe that a president, once elected, would arrange to stay in office in perpetuity by resorting to bribery, intrigue, and force. This might happen, for example, every time the presidential election was thrown into the House of Representatives because no candidate had received a majority of the votes in the electoral college, a situation that most people expected to happen frequently.

In retrospect, these concerns seem misplaced, even foolish. The power over the militia has had little significance; the election has gone to the House only twice (1800 and 1824); and though the Senate dominated the presidency off and on during the second half of the 19th century, it has not done so recently. The real sources of the expansion of presidential power—the president's role in foreign affairs, his ability to shape public opinion, his position as head of the executive branch, and his claims to have certain "inherent" powers by virtue of his office—were hardly predictable in 1787. There was nowhere in the world at that time, nor had there been at any time in history, an example of an American-style presidency. It was a unique and unprecedented institution, and the Framers and their critics can easily be forgiven for not predicting accurately how it would evolve. At a more general level, however, they understood the issue quite clearly. Gouverneur Morris of Pennsylvania put the problem of the presidency this way: "Make him too weak: the Legislature will usurp his powers. Make him too strong: he will usurp on the Legislature."

The Framers knew very well that the relations between the president and Congress and the manner in which the president is elected were of profound importance, and they debated both at great length. The first plan was for Congress to elect the president—in short, for the system to be quasi-parliamentary. But if that were done, some delegates pointed out, Congress could dominate an honest or lazy president, while a corrupt or scheming president might dominate Congress.

After much discussion, it was decided that the president should be chosen directly by voters. But by which voters? The emerging nation was large and diverse. It seemed unlikely that every citizen would be familiar enough with the candidates to cast an informed vote for a president directly. Worse, a direct popular election would give inordinate weight to the large, populous states, and no plan with that outcome had any chance of adoption by the smaller states.

The Electoral College

Thus the **electoral college** was invented, whereby each of the states would select electors in whatever manner it wished. The electors would then meet in each state capital and vote for president and vice president. Many Framers expected that this procedure would lead to each state's electors' voting for a favorite son, and thus no candidate would win a majority of the popular vote. In this event, it was decided, the House of Representatives should make the choice, with each state delegation casting one vote.

The plan seemed to meet every test: large states would have their say, but small states would be

CONSTITUTIONAL CONNECTIONS

Executive Checks and Balances

In *Federalist 70*, Alexander Hamilton famously wrote of the need for "energy in the Executive," which he defined as "unity" (a single president); "duration" (a term of office long enough for the Executive to be effective); "adequate provision for its support" (reasonable salary); and "competent powers" (the ability to fulfill the responsibilities of the office). Addressing fears that Article II of the Constitution made the Executive too powerful, Hamilton said the president would be checked by "a due dependence on the people" (elections) and "a due responsibility" (commitment to the public good). Do these checks suffice to keep the Framers' system of separation of powers/checks and balances intact, and the president accountable, in the 21st century?

Source: [Alexander Hamilton], *The Federalist No. 70: The Executive Department Further Considered*, 15 March 1788. Available online through The Avalon Project: Documents in Law, History and Diplomacy, Yale Law School.

protected by having a minimum of three electoral votes no matter how tiny their population. The small states together could wield considerable influence in the House, where, it was widely expected, most presidential elections would ultimately be decided. Of course, it did not work out quite this way: the Framers did not foresee the role that political parties would play in producing nationwide support for a slate of national candidates.

Once the manner of electing the president was settled, the question of his powers was much easier to decide. After all, if you believe the procedures are fair and balanced, then you are more confident in assigning larger powers to the president within this system. Accordingly, the right to make treaties and the right to appoint lesser officials, originally reserved for the Senate, were given to the president "with the advice and consent of the Senate."

The President's Term of Office

Another issue was put to rest soon thereafter. George Washington, the unanimous choice of the electoral college to be the first president, firmly limited himself to two terms in office (1789–1797), and no president until Franklin D. Roosevelt (1933–1945) dared to run for more (though Ulysses S. Grant tried). In 1951, the Twenty-second Amendment to the Constitution was ratified, formally limiting all subsequent presidents to two terms. The remaining issues concerning the nature of the presidency, and especially the relations between the president and Congress, have been the subject of continuing dispute. The pattern of relationships that we see today is the result of an evolutionary process that has extended over more than two centuries. The first problem was to establish the legitimacy of the presidency itself: that is, to ensure, if possible, public acceptance of the office, its incumbent, and its powers and to establish an orderly transfer of power from one incumbent to the next.

Today, we take this for granted. When Barack Obama was inaugurated in January 2009 as our 44th president, George W. Bush, the 43rd, quietly left the White House. In the world today, such an uneventful succession is unusual. In many nations, a new chief executive comes to power with the aid of military force or as a result of political intrigue; his predecessor often leaves office disgraced, exiled, or dead. At the time the Constitution was written, the Founders could only hope that an orderly transfer of power from one president to the next would occur. France had just undergone a bloody revolution; England in the not-too-distant past had beheaded a king; and in Poland the ruler was elected by a process so manifestly corrupt and so open to intrigue that Thomas Jefferson, in what may be the first example of ethnic humor in American politics, was led to refer to the proposed American presidency as a "bad edition of a Polish king."

Yet by the time Abraham Lincoln found himself at the helm of a nation plunged into a bitter, bloody civil war, 15 presidents had been elected, served their time, and left office without a hint of force being used to facilitate the process and with the people accepting the process—if not admiring all the presidents. This orderly transfer of authority occurred despite passionate opposition and deeply divisive elections (such as that which brought Jefferson to power). And it did not happen by accident.

The First Presidents

Those who first served as president were among the most prominent men in the new nation, all active either in the movement for independence or in the

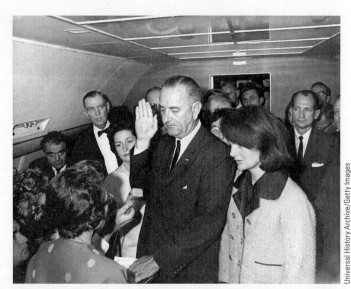

America witnessed peaceful transfers of power not only between leaders of different parties (such as Woodrow Wilson and William Howard Taft in 1913), but also after a popular leader was assassinated (Lyndon Johnson is sworn in after John F. Kennedy's death).

Founding or in both. Of the first five presidents, four (all but John Adams) served two full terms. Washington and Monroe were not even opposed. The first administration had at the highest levels the leading spokesmen for all of the major viewpoints: Alexander Hamilton was Washington's secretary of the treasury (and was sympathetic to the urban commercial interests), and Thomas Jefferson was secretary of state (and more inclined toward rural, small-town, and farming views). Washington spoke out strongly against political parties, and though parties soon emerged, there was a stigma attached to them: many people believed that it was wrong to take advantage of divisions in the country, to organize deliberately to acquire political office, or to make legislation depend upon party advantage. As it turned out, this hostility to party (or "faction," as it was more commonly called) was unrealistic: parties are as natural to democracy as churches are to religion.

Establishing the legitimacy of the presidency in the early years was made easier by the fact that the national government had relatively little to do. It had, of course, to establish a sound currency and to settle the debt accrued during the Revolutionary War. The Treasury Department inevitably became the principal federal office, especially under the strong leadership of Hamilton. Relations with England and France were important—and difficult—but otherwise government took little time and few resources.

In appointing people to federal office, a general rule of "fitness" emerged: those appointed should have some standing in their communities and be well thought of by their neighbors. Appointments based on partisanship soon arose, but community

stature could not be neglected. The presidency was kept modest. Washington clearly had not sought the office and did not relish the exercise of its then modest powers. He traveled widely so that as many people as possible could see their new president. His efforts to establish a semi-regal court etiquette were quickly rebuffed; the presidency was to be kept simple. Congress decided that not until after a president was dead might his likeness appear on a coin or on currency; no president until Eisenhower was given a pension on his retirement.

The president's relations with Congress were correct but not close. Washington appeared before the Senate to ask its advice on a proposed treaty with some Indian tribes. He got none and instead was politely told that the Senate would like to consider the matter in private. He declared that he would be "damned if he ever went there again," and he never did. Thus ended the responsibility of the Senate to "advise" the president. Vetoes were sometimes cast by the president, but sparingly, and only when the president believed the law was not simply unwise but unconstitutional. Washington cast only two vetoes; Jefferson and Adams cast none.

The Jacksonians

At a time roughly corresponding to the presidency of Andrew Jackson (1829–1837), broad changes began to occur in American politics. These changes, together with the personality of Jackson himself, altered the relations between the president and Congress and the nature of presidential leadership. As so often happens, few people at the time Jackson took office had much sense of what his presidency would be

The Granger Collection, NYC

President Andrew Jackson thought of himself as the "Tribune of the People," and he symbolized this by throwing a White House party that anyone could attend. Hundreds of people showed up and ate or carried away most of a 1,400-pound block of cheese.

like. Though he had been a member of the House of Representatives and of the Senate, he was elected as a military hero—and an apparently doddering one at that. Sixty-one years old and seemingly frail, he nonetheless used the powers of his office as no one before him had.

Jackson vetoed 12 acts of Congress, more than all his predecessors combined and more than any subsequent president until Andrew Johnson 30 years later. His vetoes were not simply on constitutional grounds but on policy ones: as the only official elected by the entire voting citizenry, he saw himself as the "Tribune of the People." None of his vetoes were overridden. He did not initiate many new policies, but he struck out against the ones he did not like. He did so at a time when the size of the electorate was increasing rapidly, and new states, especially in the West, had entered the Union. (There were then 24 states in the Union, nearly twice the original number.)

Jackson demonstrated what could be done by a popular president. He did not shrink from conflict with Congress, and the tension between the two branches of government that was intended by the Framers became intensified by the personalities of those in government: Jackson in the White House, and Henry Clay, Daniel Webster, and John Calhoun in Congress. These powerful figures walked the political stage at a time when bitter sectional conflicts—over slavery and commercial policies—were beginning to split the country. Jackson, though he was opposed to a large and powerful federal government and wished to return somehow to the agrarian simplicities of Jefferson's time, was nonetheless a believer in a strong and independent presidency. This view, though obscured by nearly a century of subsequent

congressional dominance of national politics, was ultimately to triumph—for better or for worse.

The Reemergence of Congress

With the end of Jackson's second term, Congress quickly reestablished its power, and except for the wartime presidency of Lincoln and brief flashes of presidential power under James Polk (1845–1849) and Grover Cleveland (1885–1889, 1893–1897), the presidency for a hundred years was the subordinate branch of the national government. Of the eight presidents who succeeded Jackson, two (William H. Harrison and Zachary Taylor) died in office, and none of the others served more than one term. Schoolchildren, trying to memorize the list of American presidents, always stumble in this era of the "no-name" presidents. This is hardly a coincidence: Congress was the leading institution, struggling, unsuccessfully, with slavery and sectionalism.

It was also an intensely partisan era, a legacy of Jackson that lasted well into the 20th century. Public opinion was closely divided. In nine of the 17 presidential elections between the end of Jackson's term in 1837 and Theodore Roosevelt's election in 1904, the winning candidate received less than half the popular vote. Only two candidates (Lincoln in 1864 and Ulysses S. Grant in 1872) received more than 55 percent of the popular vote.

During this long period of congressional—and usually senatorial—dominance of national government, only Lincoln broke new ground for presidential power. Lincoln's expansive use of that power, like Jackson's, was totally unexpected. He was first elected in 1860 as a minority president, receiving less than 40 percent of the popular vote in a field of four candidates. Though a member of the new Republican party, he had been a member of the Whig party, a group that had stood for limiting presidential power. He had opposed America's entry into the Mexican War and had been critical of Jackson's use of executive authority. But as president during the Civil War, he made unprecedented use of the vague powers in Article II of the Constitution, especially those that he felt were "implied" or "inherent" in the phrase "take care that the laws be faithfully executed" and in the express authorization for him to act as commander-in-chief. Lincoln raised an army, spent money, blockaded southern ports, temporarily suspended the writ of habeas corpus, and issued the Emancipation Proclamation to free the slaves—all without prior congressional approval. He justified this, as most Americans probably would have, by the emergency conditions created by civil war. In this he acted little differently from Thomas Jefferson, who while president waged undeclared war against various North African pirates.

HOW THINGS WORK

The Electoral College

Until November 2000, it was almost impossible to get a student interested in the electoral college. But in the 2000 presidential election, Florida's electoral vote hung in the balance for weeks, with Bush finally winning it and (though he had fewer popular votes than Al Gore) the presidency.

Here are the essential facts: each state gets electoral votes equal to the number of its senators and representatives (the District of Columbia also gets 3, even though it has no representatives in Congress). There are 538 electoral votes. To win, a candidate must receive at least half, or 270.

In all but two states, the candidate who wins the most popular votes wins all of the state's electoral votes. Maine and Nebraska have a different system. They allow electoral votes to be split by awarding some votes

on the basis of a candidate's statewide total and some on the basis of how the candidate did in each congressional district.

Electoral Votes per State

The distribution of electoral college votes per state is for the 2012 presidential election, based on the 2010 Census. The colors indicate which states voted Democratic and Republican in 2012.

The winning slates of electors assemble in their state capitals about six weeks after the election to cast their ballots. Ordinarily this is a pure formality. Occasionally, however, an elector will vote for a presidential candidate other than the one who carried the state. Such "faithless electors" have appeared in several elections since 1796. The state electoral ballots are opened and

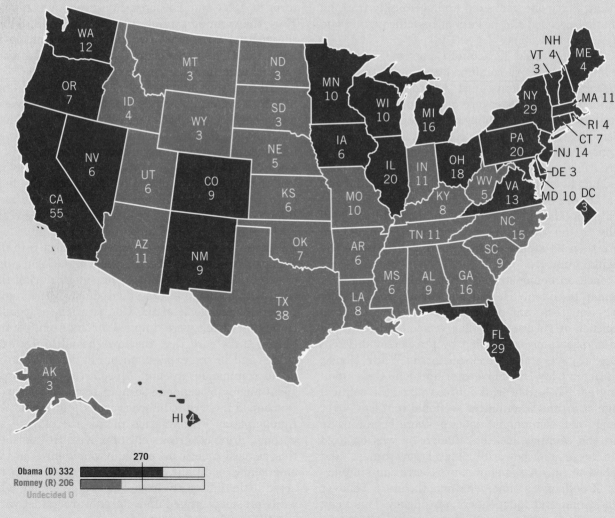

Obama (D) 332	
Romney (R) 206	
Undecided 0	

© Cengage Learning

counted before a joint session of Congress during the first week of January. The candidate with a majority is declared elected.

If no candidate wins a majority, the House of Representatives chooses the president from among the three leading candidates, with each state casting one vote. By House rules, each state's vote is allotted to the candidate preferred by a majority of the state's House delegation. If there is a tie within a delegation, that state's vote is not counted.

The House has had to decide two presidential contests. In 1800, Thomas Jefferson and Aaron Burr tied in the electoral college because of a defect in the language of the Constitution—each state cast two electoral votes, without indicating which was for president and which for vice president. (Burr was supposed to be vice president, and after much maneuvering he was.) This problem was corrected by the Twelfth Amendment, ratified in 1804. The only House decision under the modern system was in 1824, when it chose John Quincy Adams over Andrew Jackson and William H. Crawford, even though Jackson had more electoral votes (and probably more popular votes) than his rivals.

Today the winner-takes-all system in effect in 48 states makes it possible for a candidate to win at least 270 electoral votes without winning a majority of the popular votes. This happened in 2000, 1888, and 1876, and almost happened in 1960 and 1884. Today a candidate who carries the 10 largest states wins 256 electoral votes, only 14 short of a presidential victory.

This means that the candidates have a strong incentive to campaign hard in big states they have a chance of winning. In 2000, Gore worked hard in California, New York, and Pennsylvania but pretty much ignored Texas, where Bush was a shoo-in. Bush campaigned hard in Florida, Illinois, and Ohio, but not so much in New York, where Gore was an easy winner. But the electoral college can also help small states. South Dakota, for example, has 3 electoral votes (about 0.5 percent of the total), even though it casts only about 0.3 percent of the popular vote. South Dakota and other small states are thus overrepresented in the electoral college.

Most Americans would like to abolish the electoral college. But doing away with it entirely would have some unforeseen effects. If we relied just on the popular vote, there might have to be a runoff election among the two leading candidates if neither got a majority because third-party candidates won a lot of votes. This would encourage the formation of third parties (we might have a Jesse Jackson party, a Pat Buchanan party, a Pat Robertson party, and a Ralph Nader party). Each third party would then be in a position to negotiate with one of the two major parties between the first election and the runoff about favors it wanted in return for its support. American presidential politics might come to look like the multiparty systems in France and Italy.

There are other changes that could be made. One is for each state to allocate its electoral votes proportional to the popular vote the candidates receive in that state. Voters in Colorado acted on that measure in November 2004, but that proposal failed. If every state did that, several past elections would have been decided in the House of Representatives because no candidate got a majority of the popular vote.

And the electoral college serves a larger purpose: it makes candidates worry about carrying states as well as popular votes, and so heightens the influence of states in national politics.

After Lincoln, Congress reasserted its power and became, during Reconstruction and for many decades thereafter, the principal federal institution. But it had become abundantly clear that a national emergency could equip the president with great powers and that a popular and strong-willed president could expand his powers even without an emergency.

Except for the administrations of Theodore Roosevelt (1901–1909) and Woodrow Wilson (1913–1921), the president was, until the New Deal, at best a negative force—a source of opposition to Congress, not a source of initiative and leadership for it. Grover Cleveland was a strong personality, but for all his efforts he was able to do little more than veto bills that he did not like. He cast 414 vetoes— more than any other president until Franklin Roosevelt. Frequent targets of his vetoes were bills to confer special pensions on Civil War veterans.

Today we are accustomed to thinking that the president formulates a legislative program to which Congress then responds, but until the 1930s the opposite was more the case. Congress ignored the initiatives of such presidents as Grover Cleveland, Rutherford Hayes, Chester Arthur, and Calvin Coolidge. Woodrow Wilson in 1913 was the first president since John Adams to deliver personally the State of the Union address, and he was one of the first to develop and argue for a presidential legislative program.

Our popular conception of the president as the central figure of national government, devising a legislative program and commanding a large staff of advisers, is very much a product of the modern era and of the enlarged role of government. In the *bully pulpit* The president's use of his prestige and visibility to guide or enthuse the American public.

past, the presidency became powerful only during a national crisis (the Civil War, World War I) or because of an extraordinary personality (Andrew Jackson, Theodore Roosevelt, Woodrow Wilson). Since the 1930s, however, the presidency has been powerful no matter who occupied the office and whether or not there was a crisis. Because government now plays such an active role in our national life, the president is the natural focus of attention and the titular head of a huge federal administrative system (whether he is the real boss is another matter).

But the popular conception of the president as the central figure of national government belies the realities of present-day legislative-executive relations. During national policymaking from the Eisenhower years through the Reagan administration, Congress, not the president, often took the lead in setting the legislative agenda.[7] For example, the 1990 Clean Air Act, like the 1970 Clean Air Act before it, was born and bred mainly by congressional, not presidential, action. Indeed, administration officials played almost no role in the legislative process that culminated in these laws.[8] When President George H. W. Bush signed the 1990 Clean Air Act or President Clinton signed the 1996 Welfare Reform Act, each took credit for it, but in fact both bills were designed by members of Congress, not by the president.[9] Likewise, although presidents dominated budget policymaking from the 1920s into the early 1970s, they no longer do. Instead, the "imperatives of the budgetary process have pushed congressional leaders to center stage."[10] Thus, as often as not, Congress proposes, the president disposes, and legislative-executive relations involve hard bargaining and struggle between these two branches of government.

The Power to Persuade

The sketchy constitutional powers given to the president, combined with the lack of an assured legislative majority, mean that he must rely heavily on persuasion if he is to accomplish much. Here, the Constitution gives him some advantages: he and the vice president are the only officials elected by the whole nation, and he is the ceremonial head of state as well as the chief executive of the government. The president can use his national constituency and ceremonial duties to enlarge his power, but he must do so quickly: the second half of his first term in office will be devoted to running for re-election, especially if he faces opposition for his own party's nomination (as was the case with Carter and Ford).

The Three Audiences

The president's persuasive powers are aimed at three audiences. The first, and often the most important, is his Washington, D.C., audience of fellow politicians and leaders. As Richard Neustadt points out in his book *Presidential Power,* a president's reputation among his Washington colleagues is of great importance in affecting how much deference his views receive and thus how much power he can wield.[11] If a president is thought to be "smart," "sure of himself," "cool," "on top of things," or "shrewd," and thus "effective," he *will* be effective. Franklin Roosevelt had that reputation, and so did Lyndon Johnson, at least for his first few years in office. Truman, Ford, and Carter often did not have that reputation, and they lost ground accordingly. Power, like beauty, exists largely in the eye of the beholder.

A second audience is composed of party activists and officeholders outside Washington—the partisan grassroots. These persons want the president to exemplify their principles, trumpet their slogans, appeal to their fears and hopes, and help them get re-elected. Since, as we explained in Chapter 9, partisan activists increasingly have an ideological orientation toward national politics, these people will expect "their" president to make fire-and-brimstone speeches that confirm in them a shared sense of purpose and, incidentally, help them raise money from contributors to state and local campaigns.

The third audience is "the public." But of course that audience is really many publics, each with a different view or set of interests. A president on the campaign trail speaks boldly of what he will accomplish; a president in office speaks quietly of the problems that must be overcome. Citizens often are irritated at the apparent tendency of officeholders, including the president, to sound mealy-mouthed and equivocal. But it is easy to criticize the cooking when you haven't been the cook. A president learns quickly that every utterance will be scrutinized closely by the media and by organized groups here and abroad, and errors of fact, judgment, timing, or even inflection will be immediately and forcefully pointed out. Given the risks of saying too much, it is a wonder that presidents say anything at all.

Presidents have made fewer and fewer impromptu remarks in the years since Franklin Roosevelt held office and have instead relied more and more on prepared speeches from which political errors can be removed in advance. Hoover and Roosevelt held six or seven press conferences each month, but every president from Nixon through Clinton has held barely one a month. Instead, modern presidents make formal speeches. A president's use of these speeches often is called the **bully pulpit**, a phrase that means taking advantage of the prestige

WHAT'S YOUR ISSUE?

Do a President's Communication Skills Matter?

Barack Obama garnered national attention in 2004 for his eloquent keynote address at the Democratic National Convention about "the audacity of hope" (a phrase that he later used as a book title). Four years later, his speeches propelled his successful candidacy for the White House. Obama's rhetorical skills were important for his presidential campaign, but for governing, how much does a president's ability to communicate matter?

The Framers of the Constitution probably would have said, "not much." After all, they wanted to keep some distance between the president and the public, as their creation of an electoral college to select the president indicates (see box on pp. 350–351). The Constitution states that the president "shall from time to time give to the Congress Information of the State of the Union," but it does not require a presidential speech; indeed, presidents from Thomas Jefferson through William Howard Taft sent their state of the union messages in writing to Congress.

Presidential public communication has become more important since the early 20th century. Woodrow Wilson resumed the custom started by the first two presidents of delivering state of the union messages in person to Congress. Presidential scholar Richard E. Neustadt wrote in 1960 of the need for presidents to appeal to multiple constituencies, and he emphasized the importance of "public prestige," for which a president must be "effective as a teacher to the public."[1]

Political scientists and communication scholars have identified the use of public rhetoric as a political strategy by presidents in modern American politics. Samuel Kernell shows how modern presidents routinely employ a practice of "going public" to build popular support for their policies, and Jeffrey K. Tulis examines the development of the "rhetorical presidency," in which presidents use public speeches to exercise popular leadership. Mary E. Stuckey finds that advances in media technology shape what presidents say and how they do so, while Karlyn Kohrs Campbell and Kathleen Hall Jamieson evaluate how presidents use rhetorical opportunities to exercise political influence with the other institutions of government.

Despite all of the time and energy that presidents invest in their public communications, however, their efforts may not yield the results they seek. Based on extensive analysis of public opinion polls, George C. Edwards III argues that presidential speeches serve to bolster existing public views rather than to change them—the "bully pulpit," he says, falls "on deaf ears." Jeffrey E. Cohen examines media coverage of the presidency and finds that presidents can influence segments of the public through local news coverage, but that national strategies of "going public" are less successful.

Will presidents continue to devote significant resources to their public communications? Absolutely. Will doing so help them to achieve their political and policy goals? Probably not very much. The Framers appear to be correct, albeit for different reasons—they did not think presidents should "go public," and while presidents do so routinely today, they typically don't get a lot for their efforts.

[1]Richard E. Neustadt, *Presidential Power and the Modern Presidents: The Politics of Leadership from Roosevelt to Reagan* (New York: The Free Press, 1990), p. 84.

Sources: Richard E. Neustadt, *Presidential Power and the Modern Presidents: The Politics of Leadership from Roosevelt to Reagan* (New York: The Free Press, 1990); Samuel Kernell, *Going Public: New Strategies of Presidential Leadership*, 4th ed. (Washington, D.C.: CQ Press, 2007); Jeffrey K. Tulis, *The Rhetorical Presidency* (Princeton, NJ: Princeton University Press, 1987); Mary E. Stuckey, *The President as Interpreter-in-Chief* (Chatham, NJ: Chatham House Publishers, 1991); Karlyn Kohrs Campbell and Kathleen Hall Jamieson, *Presidents Creating the Presidency: Deeds Done in Words* (Chicago: University of Chicago Press, 2008); George C. Edwards III, *On Deaf Ears: The Limits of the Bully Pulpit* (New Haven, CT: Yale University Press, 2003); Jeffrey E. Cohen, *Going Local: Presidential Leadership in the Post-Broadcast Age* (New York: Cambridge University Press, 2010).

and visibility of the presidency to try to guide or mobilize the American people.

Popularity and Influence

The object of all this talk is to convert personal popularity into congressional support for the president's legislative programs (and improve chances for re-election). It is not obvious, of course, why Congress should care about a president's popularity. After all, as we saw in Chapter 13, most members of Congress are secure in their seats, and few need fear any "party bosses" who might deny them renomination. Moreover, the president cannot ordinarily provide credible electoral rewards or penalties to members of Congress. By working for their defeat in the 1938 congressional election, President Franklin Roosevelt attempted to "purge" members of

Congress who opposed his program, but he failed. Nor does presidential support help a particular member of Congress: most representatives win re-election anyway, and the few who are in trouble are rarely saved by presidential intervention. When President Reagan campaigned hard for Republican senatorial candidates in 1986, he, too, failed to have much impact.

For a while, scholars thought congressional candidates might benefit from the president's coat-tails: they might ride into office on the strength of the popularity of a president of their own party. It is true, as can be seen from Table 14.1, that a winning president will often find that his party's strength in Congress increases.

But there are good reasons to doubt whether the pattern observed in Table 14.1 is the result of presidential coattails. For one thing, there are some exceptions. Eisenhower won 57.4 percent of the vote in 1956, but the Republicans lost seats in the House and Senate. Kennedy won in 1960, but the Democrats lost seats in the House and gained but one in the Senate. When Nixon was re-elected in 1972 with one of the largest majorities in history, the Republicans lost seats in the Senate.

Careful studies of voter attitudes and of how presidential and congressional candidates fare in the same districts suggest that, whatever may once have been the influence of coattails, their effect has declined in recent years and is quite small today. The weakening of party loyalty and of party organizations, combined with the enhanced ability of members of Congress to build secure relations with their constituents, has tended to insulate congressional elections from presidential

TABLE 14.1 **Partisan Gains or Losses in Congress in Presidential Election Years**

Year	President	Party	Gains or Losses of President's Party In:	
			House	Senate
1932	Roosevelt	Dem.	+90	+9
1936	Roosevelt	Dem.	+12	+7
1940	Roosevelt	Dem.	+7	−3
1944	Roosevelt	Dem.	+24	−2
1948	Truman	Dem.	+75	+9
1952	Eisenhower	Rep.	+22	+1
1956	Eisenhower	Rep.	−3	−1
1960	Kennedy	Dem.	−20	+1
1964	Johnson	Dem.	+37	+1
1968	Nixon	Rep.	+5	+7
1972	Nixon	Rep.	+12	−2
1976	Carter	Dem.	+1	+1
1980	Reagan	Rep.	+33	+12
1984	Reagan	Rep.	+16	−2
1988	Bush	Rep.	−3	−1
1992	Clinton	Dem.	−9	+1
1996	Clinton	Dem.	+9	−2
2000	Bush	Rep.	−3	−4
2004	Bush	Rep.	+4	+4
2008	Obama	Dem.	+21	+9
2012	Obama	Dem.	+8	+2

Sources: *Updated from* Congress and the Nation, *vol. 4 (1973–1976),* 28; *Congressional Quarterly,* Guide to U.S. Elections, *928; U.S. House of Representatives website.*

FIGURE 14.1 **Presidential Popularity**

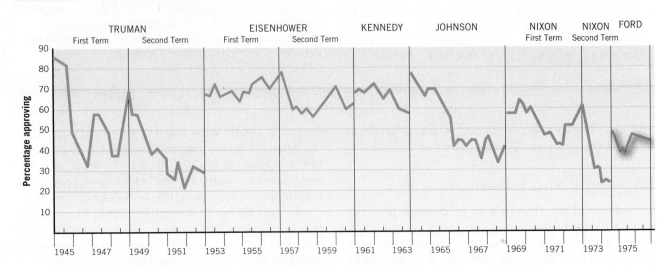

ones. When voters choose as members of Congress people of the same party as an incoming president, they probably do so out of desire for a general change and as an adverse judgment about the outgoing party's performance as a whole, not because they want to supply the new president with members of Congress favorable to him.[12] The big increase in Republican senators and representatives that accompanied the election of Ronald Reagan in 1980 was probably as much a result of the unpopularity of the outgoing president and the circumstances of various local races as it was of Reagan's coattails.

Nonetheless, a president's personal popularity may have a significant effect on how much of his program Congress passes, even if it does not affect the re-election chances of those members of Congress. Though they do not fear a president who threatens to campaign against them (or cherish one who promises to support them), members of Congress do have a sense that it is risky to oppose too adamantly the policies of a popular president. Politicians share a sense of a common fate: they tend to rise or fall together. Statistically, a president's popularity, as measured by the Gallup poll (see Figure 14.1), is associated with the proportion of his legislative proposals approved by Congress (see Figure 14.2). Other things equal, the more popular the president, the higher the proportion of his bills Congress will pass.

But use these figures with caution. How successful a president is with Congress depends not just on the numbers reported here, but on a lot of other factors as well. First, he can be "successful" on a big bill or on a trivial one. If he is successful on a lot of small matters and never on a big one, the measure of presidential victories does not tell us much. Second, a president can keep his victory

score high by not taking a position on any controversial measure. (President Carter made his views known on only 22 percent of the House votes, while President Eisenhower made his views known on 56 percent of those votes.) Third, a president can appear successful if a few bills he likes are passed, but most of his legislative program is bottled up in Congress and never comes to a vote. Given these problems, "presidential victories" are hard to measure accurately.

A fourth general caution: presidential popularity is hard to predict and can be greatly influenced by factors over which nobody, including the president, has much control. For example, when he took office in 2001, President George W. Bush's approval rating was 57 percent, nearly identical to what President Bill Clinton received in his initial rating (58 percent) in 1993. But Bush also had the highest initial *dis*approval rating (25 percent) of any president since polling began. This was undoubtedly partly due to his becoming president on the heels of the Florida vote-count controversy (see Chapter 10). Bush's approval ratings through his first six months were fairly typical for post-1960 presidents. But from the terrorist attack on the United States on September 11, 2001 through mid-2002, his approval ratings never dipped below 70 percent, and the approval ratings he received shortly after the attack (hovering around 90 percent) were the highest ever recorded. President Barack Obama's approval rating averaged 63 percent in his first six months in office, but as unemployment neared 10 percent, his popularity decreased, falling below 45 percent by the 2010 midterm elections. In 2011 and 2012, however, Obama's approval ratings typically averaged between 45 and 50 percent, and they were above 50 percent when he won re-election.

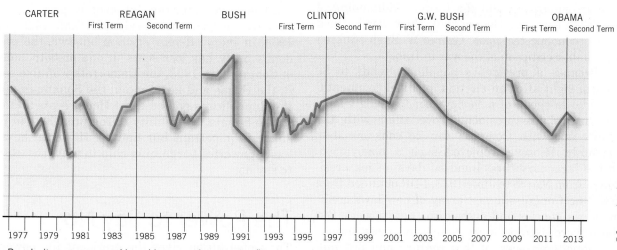

Note: Popularity was measured by asking every few months, "Do you approve of the way _____ is handling his job as president?"

Source: Thomas E. Cronin, *The State of the Presidency* (Boston: Little, Brown, 1975), 110–111. Updated with Gallup poll data, 1976 to present.

FIGURE 14.2 **Presidential Victories on Votes in Congress, 1953–2012**

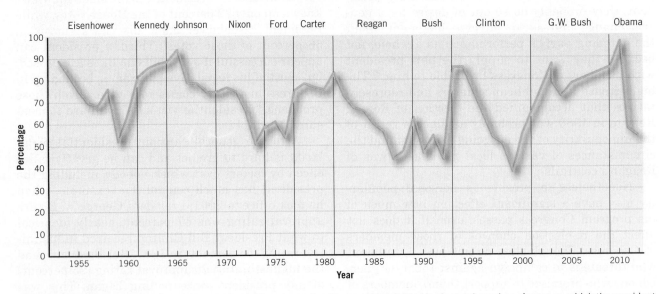

Note: Percentages indicate number of congressional votes supporting the president divided by the total number of votes on which the president has taken a position.

Source: Congressional Quarterly Weekly, various years

The Decline in Popularity

Though presidential popularity is an asset, its value tends inexorably to decline. As can be seen from Figure 14.1, every president except Eisenhower, Reagan, and Clinton lost popular support between his inauguration and the time that he left office, except when his re-election gave him a brief burst of renewed popularity. Truman was hurt by improprieties among his subordinates and by the protracted Korean War; Johnson was crippled by the increasing unpopularity of the Vietnam War; Nixon was severely damaged by the Watergate scandal; Ford was hurt by having pardoned Nixon for his part in Watergate; Carter was weakened by continuing inflation, staff irregularities, and the Iranian kidnapping of American hostages; George H. W. Bush was harmed by an economic recession. George W. Bush suffered from public criticism of the war in Iraq.

Because a president's popularity tends to be highest right after an election, political commentators like to speak of a "honeymoon," during which, presumably, the president's love affair with the people and with Congress can be consummated. Certainly, Roosevelt enjoyed such a honeymoon. In the legendary "first hundred days" of his presidency, from March to June 1933, FDR obtained from a willing Congress a vast array of new laws creating new agencies and authorizing new powers. But those were extraordinary times: the most serious economic depression of that century had put millions out of work, closed banks, impoverished farmers, and ruined the stock market. It would have

been political suicide for Congress to have blocked, or even delayed, action on measures that appeared designed to help the nation out of the crisis.

Other presidents, serving in more normal times, have not enjoyed such a honeymoon. Truman had little success with what he proposed; Eisenhower proposed little. Kennedy, Nixon, Ford, and Carter had some victories in their first year in office, but nothing that could be called a honeymoon. Only Lyndon Johnson enjoyed a highly productive relationship with Congress; until the Vietnam War sapped his strength, he rarely lost. Reagan began his administration with important victories in his effort to cut expenditures and taxes, but in his second year in office he ran into trouble.

The decay in the reputation of the president and his party in midterm is evident in Table 14.2. Since 1934, in every off-year election but two, the president's party has lost seats in one or both houses of Congress. In 1998, the Democrats won five seats in the House and lost none in the Senate; in 2002, the Republicans gained eight House seats and two in the Senate. The ability of the president to persuade is important but limited. However, he also has a powerful bargaining chip to play: the ability to say no.

The Power to Say No

The Constitution gives the president the power to veto legislation. In addition, most presidents have asserted the right of "executive privilege," or the

TABLE 14.2 **Partisan Gains or Losses in Congress in Off-Year Elections**

Year	President	Party	Gains or Losses of President's Party in:	
			House	Senate
1934	Roosevelt	Dem.	+9	+9
1938	Roosevelt	Dem.	−70	−7
1942	Roosevelt	Dem.	−50	−8
1946	Truman	Dem.	−54	−11
1950	Truman	Dem.	−29	−5
1954	Eisenhower	Rep.	−18	−1
1958	Eisenhower	Rep.	−47	−13
1962	Kennedy	Dem.	−5	+2
1966	Johnson	Dem.	−48	−4
1970	Nixon	Rep.	−12	+1
1974	Ford	Rep.	−48	−5
1978	Carter	Dem.	−12	−3
1982	Reagan	Rep.	−26	0
1986	Reagan	Rep.	−5	−8
1990	Bush	Rep.	−9	−1
1994	Clinton	Dem.	−52	−9
1998	Clinton	Dem.	+5	0
2002	G. W. Bush	Rep.	+8	+2
2006	G. W. Bush	Rep.	−30	−6
2010	Obama	Dem.	−64	−6

Sources: Norman J. Ornstein, Thomas E. Mann, and Michael J. Malbin, *Vital Statistics on Congress, 2001–2002* (Washington, D.C.: Congressional Quarterly Press, 2001), 207; web sites of U.S. House of Representatives and U.S. Senate. Note: See the Web links on the front inside cover to visit the House and Senate web sites.

right to withhold information that Congress may want to obtain from the president or his subordinates, and some presidents have tried to impound funds appropriated by Congress. These efforts by the president to say no are not only a way of blocking action but also a way of forcing Congress to bargain with him over the substance of policies.

Veto

If a president disapproves of a bill passed by both houses of Congress, he may veto it in one of two ways. One is by a **veto message**. This is a statement that the president sends to Congress accompanying the bill, within 10 days (not counting Sundays) after the bill has been passed. In it he sets forth his reasons for not signing the bill. The other is the **pocket veto**. If the president does not sign the bill within 10 days *and* Congress has adjourned within that time, then the bill will not become law. Obviously, a pocket veto can be used only during a certain time of the year—just before Congress adjourns at the end of its second session. At times, however, presidents have pocket-vetoed a bill just before Congress recessed for a summer vacation or to permit its members to campaign during an off-year election. In 1972, Senator Edward M. Kennedy of Massachusetts protested that this was unconstitutional, since a recess is not the same thing as an adjournment. In a case brought to federal court, Kennedy was upheld, and it is now understood that the pocket veto can be used only just before the life of a given Congress expires.

A bill not signed or vetoed within 10 days while Congress is still in session becomes law automatically, without the president's approval. A bill returned to Congress with a veto message can be passed over the president's objections if at least two-thirds of each house votes to override the veto. A bill that has received a pocket veto cannot be brought back to life by Congress (since Congress has adjourned), nor does such a bill carry over to the next session of Congress. If Congress wants to press the matter, it will have to start all over again by passing the bill anew in its next session, and then hope the president will sign it or, if he does not, that they can override his veto.

The president must either accept or reject the entire bill. Presidents do not have the power, possessed by most governors, to exercise a **line-item veto**, with which the chief executive can approve some provisions of a bill and disapprove others. Congress could take advantage of this by putting items the president did not like into a bill he otherwise favored, forcing him to approve those provisions along with the rest of the bill or reject the whole thing. In 1996, Congress passed a bill, which the president signed into law, that gives the president the power of "enhanced rescission." This means the president could cancel parts of a spending bill passed by Congress without vetoing the

veto message A message from the president to Congress stating that he will not sign a bill it has passed. Must be produced within 10 days of the bill's passage.

pocket veto A bill fails to become law because the president did not sign it within 10 days before Congress adjourns.

line-item veto An executive's ability to block a particular provision in a bill passed by the legislature.

entire bill. The president had five days after signing a bill to send a message to Congress rescinding some parts of what he had signed. These rescissions would take effect unless Congress, by a two-thirds vote, overturned them. Congress could choose which parts of the president's cancellations it wanted to overturn. But the Supreme Court has decided that this law is unconstitutional. The Constitution gives the president no such power to carve up a bill: he must either sign the whole bill, veto the whole bill, or allow it to become law without his signature.[13]

Nevertheless, the veto power is a substantial one, because Congress rarely has the votes to override it. From George Washington to Barack Obama, more than 2,500 presidential vetoes were cast; about 4 percent were overridden (see Table 14.3). Cleveland, Franklin Roosevelt, Truman, and Eisenhower made the most extensive use of vetoes, accounting for 65 percent of all vetoes ever cast. George W. Bush did not veto a single bill in his first term, though he issued 12 vetoes in his second term, of which four were overridden. In his first term in office, Barack Obama vetoed just two bills. Often the vetoed legislation is revised by Congress and passed in a form suitable to the president. There is no tally of how often this happens, but it is frequent enough so that both branches of government recognize that the veto, or even the threat of it, is part of an elaborate process of political negotiation in which the president has substantial powers.

Executive Privilege

The Constitution says nothing about whether the president is obliged to divulge private communications between himself and his principal advisers, but presidents have acted as if they do have that privilege of confidentiality. The presidential claim is based on two grounds. First, the doctrine of the separation of powers means that one branch of government does not have the right to inquire into the internal workings of another branch headed by constitutionally named officers. Second, the principles of statecraft and of prudent administration require that the president have the right to obtain confidential and candid advice from subordinates; such advice could not be obtained if it would quickly be exposed to public scrutiny.

For almost 200 years, there was no serious challenge to the claim of presidential confidentiality. The Supreme Court did not require the disclosure of confidential communications to or from the president.[14] Congress was never happy with this claim but until

TABLE 14.3 Presidential Vetoes, 1789–2010

	Regular Vetoes	Pocket Vetoes	Total Vetoes	Vetoes Overridden
Washington	2	—	2	—
Madison	5	2	7	—
Monroe	1	—	1	—
Jackson	5	7	12	—
Tyler	6	3	9	1
Polk	2	1	3	—
Pierce	9	—	9	5
Buchanan	4	3	7	—
Lincoln	2	4	6	—
A. Johnson	21	8	29	15
Grant	45	49	94	4
Hayes	12	1	13	1
Arthur	4	8	12	1
Cleveland	304	109	413	2
Harrison	19	25	44	1
Cleveland	43	127	170	5
McKinley	6	36	42	—
T. Roosevelt	42	40	82	1
Taft	30	9	39	1
Wilson	33	11	44	6
Harding	5	1	6	—
Coolidge	20	30	50	4
Hoover	21	16	37	3
F. Roosevelt	372	263	635	9
Truman	180	70	250	12
Eisenhower	73	108	181	2
Kennedy	12	9	21	—
L. Johnson	16	14	30	—
Nixon	26	17	43	7
Ford	48	18	66	12
Carter	13	18	31	2
Reagan	39	39	78	9
Bush	29	15	44	1
Clinton	36	1	37	2
G. W. Bush	12	0	12	4
Obama	2		2	0

Sources: Norman J. Ornstein, Thomas E. Mann, and Michael J. Malbin, Vital Statistics on Congress, 2002–2003 *(Washington, D.C.: Congressional Quarterly Press, 2003), 207; The American Presidency Project of the University of California at Santa Barbara; Office of the Clerk of the U.S. House of Representatives web site United States Senate web site*

1973 did not seriously dispute it. Indeed, in 1962, a Senate committee explicitly accepted a claim by President Kennedy that his secretary of defense, Robert S. McNamara, was not obliged to divulge the identity of Defense Department officials who had censored certain speeches by generals and admirals.

In 1974, the Supreme Court for the first time met the issue directly. A federal special prosecutor sought tape recordings of White House conversations between President Nixon and his advisers as part of his investigation of the Watergate scandal. In the case of *United States v. Nixon,* the Supreme Court, by a vote of 8 to 0 held that while there may be a sound basis for the claim of executive privilege, especially where sensitive military or diplomatic matters are involved, there is no "absolute unqualified Presidential privilege of immunity from judicial process under all circumstances."[15] To admit otherwise would be to block the constitutionally defined function of the federal courts to decide criminal cases.

Thus, Nixon was ordered to hand over the disputed tapes and papers to a federal judge so that the judge could decide which were relevant to the case at hand and allow those to be introduced into evidence. In the future, another president may well persuade the Court that a different set of records or papers is so sensitive as to require protection, especially if there is no allegation of criminal misconduct requiring the production of evidence in court. As a practical matter, it seems likely that presidential advisers will be able, except in unusual cases such as Watergate, to continue to give private advice to the president.

In 1997 and 1998, President Clinton was sued while in office by a private person, Paula Jones, who claimed he had solicited sex from her in ways that hurt her reputation. In defending himself against that and other matters, his lawyers attempted to claim executive privilege for Secret Service officers and government-paid lawyers who worked with him, but federal courts held that not only could a president be sued, but these other officials could not claim executive privilege.[16] One unhappy consequence of this episode is that the courts have greatly weakened the number of officials with whom the president can speak in confidence. It is not easy to run an organization when the courts can later compel your associates to testify about everything you said.

Impoundment of Funds

From time to time, presidents have refused to spend money appropriated by Congress. Truman did not spend all that Congress wanted spent on the armed forces, and Johnson did not spend all that Congress made available for highway construction. Kennedy refused to spend money appropriated for new weapons systems that he did not like. Indeed, the precedent for impounding funds goes back at least to the administration of Thomas Jefferson.

But what has precedent is not thereby constitutional. The Constitution is silent on whether the president *must* spend the money that Congress appropriates; all it says is that the president cannot spend money that Congress has *not* appropriated. The major test of presidential power in this respect occurred during the Nixon administration. Nixon wished to reduce federal spending. He proposed in 1972 that Congress give him the power to reduce federal spending so that it would not exceed $250 billion for the coming year. Congress, under Democratic control, refused. Nixon responded by pocket-vetoing 12 spending bills and then impounding funds appropriated under other laws that he had not vetoed.

Congress in turn responded by passing the Budget Reform Act of 1974, which, among other things, requires the president to spend all appropriated funds unless he first tells Congress what funds he wishes not to spend and Congress, within 45 days, agrees to delete the items. If he wishes simply to delay spending the money, he need only inform Congress, but Congress then can refuse the delay by passing a resolution requiring the immediate release of the money. Federal courts have upheld the rule that the president must spend, without delay for policy reasons, money that Congress has appropriated.

Signing Statements

Since at least the presidency of James Monroe, the White House has issued statements at the time the president signs a bill that has been passed by

LANDMARK CASES

Powers of the President

- **United States v. Nixon (1974):** Though the president is entitled to receive confidential advice, he can be required to reveal material related to a criminal prosecution.

- **Nixon v. Fitzgerald (1982):** The president may not be sued while in office.

- **Clinton v. Jones (1997):** The president may be sued for actions taken before he became president.

signing statement A presidential document that reveals what the president thinks of a new law and how it ought to be enforced.

Congress. These statements have had several purposes: to express presidential attitudes about the law, to tell the executive branch how to implement it, or to declare that the president thinks some part of the law is unconstitutional. President Andrew Jackson, for example, issued a statement in 1830 saying that a law designed to build a road from Chicago to Detroit should not cross the Michigan boundary (and so not get to Chicago). Congress complained, but Jackson's view prevailed and the road did not get to Chicago.

In the 20th century, these statements became common. President Reagan issued 71, President George H. W. Bush signed 141, and President Clinton inked 105. By the late 1980s, they were published in legal documents as part of the legislative history of a bill.[17] During his two terms, President George W. Bush signed more than 150, and in so doing, he challenged more than 1,200 sections of legislation, about double the number challenged by all of his predecessors. As of mid-2013, President Obama (who campaigned against the use of signing statements) had signed 23.[18]

Naturally, members of Congress are upset by this practice. To them, a **signing statement** often blocks the enforcement of a law Congress has passed and so it is equivalent to an unconstitutional line-item veto. But presidential advisers have defended these documents, arguing (as did an assistant attorney general in the Clinton administration) that they not only clarify how the law should be implemented but also allow the president to declare what part of the law is in his view unconstitutional and thus ought not to be enforced at all.[19]

While the Supreme Court has allowed signing statements to clarify the unclear legislative intent of a law, it has never given a clear verdict about the constitutional significance of such documents.[20] By 2007, the Democratic Congress was considering a challenge to the practice, and President Barack Obama issued a memo less than three months after taking office stating that he would use signing statements only to protest unconstitutional provisions on legislation, not for policy disagreements. But even with unified government, President Obama issued a few signing statements during his first year in office, and members of Congress criticized him for doing so. The struggle over signing statements is another illustration of what one scholar has called the "invitation to struggle" that the Constitution has created between the president and Congress.[21]

Presidential Character

Although all presidents share certain constitutional and political powers, every president brings to the White House a distinctive personality; the way the White House is organized and run will reflect that personality. Moreover, the public will judge the president not only in terms of what he accomplishes, but also in terms of its perception of his character. Thus, personality plays a more important role in explaining the presidency than it does in explaining Congress.

Dwight Eisenhower brought an orderly, military style to the White House. He was accustomed to delegating authority and to having careful and complete staff work done for him by trained specialists. Though critics often accused him of having a bumbling, incoherent manner of speaking, in fact much of that was a public disguise—a strategy for avoiding being pinned down in public on matters where he wished to retain freedom of action. His private papers reveal a very different Eisenhower—sharp, precise, deliberate.

John Kennedy brought a very different style to the presidency. He projected the image of a bold, articulate, and amusing leader who liked to surround himself with talented amateurs. Instead of clear, hierarchical lines of authority, there was a pattern of personal rule and an atmosphere of improvisation. Kennedy did not hesitate to call very junior subordinates directly and tell them what to do, bypassing the chain of command.

Lyndon Johnson was a master legislative strategist who had risen to be majority leader of the Senate on the strength of his ability to persuade other politicians in face-to-face encounters. He was a consummate deal maker who, having been in Washington for 30 years before becoming president, knew everybody and everything. As a result he tried to make every decision himself. But the style that served him well in political negotiations did not serve him well in speaking to the country at large, especially when trying to retain public support for the war in Vietnam.

Richard Nixon was a highly intelligent man with a deep knowledge of and interest in foreign policy, coupled with a deep suspicion of the media, his political rivals, and the federal bureaucracy. In contrast to Johnson, he disliked personal confrontations and tended to shield himself behind an elaborate staff system. Distrustful of the cabinet agencies, he tried first to centralize power in the White House and then to put into key cabinet posts former White House aides loyal to him. Like Johnson, his personality made it difficult for him to mobilize popular support. Eventually, he was forced to resign under the threat of impeachment arising out of his role in the Watergate scandal.

Gerald Ford, before being appointed vice president, had spent his political life in Congress and was at home with the give-and-take, discussion-oriented procedures of that body. He was also a genial man who liked talking to people. Thus, he preferred the circular to the pyramid system of White House organization. But this meant that many decisions were made in a disorganized fashion in which key people—and sometimes key problems—were not taken into account.

Jimmy Carter was an outsider to Washington and boasted of it. A former Georgia governor, he was determined not to be "captured" by Washington insiders. He also was a voracious reader with a wide range of interests and an appetite for detail. These dispositions led him to try to do many things and to do them personally. Like Ford, he began with a circular structure; unlike Ford, he based his decisions on reading countless memos and asking detailed questions. His advisers finally decided that he was trying to do too much in too great detail, and toward the end of his term he shifted to a pyramid structure.

Ronald Reagan was also an outsider, a former governor of California. But unlike Carter, he wanted to set the broad directions of his administration and leave the details to others. He gave wide latitude to subordinates and to cabinet officers, within the framework of an emphasis on lower taxes, less domestic spending, a military buildup, and a tough line with the Soviet Union. He was a superb leader of public opinion, earning the nickname "The Great Communicator."

George H. W. Bush lacked Reagan's speaking skills and was much more of a hands-on manager. Drawing on his extensive experience in the federal government (he had been vice president, director of the CIA, ambassador to the United Nations, representative to China, and a member of the House), Bush made decisions on the basis of personal contacts with key foreign leaders and Washington officials.

Bill Clinton, like Carter, paid a lot of attention to public policy and preferred informal, ad hoc arrangements for running his office. Unlike Carter, he was an effective speaker who could make almost any idea sound plausible. He was elected as a centrist Democrat but immediately pursued liberal policies such as comprehensive health insurance. When those failed and the Republicans won control of Congress in 1994, Clinton became a centrist again. His sexual affairs became the object of major investigations, and he was impeached by the House but acquitted by the Senate.

George W. Bush, the 43rd president, entered office as an outsider from Texas, but he was an outsider with a difference: his father had served as the 41st president of the United States, his late paternal grandfather had served as a U.S. senator from Connecticut, and he won the presidency only after the U.S. Supreme Court halted a recount of ballots in Florida, where his brother was governor. During the campaign, he focused almost entirely on domestic issues, especially cutting taxes and reforming education. A deeply religious man, he talked openly about how he had stopped drinking only after he had found God. He ran as a "compassionate conservative" concerned about America's needy children and families. Bush, who had earned an advanced degree in business administration from Harvard, ran a very tight White House ship, insisting that meetings run on time and that press contacts be strictly controlled. He turned back public doubts about his intellect through self-deprecating humor. Following the terrorist attack on America on September 11, 2001, his agenda shifted almost entirely to foreign and military affairs, the war on terror, and the issue of homeland security.

Barack Obama succeeded Bush in 2009. He was the first African American to win a major party's presidential nomination and only the third person elected to the presidency while a sitting U.S. Senator. After Harvard, he taught constitutional law part-time at the University of Chicago. After entering politics and winning an Illinois State Senate seat, he was elected to the U.S. Senate in 2004. His electrifying speech at the 2004 Democratic National Convention catapulted him to national attention. He criticized Democratic presidential candidates who had supported military action against Iraq, and he campaigned in 2008 as the candidate of change and hope ("Yes we can!" was his most popular mantra). He came to office in January 2009 amid a global economic crisis that included devastating losses in America's real-estate sector and financial markets. In his first term in office, he passed the largest budget in U.S. history and enacted legislation for comprehensive health insurance.

The Office of the President

It was not until 1857 that the president was allowed to have a private secretary paid for with public funds, and it was not until after the assassination of President McKinley in 1901 that the president was given a Secret Service bodyguard. The president was not able to submit a single presidential budget until after 1921, when the Budget and Accounting Act was passed and the Bureau of the Budget (now called the Office of Management and Budget) was created. Grover Cleveland personally answered the White *pyramid structure* A president's subordinates report to him through a clear chain of command headed by a chief of staff.

circular structure Several of the president's assistants report directly to him.

ad hoc structure Several subordinates, cabinet officers, and committees report directly to the president on different matters.

House telephone, and Abraham Lincoln often answered his own mail.

Today, of course, the president has hundreds of people assisting him, and the trappings of power—helicopters, guards, limousines—are plainly visible. The White House staff has grown enormously. (Just how big the staff is, no one knows. Presidents like to pretend that the White House is not the large bureaucracy that it in fact has become.) Add to this the opportunities for presidential appointments to the cabinet, the courts, and various agencies, and the resources at the disposal of the president would appear to be awesome. That conclusion is partly true and partly false, or at least misleading, and for a simple reason. If the president was once helpless for lack of assistance, he now confronts an army of assistants so large that it constitutes a bureaucracy he has difficulty controlling.

The ability of a presidential assistant to affect the president is governed by the rule of propinquity: in general, power is wielded by people in the room when a decision is made. Presidential appointments can thus be classified in terms of their proximity, physical and political, to the president. There are three degrees of propinquity: the White House Office, the Executive Office, and the cabinet.

The White House Office

The president's closest assistants have offices in the White House, usually in the West Wing of that building. Their titles often do not reveal the functions that they actually perform: "counsel," "counselor," "assistant to the president," "special assistant," "special consultant," and so forth. The actual titles vary from one administration to another, but in general the men and women who hold them oversee the political and policy interests of the president. As part of the president's personal staff, these aides do not have to be confirmed by the Senate; the president can hire and fire them at will. In 2012, the Obama White House had more than 460 staff members and a budget of almost $38 million.

There are essentially three ways in which a president can organize his personal staff—through the "pyramid," "circular," and "ad hoc" methods. In a **pyramid structure**, used by Eisenhower, Nixon,

Reagan, both Presidents Bush, and (after a while) Clinton, most assistants report through a hierarchy to a chief of staff, who then deals directly with the president. In a **circular structure**, used by Carter, cabinet secretaries and assistants report directly to the president. In an **ad hoc structure**, used for a while by President Clinton, task forces, committees, and informal groups of friends and advisers deal directly with the president. For example, the Clinton administration's health care policy planning was spearheaded not by Health and Human Services secretary Donna E. Shalala, but by First Lady Hillary Rodham Clinton and a White House adviser, Ira Magaziner. Likewise, its initiative to reform the federal bureaucracy (the National Performance Review) was led not by Office of Management and Budget director Leon E. Panetta, but by an adviser to Vice President Gore, Elaine Kamarck.[22]

It is common for presidents to mix methods. For example, Franklin Roosevelt alternated between the circular and ad hoc methods in the conduct of his domestic policy and sometimes employed a pyramid structure when dealing with foreign affairs and military policy.

Taken individually, each method of organization has advantages and disadvantages. A pyramid structure provides for an orderly flow of information and decisions, but does so at the risk of isolating or misinforming the president. The circular method has the virtue of giving the president a great deal of information, but at the price of confusion and conflict among cabinet secretaries and assistants. An ad hoc structure allows great flexibility, minimizes bureaucratic inertia, and generates ideas and information from disparate channels, but it risks cutting the president off from the government officials who are ultimately responsible for translating presidential decisions into policy proposals and administrative action.

All presidents claim they are open to many sources of advice, and some presidents try to guarantee that openness by using the circular method of staff organization. President Carter liked to describe his office as a wheel, with himself as the hub and his several assistants as spokes. But most presidents discover, as did Carter, that the difficulty of managing the large White House bureaucracy and of conserving their own limited supply of time and energy makes it necessary for them to rely heavily on one or two key subordinates. Carter, in July 1979, dramatically altered the White House staff organization by elevating Hamilton Jordan to the post of chief of staff, with the job of coordinating the work of the other staff assistants.

At first, President Reagan adopted a compromise between the circle and the pyramid, putting the

HOW THINGS WORK

The Myth and Reality of the White House Office

The Myth

The White House Office was created in the 1930s following recommendations made by the President's Commission on Administrative Management. The principles underlying those recommendations have been endorsed by almost every presidential chief of staff since then. The key ones are:

1. *Small is beautiful.* The presidential staff should be small. At first, there were only six assistants.

2. *A passion for anonymity.* The president's personal assistants should stay out of the limelight.

3. *Honest brokers.* The presidential staff should not make decisions for the president; it should only coordinate the flow of information to the president.

The Reality

Increasingly, the operations of the White House Office seem to reflect almost the exact opposite of these principles.

1. *Big is better.* The White House staff has grown enormously in size. Hundreds now work there.

2. *Get out front.* Key White House staffers have become household words—Henry Kissinger (under Nixon and Ford), H. R. Haldeman (under Nixon), Hamilton Jordan (under Carter), Howard Baker (under Reagan), George Stephanopoulos (under Clinton), Karl Rove (under G. W. Bush), and David Axelrod (under Obama).

3. *Be in charge.* Cabinet officers regularly complain that White House staffers are shutting them out and making all the important decisions. Congressional investigations have revealed the power of such White House aides as Haldeman, John Poindexter, and Lieutenant Colonel Oliver North.

Why the Gap Between Myth and Reality?

The answer is—the people and the government. The people expect much more from presidents today; no president can afford to say, "We're too busy here to worry about that." The government is much more complex, and so leadership requires more resources. Even conservatives such as Ronald Reagan have been activist presidents.

Source: Adapted from Samuel Kernell and Samuel L. Popkin, eds., *Chief of Staff* (Berkeley: University of California Press, 1986), 193–232.

White House under the direction of three key aides. At the beginning of his second term in 1985, however, the president shifted to a pyramid, placing all his assistants under a single chief of staff. Clinton began with an ad hoc system and then changed to one more like a pyramid. Each assistant has, of course, others working for him or her, sometimes a large number. There are, at a slightly lower level of status, "special assistants to the president" for various purposes. (Being "special" means, paradoxically, being less important.)

Typically, senior White House staff members are drawn from the ranks of the president's campaign staff—longtime associates in whom he has confidence. A few members, however, will be experts brought in after the campaign: such was the case, for example, with Henry Kissinger, a former Harvard professor who became President Nixon's assistant for national security affairs. The offices these men and women occupy often are small and crowded (Kissinger's was not much bigger than the one he had while a professor at Harvard), but their occupants willingly put up with any discomfort in exchange for the privilege (and the power) of being *in* the White

House. The arrangement of offices—their size, and especially their proximity to the president's Oval Office—is a good measure of the relative influence of the people in them.

To an outsider, the amount of jockeying among the top staff for access to the president may seem comical or even perverse. The staff attaches enormous significance to whose office is closest to the president's, who can see him on a daily as opposed to a weekly basis, who can get an appointment with the president and who cannot, and who has a right to see documents and memoranda just before they go to the Oval Office. To be sure, there is ample grist here for Washington political novels. But there is also something important at stake: it is not simply a question of power plays and ego trips. Who can see the president and who sees and "signs off" on memoranda going to the president affect in important ways who influences policy and thus whose goals and beliefs become embedded in policy.

For example, if a memo from a secretary of the treasury who believes in free trade can go directly to the president, the president may be more likely to support free trade (low tariffs). On the other hand,

cabinet The heads of the 15 executive branch departments of the federal government.

if that memo must be routed through the office of the assistant to the president for political affairs, who is worried about the adverse effects of foreign competition on jobs in the American steel industry because the votes of steelworkers are important to the president's re-election campaign, then the president may be led to support higher tariffs.

The Executive Office of the President

Agencies in the Executive Office report directly to the president and perform staff services for him but are not located in the White House itself. Their members may or may not enjoy intimate contact with him; some agencies are rather large bureaucracies. The top positions in these organizations are filled by presidential appointment, but unlike the White House staff positions, these appointments must be confirmed by the Senate.

The principal agencies in the Executive Office are:

- Office of Management and Budget (OMB)
- Director of National Intelligence (DNI)
- Council of Economic Advisers (CEA)
- Office of Personnel Management (OPM)
- Office of the U.S. Trade Representative

Of all the agencies in the Executive Office of the President, perhaps the most important in terms of the president's need for assistance in administering the federal government is the Office of Management and Budget. First called the Bureau of the Budget when it was created in 1921, it became OMB in 1970 to reflect its broader responsibilities. Today it does considerably more than assemble and analyze the figures that go each year into the national budget the president submits to Congress. It also studies the organization and operations of the executive branch, devises plans for reorganizing various departments and agencies, develops ways of getting better information about government programs, and reviews proposals that cabinet departments want included in the president's legislative program.

The OMB has a staff of more than 500 people, almost all career civil servants, many of high professional skill and substantial experience. Traditionally, OMB has been a nonpartisan agency—experts serving all presidents, without regard to party or ideology. Starting with the Reagan administration, however, OMB has played a major role in advocating policies rather than merely analyzing them. David Stockman, President Reagan's OMB director, was the primary architect of the 1981 and 1985 budget cuts proposed by the president and enacted by Congress. Stockman's proposals often were adopted over the objections of the affected department heads. In 2001, President George W. Bush's OMB director, Mitch Daniels, also participated fully in West Wing political strategy sessions; he later was elected governor of Indiana. President Obama's first OMB director, Peter Orzag, was highly active in the administration's health-care reform initiative. In President Obama's second term, he appointed Sylvia Mathews Burwell, a former executive in the Gates Foundation and former OMB staffer under President Clinton, to head OMB. Whether Burwell's appointment presaged a return to OMB's earlier tradition as a mostly nonpartisan body remains to be seen.

The Cabinet

The **cabinet** is a product of tradition and hope. At one time, the heads of the federal departments met regularly with the president to discuss matters, and some people, especially those critical of strong presidents, would like to see this kind of collegial decision making reestablished. But in fact this role of the cabinet is largely a fiction. Indeed, the Constitution does not even mention the cabinet (though the Twenty-fifth Amendment implicitly defines it as consisting of "the principal offices of the executive departments"). When Washington tried to get his cabinet to work together, its two strongest members—Alexander Hamilton and Thomas Jefferson—spent most of their time feuding. The cabinet, as a presidential committee, did not work any better for John Adams or Abraham Lincoln, for Franklin Roosevelt or John Kennedy. Dwight Eisenhower is almost the only modern president who came close to making the cabinet a truly deliberative body: he gave it a large staff, held regular meetings, and listened to opinions expressed there. But even under Eisenhower, the cabinet did not have much influence over presidential decisions, nor did it help him gain more power over the government.

By custom, cabinet officers are the heads of the 15 major executive departments. These departments, together with the dates of their creation and the approximate number of their employees, are given in Table 14.4. The order of their creation is unimportant except in terms of protocol: where one sits at cabinet meetings is determined by the age of the department that one heads. Thus, the secretary of state sits next to the president on one side and the

TABLE 14.4 The Cabinet Departments

Department	Created	Approximate Employment (2012)
State	1789	39,200*
Treasury	1789	104,100
Defense[a]	1947	761,533
Justice	1789	116,303
Interior	1849	69.702
Agriculture[b]	1889	.91,278
Commerce	1913	44,996
Labor	1913	16,816
Health and Human Services[c]	1953	86,532
Housing and Urban Development	1965	9,114
Transportation	1966	57,042
Energy	1977	15,715
Education	1979	4,294
Veterans Affairs	1989	328,088
Homeland Security	2002	197,627

[a]Formerly the War Department, created in 1789. Figures are for civilians only.

[b]Agriculture Department created in 1862; made part of cabinet in 1889.

[c]Originally Health, Education and Welfare; reorganized in 1979.

Note: Department of State figure taken from: US Census Bureau. "The 2012 Statistical Abstract: The National Data Book." Census.gov. Last modified September 30, 2011. This figure is used due to the fact that there are major discrepancies in how to count foreign service and foreign service national employees. The figure in the FedScope source is inordinately low, compared to most State Department estimates.

Source: US Office of Personnel Management. "Employment - December 2012: Cabinet-Level Agencies." *FedScope.*

secretary of the treasury next to him on the other. Down at the foot of the table are the heads of the newer departments.

The president appoints or directly controls vastly more members of his cabinet departments than does the British prime minister. The reason is simple: the president must struggle with Congress for control of these agencies, while the prime minister has no rival branch of government that seeks this power. Presidents get more appointments than prime ministers to make up for what the separation of powers denies them.

This abundance of political appointments, however, does not give the president ample power over the departments. The secretary of Health and Human Services (HHS) reports to the president and has a few hundred political appointees to assist him

or her in responding to the president's wishes. But the secretary of HHS heads an agency with more than 74,000 employees, 11 operating divisions, hundreds of grant-making programs, and a budget of approximately $900 billion (of which about $80 billion is for discretionary spending; 85 percent of the budget is for spending on Medicare and Medicaid).[23] Likewise, the secretary of Housing and Urban Development (HUD) spends most of his or her time on departmental business and vastly less on talking to the president. It is hardly surprising that the secretary is largely a representative of HUD to the president than his representative to HUD. And no one should be surprised that the secretary of HUD rarely finds much to talk about with the secretary of defense at cabinet meetings.

Having the power to make these appointments does give the president one great advantage: he has a lot of opportunities to reward friends and political supporters. In the Education Department, for example, President Clinton found jobs for onetime mayors, senators, state legislators, and campaign aides.

Independent Agencies, Commissions, and Judgeships

The president also appoints people to four dozen or so agencies and commissions that are not considered part of the cabinet and that by law often have a quasi-independent status. The difference between an "executive" and an "independent" agency is not precise. In general, it means the heads of executive agencies serve at the pleasure of the president and can be removed at his discretion. On the other hand, the heads of many independent agencies serve for fixed terms of office and can be removed only "for cause" (see box on page 367).

The president can also appoint federal judges, subject to the consent of the Senate. Judges serve for life unless they are removed by impeachment and conviction. The reason for the special barriers to the removal of judges is that they represent an independent branch of government as defined by the Constitution, and limits on presidential removal powers are necessary to preserve that independence.

One new feature of appointing top government officials is the increasing use of "acting" appointments. An acting appointee holds office until the Senate acts on his or her nomination. In 1998, acting officials held one-fifth of all of the Clinton administration's cabinet-level (or subcabinet-level)* jobs. Some were in office for many months.

Subcabinet refers to undersecretary, deputy secretary, and assistant secretaries in each cabinet department.

Many senators feel that this violates their right to consent to appointments and in particular violates the Vacancies Act passed in 1868. That law limits acting appointees to 120 days in office. If the Senate takes no action during those 120 days, the acting official may stay in office until he or she, or someone else, is confirmed for the post. Administration officials defend the practice as necessary given the slow pace of confirmations; senators attack it as an opportunity for a president to fill up his administration with unconfirmed officials.

Who Gets Appointed

As we have seen, a president can make a lot of appointments, but he rarely knows more than a few of the people whom he does appoint.

Unlike cabinet members in a parliamentary system, the president's cabinet officers and their principal deputies usually have not served with the chief executive in the legislature. Instead they come from private business, universities, think tanks, foundations, law firms, labor unions, and the ranks of former and present members of Congress as well as past state and local government officials. A president is fortunate if most cabinet members turn out to agree with him on major policy questions. President Reagan made a special effort to ensure that his cabinet members were ideologically in tune with him, but even so Secretary of State Alexander Haig soon got into a series of quarrels with senior members of the White House staff and had to resign.

The men and women appointed to the cabinet and to the subcabinet usually will have had some prior federal experience. One study of more than a thousand such appointments made by five presidents (Franklin Roosevelt through Lyndon Johnson) found that about 85 percent of the cabinet, subcabinet, and independent-agency appointees had some prior federal experience. In fact, most were in government service (at the federal, state, or local levels) just before they received their cabinet or subcabinet appointment.[24] Clearly, the executive branch is not, in general, run by novices.

Many of these appointees are what Richard Neustadt has called "in-and-outers": people who alternate between jobs in the federal government and ones in the private sector, especially in law firms and in universities. Donald Rumsfeld, before becoming secretary of defense to President George W. Bush, had been secretary of defense and chief of staff under President Ford and before that a member of Congress. Between his Ford and Bush services, he was an executive in a large pharmaceutical company. This pattern is quite different from that of parliamentary systems, where all the cabinet officers come from the legislature and typically are full-time career politicians.

At one time, the cabinet had in it many people with strong political followings of their own—former senators and governors and powerful local party leaders. Under Franklin Roosevelt, Truman, and Kennedy, the postmaster general was the president's campaign manager. George Washington, Abraham Lincoln, and other presidents had to contend with cabinet members who were powerful figures in their own right: Alexander Hamilton and Thomas Jefferson worked with Washington; Simon Cameron (a Pennsylvania political boss) and Salmon P. Chase (formerly governor of Ohio) worked for—and against—Lincoln. Before 1824, the post of secretary of state was regarded as a stepping stone to the presidency; and after that at least 10 persons ran for president who had been either secretary of state or ambassador to a foreign country.[25]

Of late, however, a tendency has developed for presidents to place in their cabinets people known for their expertise or administrative experience rather than for their political following. This is in part because political parties are now so weak that party leaders can no longer demand a place in the cabinet and in part because presidents want (or think they want) "experts." A remarkable illustration of this is the number of people with Ph.Ds who have entered the cabinet. President Nixon, who supposedly did not like Harvard professors, appointed two—Henry Kissinger and Daniel Patrick Moynihan—to important posts; Gerald Ford added a third, John Dunlop.

A president's desire to appoint experts who do not have independent political power is modified—but not supplanted—by his need to recognize various politically important groups, regions, and organizations. Since Robert Weaver became the first African American to serve in the cabinet (as secretary of HUD under President Johnson), it is clear that it would be quite costly for a president *not* to have one or more blacks in his cabinet. The secretary of labor must be acceptable to the AFL-CIO, the secretary of agriculture to at least some organized farmers. Each of the last three presidents (Bill Clinton, George W. Bush, and Barack Obama) appointed several women and minorities to his cabinet.

Because political considerations must be taken into account in making cabinet and agency appointments and because any head of a large organization will tend to adopt the perspective of that organization, there is an inevitable tension—even a rivalry—between the White House staff and the department heads. Staff members see themselves as extensions of the president's personality and policies;

HOW THINGS WORK

Federal Agencies

The following agencies are classified by whether the president has unlimited or limited right of removal.

"Executive" Agencies

Head can be removed at any time.

- Arms Control and Disarmament Agency
- Commission on Civil Rights
- Energy Research and Development Agency
- Environmental Protection Agency
- Federal Mediation and Conciliation Service
- General Services Administration
- National Aeronautics and Space Administration
- Postal Service
- Small Business Administration
- All cabinet departments
- Executive Office of the President

"Independent" or "Quasi-Independent" Agencies

Members serve for a fixed term.

- Federal Reserve Board (14 years)
- Consumer Product Safety Commission (6 years)
- Equal Employment Opportunity Commission (5 years)
- Communications Commission (7 years)
- Federal Deposit Insurance Corporation (6 years)
- Federal Energy Regulatory Commission (5 years)
- Maritime Commission (5 years)
- Federal Trade Commission (7 years)
- National Labor Relations Board (5 years)
- National Science Foundation (6 years)
- Securities and Exchange Commission (5 years)
- Tennessee Valley Authority (9 years)

Keystone-France/Gamma-Keystone/Getty Images

Chip Somodevilla/Getty Images

Secretary of Labor Frances Perkins (left), appointed by President Franklin Roosevelt, was the first woman cabinet member. When Condoleezza Rice was selected by President George W. Bush to be National Security Advisor, she became the first woman to hold that position (and later the first African American woman to be Secretary of State).

department heads see themselves as repositories of expert knowledge (often knowledge of why something will not work as the president hopes). White House staffers, many of them young men and women in their 20s or early 30s with little executive experience, will call department heads, often persons in their 50s with substantial executive experience, and tell them "the president wants" this or that or "the president asked me to tell you" one thing or another. Department heads try to conceal their irritation and then maneuver for some delay so they can develop their own counterproposals. On the other hand, when department heads call a White House staff person and ask to see the president, unless they are one of the privileged few in whom the president has special confidence, they often are told that "the president can't be bothered with that" or "the president doesn't have time to see you."

The President's Program

Imagine you have just spent three or four years running for president, during which time you have given essentially the same speech over and over again. You have had no time to study the issues in any depth. To reach a large television audience, you have couched your ideas largely in rather simple—if not simple-minded—slogans. Your principal advisers are political aides, not legislative specialists.

You win. You are inaugurated. Now you must *be* a president instead of just talking about it. You must fill hundreds of appointive posts, but you know personally only a handful of the candidates. You must deliver a State of the Union message to Congress only two or three weeks after you are sworn in. It is quite possible you have never read, much less written, such a message before. You must submit a new budget; the old one is hundreds of pages long, much of it comprehensible only to experts. Foreign governments, as well as the stock market, hang on your every word, interpreting many of your remarks in ways that totally surprise you. What will you do?

The Constitution is not much help. It directs you to report on the state of the union and to recommend "such measures" as you shall judge "necessary and expedient." Beyond that, you are charged to "take care that the laws be faithfully executed."

At one time, of course, the demands placed on a newly elected president were not very great, because the president was not expected to do very much. The president, on assuming office, might speak of the tariff, or relations with England, or the value of veterans' pensions, or the need for civil service reform, but he was not expected to have something to say (and offer) to everybody. Today he is.

Putting Together a Program

To develop policies on short notice, a president will draw on several sources, each with particular strengths and weaknesses:

- Interest groups

Strength: Will have specific plans and ideas.
Weakness: Will have narrow view of the public interest.

- Aides and campaign advisers

Strength: Will test new ideas for their political soundness.
Weakness: Will not have many ideas to test; inexperienced in government.

- Federal bureaus and agencies

Strength: Will know what is feasible in terms of governmental realities.
Weakness: Will propose plans that promote own agencies and will not have good information on whether plans will work.

- Outside, academic, and other specialists and experts

Strength: Will have many general ideas and criticisms of existing programs.
Weakness: Will not know the details of policy or have good judgment as to what is feasible.

There are essentially two ways for a president to develop a program. One, exemplified by Presidents Carter and Clinton, is to have a policy on almost everything. To do this, they worked endless hours and studied countless documents, trying to learn something about and then state their positions on, a large number of issues. The other method, illustrated by President Reagan, is to concentrate on three or four major initiatives or themes and leave everything else to subordinates.

But even when a president has a governing philosophy, as did Reagan, he cannot risk plunging ahead on his own. He must judge public and congressional reaction to this program before he commits himself fully to it. Therefore, he often will allow parts of his program to be "leaked" to the press, or "floated" as a trial balloon. Reagan's commitment to a 30 percent tax cut and larger military expenditures was so well known that it required no leaking, but he did have to float his ideas on Social Security and certain budget cuts to test popular reaction. His opponents in the bureaucracy did exactly the same thing, hoping for the opposite effect. They leaked controversial parts of the program in an effort to discredit the whole policy. This process of testing the winds by a president and his critics helps explain why so many news stories coming from Washington mention no person by name but only an anonymous "highly placed source."

In addition to the risks of adverse reaction, the president faces three other constraints on his ability to plan a program. One is the sheer limit of his time and attention span. Every president works harder than he has ever worked before. A 90-hour week is typical. Even so, he has great difficulty keeping up with all the things he is supposed to know and make decisions about. For example, Congress during an average year passes between 400 and 600 bills, each of which the president must sign, veto, or allow to take effect without his signature. Scores of people wish to see him. Hundreds of phone calls must be made to members of Congress and others in order to ask for help, to smooth ruffled feathers, or to get information. He must receive all newly appointed ambassadors and visiting heads of state and in addition have his picture taken with countless people, from a Nobel Prize winner to a child whose likeness will appear on the Easter Seal.

The second constraint is the unexpected crisis. Franklin Roosevelt obviously had to respond to a depression and to the mounting risks of world war. But most presidents get their crises when they least expect them. Consider these crises:

Kennedy

- Failure of Bay of Pigs invasion of Cuba
- Soviets put missiles in Cuba
- China invades India
- Federal troops sent to the South to protect blacks

Johnson

- Vietnam War
- Civil rights riots in major cities
- War between India and Pakistan
- Civil war in Dominican Republic
- Arab-Israeli war
- Civil rights workers murdered in South

Nixon

- Watergate scandal
- Arab-Israeli war
- Value of dollar falls in foreign trade
- Arabs raise the price of oil

Carter

- OMB director Bert Lance accused of improprieties
- Lengthy coal strike
- Seizure of American hostages in Iran
- Soviet invasion of Afghanistan

Reagan

- Poland suppresses Solidarity movement
- U.S. troops sent to Lebanon
- U.S. hostages held in Lebanon
- Civil war in Nicaragua
- Iran-Contra crisis

George H.W. Bush

- Soviet Union dissolves
- Iraq invades Kuwait

Clinton

- Civil war continues in Bosnia and other parts of the former Yugoslavia
- Investigation of possible wrongdoing of President and Mrs. Clinton in Whitewater real estate development
- Clinton impeached

George W. Bush

- Terrorist attacks on World Trade Center and Pentagon kill close to 3,000 people
- U.S.-led wars against terrorists in Afghanistan and Iraq

Obama

- Economic crisis affecting financial markets, industry, and employment

The third constraint is that the federal government and most federal programs, as well as the federal budget, can only be changed marginally, except in special circumstances. The vast bulk of federal expenditures are beyond control in any given year: the money must be spent whether the president likes it or not. Many federal programs have such strong congressional or public support that they must be left intact or modified only slightly. And this means that most federal employees can count on being secure in their jobs, whatever a president's views on reducing the bureaucracy.

The result of these constraints is that the president, at least in ordinary times, has to be selective about what he wants. He can be thought of as having a stock of influence and prestige the way that he might have a supply of money. If he wants to get the most "return" on his resources, he must "invest" that influence and prestige carefully in enterprises that promise substantial gains—in

A group of Civilian Conservation Corps workers hired by the government during the Great Depression.

public benefits and political support—at reasonable costs. Each president tends to speak in terms of changing everything at once, calling his approach a "New Deal," a "New Frontier," a "Great Society," or the "New Federalism." But beneath the rhetoric, he must identify a few specific proposals on which he wishes to bet his resources while remaining mindful of the need to leave a substantial stock of resources in reserve to handle the inevitable crises and emergencies. In recent decades, events have required every president to devote much of his time and resources to two key issues: the state of the economy and foreign affairs. What he manages to do beyond this will depend on his personal views and his sense of what the nation, as well as his re-election, requires.

And it will depend on one other thing: opinion polls. The last president who never used polls was Herbert Hoover. Franklin Roosevelt began making heavy use of them, and every president since has relied on them. Bill Clinton had voters polled about almost everything—where he should go on vacation (the West) and how to deal with Bosnia (no ground troops).

Once, when polls did not exist, politicians often believed they should do what they thought the public interest required. Now that polls are commonplace, some politicians act on the basis of what their constituents want. Scholars call the first view the trustee approach: do what the public good requires, even if the voters are skeptical. The second view is the delegate model: do what your constituents want you to do.

But there is another way of looking at polls. They may be a device not for picking a policy, but for deciding what language to use in explaining that policy. Choose a policy that helps you get re-elected or that satisfies an interest group, but then explain it with poll-tested words. President Clinton wanted to keep affirmative action (described

in the chapter titled "Civil Rights"), but knew that most voters disliked it. So he used a poll-tested phrase—"mend it but don't end it"—and then did nothing to mend it.

Finally, a president's program can be radically altered by a dramatic event or prolonged crisis. George W. Bush ran as a candidate interested in domestic issues and with little background in foreign affairs, but the terrorist attack of September 11, 2001, on the World Trade Center and the Pentagon dramatically changed his presidency into one preoccupied with foreign and military policy. Barack Obama campaigned against the war in Iraq but spent the first months of his presidency focused mainly on the country's sagging economy.

Attempts to Reorganize

One item on the presidential agenda has been the same for almost every president since Herbert Hoover: reorganizing the executive branch of government. In the wake of the terrorist attack on the United States on September 11, 2001, the president, by executive order, created a new White House Office of Homeland Security, headed by his friend and former Pennsylvania governor, Tom Ridge. In the months that followed, it became clear to all, including the president, that he had given Ridge an impossible job. For one thing, despite its obvious importance, Ridge's office, like most units with the Executive Office of the President, had only a dozen or so full-time staff, little budgetary authority, and virtually no ability to make and enforce decisions regarding how cabinet agencies operated. Nobody could meaningfully coordinate the literally dozens of administrative units that the administration's new homeland security blueprint required Ridge's office to somehow manage.

To address this problem, President Bush called for a reorganization that would create the third-largest cabinet department: encompassing 22 federal agencies, nearly 180,000 employees, and an annual budget of close to $40 billion. Among the federal agencies placed under the new Department of Homeland Security are the Coast Guard, the Customs Service, the Federal Emergency Management Agency, and the Immigration and Naturalization Service. A law authorizing the new Department of Homeland Security was enacted in November 2002, but it will take years and much effort for the new agency to become fully operational.

Important as it is, the ongoing attempt to reorganize the federal government around homeland security goals is neither the first, nor even the largest, reorganization effort made by a sitting president. With few exceptions, every president since 1928 has tried to change the structure of the staff, departments, and agencies that are theoretically subordinate to him. Every president has been appalled by the number of agencies that report to him and by the apparently helter-skelter manner in which they have grown up. But this is only one—and often not the most important—reason for wanting to reorganize. If a president wants to get something done, put new people in charge of a program, or recapture political support for a policy, it often is easier to do so by creating a new agency or reorganizing an old one than by abolishing a program, firing a subordinate, or passing a new law. Reorganization serves many objectives and thus is a recurring theme.

Legally, the president can reorganize his personal White House staff anytime he wishes. To reorganize in any important way the larger Executive Office of the President or any of the executive departments or agencies, however, Congress must first be consulted. For more than 40 years, this consultation usually took the form of submitting to Congress a reorganization plan that would take effect provided that neither the House nor the Senate passed, within 60 days, a concurrent resolution disapproving the plan (such a resolution was called a **legislative veto**). This procedure, first authorized by the Reorganization Act of 1939, could be used to change, but not create or abolish, an executive agency. In 1981, authority under that act expired, and Congress did not renew it. Two years later, the Supreme Court declared all legislative vetoes unconstitutional (see Chapter 15), and so today any presidential reorganization plan would have to take the form of a regular law, passed by Congress and signed by the president.

What has been said so far may well give the reader the impression that the president is virtually helpless. That is not the case. The *actual* power of the president can only be measured in terms of what he can accomplish. What this chapter has described so far is the office as the president finds it—the burdens, restraints, demands, complexities, and resources that he encounters on entering the Oval Office for the first time. Every president since Truman has remarked on how limited the powers of the president seem from the inside compared to what they appear to be from the outside. Franklin Roosevelt compared his struggles with the bureaucracy to punching a feather bed; Truman wrote that the power of the president was chiefly the power to persuade people to do what they ought to do anyway. After in office a year or so, Kennedy spoke to interviewers about how much more complex the world appeared than he had first supposed. Johnson and Nixon were broken by the office and the events that happened there.

Yet Franklin Roosevelt helped create the modern presidency, with its vast organizational reach, and

directed a massive war effort. Truman ordered two atomic bombs dropped on Japanese cities. Eisenhower sent American troops to Lebanon; Kennedy supported an effort to invade Cuba. Johnson sent troops to the Dominican Republic and to Vietnam; Nixon ordered an invasion of Cambodia; Reagan launched an invasion of Grenada and sponsored an antigovernment insurgent group in Nicaragua; Bush invaded Panama and sent troops to the Persian Gulf to fight Iraq; Clinton sent troops to Haiti and Bosnia; George W. Bush ordered U.S. military operations in Afghanistan and Iraq; Obama approved air strikes in Libya. Obviously Europeans, Russians, Vietnamese, Panamanians, Iraqis, and others do not think the American president is "helpless."

> *legislative veto* The authority of Congress to block a presidential action after it has taken place. The Supreme Court has held that Congress does not have this power.

Presidential Transition

No president but Franklin Roosevelt has ever served more than two terms, and since the ratification of the Twenty-second Amendment in 1951, no president will ever again have the chance. But more than tradition or the Constitution escorts presidents from office. Only about one-third of the presidents since George Washington have been elected to a second term. Of the 27 not re-elected, four died in office during their first term. But the remainder either did not seek or (more usually) could not obtain re-election.

President Reagan, moments before he was shot on March 30, 1981, by a would-be assassin. The Twenty-fifth Amendment solves the problem of presidential disability by providing for an orderly transfer of power to the vice president.

Michael Evans/The White House/National Archives and Records/Administration

Of the eight presidents who died in office, four were assassinated: Lincoln, Garfield, McKinley, and Kennedy. At least six other presidents were the objects of unsuccessful assassination attempts: Jackson, Theodore Roosevelt, Franklin Roosevelt, Truman, Ford, and Reagan. (There may have been attempts on other presidents that never came to public notice; the attempts mentioned here involved public efforts to fire weapons at presidents.)

The presidents who served two or more terms fall into certain periods, such as the Founding (Washington, Jefferson, Madison, Monroe) or wartime (Lincoln, Wilson, Roosevelt), or they happened to be in office during especially tranquil times (Monroe, McKinley, Eisenhower, Clinton), or some combination of the above. When the country was deeply divided, as during the years just before the Civil War and during the period of Reconstruction after it, it was the rare president who was re-elected.

The Vice President

Eight times a vice president has become president because of the death of his predecessor. It first happened to John Tyler, who became president in 1841 when William Henry Harrison died peacefully after only one month in office. The question for Tyler and for the country was substantial: Was Tyler simply to be the acting president and a kind of caretaker until a new president was elected, or was he to be *president* in every sense of the word? Despite criticism and despite what might have been the contrary intention of the Framers of the Constitution, Tyler decided on the latter course and was confirmed in that opinion by a decision of Congress. Ever since, the vice president has automatically become president, in title and in powers, when the occupant of the White House has died or resigned.

But if vice presidents frequently acquire office because of death, they rarely acquire it by election. Since the earliest period of the Founding, when John Adams and Thomas Jefferson were each elected president after having first served as vice president under their predecessors, there have only been three occasions when a vice president was later able to win the presidency without his president's having died in office. One was in 1836, when Martin Van Buren was elected president after having served as Andrew Jackson's vice president; the second was in 1968, when Richard Nixon became president after having served as Dwight Eisenhower's vice president eight years earlier; the third was in 1988, when George Bush succeeded Ronald Reagan. Many vice presidents who entered the Oval Office because

their predecessors died were subsequently elected to terms in their own right—Theodore Roosevelt, Calvin Coolidge, Harry Truman, and Lyndon Johnson. But no one who wishes to become president should assume that to become vice president first is the best way to get there.

The vice-presidency is just what so many vice presidents have complained about its being: a rather empty job. John Adams described it as "the most insignificant office that ever the invention of man contrived or his imagination conceived," and most of his successors would have agreed. Thomas Jefferson, almost alone, had a good word to say for it: "The second office of the government is honorable and easy, the first is but a splendid misery."[26] Daniel Webster rejected a vice-presidential nomination in 1848 with the phrase, "I do not choose to be buried until I am really dead."[27] (Had he taken the job, he would have become president after Zachary Taylor died in office, thereby achieving a remarkable secular resurrection.) For all the good and bad jokes about the vice-presidency, however, candidates still struggle mightily for it. John Nance Garner gave up the speakership of the House to become Franklin Roosevelt's vice president (a job he later cuttingly valued as "not worth a pitcher of warm spit"[†]), and Lyndon Johnson gave up the majority leadership of the Senate to become Kennedy's. Truman, Nixon, Humphrey, Mondale, and Gore all left reasonably secure Senate seats for the vice-presidency.

The only official task of the vice president is to preside over the Senate and to vote in case of a tie. Even this is scarcely time-consuming, as the Senate chooses from among its members a president pro tempore, as required by the Constitution, who (along with others) presides in the absence of the vice president. The vice president's leadership powers in the Senate are weak, especially when the vice president is of a different party from the majority of the senators. But on occasion the vice president can become very important. Right after the terrorists attacked the United States in 2001, President Bush was in his airplane while his advisers worried that he might be attacked next. Vice President Cheney was quickly hidden away in a secret, secure location so he could run the government if anything happened to President Bush. And for many months thereafter, Cheney stayed in this location in case he suddenly became president. But absent a crisis, the vice president is, at best, only an adviser to the president.

[†]The word he actually used was a good deal stronger than *SPIT*, but historians are decorous.

Problems of Succession

If the president should die in office, the right of the vice president to assume that office has been clear since the time of John Tyler. But two questions remain: What if the president falls seriously ill, but does not die? And if the vice president steps up, who then becomes the new vice president?

The first problem has arisen on a number of occasions. After President James A. Garfield was shot in 1881, he lingered through the summer before he died. President Woodrow Wilson collapsed from a stroke in 1919, became a virtual recluse for several months, and then sharply curtailed activity for the rest of his term. Eisenhower had three serious illnesses while in office; Reagan was shot during his first term and hospitalized during his second.

The second problem has arisen on eight occasions when the vice president became president owing to the death of the incumbent. In these cases, no elected person was available to succeed the new president, should he die in office. For many decades, the problem was handled by law. The Succession Act of 1886, for example, designated the secretary of state as next in line for the presidency should the vice president die, followed by the other cabinet officers in order of seniority. But this meant that a vice president who became president could pick his own successor by choosing his own secretary of state. In 1947, the law was changed to make the Speaker of the House and then the president pro tempore of the Senate next in line for the presidency. But that created still other problems: a Speaker or a president pro tempore is likely to be chosen because of seniority, not executive skill, and in any event might well be of the party opposite to that occupying the White House.

Both problems were addressed in 1967 by the Twenty-fifth Amendment to the Constitution. It deals with the disability problem by allowing the vice president to serve as "acting president" whenever the president declares he is unable to discharge the powers and duties of his office or whenever the vice president and a majority of the cabinet declare that the president is incapacitated. If the president disagrees with the opinion of his vice president and a majority of the cabinet, then Congress decides the issue. A two-thirds majority is necessary to confirm that the president is unable to serve.

The amendment deals with the succession problem by requiring a vice president who assumes the presidency (after a vacancy is created by death or resignation) to nominate a new vice president. This person takes office if the nomination is confirmed by a majority vote of both houses of Congress. When there is no vice president, then the 1947 law governs:

next in line are the Speaker, the Senate president, and the 15 cabinet officers, beginning with the secretary of state.

> *impeachment* Charges against a president approved by a majority of the House of Representatives.

The disability problem has not arisen since the adoption of the amendment, but the succession problem has. In 1973, Vice President Spiro Agnew resigned, having pleaded no contest to criminal charges. President Nixon nominated Gerald Ford as vice president, and after extensive hearings he was confirmed by both houses of Congress and sworn in. Then on August 9, 1974, Nixon resigned the presidency—the first man to do so—and Ford became president. He nominated as his vice president Nelson Rockefeller, who was confirmed by both houses of Congress—again, after extensive hearings—and was sworn in on December 19, 1974. For the first time in history, the nation had as its two principal executive officers men who had not been elected to either the presidency or the vice-presidency. It is a measure of the legitimacy of the Constitution that this arrangement caused no crisis in public opinion.

Impeachment

There is one other way—besides death, disability, or resignation—by which a president can leave office before his term expires, and that is by impeachment. Not only the president and vice president, but also all "civil officers of the United States" can be removed by being impeached and convicted. As a practical matter civil officers—cabinet secretaries, bureau chiefs, and the like—are not subject to impeachment, because the president can remove them at any time and usually will if their behavior makes them a serious political liability. Federal judges, who serve during "good behavior"‡ and who are constitutionally independent of the president and Congress, have been the most frequent objects of impeachment.

An **impeachment** is like an indictment in a criminal trial: a set of charges against somebody, voted by (in this case) the House of Representatives. To be removed from office, the impeached officer must be convicted by a two-thirds vote of the Senate, which sits as a court, is presided over by the Chief Justice, hears the evidence, and makes its decision under whatever rules it wishes to adopt. Sixteen persons have been impeached by the House, and

---

‡"Good behavior" means a judge can stay in office until he retires or dies, unless he or she is impeached and convicted.

seven have been convicted by the Senate. The last conviction was in 1989, when two federal judges were removed from office.

Only two presidents have ever been impeached—Andrew Johnson in 1868 and Bill Clinton in 1998. Richard Nixon would surely have been impeached in 1974, had he not resigned after the House Judiciary Committee voted to recommend impeachment.

The Senate did not convict either Johnson or Clinton by the necessary two-thirds vote. The case against Johnson was entirely political—Radical Republicans, who wished to punish the South after the Civil War, were angry at Johnson, a southerner, who had a soft policy toward the South. The argument against him was flimsy.

The case against Clinton was more serious. The House Judiciary Committee, relying on the report of independent counsel Kenneth Starr, charged Clinton with perjury (lying under oath about his sexual affair with Monica Lewinsky), obstruction of justice (trying to block the Starr investigation), and abuse of power (making false written statements to the Judiciary Committee). The vote to impeach was passed by the House along party lines. The Senate vote fell far short of the two-thirds required for conviction.

Why did Clinton survive? There were many factors. The public disliked his private behavior, but did not think it amounted to an impeachable offense. (In fact, right after Lewinsky revealed her sexual affair with him, his standing in opinion polls went up.) The economy was strong, and the nation was at peace. Clinton was a centrist Democrat who did not offend most voters.

The one casualty of the entire episode was the death of the law creating the office of the Independent Counsel. Passed in 1978 by a Congress that was upset by the Watergate crisis, the law directed the attorney general to ask a three-judge panel to appoint an independent counsel whenever a high official is charged with serious misconduct. (In 1993, when the 1978 law expired, President Clinton asked that it be passed again. It was.) Eighteen people were investigated by various independent counsels from 1978 to 1999. In about half the cases, no charges were brought to court.

For a long time, Republicans disliked the law because the counsels were investigating them. After Clinton came to office, the counsels started investigating him and his associates, and so the Democrats began to oppose it. In 1999, when the law expired, it was not renewed.

A problem remains, however. How will any high official, including the president, be investigated when the attorney general, who does most investigations, is part of the president's team? One answer is to let Congress do it, but Congress may be controlled by the president's party. No one has yet solved this puzzle.

Some Founders may have thought that impeachment would be used frequently against presidents, but as a practical matter it is so complex and serious an undertaking that we can probably expect it to be reserved in the future only for the gravest forms of presidential misconduct. No one quite knows what a high crime or misdemeanor is, but most scholars agree that the charge must involve something illegal or unconstitutional, not just unpopular. Unless a president or vice president is first impeached and convicted, many experts believe he is not liable to prosecution as would be an ordinary citizen. (No one is certain, because the question has never arisen.) President Ford's pardon of Richard Nixon meant that he could not be prosecuted under federal law for things he may have done while in office.

Students may find the occasions of misconduct or disability remote and the details of succession or impeachment tedious. But the problem is not remote—succession has occurred nine times and disability at least twice—and what may appear tedious goes, in fact, to the heart of the presidency. The first and fundamental problem is to make the office legitimate. That was the great task George Washington set himself, and that was the substantial accomplishment of his successors. Despite bitter and sometimes violent partisan and sectional strife, beginning almost immediately after Washington stepped down, presidential succession has always occurred peacefully, without a military coup or a political plot. For centuries, in the bygone times of kings as well as in the present times of dictators and juntas, peaceful succession has been a rare event among the nations of the world. Many of the critics of the Constitution believed in 1787 that peaceful succession would not happen in the United States either: somehow the president would connive to hold office for life or to handpick his successor. Their predictions were wrong, though their fears are understandable.

How Powerful Is the President?

Just as members of Congress bemoan their loss of power, so presidents bemoan theirs. Can both be right?

In fact, they can. If Congress is less able to control events than it once was, it does not mean that the president is thereby more able to exercise control. The federal government *as a whole* has become more constrained, so it is less able to act decisively.

The chief source of this constraint is the greater complexity of the issues with which Washington must deal.

It was one thing to pass the Social Security Act in 1935; it is quite another thing to keep the Social Security system adequately funded. It was one thing for the nation to defend itself when attacked in 1941; it is quite another to maintain a constant military preparedness while simultaneously exploring possibilities for arms control. It was not hard to give pensions to veterans; it seems almost impossible today to find the cure for drug abuse or juvenile crime.

In the face of modern problems, all branches of government, including the presidency, seem both big and ineffectual. Add to this the much closer and more critical scrutiny of the media and the proliferation of interest groups, and it is small wonder that both presidents and members of Congress feel that they have lost power.

Presidents have come to acquire certain rules of thumb for dealing with their political problems. Among them are these:

- *Move it or lose it.* A president who wants to get something done should do it early in his term, before his political influence erodes.

- *Avoid details.* President Carter's lieutenants regret having tried to do too much. Better to have three or four top priorities and forget the rest.

- *Cabinets don't get much accomplished; people do.* Find capable White House subordinates and give them well-defined responsibility; then watch them closely.[28]

POLICY DYNAMICS: INSIDE/OUTSIDE THE BOX

The Sequester: Entrepreneurial or Majoritarian Politics?

In the spring of 2013, federal spending cuts took effect because the White House and Congress did not reach a budget agreement. The cuts, known as the "sequester," were part of the 2011 agreement to increase the debt ceiling, which stated that if the federal government did not enact a plan to cut $1.5 trillion in spending over ten years, then automatic spending reductions, divided evenly between domestic and defense spending, would be enacted.

Republican leaders in Congress presented the sequester as entrepreneurial politics. Those directly affected by the spending cuts – furloughed government employees, participants in public tours of the White House (which were halted after the sequester began) – would pay, but the public as a whole would benefit from trimming the budget deficit and achieving more moderate and sustainable federal spending of public dollars over the next decade.

The White House criticized the spending cuts as draconian efforts to limit short-term government spending at the expense of our long-term economic health. The president's economic advisers defined budgetary battles as majoritarian politics: everyone would pay for deficit spending now, which would lead to greater and more sustained economic productivity, lower unemployment, and reduced budget deficits in the future. The sequester did not cut wasteful government spending, according to the White House, but cut preschool and after-school educational opportunities in the Head Start program, halted meals for senior citizens, and reduced funds for first responders nationwide. Those who most needed assistance from the federal government were harmed most by the sequester, with significant consequences for curtailing their educational and economic opportunities in the future.

How do you think the White House and Congress should decide on immediate and long-term spending priorities? What does the United States need to do in the coming years to lower budget deficits and reduce the national debt? And how should the proposals be presented to win the most public support?

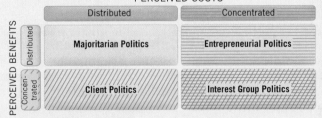

Sources: Dylan Matthews, "The Sequester: Absolutely Everything You Could Possibly Need to Know," *The Washington Post*, March 1, 2013; White House, "What You Need to Know About the Sequester," at http://www.whitehouse.gov/issues/sequester.

WHAT WOULD YOU DO?

MEMORANDUM

To: *President Sally Churchill*

From: *Office of Legislative Affairs Director Harry Washington*

Subject: *Passing budget bills under divided government*

With the opposition party in control of Congress, media pundits and other commentators are calling for the president to accept the other party's agenda for the next round of budget bills.

Arguments for:

1. With a re-election battle around the corner, the president cannot afford to get caught up in a budget battle with Congress.

2. The president's ability to gain public support for his agenda is limited, and even increased public support will not improve leverage with Congress.

3. The president should defer to Congress as the primary representative of the people in American politics.

Arguments against:

1. American politics is guided too often by campaigns, and the president will build support for re-election by acting presidential—that is, by setting the agenda for the budget and not backing down.

2. The president can build public support through speeches and other forms of communication, and

News »

Will the White House and Congress Agree on a Budget?

In the latest budget battle between the White House and Congress, the pressure on the president to accept a compromise with his political opponents is great, given the looming threat of not only a government shutdown, but also a debt default by the United States for the first time in the history of the American republic.

this support can be used as political capital to negotiate with Congress.

3. The president is the only nationally elected official in American politics (other than the vice president), and therefore is responsible for identifying and promoting public priorities, even if this means legislative battles with Congress.

Your decision:

Favor plan _____   Oppose plan _____

LEARNING OBJECTIVES

1. **How do presidents differ from prime ministers?**

   Unlike prime ministers, American presidents are elected independently of Congress, which gives them both more independence in governing and more challenges in building political coalitions.

2. **Did the Founders expect the presidency to be the most important political institution?**

   Most did not. They worried about whether the presidency would be too strong or too weak, but designed a Constitution hoping that Congress would be the most important institution. And it was, with a few exceptions, until the 20th century. Today, the strength of the presidency depends chiefly on two things: the importance of military and foreign affairs and the president's personal popularity.

3. **How have the constitutional and political powers of the presidency evolved from the founding of the United States to the present?**

Presidential power has grown significantly from its constitutional origins. Since the 1930s, the president has become the central figure in American politics, even though the president's ability to achieve political success remains highly dependent on other individuals and institutions.

4. **How do presidents make policy?**

To make policy, a president must work closely with Congress and the federal bureaucracy, while being attentive to public and political party expectations, as well as media scrutiny.

5. **Is it harder to govern when the presidency and Congress are controlled by different political parties?**

Not really. Both the Democratic and Republican parties have legislators who often vote with their party rivals. Unless the president has a big ideological majority in Congress, something that does not happen too often, he can easily lose legislative struggles. Gridlock does not in fact prevent major new pieces of legislation from being passed.

TO LEARN MORE

Official White House blog:

www.whitehouse.gov

Studies of presidents:

Miller Center of Public Affairs, University of Virginia:

www.millercenter.virginia.edu/academic/ americanpresident

The American Presidency Project, University of California at Santa Barbara:

www.presidency.ucsb.edu

Cohen, Jeffrey E. *Going Local: Presidential Leadership in the Post-Broadcast Age*. New York: Cambridge University Press, 2010. Examines how party polarization and an increasingly decentralized media have led presidents to target their public communications to local audiences over the national arena.

Corwin, Edward S. *The President: Office and Powers*, 5th ed. New York: New York University Press, 1985. Historical, constitutional, and legal development of the office.

Greenstein, Fred I. *The Presidential Difference: Leadership Style from FDR to Barack Obama*, 3rd ed. Princeton, NJ: Princeton University Press, 2009. Explores how, independent of other influences, modern presidents' respective leadership styles account for consequential changes in domestic and foreign policy decisions.

Kernell, Samuel. *Going Public: New Strategies of Presidential Leadership*, 4th ed. New Haven, CT: Yale University Press, 2007. Examines how modern presidents develop policies with an eye fixed on how best to communicate with multiple public audiences.

Neustadt, Richard E. *Presidential Power and the Modern Presidents: The Politics of Leadership from Roosevelt to Reagan*. New York: The Free Press, 1990 (original edition published in 1960). How presidents try to acquire and hold political power in the competitive world of official Washington, by a man who was both a scholar and an insider.

Peterson, Mark A. *Legislating Together: The White House and Congress from Eisenhower to Reagan*. Cambridge: Harvard University Press, 1990. Challenges the conventional view that "the president proposes, Congress disposes." Contains many excellent examples of bargaining and cooperation between Congress and the executive branch.

Polsby, Nelson W., and Aaron Wildavsky. *Presidential Elections*, 10th ed. New York: Chatham House, 2000. Excellent analysis of how campaigns and the electoral college shape the presidency.

Tulis, Jeffrey K. *The Rhetorical Presidency*. Princeton, NJ: Princeton University Press, 1987. Fascinating study of how once-powerful constitutional customs that proscribed presidents rallying the public for political support on a routine basis changed in the early 20th century.

On Franklin D. Roosevelt

Leuchtenberg, William E. *Franklin D. Roosevelt and the New Deal, 1932–1940*. New York: Harper & Row, 1963.

Maney, Richard J. *The Roosevelt Presence*. New York: Twayne, 1992.

On Harry S. Truman

Hamby, A. L. *Beyond the New Deal: Harry S. Truman and American Liberalism*. New York: Columbia University Press, 1973.

McCullough, David. *Truman*. New York: Simon and Schuster, 1984.

On Dwight D. Eisenhower

Ambrose, Stephen E. *Eisenhower*. New York: Simon and Schuster, 1984.

Greenstein, Fred I. *The Hidden-Hand Presidency: Eisenhower as Leader*. New York: Basic Books, 1982.

On John F. Kennedy

Paper, Lewis J. *The Promise and the Performance: The Leadership of John F. Kennedy*. New York: Crown, 1975.

Parmet, Herbert C. *Jack*. New York: Dial Press, 1980.

On Lyndon B. Johnson

Caro, Robert A. *The Years of Lyndon Johnson*. 3 vols. New York: Alfred Knopf, 1982–2002.

Dallek, Robert. *Lone Star Rising and Flawed Giant*. New York: Oxford University Press, 1991 and 1996.

Kearns, Doris. *Lyndon Johnson and the American Dream*. New York: Harper and Row, 1976.

On Richard M. Nixon

Ambrose, Stephen E. *Nixon*. 3 vols. New York: Simon and Schuster, 1987, 1989, 1991.

On Jimmy Carter

Bourne, Peter G. *Jimmy Carter*. New York: Scribner, 1997.

On Ronald Reagan

Cannon, Lou. *President Reagan*. New York: Simon and Schuster, 1991.

On George H. W. Bush

Han, Lori Cox. *A Presidency Upstaged: The Public Leadership of George H.W. Bush*. College Station, TX: Texas A&M University Press, 2011.

Parmet, Herbert C. *George Bush*. New York: Scribner, 1997.

On Bill Clinton

Klein, Joe. *The Natural: The Misunderstood Presidency of Bill Clinton*. New York: Doubleday, 2002.

On George W. Bush

Draper, Robert. *Dead Certain: The Presidency of George W. Bush*. New York; Free Press, 2007.

Jacobson, Gary C. *A Divider, Not a Uniter: George W. Bush and the American People*. 2d ed. (New York: Longman, 2010).

Pfiffner, James P. *Power Play: The Bush Presidency and the Constitution*. Washington, D.C.: Brookings Institution Press, 2008.

On Barack Obama

Remnick, David. *The Bridge: The Life and Rise of Barack Obama*. New York: Knopf, 2010.

Renshon, Stanley A. *Barack Obama and the Politics of Redemption*. New York: Routledge, 2011.

The Bureaucracy

1. What is "bureaucracy" and in what ways is the American bureaucracy distinctive?

2. What is "discretionary authority" and why do some bureaucrats have lots of it?

3. How does Congress exert control over the bureaucracy?

4. What happened to make the bureaucracy a "fourth branch" of American national government?

5. What are the actual size and scope of the federal bureaucracy?

6. What should be done to improve bureaucratic performance?

7. Is "red tape" all bad?

bureaucracy A large, complex organization composed of appointed officials.

There is probably not a man or woman in the United States who has not, at some time or other, complained about "the bureaucracy." Your letter was slow in getting to Aunt Minnie? The Internal Revenue Service took months to send you your tax refund? The Defense Department paid $400 for a hammer? The Occupational Safety and Health Administration told you that you installed the wrong kind of portable toilet for your farm workers? The "bureaucracy" is to blame.

For most people and politicians, *bureaucracy* is a pejorative word implying waste, confusion, red tape, and rigidity. But for scholars—and for bureaucrats themselves—*bureaucracy* is a word with a neutral, technical meaning. A **bureaucracy** is a large, complex organization composed of appointed officials. By *complex*, we mean that authority is divided among several managers; no one person is able to make all the decisions. A large corporation is a bureaucracy; so also are a big university and a government agency. With its sizable staff, even Congress has become, to some degree, a bureaucracy.

What is it about complex organizations in general, and government agencies in particular, that leads so many people to complain about them? In part, the answer is to be found in their very size and complexity. But in large measure the answer is to be found in the political context within which such agencies must operate. If we examine that context carefully, we will discover that many of the problems that we blame on "the bureaucracy" are in fact the result of what Congress, the courts, and the president do. And, if we dig just a bit deeper, we will also discover that behind just about every government bureaucracy is some set of new or old public demands. Consider, for example, Washington bureaucracies' roles with respect to keeping us safe from street criminals, cleaning up toxic waste sites, and making sure that poor children have nutritious school lunches.

THEN

The U.S. Department of Justice (USDOJ—this is bureaucracy, so enjoy all the alphabet soup) was established in 1789, but until a series of federal "crime bills" was enacted beginning in the 1960s, it had only an incidental role in crime control. For the most part, it neither funded nor worked at all closely with state and local criminal justice agencies. A USDOJ subunit, the Federal Bureau of Prisons (FBOP), was a tiny agency that held fewer inmates than many small state prison systems did.

NOW

With public support for successive federal "wars on crime" and "wars on drugs," the USDOJ and other federal agencies now spend billions of dollars each year to fund federal, state, and local agencies engaged in combating street crime, and the FBOP now runs one of the largest prison systems in the world.

THEN

Before the Environmental Protection Agency (EPA) was launched in 1970, the federal government's environmental protection activities were virtually nonexistent.

NOW

The media stories and public outcries that accompanied the discovery of lethal toxic waste sites in and around New York's Love Canal area led in 1978 to the creation of the so-called Superfund program. To administer Superfund, in 1980, the EPA expanded, and there has been an expansion in federal environmental protection efforts, and in federally directed state and local efforts as well, in most years ever since.

THEN

The first federal law providing for subsidized school lunches was passed in 1946, but it was not until the 1960s that Washington began expanding its programs in this area to include ever greater numbers of children eligible for both free (or reduced price) breakfasts and lunches.

NOW

It was only in 2010 that the U.S. Department of Agriculture (USDA)—created in 1862, made into a cabinet department in 1889, and long concerned mainly with the nation's farms and agri-businesses—was mandated by law to work with local school districts and other organizations so as to make nutritious meals (breakfasts, lunches, and snacks) available to low-income children year-round, including in the summer months when school is out.

Whatever else it may be, bureaucracy is an outgrowth of representative democracy. If people demanded that government do less or do nothing, in due course public laws would change and the agencies that exist to translate those laws into administrative action would dissolve. But that has rarely happened. Instead, six of the federal government's 15 cabinet agencies, including (next to the U.S. Department of Defense) its two largest and newest (the U.S. Department of Veterans Affairs, created in 1989, and the U.S. Department of Homeland Security, created in 2002), were created after 1964.

Distinctiveness of the American Bureaucracy

As you might expect, much the same can be said for the growth of bureaucracy in other democratic nations. Indeed, bureaucratic government has become an obvious feature of all modern societies, democratic and nondemocratic alike.

In the United States, however, three aspects of our constitutional system and political traditions give to the bureaucracy a distinctive character. First, political authority over the bureaucracy is not in one set of hands but is shared among several institutions. In a parliamentary regime, such as in the United Kingdom, the appointed officials of the national government work for the cabinet ministers, who are in turn dominated by the prime minister. In theory, and to a considerable extent in practice, British bureaucrats report to and take orders from the ministers in charge of their departments, do not deal directly with Parliament, and rarely give interviews to the press. In the United States, the Constitution permits both the president and Congress to exercise authority over the bureaucracy. Every senior appointed official has at least two masters: one in the executive branch and the other in the legislative. Often there are many more than two: Congress, after all, is not a single organization but a collection of committees, subcommittees, and individuals. This divided authority encourages bureaucrats to play one branch of government against the other and to make heavy use of the media.

Second, most of the agencies of the federal government share their functions with related agencies in state and local government. Though some federal agencies deal directly with American citizens—the Internal Revenue Service collects taxes from them, the Federal Bureau of Investigation looks into crimes for them, the Postal Service delivers mail to them—many agencies work with other organizations at other levels of government. For example, the Department of Education gives money to local school systems; the Centers for Medicare and Medicaid Services in the Department of Health and Human Services reimburses states for money spent on health care for the poor; the Department of Housing and Urban Development gives grants to cities for community development; and the Employment and Training

Administration in the Department of Labor supplies funds to local governments so that they can run job-training programs. In France, by contrast, government programs dealing with education, health, housing, and employment are centrally run, with little or no control exercised by local governments.

> **government by proxy**
> Washington pays state and local governments and private groups to staff and administer federal programs.

Third, the institutions and traditions of American life have contributed to the growth of what some writers have described as an "adversary culture," in which the definition and expansion of personal rights, and the defense of rights and claims through lawsuits as well as political action, are given central importance. A government agency in this country operates under closer public scrutiny and with a greater prospect of court challenges to its authority than in almost any other nation. Virtually every important decision of the Occupational Safety and Health Administration or of the Environmental Protection Agency is likely to be challenged in the courts or attacked by an affected party; in Sweden the decisions of similar agencies go largely uncontested.

The scope as well as the style of bureaucratic government differs. In most Western European nations, the government owns and operates large parts of the economy: the French government operates the railroads and owns companies that make automobiles and cigarettes, and the Italian government owns many similar enterprises and also the nation's oil refineries. In just about every large nation except the United States, the telephone system is owned by the government. Publicly operated enterprises account for about 12 percent of all employment in France but less than 3 percent in the United States.[1] The U.S. government regulates privately owned enterprises to a degree not found in many other countries, however. Why we should have preferred regulation to ownership as the proper government role is an interesting question to which we shall return.

Proxy Government

Much of our federal bureaucracy operates on the principle of **government by proxy**.[2] In every representative government, the voters elect legislators who make the laws, but in this country the bureaucrats often pay other people to do the work. These "other people" include state and local governments, business firms, and nonprofit organizations.

Among the programs run this way are Social Security, Medicare, much environmental protection, and the collection of income taxes by withholding

People taken by boat away from their New Orleans homes that were struck by Hurricane Katrina in 2005.

money from your paycheck. Even many military duties are contracted out.[3] In the first Gulf War in 1991, American soldiers outnumbered private contractors in the region by 60 to 1. But by 2006, there were nearly as many private workers as soldiers in Iraq. One company was paid $7.2 billion to get food and supplies to our troops there.[4]

When Hurricanes Katrina and Rita hit our Gulf Coast, the nation's response was managed by a small and weak group, the Federal Emergency Management Agency (FEMA). When the levees broke, it had only 2,600 employees; most of the help it was to provide came through "partners," such as state and local agencies, and some of these were not very competent.

Critics of our government-by-proxy system argue that it does not keep track of how the money we send to public and private agencies is used. Congress, of course, could change matters around, but it has an interest in setting policies and defining goals, not in managing the bureaucracy or levying taxes. Moreover, the president and Congress like to keep the size of the federal bureaucracy small by giving jobs to people not on the federal payroll.[5]

Defenders of government by proxy claim that the system produces more flexibility, takes advantage of private and nonprofit skills, and defends the principle of federalism embodied in our Constitution. The defenders make fair points, but the system does produce certain everyday oddities, such as the fact that many average citizens receive costly federal government services over long periods of time without ever directly interacting with civil servants. Donald F. Kettl, a University of Maryland political scientist, dubbed this the "Mildred Paradox": in her last several years of life, his aged and ill mother-in-law, Mildred, applied successfully for multiple federal health insurance programs and received several years' worth of different types of expensive institutional care and top-quality medical treatment—all

at government expense—but without ever actually encountering a single government worker.[6]

Or look a bit closer at what we noted above regarding the U.S. Department of Agriculture (USDA). As a result of a new federal law (the Healthy, Hunger-Free Kids Act of 2010), the USDA is now required to expand and improve its "food security" programs by, among other measures, seeing to it that all eligible low-income children have daily access to free meals (breakfast or lunch plus a snack) during the summer months when school is out. The new law, however, does not even begin to specify just how the USDA and its scores and scores of state and local government proxy agencies (not to mention their tens of thousands of administrative partners) are to accomplish that objective. Among big cities, Philadelphia has had the largest USDA-funded summer food program in the country (almost 4 million meals served each summer through more than 1,000 local "sites" including churches, recreation centers, and private homes on streets closed off for the purpose by local police). But the city's summer participation rate among eligible children has still been only about 50 percent.

The Growth of the Bureaucracy

The Constitution made scarcely any provision for an administrative system other than to allow the president to appoint, with the advice and consent of the Senate, "ambassadors, other public ministers and consuls, judges of the Supreme Court, and all other officers of the United States whose appointments are not herein otherwise provided for, and which shall be established by law."[7] Departments and bureaus were not mentioned.

In the first Congress, in 1789, James Madison introduced a bill to create a Department of State to assist the new secretary of state, Thomas Jefferson, in carrying out his duties. People appointed to this department were to be nominated by the president and approved by the Senate, but they were "to be removable by the president" alone. These six words, which would confer the right to fire government officials, occasioned six days of debate in the House. At stake was the locus of power over what was to become the bureaucracy. Madison's opponents argued that the Senate should consent to the removal of officials as well as their appointment. Madison responded that, without the unfettered right of removal, the president would not be able to control his subordinates, and without this control he would not be able to discharge his constitutional obligation to "take care that the laws be faithfully executed."[8] Madison won, 29 votes to 22. When the issue went to the

Senate, another debate resulted in a tie vote, broken in favor of the president by Vice President John Adams. The Department of State, and all cabinet departments subsequently created, would be run by people removable only by the president.

That decision did not resolve the question of who would really control the bureaucracy, however. Congress retained the right to appropriate money, to investigate the administration, and to shape the laws that would be executed by that administration—more than ample power to challenge any president who claimed to have sole authority over his subordinates. And many members of Congress expected the cabinet departments, even though headed by people removable by the president, to report to Congress.

The government in Washington was at first minuscule. The State Department started with only nine employees; the War Department did not have 80 civilian employees until 1801. Only the Treasury Department, concerned with collecting taxes and finding ways to pay the public debt, had much power, and only the Post Office Department provided any significant service.

The Appointment of Officials

Small as the bureaucracy was, people struggled, often bitterly, over who would be appointed to it. From George Washington's day to modern times, presidents have found appointment to be one of their most important and difficult tasks. The officials they select affect how the laws are interpreted (thus the political ideology of the job holders is important), what tone the administration will display (thus personal character is important), how effectively the public business is discharged (thus competence is important), and how strong the political party or faction in power will be (thus party affiliation is important). Presidents trying to balance the competing needs of ideology, character, fitness, and partisanship have rarely pleased most people. As John Adams remarked, every appointment creates one ingrate and 10 enemies.

Because Congress, during most of the 19th and 20th centuries, was the dominant branch of government, congressional preferences often controlled the appointment of officials. And since Congress was, in turn, a collection of people who represented local interests, appointments were made with an eye to rewarding the local supporters of members of Congress or building up local party organizations. These appointments made on the basis of political considerations—patronage—were later to become a major issue. They galvanized various reform efforts that sought to purify politics and to raise the level of competence of the public service. Many of the abuses the reformers complained about were real enough,

but patronage served some useful purposes as well. It gave the president a way to ensure that his subordinates were reasonably supportive of his policies; it provided a reward the president could use to induce recalcitrant members of Congress to vote for his programs; and it enabled party organizations to be built up to perform the necessary functions of nominating candidates and getting out the vote.

Though at first there were not many jobs to fight over, by the middle of the 19th century, there were a lot. From 1816 to 1861, the number of federal employees increased eightfold. This expansion was not, however, the result of the government's taking on new functions, but simply a result of the increased demands on its traditional functions. The Post Office alone accounted for 86 percent of this growth.[9]

The Civil War was a great watershed in bureaucratic development. Fighting the war led, naturally, to hiring many new officials and creating many new offices. Just as important, the Civil War revealed the administrative weakness of the federal government and led to demands by the civil service reform movement for an improvement in the quality and organization of federal employees. And finally, the war was followed by a period of rapid industrialization and the emergence of a national economy. The effects of these developments could no longer be managed by state governments acting alone. With the creation of a nationwide network of railroads, commerce among the states became increasingly important. The constitutional powers of the federal government to regulate interstate commerce, long dormant for want of much commerce to regulate, now became an important source of controversy.

A Service Role

From 1861 to 1901, new agencies were created, many to deal with particular sectors of society and the economy. More than 200,000 new federal employees were added, with only about half of this increase in the Post Office. The rapidly growing Pension Office began paying benefits to Civil War veterans; the Department of Agriculture was created in 1862 to help farmers; the Department of Labor was founded in 1882 to serve workers; and the Department of Commerce was organized in 1903 to assist businesspeople. Many more specialized agencies, such as the National Bureau of Standards, also came into being.

These agencies had one thing in common: their role was primarily to serve, not to regulate. Most did research, gathered statistics, dispensed federal lands, or passed out benefits. Not until the Interstate Commerce Commission (ICC) was created in 1887 did the federal government begin to regulate the economy (other than by managing the currency) in any large way. Even the ICC had, at first, relatively few powers.

laissez-faire An economic theory that government should not regulate or interfere with commerce.

There were several reasons why federal officials primarily performed a service role. The values that had shaped the Constitution were still strong: these included a belief in limited government, the importance of states' rights, and the fear of concentrated discretionary power. The proper role of government in the economy was to promote, not to regulate, and a commitment to **laissez-faire**—a freely competitive economy—was strongly held. But just as important, the Constitution said nothing about giving any regulatory powers to bureaucrats. It gave to *Congress* the power to regulate commerce among the states. Now obviously Congress could not make the necessary day-to-day decisions to regulate, for example, the rates that interstate railroads charged to farmers and other shippers. Some agency or commission composed of appointed officials and experts would have to be created to do that. For a long time, however, the prevailing interpretation of the Constitution was that no such agency could exercise such regulatory powers unless Congress first set down clear standards that would govern the agency's decisions. As late as 1935, the Supreme Court held that a regulatory agency could not make rules on its own; it could only apply the standards enacted by Congress.[10] The Court's view was that the legislature may not delegate its powers to the president or to an administrative agency.[11]

These restrictions on what administrators could do were set aside in wartime. During World War I, for example, President Woodrow Wilson was authorized by Congress to fix prices, operate the railroads, manage the communications system, and even control the distribution of food.[12] This kind of extraordinary grant of power usually ended with the war.

Some changes in the bureaucracy did not end with the war. During the Civil War, World War I, World War II, the Korean War, and the war in Vietnam, the number of civilian (as well as military) employees of the government rose sharply. These increases were not simply in the number of civilians needed to help serve the war effort; many of the additional people were hired by agencies, such as the Treasury Department, not obviously connected with the war. Furthermore, the number of federal officials did not return to prewar levels after each war. Though there was some reduction, each war left the number of federal employees larger than before.[13]

It is not hard to understand how this happens. During wartime, almost every government agency argues that its activities have *some* relation to the war effort, and few legislators want to be caught voting against something that may help that effort.

Hence in 1944, the Reindeer Service in Alaska, an agency of the Interior Department, asked for more employees because reindeer are "a valued asset in military planning."

A Change in Role

Today's bureaucracy is largely a product of two events: the depression of the 1930s (and the concomitant New Deal program of President Roosevelt) and World War II. Though many agencies have been added since then, the basic features of the bureaucracy were set mainly as a result of changes in public attitudes and in constitutional interpretation that occurred during these periods. The government was now expected to play an active role in dealing with economic and social problems. In the late 1930s, the Supreme Court reversed its earlier decisions (see Chapter 16) on the question of delegating legislative powers to administrative agencies and upheld laws by which Congress merely instructs agencies to make decisions that serve "the public interest" in some area.[14] As a result, it was possible for President Nixon to set up in 1971 a system of price and wage controls based on a statute that simply authorized the president "to issue such orders and regulations as he may deem appropriate to stabilize prices, rents, wages, and salaries."[15] The Cost of Living Council and other agencies that Nixon established to carry out this order were run by appointed officials who had the legal authority to make sweeping decisions based on general statutory language.

World War II was the first occasion during which the government made heavy use of federal income taxes—on individuals and corporations—to finance its activities. Between 1940 and 1945, total federal tax collections increased from about $5 billion to nearly $44 billion. The end of the war brought no substantial tax reduction: the country believed that a high level of military preparedness continued to be necessary and that various social programs begun before the war should enjoy the heavy funding made possible by wartime taxes. Tax receipts continued, by and large, to grow. Before 1913, when the Sixteenth Amendment to the Constitution was passed, the federal government could not collect income taxes at all (it financed itself largely from customs duties and excise taxes). From 1913 to 1940, income taxes were small (in 1940, the average American paid only $7 in federal income taxes). World War II created the first great financial boom for the government, permitting the sustained expansion of a wide variety of programs and thus entrenching a large number of administrators in Washington.[16]

Although it is still too soon to tell, a third event—the September 11, 2001, terrorist attacks on the United States—could affect bureaucracy as

CONSTITUTIONAL CONNECTIONS

Beyond Checks and Balances?

The Framers of the Constitution did not envision anything akin to today's federal bureaucracy with its several million full-time employees and its millions more part-time employees. But far more surprising to the Framers than the sheer size of today's federal bureaucracy (after all, the country and its population have grown, too) would be its scope: cabinet departments, bureaus, independent agencies, government corporations, and regulatory commissions touching virtually every facet of the nation's economic, social, and civic life—trade, banking, labor, environmental protection, broadcasting, transportation, human services, health, housing, education, energy, environmental protection, space exploration, national parks, homeland security, and more. Beyond the contemporary federal bureaucracy's size and scope, the Framers might be mystified by the "proxy government" system described on pages 381–382, and by how so many "federal" programs are actually jointly funded and administered by federal, state, and local governments in conjunction with for-profit firms and nonprofit organizations.

But would the Framers, in turn, view today's federal bureaucracy not only as a "fourth branch" of American national government but one that operates outside their system of separated powers and checks and balances, and that has transformed federalism (see Chapter 3) into Washington-controlled "intergovernmental administration"?

Some think so. They argue that federal agencies, including the Internal Revenue Service, the Environmental Protection Agency, and many others, routinely exercise not only executive powers but also lawmaking and judicial powers as well, and that state governments are required to fund or co-fund and administer many federal programs including large ones like Medicaid. Moreover, they claim, Congress now commonly passes long and complicated laws and leaves it almost entirely to the discretion of federal bureaucrats to decide what the laws mean, how to apply them, and even in some cases how much to spend on them.

Others, however, think not. They argue that through federal laws that set boundaries on administrators' authority (like the Administrative Procedures Act of 1946), routine oversight of federal agencies by congressional committees and subcommittees, and federal court decisions limiting how far Washington can go in requiring state governments to fund or administer its programs, the federal bureaucracy's powers and the discretion exercised by Washington's appointed officials normally remain duly limited. We share this view: the "fourth branch" is far bigger and broader than the Framers could ever have envisioned, but most federal government agencies most of the time are checked and balanced by Congress and by other means.

profoundly as the depression of the 1930s and World War II. A law creating a massive new cabinet agency, the Department of Homeland Security (DHS), was passed in late 2002. Within two years of its creation, the DHS had consolidated under its authority 22 smaller federal agencies with nearly 180,000 federal employees (third behind Defense and Veterans Affairs) and over $40 billion in budgets (fourth behind Defense, Health and Human Services, and Education). In addition, dozens of intergovernmental grant-making programs came under the authority of the DHS. In late 2004, Congress passed another law that promised, over time, to centralize under a single director of national intelligence the work of the more than 70 federal agencies authorized to spend money on counterterrorist activities. But even after related reforms in 2006, dozens of different agencies were still authorized to spend money on counterterrorism activities; and in 2013, the DHS faced sharp questioning from the House Subcommittee on Oversight

and Management Efficiency, and the Government Accountability Office (GAO) once again ranked the DHS, which by then employed more than 220,000 employees, among those agencies with serious management problems.[17]

The Federal Bureaucracy Today

No president wants to admit that he has increased the size of the bureaucracy. He can avoid saying this by pointing out that the number of civilians working for the federal government, excluding postal workers, has not increased significantly in recent years and is about the same today (2 million persons) as it was in 1960, and less than it was during World War II. This explanation is true but misleading, for it neglects the roughly 13 million people who work *indirectly* for Washington as employees of private firms and state or local agencies that are largely, if not entirely, supported by federal funds. There are nearly three persons earning their living indirectly from the federal government for every one earning it directly. While federal employment has remained quite stable, employment among federal contractors and consultants and in state and local governments has mushroomed. Indeed, most federal bureaucrats, like most other people who work for the federal government, live outside Washington, D.C.

As Table 15.1 shows, from 1990 to 2012, 11 of the 15 federal executive departments reduced their workforce. The U.S. Department of State grew by more than half, but that represented fewer than 15,000 new staff. The Department of Veterans Affairs expanded after 2007 as veterans from the wars in Iraq and Afghanistan began to return home. Since its creation in 2003, the Department of Homeland Security grew by about a quarter. The largest growth was in the U.S. Department of Justice (DOJ). This growth

is explained mainly by the growth in just one DOJ unit—and one of the few federal agencies anywhere in the bureaucracy that was slow to join the trend toward what we described earlier in this chapter as government by proxy—the Federal Bureau of Prisons (BOP). The BOP administers nearly 200 facilities, from maximum-security prisons to community corrections centers, all across the country. Between 1990 and 2013, its staff doubled to nearly 39,000, while the prisoner populations these federal workers supervised more than doubled to about 276,000.

The power of the federal bureaucracy cannot be measured by the number of employees, however. A bureaucracy of 5 million persons would have little power if each employee did nothing but type letters or file documents, whereas a bureaucracy of only 100 persons would have awesome power if each member were able to make arbitrary life-and-death decisions affecting the rest of us. The power of the bureaucracy depends on the extent to which appointed officials

TABLE 15.1   Federal Civilian Employment, 1990–2012

	1990	2012	Percent Change
All executive departments (in millions) (In thousands)	2.065	1.937	−6.2
State	25.2	39.2	+55.5
Treasury	158.6	110.1	−30.6
Defense	1,034	772.6	−25.3
Justice	83.9	117.9	+40.5
Interior	77.6	70.2	−9.5
Agriculture	122.5	106.9	−12.7
Commerce	69.9	56.9	−18.6
Labor	17.7	17.6	−0.6
Health and Human Services	123.9	69.8	−43.7
Housing and Urban Development	13.5	9.6	−28.9
Transportation	67.3	58.0	−1.3
Energy	17.7	16.1	−9.0
Education	4.70	4.5	−4.3
Veterans Affairs	248.1	304.7	+22.8
Homeland Security	N/A	183.5	+22.0*

*Since its creation in 2003

Source: Statistical Abstract of the United States, 2009 and 2012

Federal Bureau of Prisons	1990	2013	Percent Change
Staff	19.0	38.6	+103
Inmates	58.0	218.1	+276

Sources: Federal Bureau of Prisons Weekly Population Report and Quick Facts, available at http://www.bop.gov/locations/weekly_report.jsp; and http://www.bop.gov/news/quick.jsp#5.

have **discretionary authority**—that is, the ability to choose courses of action and to make policies not spelled out in advance by laws. As Figure 15.1 shows, the volume of regulations issued has risen much faster than the rate of government spending (relative to gross domestic product) and the number of federal employees who write the regulations and spend the money (federal employees who, as we have explained, often work mainly through state and local government employees and other administrative proxies).

By this test, the power of the federal bureaucracy has grown enormously. Congress has delegated substantial authority to

discretionary authority The extent to which appointed bureaucrats can choose courses of action and make policies not spelled out in advance by laws.

FIGURE 15.1 **The Growth of the Federal Government in Money, People, and Rules, 1940–2012**

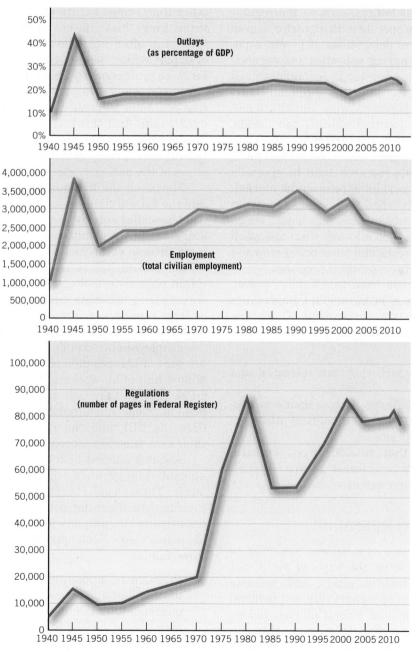

Source: Data for 2011 and 2012 compiled by Jesse Crosson from reports of the Office of Management and Budget, the U.S. Department of Labor, and the *Federal Register*.

competitive service
The government offices to which people are appointed on the basis of merit, as ascertained by a written exam or by applying certain selection criteria.

administrative agencies in three areas: (1) paying subsidies to particular groups and organizations in society (farmers, veterans, scientists, schools, universities, hospitals); (2) transferring money from the federal government to state and local governments (the grant-in-aid programs described in Chapter 3); and (3) devising and enforcing regulations for various sectors of society and the economy. Some of these administrative functions, such as grants-in-aid to states, are closely monitored by Congress; others, such as the regulatory programs, usually operate with a greater degree of independence. These delegations of power, especially in the areas of paying subsidies and regulating the economy, did not become commonplace until the 1930s, and then only after the Supreme Court decided that such delegations were constitutional. Today, by contrast, appointed officials can decide, within rather broad limits, who shall own a television station, what safety features automobiles shall have, what kinds of scientific research shall be specially encouraged, what drugs shall appear on the market, which dissident groups shall be investigated, what fumes an industrial smokestack may emit, which corporate mergers shall be allowed, what use shall be made of national forests, and what prices crop and dairy farmers shall receive for their products.

If appointed officials have this kind of power, then how they use it is of paramount importance in understanding modern government. There are, broadly, four factors that may explain the behavior of these officials:

1. The manner in which they are recruited and rewarded
2. Their personal attributes, such as their socioeconomic backgrounds and their political attitudes
3. The nature of their jobs
4. The constraints that outside forces—political superiors, legislators, interest groups, journalists—impose on their agencies

Recruitment and Retention

The federal civil service system was designed to recruit qualified people on the basis of merit, not political patronage, and to retain and promote employees on the basis of performance, not political favoritism. Many appointed federal officials belong to the **competitive service**. This means they are appointed only after they have passed a written examination administered by the Office of Personnel

Management (OPM) or met certain selection criteria (such as training, educational attainments, or prior experience) devised by the hiring agency and approved by the OPM. Where competition for a job exists and candidates can be ranked by their scores or records, the agency must usually appoint one of the three top-ranking candidates.

In recent years, the competitive service system has become decentralized, so that each agency now hires its own people without an OPM referral, and examinations have become less common. In 1952, more than 86 percent of all federal employees were civil servants hired by the competitive service; by 1996, that figure had fallen to less than 54 percent. This decentralization and the greater use of ways other than exams to hire employees were caused by three things. First, the old OPM system was cumbersome and often not relevant to the complex needs of departments. Second, these agencies had a need for more professionally trained employees—lawyers, biologists, engineers, and computer specialists—who could not be ranked on the basis of some standard exam. And third, civil rights groups pressed Washington to make the racial composition of the federal bureaucracy look more like the racial composition of the nation.

Moreover, the kinds of workers being recruited into the federal civil service have changed. For example, blue-collar employment has fallen while the federal government's white-collar workforce has become more diverse occupationally. As one expert on civil service reform has noted, the "need to recruit and retain physicists, biologists, oceanographers, nurses, statisticians, botanists, and epidemiologists, as well as large numbers of engineers, lawyers, and accountants, now preoccupies federal personnel managers."[18]

Employees hired outside the competitive service are part of the excepted service. They now make up almost half of all workers. Though not hired by the OPM, they still are typically hired in a nonpartisan fashion. Some are hired by agencies—such as the CIA, the FBI, and the Postal Service—that have their own selection procedures.

About 3 percent of the excepted employees are appointed on grounds other than or in addition to merit. These legal exceptions exist to permit the president to select, for policymaking and politically sensitive posts, people who are in agreement with his policy views. Such appointments are generally of three kinds:

1. Presidential appointments authorized by statute (cabinet and subcabinet officers, judges, U.S. marshals and U.S. attorneys, ambassadors, and members of various boards and commissions).
2. "Schedule C" appointments to jobs described as having a "confidential or policy-determining

character" below the level of cabinet or subcabinet posts (including executive assistants, special aides, and confidential secretaries).

3. Noncareer executive assignments (NEAs) given to high-ranking members of the regular competitive civil service or to persons brought into the civil service at these high levels. These people are deeply involved in the advocacy of presidential programs or participate in policymaking.

These three groups of excepted appointments constitute the patronage available to a president and his administration. When President Kennedy took office in 1961, he had 451 political jobs to fill. When President Barack Obama took office in 2009, he had more than four times that number, including nearly four times the number of top cabinet posts. Scholars disagree over whether this proliferation of political appointees has improved or worsened Washington's performance, but one thing is clear: widespread presidential patronage is hardly unprecedented. In the 19th century, practically every federal job was a patronage job. For example, when Grover Cleveland, a Democrat, became president in 1885, he replaced some 40,000 Republican postal employees with Democrats.

Ironically, two years earlier, in 1883, the passage of the Pendleton Act had begun a slow but steady transfer of federal jobs from the patronage to the merit system. It may seem strange that a political party in power (the Republicans) would be willing to relinquish its patronage in favor of a merit-based appointment system. Two factors made it possible for the Republicans to pass the Pendleton Act: (1) public outrage over the abuses of the spoils system, highlighted by the assassination of President James Garfield by a man always described in the history books as a "disappointed office seeker" (*lunatic* would be a more accurate term); and (2) the fear that

if the Democrats came to power on a wave of antispoils sentiment, existing Republican officeholders would be fired. (The Democrats won anyway.)

> ***name-request job*** A job filled by a person whom an agency has already identified.

The merit system spread to encompass most of the federal bureaucracy, generally with presidential support. Though presidents may have liked in theory the idea of hiring and firing subordinates at will, most felt that the demands for patronage were impossible either to satisfy or to ignore. Furthermore, by increasing the coverage of the merit system a president could "blanket in" patronage appointees already holding office, thus making it difficult or impossible for the next administration to fire them.

The Buddy System

The actual recruitment of civil servants, especially in middle and upper-level jobs, is somewhat more complicated, and slightly more political, than the laws and rules might suggest. Though many people enter the federal bureaucracy by learning of a job, filling out an application, perhaps taking a test, and being hired, many also enter on a "name-request" basis. A **name-request job** is one that is filled by a person whom an agency has already identified. In this respect, the federal government is not so different from private business. A person learns of a job from somebody who already has one, or the head of a bureau decides in advance whom he or she wishes to hire. The agency must still send a form describing the job to the OPM, but it also names the person whom the agency wants to appoint. Sometimes the job is even described in such a way that the person named is the only one who can qualify for it. Occasionally, this tailor-made, name-request job is offered to a person at the insistence of a member of Congress who wants a political supporter taken care of; more often it is made available because the bureaucracy itself knows whom it wishes to hire and wants to circumvent an elaborate search. This is the "buddy system."

The buddy system does not necessarily produce poor employees. Indeed, it is frequently a way of hiring people known to the agency as capable of handling the position. It also opens up the possibility of hiring people whose policy views are congenial to those already in office. Such networking is based on shared policy views, not (as once was the case) on narrow partisan affiliations. For example, bureaucrats in consumer protection agencies recruit new staff from private groups with an interest in consumer protection, such as the various organizations associated with Ralph Nader, or from academics who have a pro-consumer inclination.

Fire erupting from the offshore oil rig operated by BP in the Gulf of Mexico near American land.

U.S. COAST GUARD/UPI/Newscom

There has always been an informal "old boys' network" among those who move in and out of high-level government posts; with the increasing appointment of women to these jobs, there has begun to emerge an old girls' network as well.[19] In a later section, we will consider whether, or in what ways, these recruitment patterns make a difference.

Firing a Bureaucrat

The great majority of bureaucrats who are part of the civil service and who do not hold presidential appointments have jobs that are, for all practical purposes, beyond reach. An executive must go through elaborate steps to fire, demote, or suspend a civil servant. Realistically, this means no one is fired or demoted unless his or her superior is prepared to invest a great deal of time and effort in the attempt. In 1987, about 2,600 employees who had completed their probationary period were fired for misconduct or poor performance. That is about one-tenth of 1 percent of all federal employees. It is hard to believe that a large private company would fire only one-tenth of 1 percent of its workers in a given year. It's also impossible to believe that, as is often the case in Washington, it would take a year to fire anyone. To cope with this problem, federal executives have devised a number of stratagems for bypassing or forcing out civil servants with whom they cannot work—denying them promotions, transferring them to undesirable locations, or assigning them to meaningless work.

With the passage of the Civil Service Reform Act of 1978, Congress recognized that many high-level positions in the civil service have important policy-making responsibilities and that the president and his cabinet officers ought to have more flexibility in recruiting, assigning, and paying such people. Accordingly, the act created the Senior Executive Service (SES), about 8,000 top federal managers who can (in theory) be hired, fired, and transferred more easily than ordinary civil servants. Moreover, the act stipulated that members of the SES would be eligible for substantial cash bonuses if they performed their duties well. (To protect the rights of SES members, anyone who is removed from the SES is guaranteed a job elsewhere in the government.)

Things did not work out quite as the sponsors of the SES had hoped. Though most eligible civil servants joined it, there was only a modest increase in the proportion of higher-ranking positions in agencies that were filled by transfer from another agency; the cash bonuses did not prove to be an important incentive (perhaps because the base salaries of top bureaucrats did not keep up with inflation); and hardly any member of the SES was actually fired. Two years after the SES was created, less than one-half of 1 percent of its members had received an unsatisfactory rating, and none had been fired. Nor does the SES give the president a large opportunity to make political appointments: only 10 percent of the SES can be selected from outside the existing civil service. And no SES member can be transferred involuntarily.

The Agency's Point of View

When one realizes that most agencies are staffed by people recruited by those agencies, sometimes on a name-request basis, and virtually immune from dismissal, it becomes clear that the recruitment and retention policies of the civil service work to ensure that most bureaucrats will have an "agency" point of view. Even with the encouragement for transfers created by the SES, most government agencies are

HOW THINGS WORK

Firing a Bureaucrat

To fire or demote a member of the competitive civil service, these procedures must be followed:

1. The employee must be given written notice at least 30 days in advance that he or she is to be fired or demoted for incompetence or misconduct.

2. The written notice must contain a statement of reasons, including specific examples of unacceptable performance.

3. The employee has the right to an attorney and to reply, orally or in writing, to the charges.

4. The employee has the right to appeal any adverse action to the Merit Systems Protection Board (MSPB), a three-person, bipartisan body appointed by the president with the consent of the Senate.

5. The MSPB must grant the employee a hearing, at which the employee has the right to have an attorney present.

6. The employee has the right to appeal the MSPB decision to a U.S. court of appeals, which can hold new hearings.

dominated by people who have not served in any other agency and who have been in government service most of their lives. This fact has some advantages: it means that most top-tier bureaucrats are experts in the procedures and policies of their agencies and that there will be a substantial degree of continuity in agency behavior no matter which political party happens to be in power.

But the agency point of view has its costs as well. A political executive entering an agency with responsibility for shaping its direction will discover that he or she must carefully win the support of career subordinates. A subordinate has an infinite capacity for discreet sabotage and can make life miserable for a political superior by delaying action, withholding information, following the rule book with literal exactness, or making an "end run" around a superior to mobilize members of Congress sympathetic to the bureaucrat's point of view. For instance, when one political executive wanted to downgrade a bureau in his department, he found, naturally, that the bureau chief was opposed. The bureau chief spoke to some friendly lobbyists and a key member of Congress. When the political executive asked the congressman whether he had any problem with the contemplated reorganization, the congressman replied, "No, you have the problem, because if you touch that bureau, I'll cut your job out of the budget."[20]

Personal Attributes

A second factor that might shape the way bureaucrats use their power is their personal attributes. These include their social class, education, and personal political beliefs. The federal civil service as a whole looks very much like a cross section of American society in the education, sex, race, and social origins of its members (see Figure 15.2). But as with many other employers, African Americans and other minorities are most likely heavily represented in the lowest grade levels and tend to be underrepresented at the executive level. At the higher-ranking levels, where the most power is found—say, in the supergrade ranks of GS 16 through GS 18—the typical civil servant is a middle-aged white male with a college degree whose father was somewhat more advantaged than the average citizen. In the great majority of cases, this individual is in fact very different from the typical American in both background and personal beliefs.

Because political appointees and career bureaucrats are unrepresentative of the average American, and because of their supposed occupational self-interest, some critics have speculated that the people holding these jobs think about politics and government in ways very different from the public at large. Some surveys do find that career bureaucrats are more likely than other people to hold liberal views, to trust government, and to vote for Democrats.[21]

It is important, however, not to overgeneralize from such differences. For example, whereas Clinton appointees (virtually all of them strong Democrats) were more liberal than average citizens, Reagan appointees (virtually all of them loyal Republicans) were undoubtedly more conservative than average citizens. Likewise, career civil servants are

FIGURE 15.2 **Characteristics of Federal Civilian Employees, 1960 and 2012**

*Blacks, Native Americans, Hispanics, Asians, and Pacific Islanders

Source: Statistical Abstract of the United States, 1961, pp. 392–394; Office of Personnel Management, *Data Analysis & Documentation: Federal Employment Records*, September 30, 2012.

An Amtrak train speeding along its tracks. Amtrak service costs the federal government much more than the train earns in fares.

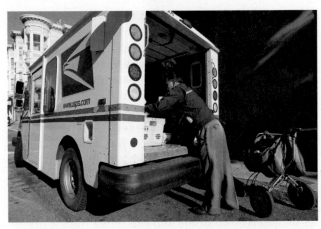

A letter carrier picks up mail; his employer, the U.S. Postal Service, is running a huge deficit.

more pro-government than the public at large, but on most specific policy questions, federal bureaucrats do not have extreme positions. Still, those employed in "activist" agencies such as the Federal Trade Commission, Environmental Protection Agency, and Food and Drug Administration tend to have more liberal views than those who work for the more "traditional" agencies such as the departments of Agriculture, Commerce, and the Treasury. Even when the bureaucrats come from roughly the same social backgrounds, their policy views seem to reflect the type of government work that they do. For example, studies dating back decades have found that Democrats and people with liberal views tend to be overrepresented in social service agencies, whereas Republicans and people with conservative views tend to be overrepresented in defense agencies.[22] But it is not clear whether such differences in attitudes are produced by the jobs that people hold or whether certain jobs attract people with certain beliefs. Probably both forces are at work.

Do Bureaucrats Sabotage Their Political Bosses?

Because it is so hard to fire career bureaucrats, it is often said that these people will sabotage any actions by their political superiors with which they disagree. And since civil servants tend to have liberal views, it has been conservative presidents and cabinet secretaries who have usually expressed this worry.

There is no doubt that some bureaucrats will drag their heels if they don't like their bosses, and a few will block actions they oppose. However, most bureaucrats try to carry out the policies of their superiors even when they personally disagree with them. When David Stockman was director of the OMB, he set out to make sharp cuts in

government spending programs in accordance with the wishes of his boss, President Reagan. He later published a book complaining about all the people in the White House and Congress who worked against him.[23] But nowhere in the book is there any major criticism of the civil servants at the OMB. It appears that whatever these people thought about Stockman and Reagan, they loyally tried to carry out Stockman's policies.

Bureaucrats tend to be loyal to political superiors who deal with them cooperatively and constructively. An agency head who tries to ignore or discredit them can be in for a tough time, however. The powers of obstruction available to aggrieved bureaucrats are formidable. Such people can leak embarrassing stories to Congress or to the media, help interest groups mobilize against the agency head, and discover a thousand procedural reasons why a new course of action won't work.

The exercise of some of those bureaucratic powers is protected by the Whistle Blower Protection Act. Passed in 1989, the law created the Office of Special Counsel, charged with investigating complaints from bureaucrats that they were punished after reporting to Congress about waste, fraud, or abuse in their agencies.

It may seem odd that bureaucrats, who have great job security, would not always act in accordance with their personal beliefs instead of in accordance with the wishes of their bosses. Bureaucratic sabotage, in this view, ought to be very common. But bureaucratic cooperation with superiors is not odd, once you take into account the nature of a bureaucrat's job.

If you are a voter at the polls, your beliefs will clearly affect how you vote (see Chapter 7). But if you are the second baseman for the Boston Red Sox, your political beliefs, social background, and education will have nothing to do with how you field ground balls. Sociologists like to call the different things that people do in their lives "roles" and to distinguish between roles that are loosely structured (such as the role of voter) and those that are highly structured (such as that of second baseman). Personal attitudes greatly affect loosely structured roles and only slightly affect highly structured ones. Applied to the federal bureaucracy, this suggests that civil servants performing tasks that are routinized (such as filling out forms), tasks that are closely defined by laws and rules (such as issuing welfare checks), or tasks that are closely monitored by others (supervisors, special-interest groups, the media) will probably perform them in ways that can only partially be explained, if at all, by their personal attitudes. Civil servants performing complex, loosely defined tasks that are not closely monitored may carry out their work in ways powerfully influenced by their attitudes.

Among the loosely defined tasks are those performed by professionals, and so the values of these people may influence how they behave. An increasing number of lawyers, economists, engineers, and physicians are hired to work in federal agencies. These men and women have received extensive training that produces not only a set of skills, but also a set of attitudes as to what is important and valuable. For example, the Federal Trade Commission (FTC), charged with preventing unfair methods of competition among businesses, employs two kinds of professionals—lawyers, organized into a Bureau of Competition, and economists, organized into a Bureau of Economics. Lawyers are trained to draw up briefs and argue cases in court and are taught the legal standards by which they will know whether they have a chance of winning a case or not. Economists are trained to analyze how a competitive economy works and what costs consumers must bear if the goods and services are produced by a monopoly (one firm controlling the market) or an oligopoly (a small number of firms dominating the market).

Because of their training and attitudes, lawyers in the FTC prefer to bring cases against a business firm that has done something clearly illegal, such as attending secret meetings with competitors to rig the prices that will be charged to a purchaser. These cases appeal to lawyers because there is usually a victim (the purchaser or a rival company) who complains to the government, the illegal behavior can be proved in a court of law, and the case can be completed rather quickly.

Economists, on the other hand, are trained to measure the value of a case not by how quickly it can be proved in court, but by whether the illegal practice imposes large or small costs on the consumer.

FTC economists often dislike the cases that appeal to lawyers. The economists feel that the amount of money that such cases save the consumer is often small and that the cases are a distraction from the major issues—such as whether IBM unfairly dominates the computer business or whether General Motors is too large to be efficient. Lawyers, in turn, are leery of big cases, because the facts are hard to prove and they may take forever to decide (one blockbuster case can drag through the courts for 10 years). In many federal agencies divergent professional values such as these help explain how power is used.

Culture and Careers

Unlike the lawyers and economists working in the FTC, the government bureaucrats in a typical agency don't have a lot of freedom to choose a course of action. Their jobs are spelled out not only by the laws, rules, and routines of their agency, but also by the informal understandings among fellow employees as to how they are supposed to act. These understandings are the *culture* of the agency.[24]

If you belong to the air force, you can do a lot of things, but only one thing really counts: flying airplanes, especially advanced jet fighters and bombers. The culture of the air force is a pilots' culture. If you belong to the navy, you have more choices: fly jet aircraft or operate nuclear submarines. Both jobs provide status and a chance for promotion to the highest ranks. By contrast, sailing minesweepers or transport ships (or worse, having a desk job and not sailing anything at all) is not a very rewarding job. The culture of the CIA emphasizes working overseas as a clandestine agent; staying in Washington as a report writer is not as good for your career. The culture of the State Department rewards skill in political negotiations; being an expert on international economics or embassy security is much less rewarding.

You can usually tell what kind of culture an agency has by asking an employee, "If you want to get ahead here, what sort of jobs should you take?" The jobs that are career enhancing are part of the culture; the jobs that are not career enhancing (NCE in bureaucratic lingo) are not part of it.

Being part of a strong culture is good—up to a point. It motivates employees to work hard in order to win the respect of their coworkers as well as the approval of their bosses. But a strong culture also makes it hard to change an agency. FBI agents for many years resisted getting involved in civil rights or organized crime cases, and diplomats in the State Department didn't pay much attention to embassy security. These important jobs were not a career-enhancing part of the culture.

POLICY DYNAMICS: INSIDE/OUTSIDE THE BOX

Postal Service Reform: Client Politics?

Article I, Section 8, of the Constitution authorized the Congress to "establish Post Offices." Today's United States Postal Service (USPS) is the second largest employer in the nation (behind Walmart). It is not taxpayer-funded and generates more than $60 billion a year in revenue for its services. It has more than 500,000 career employees. It has mail routes that cover every square mile of the nation. It delivers mail to more than 100 million addresses each week. It handles about 160 billion pieces of mail each year. It has more office buildings than the number of McDonald's, Starbucks, and Walmart stores combined. Millions of people (especially older people) and many businesses (not only "junk mail" purveyors) continue to rely heavily on "snail mail." And certain legal documents still normally get sent in paper envelopes via "regular mail."

But the USPS is in trouble. Since 2001, the volume of mail delivered by the USPS has declined by about a quarter, and its workforce has fallen by more than 300,000. In the 2012 Fiscal Year, the USPS ran a deficit that totaled about $16 billion. Facebook, email, texting, and other means of electronic communications have increasingly displaced both routine and episodic communications that once started with dropping paper into the old metal "mailbox" on the street corner. Meanwhile, for-profit shipping businesses like United Parcel Service (UPS) and Federal Express have expanded. They carry substantial portions of all "door-to-door" mail including express or "overnight" envelopes, packages, and boxes.

In recent years, Congress has considered numerous proposals to "save" or "streamline" the USPS. For instance, in 2012, Postmaster General Patrick Donahoe proposed reducing mail delivery to five days a week (eliminating most Saturday deliveries), restructuring payments for postal worker retiree health benefits, consolidating mail processing centers, and reducing "window hours" in about half of the roughly 26,000 post offices around the country. The USPS receives no taxpayer funding. In 2012, the Senate passed a bill that would have pumped billions of tax dollars into the USPS, but the House rejected the measure. In 2013, the USPS was authorized to end most Saturday deliveries effective August of that year as many more far-reaching reform bills continued to circulate in Congress.

Some have characterized the battles over USPS reform bills as, in effect, instances of client politics. Supposedly, the issue pits the labor union representing most postal workers (the American Postal Workers Union of the AFL-CIO) against a broad, bipartisan coalition, backed by majority public opinion, which favors closing more postal offices and accelerating workforce reductions. But that view is at odds with at least two facts: first, some key GOP leaders in Congress have opposed sweeping reforms to the USPS; and, second, as revealed in a major survey commissioned by the USPS Office of the Inspector General in early 2013, most Americans, including young Americans, oppose such reforms, too:

- Although three-quarters of people erroneously assume that the USPS is taxpayer-funded, four-fifths still say they want the USPS to serve all citizens in all locations even if it means that the USPS loses money.

- Three-quarters are opposed to reducing postal service hours, and three-quarters also oppose plans for three-day delivery schedules.

- Even 95 percent of young adults, a population that relies largely on online communications, say they would be adversely affected if the USPS went out of business anytime soon.

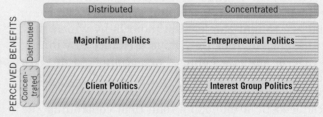

Source: "Going Postal," *The Economist: World in 2012,* p. 46; Julia Ziegler, Postmaster General Urges Quick Action n Lame Duck Session, Federal News Radio, November 1, 2012; Hope Yen, "Post Office Reports Record Loss of $15.9 Billion for Year," Federal News Radio, Associated Press, November 15, 2012; American Postal Workers Union, APWU Home Page, "Survey Says: Most Americans Oppose Plant Closures," June 4, 2013.

Constraints

The biggest difference between a government agency and a private organization is the vastly greater number of constraints on the agency. Unlike a business firm, the typical government bureau cannot hire, fire, build, or sell without going through procedures set down in laws. How much money it pays its members is determined by statute, not by the market. Not only the goals of an agency, but often its exact procedures, are spelled out by Congress.

At one time, the Soil Conservation Service was required by law to employ at least 14,177 full-time workers. The State Department has been forbidden by law from opening a diplomatic post in Antigua or Barbuda but forbidden from closing a post anywhere else. The Agency for International Development (which administers our foreign-aid program) has been given by Congress 33 objectives and 75 priorities and must send to Congress 288 reports each year. When it buys military supplies, the Defense Department must give a "fair proportion" of its contracts to small businesses, especially those operated by "socially and economically disadvantaged individuals," and must buy from American firms even if, in some cases, buying abroad would be cheaper. Some of the more general constraints include the following:

- Administrative Procedure Act (1946). Before adopting a new rule or policy, an agency must give notice, solicit comments, and (often) hold hearings.

- Freedom of Information Act (1966). Citizens have the right to inspect all government records except those containing military, intelligence, or trade secrets or revealing private personnel actions.

- National Environmental Policy Act (1969). Before undertaking any major action affecting the environment, an agency must issue an environmental impact statement.

- Privacy Act (1974). Government files about individuals, such as Social Security and tax records, must be kept confidential.

- Open Meeting Law (1976). Every part of every agency meeting must be open to the public unless certain matters (for example, military or trade secrets) are being discussed.

One of the biggest constraints on bureaucratic action is that Congress rarely gives any job to a single agency. Stopping drug trafficking is the task of the Customs Service, the FBI, the Drug Enforcement Administration, the Border Patrol, and the Defense Department (among others). Disposing of the assets of failed savings-and-loan associations is the job of the Resolution Funding Corporation, Resolution Trust Corporation, Federal Housing Finance Board, Office of Thrift Supervision in the Treasury Department, Federal Deposit Insurance Corporation, Federal Reserve Board, and Justice Department (among others).

The effects of these constraints on agency behavior are not surprising.

- The government will often act slowly. (The more constraints that must be satisfied, the longer it will take to get anything done.)

- The government will sometimes act inconsistently. (What is done to meet one constraint—for example, freedom of information—may endanger another constraint—for example, privacy.)

- It will be easier to block action than to take action. (The constraints ensure that lots of voices will be heard; the more voices heard, the more they may cancel each other out.)

- Lower-ranking employees will be reluctant to make decisions on their own. (Having many constraints means having many ways to get into trouble; to avoid trouble, let your boss make the decision.)

- Citizens will complain of red tape. (The more constraints to serve, the more forms to fill out.)

These constraints do not mean government bureaucracy is powerless, only that, however great its power, it tends to be clumsy. That clumsiness arises not from the fact that the people who work for agencies are dull or incompetent, but from the complicated political environment in which that work must be done.

The moral of the story: the next time you get mad at a bureaucrat, ask yourself, why would a rational, intelligent person behave that way? Chances are

An U.S. Air Force F-35 stealth fighter aircraft undergoes pre-flight checks before launching.

US Air Force Photo/Alamy

iron triangle A close relationship between an agency, a congressional committee, and an interest group.

you will discover there are good reasons for that action. You would probably behave the same way if you were working for the same organization.

Why So Many Constraints?

Government agencies behave as they do in large part because of the many different goals they must pursue and the complex rules they must follow. Where does all this red tape come from?

From us. From us, the people.

Every goal, every constraint, every bit of red tape, was put in place by Congress, the courts, the White House, or the agency itself responding to the demands of some influential faction. Civil rights groups want every agency to hire and buy from women and minorities. Environmental groups want every agency to file environmental impact statements. Industries being regulated want every new agency policy to be formulated only after a lengthy public hearing with lots of lawyers present. Labor unions also want those hearings so that they can argue against industry lawyers. Everybody who sells something to the government wants a "fair chance" to make the sale, and so everybody insists that government contracts be awarded only after complex procedures are followed. A lot of people don't trust the government, and so they insist that everything it does be done in the sunshine—no secrets, no closed meetings, no hidden files.

If we wanted agencies to pursue their main goal with more vigor and less encumbering red tape, we would have to ask Congress, the courts, or the White House to repeal some of these constraints. In other words, we would have to be willing to give up something we want in order to get something else we want even more. But politics does not encourage people to make these trade-offs; instead it encourages us to expect to get everything—efficiency, fairness, help for minorities—all at once.

Agency Allies

Despite these constraints, government bureaucracies are not powerless. In fact, some of them actively seek certain constraints. They do so because it is a way of cementing a useful relationship with a congressional committee or an interest group.

At one time scholars described the relationship between an agency, a committee, and an interest group as an **iron triangle**. For example, the Department of Veterans Affairs, the House and Senate committees on veterans' affairs, and veterans' organizations (such as the American Legion) would form a tight, mutually advantageous alliance. The department would do what the committees wanted and in return get political support and budget appropriations; the committee members would do what the veterans' groups wanted and in return get votes and campaign contributions. Iron triangles are examples of what are called *client politics*.

Many agencies still have important allies in Congress and the private sector, especially those bureaus that serve the needs of specific sectors of the economy or regions of the country. The Department of Agriculture works closely with farm organizations, the Department of the Interior with groups interested in obtaining low-cost irrigation or grazing rights, and the Department of Housing and Urban Development with mayors and real-estate developers.

Sometimes these allies are so strong that they can defeat a popular president. For years, President Reagan tried to abolish the Small Business Administration (SBA), arguing that its program of loans to small firms was wasteful and ridden with favoritism. But Congress, reacting to pressures from small-business groups, rallied to the SBA's defense. As a result, Reagan had to oversee an agency that he didn't want.

But iron triangles are much less common today than once was the case. Politics of late has become far more complicated. For one thing, the number and variety of interest groups have increased so much in recent years that scarcely any agency is not subject to pressures from several competing interests instead of only from one powerful interest. For another, the growth of subcommittees in Congress has meant most agencies are subject to control by many different legislative groups, often with very different concerns. Finally, the courts have made it much easier for all kinds of individuals and interests to intervene in agency affairs.

As a result, nowadays government agencies face a bewildering variety of competing groups and legislative subcommittees that constitute not a loyal group of allies, but a fiercely contentious collection of critics. The Environmental Protection Agency is caught between the demands of environmentalists and those of industry organizations, the Occupational Safety and Health Administration between the pressures of labor and those of business, and the Federal Communications Commission between the desires of broadcasters and those of cable television companies. Even the Department of Agriculture faces not a unified group of farmers, but many different farmers split into rival groups, depending on the crops they raise, the regions in which they live, and the attitudes they have toward the relative merits of farm subsidies or free markets.

Political scientist Hugh Heclo has described the typical government agency today as being embedded not in an iron triangle, but in an **issue network**.[25] These issue networks consist of people in Washington-based interest groups, on congressional staffs, in universities and think tanks, and in the mass media, who regularly debate government policy on a certain subject—say, health care or auto safety. The networks are contentious, split along political, ideological, and economic lines. When a president takes office, he often recruits key agency officials from those members of the issue network who are most sympathetic to his views.

When Jimmy Carter, a Democrat, became president, he appointed to key posts in consumer agencies people who were from that part of the consumer issue network associated with Ralph Nader. Ronald Reagan, a conservative Republican, filled these same jobs with people who were from that part of the issue network holding free-market or antiregulation views. When George Bush the elder, a more centrist Republican, took office, he filled these posts with more centrist members of the issue network. Bill Clinton brought back the consumer activists. George W. Bush reversed Clinton, and Barack Obama reversed Bush.

issue network A network of people in Washington, D.C.-based interest groups, on congressional staffs, in universities and think tanks, and in the mass media, who regularly discuss and advocate public policies.

Congressional Oversight

The main reason why some interest groups are important to agencies is that they are important to Congress. Not every interest group in the country

WHAT'S YOUR ISSUE?

Fix the Sewers First?

Debates over gun control, education funding, health care policy, and many other issues garner wide attention. But you probably have never heard, let alone led or participated in, a debate about raw sewage. Few citizens, and few elected leaders, pay much attention to "municipal waste" or "wastewater management." But there are federal, state, and local government agencies and associated professional societies (mainly engineers and lawyers) that spend all their time worrying about America's "water infrastructure." For example, in the early 1990s and again in the early 2000s, the U.S. Environmental Protection Agency (EPA) made a major push to get the more than 700 cities and towns that rely on century-old sewer systems to repair or upgrade those systems. Some cities acted, if only because the EPA pressured them to do so. For instance, in 2002, Baltimore began a 14-year, billion-dollar plan to fix broken sewer pipes that were discharging untreated wastes and raw sewage into the Chesapeake Bay.

But, in December 2011, U.S. Senate hearings revealed that such problems were growing all across the country. Each year, 25 percent of all drinking water (1.7 trillion gallons) leaks from water pipes before reaching the faucet and 900 billion gallons of raw sewage leaks into waterways. In Washington, D.C. itself, raw sewage routinely flows into the Potomac River and the 1,300 miles of water pipes that run beneath the city

are, on average, 77-years-old; they are being repaired or replaced at a rate that would take 100 years to complete. The American Society of Engineers told the Senate that to fix the sewers and waterways nationally would cost, all told, about $650 billion—and that is if we started right now. But Congress did not act and, as of mid-2013, there were no major "fix the sewers" proposals pending on Capitol Hill. "Americans," the engineers warned, "should prepare for regular disruption of water service and a jump in contamination caused by sewage bacteria."

So, what's flowing from your faucet? Do you live in a city or town where the waterways are in serious trouble? Regardless, with all the other issues and problems facing the nation, would you put fixing the sewers first on the federal policy agenda? If not first, then would you give the issue substantially more attention than it has normally received? And if $650 billion to upgrade the waterways could be obtained only by cutting other government programs (health, housing, policing, transportation, or others), which, if any, would you cut—or would you somehow try to pay for the fixes by charging (everybody? businesses?) more for water?

Source: Ashley Halsey, III, "Billions Needed to Upgrade America's Leaky Water Infrastructure," *The Washington Post*, January 2, 2012; Tom Arrandale, "Cities Take the Sewer Plunge," *Governing Magazine*, August 2002.

authorization legislation Legislative permission to begin or continue a government program or agency.

appropriation A legislative grant of money to finance a government program or agency.

trust funds Funds for government programs collected and spent outside the regular government budget.

has substantial access to Congress, but those that do and that are taken seriously by the relevant committees or subcommittees must also be taken seriously by the agency. Furthermore, even apart from interest groups, members of Congress have constitutional powers over agencies and policy interests in how agencies function.

Congressional supervision of the bureaucracy takes several forms. First, no agency may exist (except for a few presidential offices and commissions) without congressional approval. Congress influences—and sometimes determines precisely—agency behavior by the statutes it enacts.

Second, no money may be spent unless it has first been authorized by Congress. **Authorization legislation** originates in a legislative committee (such as Agriculture, Education and Labor, or Public Works) and states the maximum amount of money that an agency may spend on a given program. This authorization may be permanent, it may be for a fixed number of years, or it may be annual (that is, it must be renewed each year, or the program or agency goes out of business).

Third, even funds that have been authorized by Congress cannot be spent unless (in most cases) they are also appropriated. Appropriations usually are made annually, and they originate not with the legislative committees but with the House Appropriations Committee and its various (and influential) subcommittees. An **appropriation** (money formally set aside for a specific use) may be, and often is, for less than the amount authorized. The Appropriations Committee's action thus tends to have a budget-cutting effect. There are some funds that can be spent without an appropriation, but in virtually every part of the bureaucracy, each agency is keenly sensitive to congressional concerns at the time that the annual appropriations process is going on.

But is fidelity to the constitutional principle of separation of powers (see Chapter 2) called into question when Congress engages in oversight of agencies that are in the executive branch? Members of Congress themselves once debated that issue, but the aforementioned Administrative Procedure Act of 1946 and a dozen subsequent laws that built on it (the latest being the Data Quality Act of 2000, and all upheld when challenged in the courts) are predicated on the idea that agencies are "adjuncts for legislative functions.... Congress lacks the capacity to legislate on all matters it touches and perforce must delegate a great deal of legislative authority to the agencies."[26]

This idea was challenged during the George W. Bush presidency by administration officials and others who, especially but not exclusively with respect to military, national, and homeland security issues, argued that agencies were bound to act in accordance with the president's directives whenever they conflicted with directives from Congress. While Bush's executive-centered approach sparked many controversies, most scholars seem to think that it effected no major or lasting changes, and some suggest that it stirred Congress to pursue even more comprehensive (and aggressive) oversight policies and practices.[27]

The Appropriations Committee and Legislative Committees

The fact that an agency budget must be both authorized and appropriated means that each agency serves not one congressional master but several, and that these masters may be in conflict. The real power over an agency's budget is exercised by the Appropriations Committee; the legislative committees are especially important when a substantive law is first passed or an agency is first created, or when an agency is subject to annual authorization.

In the past, the power of the Appropriations Committee was rarely challenged: from 1947 through 1962, fully 90 percent of the House Appropriations Committee's recommendations on expenditures were approved by the full House without change.[28] Furthermore, the Appropriations Committee tends to recommend less money than an agency requests (though some specially favored agencies, such as the FBI, the Soil Conservation Service, and the Forest Service, have tended to get almost everything that they have asked for). Finally, the process of "marking up" (revising, amending, and approving) an agency's budget request gives to the Appropriations Committee, or one of its subcommittees, substantial influence over the policies that the agency follows.

Of late, the appropriations committees have lost some of their great power over government agencies. This has happened in three ways.

First, Congress has created trust funds to pay for the benefits many people receive. The Social Security trust fund is the largest of these. In 2012, it took in $729 billion in Social Security taxes and paid out $635 billion in old-age benefits. There are several other trust funds as well. **Trust funds** operate outside the regular government budget, and the appropriations committees have no control over these expenditures. They are automatic.

Second, Congress has changed the authorization of many programs from permanent or multiyear to annual authorizations. This means that every year the legislative committees, as part of the reauthorization process, get to set limits on what these agencies can spend. This limits the ability of the appropriations committees to determine the spending limits. Before 1959, most authorizations were permanent or multiyear. Now a long list of agencies must be reauthorized every year—the State Department, NASA, military procurement programs of the Defense Department, the Justice Department, the Energy Department, and parts or all of many other agencies.

Third, the existence of huge budget deficits during the 1980s and in the 2000s has meant that much of Congress's time has been taken up with trying (usually not very successfully) to keep spending down. As a result, there has rarely been much time to discuss the merits of various programs or how much ought to be spent on them; instead, attention has been focused on meeting a target spending limit. In 1981, the budget resolution passed by Congress mandated cuts in several programs before the appropriations committees had even completed their work.[29]

In addition to the power of the purse, there are informal ways by which Congress can control the bureaucracy. An individual member of Congress can call an agency head on behalf of a constituent. Most such calls merely seek information, but some result in, or attempt to obtain, special privileges for particular people. Congressional committees may also obtain the right to pass on certain agency decisions. This is called **committee clearance**, and though it usually is not legally binding on the agency, few agency heads will ignore the expressed wish of a committee chair that he or she be consulted before certain actions (such as transferring funds) are taken.

The Legislative Veto

For many decades, Congress made frequent use of the legislative veto to control bureaucratic or presidential actions. A **legislative veto** is a requirement that an executive decision must lie before Congress for a specified period (usually 30 or 90 days) before it takes effect. Congress could then veto the decision if a resolution of disapproval was passed by either house (a "one-house veto") or both houses (a "two-house veto"). Unlike laws, such resolutions were not signed by the president. Between 1932 and 1980, about 200 laws were passed providing for a legislative veto, many of them involving presidential proposals to sell arms abroad.

But in June 1983, the Supreme Court declared the legislative veto to be unconstitutional. In the *Chadha* case, the Court held that the Constitution clearly requires in Article I that "every order, resolution, or vote to which the concurrence of the Senate and House of Representatives may be necessary" (with certain minor exceptions) "shall be presented to the President of the United States," who must either approve it or return it with his veto attached. In short, Congress cannot take any action that has the force of law unless the president concurs in that action.[30] With a stroke of the pen, parts of 200 laws suddenly became invalid. At least that happened in theory. In fact, since the *Chadha* decision, Congress has passed a number of laws that contain legislative vetoes, despite the Supreme Court having ruled against them! (Someone will have to go to court to test the constitutionality of these new provisions.)

Opponents of the legislative veto hope future Congresses will have to pass laws that state much more clearly than before what an agency may or may not do. But it is just as likely that Congress will continue to pass laws stated in general terms and require that agencies implementing those laws report their plans to Congress, so that it will have a chance to enact and send to the president a regular bill disapproving the proposed action. Or Congress may rely on informal (but scarcely weak) means of persuasion, including threats to reduce the appropriations of an agency that does not abide by congressional preferences.

Congressional Investigations

Perhaps the most visible and dramatic form of congressional supervision of an agency is the investigation. Since 1792, when Congress investigated an army defeat by a Native American tribe, congressional investigations of the bureaucracy have been a regular feature—sometimes constructive, sometimes destructive—of legislative-executive relations. The investigative power is not mentioned in the Constitution, but has been inferred from the power to legislate. The Supreme Court has consistently upheld this interpretation, though it has also said that such investigations should not be solely for the purpose of exposing the purely personal affairs of private individuals and must not operate to deprive

committee clearance The ability of a congressional committee to review and approve certain agency decisions in advance and without passing a law.

legislative veto The authority of Congress to block a presidential action after it has taken place. The Supreme Court has held that Congress does not have this power.

red tape Complex bureaucratic rules and procedures that must be followed to get something done.

citizens of their basic rights.[31] Congress may compel a person to attend an investigation by issuing a subpoena; anyone who ignores the subpoena may be punished for contempt. Congress can vote to send the person to jail or can refer the matter to a court for further action. As explained in Chapter 14, the president and his principal subordinates have refused to answer certain congressional inquiries on grounds of "executive privilege."

Although many areas of congressional oversight—budgetary review, personnel controls, investigations—are designed to control the exercise of bureaucratic discretion, other areas are intended to ensure the freedom of certain agencies from effective control, especially by the president. In dozens of cases, Congress has authorized department heads and bureau chiefs to operate independent of presidential preferences. Congress has resisted, for example, presidential efforts to ensure that policies to regulate pollution do not impose excessive costs on the economy, and interest groups have brought suit to prevent presidential coordination of various regulatory agencies. If the bureaucracy sometimes works at cross-purposes, it usually is because Congress—or competing committees in Congress—wants it that way.

Bureaucratic "Pathologies"

Everyone complains about bureaucracy in general (though rarely about bureaucratic agencies that everyone believes are desirable). This chapter should persuade you that it is difficult to say anything about bureaucracy "in general"; there are too many different kinds of agencies, kinds of bureaucrats, and kinds of programs to label the entire enterprise with some single adjective. Nevertheless, many people who recognize the enormous variety among government agencies still believe they all have some general features in common and suffer from certain shared problems or pathologies.

This is true enough, but the reasons for it—and the solutions, if any—are often not understood. There are five major (or at least frequently mentioned) problems with bureaucracies: red tape, conflict, duplication, imperialism, and waste. **Red tape** refers to the complex rules and procedures that must be followed to get something done. (As early as the seventh century, legal and government documents in England were bound together with a tape of pinkish-red color. Since then *red tape* has come to mean "bureaucratic delay or confusion," especially

that accompanied by unnecessary paperwork.[32]) *Conflict* exists because some agencies seem to be working at cross-purposes with other agencies. (For example, the Agricultural Research Service tells farmers how to grow crops more efficiently, while the Agricultural Stabilization and Conservation Service pays farmers to grow fewer crops or to produce less.) *Duplication* (usually called "wasteful duplication") occurs when two government agencies seem to be doing the same thing, as when the Customs Service and the Drug Enforcement Administration both attempt to intercept illegal drugs being smuggled into the country. *Imperialism* refers to the tendency of agencies to grow without regard to the benefits that their programs confer or the costs that they entail. *Waste* means spending more than is necessary to buy some product or service.

These problems all exist, but they do not necessarily exist because bureaucrats are incompetent or power-hungry. Most exist because of the very nature of government itself. Take red tape: partly we encounter cumbersome rules and procedures because any large organization, governmental or not, must have some way of ensuring that one part of the organization does not operate out of step with another. Business corporations have red tape also; it is to a certain extent a consequence of bigness. But a great amount of governmental red tape is also the result of the need to satisfy legal and political requirements. Government agencies must hire on the basis of "merit," must observe strict accounting rules, must supply Congress with detailed information on their programs, and must allow for citizen access in countless ways. Meeting each need requires rules; enforcing the rules requires forms.

Or take conflict and duplication: they do not occur because bureaucrats enjoy conflict or duplication. (Quite the contrary!) They exist because Congress, in setting up agencies and programs, often wants to

At the world's busiest border crossing, cars line up to enter the United States in Tijuana, Mexico.

achieve a number of different, partially inconsistent goals or finds that it cannot decide which goal it values the most. Congress has 535 members and little strong leadership; it should not be surprising that 535 people will want different things and will sometimes succeed in getting them.

Imperialism results in large measure from government agencies' seeking goals so vague and so difficult to measure that it is hard to tell when they have been attained. When Congress is unclear as to exactly what an agency is supposed to do, the agency will often convert that legislative vagueness into bureaucratic imperialism by taking the largest possible view of its powers. It may do this on its own; more often it does so because interest groups and judges rush in to fill the vacuum left by Congress. As we saw in Chapter 3, the 1973 Rehabilitation Act was passed with a provision barring discrimination against people with disabilities in any program receiving federal aid. Under pressure from people with disabilities, that lofty but vague goal was converted by the Department of Transportation into a requirement that virtually every big-city bus have a device installed to lift people in wheelchairs onboard.

Waste is probably the biggest criticism that people have of the bureaucracy. Everybody has heard stories of the Pentagon's paying $91 for screws that cost 3 cents in the hardware store. President Reagan's "Private Sector Survey on Cost Control," generally known as the Grace Commission (after its chairman, J. Peter Grace), publicized these and other tales in a 1984 report. No doubt there is waste in government. After all, unlike a business firm worried about maximizing profits, in a government agency there are only weak incentives to keep costs down. If a business employee cuts costs, he or she often receives a bonus or raise, and the firm gets to add the savings to its profits. If a government official cuts costs, he or she receives no reward, and the agency cannot keep the savings—they go back to the Treasury.

But many of the horror stories are either exaggerations or unusual occurrences.[33] Most of the screws, hammers, and light bulbs purchased by the government are obtained at low cost by means of competitive bidding among several suppliers. When the government does pay outlandish amounts, the reason typically is that it is purchasing a new or one-of-a-kind item not available at your neighborhood hardware store—for example, a new bomber or missile.

Even when the government is not overcharged, it still may spend more money than a private firm in buying what it needs. The reason is red tape—the rules and procedures designed to ensure that when the government buys something, it will do so in a way that serves the interests of many groups. For

example, it often must buy from American rather than foreign suppliers, even if the latter charge a lower price; it must make use of contractors that employ minorities; it must hire only union laborers and pay them the "prevailing" (that is, the highest) wage; it must allow public inspection of its records; it frequently is required to choose contractors favored by influential members of Congress; and so on. Private firms do not have to comply with all these rules and thus can buy for less.

From this discussion, it should be easy to see why these five basic bureaucratic problems are so hard to correct. To end conflicts and duplication, Congress would have to make some policy choices and set some clear priorities, but with all the competing demands that it faces, Congress finds it difficult to do that. You make more friends by helping people than by hurting them, and so Congress is more inclined to add new programs than to cut old ones, whether or not the new programs are in conflict with existing ones. To check imperialism, some way would have to be found to measure the benefits of government, but that is often impossible; government exists in part to achieve precisely those goals—such as national defense—that are least measurable. Furthermore, what might be done to remedy some problems would make other problems worse: if you simplify rules and procedures to cut red tape, you are also likely to reduce the coordination among agencies and thus to increase the extent to which there is duplication or conflict. If you want to reduce waste, you will have to have more rules and inspectors—in short, more red tape. The problem of bureaucracy is inseparable from the problem of government generally.

Just as people are likely to say they dislike Congress but like their own member of Congress, they are inclined to express hostility toward "the bureaucracy" but goodwill for that part of the bureaucracy with which they have dealt personally. While most Americans have unfavorable impressions of government agencies and officials in general, they have quite favorable impressions about government agencies and officials with whom they have had direct contact or about which they claim to know something specific.

For example, Table 15.2 shows that wide majorities have very or somewhat favorable impressions of diverse federal government agencies. Surveys dating back decades suggest that, despite persistent public complaints about "the bureaucracy," most Americans have judged, and continue to judge, each federal agency to be fair and useful.[34] Even the tax-collecting IRS has more public fans than foes, as did the new Transportation Safety Administration (TSA), whose workers people routinely encounter at airport security checkpoints.

TABLE 15.2	How the Public Views Particular Federal Agencies		
AGENCY	**% FAVORABLE Very/ Somewhat/Total**	**% UNFAVORABLE Very/ Somewhat/Total**	**Favorable Minus Unfavorable**
Postal Service	58/31/89	5/5/10	+79
FBI	31/46/77	10/7/17	+60
Defense Department	31/34/65	15/2/17	+48
Social Security Admin.	24/40/64	19/13/32	+32
EPA	23/40/63	15/15/31	+32
CIA	22/36/58	16/14/30	+28
Homeland Security	24/36/60	17/17/34	+26
Transportation Safety	15/41/56	16/9/25	+26
Education Department	22/37/59	19/19/38	+21
IRS	14/42/56	21/18/39	+17
FEMA	16/33/49	24/26/50	−1

Percent reporting a "favorable or unfavorable impression"*

*Other response categories were "never heard of" and "can't rate," and only the newest agency, the Transportation Safety Administration, drew significant numbers in each category (9 percent for each).

Source: Adapted from results of a nationally representative Associated Press/IPSOS Public Agenda poll conducted December 17–19, 2007.

This finding helps explain why government agencies are rarely reduced in size or budget: whatever the popular feelings about the bureaucracy, any given agency tends to have many friends. Even the much-criticized FEMA, viewed unfavorably by half the public, was able to fend off budget cuts in the several years following its failed response to Hurricane Katrina.

Reforming the Bureaucracy

The history of American bureaucracy has been punctuated with countless efforts to make it work better and cost less. There were 11 major attempts in the 20th century alone. The latest was the National Performance Review (NPR)—popularly called the plan to "reinvent government"—led by Vice President Al Gore.

The NPR differed from many of the preceding reform efforts in one important way. Most of the earlier ones suggested ways of increasing central (that is, presidential) control of government agencies: the Brownlow Commission (1936–1937) recommended giving the president more assistants, the First Hoover Commission (1947–1949) suggested ways of improving top-level management, and the Ash Council (1969–1971) called for consolidating existing agencies into a few big "super departments." The intent was to make it easier for the president and his cabinet secretaries to run the bureaucracy. The key ideas were efficiency, accountability, and consistent policies.

The NPR, by contrast, emphasized customer satisfaction (the "customers" in this case being the citizens who come into contact with federal agencies). To the authors of the NPR report, the main problem with the bureaucracy was that it had become too centralized, too rule-bound, too little concerned with making programs work, and too much concerned with avoiding scandal. The NPR report contained many horror stories about useless red tape, excessive regulations, and cumbersome procurement systems that make it next to impossible for agencies to do what they were created to do. (For example, before it could buy an ashtray, the General Services Administration issued a nine-page document that described an ashtray and specified how many pieces it must break into, should it be hit with a hammer.)[35]

To solve these problems, the NPR called for less centralized management and more employee initiative, fewer detailed rules and more emphasis on customer satisfaction. It sought to create a new kind of organizational culture in government agencies, one more like that found in the more innovative, quality-conscious American corporations. The NPR was reinforced legislatively by the Government Performance and Results Act (GPRA) of 1993, which required agencies "to set goals, measure performance, and report on the results."

President George W. Bush built on the Clinton-Gore NPR efforts and the GPRA using the Performance Assessment Rating Tool (PART). The main goal of the PART was to link management reform to the budget process. During the 2008 presidential campaign, Barack Obama harkened back to

HOW WE COMPARE

Outsourcing Government

In the United States, government by proxy is the norm. Bureaucrats in Washington pay state and local governments and private groups to staff and administer most federal programs.

For instance, Medicaid, the main federal health program for low-income citizens, is administered mainly by state agencies. The federal government has co-funded nonprofit groups to lead recovery efforts in the hurricane-ravaged Gulf Coast. At points during the second Gulf War, there were nearly as many for-profit workers as U.S. soldiers in Iraq.

The Canadian and Indian central governments each administer many policies via provincial or territorial governments; and every European government uses private contractors for at least some functions.

But most other democracies restrict and regulate outsourcing more than the United States does; for example, German law directs that all persons involved in administering national policies must be directly supervised by a government official.

And no other nation follows the American practice whereby government bureaucracies give tax-exempt organizations, including local faith-based groups, grants to administer myriad health and human services programs.

Many experts argue that outsourcing and proxy government have gone too far in this country; but none is sure whether or how it can be reined in, and most admit that public administration in other democracies is also far from perfect.

Sources: Donald F. Kettl, The Next Government of the United States: Why Our Institutions Fail Us and How to Fix Them (New York: W. W. Norton, 2008); Paul R. Verkuil, Outsourcing Sovereignty: Why Privatization of Government Functions Threatens Democracy and What We Can Do About It (Cambridge: Cambridge University Press, 2007); John J. DiIulio, Jr., *"Government by Proxy: A Faithful Overview,"* Harvard Law Review, March 2003, pp. 1271–1284.

and Congress for control over the agencies or of the agencies' desire to avoid irritating influential voters. Silly as the rules for ashtrays may sound, they were written so that the government could say it had an "objective" standard for buying ashtrays. If it simply went out and bought ashtrays at a department store the way ordinary people do, it would risk being accused by the Acme Ashtray Company of buying trays from its competitor, the A-1 Ashtray Company, because of political favoritism.

The rivalry between the president and Congress for control of the bureaucracy makes bureaucrats nervous about irritating either branch, and so they issue rules designed to avoid getting into trouble, even if these rules make it hard to do their job. Matters become even worse during periods of divided government when different parties control the White House and Congress. As we saw in Chapter 14, divided government may not have much effect on *making* policy, but it can have a big effect on *implementing* it. Presidents of one party have tried to increase political control over the bureaucracy ("executive micromanagement"), and Congresses of another party have responded by increasing the number of investigations and detailed rule-making ("legislative micromanagement"). Divided government intensifies the cross fire between the executive and legislative branches, making bureaucrats dig into even deeper layers of red tape to avoid getting hurt.

This does not mean that reform is impossible, only that it is very difficult. For example, despite a lack of clear-cut successes in other areas, the NPR's procurement reforms stuck: government agencies can now buy things costing as much as $100,000 without following any complex regulations. Still, the main effect of the NPR, the GPRA, and the PART was to get federal agencies collecting far more information than in the past concerning what they do, without, however, using the information to improve the way they do it.[36]

Former Los Angeles Mayor Antonio Villaraigosa goes through a full-body scanner at Los Angeles International Airport.

the Clinton-Gore NPR but also pledged to keep but improve Bush's PART. By 2011, however, administrative reform was not widely mentioned among Obama's main priorities or accomplishments in office.

Reforming the bureaucracy is easier said than done. Most of the rules and red tape that make it hard for agency heads to do a good job are the result either of the struggle between the White House

WHAT WOULD YOU DO?

MEMORANDUM

To: *Dr. Robert Smith, president of Cybersystems Engineering*

From: *James Logan, secretary of defense*

Subject: *Becoming an assistant secretary of defense*

As both secretary and a dear old college buddy of yours, I write again to express my hope that you will accept the president's call to service. We all desperately want you aboard. Yes, conflict-of-interest laws will require you to sell your stock in your present company and drop out of its generous pension plan. No, the government won't even pay moving costs. And once you leave office, you will be barred for life from lobbying the executive branch on matters in which you were directly involved while in office, and you will be barred for two years from lobbying on matters that were under your general official authority. Your other concerns have teeth, too, but let me help you weigh your options.

Arguments for:

1. I hate to preach, but it is one's duty to serve one's country when called. Your sacrifice would honor your family and benefit your fellow Americans for years to come.

2. As an accomplished professional and the head of a company that has done business with the government, you could help the president succeed in reforming the department so that it works better and costs less.

3. Despite the restrictions, you could resume your career once your public service was complete.

Arguments against:

1. Since you will have to be confirmed by the Senate, your life will be put under a microscope, and everything (even some of our old college mischief together) will be fair game for congressional staffers and reporters.

News »

New Administration Struggling to Fill Top Posts—Cabinet Secretaries Say "The President Needs Help!"

Four months into the new administration, hundreds of assistant secretary and deputy assistant secretary positions remain unfilled. In 1960 the total number of presidential political appointees was just 450. Today the total is closer to 3,000, but sheer growth is not the whole story. Rather, say experts on federal bureaucracy, plum public service posts go unfilled because the jobs have become so unrewarding, even punishing.

2. You will face hundreds of rules telling you what you can't do and scores of congresspersons telling you what you should do. Old friends will get mad at you for not doing them favors. The president will demand loyalty. The press will pounce on your every mistake, real or imagined.

3. Given the federal limits on whom in the government you can deal with after you leave office, your job at Cybersystems may well suffer.

Your decision:

Accept position _____

Reject position _____

It might be easier to make desirable changes if the bureaucracy were accountable to only one master—say, the president—instead of to several. But that situation, which exists in many parliamentary democracies, creates its own problems. When the bureaucracy has but one master, it often ends up having none: it becomes so powerful that it controls the prime minister and no longer listens to citizen complaints. A weak, divided bureaucracy, such as exists in the United States, may strike us as inefficient, but that very inefficiency may help protect our liberties.

LEARNING OBJECTIVES

1. What is "bureaucracy" and in what ways is the American bureaucracy distinctive?

A bureaucracy is a large, complex organization composed of appointed officials. American bureaucracy is distinctive in three ways: political authority over the bureaucracy is shared by several institutions; most national government agencies share their functions with state and local government agencies; and government agencies are closely scrutinized and frequently challenged by both individuals and nongovernmental groups.

2. What is "discretionary authority" and why do some bureaucrats have lots of it?

Discretionary authority refers to the extent to which appointed bureaucrats can choose courses of action and make policies not spelled out in advance by laws. It is impossible for Congress to specify every last detail regarding how a law it passes is to be implemented. Many laws are administered by persons with special information and expertise, and many private citizens administer public laws by working as government contractors or grantees.

3. How does Congress exert control over the bureaucracy?

Congress exerts control over the bureaucracy in many different ways. It decides whether an agency may exist and how much money an agency spends. It can hold oversight hearings and launch investigations into just about any aspect of agency decision making or operations it chooses. And it traditionally has enjoyed wide latitude from the president in exercising its oversight functions.

4. What happened to make the bureaucracy a "fourth branch" of American national government?

The Constitution made no provision for an administrative system other than to allow the president to appoint, with the advice and consent of the Senate, ambassadors, Supreme Court judges, and "all other officers … which shall be provided by law." By the early 20th century, however, Washington's role in making, administering, and funding public policies had already grown far beyond what the Framers had contemplated. Two world wars, the New Deal, and the Great Society each left the government with expanded powers and requiring new batteries of administrative agencies to exercise them. Today, the federal bureaucracy is as vast as most people's expectations about Washington's responsibility for every public concern one can name. It is the appointed officials—the bureaucrats—not the elected officials or policymakers, who command the troops, deliver the mail, audit the tax returns, run the federal prisons, decide who qualifies for public assistance, and do countless other tasks. Unavoidably, many bureaucrats exercise discretion in deciding what public laws and regulations mean and how to apply them. Still, the president, cabinet secretaries, and thousands of political appointees are ultimately their bosses. Congress and the courts have ample, if imperfect, means of checking and balancing even the biggest bureaucracy, old or new.

5. What are the actual size and scope of the federal bureaucracy?

A few million civil servants work directly for the federal government, but more than five times as many people work indirectly for Washington as employees of business firms or of nonprofit organizations that receive federal grants or contracts, or as state and local government employees working under federal mandates. For example, the U.S. Department of Health and Human Services (HHS) has about 70,000 employees, runs more than 300 different programs, and makes more than 60,000 grants a year. But millions more people work indirectly for the HHS—as state and local government employees whose entire jobs involve the administration of one or more HHS programs (for example, Medicaid), and as people who work for community-serving nonprofit organizations that receive HHS grants to administer social services.

6. What should be done to improve bureaucratic performance?

There have been numerous efforts to make the bureaucracy work better and cost less, including 11 presidential or other major commissions in the 20th century. Among the latest was the National Performance Review (NPR), popularly called the plan to "reinvent government." Vice President Gore led the NPR during the two terms of the Clinton administration. The NPR was predicated on the view that bureaucracy had become too centralized, too rule-bound, too little concerned with program results, and too much concerned with avoiding scandal. In the end, the NPR produced certain money-saving changes in the federal procurement process (how government purchases goods and services from private contractors), and it also streamlined parts of the federal personnel process (how Washington hires career employees). Most experts, however, gave the NPR mixed grades. The Bush Administration abolished the NPR but began the Performance Assessment Rating Tool (PART). Most experts judged the PART to be only mildly successful.

7. Is "red tape" all bad?

No, not all. Red tape refers to the complex rules and procedures that must be followed to get something done. All large organizations, including business firms, have some red tape. Some red tape in government agencies is silly and wasteful (or worse), but try imagining government without any red tape at all. Imagine no rules about hiring on the basis of merit, no strict financial accounting procedures, and no regulations concerning citizen access to information or public record keeping. As the Yale political scientist Herbert Kaufman once quipped, one citizen's "red tape" often is another's "treasured procedural safeguard."

TO LEARN MORE

For addresses and reports of various cabinet departments:

Web addresses: **www.whitehouse.gov**

Documents and bulletin boards: **http://fedworld.ntis.gov**

National Partnership for Reinventing Government:
   http://govinfo.library.unt.edu/npr/index.htm

A few specific Web sites of federal agencies:

Department of Defense: **www.defenselink.mil**

Department of Education: **www.ed.gov**

Department of Health and Human Services:
   www.dhhs.gov

Department of State: **www.state.gov**

Federal Bureau of Investigation: **www.fbi.gov**

Department of Labor: **www.dol.gov**

Burke, John P. *Bureaucratic Responsibility*. Baltimore: Johns Hopkins University Press, 1986. Examines the problem of individual responsibility—for example, when to be a whistle blower—in government agencies.

Downs, Anthony. *Inside Bureaucracy*. Boston: Little, Brown, 1967. An economist's explanation of why bureaucrats and bureaus behave as they do.

Durant, Robert F., ed. *The Oxford Handbook of American Bureaucracy*. New York: Oxford University Press, 2010. Thirty-three largely up-to-date academic essays covering just about every facet of the subject.

Halperin, Morton H. *Bureaucratic Politics and Foreign Policy*. Washington, D.C.: Brookings Institution, 1974. Insightful account of the strategies by which diplomatic and military bureaucracies defend their interests.

Heclo, Hugh. *A Government of Strangers*. Washington, D.C.: Brookings Institution, 1977. Analyzes how political appointees attempt to gain control of the Washington bureaucracy and how bureaucrats resist those efforts.

Kettl, Donald F. *Government by Proxy*. Washington, D.C.: Congressional Quarterly Press, 1988. An account of how the federal government pays others to staff and run its programs.

Kettl, Donald F. *The Next Government of the United States: Why Our Institutions Fail Us and How to Fix Them*. New York: W. W. Norton, 2008. A masterful study of how proxy government functions and often fails today, and what might be done to remedy its worst failures.

Moore, Mark H. *Creating Public Value: Strategic Management in Government*. Cambridge: Harvard University Press, 1995. A thoughtful account of how wise bureaucrats can make government work better.

Parkinson, C. Northcote. *Parkinson's Law*. Boston: Houghton Mifflin, 1957. Half-serious, half-joking explanation of why government agencies tend to grow.

Wilson, James Q. *Bureaucracy: What Government Agencies Do and Why They Do It*. New York: Basic Books, 1989. A comprehensive review of what we know about bureaucratic behavior in the United States.

Mladen Antonov/AFP/Getty Images

The Judiciary

LEARNING OBJECTIVES

1. Where in the Constitution does it say that the Supreme Court has the power of judicial review?

2. What is meant by an "Article III" federal judge?

3. What is the difference between original and appellate jurisdiction?

4. Why should federal judges serve for life?

5. Why should federal courts be able to declare laws unconstitutional?

6. Should federal judges only interpret existing laws or should they be able to create new laws?

THEN

When the states were debating the ratification of the Constitution, Alexander Hamilton wrote in *Federalist* paper No. 78 that the new system of federal courts would be "the least dangerous" branch of government because, unlike the president, it would not command the sword and, unlike Congress, it would not control the purse strings. The courts, he argued, could take "no active resolution whatever." Nowhere in the Constitution was the Supreme Court given the right to declare laws of Congress or decisions of the president to be unconstitutional, though Hamilton argued that such a power was necessary. That document was our fundamental law and expressed the will of the people, and so it ought to be preferred to a law passed by Congress if there were an "irreconcilable variance between the two."

NOW

Within a few years after the Constitution was ratified, the Supreme Court took Hamilton's position by asserting that the Court could decide if a law was unconstitutional. A dozen years later, the same Court said that Congress could not only pass laws on the basis of powers explicitly given it by the Constitution, but also do things that were "necessary and proper" in order to implement those powers. By the middle of the 19th century, the Supreme Court had begun to declare many federal and scores of state laws to be unconstitutional.

As a result of its newfound powers, justices began serving on the Supreme Court for much longer periods. The 11 justices nominated by President George Washington served, on average, seven years, while the five nominated 40 years later by President Andrew Jackson served on average 20 years. The Court had become not the least dangerous branch, but a powerful one.

In time, the identity of the justices became an important political issue. Until recently, most justices were confirmed by the Senate, and from 1947 to 1985, almost all persons nominated to be a federal appeals court judge were approved. But of late, these nominations have had a less certain reception in the Senate.

When President Ronald Reagan nominated Antonin Scalia for the Supreme Court, he was confirmed by the Senate in 1986 by a vote of 98–0. But one year later, when President Reagan nominated Robert Bork, he was rejected by the Senate. Four years after that, Clarence Thomas barely survived a confirmation vote (52 to 48). In 2006, President George W. Bush's nominee Samuel Alito won confirmation by a vote of 58 to 42 after Senate Democrats tried to block the vote by means of a filibuster. During President Barack Obama's first term, each of his two nominees won confirmation: Sonia Sotomayor won confirmation in 2009 by a vote of 68 to 31, and Elena Kagan won confirmation in 2010 by a vote of 63 to 37. But in each case many Republicans voted against the nominee.

Beyond the Supreme Court, there has been a sharp drop in the percentage of nominees to federal appeals courts who are confirmed. From 1945 until 1970, almost every appeals court nominee was confirmed, but by 1995 only about half got through the Senate and by 2000 it was less than 40 percent. Table 16.1 shows a decline in the confirmation rate for the federal appeals courts that occurred from the Carter administration (92 percent) to the George W. Bush administration (71 percent). During President Obama's first term, the confirmation rate for his nominees to the federal appeals courts was 71 percent, slightly higher than the confirmation rate (67 percent) for the preceding administration.[1] Nominees to the federal district court are much less controversial than nominees to the federal appeals courts because the president rarely nominates for a federal district court someone who is not known to and supported by the nominee's two home state senators. Still, the confirmation rate for President Obama's nominees to the federal district courts (78 percent) was well below the confirmation rate (95 percent) for the preceding administration.[2] Also, as Table 16.2 shows, over the last three presidencies, the average number of days between a nominee's Senate hearings and his or her confirmation has increased steeply for both federal appeals court nominees and for federal district court nominees.

Why the changes? One reason is that the federal judiciary has played an increasingly important role

TABLE 16.1 **Judicial Nominations and Confirmations**

U.S. Court of Appeals

Presidency	Nominations	Confirmations	Confirmation Rate
Jimmy Carter	61	56	92%
Ronald Reagan	94	83	88
George H.W. Bush	53	42	79
Bill Clinton	90	66	73
George W. Bush	84	60	71

Source: Adapted from Russell Wheeler, *Judicial Nominations and Confirmations in the 11th Senate and What to Look for in the 112th*, Governance Studies, Brookings Institution, January 4, 2011, p. 2.

TABLE 16.2 **Federal Court Nominees, Time From Hearings to Confirmation**

Presidency	U.S. District Court Nominees	U.S. Appeals Court Nominees
	Average Number of Days	
Bill Clinton	30	43
George W. Bush	54	63
Barack Obama (first term)	139	177

Source: Adapted from Russell Wheeler, *Judicial Nominations and Confirmations in Obama's First Term*, Governance Studies, Brookings Institution, December 13, 2012, p. 9.

in making public policy. It, and not Congress, decided that abortions should be legal, settled the closely contested 2000 presidential election, and allowed private homes to be seized in order to build a residential hotel and other private structures aimed at affluent clientele. In these and many other cases, the federal courts have become major political actors; as a result, Congress has become concerned about who will be federal judges. Especially during certain periods of divided government (see Chapter 14), the increased partisan polarization in Congress (see Chapter 13) has made its mark on the Senate's confirmation process. For example, during President Clinton's first two years in office, a period of unified government, 86 percent of his nominees for the U.S. Court of Appeals were confirmed; but, during his second two years in office, a period of divided government, the confirmation rate dropped to 55 percent.[3]

As federal judges make more policy decisions, and as partisan rancor over those decisions rises, the process by which the Senate considers nominees for the federal bench has become longer, more ideologically charged, and less certain to result in confirmations. By long-standing tradition, senators from the home state of an appeals court nominee are allowed to file a private objection—what is called registering a negative "blue slip" complaint. If filed by a Judiciary Committee member, this will prevent a hearing on the nominee from being held. Sometimes these blue slips indicate that a senator doesn't like the nominee's political views, but other times it can mean that the senator is blocking a judicial appointment as a way of inducing the president to do something he or she wants on a totally unrelated matter. But, over the last three presidencies, that tradition has been used ever more as just another tool of partisan politics.

Judicial Review

One aspect of the power of the federal courts is **judicial review**— the right of the federal courts to declare laws of Congress and acts of the executive branch void and unenforceable if they are judged to be in conflict with the Constitution. Since 1789, the Supreme Court has declared more than 160 federal

laws to be unconstitutional. In Britain, by contrast, Parliament is supreme. The UK Supreme Court, established quite recently by the Constitutional Reform Act of 2005, started work in 2009 and is much more limited in its powers of judicial review. It cannot overturn primary legislation made by Parliament. As the second earl of Pembroke supposedly said, "A parliament can do anything but make a man a woman and a woman a man." All that prevents Parliament from acting contrary to the (unwritten) constitution of Britain are the consciences of its members and the opinions of the citizens.

About 60 nations do have something resembling judicial review, but in only a few cases does this power mean much in practice. Where it means something—in Australia, Canada, Germany, India, and some other nations—one finds a stable, federal system of government with a strong tradition of an independent judiciary.[4] Some other nations—France, for example—have special councils, rather than courts, that can under certain circumstances decide that a law is not authorized by the constitution.

Judicial review is the federal courts' chief weapon in the system of checks and balances on which the American government is based. Today, few people would deny to the courts the right to decide that a legislative or executive act is unconstitutional, though once that right was controversial. What remains controversial is the method by which such review is conducted.

There are two competing views, each ardently pressed during the fight to confirm Clarence Thomas. The first holds that judges should only judge—that is, they should confine themselves to applying those rules stated in or clearly implied by the language of the Constitution. This often is called the **judicial restraint approach**. The other argues that judges should discover the general principles underlying

judicial review
The power of courts to declare laws unconstitutional.

judicial restraint approach The view that judges should decide cases strictly on the basis of the language of the laws and the Constitution.

activist approach The view that judges should discern the general principles underlying laws or the Constitution and apply them to modern circumstances.

the Constitution and its often vague language, amplify those principles on the basis of some moral or economic philosophy, and apply them to cases. This is sometimes called the **activist approach**.

Note that the difference between activist and strict-constructionist judges is not necessarily the same as the difference between liberals and conservatives. Judges can be political liberals and still believe they are bound by the language of the Constitution. A liberal justice, Hugo Black, once voted to uphold a state law banning birth control because nothing in the Constitution prohibited such a law. Or judges can be conservative and still think they have a duty to use their best judgment in deciding what is good public policy. Rufus Peckham, one such conservative, voted to overturn a state law setting maximum hours of work because he believed the Fourteenth Amendment guaranteed something called "freedom of contract," even though those words are not in the amendment. Seventy years ago, judicial activists tended to be conservatives and strict-constructionist judges tended to be liberals; today the opposite usually is the case.

TABLE 16.3 Chief Justices of the United States

Chief Justice	Appointed by	Years of Service
John Jay	Washington	1789–1795
Oliver Ellsworth	Washington	1796–1800
John Marshall	Adams	1801–1835
Roger B. Taney	Jackson	1836–1864
Salmon P. Chase	Lincoln	1864–1873
Morrison R. Waite	Grant	1874–1888
Melville W. Fuller	Cleveland	1888–1910
Edward D. White	Taft	1910–1921
William Howard Taft	Harding	1921–1930
Charles Evans Hughes	Hoover	1930–1941
Harlan Fiske Stone	F. Roosevelt	1941–1946
Fred M. Vinson	Truman	1946–1953
Earl Warren	Eisenhower	1953–1969
Warren E. Burger	Nixon	1969–1986
William H. Rehnquist	Reagan	1986–2005
John G. Roberts, Jr.	Bush	2005–present

Note: Omitted is John Rutledge, who served for only a few months in 1795 and who was not confirmed by the Senate.

© Cengage Learning

The Development of the Federal Courts

Most of the Founders probably expected the Supreme Court to have the power of judicial review (though they did not say that in so many words in the Constitution), but they did not expect federal courts to play so large a role in making public policy. The traditional view of civil courts was that they judged disputes between people who had direct dealings with each other—they had entered into a contract, for example, or one had dropped a load of bricks on the other's toe—and decided which of the two parties was right. The court then supplied relief to the wronged party, usually by requiring the other person to pay him or her money ("damages").

This traditional understanding was based on the belief that judges would find and apply existing law. The purpose of a court case was not to learn what the judge believes but what the law requires. The later rise of judicial activism occurred when judges questioned this traditional view and argued instead that judges do not merely find the law, they make the law.

The view that judges interpret the law, not make policy, made it easy for the Founders to justify the power of judicial review. It also led them to predict that the courts would play a relatively neutral, even passive, role in public affairs. Alexander Hamilton, writing in *Federalist* No. 78, described the judiciary as the branch "least dangerous" to political rights. The president is commander in chief and thus holds the "sword of the community"; Congress appropriates money and thus "commands the purse" as well as decides what laws shall govern. But the judiciary "has no influence over either the sword or the purse" and "can take no active resolution whatever." It has "neither force nor will but merely judgment," and thus is "beyond comparison the weakest of the three departments of power." As a result, "liberty can have nothing to fear from the judiciary alone." Hamilton went on to state clearly that the Constitution intended to give to the courts the right to decide whether a law is contrary to the Constitution. But this authority, he explained, was designed not to enlarge the power of the courts but to confine that of the legislature.

Obviously, things have changed since Hamilton's time. The evolution of the federal courts, especially the Supreme Court, toward the present level of activism and influence has been shaped by the political, economic, and ideological forces of three historical eras. From 1787 to 1865, nation building, the legitimacy of the federal government, and slavery were the great issues; from 1865 to 1937, the great issue was the relationship between the government and the economy; from 1938 to the present, the major issues confronting the Court have involved personal liberty and social equality and the potential conflict between the two. In the first period, the Court asserted the supremacy of the federal government; in the second, it placed important restrictions on the powers of that government; and in the third, it enlarged the scope of personal freedom and narrowed that of economic freedom.

National Supremacy and Slavery

"From 1789 until the Civil War, the dominant interest of the Supreme Court was in that greatest of all the questions left unresolved by the Founders—the nation-state relationship."[5] The answer the Court gave, under the leadership of Chief Justice John Marshall, was that national law was in all instances the dominant law, with state law having to give way, and that the Supreme Court had the power to decide what the Constitution meant. In two cases of enormous importance—*Marbury v. Madison* in 1803 and *McCulloch v. Maryland* in 1819—the Court, in decisions written by Marshall, held that the Supreme Court could declare an act of Congress unconstitutional; that the power granted by the Constitution to the federal government flows from the people and thus should be generously construed (and thus any federal laws that are "necessary and proper" to the attainment of constitutional ends are permissible); and that federal law is supreme over state law, even to the point that a state may not tax an enterprise (such as a bank) created by the federal government.[6]

The supremacy of the federal government was reaffirmed by other decisions as well. In 1816, the Supreme Court rejected the claim of the Virginia courts that the Supreme Court could not review the decisions of state courts. The Virginia courts were ready to acknowledge the supremacy of the U.S. Constitution but believed they had as much right as the U.S. Supreme Court to decide what the Constitution meant. The Supreme Court felt otherwise, and in this case and another like it, the Court asserted its own broad powers to review any state court decision if that decision seemed to violate federal law or the federal Constitution.[7]

The power of the federal government to regulate commerce among the states was also established. When New York gave to Robert Fulton, the inventor of the steamboat, the monopoly right to operate his steamboats on the rivers of that state, the Marshall Court overturned the license because the rivers connected New York and New Jersey and thus trade on those rivers would involve *inter* state commerce, and federal law in that area was supreme. Since there was a conflicting federal law on the books, the state law was void.[8]

All of this may sound rather obvious to us today, when the supremacy of the federal government is largely unquestioned. In the early 19th century, however, these were almost revolutionary decisions. The Jeffersonian Republicans were in power and had become increasingly devoted to states' rights; they were aghast at the Marshall decisions. President Andrew Jackson attacked the Court bitterly for defending the right of the federal government to create a national bank and for siding with the Cherokee Indians in a dispute with Georgia. In speaking of the latter case, Jackson is supposed to have remarked, "John Marshall has made his decision; now let him enforce it!"[9]

Though Marshall seemed to have secured the supremacy of the federal government over the state governments, another even more divisive issue had arisen; that, of course, was slavery. Roger B. Taney succeeded Marshall as chief justice in 1836. He was deliberately chosen by President Jackson because he was an advocate of states' rights, and he began to chip away at federal supremacy, upholding state claims that Marshall would have set aside. But the decision for which he is famous—or infamous—came in 1857 when, in the *Dred Scott* case, he wrote perhaps the most disastrous judicial opinion ever issued. A slave, Dred Scott, had been taken by his owner to a territory (near what is now St. Paul, Minnesota) where slavery was illegal under federal law. Scott claimed that since he had resided in a free territory, he was now a free man. Taney held that Negroes were not citizens of the United States and could not become so, and that the federal law—the Missouri Compromise—prohibiting slavery in northern territories was unconstitutional.[10] The public outcry against this view was enormous, and the Court and Taney were discredited in the North, at least. The Civil War was ultimately fought over what the Court mistakenly had assumed was a purely legal question.

Government and the Economy

The supremacy of the federal government may have been established by John Marshall and the Civil War, but the scope of the powers of that government or even of the state governments was still to be defined. During the period from the end of the Civil War to the early years of the New Deal, the dominant issue the Supreme Court faced was deciding when the economy would be regulated by the states and when by the nation.

The Court revealed a strong though not inflexible attachment to private property. In fact, that attachment had always been there: the Founders thought political and property rights were inextricably linked, and Marshall certainly supported

LANDMARK CASES

Marbury v. Madison

The story of *Marbury v. Madison* is often told, but it deserves another telling because it illustrates so many features of the role of the Supreme Court—how apparently small cases can have large results, how the power of the Court depends not simply on its constitutional authority but also on its acting in ways that avoid a clear confrontation with other branches of government, and how the climate of opinion affects how the Court goes about its task.

When President John Adams lost his bid for re-election to Thomas Jefferson in 1800, he—and all members of his party, the Federalists—feared that Jefferson and the Republicans would weaken the federal government and turn its powers to what the Federalists believed were wrong ends (states' rights, an alliance with the French, hostility to business). Feverishly, as his hours in office came to an end, Adams worked to pack the judiciary with 59 loyal Federalists by giving them so-called midnight appointments before Jefferson took office.

John Marshall, as Adams's secretary of state, had the task of certifying and delivering these new judicial commissions. In the press of business, he delivered all but 17; these he left on his desk for the incoming secretary of state, James Madison, to send out. Jefferson and Madison, however, were furious at Adams's behavior and refused to deliver the 17. William Marbury and three other Federalists who had been promised these commissions hired a lawyer and brought suit against Madison to force him to produce the documents. The suit requested the Supreme Court to issue a writ of mandamus (from the Latin, "we command") ordering Madison to do his duty. The right to issue such writs had been given to the Court by the Judiciary Act of 1789.

Marshall, the man who had failed to deliver the commissions to Marbury and his friends in the first place, had become the chief justice and was now in a position to decide the case. These days, a justice who had been involved in an issue before it came to the Court would probably disqualify himself or herself, but Marshall had

no intention of letting others decide this question. He faced, however, not simply a partisan dispute over jobs but what was nearly a constitutional crisis. If he ordered the commission delivered, Madison might still refuse, and the Court had no way—if Madison was determined to resist—to compel him. The Court had no police force, whereas Madison had the support of the president of the United States. And if the order were given, whether or not Madison complied, the Jeffersonian Republicans in Congress would probably try to impeach Marshall. On the other hand, if Marshall allowed Madison to do as he wished, the power of the Supreme Court would be seriously reduced.

Marshall's solution was ingenious. Speaking for a unanimous Court, he announced that Madison was wrong to withhold the commissions, that courts could issue writs to compel public officials to do their prescribed duty—*but* that the Supreme Court had no power to issue such writs in this case because the law (the Judiciary Act of 1789) giving it that power was unconstitutional. The law said the Supreme Court could issue such writs as part of its "original jurisdiction"—that is, persons seeking such writs could go *directly* to the Supreme Court with their request (rather than go first to a lower federal court and then, if dissatisfied, appeal to the Supreme Court). Article III of the Constitution, Marshall pointed out, spelled out precisely the Supreme Court's original jurisdiction; it did not mention issuing writs of this sort and plainly indicated that on all matters not mentioned in the Constitution, the Court would have only appellate jurisdiction. Congress may not change what the Constitution says; hence, the part of the Judiciary Act attempting to do this was null and void.

The result was that a showdown with the Jeffersonians was avoided—Madison was not ordered to deliver the commissions—but the power of the Supreme Court was unmistakably clarified and enlarged. As Marshall wrote, "It is emphatically the province and duty of the judicial department to say what the law is." Furthermore, "a law repugnant to the Constitution is void."

---

the sanctity of contracts. But now, with the muting of the federal supremacy issue and the rise of a national economy with important unanticipated effects, the property question became the dominant one. In general, the Court developed the view that the Fourteenth Amendment, adopted in 1868 primarily to protect African American claims to citizenship from hostile state action, also protected private property and the corporation from unreasonable

state action. The crucial phrase was this: no state shall "deprive any person of life, liberty, or property, without due process of law." Once it became clear that a "person" could be a firm or a corporation as well as an individual, business and industry began to flood the courts with cases challenging various government regulations.

The Court quickly found itself in a thicket: it began ruling on the constitutionality of virtually every effort by any government to regulate any aspect of business or labor, and its workload rose sharply. Judicial activism was born in the 1880s and 1890s as the Court set itself up as the arbiter of what kind of regulation was permissible. In the first 75 years of this country's history, only two federal laws were held to be unconstitutional; in the next 75 years, 71 were.[11] Of the roughly 1,300 state laws held to be in conflict with the federal Constitution since 1789, about 1,200 were overturned after 1870. In one decade alone—the 1880s—five federal and 48 state laws were declared unconstitutional.

Many of these decisions provided clear evidence of the Court's desire to protect private property: it upheld the use of injunctions to prevent labor strikes,[12] struck down the federal income tax,[13] sharply limited the reach of the antitrust law,[14] restricted the powers of the Interstate Commerce Commission to set railroad rates,[15] prohibited the federal government from eliminating child labor,[16] and prevented the states from setting maximum hours of work.[17] In 184 cases between 1899 and 1937, the Supreme Court struck down state laws for violating the Fourteenth Amendment, usually by economic regulation.[18]

But the Court also rendered decisions that authorized various kinds of regulation. It allowed states to regulate businesses "affected with a public interest,"[19] changed its mind about the Interstate Commerce Commission and allowed it to regulate railroad rates,[20] upheld rules requiring railroads to improve their safety,[21] approved state antiliquor laws,[22] approved state mine safety laws,[23] supported state workers' compensation laws,[24] allowed states to regulate fire-insurance rates,[25] and in time upheld a number of state laws regulating wages and hours. Indeed, between 1887 and 1910, in 558 cases involving the Fourteenth Amendment, the Supreme Court upheld state regulations over 80 percent of the time.[26]

To characterize the Court as pro-business or antiregulation is both simplistic and inexact. More accurate, perhaps, is to characterize it as supportive of the rights of private property but unsure how to draw the lines that distinguish "reasonable" from "unreasonable" regulation. Nothing in the Constitution clearly differentiates reasonable from unreasonable regulation, and the Court has been able to invent no consistent principle of its own to make this determination. For example, what kinds of businesses are "affected with a public interest"? Grain elevators and railroads are, but are bakeries? Sugar refineries? Saloons? And how much of commerce is "interstate"—anything that moves? Or only something that actually crosses a state line? The Court found itself trying to make detailed judgments that it was not always competent to make and to invent legal rules where no clear legal rules were possible.

In one area, however, the Supreme Court's judgments were clear: the Fourteenth and Fifteenth Amendments were construed so narrowly as to give African Americans only the most limited benefits of their provisions. In a long series of decisions, the Court upheld segregation in schools and on railroad cars and permitted blacks to be excluded from voting in many states.

Government and Political Liberty

After 1936, the Supreme Court stopped imposing any serious restrictions on state or federal power to regulate the economy, leaving such matters in the hands of the legislatures. From 1937 to 1974, the Supreme Court did not overturn a single federal law designed to regulate business but did overturn 36 congressional enactments that violated personal political liberties. It voided as unconstitutional laws that restricted freedom of speech,[27] denied passports to communists,[28] permitted the government to revoke a person's citizenship,[29] withheld a person's mail,[30] or restricted the availability of government benefits.[31]

This new direction began when one justice changed his mind, and it continued as the composition of the Court changed. At the outset of the New Deal, the Court was by a narrow margin dominated by justices who opposed the welfare state and federal regulation based on broad grants of discretionary authority to administrative agencies. President Franklin Roosevelt, who was determined to get just such legislation implemented, found himself powerless to alter the composition of the Court during his first term (1933–1937); because no justice died or retired, he had no vacancies to fill. After his overwhelming re-election in 1936, he moved to remedy this problem by "packing" the Court.

Roosevelt proposed a bill that would have allowed him to appoint one new justice for each one over the age of 70 who refused to retire, up to a total membership of 15. Since there were six men in this category then on the Supreme Court, he would have been able to appoint six new justices, enough to ensure a comfortable majority supportive of his economic policies. A bitter controversy ensued, but before the bill could be voted on, the Supreme Court, perhaps reacting to Roosevelt's big win in the 1936 election, changed its mind. Whereas it had been striking down several New Deal measures by votes of 5 to 4, now it started approving them by the same vote. One justice, Owen Roberts, had switched his position. This was called the "switch in time that saved nine," but in fact Roberts had changed his mind *before* the FDR plan was announced.

CONSTITUTIONAL CONNECTIONS

The "Exceptions" Clause

Article III, Section II of the Constitution provides that "the Supreme Court shall have appellate Jurisdiction, both as to Law and Fact, with such Exceptions, and under such Regulations as the Congress shall make." In the 1868 case of *Ex Parte McCardle*, the Court unanimously agreed that the "Exceptions" clause gives Congress the power to restrict the Court's appellate jurisdiction. Since then, many noted jurists and scholars have taken serious issue with that interpretation; but, the prevailing view is that, at least on an issue by issue basis, the exceptions clause gives Congress broad, if not unlimited, power to prohibit the federal courts, including the Supreme Court, from exercising judicial review.

Over the last several decades, each session of Congress has witnessed proposals to deny the federal courts appellate jurisdiction. There have been such proposals on abortion rights, busing to achieve racial balance in schools, school prayer, prisoners'

rights, same-sex marriage, and many other issues. Some exception-clause proposals have become bills and made it into federal law; for example, the Illegal Immigration Reform and Immigrant Responsibility Act of 1996 prohibited the federal courts from hearing appeals regarding certain decisions by the U.S. Immigration and Naturalization Service.

Typically, however, even exception clause-related bills that come to a vote never make it into law. For example, in each of several post-2000 sessions, the House approved a bill prohibiting federal courts from exercising appellate jurisdiction in cases involving the invocation of "under God" in the Pledge of Allegiance. But none of these bills made it through the Senate. Likewise, in 2011, Rep. Ron Paul (R-TX) sponsored the Sanctity of Life Act, which would have stripped the federal courts of the authority to hear abortion cases; but that was just the latest in a series of such exception-clause bills on abortion that were much-debated but never enacted.

LANDMARK CASES

Power of the Supreme Court

- *Marbury v. Madison* (1803): Upheld judicial review of congressional acts.

- *Martin v. Hunter's Lessee* (1816): The Supreme Court can review the decisions of the highest state courts if they involve a federal law or the federal Constitution.

- *McCulloch v. Maryland* (1819): Ruled that creating a federal bank, though not mentioned in the Constitution, was a "necessary and proper" exercise of the government's right to borrow money.

- *Ex parte McCardle* (1869): Allowed Congress to change the appellate jurisdiction of the Supreme Court.

The "Court-packing" bill was not passed, but it was no longer necessary. Justice Roberts had yielded before public opinion in a way that Chief Justice Taney a century earlier had not, thus forestalling an assault on the Court by the other branches of government. Shortly thereafter, several justices

stepped down, and Roosevelt was able to make his own appointments (he filled seven seats during his four terms in office). From then on, the Court turned its attention to new issues—political liberties and, in time, civil rights.

With the arrival in office of Chief Justice Earl Warren in 1953, the Court began its most active period yet. Activism now arose to redefine the relationship of citizens to the government and especially to protect the rights and liberties of citizens from governmental trespass. Although the Court has always seen itself as protecting citizens from arbitrary government, before 1937 that protection was of a sort that conservatives preferred; after 1937, it was of a kind that liberals preferred.

The Revival of State Sovereignty

For many decades, the Supreme Court allowed Congress to pass almost any law authorized by the Constitution, no matter how it affected the states. As we saw in Chapter 3, the Court had long held that Congress could regulate almost any activity if it affected interstate commerce, and in the Court's opinion virtually every activity did affect it. The states were left with few rights to challenge federal power. But since around 1992, the Court has backed away from this view. By narrow majorities, it has

FIGURE 16.1 **Economics and Civil Liberties Laws Overturned by the U.S. Supreme Court, by Decade, 1900–2006**

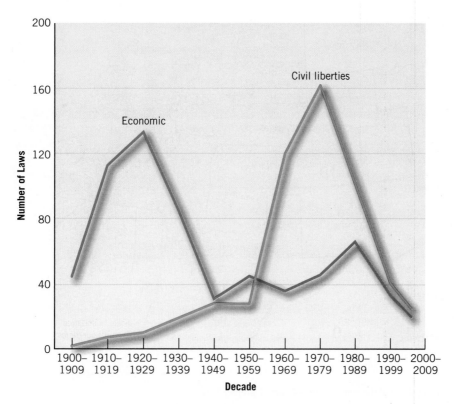

Note: Civil liberties category does not include laws supportive of civil liberties. Laws include federal, state, and local.

Source: Data adapted from Harold W. Stanley and Richard G. Niemi, *Vital Statistics on American Politics*, 2007–2008, 5th ed., p. 302 (Washington, D. C.: CQ Press, 2008).

begun to restore the view that states have the right to resist some forms of federal action.

When Congress passed a bill that forbade anyone from carrying a gun near a school, the Court held that carrying guns did not affect interstate commerce, and so the law was invalid.[32] One year later, it struck down a law that allowed Indian tribes to sue the states in federal courts, arguing that Congress lacks the power to ignore the "sovereign immunity" of states—that is, the right, protected by the Eleventh Amendment, not to be sued in federal court. (It has since upheld that view in two more cases.) And the next year, it held that the Brady gun control law could not be used to require local law enforcement officers to do background checks on people trying to buy weapons.[33] These cases are all hints that there are some real limits to the supremacy of the federal government created by the existence and powers of the several states.

After the enactment of President Obama's health care plan in 2010, several states argued that its requirement that everyone purchase health

insurance was unconstitutional. Some district courts agreed with the claims and others disagreed. The issue was whether Congress's authority to levy taxes or to regulate interstate commerce gave it the right to require citizens to purchase a product. In addition, some state officials questioned the constitutionality of provisions requiring state governments to expand health care coverage for low-income citizens via the federal-state Medicaid program or risk losing all existing federal funding for that program.

In *National Federation of Independent Business v. Sebelius* (2012), the Supreme Court decided these issues. It upheld the law's "individual mandate" to purchase "minimum essential" health insurance, ruling that the monetary "penalty" to be levied by the Internal Revenue Service on anyone that does not purchase insurance as required by the law is tantamount to a constitutionally permissible federal "tax."

But, in the same decision, the Court struck down the law's mandate that state governments expand Medicaid coverage by 2014, ruling that the provision "violates the Constitution" by impermissibly

MAP 16.1 **U.S. District and Appellate Courts**

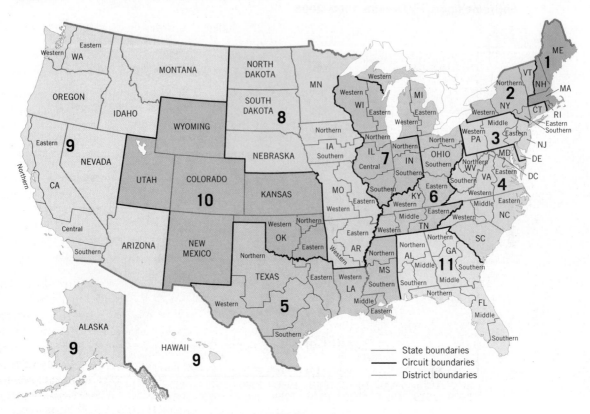

Source: Administrative Office of the United States Courts (January 1983).

Note: Washington, D.C., is in a separate court. Puerto Rico is in the first circuit; the Virgin Islands are in the third; Guam and the Northern Mariana Islands are in the ninth. The Court of Appeals for the Federal Circuit, located in Washington, D.C., is a Title 3 court that hears appeals regarding patents, trademarks, international trade, government contracts, and from civil servants who claim they were unjustly discharged.

constitutional court A federal court authorized by Article III of the Constitution that keeps judges in office during good behavior and prevents their salaries from being reduced. They are the Supreme Court (created by the Constitution) and appellate and district courts created by Congress.

"threatening States with the loss of their existing" federal funding for the program. This part of the decision had important consequences for the law's implementation (see the "States and Health Exchanges" feature on page 53), and it could in time have far-reaching implications for how the federal courts handle cases concerning intergovernmental programs (see Chapter 3):

Congress has no authority to order the States to regulate according to its instructions. Congress may offer the States grants and require the States

to comply with accompanying conditions, but the States must have a genuine choice whether to comply.

The Structure of the Federal Courts

The only federal court the Constitution requires is the Supreme Court, as specified in Article III. All other federal courts and their jurisdictions are creations of Congress. Nor does the Constitution indicate how many justices shall be on the Supreme Court (there were originally six, now there are nine) or what its appellate jurisdiction shall be.

Congress has created two kinds of lower federal courts to handle cases that need not be decided by the Supreme Court: constitutional and legislative courts. A **constitutional court** is one exercising the judicial powers found in Article III of the

Fotosearch/Archive Photos/Getty Images

Louis Brandeis, creator of the "Brandeis Brief" that developed court cases based on economic and social more than legal arguments, became the first Jewish Supreme Court justice. He served in the Court from 1916 until 1939.

Constitution, and therefore its judges are given constitutional protection: they may not be fired (they serve during "good behavior"), nor may their salaries be reduced while they are in office. The most important of the constitutional courts are the **district courts** (a total of 94, with at least one in each state, the District of Columbia, and the commonwealth of Puerto Rico) and the **courts of appeals** (one in each of 11 regions, plus one in the District of Columbia and one federal circuit). There are also various specialized constitutional courts, such as the Court of International Trade.

Legislative courts are those set up by Congress for some specialized purpose and staffed with people who have fixed terms of office and can be removed or have their salaries reduced. Legislative courts include the Court of Military Appeals and the territorial courts.

Selecting Judges

Party background makes a difference in how judges behave. An analysis has been done of more than 80 studies of the link between party and either liberalism or conservatism among state and federal judges in cases involving civil liberties, criminal justice, and economic regulation. It shows that judges who are Democrats are more likely to make liberal decisions and Republican judges are more likely to make conservative ones.[*] The party effect is not small.[34] We should not be surprised by this, since we have already seen that among political elites (and judges are certainly elites), party identification influences personal ideology.

But ideology does not entirely determine behavior. So many other things shape court decisions—the facts of the case, prior rulings by other courts, the arguments presented by lawyers—that there is no reliable way of predicting how judges will behave in all matters. Presidents sometimes make the mistake of thinking they know how their appointees will behave, only to be surprised by the facts. Theodore Roosevelt appointed Oliver Wendell Holmes to the Supreme Court, only to remark later, after Holmes had voted in a way that Roosevelt did not like, that "I could carve out of a banana a judge with more backbone than that!" Holmes, who had plenty of backbone, said he did not "give a damn" what Roosevelt thought. Richard Nixon, an ardent foe of court-ordered school busing, appointed Warren Burger chief justice. Burger promptly sat down and wrote the opinion upholding busing. Another Nixon appointee, Harry Blackmun, wrote the opinion declaring the right to an abortion to be constitutionally protected.

Federal judges tend to be white, male, and Protestant, and increasingly have been judges on some other court. There has been a decline in the proportion of Supreme Court justices who come directly from private law practice; almost all have been promoted from a lower-ranking judgeship. For example, of the nine justices chosen by President Franklin D. Roosevelt, only two had been judges, while of the 12 nominated by presidents Ronald Reagan, George H. W. Bush, Bill Clinton, George W. Bush, and Barack Obama, ten had been judges. Sex, race, and ethnicity

district courts The lowest federal courts; federal trials can be held only here.

courts of appeals Federal courts that hear appeals from district courts; no trials.

Legislative courts Courts created by Congress for specialized purposes whose judges do not enjoy the protections of Article III of the Constitution.

---

[*]A "liberal" decision is one that favors a civil right, a criminal defendant or an economic regulation; a "conservative" one opposes the right or the regulation or supports the criminal prosecutor.

also have become important factors in selecting judges. As is evident in Figure 16.2, Democratic presidents since President Lyndon Johnson have appointed higher percentages of women, blacks, and Hispanics than Republican presidents have, including a record-shattering fraction of female appointees during President Obama's first term.

Senatorial Courtesy

In theory, the president nominates a "qualified" person to be a judge, and the Senate approves or rejects the nomination based on those "qualifications." In fact, the tradition of *senatorial courtesy* gives heavy weight to the preferences of the senators from the state where a federal district judge

FIGURE 16.2 **Female and Minority Judicial Appointments, 1963–2013**

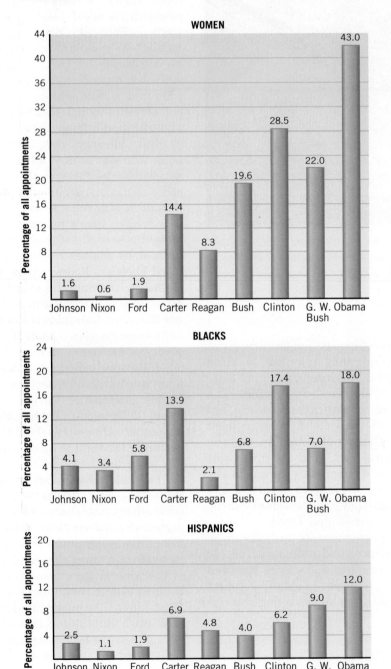

Source: Updated from Harold W. Stanley and Richard G. Niemi, *Vital Statistics on American Politics, 2005–2006* (Washington, D.C. : Congressional Quarterly, 2006), Table 7.5.

is to serve. Ordinarily, the Senate will not confirm a district court judge if the senior senator from the state where the district is located objects (if he is of the president's party). The senator can exercise this veto power by means of the "blue slip"—a blue piece of paper on which the senator is asked to record his or her views on the nominee. A negative opinion, or even failure to return the blue slip, usually kills the nomination. This means that as a practical matter the president nominates only persons recommended to him by that key senator. Someone once suggested that, at least with respect to district judges, the Constitution has been turned on its head. To reflect reality, he said, Article II, section 2, ought to read: "The senators shall nominate, and by and with the consent of the President, shall appoint" federal judges.

The "Litmus Test"

Of late, presidents have tried to exercise more influence on the selection of federal district and appellate court judges by getting the Justice Department to find candidates that not only are supported by their party's senators, but also reflect the political and judicial philosophy of the president. Presidents Carter and Clinton sought out liberal, activist judges; President Reagan sought out conservative, strict-constructionist ones. The party membership of federal judges makes a difference in how they vote.[35]

Because different courts of appeals have different combinations of judges, some will be more liberal than others. For example, there are more liberal judges in the court of appeals for the ninth circuit (which includes most of the far western states) and more conservative ones in the fifth circuit (Texas, Louisiana, and Mississippi). The ninth circuit takes liberal positions, the fifth more conservative ones. Since the Supreme Court does not have time to settle every disagreement among appeals courts, different interpretations of the law may exist in different circuits. In the fifth, for instance, it was for a while unconstitutional for state universities to have affirmative action programs, but in the ninth circuit that was permitted.

These differences make some people worry about the use of a political **litmus test**—a test of ideological purity—in selecting judges. When conservatives are out of power, they complain about how liberal presidents use such a test; when liberals are out power, they complain about how conservative presidents use it. Many people would like to see judges picked on the basis of professional qualifications, without reference to ideology, but the courts are now so deeply involved in political issues that it is hard to imagine what an ideologically neutral set of professional qualifications might be.

A judicial nominee's view on abortion is the chief motive for using the litmus test. Since it is easy to mount a filibuster and it takes 60 votes to end one, the nominee usually must be assured of 60 Senate votes to be confirmed. In theory, the Senate could adopt a rule preventing filibusters of nominations—but it never has. In 2005, a group of 14 senators, half from each party, agreed they would vote to block a filibuster on court nominees unless there were "extraordinary circumstances." This group—called the Gang of Fourteen—made it possible for several nominees (including Samuel Alito) to be confirmed even though they had fewer than 60 votes (but still, of course, more than 50).

The litmus test issue is of greatest importance in selecting Supreme Court justices. Here, there is no tradition of senatorial courtesy. The president takes a keen personal interest in the choices and, of late, has sought to find nominees who share his philosophy. In the Reagan administration, there were bruising fights in the Senate over the nomination of William Rehnquist to be chief justice (he won) and Robert Bork to be an associate justice (he lost), with liberals pitted against conservatives. When President George H. W. Bush nominated David Souter, there were lengthy hearings as liberal senators tried to pin down Souter's views on issues such as abortion. Souter refused to discuss matters on which he might later have to judge, however. Clarence Thomas, another Bush nominee, also tried to avoid the litmus test by saying he had not formed an opinion on prominent abortion cases. In his case, however, the litmus test issue was overshadowed by sensational allegations from a former employee, Anita Hill, that Thomas had sexually harassed her.

Of the 160 Supreme Court nominees presented to it, the Senate failed to confirm 36 of them. From the presidency of Harry Truman through the first term of President Barack Obama, 29 of 34 nominees have been confirmed. Of the five that were not confirmed, three (two nominated by President Richard Nixon, and one nominated by President Ronald Reagan) were voted on and rejected by a Senate majority, and two (one nominated by President Lyndon Johnson, and one nominated by President George W. Bush) withdrew before any Senate vote on the nomination. The reasons for rejecting a Supreme Court nominee are complex—each senator may have a different reason—but have involved such matters as the nominee's alleged hostility to civil rights, questionable personal financial dealings, a poor record as a lower-court judge, and Senate opposition to

> **litmus test** An examination of the political ideology of a nominated judge.

federal-question cases Cases concerning the Constitution, federal laws, or treaties.

diversity cases Cases involving citizens of different states who can bring suit in federal courts.

the nominee's political or legal philosophy. As we indicated earlier, nominations of district court judges are rarely defeated, because typically no nomination is made unless the key senators approve in advance.

The Jurisdiction of the Federal Courts

We have a dual court system—one state, one federal—and this complicates enormously the task of describing what kinds of cases federal courts may

hear and how cases beginning in the state courts may end up before the Supreme Court. The Constitution lists the kinds of cases over which federal courts have jurisdiction (in Article III and the Eleventh Amendment) by implication; all other matters are left to state courts. Federal courts (see Figure 16.3) can hear all cases "arising under the Constitution, the laws of the United States, and treaties" (these are **federal-question cases**), and cases involving citizens of different states (called **diversity cases**).

Some kinds of cases can be heard in either federal or state courts. For example, if citizens of different states wish to sue one another and the matter involves more than $75,000, they can do so in either a federal or a state court. Similarly, if someone robs a federally insured bank, he or she has broken both state and federal law and thus can be prosecuted in state or federal courts, or both. Lawyers have become quite sophisticated in deciding whether, in

FIGURE 16.3 **The Jurisdiction of the Federal Courts**

© Cengage Learning

Sonia Sotomayor answers questions before the Senate committee considering her nomination to be a Supreme Court justice.

a given civil case, their clients will get better treatment in a state or federal court. Prosecutors often send a person who has broken both federal and state law to whichever court system is likelier to give the toughest penalty.

Sometimes defendants may be tried in both state and federal courts for the same offense. In 1992, four Los Angeles police officers accused of beating Rodney King were tried in a California state court and acquitted of assault charges. They were then prosecuted in federal court for violating King's civil rights. This time, two of the four were convicted. Under the dual sovereignty doctrine, state and federal authorities can prosecute the same person for the same conduct. The Supreme Court has upheld this doctrine on two grounds: first, each level of government has the right to enact laws serving its own purposes.[36] As a result, federal civil rights charges could have been brought against the officers even if they had already been convicted of assault in state court (though as a practical matter this would have been unlikely). Second, neither level of government wants the other to be able to block prosecution of an accused person who has the sympathy of the authorities at one level. For example, when certain southern state courts were in sympathy with whites who had lynched blacks, the absence of the dual sovereignty doctrine would have meant that a trumped-up acquittal in state court would have barred federal prosecution.

Furthermore, a matter that is exclusively within the province of a state court—for example, a criminal case in which the defendant is charged with violating only a state law—can be appealed to the U.S. Supreme Court under certain circumstances (described below). Thus federal judges can overturn state court rulings even when they had no jurisdiction over the original matter. Under what circumstances this should occur has been the subject of long-standing controversy between the state and federal courts.

Some matters, however, are exclusively under the jurisdiction of federal courts. When a federal criminal law is broken—but not a state one—the case is heard in federal district court.

> **writ of certiorari** An order by a higher court directing a lower court to send up a case for review.

If you wish to appeal the decision of a federal regulatory agency, such as the Federal Communications Commission, you can do so only before a federal court of appeals. And if you wish to declare bankruptcy, you do so in federal court. If there is a controversy between two state governments—say, California and Arizona sue each other over which state is to use how much water from the Colorado River—the case can be heard only by the Supreme Court.

The vast majority of all cases heard by federal courts begin in the district courts. The volume of business there is huge. In 2009, the 667 district court judges received 276,397 cases (more than 400 per judge). Most of the cases heard in federal courts involve rather straightforward applications of law; few lead to the making of new public policy. Cases that do affect how the law or the Constitution is interpreted can begin with seemingly minor events. For example, a major broadening of the Bill of Rights—requiring for the first time that all accused persons in *state* as well as federal criminal trials be supplied with a lawyer, free if necessary—began when impoverished Clarence Earl Gideon, imprisoned in Florida, wrote an appeal in pencil on prison stationery and sent it to the Supreme Court.[37]

The Supreme Court does not have to hear any appeal it does not want to hear. At one time, it was required to listen to certain appeals, but Congress has changed the law so that now the Court can pick the cases it wants to consider. It does this by issuing a **writ of certiorari**. *Certiorari* is a Latin word meaning, roughly, "made more certain"; lawyers and judges have abbreviated it to *cert*. It works this way: the Court considers all the petitions it receives to review lower-court decisions. If four justices agree to hear a case, cert is issued and the case is scheduled for a hearing.

In deciding whether to grant certiorari, the Court tries to reserve its time for cases decided by lower federal courts or by the highest state courts in which a significant federal or constitutional question has been raised. For example, the Court often will grant certiorari when one or both of the following is true:

- Two or more federal circuit courts of appeals have decided the same issue in different ways.

- The highest court in a state has held a federal or state law to be in violation of the Constitution or has upheld a state law against the claim that it is in violation of the Constitution.

In a typical year, the Court may consider more than 7,000 petitions asking it to review decisions of lower or state courts. It rarely accepts more than about 100 of them for full review.

In exercising its discretion in granting certiorari, the Supreme Court is on the horns of a dilemma. If it grants it frequently, it will be inundated with cases. As it is, the Court's workload has quintupled in the last 50 years. If, on the other hand, the Court grants certiorari only rarely, then the federal courts of appeals have the last word on the interpretation of the Constitution and federal laws, and since there are 12 of these, staffed by about 167 judges, they may well be in disagreement. In fact this has already happened: because the Supreme Court reviews only about 1 or 2 percent of appeals court cases, applicable federal law may be different in different parts of the country.[38] One proposal to deal with this dilemma is to devote the Supreme Court's time entirely to major questions of constitutional interpretation and to create a national court of appeals that would ensure

Clarence Earl Gideon studied law books while in prison so that he could write an appeal to the Supreme Court. His handwritten sked that his conviction be set aside because he had not been provided with an attorney. His appeal was granted.

WHAT'S YOUR ISSUE?

A "PRISM" on Internet Surveillance

"U.S., British Intelligence Mining Data from Nine U.S. Internet Companies in Broad Secret Program." That was the headline of a June 6, 2013 story in *The Washington Post*. The story revealed how the National Security Agency (NSA) and the Federal Bureau of Investigation (FBI) had since 2007 conducted a secret surveillance program, code-named PRISM. The program, conducted by the NSA and the FBI in concert with British intelligence agencies, gathered, tracked, and analyzed massive amounts of "private" data (audio and video chats, emails, and more) by directly searching the central servers of Microsoft, Yahoo, Google, Facebook, PalTalk, AOL, Skype, YouTube, and Apple.

The story and subsequent reports on the program sparked much public controversy. Somewhat lost in the first waves of reaction to the news was the legislative and judicial history surrounding the program. Under the Foreign Intelligence Service Act of 1978, as amended in 2008, the NSA submits requests to conduct secret electronic surveillance to the (until the 2013 story broke) little-known U.S. Foreign Intelligence Surveillance Court, or FISC, which is composed of 11 specially selected U.S. district court judges from seven different judicial circuits (at least three of whom must live within 20 miles of the District of Columbia). A January 24, 2007 report by the Congressional Research Service outlined how the FISC is supposed to work (membership, structure, jurisdiction, and review

of its decisions by a special Court of Review). Under the Protect America Act of 2007, Congress immunized from private lawsuits internet companies that participate in government-directed surveillance programs.

When President Barack Obama addressed the controversy regarding PRISM, he characterized the program as secret to the public but well known to the Congress and conducted as an anti-terrorism effort, adding "No one is listening to your phone calls." On June 6, 2013, the day after the story broke, the normally pro-Obama *New York Times* editorialized strongly against what it called "President Obama's Dragnet," while the normally anti-Obama *Wall Street Journal* endorsed the president's view in an editorial entitled "Thank You for Data-Mining."

What is your stake and what is your take on PRISM? Whether court-sanctioned and congressionally-authorized or not, what civil liberties (see Chapter 5) issues do you think are raised by any such broad secret surveillance program?

Source: Barton Gellman and Laura Poitras, "U.S., British Intelligence Mining Data from Nine U.S. Internet Companies in Broad Secret Program," *The Washington Post*, June 6, 2013; Elizabeth B. Bazan, CRS Report for Congress: The U.S. Foreign Intelligence Surveillance Court and the U.S. Foreign Intelligence Surveillance Court of Review: An Overview, Congressional Research Service, January 24, 2007.

that the 12 circuit courts of appeals are producing uniform decisions.[39]

Because the Supreme Court has a heavy workload, the influence wielded by law clerks has grown. These clerks—recent graduates of law schools hired by the justices—play a big role in deciding which cases should be heard under a writ of certiorari. Indeed, some of the opinions written by the justices are drafted by the clerks. Since the reasons for a decision may be as important as the decision itself, and since these reasons are sometimes created by the clerks, the power of the clerks can be significant.

Getting to Court

In theory, the courts are the great equalizer in the federal government. To use the courts to settle a question, or even to fundamentally alter the accepted interpretation of the Constitution, one need not be elected to any office, have access to the mass media, be a member of an interest group, or be otherwise powerful or rich. Once the contending parties are before the courts, they are legally equal.

It is too easy to believe this theory uncritically or to dismiss it cynically. In fact, it is hard to get before the Supreme Court: it rejects over 96 percent of the applications for certiorari that it receives. And the costs involved in getting to the Court can be high. To apply for certiorari costs only $300 (plus 40 copies of the petition), but if certiorari is granted and the case is heard, the costs—for lawyers and for copies of the lower-court records in the case—can be very high. And by then one has already paid for the cost of the first hearing in the district court and probably one appeal to the circuit court of appeals. Furthermore, the time it takes to settle a matter in federal court can be quite long.

But there are ways to make these costs lower. If you are indigent—without funds—you can file and be heard as a pauper for nothing; about half the petitions arriving before the Supreme Court are **in forma pauperis** (such as the one from Gideon, described earlier). If your case began as a criminal trial in the district courts and you are poor, the government will supply you with a lawyer at no charge. If the matter is not a criminal case and you cannot afford to hire a lawyer, interest groups representing a wide spectrum of opinion sometimes are willing to take up the cause if the issue in the case seems sufficiently important. The American Civil Liberties Union (ACLU), a liberal group, represents some people who believe their freedom of speech has been abridged or their constitutional rights in criminal proceedings have been violated. The Center for Individual Rights, a conservative group, represents some people who feel that they have been victimized by racial quotas.

But interest groups do much more than just help people pay their bills. Many of the most important cases decided by the Court got there because an interest group organized the case, found the plaintiffs, chose the legal strategy, and mobilized legal allies. The NAACP has brought many key civil rights cases on behalf of individuals. Although in the past most such cases were brought by liberal interest groups, of late conservative interest groups have entered the courtroom on behalf of individuals. One helped sue CBS for televising a program that allegedly libeled General William Westmoreland, once the American commander in Vietnam. (Westmoreland lost the case.) And many important issues are raised by attorneys representing state and local governments. Several price-fixing cases have been won by state attorneys general on behalf of consumers in their states.

Fee Shifting

Unlike what happens in most of Europe, each party to a lawsuit in this country must pay its own way. (In England, by contrast, if you sue someone and lose, you pay the winner's costs as well as your own.) But various laws have made it easier to get someone else to pay. **Fee shifting** enables the **plaintiff** (the party that initiates the suit) to collect its costs from the defendant if the defendant loses, at least in certain kinds of cases. For example, if a corporation is found to have violated the antitrust laws, it must pay the legal fees of the winner. If an environmentalist group sues the Environmental Protection Agency and wins, it can get the EPA to pay the group's legal costs. Even more important to individuals, Section 1983 of Chapter 42 of the *United States Code* allows a citizen to sue a state or local government official—say, a police officer or a school superintendent—who has deprived the citizen of some constitutional right or withheld some benefit to which the citizen is entitled. If the citizen wins, he or she can collect money damages and lawyers' fees from the government. Citizens, more aware of their legal rights, have become more litigious, and a flood of such "Section 1983" suits has burdened the courts. The Supreme Court has restricted fee shifting to cases authorized by statute,[40] but it is clear that the drift of policy has made it cheaper to go to court—at least for some cases.

in forma pauperis A method whereby a poor person can have his or her case heard in federal court without charge.

fee shifting A rule that allows a plaintiff to recover costs from the defendant if the plaintiff wins.

plaintiff The party that initiates a lawsuit.

standing A legal rule stating who is authorized to start a lawsuit.

sovereign immunity The rule that a citizen cannot sue the government without the government's consent.

class-action suit A case brought by someone to help both himself or herself and all others who are similarly situated.

Standing

There is, in addition, a nonfinancial restriction on getting into federal court. To sue, one must have **standing**, a legal concept that refers to who is entitled to bring a case. It is especially important in determining who can challenge the laws or actions of the government itself. A complex and changing set of rules governs standings; some of the more important ones are these:

- There must be an actual controversy between real adversaries. (You cannot bring a "friendly" suit against someone, hoping to lose in order to prove your friend right. You cannot ask a federal court for an opinion on a hypothetical or imaginary case or ask it to render an advisory opinion.)

- You must show that you have been harmed by the law or practice about which you are complaining. (It is not enough to dislike what the government or a corporation or a labor union does; you must show that you were actually harmed by that action.)

- Merely being a taxpayer does not ordinarily entitle you to challenge the constitutionality of a federal governmental action. (You may not want your tax money to be spent in certain ways, but your remedy is to vote against the politicians doing the spending; the federal courts will generally require that you show some other personal harm before you can sue.)

Congress and the courts have recently made it easier to acquire standing. It has always been the rule that a citizen could ask the courts to order federal officials to carry out some act that they were under a legal obligation to perform or to refrain from some action that was contrary to law. A citizen can also sue a government official personally to collect damages if the official acted contrary to law. For example, it was for long the case that if an FBI agent broke into your office without a search warrant, you could sue the agent and, if you won, collect money. However, you cannot sue the government itself without its consent. This is the doctrine of **sovereign immunity**. For instance, if the army accidentally kills your cow while testing a new cannon, you cannot sue the government to recover the cost of the cow unless the government agrees to be sued. (Since testing cannons is legal, you cannot sue the army officer who fired the cannon.) By statute, Congress has given its consent for the government to be sued in many cases involving a dispute over a contract or damage done as a result of negligence (for example, the dead cow). Over the years, these statutes have made it easier to take the government into court as a defendant.

Even some of the oldest rules defining standing have been liberalized. The rule that merely being a taxpayer does not entitle you to challenge in court a government decision has been relaxed where the citizen claims that a right guaranteed under the First Amendment is being violated. The Supreme Court allowed a taxpayer to challenge a federal law that would have given financial aid to parochial (or church-related) schools on the grounds that this aid violated the constitutional requirement of separation between church and state. On the other hand, another taxpayer suit to force the CIA to make public its budget failed because the Court decided that the taxpayer did not have standing in matters of this sort.[41]

Class-Action Suits

Under certain circumstances, a citizen can benefit directly from a court decision, even though the citizen himself or herself has not gone into court. This can happen by means of a **class-action suit**: a case brought into court by a person on behalf not only of himself or herself, but of all other persons in similar circumstances. Among the most famous of these was the 1954 case in which the Supreme Court found that Linda Brown, a black girl attending the fifth grade in the Topeka, Kansas, public schools, was denied the equal protection of the laws (guaranteed under the Fourteenth Amendment) because the schools in Topeka were segregated. The Court did not limit its decision to Linda Brown's right to attend an unsegregated school but extended it—as Brown's lawyers from the NAACP had asked—to cover all "others similarly situated."[42] It was not easy to design a court order that would eliminate segregation in the schools, but the principle was clearly established in this class action.

Since the *Brown* case, many other groups have been quick to take advantage of the opportunity created by class-action suits. By this means, the courts could be used to give relief not simply to a particular person but to all those represented in the suit. A landmark class-action case challenged the malapportionment of state legislative districts (see Chapter 13).[43] There are thousands of class-action suits in the federal courts involving civil rights, the rights of prisoners, antitrust suits against corporations, and other matters. These suits became more common partly because people were beginning to have new concerns that were not being met by Congress and partly because some class-action suits became quite profitable. The NAACP got no money from Linda Brown or from the Topeka Board of Education in compensation for its long and expensive labors, but, beginning in the 1960s, court rules were changed to make it financially attractive for lawyers to bring certain kinds of class-action suits.

Suppose, for example, that you think your telephone company overcharged you by $75. You could try to hire a lawyer to get a refund, but not many lawyers would take the case, because there would be no money in it. Even if you were to win, the lawyer would stand to earn no more than perhaps one-third of the settlement, or $25. Now suppose you bring a class action against the company on behalf of everybody who was overcharged. Millions of dollars might be at stake; lawyers would line up eagerly to take the case, because their share of the settlement, if they won, would be huge. The opportunity to win profitable class-action suits, combined with the possibility of having the loser pay the attorneys' fees, led to a proliferation of such cases.

In response to the increase in its workload, the Supreme Court decided in 1974 to drastically tighten the rules governing these suits. It held that it would no longer hear (except in certain cases defined by Congress, such as civil rights matters) class-action suits seeking monetary damages unless each and every ascertainable member of the class was individually notified of the case. To do this often

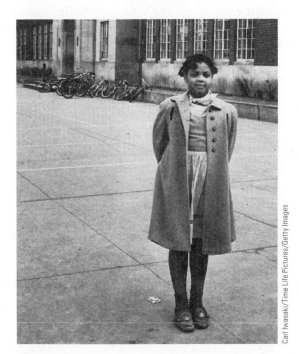

Linda Brown was refused admission to a white elementary school in Topeka, Kansas. On her behalf, the NAACP brought a class-action suit that resulted in the 1954 landmark Supreme Court decision Brown v. Board of Education.

Carl Iwasaki/Time Life Pictures/Getty Images

is prohibitively expensive (imagine trying to find and send a letter to every customer that may have been overcharged by the telephone company!), and so the number of such cases declined and the number of lawyers seeking them out dropped.[44]

> *brief* A written statement by an attorney that summarizes a case and the laws and rulings that support it.

But it remains easy to bring a class-action suit in most state courts. State Farm automobile insurance company was told by a state judge in a small Illinois town that it must pay over $1 billion in damages on behalf of a "national" class, even though no one in this class had been notified. Big class-action suits powerfully affect how courts make public policy. Such suits have forced into bankruptcy companies making asbestos and silicone breast implants and have threatened to put out of business tobacco companies and gun manufacturers. (Ironically, in some of these cases, such as the one involving breast implants, there was no scientific evidence showing that the product was harmful.) Some class-action suits, such as the one ending school segregation, are good, but others are frivolous efforts to get companies to pay large fees to the lawyers who file the suits.

In sum, getting into court depends on having standing and having resources. The rules governing standing are complex and changing, but generally they have been broadened to make it easier to enter the federal courts, especially for the purpose of challenging the actions of the government. Obtaining the resources is not easy, but has become easier because laws in some cases now provide for fee shifting, private interest groups are willing to finance cases, and it is sometimes possible to bring a class-action suit that lawyers find lucrative.

The Supreme Court in Action

If your case should find its way to the Supreme Court—and of course the odds are that it will not—you will be able to participate in one of the more impressive, sometimes dramatic ceremonies of American public life. The Court is in session in its white marble building for 36 weeks out of each year, from early October until the end of June. The nine justices read briefs in their individual offices, hear oral arguments in the stately courtroom, and discuss their decisions with one another in a conference room where no outsider is ever allowed.

Most cases, as we have seen, come to the Court on a writ of certiorari. The lawyers for each side may then submit their briefs. A **brief** is a document that sets forth the facts of the case, summarizes the

TABLE 16.4 **Supreme Court Justices in Order of Seniority**

Name (Birth Date)	Home State	Prior Experience	Appointed by (Year)
John G. Roberts, Jr., Chief Justice (1955)	Maryland	Federal judge	G. W. Bush (2005)
Antonin Scalia (1936)	Virginia	Federal judge	Reagan (1986)
Anthony Kennedy (1936)	California	Federal judge	Reagan (1988)
Clarence Thomas (1948)	Georgia	Federal judge	G. H. W. Bush (1991)
Ruth Bader Ginsburg (1933)	New York	Federal judge	Clinton (1993)
Stephen Breyer (1938)	Massachusetts	Federal judge	Clinton (1994)
Samuel Alito (1950)	New Jersey	Federal judge	G. W. Bush (2006)
Sonia Sotomayor (1954)	New York	Federal judge	Obama (2009)
Elena Kagan (1960)	New York	Law school dean	Obama (2010)

© Cengage Learning

amicus curiae A brief submitted by a "friend of the court."

per curiam opinion A brief, unsigned court opinion.

lower-court decision, gives the arguments for the side represented by the lawyer who wrote the brief, and discusses the other cases that the Court has decided bear on the issue. Then the lawyers are allowed to present their oral arguments in open court. They usually summarize their briefs or emphasize particular points in them, and they are strictly limited in time—usually to no more than a half hour. (The lawyer speaks from a lectern that has two lights on it. When the white light goes on, the attorney has five minutes remaining; when the red flashes, he or she must stop—instantly.) The oral arguments give the justices a chance to question the lawyers, sometimes searchingly.

Since the federal government is a party—as either plaintiff or defendant—to about half the cases that the Supreme Court hears, the government's top trial lawyer, the solicitor general of the United States, appears frequently before the Court. The solicitor general is the third-ranking officer of the Department of Justice, right after the attorney general and deputy attorney general. The solicitor general decides what cases the government will appeal from lower courts and personally approves every case the government presents to the Supreme Court. In recent years, the solicitor general often has been selected from the ranks of distinguished law school professors.

In addition to the arguments made by lawyers for the two sides in a case, written briefs and even oral arguments may also be offered by "a friend of the court," or **amicus curiae**. An amicus brief is from an interested party not directly involved in the suit. For example, when Allan Bakke complained that he had been the victim of "reverse discrimination" when he

was denied admission to a University of California medical school, 58 amicus briefs were filed supporting or opposing his position. Before such briefs can be filed, both parties must agree or the Court must grant permission. Though these briefs sometimes offer new arguments, they are really a kind of polite lobbying of the Court that declare which interest groups are on which side. The ACLU, the NAACP, the AFL-CIO, and the U.S. government itself have been among the leading sources of such briefs.

These briefs are not the only source of influence on the justices' views. Legal periodicals such as the *Harvard Law Review* and the *Yale Law Journal* are frequently consulted, and citations to them often appear in the Court's decisions. Thus the outside world of lawyers and law professors can help shape, or at least supply arguments for, the conclusions of the justices.

The justices retire every Friday to their conference room, where in complete secrecy they debate the cases they have heard. The chief justice speaks first, followed by the other justices in order of seniority. After the arguments they vote, traditionally in reverse order of seniority: the newest justice votes first, the chief justice last. By this process an able chief justice can exercise considerable influence—in guiding or limiting debate, in setting forth the issues, and in handling sometimes temperamental personalities. In deciding a case, a majority of the justices must be in agreement: if there is a tie, the lower-court decision is left standing. (There can be a tie among nine justices if one is ill or disqualifies himself or herself because of prior involvement in the case.)

Though the vote is what counts, by tradition the Court usually issues a written opinion explaining its decision. Sometimes the opinion is brief and unsigned (called a **per curiam opinion**); sometimes it is quite long and signed by the justices agreeing with it. If the chief justice is in the majority, he will either write the opinion or assign the task to a justice who agrees with him. If he is in the minority, the senior justice on the winning side will decide who writes the Court's opinion. There are three kinds of opinions—an **opinion of the Court** (reflecting the majority's view), a **concurring opinion** (an opinion by one or more justices who agree with the majority's conclusion but for different reasons that they wish to express), and a **dissenting opinion** (the opinion of the justices on the losing side). Each justice has three or four law clerks to help him or her review the many petitions the Court receives, study cases, and write opinions.

Many Supreme Court decisions, perhaps two-fifths of them, are decided unanimously. In these cases, the law is clear and no difficult questions of interpretation exist. But for the remaining ones, there appear to be two main blocs and one swing vote on today's Court:

- A conservative bloc of Samuel Alito, John Roberts, Antonin Scalia, and Clarence Thomas

- A liberal bloc of Stephen Breyer, Ruth Bader Ginsburg, Elena Kagan, and Sonia Sotomayor.

- A swing vote of Anthony Kennedy. He often votes with the conservatives on criminal law but on some other cases (abortion, gay rights, and foreign combatants detained at Guantanamo Bay) votes with the liberals.

The Power of the Federal Courts

The great majority of the cases heard in the federal courts have little or nothing to do with changes in public policy: people accused of bank robbery are tried, disputes over contracts are settled, personal-injury cases are heard, and patent law is applied. In most instances, the courts are simply applying a relatively settled body of law to a specific controversy.

The Power to Make Policy

The courts make policy whenever they reinterpret the law or the Constitution in significant ways, extend the reach of existing laws to cover matters not previously thought to be covered by them, or design remedies for problems that involve the judges' acting in administrative or legislative ways. By any of these tests the courts have become exceptionally powerful.

One measure of that power is the fact that more than 160 federal laws have been declared unconstitutional. And as we shall see, on matters where Congress feels strongly, it can often get its way by passing slightly revised versions of a voided law.

Another measure, and perhaps a more revealing one, is the frequency with which the Supreme Court changes its mind. An informal rule of judicial decision making has been **stare decisis**, meaning "let the decision stand." It is the principle of precedent:

opinion of the Court A signed opinion of a majority of the Supreme Court.

concurring opinion A signed opinion in which one or more members agree with the majority view but for different reasons.

dissenting opinion A signed opinion in which one or more justices disagree with the majority view.

stare decisis "Let the decision stand," or allowing prior rulings to control the current case.

The nine members of the U.S. Supreme Court are: Front row – Justices Clarence Thomas and Antonin Scalia, Chief Justice John Roberts, Justices Anthony Kennedy and Ruth Bader Ginsburg; second row – Justices Sonia Sotomayor, Stephen Breyer, Samuel Alito, and Elena Kagan.

Steve Petteway, Collection of the Supreme Court of the United States *political question* An issue the Supreme Court will allow the executive and legislative branches to decide.

remedy A judicial order enforcing a right or redressing a wrong.

a court case today should be settled in accordance with prior decisions on similar cases. (What constitutes a similar case is not always clear; lawyers are especially gifted at finding ways of showing that two cases are different in some relevant way.) There are two reasons why precedent is important. The practical reason should be obvious: if the meaning of the law continually changes, if the decisions of judges become wholly unpredictable, then human affairs affected by those laws and decisions become chaotic. A contract signed today might be invalid tomorrow. The other reason is at least as important: if the principle of equal justice means anything, it means that similar cases should be decided in a similar manner. On the other hand, times change, and the Court can make mistakes. As Justice Felix Frankfurter once said, "Wisdom too often never comes, and so one ought not to reject it merely because it comes late."[45]

However compelling the arguments for flexibility, the pace of change can become dizzying. By one count, the Court has overruled its own previous decisions in more than 260 cases since 1810.[46] In fact, it may have done it more often, because sometimes the Court does not say that it is abandoning a precedent, claiming instead that it is merely distinguishing the present case from a previous one.

A third measure of judicial power is the degree to which courts are willing to handle matters once left to the legislature. For example, the Court refused for a long time to hear a case about the size of congressional districts, no matter how unequal their populations.[47] The determination of congressional district boundaries was regarded as a **political question**—that is, as a matter that the Constitution left entirely to another branch of government (in this case, Congress) to decide for itself. Then in 1962, the Court decided that it was competent after all to handle this matter, and the notion of a "political question" became a much less important (but by no means absent) barrier to judicial power.[48]

By all odds the most powerful indicator of judicial power can be found in the kinds of remedies that the courts will impose. A **remedy** is a judicial order setting forth what must be done to correct a situation that a judge believes to be wrong. In ordinary cases, such as when one person sues another, the remedy is straightforward: the loser must pay the winner for some injury that he or she has caused, the loser must agree to abide by the terms of a contract he or she has broken, or the loser must promise not to do some unpleasant thing (such as dumping garbage on a neighbor's lawn).

Today, however, judges design remedies that go far beyond what is required to do justice to the individual parties who actually appear in court. The remedies now imposed often apply to large groups and affect the circumstances under which thousands or even millions of people work, study,

Kevork Djansezian/Getty Images

The activism of federal courts is exemplified by the sweeping orders they have issued to correct such problems as overcrowded prisons.

or live. For example, when a federal district judge in Alabama heard a case brought by a prison inmate in that state, he issued an order not simply to improve the lot of that prisoner but to revamp the administration of the entire prison system. The result was an improvement in the living conditions of many prisoners, at a cost to the state of an estimated $40 million a year. Similarly, a person who feels entitled to welfare payments that have been denied him or her may sue in court to get the money, and the court order will in all likelihood affect all welfare recipients. In one case certain court orders made an additional 100,000 people eligible for welfare.[49]

The basis for sweeping court orders can sometimes be found in the Constitution; the Alabama prison decision, for example, was based on the judge's interpretation of the Eighth Amendment, which prohibits "cruel and unusual punishments."[50] Others are based on court interpretations of federal laws. The Civil Rights Act of 1964 forbids discrimination on grounds of "race, color, or national origin" in any program receiving federal financial assistance. The Supreme Court interpreted that as meaning the San Francisco school system was obliged to teach English to Chinese students unable to speak it.[51] Since a Supreme Court decision is the law of the land, the impact of that ruling was not limited to San Francisco. Local courts and legislatures elsewhere decided that that decision meant that classes must be taught in Spanish for Hispanic children. What Congress meant by the Civil Rights Act is not clear; it may or may not have believed that teaching Hispanic children in English rather than Spanish was a form of discrimination. What is important is that it was the Court, not Congress, that decided what Congress meant.

Views of Judicial Activism

Judicial activism has, of course, been controversial. Those who support it argue that the federal courts must correct injustices when the other branches of the federal government, or the states, refuse to do so. The courts are the institution of last resort for those without the votes or the influence to obtain new laws, and especially for the poor and powerless. After all, Congress and the state legislatures tolerated segregated public schools for decades. If the Supreme Court had not declared segregation unconstitutional in 1954, it might still be law today.

Those who criticize judicial activism rejoin that judges usually have no special expertise in matters of school administration, prison management, environmental protection, and so on; they are lawyers, expert in defining rights and duties but not in designing and managing complex institutions.

Furthermore, however desirable court-declared rights and principles may be, implementing those principles means balancing the conflicting needs of various interest groups, raising and spending tax monies, and assessing the costs and benefits of complicated alternatives. Finally, federal judges are not elected; they are appointed and are thus immune to popular control. As a result, if they depart from their traditional role of making careful and cautious interpretations of what a law or the Constitution means and instead begin formulating wholly new policies, they become unelected legislators.

Some people think we have activist courts because we have so many lawyers. The more we take matters to courts for resolution, the more likely it is that the courts will become powerful. It is true that we have more lawyers in proportion to our population than most other nations. There is one lawyer for every 325 Americans, but only one for every 970 Britons, every 1,220 Germans, and every 8,333 Japanese.[52] But that may well be a symptom, not a cause, of court activity. As we suggested in Chapter 4, we have an adversary culture based on an emphasis on individual rights and an implicit antagonism between the people and the government. Generally speaking, lawyers do not create cases; contending interests do, thereby generating a demand for lawyers.[53] Furthermore, we had more lawyers in relation to our population in 1900 than in 1970, yet the courts at the turn of the 20th century were far less active in public affairs. In fact, in 1932 there were more court cases per 100,000 people than there were in 1972.

A more plausible reason for activist courts has been the developments discussed earlier in this chapter that have made it easier for people to get standing in the courts, to pay for the costs of litigation, and to bring class-action suits. The courts and Congress have gone a long way toward allowing private citizens to become "private attorneys general." Making it easier to get into court increases the number of cases being heard. For example, in 1961, civil rights cases, prisoners' rights cases, and cases under the Social Security laws were relatively uncommon in federal court. Between 1961 and 1990, the increase in the number of such matters was phenomenal: civil rights cases rose more than sixtyfold and prisoners' petitions more than fortyfold. Such matters are the fastest-growing portion of the courts' civil workload.

Legislation and the Courts

An increase in cases will not by itself lead to sweeping remedies. For that to occur, the law must be sufficiently vague to permit judges wide latitude in interpreting it, and the judges must want to exercise that opportunity fully. The Constitution is filled with words of seemingly ambiguous meaning—"due process of law," the "equal protection of the laws," the "privileges or immunities of citizens." Such phrases may have been clear to the Framers, but to the Supreme Court they have become equivocal or elastic. How the Court has chosen to interpret such phrases has changed greatly over the last two centuries in ways that can be explained in part by the personal political beliefs of the justices.

Increasingly, Congress has passed laws that also contain vague language, thereby adding immeasurably to the courts' opportunities for designing remedies. Various civil rights acts outlaw discrimination but do not say how one is to know whether discrimination has occurred or what should be done to correct it if it does occur. That is left to the courts and the bureaucracy. Various regulatory laws empower administrative agencies to do what the "public interest" requires but say little about how the public interest is to be defined. Laws intended to alleviate poverty or rebuild neighborhoods speak of "citizen participation" or "maximum feasible participation" but do not explain who the citizens are that should participate, or how much power they should have.

In addition to laws that require interpretation, other laws induce litigation. Almost every agency that regulates business will make decisions that cause the agency to be challenged in court—by business firms if the regulations go too far, by consumer or labor organizations if they do not go far enough.

One study showed that the federal courts of appeals heard more than 3,000 cases in which they had to review the decision of a regulatory agency. In two-thirds of them, the agency's position was supported; in the other third, the agency was overruled.[54] Perhaps one-fifth of these cases arose out of agencies or programs that did not even exist in 1960. The federal government today is much more likely to be on the defensive in court than it was 20 or 30 years ago.

POLICY DYNAMICS: INSIDE/OUTSIDE THE BOX

Telecommunications and "Decency": Interest Group Politics

In the more than six decades that separated the Communications Act of 1934 from the Telecommunications Act of 1996, radio, television, and the internet became everyday features of American life. The 1996 overhaul of the 1934 law was a clear-cut case of interest group politics. The political pitched battles over the bills that preceded the 1996 act were fought out mainly among and between economically self-interested groups. For instance, television broadcasters fought cable companies over who may send what kinds of signals to which homes. Telephone companies fought firms in other industries as well as each other.

As is often the case with interest group politics, the telecommunications policy debates involved issues that most average citizens did not understand (in this case, "spectrum allotment," "intra-modal competition," and others) but which interest group members lived and breathed. When the interest group politics dust settled, the complex law deregulated the industry and fostered competition, but it also made possible cross-media mega-corporations like those that now dominate cable broadcasting and telecommunications services in many regions.

In the mid-1990's, the general public and the media focused less on how an overhaul of the 1934 law might affect most people as consumers and more on Title V of the 1996 bill, which sought to restrict internet and cable television pornography. The bill's "communications decency" provisions made it into law; but, a year later, in *Reno v. ACLU* (1997), the Supreme Court declared that the provisions were unconstitutional.

In 2008, the Federal Communications Commission launched investigations into the pricing policies of cable television companies. The effort resulted in few changes to industry practices. In 2012, an interfaith coalition of religious leaders publicly petitioned five leading national hotel chains to stop offering on-demand "adult" cable service. None complied. During the 2011-2012 national election cycle, telecommunications companies contributed millions of dollars to candidates of both parties; they also maintained a huge lobbying presence on Capitol Hill, and skirmished with each other over proposed tweaks to this or that provision of the 1996 law.

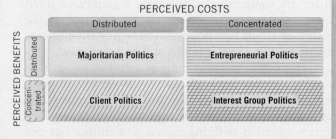

Finally, the attitudes of the judges powerfully affect what they will do, especially when the law gives them wide latitude. Their decisions and opinions have been extensively analyzed—well enough, at least, to know that different judges often decide the same case in different ways. Conservative southern federal judges in the 1950s, for example, often resisted plans to desegregate public schools, while judges with a different background authorized bold plans.[55] Some of the greatest disparities in judicial behavior can be found in the area of sentencing criminals.[56]

Checks on Judicial Power

No institution of government, including the courts, operates without restraint. The fact that judges are not elected does not make them immune to public opinion or to the views of the other branches of government. How important these restraints are varies from case to case, but in the broad course of history they have been significant.

One restraint exists because of the very nature of courts. A judge has no police force or army; decisions that he or she makes can sometimes be resisted or ignored, *if* the person or organization resisting is not highly visible and is willing to run the risk of being caught and charged with contempt of court. For example, long after the Supreme Court's controversial decisions that praying and Bible reading could not take place in public schools,[57] schools all over the country were still allowing prayers and Bible reading.[58] Years after the Court declared segregated schools to be unconstitutional, scores of school systems remained segregated. On the other hand, when a failure to comply is easily detected and punished, the courts' power is usually unchallenged. When the Supreme Court declared the income tax to be unconstitutional in 1895, income tax collections promptly ceased. When the Court in 1952 declared illegal President Truman's effort to seize the steel mills in order to stop a strike, the management of the mills was immediately returned to their owners.

Congress and the Courts

Congress has a number of ways of checking the judiciary. It can gradually alter the composition of the judiciary by the kinds of appointments the Senate is willing to confirm, or it can impeach judges it does not like. Fifteen federal judges have been the object of impeachment proceedings in our history, and nine others have resigned when such proceedings seemed likely. Of the 15 who were impeached, seven were acquitted, four were convicted, and one resigned. The most recent

HOW WE COMPARE

Judicial Review in Canada and Europe

Courts outside the United States can declare laws to be unconstitutional, but most can do so in ways that are very different from those in the United States.

Canada: The highest court can declare a law unconstitutional, but not if the legislature has passed it with a special provision that says the law will survive judicial scrutiny notwithstanding the country's Charter of Rights. Such laws must be renewed every five years.

Europe: The European Court of Human Rights in Strasbourg can decide human rights cases that begin in any of the nations that make up the European Community.

France: Its Constitutional Council can declare a law unconstitutional, but only if asked to do so by government officials and only before (not after) the law goes into effect.

Germany: The Federal Constitutional Court can declare in an advisory opinion, before a case has emerged, that a law is unconstitutional, and it can judge the constitutionality of laws when asked to do so by a lower court (which itself cannot rule a law unconstitutional). The Federal Constitutional Court may hold an administrative or judicial action to be unjustified when a citizen, having exhausted all other remedies, files a petition.

convictions were those of Alcee Hastings of Florida and Walter Nixon of Mississippi, both in 1989.[59] In practice, however, confirmation and impeachment proceedings do not make much of an impact on the federal courts because simple policy disagreements are not generally regarded as adequate grounds for voting against a judicial nominee or for starting an impeachment effort.

Congress can alter the number of judges, though, and by increasing the number sharply, it can give a president a chance to appoint judges to his liking. As described above, a "Court-packing" plan was proposed (unsuccessfully) by Franklin Roosevelt in 1937 specifically to change the political persuasion of the Supreme Court. In 1978, Congress passed a bill creating 152 new federal district and appellate judges to help ease the workload of the federal judiciary. This bill gave President Carter a chance to appoint over 40 percent of the federal bench. In 1984, an additional 84 judgeships were created; by 1988, President Reagan had appointed about half of all federal judges. In 1990, an additional 72 judges were authorized. During and after the Civil War, Congress may have been trying to influence Supreme Court decisions when it changed the size of the Court three times in six years (raising it from nine to 10 in 1863, lowering it again from 10 to seven in 1866, and raising it again from seven to nine in 1869).

Congress and the states can also undo a Supreme Court decision interpreting the Constitution by amending that document. This happens, but rarely: the Eleventh Amendment was ratified to prevent a citizen from suing a state in federal court; the Thirteenth, Fourteenth, and Fifteenth were ratified to undo the *Dred Scott* decision regarding slavery; the Sixteenth was added to make it constitutional for Congress to pass an income tax; and the Twenty-sixth was added to give the vote to 18-year-olds in state elections.

On more than 30 occasions, Congress has merely repassed a law that the Court has declared unconstitutional. In one case, a bill to aid farmers, voided in 1936, was accepted by the Court in slightly revised form three years later.[60] (In the meantime, of course, the Court had changed its collective mind about the New Deal.)

One of the most powerful potential sources of control over the federal courts, however, is the authority of Congress, given by the Constitution, to decide what the entire jurisdiction of the lower courts and the appellate jurisdiction of the Supreme Court shall be. In theory, Congress could prevent matters on which it did not want federal courts to act from ever coming before the courts. This happened in 1868. A Mississippi newspaper editor named McCardle was jailed by federal military authorities who occupied the defeated South. McCardle asked the federal district court for a writ of habeas corpus to get him out of custody; when the district court rejected his plea, he appealed to the Supreme Court. Congress at that time was fearful that the Court might find the laws on which its Reconstruction policy was based (and under which McCardle was in jail) unconstitutional. To prevent that from happening, it passed a bill withdrawing from the Supreme Court appellate jurisdiction in cases of this sort. The Court conceded that Congress could do this and thus dismissed the case because it no longer had jurisdiction.[61]

Congress has threatened to withdraw jurisdiction on other occasions, and the mere existence of the threat may have influenced the nature of Court decisions. In the 1950s, for example, congressional opinion was hostile to Court decisions in the field of civil liberties and civil rights, and legislation was proposed that would have curtailed the Court's jurisdiction in these areas. It did not pass, but the Court may have allowed the threat to temper its decisions.[62] On the other hand, as congressional resistance to the Roosevelt Court-packing plan shows, the Supreme Court enjoys a good deal of prestige in the nation, even among people who disagree with some of its decisions, and so passing laws that would frontally attack it would not be easy except perhaps in times of national crisis.

Furthermore, laws narrowing jurisdiction or restricting the kinds of remedies that a court can impose often are blunt instruments that might not achieve the purposes of their proponents. Suppose that you, as a member of Congress, would like to prevent the federal courts from ordering schoolchildren to be bused for the purpose of achieving racial balance in the schools. If you denied the Supreme Court appellate jurisdiction in this matter, you would leave the lower federal courts and all state courts free to do as they wished, and many of them would go on ordering busing. If you wanted to attack that problem, you could propose a law that would deny to all federal courts the right to order busing as a remedy for racial imbalance. But the courts would still be free to order busing (and of course a lot of busing goes on even without court orders), provided that they did not say that it was for the purpose of achieving racial balance. (It could be for the purpose of "facilitating desegregation" or making possible "redistricting.") Naturally, you could always make it illegal for children to enter a school bus for any reason, but then many children would not be able to get to school at all. Finally, the Supreme Court might well decide that if busing were essential to achieve a constitutional right, then any congressional law prohibiting such busing would itself be unconstitutional. Trying to think through how *that* dilemma would be resolved is like trying to visualize two kangaroos simultaneously jumping into each other's pouches.

Public Opinion and the Courts

Though they are not elected, judges read the same newspapers as members of Congress, and thus they, too, are aware of public opinion, especially elite opinion. Though it may be going too far to say the Supreme Court follows the election returns, it is nonetheless true that the Court is sensitive to certain bodies of opinion, especially of those elites—liberal or conservative—to which its members happen to be attuned. The justices will keep in mind historical cases in which their predecessors, by blatantly disregarding public opinion, very nearly destroyed the legitimacy of the Court itself. This was the case with the *Dred Scott* decision, which infuriated the North and was widely disobeyed. No such crisis exists today, but it is altogether possible that changing political moods affect the kinds of remedies that judges will think appropriate.

Opinion not only restrains the courts; it may also energize them. The most activist periods in Supreme Court history have coincided with times when the political system was undergoing profound and lasting changes. The assertion by the Supreme Court, under John Marshall's leadership, of the principles of national supremacy and judicial review occurred at the time when the Jeffersonian Republicans were coming to power and their opponents, the Federalists, were collapsing as an organized party. The pro-slavery decisions of the Taney Court came when the nation was so divided along sectional and ideological lines as to make almost any Court decision on this matter unpopular. Supreme Court review of economic regulation in the 1890s and 1900s came at a time when the political parties were realigning and the Republicans were acquiring dominance that would last for several decades. The Court decisions of the 1930s corresponded to another period of partisan realignment. (The meaning of a realigning election was discussed in Chapter 10.)

Pollsters have measured changes in public perceptions of how well the Supreme Court is handling its job. The results are shown in Figure 16.4. The percentage of people saying that they approve of how the Court is handling its job has fluctuated over the last 40 years. In the last half-decade, public approval of the Court's performance has been as high as 61 percent (in 2009) and as low as 46 percent (in 2011). These movements do not reflect any obvious swings

in how the public perceives the Court's ideological tilt. Gallup polls and other opinion surveys indicate that, for most of the last decade, about four-fifths to half of the public thought the Court was neither too liberal nor too conservative, about a third thought the Court was too liberal, and about a fifth thought it was too conservative. Rather, the shifts in opinion seem to reflect the public's reaction not only to what the Court does but also to what the government as a whole is doing. The upturn in the early 1970s was probably caused by the Watergate scandal, an episode that simultaneously discredited the presidency and boosted the stock of those institutions (such as the courts) that seemed to be checking the abuses of the White House. The gradual upturn in the 1980s may have reflected a general restoration of public confidence in government during that decade.[63]

Though popular support for the Court sometimes declines, these drops have so far not resulted in any legal checks placed on it. As explained in this chapter's **Constitutional Connections** feature (see page 414), each Congress witnesses many proposals that restrict the jurisdiction of federal courts and prohibit them from exercising judicial review in relation to given issues, but these proposals almost never become bills that make their way into law. The changes that have occurred in the Court have been caused by changes in its personnel. Presidents Nixon and Reagan attempted to produce a less activist Court by appointing justices who were more inclined to be strict constructionists and conservatives. To some extent, they succeeded: Justices Kennedy, O'Connor, Rehnquist, and Scalia were certainly less inclined than Justice Thurgood Marshall to find new rights in the Constitution or to overturn the

FIGURE 16.4 **Public Approval of the Supreme Court's Performance, 1974–2011**

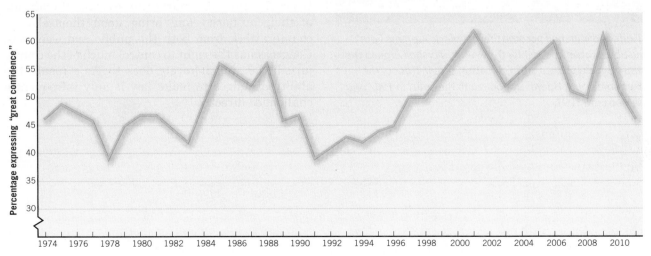

Source: Gallup polls

decisions of state legislatures. But as of yet, there has been no wholesale retreat from the positions staked out by the Warren Court. As noted above, a Nixon appointee, Justice Blackmun, wrote the decision making antiabortion laws unconstitutional; and another Nixon appointee, Chief Justice Burger, wrote the opinion upholding court-ordered school busing to achieve racial integration. A Reagan appointee, Justice O'Connor, voted to uphold a right to an abortion. The Supreme Court has become somewhat less willing to impose restraints on police practices, and it has not blocked the use of the death penalty.

But in general, the major features of Court activism and liberalism during the Warren years—school integration, sharper limits on police practice, greater freedom of expression—have remained intact, as has the Court's deference to Congress and the presidency when they have established new agencies or expanded federal programs. The Warren E. Burger Court (1969–1986) was succeeded by Courts with conservative Chief Justices, namely William H. Rehnquist (1986–2005) and John G. Roberts (2005–present).

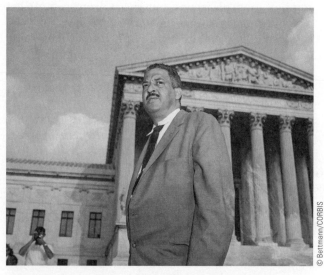

Thurgood Marshall became the first black Supreme Court justice. As chief counsel for the NAACP, Marshall argued the 1954 Brown v. Board of Education *case in front of the Supreme Court. He was appointed to the Court in 1967 and served until 1991.*

The aforementioned 2012 Court decision upholding the constitutionality of all (save the Medicaid expansion provision) of the 2010 health care reform law was written by Chief Justice Roberts.

The reasons for the growth in court activism are clear. One is the sheer growth in the size and scope of the government as a whole. The courts have come to play a larger role in our lives because Congress, the bureaucracy, and the president have come to play larger ones. In 1890, hardly anybody would have thought of asking Congress—much less the courts—to make rules governing the participation of women in college sports or the district boundaries of state legislatures. Today such rules are commonplace, and the courts are inevitably drawn into interpreting them. And when the Court decided how the vote in Florida would be counted during the 2000 presidential election, it created an opportunity in the future for scores of new lawsuits challenging election results.

The other reason for increased activism is the acceptance by a large number of judges, conservative as well as liberal, of the activist view of the function of the courts. If courts once existed solely to "settle disputes," today they also exist in the eyes of their members to "solve problems."

Though the Supreme Court is the pinnacle of the federal judiciary, most decisions, including many important ones, are made by the several courts of appeals and the 94 district courts. The Supreme Court can control its own workload by deciding when to grant certiorari. It has become easier for citizens and groups to gain access to the federal courts (through class-action suits, by amicus curiae briefs, by laws that require government agencies to pay legal fees).At the same time, the courts have widened the reach of their decisions by issuing orders that cover whole classes of citizens or affect the management of major public and private institutions. However, the courts can overstep the bounds of their authority and bring upon themselves a counterattack from both the public and Congress. Congress has the right to control much of the courts' jurisdiction, but it rarely does so. As a result, the ability of judges to make law is only infrequently challenged directly.

WHAT WOULD YOU DO?

MEMORANDUM

To: *Senator Ann Gilbert*

From: *Amy Wilson, legislative assistant*

Re: *Federal law legalizing assisted suicide*

The Supreme Court has held that the attorney general cannot use his authority over federally controlled drugs to block the implementation of the Oregon "Death with Dignity" law. Now some of your colleagues want to enact a federal equivalent of that law that would allow physicians to prescribe deadly drugs to patients who request them.

Arguments for:

1. The law respects the people's right to choose the time and place of their own death.

2. It is already permissible to post "Do Not Resuscitate" orders on the charts of terminally ill patients.

3. Physicians can be held to high standards in implementing the law.

Arguments against:

1. The law will corrupt the role of doctors, as many think has happened in Holland, where a similar law

News »

Legalizing Assisted Suicide

Congress is discussing a federal law that would allow physicians to administer drugs that will lead to the death of patients who request them. Oregon already has a "Death with Dignity" statute.

has led some physicians to kill patients prematurely or without justification.

2. Such a law will lead some physicians to neglect or ignore the desires of the patient.

3. This law will undermine the more important goal of helping patients overcome pain and depression.

Your decision:

Support the law_____   Oppose the law_____

LEARNING OBJECTIVES

1. Where in the Constitution does it say that the Supreme Court has the power of judicial review?

Nowhere in the Constitution does it say that the Supreme Court has the power of judicial review. The Constitution is silent on this matter, but the Court has asserted, and almost every scholar has agreed, that our system of separated powers means that the Court must be able to defend the Constitution. Otherwise, Congress and the president would be free to ignore it.

2. What is meant by an "Article III" federal judge?

An "Article III" federal judge is a federal judge who benefits from Article III of the Constitution, which guarantees judges that they can serve during good behavior. The Supreme Court, courts of appeal, and all district courts are all Title 3 courts. Congress has also established "legislative" courts whose members serve for fixed terms. Examples are the Tax Court and the Court of Appeals for the Armed Forces.

3. What is the difference between original and appellate jurisdiction?

Original jurisdiction refers to a trial held before a court; appellate jurisdiction refers to an appeal a court hears from a trial in another court. Even the Supreme Court has original jurisdiction. For example, it will hear a trial involving ambassadors or a controversy between two or more states.

4. Why should federal judges serve for life?

Strictly speaking, they serve during "good behavior," but that means they would have to be impeached and convicted in order to be removed. The reason for this protection is clear: the judiciary cannot be independent of the other two branches of government if judges could be easily removed by the president or Congress, and this independence ensures that they are a separate branch of government.

5. Why should federal courts be able to declare laws unconstitutional?

Though the Constitution does not explicitly give them that power, they have acquired it on the reasonable assumption that the Constitution would become meaningless if the president and Congress could ignore its provisions. The Constitution, after all, states that it shall be the "supreme law of the land."

6. Should federal judges only interpret existing laws or should they be able to create new laws?

The federal courts rarely think their decisions create entirely new laws, but in fact their interpretations sometimes come close to just that. One reason is that many provisions of the Constitution are vague. What does the Constitution mean by "respecting an establishment of religion," the "equal protection of the law," or a "cruel and unusual punishment"? The courts must give concrete meaning to these phrases. But another reason is the personal ideology of judges. Some think a free press is more important than laws governing campaign finance, while others think a free press must give way to such laws. Some believe the courts ought to use federal law to strike down discrimination, but judges disagree about what types of affirmative action program must be put in place.

TO LEARN MORE

Federal Judicial Center: **www.fjc.gov**

Federal courts: **www.uscourts.gov**

Supreme Court decisions: **www.law.cornell.edu**

Finding laws and reports: **www.findlaw.com**

Abraham, Henry J. *The Judicial Process*, 7th ed. New York: Oxford University Press, 1998. An excellent, comprehensive survey of how the federal courts are organized and function.

Abraham, Henry J., and Barbara A. Perry. *Freedom and the Court*, 8th ed. Lawrence, KS: University of Kansas Press, 2003. Careful summary of civil liberties and civil rights cases.

Cardozo, Benjamin N. *The Nature of the Judicial Process*. New Haven, CT: Yale University Press, 1921. Important statement of how judges make decisions, by a former Supreme Court justice.

Ely, John Hart. *Democracy and Distrust*. Cambridge: Harvard University Press, 1980. Effort to create a theory of judicial review that is neither strict-constructionist nor activist.

Greenburg, Jan Crawford. *Supreme Conflict*. New York: Penguin, 2007. A fascinating journalistic account of how the Supreme Court operates.

Hall, Kermit L., and James W. Ely, Jr., eds. *The Oxford Guide to the United States Supreme Court Decisions*, 2nd ed. New York: Oxford University Press, 2009. Summarizes the 440 most important decisions of the Supreme Court and includes a comprehensive bibliography of books about the Court.

Lasser, William. *The Limits of Judicial Power*. Chapel Hill: University of North Carolina Press, 1988. Shows how the Court through history has withstood the political storms created by its more controversial decisions.

McCloskey, Robert G. *The American Supreme Court*, 4th ed. Edited by Sanford Levinson. Chicago: University of Chicago Press, 2005. Superb brief history of the Supreme Court, updated by one of McCloskey's former students who now teaches law at the University of Texas.

Rabkin, Jeremy. *Judicial Compulsions*. New York: Basic Books, 1989. Explains (and argues against) the extensive Court intervention in the work of administrative agencies.

Wolfe, Christopher. *The Rise of Modern Judicial Review*. New York: Basic Books, 1986. An excellent history of judicial review from 1787 to the present.

PART

4

Public Policy and American Democracy

In the extended republic of the United States, and among the great variety of interests, parties, and sects, which it embraces, a coalition of a majority of the whole society could seldom take place on any other principles than those of justice and the general good.

—FEDERALIST NO. 51

17

Domestic Policy

LEARNING OBJECTIVES

1. What types of politics may matter to whether and how government acts on any given issue?

2. How do America's social welfare policies and programs differ from those of many other modern democracies?

3. Why are some social welfare policies and programs politically protected while others are politically imperiled?

4. Is there a political consensus about how to address the solvency challenges facing major social welfare programs?

5. Why have government regulations on certain big businesses been imposed over the objections of those industries?

6. Why are environmental policies designed and enforced differently in America than in other industrialized nations?

7. Does just one type of politics drive environmental policies and programs?

As we explained in Chapter 1, understanding any political system means being able to give reasonable answers to each of two separate but related questions about it: who governs, and to what ends? The preceding chapters should be especially helpful to you in discovering "who governs" while this chapter and the next two chapters should be especially helpful to you in discerning "to what ends."

The primary puzzles about public policy in America concern the nation's political agenda (see pages 10–13). How do people come to believe that certain issues require governmental action? What explains why some issues are on the political agenda while others are not? Why are some issues more prominent on today's political agenda than they were either in previous historical periods or just a few years ago, and why are other issues less prominent than they once were? Why do elected officials sometimes suddenly shift attention away from some issues and toward others? What explains the timing and character of government action (or inaction) on any given issue?

The causes, contours, and consequences of government action or inaction on any given issue or any class of issues (domestic policy, economic policy, or foreign policy) are not easily explained. What at first glance may appear to be simple and stable policymaking patterns often turn out upon closer inspection to be more complex and dynamic than they seemed. For instance, consider what has happened in each of three domestic policy domains—social welfare policy, business regulation policy, and environmental protection policy.

Social Welfare Policy

THEN

Before the 1960s, neither most Washington lawmakers nor most citizens believed that the federal government should ensure that all retirees, whatever their work history, have enough money to live on; that all veterans of foreign wars have grants for college and subsidized medical care for life; that all poor children are guaranteed free or reduced price meals in schools and during summers; that all physically, mentally, or developmentally disabled people, like all people with life-threatening medical maladies, are insured for hospital stays and treatment including long-term nursing care; that all low-wage workers receive tax credits that effectively boost their wages; that all citizens who may need it have access to affordable housing; that all low-income children are able to attend preschools; that all special needs children receive special education; and that all full-time workers who lose their jobs receive unemployment benefits and (in many cases) job training. If they existed at all, national laws touching on these social welfare matters were few and thin, and federal departments, bureaus, or programs to fund or administer such social welfare benefits were virtually nonexistent.

NOW

Washington sets, funds, and implements policies on all these social welfare matters and others besides. By 2010, three giant programs—the Social Security (established in 1935) plus Medicare and Medicaid (each established in 1965)—together accounted for over 40 percent of the federal budget (double what was spent on national defense). They were flanked by scores of smaller federal social welfare programs, most of them either established or expanded since 1965. The U.S. Department of Health and Human Services and the U.S. Department of Veterans Affairs are two of the main bureaucracies responsible for federal social welfare policies and programs, but benefits also emanate from several other federal departments. For instance, the U.S. Department of Justice has supported myriad programs for "at-risk youth" including ones that provide mentors to the children of prisoners and "second chance" job training to young adult ex-prisoners. But, in recent years, as policymakers have struggled with big annual budget deficits and a growing public debt (see Chapter 18), the future of many social welfare policies and programs, including the largest entitlement programs like Social Security and Medicare, has for the first time in more than a generation been placed in some serious doubt.

Business Regulation Policy

THEN

Big oil companies were once able to persuade the government to sharply restrict the amount of foreign oil imported into the United States, to give them preferential tax treatment, and to permit them to drill for new oil just about anywhere they liked. Automobile manufacturers once faced virtually no federal controls on the products they manufactured. Well into the 1990's, communications and broadcasting companies were regulated under a 1934 federal law that was debated and developed at a time when most Americans neither owned radios nor had ever even heard of television. Certain telephone companies were free to function as monopolies.

NOW

Today, the restrictions on foreign oil imports have ended, the tax breaks the oil companies enjoyed have been reduced considerably (though they still exist), and the freedom of oil companies to drill in certain places, particularly offshore locations, has been restricted. Auto companies are heavily regulated regarding the safety of the vehicles they make, and two of them (GM and Chrysler) have been partially owned by the federal government. In 1996, a new federal communications act took effect, and the industry now features not only more broadcasting companies, stricter rules governing what cable service providers can charge, and no telephone company monopolies, but also fewer regulations to keep corporate conglomerates from dominating certain rapidly changing "telecommunications" markets.

Environmental Policy

THEN

Environmental policies in the United States gained widespread public attention in the 1960s and 1970's, when reports of water and air pollution, pesticide use, and other threats to natural resources prompted the passage of legislation to control such activity. The Environmental Protection Agency was created in 1970 to set standards for environmental safety, track violations, and enforce compliance. Since then, the field has expanded to encompass concerns about broader national and international environmental issues such as global warming. In the 2008 presidential race, environmental politics was a major concern for the electorate, particularly young voters. A CBS News/MTV poll in the spring of 2008 found that 18 percent of voters aged 18–29 viewed environmental problems as the biggest challenge in the coming years, exceeded only by the economy, which was ranked first by 34 percent of voters in that age group. Both presidential candidates discussed the need to protect the environment for future generations: Barack Obama declared that the country faced a "defining moment in our history: Our nation is at war. The planet is in peril," while John McCain called for the need to "restore the health of our planet."[1]

NOW

Since the 2008 presidential race, and even after the disastrous oil spill in the Gulf of Mexico in May 2010, environmental issues have received less attention from federal policymakers. In the 2012 presidential race, environmental issues were less prominent than they were during the 2008 presidential race. Prior to 2008, Gallup polls stretching back to the 1980s found most Americans agreed that the environment should be given priority "even at the risk of curbing economic growth;" but, in 2013, for the fifth consecutive year, and "with the exception of a poll

conducted shortly after" the aforementioned oil spill in the Gulf of Mexico, "support for the environment on this question...remained the minority view."[2] Over the same period, however, the percentage of the public expressing a "great deal" of concern about various environmental issues fell only slightly. For example, from 2008 to 2013, the slight dips in deep public concern included pollution of rivers, lakes, and reservoirs (50 to 46 percent), air pollution (43 to 40 percent), loss of the tropical rain forests (40 to 36 percent), and global warming (37 to 33 percent).[3]

To begin to understand policy dynamics, to help explain both short-term shifts and long-term trends in what issues are on the political agenda and how government acts on these issues (or doesn't), we need some theory of policymaking. After defining key terms ranging from "politics" to "representative democracy" (see pages 4 and 6, respectively) and explaining five different views of "power in America" (see pages 7–9), the first chapter of this book outlined a theory of policymaking involving four different types of politics: majoritarian, client, interest group, and entrepreneurial (see pages 14–17). In half of the preceding chapters, a *Policy Dynamics: Inside/Outside the Box* feature invited you to reflect on how diverse issues—health care reform (Chapter 1), same-sex marriage (Chapter 6), the auto industry bailout (Chapter 9), immigration reform (Chapter 11), national service (Chapter 13), sequestered budget cuts (Chapter 14), postal service reform (Chapter 15), and telecommunications (Chapter 16)—might be understood in relation to one or more of the four types of politics. In the next section of this chapter, we reiterate the theory and its key terms, but this would be a good time to review Chapter 1 and revisit the *Policy Dynamics* features in other chapters, too.

This chapter will elaborate and apply the theory of policymaking outlined in Chapter 1 to domestic policy dynamics on issues in social welfare policy, business regulation policy, and environmental policy. Each area of domestic policy has issues and policy dynamics all its own. But in social welfare, business regulation, and environmental policy, as in education, housing, homeland security, transportation, and other domestic policy domains, each of the four types of policymaking politics can be found. In Chapter 18, we will explore the politics of economic policy, and in Chapter 19 we will examine the politics of foreign and military policy.

Policymaking Politics Revisited

How are public policies proposed and then passed, rejected, or modified? Let us revisit our simple way of classifying the politics of policymaking. Once more, we begin by observing that each policy has a **cost** and a **benefit**. A cost is the burden of a program, whether it is financial or social, that is placed on people. It includes taxes, unpleasant regulations, or social stigma. A benefit is the gain, whether financial or social, that flows to people. This includes payments, subsidies, tax reductions, government contracts, or heightened prestige.

Remember, these are *perceived* costs and benefits. For example, some people may think the nation benefits by massive military and other defense spending. Others disagree and believe the country is better served by social spending. By the same token, some people may think that a government regulation is a cost, whereas others may think it is a benefit. It is also important to understand that people differ in their beliefs about who gets a benefit and who pays a cost. Those beliefs are about the **legitimacy** of various groups. For example, some people may think that public assistance to the needy is legitimate. Others believe that it is not legitimate for the needy to receive such benefits.

Perceived costs and benefits can be widely distributed or narrowly concentrated, giving us the by-now familiar (we hope!) four types of politics depicted by our four-box diagram (see Figure 17.1):

- Widely distributed benefits and widely distributed costs, or **majoritarian politics**. This means that all or most people benefit and all or most people pay.

- Narrowly concentrated benefits and widely distributed costs, or **client politics**. A few people, or some particular community or organization benefits, but most people pay for what they get.

- Narrowly concentrated benefits and narrowly concentrated costs, or **interest-group politics**. A few people, communities, or organizations benefit, and a few people, communities, or organizations pay.

- Widely distributed benefits and narrowly concentrated costs or **entrepreneurial politics**. Almost everybody benefits, but only a few people, communities, or organizations pay the costs.

Now, after in each case first learning some basic history and background facts about the policies and programs, let's try to apply our theory to domestic policy dynamics in three areas: social welfare, business regulation, and environmental policy. We begin with social welfare policy and consider each of four federal social welfare programs. As we shall see, Social Security and Medicare seem to exemplify majoritarian politics; but Temporary Assistance to Needy Families (TANF), like the program that it succeeded, Aid to Families with Dependent Children (AFDC), has played out more as a client politics issue; and, finally, Medicaid, the large federal–state health care program, would seem to belong partly in the majoritarian politics box and partly in the client politics box.

cost A burden that people believe they must bear if a policy is enacted.

benefit A satisfaction that people believe they will enjoy if a policy is adopted.

legitimacy Political authority conferred by law or by a state or national constitution.

Social Welfare Policy

Among the reasons given in the Preamble to the United States Constitution for establishing the national government is a desire to "promote the general Welfare." Article I, Section 8 of the Constitution states the power of Congress to "provide for the… general Welfare."

From the first, however, the Constitution's defenders disagreed about what the phrase was

FIGURE 17.1   A Way of Classifying and Explaining the Politics of Different Policy Issues

PERCEIVED COSTS

	Distributed	Concentrated
Distributed	Majoritarian Politics	Entrepreneurial Politics
Concentrated	Client Politics	Interest Group Politics

PERCEIVED BENEFITS

© Cengage Learning

supposed to mean. Some, like James Madison, argued that it was meant to restrict Congress to taxing and spending only for things that the Constitution specifically empowered Congress to do (like regulating interstate commerce or maintaining the military). Others, like Alexander Hamilton, argued for a broader meaning that would allow Congress to tax and spend for things that it was not specifically empowered by the Constitution to do, but which might reasonably be expected to meet national needs and benefit some or all citizens.

In the 1930s, asserting a constitutional authority to advance the "general welfare," Congress enacted a host of new national policies and programs in response to the economic hardships wrought by the Great Depression. The biggest was the Social Security Act of 1935. Among other provisions, the law created a national system of old-age pensions and, to pay for it, imposed an income tax on workers that was deducted from their wages and paid by their employers. In 1937, in the case of *Helvering v. Davis*, the U.S. Supreme Court upheld the constitutionality of that provision, ruling that Congress has broad discretion to tax and spend "in aid of the 'general welfare,'" including policies and programs designed to ease the "plight of men and women" who lose their jobs and provide for others who are either temporarily or permanently "needy and dependent." Nobody, however, foresaw just how far Congress would go in exercising that power, or where doing so would lead.

LANDMARK CASES

Federal Laws About "General Welfare"

- *United States v. Butler* (1936): Found particular federal regulations on agricultural production to be unconstitutional, but proclaimed that Congress has wide power to tax and spend for whatever it deems to be for the "general welfare."

- *Helvering v. Davis* (1937): Upheld key provisions of the Social Security Act of 1935, and declared that Congress has broad discretion to tax and spend "in aid of the 'general welfare.'"

- *South Dakota v. Dole* (1987): Ruled that Washington could condition the receipt of federal highway funds on a state's compliance with a 21-year-old drinking age, and declared that Congress's power to define the "general welfare" and to spend in pursuit of it is virtually unlimited.

From the New Deal to the New Health Care Law

The first major steps toward today's social welfare policies and programs were taken after the election of 1932. At the time the Great Depression began in 1929, the job of providing relief (food, money, medicine, and other services) to needy people fell almost entirely to state and local governments or to private charities, and even these sources were primarily concerned with widows, orphans, and the elderly.[4] Hardly any state had a systematic program for supporting the unemployed, though many states provided some kind of help if it was clear that the person was out of work through no fault of his or her own. When the economy suddenly ground to a near standstill and the unemployment rate rose to include one-fourth of the workforce, private charities and city relief programs nearly went bankrupt. Americans sung the 1931 song "Brother, Can You Spare a Dime?" But, with families, neighbors, local churches, charities, and city agencies all unable to meet the economic crisis despite their best efforts, on the eve of the 1932 presidential election, ever more citizens had come to feel that it was time for Uncle Sam to lend a hand.

That election produced an overwhelming congressional majority for the Democrats and placed Franklin D. Roosevelt in the White House. Almost immediately, a number of emergency measures were adopted to cope with the depression by supplying federal cash to bail out state and local relief agencies and by creating public works jobs under federal auspices. These measures were recognized as temporary expedients, however, and were unsatisfactory to those who believed the federal government had a permanent and major responsibility for welfare.

In 1932, unemployed workers line up at a soup kitchen during the Great Depression.

Roosevelt created the Cabinet Committee on Economic Security to consider long-term policies. The committee drew heavily on the experience of European nations and on the ideas of various American scholars and social workers, but it understood that it would have to adapt these proposals to the realities of American politics. Chief among these was the widespread belief that any direct federal welfare program might be unconstitutional. The Constitution nowhere explicitly gave to Congress the authority to set up an unemployment compensation or old-age retirement program. And even if a welfare program were constitutional, many believed, it would be wrong because it violated the individualistic creed that people should help themselves unless they were physically unable to do so.

But failure by the Roosevelt administration to produce a comprehensive social security program, his supporters felt, might make the president vulnerable in the 1936 election to the leaders of various radical social movements. Huey Long of Louisiana was proposing a "Share Our Wealth" plan; Upton Sinclair was running for governor of California on a platform calling for programs to "End Poverty in California"; and Dr. Francis E. Townsend was leading an organization of hundreds of thousands of elderly people on whose behalf he demanded government pensions of $200 a month.

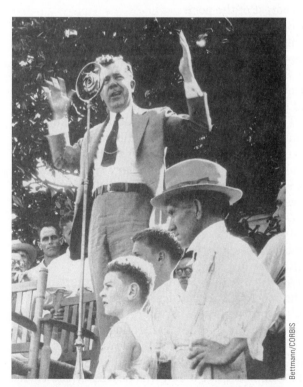

Bettmann/CORBIS

In 1934, Huey Long, the popular governor of Louisiana, claimed that Roosevelt was not doing enough to help the common man. But before he could become a serious threat to Roosevelt in the 1936 election, Long was assassinated in 1935.

The plan that emerged from the cabinet committee was carefully designed to meet popular demands within the framework of constitutional understandings. It called for two kinds of programs: (1) an **insurance program** for the unemployed and elderly, to which workers would contribute and from which they would benefit when they became unemployed or retired; and (2) an **assistance program** for the blind, dependent children, and the aged. (Giving assistance as well as providing "insurance" for the aged was necessary because for the first few years the insurance program would not pay out any benefits.) The federal government would use its power to tax to provide the funds, but all of the programs (except for old-age insurance) would be administered by the states. Everybody, rich or poor, would be eligible for the insurance programs. Only the poor, as defined by a **means test** (a measure to determine that incomes are below a certain level), would be eligible for the assistance programs. Though bitterly opposed by some, the resulting Social Security Act passed swiftly and virtually unchanged through Congress. It was introduced in January 1935 and signed by President Roosevelt in August of that year.

The Social Security Act became a cornerstone of Roosevelt's New Deal. But many of the act's supporters also wanted Washington to guarantee all citizens including the elderly and the poor a certain minimum level of health care. The idea of having the government pay the medical and hospital bills of the elderly and the poor had been discussed in Washington since the drafting of the Social Security Act. President Roosevelt and his Committee on Economic Security sensed that medical care would be very controversial, and so health programs were left out of the 1935 bill in order not to jeopardize its chances of passage.[5] The proponents of the idea did not abandon it, however. Working mostly within the executive branch, they continued to press, sometimes publicly, sometimes behind the scenes, for a national health care plan. Democratic presidents, including Truman, Kennedy, and Johnson, favored it; Republican president Eisenhower opposed it;

insurance program A self-financing government program based on contributions that provide benefits to unemployed or retired persons.

assistance program A government program financed by general income taxes that provides benefits to poor citizens without requiring contribution from them.

means test An income qualification program that determines whether one is eligible for benefits under government programs reserved for lower-income groups.

Congress was deeply divided on it. The American Medical Association attacked it as "socialized medicine." For 30 years, key policy entrepreneurs, such as Wilbur Cohen, worked to find a formula that would produce a congressional majority.

The first and highest hurdle to overcome, however, was not Congress as a whole but the House Ways and Means Committee, especially its powerful chairman from 1958 to 1975, Wilbur Mills of Arkansas. A majority of the committee members opposed a national health care program. Some members believed it wrong in principle; others feared that adding a costly health component to the Social Security system would jeopardize the financial solvency and administrative integrity of one of the most popular government programs. By the early 1960s, a majority of the House favored a health care plan, but without the approval of Ways and Means it would never reach the floor.

The 1964 elections changed all that. The Johnson landslide produced such large Democratic majorities in Congress that the composition of the committees changed. In particular, the membership of the Ways and Means Committee was altered. Whereas before it had three Democrats for every two Republicans, after 1964 it had two Democrats for every one Republican. The House leadership saw to it that the new Democrats on the committee were strongly committed to a health care program. Suddenly the committee had a majority favorable to such a plan, and Mills, realizing that a bill would pass and wanting to help shape its form, changed his position and became a supporter of what was to become Medicare.

Medicare became a cornerstone of Johnson's Great Society. The policy entrepreneurs in and out of the government who drafted the Medicare plan attempted to anticipate the major objections to it. First, the bill would apply only to the aged—those eligible for Social Security retirement benefits. This would reassure legislators worried about the cost of providing tax-supported health care for everybody. Second, the plan would cover only hospital expenses, not doctors' bills. Since doctors were not to be paid by the government, they would not be regulated by it; thus, presumably, the opposition of the American Medical Association would be blunted.

Unexpectedly, however, the Ways and Means Committee broadened the coverage of the plan beyond what the administration had thought was politically feasible. It added sections providing medical assistance, called Medicaid, for the poor (defined as those already getting public assistance payments) and payment of doctors' bills for the aged (a new part of Medicare). The new, much-enlarged bill passed both houses of Congress with ease. The key votes pitted a majority of the Democrats against a majority of the Republicans.

Johnson's Great Society programs and "war on poverty" went far beyond Roosevelt's New Deal programs. But neither the chief political architects of Social Security in 1935 nor the main political movers behind Medicare and Medicaid in 1965 ever envisioned scores of millions of Americans receiving food, money, medicine, and other benefits through programs funded largely by the federal government. And no one contemplated that middle-class and even upper-income citizens would one day become as likely to receive federally financed health care as the poorest of the poor.

But that day has long since arrived. In 2010, about 60 million Americans received Medicaid benefits, 54 million Americans received Social Security benefits, and 52 million Americans (45 million senior citizens and 7 million younger adults with permanent disabilities) received Medicare benefits.

The two largest federal social welfare programs, Social Security and Medicare, are bound for big increases in beneficiaries over the next several decades as the primary beneficiary population each program serves, persons age 65 and older, grows and grows. And Medicaid, for several decades now the largest program co-funded by the federal government and the states, is now being further expanded in most states in accordance with the latest federal health care law.

As discussed in several previous chapters, one of the most heated political controversies of recent years concerned social welfare policy, namely, the passage of the Patient Protection and Affordable Care Act of 2010. Dubbed by certain of its critics (and eventually called by President Obama himself) "Obamacare," the bill was passed by the House and Senate without a single Republican vote. Only 34 Democrats in the House and three in the Senate voted against it.[6] When it passed, public opinion polls indicated the plan was not popular. Its defenders argued that as the law took effect it would win

President Lyndon Johnson signs the Medicare Act in 1965.

Lyndon Baines Johnson Library/MCT/Newscom

President Barack Obama signs the Affordable Health Care for America Act in 2010 .

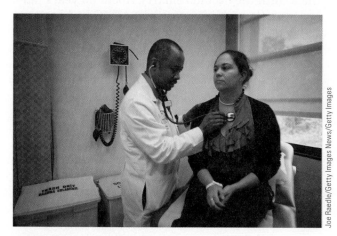

The Affordable Care Act guarantees that all Americans will have access to health care.

over most people and that in time its cost would go down. Its critics claimed that it would stifle health care by heavy regulations and rapidly rising costs. In the November 2010 congressional elections, the law was not popular and may have contributed to large Republican gains in the House and Senate. A case challenging the law's constitutionality made it to the Supreme Court.

In 2012, the Supreme Court upheld the law's constitutionality, excepting its provisions requiring states to expand Medicaid coverage.[7] In 2013, a re-elected President Obama began his second term, public opinion on the law became more favorable, and the debate among federal policymakers shifted somewhat from disputes about the law's overall desirability to immediate concerns about its administrative workability and doubts about its long-term potential to contain costs.[8] Its key benefits are summarized in the *How Things Work* feature on this page.

majoritarian politics A policy in which almost everybody benefits and almost everybody pays.

Two Kinds of Social Welfare Programs

Today, some eight decades after Social Security was first debated, two kinds of social welfare programs exist in this country: those that benefit most or all of the people and those that help only a small number of them. In the first category are Social Security and Medicare, programs that provide retirement benefits or medical assistance to almost every citizen who has reached a certain age. In the second are programs such as Temporary Assistance to Needy Children (TANF) and the Supplemental Nutrition Assistance Program (SNAP, which encompasses Food Stamps) that offer help only to people with low incomes. The *How Things Work* feature on page 446 briefly describes these and other major social welfare programs.

Legally, the difference between the two kinds of social welfare programs is that the first have no *means test* (they are available to everyone without regard to income) while the second are *means tested* (you must fall below a certain income level to enjoy them). Politically, the programs differ in how they get money from the government. The first kind of welfare program represents **majoritarian politics**: nearly

HOW THINGS WORK

Patient Protection and Affordable Care Act of 2010, Major Provisions

- Extends health care insurance to some 32 million uninsured Americans

- Provides federal subsidies to people who have trouble paying

- Imposes a "tax" penalty on people who do not buy health insurance

- Dependent children under age 26 are covered by parent's insurance

- Adds more people to Medicaid

- Levies fees and taxes on medical devices, drugs, high-cost health insurance plans, health insurers *client politics* A policy in which one small group benefits and almost everybody pays.

everyone benefits, nearly everyone pays. The second kind represents **client politics**: a (relatively) low number of people benefit, but almost everyone pays. The biggest problem facing majoritarian welfare programs is their cost: who will pay, and how much will they pay? The biggest problem facing client-oriented programs is their legitimacy: who should benefit, and how should they be served?

This political difference between these programs has a huge impact on how the government acts in regard to them. Social Security and Medicare are sacrosanct. The thought of making any changes that might lower the benefits these programs pay is so politically risky that most politicians never even discuss them. As we will discuss in the next section, because of rising senior citizen populations, rising expenses, and rising demands for more benefits, Medicare is in deep financial trouble today, and Social Security will face high financial hurdles in a few decades. Federal policymakers are scrambling to look for ways of maintaining benefits while hiding the rising costs or postponing dealing with them. No politician wants to raise taxes or cut benefits, so they adopt a variety of halfhearted measures (like slowly increasing the age at which people can get

these benefits) designed to postpone the tough decisions until they are out of office.

Client-based welfare programs—those that are means tested—are a very different matter. Like many other client-based programs, their political appeal changes as popular opinion about them changes. Take the old Aid to Families with Dependent Children (AFDC) program. When it was started in 1935, people thought of it as a way of helping poor women whose husbands had been killed in war or had died in mining accidents. The goal was to help these women support their children, who had been made fatherless by death or disaster. Most people thought of these women as the innocent victims of a tragedy. No one thought that they would take AFDC for very long. It was a program to help smooth things over for them until they could remarry. About 30 years later, however, the public's opinion of AFDC had begun to change. People started to think AFDC was paying money to women who had never married and had no intention of marrying. The government, according to this view, was subsidizing single-parent families, encouraging out-of-wedlock births, and creating social dependency. From the mid-1960s, through the mid-1990s, these views became stronger. AFDC had lost the legitimacy it needed, as a client program, to survive politically. As we shall discuss in more detail later in this chapter, even though it never accounted for as much as 1 percent of total federal spending,

HOW THINGS WORK

Major Social Welfare Programs

Insurance, or "Contributory," Programs

Old Age, Survivors, and Disability Insurance (OASDI) Monthly payments to retired or disabled people and to surviving members of their families. This program, popularly called Social Security, is paid for by a payroll tax on employers and employees. *No means test.*

Medicare Federal government pays for part of the cost of medical care for retired or disabled people covered by Social Security. Paid for by payroll taxes on employees and employers. *No means test.*

Assistance, or "Noncontributory," Programs

Unemployment Insurance (UI) Weekly payments to workers who have been laid off and cannot find work. Benefits and requirements determined by states. Paid for by taxes on employers. *No means test.*

Temporary Assistance for Needy Families (TANF) Payments to needy families with children. Replaced the old AFDC program. Partially paid for by block grants from the federal government to the states. *Means test.*

Supplemental Security Income (SSI) Cash payments to aged, blind, or disabled people whose income is below a certain amount. Paid for from general federal revenues. *Means test.*

Food Stamps (now part of the **Supplemental Nutrition Assistance Program, SNAP**) Vouchers, given to people whose income is below a certain level, that can be used to buy food at grocery stores. Paid for out of general federal revenues. *Means test.*

Medicaid Pays medical expenses of persons receiving TANF or SSI payments. *Means test.*

Earned Income Tax Credit Pays cash or tax credit to poor working families. *Means test.*

in 1996, AFDC suffered a fate that few decades-old federal programs of any type ever do, and that far more costly majoritarian social welfare programs never do: it was abolished.

Now, however, let's take a closer look at Washington's two biggest social welfare programs, Social Security and Medicare, and how the majoritarian politics surrounding each program helps to explain what federal policymakers are (or, more to the point, are not) doing as each program faces severe financial stresses.

Social Security and Medicare: *Majoritarian Politics*

When Social Security began in 1935 and Medicare in 1965, many people benefited and the cost was small. In the late 1930s, an old-age check for a retired person on Social Security was paid for by taxes levied on 42 workers; today, only about 3 workers pay for each retired program beneficiary. The current Social Security tax is 12.4 percent of a person's earnings (half of this is paid by the employer). This money is used to make payments to current retirees, with the leftover funds invested in government bonds owned by the Treasury Department.

But that system is breaking down as millions more Americans retire and depend on Social Security for some or all of their income. By 2030, nearly one in five Americans will be 65 or older; each day, about 10,000 baby boomers (Americans born 1946 to 1964) turn 65. In 2012, Social Security paid benefits of about $775 billion to around 57 million people. In its 2013 report, the Social Security Board of Trustees projected that by 2033, if Congress does not act before then, Social Security will be able to pay only 77 percent of scheduled benefits.

Still, for at least three reasons, the program's prospects for remaining solvent are pretty good. First, Social Security is well run, costing less than 1 percent of total annual expenditures to administer. Second, the program remains highly popular with the public, and most people are aware that it faces a solvency problem. Third, and most importantly, Congress, as it has done in the past when the program's finances were faltering, will almost certainly act well before 2033 to increase future funding so that all scheduled benefits get paid.

Like Social Security, Medicare is a widely popular program. Medicare, however, poses a more formidable financial challenge than Social Security does. In 1965, supporters of Medicare said it would not cost more than $8 billion a year. Today, Medicare costs more than $550 billion a year. Even when adjusted for inflation (a dollar in 1965 bought what about $7.38 did in 2013), that is about 75 times what the program cost when it started. Medicare now has more

HOW WE COMPARE

Social Security

Most European democracies began social security systems earlier than the United States did. Even for its time, the U.S. Social Security program that began in 1935 was a relatively modest insurance-based retirement program.

Today, nearly eight decades later, the U.S. Social Security program has grown dramatically and covers more than "old age, disability, and survivors." Still, European nations not only started sooner but have developed far more comprehensive—and expensive—social security systems than America has yet known.

In many European countries, social security programs extend well beyond retirement benefits or pensions to funding for work-related injury, sickness, maternity leave, and more; the retirement age for eligibility is lower than it is in the United States; and the benefits are, on average, greater.

For example, while the average American has received maybe half of his or her working-life income in benefits, a typical French or German worker has retired several years earlier and received as much as 70 percent of his or her working-life income in benefits. Social security benefits here are earnings-related, but many European nations (Ireland, Switzerland, and the United Kingdom, to name just three) provide a flat-rate pension independent of earnings.

Nothing is free: Europeans have paid two to three times as much as Americans in program-related taxes. And, unlike some European and other nations, the United States has avoided "dual Social Security taxation" via bilateral agreements and policies that do not require either foreign workers in America or Americans who work abroad to pay social security to both countries.

Sources: US Social Security Administration, *Social Security Programs Throughout the World*, September 2008, and "U.S. International Social Security Agreements," 2009, accessed May 27, 2010 at www.ssa.gov/international/agreements_overview.html.

than 50 million beneficiaries (about 45 million senior citizens and most of the rest younger citizens with disabilities). The number of Medicare beneficiaries is expected to grow by about 50 percent over the next 20 years, reaching about 80 million in the early 2030s.

As presently structured, Medicare allows beneficiaries to visit the doctor or go to the hospital pretty much whenever they feel they need to do so. The doctor or hospital is paid a fee for each visit. This creates three problems: some people use medical services when they don't really need them; some doctors and hospitals overcharge the government for their services; and doctors and hospitals are paid on the basis of a government-approved payment plan that can change whenever the government wants to save money.

The health care reform law that was enacted in 2010 has scores of different provisions that affect Medicare. A number of these provisions are intended to make Medicare work better and cost less by instituting more sophisticated systems for tracking differences in pricing for given medical services. By 2013, it had already been discovered that for-profit hospitals billed Medicare at a 29 percent higher rate, on average, than nonprofit or government-owned hospitals.[9] To treat a Medicare patient with a simple case of pneumonia (no complications), Medicare paid $124,051 in Philadelphia, $5,093 in Water Valley, Mississippi, and, on average, $24,549 nationally.[10] Even within a given city, hospitals just blocks apart charged Medicare widely different prices for the same services (lower joint replacements, treating complicated cases of asthma or bronchitis, and many others).[11]

Whether efforts to make Medicare beneficiaries more cost-conscious and Medicare providers less prone to overbill will do much to contain costs or improve services remains to be seen. In its 2012 report, the Medicare Board of Trustees forecast that, even given favorable economic assumptions, including projected savings to be wrought by just such measures, the program's trust fund will run out of money in 2024.[12] Medicare's long-term liability is estimated to be more than $40 trillion. The program's administrative overhead costs are relatively low (about 5 percent of annual expenditures), but a 2011 report by the Government Accountability Office estimated that each year Medicare makes at least $48 billion in "improper payments" to doctors, hospitals, medical equipment companies, and other organizations and individuals that it pays or reimburses.

Federal policymakers at both ends of Pennsylvania Avenue and in both parties have struggled to solve each major social welfare program's problems. For instance, in 2001, the bipartisan Commission to Strengthen Social Security suggested, and President Bush proposed, modifying Social Security by allowing people to invest a portion of their tax contributions into private mutual funds that generate higher returns than what the government can pay. The commission provided this example: If the average worker paid 1 percent of his or her income, matched by 1 percent contributed by the government, into a mutual fund that held both stocks and bonds, and he or she worked from age 21 to 65, that person at age 65 would have more than $500,000, in addition to Social Security. If both husband and wife worked all of these years, they would have more than $1 million. Congress, however, did not agree, and since 2001 similar proposals have gone nowhere in Washington.

In 2003, a new Medicare bill was passed, designed in part to change the system by allowing people to save, tax free, money for medical expenses.

HOW THINGS WORK

Medicare ABCDs

Medicare is a federal health insurance program that covers most senior citizens 65 or older, some younger people with disabilities, and people with end-stage renal disease. Today, it covers more than 50 million elderly and disabled persons.

Part A: Hospital Insurance

It covers inpatient care in hospitals, and also helps cover skilled nursing facility care, hospice care, and home health care. Some people pay a monthly premium; others do not.

Part B: Medical Insurance

It covers doctors' services, hospital outpatient care, and some preventive services. The standard monthly premium in 2009 was $96.40. It gets deducted automatically from your Social Security check.

Part C: Medicare Advantage Plus

Basically, it sets the terms under which companies that contract with the Medicare program must provide benefits.

Part D: Prescription Drug Coverage

Participation is voluntary, and the monthly premium depends on how much coverage you have.

TABLE 17.1 **Opinion on Social Security and Medicare Proposals, By Generation**

	Millennial (18–29)	Gen X (30–43)	Boomer (45–63)	Silent (64–81)
	Percent Who Favor			
Changing Social Security to let younger workers put Social Security taxes into private accounts	86	69	58	52
Changing Medicare so people can use benefits toward purchasing private health insurance	74	60	61	48

Source: Adapted from Andrew Kohut, "Debt and Deficit: A Public Opinion Dilemma," Pew Research Center for the People & the Press, June 14, 2012.

But the gains this produced would be partially offset by a huge new benefit to retired persons that was the law's real centerpiece: payments for prescription drugs, or, as it became officially known, Medicare Part D (see the **How Things Work** feature on page 448). In 2011, Senator Ron Wyden (D-OR) and Representative Paul Ryan (R-WI) introduced a Medicare reform plan. Among other provisions, the Wyden-Ryan plan reduced benefits for the wealthiest senior citizens. It featured a "premium support" (voucher-type) option under which beneficiaries could choose either a traditional Medicare plan or a Medicare-approved private plan. Total out-of-pocket Medicare costs were to be capped at $6,000 per person, and low-income citizens who could not pay the cap would receive a subsidy from the government. The bipartisan proposal generated much election-year debate but resulted in no far-reaching Medicare reform legislation.

As we learned in Chapter 7 (see pages 156–160), there are several significant inter-generational gaps in public opinion. "Millennial generation" Americans (ages 18 to 29) differ from senior citizens on issues ranging from same-sex marriage to immigration. There is a similar age gap in opinion on what to do about Social Security and Medicare. Unlike older Americans, most voters under age 30 favor putting Social Security taxes into private accounts and using Medicare benefits to purchase private health insurance (see Table 17.1).

But, as we learned in Chapter 8, older Americans vote at much higher rates than young Americans do, most especially in mid-term congressional elections. Besides, even after years of serious to dire public warnings by present and former lawmakers and blue-ribbon bodies of experts, in 2011, only 8 percent of the public was willing to entertain "major reductions in benefits" for either program, only a quarter (Social Security) and a third (Medicare) was willing to consider "minor reductions in benefits," and a majority in each case opposed increasing taxes to pay for benefits (see Table 17.2).

It may be tempting to see the politics of Social Security and Medicare as a species of client politics in which older citizens benefit and young and middle-aged citizens pay. But resist that temptation. It is true that older citizens vote at higher rates than young ones do. It is also true that interest groups like the AARP that advocate or lobby for the elderly and retirees have great influence in Washington. But most citizens, young and old alike, support the programs; and most oppose trimming benefits and tinkering too much with how the programs presently work. Each program is widely perceived as one into which all people pay and from which all people can and should benefit. The fact that many people receive more in benefits than they ever pay in, like the fact that the programs' massive unfunded liabilities do not fall equally on people of all ages (and will

TABLE 17.2 **Public Opinion on Changing Medicare and Social Security**

	Support (%)
Social Security	
Major Reduction in Benefits	8
Minor Reduction in Benefits	27
Raise Retirement Age from 67 to 68	42
Increase Program Tax Rates	35
Increase Benefits at a Slower Rate	45
Medicare	
Major Reduction in Benefits	8
Minor Reduction in Benefits	35
Raise Eligibility Age from 67 to 70	32
Increase Program Tax Rates	49
Replace Program with a Voucher System	35

Source: ABC News/Washington Post Poll, March 10–13, 2011; Kaiser Family Foundation/Harvard School of Public Health Poll, January 4–14, 2011; and School of Public Policy, University of Maryland and Center on Policy Attitudes, "How Americans Would Deal with the Budget Deficit," February 3, 2011, p. 49.

also be borne by citizens yet to be born), would seem to have little bearing on popular attitudes toward these highly popular programs.

Apparently, most federal policymakers also feel that way about the programs; regardless, even those that may feel differently know that they would court real re-election troubles if they publicly prescribed deep cuts in benefits or steep tax increases for either program. For instance, the first lines of the aforementioned Wyden-Ryan Medicare reform plan read like a majoritarian politics rhapsody: the goal was to "strengthen Medicare and health security for all," with "no changes for those in or near retirement," and guaranteeing that Americans age 56 and older "would see no changes to the structure of their benefits" save any changes they might voluntarily opt to make.

Social Welfare Policy in America: Four Distinctive Features

But not all social welfare policies and programs are so supported by majoritarian politics. Here is a little thought experiment: try imagining federal policymakers in both parties, as they head into a presidential election season, fighting with each other for recognition by voters as having led the charge to "end Social Security as we know it" or "end Medicare as we know it." That's impossible to imagine. Yet, with respect to claiming credit for "ending welfare as we know it"—specifically, ending the Aid to Families with Dependent Children (AFDC) program, which provided cash assistance and other benefits to eligible low-income families with children—that is what happened during the 1996 elections. Republicans led by House Speaker Newt Gingrich (R-GA), and Democrats led by President Bill Clinton (who coined the phrase), each claimed credit for eliminating the program and replacing it with a "work-based welfare" program, Temporary Assistance to Needy Families (TANF).

Before describing the particular client politics that led to AFDC's demise and TANF's rise, it is first necessary to understand that social welfare policy in the United States, most especially as it relates to antipoverty programs designed primarily to benefit low-income children and families, is shaped by four factors that make it different from what exists in many other nations. First, Americans generally have taken a more restrictive view of who is entitled to government assistance. Second, America has been slower than other countries to embrace "the welfare state." Third, Americans have insisted that the states play a large role in running social welfare programs. Fourth, nongovernmental organizations (both for-profit businesses and nonprofit groups) play a large role in administering social welfare policies.

The first distinctive feature of the American welfare state involves who benefits. The way most Americans have seen it, who benefits has been a question of who *deserves* to benefit. Americans usually have insisted that public support be given only to those who cannot help themselves. But what does it mean to say that a person cannot help himself or herself? Surely a disabled, blind, elderly woman deserted by her family cannot do much to help herself, but would she still be deserving of public aid were she merely disabled or merely elderly? And to what extent should government require that her family support her? Social welfare policy since the 1930s has been fundamentally shaped by a slow but steady change in how Americans and their elected leaders have separated the "deserving" from the "undeserving" poor.

That most Americans have thought this way may make us forget there are other ways of thinking about government assistance. The major alternative view is to ask not who deserves help but what each person's "fair share" of the national income is. Seen this way, the role of government is to take money from those who have a lot and give it to those who have only a little, until each person has, if not the same amount, then at least a fair share. But defining a "fair share" is even more difficult than defining the "deserving poor." Moreover, Americans have generally felt that giving money to people who are already working, or who could work if they chose to, is unfair. In some nations—Sweden is an example—government policy is aimed at redistributing income from better-off to not-so-well-off persons, without regard to who "deserves" the money.

Thus Americans base antipoverty policy on the concept of "help for the deserving poor" rather than "redistribution to produce fair shares."[13] They have done so because, as most surveys continue to suggest, they believe citizens should be encouraged to be self-reliant, people who work hard will get what they deserve, and giving money to people who could help themselves will produce a class of "chiselers," subsidize "welfare dependency," and encourage "voluntary non-work" and other behaviors that they think it best to discourage. If Americans believed success at work was a matter of luck rather than effort or was dictated by forces over which they had no control, they might support a different approach, one closer to that followed in many European democracies. The very title of the 1996 federal law that abolished AFDC reflects this view. It was named "The Personal Responsibility and Work Opportunity Reconciliation Act."

Moreover, Americans have always been a bit uneasy about giving money to people. That remains true even today when middle-class Americans, through programs like Social Security, receive the largest share of social welfare dollars. Though they recognize that many people through no fault of their own cannot buy groceries and thus need funds, they would still prefer that, to the extent possible, adults that need help because they are sick, disabled, unemployed, or have a job that pays too little to cover basic life necessities, be given *services* (education, training, medical care) rather than money. Throughout much of American history, social welfare policies have reflected a general philosophical disposition in favor of providing services rather than money to adults deemed deserving of government assistance.

The second striking fact about American social welfare policy is how late in our history it arrived (at least at the national level) compared to other nations. By 1935, when Congress passed the Social Security Act, at least 22 European nations already had similar programs, as did Australia and Japan.[14] Germany was the first to create a nationwide social security program when it developed sickness and maternity insurance in 1883. Six years later, it added old-age insurance and in 1927 unemployment insurance.

The United Kingdom offers perhaps the clearest contrast with the United States. In 1908, a national system of old-age pensions was set up, followed three years later by a plan for nationwide health and unemployment insurance.[15] The United Kingdom had a parliamentary regime in which a political party with liberal sentiments and a large majority had come to power. With authority concentrated in the hands of the prime minister and his cabinet, there was virtually no obstacle to instituting measures, such as welfare programs, that commended themselves to party leaders on grounds of either principle or party advantage. Furthermore, the British Labour party was then beginning to emerge. Though the party was still small (it had only 30 seats in Parliament in 1908), its leaders included people who had been influential in formulating social welfare programs that the leaders of the dominant Liberal party backed. And once these programs were approved, they were in almost all cases nationally run: there were no state governments to which authority had to be delegated or whose different experiences had to be accommodated.

Moreover, the British in 1908 were beginning to think in terms of social classes, to accept the notion of an activist government, and to make welfare the central political issue. Americans at that time also had an activist leader, Theodore Roosevelt; there was a progressive movement; and labor was well along in its organizing drives. But the issues were defined differently in the United States. Progressives, or at least most of them, emphasized the reform of the political process—by eliminating corruption, by weakening the parties, and by improving the civil service—and attacked bigness by breaking up industrial trusts.

Though some progressives favored the creation of a welfare state, they were a distinct minority. They had few allies in organized labor (which was skeptical of public welfare programs) and could not overcome the general distrust of big government and the strong preference for leaving matters of welfare in state hands. In sum, what ordinary politics brought to England in 1908–1911, only the crisis politics of 1935 would bring to the United States. But once started, the programs grew. By 1983, almost one-third of all Americans received benefits from one or more social welfare programs, and today some estimates put the fraction closer to one-half.

The third factor involves the degree to which federalism has shaped national social welfare policy. Since the Constitution was silent on whether Congress had the power to spend money on welfare and since powers not delegated to Congress were reserved to the states, it was not until the constitutional reinterpretation of the 1930s (see Chapter 16) that it became clear that the federal government could do anything in the area of social policy. At the same time, federalism meant that any state so inclined could experiment with welfare programs. Between 1923 and 1933, 30 states enacted some form of an old-age pension. By 1935 all but two states had adopted a "mother's pension"—a program whereby a widow with children was given financial assistance, provided that she was a "fit mother" who ran a "suitable home." The poor were given small doles by local governments, helped by private charities, or placed in almshouses. Only one state, Wisconsin, had an unemployment insurance program.

Politically the state programs had a double-edged effect: they provided opponents of a federal welfare system with an argument (the states were already providing welfare assistance), but they also supplied a lobby for federal financial assistance (state authorities would campaign for national legislation to help them out). Some were later to say that the states were the laboratories for experimentation in welfare policy. When the federal government entered the field in 1935, it did so in part by spending money through the states, thereby encouraging the formation in the states of a strong welfare bureaucracy whose later claims would be difficult to ignore.

A fourth distinctive feature of social welfare policy in the United States is that much of it is administered via grants and contracts to nongovernmental institutions, both for-profit firms and nonprofit organizations. For example, many large national nonprofit organizations, such as Big Brothers Big Sisters of America, Youth Build, Jewish Federation, and Catholic Charities, have received large federal grants and long participated in the administration of federal social welfare programs. The 1996 law that abolished the AFDC program contained a provision (Section 104) *charitable choice* Name given to four federal laws passed in the late 1990s specifying the conditions under which nonprofit religious organizations could compete to administer certain social service delivery and welfare programs.

directing that religious nonprofit organizations, including small community-based groups, be permitted to compete for government grants with which to administer federal welfare-to-work and related policies. The provision, known as **charitable choice**, enjoyed bipartisan support. The provision prohibited religious organizations from using any public funds for proselytizing, religious instruction, or worship services, but also prohibited the government from requiring them to remove religious art or iconography from buildings where social service delivery programs funded in whole or in party by Washington might be administered.

During the 2000 presidential race, both Vice President Al Gore and Governor George W. Bush endorsed charitable choice and called for expanding government grants to qualified religious nonprofit organizations. In 2001, President Bush created a White House "faith-based" office with centers in five cabinet agencies. In 2009, President Obama renamed but retained that White House office and expanded its centers to all federal cabinet agencies as well as the Corporation for National and Community Services (the agency responsible for most national

service programs funded by Washington). During President Obama's first term, federal grants to religious nonprofit organizations increased, and new "faith-based and neighborhood partnership" initiatives were launched, like one that expanded the U.S. Department of Agriculture's capacity to deliver free meals to needy children in the summer months.

From AFDC to TANF: Client Politics

All four distinctive features of social welfare policy in the United States are evident in the story of what came to be called Aid to Families with Dependent Children (AFDC). The program began as part of the Social Security Act of 1935. It was scarcely noticed at the time. In response to the Great Depression, the federal government promised to provide aid to states that in many cases were already running programs to help poor children who lacked a father.

Because AFDC involved giving federal aid to existing state programs, it allowed the states to define what constituted "need," to set benefit levels, and to administer the program. Washington did set (and, over the years, continued to increase) a number of rules governing how the program would work, however. Washington told the states how to calculate applicants' incomes and, after 1965, required the states to give Medicaid to AFDC recipients (a fact that we will return to in the next section when we parse Medicaid's policy dynamics). The states had to establish mandatory job-training programs for many AFDC recipients and to provide

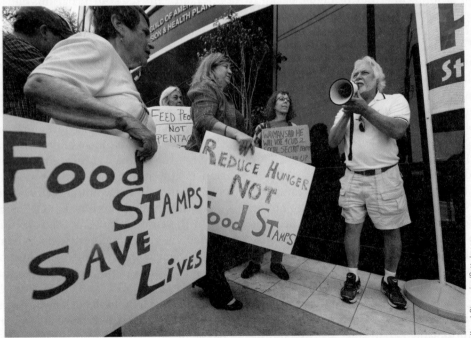

People rally against funding cuts for the Supplemental Nutrition Assistance Program (SNAP), popularly known as food stamps.

Kevork Djansezian/Getty Images

child-care programs for working AFDC parents. Washington also required that women on AFDC identify their children's fathers. In addition to the growing list of requirements, Washington created new programs for which AFDC recipients were eligible, such as Food Stamps, the Earned Income Tax Credit (EITC—a cash grant to poor parents who were working), free school meals, various forms of housing assistance, and certain other benefits. But while all this was happening, public opinion moved against the AFDC program.

By the time that abolishing AFDC was being debated in Congress, opinion surveys found more than 70 percent of the public agreed that people "abuse the system by staying on too long," more than 60 percent agreed that the system "gives people benefits without requiring them to do work" and also permits people "to cheat and commit fraud to get welfare benefits," and about 60 percent agreed that the program encourages out-of-wedlock births.[16] The combination of souring public opinion, increasing federal regulations, and a growing roster of benefits produced a program that lost many one-time supporters. The states disliked having to conform to a growing list of federal regulations. The public disliked the program because over time it came to be viewed as weakening the family by encouraging out-of-wedlock births (since AFDC recipients received additional benefits for each new child). The public worried that AFDC recipients were working covertly on the side; the data proved that this was true of at least half of them in several large cities. AFDC recipients saw that the actual (inflation-adjusted) value of their AFDC checks was going down. Critics countered that if you added together all the benefits they were receiving (Food Stamps, Medicaid, housing assistance, and so on), benefit levels were actually going up. Politicians complained that healthy parents were living off AFDC instead of working. The AFDC law was revised many times, including in 1988 (just eight years before AFDC was abolished). But the program was never revised in a way that satisfied all, or even most, of its critics. Though AFDC recipients were only a small fraction of all Americans, they had become a large political problem.

What made the political problem worse was that the composition of the people in the program had changed. In 1970, about half of the mothers on AFDC were there because their husbands had died or divorced them; only a quarter had never been married. By 1994, the situation had changed dramatically: only about a quarter of AFDC mothers were widowed or divorced, and over half had never been married at all. And though most women on AFDC for the first time got off it after just a few years, almost two-thirds of the women on AFDC at any given moment had been on it for eight years or more.

These facts, combined with the increased proportion of out-of-wedlock births in the country as a whole, made it virtually impossible to sustain political support for what had begun as a noncontroversial client program. In 1996 AFDC was abolished. It was replaced by Temporary Assistance for Needy Families (TANF), a block grant program that set strict federal requirements about work and limited how long families can receive federally funded benefits. In 2002, during the largely consensual congressional debate over reauthorizing TANF, even many who had opposed these strategies in 1996 (when TANF replaced AFDC) now supported them. By 2006, a decade after abolishing AFDC, welfare caseloads nationally had declined by 62 percent. "Ending welfare as we know it," as in ending AFDC, was widely, albeit no means universally, viewed as a success.

During President Obama's first term, critics charged that the administration was weakening TANF's work requirements and permitting TANF recipients to receive benefits longer than the program's rules allowed. The facts, however, told a different tale: TANF recipients, like most Americans generally, were simply having ever greater trouble finding or keeping work amidst the nation's deep economic downturn. Similarly, the number of people receiving Food Stamps increased from about 28 million in 2008 to about 47 million in 2012. Even though most new Food Stamp recipients entered the program after losing jobs or having other financial problems that reduced their incomes, during the 2012 presidential campaign, a debate began over the estimated 2 million or so "able-bodied" Food Stamp recipients that did not meet all the usual program eligibility criteria, and over allegations concerning widespread "waste, fraud, and abuse" in the program. Again, the facts told a different tale: about 40 percent of all Food Stamps beneficiaries were children, about 8 percent were senior citizens, and nearly half of all persons receiving benefits lived in a household where someone worked for low wages.

In sum, although they may be quite controversial when they are first proposed and debated, social welfare programs like Social Security and Medicare that are perceived to benefit wide classes of citizens at a cost that is shared by most people (majoritarian politics) become politically sacrosanct even though, as is presently true for both Social Security and Medicare, they have huge costs, pose present and future financial burdens, make billions of dollars in improper payments, and pay out to most beneficiaries more than those beneficiaries ever pay in. In stark contrast, although they may stir little controversy or go virtually unnoticed when they are first proposed and debated, social welfare programs like the late AFDC that are perceived to benefit only certain groups of citizens at a cost that is shouldered by most people (client politics) will be established and remain politically protected only if the cost to the public at large is not perceived to be great *and* if the people receiving the benefit are widely deemed "deserving."

Medicaid: Client and Majoritarian

At first glance, Medicaid may seem closer to the old AFDC program and the present TANF program than it does to Social Security and Medicare. As explained earlier in this chapter, in 1965, Medicaid was enacted into law in the eleventh hour of Medicare's approval so that at least some low-income persons who were not Medicare-eligible senior citizens might receive some health care coverage. Today, Medicaid is still a means-tested program that pays the medical expenses of persons receiving TANF payments, mainly TANF-eligible low-income adults and their dependent children.

But now look closer. Medicaid also pays medical expenses of persons receiving Social Security benefits, including senior citizens that have spent down their life savings and require long-term medical care, people with permanent or total disabilities, and others, including certain Medi*care* enrollees. It is true that about two-thirds of all Medicaid beneficiaries are low-income children plus non-disabled low-income adults; the other third are non-elderly disabled adults plus low-income or disabled senior citizens. But it is also true that about two-thirds of Medicaid dollars are spent on the one-third of the Medicaid beneficiaries that are elderly or disabled. The other third or so of Medicaid dollars are spent on the roughly two-thirds of the Medicaid beneficiaries that are TANF-eligible non-disabled low-income adults or low-income children. The average annual per capita Medicaid expenditure for disabled and elderly beneficiaries has been more than four times the average annual per capita Medicaid expenditure for non-disabled adult or low-income child beneficiaries.

In the mid-1990s, when AFDC was being dismantled, more than five times as much public money was being spent on Medicaid as was being spent on AFDC, and a majority of Medicaid beneficiaries were also AFDC beneficiaries. But Medicaid has had, and continues to have, a beneficiary population that AFDC did not, namely, senior citizens and disabled persons. Today, just as it was some two decades ago when Congress was about the business of ending AFDC, Medicaid is the main source of public funding for long-term care, accounting for more than half of all government spending on nursing homes, intermediate-care facilities, and medical home-care services. In Congress as well as in state legislatures, Medicaid has had political support from interest groups beyond those advocating directly for its various beneficiaries,

namely, the for-profit firms and nonprofit organizations that receive billions of dollars each year to supply nursing home care and other services.

Thus it is that the policy dynamics surrounding Medicaid mix client politics with majoritarian politics. Over the last two decades, most proposals to "cut Medicaid" have actually been proposals to trim program benefits for the program's TANF-eligible adult, non-disabled populations. Almost nobody thinks of poor senior citizens, poor children, or disabled persons as "undeserving." Since the late 1990s, while Medicaid benefits for TANF-eligible adults have remained flat or been reduced in some states, Medicaid benefits for the program's youngest and oldest beneficiaries, as well for its disabled beneficiaries, have remained stable or grown just about everywhere, including through related policies and programs like the State Children's Health Insurance Program, known as S-CHIP.

In sum, because of its client politics components, Medicaid is not as politically sacrosanct as either Social Security or Medicare each are; but, because of its majoritarian politics components, Medicaid, unlike AFDC, has survived every major push for program-wide cuts while preserving most benefits for TANF-eligible non-disabled adults and expanding benefits for low-income children; and there is not now nor has there ever been any politically significant constituency for "ending Medicaid as we know it." Still, it is too soon to know how Medicaid's politics might change as the now roughly $400 billion a year federal–state program continues to expand, or whether the state-to-state differences in benefit levels for some or all of its beneficiary populations will shrink or widen as the new federal health care policy is implemented.

Business Regulation Policy

Efforts by government to regulate business not only illustrate the four kinds of policymaking politics, but also shed light on a facet of political life that many people think is fundamental to understanding who governs and to what ends—namely, the relationship between wealth and power.

To some observers, the very existence of large corporations is a threat to popular rule. Economic power will dominate political power, they believe, for one or more of three reasons: first, because wealth can be used to buy influence; second, because politicians and business leaders have similar class backgrounds and thus similar beliefs about public policy; and third, because elected officials must defer to the preferences of business so as to induce corporations to keep the economy healthy and growing. Karl Marx, of course, proposed the most sweeping version of the view that economics controls politics;

for him the state in a capitalist society was nothing more than the executive committee of the propertied classes.[17] But there are other non-Marxist or neo-Marxist versions of the same concern.[18]

To other observers, politics, far from being subordinate to economic power, is a threat to the very existence of a market economy and the values—economic growth, private property, personal freedom—that they believe such an economy protects. In this view, politicians will find it in their interest, in their struggle for votes, to take the side of the nonbusiness majority against that of the business minority. The heads of large corporations, few in number but great in wealth, fear that they will be portrayed as a sinister elite on whom politicians can blame war, inflation, unemployment, and pollution. Defenders of business worry that corporations will be taxed excessively to pay for social programs that in turn will produce more votes for politicians. Just as bad, in this view, is the tendency of universities (on which corporations must rely for technical experts) to inculcate antibusiness values in their students.[19]

As the theory of the policymaking process presented in this book should suggest, neither of these two extreme views of business-government relations is entirely correct. These relations depend on many things, including the *kind* of business regulation policy proposed. Instead of clenching our fists and shouting pro-business or antibusiness slogans at each other, we should be able, after applying this theory to the available facts, to make more careful and exact statements of the following sort: "If certain conditions exist, then business regulation policy will take certain forms."

Antitrust Laws: Majoritarian Politics

Not all efforts to regulate business pit one group against another. From time to time, laws are passed that reflect the views of a majority of voters that is neither imposing its will on a hostile business community nor acceding to the desires of a privileged industry.

Much of the antitrust legislation passed in this country, including the Sherman Act (1890), parts of the Federal Trade Commission Act (1914), and the Clayton Act (1914), has been the result of majoritarian politics. Toward the end of the 19th century, a broadly based criticism arose of business monopolies (then called trusts) and, to a lesser extent, of large corporations, whether or not they monopolized trade. The Grange, an organization of farmers, was especially outspoken in its criticism, and popular opinion generally—insofar as we can know it in an era without pollsters—seems to have been indignant about trusts and in favor of "trust-busting." Newspaper editorials and magazine articles frequently dwelt on the problem.[20]

But though antitrust feeling was strong, it was also relatively unfocused: no single industry was the special target of this criticism (the oil industry, and especially the Standard Oil Company, came as close as any), and no specific regulation was proposed. In fact, there was no general agreement about how to define the problem: for some it was monopoly; for others sheer bigness; and for still others the legal basis of the modern corporation. The bill proposed by Senator John Sherman did not clarify matters much: while it made it a crime to "restrain" or "monopolize" trade, it did not define these terms, nor did it create any new regulatory agency charged with enforcing the law.[21]

No doubt some large corporations worried about what all this would mean for them, but few felt sufficiently threatened to try very hard to defeat the bill. It passed the Senate by a voice vote and the House by a vote of 242 to 0.

Laws are not self-executing, and vague laws are especially likely to lie dormant unless political leaders work hard at bringing them to life. For the first decade or so after 1890, only one or two antitrust cases a year were filed in the courts. In 1904, President Theodore Roosevelt persuaded Congress to provide enough money to hire five full-time lawyers, and soon the number of prosecutions increased to about seven a year. Then in 1938, President Franklin Roosevelt appointed as head of the Antitrust Division of the Justice Department a vigorous lawyer named Thurman Arnold, who began bringing an average of 50 cases a year.[22] Today, more than 400 lawyers in the division sift through complaints alleging monopolistic or other unfair business practices. Though controversy exists over the kinds of cases that should be brought, there is no serious effort among either politicians or business leaders to abandon the commitment to a firm antitrust policy, the strongest such policy found in any industrial nation.

The antitrust laws were strengthened in 1914 by bills that created the Federal Trade Commission and made (via the Clayton Act) certain specific practices, such as price discrimination, illegal. As with the earlier Sherman Act, the advocates of these measures had a variety of motives. Some proponents favored these laws because they would presumably help consumers (by preventing unfair business practices); other proponents supported them because they might help business (by protecting firms against certain tactics that competitors might employ).

President Woodrow Wilson endorsed both of these bills and helped create a broad coalition on behalf of the legislation; the Federal Trade Commission Act and the Clayton Act passed Congress by lopsided majorities.[23]

As with the Sherman Act, there has been continual controversy about how these laws should be administered. But this controversy, like the debate over the initial passage of the laws, has not been dominated by interest groups.[24] The reason for the relative absence of interest group activity is that these laws do not divide society into permanent and identifiable blocs of proponents and opponents. Any given business firm can be either helped or hurt by the enforcement of the antitrust laws. One year, the XYZ Widget Company may be sued by the government to prevent it from unfairly advertising its widgets, and the next year the same XYZ Company may ask the government to prosecute its competitor for trying to drive XYZ out of business by selling widgets at prices below cost.

The amount of money the federal government devotes to antitrust enforcement and the direction those enforcement efforts take are determined more by the political ideology and personal convictions of the administration in power than by interest group pressures. For example, the Reagan administration decided the benefits of trying to break up IBM were not worth the costs, and thus it ended its antitrust prosecution of the giant computer firm. At the same time, however, it decided it was desirable to break up American Telephone and Telegraph (AT&T), making the local phone companies independent of AT&T and forcing AT&T to compete with other long-distance service providers. In the 1990s, the Clinton administration brought an antitrust suit against computer software giant Microsoft.

Between 2001 and 2008, the Bush administration, through a high-level White House task group led by Vice President Dick Cheney, reversed many Clinton-era policies and reinstated Reagan-era ones. Then, in 2009, with the country beset by a major economic crisis, the Obama administration proposed overhauling antitrust policies yet again, folding its plan into a proposal that would centralize all relevant financial regulatory powers in just a few federal agencies. And Christine Varney, a strong antitrust enforcement advocate, was appointed to head the new administration's antitrust investigations within the U.S. Department of Justice.

In sum, as with most majoritarian policies, antitrust regulation tends to reflect broad philosophies of governance more than interest group activity.

Labor and Occupational Health and Safety: Interest Group Politics

Organized interest groups are very powerful, however, when the regulatory policies confer benefits on a particular group and costs on another, equally distinct group.

In 1935, labor unions sought government protection for their right to organize, to bargain collectively with industry, and to compel workers in unionized industries to join the unions. Business firms opposed these plans. The struggle was fought out in Congress, where the unions won. The Wagner Act, passed that year, created the National Labor Relations Board (NLRB) to regulate the conduct of union organizing drives and to hear complaints of unfair labor practices brought by workers against management.

But the struggle was far from over. In 1947, management sought to reverse some of the gains won by unions by pressing for a law (the Taft-Hartley Act) that would make illegal certain union practices (such as the closed shop and secondary boycotts) and would authorize the president to obtain a court order blocking for up to eighty days any strike that imperiled the "national health or safety." Business won.

Business and labor fought round three in 1959 over a bill (the Landrum-Griffin Act) intended to prevent corruption in unions, to change the way in which organizing drives were carried out, and to prohibit certain kinds of strikes and picketing. Business won.

In each of these cases, the struggle was highly publicized. The winners and losers were determined by the partisan composition of Congress (Republicans and southern Democrats tended to support business, northern Democrats to support labor) and by the existence of economic conditions (a depression in 1935, revelations of labor racketeering in 1959) that affected public opinion on the issue.

But the interest group struggle did not end with the passage of the laws; it continued throughout their administration. The National Labor Relations Board, composed of five members appointed by the president, had to adjudicate countless disputes between labor and management over the interpretation of these laws. The losing party often appealed the NLRB decision to the courts, where the issue was fought out again. Moreover, each president has sought to tilt the NLRB in one direction or another by means of whom he appoints to it. Democratic presidents favor labor and thus tend to appoint pro-union board members; Republican presidents favor business and thus tend to appoint pro-management members. Since NLRB members serve five-year terms, a new president cannot immediately appoint all of the board's members; thus there is often a split on the board between two factions.

But one vote can make a difference. When President Obama appointed a Democrat to the NLRB, it acquired a Democratic majority. The Board then issued an order that would prevent Boeing from building its 787 aircraft in South Carolina, a state with a "right to work" law that prevents workers from being required to join a union. The issue was, of course, appealed. In December 2011, the NLRB rescinded the order after the Machinists Union ratified a new contract with Boeing.

A similar pattern of interest group influence is revealed by the history of the Occupational Safety and Health Act, passed in 1970. Labor unions wanted a strict bill with tough standards set by a single administrator; business organizations wanted a more flexible bill with standards set by a commission that would include some business representatives. After a long struggle, labor prevailed, and the Occupational Safety and Health Administration (OSHA), headed by a single administrator, was set up inside the Department of Labor.

As with the NLRB, conflict did not end with the passage of the law, and OSHA decisions were frequently appealed to the courts. The politics swirling about OSHA were all the more contentious because of the vast mandate of the agency: it is supposed to determine the safe limits for worker exposure to hundreds of chemicals and to inspect tens of thousands of workplaces to see whether they should be cited for violating any standards. During the Carter administration, an appointed OSHA administrator was sympathetic to the labor view and thus set many standards and issued many citations; during the Reagan administration, the selected administrator was admired by business because he set fewer standards and issued fewer citations.

Agriculture Subsidies: Client Politics

Many people suppose that when government sets out to regulate business, the firms that are supposed to be regulated will in fact "capture" the agency that is supposed to do the regulating. But as we have already seen, certain kinds of policies—those that give rise to majoritarian and interest group politics—do not usually lead to capture, because the agency either faces no well-organized, enduring opponent (as with majoritarian politics) or is caught in a crossfire of competing forces (as with interest group politics).

But when a policy confers a benefit on one group at the expense of many other people, client politics arises, and so agency "capture" is likely. More precisely, nothing needs to be captured at all, since the agency will have been created from the outset to serve the interests of the favored group. We sometimes think regulations are always resisted. But a regulation need not be a burden; it can be a great benefit.

How this works can be seen close to home. State and city laws regulate the practice of law and medicine as well as a host of other occupations—barbers, beauticians, plumbers, dry cleaners, taxi drivers, and undertakers. These regulations are sometimes designed and always defended as ways of preventing fraud, malpractice, and safety hazards. But they also have the effect of restricting entry into the regulated occupation, thereby enabling its members to charge higher prices than they otherwise might.[25] Ordinarily, citizens do not object to this, in part because they believe, rightly or wrongly, that the regulations in fact protect them, and in part because the higher prices are spread over so many customers as to be unnoticed.

Much the same thing can be found at the national level. In the early 1930s, the American dairy industry was suffering from rapidly declining prices for milk. As the farmers' incomes fell, many could no longer pay their bills and were forced out of business. Congress responded with the Agricultural Adjustment Act, which authorized an agency of the Department of Agriculture to regulate the milk industry. This agency, the Dairy Division of the Agricultural Marketing Service, would issue "market orders" that had the effect of preventing price competition among dairy farmers and thus kept the price of milk up. If this guaranteed minimum price leads to the production of more milk than people want to drink, then another part of the Agriculture Department—the Commodity Credit Corporation—stands ready to buy up the surplus with tax dollars.[26]

Consumers wind up paying more for milk than they otherwise would, but they have no way of knowing the difference between the regulated and unregulated price of milk.[27] Consumers have little incentive to organize politically to do much about it. The total cost, however, can be very high; in 2006 it was over $4 billion. Although consumers are not helped by high prices, not every dairy farmer is helped either. More milk is produced than people will buy, and so many dairy farmers have gone out of business.

A similar system works with sugar. Sugar produced abroad, in countries such as Brazil and the Philippines, costs much less than sugar produced here, in states such as Louisiana. To keep the incomes of U.S. sugar producers high, Congress decided to restrict the importation of cheap foreign sugar by

Dairy farmers get government subsidies for their milk production.

imposing quotas. By 1990, this cost American consumers real money—maybe as much as $3 billion a year—but the extra cost per pound of sugar was not noticeable to each individual consumer.[28]

From time to time, various officials attempt to change the regulations that benefit a client group. But they must confront some sobering political facts. Dairy farmers are found scattered through scores of congressional districts; sugar beet growers are concentrated in southern states important in any presidential election. Efforts have been made in Congress to cut milk subsidies and sugar quotas, but with only limited success.

In 1996, Congress passed and President Clinton signed a bill that began, at least for wheat and corn crops, to phase out the practice of paying farmers the difference between what they can sell their crops for and what the government thinks the crops ought to be worth. It replaced these crop subsidies with direct cash payments to farmers that they can use for anything, farming or otherwise.

But the 1996 plan to lure farmers into a free-market economy did not last. Between 1996 and 2001, the subsidies they got increased rather than decreased. In 2002, President Bush signed a new farm bill that did away with the 1996 law and authorized paying farmers $171 billion in new subsidies by 2012. Though defended as a way of protecting "the little farmer," most of the money will go to big farmers who produce wheat, corn, rice, cotton, and soybeans (but not to those who produce cattle, hogs, poultry, fruits, or vegetables).

Farm subsidies are justified by the fact that the prices farmers earn swing wildly, but subsidies don't go to people who make computer chips or raise cattle even though they also experience big swings in the prices they can charge. The existence of farm subsidies is the result of history (a legacy of the time, during the Great Depression, when the government wanted to help nearly one-fourth of all employed Americans who then worked on farms) and politics (farmers are key and changeable voters in many important states). Today, there is a small but growing movement to focus farm subsidies more on individual or small farms (including "urban farms" in big cities) that employ sustainable food cultivation strategies, create local jobs, and promote healthier eating habits.[29]

Client politics has become harder to practice in this country unless a group is widely thought to be a "deserving" client. Dairy farmers, sugar producers, and tobacco growers struggle (sometimes successfully, sometimes unsuccessfully) to keep their benefits, but the struggle relies on "insider politics"—that is, on dealing with key Washington decision makers and not on building widespread public support. By contrast, when a devastating flood, tornado, earthquake, or hurricane strikes a community, the victims are thought to be eminently deserving of help. After all, people say, it was not their fault that their homes were destroyed. (In some cases, it was because they built homes in areas they knew were at high risk for hurricanes or floods.) They receive client benefits.

Although client politics for "special interests" seems to be on the decline, that is true mostly for programs that actually send certain groups money. Pietro Nivola reminds us of a different form of client politics: using regulations instead of cash to help groups. For example, regulations encourage the use of ethanol (a kind of alcohol made from corn) in gasoline, which benefits corn farmers and ethanol manufacturers. Clients that might not be thought legitimate increasingly get their way by means of regulations rather than subsidies.[30]

But regulation that starts out by trying to serve a client can end up hurting it. Radio broadcasters supported the creation of the Federal Communications Commission (FCC), which would, broadcasters and telephone companies thought, bring order and stability to their industries. It did. But then it started doing a bit more than the industries had hoped for. It began reviewing efforts by companies to merge. When one telephone company tried to merge with another, the FCC said it would have to review the consolidation even though the law did not give it the power to do so. After long (and secret) negotiations, it extracted concessions from the companies as a condition of their merger. Because there was no law requiring such concessions, the firms accepted them "voluntarily." But if they had not agreed, they would have been in deep trouble with the FCC in the future.

Regulatory agencies created to help clients can become burdens to those clients when the laws the agencies enforce are sufficiently vague so as to provide freedom of action for the people who run them. For a long time, most of these laws were hopelessly vague. The FCC, for example, was told to award licenses as "the public interest, convenience, and necessity" required. In time, such language can give an agency powers that are wide and undefined.

Consumer and Environmental Protection: Entrepreneurial Politics

During the 1960s and 1970s some two dozen consumer and environmental protection laws were passed, including laws that regulated the automobile industry, oil companies, toy manufacturers, poultry producers, the chemical industry, and pharmaceutical companies.[31]

When measures such as these become law, it is often because a policy entrepreneur has dramatized an issue, galvanized public opinion, and mobilized congressional support. Sometimes that entrepreneur is in the government (a senator or an outspoken bureaucrat); sometimes that entrepreneur is a private person (the best known, of course, is Ralph Nader). The motives of such entrepreneurs can be either self-serving or public-spirited; the policies they embrace may be either good or bad. (Just because someone succeeds in regulating business does not mean that the public will necessarily benefit; by the same token, just because business claims that a new regulation will be excessively costly does not mean that business will in fact have to pay those costs.)

An early example of a policy entrepreneur inside the government was Dr. Harvey Wiley, a chemist in the Department of Agriculture, who actively campaigned for what was to become the Pure Food and Drug Act of 1906. Later, Senator Estes Kefauver held hearings that built support for the 1962 drug laws (and incidentally for his presidential bid), and Senator Edmund Muskie called attention to the need for air and water pollution control legislation (and incidentally to his own 1972 presidential aspirations).

When a policy entrepreneur is outside the government, he or she will need a sympathetic ear within it. Occasionally, the policy needs of the entrepreneur and the political needs of an elected official coincide. When Ralph Nader was walking the corridors of the Capitol looking for someone interested in auto safety, he found Senators Abraham Ribicoff and Warren Magnuson, who themselves were looking for an issue with which they could be identified.

The task of the policy entrepreneur is made easier when a crisis or scandal focuses public attention on a problem. Upton Sinclair's book *The Jungle*[32] dramatized the frightful conditions in meat-packing plants at the turn of the century and helped pave the way for the Meat Inspection Act of 1906. The stock market collapse of 1929 helped develop support for the Securities and Exchange Act. When some people who had taken a patent medicine (elixir of sulfanilamide) died as a result, the passage of the 1938 drug laws became easier. Oil spilled on the beaches of Santa Barbara, California, drew attention to problems addressed by the Water Quality Improvement Act of 1970.

The dramatic event need not be an actual crisis; in some cases, a political scandal will do. Highway fatalities were not a matter of great concern to most citizens when Congress began considering the auto safety act in 1965–1966, but support for the bill grew when it was revealed that General Motors had hired a private detective who made a clumsy effort to collect (or manufacture) gossip harmful to Ralph Nader, whose 1965 book *Unsafe at Any Speed: The Designed-In Dangers of the American Automobile*[33] had criticized the safety of certain GM cars.

In some cases, no dramatic event at all is required for entrepreneurial politics to succeed. Most of the air and water pollution control bills were passed despite the absence of any environmental catastrophe.[34] Support for such measures was developed by holding carefully planned committee hearings that were closely followed by the media. For example, by drawing attention to the profits of the pharmaceutical companies, Senator Kefauver was able to convince many people that these firms were insensitive to public needs. By drawing on information made available to him by environmentalists, Senator Muskie was able to capitalize on and help further a growing perception in the country during the early 1970s that nature was in danger.

Because political resistance must be overcome without the aid of a powerful economic interest group, policy entrepreneurs seeking to regulate an industry often adopt a moralistic tone, with their opponents portrayed as devils, their allies viewed with suspicion, and compromises fiercely resisted. When Senator Muskie was drafting an air pollution bill, Ralph Nader issued a highly publicized report *attacking* Muskie, his nominal ally, for not being tough enough. This strategy forced Muskie—who wanted acclaim, not criticism, for his efforts—to revise the bill so that it imposed even more stringent standards.[35] Other allies of Nader, such as Dr. William Haddon, Jr., and Joan Claybrook, got the same treatment when they later became administrators of the National Highway Traffic Safety Administration. They came under attack not only from the auto industry for designing rules that the companies thought were too strict, but also from Nader, for devising rules that he thought were not strict enough.

Once a policy entrepreneur manages to defeat an industry that is resisting regulation, he or she

Entrepreneurial politics: Upton Sinclair's book The Jungle, *published in 1906, shocked readers with its description of conditions in the meat-packing industry and helped bring about passage of the Meat Inspection Act of 1906.*

Bettman/CORBIS

AP Photos

WHAT WOULD YOU DO?

MEMORANDUM

To: *J. Peter, assistant to the president*

From: *Daniel Gilbert, special assistant to the president*

Subject: *Department of Energy nuclear waste plan*

The president must decide whether to sign the bill allowing the department to establish a safe repository for the nation's nuclear waste beneath mountains in Nevada. The waste is produced mainly by 131 commercial nuclear reactors and by national defense weapons programs. It is presently stored at 126 sites in more than three dozen states.

Arguments for:

1. For more than 50 years, radioactive waste that remains deadly to humans for 10,000 years has been accumulating in cities and towns throughout the country.

2. According to many experts, encasing the waste in well-engineered tunnels beneath mountains in remote locations is both safer and more cost-effective than such alternatives as storing it in ocean tunnels or propelling it into space.

3. The bill achieved a bipartisan majority. Polls find that most people know little about the problem but believe that something should be done to increase safety.

Arguments against:

1. The department admits that transporting nuclear waste to the Nevada site through dozens of states on trucks, trains, and barges would take decades and pose safety risks.

News »

Congress Approves Plan to Store Nuclear Waste in Nevada

Yesterday the U.S. Congress approved a bill allowing the U.S. Department of Energy to proceed with a plan to site 70,000 tons of highly radioactive nuclear waste in Nevada. Under the plan, beginning in three years, irradiated fuel from nuclear reactors would be shipped to Nevada from cities all over the country.

2. Some experts argue that constructing a 100-mile network of tunnels that safely stores nuclear waste in disposal canisters for 10,000 years will prove technologically difficult and financially burdensome.

3. The plan is strongly opposed by many elected officials in Nevada and surrounding states, and a coalition of environmental groups is threatening to challenge it in court.

Your decision:

Advise president to sign _____

Advise president not to sign _____

creates—at least for a while—a strong impetus for additional legislation of the same kind. A successful innovator produces imitators, in politics as in rock music. After the auto safety law was passed in 1966, it became easier to pass a coal mine safety bill in 1969 and an occupational safety and health bill in 1970.

The great risk faced by policy entrepreneurs is not that their hard-won legislative victories will later be reversed, but that the agency created to do the regulating will be captured by the industry it is supposed to regulate. The Food and Drug Administration (FDA), which regulates the pharmaceutical industry, has fallen victim during much of its history to precisely this kind of capture. Once the enthusiasm of its founders had waned and public attention had turned elsewhere, the FDA seemed to develop a cozy and rather uncritical attitude toward the drug companies. (In 1958, the head of the Pharmaceutical Manufacturers' Association received an award from the FDA.)[36] In the mid-1960s, under the spur of renewed congressional and White House attention, the agency was revitalized. During the Reagan administration, environmentalists worried that the leadership of the Environmental Protection Agency had been turned over to persons who were unduly sympathetic to polluters.

There are at least five reasons, however, why the consumer and environmental protection agencies may not be as vulnerable to capture as some critics contend. First, these agencies often enforce laws that impose specific standards in accordance with strict timetables, and so they have relatively little discretion. (The Environmental Protection Agency, for example, is required by law to reduce certain pollutants by a fixed percentage within a stated number of years.) Second, the newer agencies, unlike the FDA, usually regulate many different industries and so do not confront a single, unified opponent. The Occupational Safety and Health Administration, for example, deals with virtually every industry. Third, the very existence of these agencies has helped strengthen the hand of the "public-interest" lobbies that initially demanded their creation. Fourth, these lobbies can now call upon many sympathetic allies in the media who will attack agencies thought to have a pro-business bias.

Finally, as explained in Chapter 16, it has become easier for groups to use the federal courts to put pressure on the regulatory agencies. These groups do not have to be large or broadly representative of the public; all they need are the services of one or two able lawyers. If the Environmental Protection Agency (EPA) issues a rule disliked by a chemical company, the company will promptly sue the EPA; if it issues a ruling that pleases the company, the Environmental Defense Fund will sue.

Environmental Policy

Since 1963, more than three dozen major federal environmental laws have been enacted. When an offshore well spewed thousands of gallons of oil onto the beaches of Santa Barbara, California, at the very time (January 1969) when protest politics was in the air, it became difficult or impossible for the government or business firms to resist the demand that threats to our natural surroundings be curtailed. The emerging environmental movement created an

"Yeah, yeah, maybe it's cyclical but I don't feel any better."

occasion—Earth Day, first celebrated on April 22, 1970—to celebrate its beginning.

The movement was hugely successful. In 1970, President Nixon created the Environmental Protection Agency (EPA) and Congress toughened the existing Clean Air Act and passed the Water Quality Improvement Act. Two years later, it passed laws designed to clean up the water; three years later, it adopted the Endangered Species Act. New laws were passed right into the 1990s. Existing environmental organizations grew in size, and new ones were formed. Public opinion rallied around environmental issues.

The Politics of "Cap and Trade"

Of course, as on virtually all other issues, public sentiments on environmental policy are not perfectly stable. For instance, as we indicated at the start of this chapter, when the public is asked which should be more important, economic growth or environmental protection, they are today less prone to prefer environmental protection than they were just a half-decade ago. Still, overall, most Americans are now environmentalists first, including on the single most interesting and important environmental policy issue of our time, global warming.

Global warming occurs when gases, such as carbon dioxide, produced by people when they burn fossil fuels—wood, oil, or coal—get trapped in the atmosphere and cause the earth's temperature to rise. When the temperature goes up, bad things happen—floods on coastal areas as the polar ice caps melt, wilder weather as more storms are created, and the spread of tropical diseases. The policy dynamics of global warming have involved all four types of politics. The issue might be safely majoritarian by now were it not for partisan differences in how people understand it (see Table 17.3).

Despite the partisan divide, bipartisan efforts to address the issue have been made in each of the last

TABLE 17.3 **Partisan Differences on Global Warming**

	Percentage that Agree		
	Republicans	**Democrats**	**Independents**
There is solid evidence the earth is warming	38	79	56
Global warming is a "very serious" problem	14	50	30
The problem requires immediate action	24	68	44
The problem results from human activity	30	59	41

Source: Adapted from "Wide Partisan Differences on Global Warming," Pew Research Center, October 27, 2010.

several sessions of Congress. For example, the House of Representatives in mid-2009 passed the American Clean Energy and Security Act. The bill, however, did not make it through the Senate. It featured a "cap and trade" provision that would set maximum emissions of carbon dioxide for most large firms. The emissions allowed by these caps would decline as the years passed. If a firm produced less than the maximum emissions, it could sell part of its permit to another firm. The theory was that firms would take the least costly way to meet the standards: either lowering their emissions or, if that was too expensive, buying an additional permit from another firm. This strategy was used in the 1990s to reduce the emission of sulfur dioxide that people believed caused acid rain. This plan was similar to the cap-and-trade requirements imposed by the Kyoto Treaty of 1997, but the Senate had never ratified that bill in part because China, India, and other growing economies were not bound by it.

Some critics of the 2009 bill argued that it allowed firms to pay money in order to pollute and was not an efficient method to reduce pollution. Many of them argued that it should be replaced by a tax on carbon. Other critics said it would only work if the permits were auctioned off (instead, the plan allowed the government to give most away), that it required an unrealistically large decrease in carbon dioxide (85 percent by 2050), and that the decreased emissions would impose taxes on Americans and slow economic growth.

Despite the efforts of a small bipartisan group of senators, the bill did not come to a vote in their chamber. The White House was focused on passing health care reform, and the president's advisers were divided over how much the president should engage in the legislative negotiations about the environmental bill. Then the Senate majority leader, Democrat Harry Reid of Nevada, declared that immigration reform needed to pass before environmental reform, in an effort to win support from immigration activists in his home state, where he faced a tough (though ultimately successful) re-election campaign. Finally, the disastrous oil spill in the Gulf of Mexico doomed any prospects of passing legislation that had promised (with White House support) an expansion of offshore oil drilling in return for capping carbon emissions.[37]

After his failure to make headway on one of his signature campaign issues, President Obama, like his recent predecessors, has pursued environmental reforms through regulation instead of legislation. For example, the EPA has imposed stricter guidelines for coal mines to receive permits in compliance with the Clean Water Act. In 2011, the U.S. Fish and Wildlife Service debated whether a small desert lizard belonged on its endangered species list, which would mean prohibiting oil and gas production in the areas where the lizard resides. Interest group politics typically dominate regulatory efforts, while large-scale reform more often requires majoritarian support, which is more difficult for the administration to build in a time of economic turmoil.

Over the last four decades, the United States has constructed the most comprehensive and complicated body of environmental laws and regulations in the world. On such issues as endangered species (entrepreneurial), auto pollution (majoritarian), acid rain (interest group), and agricultural pesticides (client), environmental policies arose, persisted, and changed through one or more of the four types of politics we have been discussing. But before turning to explore each example, it is important to understand how environmental policy in America differs from environmental policy in many other modern democracies.

Environmental Policy in America: Three Distinctive Features

First, environmental policymaking in the United States is much more adversarial than it is in most European nations. In this country, there have been bitter and lasting conflicts over the contents of the Clean Air Act. Minimum auto emissions standards are uniform across the nation, regardless of local conditions (states can set higher standards if they wish). Many rules for improving air and water quality have strict deadlines and require expensive technology. Hundreds of inspectors enforce these rules,

HOW THINGS WORK

Major Environmental Laws

Smog Clean Air Act (passed in 1970; amended in 1977 and 1990)

- **Stationary sources:** EPA sets national air quality standards; states must develop plans to attain them. If the state plan is inadequate, EPA sets a federal plan. Local sources that emit more than a certain amount of pollutants must install pollution control equipment.

- **Gasoline-powered vehicles:** Between 1970 and 1990, pollution from cars was cut by between 60 and 80 percent. Between 1991 and 1998 there was another 30 percent reduction. All states must have an auto pollution inspection system.

- **Cities:** Classifies cities in terms of how severe their smog problem is and sets deadlines for meeting federal standards.

Water Clean Water Acts of various years state that there is to be no discharge of wastewater into lakes and streams without a federal permit; to get a permit, cities and factories must meet federal discharge standards.

Toxic wastes EPA is to clean up abandoned dump sites with money raised by a tax on the chemical and petroleum industries and from general revenues. (Many thousands of such sites exist.)

Environmental impact statements Since 1969, any federal agency planning a project that would significantly affect the human environment must prepare in advance an environmental impact statement (EIS).

Acid rain The Clean Air Act of 1990 requires a reduction of 10 million tons of sulphur dioxide (mostly from electric-generating plants that burn coal) by 1995. The biggest sources must acquire government allowances (which can be traded among firms) setting emission limits.

and hundreds of lawyers bring countless lawsuits to support or challenge this enforcement. Government and business leaders have frequently denounced each other for being unreasonable or insensitive. So antagonistic are the interests involved in environmental policy that it took 13 years, from 1977 to 1990, to agree on a congressional revision of the Clean Air Act.

In the United Kingdom, by contrast, rules designed to reduce air pollution were written by

An EPA environmental scientist surveys a Superfund site in Houston, TX, where bacteria is used to clean up toxic industrial waste.

government and business leaders acting cooperatively. The rules are neither rigid nor nationally uniform; they are flexible and allow plenty of exceptions to deal with local variations in business needs. Compliance with the rules depends mostly on voluntary action, not formal enforcement. Lawsuits are rare. You might think all this sweetness and light were the result of having meaningless rules, but not so. As David Vogel has shown, by the early 1980s the British government had implemented an impressive and effective array of regulations intended to improve the nation's air and water quality.[38] Second, environmental policy here, as in so many other policy areas, depends heavily on the states. Though there are uniform national air quality standards, how those standards are achieved is left to the states (subject to certain federal controls). Though sewage treatment plants are in large measure paid for by Washington, they are designed, built, and operated by state and local governments.

Though the federal government decrees that radioactive waste must be properly disposed of somewhere, the states have a big voice in where that is. Federalism reinforces adversarial politics: one of the reasons environmental issues are so contentious in this country is that cities and states fight over what standards should apply where.

Third, the separation of powers guarantees that almost anybody who wants to wield influence over environmental policy will have an opportunity to do so. In the United Kingdom and in most European nations, the centralized, parliamentary form of government means that the opponents of a policy have less leverage. Here, environmental pressures are brought by interest groups; in Europe, where such groups have less influence, environmentalists form political parties, such as the Green party, so as to be represented in the legislature.

The distinctive features of environmental policy in America are evident in the policy dynamics history of each of four different issues: endangered species, pollution from automobiles, acid rain, and agricultural pesticides.

Endangered Species: Entrepreneurial Politics

Passed in 1973, the Endangered Species Act (ESA) forbids buying or selling a bird, fish, animal, or plant the government regards as "endangered"—that is, likely to become extinct unless it receives special protection—or engaging in any economic activity (such as building a dam or running a farm) that would harm an endangered species. There have been more than 600 species on the protected list; about half are plants. The regulations forbid not only killing a protected species but also adversely affecting its habitat.

The ESA is run by the Fish and Wildlife Service and the National Oceanic and Atmospheric Administration. They can add species to the endangered or threatened list on their own accord or in response to a private petition. Trafficking in an endangered species can lead to criminal penalties; fines may be imposed for managing private land in ways that might harm a species. Several species (such as bald eagles, grizzly bears, gray wolves, and sea otters) have increased in number since being listed and a few (such as bald eagles and gray wolves) have been taken off the list.

Firms and government agencies that wish to build a dam, bridge, factory, or farm in an area where an endangered species lives must comply with federal regulations. The complaints of such clients about these regulations are outweighed by the public support for the law. Sometimes the law preserves a creature, such as the bald eagle, that almost everyone admires; sometimes it protects a creature, such as the snail darter, that almost no one has ever heard of.

Wood product companies and loggers want access to forests under the control of the U.S. Forest Service. Though only a small fraction of all cut timber comes from these forests and most of the U.S. forest system is already off-limits to logging, environmentalists want further restrictions, especially to prevent clear-cutting (cutting down all the trees in a given area) and to prevent harvesting trees from the old-growth forests of Oregon and Washington. But Congress has generally supported the timber industry, ordering the Forest Service to sell harvesting rights at below-market prices, in effect subsidizing the industry. Some activists have worked to convert this client politics into entrepreneurial politics by demanding that clear-cutting in certain forests be stopped in order to protect endangered species, such as the spotted owl.

Pollution from Automobiles: Majoritarian Politics

The Clean Air Act of 1970 imposed tough restrictions on the amount of pollutants that could come out of automobile tailpipes. Indeed, most of the debate over that bill centered on this issue.

Initially, the auto emissions control rules followed the pattern of entrepreneurial politics: an aroused public with media support demanded that automobile companies be required to make their cars less polluting. It seemed to be "the public" against "the interests," and the public won: by 1975, new cars would have to produce 90 percent less of two pollutants (hydrocarbons and carbon monoxide), and by 1976 achieve a 90 percent reduction in another (nitrous oxides). This was a tall order. There was no time to redesign automobile engines or to find an alternative to the internal combustion engine; it would be necessary to install devices (called catalytic converters) on exhaust pipes that would transform pollutants into harmless gases.

But a little-noticed provision in the 1970 law soon shoved the battle over automobile pollution into the arena of majoritarian politics. That provision required states to develop land-use and transportation rules to help attain air quality standards. What that meant in practice was that in any area where smog was still a problem, even after emission controls had been placed on new cars, there would have to be rules restricting the public's use of cars. There was no way for cities such as Denver, Los Angeles, and New York to get rid of smog just by requiring people to buy less-polluting cars—the increase in the number of cars or in the number of miles driven in those places outweighed the gain from making the average car less polluting. That meant the government would have to impose such unpopular measures as bans on downtown parking, mandatory use of buses and carpools, and even gasoline rationing. But efforts to do this failed. Popular opposition to such rules was too great, and the few such rules put into place didn't work. Congress reacted by postponing the deadlines by which air quality standards in cities would have to be met; the EPA reacted by abandoning any serious effort to tell people when and where they could drive.[39]

Even the effort to clean up the exhausts of new cars ran into opposition. Some people didn't like the higher cost of cars with catalytic converters; others didn't like the loss in horsepower these converters caused (many people disconnected them). The United Auto Workers union began to worry that antismog rules would hurt the U.S. auto industry and cost them their jobs. Congress took note of these complaints and decided that despite a lot of effort, new cars could not meet the 90 percent emission reduction standard by 1975–1976, and so in 1977 it amended the Clean Air Act to extend these deadlines by up to six years.

The Clean Air Act, when revised again in 1990, set new, tougher auto emission control standards—but it pushed back the deadline for compliance. It reiterated the need for getting rid of smog in the smoggiest cities and proposed a number of ways to do it—but it set the deadline for compliance in the worst area (Los Angeles) at 20 years in the future.

Most clean-air laws passed since 1990 have targeted particular industries. For example, in 2004 the Bush administration approved a new measure to dramatically reduce emissions from heavy-use diesel engines used in construction, agricultural, and other industrial machinery. The public will support such tough environmental laws when somebody else pays or when the costs are hidden (as in the price of a car); it will not give as much support when it believes it is paying, especially when the payment takes the form of changing how and when it uses the family car. Here are more examples of each kind of majoritarian politics.

Majoritarian Politics When People Believe the Costs Are Low

The National Environmental Policy Act (NEPA), passed in 1969, contained a provision requiring that an **environmental impact statement** (EIS) be written before any federal agency undertakes an activity that will "significantly" affect the quality of the human environment. (Similar laws have been passed in many states, affecting not only what government does but also what private developers do.) Because it required only a "statement" rather than some specific action and because it was a pro-environment law, NEPA passed by overwhelming majorities.

As it turned out, the EIS provision was hardly innocuous. Opponents of virtually any government-sponsored project have used the EIS as a way of blocking, changing, or delaying the project. Hundreds of lawsuits have been filed to challenge this or that provision of an EIS or to claim that a project was not supported by a satisfactory EIS. In this way, environmental activists have challenged the Alaska pipeline, a Florida canal, and several nuclear power plants, as well as countless dams, bridges, highways, and office buildings. Usually the agency's plan is upheld, but this does not mean the EIS is unimportant: the EIS induces the agency to think through what it is doing, and it gives critics a chance to examine, and often to negotiate, the content of those plans.

> **environmental impact statement** A report required by federal law that assesses the possible effect of a project on the environment if the project is subsidized in whole or part by federal funds.

Despite the grumbling of many people adversely affected by fights over an EIS (someone once complained that Moses would never have been able to part the Red Sea if he had had to file an EIS first), popular support for it remains strong because the public at large does not believe it is paying a high price and does believe it is gaining a significant benefit.

Majoritarian Politics When People Believe the Costs Are High

From time to time, someone proposes that gasoline taxes be raised sharply. Such taxes would discourage driving, and this not only would conserve fuel but

LANDMARK CASES

Government and the Environment

- ***Union Electric Co. v. Environmental Protection Agency* (1976):** EPA rules must be observed without regard to their cost or technological feasibility.

- ***Chevron v. National Resources Defense Council* (1984):** States should comply with EPA decisions, even if not explicitly authorized by statute, provided they are reasonable efforts to attain the goal of the law.

- ***Whitman v. American Trucking Associations* (2001):** Allows Congress to delegate broad authority to regulatory agencies.

- ***Massachusetts v. Environmental Protection Agency* (2007):** The EPA must hear a petition asking it to regulate greenhouse gases.

also would reduce smog. Almost everyone would pay, but almost everyone would benefit. However, it is only with great difficulty that the public can be persuaded to support such taxes. The reason is that the people pay the tax first, and the benefit, if any, comes later, and may be a general, rather than individual, result. Unlike Social Security, where the taxes we pay now support cash benefits we get later, gasoline taxes support noncash benefits (cleaner air, less congestion) that many people doubt will ever appear or, if they do, may not be meaningful to them.[40]

When gasoline taxes have been raised, it has usually been because the politicians did not push the tax hike as an environmental measure. Instead, they promised that in return for paying higher taxes the public would receive some concrete benefits—more highways, more buses, or a reduction in the federal deficit (as happened with the gas tax hike of 1990 and again in 1993).

Since it cannot easily cut gasoline use by raising taxes, the government has turned to other approaches. One is to provide tax breaks and other incentives to companies that seek to develop alternative energy sources. Another is to offer incentives to car manufacturers to build vehicles that consume less fuel by relying in whole or in part on electricity.

Acid Rain: Interest Group Politics

Sometimes the rain, snow, or dust particles that fall onto the land are acidic. This is called *acid rain*. In the 1970s, policymakers began to debate policies to deal with it. As everyone acknowledged, one source of acid precipitation is burning fuel such as certain types of coal that contain a lot of sulfur. Some of the sulfur (along with nitrogen) will turn into sulfuric (or nitric) acid as it comes to earth. Steel mills and electric power plants that burn high-sulfur coal are concentrated in the Midwest and Great Lakes regions of the United States. The prevailing winds tend to carry those sulfurous fumes eastward, where some fall to the ground.

That much was certain. Everything else about the issue, however, was surrounded by controversy. Many lakes and rivers in the eastern United States and in Canada had become more acidic, and some forests in these areas had died back. Some part of this was the result of acid rain from industrial smokestacks, but some part of it was also the result of naturally occurring acids in the soils and rainfall. How much of the acidification is man-made and how much is a result of the actions of Mother Nature was a matter of dispute. Some lakes were not affected by acid rain; some were. Why were some affected more than others? Each side in the debate mustered its favorite experts. They provided some support for each side in what became a fierce interest group battle. Residents of

Canada and New England have complained bitterly of the loss of forests and the acidification of lakes, blaming it on Midwestern smokestacks. Midwestern businesses, labor unions, and politicians denied that their smokestacks were the major cause of the problem (if, indeed, there was a problem) and argued that, even if they were the cause, they shouldn't have to pay the cost of cleaning up the problem.

An attempt to deal with the issue in 1977 reflected the kind of bizarre compromises that sometimes result when politically opposed forces have to be reconciled. There were essentially two alternatives. One was to require power plants to burn low-sulfur coal. This would undoubtedly cut back on sulfur emissions, but it would cost money, because low-sulfur coal is mined mostly in the West, hundreds of miles away from the Midwestern coal-burning industries. The other way would be to require power plants to install scrubbers—complicated and very expensive devices that would take sulfurous fumes out of the gas before it came out of the smokestack. In addition to their cost, the trouble with scrubbers was that they didn't always work and that they generated a lot of unpleasant sludge that would have to be hauled away and buried somewhere. Their great advantage, however, was that they would allow Midwestern utilities to continue their practice of using cheap, high-sulfur coal.

Congress voted for the scrubbers for all new coal-burning plants, even if they burned low-sulfur coal. In the opinion of most economists, this was the wrong decision,[41] but it had four great political advantages. First, the jobs of miners in high-sulfur coal mines would be protected. They had powerful allies in Congress. Second, environmentalists liked scrubbers, which they seemed to regard as a definitive, technological "solution" to the problem, an approach far preferable to relying on incentives to induce power plants to buy low-sulfur coal. Third, scrubber manufacturers liked the idea, for obvious reasons. Finally, some eastern governors liked scrubbers because if all new plants had to have them, it would be more costly, and thus less likely, for existing factories in their states to close down and move into the West.

The 1977 law in effect required scrubbers on all new coal-burning plants—even ones located right next to mines where they could get low-sulfur coal. As two scholars later described the law, it seemed to produce "clean coal and dirty air."[42] The 1977 bill did not solve much. Many of the scrubbers, as predicted, didn't work very well. And there remained the question of what to do about existing power plants and factories.

When a solution was finally agreed upon, it was a compromise. President Bush the elder proposed a two-step regulation. In the first phase, 111 power plants would be required to reduce their emission of sulfur by a fixed amount. They could decide for themselves how to do it: buy low-sulfur coal, install scrubbers, or use some other technology. This would be done by 1995. In the second phase, with a deadline in the year 2000, there would be sharper emission reductions for many more plants, and this would probably require the use of scrubbers. To create some flexibility in how much each utility must cut its emissions, a system of sulfur dioxide allowances that could be bought and sold was established. This compromise became part of the Clean Air Act of 1990.

In the mid-2000s, interest groups, advocates, and experts on all sides of the issue were once again poised to battle each other over new and proposed changes to the relevant parts of several different environmental laws. They did, but by 2010, the groups arguing for maintaining the policies were supported by longitudinal data from the national program that monitors the composition of precipitation. The data indicated that, though the problem was still far from solved, since 1994 there had been a dramatic decrease in acid rain falling in the parts of the country where the problem had been most severe, and that decrease was achieved largely without the adverse economic and other impacts that the critics had been predicting since the 1977 law took effect.[43] Still, the interest group politics of the issue continued just the same, including but not limited to political battles in 2011 over efforts by the EPA to bolster anti-acid rain regulatory enforcement.

Agricultural Pesticides: Client Politics

Some client groups have so far escaped this momentum. One such group is organized farmers, who have more or less successfully resisted efforts to restrict the use of pesticides or to control the runoff of pesticides from farmlands.

For a while, it seemed as though farmers would also fall before the assaults of policy entrepreneurs. When Rachel Carson published *Silent Spring* in 1962,[44] she set off a public outcry about the harm to wildlife caused by the indiscriminate use of DDT, a common pesticide. In 1972, the EPA banned the use of DDT.

That same year, Congress directed the EPA to evaluate the safety of *all* pesticides (herbicides, insecticides, fungicides, and others) on the market; unsafe ones were to be removed. However, that was easier said than done. By the late 1970s, there were more than 50,000 pesticides in use, with 5,000 new ones introduced every year.[45] Testing all of these chemicals proved to be a huge, vastly expensive, and very time-consuming job, especially since any health effects on people could not be observed for several years. Pesticides have many beneficial uses; therefore, the EPA had to balance the gains and the risks of using a given pesticide and compare the relative gains and risks of two similar pesticides.

In 2004, Congress directed the EPA to expand and improve its pesticides regulation. Again, that would be a tall order. As summarized in a 2011 EPA report, today in America there are some 112 pesticides producers and about 13,000 pesticides distributors; and about $12 billion a year is spent on pesticides by about 78 million households and 1.2 million farms.[46]

The client politics of the issue makes the EPA's huge regulatory task even harder. American farmers are the most productive in the world, and most of them believe they cannot achieve that output (and thus their present incomes) without using pesticides. These farmers are well organized to express their interests and well represented in Congress (especially on the House and Senate Agricultural Committees). Complicating matters is the fact that the subsidies the taxpayers give to farmers often encourage them to produce more food than they can sell and thus to use more pesticides than they really need. Though many of these chemicals do not remain in the crops harvested, large amounts sink into the soil, contaminating water supplies. But these problems are largely invisible to the public and are much harder to dramatize than the discovery of a toxic waste dump like that at Love Canal, New York.

Though opposed by environmental organizations, farm groups have been generally successful at practicing client politics. Even with the aforementioned 2004 mandate to expand and improve pesticides regulation, now, as when the effort began, the EPA's budget for reviewing pesticides has been kept small. Very few pesticides have been taken off the market, and those that have been removed have tended to be ones that, because they were involved in some incident receiving heavy media coverage (such as the effect of DDT on birds), were decided through entrepreneurial politics.

Beyond Domestic Policy

Challenge yourself to learn more about some or all of the various domestic issues, policies, and programs discussed in this chapter. In each case, ask yourself how, if at all, what you have learned tells you about the type (or types) of policymaking politics that is (or was) most important to whether, when, and how government acted (or failed to act). The next chapter explores economic policy and examines which type of politics has mattered most on such issues as what to do about budget deficits and the public debt. Economic policy is sometimes discussed as if it were all about political battles among and between competing, economically self-interested groups. Chapter 19 explores foreign and military policy and examines which type of politics has mattered most on such issues as international trade and decisions to commit troops abroad. Foreign and military policy is sometimes discussed as if it were all about majoritarian politics that "stops at the water's edge." But, as we shall see, economic policy is hardly all about interest group politics, foreign and military policy is far from uniformly majoritarian, and both "who governs" and "to what ends" vary lots from issue to issue.

LEARNING OBJECTIVES

1. What types of politics may matter to whether and how government acts on any given issue?

Four types of politics matter, each based on how most people perceive the distribution of monetary and other costs and benefits associated with the policy or program: majoritarian (everybody benefits, everybody pays), interest group (one small group pays, another small group benefits), client (almost everybody pays, one small group benefits), and entrepreneurial (almost everybody benefits, one small group pays).

2. How do America's social welfare policies and programs differ from those of many other modern democracies?

They differ in four main ways. First, Americans have taken a more restrictive view of who is entitled to or "deserves" to benefit from government assistance. Second, America was slower to embrace the need for "the welfare state," and, in turn, slower to adopt and enact relevant policies and programs. Third, state governments have played a large role in administering or co-funding many "national" social welfare measures (like, for example, Medicaid). Fourth, nongovernmental organizations, both for-profit firms and nonprofit groups (secular as well as religious) have played a large role in administering Washington's social welfare initiatives.

3. Why are some social welfare policies and programs politically protected while others are politically imperiled?

The answer relates mainly to who benefits directly, or who is perceived to benefit directly, from given social welfare policies and programs. For example, Social Security and Medicare benefit almost all people who have reached a certain age, while the Food Stamps program, like the old AFDC program's successor, TANF, benefits only people with low incomes. The first type of social welfare program has no means test (they are available to everyone without regard to income), while the second type is means-tested (only people who fall below a certain income level are eligible). The first type represents majoritarian politics and is almost always politically protected; the second type represents client politics and is often politically imperiled. Medicaid, the federal–state health program, is means-tested, but it has as beneficiaries not only low-income persons but also the aged and the disabled. It mixes majoritarian and client politics, making it less politically sacrosanct than Social Security or Medicare, but more so than the Food Stamps program, TANF, and other means-tested programs.

4. Is there a political consensus about how to address the solvency challenges facing major social welfare programs?

No, not unless one counts as the "political consensus" on these issues the persistent public majority opposed to making either major or minor cuts to each program. Even the ostensibly far-reaching, bipartisan plans offered in recent sessions of Congress have been predicated on preserving (or expanding) all extant benefits to all present-day and near-term beneficiaries without raising taxes and without reducing services. For good or for ill, their majoritarian politics forbid any truly far-reaching reforms.

5. Why have government regulations on certain big businesses been imposed over the objections of those industries?

There were several reasons, but the most important reasons had to do with entrepreneurial politics. Big oil companies, auto manufacturing companies, drug companies, pesticides producers, and other corporations that once had, or were perceived to have, cozy relationships with government were challenged by consumer advocates or environmental activists. A half-century or so ago, policy entrepreneurs outside government like Ralph Nader and Rachel Carson dramatized how existing public policies and programs helped the companies to profit but hurt most people in the pocketbook, jeopardized public health and safety, or both. By the 1970s and 1980s, policy entrepreneurs inside government, like those at the Environmental Protection Agency (founded in 1970), began regulating the businesses even more closely than they had in the past. Although business regulation policy still generates much controversy and many debates over its cost-effectiveness, most people now favor diverse regulations on big oil companies and other large-scale businesses.

6. Why are environmental policies designed and enforced differently in America than in other industrialized nations?

The adversarial nature of American politics, as well as the system of federalism, complicates policymaking in America, as illustrated by efforts to pass and enforce legislation on automobile emissions, clean air and water, and other environmental issues.

7. Does just one type of politics drive environmental policies and programs?

No. While entrepreneurial politics figure prominently in environmental policy dynamics, including on an issue like protecting endangered species, there are environmental issues in each "box," like pollution from automobiles (majoritarian), acid rain (interest group), and agricultural pesticides (client politics). The same can be said for social welfare, business regulation, and other domestic policies and programs.

TO LEARN MORE

Nonpartisan reviews of public policy issues

www.publicagenda.org

www.people-press.org

Selected social welfare programs

Social Security: www.ssa.gov

Medicare and Medicaid: www.cms.gov

TANF: www.acf.hhs.gov/programs/ofa

Selected federal agencies

Environmental Protection Agency: www.epa.gov

National Labor Relations Board: www.nlrb.gov

Occupational Safety and Health Administration: www.osha.gov

Allen, Will. *The Good Food Revolution: Growing Healthy Food, People, and Communities*. New York: Gotham, 2012. Account by a former professional basketball player and fast-food executive who built an "urban farm" program that employs sustainable food cultivation strategies, creates local jobs, promotes healthier eating habits, and has been replicated in many cities all across the country.

Derthick, Martha. *Policymaking for Social Security*. Washington, D.C.: Brookings Institution, 1979. A detailed analysis of how the Social Security program grew during its first four decades.

Gore, Al. *Earth in the Balance*. Boston: Houghton Mifflin, 2000. Revised edition of the book on the environment first written when Gore was a senator.

Heclo, Hugh. *Modern Social Politics in Britain and Sweden*. New Haven, CT: Yale University Press, 1974. Classic comparative analysis of how social welfare programs came to Britain and Sweden.

Kingdon, John W. *Agendas, Alternatives, and Public Policies*. Boston: Little, Brown, 1984. An insightful account of how domestic issues, especially those involving health and transportation, get on (or drop off) Washington's political agenda.

Mead, Lawrence M. *From Prophecy to Charity: How to Help the Poor*. Washington, D.C.: American Enterprise Institute, 2011. Argues that the work-based welfare reform programs that succeeded AFDC have been largely successful and prescribes more "paternalistic programs" plus a wider role for charities in administering anti-poverty policies.

Monsma, Stephen V. *Putting Faith in Partnerships: Welfare-to-Work in Four Cities*. Ann Arbor: University of Michigan Press, 2004. Careful study of the six different types of organizations that administer welfare-to-work programs in big cities.

Rosenbaum, Walter A. *Environmental Politics and Policy*, 8th ed. Washington, D.C.: Congressional Quarterly Press, 2010. Analyses of the politics of air and water pollution, the use of chemicals, and other environmental issues.

Vogel, David. *National Style of Regulation: Environmental Policy in Great Britain and the United States*. Ithaca, NY: Cornell University Press, 1986. An explanation of why environmental politics in America tends to be adversarial.

Washington Post Staff. *Landmark: The Inside Story of America's New Health Care Law and What It Means for All of Us*. New York: Public Affairs, 2010. A lively journalistic account of the politics that produced the Patient Protection and Affordable Care Act of 2010.

Wilson, James Q., ed. *The Politics of Regulation*. New York: Basic Books, 1980. Analyzes regulatory politics in nine agencies and provides a more detailed statement of the theory of policymaking politics presented in the text.

OUR NATIONAL DEBT:

15,759,278,284,062

OUR *Family share* 133,285.

THE NATIONAL DEBT CLOCK

Viviane Moos/Corbis

Economic Policy

LEARNING OBJECTIVES

1. How do you define "deficit," "national debt," and "gross domestic product"?

2. What makes the politics of taxing and spending so difficult?

3. On which programs does the federal government spend most of its money?

4. Who in the federal government can make our economy strong?

5. Why does the federal government ever have a budget deficit?

Like most Americans, you probably think about the way the government spends its money the same way you think about how you ought to spend yours. If you spend more than you earn, you will have to borrow money and pay it back to the bank. If you want to buy a car or a house, you will have to get a loan and make monthly payments on it. It you run up so many charges on your credit card that it is maxed out, you won't be able to charge anything more on it. If you keep spending more than you earn, you will have to declare bankruptcy. Surely, the government ought to work the same way: spend no more than it earns and pay back its loans.

But it doesn't. With just a few exceptions, the government has spent more money than it takes in every year since at least 1960. The amount it spends in excess of what it takes in each year is called the **deficit** (see Figure 18.1). It is financed by selling government bonds, issued by the Treasury Department, to Americans and foreigners. The total amount of all deficits is the **national debt**. In 2012, the national debt rose to over $16 trillion, and it was widely projected to reach nearly $22 trillion by 2015.

For the last four decades, the government in Washington got away with routine deficit spending and nonstop increases in the national debt. But over the last several years, for both economic and political reasons, this has begun to change rather dramatically.

THEN

Deficits that result in debt are important economically only insofar as the government cannot make the payments on its bonds in a currency that people regard as stable and valuable. Happily, almost everybody around the world has regarded the American dollar as stable and valuable. As a result, people have lined up to buy U.S. Treasury bonds whenever they are sold. But to keep our currency stable, people must believe that the dollar will always be valuable and that the government is not borrowing more than it can pay back. Prior to 1980, annual deficit spending was relatively minor and large deficits occurred only during wartime. Washington began its deficit spending and debt accumulation spree in the mid-1970s, interrupted only by several years during the 1990s when the government ran surpluses. Despite the huge deficits and mounting debt, most people, including most major domestic and foreign investors and experts on public finances, nonetheless considered America to be a good credit risk. In particular, concerns about "too much debt" were often dismissed as unduly alarmist, and presidents and

deficit The result of when the government in one year spends more money than it takes in from taxes.

national debt The total deficit from the first presidency down to the present.

FIGURE 18.1 **Federal Budget Deficit (or Surplus), FY1960–2013 in Billions of Constant FY 2005 Dollars (President's Proposals)**

Source: Office of Management and Budget, *Historical Tables.*

gross domestic product The total of all goods and services produced in the economy during a given year.

congressional leaders in both parties quietly and consistently increased the national debt ceiling so that Washington could keep right on spending and borrowing.

NOW

In April 2011, Standard & Poor's, a credit ratings agency that has been grading U.S. Treasury bonds since the 1930s, issued a first-ever warning about America's national debt, downgrading it from "stable" to "negative," and forecasting a one-third chance that the country would lose its "triple-A" credit rating before 2014. It did not take that long. In August 2011, Standard & Poor's itself downgraded the United States to "double-A" status. The annual federal deficit topped a trillion dollars for the first time in 2009, and in 2010 another trillion-dollar deficit was recorded. In December 2010, members of a bipartisan presidential commission, the National Commission on Fiscal Responsibility and Reform, proclaimed that dire, long-term economic consequences would follow unless Washington acted at once to rein in deficit spending and slow debt accumulation. For example, the total value of all the goods and services the nation produces each year is called **gross domestic product**, or GDP. The Commission warned that the national debt would soon exceed the nation's annual GDP, and that annual interest payments on the national debt could rise to almost 4 percent of GDP (from about 2.3 percent of GDP in 2012) over the next decade. In 2011, several competing deficit and debt reduction plans were circulated by members of Congress and by the White House, but bitterly partisan and ideological politics greeted each plan, and a heated public debate ensued regarding the once-routine business of raising the national debt ceiling. In accordance with key provisions of the final bipartisan deal that raised the debt ceiling, in August 2011, a dozen members of Congress (half from the House and half from the Senate, half Democrats and half Republicans) were appointed to a "super committee" and charged with identifying $1.5 trillion in additional debt reduction; if they failed to agree, or if Congress rejected their plan, then across-the-board spending cuts (half in defense and half in domestic programs) were to be "triggered." They failed, but various measures were adopted to avoid making all the "automatic" cuts.

Today's debates about deficit spending and debt accumulation are so rancorous in part because they have taken shape in the midst of a weak economy. A serious recession occurs when businesses fail, unemployment rises, and economic growth stops. This happened, starting in 2007 and continuing through 2010 and (depending on which economists one believes) perhaps beyond. The debates are also made more intense by the fiscal challenges that policymakers see just over the horizon. One such challenge is that our population is getting older. This creates huge new demands for Social Security retirement benefits and medical payments under Medicare and the part of Medicaid that covers long-term care (see Chapter 17). When a recession and an older population occur together, our national debt and interest payments to support it will shoot up.

But the core reason why ongoing debates over economic policy are so divisive is that people disagree, often fundamentally, not so much over the sheer size of our national debt, but over what we buy with all this borrowed money. Most families borrow to buy long-lasting items, like a home, a new car, or a college education. We don't really know what the federal debt is used for. It would be nice if we knew that we borrowed only to pay for long-lasting things that enhance security and economic growth, such as schools, aircraft carriers, and basic health care research. But our government borrows whenever it needs the money, without much regard for what it gets.

It should not be surprising that politicians typically avoid seriously debating, let alone making, hard choices on economic policy. Since they know the public is opposed to the government going into debt, politicians will also oppose the debt, but they offer two opposed ways to combat it. One, advanced mainly by conservatives, is by cutting spending; the other, offered mainly by liberals, is raising taxes. But since the people do not want less spending on programs they favor and certainly don't want higher taxes, these contradictory political strategies are hard to reconcile, maybe now more than ever. National polls in 2010 and 2011 found that most Americans thought that big government and big business work together against them, doubted that cuts to huge and hugely popular programs like Medicare were really necessary to rein in deficits and debt, and believed that eliminating government "waste, fraud, and abuse" could pretty nearly set things right. Thus, any truly far-reaching fiscal reforms will require politicians in both parties to win back public trust while telling the people what few care to hear.

The Politics of Economic Prosperity

In more normal economic times, however, economic policy is not nearly so hard for politicians to fashion without fighting big legislative battles or risking public ire. The health of the American economy creates majoritarian politics. Hardly anyone wants inflation or unemployment; everyone wants rapid increases in income and wealth. But this fact is a bit puzzling. You might think that people would care about their own jobs and worry only about avoiding their own unemployment. If that were the case, they would vote for politicians who promised to award contracts to firms that would hire them or who would create programs that would benefit them, regardless of how well other people were getting along. In fact, though, people see connections between their own well-being and that of the nation, and they tend to hold politicians responsible for the state of the country.

Everybody knows that just before an election, politicians worry about the *pocketbook issue.* We have seen in Chapter 10 that economic conditions are strongly associated with how much success the incumbent party has in holding on to the White House and to the seats held by the White House's party in Congress. But whose pocketbook are voters worried about?

In part, of course, it is their own. We know that low-income people are more likely to worry about unemployment and to vote Democratic, and higher-income people are more likely to worry about inflation and to vote Republican.[1] We also know that people who tell pollsters that their families' finances have gotten worse are more likely than other people to vote against the incumbent president.[2] In 1980, about two-thirds of those who said they had become worse off economically voted for Ronald Reagan, the challenger, while over half of those who felt they had become better off voted for Jimmy Carter, the incumbent.[3] In 1992, people who felt economically pinched were more likely to vote for Clinton than for Bush. Clinton campaign aides often reminded each other, "It's the economy, stupid!"

But people do not simply vote their own pocketbooks. In any recession, the vast majority of people still have jobs; nevertheless, these people say unemployment is the nation's biggest problem, and many of them vote accordingly—against the incumbent during whose watch unemployment went up.[4] Why should employed people worry about other people's unemployment?

By the same token, younger voters—whose incomes tend to go up each year—often worry less about inflation than retired people living on fixed incomes, the purchasing power of which goes down with inflation.[5] In presidential elections, those who think national economic trends are bad are much more likely to vote against the incumbent, *even when* their own personal finances have not worsened.[6]

In technical language, voting behavior and economic conditions are strongly correlated at the national level but not at the individual level, and this is true both in the United States and in Europe.[7] Such voters are behaving in an "other-regarding" or "sociotropic" way. In ordinary language, voters seem to respond more to the condition of the national economy than to their own personal finances.

It is not hard to understand why this might be true. Part of the explanation is that people understand what government can and cannot be held accountable for. If you lose your job at the aircraft plant because the government has not renewed the plant's contract, you will be more likely to hold the government responsible than if you lose your job because you were always showing up drunk or because the plant moved out of town.

And part of the explanation is that people see general economic conditions as having indirect effects on them even when they are still doing pretty well. They may not be unemployed, but they may have friends who are, and they may worry that if unemployment grows worse, they will be the next to lose their jobs.

What Politicians Try to Do

Elected officials, who have to run for re-election every few years, are strongly tempted to take a short-run view of the economy and to adopt those policies that will best satisfy the self-regarding voter. They would dearly love to produce low unemployment rates and rising family incomes just before an election. Some scholars think that they do just this.

Since the 19th century, the government has used money to affect elections. At first this mostly took the form of patronage passed out to the party faithful and money benefits given to important blocs of voters. The massive system of Civil War pensions for Union army veterans was run in a way that did no harm to the political fortunes of the Republican party. After the Social Security system was established, Congress voted to increase the benefits in virtually every year in which there was an election (see Chapter 17).

But it is by no means clear that the federal government can or will do whatever is necessary to reduce unemployment, cut inflation, lower interest rates, and increase incomes just to win an election. For one thing, the government does not know how to produce all of these desirable outcomes. Moreover, doing one of these things often may be possible only at the cost of not doing another. For example, reducing inflation can, in many cases, require the government to raise interest rates, and this in turn can slow down the economy by making it harder to sell houses, automobiles, and other things purchased with borrowed money.

If it were easy to stimulate the economy just before an election, practically every president would serve two full terms. But because of the uncertainties and complexities of the economy, presidents can lose elections over economic issues they do not manage to the satisfaction of voters. Ford lost in 1976, Carter in 1980, and George H. W. Bush in 1992. In all cases, economic conditions played a major role.

In 2012, however, Barack Obama won re-election despite widespread concerns about the economy's performance. Indeed, Obama is the first president since Franklin Delano Roosevelt in 1940 to be re-elected despite an unemployment rate on election day that was higher than the unemployment rate on the day of his first inaugural.

All this means that politicians must make choices about economic policy, choices affected by uncertainty and ignorance. Those choices are shaped significantly by the ideological differences between the two political parties over what ought to be the principal goal of economic policy. Democrats and Republicans alike would prefer to have low unemployment and no inflation, but if they must choose (and choose they must), then the Democrats mainly attempt to reduce unemployment and the Republicans chiefly attempt to reduce inflation.[8]

This tendency mirrors to some degree what Democratic and Republican voters want their parties to do. Polls regularly show that those who think of themselves as Democrats are much more worried about unemployment than those who think of themselves as Republicans.[9] (There is not as much of a difference between Democratic and Republican voters in worrying about inflation.) Because of these beliefs, voters concerned about unemployment not only are more likely to vote against the incumbent but also are more likely to vote Democratic.

The Politics of Taxing and Spending

People want prosperity, but they also want no tax increases, no government deficit, and continued (or higher) government spending on the things they like, such as education, medical care, the environment, and retirement benefits. Politicians confront two inconsistent kinds of majoritarian politics: everybody wants general prosperity, and large majorities want more government spending on popular programs. But the more the government spends on popular programs, the more money it requires, and the more it takes in, the less that is left over for private investment that produces prosperity.

Most voters would like to have all three things—lower taxes, less debt, and new programs. But the difficulty with this is that the policies endorsed are inconsistent with one another. We cannot have lower taxes, no debt, and higher spending on politically popular programs such as health care, education, the environment, and retirement benefits. If we have more spending, we have to pay for it, either with higher taxes or with more borrowing.

People who want new programs have to either cut existing programs, let the government go deeper in debt, or raise taxes. But how do you raise taxes without alienating voters? The answer is that you raise taxes on *other people*.

The "other people" are always a minority of the voters. For example, if you want to put more money into medical research (something that everybody likes), you raise taxes on cigarettes (only a minority smoke them). If you want to pay for new education programs or bigger environmental programs, you raise taxes on affluent voters. In this way, you can find a majority of voters who will support—or at least not oppose very strongly—tax increases on a small group of voters—cigarette smokers or high-income people.

Tea Party activists protest in Washington after a government audit reveals that the Internal Revenue Service (IRS) targeted for special scrutiny applications by politically conservative groups for tax-exempt status.

Legislators who like high rates say that "people who can afford it should pay a lot." Legislators who want low rates say that their opponents are trying to "soak the rich" by denying tax cuts to the people who now pay the biggest share of taxes.

Economic Theories and Political Needs

There are four main theories about how to improve the economy. When presidents select economic advisers, they often choose people who identify with one of these theories. In general, conservative economists tend to support monetarism and supply-side economics, while liberal economists are more likely to embrace Keynesianism and planning. Here, we give a highly simplified account of them and what each implies about ending a recession.

Monetarism

A monetarist, such as the late economist Milton Friedman, believes that inflation occurs when too much money chases too few goods. The federal government has the power to create money (in ways to be described on page 478); according to monetarists, inflation occurs when it prints too much money. When inflation becomes rampant and government tries to do something, it often cuts back sharply on the amount of money in circulation. Then a recession will occur, with slowed economic growth and an increase in unemployment. Since the government does not understand that economic problems result from its own start-and-stop habit of issuing new money, it will try to cure some of these problems with policies that make matters worse—such as having an unbalanced budget or creating new welfare programs. **Monetarism** suggests that the proper thing for government to do is to have a steady, predictable increase in the money supply at a rate about equal to the growth in the economy's productivity. When the economy goes into a recession, however, many monetarists think the Federal Reserve Bank ("the Fed") should cut interest rates to make it easier for people and businesses to borrow money. That is what the Fed did during 2008.

Keynesianism

John Maynard Keynes, an English economist who died in 1946, believed that the market will not automatically operate at a full-employment, low-inflation level. Its health depends on what fraction of people's incomes they save or spend. If they save too much, there will be too little demand, production will decline, and unemployment will rise. If they spend too much, demand will rise too fast, prices will go up, and shortages will develop. According to **Keynesianism**, the key is to create the right level of demand. This is the task of government. When demand is too little, the government should pump more money into the economy (by spending more than it collects in taxes and by creating public-works programs). When demand is too great, the government should take money out of the economy (by increasing taxes or cutting federal expenditures). There is no need for the government's budget to be balanced on a year-to-year basis; what counts is the performance of the economy.

Planning

Some economists have too little faith in the workings of the free market to be pure Keynesians, much less monetarists. They believe the government should plan, in varying ways, some part of the country's economic activity. One form of **economic planning** is price and wage controls, as advocated by John Kenneth Galbraith and others. In this view, big corporations can raise prices because the forces of competition are too weak to restrain them, and labor unions can force up wages because management finds it easy to pass the increases along to consumers in the form of higher prices. Thus, during inflationary times, the government should regulate the maximum prices that can be charged and wages that can be paid, at least in the larger industries.

Planning has never been popular in America, but when the TARP program began investing in banks, some people began to suggest that perhaps the government should own the banks. That way, they said, the government might get back some of the money it had spent on them. The government was already the largest single stockholder in Bank of America and Citigroup (though in each case it owned less than half the stocks).

Supply-Side Tax Cuts

Exactly the opposite remedy for declining American productivity is suggested by people who call themselves supply-siders. The view of economists such as Arthur Laffer and Paul Craig Roberts is that the market, far from having failed, has not been given an adequate chance. According to **supply-side theory**, what is needed is not more planning but less government

monetarism The belief that inflation occurs when too much money is chasing too few goods.

Keynesianism The belief the government must manage the economy by spending more money when in a recession and cutting spending when there is inflation.

economic planning The belief that government plans, such as wage and price controls or the direction of investment, can improve the economy.

supply-side theory The belief that lower taxes and fewer regulations will stimulate the economy.

HOW THINGS WORK

Washington Tries to Stimulate the Economy

First Stimulus Bill (February 2008)

- $125 billion paid to people in checks of $600 each

Troubled Asset Relief Program (October 2008)

- $700 billion invested
- Buy shares in troubled banks and insurance companies
- Make loans to Chrysler and General Motors
- Make payments to troubled mortgage owners

American Recovery and Reinvestment Act (February 2009)

- $787 billion (over 11 years)
- Tax cuts and benefit checks for people earning less than $75,000 (total = $237 billion)
- Tax cuts for some businesses (total = $51 billion)
- Paying for unemployment benefits, health insurance, food stamps, etc. (total = $322 billion)

- Grants to states for Medicaid, highways, school construction, etc. (total = $155 billion)
- Money to repair or manage federal facilities (total = $57 billion).

Federal Reserve Board

- Federal Reserve spending $1.8 trillion (The Fed can create money by writing a check).
- Fed will help banks borrow money at low rates, purchase some corporate debt, and help bail out some investment houses and insurance companies (AIG).

Public-Private Investment Program (March 23, 2009)

- A program to help banks and others get rid of bad loans
- An auction will be held in which investors can buy up bad loans at low prices, with the federal government paying for much of the cost.

Source: Updated from "Sorting Out the Bailouts," *Congressional Quarterly Weekly* (February 23, 2009).

---

interference. In particular, sharply cutting taxes will increase people's incentive to work, save, and invest. Greater investments will then lead to more jobs, and if the earnings from these investments and jobs are taxed less, it will lessen the tendency of many individuals to shelter their earnings from the tax collector by taking advantage of various tax loopholes or cheating on their income tax returns. The greater productivity of the economy will produce more tax revenue for the government. Even though tax *rates* will be lower, the total national income to which these rates are applied will be higher.

LANDMARK CASES

Federal Laws About Commerce

- *Lochner v. New York* (1905): Struck down as unconstitutional a New York law limiting the number of hours that may be worked by bakers.
- *Muller v. Oregon* (1980): Upheld as constitutional an Oregon law limiting the number of hours worked by women; in effect, it overruled the *Lochner* decision.
- *West Coast Hotel Co. v. Parrish* (1937): Upheld as constitutional a Washington State minimum wage law for women.
- *Youngstown Sheet & Tube Co. v. Sawyer* (1952): The president does not have the authority to seize private steel mills even in wartime.

The Machinery of Economic Policymaking

Predicting what will happen to the economy is very hard. Few economists, for example, foresaw the recession that began in 2007. But even if the president knew exactly the right thing to do, he would still have to find some way of doing it. In our government, that is no easy task. The machinery for making decisions about economic matters is complex and not under the president's full control. Within the executive branch, three people other than the president are of special importance. Sometimes called the troika,* these are the chairman of the Council of

---

*From the Russian word for a carriage pulled by three horses.

Milton Friedman

John Maynard Keynes

John Kenneth Galbraith

Arthur B. Laffer

Economic Advisers (CEA), the director of the Office of Management and Budget (OMB), and the secretary of the treasury.

The CEA, composed of three professional economists plus a small staff, has existed since 1946. In theory, it is an impartial group of experts responsible for forecasting economic trends, analyzing economic issues, and helping prepare the economic report that the president submits to Congress each year. Though quite professional in tone, the CEA is not exactly impartial in practice, since each president picks members sympathetic to his point of view. Kennedy picked Keynesians; Reagan picked supply-siders and monetarists. But whatever its philosophical tilt, the CEA is seen by other executive agencies as the advocate of the opinion of professional economists, who despite their differences generally tend to favor reliance on the market.

The OMB originally was the Bureau of the Budget, which was created in 1921 and made part of the executive office of the president in 1939; in 1970, it was renamed the Office of Management and Budget. Its chief function is to prepare estimates of the amount that will be spent by federal agencies, to negotiate with other departments over the size of their budgets, and to make certain (insofar as it can) that the legislative proposals of these other departments are in accord with the president's program. Of late it has acquired something of a split personality; it is in part an expert, nonpartisan agency that analyzes spending and budget patterns and in part an activist, partisan organization that tries to get the president's wishes carried out by the bureaucracy.

The secretary of the treasury often is close to or drawn from the world of business and finance and is expected to argue the point of view of the financial community. (Since its members do not always agree, this is not always easy.) The secretary provides estimates of the revenue that the government can expect from existing taxes and what will be the result of changing tax laws. He or she represents the United States in its dealings with the top bankers and finance ministers of other nations.

A good deal of pulling and hauling takes place among members of the troika, but if that were the extent of the problem, presidential leadership would be fairly easy. The problem is far more complex. One study found 132 separate government bureaus engaged in formulating economic policy. They regulate business, make loans, and supply subsidies. For example, as foreign trade becomes increasingly important to this country, the secretary of state (among many others) acquires an interest in economic policy. One-third of corporate profits come from overseas investments, and one-fourth of farm output is sold abroad.

monetary policy Managing the economy by altering the supply of money and interest rates.

The Fed

Among the most important of these other agencies is the board of governors of the Federal Reserve System (the "Fed"). Its seven members are appointed by the president, with the consent of the Senate, for 14-year, nonrenewable terms and may not be removed except for cause. (No member has been removed since it was created in 1913.) The chairperson serves for four years. In theory, and to some degree in practice, the Fed is independent of both the president and Congress. Its most important function is to regulate, to the extent possible, the supply of money (both in circulation and in bank deposits) and the price of money (in the form of interest rates). The Fed sets **monetary policy**, that is, the effort to shape the economy by controlling the amount of money and bank deposits and the interest rates charged for money. The box on page 478 shows how the Fed does this. In 2001, it lowered interest rates 11 times in *fiscal policy* Managing the economy by the use of tax and spending laws.

order to help reduce the recession. From 2004 to 2007, it raised these rates 17 times in order to prevent inflation.

Just how independent the Fed is can be a matter of dispute. During the 1980 election, Fed policies helped keep interest rates at a high level, a circumstance that did not benefit President Carter's re-election bid. On the other hand, whenever a president is determined to change monetary policy, he usually can do so. For example, the term of Fed chairman Arthur F. Burns, appointed by President Nixon, came up for renewal in 1978. President Carter, seeking to influence Burns's decisions, held out the prospect of reappointing him chairman. When Burns balked, he was passed over, and G. William Miller was appointed in his stead. Presidents Truman, Johnson, and Nixon were all able to obtain changes in monetary policy. Alan Greenspan, a conservative, became Fed chairman in 1987 under President Reagan; he was so successful in curbing inflation that he was reappointed by President Clinton, a Democrat.

Congress

The most important part of the economic policy-making machinery, of course, is Congress. It must approve all taxes and almost all expenditures; there can be no wage or price controls without its consent; and it has the ability to alter the policy of the nominally independent Federal Reserve Board by threatening to pass laws that would reduce its powers. And Congress itself is fragmented, with great influence wielded by the members of key committees, especially the House and Senate Budget Committees, the House and Senate Appropriations Committees, the House Ways and Means Committee, and the Senate Finance Committee. The decisions Congress makes about how high taxes should be and how much money the government should spend create the nation's **fiscal policy**.

In sum, no matter what economic theory the president may have, if he is to put that theory into effect he needs the assistance of many agencies within the executive branch, such independent agencies as the

HOW THINGS WORK

The Federal Reserve Board

The Tools by Which the Fed Implements Its Monetary Policy

1. **Buying and selling federal government securities** (bonds, Treasury notes, and other pieces of paper that constitute government IOUs). When the Fed buys securities, it in effect puts more money into circulation and takes securities out of circulation. With more money around, interest rates tend to drop, and more money is borrowed and spent. When the Fed sells government securities, it in effect takes money out of circulation, causing interest rates to rise and making borrowing more difficult.

2. **Regulating the amount of money that a member bank must keep in hand as reserves** to back up the customer deposits it is holding. A bank lends out most of the money deposited with it. If the Fed says that it must keep in reserve a larger fraction of its deposits, then the amount that it can lend drops, loans become harder to obtain, and interest rates rise.

3. **Changing the interest charged to banks** that want to borrow money from the Federal Reserve System. Banks borrow from the Fed to cover short-term needs. The interest that the Fed charges for this is called the *discount* rate. The Fed can raise or lower

that rate; this will have an effect, though usually rather a small one, on how much money the banks will lend.

Federal Reserve Board (7 members)

- Determines how many government securities will be bought or sold by regional and member banks.

- Determines interest rates to be charged by regional banks and amount of money member banks must keep in reserve in regional banks.

Regional Federal Reserve Banks (12)

- Buy and sell government securities.

- Loan money to member banks.

- Keep percentage of holdings for member banks.

Member Banks (6,000)

- Buy and sell government securities.

- May borrow money from regional banks.

- Must keep percentage of holdings in regional banks.

- Interest rates paid to regional banks determine interest rates charged for business and personal loans and influence all bank interest rates.

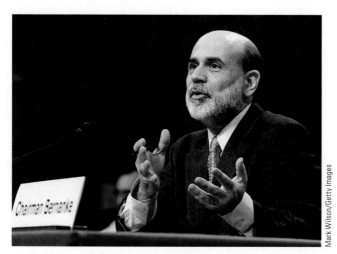

Ben Bernanke, who served as Chairman of the Federal Reserve during the 2008 financial crisis, speaks to a congressional committee.

Mark Wilson/Getty Images

Federal Reserve Board, and the various committees of Congress. Though members of the executive and legislative branches are united by their common desire to get re-elected (and thus have a common interest in producing sound economic growth), each part of this system may also be influenced by different economic theories and will be motivated by the claims of interest groups.

The effect of these interest group claims is clearly shown in the debate over trade restriction. Usually the economic health of the nation affects everyone in pretty much the same way—we are all hurt by inflation or helped by stable prices; the incomes of all of us tend to grow (or remain stagnant) together. In these circumstances, the politics of economic health is majoritarian.

Suppose, however, that most of us are doing pretty well, but that the people in a few industries or occupations are suffering. That is sometimes the result of foreign competition. In many countries, labor costs are much lower than in the United States. That means these countries can ship goods—such as shoes, textiles, and beef— to American buyers that sell at much lower prices than American producers can afford to charge. By contrast, if the price of a product is based chiefly on having advanced technology rather than low labor costs, American manufacturers can beat almost any foreign competitor.

When Congress passes laws governing foreign trade, it is responding to interest group politics. Industries that find it easy to sell American products abroad want free trade—that is, they want no taxes or restrictions on international exchanges. Industries that find it hard to compete with foreign imports oppose free trade—that is, they want tariffs and other limitations on imports.

When the North American Free Trade Agreement (NAFTA) was passed by Congress in 1993, the free traders won, and tariffs on our commerce with Canada and Mexico were largely abolished. But when the government later suggested creating free trade with all of Latin America, the critics of free trade opposed the idea, and it died. This is a good example of how people who bear the costs of a policy are often much more effective in influencing the votes on it than are those who stand to benefit from it.

globalization The growing integration of the economies and societies of the world.

Not only has the United States not extended the NAFTA idea to other countries, but it has done things that reward certain economic interest groups. Even though Republicans tend to support free trade, President George W. Bush imposed sharp increases in the taxes that must be paid on imported steel. The reason is not hard to find. Steel is produced in certain states, such as Ohio and Pennsylvania, that the president wanted to carry in 2004.

Globalization

Trying to block free trade is a part of the opposition of some people to **globalization**, the growing integration of the economies and societies of the world. You can experience globalization easily: if your computer develops a problem and you call technical support, you are likely to speak with a technician based in India.

Supporters of globalization argue that it has increased the income, literacy, and standard of living of people in almost every country involved in the worldwide process of economic growth. These supporters favor free trade because it makes products cheaper. Opponents of globalization make several different and not always consistent arguments. Some (such as labor union leaders) argue that free trade undercuts the wages of American workers as less expensive foreign workers make things that are sold here. Others argue that globalization is driven by selfish corporate interests that exploit people in poor countries when they work for American firms. Still others feel that globalization means imposing one culture on everyone in ways that hurt local cultures.

Spending Money

If only the economic health of the nation mattered, then majoritarian politics would dominate, and the president and Congress would both work to improve economic conditions. Although they still might work at cross-purposes because they held to different economic theories, the goal would be the same.

But the government must also respond to the demands of voters and interest groups. While these *budget* A document that states tax collections, spending levels, and the allocation of spending among purposes.

fiscal year For the federal government, October 1 through the following September 30.

budget resolution A congressional decision that states the maximum amount of money the government should spend.

entitlements A claim for government funds that cannot be changed without violating the rights of the claimant.

demands are no less legitimate than the voters' general interest in economic health, they produce not majoritarian but client and interest group politics.

The sources of this conflict can be seen in public opinion polls. Voters consistently say they want a balanced budget and lower government spending. They believe the government spends too much and that if it wanted to, it could cut spending. When the government runs a deficit, the reason in the voters' eyes is that it is spending too much, not that it is taxing too little. But these same polls show that the voters believe the government should spend more on education, homelessness, child care, and crime control.

The voters are not irrational, thinking they can have more spending and less spending simultaneously. Nor are they selfish or hypocritical, wanting less spending overall but more for programs that benefit them. They are simply expressing a variety of concerns. They want a limited government with no deficit; they also want good schools, cleaner air, better health care, and less crime. They believe a frugal government could deliver what they want by cutting out waste.

What this means for the government is easy to imagine. Politicians have an incentive to make two kinds of appeals: The first is, "Vote for me and I will keep government spending down and cut the deficit." The second is, "Vote for me and I will make certain that your favorite program gets more money." Some people will vote for the candidate because of the first appeal; some will vote for him or her because of the second. But acting on these two appeals is clearly going to lead to inconsistent policies. These inconsistencies become evident in the budget.

The Budget

A **budget** is a document that announces how much the government will collect in taxes and spend in revenues and how those expenditures will be allocated among various programs. (Each budget covers a **fiscal year**, which runs from October 1 of one year through September 30 of the next. A fiscal year is named after

the year in which it *ends:* thus, "fiscal 2013" or "FY 2013" means the year ending on September 30, 2013.

In theory, the federal budget should be based on *first* deciding how much money the government is going to spend and *then* allocating that money among different programs and agencies. That is the way a household makes up its budget: "We have this much in the paycheck, and so we will spend *X* dollars on rent, *Y* dollars on food, and *Z* dollars on clothing, and what's left over on entertainment. If the amount of the paycheck goes down, we will cut something out—probably entertainment."

In fact, the federal budget is a list of everything the government is going to spend money on, with only slight regard (sometimes no regard at all) for how much money is available to be spent. Instead of being a way of *allocating* money to be spent on various purposes, it is a way of *adding up* what is being spent.

Indeed, there was no federal budget at all before 1921, and there was no unified presidential budget until the 1930s. Even after the president began submitting a single budget, the committees of Congress acted on it separately, adding to or subtracting from the amounts he proposed. (Usually they followed his lead, but they were certainly free to depart from it as they wished.) If one committee wanted to spend more on housing, no effort was made to take that amount away from the committee that was spending money on health (in fact, there was no machinery for making such an effort).

The Congressional Budget Act of 1974 changed this somewhat. Now after the president submits his budget in February, two budget committees—one in the House, one in the Senate—study his overall package and obtain an analysis of it from the Congressional Budget Office (CBO). Each committee then submits to its house a **budget resolution** that proposes a total budget ceiling and a ceiling for each of several spending areas (such as health or defense). Each May, Congress is supposed to adopt, with some modifications, these budget resolutions, intending them to be targets to guide the work of each legislative committee as it decides what should be spent in its area. During the summer Congress then takes up the specific appropriations bills, informing its members as it goes along whether or not the spending proposed in these bills conforms to the May budget resolution. The object, obviously, is to impose some discipline on the various committees. After each committee approves its appropriations bill and Congress passes it, it goes to the president for his signature.

These appropriations bills, however, can rarely make big changes in government spending. About two-thirds of what the government spends is mandatory—that is, the money goes to people who are entitled to it. **Entitlements** include Social Security and Medicare payments, veterans' benefits, Food

Stamps, and money the government owes investors who have bought Treasury bonds (that is, the interest on the national debt). In theory, the government could change these entitlements by, for example, cutting Social Security payments, but that would be a political disaster. In reality, the government can change only about one-third of federal spending in any year.

There is a big loophole in the current budget process: nothing in the process requires Congress to tighten the government's financial belt. It can pass a budget resolution authorizing spending that is more or less than what the president has proposed. Nonetheless, the process has made a difference. Congress is now conscious of how its spending decisions match up with estimates of tax revenues.

When President Reagan took office, he and his allies in Congress took advantage of the Congressional Budget Act to start the controversial process of cutting federal spending. The House and Senate budget committees, with the president's support, used the first budget resolution in May 1981 not simply to set a budget ceiling that, as in the past, looked pretty much like the previous year's budget, but to direct each committee of Congress to make *cuts*—sometimes deep cuts—in the programs for which it was responsible. These cuts were to be made in the authorization legislation (see Chapter 15) as well as in the appropriations.

The object was to get members of Congress to vote for a total package of cuts before they could vote on any particular cut. Republican control of the Senate and an alliance between Republicans and conservative southern Democrats in the House allowed this strategy to succeed. The first budget resolution ordered Senate and House committees to reduce federal spending during fiscal 1982 by about $36 billion—less than the president had first asked, but a large sum nonetheless. Then the individual committees set to work trying to find ways of making these cuts.

Note how the *procedures* used by Congress can affect the *policies* adopted by Congress. If the Reagan plan had been submitted in the old piecemeal way, it is unlikely that cuts of this size would have occurred in so short a time, or at all. The reason is not that Congress would have wanted to ignore the president, but that, then as now, Congress reflects public opinion on economic policy. As stated at the beginning of the chapter, the public wants less total federal spending but more money spent on specific federal programs. Thus, if you allow the public or Congress to vote first on specific programs, spending is bound to rise. But if you require Congress to vote first on a budget ceiling, then (unless it changes its mind as it goes along) total

spending will go down, and tough choices will have to be made about the component parts of the budget. That, at least, is the theory. It worked once, in 1981, but it did not work very well thereafter.

sequester Automatic spending cuts.

discretionary spending Spending that is not required to pay for contracts, interest on the national debt, or entitlement programs such as Social Security.

Reducing Spending

Because the 1974 Congressional Budget Act did not automatically lead to spending cuts, people concerned about the growing federal deficit decided to find ways to put a cap on spending. The first such cap was the Balanced Budget Act of 1985, called the Gramm-Rudman Act after two of its sponsors, Senators Phil Gramm (R-Tex.) and Warren Rudman (R-N.H.). The law required that each year from 1986 to 1991 the budget would automatically be cut until the federal deficit had disappeared. What made the cuts automatic, its authors hoped, was a provision in the bill, called a **sequester**, that required across-the-board percentage cuts in all federal programs (except for entitlements) if the president and Congress failed to agree on a total spending level that met the law's targets.

But nobody much liked the idea, and the plan failed. By various devices that people began to call "smoke and mirrors," Congress and the president found ways to get new spending that was higher than the targeted amounts. By 1990, it was evident that a new strategy was needed if the government was going to help eliminate the deficit.

That strategy had two parts. First, Congress voted for a tax increase. Second, it passed the Budget Enforcement Act of 1990 that set limits on **discretionary spending**. This phrase refers to those government expenditures that are not required by existing contracts, payments on the national debt, or entitlement programs such as Social Security. As Figure 18.2 indicates, today less than a fifth of the budget involves discretionary spending, but back when the 1990 act was debated, the fraction was closer to a third. According to the 1990 act, if Congress were to spend more on a discretionary program, it would have to cut spending on another discretionary program or raise taxes. The law expired in 2001. As Figure 18.3 makes clear, something has to be done to manage huge future increases in spending on Social Security and Medicare; however, as we explained in Chapter 17, even though their respective financial challenges are widely acknowledged, these majoritarian politics programs have proven very hard to reform.

FIGURE 18.2 **Federal Revenues in 2012**

Federal Outlays in 2012

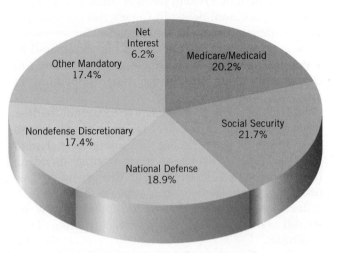

Source: Adapted from Office of Management and Budget, *Historical Tables.*

FIGURE 18.3 **Social Security and Medicare Cost as a Percentage of GDP**

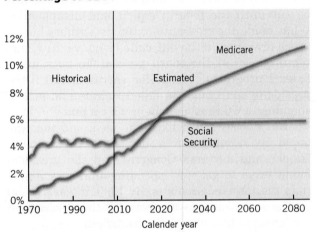

Source: Trustees' Report, 2009.

Levying Taxes

Tax policy reflects a mixture of majoritarian politics ("What is a 'fair' tax law?") and client politics ("How much is in it for me?"). In the United States, a fair tax law generally has been viewed as one that keeps the overall tax burden rather low, requires everyone to pay something, and requires the better-off to pay at a higher rate than the less-well-off. The law, in short, was viewed as good if it imposed modest burdens, prevented cheating, and was mildly progressive.

Americans have had their first goal satisfied. The tax burden in the United States is lower than it is in most other democratic nations (see **How We Compare** on page 484). There is some evidence that they have also had their second goal met—there

is reason to believe that Americans evade their income taxes less than do citizens of, say, France or Italy. (That is one reason why many nations rely more on sales taxes than we do—they are harder to evade.) And federal income taxes here are progressive: the three-quarters of Americans who earn the least money pay about 12.5 percent of all individual income taxes, while the 10 percent who earn the most money pay about 70 percent of all individual income taxes.

Keeping the burden low and the cheating at a minimum are examples of majoritarian politics: most people benefit, most people pay. The loopholes, however, are another matter—all manner of special interests can get some special benefit from the tax law that the rest of us must pay for but, given the complexity of the law, rarely notice. Loopholes are client politics par excellence.

Because of that, hardly any scholars believed tax reform (dramatically reducing the loopholes) was politically possible. Every interest that benefited from a loophole—and these included not just corporations but universities, museums, states, cities, and investors—would lobby vigorously to protect it.

Nevertheless, in 1986 a sweeping tax reform act was passed. Many of the most cherished loopholes were closed or reduced. What happened? It is as if scientists who had proved that a bumblebee could not fly got stung by a flying bumblebee.

The Rise of the Income Tax

To understand what happened in 1986, one must first understand the political history of taxation in the United States. Until almost the end of the 19th century, there was no federal income tax (except for a brief period during the Civil War). The money the

FIGURE 18.4 **Federal Taxes on Income, Top Percentage Rates, 1913–2013**

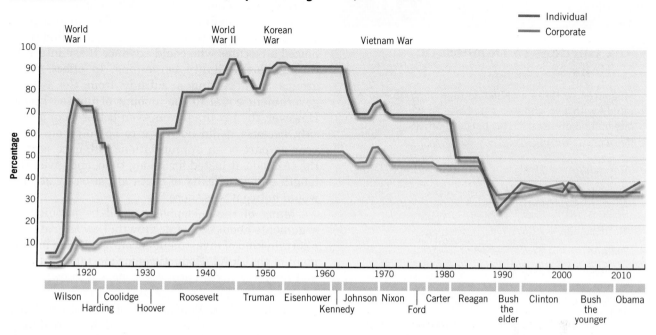

Source: Internal Revenue Service, *Tax Tables, 2013.*

government needed came mostly from tariffs (that is, taxes on goods imported into this country). And when Congress did enact a peacetime income tax, the Supreme Court in 1895 struck it down as unconstitutional.[10] To change this, Congress proposed, and in 1913 the states ratified, the Sixteenth Amendment, which authorized such a tax.

For the next 40 years or so, tax rates tended to go up during wartime and down during peacetime (see Figure 18.4). The rates were progressive—that is, the wealthiest individuals paid at a higher rate than the less affluent. For example, during World War II incomes in the highest bracket were taxed at a rate of 94 percent. (The key tax rate is called by economists the "marginal rate." This is the percentage of the last dollar you earn that must be paid out in taxes.)

An income tax offers the opportunity for majoritarian politics to become class politics. The majority of the citizenry earn average incomes and control most of the votes. In theory there is nothing to prevent the mass of people from voting for legislators who will tax only the rich, who, as a minority, will always be outvoted. During the early decades of the 20th century, that is exactly what the rich feared would happen. Since the highest marginal tax rate was 94 percent, you might think that is in fact what did happen.

You would be wrong. Offsetting the high rates were the deductions, exemptions, and exclusions by which people could shelter some of their income from taxation. These loopholes were available for everyone, but they particularly helped the well-off.

In effect, a political compromise was reached during the first half of the 20th century. The terms were these: the well-off, generally represented by the Republican party, would drop their bitter opposition to high marginal rates provided that the less-well-off, generally represented by the Democratic party, would support a large number of loopholes. The Democrats (or more accurately, the liberals) were willing to accept this compromise because they feared that if they insisted on high rates with no loopholes, the economy would suffer as people and businesses lost their incentive to save and invest.

For at least 30 years after the adoption of the income tax in 1913, only a small number of high-income people paid any significant amount in federal income taxes. The average citizen paid very little in such taxes until World War II. After the war, taxes did not fall to their prewar levels.

Most people did not complain too much, because they, too, benefited greatly from the loopholes. They could deduct from their taxable income the interest they paid on their home mortgages, the state and local taxes they paid, much of what they paid in medical insurance premiums, and the interest they paid on consumer loans (such as those used to buy automobiles). On the eve of the Tax Reform Act of 1986, an opinion poll showed that more people favored small cuts in tax rates coupled with many large deductions than favored big cuts in tax rates coupled with fewer and smaller deductions.[11]

Interest groups organized around each loophole. Home builders organized to support the

HOW WE COMPARE

Tax Burdens in Democratic Nations

Measured by taxes as a percentage of income of a family with two children, America as of 2008 had one of the lightest such tax burdens anywhere in the democratic world.

Denmark	28.8%
Turkey	25.7%
Greece	25.4%
Netherlands	22.6%
Finland	22.6%
Norway	21.8%
Germany	20.8%
Belgium	20.2%
UK	18.5%
Sweden	17.9%
Poland	17.8%
France	17.1%
Italy	15.1%
Japan	13.8%
Spain	12.0%
Canada	8.8%
Australia	8.6%
Switzerland	8.1%
U.S.	5.2%

Source: U.S. Bureau of the Census, reporting data from Organization for Economic Cooperation and Development (OECD), Comparative Table 1361, 2010.

but not as important as tax loopholes. "Loophole politics" was client politics. When client groups pressed for benefits, they could take advantage of the decentralized structure of Congress to find well-placed advocates who could advance these interests through low-visibility bargaining. In effect, these groups were getting a subsidy from the federal government equal to the amount of the tax break. However, the tax break was even better than a subsidy, because it did not have to be voted on every year as part of an appropriations bill: once part of the tax code, it lasted for a long time, and given the length and complexity of that code, scarcely anyone would notice it was there.

Many of these loopholes could be justified by arguments about economic growth. Low tax rates on a certain kind of investment encouraged more investment of that kind. Deductions for mortgage interest and property taxes encouraged people to own their own homes and boosted the construction industry.

Then the Tax Reform Act of 1986 turned the decades-old compromise on its head: instead of high rates with big deductions, we got low rates with much smaller deductions. The big gainers were individuals; the big losers were businesses.

But soon the old system began to reassert itself. Not long after the 1986 bill became law, tax rates started to go up again, this time with far fewer of the deductions that had once made it easy for affluent citizens to keep their effective rates low. In 1990, President Bush, after having campaigned on the slogan "Read my lips, no new taxes," signed a tax increase. The top rate was 31 percent. In 1993 President Clinton proposed another tax increase, one that would raise the top rate to over 39 percent (it had been 28 percent in 1986) and make most Social Security benefits taxable for upper-income retirees. His bill narrowly passed by a vote of 218 to 216 in the House, a vote of 51 to 50 in the Senate, with Vice President Al Gore casting the deciding vote. Not a single Republican voted for it. It was the first time since 1945 that the majority party in Congress had passed a major bill without one vote from the minority party.

When President George W. Bush got his tax cut plan through Congress in 2002, many Democrats as well as most Republicans voted for it. The next issue was clear: Should the tax cuts, now expiring at the end of 2010, be made permanent? The issue deeply divided the parties in Congress. But, in December 2010, President Barack Obama signed into law a compromise bill featuring a two-year extension of the Bush tax cuts (favored by most Republicans) as well as additional money for unemployment insurance (favored by most Democrats). Under the American Taxpayer Relief Act of 2012, the top individual tax rate reverted back to its pre-Bush level, 39.6 percent, but the lower, Bush-era tax rates for many other income levels were retained.

mortgage-interest deduction; universities supported the charitable-contribution deduction; insurance companies supported the deduction for medical insurance premiums; and automakers supported the deduction for interest on consumer loans.

In addition to these well-known loopholes, there were countless others, not so well known and involving much less money, that were defended and enlarged through the efforts of other interest groups: for instance, oil companies supported the deduction for drilling costs, heavy industry supported the investment tax credit, and real estate developers supported special tax write-offs for apartment and office buildings.

Until 1986, the typical tax fight was less about rates than about deductions. Rates were important,

WHAT WOULD YOU DO?

MEMORANDUM

To: *Elizabeth Gilbert, chairperson, Council of Economics*

From: *Edward Larson, White House speechwriter*

Subject: *Flat tax proposal*

The President would like your advice on whether to endorse a flat tax. His likely opponent is pushing this issue.

Arguments for:

1. A flat tax is fair because it treats all income groups the same. We could leave the lowest income group with no taxes.

2. With a flat tax, we could eliminate almost all deductions and loopholes from the tax code.

3. Countries with a flat tax, such as Lithuania, have achieved great economic prosperity.

Arguments against:

1. A flat tax is unfair because it treats all income groups the same. The rich should be taxed more heavily.

News »

Should We Have a Flat Tax?

White House candidate David Wilson declared yesterday that he would seek a fundamental overhaul of the nation's tax system by creating a single rate for all taxpayers. The President is expected to respond to this in his State of the Union address.

2. Many tax deductions, such as the one for home mortgages, are desirable.

3. We could eliminate undesirable tax loopholes without creating a flat tax.

Your decision:

Support _____   Oppose _____

LEARNING OBJECTIVES

1. How do you define "deficit," "national debt," and "gross domestic product"?

The deficit is what results when the government in one year spends more money than it takes in from taxes. The national debt is the total deficit from the first presidency down to the present. The gross domestic product, or GDP, is the total of all goods and services produced in the economy during a given year. In recent years, deficits and the national debt, both in absolute terms and relative to GDP, have reached record highs.

2. What makes the politics of taxing and spending so difficult?

The politics of taxing and spending are so difficult mainly because most people don't like being taxed but do value government-funded programs that benefit themselves, their families and communities, and other citizens more generally. Most voters want lower taxes, less debt, and new programs, but if we have more spending, we have to pay for it, either with higher taxes or with more borrowing (and hence more, not less, debt). The recession that began in

2007 lingered. Both deficits and the national debt hit new highs in 2008 and 2009. In 2011, for the first time, America's top credit rating was called into serious question. Thus, it has become harder and harder for politicians to avoid debating and making hard economic policy choices.

3. On which programs does the federal government spend most of its money?

The federal government now spends about a fifth of its money on each of four things: Social Security, health care (Medicare and Medicaid), national defense, and nondefense programs. It spends the remaining fifth on other things including interest on the national debt.

4. Who in the federal government can make our economy strong?

Nobody. The president, the Congress, the Federal Reserve Board, and countless small agencies play a role. And opinions as to what is the correct course of action (cut or increase taxes, decrease or increase regulations, spend more or less money) are deeply divided. The party that controls the White House usually must take the blame if the economy is in bad shape, but it is limited in what it can do to make it better.

5. Why does the federal government ever have a budget deficit?

It is not because politicians like deficits; it is because events may cause them while leaders disagree over how to fix them. Since the 1930s we have had deficits whenever the economy went into a depression or we had to take part in a war. In fact, a lot of things the government buys, such as new buildings and military supplies, ought to be considered as investments to be paid for over time, just as when private citizens buy cars and houses. And when the deficit goes up, some politicians will want to cut it by raising taxes while others will prefer cutting spending.

TO LEARN MORE

Internal Revenue Service: **www.irs.gov**

Tax Foundation: **www.taxfoundation.org**

Birnbaum, Jeffrey H., and Alan S. Murray. *Showdown at Gucci Gulch*. New York: Random House, 1987. Lively journalistic account of the passage of the Tax Reform Act of 1986.

Kiewiet, D. Roderick. *Macroeconomics and Micropolitics*. Chicago: University of Chicago Press, 1983. Argues that citizens vote on the basis of their estimate of national economic conditions as well as their own financial circumstances.

Morgenson, Gretchen, and Joshua Rosner. *Reckless Endangerment: How Outside Ambition, Greed, and Corruption Led to Economic Armageddon*. New York: Times Books/Henry Holt, 2011. The subtitle says it all.

Samuelson, Robert J. *The Good Life and Its Discontents*. New York: Times Books/Random House, 1995. A readable, intelligent account of American economic life since the Second World War.

Schick, Allen. *The Federal Budget*. Washington, D.C.: Brookings Institution, 2000. Excellent overview of how Washington allocates money.

Sorkin, Andrew Ross. *Too Big to Fail: The Inside Story of How Wall Street and Washington Fought to Save the Financial System—and Themselves*. New York: Viking, 2009. The captivating tale of how certain top Washington officials and Wall Street leaders reacted to the near-collapse of the financial system.

Stein, Herbert, and Murray Foss. *The New Illustrated Guide to the American Economy*, 3rd ed. Washington, D.C.: American Enterprise Institute, 1999. A vivid collection of graphs, all clearly explained, that describes the American economy and government spending from the 1950s through the 1990s.

US Army Photo / Alamy

Foreign and Military Policy

LEARNING OBJECTIVES

1. Is American foreign policy set by public opinion or elite views?

2. If only Congress can declare war, why has the president become so powerful in military affairs?

3. Should our foreign policy be based on American interests or some conception of human rights?

Every American knows we struggle against terrorists—that is, against private groups that attack unarmed civilians. But this is not a recent development.

THEN

Between 1801 and 1805 President Thomas Jefferson sent our navy to fight the Barbary Pirates who operated out of various North African countries against merchant shipping in the Mediterranean. They were sponsored by the Ottoman Empire, a Muslim organization based in Turkey. In the 19th century, American warships did battle with pirates in the Caribbean and along our Atlantic coast. Some terrorists operated inside the country. John Brown fought against slavery by raiding the supplies of the American military at Harper's Ferry. One might sympathize with his antislavery views, but he and his followers killed innocent civilians. He was caught and hanged.

After the Civil War, the Ku Klux Klan (KKK) was formed to block the emancipation of blacks by lynching them and shooting into their homes as well as those of sympathetic whites. The first KKK, created in the 19th century, was replaced by a second one created in the 20th; each of them enrolled several million members and continued the policy of harassment and murder. Although a KKK still exists, it only has a few thousand members and rarely commits an illegal act. To defeat the Klan, in 1871 Congress passed the "Klan Act" that gave the president the power to suspend the writ of habeas corpus in any state where ordinary law enforcement procedures were unavailable and afforded people the right to sue officials who violated their rights.

In the 1960s and 1970s, the Weather Underground, a radical leftist organization, bombed police stations, the Pentagon, and a townhouse; threw Molotov cocktails through a judge's window; and robbed a Brink's armored car. Though several of its leaders have abandoned radical action and taken respectable jobs, they denounce conservatives in and out of government in the strongest language.

NOW

The 9/11 attacks by hijacked aircraft against the World Trade Center and the Pentagon ushered in a new phase and represented a much more deadly form of terrorism than what we have encountered in the past. The evidence suggests that this attack, as well as the bombing of two American embassies and the suicide attack on the USS *Cole,* were carried out by al Qaeda, a radical Islamic group founded by Osama bin Laden and his colleagues. ("Al Qaeda" means "the base.") But these attacks were different from that on Pearl Harbor: the latter attack had, so to speak, a return address—we knew who did it and where they lived. But 9/11 had no return address: it was a terrorist attack waged by small groups that could be located anywhere.

In response, the United States launched an attack on Afghanistan, where the ruling party, the Taliban, had supported and helped train al Qaeda,

In May 2011 Osama bin Laden was killed by U.S. special forces in the house behind this wall, located in Abbottabad, Pakistan.

and passed the Patriot Act, which improved cooperation among intelligence and law enforcement agencies. The federal government amended the Foreign Intelligence Surveillance Act (FISA) that makes it possible for the government to eavesdrop on communications that cross our national borders. In 2011, Osama bin Laden, the founder of al Qaeda, was found in Pakistan and killed by American special forces operatives.

Such choices must be made in a democracy, and some observers think democratic politics makes managing foreign and military policy harder. Tocqueville said the conduct of foreign affairs requires precisely those qualities most lacking in a democratic nation: "A democracy can only with great difficulty regulate the details of an important undertaking, persevere in a fixed design, and work out its execution in spite of serious obstacles. It cannot combine its measures with secrecy or await their consequences with patience."[1] In plain language, a democracy is forced to play foreign policy poker with its cards turned up. As a result, aggressors from Hitler to Saddam Hussein can bluff a democracy, but the reverse is far more difficult.

But other writers disagree with Tocqueville. To them, the strength of democracy is that, though it rarely if ever wages an unjustified war on another country, its people, when mobilized by the president, will support our overseas engagements even when many deaths occur.[2]

Kinds of Foreign Policy

The majoritarian component of foreign policy includes those decisions (and non-decisions) perceived to confer widely distributed benefits and impose widely distributed costs. The decision to go to war is an obvious example of this. So, too, are the establishment of military alliances with Western Europe, the negotiation of a nuclear test ban treaty or a strategic arms limitation agreement, the response to the placement of Soviet offensive missiles in Cuba, and the opening up of diplomatic relations with the People's Republic of China. These may be good or bad policies, but the benefits and costs accrue to the nation generally.

Some argue that the costs of many of these policies are in fact highly concentrated—for example, soldiers bear the burden of a military operation— but that turns out, on closer inspection, not to shape the positions that people take on issues of war and peace. Though soldiers and their immediate families may feel the costs of war to an especially high degree, public opinion surveys taken during the Vietnam War showed that having a family member in the armed forces did not significantly affect how people evaluated the war.[3] There is a sense that, during wartime, we are all in this together.

Foreign policy decisions may also reflect interest group politics. Tariff decisions confer benefits on certain business firms and labor unions and impose costs on other firms and unions. If the price of Japanese steel imported into this country is increased by tariffs, quotas, or other devices, this helps the American steel industry and the United Steel Workers of America. On the other hand, it hurts those firms (and associated unions) that had been purchasing the once-cheap Japanese steel.

Examples of client politics also occur in foreign affairs. Washington often provides aid to American corporations doing business abroad because the aid helps those firms directly without imposing any apparent costs on an equally distinct group in society. Americans support Israel partly because Jewish organizations back her and partly because they admire that embattled democracy. Arab Americans have begun to organize and to press concerns on the government that are very different from the pro-Israel arguments.

Who has power in foreign policy depends very much on what kind of foreign policy we have in mind. Where it is of a majoritarian nature, the president is clearly the dominant figure, and much, if not everything, depends on his beliefs and skills and on those of his chief advisers. Public opinion will ordinarily support this presidential leadership, but it will not guide it. Woe to the president who by his actions forfeits that trust.

When interest group or client politics is involved, Congress plays a much larger role. Although Congress has a subsidiary role in the conduct of foreign diplomacy, the decision to send troops overseas, or the direction of intelligence operations, it has a large one in decisions involving foreign economic aid, the structure of the tariff system, the shipment of weapons to foreign allies, the creation of new weapons systems, and the support of Israel.

And Congress is the central political arena on those occasions when entrepreneurial politics shapes foreign policy. If a multinational corporation is caught in a scandal, congressional investigations shake the usual indifference of politicians to the foreign conduct of such corporations. If presidential policies abroad lead to reversals, as when in 1986 presidential aides sought to trade arms for U.S. hostages in Iran and then use some profits from the arms sales to support the anti-Marxist contras fighting in Nicaragua, Congress becomes the forum for investigations and criticism. At such moments Congress often seeks to expand its power over foreign affairs.

In this chapter, we will be chiefly concerned with foreign policy insofar as it displays the characteristics of majoritarian politics. Limiting the discussion in this way permits us to focus on the grand issues

Mohsen Shandiz/Corbis

A nuclear power plan in Iran raises concerns for the United States about potential threats to regional and international security.

of foreign affairs—war, peace, and global diplomacy. It allows us to see how choices are made in a situation in which public majorities support but do not direct policy, in which opinion tends to react to events, and in which interest groups are relatively unimportant.

The Constitutional and Legal Context

The Constitution defines the authority of the president and of Congress in foreign affairs in a way that, as Edward Corwin put it, is an "invitation to struggle."[4] The president is commander-in-chief of the armed forces, but Congress must authorize and appropriate money for those forces. The president appoints ambassadors, but they must be confirmed by the Senate. The president may negotiate treaties, but the Senate must ratify these by a two-thirds vote. Only Congress may regulate commerce with other nations and "declare" war. (In an early draft of the Constitution, the Framers gave Congress the power to "make" war but changed this to "declare" so that the president, acting without Congress, could take military measures to repel a sudden attack.) Because power over foreign affairs is shared by the president and Congress, conflict between them is to be expected.

Yet almost every American thinks instinctively that the president is in charge of foreign affairs, and what popular opinion supposes, the historical record confirms. Presidents have asserted the right to send

troops abroad on their own authority in more than 125 instances. Only five of the 11 major wars that this country has fought have followed a formal declaration of war by Congress.[5] The State Department, the Central Intelligence Agency, and the National Security Agency are almost entirely "presidential" agencies, with only modest congressional control. The Defense Department, though keenly sensitive to congressional views on weapons procurement and the location of military bases, is very much under the control of the president on matters of military strategy. While the Senate has since 1789 ratified well over 1,000 treaties signed by the president, the president during this period also has signed around 7,000 executive agreements with other countries that did not require Senate ratification and yet have the force of law.[6]

Presidential Box Score

When the president seeks congressional approval for foreign policy matters, he tends to win more often than when he asks for support on domestic matters. One student of the presidency, Aaron Wildavsky, concluded that the American political system has "two presidencies"—one in domestic affairs that is relatively weak and closely checked, and another in foreign affairs that is quite powerful.[7] As we shall see, this view considerably overstates presidential power in certain areas.

When it comes to international diplomacy and the use of American troops, the president is indeed strong, much stronger than the Framers may have intended and certainly stronger than many members of Congress would prefer. Examples abound:

- 1861: Abraham Lincoln blockaded southern ports and declared martial law.

- 1940: Franklin D. Roosevelt sent 50 destroyers to England to be used against Germany, with which we were then technically at peace.

- 1950: Harry Truman sent American troops into South Korea to help repulse a North Korean attack on that country.

- 1960s: John F. Kennedy and Lyndon Johnson sent American forces into South Vietnam without a declaration of war.

- 1983: Ronald Reagan sent troops to overthrow a pro-Castro regime in Grenada.

- 1989: George H. W. Bush ordered the U.S. invasion of Panama to depose dictator Manuel Noriega.

- 1990: Bush ordered troops to Saudi Arabia in response to Iraq's invasion of Kuwait.

- 1999: Bill Clinton ordered the military to attack, with bombs and cruise missiles, Serbian forces that were trying to control Kosovo.

- 2001: George W. Bush sent U.S. troops to liberate Afghanistan from the Taliban, a regime supportive of Osama bin Laden, the architect of the September 11 terrorist attacks.

- 2003: Bush, with some allies, invaded Iraq.

- 2011: President Obama secured a UN Security Council resolution (but not congressional authorization) to give military support to rebels in Libya, who successfully overturned the repressive regime of Muammar Gaddafi.

However, by the standards of other nations, even other democratic ones, the ability of an American president to act decisively often appears rather modest. The United Kingdom was dismayed at the inability of Woodrow Wilson in 1914–1915 and Franklin Roosevelt in 1939–1940 to enter into an alliance when the Britons were engaged in a major war with Germany. Wilson was unable to bring the United States into the

---

HOW THINGS WORK

Shifting Patterns of Leadership in Foreign Policy

Depending on the personalities, skills, and interests of those involved, leadership in making American foreign policy may be found centered in the White House (the president and his national security adviser) or in the State Department (the secretary of state).

Periods of White House Dominance

President	Secretary of State
Franklin D. Roosevelt	Cordell Hull (1933–1944)
John F. Kennedy (and National Security Adviser McGeorge Bundy)	Dean Rusk (1961–1969)
Richard M. Nixon (and National Security Adviser Henry A. Kissinger)	William P. Rogers (1969–1973)

Periods of Leadership by the Secretary of State

Secretary of State	President
George C. Marshall (1947–1949) and Dean Acheson (1949–1953)	Harry S. Truman
John Foster Dulles (1953–1959)	Dwight D. Eisenhower
Henry A. Kissinger (1973–1977)	Gerald R. Ford
Warren Christopher (1993–1996)	Bill Clinton
Condoleezza Rice (2005–2009)	George W. Bush (and National Security Adviser Stephen J. Hadley)
Hillary Rodham Clinton (2009–2013)	Barack Obama (and National Security Advisers James Jones and Tom Donilon)

Periods of Tension between the White House and Secretary of State

President	Secretary of State
Jimmy Carter	Cyrus Vance (1977–1980)
Ronald Reagan	George Shultz (1982–1989)
George W. Bush	Colin Powell (2001-2005)

League of Nations. Gerald Ford could not intervene covertly in Angola in support of an anti-Marxist faction. Ronald Reagan was heavily criticized in Congress for sending 55 military advisers to El Salvador and a few hundred Marines to Lebanon. After George H. W. Bush sent U.S. troops to the Persian Gulf in 1990, he began a long debate with Congress over whether he would need a formal declaration of war before the troops were sent into combat. George W. Bush's decision to invade Iraq in 2003 became bitterly controversial in the 2004, 2006, and 2008 elections.

Furthermore, a treaty signed by the president is little more than his promise to try to get the Senate to go along. He can sign executive agreements without Senate consent, but most of these are authorized in advance by Congress.[8]

By contrast, the leaders of other democratic nations (to say nothing of totalitarian ones) often are able to act with much greater freedom. While Reagan was arguing with Congress over whether we should assign any military advisers to El Salvador, the president of France, François Mitterrand, ordered 2,500 combat troops to Chad with scarcely a ripple of opposition. A predecessor of Mitterrand, Charles de Gaulle, brought France into the European Common Market over the explicit opposition of the French Assembly and granted independence to Algeria, then a French colony, without seriously consulting the Assembly.[9] British prime minister Edward Heath brought his country into the Common Market despite popular opposition, and the prime minister can declare war without the consent of Parliament.[10]

Evaluating the Power of the President

Whether one thinks the president is too strong or too weak in foreign affairs depends not only on whether one holds a domestic or international point of view but also on whether one agrees or disagrees with his policies. Historian Arthur M. Schlesinger, Jr., thought that President Kennedy exercised commendable presidential vigor when he made a unilateral decision to impose a naval blockade on Cuba to induce the Soviets to remove missiles installed there. However, he viewed President Nixon's decision to extend U.S. military action in Vietnam into neighboring Cambodia as a deplorable example of the "imperial presidency."[11] To be sure, there were important differences between these two actions, but that is precisely the point: an office strong enough to do something that one thinks proper is also strong enough to do something that one finds wrong.

The Supreme Court has fairly consistently supported the view that the federal government has powers in the conduct of foreign and military policy beyond those specifically mentioned in the Constitution. The leading decision, rendered in 1936,

holds that the right to carry out foreign policy is an inherent attribute of any sovereign nation:

> *The power to declare and wage war, to conclude peace, to make treaties, to maintain diplomatic relations with other sovereignties, if they had never been mentioned in the Constitution, would have vested in the Federal Government as necessary concomitants of nationality.*[12]

The individual states have few rights in foreign affairs.

Moreover, the Supreme Court has been reluctant to intervene in disputes over the conduct of foreign affairs. When various members of Congress brought suit challenging the right of President Nixon to enlarge the war in Vietnam without congressional approval, the court of appeals handled the issue, as one scholar was later to describe it, with all the care of porcupines making love. The Court said it was a matter for the president and Congress to decide and that if Congress was unwilling to cut off the money to pay for the war, it should not expect the courts to do the job for it.[13]

The Supreme Court upheld the extraordinary measures taken by President Lincoln during the Civil War and refused to interfere with the conduct of the Vietnam War by Presidents Johnson and Nixon.[14] After Iran seized American hostages in 1979, President Carter froze Iranian assets in this country. To win the hostages' freedom the president later agreed to return some of these assets and to nullify claims on them by American companies. The Court upheld the nullification because it was necessary for the resolution of a foreign policy dispute.[15]

How great the deference to presidential power may be is vividly illustrated by the actions of President Franklin Roosevelt in ordering the army to move more than 100,000 Japanese Americans—the great majority

In 1962 President Kennedy forced the Soviet Union to withdraw the missiles it had placed in Cuba after their presence was revealed by aerial photography.

of them born in this country and citizens of the United States—from their homes on the West Coast to inland "relocation centers" for the duration of World War II. Though this action was a wholesale violation of the constitutional rights of U.S. citizens and was unprecedented in American history, the Supreme Court decided that with the West Coast vulnerable to attack by Japan, the president was within his rights to declare that people of Japanese ancestry might pose a threat to internal security; thus the relocation order was upheld.[16] (No Japanese American was ever found guilty of espionage or sabotage.) One of the few cases in which the Court denied the president broad wartime powers occurred in 1952, when by a 5-to-4 vote it reversed President Truman's seizure of the steel mills—a move that he had made in order to avert a strike that, in his view, would have imperiled the war effort in Korea.[17]

Checks on Presidential Power

If there is a check on the powers of the federal government or the president in foreign affairs, it is chiefly political rather than constitutional. The most important check is Congress's control of the purse strings. In addition, Congress has imposed three important kinds of restrictions on the president's freedom of action, all since Vietnam.

Limitations on the President's Ability to Give Military or Economic Aid to Other Countries

For example, between 1974 and 1978 the president could not sell arms to Turkey because of a dispute between Turkey and Greece over control of the island of Cyprus. The pressure on Congress from groups supporting Greece was much stronger than that from groups supporting Turkey. In 1976, Congress prevented President Ford from giving aid to the pro-Western faction in the Angolan civil war. Until the method was declared unconstitutional, Congress for many years could use a legislative veto, a resolution disapproving of an executive decision (see Chapter 15), to block the sale by the president of arms worth more than $25 million to another country.

The War Powers Act

Passed in 1973 over a presidential veto, this law placed the following restrictions on the president's ability to use military force:

- He must report in writing to Congress within 48 hours after he introduces U.S. troops into areas where hostilities have occurred or are imminent.

Following the attack on Pearl Harbor, in 1942 President Roosevelt ordered that all Japanese Americans living on the West Coast be interned in prison camps.

- Within 60 days after troops are sent into hostile situations, Congress must, by declaration of war or other specific statutory authorization, provide for the continuation of hostile action by U.S. troops.

- If Congress fails to provide such authorization, the president must withdraw the troops (unless Congress has been prevented from meeting as a result of an armed attack).

- If Congress passes a concurrent resolution (which the president may not veto) directing the removal of U.S. troops, the president must comply.

Until recently the War Powers Act has had very little influence on American military actions. Since its passage every president—Ford, Carter, Reagan, Bush the elder, Clinton, Bush the younger, and Obama—has sent American forces abroad without any explicit congressional authorization. (Bush the elder asked for that support when he attacked Iraq and, by a narrow margin, received it.) No president has acknowledged that the War Powers Act is constitutional. In its 1983 decision in the *Chadha* case, the Supreme Court struck down the legislative veto, which means that this section of the act is already in constitutional trouble.[18]

Even if the act is constitutional, politically it is all but impossible to use. Few members of Congress would challenge a president who carried out a successful military operation (for example, those in Grenada, Panama, and Afghanistan). More might challenge the president if, after a while, the military action were in trouble, but the easiest way to do that would be to cut off funding for the operation. But even during the Vietnam War, a conflict that preceded the War Powers Act, Congress, though it contained many critics of U.S. policy, never stopped military appropriations.

In 2011, however, after the United States, working with the North Atlantic Treaty Organization (NATO), used military resources in support of rebels attacking the despotic regime of Muammar Gaddafi in Libya, Republicans in Congress (who in the past had shown little interest in the War Powers Act) attacked President Obama over his failure to comply with it.

Intelligence Oversight

Owing to the low political stock of President Nixon during the Watergate scandal and the revelations of illegal operations by the Central Intelligence Agency (CIA) within the United States, Congress required that the CIA notify appropriate congressional committees about any proposed covert action (between 1974 and 1980 it had to notify *eight* different committees). Today it must keep two groups, the House and the Senate Intelligence Committees, "fully and currently informed" of all intelligence activities, including covert actions. The committees do not have the authority to disapprove such actions.

However, from time to time Congress will pass a bill blocking particular covert actions. This happened when the Boland Amendment (named after its sponsor, Representative Edward Boland) was passed on several occasions between 1982 and 1985. Each version of the amendment prevented, for specifically stated periods, intelligence agencies from supplying military aid to the Nicaraguan contras.

The 9/11 terrorist attacks left everyone wondering why our intelligence agencies had not foreseen them. After the attacks, there was an investigation to find out why the CIA had not warned the country of this risk. In an effort to improve matters, Congress passed and President Bush signed a law creating the Office of the Director of National Intelligence (DNI). It was designed to coordinate the work of the CIA, the FBI, the Defense Intelligence Agency (DIA), and the intelligence units of several other government agencies. The DNI replaced the director of the CIA as the president's chief adviser. It is too early to tell how much real coordination will occur; the DNI's office is another large bureaucracy placed on top of other big ones.

The Machinery of Foreign Policy

From the time that Thomas Jefferson took the job in Washington's first administration until well into the 20th century, foreign policy was often made and almost always carried out by the secretary of state. No more. When America became a major world power during and after World War II, our commitments overseas expanded dramatically. With that expansion two things happened. First, the president began to put foreign policy at the top of his agenda and to play a larger role in directing it. Second, that policy was shaped by the scores of agencies (some brand-new) that had acquired overseas activities.

Today Washington, D.C., has not one State Department but many. The Defense Department has military bases and military advisers abroad. The Central Intelligence Agency has intelligence officers abroad, most of them assigned to "stations" that are part of the American embassy but not under the full control of the American ambassador there. The Departments of Agriculture, Commerce, and Labor have missions abroad. The Federal Bureau of Investigation and the Drug Enforcement Administration have agents abroad. The Agency for International Development has offices to dispense foreign aid in host countries. The U.S. Information Agency runs libraries, radio stations, and educational programs abroad.

HOW THINGS WORK

Rivalry Versus Cooperation: The President and the Senate

Because the Senate must ratify treaties and consent to the appointment of ambassadors and other high foreign policy officials, it has the opportunity to play a large role in the conduct of foreign affairs. The key figure in the Senate is usually the chairman of the Senate Foreign Relations Committee.

Depending on personalities and circumstances, the president and the chairman have sometimes been able to work together closely, but at other times have been bitter, outspoken rivals. In general, cooperation occurs when there is a widely shared foreign policy worldview; rivalry erupts when worldviews diverge.

Periods of Shared Worldviews and Political Cooperation

President	Chairman of Foreign Relations Committee
Franklin D. Roosevelt	Tom Connally (1941–1947, 1949–1953)

President	Chairman of Foreign Relations Committee
Harry S. Truman	Arthur H. Vandenberg (1947–1949)

Periods of Competing Worldviews and Political Rivalry

President	Chairman of Foreign Relations Committee
Woodrow Wilson	Henry Cabot Lodge (1919–1924)
Lyndon B. Johnson	J. William Fulbright (1959–1975)
Richard M. Nixon	J. William Fulbright (1959–1975)
Bill Clinton	Jesse Helms (1995–1999)

Every new secretary of state bravely announces he or she is going to "coordinate" and "direct" this enormous foreign policy establishment. He or she never does. The reason is partly that the job is too big for any one person and partly that most of these agencies owe no political or bureaucratic loyalty to the secretary of state. If anyone is to coordinate them, it will have to be the president. But the president cannot keep track of what all these organizations are doing in the more than 190 nations and 50 international organizations where we have representatives, or in the more than 800 international conferences that we attend each year.

So he has hired a staff to do the coordinating for him. That staff is part of the National Security Council (NSC), a committee created by statute and chaired by the president, whose members include by law the vice president and the secretaries of state and defense, by custom the director of national intelligence (DNI), the chairman of the Joint Chiefs of Staff, and often the attorney general. Depending on the president, the NSC can be an important body in which to hammer out foreign policy. Attached to it is a staff headed by the national security adviser. That staff, which usually numbers a few dozen men and women, can be (again, depending on the president) an enormously powerful instrument for formulating and directing foreign policy.

Presidents Truman and Eisenhower made only limited use of the NSC staff, but beginning with President Kennedy it has grown greatly in influence. Its head, the national security adviser, has come to rival the secretary of state for foreign policy leadership, especially when the adviser is a powerful personality such as Henry Kissinger. President Reagan attempted to downgrade the importance of the national security adviser, but ironically it was one of his relatively low-visibility advisers, Admiral John Poindexter, and his subordinate, Lieutenant Colonel Oliver North, who precipitated the worst crisis of the Reagan presidency when, allegedly without informing the president, they tried to use cash realized from the secret sale of arms to Iran to finance guerrillas fighting against the Marxist government of Nicaragua. The sale and the diversion became known, North was fired, a congressional investigation ensued, criminal charges were filed against Poindexter and North, and the president's political position was weakened. But even in ordinary times the NSC staff has been the rival of the secretary of state, except during that period in the Ford administration when Henry Kissinger held *both* jobs.

The way in which the machinery of foreign policymaking operates has two major consequences for the substance of that policy. First, as former secretary of state George Shultz asserted, "It's never over." Foreign policy issues are endlessly agitated, rarely settled. The reason is that the rivalries *within* the executive branch intensify the rivalries *between* that branch and Congress. In ways already described, Congress has steadily increased its influence over the conduct of foreign policy. Anybody in the executive branch who loses out in a struggle over foreign policy can take his or her case (usually by means of a well-timed leak) to a sympathetic member of Congress, who then can make a speech, hold a hearing, or introduce a bill.

Second, the interests of the various organizations making up the foreign policy establishment profoundly affect the positions that they take. Because the State Department has a stake in diplomacy, it tends to resist bold or controversial new policies that might upset established relationships with other countries. Part of the CIA has a stake in gathering and analyzing information; that part tends to be skeptical of the claims of other agencies that their overseas operations are succeeding. Another part of the CIA conducts covert operations abroad; it tends to resent or ignore the skepticism of the intelligence analysts. The air force flies airplanes and so tends to be optimistic about what can be accomplished through the use of air power in particular and military power in general; the army, on the other hand, which must fight in the trenches, is often dubious about the prospects for military success. During the American war in Iraq, the conflict between the CIA and the Defense Department was great, with each side leaking information to the press.

Americans often worry that their government is keeping secrets from them. In fact, there are no secrets in Washington—at least not for long.

Foreign Policy and Public Opinion

These organizational conflicts shape the details of foreign policy, but its broad outlines are shaped by public and elite opinion.

World War II was the great watershed event in American foreign policy. Before that time, a clear majority of the American public opposed active involvement in world affairs. The public saw the costs of such involvement as being substantially in excess of the benefits, and only determined, skillful leaders were able, as was President Roosevelt during 1939–1940, to affect in even a limited fashion the diplomatic and military struggles then convulsing Europe and Asia.

In 1937, 94 percent of the American public preferred the policy of doing "everything possible to keep out of foreign wars" to the policy of doing "everything possible to prevent war, even if it means threatening to fight countries that fight wars." In 1939, after World War II had begun in Europe but before Pearl Harbor was attacked, only 13 percent of Americans polled thought that we should enter the war against Germany. Just a month before Pearl Harbor, only 19 percent felt that the United States should take steps, at the risk of war, to prevent Japan from becoming too powerful.[19] Congress reflected the noninterventionist mood of the country: in the summer of 1941, with war breaking out almost everywhere, the proposal to continue the draft passed the House of Representatives by only one vote.

The Japanese attack on Pearl Harbor on December 7 changed all that. Not only was the American war effort supported almost unanimously, not only did Congress approve the declaration of war with only one dissenting vote, but World War II—unlike World War I—produced popular support for an active assumption of international responsibilities that continued after the war had ended.[20] Whereas after World War I a majority opposed U.S. entry into the League of Nations, after World War II a clear majority favored our entry into the United Nations.[21]

This willingness to see the United States remain a world force persisted. Even during the Vietnam War, the number of people thinking that we should "keep independent" in world affairs as opposed

---

LANDMARK CASES

Foreign Affairs

- *Curtiss-Wright Export Corp. v. United States* (1936): American foreign policy is vested entirely in the federal government where the president has plenary power.

- *Korematsu v. United States* (1944): Sending Japanese Americans to relocation centers during World War II was based on an acceptable military justification.

- *Youngstown Sheet & Tube Co. v. Sawyer* (1952): The president may not seize factories during wartime without explicit congressional authority even when they are threatened by a strike.

- *Hamdi v. Rumsfeld* (2004): An American citizen in jail because he allegedly joined the Taliban extremist group should have access to a "neutral decision maker."

- *Rasul v. Bush* (2004): Foreign nationals held at Guantanamo Bay because they are believed to be terrorists have a right to bring their cases before an American court.

to "working closely with other nations" rose from 10 percent in 1963 to only 22 percent in 1969.²² In 1967, after more than two years of war in Vietnam, 44 percent of Americans believed that this country had an obligation to "defend other Vietnams if they are threatened by communism."²³

Before 9/11, hardly any American thought we should fight a war in Afghanistan, but after that attack we fought exactly that war in order to get rid of the Taliban regime. The Taliban, a group of radical young Muslims, had taken control of that country and allowed Osama bin Laden, the head of al Qaeda, to use the nation as a place to train and direct terrorists. Though al Qaeda designed and carried out the 9/11 attacks on America, it is not a single organization located in one place and thus easily defeated. It is instead a network of terrorist cells found all over the world that is allied with other terrorist groups.

But the support for an internationalist American foreign policy was, and is, highly general and heavily dependent on the phrasing of poll questions, the opinions expressed by popular leaders, and the impact of world events. Public opinion, while more internationalist than once was the case, is both mushy and volatile. Just prior to President Nixon's decision to send troops into Cambodia, only 7 percent of the people said they supported such a move. After the troops were sent and Nixon made a speech explaining his move, 50 percent of the public said they supported it.²⁴ Similarly, only 49 percent of the

people favored halting the American bombing of North Vietnam before President Johnson ordered such a halt in 1968; afterward 60 percent of the people said they supported such a policy.²⁵

Backing the President

Much of this volatility in specific opinions (as opposed to general mood) reflects the already-mentioned deference to the "commander-in-chief" and a desire to support the United States when it confronts other nations. Table 19.1 shows the proportion of people who said that they approved of the way the president was doing his job before and after various major foreign policy events. Almost every foreign crisis increased the level of public approval of the president, often dramatically. The most vivid illustration of this was the Bay of Pigs fiasco: an American-supported, American-directed invasion of Cuba by anti-Castro Cuban émigrés was driven back into the sea. President Kennedy accepted responsibility for the aborted project. His popularity *rose*. (Comparable data for domestic crises tend to show no similar effect.)

This tendency to "rally round the flag" operates for some but not all foreign military crises.²⁶ The rally not only helped Kennedy after the Bay of Pigs, but it also helped Ronald Reagan when he invaded Grenada and George Bush the elder when he sent troops to fight Iraq. But it did not help Bill Clinton

---

TABLE 19.1 **Popular Reactions to Foreign Policy Crises**

Percentage of public saying that they approve of the way the president is handling his job

Foreign Policy Crisis		Before	After
1960	American U-2 spy plane shot down over Soviet Union	62%	68%
1961	Abortive landing at Bay of Pigs in Cuba	73	83
1962	Cuban missile crisis	61	74
1975	President Ford sends forces to rescue the American ship	40	51
1979	American embassy in Tehran seized by Iranians	32	61
1980	Failure of military effort to rescue hostages in Iran	39	43
1983	U.S. invasion of Grenada	43	53
1989	U.S. invasion of Panama	71	80
1990	U.S. troops to Persian Gulf	60	75
1995	U.S. troops to Bosnia	59	54
1999	U.S. troops to Kosovo	55	51
2001	U.S. combat in Afghanistan	51	86
2003	U.S. invasion of Iraq	58	71
2011	U.S. kills Osama bin Laden	46	52
2011	NATO intervention in Libya; Muammar Gaddafi killed	48	45

Source: Updated from Theodore J. Lowi, *The End of Liberalism* (New York: Norton, 1969), p. 184. Poll data are from Gallup poll and realclearpolitics. com. Time lapse between "before" and "after" samplings of opinion was in no case more than one month.

when he sent forces to Bosnia or launched bombing attacks on Iraq. If there is an attack on America, then the public typically unites in support of the president. Just before September 11, 2001, George Bush's favorability rating was 51 percent; just after the attack, it was 86 percent.

Sometimes people argue that whatever support a president gets during a military crisis will disappear once dead soldiers in body bags begin returning home. There are two things wrong with this statement. First, dead soldiers do not come home in body bags; they come home in coffins. Second, a close study of how casualty rates affect public opinion showed that although deaths tend to reduce how "favorable" people are toward a war, what they then support is not withdrawal but an *escalation* in the fighting so as to defeat the enemy more quickly. This was true during Korea, Vietnam, and the Persian Gulf War.[27]

In sum, people tend to be leery of overseas military expeditions by the United States—until they start. Then they support them and want to win, even if it means more intense fighting. When Americans began to dislike our involvement in Korea and Vietnam,[28] they did not conclude that we should pull out; they concluded instead that we should do whatever was necessary to win. The invasion of Iraq did not raise large questions for many Americans until terrorist attacks on the American military continued after the Iraqi army had been defeated.

Despite the tendency for most Americans to rally round the flag, there has been for many decades some public opposition to almost any war in which the United States participates. About one-fifth of Americans opposed our invading Iraq, about the same level of opposition to our wars in Korea and Vietnam. Opposition has generally been highest among Democrats, African Americans, and people with a postgraduate degree.[29] For the U.S. intervention in Libya in 2011, just 47 percent of Americans approved of this military action, with 37 percent in opposition.[30]

Mass versus Elite Opinion

The public is poorly informed about foreign affairs. It probably has only a vague idea where Kosovo is, how far it is from Baghdad to Kuwait, or why the Palestinians and the Jews disagree about the future of Israel. But that is to be expected. Foreign affairs are, well, foreign. They do not have much to do with the daily lives of American citizens, except during wartime. But the public, since World War II, has consistently felt that the United States should play an important international role.[31] And if our troops go abroad, it is a foolish politician who will try to talk the public out of supporting them.

Political elites, however, have a different perspective. They are better informed about foreign policy issues, but their opinions are more likely to change rapidly. Initially, college-educated people gave *more* support to the war in Vietnam than those without college training; by the end of the war, however, that support had decreased dramatically. Whereas the average citizen was upset when the United States seemed to be on the *defensive* in Vietnam, college-educated voters tended to be more upset when the United States was on the *offensive*.[32]

Though the average citizen did not want our military in Vietnam in the first place, he or she felt that we should support our troops once they were there. The average person also was deeply opposed to the antiwar protests taking place on college campuses. When the Chicago police roughed up antiwar demonstrators at the 1968 Democratic convention, public sentiment was overwhelmingly on the side of the police.[33] Contrary to myths much accepted at the time, younger people were *not* more opposed to the war than older ones. There was no "generation gap."

By contrast, college-educated citizens, thinking at first that troops should be involved, soon changed their minds, decided that the war was wrong, and grew increasingly upset when the United States seemed to be enlarging the war (by invading Cambodia, for example). College students protested against the war largely on moral grounds, and their protests received more support from college-educated adults than from other citizens.

Elite opinion changes more rapidly than public opinion. During the Vietnam War, upper-middle-class people who regularly read several magazines and newspapers underwent a dramatic change in opinion between 1964 (when they supported the war) and 1968 (when they opposed it). But the views of blue-collar workers scarcely changed at all.[34]

The cleavage between mass and elite opinion is even wider if you restrict the definition of *elite* to only those involved in making foreign policy rather than including all college-educated people. In Figure 19.1, we see the differences in foreign policy views of a cross section of American citizens and a group of 450 leaders active in government, academia, the mass media, and various organizations concerned with foreign affairs.[35]

In general the leaders have a more liberal and internationalist outlook than the public: they are more likely to favor giving economic aid to other countries and defending our allies. The public, on the other hand, wants the United States to be less active overseas and worries about protecting the jobs of American workers. Accordingly, it wants the United States to protect American jobs from foreign competition and give less economic aid to other nations.

FIGURE 19.1   **Public's View of America as World Leader**

Public's View of America's Role as World Leader

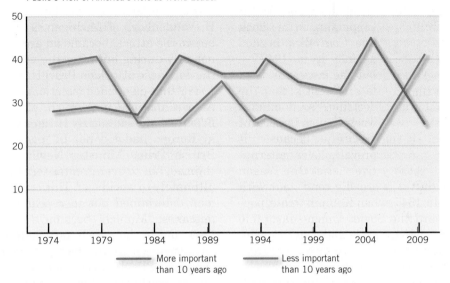

Source: Pew Research Center for the People & the Press, "U.S. Seen As Less Important, China as More Powerful: Isolationist Sentiment Surges to Four-Decade High," 3 December 2009.

Cleavages among Foreign Policy Elites

As we have seen, public opinion on foreign policy is permissive and a bit mushy: it supports presidential action without giving it much direction. Elite opinion therefore acquires extraordinary importance. Of course events and world realities are also important, but since events have no meaning except as they are perceived and interpreted by people who must react to them, the attitudes and beliefs of those people in and out of government who are actively involved in shaping foreign policy often assume decisive importance.

Contrary to the views of people who think that some shadowy, conspiratorial group of insiders runs our foreign policy, the foreign policy elite in this country is deeply divided. That elite consists not only of those people with administrative positions in the foreign policy field—the senior officials of the State Department and the staff of the National Security Council—but also the members and staffs of the key congressional committees concerned with foreign affairs (chiefly the Senate Foreign Relations Committee and the House International Relations Committee) and various private organizations that help shape elite opinion, such as the members of the Council on Foreign Relations and the editors of two important publications, *Foreign Affairs* and *Foreign Policy*. To these must be added influential columnists and editorial writers whose work appears regularly in the national press. One could extend the list by adding ever-wider circles of people with some influence (lobbyists, professors, leaders of veterans' organizations);

this would complicate without changing the central point: elite beliefs are probably more important in explaining foreign policy than in accounting for decisions in other policy areas.

worldviews
A comprehensive opinion of how the United States should respond to world problems.

How a Worldview Shapes Foreign Policy

These beliefs can be described in simplified terms as **worldviews** (or, as some social scientists put it, as paradigms)—more or less comprehensive mental pictures of the critical problems facing the United States in the world and of the appropriate and inappropriate ways of responding to these problems. The clearest, most concise, and perhaps most influential statement of one worldview that held sway for many years was in an article published in 1947 in *Foreign Affairs*, titled "The Sources of Soviet Conduct."[36] Written by a "Mr. X" (later revealed to be George F. Kennan, director of the Policy Planning Staff of the State Department and thereafter ambassador to Moscow), the article argued that the Russians were pursuing a policy of expansion that could only be met by the United States' applying "unalterable counterforce at every point where they show signs of encroaching upon the interests of a peaceful and stable world." This he called the strategy of "containment," and it became the governing principle of American foreign policy for at least two decades.

isolationism The opinion that the United States should withdraw from world affairs.

containment The belief that the United States should resist the expansion of aggressive nations, especially the former Soviet Union.

There were critics of the containment policy at the time—Walter Lippmann, in his book *The Cold War,* argued against it in 1947[37]—but the criticisms were less influential than the doctrine. A dominant worldview is important precisely because it prevails over alternative views. One reason why it prevails is that it is broadly consistent with the public's mood. In 1947, when Kennan wrote, popular attitudes toward the Soviet Union—favorable during World War II when Russia and America were allies—had turned quite hostile. In 1946, less than one-fourth of the American people believed Russia could be trusted to cooperate with this country,[38] and by 1948 over three-fourths were convinced the Soviet Union was trying not simply to defend itself, but to become the dominant world power.[39]

Such a worldview was also influential because it was consistent with events at the time: Russia had occupied most of the previously independent countries of Eastern Europe and was turning them into puppet regimes. When governments independent of both the United States and the Soviet Union attempted to rule in Hungary and Czechoslovakia, they were overthrown by Soviet-backed coups. A worldview also becomes dominant when it is consistent with the prior experiences of the people holding it.

Four Worldviews

Every generation of political leaders comes to power with a foreign policy worldview shaped, in large measure, by the real or apparent mistakes of the previous generation.[40] This pattern can be traced back, some have argued, to the very beginnings of the nation. Frank L. Klingberg traces the alteration since 1776 between two national "moods" that favored first "extroversion" (or an active, internationalist policy) and then "introversion" (a less active, even isolationist posture).[41]

Since the 1920s, American elite opinion has moved through four dominant worldviews: isolationism, containment (or antiappeasement), disengagement, and human rights. **Isolationism** was the view adopted as a result of our unhappy experience in World War I. Our efforts to help European allies had turned sour: thousands of American troops had been killed in a war that had seemed to accomplish little and certainly had not made the world, in Woodrow Wilson's words, "safe for democracy." As a result, in the 1920s and 1930s elite opinion (and popular opinion) opposed U.S. involvement in European wars.

The **containment** (or antiappeasement) paradigm was the result of World War II. Pearl Harbor was the death knell for isolationism. Senator Arthur H. Vandenberg of Michigan, a staunch isolationist before the attack, became an ardent internationalist not only during but after the war. He later wrote of the Japanese attack on Pearl Harbor on December 7, 1941, "that day ended isolationism for any realist."[42] At a conference in Munich, efforts of British and French leaders to satisfy Hitler's territorial demands in Europe had led not to "peace in our time," as British Prime Minister Neville Chamberlain had claimed, but to ever-greater territorial demands and ultimately to world war. This crisis brought to power men determined not to repeat their predecessors' mistakes: "Munich" became a synonym for weakness, and leaders such as Winston Churchill made antiappeasement the basis of their postwar policy of resisting Soviet expansionism. Churchill summed up the worldview that he had acquired from the Munich era in a famous speech delivered in 1946 in Fulton, Missouri, in which he coined the term *iron curtain* to describe Soviet policy in Eastern Europe.

The events leading up to World War II were the formative experiences of those leaders who came to power in the 1940s, 1950s, and 1960s. What they took to be the lessons of Pearl Harbor and Munich were applied repeatedly—in building a network of

A meeting that named an era: In Munich in 1938, British prime minister Neville Chamberlain attempted to appease the territorial ambitions of Hitler. Chamberlain's failure brought World War II closer.

defensive alliances in Europe and Asia during the late 1940s and 1950s, in operating an airlift to aid West Berlin when road access to it was cut off by the Russians, in coming to the aid of South Korea, and finally in intervening in Vietnam. Most of these applications of the containment worldview were successful in the sense that they did not harm American interests, they proved welcome to allies, or they prevented a military conquest.

The **disengagement** (or "Vietnam") view resulted from the experience of the younger foreign policy elite that came to power in the 1970s. Unlike previous applications of the antiappeasement view, our entry into Vietnam had led to a military defeat and a domestic political disaster. There were three ways of interpreting that crisis: (1) we applied the correct worldview in the right place but did not try hard enough; (2) we had the correct worldview but tried to apply it in the wrong place under the wrong circumstances; (3) the worldview itself was wrong. By and large, the critics of our Vietnam policy tended toward the third conclusion, and thus when they supplanted in office the architects of our Vietnam policy, they inclined toward a worldview based on the slogan "no more Vietnams." Critics of this view called it the "new isolationism," arguing that it would encourage Soviet expansion.

The debates over the Vietnam War colored many subsequent discussions of foreign policy. Almost every military initiative since then has been debated in terms of whether it would lead us into "another Vietnam": sending the Marines to Lebanon, invading Grenada, dispatching military advisers to El Salvador, supporting the contras in Nicaragua, helping South American countries fight drug producers, and sending troops to invade Iraq.

How elites thought about Vietnam affected their foreign policy views for many years. If they thought the war was "immoral," they were reluctant to see American military involvement elsewhere. These elites played a large role in the Carter administration, but were replaced by rival elites—those more inclined to a containment view—during the Reagan presidency.[43] When George H. W. Bush sought to expel Iraqi troops from Kuwait, the congressional debate pitted those committed to containment against those who believed in disengagement. The Senate vote on Bush's request for permission to use troops was narrowly carried by containment advocates.

When Clinton became president in 1992, he brought to office a lack of interest in foreign policy coupled with advisers who were drawn from the ranks of those who believed in disengagement. His strongest congressional supporters were those who had argued against the Gulf War. But then a remarkable change occurred. When Slobodan Milosevic, the Serbian leader, sent troops into neighboring Kosovo to suppress the ethnic Albanians living there, the strongest voices for American military intervention came from those who once advocated disengagement. During the Gulf War, 47 Senate Democrats voted to oppose U.S. participation. A few years later, 42 Senate Democrats voted to support our role in Kosovo.

What had happened? The change was inspired by the view that helping the Albanians was required by the doctrine of **human rights**. Liberal supporters of U.S. air attacks on Serbian forces believed that we were helping Albanians escape mass killing. By contrast, many conservative members of Congress who had followed a containment policy in the Gulf War now felt that disengagement ought to be followed in Kosovo. Of course, politics also mattered. Clinton was a Democratic president; Bush had been a Republican one.

But politics was not the whole story. Advocates of intervention declared that the attack in Kosovo resembled the genocide—that is, the mass murder of people because of their race or ethnicity—that the Jews had suffered in Nazi Germany. They held that we must "never again" permit a whole people to be killed. Anti-interventionists said if American foreign policy were guided by human rights, then the United States would have to send troops to many places. How would military action resolve a conflict that had gone on for centuries?

> **disengagement** The belief that the United States was harmed by its war in Vietnam and so should avoid supposedly similar events.
>
> **human rights** The view that we should try to improve the lives of people in other countries.

The battleship USS West Virginia *burns after being hit by Japanese warplanes at Pearl Harbor on December 7, 1941.*

polarization A deep and wide conflict over some government policy.

In the aftermath of 9/11, a new issue has arisen that may divide foreign policy elites in the future. Should the United States "go it alone" against its enemies abroad, or do so only on the basis of a broad coalition of supporting nations? President Bush the elder assembled just such a coalition to force Iraq out of Kuwait, but President Bush the younger acted without UN support in invading Afghanistan and later Iraq, though he received crucial support from the United Kingdom, Australia, and Poland.

Political Polarization

For as long as we have records, public opinion has been slow to favor our military actions overseas in the abstract but quick to support them once they occur. However, that pattern ended with our invasion of Iraq in 2003. Public opinion became deeply divided about that war, with most Democrats strongly opposing it and most Republicans favoring it.

That was not how things worked out during our wars in Korea and Vietnam. The war in Korea produced angry divisions in Congress, especially after General Douglas MacArthur, the allied commander in Korea, was fired in 1951 for having disobeyed the president. He received a hero's welcome when he returned to this country and gave an emotional speech to a joint session of Congress. Many Republicans demanded that President Truman be impeached. Despite this public support for MacArthur and these angry congressional words, the country was not split along partisan lines. Slightly more Republicans than Democrats said the war was a mistake (roughly half of each party), but the differences between these voters was not great.

The war in Vietnam split American political elites even more deeply. Journalists and members of Congress took sharply opposing sides, and some Americans traveled to North Vietnam to express their support for the Communist cause. When the North Vietnamese launched a major offensive to destroy American and South Vietnamese troops during the Tet holidays in 1968, it failed, but the American press reported it as a Communist victory, and demands to bring our troops home were heard during the presidential campaign that year. But public opinion did not divide along party lines; in 1968, Democratic and Republican voters had just about the same views (a little over half thought the war was a mistake, about a third thought it wasn't).

Our invasion of Iraq was a different story. From the very first, Democratic voters strongly opposed it and Republican ones favored it. By 2006, 76 percent of Democrats said we should have stayed out of Iraq, while 71 percent of Republicans said that the invasion was the right thing to do.[44]

American public opinion has become more polarized by our foreign policy. **Polarization** means a deep and wide conflict, usually along party lines, over some government policy. It has replaced the bipartisan foreign policy of the Second World War and the modest differences in public opinion during Korea and Vietnam.[45]

It is clear from Table 19.2 that what political party we belong to is strongly linked to our views on foreign policy. The public is deeply divided about these matters, and so, we think, will be the people for whom they vote.

TABLE 19.2 Foreign Policy Goals

Percentage who think each of the following is a "very important" foreign policy goal of the United States.

	Republican	Democrat	Independent
Protecting the jobs of American workers	84	84	82
Reducing U.S. dependence on foreign oil	78	77	73
Preventing the spread of nuclear weapons	76	74	67
Combating international terrorism	73	64	57
Maintaining superior military power worldwide	68	48	46
Controlling and reducing illegal immigration	70	43	48
Combating world hunger	31	54	40
Strengthening the United Nations	28	46	29
Limiting climate change	16	46	33
Helping to bring a democratic form of government to other nations	11	21	10

Source: Chicago Council on Global Affairs, "Foreign Policy in the New Millennium: Results of the 2012 Chicago Council Survey of American Public Opinion and U.S. Foreign Policy," Table 5.2, "Foreign Policy Goals," p. 43.

The Use of Military Force

Foreign policy takes many forms—discussions are held, treaties are signed, organizations are joined—but in many cases it depends on the ability to use military force. Troops, ships, and aircraft are not the only ways of influencing other countries; international trade and foreign aid are also useful. But in modern times, as in the past, the nations of the world know the difference between a "great power" (that is, a heavily armed one) and a weak nation.

With the collapse of the Soviet Union and the end of the cold war, one might think that military power has become less important. But in fact it remains as important as ever. Since the Soviet Union was dissolved and the Berlin Wall came down in 1989, the United States has used military force to attack Iraq, maintain order in Bosnia, defend Kosovo, and go to war in Afghanistan. Various rogue nations, such as Iran and North Korea, have acquired or are about to acquire long-range rockets and weapons of mass destruction (that is, nuclear, chemical, and biological

arms). Many nations that feel threatened by their neighbors, such as China, India, Pakistan, and Israel, have nuclear bombs. And Russia still has many of the nuclear weapons that the old Soviet Union built. It would be foolish to assume that the end of the cold war means the end of war.

There are two views about the role of the military in American life. One is majoritarian: the military exists to defend the country or to help other nations defend themselves. When troops are used, almost all Americans benefit and almost all pay the bill. (Some Americans, such as those who lose a loved one in war, pay much more than the rest of us.) The president is the commander-in-chief, and Congress plays a largely supportive role.

Although the other view does not deny that the armed forces are useful, it focuses on the extent to which the military is a large and powerful client. The real beneficiaries of military spending are the generals and admirals, as well as the big corporations and members of Congress whose districts get fat defense contracts. Everyone pays, but these clients get most of the

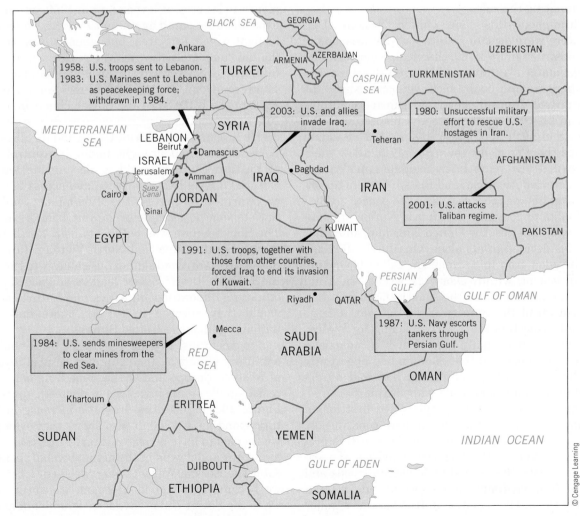

U.S. Military Intervention in the Middle East

military-industrial complex An alleged alliance between military leaders and corporate leaders.

benefits. What we spend on defense is shaped by the **military-industrial complex**, a supposedly unified bloc of Defense Department leaders and military manufacturers.

War in Iraq

After the Iraqi army under Saddam Hussein had invaded neighboring Kuwait in 1990, the United Nations passed a resolution demanding that Iraq withdraw and authorizing force to expel it. In January 1991, the United States led a coalition of forces from several nations that attacked Iraq; within 100 days, the Iraqi army had retreated from Kuwait and fled home. The U.S.-led military forces ended their attack, allowing Saddam to remain in power in Baghdad, the Iraqi capital.

After the war, a no-fly zone was established under which Iraqi flights in certain areas were prohibited. This ban was enforced for 12 years by U.S., British, and French planes that shot down Iraqi aircraft violating the rule.

Throughout this time, United Nations (UN) inspectors were sent to Iraq to look for weapons of mass destruction (WMDs): chemical, biological, and nuclear materials that could be used to attack others. There was no doubt such weapons existed, as Saddam had dropped chemical weapons on people living in his own country. The UN inspectors found evidence of such a program, but in 1997 Saddam expelled them from his country, only to allow them to return a few years later. Saddam's misleading statements led American and British leaders to conclude that his regime was a threat to peace.

Unable to convince the United Nations to support a war, America, the United Kingdom, and other countries decided to act alone. On March 30, 2003, they invaded Iraq in a campaign called Operation Iraqi Freedom; within about six weeks, the Iraqi army was defeated and the American-led coalition occupied all of the country. After the war, a large group of inspectors toured Iraq looking for WMDs, but they found virtually none. Later, a bipartisan commission concluded that Saddam had apparently cancelled his WMD program, but had told hardly any of his own military leaders about this.[46]

The newly freed Iraqi people voted first for an interim parliament, then for a new constitution, and finally for a regular government. But this process was offset by the terrorist activities of various insurgents, first aimed at American troops and later at Iraqi civilians, killing several tens of thousands of them. The situation in Iraq became a major American political issue, contributing to the loss of the Republican congressional majority in the 2006 elections. As we shall see later in this chapter, a new military strategy began in 2007 than improved conditions in Iraq.

The Defense Budget

There are two important things to know: how much money we spend and how it is divided up. The first reflects majoritarian politics, the second, interest group bargaining.

Total Spending

Throughout most of our history the United States has not maintained large military forces during peacetime. For instance, the percentage of the gross national product (GNP) spent on defense in 1935, on the eve of World War II, was about the same as it was in 1870, when we were on the eve of nothing in particular. We armed when a war broke out, then we disarmed when the war ended.

But all of that changed after World War II, when defense spending declined sharply but did not return to its prewar levels. And in 1950, our defense expenditures soared again. In that year, we rearmed to fight a war in Korea, but when it was over, we did not completely disarm. The reason was our containment policy toward the Soviet Union. For about 40 years—from the outbreak of the Korean War in 1950 to the collapse of the Soviet Union in 1991—American military spending was driven by our desire to contain the Soviet Union and its allies. The Soviet Union had brought under its control most of Eastern Europe; would it also invade Western Europe? Russia had always wanted access to the oil and warm-water ports of the Middle East; would the Soviets someday invade or subvert Iran or Turkey? The Soviet Union was willing to help North Korea invade South Korea and North Vietnam to invade South Vietnam; would it next use an ally to threaten the United States? Soviet leaders supported "wars of national liberation" in Africa and Latin America; would they succeed in turning more and more nations against the United States?

To meet these threats, the United States built up a military system designed to repel a Soviet invasion of Western Europe and at the same time help allies resist smaller-scale invasions or domestic uprisings. Figure 19.2 depicts the dramatic increase in military spending in 1950. It also shows that even after we decided to have a large military force, there were many ups and downs in the actual level of spending. After the Korean War was over, we spent less; when we became involved in Vietnam, we spent more; when the Soviet Union invaded Afghanistan and we invaded Iraq, we spent more again. These changes in

U.S. Military Intervention in Central America and the Caribbean Since 1950

spending tended to reflect changes in public opinion about the defense budget.

As Figure 19.3 shows, a majority of Americans have said that our defense program is either "about right" or "not strong enough," but other studies show that popular support for spending more money on defense changes from year to year.

After the collapse of the Soviet Union, there has been a debate about defense strategy. Liberals demanded sharp cuts in defense spending, weapons

FIGURE 19.2 Trends in Military Spending (outlays in constant dollars)

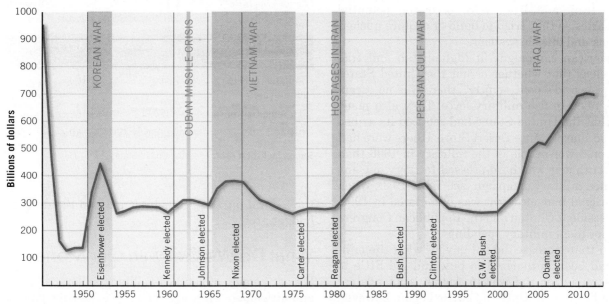

Source: Office of the Under Secretary of Defense (Comptroller), National Defense Budget Annual Estimates and Reports."

FIGURE 19.3   **Most Americans Think National Defense Is Either "About Right" or "Not Strong Enough"**

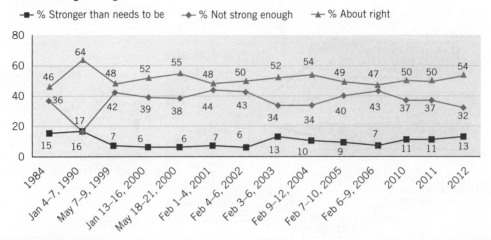

Source: Gallup Poll.

procurement, and military personnel, arguing that with the Soviet threat ended, it was time to collect our "peace dividend" and divert funds from the military to domestic social programs. Conservatives agreed that some military cuts were in order, but they argued that the world was still a dangerous place and therefore that a strong (and well-funded) military remained essential to the nation's defense. This disagreement reflected different predictions about what the future would be like. Many liberals (and some conservatives, such as Pat Buchanan, who believed that America should "stay at home") argued that we could not afford to be the "world's policeman." Many conservatives (and some liberals) responded by saying that Russia was still a military powerhouse that might once again fall under the control of ruthless leaders and that many other nations hostile to the United States (such as North Korea, Iran, and Iraq) were becoming potential adversaries as they tried to build or acquire nuclear weapons and missile systems.

American campaigns in Afghanistan and Iraq made clear that whether or not the United States was the "world's police officer," there was no escaping its need to use military force. They also made clear that the United States had reduced its armed forces so sharply since Desert Storm (there were half a million fewer people in the military in 1996 than in 1991) that it was hard-pressed to carry out any sustained military campaign (see Table 19.3). When the national budget deficit was eliminated in 1999, both President Clinton and the Republican Congress called for more military spending.

But that increase did not pay for what the military had been authorized to buy, and did little to get us ready for the war in Afghanistan against Osama bin Laden. Once the battle began, however,

TABLE 19.3   **U.S. Military Forces Before and After the Breakup of the Soviet Union**

Service	Before 1991	End FY 1998
Army		
Active divisions	18	10
National Guard divisions	10	8
Navy		
Aircraft carriers	15	11
Training carriers	1	2
Ships	546	346
Air Force		
Active fighter wings	24	13
Reserve fighter wings	12	7
Marine Corps		
Active divisions	3	3
Reserve divisions	1	1
Strategic Nuclear Forces		
Ballistic missile submarines	31	18
Strategic bombers	324	182
ICBMs	1,000	550

Source: Statistical Abstract of the United States, 1998, *363*.

the federal purse strings loosened and the defense budget grew.

What Do We Get with Our Money?

We get people, of course—soldiers, sailors, airmen, and airwomen. They are the most expensive part of the defense budget. Then we get hardware of roughly two kinds—big-ticket items, like aircraft carriers and bombers, and small-ticket items, like hammers and screwdrivers. Each of these kinds of hardware has its own politics. Finally, we get "readiness"—training, supplies, munitions, fuel, and food.

Personnel

Efforts to develop our military forces before World War II reflected the considerable American discomfort with a strong central government. The United States did not institute a peacetime draft until 1940, when the rest of the world was already at war, and the draft was renewed the following year (only a few months before Pearl Harbor) by only a one-vote margin in the House. Until 1973, the United States relied on the draft to obtain military personnel. Then, at the end of the Vietnam War, it replaced the draft with the all-volunteer force (AVF). After getting off to a rocky start, the AVF began to improve thanks to increases in military pay and rising civilian unemployment. Abolishing the draft had been politically popular: nobody likes being drafted, and even in congressional districts that otherwise are staunch supporters of a strong defense, voters tell their representatives that they do not want to return to the draft (and many military leaders agree).

There has been a steady increase in the percentage of women in the military (in 2011, they constituted 14.5 percent of the total). For a long time, however, women were barred by law from serving in combat roles. (What constitutes a "combat role" is a bit difficult to say, since even personnel far from the main fighting can be hit by an enemy bomb or artillery shell.) In 1993 Congress ended the legal ban on assigning women to navy combat ships and air force fighter jets, and soon women were serving on three aircraft carriers. Twenty years later, the Pentagon lifted its official ban on women serving in combat. The military's rules on sexual orientation and military service also have changed significantly in the past two decades. Until 1993, it was the long-standing policy of the U.S. armed forces to bar gay and lesbian soldiers from entering the military and to discharge them if they were discovered when serving. Gay and lesbian rights organizations had long protested this exclusion. In 1993, a gay soldier won a lawsuit against the army for having discharged him; he settled for back pay and retirement benefits in exchange for a promise not to re-enlist. In 1993, a judge ordered the navy to reinstate a discharged sailor who had revealed on national television that he was gay. In response to the growing controversy, presidential candidate Bill Clinton promised to lift the official ban on gays and lesbians serving in the military if he were elected to office.

Once in office, he discovered that it was not that easy. Many members of the armed forces believed that knowingly serving alongside and living in close quarters with gays and lesbians would create unnecessary tension and harm military morale and troop solidarity. The Joint Chiefs of Staff opposed lifting the ban, and several key members of Congress said they would try to pass a law reaffirming it. President Clinton was forced to settle for a compromise: "don't ask, don't tell." Under this policy, persons entering or serving in the military would not be asked to reveal their sexual orientation and would be allowed to serve, provided they did not engage in homosexual conduct. If a person stated that he or she was gay, that would not have been automatic grounds for discharge, but it may have been grounds for launching an investigation to determine whether rules against homosexual conduct had been violated.

In 1994, the new Pentagon rules designed to implement "don't ask, don't tell" went into effect, but the challenges of implementation soon prompted calls for ending altogether the prohibition on soldiers revealing their sexual orientation. President Obama signed a law repealing "don't ask, don't tell" in 2010 with the strong support of his secretary of defense and chairman of the Joint Chiefs, who said this would not harm military readiness.

The United States has tried to decide whether to build interceptors like this one to shoot down incoming missiles from enemies.

cost overruns When the money actually paid to military suppliers exceeds the estimated costs.

gold plating The tendency of Pentagon officials to ask weapons contractors to meet excessively high requirements.

Big-Ticket Items

Whenever the Pentagon buys a new submarine, airplane, or missile, we hear about **cost overruns**. In the 1950s, actual costs were three times greater than estimated costs; by the 1960s, things were only slightly better—actual costs were twice estimated costs.

There are five main reasons for these overruns. First, it is hard to know in advance what something that has never existed before will cost once you build it. People who have remodeled their homes know this all too well. So do government officials who build new subways or congressional office buildings. It is no different with a B-2 bomber.

Second, people who want to persuade Congress to appropriate money for a new airplane or submarine have an incentive to underestimate the cost. To get the weapon approved, its sponsors tell Congress how little it will cost; once the weapon is under construction, the sponsors go back to Congress for additional money to cover "unexpected" cost increases.

Third, the Pentagon officials who decide what kind of new aircraft they want are drawn from the ranks of those who will fly it. These officers naturally want the best airplane (or ship or tank) that money can buy. As air force General Carl "Tooey" Spaatz once put it, "A second-best aircraft is like a second-best poker hand. No damn good."[47] But what exactly is the "best" airplane? Is it the fastest one? Or the most maneuverable one? Or the most reliable one? Or the one with the longest range? Pentagon officials have a tendency to answer, "All of the above." Of course, trying to produce all of the above is incredibly expensive (and sometimes impossible). But asking for the expensive (or the impossible) is understandable, given that the air force officers who buy it will also fly it. This tendency to ask for everything at once is called **gold plating**.

Fourth, many new weapons are purchased from a single contractor. This is called sole-sourcing. A contractor is hired to design, develop, and build an airplane. As a result there is no competition, and so the manufacturer has no strong incentive to control costs. And if the sole manufacturer gets into financial trouble, the government, seeking to avoid a shutdown of all production, has an incentive to bail the company out.

Fifth, when Congress wants to cut the military budget, it often does so not by canceling a new weapons system but by stretching out the number of years during which it is purchased. Say that Congress wants to buy one hundred F-22s, twenty-five a year for four years. To give the appearance of cutting the budget, it will decide to buy only fifteen the first year and take five years to buy the rest. Or it will authorize the construction of twenty now and then ask again next year for the authority to build more. But start-and-stop production decisions and stretching out production over more years drives up the cost of building each unit. If Toyota built cars this way, it would go broke.

There are ways to cope with four of these five problems. You cannot do much about the first, ignorance, but you can do something about low estimates, gold plating, sole-sourcing, and stretch-outs. If the Pentagon would give realistic cost estimates initially (perhaps verified by another agency); if it would ask for weapons that meet a few critical performance requirements instead of every requirement that can be thought of; if two or more manufacturers were to compete in designing, developing, and manufacturing new weapons; and if Congress were to stop trying to "cut" the budget using the smoke-and-mirrors technique of stretch-outs, then we would hear a lot less about cost overruns.

Some of these things are being done. There is more competition and less sole-sourcing in weapons procurement today than once was the case. But the political incentives to avoid other changes are very powerful. Pentagon officers will always want "the best." They will always have an incentive to understate costs. Congress will always be tempted to use stretch-outs as a way of avoiding hard budget choices.

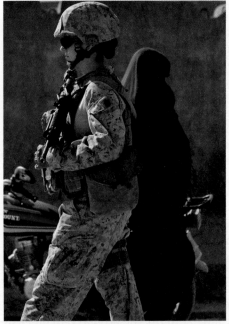

A U.S. Marine goes on patrol in Afghanistan.

Retired Navy commander Zoe Dunning (2nd from left) and her friends celebrate the end of "Don't Ask, Don't Tell" in San Francisco.

Readiness

Presumably, we have a peacetime military so that we will be ready for wartime. Presumably, therefore, the peacetime forces will devote a lot of their time and money to improving their readiness.

Not necessarily. The politics of defense spending is such that readiness often is given a very low priority. Here is why.

Client politics influences the decision. In 1990, Congress was willing to cut almost anything, provided it wasn't built or stationed in some member's district. That doesn't leave much. Plans to stop producing F-14 fighters for the navy were opposed by members from Long Island, where the Grumman manufacturing plant was located. Plans to kill the Osprey aircraft for the Marines were opposed by members from the places where it was to be built. Plans to close bases were opposed by every member with a base in his or her district.

That leaves training and readiness. These things, essential to military effectiveness, have no constituencies and hence few congressional defenders. When forced to choose, the services themselves often prefer to allocate scarce dollars to developing and buying new weapons than to spending for readiness. Moreover, the savings from buying less fuel or having fewer exercises shows up right away, while the savings from canceling an aircraft carrier may not show up for years. Not surprisingly, training and readiness are usually what get the ax.

Bases

At one time, the opening and closing of military bases was pure client politics, which meant that a lot of bases were opened and hardly any were closed. Almost every member of Congress fought to get a base in his or her district, and *every* member fought to keep an existing base open. Even the biggest

congressional critics of the U.S. military, people who would vote to take a gun out of a soldier's hand, would fight hard to keep bases in their districts open and operating.

In 1988, Congress finally concluded that no base would ever be closed unless the system for making decisions was changed. It created a Commission on Base Realignment and Closure (BRAC), consisting of private citizens (originally 12, later 8) who would consider recommendations from the secretary of defense. By law Congress would have to vote within 45 days for or against the commission's list as a whole, without having a chance to amend it. Since 1988, there have been five BRAC reports. Congress approved each one, resulting in the closing of more than 350 bases.

Congress, it appears, has finally figured out how to make some decisions that most members know are right but that each member individually finds it politically necessary to oppose.

The Structure of Defense Decision Making

The formal structure within which decisions about national defense are made was in large part created after World War II, but it reflects concerns that go back at least to the time of the Founding. Chief among these is the persistent desire by citizens to ensure civilian control over the military.

The National Security Act of 1947 and its subsequent amendments created the Department of Defense. It is headed by the secretary of defense, under whom serve the secretaries of the army, the air force, and the navy as well as the Joint Chiefs of Staff. The secretary of defense, who must be a civilian (though one former general, George C. Marshall, was allowed by Congress to be the secretary), exercises, on behalf of the president, command authority over the defense establishment. The secretary of the army, the secretary of the navy,[*] and the secretary of the air force also are civilians and are subordinate to the secretary of defense. Unlike him, they do not attend cabinet meetings or sit on the National Security Council. In essence, they manage the "housekeeping" functions of the various armed services, under the general direction of the secretary of defense and his deputy and assistant secretaries of defense.

The four armed services are separate entities; by law, they cannot be merged or commanded by a single military officer, and each has the right to communicate directly with Congress. There are two reasons

[*]The secretary of the navy manages two services, the navy and the Marine Corps.

for having separate uniformed services functioning within a single department: the fear of many citizens that a unified military force might become too powerful politically, and the desire of each service to preserve its traditional independence and autonomy. The result, of course, is a good deal of interservice rivalry and bickering, but this is precisely what Congress intended when it created the Department of Defense. Rivalry and bickering, it was felt, would ensure that Congress would receive the maximum amount of information about military affairs and would enjoy the largest opportunity to affect military decisions.

Since the end of World War II, Congress has aimed both to retain a significant measure of control over the military's decision making and to ensure the adequacy of the nation's defenses. Congress does not want a single military command headed by an all-powerful general or admiral, but neither does it want the services to be so autonomous or their heads so equal that coordination and efficiency suffer. In 1986, Congress passed and the president signed a defense reorganization plan known as the Goldwater-Nichols Act, which increased the power of the officers who coordinate the activities of the different services. The 1947 structure was left in place, but with revised procedures.

Joint Chiefs of Staff

The Joint Chiefs of Staff (JCS) is a committee consisting of the uniformed heads of each of the military services (the army, navy, air force, and Marine Corps), plus a chairman and a (nonvoting) vice chairman, also military officers, who are appointed by the president and confirmed by the Senate. The JCS does not have command authority over troops, but it plays a key role in national defense planning. Since 1986, the chairman of the joint chiefs has been designated the president's principal military adviser, in an effort to give him more influence over the JCS.

Assisting the JCS is the Joint Staff, consisting of several hundred officers from each of the four services. The staff draws up plans for various military contingencies. Before 1986, each staff member was loyal to the service whose uniform he or she wore. As a result, the staff was often "joint" in name only, since few members were willing to take a position opposed by their service for fear of being passed over for promotion. The 1986 law changed this in two ways: first, it gave the chairman of the JCS control over the Joint Staff; now it works for the chairman, not for the JCS as a group. Second, it required the secretary of defense to establish guidelines to ensure that officers assigned to the Joint Staff (or to other interservice bodies) are promoted at the same rate as officers whose careers are spent entirely with their own services.

The Services

Each military service is headed by a civilian secretary—one for the army, the navy (including the Marine Corps), and the air force—plus a senior military officer: the chief of staff of the army, the chief of naval operations, the commandant of the Marine Corps, and the chief of staff of the air force. The civilian secretaries are in charge of purchasing, auditing, congressional relations, and public affairs. The military chiefs oversee the discipline and training of their uniformed forces and in addition represent their services on the Joint Chiefs of Staff.

The Chain of Command

Under the Constitution the president is the commander-in-chief of the armed forces. The chain of command runs from him to the secretary of defense (also a civilian), and from him to the various unified and specified commands. These orders may be transmitted through the Joint Chiefs of Staff or its chairman, but by law the chairman of the JCS does not have command authority over the combat forces. Civilians are in charge at the top to protect against excessive concentration of power.

No one yet knows how well the 1986 changes will work, though many analysts viewed the quick victory in the 1991 Persian Gulf War as evidence of its success. Critics of the Pentagon have been urging changes along these lines at least since 1947. But others say that unless the armed services are actually merged, interservice rivalry will continue. Still others argue that even the coordination achieved by the 1986 act is excessive. The country, in their view, is better served by having wholly autonomous services. What is striking is that so many members of Congress who once would have insisted on the anticoordination view voted for the 1986 law, thereby indicating a greater willingness to permit some degree of central military leadership.

The New Problem of Terrorism

Since 9/11, both our foreign policy and our military policy have had to focus on terrorism and what to do with nations we have conquered that harbored terrorists. During the cold war, this was easy. For a half century, each president, operating through the National Security Council, made it clear that our chief goal was to prevent the Soviet Union from overrunning Western Europe, bombing the United States, or invading other nations.

But the Soviet Union has disappeared and no other nation has acquired the power to take its place. During the cold war, we lived in a **bipolar world** made up of two superpowers. Now we live in a **unipolar world** made up of the United States as the only superpower. But our superpower status, though it means no other country can challenge us militarily, still leaves us vulnerable here and abroad to terrorist attacks, as 9/11 amply confirms.

To respond, President George W. Bush in September 2002 issued a document that emphasized a new view of our policies. Instead of waiting to be attacked, the president said that

> *bipolar world* A political landscape with two superpowers.
>
> *unipolar world* A political landscape with one superpower.

WHAT WOULD YOU DO?

MEMORANDUM

To: *President Grace Smith*

From: *National security adviser Arjun Luce*

Subject: *Hostages*

The six Americans held hostage in the Middle East are beginning their second year of captivity. One, a CIA officer, is undergoing torture. It has been the policy of this administration not to negotiate with terrorists. Criticism of this refusal is being heard from hostage families and their sympathizers. The terrorist groups are demanding that we end our support of Israel. A government in the region has secretly indicated that, in exchange for military supplies, it may be able to help win the release of "some" hostages.

Your options:

1. Maintain the "no-negotiations" policy but use quiet diplomacy with friendly nations in the region to see whether they can intercede with the terrorist groups on behalf of the hostages.
   Advantages: (a) Our "no-negotiations" policy remains credible, and this will deter other terrorist groups from thinking that they can win concessions by capturing Americans. (b) This policy is consistent with our insistence that U.S. allies not negotiate with terrorists.
   Disadvantages: (a) There is no evidence that our traditional policy will get the hostages released. (b) Public sympathy for the hostages may increase, and this will lead to more criticism of this administration for failing to free captive Americans.

2. Secretly exchange arms for the release of Americans.

News »

American Hostages Begin Second Year of Captivity

Families Urge President to Negotiate Freedom

The families of the six American hostages held captive in the Middle East today criticized the president for failing to win their release.

Advantages: (a) Some or all hostages may be released. (b) We may earn the goodwill of more moderate elements in the area and thereby increase our influence there.
Disadvantages: (a) We may deliver arms and no hostages will be released. (b) If secret arms deliveries become public, we will be heavily criticized for abandoning our "no-negotiations" policy.

3. Use military units to find and free the hostages.
   Advantage: The hostages may be freed without our having to make any concessions.
   Disadvantages: (a) The military is not optimistic that it can find and free the hostages, who are being kept in hidden, scattered sites. (b) The hostages may be killed during the rescue effort.

Your decision:

Option 1 _____   Option 2 _____   Option 3 _____

America "will act against such emerging threats before they are fully formed" because we "cannot defend America and our friends by hoping for the best." We will identify and destroy a terrorist threat "before it reaches our borders" and "we will not hesitate to act alone."[48] In the case of Iraq, this meant a commitment to "regime change"; that is, getting rid of a hostile government, even if the United Nations did not support us.

This has been called a doctrine of preemption; that is, of attacking a determined enemy before it can launch an attack against us or an ally. In fact, it is not really new. President Bill Clinton launched cruise missile strikes against training camps that followers of Osama bin Laden were using in the aftermath of their bombing of American embassies in Kenya and Tanzania in 1998. President Bush elevated the policy of preemption into a clearly stated national doctrine.

Supporters of this view hailed it as a positive step to defeat terrorists abroad before they could attack us at home. Critics attacked the argument as justifying preemptive and possibly unjust wars and abandoning the United Nations. This debate has divided Congress in a way that puts an end to the old adage that partisanship ends at the water's edge.

Since the end of the cold war, we have not had a common enemy that, in the opinion of critics of our overseas efforts, should justify a nonpartisan view. Most liberal Democrats opposed both our effort to get Iraq out of Kuwait in 1991 and our invasion of Iraq in 2003; most Republicans supported both efforts.[49] But when President Clinton launched attacks on hostile forces in Kosovo, he was supported by many liberal Democrats and opposed by many conservative Republicans.[50] Party differences and political ideology now make a big difference in foreign policy.

Sometimes we have sought and obtained United Nations support, as we did when going to war in Korea (1950) and in launching our effort to force Iraqi troops out of Kuwait (1991). We did not seek it in fighting against North Vietnam (in the 1960s), in occupying Haiti (1994), or in going to the assistance of friendly forces in Bosnia (1994) or Kosovo (1999). When we invaded Iraq in 2003, we asked for but did not get UN support; we went anyway, aided by allies such as the United Kingdom and Australia.

After we conquered Afghanistan and Iraq, we faced the problem of rebuilding these nations. The United States has had a lot of experience, some good and some bad, with this problem. We helped put Germany and Japan back on their feet after World War II. From 1992 to 1994, we tried to bring peace among warring factions to Somalia. From 1994 to 1996, we worked to install a democratically elected president and rebuild the local police force in the Caribbean country Haiti. Starting in 1995, we worked with European allies to restore order to Bosnia and Kosovo, located in what used to be Yugoslavia. In 2001, we began helping Afghans create a new government and economy, and in 2003 we started doing the same thing in Iraq.

We succeeded in Germany and Japan, failed in Somalia and Haiti, and made progress in Bosnia and Kosovo.[51]

Iraq and Afghanistan

After easily defeating the Iraqi army in 2003, we tried to bring stability and democracy to the country in mistaken ways. We abolished the Iraqi army (and so had no native defense force), relied on too few American troops (and so could not pacify the country),

HOW THINGS WORK

The Paradoxes of Fighting Insurgents

The U.S. Army Field Manual lists some paradoxes of fighting terrorists and insurgents. It was the manual used during the Iraq War.

Sometimes, the more you protect your force, the less secure you are.

You may be safe staying barricaded in compounds, but you lose contact with the people.

Some of the best weapons for fighting insurgents do not shoot.

Diplomacy, communications, and economic development can be more effective than guns.

Many important decisions are not made by generals.

Teaching lower-ranking personnel how to think and adapt is more important than teaching them what to think.

Sometimes the more force is used, the less effective it is.

Using too much force can hurt civilians and generate sympathy for insurgents.

and kept these troops when they were not fighting in American compounds (thus leaving Iraqi civilians unprotected). Iran funneled arms and terrorists into the country to help attack American soldiers. Public opinion in this country, though deeply divided along party lines, became hostile to our efforts there.

To deal with this problem, President Bush (over the objections of many subordinates) announced a new strategy. We would send another 30,000 troops to Iraq (the "surge") and instruct these troops to work in Iraqi neighborhoods and build alliances with local groups. He assigned General David Petraeus to be our military leader.

The surge worked. Deaths of American forces and Iraqi civilians fell dramatically, an elected Iraqi government began to function effectively, and new Iraqi elections in 2009 were held peacefully. The American government negotiated an agreement with Iraqi leaders that called for withdrawing most American troops from the country by 2011. Because of this progress and because our economy went into a recession, American public opinion began to lose interest in Iraq.

Afghanistan is a more difficult problem. Unlike Iraq, it has never been a unified nation and lacks a large middle class or many populous cities. We easily defeated the Taliban regime and managed to put in office a moderate leader. Troops from other nations arrived to help out. But creating an effective central government in a country that has rarely had one and ending terrorist attacks has proved to be a difficult assignment. During the 2008 presidential campaign, Barack Obama promised to send more forces to that country, and beginning in 2009 he did so. By the middle of the year we had 60,000 troops there, but they were not enough. In 2009, the general leading our forces there asked President Obama for another 40,000 troops; the president sent 30,000. In 2011, the Obama administration began to draw down its "surge" in Afghanistan, with plans for withdrawal of most troops by 2014, but the prospects for long-term stability there remained uncertain.

LEARNING OBJECTIVES

1. **Is American foreign policy set by public opinion or elite views?**

   Elite views matter greatly because most Americans pay little attention to foreign affairs most of the time. And on many key issues, the public disagrees with the elite. But when the president sends troops overseas to fight, the public will rally around him.

2. **If only Congress can declare war, why has the president become so powerful in military affairs?**

   The Constitution makes him the commander-in-chief of the military, and the Supreme Court has made it clear that he has great powers on foreign affairs. The president often has sent troops to fight without a declaration of war, but Congress has invariably supported him. Technically, he should get Congress's approval under the War Powers Act, but if Americans are already fighting it would be very hard for Congress to say no.

3. **Should our foreign policy be based on American interests or some conception of human rights?**

   Sometimes this is not a problem because in a few cases a threat to our interests and a violation of human rights coincide. But at other times, they do not. This is a continuing issue that divides American foreign policy elites. In Congress, liberal members supported and conservative ones opposed our intervention in Bosnia and Kosovo even though neither country threatened us; in Iraq, conservative ones supported and many liberal ones opposed our intervention.

TO LEARN MORE

U.S. Army: **www.army.mil**

U.S. Air Force: **www.af.mil**

U.S. Navy: **www.navy.mil**

Central Intelligence Agency: **www.cia.gov**

Department of State: **www.state.gov**

Allison, Graham T. *Essence of Decision: Explaining the Cuban Missile Crisis*. Boston: Little, Brown, 1971. Shows how the decision made by a president during a major crisis was shaped by bureaucratic and organizational factors.

Barnett, Thomas P. M. *The Pentagon's New Map: War and Peace in the Twenty-First Century*. New York: Berkley

Books, 2004. Discusses what America's foreign and military policy should be in the global war against terror.

Commission on the Intelligence Capabilities of the United States Regarding Weapons of Mass Destruction. *Report to the President of the United States.* Washington, D.C.: Government Printing Office, 2005. Thorough examination by a bipartisan group of why American intelligence agencies did not understand Iraq's WMD efforts.

Kissinger, Henry. *White House Years.* Boston: Little, Brown, 1979. A brilliant insider's account of the politics

and tactics of "high diplomacy" during the Nixon administration.

Mead, Walter Russell. *Special Providence.* New York: Knopf, 2001. Argues that American foreign policy, though often criticized, has been remarkably successful.

Mueller, John E. *War, Presidents, and Public Opinion.* New York: Wiley, 1973. Best summary of the relationship between presidential foreign policy decisions and public opinion.

Robyn Beck/AFP/Getty Images

American Democracy, Then and Now

20

LEARNING OBJECTIVES

1. Name three things that for many years kept the agenda of the federal government short.

2. Name three things that have expanded the agenda of the federal government.

3. Contrast three features of the Old System versus the New System of American government.

4. How has the challenge of political leadership changed since the days of the Constitutional Convention?

Like most Americans, you probably worry about some social problems. These might include abortion, crime, drug abuse, civil rights, gun control, homelessness, or school quality. Maybe you have argued about these matters with your friends, discussing what Washington should do about these things. While you argue, remember this: until the mid-20th century all of this talk would have been nonsense. None of these things were matters that people believed the federal government could or should do anything about.

THEN: Restraints on the Growth of Government

When Dwight Eisenhower was president, none of these issues except civil rights was even thought to be a matter for federal policy, and on civil rights Congress didn't do very much. Our national political agenda was very short. During the Eisenhower administration, we decided to build an interstate highway system, admit Alaska and Hawaii into the union, and fight over the power of labor unions. For *eight years,* these were about the only major domestic political issues. The rest of the time, Washington worried about foreign affairs.

This was about what the Founders had expected, though many of them would have objected to some things that were done in the Eisenhower administration. Some would have thought Washington shouldn't build any highways because the Constitution did not authorize Congress to make laws about such matters. The federal government, in their view, should limit itself to war, peace, interstate commerce, establishing a national currency, and delivering the mail. And for a long time, the prevailing interpretation of the Constitution sharply limited what policies the federal government could adopt. The Supreme Court restricted the authority of the government to regulate business and prevented it from levying an income tax. Most important, the Supreme Court refused, with some exceptions, to allow the delegation of broad discretionary power to administrative agencies.

The Supreme Court could not have maintained this position for as long as it did if it had acted in the teeth of popular opposition. But popular opinion was also against the growth of government. It was not thought legitimate for the federal government to intervene deeply in the economy (even the American Federation of Labor, led by Samuel Gompers, resisted federal involvement in labor-management issues). It was certainly not thought proper for Washington to upset racial segregation as it was practiced in both the North and the South. It took constitutional amendments to persuade Congress that it had the authority to levy an income tax or to prohibit the sale of alcoholic beverages. Even in the 1930s, public

opinion polls showed that as many as half the voters were skeptical of a federal unemployment compensation program.

That was the Old System. Today, under the New System, federal politics is not about some small list of problems thought to be truly national; it is about practically everything. It is almost impossible to think of a problem about which Washington has no policy at all or around which it does not carry on intense debates. Listen to radio talk shows, and you will hear discussions about why Washington has a good or bad policy on almost any issue you can imagine.

What is puzzling about this change from the Old System to the New System is that the Constitution is filled with arrangements designed to make it hard, not easy, for the federal government to act. The separation of powers permits the president, Congress, and the courts to check one another; federalism guarantees that states will have an important role to play; and the division of legislative authority between the House and the Senate ensures that each body will be inclined to block the other. To get a new law passed, you have to please a large number of political actors; to get a new one blocked, you only have to convince one congressional committee.

That system made the national government relatively unimportant for many decades. Until well into the 20th century, governors and mayors were more important than the president. Most members of Congress did not serve more than one or two terms in Washington; there didn't seem to be much point in becoming a career legislator because Congress didn't do much, didn't pay much, and wasn't in session for very long.

NOW: Relaxing the Restraints

As we have said, the constraints on federal action have now weakened or disappeared altogether. First, the courts have altered their interpretation of the Constitution in ways that have not only permitted but sometimes even required government action. The Bill of Rights has been extended so that almost all its important provisions are now regarded as applying to the states (by having been incorporated into the due process clause of the Fourteenth Amendment). This means that a citizen can use the federal courts to alter state policy to a greater degree than ever before. (Overturning state laws that ban abortions or require racially separate schools are two important examples of this change.) The special protection the courts once granted property rights has been substantially reduced so that business can be regulated to a greater degree than previously. The Court has permitted Congress to give broad discretionary powers to administrative agencies, allowing bureaucrats to make decisions that once only Congress could make.

Second, public opinion has changed in ways that support an expanded role for the federal government. The public demanded action to deal with the Great Depression (the programs that resulted, such as Social Security, survived in part because the Supreme Court changed its mind about the permissible scope of federal action). Political elites changed their minds faster than the average citizen. Well-educated, politically active people began demanding federal policies regarding civil rights, public welfare, environmental protection, consumer safety, and foreign aid well before the average citizen became concerned with such things.

Once in place, most of these programs proved popular, so their continuance was supported by mass as well as elite opinion. The cumulative effect of this process was to blur, if not erase altogether, the line that once defined what the government had the authority to do. At one time, a new proposal was debated in terms of whether it was *legitimate* for the federal government to do it all. Federal aid to education, for example, usually was opposed because many people feared it would lead to federal control of local schools. But after so many programs (including federal aid to education) had been passed, people stopped arguing about whether a certain policy was legitimate and argued instead about whether it was *effective*.

Third, political resources have become more widely distributed. The number and variety of interest groups have increased enormously. The funds available from foundations for organizations pursuing specific causes have grown. It is now easier to get access to the federal courts than formerly was the case, and once in the courts the plaintiffs are more likely to encounter judges who believe that the law and the Constitution should be interpreted broadly to permit particular goals (for example, prison reform) to be attained by legal rather than legislative means. Hundreds of magazines, newsletters, and web sites have arisen to provide policy information to specialized segments of opinion. The techniques of mass protest, linked to the desire of television to show visually interesting accounts of social conflict, have been perfected in ways that convey the beliefs of a few into the living rooms of millions.

Campaign finance laws and court rulings have given legal status and constitutional protection to thousands of political action committees (PACs) that raise and spend tens of millions of dollars from millions of small-time contributors. College education, once the privilege of a tiny minority, has become the common experience of millions of people, so that the effects of college—in encouraging political participation and in shaping political beliefs (usually in a

liberal direction)—are now widely shared. The ability of candidates to win nomination for office no longer depends on their ability to curry favor with a few powerful bosses; it now reflects their skill at raising money, mobilizing friends and activists, cultivating a media image, and winning a primary election.

So great have been the changes in the politics of policymaking in this country starting in the 1930s that we can refer, with only slight exaggeration, to one policymaking system having been replaced by another (see Table 20.1).

The Old System

The Old System had a small agenda. Though people voted at a high rate and often took part in torch-light parades and other mass political events, political leadership was professionalized in the sense that the leadership circle was small, access to it was difficult, and the activists in social movements generally were kept out. Only a few major issues were under discussion at any time. A member of Congress had a small staff (if any at all), dealt with his or her colleagues on a personal basis, deferred to the prestige of House and Senate leaders, and tended to become part of some stable coalition (the farm bloc, the labor bloc, the southern bloc) that persisted across many issues.

When someone proposed adding a new issue to the public agenda, a major debate often arose over whether it was legitimate for the federal government to take action at all on the matter. A dominant theme in this debate was the importance of "states' rights." Except in wartime, or during a very brief period when the nation expressed interest in acquiring colonies, the focus of policy debate was on domestic affairs. Members of Congress saw these domestic issues largely in terms of their effect on local constituencies. The presidency was small and

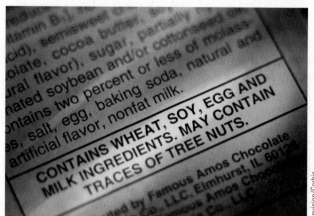

Food products now contain health warnings, such as one for nuts in this package of cookies.

TABLE 20.1 **How American Politics Has Changed**

Old System	Congress	New System
Chairs relatively strong		Chairs relatively weak
Small staffs		Large staffs
Few subcommittees		Many subcommittees
	Interest Groups	
A few large blocs (farmers, business, labor)		Many diverse interests that form ad hoc coalitions
Rely on "insider" lobbying		Mobilize grassroots
	Presidency	
Small staff		Large staff
Reaches public via press conferences		Reaches public via radio, television, and internet
	Courts	
Allow government to exercise few economic powers		Allow government to exercise broad economic power
Take narrow view of individual freedoms		Take broad view of individual freedoms
	Political Parties	
Dominated by state and local party leaders meeting in conventions		Dominated by activists chosen in primaries and caucuses
	Policy Agenda	
Brief		Long
	Key Question	
Should the federal government enter a new policy area?		How can we fix and pay for an existing policy?
	Key Issue	
Would a new federal program abridge states' rights?		Would a new federal program prove popular?

© Cengage Learning

somewhat personal; there was only a rudimentary White House staff. The president would cultivate the press, but there was a clear understanding that what he said in a press conference was never to be quoted directly.

For the government to take bold action under this system, the nation usually had to be facing a crisis. War presented such crisis, and so the federal government during the Civil War and World Wars I and II acquired extraordinary powers to conscript soldiers, control industrial production, regulate the flow of information to citizens, and restrict the scope of personal liberty. Each succeeding crisis left the government bureaucracy somewhat larger than it had been before, but when the crisis ended, the exercise of extraordinary powers ended. Once again, the agenda of political issues became small, and legislators argued about whether it was legitimate for the government to enter some new policy area, such as civil rights or industrial regulation.

The New System

The New System began in the 1930s but did not take its present form until the 1970s. It is characterized by a large policy agenda, the end of the debate over the legitimacy of government action (except in the area of First Amendment freedoms), the diffusion and decentralization of power in Congress, and the multiplication of interest groups. The government has grown so large that it has a policy on almost every conceivable subject, and so the debate in Washington is less often about whether it is right and prudent to take some bold new step and more often about how the government can best cope with the strains and problems that arise from implementing existing policies. As someone once said, the federal government is now more concerned with managing than with ruling.

For example, in 1935 Congress debated whether the nation should have a Social Security system at all; in the 1980s, it debated whether the system could best be kept solvent by raising taxes or by cutting benefits; in 2004 and 2005, it debated whether some part of each person's Social Security payments could be invested in the stock market. In the 1960s, Congress argued over whether there should be any federal civil rights laws at all; by the 1980s and 1990s, it was arguing over whether those laws should be administered in a way that simply eliminated legal barriers to equal opportunity for racial minorities or in a way (by affirmative action) that made up for the disadvantages that burdened such minorities in the past. As late as the 1950s, the president and Congress argued over whether it was right to adopt a new program if it meant the government had to borrow money to pay for it. As late as the 1960s, many members of Congress believed the federal government had no business paying for the health care of its citizens; today hardly anyone argues against having Medicare, but many worry about how best to control its rising cost.

The differences between the Old and New Systems should not be exaggerated. The Constitution still makes it easier for Congress to block the proposals of the president, or for some committee of Congress to defeat the preferences of the majority of Congress, than in almost any other democratic government. The system of checks and balances operates as before. The essential differences between the Old and the New Systems are these:

1. Under the Old System, the checks and balances made it difficult for the federal government to *start* a new program, and so the government remained relatively small. Under the New System, these checks and balances have made it hard to *change* what the government is already doing, and so the government has remained large.

2. Under the Old System, power was *somewhat centralized* in the hands of party and congressional leaders. There was still plenty of conflict, but the number of people who had to agree before something could be done was not large. Under the New System, power is much more *decentralized,* and so it is harder to resolve conflict because so many more people—party activists, interest group leaders, individual members of Congress, heads of government agencies—must agree.

The transition from the Old to the New System occurred chiefly during two periods in American politics. The first was in the early 1930s, when a catastrophic depression led the government to explore new ways of helping the needy, regulating business, and preventing a recurrence of the disaster. Franklin Roosevelt's New Deal was the result. The huge majorities enjoyed by the Democrats in Congress, coupled with popular demands to solve the problem, led to a vast outpouring of new legislation and the creation of dozens of new government agencies. Though initially the Supreme Court struck down some of these measures as unconstitutional, a key member of the Court changed his mind and others retired from the bench; by the late 1930s, the Court had virtually ceased opposing any economic legislation.

The second period was in the mid-1960s, a time of prosperity. There was no crisis akin to the Great Depression or World War II, but two events helped change the face of American politics. One was an intellectual and popular ferment that we now refer to as the spirit of "the sixties"—a militant civil rights movement, student activism on college campuses aimed at resisting the Vietnam War, growing concern about threats to the environment, the popular appeal of Ralph Nader and his consumer protection movement, and an optimism among many political and intellectual leaders that the government could solve whatever problems it was willing to address. The other was the 1964 election that returned Lyndon Johnson to the presidency with a larger share of the popular vote than any other president in modern times. Johnson swept into office, and with him came liberal Democratic majorities in both the House and Senate.

The combination of organized demands for new policies, elite optimism about the likely success of those policies, and extraordinary majorities in Congress meant that President Johnson was able, for a few years, to get almost any program he wanted enacted into law. So large were his majorities in Congress that the conservative coalition of Republicans and southern Democrats was no longer large enough to block action; northern Democratic liberals were sufficiently numerous in the House and Senate to take control of both bodies. Consequently, much of Johnson's "Great Society" legislation became law. This included the passage of Medicare (to help pay the medical bills of retired people) and Medicaid (to help pay the medical bills of people on welfare); greatly expanded federal aid to the states (to assist them in fighting crime, rebuilding slums, and running transit systems); the enactment of major civil rights laws and of a program to provide federal aid to local schools; the creation of a "War on Poverty" that included various job-training and community-action agencies; and the enactment of a variety of laws regulating business for the purpose of reducing auto fatalities, improving the safety and health of industrial workers, cutting back on pollutants entering the atmosphere, and safeguarding consumers from harmful products.

These two periods—the early 1930s and the mid-1960s—changed the political landscape in America. Of the two, the latter was perhaps the more

The federal government bailed out the U.S. automobile industry in 2009 to help companies avoid bankruptcy.

important, for not only did it witness the passage of so much unprecedented legislation, but also it saw major changes in the pattern of political leadership. It was during this time that the great majority of the members of the House of Representatives came to enjoy relatively secure seats, the primary elections came to supplant party conventions as the decisive means of selecting presidential candidates, interest groups increased greatly in number, and television began to play an important role in shaping the political agenda and perhaps influencing the kinds of candidates nominated.

Consequences of Government Growth

One way of describing the New System is to call it an "activist" government. It is tempting to make a sweeping judgment about such a government, either praising it because it serves a variety of popular needs or condemning it because it is a bureaucratic affliction. Such generalizations are not entirely empty, but neither are they very helpful. The worth of any given program, or of any collection of programs, can be assessed only by a careful consideration of its costs and benefits, of its effects and side effects. But we may discover some general political consequences of the enlarged scope of government activity.

First, as the government gets bigger, its members must spend more time managing the

consequences—intended and unintended—of existing programs and less time debating at length new ideas. As a result, all parts of the government, not just the executive agencies, become more bureaucratized. The White House Office and the Office of Management and Budget (OMB) grow in size and influence, as do the staffs of Congress. At the same time, private organizations (corporations, unions, universities) that deal with the government must also become more bureaucratic. The government hires more people when it is running 80 programs concerned with employment than when it is running two. By the same token, a private employer will hire (and give power to) more people when it is complying with 80 sets of regulations than when it is complying with two.

Second, the more government does, the more it will appear to be acting in inconsistent, uncoordinated, and cumbersome ways. When people complain of red tape, bureaucracy, stalemates, and confusion, they often assume these irritants are caused by incompetent or self-seeking public officials. There is incompetence and self-interest in government just as in every other part of society, but these character traits are not the chief cause of the problem. As citizens, we want many different and often conflicting things. The result is the rise of competing policies, the division of labor among separate administrative agencies, the diffusion of accountability and control, and the multiplication of paperwork. And because Americans are especially energetic about asserting their rights, we must add to the above list of problems the regular use of the courts to challenge policies that we do not like.

Third, an activist government is less susceptible to control by electoral activity than a passive one. When the people in Washington did little, elections made a larger difference in policy than when they began to do a lot. We have pointed out in this book the extent to which both political parties and voter turnout have declined. There are many reasons for this, but an important one often is forgotten. If elections make less of a difference—because the few people for whom one votes can do little to alter the ongoing programs of government—then it may make sense for people to spend less time on party or electoral activities and more on interest group activities aimed at specific agencies and programs.

The rapid increase in the number and variety of interest groups and their enlarged role in government are not pathological. They are a rational response to the fact that elected officials can tend to only a few things, and therefore we must direct our energies at the appointed officials (and judges) who tend to all other government matters. Every president tries to accomplish more, usually by trying to reorganize the executive branch. But no president and no reorganization plan can affect more than a tiny fraction of the millions of federal employees and thousands of government programs. "Coordination" from the top can at best occur selectively, for a few issues of exceptional importance.

Ronald Reagan learned this when he took office in 1981 after promising to reduce the size of government. He did persuade Congress to cut taxes and increase defense spending, but his plans to cut domestic spending resulted in only small declines in some programs and actual increases in many others. Though some programs, such as public housing, were hard hit, most were not, and agricultural subsidies increased dramatically.

When George W. Bush became president in 2001, his philosophy was summarized by the phrase "compassionate conservatism," words that implied that, though he was a conservative, he was not much interested in simply cutting the size of the federal government. And while in office, he proposed policies that would increase spending on many programs. His actions suggest a fact: cutting down on what Washington does is virtually impossible because the people want so much of what it does.

Finally, the more government tries to do, the more things it will be held responsible for and the greater the risk of failure. From time to time in the 19th century, the business cycle made many people unhappy with the federal government—recall the rise of various protest parties—though then the government did very little. If federal officials were lucky, popular support would rise as soon as economic conditions improved. If they were unlucky and a depression lasted into the election campaign, they would be thrown out of office. Today, however, the government—and the president in particular—is held responsible for crime, drug abuse, abortion, civil rights, the environment, the elderly, the status of women, the decay of central cities, the price of gasoline, and international tensions in half a dozen places around the globe.

No government and no president can do well on all or even most of these matters most of the time. Indeed, most of these problems, such as crime, may be totally beyond the reach of the federal government, no matter what its policy. It should not be surprising, therefore, that opinion surveys taken since the early 1960s have shown a steep decline in public confidence in government. There is no reason to believe that this represents a loss of faith in our form of government or even in the design of its institutions, but it clearly reflects a disappointment in, and even cynicism about, the performance of government.

It is too soon to know how, if at all, public sentiments about the performance of government will change as Washington (in response to the 2008–2009 economic crisis) has expanded government activity faster than it has grown in any periods since the late 1930s and the mid-1960s. President Barack Obama proposed a budget for Fiscal Year 2012 that contemplated a deficit of $1.645 trillion. Congressional Republicans, who won control of the House in 2010, objected. After long negotiations with the White House, the two sides agreed on a compromise that made some cuts in spending, thereby avoiding a shutdown of the federal government until November 2011. The large spending increases, however, are only half the story. The other half concerns the federal government taking on new responsibilities and challenges: It has become the majority stockholder in what was once the world's largest automotive company, General Motors; it has more closely controlled dozens of other companies and diverse financial markets; and it has enacted a large, new government-regulated health care system.

University of Maryland political scientist Donald F. Kettl has argued that the "financial meltdown accelerated our expectations that government will keep us safe. ... We've gone from debates over privatizing the public sector to big steps toward governmentalizing the private sector."[1] The far-reaching changes include "more public money in the private economy, more rules to shape how the private sector behaves, and more citizen expectations that government will manage the risks we face."[2]

We cannot yet say whether multi-trillion-dollar budget deficits and policies that betoken

WHAT WOULD YOU DO?

MEMORANDUM

To: *President Daniel Gilbert*

From: *Fowler Brown, legislative liaison*

Subject: *Replacing Social Security*

You face a difficult decision. Despite past reforms, the program can no longer be funded without large tax increases. Here are the arguments for and against allowing workers to invest their taxes in private mutual funds.

Arguments for:

1. Workers pay 15 percent of their salary to Social Security, with no guarantee that they will get their money back when they retire.

2. There are only two workers for every retired person (in the 1930s, there were 16 for every retiree). People must be encouraged to invest in their own retirement.

3. The federal government spends a quarter of its budget on Social Security, far more than it devotes to national defense.

News »

Policies for the Future

The President will make a major announcement about Social Security in his 2021 State of the Union message next week. The program, while popular, is running out of money.

Arguments against:

1. Workers will have no guarantee that the mutual funds in which they put their tax money will earn them enough.

2. We should raise taxes on all high-income workers to save Social Security.

3. Social Security is more important than national defense.

Your decision:

Approve _____   Oppose _____

---

government-guaranteed corporate capitalism will persist for years to come. But it seems a fair bet that the New System is entering a new era which, not unlike the expansion that began in the late 1930s, has been fueled by economic problems that have afflicted or threatened most Americans.

It also seems likely that, if anything, public disenchantment with government performance will continue to grow along with government's role in people's lives. Such disenchantment is hardly unique to the United States; it appears to be a feature of almost every democratic political system. The disenchantment is in fact probably greater elsewhere. Americans who complain of high taxes might feel somewhat differently if they lived in Sweden, where taxes are nearly twice as high as here. Those who grouse about bureaucrats in this

country probably have never dealt with the massive, centralized bureaucracies of Italy or France. People who are annoyed by congestion, pollution, and inflation ought to arrange a trip to Beijing, Mexico City, or Tokyo. However frustrating private life and public affairs may be in this country, every year thousands living in other nations immigrate to this country. Few Americans choose to migrate to other places.

The enormous expansion of the scope and goals of the federal government has not been random or unguided. The government has tended to enlarge its powers more in some directions than in others; certain kinds of goals have been served more frequently than others. Though many factors shape this process of selection, two are of special importance. One is our constitutional structure, and the other our political culture.

The 2009 stimulus bill allowed people to get money if they traded in an old car that burned a lot of gas.

The Influence of Structure

To see the influence of structure, it is necessary to perform a mental experiment. Suppose the Founders had adopted a centralized, parliamentary regime instead of a decentralized, congressional one. They had the British model right before their eyes. Every other European democracy adopted it. What difference would it have made had we followed the British example?

No one can be certain, of course, because the United States and the United Kingdom differ in many ways, and not just in their political forms. At best, our mental experiment will be an educated guess. But the following possibilities seem plausible.

A parliamentary regime of the British sort centralizes power in the hands of an elected prime minister with a disciplined partisan majority in the legislature and frees him or her from most of the constraints created by independent congressional committees or independent, activist courts. Had the Framers adopted a parliamentary system, we might see these features in the political life of the United States today:

- *Quicker adoption of majoritarian policies, such as those in the area of social welfare.* Broad popular desires would be translated sooner into national policy when they are highly salient and conform to the views of party leaders.

- *More centralization of bureaucratic authority—more national planning, and less local autonomy.* More decisions would be made bureaucratically, both because bureaucracies would be proportionately larger and because they would have wider discretionary authority delegated to them. (If the prime minister heads *both* the executive branch and the legislature, he or she sees no reason why decisions cannot be made as easily in one place as

the other.) Local authorities would not have been able to prevent groups of citizens (such as African Americans) from voting or otherwise participating in public life by maintaining segregated facilities at the local level.

- *Fewer opportunities for citizens to challenge or block government policies of which they disapprove.* Without independent and activist courts, without local centers (state and city) of autonomous power, U.S. citizens would have less of a chance to organize to stop a highway or an urban-renewal project, for example, and hence fewer citizen organizations with these and similar purposes would exist.

- *Greater executive control of government.* If a situation like Watergate occurred, we would never know about it. No legislative investigating committees would be sufficiently independent of executive control to be able to investigate claims of executive wrongdoing.

- *Similar foreign policy.* We probably would have fought in about the same number of wars and under pretty much the same circumstances.

- *Higher and more centralized taxation.* Taxes would be higher, and a larger share of our tax money would be collected at the national level. Thus we would find it harder to wage a "tax revolt" (since it is easier to block local spending decisions than national ones).

If this list of guesses is even approximately correct, it means that you would get more of some things that you want and less of others. In general, it would be easier for temporary majorities to govern and harder for individuals and groups to protect their interests.

The Founders would probably not be surprised at this list of differences. Though they could not have foreseen all the events and issues that would have led to these outcomes, they would have understood them, because they thought they were creating a system designed to keep central power weak and to enhance local and citizen power. They would have been amazed, of course, at the extent to which central power has been enhanced and local power weakened in the United States, but if they visited Europe, they would learn that, by comparison, American politics remains far more sensitive to local concerns than does politics abroad.

The Influence of Ideas

The broadly shared political culture of Americans has also influenced the policies adopted by the U.S. government. Paramount among these attitudes is the preoccupation with rights. More than the citizens of perhaps any other nation, Americans define their relations with one another and with political authority in terms of rights. The civil liberties protected by the Bill of Rights have been assiduously defended and their interpretation significantly broadened even while the power of government has been growing.

For example, we expect that the groups affected by any government program will have a right to play a role in shaping and administering that program. In consequence, interest groups have proliferated. We think citizens should have the right to select the nominees of political parties as well as to choose between the parties; hence primary elections have largely replaced party conventions in selecting candidates. Individual members of Congress assert their rights, and thus the power of congressional leaders and committee chairs has steadily diminished. We probably use the courts more frequently than the citizens of any other nation to make or change public policy; in doing so, we are asserting one set of rights against a competing set. The procedural rules that set forth how government is to act—the Freedom of Information Act, the Privacy Act, the Administrative Procedure Act—are more complex and demanding than the rules under which any other democratic government must operate. Each rule exists because it embodies what somebody has claimed to be a right: the right to know information, to maintain one's privacy, to participate in making decisions, and to bring suit against rival parties.

The more vigorously we assert our rights, the harder it is to make government decisions or to manage large institutions. We recognize this when we grumble about red tape and bureaucratic confusion, but we rarely give much support to proposals to centralize authority or simplify decision making. We seem to accept whatever it costs in efficiency or effectiveness in order to maintain the capacity for asserting our rights.

We do not always agree on which rights are most important, however. In addition to the influence of the widely shared commitment to rights generally, government is also shaped by the views that certain political elites have about which rights ought to be given the highest priority. Elite opinion tends to favor freedom of expression over freedom to manage or dispose of property. Mass opinion, though it has changed a good deal in the last few decades, is less committed to the preferred position of freedom of expression. Rank-and-file citizens often complain that what the elite calls essential liberty should instead be regarded as excessive permissiveness. People who own or manage property often lament the extent to which the rights governing its use have declined.

The changes in the relative security of personal and property freedom are linked to a fundamental and enduring tension in American thought. Tocqueville said it best: Americans, he wrote, "are far more ardently and tenaciously attached to equality than to freedom." Though democratic communities have a "natural taste for freedom," that freedom is hard to preserve, because its excesses are immediate and obvious and its advantages are remote and uncertain. The advantages of equality, on the other hand, are readily apparent, and its costs are obscure and deferred.[3] For example, Americans believe in free speech, but most of us rarely take advantage of that right and notice the problem only when somebody says something we don't like. We have to remind ourselves that freedom has to be protected even when it does not help us directly. By contrast, we notice equality immediately, as when everybody of a certain age gets Social Security even when they are already rich. Equality makes us feel comfortable even if a few people don't need the benefits they are getting.

Tocqueville, however, may have underestimated the extent to which political liberties would endure, because he did not foresee the determination of the courts to resist, in the long run if not the short, the passions of temporary majorities seeking to curtail such liberties. But he did not underestimate the extent to which in the economic and social realms Americans would decide that improving the conditions of life would justify restrictions on the right to dispose of property and to manage private institutions. At first, the conflict was between liberty and equality of opportunity; more recently it has become a conflict—among political elites if not within the citizenry itself—between equality of opportunity and equality of results.

The fact that decisions can be influenced by opinions about rights indicates that decisions can be influenced by opinions generally. As the political system has become more fragmented and more individualized as a result of our collective assertion of rights, it has come more under the sway of ideas. When political parties were strong and congressional leadership was centralized (as in the latter part of the 19th and the early part of the 20th centuries), gaining access to the decision-making process in Washington was difficult, and the number of new ideas that stood a chance of adoption was small. However, those proposals that could command leadership support were more easily adopted: though there were powerful organizations that could say no, those same organizations could also say yes.

Today, these and other institutions are fragmented and in disarray. Individual members of Congress are far more important than congressional leaders. Political parties no longer control

HOW WE COMPARE

Deficit Spending in America and Europe

From 1800 to 1932, the federal government had an annual budget deficit about one-third of the time. In that 132-year stretch, the federal government had large and consecutive annual budget deficits only during the Civil War and again during World War I. From the dawn of the New Deal in 1933 to the eve of the Great Society in 1964, the federal government had an annual budget deficit about five-sixths of the time. Deficit spending soared during World War II, and it was only in each of five subsequent pre-1965 years (1947, 1948, 1956, 1957, and 1960) that the federal budget was in surplus. From 1965 to 2013, a 49-year period, the federal government had an annual budget surplus in each of only two years (1999 and 2000).

America is not the only modern democracy to have settled into a persistent pattern of annual deficit spending, or to run annual deficits that are large relative to the nation's economy. For instance, in 2010, the federal deficit was about 10.7 percent of U.S. Gross Domestic Product. Here are that year's comparable figures for a host of European democracies:

Nation	Deficit as a percentage of Gross Domestic Product
Ireland	32.4%
Greece	10.5
United Kingdom	10.5
Spain	9.2
Portugal	9.1
Poland	7.9
France	7.0
Denmark	2.7
Finland	2.4
Sweden	0.0

Source: Office of Management and Budget, *Historical Tables: Fiscal Year 2011*, Table 1.1, pp. 21–23; "EU States with the Biggest Deficits and Debts," *Telegraph*, April 26, 2011, reporting data from Eurostat.

spending money. Forming new, issue-oriented lobbying groups is much easier today than formerly, thanks to the capability of computers and direct-mail advertising.

These idea-based changes in institutions affect how policy is made. When there is widespread enthusiasm for an idea—especially among political elites but also in the public at large—new programs can be formulated and adopted with great speed. This happened when Lyndon Johnson's Great Society legislation was proposed, when the environmental and consumer protection laws first arrived on the public agenda, and when campaign finance reform was proposed in the wake of Watergate. So long as such symbols have a powerful appeal, so long as a consensus persists, change is possible. But when these ideas lose their appeal—or are challenged by new ideas—the competing pressures make change extremely difficult. Environmentalism today is challenged by concerns about creating jobs and economic growth; social legislation is challenged by skepticism about its effectiveness and concern over its cost; campaign finance reforms are, to some critics, merely devices for protecting incumbents.

This may all seem obvious to a reader raised in the world of contemporary politics. But it is different in degree if not in kind from the way in which politics was once carried out. In the 1920s, the 1930s, the 1940s, and even the 1950s, people described politics as a process of bargaining among organized interests, or "blocs," representing business, farming, labor, ethnic, and professional groups. With the expansion of the scope of government policy, there are no longer a few major blocs that sit astride the policy process. Instead, thousands of highly specialized interests and constituencies seek above all to protect whatever benefits, intangible as well as tangible, they get from government.

American Democracy—Then, Now, and Next

We have a large government—and large expectations about what it can achieve. But the government finds it increasingly difficult to satisfy those expectations. The public's acceptance of a larger and larger role for government has been accompanied by a decline in public confidence in those who lead and manage that government. We expect more and more from government but are less and less certain that we will get it, or get it in a form and at a cost that we find acceptable. This perhaps constitutes the greatest challenge to political leadership in the years ahead: to find a way to serve the true interests of the people while restoring and retaining

nominations for office. The media have given candidates direct access to the voters; campaign finance laws have restricted, but not eliminated, the influence that interest groups can wield by their confidence in the legitimacy of government itself. We might begin by challenging the increasingly popular notion that present-day American democracy's problems are so deep because its political leaders are so shallow, not least by comparison to the nation's first leaders.

THEN

When the Constitution was created and ratified, national leaders beholden only to their own consciences could meet in secret to debate and decide even the most controversial and consequential questions about government. They could belittle, berate, or battle each other one day, and beseech, bargain, or broker deals with each other the next day, all without their words or deeds (or misdeeds) being a matter of public record or widely known at all.

NOW

In stark contrast, the political leaders that today hold office under the terms of that same Constitution, amended only 27 times in more than 220 years, must deliberate and legislate while the whole world—friend and foe alike—is listening and watching. Contemporary presidents and congresspersons face the challenge of leading a large and diverse population, coping with an all-pervasive mass communications media, and steering a federal government that is far bigger, and administered in a way that is far more complicated, than any of the Constitution's authors ever envisioned.

As a class, today's elected officials at both ends of Pennsylvania Avenue and in both parties are often much-maligned, not only, at times, by each other and by their other respective partisan and ideological opponents, but by the public at large, with majorities disparaging the "politicians" about as readily as they denounce the "bureaucrats." But now reflect seriously on questions like the following:

- How do you suppose James Madison, George Washington, or the other authors of the Constitution would have fared if they had led, not a slave-holding society of barely 4 million people, but a demographically diverse and free society of more than 300 million people?

- How do you think the nation's early political leaders, bitterly divided over the Constitution as they were (see Chapter 2), would have held up had they faced anything like the incessant public stare and media glare that Democratic President Barack Obama and Republican President George W. Bush, Republican House Speaker John Boehner and Democratic House Speaker Nancy Pelosi,

and other present-day national political leaders now routinely face even when not battling with each other?

- Do you believe that American democracy's first generation of leaders would in our present-day context come any closer than today's leaders have come to forging a national consensus and getting decisive action on difficult issues like the federal government's annual budget deficits and the growing national debt?

- As contentious and complicated as the debates over federalism (see Chapter 3) were when the republic was founded, do you think that those who forged the compromises that then defined federal–state relations would be significantly more effective than today's federal, state, and local public officials are when it comes to ensuring that the more than $600 billion a year that Washington now spends on grants to state and local governments for social welfare (see Chapter 17) and other public purposes is all money well spent?

- And do you suppose that earlier generations of leaders would be any more adept than today's leaders are when it comes to ensuring that the private, for-profit firms and nonprofit organizations that are a big part of today's proxy-government system of public administration (see Chapter 15) serve the public well?

We suspect that Madison himself, if he were returned to our political moment in time, might conclude that exercising effective leadership now is even harder than it was then.

Regardless, the next chapters in the still-unfolding story of American democracy remain to be written by the nation's next generation of leaders including, we hope, some students whose interest in politics, government, and public policy was stirred in part by this book.

- At each level of government, whatever one's party or policy preferences, to be a public-spirited "politician" that wins elected office and participates in the democratic legislative process, or to be a judge responsible for interpreting and applying laws including in cases that involve civil liberties (see Chapter 5) and civil rights (see Chapter 6), is to live a truly noble calling.

- To be a "bureaucrat"—a career public servant—that serves the public by responsibly translating democratically enacted laws on health, housing, trade, transportation, education, environmental protection, nuclear energy, or any other policy area into administrative action is a truly noble calling, too.

- And, for those who, like most people, are called instead to careers in business, the arts, or other fields, to yet be an engaged citizen of American democracy, to seek to know ever more about American government, political institutions, and public policies, is a most worthy intellectual and civic pastime.

So, we end with words from *Federalist* No. 51 that should remind us all why the subject you have been studying with the aid of this book is so important:

Justice is the end of government. It is the end of civil society. It ever has been and ever will be pursued until it be obtained, or until liberty be lost in the pursuit.

LEARNING OBJECTIVES

1. Name three things that for many years kept the agenda of the federal government short.

The Supreme Court restricted the ability of Congress to delegate broad discretionary powers to administrative agencies.
Public opinion supported the idea of a limited federal government.
Washington could not levy an income tax.

2. Name three things that have expanded the agenda of the federal government.

The Supreme Court has allowed the delegation of broad discretionary powers to top administrative agencies.
Public opinion has supported a more activist government.
The Constitution has been amended to allow for an income tax.

3. Contrast three features of the Old System versus the New System of American government.

Old: Congress had strong committee chairpersons, small staffs, and few subcommittees. New: Congress has weak committee chairpersons, large staffs, and many subcommittees.
Old: The courts allowed government to exercise few economic powers and took a narrow view of individual freedoms. New: The courts allow the government many economic powers and take a broad view of individual freedoms.
Old: Political parties were dominated by local party leaders meeting in conventions. New: Political parties are dominated by activists chosen in primaries and caucuses.

4. How has the challenge of political leadership changed since the days of the Constitutional Convention?

In at least some respects, it has become harder. Unlike the authors of the Constitution and most other previous generations of political leaders, today's presidents and members of Congress make important decisions under intense public scrutiny. They lead a demographically diverse and free society of more than 300 million citizens, with a government that constitutes a much larger share of the nation's economy than any of the Framers ever envisioned, and that touches virtually every facet of contemporary economic, social, and civic life.

Correlation for U.S. Government and Politics to *American Government: Institutions and Policies, 14th Edition*

TOPIC	CORRELATION TO *American Government: Institutions and Policies, 14th Edition*
I. Constitutional Underpinnings of United States Government	
A. Considerations that influenced the formulation and adoption of the Constitution	Pages 23–41, 96, 307–309, 516
B. Separation of powers	Pages 28, 33–35, 41–43, 154, 303, 305, 332–333, 342, 347, 358, 365, 398, 516
C. Checks and balances	Pages 34, 303, 305, 342–343, 347, 385, 409, 431–434, 519
D. Federalism	Pages 33–35, 50–75, 154, 191, 303
E. Theories of democratic government	Pages 5–10, 28–48, 79–80, 82–83, 91

TOPIC	CORRELATION TO *American Government: Institutions and Policies, 14th Edition*
II. Political Beliefs and Behaviors	
A. Beliefs that citizens hold about their government and its leaders	Pages 3–14, 35, 76–94, 153–154, 156–168
B. Processes by which citizens learn about politics	Pages 156–160, 219–221, 230–233, 276–300
C. The nature, sources, and consequences of public opinion	Pages 151–170, 247–249, 26, 432–434
D. The ways in which citizens vote and otherwise participate in political life	Pages 171–187, 241–244, 251–275
E. Factors that influence citizens to differ from one another in terms of political beliefs and behaviors	Pages 4, 10-14, 76–94, 97–100, 121–150, 155–168, 227–233, 251–275

TOPIC	CORRELATION TO *American Government: Institutions and Policies, 14th Edition*
III. Political Parties, Interest Groups, and Mass Media	
A. Political parties and elections	
1. Functions	Pages 189–192, 241–247
2. Organization	Pages 198–211, 221–241
3. Development	Pages 176–181, 192–206
4. Effects on the political process	Pages 188–217, 247–249
5. Electoral Laws and systems	Pages 211–213, 218–250
B. Interest groups, including political action committees (PACs)	
1. The range of interests represented	Pages 252–263
2. The activities of interest groups	Pages 263–271
3. The effects of interest groups on the political process	Pages 9–12, 97–98, 252–275, 396–397, 14–17, 456–457, 466–467
4. The unique characteristics and roles of PACs in the political process	Pages 223, 233–241, 252, 261–262, 265–269
C. The mass media	
1. The functions and structure of the news media	Pages 279–287
2. The impact of the news media on politics	Pages 166, 277–282, 287–297
3. The news media industry and its consequences	Pages 279–297

TOPIC	CORRELATION TO *American Government: Institutions and Policies, 14th Edition*
IV. Institutions of National Government: The Congress, the Presidency, the Bureaucracy, and the Federal Courts	
A. The major formal and informal institutional arrangements of power	Pages 4–10, 32–34, 53–67, 301–337, 338–378, 379–406, 407–436
B. Relationships among these four institutions and varying balances of power	Pages 32–34, 41–43, 53–57, 301–305, 341–345, 352–360, 365–374, 396–400, 408–410, 417–420, 427–434, 492–494, 516–520
C. Linkages between institutions and the following:	
1. Public opinion and voters	Pages 151–170, 181–184, 247–249, 265, 352, 432–434
2. Interest groups	Pages 233–241, 251–275
3. Political parties	Pages 189–192, 241–243, 305–307, 315–322
4. The media	Pages 219–222, 228–233, 276–300
5. State and local governments	Pages 51–75, 176–179, 202–206

TOPIC	CORRELATION TO *American Government: Institutions and Policies, 14th Edition*
V. Public Policy	
A. Policymaking in a federal system	Pages 10–20, 325–332, 437–469, 470–486, 487–514
B. The formation of policy agendas	Pages 10–20, 77–82, 166–168, 211–212, 440–447, 479–484, 516–520
C. The role of institutions in the enactment of policy	Pages 322–332, 341–343, 368–371, 379–406, 409–416, 427–429
D. The role of the bureaucracy and the courts in policy implementation and interpretation	Pages 379–406, 407–436
E. Linkages between policy processes and the following:	
1. Political institutions and federalism	Pages 51–53, 59–63, 10–13
2. Political parties	Pages 189–192, 241–243, 474, 502
3. Interest groups	Pages 251–275, 11–12, 15, 456–457, 466–467, 479, 489
4. Public opinion	Pages 11, 89–93, 164–168, 352–356, 432–434
5. Elections	Pages 12, 241–244, 247–249, 345–347, 352–356, 473, 520–521
6. Policy networks	Pages 396-397, 458–459

TOPIC	CORRELATION TO *American Government: Institutions and Policies, 14th Edition*
VI. Civil Rights and Civil Liberties	
A. The development of civil liberties and civil rights by judicial interpretation	Pages 6, 37–39, 68–69, 97–119, 125–131, 136–137, 139, 144, 145, 408–414, 424–427
B. Knowledge of substantive rights and liberties	Pages 37–39, 80–81, 96–119, 122–148
C. The impact of the Fourteenth Amendment on the constitutional development of rights and liberties	Pages 38–39, 96, 97, 102, 119, 125–129, 134–144, 409–413

Preparing for the AP® Exam

Advanced Placement can be exhilarating. Whether you are taking an AP course at your school or you are working on AP independently, the stage is set for a great intellectual experience. As the school year progresses and you burrow deeper and deeper into the course work, you will begin to make connections between the ideas and concepts that form the basis of government and politics in the United States. Fleshing out those concepts is exciting. More exciting still is recognizing examples of these concepts in the media. More importantly, this course will prepare you to become a participatory citizen and informed voter.

But sometime after New Year's Day, when the examination begins to loom on a very real horizon, Advanced Placement can seem downright intimidating—in fact, offered the opportunity to take the examination for a lark, even adults long out of high school refuse. If you dread taking the test, you are in good company.

The best way to deal with an AP examination is to master it, not let it master you. If you can think of these examinations as a way to show off how your mind works, you have a leg up: attitude *does* help. If you are not one of those students, there is still a lot you can do to sideline your anxiety. Focused review and practice time will help you master the examination so that you can walk in with confidence and get a 5.

Before The Examination

By February, long before the exam, you need to make sure that you are registered to take the test. Many schools take care of the paperwork and handle the fees for their AP students, but check with your teacher or the AP coordinator to make sure that you are on the list. This is especially important if you have a documented disability and need test accommodations. If your family cannot afford to pay the full testing fee, do not be shy. Inform your AP coordinator. Reduced fees are available for those students who qualify. If you are studying AP independently, call AP Services at the College Board for the name of the local AP coordinator, who will help you through the registration process.

The evening before the exam is not a great time for partying. Nor is it a great time for cramming. If you like, look over class notes or drift through your textbook, concentrating on the broad outlines, not the small details, of the course.

The evening before the exam *is* a great time to get your things together for the next day. Sharpen a fistful of no. 2 pencils with good erasers for the multiple-choice section; set out several black or dark-blue ballpoint pens for the free-response questions; get a watch, as cell phones are not allowed in the testing room; get a piece of fruit or a power bar and a bottle of water for the break; make sure you have your Social Security number and whatever photo identification and admission ticket are required. Then relax. And get a good night's sleep.

On the day of the examination it is wise not to skip breakfast—studies show that students who eat a hot breakfast before testing get higher grades. Be careful not to drink a lot of liquids, necessitating a trip to the bathroom during the test. Breakfast will give you the energy you need to power you through the test—and more. You will spend some time waiting while everyone is seated in the right room for the right test, so prepare to be patient. Bring a high-energy snack to eat during the short break between Section I and Section II. The U.S. Government and Politics exam lasts for over two and a half hours. So be prepared for a long morning. You do not want to be distracted by a growling stomach or hunger pangs.

Leave your cell phone at home or in your locker. Be sure to wear comfortable clothes, taking along a sweater in case the heating or air-conditioning is erratic. Be sure, too, to wear clothes you like—everyone performs better when they think they look better—and by all means wear your lucky socks.

Now go get a 5.

Taking the AP® U.S. Government and Politics Exam

The AP U.S. Government and Politics examination consists of two sections: Section I has 60 multiple-choice questions; Section II has four free-response questions. You will have 45 minutes for the multiple-choice portion. The questions are collected, and you will be given a short break. You then have 100 minutes for the free-response portion. You must write an essay for each of the four questions—some AP examinations allow you to choose among the free-response questions, but this is not one of them. Keep an eye on your watch and devote 25 minutes to each free-response question. Watch alarms are not allowed.

Strategies For The Multiple-Choice Section

Here are some rules of thumb to help you work your way through the multiple-choice questions:

- Answer every question There are five possible answers for each question. Each correct answer is worth 1 point. There is no penalty for incorrect answers, so you should answer every question, even if you have to guess. Some students like to go through the exam quickly and answer the questions they know, and then go back to the more difficult questions. If you do this, be sure you mark the correct line on the answer sheet.

- Read the question carefully Pressured for time, many students make the mistake of reading the questions too quickly or merely skimming them. By reading a question carefully, you may already have some idea about the correct answer. You can then look for it in the responses. Careful reading is especially important in EXCEPT questions.

- Eliminate any answer you know is wrong You can write on the multiple-choice questions in the test book. As you read through the responses, draw a line through any answer you know is wrong.

- Read all of the possible answers, then chose the most accurate response AP examinations are written to test your precise knowledge of a subject. Sometimes there are a few probable answers but one of them is more specific. For example, the Fifteenth Amendment gave the vote to African Americans, but only men could vote at that time. An answer that referred to black men would be more correct than an answer that referred to all African Americans.

- Avoid absolute responses These answers often include the words "always" or "never." For example, the statement "Voter turnout in presidential elections is always slightly above 50 percent" is incorrect because in the 1996 presidential election, turnout was a little below 50 percent.

- Mark and skip tough questions If you are hung up on a question, mark it in the margin of the question book. You can come back to it later if you have time. Make sure you skip that question on your answer sheet too.

Types of Multiple-Choice Questions

There are various kinds of multiple-choice questions. Here are some suggestions for how to approach each kind:

Classic/Best Answer Questions

This is the most common type of multiple-choice question. It simply requires you to read the question and select the most correct answer. For example:

1. How is the president of the United States usually selected?
   (A) by direct vote of the populace
   (B) by the House of Representatives
   (C) by the Senate
   (D) in a runoff election between the top two vote getters
   (E) by the Electoral College

ANSWER: E. The Electoral College usually selects the president, although the House of Representatives decides on the rare occasion when no candidate receives a majority of Electoral College votes. The word "usually" is very important in this question. This is a standard question that has one correct answer.

EXCEPT Questions

In the EXCEPT question, all of the answers are correct but one. The best way to approach these questions is as true/false. Mark a T or F in the margin next to each possible answer. There should be only one false answer, and that is the one you should select. For example:

1. Congress has the express power to do all of the following EXCEPT
   (A) lay and collect taxes
   (B) regulate interstate commerce
   (C) establish uniform standards for weights and measures
   (D) declare war
   (E) regulate intrastate commerce

ANSWER: E. Congress does not have the power to regulate intrastate commerce, so that is a false statement. You should have put an "F" next to it. All of the other statements are true.

List and Group Questions

In this type of question, there is a list of possible answers, and you must select the answer that contains the correct group of responses. These questions look hard, but you can simplify them by crossing out items from the list and then eliminating them in the answers below. For example:

1. According to the Constitution, as amended, which of the following is elected directly?

To approach the question, draw a line through choice I, because the president and vice president are not elected directly but are chosen by the Electoral College. Then cross out any response that contains choice I.

   I. the president and vice-president
   II. members of the House of Representatives
   III. justices of the Supreme Court
   IV. senators
   (A) I and II
   (B) II and III
   (C) I, II, and III
   (D) I and IV
   (E) II and IV

Continue to cross out items that are wrong and the responses that contain them. Justices of the Supreme Court are appointed, not elected. Draw a line through III and answer (B), which contains choice III, as well as through (C), which also contains choice III. Now you have narrowed down the possible responses.

ANSWER: E. Under the Constitution, including the Seventeenth Amendment, which provides for the direct election of senators, members of the House of Representatives and Senate are elected directly.

Chart/Graph Questions

These questions require you to examine the data on a chart or graph. While these questions are not difficult, spending too much time interpreting a chart or graph may slow you down. If a chart or graph is particularly difficult or detailed, consider skipping it and coming back to it later. Make sure you skip the question on your answer sheet as well. However, many graphs and charts are easy to decipher. First read the question and all of the possible

Characteristics of Federal Civilian Employees, 1960 and 2012

Total number of employees　1960　2.2 million
　　　　　　　　　　　　　　2012　2.7 million

Sex

1960 — Male 75% | Female 25%

2012 — Male 56.4% | Female 43.4%

Race

1960　White/Minority data for 1960 unavailable

2012 — White 66% | Minority* 34%

Employing Agency

1960 — Defense Department 44% | All other 56%

2012 — Defense Department 35.9% | All other 64.1%

*Blacks, Native Americans, Hispanics, Asians, and Pacific Islanders

Sources: *Statistical Abstract of the United States, 1961*, 392–394; *Statistical Abstract of the United States, 2009*, Table 482.

answers so that you know what you are looking for. Before you look at the chart, you may be able to eliminate some obviously incorrect responses. For example:

1. Which of the following statements does the figure above best support?

   (A) Due to affirmative action, ethnic minorities in the civil service are represented according to their percentage in the general population.

   (B) The percentage of civil servants working in the Defense Department increased from 1960 to 2012.

   (C) Because of gender discrimination, women are underrepresented in the bureaucracy.

   (D) The percentage of females in the bureaucracy has increased from 1960 to 2012.

   (E) There are more minorities in the bureaucracy than in any other branch of the federal government.

After reading the question and the responses, you could eliminate answer (A) without even reading the table; there is no affirmative action program that requires the federal civil service to reflect the population as a whole. After reading the table, eliminate choice (C) immediately—while discrimination may play a role, it is not addressed in the table, and the question requires you to find your answer from the table. You can eliminate answer (E) for the same reason—while there are more minorities in the bureaucracy than in any other branch of the federal government, the table does not contain information about the other branches, and you must answer the question using information from this table. Answer (B) is wrong because the percentage of civil servants working the Defense Department decreased.

ANSWER: D. As the table shows, the number of female civil servants increased from 25% in 1960 to 43.4% in 2012.

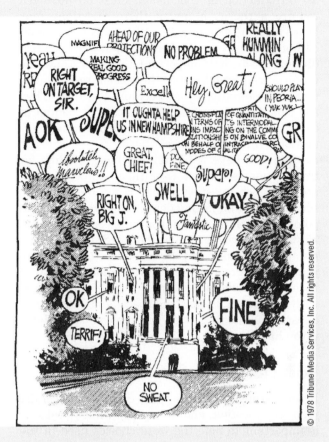

Political Cartoon Questions

These questions require you to interpret a political cartoon. Every political cartoon contains symbolism and a point of view. Examine the cartoon before you read the question and possible responses to determine what each part of the drawing represents and to identify the artist's viewpoint. For example:

1. What is the viewpoint expressed in the cartoon on this page

    (A) One barrier to improving congressional control of the bureaucracy is the large number of federal agencies.

    (B) One barrier to improving presidential control of the federal bureaucracy is that even the White House has become a large bureaucracy.

    (C) The budget grows incrementally each year, and the result is a larger and larger bureaucracy.

    (D) Although the bureaucracy has become very large, there are many people on the White House staff who would approve of cutting the bureaucracy.

    (E) Neither the president nor his staff has any meaningful incentive to control the size of the federal bureaucracy.

ANSWER: B. The box on the left symbolizes the presidency (the president is speaking from the White House). The box on the right symbolizes the federal employees who work at the White House (all of the reactions to his comments are also coming from the White House). The viewpoint of the cartoonist is that although White House employees may claim to agree that the bureaucracy is hard to control, they are part of the problem.

Free-Response Questions

There are four mandatory free-response questions on the U.S. Government and Politics examination. At least one of the questions may require interpretation of a chart or graph. Essays for free-response questions can be written in any order. Whether you write the essays in or out of order, make sure you put the number of the question in the corner of each page of your essay booklet. Each free response question begins with a short introductory sentence. In the interest of time, do not re-write this on your paper. Following the introduction, free-response questions are broken into parts, such as (a), (b), (c), and (d). Label each part of your response.

Usually these are not traditional essay questions. Most free-response questions do not require an introduction or conclusion. Most do not even require a thesis. Many of these questions may be written in a bulleted or short-answer format. Although this may sound easier than writing a traditional essay, it is important that you know the material very well because these are targeted questions. Examination readers want specifics. They are looking for accurate information presented in clear, concise prose. You cannot mask vague information with elegant prose.

You will have a 100-minute block of time for this section, so watch your time. Allow 25 minutes for each question. Spend 5 minutes reading the question and jotting down a few words on each point you want to cover in your answer. Then spend 15 minutes writing your response. Save the last 5 minutes to read over your response to make sure you have covered each point with enough detail. If 25 minutes have passed and you are not finished with a question, leave some space, and start a new question on the next page. You can come back later if you have time.

Vocabulary

In answering the free-response questions, carefully read the question, and do exactly what it asks. It is important to note the word choices used in the questions:

- **Define**: to state the meaning of a word or phrase or to give a specific example. For instance, if a question asks you to define "iron triangle," the response is "An iron triangle is a close, advantageous relationship between an interest group, a congressional committee, and an administrative agency." Definitions are usually just one sentence.

- **Identify**: to select a factor, person, or idea and give it a name. For instance, if a question asks you to identify one advantage of incumbency, one possible response is "One advantage of incumbency is the opportunity to do *casework* for constituents."

- **Explain why/explain how**: to give a cause or reason. Explanations usually include the word *because*. For instance, if a question asks you why the ability to do casework gives incumbents an advantage, one possible response is "By doing casework, such as helping a constituent get her Social Security check, members of Congress are able to leave a favorable impression on members of their district. This increases their chances of reelection *because* they are able to get positive results for their constituents, who will vote for them in the next election."

Scoring For Free-Response Questions

These questions are scored using a rubric that assigns points for each part of the answer. For example, if Part (a) requires you to identify and explain two factors, that part of the response will be worth 4 points (1 point for each identification and 1 point for each explanation). If Part (b) requires you to identify and explain one factor, that part of the response will be worth 2 points (1 point for the identification and 1 point for the explanation), for a total of 6 points possible on the question.

For the following free-response question you will find three sample responses—one excellent, one mediocre, and one poor—and an explanation of how the responses were scored.

QUESTION Congress has several ways of checking the power of the executive branch.

a. Identify and explain TWO formal powers that Congress may use to limit executive authority.

b. Identify and explain ONE informal power that Congress may use to limit executive authority.

Sample Essay 1

Part (a): The Constitution provides several formal, expressed powers that Congress can use to limit executive authority. One is by overriding a veto. When the president vetoes a bill passed by Congress, that bill does not usually become law. However, Congress may override a presidential veto by a two-thirds vote in each house. This limits presidential power, because the president does not have the final say over legislation. If enough members of Congress feel strongly enough about the legislation, it can still become law. Sometimes presidents are aware that their vetoes will be overridden and will sign bills they do not support in order to avoid the negative press that may come later with a defeat in Congress.

Another formal power that Congress has to limit executive authority is that Congress has the power to declare war. The president is commander in chief and has substantial authority in foreign affairs. He may commit troops for sixty days without congressional approval under the War Powers Act. However, for prolonged conflict, the president must turn to Congress to get an official declaration of war.

Part (b): An informal power that Congress has to limit executive authority is legislative oversight. Congress can conduct investigations and hold hearings to supervise the activities of the executive branch. This may pressure the executive to make changes in those agencies. For example, after Hurricane Katrina, Congress held hearings to investigate the effectiveness of the nation's disaster relief agencies.

SCORING 6/6. *In Part (a) the response identifies overriding a veto as a formal power of Congress (1 point for identification). The essay explains that by overriding a veto, presidential power is limited because the president does not have the final say over legislation (1 point for explanation).*

The student also identifies the power to declare war as a check on the presidency (1 point for identification). The essay explains that presidential power is limited because the president must turn to Congress in prolonged conflicts (1 point for explanation). Part (a) earns all 4 points.

In Part (b) the essay identifies legislative oversight as an informal limit on the power of the executive (1 point for identification). The essay explains that this limits the power of executive agencies because their activities are investigated and their effectiveness may be challenged (1 point for explanation). Part (b) earns 2 points.

Sample Essay 2

Part (a): Under the Constitution, all appropriations bills must originate in the House. This means that the House has the power of the purse over executive proposals. This limits executive authority because Congress may reduce or eliminate funding altogether for presidential initiatives. Likewise, Congress must approve the budget. This limits executive authority because the president may not get everything he wants in his budget. This happened in 2004, when Congress cut President Bush's budget before it passed.

In addition, Congress may limit executive authority, because the Senate must ratify treaties. Although the executive branch negotiates treaties, often through the State Department, the Senate must ratify them in order to become law.

Part (b): One informal power that Congress has over the executive branch is the ability to go to the press. If Congress does not like a presidential proposal, a press conference can be held to get the public to oppose the president's policies.

SCORING 3/6. *In Part (a) the student is awarded 3 points. The essay identifies the power of the purse as a limitation on the executive (1 point for* identification). *The response explains that Congress can limit executive power by refusing to fund presidential initiatives by cutting the budget proposed by the president (1 point for explanation).*

The student also identifies Senate ratification of treaties as a limit on executive power (1 point for identification), but there is no meaningful explanation of how this limits presidential power.

In Part (b) the student does not receive any points. While congressional leaders may call press conferences as a way to put public pressure on the president, Congress is made up of 535 members. Congress as a whole cannot appeal to the press.

Sample Essay 3

Part (a): One formal power of Congress that limits the executive branch is the power to declare war. However, the president is the commander in chief. As a result, he is able to commit troops to foreign conflicts without a formal declaration of war. This is what Lyndon Johnson did during the Vietnam conflict.

Another formal power of Congress is the power to regulate interstate commerce. This gives Congress the power to enact laws affecting the economy. Such laws have been used to provide civil rights to African Americans, as well as to provide consumer protection nationwide.

Part (b): One informal power of Congress is the ability to support a president's reelection campaign. If the president does not do what Congress wants, it can oppose his reelection.

SCORING 1/6. *The student identifies the power to declare war as a limit on the executive (1 point for identification). However, the essay does not explain how this power limits the president. Instead, it discusses how the president has not been limited by this power.*

While the power to regulate interstate commerce is a power of Congress, it does not generally limit the power of the presidency. The student does not earn any points for the rest of Part (a).

In Part (b) the response indicates that Congress may not support a president's reelection. While this may be true of individual members of Congress, it is not true of Congress as a whole. The student earns no points for Part (b).

A Diagnostic Test

This diagnostic test will you give some indication of how you might score on the multiple-choice portion of the AP U.S. Government and Politics exam. Of course, the exam changes every year, so it is never possible to predict a student's score with certainty. This test will also pinpoint strengths and weaknesses on the key content areas.

UNITED STATES GOVERNMENT AND POLITICS

Section I

Time: 45 minutes 60 Questions

Multiple Choice Questions

1. What is the significance of *McCulloch v. Maryland*?

   (A) applied the Thirteenth Amendment to Maryland

   (B) provided for selective incorporation of the Bill of Rights

   (C) established a broad interpretation of the Elastic Clause

   (D) created judicial review

   (E) overturned *Dred Scott v. Sanford*

2. James Madison believed that various groups, or factions, would compete within our democratic system. The result would be effective policymaking. Madison's theory can best be described as

   (A) pluralism

   (B) Marxism

   (C) bureaucratic elitism

   (D) hyperpluralism

   (E) elitism

3. Which of the followings statements best describes most of the Founding Fathers?

   (A) They were older, wealthy, and very experienced politicians.

   (B) They were relatively young, wealthy, and well educated.

   (C) They were representative of the population as a whole.

   (D) They were radicals who favored states' rights and the protection of individual liberties.

   (E) They were young and inexperienced.

4. What is the result of the Great Compromise?

   (A) Both the House of Representatives and the Senate directly represent the population as a whole.

   (B) The House of Representatives represents the interests of the states, while the Senate represents individuals within a district.

   (C) The Senate represents state interests, while the House of Representatives mirrors the population proportionally.

   (D) The electoral college vote does not always mirror the popular vote.

   (E) Large states have more power in the Senate than small states.

5. The president nominates Supreme Court justices, who must be confirmed by the Senate. Once appointed, those justices usually serve for life terms. This is an example of

   I. separation of powers

   II. federalism

   III. checks and balances

   IV. judicial review

   (A) I and II

   (B) I and III

   (C) II and III

   (D) III and IV

   (E) I, II, and IV

6. The United States is characterized by cooperative federalism, whereby the national government shares money with the states through grants. Which of the following is most favored by the states?

   (A) categorical grants, because the states can spend the money on broad categories of projects

   (B) categorical grants, because the states can spend the money for any purpose

   (C) categorical grants, because they rarely have any strings attached

TABLE 7.6 Gender Gaps in Presidential Voting, 1992–2012

	Men			Women		
	Rep %	Dem %	D–R diff	Rep %	Dem %	D–R diff
2012	54	46	−8	44	56	+12
2008	50	50	0	43	57	+14
2004	44	56	−12	48	52	+4
2000	45	52	−7	45	53	+8
1996	45	44	+1	39	54	+15
1992	41	37	+4	38	46	+8

Source: Gallup Organization, *Gender Gap in 2012 is Largest in Gallup Survey's History*, November 9, 2012.

(D) block grants, because they give states considerable freedom in deciding how to spend the money

(E) categorical grants, because the states can compete to build specific projects, such as libraries and airports

7. All of the following characterize American beliefs about the political system EXCEPT

(A) Americans believe that, barring a disability, people should be responsible for their own actions and well-being

(B) Americans believe government officials should be accountable to the people

(C) Americans believe that they ought to engage in civic participation and help out their communities when they can

(D) Americans believe that everybody should have an equal vote and an equal chance to participate and succeed

(E) Americans believe that the government should try to equalize wealth so that there is less conflict among citizens

8. When citizens have a political culture that allows the discussion of ideas and the selection of rulers in an atmosphere reasonably free of oppression, there is a high degree of

(A) political agreement
(B) political socialization
(C) political effectiveness
(D) political tolerance
(E) civic duty

9. Which of the following examples best illustrates the concept of political efficacy?

(A) feminists organizing a march in favor of the Equal Rights Amendment

(B) Protestants holding a revival meeting

(C) atheists preaching against organized religion

(D) a civic group collecting canned goods for the homeless

(E) all of the above activities

10. Which of the following statements best describes the factors that influence political socialization?

(A) Young adults identify with the political party supported by their peer group.

(B) The majority of young people identify with their parents' political party.

(C) Republicans socialize their children more than Democrats.

(D) Children tend to follow their parents' political ideology, but a majority of them stray from those beliefs when they become young adults.

(E) Teenagers are more likely to identify themselves as Republicans than as Democrats.

11. The table above supports which of the following conclusions?

(A) The gender gap steadily increased from 1992 to 2008.

(B) Men always prefer Republican candidates to Democrats.

(C) There is a greater gender gap among women than among men.

(D) The gender gap is larger among younger voters than older voters.

(E) The largest difference in party support occurred in 1996 among women.

FIGURE 9.2 Split-Ticket Voting for President/House, 1952–2008

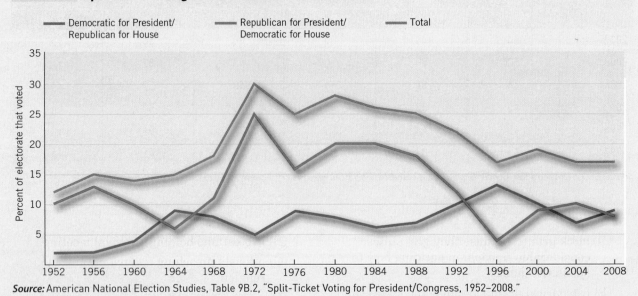

Democratic for President/Republican for House
Republican for President/Democratic for House
Total

Source: American National Election Studies, Table 9B.2, "Split-Ticket Voting for President/Congress, 1952–2008."

12. A person who holds a consistent conservative political ideology would support which of the following?

    I. support for a market economy with few government regulations

    II. keeping taxes low

    III. cutting back on the welfare state

    IV. locking up criminals to prevent recidivism

    (A) I and II

    (B) I, II, and III

    (C) I, III, and IV

    (D) III and IV

    (E) I, II, III, and IV

13. What was the impact of the Motor Voter law of 1993?

    (A) It increased voter turnout significantly, especially in the 18-to 21-year-old age group.

    (B) It increased voter registration but did not significantly increase voter turnout.

    (C) It was widely evaded, especially in southern states.

    (D) It had no significant impact on either voter registration or voter turnout.

    (E) It increased voter registration and voter turnout in all age categories.

14. All of the following are true about voter turnout in the United States EXCEPT:

    (A) educated people vote more than the uneducated

    (B) wealthy people vote more than the poor

    (C) African Americans vote more than whites, when adjusted for income

    (D) whites vote more than African Americans

    (E) men vote more often than women

15. The chart above supports which of the following conclusions?

    (A) Split-ticket voting rose between 1952 and 1972 and declined somewhat after 1992.

    (B) Split-ticket voting rarely occurred prior to 1920.

    (C) Because of split-ticket voting, policy gridlock occurs.

    (D) From 1952 until 2008, there was a steady increase in split-ticket voting.

    (E) Split-ticket voting increases during periods of economic decline.

16. What is the impact of third parties on the American political system?

    (A) Minor parties develop ideas that the major parties later come to adopt.

    (B) Minor parties create new coalitions within the major parties, often resulting in party realignment.

    (C) Minor parties tend to develop around charismatic personalities, who are recruited as candidates by the major parties.

    (D) Minor parties usually get enough votes to prevent a majority vote in the electoral college.

    (E) Minor parties have had no significant impact on the American political system.

17. All of the following are examples of interest groups EXCEPT

(A) Greenpeace

(B) Right to Life

(C) Christian Coalition

(D) Libertarians

(E) National Organization of Women

18. How do interest groups differ from PACs?

(A) Interest groups donate money to candidates, while PACs hire lobbyists to influence policy-making.

(B) Interest groups can hire PACs to help them conduct polls, create direct mail solicitations, and produce TV ads.

(C) PACs are committees, often set up by interest groups, to raise and spend money on campaigns and causes.

(D) Interest groups are required to register with the Federal Election Commission, but there are no registration requirements for PACs.

(E) PACs run candidates for election, while interest groups do not.

19. Which of the following groups have led a social movement?

I. labor union members

II. women's rights advocates

III. environmentalists

IV. opponents of nuclear energy

(A) I and II

(B) I, II, and III

(C) II and III

(D) II, III, and IV

(E) I, II, III, and IV

20. A primary in which voters must declare a political affiliation before the election is

(A) a blanket primary

(B) a closed primary

(C) an open primary

(D) a runoff primary

(E) a party primary

21. How has broadcast journalism changed news coverage?

(A) It has become more detailed, with more in-depth discussion of political issues.

(B) It has become less sensationalized, with visual images replacing lurid written descriptions.

(C) It has become more biased, with newscasters frequently giving their own viewpoints.

(D) It has become more like a headline service, with the length of the average sound bite dropping to less than ten seconds.

(E) It has resulted in more coverage of Congress and less coverage of the president, because large numbers of reporters can now cover the capitol.

22. Which of the following is the best predictor of who will win a Congressional election?

(A) presidential endorsement

(B) fund-raising

(C) party affiliation

(D) incumbency status

(E) prior office

23. How does regulation of radio and television broadcasts differ from the treatment of newspapers and magazines?

(A) Newspapers are not subject to libel and slander laws, while broadcasters are.

(B) The FCC regulates broadcasters but not newspapers.

(C) Because of the First Amendment, broadcasters and newspapers have equal free-speech rights.

(D) Newspapers do not need to be regulated because their content is rarely controversial; most papers simply report the news as it happens.

(E) Both newspapers and television stations must be licensed.

24. How do the rules governing conduct of the House of Representatives compare with the rules governing conduct of the Senate?

(A) There are fewer rules governing the conduct of the House of Representatives because it is the lower house and has less power.

(B) There are fewer rules governing the conduct of the House of Representatives because the House is so big that its individual members lack power.

(C) There are fewer rules governing the conduct of the Senate because its smaller size makes it more manageable.

(D) There are fewer rules governing the conduct of the Senate because of its strong leadership structure.

(E) The same rules of conduct govern both the House and the Senate.

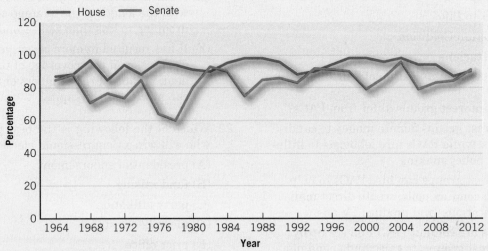

FIGURE 13.1 Re-election Rates for House and Senate Incumbents, 1964–2012

Sources: For 1964–2008 data, The Center for Responsive Politics; 2010 data compiled by author; and 2012 data drawn from The Center for Responsive Politics, OpenSecrets.org, accessed by Jesse Crosson, May 28, 2013.

25. The graph above supports which of the following conclusions?

    (A) Incumbency is a more important factor for re-election in the House than in the Senate.

    (B) From 1964 to 2012, most incumbents in the Senate were re-elected with more than 80 percent of the vote.

    (C) The percentage of incumbent senators re-elected is very consistent over time.

    (D) A challenger would be more likely to win in the House than in the Senate.

    (E) Because members of the House run for re-election every two years, they have more name recognition with voters.

26. Which of the following advantages does the majority party have regarding committees?

    I.   Committees usually reflect the party affiliations of the House or Senate as a whole.

    II. Committee chairs are appointed by the majority party.

    III. The majority leadership decides which bills to assign to a particular committee.

    IV. The majority party often creates committees that have no members from the minority party.

    (A) I and II

    (B) II and III

    (C) I, II, and III

    (D) II, III, and IV

    (E) I, II, III, and IV

27. What is a congressional caucus?

    (A) members of Congress who meet in their individual states during primary season to help select the party's presidential nominee

    (B) a subcommittee created to oversee an executive agency

    (C) an informal meeting of members of Congress to "logroll" pending legislation

    (D) a meeting between members of the House and Senate to revise language when a bill passes both houses in different forms

    (E) an association of members of Congress with similar characteristics or ideology, which acts like an interest group within Congress

28. After a bill is introduced in the House or Senate, which of the following is the most likely outcome?

    (A) passed in one house only

    (B) passed in both houses and becomes law without presidential signature

    (C) vetoed by the president

    (D) died in committee

    (E) subjected to the line-item veto

29. The Foreign Investors Act, a bill designed to solve the balance-of-payments problem, had riders added to it giving assistance to hearse owners, the mineral ore business, importers of scotch whiskey, and presidential candidates. This is an example of a
    (A) Christmas tree bill
    (B) revenue bill
    (C) authorization bill
    (D) concurrent resolution
    (E) reconciliation bill

30. The majority party in the Senate enjoys all of the following EXCEPT:
    (A) select committee chairs
    (B) set the legislative agenda
    (C) select the Senate President
    (D) select the whip
    (E) assign its members to Senate committees

31. Which of the following is the principal advisory group to the president?
    (A) White House Staff
    (B) National Committee
    (C) Cabinet
    (D) Senate
    (E) Council of Governors

32. Political scientist David Mayhew studied important laws and found that significant legislation was as likely to be enacted in times of divided government as in periods of unified government. What is the best explanation for this phenomenon?
    (A) The Constitution ensures that the president and Congress will be rivals for power. Divided government is simply an example of separation of powers in action.
    (B) Most presidents have so much political clout that they are able to convince members of the opposing party to support their key legislative proposals.
    (C) Legislation is passed during periods of divided government because Congress frequently overrides presidential vetoes.
    (D) Legislation is passed in times of divided government because presidents tend to present noncontroversial proposals to Congress.
    (E) Divided government occurs most frequently in wartime. Congress is forced to pass legislation in order to meet the needs of the nation.

33. What would be the most likely effect of the elimination of the Electoral College?
    (A) a reduction in overall campaign costs
    (B) a reduction in campaign costs in "battleground" states only
    (C) an increase in overall campaign costs
    (D) an increase in campaign costs in "battleground" states only
    (E) there would be no effect

34. All of the following are powers of the President EXCEPT
    (A) appoint judges
    (B) set the agenda for Congress
    (C) rewrite legislation
    (D) pardon
    (E) commission military officers

TABLE 14.4   The Cabinet Departments

Department	Created	Approximate Employment (2012)
State	1789	39,200*
Treasury	1789	104,100
Defense[a]	1947	761,533
Justice	1789	116,303
Interior	1849	69.702
Agriculture[b]	1889	91,278
Commerce	1913	44,996
Labor	1913	16,816
Health and Human Services[c]	1953	86,532
Housing and Urban Development	1965	9,114
Transportation	1966	57,042
Energy	1977	15,715
Education	1979	4,294
Veterans Affairs	1989	328,088
Homeland Security	2002	197,627

[a]Formerly the War Department, created in 1789. Figures are for civilians only.
[b]Agriculture Department created in 1862; made part of cabinet in 1889.
[c]Originally Health, Education and Welfare; reorganized in 1979.

Note: Department of State figure taken from: US Census Bureau. "The 2012 Statistical Abstract: The National Data Book." Census.gov. Last modified September 30, 2011. This figure is used due to the fact that there are major discrepancies in how to count foreign service and foreign service national employees. The figure in the FedScope source is inordinately low, compared to most State Department estimates.

Source: US Office of Personnel Management. "Employment - December 2012: Cabinet-Level Agencies." *FedScope.*

35. How is the Federal Reserve Board classified?

(A) as an executive agency, because the chairman can be removed by the president at any time

(B) as an executive agency, because the president appoints the chairman

(C) as an independent agency, because the chairman serves for a fixed term, subject to reappointment by the president

(D) as a government corporation, because it regulates banks

(E) as an independent regulatory commission, because its chairman is selected from its board

36. Table 14.4 on the facing page best supports which of the following conclusions?

(A) The older the cabinet department, the more employment opportunities.

(B) Energy and education are of top concerns for cabinet members.

(C) Defense, veteran services, and security are primary concern.

(D) Newer Cabinet departments have lower employment rates.

(E) Where one sits at cabinet meetings has no regard to the age of the department.

37. What was the intent of Congress in passing the Budget Reform Act of 1974?

(A) to keep presidents from submitting budget proposals that contained deficits

(B) to prevent presidents from presenting budgets that raise taxes greater than the rate of inflation

(C) to require presidents to submit balanced budgets

(D) to require across-the-board cuts in three categories of spending (discretionary, domestic, and military) in order to balance the budget

(E) to require presidents to spend all appropriated funds unless Congress agrees to delete the items within 45 days

38. When candidates run for office, they often promise to present certain legislative programs once elected. Why is it difficult for presidents to get these promised programs passed?

I. Unexpected crisis may divert attention from previous plans.

II. Controversial aspects of a program may face adverse and well-publicized reactions.

III. The presidency is characterized by long hours and hundreds of activities, which make it difficult to concentrate on specific programs.

IV. The public rarely expects politicians to deliver on their promises, so they are frequently abandoned.

(A) I and II

(B) II and III

(C) II, III, and IV

(D) I, II, and IV

(E) I, II, and III

39. The presidential veto can be applied to which of the following?

(A) legislation from states

(B) judicial decisions

(C) parts of treaties

(D) legislation from Congress

(E) regulations from bureaucratic agencies

40. What was the Supreme Court's ruling in *United States v. Nixon*?

(A) There is not an absolute, unqualified, claim of executive privilege in criminal investigations.

(B) There is not an absolute, unqualified, claim of executive privilege unless national security is involved.

(C) Confidential communications between a president and his staff are privileged.

(D) Written communications are privileged, but taped conversations are not protected from judicial subpoenas.

(E) There is an absolute, unqualified, executive privilege for all written and oral communications in the White House between the president and his staff.

41. What is the process for impeachment and removal of the president?

(A) The House must vote to impeach a president by a two-thirds vote, and the president is tried in the Senate, which must vote to convict by a three-fourths vote.

(B) The House must vote to impeach a president by a majority vote, and the president is tried in the Senate, which must vote to convict by a two-thirds vote.

(C) Both houses of Congress must vote on impeachment charges, and the Supreme

Court has original jurisdiction to hear the case.

    (D) The House votes on articles of impeachment, a trial is held in the Senate, and then the case is sent back to the House for a final vote on conviction.

    (E) The House and Senate appoint members to a joint committee on impeachment, which then holds hearings and makes a final recommendation to the Congress as a whole.

42. What gives the American bureaucracy its distinctive character in comparison with most other nations?

    (A) Both Congress and the president exercise authority over the bureaucracy.

    (B) Bureaucrats report to and take orders from the heads of their departments.

    (C) Most agencies of the federal government do not have to share authority with state or local agencies.

    (D) Bureaucratic agencies are able to operate with little public scrutiny.

    (E) The bureaucracy regulates large sectors of the economy.

43. Which of the following was responsible for the creation of the merit system?

    (A) Hatch Act

    (B) Smith Act

    (C) Pendleton Act

    (D) Sherman Clayton Act

    (E) McCain Feingold Act

44. How are most members of the federal bureaucracy selected?

    (A) The president, often on the basis of party loyalty, appoints them.

    (B) They are selected by the Congressional Committee on Hiring and usually reflect the political affiliations of Congress.

    (C) They are appointed after they have passed a written exam or have met certain selection criteria.

    (D) Federal positions are filled using strict affirmative action guidelines that require the bureaucracy to mirror the population as a whole.

    (E) They are interviewed by the OPM, and the top three candidates are sent to the agency head, who makes the final selection.

45. Which of the following is the BEST definition of legislative oversight?

    (A) the ability of Congress to review action of the president

    (B) the ability of Congress to review actions of the bureaucracy

    (C) the president's ability to oversee the legislative branch using the veto

    (D) the ability of the judiciary to review the actions of Congress

    (E) the ability of congressional leadership to oversee the committee process

46. What is judicial review?

    (A) the right of the Supreme Court to rewrite a federal law to make it constitutional

    (B) the right of the Supreme Court to review the evidence in a trial and hear new testimony

    (C) the right of the Supreme Court to hear appeals in cases involving constitutional issues

    (D) the right of the Supreme Court to declare a state or federal law void if it violates the Constitution

    (E) the right of the Supreme Court to reduce a defendant's criminal sentence upon review if that sentence is excessive

47. In which way would a special interest group attempt to influence the selection of federal judges?

    (A) make campaign contributions to the judge

    (B) lobby the Supreme Court appointment of a judge

    (C) testify before the House Judiciary Committee about a potential judge's qualifications

    (D) attempt to influence the Vice President in his capacity as Senate President

    (E) pressure key senators to vote against confirmation

48. What is a likely outcome of divided government?

    (A) an increase in presidential power

    (B) the inability of the Federal Reserve to function

    (C) a "co-leadership" system for congressional committees

    (D) delays in judicial confirmation

    (E) the inability of the House and Senate to work together

49. Those who dramatize issues, galvanize public opinion, and mobilize congressional support can best be described as

(A) policy entrepreneurs

(B) policy specialists

(C) interest groups

(D) issue networks

(E) PACs

50. Some laws both regulate and help business. Antitrust laws are one example. They prevent businesses from becoming so large that they can control the market. This may hinder the growth of large businesses, but at the same time, it protects businesses from unfair competition. One example of this is

(A) the Clayton Act

(B) the Pendleton Act

(C) the Taft-Hartley Act

(D) the Bipartisan Campaign Finance Reform Act

(E) the Administrative Procedures Act

51. What is the difference between monetary policy and fiscal policy?

(A) Monetary policy involves taxing, and fiscal policy involves spending.

(B) Fiscal policy occurs when there is a deficit, and monetary policy is used when there is a surplus.

(C) Fiscal policy uses tax cuts to stimulate the economy, while monetary policy uses government spending to stimulate the economy.

(D) Fiscal policy involves the budget, and monetary policy involves interest rates and the money supply.

(E) There is no difference; these terms are synonymous.

52. The economic theory that emphasizes deregulation and tax cuts is

(A) Keynesianism

(B) supply-side economics

(C) monetarism

(D) fiscal federalism

(E) New Deal activism

53. Who is responsible for setting monetary policy?

(A) Congress and the President

(B) Office of Management and Budget

(C) Treasury Department

(D) Federal Reserve

(E) Appropriations Committee

54. All of the following are classified as mandatory expenditures EXCEPT

(A) Social Security

(B) Medicare

(C) interest on the national debt

(D) National Defense

(E) Medicaid

55. Which of the following statements best describes the difference between Aid to Families with Dependent Children (AFDC) and Temporary Assistance for Needy Families (TANF)?

(A) AFDC was means tested, while TANF is not.

(B) Most recipients of AFDC received benefits for less than one year.

(C) TANF set limits on how long families could receive federally funded benefits.

(D) AFDC was more successful in moving people from welfare to work.

(E) AFDC had more popular support than TANF.

56. Which of the following would present a "clear and present danger" and thus not be protected by the Constitution?

(A) members of the Ku Klux Klan holding a rally

(B) members of the Communist Party distributing literature

(C) antiwar protesters

(D) a parade held by the American Nazi party

(E) encouraging the violent overthrow of the government of the United States

57. Which of the following is part of the "Lemon Test" established in the case of *Lemon v. Kurtzman*?

(A) Neutral Effect

(B) Separation of Church and State

(C) Non-Establishment

(D) Free Exercise of Religion

(E) Entanglement Prohibited

58. What is the effect of exclusionary rule?
   (A) Illegally obtained evidence is not admissible.
   (B) Presidential candidates who have not served in other offices are not permitted to run.
   (C) Police officers obtaining evidence illegally are subject to disciplinary action.
   (D) Persons under 18 at the time of their crimes are exempt from the death penalty.
   (E) The process of selective incorporation excludes parts of the Bill of Rights.

59. What was the Court's decision in *Bakke v. University of California*?
   (A) Affirmative action programs are reverse discrimination and violate the Fourteenth Amendment.
   (B) Affirmative action programs were designed to provide racial equality and are required by the Fourteenth Amendment.
   (C) Schools can take race into account in making admissions decisions, but the use of quotas will be viewed with strict scrutiny.
   (D) Schools can take race into account in making admissions decisions, and using quotas is the best way to accomplish this.
   (E) Affirmative action programs are permissible but not required; states may abolish them if they wish.

60. What is the significance of the Supreme Court's decision in *Griswold v. Connecticut*?
   (A) The court affirmed major provisions of the Civil Rights Act of 1964.
   (B) The court overturned a state ban on political speech.
   (C) The court declared that there is a right to privacy.
   (D) The court required that indigent defendants must have a state provided attorney.
   (E) The court held that it has the right to review actions of administrative agencies.

STOP

END OF SECTION I

IF YOU FINISH BEFORE TIME IS CALLED, YOU MAY CHECK YOUR WORK ON THIS SECTION. DO NOT GO ON TO SECTION II UNTIL YOU ARE TOLD TO DO SO.

UNITED STATES GOVERNMENT AND POLITICS

Section II

Time: 100 minutes

Free Response Questions

Directions You have 100 minutes to answer all four of the following questions. Unless the directions indicate otherwise, respond to all parts of each question. It is recommended that you take a few minutes to plan and outline each answer. Spend approximately 25 minutes on each question. Support your essay with specific examples where appropriate. Be sure to number each of your answers.

1. The due-process clause of the Fourteenth Amendment has been used by the Supreme Court to protect individuals from state actions that violate fundamental rights. These Supreme Court cases include:
   Mapp v. Ohio
   Miranda v. Arizona
   Roe v. Wade
   a. Pick one of the cases listed above. Identify the issue the Court was asked to resolve, and describe the Court's ruling.
   b. For the case you discussed in (a), explain how the ruling expanded individual rights.
   c. Pick another case from the list above. Identify the issue the Court was asked to resolve, and describe the Court's ruling. Explain how the ruling expanded individual rights.

2. The United States has a federal system of government. This system provides a division of power between the national government and the states. Identify and explain three ways in which the power of the national government has increased over the last 200 years.

FIGURE 14.2 Presidential Victories on Votes in Congress, 1953–2012

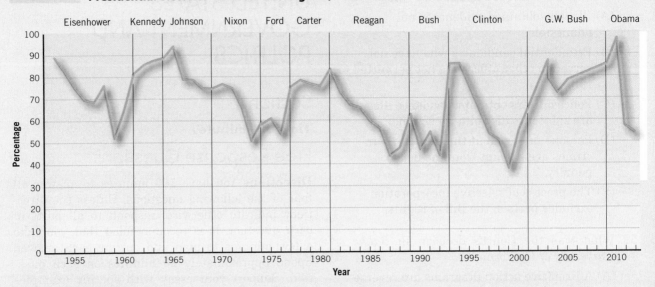

Note: Percentages indicate number of congressional votes supporting the president divided by the total number of votes on which the president has taken a position.

Source: Congressional Quarterly Weekly, various years

3. Using the information in the figure above and your knowledge of United States politics, complete the following tasks.

   a. Identify one trend with regard to presidential victories in Congress.

   b. Identify and explain two relevant factors that have affected presidential victories in Congress.

4. In any election not all of the candidates are equally matched. Typically incumbents have significant advantages over challengers. Identify and explain three advantages that congressional incumbents have over challengers.

END OF EXAMINATION

Scoring This Diagnostic Test

Using the table below, score your test. Determine how many you answered correctly and how many you answered incorrectly.

1. C	6. D	23. B	40. A
2. A	7. E	24. C	41. B
3. B	8. D	25. A	42. A
4. C	9. A	26. C	43. C
5. B	10. B	27. E	44. C
11. E	28. D		
12. E	29. A		
13. B	30. C		
14. E	31. A		
15. A	32. A		
16. A	33. C		
17. D	34. C		
18. C	35. C		
19. B	36. C		
20. B	37. E		
21. D	38. E		
22. D	39. D		

45. B	53. D
46. D	54. D
47. E	55. C
48. D	56. E
49. A	57. A
50. A	58. A
51. D	59. C
52. B	60. C

CALCULATE YOUR SCORE
Number answered correctly _____

WHAT YOUR SCORE MEANS
Your score will give you some idea of how well you might do on the AP exam. Keep in mind that your essays will count for 50 percent and will also determine your score.

Answer Key

The AP exam covers key content areas in certain percentages. This answer key will give you an indication of how much weight each area is given and your knowledge of each of the important content areas. Page numbers at the end of each answer refer to the pages in *American Government,* 14th ed., where that issue is discussed.

Multiple Choice Answers

Questions 1–6 are about Constitutional Underpinnings (covered in American Government, *14th ed.), which will be 5–15 percent of the multiple-choice portion of the AP exam.*

1. **(C)** McCulloch is a landmark case because in this case the Court interpreted the Supremacy Clause in a manner that prohibited state interference in a function of the national government. Further, the Court also interpreted the Elastic Clause "loosely," thus increasing the power of the national government. (*American Government*, 14th ed., pages **55–56**).
2. **(A)** Pluralism is the belief that groups compete within a democratic system. Because no single group can dominate the policy-making process, the result is that all relevant interests can affect policy-making (*American Government*, 14th ed., page **9**).

3. **(B)** The Founding Fathers were relatively young but politically experienced. They were wealthier and more educated than the general public (*American Government*, 14th ed., pages **28–29**).
4. **(C)** There are two senators per state. Thus states are represented equally in the Senate. Seats in the House are awarded based on a state's population, as determined by the census. Thus the number of members in the House of Representatives reflects a state's population (*American Government*, 14th ed., pages **31–32**).
5. **(B)** The appointment process for the Supreme Court is an example of both separation of powers and checks and balances. The executive and legislative branches have distinct roles. By confirming presidential nominees, Congress has a check on the presidency. Lifetime tenure is a check on both the executive and the legislature, because justices cannot be removed for political reasons (*American Government*, 14th ed., pages **34–35**).
6. **(D)** States prefer block grants because, in theory, they allow states more freedom in deciding how to spend the money. However, in practice, the federal government has been increasing the number of strings attached to supposedly unrestricted grants (*American Government*, 14th ed., page **66**).

Questions 7–14 are about Political Beliefs and Behavior (covered in American Government, *14th ed., Chapters 4, 7, 8), which will be 10–20 percent of the multiple-choice portion of the AP exam.*

7. **(E)** Americans believe in equality, personal responsibility, and civic participation. They also believe government officials should be held accountable for their actions. Equalizing income is not a goal of most Americans, who believe that those who work hard or are better educated should receive higher salaries (*American Government*, 14th ed., page **79**).
8. **(D)** Not all behavior is acceptable. However, political tolerance requires that citizens be able to discuss and disagree about controversial issues in an atmosphere that is fairly free of oppression (*American Government,* 14th ed., page **91**).
9. **(A)** Political efficacy is the belief that a citizen has the capacity to understand and influence political events. The feminists who are protesting believe that they can influence the passage of the Equal Rights Amendment. The other examples do not involve an attempt to influence the government's policy-making processes (*American Government*, 14th ed., page **256**).

10. **(B)** The majority of young people identify with their parents' political party. This is a result of political socialization (*American Government*, 14th ed., pages **156–158**).

11. **(E)** The largest difference in party preference occurred among young women in the 2008 election. Sixty-three percent voted for Obama while twenty-eight percent supported McCain. This is a thirty-five percent difference (*American Government*, 14th ed., page **160**).

12. **(E)** Conservatives support the free market and tax cuts. They want to reduce the welfare state and lock up criminals to prevent them from committing other crimes (*American Government*, 14th ed., pages **164–165**).

13. **(B)** The Motor Voter Act of 1993 increased voter registration but not voter turnout. For example, in the 1996 presidential election (the first presidential election following the enactment), voter turnout fell to slightly below 50 percent (*American Government*, 14th ed., page **174**).

14. **(E)** Most recent research indicates that men and women vote at the same level. Some research indicates the women vote more often than men. There is virtually no data to suggest that men vote more often than women. (*American Government*, 14th ed., page **160**).

Questions 15–23 are about Political Parties, Interest Groups, and the Media (covered in American Government, *14th ed., Chapters 9–12), which will be 10–20 percent of the multiple-choice portion of the AP exam.*

15. **(A)** Split-ticket voting increases during midterm congressional election years, when the president's party usually loses seats in Congress (*American Government*, 14th ed., page **197**).

16. **(A)** The conventional wisdom is that minor parties develop ideas that the major parties later adopt. For example, in 1996, Ross Perot emphasized campaign finance reform, an issue later adopted by both the Republicans and the Democrats (*American Government*, 14th ed., pages **208–211**).

17. **(D)** An interest group is any organization that seeks to influence public policy. In America, these groups do not usually run candidates for office. The Libertarians are best described as a political party, rather than an interest group, because they hold positions on a variety of issues and frequently run candidates for office (*American Government*, 14th ed., page **252**).

18. **(C)** Political Action Committees are set up by and represent a corporation, labor union, or special-interest group. They raise and spend campaign contributions on behalf of candidates or causes (*American Government*, 14th ed., page **252**).

19. **(B)** Feminists, labor union members, and environmentalists have all led social movements—widely shared demands for change in some aspect of the social or political order. While some groups oppose nuclear energy, they have not grown into a larger social movement (*American Government*, 14th ed., pages **259–260**).

20. **(B)** In a closed primary, a voter must declare in advance (sometimes several weeks in advance) that he or she is a member of a specific political party. Voters may vote only in the primary of the party to which they have registered (*American Government*, 14th ed., page **230**).

21. **(D)** Broadcast journalism has changed the way politicians get their message across. Because viewers can easily turn off the TV set, speeches must be boiled down to very interesting, short catchphrases that can be captured in sound bites (*American Government*, 14th ed., page **280–281**).

22. **(D)** Incumbents, persons who currently hold the office, stand the best chance of being elected. This is called incumbency advantage (*American Government*, 14th ed., page **222**).

23. **(B)** The FCC regulates broadcasters, because the content of their programs is available to the general public, including children, over the airwaves (*American Government*, 14th ed., page **283, 286**).

Questions 24–48 are about Institutions, including Congress, the Presidency, the Courts, the Bureaucracy, and the Budget (covered in American Government, *14th ed., Chapters 13–16), which will be 35–45 percent of the multiple-choice portion of the AP exam.*

24. **(C)** There are fewer rules governing the conduct of the Senate because it has only 100 members, compared to 435 members in the House of Representatives. As a result, it is easier to manage (*American Government*, 14th ed., page **319**).

25. **(A)** A greater percentage of incumbents in the House is re-elected than in the Senate (*American Government*, 14th ed., page **313**).

26. **(C)** Committees usually reflect party membership in the chamber as a whole. Chairs are appointed by the majority party, which also decides which bills will be sent to particular committees. Although there have been occasions when the majority takes extra seats on

a committee, they do not take all of the seats (*American Government*, 14th ed., page **322**).

27. **(E)** A congressional caucus is made up of members of Congress who share certain characteristics (for example, there is a women's caucus) or ideology. They advocate for their interests within Congress (*American Government*, 14th ed., pages **321–322**).

28. **(D)** Most bills introduced in Congress die in committee (*American Government*, 14th ed., page **327**).

29. **(A)** A bill with a large number of unrelated riders attached, many of which provide "pork," is known as a Christmas tree bill (*American Government*, 14th ed., page **328**).

30. **(C)** The president of the Senate is the Vice President of the United States. As such, this position is selected by the Electoral College (*American Government*, 14th ed., page **318**).

31. **(A)** The White House Staff is the principal advisory group to the president and has been since the middle of the 20th century. While certain cabinet members are important, the cabinet as a whole is not. (*American Government*, 14th ed., page **362**).

32. **(A)** Divided government is separation of powers and checks and balances in action. Opposing parties must compromise to pass legislation (*American Government*, 14th ed., page **331**).

33. **(C)** The Electoral College, when combined with winner take all, results in the creation of only a few truly competitive states. These states become the focal point of the campaign. The elimination of the Electoral College would result in a candidate having to campaign all over the United States, thus increasing costs (*American Government*, 14th ed., pages **350–351**).

34. **(C)** The President does not have the power to rewrite legislation. The President may suggest changes while Congress considers the bill. If the President vetoes the bill, he is required to inform Congress of his objections (*American Government*, 14th ed., page **357**).

35. **(C)** The Chairman of the Federal Reserve Board is appointed by the president and serves for a fourteen-year term. During this time, the chairman is not generally subject to removal. The Federal Reserve Board is an independent federal agency (*American Government*, 14th ed., page **367**).

36. **(C)** Defense employs 761,533 individuals along with Veteran Affairs (328,000) and Homeland Security (almost 200,000). (*American Government*, 14th ed., page **365**).

37. **(E)** The Budget Reform Act was a response to presidents who refused to spend money appropriated by Congress. It requires that the money be spent unless notice is given to Congress within 45 days and the items are deleted from the budget (*American Government*, 14th ed., page **359**).

38. **(E)** People expect presidents to deliver on their promises. However, presidential programs may face negative reactions, crises may erupt, and a president's hectic schedule may impair his ability to deliver a program (*American Government*, 14th ed., pages **368–371**).

39. **(D)** The veto serves as a President's primary check on Congress. The veto can only be applied to the bill in its entirety. The United States President does not have a line-item veto. (*American Government*, 14th ed., pages **356–358**).

40. **(A)** In *United States v. Nixon*, the Supreme Court ruled that taped conservations were not protected by a broad executive privilege because such a privilege would block the function of the federal courts in criminal cases (*American Government*, 14th ed., page **359**).

41. **(B)** The House votes, by a simple majority, on impeachment charges. The Senate holds an impeachment trial. A conviction requires a two-thirds vote in the Senate (*American Government*, 14th ed., pages **373–374**).

42. **(A)** One distinctly American feature of the bureaucracy is that both Congress and the president exercise authority over it. In parliamentary systems, bureaucrats do not report directly to the legislature (*American Government*, 14th ed., page **381**).

43. **(C)** The Pendleton Act, passed during the Progressive Period of American history, was responsible for the beginning of the merit system (*American Government*, 14th ed., page **389**).

44. **(C)** Most bureaucrats serve in the competitive service, in which positions are filled through written examinations or are based upon certain selection criteria (*American Government*, 14th ed., page 388).

45. **(B)** Legislative oversight is the ability of Congress to oversee the bureaucracy. Congress has several tools it can use including funding and structure (*American Government*, 14th ed., pages **397–400**).

46. **(D)** In *Marbury v. Madison*, the Supreme Court asserted its authority to invalidate state and federal laws that violate the Constitution (*American Government*, 14th ed., page **412**).

47. **(E)** Federal judges are appointed by the President and confirmed by the Senate.

Pressuring key senators, such as the majority party's leadership, could very well impact the result of the confirmation vote (*American Government*, 14th ed., page **409**).

48. **(D)** Divided government is when the president and at least one house of Congress are of opposite political parties. In this event the president's legislative agenda and nominees are subjected to greater scrutiny, which results in delays (*American Government*, 14th ed., page **409**).

Questions 49–54 are about Public Policy (covered in American Government, *14th ed., Chapters 1, 17–19), which will be 5–15 percent of the multiple-choice portion of the AP exam.*

49. **(A)** Policy entrepreneurs are those, both in and out of government, who find ways of pulling together a legislative majority on behalf of interests that are not well represented in government (*American Government*, 14th ed., page **16**).

50. **(A)** The Clayton Antitrust Act prevents a business from gaining control of the market. This encourages competition (*American Government*, 14th ed., page **455**).

51. **(D)** Monetary policy involves government decisions that control interest rates and the money supply. Fiscal policy concerns the budget (*American Government*, 14th ed., pages **477–478**).

52. **(B)** Supply-side economists favor less government planning, more deregulation, and tax cuts to stimulate economic growth (*American Government,* 14th ed., pages **475–476**).

53. **(D)** Monetary policy is concerned with the amount of money in circulation. This amount is manipulated in an attempt to control its value. The Board of Governors of the Federal Reserve is charged with setting monetary policy (*American Government*, 14th ed., page **477**).

54. **(D)** Mandatory expenditures occur automatically. Under prior legislation money is taken from the treasury and spent according to law. No further congressional action is required. National Defense spending is the result of the regular appropriations process that occurs annually (*American Government*, 14th ed., page **480**).

55. **(C)** TANF replaced ADFC, partly due to the public's dissatisfaction with the number of unwed mothers who remained on the welfare rolls. TANF limits the number of years families can receive federally funded benefits (*American Government*, 14th ed., page **450**).

Questions 55–60 are about Civil Rights and Civil Liberties (covered in American Government, *14th ed., Chapters 5–6), which will be 5–15 percent of the multiple-choice portion of the AP exam.*

56. **(E)** Encouraging the violent overthrow of the government of the United States presents a clean and present danger and is thus not protected speech. All of the others are protected forms of expression (*American Government*, 14th ed., page **102**).

57. **(A)** *Lemon v. Kurtzman* created a three-part test for government aid to religious institutions: Secular Purpose, Neutral Effect, and no Excessive Entanglement (*American Government*, 14th ed., pages **110–111**).

58. **(A)** The exclusionary rule prohibits the use of illegally obtained evidence in criminal trials. It was applied to the states in *Mapp v. Ohio* (*American Government*, 14th ed., page **112**).

59. **(C)** In the *Bakke* case, the University of California's racial quota system was found to violate the prohibition against race discrimination in the Fourteenth Amendment. The Court did not abolish affirmative action, stating that race can be a factor in admissions decisions (*American Government*, 14th ed., page **142**).

60. **(C)** *Griswold* is the first major privacy case. The Court held that there is an inherent right to privacy found in the Ninth Amendment (*American Government*, 14th ed., page **139**).

Free Response Answers

QUESTION 1

This question required you to write about TWO of the following three cases:

Part (a): In *Mapp v. Ohio*, the Supreme Court was asked to consider whether evidence obtained in an illegal search could be used against a defendant at trial. Police broke into Mapp's home in search of drugs. They did not find any drugs, but they found pornography. The police had plenty of time to obtain a search warrant, but they did not get one. The Supreme Court held that the evidence could not be used in Mapp's trial. This established the exclusionary rule. The exclusionary rule protects defendants from having illegally obtained evidence used against them in court. The right being protected is provided in the Fourth Amendment, which prohibits unreasonable searches and seizures. This right is protected to make sure police will be diligent in getting proper warrants (*American Government*, 14th ed., pages **112–113, 118**).

Part (b): In *Miranda v. Arizona*, the Supreme Court considered whether a suspect's confession could be used in court if he was not informed of his rights. Miranda was arrested for kidnapping and rape. Police did not inform him that he had the right to remain silent, that his statements could be used against him, or that he had a right to have an attorney present during questioning. Miranda confessed. The Supreme Court threw out the confession because defendants have a right to be protected against self-incrimination.

Part (c): The *Miranda* decision expanded the rights of those accused of crimes. The right to remain silent is meaningful only when suspects are fully aware of their rights. As a result of this ruling, it is now standard police procedure to read from a "Miranda card" when taking suspects into custody (*American Government*, 14th ed., page **118**). (*Alternate a*) The *Roe v. Wade* case is one of the most controversial decisions of the Supreme Court. A Texas law outlawed abortion, except when the woman's life is threatened. Roe, a pregnant woman, challenged the law. The issue was whether laws prohibiting abortion were a violation of the right of privacy implied in the Fourth Amendment. The Court overturned the Texas law and ruled that states may not outlaw abortion during the first two trimesters of pregnancy. (*Alternate b*) The impact of the Court's ruling in *Roe v. Wade* was to expand the right of privacy by legalizing abortion (before the fetus is viable) nationwide. Women can make individual decisions about their pregnancies. Later Court decisions allow states to regulate the procedure, as long as those regulations do not impose an undue burden on the woman (*American Government*, 14th ed., pages **138–139**).

Scoring

This essay is worth 8 points. The discussion of each of the two cases you choose is worth 4 points.

Part (a) is worth 1 point for identifying the issue. The issue in *Mapp v. Ohio* was whether illegally obtained evidence can be used in court. In *Miranda v. Arizona*, the issue was whether the use in court of a confession made when the suspect has not been read his rights violates the prohibition against self-incrimination. In *Roe v. Wade*, the issue was whether state laws prohibiting abortion violate the right of privacy.

Part (b) is worth 1 point for explaining the Court's decision. In *Mapp*, the Court established the exclusionary rule. In *Miranda*, the Court held that confessions cannot be used in court if the suspect has not been read his rights. In *Roe*, the Court held that state laws banning abortion during the first two trimesters violate the Fourth Amendment.

Part (c) is worth 2 points for explaining how the decision expands rights. An incomplete but correct explanation would receive 1 point. In *Mapp*, the exclusionary rule protects people from illegal searches (1 point) because police will be more diligent (1 point). In *Miranda*, suspects will be protected from self-incrimination (1 point) because police now read Miranda cards when taking suspects into custody (1 point). In *Roe*, women have a right to privacy (1 point), because they can make decisions about a pregnancy without substantial state interference (1 point).

QUESTION 2

The power of the national government in the United States has increased in several significant ways over the law 200 years. Any three of the following identifications and explanations are acceptable.

Loose Interpretation of the Elastic Clause - The Elastic Clause, also known as the Necessary and Proper Clause, allows Congress to pass laws related to the expressed powers listed in the Constitution. The Supreme Court in the case of *McCulloch v Maryland* established that the clause should be interpreted loosely. This has allowed for the power of the national government to grow over time (*American Government*, 14th ed., pages **55–56, 59, 411**).

Loose Interpretation of the Commerce Clause - The Commerce Clause allows the national government to regulate interstate commerce. Depending on how broad that definition is, the power of the national government will increase. Through a series of decisions, the Court has interpreted the Commerce Clause to cover virtually all business activity even if it is only tangentially connected to interstate commerce. The combined effect of these decisions has been an increase in the scope of the national government (*American Government*, 14th ed., pages **57–59**).

Fiscal Federalism - The Constitution gives the national government the power to lay and collect taxes to "promote the general welfare." The national government has used this taxing power to generate large sums of money that are then given to state and local governments through various grants. These grants frequently come with conditions and mandates. This process allows the national government to effectively make policy over topics that would otherwise be restricted to the states (*American Government*, 14th ed., pages **63–70**).

The Fourteenth Amendment - The Fourteenth Amendment has increased the power of the national government in two ways. First, the Due

Process Clause has been used to selectively apply parts of the Bill of the Rights to the states. This allows the national judiciary to determine the minimal standards for civil liberties. Second, the Equal Protection Clause required that states treat members of the suspect classes in an essentially equal manner. States are no longer free to regulate civil rights in any manner they choose (*American Government*, 14th ed., pages **39, 99–100**).

Scoring

This essay is worth 6 points. One point is awarded for each correct identification. One point is awarded for each correct explanation.

QUESTION 3

Part (a): The figure demonstrates that most presidents are more successful in Congress at the beginning of their terms (*American Government*, 14th ed., pages **355–356**).

Part (b): One factor that impacts presidential victories in Congress is the honeymoon period immediately following an election. Presidents are often most popular right after an election, and they can use the public's optimism to persuade Congress to enact legislation. This is called a honeymoon period. Franklin Roosevelt took advantage of this period to get much of his first New Deal programs enacted. Because times were hard, it would have been political suicide for Congress to reject his plans. President Reagan also benefited from a honeymoon period and was able to pass tax cuts shortly after taking office. Another factor affecting presidential victories in Congress is whether government is divided or unified. Divided government occurs when one or both houses of Congress are controlled by the political party opposite the president's. An example of this occurred during President Clinton's first term in office. In 1994, Congress became Republican and thereafter blocked much of his proposed legislation. The federal government even "shut down" because Clinton and Congress could not agree on a budget. Conversely, when there is unified government (when both houses of Congress and the president share the same political party), it may be easier for the president to get his program of legislation passed. This was true for George W. Bush from 2002 until 2006 and for Barack Obama from 2008 until 2010 (*American Government*, 14th ed., pages **355–356**).

Scoring

This essay is worth 5 points.

Part (a) is worth 1 point for describing what the figure demonstrates (presidents are more successful in the beginning of their terms). Points would be awarded for other trends, such as a decline in victories over time.

Part (b) is worth 4 points, with 1 point awarded for identifying each factor affecting presidential victories in Congress (honeymoon period, divided government), and 1 point awarded for each explanation (Congress supports the president because he has popular approval and divided government makes it difficult for the president to get his program enacted). Points would be awarded for other factors, such as a crisis, that would cause Congress to support the president's program.

QUESTION 4

Incumbent members of Congress enjoy significant advantages over challengers. Any three of the following identifications and explanations are acceptable.

Name Recognition - Incumbent members of Congress typically have higher name recognition than do challengers. There is a high degree of correlation between name recognition and electoral success.

Ease of Fundraising - Incumbent members of Congress usually are able to raise more money than are challengers. In fact, most PAC money goes to incumbents.

Ombudsman - Incumbent members of Congress are able to use the power and influence of their offices to help individuals from their states and districts to navigate the labyrinth that is the national government. For example, this may take the form of helping a retired person who is having difficulties with the Social Security Administration. These favors translate into votes for the member.

Pork - Members of Congress are able to influence the appropriation process. This can take the form of trying to increase federal spending in their states and districts. Infrastructure, military installations, and scientific research are all examples of the federal spending in a district. This spending increases economic activity, which improves the lives of constituents (*American Government*, 14th ed., pages **222, 314**).

Scoring

This essay is worth 6 points. One point is awarded for each correct identification. One point is awarded for each correct explanation.

Calculating your score on the AP Exam

SECTION 1: MULTIPLE-CHOICE QUESTIONS

Total number answered correctly _____

SECTION II: FREE-RESPONSE QUESTIONS

Question 1 ____ × 1.875 equals _____

Out of 8   do not round

Question 2 ____ × 2.5 equals _____

Out of 6   do not round

Question 3 ___ × 3.0 equals _____

Out of 5   do not round

Question 4 ___ × 2.5 equals _____

Out of 6   do not round

TOTAL FOR SECTION II ___

COMPOSITE SCORE:

_____ + _____ = _____

Section I   Section II   Composite Score

Student scores are weighted differently each year to determine the final AP score. The conversion chart below is according to the weighting on the 2009 exam:

COMPOSITE SCORE RANGE	AP GRADE
93–120	5
82–92	4
66–81	3
48–65	2
0–47	1

Unit I: The Constitution

Correlates to Chapter 2 in *American Government, 14th Edition*

When delegates reached Philadelphia in 1787 with the charge of revising the Articles of Confederation, none could have imagined the momentous outcomes their meetings would have. While the Articles had established a government for the new nation, their failings were apparent to most. The delegates brought with them a host of historical and philosophical concerns that would shape a new constitution.

Key Terms

amendment
Antifederalists
Articles of Confederation
bill of attainder
Bill of Rights
checks and balances
coalition
concurrent powers
Constitutional Convention
enumerated powers
ex post facto law
faction
federalism
Federalists
Great Compromise
habeas corpus
judicial review
line-item veto
New Jersey Plan
republic
reserved powers
separation of powers
Shays's Rebellion
unalienable
Virginia Plan

Key Concepts

- The Bill of Rights is adopted soon after the ratification of the Constitution to address many of the fears of the Antifederalists.

- Most of the founders feared factions, in particular Madison. He believed the causes of faction are "sown in the nature of man." If unchecked, these factions would tear apart the country, as each group vied for control of the government.

- The framers agreed that a separation of powers would be the best way to protect liberty and control the evils of factions.

- The framers defined a democracy as a rule by the people. In today's terms, it would be called direct democracy. A republic is a political system where the people exercise power through elected representatives. Under the U.S. Constitution, as originally written, only the House of Representatives was to be directly elected by the people.

- Thomas Hobbes viewed democracy as impossible because people would always pursue self-interest. This would result in what he termed the "war of all against all." John Locke believed that democracy was possible if people consented to the government and it expressed the will of the majority.

- Most framers viewed the Congress as the most important and most powerful branch of government. Over time, the power of the other branches has grown. There is tension between the branches today. Congress remains, for the most part, the focal point of policy making.

- Generally speaking, the goals in the preamble to the Constitution are vague. Therefore the government is free to set its own goals.

- The Constitution was designed to protect the political rights of the dominant group at time, white men who owned property. The rights of women were not mentioned. Native Americans were treated much like foreign nations. Finally, the institution of slavery was protected. Over time these groups have been enfranchised.

For a full discussion of the Constitution, see *American Government*, 14th ed., Chapter 2.

AP Tip

The solution to the problem of representation at the Constitutional Convention still resonates within our government. The Great Compromise led to the creation of the House of Representatives and the Senate, each with its own responsibilities and powers. Representation is likely to appear on the AP exam.

Multiple Choice Questions

1. All of the following were weaknesses of the Articles of Confederation EXCEPT

   (A) the national government could not resolve state boundary disputes

   (B) currency was not accepted outside of local areas

   (C) the military could not put down even small rebellions

   (D) the national government had too much power

   (E) there was no national judicial system

2. What was the result of the Great Compromise?

   (A) States were represented in the upper house, and individuals were represented in the lower house.

   (B) Individuals were represented in the upper house, and states were represented in the lower house.

   (C) Individuals were given proportional representation in both the House of Representatives and the Senate.

   (D) All members of Congress were selected by direct election.

   (E) Slaves were not counted in the census.

3. All of the following are part of the amendment process EXCEPT

   (A) a proposal accepted by a two-thirds vote of Congress

   (B) a proposal accepted at a national convention called by Congress as requested by two-thirds of the states

   (C) a national referendum (by popular vote) with two-thirds voter approval

   (D) ratification by three-fourths of state legislatures

   (E) ratification by three-fourths of states in special conventions

4. How does the Constitution provide an executive check on the judicial branch?

   (A) by allowing the president to remove Supreme Court justices from office

   (B) by permitting bureaucrats to ignore a decision of the Supreme Court

   (C) by allowing the president to propose a bill to Congress to overturn a decision by the Supreme Court

   (D) by nominating federal judges, subject to Senate confirmation

   (E) by appointing federal judges

5. How did the Antifederalists differ from the Federalists?

   (A) The Antifederalists wanted a stronger central government.

   (B) The Federalists wanted to protect state sovereignty.

   (C) The Antifederalists had a more positive view of human nature.

   (D) The Antifederalists believed that a strong central government would be too distant from the people.

   (E) The Antifederalists were opposed to representative democracy.

6. Which of the following guarantees of individual liberties is found in the original Constitution?

   (A) freedom of speech, press, and assembly

   (B) no official state religion

   (C) a prohibition against double jeopardy

   (D) no unreasonable searches and seizures

   (E) no religious tests to hold office

7. Which of the following is NOT a criticism of separation of powers?

   (A) It creates gridlock in policy-making.

   (B) It makes it difficult for the government to act decisively in times of crisis.

   (C) It results in prompt, but hasty, decision-making.

   (D) It makes it difficult to stimulate economic growth.

   (E) It damages our position of international leadership.

8. What would be the impact of the line-item veto on the separation of powers?

   (A) It would weaken the presidency and strengthen Congress.

   (B) It would strengthen the presidency in relation to Congress.

   (C) It would prevent the Supreme Court from using judicial review.

(D) It would strengthen the power of the states.

(E) It is not clear how the line-item veto would affect the separation of powers.

9. All of the following were arguments by the Federalists in support of the Constitution EXCEPT

(A) representative democracy would be preferable to direct democracy

(B) a large republic would be preferable to a small republic

(C) the new Constitution would eliminate factions

(D) a diversity of interests would be represented in the new government

(E) the majority interests would be less able to persecute minority interests

10. Which of the following best describes judicial review?

(A) The Supreme Court may amend the Constitution.

(B) The Supreme Court may nullify state laws if they provide more rights than are contained in the federal Bill of Rights.

(C) The Supreme Court may remove state government officials who violate the Constitution.

(D) The Supreme Court may recommend impeachment proceedings against the president.

(E) The Supreme Court may nullify government acts that conflict with the Constitution.

11. All of the following were features of the New Jersey plan EXCEPT:

(A) Equal representation in the national legislature

(B) Power to regulate interstate commerce vested in the national government

(C) Bicameral Legislature

(D) Plural Executive

(E) Executive elected by Congress

12. How can the President check the power of the other branches?

(A) Dissolve Congress and call for new elections

(B) Remove Judges who commit serious crimes

(C) Bypass Congress by submitting proposed Constitutional amendments to the states

(D) Vetoing judicial decisions

(E) Nominating federal judges

13. The Bill of Rights, as originally adopted in 1791 applied to:

(A) Both state and national governments

(B) The Congress and the President, but not the courts

(C) Only the national government

(D) Only the States

(E) The Congress only, but not the President and the courts

14. Under the original text of the Constitution, which of the following rights were protected:

(A) Free speech

(B) Right to a jury trial

(C) Freedom of religion

(D) Right to privacy

(E) Prohibition of unreasonable searches and seizures

15. Which of the following institutions did the people have a right to elect under the Constitution as originally written:

(A) President

(B) House of Representatives

(C) Senate

(D) Judiciary

(E) Bureaucracy

Free Response Questions

1. While the Federalists supported ratification of the Constitution, the Antifederalists were opposed to ratification.

(a) Identify and explain TWO arguments made by the Federalists in support of the Constitution.

(b) Explain how the Antifederalists countered each of the arguments you discussed in part

2. The Constitution of the United States as originally written contained no "bill of rights." It was not until after the ratification of the Constitution and the beginning of the first session of Congress that one was drafted and submitted to the states for approval. Identify and explain three reasons why the Constitution did not contain a "bill of rights."

Answers

Multiple Choice Answers

1. (D) Most of the power under the Articles of Confederation was given to the states (*American Government*, 14th ed., page **27**).

2. (A) Under the Great Compromise, the House of Representatives is proportional and elected directly, and there are two senators per state. Senators were originally chosen by state legislators; they are now chosen by direct election (*American Government*, 14th ed., page **31**).

3. (C) A proposed amendment must receive a two-thirds vote in Congress or in a specially held national convention. It must then be approved by a three-fourths vote in state legislatures or through special state ratifying conventions (*American Government*, 14th ed., page **33**).

4. (D) The president nominates federal judges. Judges must be confirmed by the Senate.

5. (D) The Antifederalists argued that a strong national government would be too distant from the people and would take away powers that belong to the states (*American Government*, 14th ed., page **36**).

6. (E) Under the original Constitution, there may be no religious qualification or test to hold office. The rest of the protections are contained in the Bill of Rights (*American Government*, 14th ed., page **37**).

7. (C) Separation of powers results in slow and deliberate decision-making. This can make it difficult to act quickly regarding foreign affairs, crises, and the economy (*American Government*, 14th ed., pages **41–42**).

8. (B) The line-item veto would strengthen the president by allowing him to veto a part of a bill. The president does not have line-item veto power (*American Government*, 14th ed., pages **45–46**).

9. (C) The Founders argued in favor of representative democracy and large republics. While they did not believe the Constitution would eliminate factions, they believed that it was structured to control the "mischiefs of faction" (*American Government*, 14th ed., page **35**).

10. (E) Judicial review is the Supreme Court's power to interpret the Constitution and nullify state and federal laws that conflict with it (*American Government*, 14th ed., page **33**).

11. (C) The New Jersey plan only called for minor amendments to the Articles of Confederation. The plan retained the idea of equal representation in a unicameral legislature (*American Government*, 14th ed., pages **30–31, 35**).

12. (E) The president has the power of nominate federal judges with the "advice and consent of the Senate" (*American Government*, 14th ed., page **32**).

13. (C) The Bill of Rights was only intended to restrict the actions of the national government. States were restricted by their bills of rights. Only later, through the process of selected incorporation, did the Bill of Right become binding upon the states and even then not in its entirety (*American Government*, 14th ed., pages **38–39**).

14. (B) The right to a jury trial in criminal cases is protected in the original text of the Constitution. It is augmented by the Sixth Amendment (*American Government*, 14th ed., pages **37, 44**).

15. (B) Only the House of Representatives was directly elected by the people.

Free Response Answers

1. (a) The Federalists argued that large republics were more capable of protecting against factions. In a large republic, factions would compete with other factions, which would make it more difficult for one self-interested group to gain control of the government. The Federalists also argued that separation of powers and checks and balances would prevent tyranny by any group or individual. By providing different levels of government, no branch or group could become too powerful (*American Government*, 14th ed., page **35**).

   (b) The Antifederalists countered that a large, strong national government would be too distant from the people and would not be able to represent the will of the citizens. They also argued that different levels of government would not ensure democracy unless individual liberties received specific protections. The Antifederalists wanted a Bill of Rights to protect states and individuals from overreaching by the national government (*American Government*, 14th ed., page **36**).

2. The original text of the Constitution did not contain a "bill of rights" for three reasons. (1) The original text did contain provisions for protecting some individual liberties, such as habeas corpus, no bills of attainders, and trial by jury. (2) Most states had bills of rights at the time. When the inclusion of a bill of rights was suggested at the convention, many thought that the protections found at the state level would be sufficient. (3) The national government is a government of specific or limited powers. If the national government does not possess the power to, for example, establish a national church, then is it not permitted to do so. Therefore many framers felt that a specific prohibition would be redundant (*American Government*, 14ᵗʰ ed., pages **37–38**).

Unit II: Federalism

Correlates to Chapter 3 in *American Government, 14ᵗʰ Edition*

Federalism is a philosophy of government based on the division of power between state and federal government. In the United States, it has been a persistent source of political conflict.

Key Terms

categorical grants
conditions of aid
dual federalism
federalism
grants in aid
initiative
mandates
"necessary and proper"
nullification
police power
recall
referendum
waiver

Key Concepts

- The United States uses a federal system to balance the power of the national government with the power of the state governments.

- Federalism in the United States is a dynamic force, with power shifting between the national and state governments over time.

- Federalism allows each level of government (national and state) to dominate in its own sphere of influence.

- In the American political system, sovereignty is not vested exclusively in either the national or the state governments.

- Political power in the United States is not neatly divided between the national and state government. Originally, most political power was vested with the states. Over time power shifted the national government. Most recently some power has "devolved" back to the states.

- Federalism in the United States implies that people in different parts of the county will be treated differently as different states are free to enact different policies. Federalism also tends to increase the opportunities for citizen participation.

- The U.S. Constitution spells out the power of the national government and reserves other powers to the states. However, these guidelines are subject to interpretation by the U.S. Supreme Court.

For a full discussion of federalism, see *American Government,* 14ᵗʰ ed., Chapter 3.

AP Tip

It is important to know the difference between categorical and block grants. Because conditions of aid and mandates are the primary ways that the federal government pressures state governments to do what it wants, they are a significant aspect of federalism and are likely to appear on the AP exam.

Multiple Choice Questions

1. Which of the following is the best example of devolution?
   - (A) the No Child Left Behind law, which provides states with monetary incentives for meeting national educational guidelines
   - (B) the *McCullough v. Maryland* case, which allowed the federal government to maintain a national bank
   - (C) civil rights legislation mandating that states not discriminate
   - (D) block grants, by which money from the national government is given to the states for discretionary use with broad guidelines
   - (E) the federal tax code, which provides deductions for local charities

2. The Founding Fathers devised a federal system for all of the following reasons EXCEPT
   - (A) federalism is one method for checking government's power and protecting personal liberty
   - (B) concentrating power in a single entity might create tyranny
   - (C) under the Articles of Confederation, the national government was too dependent on the states for survival
   - (D) a federal system provides balance of power between the state and national governments
   - (E) federal systems were common throughout the world and were proven to be effective

3. Which of the following statements best describes the impact of the Tenth Amendment?

   (A) It has been effective in protecting and expanding the powers of the states.

   (B) It had little impact at first but has been expanded over time to protect state powers.

   (C) It has rarely had much practical significance.

   (D) The Supreme Court has interpreted it consistently over time.

   (E) It has protected the powers of the states, but not those of individual citizens.

4. Which of the following Constitutional provisions has been interpreted as weakening the Tenth Amendment?

   (A) the full faith and credit clause

   (B) the supremacy clause

   (C) the Ninth Amendment

   (D) the necessary and proper clause

   (E) the extradition clause

5. The concept that the national government is supreme in its own sphere while the states are equally supreme in theirs is known as

   (A) cooperative federalism

   (B) balanced federalism

   (C) home rule

   (D) emerging federalism

   (E) dual federalism

6. Figure 3.2 supports which of the following conclusions?

   (A) The amount of federal grant money given to states more than doubled between 1960 and 2011.

   (B) The category in which federal grant money increased the most from 1960 until 2011 is health.

   (C) Because the interstate highway system was built by 2011, spending on transportation dropped.

   (D) Most of the money given to states for education and training comes in the form of block grants.

   (E) Devolution has taken place for all categories of federal grants.

7. States have found federal funding attractive for all of the following reasons EXCEPT

   (A) in the late 19th and early 20th centuries, the national government had surplus money to spend on the states

FIGURE 3.2 The Changing Purpose of Federal Grants to State and Local Governments

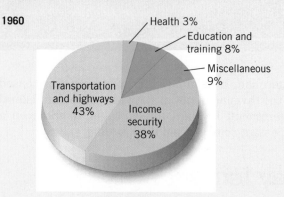

1960

Health 3%
Education and training 8%
Miscellaneous 9%
Transportation and highways 43%
Income security 38%

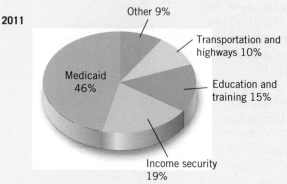

2011

Other 9%
Transportation and highways 10%
Medicaid 46%
Education and training 15%
Income security 19%

Source: Congressional Budget Office, *Federal Grants to State and Local Governments*, March 2013, pp. 2-4.

   (B) in the late 20th century, the income tax provided a flexible source of federal grant money

   (C) the federal government can print money when it is needed to fund programs

   (D) federal grants rarely come with strings attached

   (E) state politicians can get federal money without having to take the unpopular political position of supporting expanding government

8. Why do states prefer block grants to categorical grants?

   (A) Categorical grants require the states to spend matching funds.

   (B) Block grants allow states to spend funds on any governmental purpose.

   (C) Categorical grants are often rescinded.

   (D) The amounts given in block grants are stable from year to year.

   (E) Block grants allow local officials to satisfy the needs of interest groups.

TABLE 3.1 Federal Grants to State and Local Governments (2011)

The federal government spent more than $625 billion on grants to states in 2011.	
Among the biggest items:	
Medicaid	$276.2 billion
Income Security	$116.4 billion
Education and training	$101.4 billion
Transportation	$61 billion
Community development	$18.6 billion

Source: U.S. Census Bureau, *Statistical Abstract of the United States*: 2012, Table 432, p. 269.

9. Suppose the state of Nevada receives federal money to renovate McCarran International Airport. What term best describes this?

    (A) a categorical grant

    (B) a formula grant

    (C) a block grant

    (D) a condition of aid

    (E) a mandate

10. The table above supports which of the following conclusions?

    (A) Most federal grant money goes to support infrastructure, like roads and bridges.

    (B) States spend very little of their own money on health care.

    (C) Federal grants for Medicaid are more than double the spending on any other program.

    (D) States with a high percentage of poor citizens are more likely to receive federal grant money.

    (E) Federal grant money is distributed unevenly, with a few states receiving the bulk of the funds.

11. The significance of *United States v. Lopez* and *United States v. Morrison* is:

    (A) There is a limit to the power of the national government to claim "interstate commerce" as a justification for a policy.

    (B) The fundamental supremacy of the national government was upheld.

    (C) Congress may use the Commerce Clause as a justification for the expansion of national power if it demonstrates a "compelling government interest."

    (D) States are prohibited from interfering in a primary function of the national government.

    (E) The doctrine of "dual sovereignty" is fundamentally enshrined in the original text of the United States Constitution.

12. Federalism has what impact on the cost of political participation?

    (A) It tends to increase the cost of political participation at the national level.

    (B) It tends to increase the cost of political participation for large groups.

    (C) It tends to lower the cost of political participation for most all groups.

    (D) It tends to lower the cost of political participation for minority groups only.

    (E) It tends to increase the cost of political participation at the state level.

13. Under the United States Constitution, cities and other municipalities are:

    (A) protected by the Ninth Amendment and the Tenth Amendment

    (B) creatures of the states

    (C) created by the national government and subject to its direct control

    (D) sovereign creations of the people

    (E) accountable only to their residents

14. Which of the following is the best example of an intergovernmental lobby?

    (A) The mayor of New York City filing a lawsuit challenging the constitutionality of a national law.

    (B) The governor of Oklahoma negotiating with the governor of Arkansas an interstate compact regulating the water usage on the Arkansas River.

    (C) The mayor of Philadelphia arguing before a congressional committee for increased funding for transportation.

    (D) The secretary of education encouraging congress to increased funding for after-school programs.

    (E) The president of the United States delivering his state of the union message to Congress.

15. Which of the following is most clearly a condition of aid:

    (A) The Supreme Court ordering school desegregation.

    (B) Congress requiring the Defense Department to purchase a new weapons system.

(C) The president issuing an executive order establishing affirmative action in the awarding of government contracts.

(D) Congress requiring states to set their drinking age at 21 in exchange for highway funding.

(E) The Food and Drug Administration prohibiting the sale of untested drugs.

Free Response Questions

1. One way for the national government to influence the states is through the grant process.
   (a) Define one of the terms from the list of terms below.
   (b) Explain how it affects policy making, giving an example.
   (c) Define another term from the list below.
   (d) Explain how it affects policy making, giving an example.
   Terms: categorical grants, block grants, mandates.

2. Federalism in the United States is division of power between the national government and the states. However, this division is constantly changing. Since the ratification of the U.S. Constitution there has been a general increase in the power of the national government.
   (a) Identify 3 factors that have contributed to the growth of the power of the national government relative to the power of the states since the ratification of the U. S. Constitution.
   (b) For each factor you have identified in (a) explain *how* that factor has increased the power of the national government

Answers
Multiple Choice Answers

1. (D) Devolution is an effort by the national government to return some powers to the states. Block grants, which allow states to spend federal money using some discretion, are an example of devolution (*American Government*, 14th ed., pages **70–72**).
2. (E) Federal systems were uncommon when the Constitution was written and they are relatively rare today. There are only eleven countries with federal systems (*American Government*, 14th ed., pages **53, 61**).
3. (C) The Supreme Court has tried to interpret the Tenth Amendment as giving the states certain powers beyond the reach of the federal government, but there is a pattern of contradictory decisions by the Supreme Court over time. As a result, the Tenth Amendment has rarely had much practical significance (*American Government*, 14th ed., pages **53–54**).
4. (D) The Necessary and Proper Clause, also known as the Elastic Clause, gives to the national government any power important for carrying out its expressed powers. As a result, the power of the national government was expanded relative to state power (*American Government*, 14th ed., pages **55–56**).
5. (E) Dual federalism is the idea that the national and state governments are supreme in their own respective spheres. This has been replaced with cooperative federalism, with each level of government sharing overlapping powers (*American Government*, 14th ed., pages **57, 72**).
6. (B) In 1960, about 3 percent of federal grants to state and local governments were for health care. Today, however, one federal-state health care program alone, Medicaid, accounts for nearly half of all federal grants (*American Government*, 14th ed., page **65**).
7. (D) While federal funding has historically provided states with significant resources, it often comes with provisions regarding how the money must be spent (*American Government*, 14th ed., pages **64–65**).
8. (B) Block grants allow states to spend federal money on any governmental purpose, although lately, they are coming with more strings attached. Categorical grants require the states to spend the money on a specific purpose, like building an airport (*American Government*, 14th ed., pages **66–67**).
9. (A) Categorical grants are used by states for specific purposes, like building an airport (*American Government*, 14th ed., pages **66–67**).
10. (C) Grant money for Medicaid, which provides health care for the poor, amounts to $276.2 billion. This is more than double the $116.4 billion spent on income security programs and more than triple the amount spent on other programs (*American Government*, 14th ed., page **64**).
11. (A) From the 1930s until the 1990s the Supreme Court allowed Congress to use the Commerce Clause as a justification for increased national power. *United States v. Lopez* and *United States v. Morrison* signaled an end to this policy (*American Government*, 14th ed., pages **57–58**).
12. (C) Federalism tends to decrease to cost of political participation because it decentralizes the decision making in policy areas to the states (*American Government*, 14th ed., pages **62**).
13. (B) Cities and towns are entirely creatures of the states. They derive their legal authority

from the state and are subject to its regulation (*American Government*, 14th ed., pages **63**).

14. (C) Intergovernment lobbying is when state and local official pressure the national government for increased resources and favorable policy. There has been an increase in intergovernmental lobbing since the New Deal. However, the success of these efforts has been limited since the 1980s (*American Government*, 14th ed., pages **66**).

15. (D) A condition of aid is a requirement imposed on the states by the national government as a prerequisite to the distribution of funding. In the 1980s the national government required states to raise their drinking age to 21 or be subject to a reduction in highway funding.

Free Response Answers

1. (a) Categorical grants are given to the states to be used for a specific purpose defined by federal law (*American Government*, 14th ed., page **66**).

   (b) This affects policy making within the states because it restricts the states' ability to make new policy. States must spend the money in relatively narrowly defined ways, as prescribed by the federal government, such as building a new airport (*American Government*, 14th ed., pages **66**).

   (c) Block grants are devoted to some general programs with few restrictions on their use (*American Government*, 14th ed., pages **66–67**).

   (d) This enables states to create policies to address issues identified by the national government in ways that will most benefit their unique circumstances. Welfare money, for example, is given to states in a block grant. (*Alternate answer*): Mandates are laws enacted by the national government that the states must follow. Sometimes mandates require the states to spend money, and when the federal government does not accompany the requirement with funding, this is called an "unfunded mandate." (*Alternate answer*): Mandates make states act in a certain way. Often they cost money, which could be spent on other programs, and this limits policy-making by the states (*American Government*, 14th ed., pages **68–69**).

2. (a) Any three of the following factors are acceptable: Commerce Clause, Elastic Clause, Fourteenth Amendment Due Process Clause, Fourteenth Amendment Equal Protection Clause, the Taxing Clause (or Fiscal Federalism).

   (b) A loose interpretation of the Commerce Clause beginning with the case of *Gibbons v. Ogden*.

Unit III: Theories of Democratic Government

Correlates to Chapter 1 in *American Government, 14th Edition*

Americans regularly use terms such as *democracy*, *power*, and *authority*. Few take the time, however, to analyze the shades of meaning behind these critical words and their implications for understanding government. Political scientists devote their careers to considering two basic questions drawn largely from these concepts: Who governs? To what ends?

Key Terms

authority
benefit
bureaucratic view
class view
client politics
cost
creedal passion view
democracy
direct or participatory democracy
elite
entrepreneurial politics
interest group politics
issue
legitimacy
log-rolling
majoritarian politics
pluralist view
policy entrepreneur
political agenda
politics
pork-barrel legislation
power
power elite view
representative democracy

Key Concepts

- Politics is the process by which issues are settled in a political system.

- Democracy can viewed as either a system where citizens participate in the political process on a first-hand basis (direct or participatory democracy) or through the selection of representatives (representative democracy).

- There are six major theories that explain how political power is distributed in the United States (elite, class view, power elite, bureaucratic, pluralist, and creedal passion view).

- A political agenda is a set of issues that citizens believe the government should address.

- Political issues can be classified based upon who benefits and who bears the costs.

For a full discussion of theories of democratic government, see *American Government,* 14th ed., Chapter 1.

AP Tip

The political elite influence policymaking. The AP exam may ask about policymaking and how the political elite, including the bureaucracy, members of Congress, interest groups, and political parties, impacts it.

Multiple Choice Questions

1. All of the following statements about the beliefs of the framers of the Constitution are true EXCEPT

    (A) they favored representative democracy over direct democracy

    (B) they believed that most citizens did not have the time, information, and expertise to make informed choices

    (C) they believed that government decisions should mirror popular viewpoints

    (D) they recognized that representative democracy would proceed slowly

    (E) they insisted on the protection of civil rights and civil liberties

2. Which of the following statements best represents pluralist theory?

    (A) The class that dominates the economy also controls the government.

    (B) The most important policies are set by a loose coalition of three groups—corporate leaders, top military officers, and key political leaders.

(C) Leaders outside of the government structure dominate government.

(D) Unelected bureaucrats who run agencies dominate the government.

(E) There are so many groups that none of them can dominate the political process.

3. Which of the following is an example of political beliefs changing over time?

(A) Americans have come to believe that the federal government should play a bigger role in our lives.

(B) Americans have come to believe that the federal government should play less of a role in regulating the economy than it did when the country was founded.

(C) Americans wanted the federal government to play a bigger role in our lives until the 1980s, when this trend reversed.

(D) Americans have held relatively consistent views about the role of the federal government over time.

(E) Americans have become more convinced of the importance of political participation over the last fifty years.

4. What is one of the best barometers for measuring changes in who governs?

(A) public opinion polls

(B) an analysis of the topics covered in campaign speeches

(C) an examination of the amount of coverage given by the media

(D) an analysis of the policy process and changes in the laws

(E) there is no real way of measuring political change

5. What is the most basic definition of democracy?

(A) rule by the many

(B) rule by representatives who are directly elected

(C) any system of government with elections

(D) any system of government with a written constitution

(E) any system where citizenship is widely extended by most adults

6. In the United States, government agencies make a variety of regulations that impact the day-to-day life of Americans. According to the bureaucratic view of government, who holds most of the power in the American government?

(A) Congress, because it makes laws that are then translated into regulations by the bureaucracy.

(B) State governments, because they make most of the rules that impact a citizen's daily life.

(C) Appointed officials and career government workers, because they translate public laws into administrative actions.

(D) No one, because our government is so tangled in red tape it is difficult to determine who holds power.

(E) The courts, because they make policy and are unelected and serve for life.

7. What best explains the legitimacy of the United States government?

(A) The government has been in existence for more than two hundred years.

(B) Elections are frequent, and their outcome is rarely in doubt.

(C) Citizens may use the initiative process to change the law.

(D) The Constitution is widely accepted as the source of authority.

(E) All citizens have the right to vote and hold office.

8. Some argue that the government is dominated by business owners. Which of the following terms does this best describe?

(A) power elite view

(B) class view

(C) pluralism

(D) bureaucratic view

(E) prestige view

9. All of the following are arguments against direct democracy EXCEPT

(A) most people are not interested in government or politics

(B) it is impractical because of limited time, information, and energy

(C) most people do not have enough expertise to make good decisions on complicated policies

(D) direct democracy leads to bad decisions because people act according to their passions

(E) people might fall under the influence of charismatic speakers

10. Some argue that appointed officials actually run the government, despite the efforts of elected officials to control them. This belief is consistent with which theory of government?

    (A) bureaucratic view
    (B) pluralism
    (C) class view
    (D) indirect democracy
    (E) power elite view

11. Which view of government would hold that public policy is the product of the clash of special interests?

    (A) Bureaucratic
    (B) Class
    (C) Elite
    (D) Pluralist
    (E) Creedal passion

12. Which of the following is true of the political agenda?

    (A) It is controlled exclusively the political elite.
    (B) It is composed of issues of concern to citizens.
    (C) The Constitution restricts its consideration during wartime.
    (D) Presidents use it to manage the states.
    (E) It is set at the national conventions of the two major political parties.

13. Making appeals to large segments of the society is an example of

    (A) General politics
    (B) Majoritarian politics
    (C) Distributed politics
    (D) Interest group politics
    (E) Client politics

14. Entrepreneurial politics is characterized by

    (A) Distributed benefits, concentrated costs
    (B) Concentrated benefits, distributed costs
    (C) Limited benefits, concentrated costs
    (D) Limited benefits, limited costs
    (E) Concentrated benefits, limited costs

15. The primary source of legitimacy in the United States political system is derived from

    (A) State constitutions
    (B) The U.S. Constitution
    (C) Popularity
    (D) The bible
    (E) Congressional acts

Free Response Questions

1. The political agenda can be defined as the set of issues of concern to citizens. There are several political actors that could be defined as agenda setters.

   (a) Identify 3 agenda setters.
   (b) For each agenda setter identified in (a), explain how that actor sets or impacts the political agenda.

2. Political scientists have developed various theories to explain who rules the government. These theories include class view, power elite view, bureaucratic view, and pluralism.

   (a) Describe one theory from the list above. Explain the theory's beliefs about who rules the government.
   (b) Describe a second theory from the list above. Explain the theory's beliefs about who rules the government.

Answers
Multiple Choice Answers

1. (C) The framers believed that government should mediate, not mirror, popular views (*American Government*, 14th ed., page **6**).
2. (E) Pluralism is the belief that competition among all affected interests shapes public policy (*American Government*, 14th ed., page **9**).
3. (C) During the 1980s taxes were cut, along with government services, as many citizens thought government had grown too big.
4. (D) The authors of *American Government*, Wilson and DiIulio, contend that one of the best barometers of changes in who governs is the policy-making process (*American Government*, 14th ed., page **19**).
5. (A) Aristotle's basic definition of democracy is "rule of the many" (*American Government*, 14th ed., page **6**).
6. (C) The bureaucratic view is that the government is dominated by appointed officials who have a significant amount of power to make policy (*American Government*, 14th ed., pages **8–9**).
7. (D) The Constitution today is widely accepted as a source of legitimate authority (*American Government*, 14th ed., page **5**).
8. (B) Class view emphasizes the power in government of the rich or of multinational corporations. This view is inspired by the philosophy of Karl Marx (*American Government*, 14th ed., page **8**).

9. (A) Those opposed to direct democracy argue that citizens are limited by time, information, energy, and expertise and might fall under the influence of fleeting passions or demagogues (*American Government*, 14th ed., page **6**).

10. (A) The bureaucratic view, first set forth by Max Weber, contends that in modern states, appointed bureaucrats manage complex government affairs and actually make policy (*American Government*, 14th ed., pages **8–9**).

11. (D) The pluralist view states that public policy is the product of the interaction and competition of various interests in a political system (*American Government*, 14th ed., page **9**).

12. (B) The political agenda are those issues that citizens believe should be addressed by governmental action (*American Government*, 14th ed., pages **10–11**).

13. (B) Majoritarian politics involves convincing large segments of society that an issue or cause is worthy of support (*American Government*, 14th ed., pages **14–15**).

14. (A) Entrepreneurial politics are described to be in play when a large segment of society benefits from a policy, but the costs are borne by a much smaller segment of society (*American Government*, 14th ed., pages **16–17**).

15. (B) The U.S. Constitution is the source of legitimate political power in the United States as it draws its authority from the people (*American Government*, 14th ed., page **5**).

Free Response Answers

1. (a) Mentioning any three of the following is acceptable: groups (parties or interest groups), institutions (Congress, president bureaucracy, courts), media, or states (*American Government*, 14th ed., pages **11–13**).

   (b) Groups act as agenda setters by what policies they pursue through the political process. Institutions act as agenda setters by advancing or creating a policy. For example, a president can advocate for passage of a bill or issue and executive order. The media can act as an agenda setter by highlighting issues to the public. Finally, states can act as an agenda setter by make policy in concert with each other or by pursuing action through the judiciary (*American Government*, 14th ed., pages **12–13**).

2. (a) Class view is the theory, first developed by Karl Marx, that government is a reflection of economic forces and that class struggle between workers and capitalists dominates the economy. According to Marx, in a capitalist system, the elite property owners dominate government. The modern version of class theory emphasizes the power of the rich and multinational corporations (*American Government*, 14th ed., page **8**).

   (b) The power elite view contends that corporate leaders, top military officers, and a handful of key political leaders control government, although they do not hold elective office. These leaders dominate a country and are not representative of the population as a whole. (*Alternate answer*): The bureaucratic view contends that those who operate governmental agencies from day to day actually control policy-making. Unlike Marx's, this theory, proposed by Max Weber, emphasizes social and political factors. The specialization and expertise of bureaucrats enables them to control key government functions, often making policy. (*Alternate answer*): Pluralism is the theory that political resources, such as money, prestige, expertise, organizational position, and access to the mass media, are widely dispersed in our society. Therefore, one group cannot control policy. Groups compete for power. Pluralists acknowledge that political resources are not distributed evenly (*American Government*, 14th ed., pages **7–9**).

Unit IV: American Political Culture

Correlates to Chapter 4 in *American Government, 14th Edition*

Many developing nations have adopted the American constitutional model, hoping to institute features such as federalism, an elected president, a bicameral legislature, and separation of powers. Most of these have experienced brief periods of democracy interrupted by military takeovers, the rise of demagogues, and wholesale corruption. It is the American political culture that has allowed the American model to endure in the United States.

Key Terms

civic competence
civic duty
civil society
class consciousness
orthodox
political culture
progressive

Key Concepts

- American political culture refers to the long-standing patterns in how people view government, politics and the economy.

- American political culture refers to views about how government should function and its guiding principles, whereas political ideology refers to specific views about which programs and policies government should pursue.

- American "exceptionalism" is the idea that American views on government, politics, religion, and economics are distinctly different from the views held by citizens in other countries. This idea of "exceptionalism" is debated by social scientists and historians.

- Today, there is less trust in the government when compared to the 1950s. However, Americans are much more patriotic and religious than most Europeans and also have a great deal of trust in the Constitution.

- Americans generally believe in equality of opportunity and not equality of results.

- America's political culture has imbued it with more tolerance and a greater respect for orderly procedures and personal rights than can be found in nations with constitutions like ours. Therefore it is possible for political systems with similar laws and constitutions to those of the United States to function quite differently.

For a full discussion of American political culture, see *American Government,* 14th ed., Chapter 4.

AP Tip

American political and economic assumptions are fundamental to the political culture that allows the American system of government to work. Concepts such as liberty, equality, and individualism permeate our system and may appear on the AP exam.

Multiple Choice Questions

1. All of the following are important elements in the American view of the political system EXCEPT
   (A) Americans believe they should be able to do pretty much as they please
   (B) Americans think government officials should be accountable to the people
   (C) Americans believe that individuals are responsible for their own actions
   (D) Americans believe that government should try to equalize the property and living conditions of citizens
   (E) Americans feel people ought to help out in their communities

2. Which of the following best defines "civil society"?
   (A) a society that has manners, where people are generally respectful of one another's feelings
   (B) a society that uses a merit principle in awarding government jobs
   (C) a government that has a large number of civil servants working in various agencies
   (D) a collection of governmental and nongovernmental groups that work together in making policies
   (E) a collection of private, voluntary groups that make cooperation easier and hold the government accountable

3. One core American attitude about the economic system is
   (A) a widely held commitment to individualism and personal responsibility
   (B) the belief that social welfare policies should be expanded
   (C) the belief that women and minorities should have preferential treatment in hiring
   (D) a commitment to help all citizens, whether or not they are truly in need
   (E) the belief that wages should be based on economic need, as well as hard work

4. In comparison with most other nations,
   (A) Americans have less confidence in public and private institutions
   (B) Americans have less confidence in private institutions and more confidence in public institutions
   (C) Americans have more confidence in both public and private institutions
   (D) Americans have less confidence in public institutions and more confidence in private institutions
   (E) this is impossible to measure because Americans' views are so diverse

5. Which of the following statements about civic duty is most accurate?
   (A) Americans vote less and have a weaker sense of civic duty than their European counterparts.
   (B) Americans are less active in their local communities than citizens of Europe.
   (C) Most Americans believe that participating in government activities should be optional and that there should be no duty to participate.
   (D) Most Americans do not believe that their actions can have an impact on government policies.
   (E) Americans have a stronger sense of civic duty than citizens of the United Kingdom or Mexico.

6. Which of the following statements best describes the trend in Americans' trust in government?
   (A) Americans have had a high level of trust in government officials since World War II.
   (B) Americans now trust government officials more than they did during the 1950s.
   (C) Beginning with the Watergate scandal, there has been a steady decline in Americans' trust in government officials.

(D) Americans' trust in government officials has declined at a fairly steady rate since the 1950s.
(E) Americans' trust in government officials drops in wartime and rises in peacetime.

7. Citizens who believe they can influence political events have a high sense of civic
   (A) effectiveness
   (B) culture
   (C) competence
   (D) socialization
   (E) legitimacy

8. All of the following are true about political tolerance in America EXCEPT
   (A) Americans are more tolerant of members of different religious groups than they are of atheists.
   (B) Lawyers and judges are more tolerant of specific political activities than are most citizens.
   (C) Americans are willing to allow many people with whom they disagree to participate in the political process.
   (D) Americans have become more tolerant over the years.
   (E) Americans will support liberties for all groups both in theory and in practice.

9. Which of the following is the best example or description of civil society?
   (A) businesses and labor unions working together to reach a bargaining agreement
   (B) political parties running campaigns to get their candidate elected
   (C) voluntary associations outside of government control
   (D) a political culture where citizens respect each other's rights and viewpoints
   (E) members of Congress from both political parties working on bipartisan legislation

10. All of the following are part of American political culture EXCEPT
   (A) Americans believe in the protection of rights
   (B) Americans believe in political equality
   (C) Americans do not support programs to help those truly in need
   (D) Americans think government officials should be accountable
   (E) Americans believe citizens should become involved in their communities

TABLE 4.1   **Attitudes in the USA and Other Democracies**

	Pride	Outside Control	Teach Value of Work	God and Morality
USA	71%	32%	60%	58%
Canada	66	35	51	30
Britain	45	48	38	25
France	38	54	50	13
Germany	21	68	22	33
Italy	38	66	Na	27

Key to columns:

Pride: "I am very proud to be a member of [country]"

Outside Control: "Success in life is determined by forces outside our control"

Teach Value of Work: "Children should be taught the value of hard work"

God and Morality: "It is necessary to believe in God to be moral"

Source: © 2006 by Andrew Kohut and Bruce Stokes. Reprinted by permission of Henry Holt and Company, LLC and the Pew Research Center.

11. As of 2010, the fastest-growing ethnic group in the United States was:

   (A) Asians

   (B) Blacks

   (C) Hispanics

   (D) Native Americans

   (E) Whites

12. Based on the information in the above table, which of the following is likely true:

   (A) Americans have less pride in their country than the French.

   (B) Americans are more likely to believe that factors outside of their control determine their achievement than do citizens in other countries.

   (C) Americans tend to be more religious than people in other countries.

   (D) Both Americans and Germans think it is important to teach the value of work.

   (E) Americans' pride in their country has been increasing over time.

13. The political culture of the United States most likely would support which of the following statements?

   (A) Religion has a negative impact on society.

   (B) The government should intervene to ensure that income disparities are eliminated.

   (C) It is acceptable that the wealthy have a greater impact on the political system than do the poor.

   (D) The American system of government is sound.

   (E) Equality before the law is NOT as important as economic equality.

14. The primary vehicle for the transmission of political culture in the United States is:

   (A) Family

   (B) Peer group

   (C) School

   (D) State

   (E) Religious Institutions

15. Civil society is best defined as:

   (A) governmental institutions that regulate interactions between citizens

   (B) a society that promotes civil rights

   (C) a society that is tolerant of diverse viewpoints

   (D) a set of non-governmental institutions that promote cooperation

   (E) commercial and governmental institutions that promote economic activity

Free Response Questions

1. American political culture differs from many West European nations with respect to beliefs about the economic system.

   (a) Explain one way in which Americans' beliefs about the economic system differ from the political beliefs of citizens in Western European countries.

   (b) Explain one reason for the difference in beliefs that you identified in part (a).

Answers

Multiple Choice Answers

1. (D) Americans believe everybody should have an equal chance to participate and succeed. Most Americans do not support equality of outcomes or living conditions (*American Government*, 14th ed., pages **80–81**).

2. (E) Civil society is a collection of groups outside of government that teach people how to cooperate. Many political scientists believe a strong civil society is necessary for a thriving democracy (*American Government*, 14th ed., pages **90–91**).

3. (A) There is a widely—but not universally—shared commitment to economic individualism and personal responsibility as the key determinants of economic success (*American Government*, 14th ed., pages **81–82**).

4. (C) Today, people have less confidence in government than they once did. However, compared to most countries, Americans have more confidence in public and private institutions (*American Government*, 14th ed., pages **83**).

5. (E) Americans have a strong sense of civic duty. In addition, they have a stronger sense of civic competence—the belief that they can impact government policies (*American Government*, 14th ed., page **83**).

6. (D) Since the 1950s, there has been a more or less steady decline in the proportion of Americans who say they trust the government in Washington to do the right thing (*American Government*, 14th ed., pages **89–90**).

7. (C) Civic competence is the belief that a citizen can influence government (*American Government*, 14th ed., pages **83**).

8. (E) Americans are generally tolerant. However, for most of us, there is some group or cause from which we are willing to withhold political liberties—even though we endorse those liberties in the abstract (*American Government*, 14th ed., pages **91–92**).

9. (C) Civil society is the collection of private, voluntary groups, independent of the government (*American Government*, 14th ed., pages **90–91**).

10. (C) Americans support individual liberty, political equality, government accountability, and civic duty. While most Americans believe in personal responsibility, they support helping those truly in need (*American Government*, 14th ed., pages **81–82**).

11. (C) Hispanics are now the fastest-growing minority in the United States (*American Government*, 14th ed., page **81**).

12. (C) The table supports the conclusion that Americans are more religious that people in other countries. According to the table, 58 percent believe that religious belief is necessary for morality. American are more likely to be religious that are Europeans (*American Government*, 14th ed., page **82**).

13. (D) American political culture reflects the belief that Americans have a great deal of trust in their system of government, that is to say the rules and institutions. American's trust in the government, especially governmental officials, has varied over time (*American Government*, 14th ed., pages **83–84**).

14. (A) Family is the primary agent of cultural transmission or "socialization." The other agents do make an impact, but not to the degree that the family does (*American Government*, 14th ed., page **87**).

15. (D) Civil society is the nongovernmental, noncommercial voluntary associations in which people engage. Most political scientists believe that a strong civil society is necessary for democratic government. (*American Government*, 14th ed., pages **90–91**).

Free Response Answers

1. (a) Americans do not support giving all workers in a particular industry equal pay, and they are more willing than their Western European counterparts to tolerate economic inequality. Furthermore, Americans are willing to accept a larger difference between the salaries of workers and those of managers. For example, hardly anyone is upset that Bill Gates has become such a wealthy man.

   (b) One reason for this difference in political culture between Americans and Europeans is that Americans value freedom over economic equality. They support higher pay for hard work. Despite their belief in personal responsibility, Americans support education and training programs to help disadvantaged people get ahead. However, Americans are less likely to support a federal guarantee of a basic income. As a result of the policies that stem from these beliefs, the United States has a greater income gap than most European countries (*American Government,* 14th ed., pages **77–78**).

Unit V: Public Opinion and Political Beliefs

Correlates to Chapter 7 in *American Government, 14th Edition*

Government action and inaction do not always match public opinion. This apparent contradiction to the principle of democratic government occurs for several reasons. First, the framers of the Constitution set up a government that does not always give the majority what they want. Measuring public opinion is also very difficult. Finally, active participants in government are more apt to achieve their goals than is the uninvolved general public.

Key Terms

elite
exit polls
gender gap
norm
political elites
political ideology
political socialization
poll
public opinion
random sample
sampling error

Key Concepts

- Public opinion refers to people's attitudes about various political and nonpolitical issues. It is measured by random sampling.

- The Framers of the Constitution believed that public opinion should have a limited role in government.

- Political socialization is the process by which political values and cultures are transmitted from one generation to the next.

- Political ideology is a set of beliefs about what policies that government should enact. Elites are typically more concerned with ideology than is the rest of the population. However, there is evidence that average Americans are becoming more ideological.

- There are divisions or cleavages in public opinion. These cleavages follow racial, gender, and economic lines.

- Most people will self-identify as liberal, moderate, or conservative. However, these labels often do not fully explain their complex viewpoints.

For a full discussion of public opinion and political beliefs, see *American Government*, 14th ed., Chapter 7.

AP Tip

The importance of family as an agent of political socialization is a widely known fact and would likely be part of any AP question regarding political socialization.

Multiple Choice Questions

1. Which of the following voters will most likely prefer a Republican candidate?
   (A) a black woman with a college degree and high income
   (B) a middle-class Asian man who belongs to a labor union
   (C) a southern white male business owner
   (D) an Hispanic employee of the federal government
   (E) a white "soccer mom" who lives in the suburbs

2. What is the effect of a social class on political attitudes?
   (A) In the United States, there is little correlation between social class and voting patterns.
   (B) People who run their own businesses tend to vote more as independents because they think more ideologically.
   (C) There is a growing gap between the voting pattern of the upper and lower classes.
   (D) Working class people tend to describe themselves as liberal.
   (E) Professionals tend to be socially conservative and support Republicans.

TABLE 7.2 Opinion Gaps Between Young Adults and Senior Citizens in 2012

	Age 18 to 29 %	Age 65 and Older %	Gap
Social Change			
Favor allowing gay and lesbian couples to marry	65	31	+34
Believe one parent can bring up a child as well as two parents together	65	36	+29
It's all right for blacks and whites to date each other	95	68	+27
Religiosity			
Prayer is an important part of my daily life	61	85	−24
I never doubt the existence of God	67	87	−20
Government			
The Constitution should be interpreted in terms of what it means in modern times*	62	35	+27
A free market economy needs government regulation in order to best serve the public interest	74	57	+17
When something is run by the government it is usually inefficient and wasteful	47	69	−22
Immigrants			
Newcomers from other countries threaten traditional American customs and values	43	58	−15
It bothers me when I come in contact with immigrants who speak little or no English	30	44	−14
Civic Engagement			
I'm Interested in keeping up with national affairs (completely agree)	46	63	−17
I feel it's my duty as a citizen to always vote	84	98	−14

Source: Pew Research Center, "Partisan Polarization Surges in Bush, Obama Years: Trends in American Values, 1987–2012," June 2012, with one point (*) from Pew Research Center, "Ideological Chasm Over Interpreting Constitution," June 2011.

3. Table 7.2 supports which of the following conclusions?

(A) Support for same-sex marriage represents the smallest gap in opinions.

(B) Adults under age 30 differ markedly from senior citizens (persons age 65 or older) in their opinions on many issues pertaining to social change, religiosity, government, immigration, and civic engagement.

(C) Adults 65 and older tend to be more in favor of issues of social change than those 18–29 year olds.

(D) Keeping up with national affairs is greatly important to young adults (18–29).

(E) Age-related opinion gaps are wider today than they were in the past.

4. Table 7.1 supports which of the following conclusions about the viewpoints of young adults?

(A) Most 18–24-year-olds believe politics has become too partisan.

(B) Most young people do not trust politicians.

TABLE 7.1 Young Adults on Politics and Politicians (2010)

Percent of 18- to 29-year-olds who agree that:	
politics has become too partisan	46%
elected officials don't have the same priorities I have	51%
getting involved in politics is an honorable thing to do	31%
people like me don't have any say about what government does	36%
it is difficult to find ways to be involved in politics	22%
politics is not relevant to my life right now	21%

Source: Institute of Politics, *The 17th Biannual Youth Survey on Politics and Public Service,* John F. Kennedy School of Government, Harvard University, Spring 2010.

(C) Most young people view politics as an honorable profession.

(D) The majority of 18–24-year-olds believe that elected officials do not share their priorities.

(E) Young people would become more involved in politics if it was easier to volunteer for a campaign.

5. A conservative would support which of the following measures?

    I. less government regulation of the economy

    II. affirmative action programs for underrepresented groups

    III. increased spending on social programs, such as welfare

    IV. the death penalty

(A) I and II

(B) I, II, and IV

(C) II and IV

(D) II, III, and IV

(E) I and IV

6. A public opinion poll asks whether or not people agree with the following statement: "The federal government should see to it that all people have adequate housing." Which of the following statements best describes the accuracy of the poll?

(A) It will not be accurate because a random sample was not used.

(B) It will not be accurate because the statement is loaded.

(C) It will not be accurate because of sampling error.

(D) It may be accurate depending upon how many people are polled.

(E) There is no way to determine the accuracy of the poll.

7. Most people believe there should be a limit on the number of terms to which members of Congress can be elected, but Congress has not approved term limits. Which of the following principles does this best illustrate?

(A) Public opinion polling should be used to make important government decisions.

(B) Most Americans do not pay much attention to Supreme Court opinions.

(C) Members of the Supreme Court are generally unaware of public opinion polls.

(D) Public opinion polls are not important in government policy making.

(E) Sometimes government policies go against what the public wants.

8. What is political socialization?

(A) a person's identification as a liberal or conservative

(B) the distribution of the public's beliefs about an issue over time

(C) the process by which people acquire their political values

(D) an informal meeting of people who share the same political ideology

(E) the official position taken by the government on any important issue

9. Which of the following has the greatest impact on political socialization?

(A) peers

(B) the media

(C) the community

(D) parents

(E) college professors

10. All of the following are true of political elites EXCEPT

(A) they are more likely to be activists

(B) they are better informed about politics than the general public

(C) they tend to associate with people who agree with them

(D) they tend to be ideologically consistent

(E) they tend to have moderate political beliefs

11. Which of the following would indicate that a national poll's results would not be reliable?

(A) polling 300 persons

(B) using a random sample

(C) avoiding leading questions

(D) polling 1500 persons

(E) asking questions that evoke an intellectual response

12. Which of the following agents of socialization will have the biggest impact on a person's party identification?

(A) friends

(B) religious institutions

(C) the media

(D) family

(E) peers

13. Which of the following is reflective of the gender gap in American politics?

(A) Men are more likely to support activist government than women

(B) Men are more likely to favor same-sex marriage than women

(C) Women are more likely to favor limited government than men

(D) Men are more likely to vote than women

(E) Women are more likely to support Democrats than men

14. Which of the following is an accurate reflection of current public opinion?

    (A) There is a sharp divide in ideology between social classes.

    (B) Hispanics are uniformly liberal.

    (C) More Americans self-identify as moderate than liberal.

    (D) Older Americans are more likely to favor governmental intervention in the economy.

    (E) Religion has a profound impact on all political issues.

15. Which of the following persons is most likely to prefer a Republican candidate?

    (A) White, Evangelical, Middle Class, Female

    (B) White, Protestant, Wealthy, Male

    (C) African American, Protestant, Government Employed, Female

    (D) Latino, Catholic, Working Class, Male

    (E) African American, Protestant, Wealthy, Female

Free Response Questions

1. Specific political beliefs and behaviors develop from a number of sources.

    (a) Identify one factor that impacts political beliefs and behaviors and explain how the factor you identified impacts political ideology.

    (b) Identify a second factor that impacts political beliefs and behaviors, and explain how the factor you identified impacts political ideology.

2. (a) Public opinion, as measured by a valid poll, can impact the political process. Explain how each of the following can affect the validity of a poll.

    • Random Sample

    • Sample Size

    • Question Bias

    (b) While polling can impact the political process, there are factors that can mitigate the impact of a poll. Explain how each of the following can decrease the effect of an opinion poll on a member of Congress' positions on issues.

    • Political Parties

    • Special Interest Groups

Answers

Multiple Choice Answers

1. (C) While many of the voters mentioned have some factors that influence conservative voting, the southern white male business owner has the most. He is white and male. In addition, many business owners prefer to vote Republican, as do southerners (*American Government*, 14th ed., page **158**).

2. (D) Working class people are more likely to describe themselves as liberal (*American Government*, 14th ed., page **161**).

3. (B) According to the table, adults under age 30 differ markedly from senior citizens (persons age 65 or older) in their opinions on many issues pertaining to social change, religiosity, government, immigration, and civic engagement (*American Government*, 14th ed., page **165**).

4. (D) Fifty-one percent of 18–24-year-olds believe politicians do not have the same priorities that they have.

5. (E) Conservatives tend to oppose affirmative action and increased social spending. They tend to support the death penalty. They prefer less government regulation of the economy.

6. (B) The statement is one-sided. Accurate public opinion polling requires that questions be worded fairly (*American Government*, 14th ed., page **155**).

7. (E) Although public opinion polls influence policy making, sometimes policymakers are not responsive to public opinion (*American Government*, 14th ed., page **166**).

8. (C) Political socialization is the complex process by which people acquire their political beliefs (*American Government*, 14th ed., pages **156–158**).

9. (D) Parents shape their children's ideology. This is especially true when both parents share the same party identification (*American Government*, 14th ed., pages **156–158**).

10. (E) Political elites are more ideological, and thus less likely to be moderate, than the average voter (*American Government*, 14th ed., pages **165–166**).

11. (A) Most pollsters will use a sample size of 1000 to 1500 persons (*American Government*, 14th ed., page **155**).

12. (D) Family, particularly parents, have the biggest influence on a person's party identification (*American Government*, 14th ed., pages **155–158**).

13. (E) Women are more likely to be Democrats than are men. Women are also slightly more likely to vote than men. Also, women are more liberal than men. (*American Government*, 14th ed., pages **159–160**).

14. (C) Over the last four decades, the number of people who self-identify as liberal has declined to about 20 percent. Approximately 40 percent of people self-identify as moderate (*American Government*, 14th ed., page **164**).

15. (B) All four variables point to an increased likelihood of preferring Republican candidates (*American Government*, 14th ed., pages **159–161**).

Free Response Answers

1. (a) One source of political opinion is the family. The vast majority of young people know their parents' political beliefs, and the majority share those beliefs. In some families, the dinner table is a political classroom where families discuss and share their values. However, on issues of civil liberties and race, young people tend to be more liberal than their parents (*American Government*, 14th ed., pages **156–158**).

   (b) Another source of political beliefs and behaviors is religion. Catholics and Jews tended to support the Democratic Party in the past, although that allegiance is weakening for Catholics. The Jewish religion has emphasized social justice, which may explain why many Jews vote Democratic. On the other hand, conservative Christians emphasize personal salvation and responsibility and have become a cornerstone of support for the Republican Party. (*Alternate answer*): Gender also influences political attitudes. A gender gap in voting signals that men and women see political issues differently. Men are more likely to support defense spending, while women are more likely to support social programs. As a result, more women than men vote for the Democratic Party (*American Government*, 14th ed., pages **158–159**).

2. (a) Random Sample – For an opinion poll to be valid, every member of the universe, that is the population to be measured, must have an equal opportunity to be polled. In the absence of this, the poll is simply a reflection of those who participated and not a reflection of the overall population.

   Sample Size – The sample size must be large enough to decrease the margin of error. Typically, national pollsters will use a sample of 1000 to 1500 persons.

   Question Bias – The questions must be worded in a manner that does not illicit a "non attitudinal answer." Any question that is designed to evoke an emotional response will be less likely to produce valid results (*American Government*, 14th ed., page 155).

   (b) Political Parties – Parties can influence the opinion of a member of Congress if he is running for re-election. If he is from a district that is heavily comprised of one party then the opinion of a national poll will have little impact. This is important due to districts that are increasingly gerrymandered to maximize the election of particular party. Further, party leadership in Congress can put pressure on Senators and representatives to vote in a manner that goes against public opinion. This is done through the use of rewards, such as choice committee assignments, or punishments, such as thwarting a member's legislative agenda.

   Special Interest Groups – Interest groups can influence a member of Congress because they possess specialized knowledge that may not be widely available or understood by the public. Further, interest groups can use their money to buy access to members. While it is highly unlikely that a member of Congress' vote can be bought with a contribution, the interest group can influence the member's actions regarding the content of legislation. For example, a member of Congress may be persuaded to change the wording of an otherwise popular bill that is detrimental to a special interest group. Such a change could preserve the overall content of the legislation but soften the negative impact on the special interest group.

Unit VI: Political Participation

Correlates to Chapter 8 in *American Government, 14ᵗʰ Edition*

The low rate of participation in national elections in comparison with European democracies is a source of great embarrassment to the United States. However, the problem might be based less on apathy and more on problems of voter registration. Americans participate in ways other than voting to a much greater extent than other democracies.

Key Terms

activists
Australian ballot
grandfather clause
literacy test
political participation
poll tax
registered voters
voting-age population (VAP)
voting-eligible population (VEP)
white primary

Key Concepts

- While voting is a common form of participation, the term encompasses many other forms of participation. Examples include volunteering for campaigns, protesting, and contacting elected officials, to name a few.

- There are different ways to measure voter turnout. One way is to look at the percentage of people who are aged 18 and above that vote. The other is to exclude those individuals who are ineligible to vote, such as felons.

- Most citizens participate in the political process at least occasionally. However, the percentage of citizens who participate on a regular basis is small.

- There are several demographic variables that correlate to voter turnout. These include age, education and race.

- There are differences between the participation levels of these groups for a variety of factors. Some groups perceive a value to participation. Other groups may not vote due to difficulty with registration or the voting process itself.

- The Framers of the Constitution believed that citizens should be involved in the political process, but thought that this participation should be limited. As a result, under the original text of

the Constitution, the people could only participate directly in the election of members of the House of Representatives.

- College-age citizens in the United States typically participate at low levels.

For a full discussion of political participation, see *American Government*, 14ᵗʰ ed., Chapter 8.

AP Tip

The AP exam might contain a question about the demographic factors (age, race, income, education, or region) that make someone more or less likely to vote.

Multiple Choice Questions

1. Figure 8.1 below supports which one of the following statements?

    (A) The easiest way to register to vote is through a government registration office.

    (B) The majority of Americans do not know where to go to register to vote.

    (C) One fifth of voters register at their motor vehicle office.

FIGURE 8.1 Method of Registration to Vote, 2010 Percent Distribution of Registered Voters

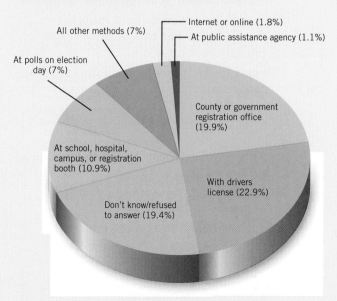

Source: U.S. Bureau of the Census, Current Population Survey, "Voting and Registration," November 2010.

(D) The main reason for not registering to vote is apathy.

(E) Methods of registration are becoming more numerous and convenient.

2. All of the following were used to keep blacks from voting EXCEPT

(A) segregation

(B) literacy tests

(C) poll taxes

(D) grandfather clauses

(E) intimidation and threats

3. The electorate has expanded as a result of all of the following EXCEPT

(A) the voting age has been lowered to 18

(B) states may not require residency of more than 30 days

(C) areas with significant non-English-speaking populations must provide ballots written in other languages

(D) residents of the District of Columbia may vote in presidential elections

(E) state standards now govern almost every aspect of voter eligibility

4. What is the most accurate way of comparing voter turnout in the United States with voter turnout in other counties?

(A) compare the percentages of citizens who vote

(B) compare the percentages of residents who vote

(C) compare the number of registered voters with the percentage of voters who cast ballots

(D) analyze how voter turnout rates have changed over time to determine trends in voter turnout rates

(E) compare the turnout among the voting-age population

5. Which of the following citizens is most likely to vote?

(A) a 65-year-old African American high school graduate

(B) a 35-year-old white college-educated woman

(C) a 70-year-old white college professor

(D) a 40-year-old Hispanic with an associate's degree

(E) an 18-year-old African American just starting college

6. What is the impact of religion on political participation?

(A) Religious people are less likely to vote, because they put their faith in a higher power.

(B) Religious people are more likely to give money to charities, but less likely to vote.

(C) Being active in a religious organization increases the likelihood of charitable volunteer work as well as voting.

(D) Being active in a religious organization increases participation in nonpolitical activities but does not increase the likelihood of voting.

(E) Religion has no measurable impact on the likelihood of voting.

7. How did voter turnout among young people (citizens under age 34) in the 2010 midterm elections compare with previous midterm elections?

(A) Voter registration in this group continued to increase dramatically.

(B) Voter turnout increased.

(C) Voter turnout decreased substantially.

(D) Voter turnout remained much the same as the previous election year.

(E) Voter turnout among young people surpassed the turnout for aged 65+ voters.

8. Table 8.3 supports which of the following statements?

(A) Citizens are more likely to register and vote as they age.

(B) Few people who register actually vote.

(C) Voter turnout in midterm elections is consistently higher than voter turnout in presidential elections.

(D) Voter registration always increases between elections.

(E) Voter turnout among those 25 to 34 years old has consistently increased from 1996 to 2008.

TABLE 8.3 Voter Registration and Turnout by Age

Age	Percent Registered/Voted, Midterm Elections				
	1994	1998	2002	2006	2010
18–20	37/17	32/14	33/15	37/17	34/16
21–24	46/22	35/19	43/19	45/22	47/22
25–34	52/32	52/28	50/27	50/28	50/27
65+	76/61	75/60	76/61	75/61	73/59

Age	Percent Registered/Voted, Presidential Elections				
	1996	2000	2004	2008	
18–20	46/31	41/28	51/41	53/44	
21–24	51/33	49/35	52/43	62/52	
25–34	57/43	55/44	56/47	66/57	
65+	77/67	76/68	77/69	77/70	

Source: Adapted from U.S. Bureau of the Census, *Current Population Reports*, June 2008, Table 400, and *Statistical Abstract of the United States: 2012*, Table 399, p. 246.

9. Which of the following citizens is most likely to participate in politics?

 (A) a 65-year-old male high school graduate

 (B) a 35-year-old college-educated woman

 (C) a 70-year-old female college professor

 (D) a 40-year-old man with an associate's degree

 (E) an 18-year-old woman starting college

10. In the 2008 presidential election, voter turn-out reached approximately 62 percent. Which of the following statements best describes this turnout rate?

 (A) It is the highest in recent decades and is higher than turnout in most European countries.

 (B) It is lower than turnout in most decades but higher than turnout in most European countries.

 (C) Voter turnout in the United States has not changed much in the past forty years, and it is lower than turnout in most European countries.

 (D) Voter turnout in the 2008 presidential election was nearly double what it has been over the past forty years.

 (E) It is the highest in recent decades but is still lower than turnout rates in most European countries.

11. Of the following, which group typically has the lowest voter turnout?

 (A) whites

 (B) 18–25 year olds

 (C) persons with graduate degrees

 (D) wealthy persons

 (E) persons with high political efficacy

12. In most European countries, voter turnout is higher than in the United States. Which of the following is a contributing factor to this?

 (A) lower voting ages

 (B) restrictive registration requirements

 (C) "same day" registration

 (D) automatic registration in those countries

 (E) enfranchisement of noncitizens

13. Many political scientists speculate that low voter turnout in the United States may indicate

 (A) profound distrust with all political leaders.

 (B) high levels of political knowledge.

 (C) a rather homogeneous population.

 (D) the existence of authoritarian tendencies.

 (E) relative satisfaction with the overall state of affairs.

14. What is the significance of *Smith v. Allwright*?

 (A) prohibited discrimination in voting based on sex

 (B) required states to offer registration when a person obtains a drivers license

 (C) declared the poll tax unconstitutional

 (D) declared the "white primary" unconstitutional

 (E) prohibited discrimination in voting based on age

15. The primary purpose behind voter registration in the United States is

(A) decrease voter turnout

(B) reduce voter fraud

(C) increase voter turnout

(D) increase the amount of information voters have

(E) decrease incumbency advantage

Free Response Questions

1. Americans participate in the political process in a number of ways.

   (a) Identify and explain one method, other than voting, of participating in the political process.

   (b) Identify and explain another method, other than voting, of participating in the political process.

2. Voter turnout in the United States is generally lower than most other liberal democracies.

   (a) Identify two demographic characteristics associated with low voter turnout.

   (b) Describe two constitutional amendments that were designed to increase political participation.

   (c) Identify one policy of the national or of a state government designed to increase voter turnout.

Answers

Multiple Choice Answers

1. (C) 22.9 percent, or one fifth, of voters registered through their motor vehicle office. This is a result of the motor-voter law, passed in 1993 (*American Government*, 14th ed., page **174**).

2. (A) Literacy tests, poll taxes, grandfather clauses, the all-white primary, and intimidation and threats were used to keep blacks from exercising their rights to vote. Jim Crow laws were used to segregate the races in public places (*American Government*, 14th ed., pages **177–178**).

3. (E) While the states originally set most of the standards for voter eligibility, the federal government now governs almost all aspects of this process (*American Government*, 14th ed., page **172**).

4. (E) Voting-age population measures the number of citizens who are eligible to vote. Countries can be compared accurately by looking at the turnout rates among voting-age citizens. The United States ranks last among well-established democracies in voter turnout rates (*American Government*, 14th ed., pages **173–175**).

5. (C) Voter turnout increases with age and educational level. Turnout rates are highest for whites, followed by blacks and Hispanics. Some political scientists believe this may be related more to socioeconomic class than to race (*American Government*, 14th ed., pages **172–175**).

6. (C) The majority of religious people participate in several forms of nonpolitical activities, including joining organizations, attending church services, and making charitable and church contributions. In addition, religious people are more likely to vote (*American Government*, 14th ed., page **183**).

7. (D) Although candidates had hoped to appeal to young people, turnout in the 2010 midterm election was roughly the same as that in the 2006 midterm election (*American Government*, 14th ed., page **174**).

8. (A) Voter registration and turnout increase with age. Voters 65 years of age or older had the highest levels of registration, at 75 percent in 2006, and turnout, at 61 percent in 2006 (*American Government*, 14th ed., page **174**).

9. (C) Voter turnout increases with age and educational level. Women vote at slightly higher rates than men do (*American Government*, 14th ed., pages **182–184**).

10. (E) Voter turnout in the 2008 presidential election was the highest it has been since 1960. However, it was still lower than the turnout in most European countries (*American Government*, 14th ed., page **173**).

11. (B) 18–24 year olds consistently have low voter turnout (*American Government*, 14th ed., page **172**).

12. (D) Most liberal democracies have automatic registration. The citizen does not have to do anything. Many experts see voter registration as a barrier to voting in the United States (*American Government*, 14th ed., page **174**).

13. (E) Many political scientists speculate that low voter turnout possibly could be a reflection of relative satisfaction. In many stable democracies the voter turnout is low (*American Government*, 14th ed., page **175**).

14. (D) The white primary was a mechanism to disenfranchise African Americans. The U.S. Supreme Court declared it unconstitutional in 1944 (*American Government*, 14th ed., page **178**).

15. (B) Registration was originally instituted during the progressive period as a means to combat voter fraud (*American Government*, 14th ed., page **180**).

Free Response Answers

1. (a) One method of participating in the political process is joining a civic association. By joining groups that provide services and do good works in the community, citizens can identify problems in their communities, lobby public officials, and even take steps to alleviate those problems themselves.

    (b) Another way to participate in the political process is by supporting social movements. People who have traditionally been the victims of discrimination may band together to work for change. One of the best examples of this is African American civil rights leaders, who worked to end segregation and lobbied for the passage of civil rights legislation. (*Alternate answer*): Writing letters or sending e-mail to legislators is another form of political participation. Members of Congress have people on staff who read letters and respond to them. Such letters can be effective in getting the attention of Congress if individual letters are persuasive or enough letters are sent on a particular issue. One example is the 1981 Reagan tax cuts. Reagan asked for the public's support, and Congress was flooded with letters favoring the bill (*American Government*, 14th ed., pages **172, 175**).

2. (a) Among many others, the following demographic characteristics are associated with low voter turnout: Nonwhite, young, low-income, and limited education. (*American Government*, 14th edition, page **181**)

    (b) The following amendments have been added to the U.S. Constitution to expand opportunities for voting: The Fifteenth Amendment prohibited states from discriminating based on race. This amendment was largely ignored until passage of the Voting Rights Act of 1965. The Seventeenth Amendment allowed citizens the right to vote for their U.S. senators. Prior to this amendment, senators were selected by state legislatures. The Nineteenth Amendment prohibited states from discriminating in voting based on sex. Some women were voting prior to this amendment. This was possible because states set voting requirements. The Twenty-Third Amendment allowed residents of the District of Columbia to elect presidential electors. Before this amendment, residents of the District of Columbia had no voice in the selection of the president because the District of Columbia is not a state. The Twenty-Fourth Amendment prohibited poll taxes. Poll taxes have a disproportionate impact on the poor. The Twenty-Sixth Amendment allowed 18-year-olds the right to vote. The Vietnam War was the rationale behind passage of this amendment (*American Government*, 14th edition, pages **172, 177**).

    (c) The national government has passed "Motor Voter." This law requires states to offer voter registration to eligible persons when they obtain or renew their driver's license. Many state governments have passed same day voter registration. This allows voters to register on the same day as the elections. As such, it removes registration as a barrier to voting (*American Government*, 14th ed., pages **172, 175**).

Unit VII: Elections and Campaigns

Correlates to Chapter 10 in *American Government, 14th Edition*

American campaigns are unique. Running for national office requires an *individual* effort—in many other democracies, running for national office requires a party effort. The candidate decides to run, raises money, and appeals to voters on the basis of personality and definition of issues. Political parties are playing a decreased role in American elections.

Key Terms

527 organizations
blanket primary
closed primary
clothespin vote
coattails
general election
gerrymandering
incumbent
independent expenditures
malapportionment
open primary
political action committee (PAC)
position issue
primary election
prospective voting
retrospective voting
runoff primary
soft money
sophomore surge
valence issue

Key Concepts

- Party nominees are selected during a primary election. The general election is used to select the person who wins the office.

- The federal government makes available funds for qualified presidential candidates. There is no federal funding for congressional candidates.

- Voters vote for candidates based on prospective and retrospective voting.

- American elections are based more on the personal qualities of the candidates rather than on party affiliation. The ideology of candidates can have more of an impact than their party identification.

- Party identification on the part of voters is a good predictor of voter behavior. Typically, only 10 to 20 percent of voters are up for grabs during any election. For those voters issues such as war and the economy are more important than their party identification.

- Who gets elected impacts the policies that are implemented.

For a full discussion of elections and campaigns, see *American Government*, 14th ed., Chapter 10.

AP Tip

Campaign finance continues to be a hotly contested political issue. The Federal Election Campaign Act of 1974 and Bipartisan Campaign Finance Reform Act of 2002 are likely targets for the AP exam.

Multiple Choice Questions

1. Presidential and congressional races differ in all of the following ways EXCEPT

    (A) presidential races are more competitive than races for the House of Representatives

    (B) a much smaller proportion of people vote in congressional races in nonpresidential election years

    (C) members of Congress can get credit for the constituent service they provide

    (D) candidates for Congress can disassociate themselves from what is going on in Washington, D.C.

    (E) congressional elections receive more national funding than presidential elections

2. Which of the following is the most accurate statement about the impact of party identification on voting behavior?

    (A) Party identification is only one factor in choosing a candidate.

    (B) Only a third of the electorate identifies with one of the major parties.

    (C) Party identification plays a key role in voting choices.

    (D) Party identification plays a key role in deciding whether or not to vote.

    (E) Independent voters are more likely to strongly favor one candidate over another.

3. Which of the following is a valid criticism of the caucus system?

(A) Everyday citizens are not welcome to participate.

(B) Caucuses are not held in convenient locations.

(C) The first caucus is in Iowa, which is not representative of the population as a whole.

(D) The first caucus is held in New Hampshire, which is not representative of the population as a whole.

(E) Caucuses often last several days and become endurance contests.

4. Which of the following is most likely to help an incumbent president get re-elected?

(A) good economic times

(B) a strong vice president

(C) his stance on abortion

(D) the addition of new groups of voters

(E) favorable reporting by the press

5. Table 10.2 supports which of the following conclusions?

(A) Congressional and presidential receipts have followed the same downward decline over recent years.

(B) Presidential campaign costs aren't affected by the number of candidates.

(C) By the end of the decade, we will witness $8 billion national election cycles.

(D) Presidential campaign fundraising and expenditures more than doubled between 2000 and 2012.

(E) Choices A and B are both correct.

6. Which type of voters has the most impact on an election?

(A) prospective voters, who cast their ballots for the person they think has the best ideas for handling matters in the future

(B) ideological voters, who carefully match the candidates with their own views on the issues

TABLE 10.2 2004–2012 Campaign Receipts

Presidential Candidates	Number of candidates/Total receipts
2012	14/$1.37 billion
2008	20/$1.67 billion
2004	12/$904 billion
2000	17/$578 million
Congressional Candidates	
2012	$1.87 billion
2010	$1.86 billion
2008	$1.41 billion
2006	$1.44 billion
2004	$1.29 billion
2002	$979 million

Source: Federal Election Commission, FEC Summary of the 2011–2012 Election Cycle, April 19, 2013.

(C) split-ticket voters, who vote for one party for Congress and the other party for the presidency

(D) retrospective voters, who look at how things have gone in the recent past

(E) voters who are more interested in foreign affairs than in domestic policy

7. Which of the following best describes those who vote in primary elections?

(A) voters from both parties who tend to be moderate in their beliefs

(B) Democrats who tend to be more conservative in their beliefs

(C) Republicans who tend to be more liberal in their beliefs

(D) voters in both parties who tend to be more active in party politics

(E) those who vote in primaries suffer from voter fatigue and are less likely to vote in the general election

Includes spending by presidential candidates, parties, and political action committees

(rounded to nearest $1 million)

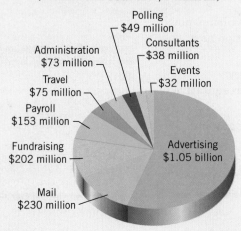

Polling
$49 million

Consultants
$38 million

Administration
$73 million

Events
$32 million

Travel
$75 million

Payroll
$153 million

Fundraising
$202 million

Advertising
$1.05 billion

Mail
$230 million

Source: Federal Election Commission Reports, December 2012, as compiled by *The Washington Post*, 2012 Campaign Finance Explorer, December 7, 2012.

8. Figure 10.1 best supports which of the following statements?

   (A) The majority of campaign spending is on advertising.

   (B) Payroll is a growing concern in campaign spending.

   (C) Mailings are becoming a thing of the past.

   (D) Campaigns take little into account in terms of new digital media and social networking.

   (E) Advertising is less important than fundraising.

9. Figure 10.2 below best supports which of the following statements?

   (A) The number of PACs has increased at a steady rate from 1979 to 2010.

   (B) Since 2007, there are more than five times as many corporate PACs as labor PACs.

   (C) Corporate and trade PACs have much more influence in the political system than labor PACs.

   (D) PAC donations to political campaigns have grown steadily from 1979 to 2010.

   (E) Campaign finance laws have been effective in reducing the number and influence of PACs.

FIGURE 10.2   Growth of PACs 1979–2010

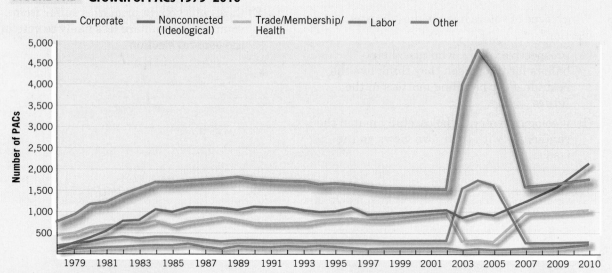

Source: Federal Election Commission.

TABLE 10.7 **Percentage of Various Groups Saying They Voted for the Democratic Presidential Candidate, 1964–2012**

		1964	1968[a]	1972	1976	1980[b]	1984	1988	1992[c]	1996	2000	2004	2008	2012
Sex	Men	60	41	37	53	37	37	41	41	43	42	45	49	45
	Women	62	45	38	48	45	42	49	46	54	54	52	56	55
Race	White	59	38	32	46	36	34	40	39	44	45	42	43	40
	Black	94	85	87	85	82	90	86	82	84	90	89	95	93
Education	College	52	37	37	42	35	40	43	44	44	45	47	49	47
	Grade school	66	52	49	58	43	49	56	55	59	52	51	63	63
Age	Under 30	64	47	48	53	43	41	47	44	53	48	54	66	60
	50 and over	59	41	36	52	41[d]	39	49	50	48	48	46	48	47
Religion	Protestant	55	35	30	46	na	na	33[e]	38	41	42	41	45	42
	Catholic	76	59	48	57	40	44	47	42	53	50	48	54	50
	Jewish[f]	89	85	66	68	45	66	64	68	78	79	76	78	69
Southerners		52	31	29	54	47	36	41	42	na	na	41	na	na

[a]1968 election had three major candidates (Humphrey, Nixon, and Wallace).
[b]1980 election had three major candidates (Carter, Reagan, and Anderson).
[c]1992 election had three major candidates (Clinton, George H. W. Bush, and Perot).
[d]For 1980–1992 and 2004, refers to age 60 and over.
[e]For 1988, white Protestants only.
[f]Jewish vote estimated from various sources; because the number of Jewish persons interviewed is often less than 100, the error in this figure, as well as that for nonwhites, may be large.
na, not available.

Source: Gallup poll data as tabulated in Jeane J. Kirkpatrick, "Changing Patterns of Electoral Competition," in Anthony King, ed., *The New American Political System* (Washington, D.C.: American Enterprise Institute, 1978), pp. 264–265. 1980, 1984, 1988, 1992, 1996, 2000, 2004, and 2008 data from CBS News/New York Times survey and CNN poll. 2012 data on Protestant, Catholic, and Jewish, Prof. John Lapinski, University of Pennsylvania, other 2012 data from NEP exit poll data 2012 as reported in Wall Street Journal, November 8, 2012.

10. All of the following statements about the 2012 election are supported by the table above EXCEPT

(A) More women than men voted for Obama.

(B) The highest percentage of support for Obama came from nonwhite voters.

(C) Those who attended graduate school were more likely to vote for Obama than for Romney.

(D) Jewish voters were less likely to support Obama than Catholic voters.

(E) Protestants were more likely to support Romney than Obama.

11. In which case did the Court declare the campaign spending is a form of constitutionally protected free speech?

(A) *Buckley v. Valeo*

(B) *McConnell v. Federal Election Commission*

(C) *Gideon v. Wainwright*

(D) *Schneck v. United States*

(E) *United States v. Nixon*

12. What are presidential "coattails"?

(A) the tendency for voters to select congressional candidates based on their choice for president

(B) the ability for a presidents to select the chair of their national party

(C) the influence presidents have on who is nominated for vice president

(D) the tendency for voters to "punish" presidents during midterm elections by voting out members of their parties

(E) the ability of presidents to influence gubernatorial nominations

13. Which type of election is restricted to registered party members?

(A) open primary

(B) closed primary

(C) blanket primary

(D) general election

(E) presidential election

14. What is the largest source of funding for congressional elections?

    (A) the federal government

    (B) Political Action Committees

    (C) political parties

    (D) individual donors

    (E) the candidates themselves

15. What is the significance of *Citizens United v. Federal Election Commission*?

    (A) led to the creation of PACs

    (B) led to the creation of 527s

    (C) led to the creation of candidate-centered campaigns

    (D) led to the creation of Super PACs

    (E) outlawed federal funding of presidential campaigns

Free Response Questions

1. In the United States, there are several different kinds of elections, and candidates use different strategies depending upon the kind of election.

    a. Define primary election.

    b. Define party caucus.

    c. Explain one difference between how candidates campaign in a primary or caucus and in a general election. Be sure to include a definition of general election in your discussion.

2. Financing American political campaigns is a controversial topic. There have been various attempts at reform with numerous unintended consequences.

    Describe the role of the following on American political campaigns:

    • Political Action Committees

    • 527s

    • Super PACs

Explain how the Court's reasoning in the case of *Buckley v. Valeo* has made it difficult to enact significant campaign finance reform.

Answers

Multiple Choice Answers

1. (E) All of the statements are true except the last one. Only qualifying presidential candidates receive federal funding (*American Government*, 14th ed., page **233**).

2. (C) Party identification plays a major role in voters' choices. Those who strongly identify with a party are more likely to favor that party's candidate (*American Government*, 14th ed., page **241**).

3. (C) Iowa receives a disproportionate share of attention from the media and candidates because it holds the first caucus. This state is not representative of the population as a whole (*American Government*, 14th ed., page **227**).

4. (A) In good economic times, the party holding the White House normally does well. This is called the "pocketbook" vote (*American Government*, 14th ed., page **239**).

5. (D) Presidential campaign fundraising and expenditures went from $578 million in 2000 to $1.37 billion in 2012 (*American Government*, 14th ed., page **220**).

6. (D) Retrospective voters, who look at how things have gone in the recent past, decide elections. They vote for the party in the White House if they like what happened and vote against that party if they don't like what occurred (*American Government*, 14th ed., pages **243–244**).

7. (D) Voters in primaries tend to be party activists (*American Government*, 14th ed., page **227**).

8. (A) Advertising totaled over $1 billion in the 2012 election campaign. (*American Government*, 14th ed., page **220**).

9. (B) In 2007, there were 1,586 corporate PACs and 273 labor PACS. In 2009, these numbers were 1,598 and 272 respectively. This means there are five times more corporate PACs than PACs representing labor (*American Government*, 14th ed., page **235**).

10. (D) 78 percent of Jewish voters supported Obama, while his support among Catholic voters was 54 percent (*American Government*, 14th ed., page **246**).

11. (A) In the *Buckley* decision, the Court held that how people spend their money is a form of constitutionally protected expression (*American Government*, 14th ed., pages **236–237**).

12. (A) Coattails are the effects of races on the top of a ballot on races on the bottom of the ballot. While diminishing in impact in recent years, coattails can still impact close races (*American Government*, 14th ed., page **222**).

13. (B) During a closed primary only registered members of a party may participate (*American Government*, 14th ed., page **230**).

14. (D) The largest source of campaign funding is individual donors, not political action committees. (*American Government*, 14th ed., page **234**).

15. (D) *Citizens United*, along with several other rulings, led to the creation of Super PACs. These organizations can raise and spend unlimited amounts of money as long as there is no "coordination" with a candidate (*American Government*, 14th ed., page **235**).

Free Response Answers

1. (a) Primaries and caucuses are used to select a party's candidate for office. A primary involves individual voters going to the polls to make a selection of their party's candidate.

    (b) A caucus is a meeting of voters to discuss and decide upon their party's candidate.

    (c) A general election determines who will be the final winner and officeholder from among each party's candidates. In general elections, candidates concentrate their efforts on big states with large numbers of electoral college votes. Before the national conventions, Iowa and New Hampshire receive a disproportionate amount of attention because they are the first states to hold caucuses and primaries, respectively. This focuses the candidates on states with populations not very representative of the population as a whole. In addition, the people who participate in the primaries and caucuses are more extreme ideologically than the rest of the population (*American Government*, 14ᵗʰ ed., pages **223–224, 227–228**).

2. Political Action Committees – PACs formed after the passage of the 1974 amendments to the Federal Election Campaign Act. PACs are considered either "aligned" or "non aligned". Aligned PACs are associated with an interest group. Through a PAC, an interest group can make direct contributions to political candidates. The tactic is typically to give money to incumbents in an attempt to buy access to the decision-making process and not in an attempt to buy the member's vote. Nonaligned PACs are not associated with an interest and are usually used by members of Congress in leadership positions. Leadership uses these PACs in an attempt to distribute campaign money to fellow members in an attempt to curry favor. These PACs are also known as leadership PACs (*American Government*, 14th ed. pages **233–234**).

    527s – A 527 is a group that raises and spends money to advance a set of "issues." They are distinct in that they do not distribute money to candidates or expressly advocate for or against a candidate. Swift Boat Veterans for Truth was the first such 527. It ran an effective attack ad against John Kerry's war record in the 2004 campaign cycle (*American Government*, 14th ed. page **239**).

    Super PACs – A super PAC is an organization that can raise and spend unlimited amounts of money. Super PACs came into existence as a result of several Supreme Court decisions including *Citizens United v. FEC*. They expressly advocate for a candidate. The primary restriction on a Super PAC is that it cannot directly coordinate with the candidate's campaign organization (*American Government*, 14th ed. page **235**).

    Buckley v. Valeo – In the Buckley decision the Court held effectively that "money is speech." How people spend their money to express their political views is a form of constitutionally protected speech. Because of this ruling overall spending by a candidate cannot be capped, and independent expenditures, such as by super PACs, cannot be limited. In essence there is no real limit money in politics as along as it is funneled through the right organization (*American Government*, 14th ed. pages **236–237**).

Unit VIII: Political Parties

Correlates to Chapter 9 in *American Government, 14ᵗʰ Edition*

American political parties are among the oldest in the world. At one time parties could mobilize voters in a way that gave local machines enormous power. Today, parties are relatively weak because the laws and rules under which they operate have taken away much of their power. In addition, many Americans have lost their sense of commitment to any particular party.

Key Terms

caucus
congressional campaign committee
critical or realignment period
ideological party
mugwumps or progressives
national chair
national committee
national convention
office-bloc ballot
party-column ballot
personal following
plurality system
political machine
political party
solidary incentives
split ticket
sponsored party
straight ticket
superdelegates
two-party system

Key Concepts

- A political party is an organization that attempts to influence public policy by getting its members elected or appointed to governmental office. Many of the Framers were concerned that political parties or "factions" would control the government to the detriment of the public good.

- The United States has a two party system because of its electoral system—single member district, plurality election.

- The prospects for a viable third party are very slim. This is due to the structure of the electoral system.

- Originally, political parties were stronger and functioned similar to today's European parties. Over time, political parties have weakened.

- Party registration and identification is a predictor of voter behavior. However, this is not as much the case today as in the past. There are increasing numbers of independents and people who vote a split ticket.

- The Framers, particularly Washington, were wary of political parties. Washington warned of the perils of parties in his Farewell Address.

- Many call for reform of the two party system. Possible reforms include being more receptive to popular influences and changing the electoral system to allow for the possibility of third parties.

For a full discussion of political parties, see *American Government*, 14ᵗʰ ed., Chapter 9.

AP Tip

The number of voters who practice ticket splitting continues to increase. Divided government is a direct result of ticket splitting. Both ticket splitting and divided government are likely to appear on the AP exam.

Multiple Choice Questions

1. How do American political parties compare with political parties in Europe?
   (A) American parties are stronger and have more loyal members.
   (B) American parties are more centralized, with more control by the national party organizations.
   (C) Because of federalism, American political parties are decentralized, with significant power at the state and local levels.
   (D) For the past three decades, the party that controls Congress has usually controlled the presidency.
   (E) National law regulates European parties heavily.

2. All of the following characterize a period of critical realignment EXCEPT
   (A) a sharp and lasting shift in the coalitions supporting the political parties
   (B) a series of crises, resulting in a reaction against the two major parties

TABLE 9.2 Historical Convention Bounces, 1964-2012 Gallup Polls, Registered Voters (in percentage points)

	Democratic Candidate	Post-Dem. Convention bounce	Republican candidate	Post-Rep. convention bounce
2012	Obama	3	Romney	−1
2008	Obama	4	McCain	6
2004	Kerry	−1	G.W. Bush	2
2000	Gore	8	G.W. Bush	8
1996	Clinton	5	Dole	3
1992	Clinton	16	G.H.W. Bush	5
1988	Dukakis	7	G.H.W. Bush	6
1984	Mondale	9	Reagan	4
1980	Carter	10	Reagan	8
1976	Carter	9	Ford	5
1972	McGovern	0	Nixon	7
1968	Humphrey	2	Nixon	5
1964	Johnson	3	Goldwater	5

Source: Various Gallup Polls: *Candidate Support Typically Up Five Points After Convention,* August 23, 2012: http://www.gallup.com/poll/156845/candidate-support-typically-five-points-convention.aspx; Romney Gets No Bounce From Last Week's GOP Convention, September 4, 2012: http://www.gallup.com/poll/157262/romney-gets-no-bounce-last-week-gop-convention.aspx; and Obama Gets Three-Point Convention Bounce, September 11, 2012: http://www.gallup.com/poll/157406/obama-gets-three-point-convention-bounce.aspx

(C) the major defeat of a party, with another party taking its place

(D) when a new issue of importance to voters cuts across existing party divisions

(E) when voters become apathetic and turnout falls below 50 percent

3. In the 1970s and 1980s, the Democratic party made reforms that unintentionally led to it becoming more fragmented. What was the original purpose of these reforms?

(A) to include more union members as delegates to the Democratic convention

(B) to improve the fund-raising efforts of the Democratic party

(C) to make the delegations from both parties more reflective of the population as a whole

(D) to make the Republican party delegations more reflective of the population as a whole

(E) to make the Democratic party delegations more reflective of the population as a whole

4. Who are superdelegates?

(A) powerful members of political parties and elected officials who become delegates without having to run in primaries or caucuses

(B) delegates who have more than one vote

(C) delegates who have veto power over the party's choice of candidates

(D) delegates who write the party's platform and have a major influence over the issues emphasized

(E) delegates, like movie stars, who have national recognition and, as a result, have great influence in choosing candidates

5. All of the following were problems with political machines EXCEPT

(A) they traded votes for favors

(B) the federal bureaucracy grew with unnecessary jobs

(C) unqualified people were given important government jobs

(D) they rarely delivered on their promises to help new immigrants

(E) they engaged in fraudulent practices in voting and government contracting

6. Long-standing third parties, such as the Socialist, Libertarian, and Green parties, are examples of

(A) ideological parties

(B) one-issue parties

(C) economic-protest parties

(D) factional parties

(E) candidate-centered parties

7. All of the following statements are supported by the table above EXCEPT

(A) The last time a winning presidential candidate experienced a double-digit post-convention bounce in approval ratings was Bill Clinton in 1992.

(B) Mitt Romney saw no post-convention bounce in approval ratings in 2012.

(C) Presidential nominating conventions are often useful to candidates in rallying party activists and increasing approval ratings.

(D) The recipient of the highest post-convention bounce has historically always won the presidential election.

(E) In the last thirty years, incumbents have received a smaller post-convention bounce in their race for a second term.

8. What is the major difference between a primary and a caucus?

(A) Primaries choose delegates, while caucuses choose candidates.

(B) Primaries are open only to voters who are registered with a party.

(C) Caucuses are meetings of high-ranking party leaders.

(D) Caucuses are meetings of party members, and primaries are elections.

(E) Primaries have been replaced with caucuses in most states.

9. In the 1824 election, Jackson won more of the popular and electoral college vote, but he lost the election. Which of the following statements best explains why this occurred?

(A) Most states use a winner-take-all system in awarding electoral college votes.

(B) Most states use a plurality system in awarding electoral college votes.

(C) When there is no majority winner in the electoral college, the House of Representatives decides the election.

(D) This result occurs when there are just two candidates in the race.

(E) This result occurs when members of the electoral college ignore the wishes of their states' citizens and vote their conscience instead.

10. Which term best describes a gathering of delegates of a single political party from across the country to choose candidates for president and vice president?

(A) national caucus

(B) national primary

(C) national convention

(D) party platform

(E) general election

11. The rise of the direct primary has

(A) strengthened America political parties

(B) strengthened the authority of party leaders

(C) increased the power of the voters

(D) decreased campaign costs

(E) had little effect on the political process

12. American political parties are, by their nature

(A) highly centralized, with power concentrated in the top levels

(B) totally ineffective in today's political climate

(C) decentralized organizations, with power fragmented

(D) dominated by party bosses

(E) controlled by elected government officials

13. The purpose of a party's national committee is to

(A) nominate candidates for president and vice president

(B) run congressional campaigns

(C) adopt a party platform

(D) coordinate policy between a president and his party members in Congress

(E) run the affairs of the party

14. An organization that make extensive use of patronage, exercises a high degree of discipline over members, and seeks to control government by dominating elections is

(A) a campaign committee

(B) a political machine

(C) a convention

(D) the national committee

(E) caucus

15. The decline of political parties has contributed to which of the following?

(A) decrease in ticket splitting

(B) decrease in campaign costs

(C) candidate-centered campaigns

(D) more political machines

(E) increase in voter turnout

Free Response Questions

1. Political parties have changed since the nation was founded.

(a) Explain one way political parties have changed over time, and discuss the results of this change.

(b) Explain another way political parties have changed over time, and discuss the results of this change.

2. Political parties have been an enduring part of American politics.

   (a) Identify and explain the principal reason that the United States has a two party system

   (b) Describe the functions of the National Committee and the National Convention

   (c) Explain the effect of the direct primary on American political parties.

Answers

Multiple Choice Answers

1. (C) Because of federalism, many important governmental decisions are made at the state and local levels. This gives state and local parties more authority, weakens the national party organizations, and decentralizes power (*American Government*, 14th ed., page **191**).

2. (E) Realignment occurs when there is a major shift in voting patterns. This can be caused by the formation of new coalitions, the major defeat of a party (such as the Federalists), a series of crises (such as economic depression), or an issue of importance (slavery) (*American Government*, 14th ed., pages **195–197**).

3. (E) The McGovern Commission reforms were intended to make the Democratic party more reflective of the population as a whole by including more women and minorities as delegates and changing the rules for delegate selection (*American Government*, 14th ed., pages **200–201**).

4. (A) Superdelegates are powerful members of political parties and elected officials. They may attend the convention as a result of their status and are not required to run in primaries or caucuses. They are powerful within the party in selecting candidates (*American Government*, 14th ed., page **201**).

5. (D) Political machines exchanged votes for favors, particularly for new immigrants. As a result, they were able to help immigrants with social services and employment. However, their practices were fraudulent, unqualified people were put into the federal government, and the bureaucracy grew (*American Government*, 14th ed., pages **202–203**).

6. (A) Ideological parties profess a comprehensive view of American society and government that is radically different from that of the established parties. Ideological parties tend to last longer than the other types of third parties (*American Government*, 14th ed., page **203**).

7. (D) The candidate with the higher post-convention bounce in approval ratings does not always win the election, as was the case in 2008, 1988, 1984, 1980, and 1964 (*American Government*, 14th ed., page **213**).

8. (D) A caucus is a meeting of party followers at which party delegates are picked. A primary is an election prior to a general election in which voters select the candidates who will run on each party's ticket (*American Government*, 14th ed., pages **192–194**).

9. (C) When there is no majority in the electoral college, the House of Representatives decides, with one vote per state. In 1824, the House selected John Quincy Adams, even though Andrew Jackson received more electoral and popular votes (*American Government*, 14th ed., pages **192–193**).

10. (C) A national convention is when a party chooses delegates from all over the country to gather, select the presidential and vice-presidential candidates, and draft a party platform (*American Government*, 14th ed., pages **199–201**).

11. (C) The general effect of the direct primary has been to weaken political parties. This is because the party, as committed group of people, no long chooses their candidates. This power has been given to the voters grew (*American Government*, 14th ed., page **194**).

12. (C) American political parties have very decentralized. Most state parties are largely autonomous (*American Government*, 14th ed., page **190**).

13. (E) The national committee runs the affairs of the party in between meetings of the national convention every four years grew (*American Government*, 14th ed., page **199**)

14. (B) Political machines were once powerful features of urban centers. They controlled city politics though the use of patronage (*American Government*, 14th ed., pages **194–196**).

15. (C) Since the decline of political parties, the focus of campaigns is on the candidates rather than on the party (*American Government*, 14th ed., pages **204–205**).

Free Response Answers

1. (a) The Jacksonian Democrats replaced the caucus with the nominating convention. This system was developed as a reform measure, and it changed the system by giving local officials some measure of control over the nominating process (*American Government*, 14th ed., pages **192–193**).

   (b) Following the Civil War, sectional divisions characterized the party system. Republicans were strong in the North and West; the South was a Democratic stronghold. This split had a profound effect on how parties were organized. Most states were one-party states. Parties used political machines to build loyalty and exchange votes for favors. (*Alternate answer*): During the progressive era, reforms such as the secret ballot and the direct election of senators weakened political machines. Political parties were less able to hold officeholders accountable, and power became more fragmented. Party organizations were weakened. (*Alternate answer*): In recent decades there has been a rise in split-ticket voting, and this weakens parties. This occurs when voters elect one party to Congress and another to the presidency. As a result, it is more difficult for either party to get things done (*American Government*, 14ᵗʰ ed., pages **193–194, 197–198**).

2. (a) The United States has a two party system because of its electoral system. Single member district, plurality election lends itself to two political parties.

This is because there is no reward for second place, as in proportional systems. Therefore, political parties attempt to build a "big tent" of supporters. Smaller parties are either absorbed by larger parties or die off (*American Government*, 14ᵗʰ ed., page **215**).

(b) A party's national committee runs the affairs of the party between meetings of the national convention. The national committee plans the national convention and elects national officers. The national convention nominates candidates for president and vice president and approves a platform (*American Government*, 14ᵗʰ ed., page **199**).

(c) The direct primary has had a negative impact on American political parties. The party as a committed organization no longer picks its candidates. This is further exacerbated by the decline in party identification in the electorate (*American Government*, 14ᵗʰ ed., page **194**).

Unit IX: Interest Groups

Correlates to Chapter 11 in *American Government, 14th Edition*

The United States is a country of diverse interests. The American constitutional system provides for many points where citizens and groups can access the government, including the president, the courts, and Congress. In addition, political parties have become relatively weak. These factors have made the United States ripe for the emergence of thousands of interest groups.

Key Terms

earmark
ideological interest groups
incentive
interest group
lobbyist
material incentives
political action committee (PAC)
political cue
public-interest lobby
purposive incentives
ratings
social movement
solidary incentives

Key Concepts

- An interest group is a group of people who share a common interest or goal with regard to public policy. They have arisen at different times; most recently there was a substantial growth in the 1960s.

- There are several different types of interest groups. There has recently been significant growth in business lobbies.

- People join interest groups for a variety of reasons. Among these reasons are members' only benefits and ideology.

- Interest groups attempt to influence policy through a variety of means such as providing information.

- The opinion that people have about interest groups may depend on whether interest groups benefit them.

- The activities of interest groups are regulated by the national government.

For a full discussion of interest groups, see *American Government*, 14th ed., Chapter 11.

AP Tip

Interest groups use different tactics, depending on their ideology, membership, and goals. Each tactic has advantages. The types of tactics used by interest groups may appear on the AP exam.

Multiple Choice Questions

1. All of the following explain the proliferation of interest groups EXCEPT
    (A) America is diverse, with countless immigrants, races, and religions
    (B) because of its federal system, there are multiple points of access to government
    (C) political authority is shared by several branches of government, each of which might be targeted by interest groups
    (D) interest groups often run candidates for office to give their supporters a voice in government
    (E) political parties are relatively weak, which helps explain the strength and number of interest groups

2. Throughout American history, which of the following conditions has led to an increase in interest groups' activity?
    I.   a strong economy with low inflation
    II. the rise of professional societies, such as the American Medical Association (AMA)
    III. government policies that create new groups, such as veterans
    IV. leaders who are willing to make personal sacrifices
    (A) I and II
    (B) I, II, and III
    (C) II, III, and IV
    (D) I, II, and IV
    (E) III and IV

3. "Free riders" occur when interest groups fight for benefits to the public as a whole, such as consumer protection. How can interest groups prevent the free-rider problem?
    (A) by ensuring that the benefits they seek will help only their members

(B) by providing people an incentive to join the interest group, such as a subscription to a magazine

(C) by limiting membership to a few carefully screened members

(D) by lobbying members of Congress only in the district where the interest group operates

(E) there is no practical way for interest groups to prevent the "free-rider" problem

4. Environmentalists, women, and union members have worked over the years to advance their interests. What is the best description of these causes?

(A) They are social movements that have spawned several related interest groups.

(B) They are PACs, which give money to political campaigns.

(C) They are social movements because all of them have liberal goals.

(D) They are interest groups because they lobby Congress for favorable legislation.

(E) They are social movements because they do not take strong positions and tend to support moderate policies.

5. Why are lobbyists useful to members of Congress in considering legislation?

(A) because most lobbyists are lawyers and can draft bills using technical legal language

(B) because lobbyists have bigger research staffs than members of Congress

(C) because lobbyists are policy generalists who have knowledge about a broad range of topics

(D) because members of Congress must listen to lobbyists in order to get electoral support

(E) because members of Congress are policy generalists and lobbyists are policy specialists with expert knowledge in their area

6. An interest group would use grassroots lobbying on all of the following issues EXCEPT

(A) abortion

(B) Medicare

(C) Social Security

(D) complex tax legislation affecting a few people

(E) affirmative action

7. Which of the following is a concern about the influence of lobbyists on government?

(A) Many lobbyists are former federal officials who gave up their positions in government to work for interest groups.

(B) Many lobbyists are attorneys who have undue influence because of their legal expertise.

(C) Many lobbyists also work as congressional staff members.

(D) Many members of Congress are former lobbyists who still have strong connections with interest groups.

(E) Because lobbyists do not have to register with the government, it is difficult to control their activities.

8. Which of the following is a restriction on the interaction between members of Congress and interest groups?

(A) Members of interest groups may not provide members of Congress with information regarding pending legislation.

(B) Members of Congress may not accept gifts of any value from registered lobbyists.

(C) Retired members of Congress may not work as lobbyists for interest groups.

(D) Members of Congress must retain records of all email, text, and phone messages from lobbyists.

(E) Interest groups may not run ads on behalf of members of Congress.

9. Which of the following best describes an earmark?

(A) an entire piece of legislation that is written to provide benefits to a small group of people

(B) a provision in a law that provides a direct benefit to a client without being reviewed on the merits by all members of Congress

(C) a provision in a law that is wasteful and expensive

(D) a provision in a law that provides a subsidy to farmers or ranchers

(E) a piece of legislation containing several unrelated provisions that benefit a few states

10. All of the following statements about political actions committees (PACs) are true EXCEPT

(A) they are formed by groups of like-minded people

(B) they must have at least fifty individual members

(C) they can give an unlimited amount of soft money to political parties

(D) PAC donations to individual candidates are limited to $5,000

(E) labor PACs give most of their money to Democrats

11. Of all of the activities that are employed by interest groups the most significant one is
    (A) running candidates for office
    (B) organizing protests
    (C) providing information
    (D) offering campaign contributions
    (E) grassroots mobilization

12. An organization that raises money and then contributes it to candidates is called a
    (A) Political Action Committee
    (B) Fund Raising Committee
    (C) Issue Finance Organization
    (D) Citizen Action Fund
    (E) Special Interest Commission

13. Which of the following amount is reflective of the most common PAC donation?
    (A) approximately $100
    (B) approximately $300
    (C) approximately $1000
    (D) approximately $5000
    (E) over $10,000

14. The phenomenon of people leaving government to take jobs in the economic sector that they regulated is called.
    (A) the revolving door
    (B) the glass ceiling
    (C) the golden parachute
    (D) the silver lining
    (E) the slippery slope

15. Protection for the activities of interest groups can be found in
    (A) the original text of the Constitution
    (B) the First Amendment
    (C) the Fifth Amendment
    (D) the Declaration of Independence
    (E) Washington's Farewell Address

Free Response Questions

1. Interest groups attempt to influence the policy-making process in a number of ways and through multiple access points. Tactics used by interest groups include
    i. litigation
    ii. donating money through PACs
    iii. grassroots lobbying/public pressure

(a) Pick one technique from the list above and explain how interest groups use this technique to advance their cause, giving a specific example.

(b) Pick another technique from the list above and explain how interest groups use this technique to advance their cause, giving a specific example.

2. Political parties and special interest groups are both features of the American political landscape. Both attempt to influence public policy in a variety of ways.

(a) Describe the primary difference between political parties and special interest groups.

(b) Describe two ways in which special interest groups attempt to influence policy making in Congress.

(c) Explain two reasons why a citizen would prefer to work through a special interest group to obtain his or her policy goals rather than through a political party.

Answers
Multiple Choice Answers

1. (D) Interest groups occur because of diversity. They target all levels of government. American political parties are weaker than in many other countries, but interest groups may be stronger. However, interest groups do not usually run candidates for office (*American Government*, 14th ed., page **252**).

2. (C) Interest groups have been created by professional organizations, such as the AMA, and new government policies, such as wars that create veterans. Interest groups often have a strong leader—historically, the NAACP has had many—who is willing to make personal sacrifices. Interest groups are less likely to arise in good economic times (*American Government*, 14th ed., pages **253–254**).

3. (B) Interest groups, such as the AARP, often provide incentives to their members, such as magazines and travel discounts. This encourages people to pay a fee to become members of the group (*American Government*, 14th ed., pages **257–258**).

4. (A) A social movement is a widely shared demand for change in some aspect of the social or political order. These movements, such as those led by environmentalists, women, and unions, often result in the creation of several related interest groups (*American Government*, 14th ed., pages **259–263**).

5. (E) Members of Congress are policy generalists who must decide about a broad range of issues. Lobbyists have expertise in specific fields. Members of Congress need credible information and often rely on lobbyists to provide it (*American Government*, 14th ed., page **263**).

6. (D) Not every issue lends itself to grass-roots lobbying, which encourages individual interest group members to contact members of Congress. The more people are directly affected by a policy, the more likely an interest group will use grassroots lobbying (*American Government*, 14th ed., page **265**).

7. (A) Many people worry about the "revolving door," the practice of officials leaving their government positions to accept more lucrative jobs as lobbyists. This may give them undue influence over policy-making (*American Government*, 14th ed., pages **269–270**).

8. (B) Beginning March 1, 2007, new regulations took effect to reform the practices of interest groups and lobbyists. Members of Congress may not accept gifts (including free travel) from interest groups or registered lobbyists (*American Government*, 14th ed., page **271**).

9. (B) An earmark is a provision in a law that provides a direct benefit to a particular client, without that benefit being reviewed by most members of Congress (*American Government*, 14th ed., page **264**).

10. (C) The Bipartisan Campaign Finance Reform Act of 2002 (McCain-Feingold) closed the "soft money loophole." PAC donations to political parties are limited to $15,000 on the national level and $5,000 on the state level.

11. (C) According to most scholars, providing credible information is perhaps the most effective way to influence policy (*American Government*, 14th ed., page **263**).

12. (A) Political Action Committees raise money to contribute to campaigns. PACs grew as a result of reform legislation in the early 1970s (*American Government*, 14th ed., pages **265–269**).

13. (B) The most common PAC contribution is a few hundred dollars per House candidate (*American Government*, 14th ed., page **267**).

14. (A) The revolving door is when a former federal employee begins to work for the private sector in a closely related field. An example would be an employee of the defense department retiring and then working for a defense contractor. (*American Government*, 14th ed., pages **269–270**).

15. (B) The First Amendment protects the activities of interest groups. The amendment specificity protects speech, press, assembly and petition. Special interest groups engage in all of these activities (*American Government*, 14th ed., page **253**).

Free Response Answers

1. (a) Litigation means the bringing of a lawsuit. Interest groups go to the courts to advance their causes. This may happen when Congress is not responsive to the interest group's demands. For example, during the 1950s, civil rights groups supported legislation to bring equal rights to African Americans. However, these efforts were frequently blocked in Congress, sometimes through filibusters in the Senate. So the NAACP turned to the courts to end segregation. In *Brown v. Board of Education,* the Supreme Court ruled that school segregation violated the Constitution (*American Government*, 14th ed., pages **258–259**).

   (b) Interest groups may contribute money to candidates and causes through political action committees (PACs). Some people worry that the sea of all this political money has resulted in our having "the finest Congress that money can buy." This concern was raised during the savings and loan scandal when it was found that the same congressmen who delayed the investigation of the savings and loan industry had received substantial campaign contributions from these very institutions. However, so much PAC money is available on so many issues that members of Congress may be able to vote freely. (*Alternate answer*): Grassroots lobbying is designed to generate public pressure directly on government officials. Interest groups contact their members, asking that they contact the members of Congress representing their district or state. Modern technology has made this even easier with email. No one enjoys dealing with people who are upset, and members of Congress want to satisfy their constituents. An example of this is the American Association of Retired Persons and its use of grassroots lobbying in support of a prescription drug benefit (*American Government*, 14th ed., pages **265–269**).

   (a) The primary difference between interest groups and political parties is that political parties run candidates for office and special interest groups do not.

   (b) Special interest groups attempt to influence congressional policy making by providing information and making campaign contributions. Interest groups provide specialized information to members of congress and their staffs. A common misconception is that this information is unreliable. This is not the case. If a lobbyist is to be influential, he or she must be trusted. Interest groups provide campaign contributions to members of Congress. These contributions are not an attempt to "buy a vote," but rather an attempt to gain access to the member. Once access is obtained, the lobbyist can attempt to influence the member. In aggregate, these contributions can account for a significant portion of an incumbent's re-election funds (*American Government*, 14th ed., page **263**).

(c) Citizens frequently choose to work through interest groups for several reasons. First, special interest groups are narrowly focused and political parties are more broadly focused. A citizen is less likely to disagree with a policy stance that a special interest group has taken as opposed to his or her political party. Second, many special interest groups provide "members only benefits" that political parties do not. These benefits, such as insurance and discounts on retail purchases, can be a powerful incentive to contribute to and work through an interest group. Political parties do not provide these benefits (*American Government*, 14th ed., pages **257–258**).

Unit X: Mass Media

Correlates to Chapter 12 in *American Government, 14th Edition*

The media in the United States enjoy a degree of freedom greater than that in virtually any other nation. Nowadays, government officials have a love-hate relationship with the media. Politicians need the media to advance their careers, but they fear the media's power to criticize, expose, and destroy.

Key Terms

adversarial press
background
blog
equal time rule
feature stories
horse-race journalism
insider stories
loaded language
routine stories
selective attention
sound bite
trial balloon

Key Concepts

- The media performs several functions in American politics. Among these are gatekeeper, scorekeeper, and watchdog.

- The First Amendment prohibits virtually all governmental restrictions on the media.

- The media is a powerful force in American politics in that it presents information to the electorate.

- Technology has altered the interactions between public officials and the media. With the advent of the internet, politicians can bypass the media and appeal directly to the voters. Further, the development of the 24-hour news cycle on cable television has eroded what would once have been considered the private lives of governmental officials.

- There is some evidence that the media has a liberal bias, and this may affect what is published.

For a full discussion of mass media, see *American Government*, 14th ed., Chapter 12.

AP Tip

Although the United States has a free press, it is subject to regulation through the FCC. These regulations may appear on the AP exam.

Multiple Choice Questions

1. How do American media outlets differ from the media in most other countries?
   (A) Almost all American radio and television stations are privately owned.
   (B) The United States government has little power to regulate broadcasters.
   (C) The United States has very strict libel laws, and untruths about public officials usually result in fines.
   (D) Most other countries have a Freedom of Information Act that permits the media to request information about the government.
   (E) Because of federal grants and special funding, the media in the United States do not have to worry much about profit.

2. Broadcast journalism changed the media's coverage of politics in all of the following ways EXCEPT
   (A) a broadcast allows public officials to speak directly to audiences without their remarks being filtered through editors
   (B) politicians can reach voters on a national scale without the support of political parties
   (C) people could easily ignore a speech by changing the channel
   (D) citizens get more detailed and specific information about programs and policies than they could get from the print media
   (E) public officials must do something bold or sufficiently colorful to gain free access to the broadcast media

3. The government can use all of the following tools to encourage positive stories and constrain negative stories written by journalists EXCEPT
   (A) "spinning" a story by attacking a politician's critics
   (B) closing the "leaks" given to particular reporters
   (C) revoking the licenses of stations that give unfavorable coverage
   (D) using the press corps to release favorable stories
   (E) refusing to give important background information

4. Which of the following is the best example of a trial balloon?

(A) A candidate for office runs ads in one state on a single issue to see how the public will react.

(B) An anonymous White House source makes a statement that is then reported on the news.

(C) A newspaper covers the flooding in a neighboring state and chooses to delete stories of local interest.

(D) A TV special report covers drug dealers in a community but does not cover efforts to end drug abuse.

(E) The president holds a news conference to announce a new program to stop the spread of AIDS.

5. Why is there more news coverage of the president than of Congress or the courts?

(A) because the president is one person and is viewed by the public as the center of government

(B) because the president has the ability to call news conferences, whereas members of Congress must act through their leaders

(C) because the courts issue opinions that are difficult to understand, and it is difficult for the press to explain court decisions clearly

(D) because congressional committee hearings are usually closed to the press and the public

(E) the statement is inaccurate; Congress actually gets as much press coverage as the president does

6. What best explains the reason for bias in newspapers?

(A) A newspaper's bias tends to reflect the political views of its readers.

(B) Reporters tend to be liberal, and the stories they write have a liberal bias.

(C) Newspapers are privately owned, so publishers can print whatever they choose.

(D) Corporate owners are conservative, and this bias is reflected in their newspapers.

(E) Newspapers in the United States are generally very neutral, with few papers reflecting any kind of ideological bias.

7. Since the early 1970s, how has the relationship between the president and the press changed?

(A) It has become friendlier because presidents are now more willing to answer questions.

(B) It has become more adversarial, partly as a result of the Vietnam War and Watergate.

(C) It has become more adversarial because embarrassing stories sell more newspapers.

(D) It has not changed, because we have always had a free press.

(E) It has become less critical of the president because surveys show that people do not like the cynicism of the media.

8. All of the following are examples of horse-race journalism EXCEPT

(A) which candidate is ahead in the polls

(B) which candidate is raising the most money

(C) which candidate opposed off-shore drilling

(D) which candidate had the most TV ads

(E) which candidate received a celebrity endorsement

9. The internet has affected politics in all of the following ways EXCEPT

(A) it makes it easier to raise money in small donations

(B) it makes it easier to organize people to attend meetings

(C) it makes it easier for campaigns to identify the names of people they should contact

(D) it makes it easier for a candidate to disseminate negative information about an opponent

(E) it contains less biased and more detailed information than the newspapers

10. The decline in newspaper circulation is troubling to many political scientists because

(A) Americans are listening more frequently to talk radio, which has a conservative bias

(B) fewer people are reading newspapers, which are an important source of in-depth coverage about politics

(C) Americans are beginning to avoid the news altogether

(D) Americans are falling behind citizens of other countries in their understanding of world affairs

(E) unbiased newspapers are being replaced with more biased sources of information, like television and the Internet

11. The American government has a system of checks and balances, when one branch of government can "check" or counteract the actions

of another. The media is often said to act as an additional check. This is a description of which function of the media in American politics?

(A) fact checker

(B) talent scout

(C) spotlight

(D) monitor

(E) watchdog

12. Which of the following statements is true regarding governmental censorship of the press?

(A) The government may never censor the press.

(B) The government may censor the press if it is publishing false information.

(C) The government may censor the press if it is publishing something that is offensive to a minority group.

(D) The government may censor the press for the sake of national security.

(E) The government may censor the press to prevent it from influencing an election.

13. In which of the following roles does the media act as a "talent scout," identifying promising politicians and then giving them increased attention?

(A) watchdog

(B) horse racer

(C) scorekeeper

(D) spotlight

(E) examiner

14. What is the significance of *Near v. Minnesota*?

(A) States cannot impose prior restraint.

(B) States can require "preclearance" of controversial stories.

(C) States can prohibit libelous publications.

(D) The national government cannot regulate broadcast media.

(E) The national government must ensure fair coverage of political events.

15. What is the function of a "shield law"?

(A) States may prohibit the publication of inflammatory material.

(B) Journalists may keep sources confidential.

(C) The national government may regulate broadcast media.

(D) The FCC may prohibit obscene material.

(E) Offended parties may require newspapers to print multiple points of view.

Free Response Questions

1. According to the text, "Important changes in the nature of American politics have gone hand in hand with major changes in the organization and technology of the press."

(a) Identify one change that has occurred as a result of technology, and describe the impact of that change on the media's coverage of politics.

(b) Identify another change that has occurred as a result of technology, and describe the impact of that change on the media's coverage of politics.

2. (a) Identify and explain two roles that the media plays in the United States political system.

(b) Identify and explain one limitation placed on media in the United States political system.

Answers
Multiple Choice Answers

1. (A) Almost all American radio and television stations are privately owned. Because they need to make a profit, they must satisfy a variety of interests (*American Government*, 14th ed., page **278**).

2. (D) Although the broadcast media reach a large audience, their coverage of the issues is generally less detailed than coverage in the print media (*American Government*, 14th ed., pages **280–282**).

3. (C) The FCC cannot revoke a station's license simply for giving a government official unfavorable press coverage. However, government officials can spin a story to their advantage, close information leaks, and refuse to give background information. In addition, the press corps can release favorable stories about White House officials (*American Government*, 14th ed., pages **296–297**).

4. (B) A "trial balloon" is a statement issued by an unnamed source to test the public's reaction (*American Government*, 14th ed., page **288**).

5. (A) It is easier to cover the president because he is one person and is seen as the center of government. There are 535 members of Congress, which makes it difficult to cover. Although there are only nine justices on the Supreme Court, it is difficult for the press to cover them because they are not allowed to discuss current cases (*American Government*, 14th ed., pages **292–293**).

6. (A) Newspapers are privately owned, and each paper's style is tailored to its own market. A newspaper's bias tends to reflect the political views of its readers (*American Government*, 14th ed., page **290**).

7. (B) After the Vietnam War, Watergate, and the Iran-Contra affair, the press became more adversarial with presidents. Although the public does not like this negative coverage, the relationship between the president and the press remains more adversarial than it was in the past (*American Government*, 14th ed., pages **294–295**).

8. (C) Horse-race journalism emphasizes who is ahead rather than focusing on national issues (*American Government*, 14th ed., page **287**).

9. (E) While the internet has made campaigning more efficient, it is not entirely trustworthy. The open access of the internet means that not all of the information conveyed comes from credible sources (*American Government*, 14th ed., page **277**).

10. (B) As the percentage of people who get their news from newspapers declines, they begin get their information from other sources. Increasing, people rely on broadcast and other forms of electronic media. This is troublesome because the print media often cover stories in more depth than the electronic media do (*American Government*, 14th ed., page **284**).

11. (E) The term "watchdog" describes the media's role in monitoring the actions of government and reporting back to the public (*American Government*, 14th ed., page **284**).

12. (D) The Supreme Court has ruled that it is acceptable for the government to censor the press if national security is at stake. However, these instances are very rare. Generally, the Court is highly suspicious of any limitations on the media (*American Government*, 14th ed., page **294**).

13. (C) In the scorekeeper role, the media will identify up-and-coming individuals and highlight them. This attention will eventually turn more critical as the media's role shifts to that of a watchdog (*American Government*, 14th ed., page **284**).

14. (A) The Supreme Court incorporated the First Amendment requirements for free press. Therefore states must now abide by national standards with regard to free press. In this case prior restraint was prohibited (*American Government*, 14th ed., page **285**).

15. (B) A shield law allows journalists to keep their sources confidential. Journalists claim that the promise of confidentiality is necessary to obtain information about governmental corruption. They hold that without it, their function as a watchdog is diminished. There is no constitutional basis for shield laws. However, over thirty states have created one statutorily for their state. There is no national shield law (*American Government*, 14th ed., pages **285, 298**).

Free Response Answers

1. (a) One change in the media was the development of the high-speed press. By the mid-nineteenth century, the high-speed press made it possible to print large quantities of newspapers quickly and cheaply. Wire services, such as the Associated Press, allowed national news to reach most Americans the same day it happened. Mass readership of newspapers developed. As political parties no longer controlled the press, press bias came to be a reflection of the market. Publishers designed papers to reflect the views of their target audiences, not political parties (*American Government*, 14th ed., page **279**).

   (b) Another change in the media was broadcast journalism— radio, television, and the internet. Broadcast journalism reaches a large audience, and it precipitated a major change in the way news was gathered. Public officials could speak directly to audiences, but people could just as easily turn off the broadcasts. This led the media to feature exciting stories to catch and keep the viewers' attention. The news again became sensationalized, and complex stories were reduced to sound bites that oversimplified coverage of the political process. The internet allows journalists to reach their audiences very quickly, and politicians can speak directly to the public through their web sites (*American Government*, 14th ed., pages **280–282**).

2. (a) Any two of the following identifications and explanations:

   Gatekeeper – In the gatekeeper role the media acts as an agenda setter. By selecting which issues to highlight and which issues to ignore, the media decides, along with other agenda setters, what issues are important and deserve the attention of the government (*American Government*, 14th ed., page 284).

   Scorekeeper – The scorekeeper role has the media identifying which politics and other public figures deserve attention. This function is particularly evident in presidential contests (*American Government*, 14th ed., page **284**).

Watchdog – This function has the media reporting to the public on governmental activities. A free press is critical in a democratic system where people hold their government accountable (*American Government*, 14th ed., page **284**).

(b) One of the two following identifications and explanations:

Threats to National Security – The government has the ability to prevent publication of information that would be damaging to national security. In such a situation prior restraint would be permissible. The burden of proof would be on the government in this instance (*American Government*, 14th ed., pages **294, 298**).

Broadcast Media – The government can impose more restrictions on broadcast media than on print media. This is because the broadcast is on the public airwaves. The government regulates broadcast media via the FCC. Recently the government has loosened many of its previous restrictions (*American Government*, 14th ed., page **278**).

Unit XI: Congress

Correlates to Chapter 13 in *American Government, 14th Edition*

Congress was given significant constitutional powers, making it the "first branch" in the minds of the Founders. It has the power over the federal budget, can override a presidential veto, and can alter the way laws are administered.

Key Terms

bicameral legislature
caucus
closed rule
cloture rule
concurrent resolution
conference committees
conservative coalition
discharge petition
divided government
division vote
double tracking
earmarks
filibuster
franking privilege
joint committees
joint resolution
majority leader
marginal districts
minority leader
open rule
party polarization
party vote
pork-barrel legislation
quorum
restrictive rule
riders
roll-call vote
safe districts
select committees
simple resolution
Speaker
standing committees
teller vote
unified government
veto
voice vote
whip

Key Concepts

- Congress is considered the "first branch" in American politics because of its central role in the American political system.

- Congress is also considered by many to be the "broken branch." This is because in view of many, Congress is ineffective in problem solving. Its low approval rating adds credence to this point of view.

- Congress differs from a parliament in several ways. First, in a parliamentary system the legislative branch typically selects the executive. Second, parliamentary systems typically have strong political parties.

- Legislative productivity, measured in number of bills passed, has fluctuated over time. Scholars disagree if this is even a valid measure of Congress.

- While Congress has become more divided in partisan and ideological terms, political scientists disagree about whether the same can be said of the electorate.

- Congress is not representative of the American people demographically. In addition, its members are further to the political left and right than is the electorate.

- Generally speaking, the legislation passed by Congress is reflective of public opinion. However, on several issues there is a disconnect.

- The strength of congressional leadership has varied over time.

- While on occasion Congress can act expeditiously, the Framers envisioned a legislature that would be deliberative in nature. Therefore, by design, Congress typically acts slowly. This has recently been exacerbated by increased partisanship.

For a full discussion of Congress, see *American Government,* 14th ed., Chapter 13.

AP Tip

The advantages of being an incumbent are important in understanding the dynamics of Congress. The AP exam may ask about the factors that lead to a high re-election rate for incumbents.

Multiple Choice Questions

1. All of the following make it difficult for Congress to make policy EXCEPT

    (A) Congress must worry about voters' preferences, so it engages in arguments on important issues

    (B) Congress does not choose the president, so there is no guarantee a bill will become law

(C) Congress operates through coalitions of several political parties, each of which represents different interests

(D) Congress is bicameral, and a bill must pass both houses

(E) each member of Congress faces re-election, and the interests of the members of his or her district must be considered

2. How did the composition of Congress change between 1950 and 2011?

(A) There was no change in the number of ethnic minorities, but the number of women increased.

(B) There was no change in the number of women, but the number of African Americans increased.

(C) The percentage of African Americans in Congress is similar to the percentage of African Americans in the country as a whole.

(D) There are fewer Hispanics but more African Americans and women.

(E) Although representation does not mirror the population as a whole, there are more minorities and women.

3. The representational view of Congress is based on the assumption that members want to get re-elected and therefore vote to please their constituents. Under what circumstances is a member of Congress most likely to vote according to this view?

(A) when a bill will bring "pork" to the congressman's district

(B) when constituents have a clear view on some issue and the issue has attracted attention

(C) when constituents have a clear view on an issue and the member of Congress agrees with constituents' views

(D) when there is a close race for re-election and a member of Congress is eager to please constituents

(E) when a small group of constituents goes to great lengths to make its views known to their senator or representative

4. Of the following members of Congress, who will most likely be chosen to head the House Appropriations Committee when the majority is Republican?

Rep.	Party	Years in Congress	Years on Appropriations Committee
Smith	R	18	2
Jones	R	5	5
Gonzales	D	22	8
Wilson	D	26	4
Jefferson	I	12	12

(A) Smith
(B) Jones
(C) Gonzales
(D) Wilson
(E) Jefferson

5. A congressional committee was created to investigate any intelligence failures that might have occurred prior to the terrorist attacks of September 11, 2001. What kind of committee does this represent?

(A) standing
(B) joint
(C) select
(D) conference
(E) oversight

6. The House Rules Committee does all of the following EXCEPT

(A) adopts procedures under which the House will consider a bill

(B) sets time limits on debate

(C) permits or forbids certain amendments on the floor

(D) reviews bills and places them on a calendar

(E) establishes the number of votes needed for a bill to pass in the House

7. A filibuster in the Senate can be used to talk a bill to death. A cloture vote can end a filibuster. Taken together, what is the impact of these practices?

(A) Neither political party can control the Senate unless it has at least sixty votes.

(B) A party with fifty-one votes can get most of its legislative agenda passed.

(C) The Senate rarely passes legislation on controversial issues.

(D) Most important decisions are made in committees because it is difficult to pass a bill in the Senate as a whole.

(E) The president's party has a significant advantage because the vice president of the United States can vote to break a tie in the Senate.

8. All of the following are powers of the Senate EXCEPT

(A) approving the appointment of cabinet heads
(B) initiating all revenue bills
(C) approving treaties with foreign nations
(D) holding impeachment trials
(E) approving appointments to the federal judiciary

9. Where does most of the work of Congress take place?

(A) on the floor of the House of Representatives

(B) on the floor of the Senate

(C) in committees

(D) in oversight hearings

(E) in the White House, where members of Congress meet with the president

10. Which of the following statements best describes the impact of divided government on Congress?

(A) Divided government occurs when the president and Congress disagree about an issue. Therefore, it is more likely that the president will veto legislation.

(B) Divided government occurs when the majority of one or both houses of Congress are from a party different from the president's. This slows the passage of the most far-reaching and costly legislation.

(C) Divided government has little effect on the ability of Congress to pass legislation.

(D) Divided government occurs when the majority of one or both houses of Congress are from a party different from the president's. This makes it very difficult for any legislation to pass.

(E) Divided government rarely occurs. Therefore, it is easy for Congress to pass a wide variety of new laws, expanding government programs.

11. The most powerful member of the Senate is

(A) the Senate President Pro Tempore

(B) the Majority Leader

(C) the Minority Whip

(D) the Senate President

(E) the chairman of the committee on rules and administration

12. A newly elected Democratic member of the House of Representatives seeking membership on key legislative committees would do well to curry favor from the

(A) Committee on Committees

(B) Majority Whip

(C) Steering and Policy Committee

(D) Rules Committee

(E) Committee on Organization and Administration

13. A significant difference between the Senate and House is

(A) the House has a powerful Rules Committee, the Senate does not

(B) the Senate has powerful leadership, the House does not

(C) House committees are easily bypassed, Senate committees are not

(D) the House had unlimited debate, the Senate does not

(E) the Senate members tend to be policy specialists, House members tend to be policy generalists

14. The process by which a filibuster is ended in the Senate is known as

(A) a closed rule

(B) double tracking

(C) the franking privilege

(D) cloture

(E) seniority

15. Where will the final version of a bill be written?

(A) House standing committee

(B) Senate standing committee

(C) House floor

(D) Rules Committee

(E) conference committee

Free Response Questions

1. (a) Identify and explain TWO ways party leaders (Speaker of the House, president pro tempore of the Senate, majority leaders, minority leaders, and whips) influence members of their party in Congress.

(b) Identify and explain ONE factor that makes it difficult for party leadership to influence members of their party in Congress.

2. Despite widespread disapproval of Congress as in institution, members of Congress are re-elected at rather high rates.

(a) Define incumbency advantage

(b) Identify the rate of re-election for both members of the House and Senate

(c) Identify and explain two factors that contribute to high re-election rates in Congress.

Answers

Multiple Choice Answers

1. (C) Each member of Congress must consider the preferences of the voters in his or her district. This can lead to arguments over policy. In addition, a bill must pass both houses of Congress and be signed by the president (or have a veto overridden) to become law. Unlike many countries, the United States has a two-party system that does not require party coalitions (*American Government*, 14th ed., page **303**).

2. (E) Congress has gradually become less white and less male (*American Government*, 14th ed., page **311**).

3. (B) Congressmen act according to the representational view when constituents have a clear view on an issue that has attracted attention (*American Government*, 14th ed., pages **316–317**).

4. (B) Although this rule is not always followed, the chairman of the committee is usually the member who has served the longest on that committee from the majority party (*American Government*, 14th ed., page **322**).

5. (C) A select committee is a group appointed for a limited purpose and lasting for only a few Congresses (*American Government*, 14th ed., page **322**).

6. (E) The House rules committee reviews bills and puts them on the agenda. It sets time limits and can limit the kinds of amendments allowed. Bills must pass the House of Representatives by majority vote (*American Government*, 14th ed., page **327**).

7. (A) It takes sixty votes to end a filibuster. This means that neither party can control the Senate unless it has sixty votes. Otherwise, the minority party can use the filibuster to block legislation sponsored by the majority party (*American Government*, 14th ed., page **328**).

8. (B) The Senate approves treaties and major presidential appointments. It holds impeachment trials. Revenue bills must be initiated in the House (*American Government*, 14th ed., pages **308–311**).

9. (C) Most of the work of Congress takes place in committees (*American Government*, 14th ed., page **306**).

10. (B) Divided government occurs when one or both houses of Congress are controlled by a party different from the president's party. Because a bill must pass both houses of Congress and be signed by the president to become law, divided government slows the passage of far-reaching legislation (*American Government*, 14th ed., page **331**).

11. (B) The majority leader is the true leader of the Senate. Presiding over the Senate is not a source of power and influence. The Senate President (Vice President of the United States) usually only presides during ceremonial occasions (*American Government*, 14th ed., page **318**).

12. (C) The Steering and Policy Committee is responsible for assigning Democratic members to House committees (*American Government*, 14th ed., page **319**).

13. (A) The House Rules Committee is the most powerful committee in the House. It sets the conditions under which the House will consider a bill. Further, it significantly impacts the legislative schedule. The Senate does not have a committee this powerful. The Senate committee on Rules and Administration plays a very minor role in the administration of the Senate (*American Government*, 14th ed., pages **323, 327**).

14. (D) Cloture is the procedure that is used to end a filibuster. Sixty votes are required to invoke cloture (*American Government*, 14th ed., page **328**).

15. (E) A conference committee is the place where the House and Senate versions of a bill are reconciled. As such, the conference committee will write the final version of the bill that the House and Senate will vote on (*American Government*, 14th ed., page **330**).

Free Response Answers

1. (a) The Speaker is the most important person in the House. He or she is elected by the majority party and presides over all House meetings. The Speaker decides which bills will be assigned to which committees. This is one way he or she can use party leadership to influence members of their party in Congress. If a wayward member is sponsoring a bill, the Speaker may assign that bill to a committee where the bill is likely to get an unfavorable reception and be killed. Conversely, the Speaker can assign the bill to a safe committee where the bill will receive a favorable reception in exchange for the sponsor's party loyalty.

   In addition, party leadership assigns members to committees. These assignments are especially important for newly elected members in Congress. Their political careers, opportunities for favorable press coverage, and chances for helping their states with important issues and "pork" all depend upon being assigned to the right committees.

   (b) Despite the importance of party leadership, members of Congress represent their states or districts, and they want to be re-elected by their constituents. This means that they do not always act in accordance with their party's platform. Sometimes they run for office as outsiders who will "clean up the mess in Washington." As a result, they are independent actors, and it is difficult for their political parties to control their votes on particular issues (*American Government*, 14th ed., pages **308–309**).

2. (a) Incumbency advantage is the high likelihood that a current officeholder, the incumbent, will defeat a challenger, and thus be re-elected.

   (b) Incumbents in both the House and Senate have high re-election rates. Members of Congress enjoy re-elections rates that are typically 85 to 90 percent. House members have slightly higher re-election rates than do members of the Senate (*American Government*, 14th ed., page **303**).

   (c) Any two of the following identifications and explanations:

   Franking privilege – Members of Congress have free use of the mail. This allows them to send information to their constituents. The effect of this is higher name recognition, which is directly linked to higher chances of re-election (*American Government*, 14th ed., page **307**).

   Ease of Fundraising – Members of Congress have better access to lobbyists and their associated PAC contributions. There is a direct positive correlation between the amount of money raised and the likelihood of electoral victory (*American Government*, 14th ed., page **306**).

   Committee Assignments – Members of Congress are frequently able to gain membership on committees that consider legislation that has a direct impact on their states or districts. As members of these committees, they are better able to look after the interests of their constituents, contributing to higher chances of re-election (*American Government*, 14th ed., pages **306, 317**).

   Gerrymandering – Members of the House are usually able to pressure state legislatures to draw congressional districts lines in a manner designed to maximize the number of supporters in the district while minimizing the number of people likely to vote against the representative. The effect of this is high re-election rates for members of the House.

Unit XII: The Presidency

Correlates to Chapter 14 in *American Government, 14th Edition*

The American presidency is a unique office. Presidents can send the most formidable military forces of the world into combat, but can also have Congress reject their most treasured programs. The key to understanding this paradox is found in the system of separation of powers.

Key Terms

ad hoc structure
bully pulpit
cabinet
circular structure
divided government
electoral college
gridlock
impeachment
legislative veto
line-item veto
pocket veto
pyramid structure
signing statement
unified government
veto message

Key Concepts

- Unlike prime ministers, presidents are elected independent of Congress.

- The Founders did not envision the office of president being as powerful and central to the political process as it is today.

- Presidential power has grown significantly since the founding of the country. However, much of this power is dependent on a president's ability to influence others.

- Presidential policymaking is tied to his or her ability to work with other institutions both in and out of government.

- Divided government does not prevent a president from governing.

For a full discussion of the presidency, see *American Government*, 14th ed., Chapter 14.

AP Tip

The AP exam focuses on interactions between institutions. Several AP exam questions have asked about the relationship between the president, Congress, the bureaucracy, and the courts. It is important to understand the president's authority, and the limits of that authority, over other institutions of government.

Multiple Choice Questions

1. Why is it more difficult for an American president to get his program enacted in comparison with a prime minister in a parliamentary system?

    (A) because of divided government, when one or both houses of Congress differ from the president's political party

    (B) because the president has fewer constitutional powers than a prime minister

    (C) because the president has less control over the cabinet than a prime minister

    (D) because prime ministers can enact their programs without the approval of parliament

    (E) because the Supreme Court in the United States frequently uses judicial review to overturn presidential programs

2. All of the following are features of the electoral college system EXCEPT

    (A) there is a winner-take-all system in forty-eight states

    (B) if no one wins a majority of electoral college votes, the election is decided by the House of Representatives

    (C) when the House of Representatives decides an election, each member has one vote

    (D) state electoral ballots are opened and counted before a joint session of Congress

    (E) on rare occasions an elector will vote for a presidential candidate other than the one who carried his or her state

3. President Cleveland used federal troops to break up a labor strike, and President Eisenhower sent federal troops to desegregate Central High School in Little Rock, Arkansas. Which clause of the Constitution gave them this power?

    (A) serve as commander-in-chief of the armed forces

    (B) convene Congress in special sessions

(C) commission officers in the armed forces

(D) take care that the laws be faithfully executed

(E) wield the "executive power"

4. One of the criticisms of President Carter was that he was so involved with the minor details of policies that he "couldn't see the forest for the trees." How did President Carter structure his White House staff?

(A) ad hoc

(B) circular

(C) bureaucratic

(D) pyramid

(E) business model

5. How are cabinet secretaries and the attorney general selected and removed?

(A) The president appoints cabinet secretaries and the attorney general, subject to Senate confirmation, and they serve at his will.

(B) The president usually retains his predecessor's cabinet secretaries and attorney general.

(C) The president appoints cabinet secretaries and the attorney general for fixed fourteen-year terms of office.

(D) Cabinet secretaries and the attorney general are appointed by the president and can be removed by Congress at will.

(E) The president appoints cabinet secretaries and the attorney general, and they must resign at the end of the presidential term.

6. Which of the following statements most accurately describes the president's power to get his programs enacted?

(A) Presidents often rule by decree and executive order; as a result, much of their program becomes law.

(B) Presidents often have a majority of both houses of Congress; as a result, many of their proposals are adopted.

(C) The president must rely heavily on persuasion to get things done.

(D) Because the president can always call a press conference, he often uses the media to his advantage to get his program passed.

(E) The president has more power to get things done in the second half of his term because by then he has established himself in office.

TABLE 14.2 Partisan Gains or Losses in Congress in Off-Year Elections

Year	President	Party	Gains or Losses of President's Party in:	
			House	Senate
1934	Roosevelt	Dem.	+9	+9
1938	Roosevelt	Dem.	−70	−7
1942	Roosevelt	Dem.	−50	−8
1946	Truman	Dem.	−54	−11
1950	Truman	Dem.	−29	−5
1954	Eisenhower	Rep.	−18	−1
1958	Eisenhower	Rep.	−47	−13
1962	Kennedy	Dem.	−5	+2
1966	Johnson	Dem.	−48	−4
1970	Nixon	Rep.	−12	+1
1974	Ford	Rep.	−48	−5
1978	Carter	Dem.	−12	−3
1982	Reagan	Rep.	−26	0
1986	Reagan	Rep.	−5	−8
1990	Bush	Rep.	−9	−1
1994	Clinton	Dem.	−52	−9
1998	Clinton	Dem.	+5	0
2002	G. W. Bush	Rep.	+8	+2
2006	G. W. Bush	Rep.	−30	−6
2010	Obama	Dem.	−64	−6

Sources: Norman J. Ornstein, Thomas E. Mann, and Michael J. Malbin, *Vital Statistics on Congress, 2001–2002* (Washington, D.C.: Congressional Quarterly Press, 2001), 207; web sites of U.S. House of Representatives and U.S. Senate. Note: See the Web links on the front inside cover to visit the House and Senate web sites.

7. Table 14.2 above supports which of the following conclusions?

(A) Democratic presidents have partisan gains in the House, while Republican presidents have partisan gains in the Senate.

(B) When a president's party gains seats in Congress, it always gains more seats in the House than in the Senate.

(C) President Truman received the most partisan gains in Congress of all the presidents on the chart.

(D) The president's party usually loses seats in Congress in mid-term elections.

(E) The president's party always loses more seats in the House than in the Senate.

8. What happens to a bill that is not signed or vetoed within ten days while Congress is still in session?

(A) It becomes law automatically, without the president's approval.

(B) It is "pocket vetoed" and does not become law.

(C) It becomes law as soon as Congress adjourns; until then, the president may veto it.

(D) It is held over until the next session of Congress.

(E) It becomes law if 60 percent of both houses of Congress approve it.

9. There is a difference between elite opinion and the opinion of the American electorate as a whole. Which of the following statements best describes this difference?

(A) Elite ideologies are often radical, while the typical American voter is a moderate.

(B) The political elite are less likely to believe that they can influence government decision making.

(C) The American electorate is more consistent in its voting patterns than the elite, who tend to favor candidates on a case-by-case basis.

(D) Polling data has more influence on elites than on the average American voter.

(E) Political elites have greater political knowledge and more consistent ideologies.

10. All of the following are normally duties of the vice president EXCEPT

(A) attending the funeral of a third-world dictator

(B) presiding over the Senate each day, as the leader of the majority party

(C) campaigning on behalf of his political party

(D) reviewing a key policy area, such as energy policy

(E) providing the president with perspective from his region of the country

11. Which group comprises the closest advisors to the president?

(A) Cabinet

(B) White House Office

(C) Senate

(D) Executive Office of the President

(E) Council of Governors

12. Which of the following is true with regard to presidential popularity?

(A) It increases over time.

(B) It decreases when the Supreme Court make a controversial ruling.

(C) It remains relatively constant over time.

(D) It increases over the course of a war.

(E) It decreases over time.

13. What is the significance of *United States v. Nixon* (1974)?

(A) A president may not wage an undeclared war.

(B) A president may not veto part of a bill.

(C) A president must secure the approval of the Senate to fire a cabinet appointee.

(D) A president does not have an unlimited right to executive privilege.

(E) A president may not impound funds appropriated by Congress.

14. Which of the following is NOT a constitutional power of the president?

(A) declare war

(B) recommend legislation to Congress

(C) appoint diplomats

(D) negotiate treaties

(E) veto part of a bill

15. The term "divided government" means which of the following?

(A) a president and a judiciary of different political parties

(B) a president and a vice president of different political parties

(C) a disagreement between the Supreme Court and the Congress

(D) a cabinet of composed of members of different political parties

(E) a president and congress of different political parties

Free Response Questions

1. There are several constraints that make it difficult for a president to develop a program. These constraints include crisis, the federal budget, and adverse popular reaction.

(a) Identify a specific example of one of the constraints listed above and explain why it made it difficult for a president to get his program enacted.

(b) Identify a specific example of another of the constraints from the list above, and explain why it made it difficult for a president to get his program enacted.

2. The last half of the 20th century saw a shift in power and influence from cabinet to the White House Office.

(a) Define presidential cabinet.

(b) Define White House Office.

(c) Identify and explain two reasons why power has shifted from the cabinet to the White House Staff.

Answers

Multiple Choice Answers

1. (A) Divided government occurs when at least one house of Congress differs from the political party of the president. This makes it difficult for a president to get his programs passed. In parliamentary systems, the prime minister is a member of the biggest party in parliament, and divided government does not occur (*American Government*, 14th ed., pages **341–342**).

2. (C) Each state's vote is allotted to the candidate preferred by a majority of the state's House delegation. Each state has one vote in the event the House of Representatives decides a presidential election (*American Government*, 14th ed., pages **346–347**).

3. (D) The president's duty to "take care that the laws be faithfully executed" has become one of the most elastic phrases in the Constitution. Both Cleveland and Eisenhower interpreted this broadly in deploying federal troops (*American Government*, 14th ed., page **349**).

4. (B) Carter used a circular (or wheel-and-spokes) model. While this model guarantees openness to many sources of advice, it makes it difficult to manage the complexities of the government (*American Government*, 14th ed., page **361**).

5. (A) Cabinet officers are the heads of the fifteen major executive departments. The attorney general runs the Justice Department. Upon taking office, presidents can appoint all new cabinet heads and a new attorney general. Sometimes they retain some of the existing cabinet secretaries. They serve at the will of the president (*American Government*, 14th ed., pages **364–365**).

6. (C) Because the constitutional powers of the president are subject to interpretation, he must rely predominantly on persuasion, rather than power, to get things done (*American Government*, 14th ed., page **352**).

7. (D) The president's party usually loses seats in mid-term congressional elections. As a general rule, losses are greater in the House of Representatives, although this is not always the case. In the 2010 mid-term elections, Democrats lost 64 seats in the House and 6 seats in the Senate (*American Government*, 14th ed., page **354**).

8. (A) A bill that is not signed by the president within ten days while Congress is in session automatically becomes law. If Congress adjourns within ten days, the bill is "pocket vetoed" (*American Government*, 14th ed., pages **356–357**).

9. (E) Elites know more about politics, and their views on policy are more consistent than the ideologies and viewpoints of the average American.

10. (B) Although the vice president may be called on to break a tie vote in the Senate, he is not a member of the Senate and does not attend its proceedings (*American Government*, 14th ed., page **372**).

11. (B) The White House Office is the principal advisory group to the president. The cabinet was replaced by the White House Office as the principal advisory group in the middle of the 20th century (*American Government*, 14th ed., pages **362–364**).

12. (E) Presidential popularity generally decreases over time. This is an important concept because a president's ability to shape public opinion is correlated with presidential popularity (*American Government*, 14th ed., pages **353–354**).

13. (D) The Supreme Court ruled in *United States v. Nixon* that while presidents have a right to executive privilege, that right is not unlimited (*American Government*, 14th ed., page **359**).

14. (E) Presidents, unlike most state governors, do not have the "line item veto." Congress attempted, legislatively, to create a line item veto for the president. The Supreme Court in *Clinton v. New York City* declared this unconstitutional (*American Government*, 14th ed., pages **357–358**).

15. (E) A divided government exists when the president and one or both houses of Congress are of different political parties (*American Government*, 14th ed., pages **341–342**).

Free Response Answers

1. (a) One constraint that makes it difficult for a president to pursue his programs is crisis. For example, President Johnson proposed a number of social programs as part of the Great Society. He even declared war on poverty. However, the growing crisis in

Vietnam and the war's increasing unpopularity took much of his attention. Although much of Johnson's social welfare program was enacted, it soon took a back seat to the war in Vietnam (*American Government*, 14th ed., page **369**).

(b) Another constraint that stands in the way of a president's programs is the federal budget. The budget contains certain uncontrollable expenditures. These are programs, like Social Security, that have been promised to a large sector of the population. Eliminating these programs would be political suicide, and they must be accounted for in the federal budget. Although President George H. W. Bush promised not to raise taxes, he was forced to break that promise in light of a slow economy and budgetary concerns. An economic crisis at the end of George W. Bush's term may make it difficult for President Obama to pursue the programs he promised in his campaign (*American Government*, 14th ed., page **369**).

(*Alternate response*): Adverse popular reaction also may prevent a president from enacting his program. For example, President Reagan proposed tax cuts, larger military expenditures, adjustments to Social Security, and certain budget cuts. When these proposals became public, the first two were popular, but the last two met with resistance. As a result of this adverse reaction, the unpopular proposals were scaled back. Both President Clinton and President Obama struggled to develop a health care program popular enough with the public to be enacted by Congress (*American Government*, 14th ed., pages **368–369**).

2. (a) The president's cabinet is comprised of the heads of the 15 executive departments (*American Government*, 14th ed., page **340**).

(b) The White House Office is the group of presidential advisors that are closest to the president. They have offices in the White House (*American Government*, 14th ed., page **362**).

(c) Divided loyalty – Frequently members of cabinet departments begin to be advocates for the needs and views of their departments rather than being advocates for the policies of the administration (*American Government*, 14th ed., pages **364–365**).

Patronage – While patronage has been greatly reduced by the growth of the merit system, it still exists. Presidents use appointments to executive departments as a way of rewarding supporters. Appointments to the White House Office are usually motivated by loyalty, the ability to provide advice, and the ability to be an effective advocate for the president's agenda (*American Government*, 14th ed., page **365**).

Unit XIII: The Bureaucracy

Correlates to Chapter 15 in *American Government, 14ᵗʰ Edition*

The federal bureaucracy is a complex web of federal agencies with overlapping jurisdictions. Most people think of the bureaucracy as wasteful, confusing, and rigid. Because the bureaucracy has such a large and complex organization, it is easy to find examples supporting this view. A closer look at the bureaucracy reveals that there is satisfaction with many aspects of government services and that many of the bureaucracy's problems are the result of actions taken by Congress, the courts, and the president.

Key Terms

appropriation
authorization legislation
bureaucracy
committee clearance
competitive service
discretionary authority
government by proxy
iron triangle
issue network
laissez-faire
legislative veto
name-request job
red tape
trust funds

Key Concepts

- The bureaucracy is the organization composed of appointed officials.

- The bureaucracy is vested with the power to make policy within the guidelines specified by Congress.

- Congress can exercise control over the bureaucracy in several ways, including setting its budget.

- The bureaucracy is often considered the "fourth branch" because of its functional independence from the rest of the government. This is the product of historical events and legislation passed by Congress.

- The federal bureaucracy is massive in size, consisting of several million workers.

- Attempts to reform the bureaucracy have been ongoing. These have included at least 11 major attempts in the twentieth century alone.

- "Red tape" refers to the numerous rules that have been created by the bureaucracy. Those rules are viewed as either positive or negative, depending on whether a person sees them as protections or burdens.

For a full discussion of the bureaucracy, see *American Government*, 14th ed., Chapter 15.

AP Tip

Congressional oversight of the bureaucracy is fundamental to the system of checks and balances. Nevertheless, the bureaucracy can be difficult to control. Both of these concepts may appear on the AP exam.

Multiple Choice Questions

1. Which of the following statements best describes how the bureaucracy is controlled?

   (A) There is very little control over the bureaucracy because agencies make regulations that have the force of law.

   (B) The executive branch controls the bureaucracy by appointing all federal employees.

   (C) Congress controls the bureaucracy because it has the power to fire agency heads after oversight hearings and for cause.

   (D) The judicial branch controls the bureaucracy by reviewing regulations to make sure they are constitutional before they go into effect.

   (E) Both Congress and the executive branch have controls over the bureaucracy.

2. A postal clerk asks a customer if her package contains anything flammable. The customer responds that she is mailing a bottle of nail polish to her elderly aunt, who lives across town. The postal service employee allows the package to be mailed. The clerk's decision is an example of

   (A) discretionary authority

   (B) standard operating procedures

   (C) standard deviation

   (D) abuse of power

   (E) complexity and red tape

3. Which of the following has been a criticism of the process for firing a bureaucrat?

(A) It is too political, and bureaucrats are often terminated for expressing their political beliefs.

(B) Although bureaucrats must be given written warnings before they are terminated, there is not enough time given for them to improve their performance.

(C) It is too difficult to fire bureaucrats because the process is elaborate and time-consuming.

(D) Many good people do not enter the bureaucracy because most federal bureaucrats are fired when a new president takes office.

(E) The process for terminating an employee differs from agency to agency, making the firing process too inconsistent.

4. How does the bureaucracy compare with the rest of the government in employing women and minorities?

(A) Women and minorities mirror the population as a whole at all levels of the bureaucracy.

(B) There are more women and minorities in Congress (including congressional staffs) than in the bureaucracy.

(C) There are more women in the bureaucracy than in the rest of the government, but there are fewer minorities than in the population as a whole.

(D) There are more women and minorities in the bureaucracy, but they are clustered in lower level jobs.

(E) The bureaucracy is overwhelmingly white and male.

5. From the standpoint of a federal agency, what is the advantage of an iron triangle?

(A) It gives the agency allies in Congress, as well as in the private sector.

(B) It allows federal agencies to receive funding directly from interest groups.

(C) It provides agency heads with access to the media, so they can publicize their programs.

(D) It gives the federal agency a direct link to the White House staff.

(E) It prevents Congress from using oversight hearings as a means of cutting agency budgets.

6. The Department of Homeland Security was established to coordinate policies among the Federal Bureau of Investigation, the Transportation Security Administration, and the Central Intelligence Agency, as well as other federal agencies. What is the most serious problem that the creation of this department attempted to resolve?

(A) red tape

(B) imperialism

(C) duplication

(D) waste

(E) conflict and lack of coordination among agencies

7. In general, what is the opinion of the American public regarding the bureaucracy?

(A) When people have personal dealings with bureaucrats, they generally have positive experiences, although they have a less favorable attitude about the federal bureaucracy as a whole.

(B) When people have personal dealings with bureaucrats, they generally have negative experiences, although they have a favorable attitude about the federal bureaucracy as a whole.

(C) People have negative experiences with individual bureaucrats and feel negatively about the bureaucracy as a whole.

(D) People have positive experiences with individual bureaucrats and feel positively about the bureaucracy as a whole.

(E) People believe that bureaucrats try to be helpful, but they believe that the bureaucracy is too small to provide services effectively.

8. Which of the following statements most accurately describes the federal civil service?

(A) It provides a wide variety of diverse services and employs people in hundreds of different occupations.

(B) It employs nearly 10 percent of the American workforce.

(C) Most jobs in the civil service are filled based on political affiliation and faithful service to a political party.

(D) Most federal civil servants work in Washington, D.C.

(E) Americans reject the stereotype of civil servants as faceless pencil pushers.

TABLE 15.2   How the Public Views Particular Federal Agencies

AGENCY	% FAVORABLE Very/Somewhat/Total	% UNFAVORABLE Very/Somewhat/Total	Favorable Minus Unfavorable
Postal Service	58/31/89	5/5/10	+79
FBI	31/46/77	10/7/17	+60
Defense Department	31/34/65	15/2/17	+48
Social Security Admin.	24/40/64	19/13/32	+32
EPA	23/40/63	15/15/31	+32
CIA	22/36/58	16/14/30	+28
Homeland Security	24/36/60	17/17/34	+26
Transportation Safety	15/41/56	16/9/25	+26
Education Department	22/37/59	19/19/38	+21
IRS	14/42/56	21/18/39	+17
FEMA	16/33/49	24/26/50	−1

Percent reporting a "favorable or unfavorable impression"*

*Other response categories were "never heard of" and "can't rate," and only the newest agency, the Transportation Safety Administration, drew significant numbers in each category (9 percent for each).

Source: Adapted from results of a nationally representative Associated Press/IPSOS Public Agenda poll conducted December 17–19, 2007.

9. The table above supports all of the following statements EXCEPT
   (A) social services agencies are viewed more favorably than defense and security agencies
   (B) the Postal Service is viewed favorably by a wide majority of Americans
   (C) contrary to popular belief, Americans view most agencies favorably
   (D) the services provided by federal agencies are diverse
   (E) the FBI is viewed more favorably than the CIA

10. The table above best supports which of the following?
    (A) The Internal Revenue Service is disliked by most Americans.
    (B) FEMA's favorability rating is a result of the aftermath of Hurricane Katrina.
    (C) The crisis in Social Security funding causes most Americans to view that agency negatively.
    (D) The No Child Left Behind Act has negatively impacted the public's perception of the Department of Education.
    (E) The war in Iraq has negatively impacted the public's perception of the Defense Department.

11. Who is responsible for determining the appropriations that bureaucratic agencies receive?
    (A) the president
    (B) Congress
    (C) the Office of Management and Budget
    (D) the Treasury Department
    (E) the Cabinet

12. What is the significance of the Pendleton Act?
    (A) It replaced the cabinet with the White House Staff as the principal advisory group to the president.
    (B) It authorizes the president to reorganize the executive branch.
    (C) It began the process of implementing the merit system.
    (D) It made it easier to remove a bureaucrat from office.
    (E) It prohibited partisan political activity by federal workers.

13. What is the function of a legislative veto?
    (A) allow Congress of override a presidential veto
    (B) allow Congress to counteract a judicial decision
    (C) allow the president to overturn an act of Congress
    (D) allow Congress to invalidate a regulation made by the bureaucracy
    (E) allow the bureaucracy to override a law made by Congress

14. Why is there so much "red tape?"

(A) to supplement the system of checks and balances

(B) to protect the president from political attacks

(C) to protect individuals and execute Congressional directives

(D) to prevent Congress from exercising the legislative veto

(E) to direct the judiciary in how to interpret laws passed by Congress

15. To whom is the bureaucracy accountable?

(A) the president and Congress

(B) Congress alone

(C) the president alone

(D) the executive branch alone

(E) the judiciary alone

Free Response Questions

1. The role of the federal bureaucracy has expanded over time. Nevertheless, there are restraints on the growth of the bureaucracy.

(a) Identify and explain two factors that have increased the role of the bureaucracy over time.

(b) Identify and explain one factor that restrains the growth of the bureaucracy.

2. (a) Define legislative oversight.

(b) Identify and explain two tools of legislative oversight.

Answers

Multiple Choice Answers

1. (E) Both Congress and the executive branch have control over the bureaucracy. The executive appoints agency heads and proposes agency budgets. Congress must approve budget proposals and can hold oversight hearings (*American Government*, 14th ed., page **381**).

2. (A) Street-level bureaucrats have discretionary authority when rules are not spelled out clearly (*American Government*, 14th ed., page **384**).

3. (C) The process for firing a bureaucrat is elaborate and time consuming, often taking more than a year (*American Government*, 14th ed., page **390**).

4. (D) There are more women and minorities in the bureaucracy than in the other branches of government. However, they are clustered in lower paying, lower level jobs (*American Government*, 14th ed., page **391**).

5. (A) Iron triangles consist of a federal agency, interest groups, and a congressional committee or subcommittee involved in a specific policy area. Iron triangles are important links between the agency, Congress, and the private sector (*American Government*, 14th ed., page **396**).

6. (E) Although the Department of Homeland Security was established to reduce a number of problems, the most serious was conflict and lack of coordination among agencies (*American Government*, 14th ed., page **398**).

7. (A) In general, people have good experiences with street-level bureaucrats, but they have a less favorable attitude about the bureaucracy as a whole (*American Government*, 14th ed., page **398**).

8. (A) The federal civil service includes hundreds of diverse occupations. Some civil service jobs, like FBI agents, are glamorous. Others are more commonplace, like plumbers (*American Government*, 14th ed., page **398**).

9. (A) All but one of the agencies shown on the chart have positive favorability ratings. This is true of both social service and defense/security agencies. For example, the Defense Department has a 48 percent favorability rating, while the Social Security Administration has a rating of 32 percent (*American Government*, 14th ed., page **402**).

10. (B) FEMA is the only agency shown on the chart with a negative favorability rating, although the difference between total negative and positive ratings is only 1 percent. This is a result of the agency's perceived ineffectiveness in the aftermath of Hurricane Katrina, which devastated New Orleans (*American Government*, 14th ed., page **402**).

11. (B) Congress is the correct answer. While there are several actors in the budget making process, Congress is ultimately responsible for the appropriation of money to the agencies (*American Government*, 14th ed., page **383**).

12. (C) The Pendleton Act was the first real attempt at serious civil service reform. It was the first time that "merit" was used, in any significant way, to determine federal employment (*American Government*, 14th ed., page **389**).

13. (D) The legislative veto is an action where Congress overturns or invalidates an administrative regulation issued by the bureaucracy. The one-house legislative veto was declared unconstitutional in *INS v. Chadha* (*American Government*, 14th ed., page **399**).

14. (C) Complicated regulations are issued to protect the rights of individuals and to enforce legislation that is frequently vague (*American Government*, 14th ed., page **396**).

15. (A) The bureaucracy is accountable to many political actors, including the president and Congress (*American Government*, 14th ed., pages **396–399**).

Free Response Answers

1. (a) The bureaucracy has grown from three cabinet departments into the "fourth branch" of government. One factor that caused this is a change in public attitude. As a result of the New Deal, people expect the government to play an active role in dealing with economic and social problems. For example, President Nixon established agencies that implemented wage and price controls. The regulations created by these agencies expanded the role of the federal government in controlling the economy. Terrorist attacks have also led to growth in the bureaucracy. After the September 11th attack, a new agency, the Department of Homeland Security, was created. This large agency consolidated many smaller ones, and its role in gathering intelligence and preventing terrorism may expand in the future (*American Democracy*, 14th ed., pages **384–385**).

   (b) One factor that restrains the growth of the bureaucracy is legislative oversight. Although tales of wasteful spending may be exaggerated, Congress is sensitive to the public's perception that the bureaucracy does not spend money wisely and is mired in red tape. Oversight hearings are held to determine whether the bureaucracy is operating efficiently and effectively. If Congress believes that an agency's budget is bloated, it can cut funding to that agency when it passes appropriations bills in the next session (*American Government*, 14th ed., pages **397–400**).

2. (a) Legislative oversight is the process of evaluating the performance of the bureaucracy.

   (b) Any two of the following identifications and explanations.
   - Funding – Congress controls the budget of the bureaucracy and can use this power to manipulate the function of the bureaucracy. Congress can fund activities it likes and can "defund" activities and actions that it dislikes.
   - Structure – Congress controls the structure of the bureaucracy. Only Congress can reorganize the executive branch.
   - Confirmation – The officials that run the bureaucracy are appointed by the president and approved by the Senate.
   - Support Staff – Congress has created agencies that help them supervise the bureaucracy. The Congressional Budget Office and the Government Accountability Office (formerly the General Accounting Office) were created by Congress to aid it in the supervision of the bureaucracy. (*American Government*, 14th ed., pages **397–400**).

Unit XIV: The Federal Courts

Correlates to Chapter 16 in *American Government, 14th Edition*

The judicial branch plays a large role in making public policy. The major power that the federal courts have is judicial review, the right to declare laws of Congress and acts of the president unconstitutional.

Key Terms

activist approach
amicus curiae
brief
class-action suit
concurring opinion
constitutional court
courts of appeals
dissenting opinion
district court
diversity cases
federal-question cases
fee shifting
in forma pauperis
judicial restraint approach
judicial review
legislative courts
litmus test
opinion of the Court
per curiam opinion
plaintiff
political question
remedy
sovereign immunity
standing
stare decisis
writ of certiorari

Key Concepts

- While judicial review is not specifically mentioned in the Constitution, virtually every scholar recognizes that judicial review is authorized by the Constitution.

- There are two different types of judges. Judges who are appointed according to Article III of the Constitution and serve for life and judges who are appointed according to Article I and serve for a fixed term.

- The United Kingdom did not have a supreme court until 2009. Before that, 12 members of the House of Lords served as a sort of supreme court. The UK Supreme Court's power of judicial review is limited.

- Original jurisdiction is the authority to hear a case first. Appellate jurisdiction is the authority to hear a case on appeal.

- Most federal judges have a lifetime term of office. This is to insulate them from political pressures that might impact their decision making.

- If the Constitution is to be the "supreme law of the land," then some official or institution must be empowered to invalidate policies that violate the Constitution.

- The judiciary is a policy-making institution. It is impossible for the judiciary not to make policy, because the decisions it renders serve as precedent for future cases.

For a full discussion of the federal courts, see *American Government,* 14th ed., Chapter 16.

AP Tip

Judicial review is an important power of the federal courts and serves as a check on Congress and the president. The topic is likely to appear on the AP exam in some form.

Multiple Choice Questions

1. Using the power of judicial review, the Supreme Court can do all of the following EXCEPT
    (A) declare a law passed by Congress unconstitutional
    (B) declare a law passed by a state unconstitutional
    (C) declare acts of the executive branch unconstitutional
    (D) determine the meaning and application of the Constitution
    (E) overturn a Constitutional amendment as a violation of civil rights

2. Justice Clarence Thomas believes that the Constitution should be interpreted according to its clear language. This judicial philosophy can best be described as:
    (A) strict construction
    (B) judicial activism
    (C) conservatism
    (D) liberalism
    (E) constitutionalism

3. The federal courts have jurisdiction over all of the following cases EXCEPT
   (A) civil suits between citizens of different states in which the amount exceeds $50,000
   (B) criminal cases involving violations of laws passed by Congress
   (C) bankruptcy cases
   (D) state appeals cases in which the defendant alleges his or her constitutional rights were violated
   (E) prosecutions under state criminal law

4. National supremacy over the states was expanded by the Supreme Court in cases involving all of the following issues EXCEPT
   (A) railroad regulations issued by the Interstate Commerce Commission
   (B) the creation of a national bank
   (C) the use of injunctions to prevent labor strikes
   (D) laws regulating wages and hours
   (E) state laws regarding marriage and divorce

5. All of the following make it difficult to get a case to the Supreme Court EXCEPT
   (A) the Supreme Court does not take all cases
   (B) appeals cost money for lawyers and paperwork
   (C) by the time a case gets to the Supreme Court, the case has already gone through an expensive trial and appeals process
   (D) it can take a long time to settle a matter in federal court
   (E) the government does not supply lawyers for the appeals court process

6. Long after the Supreme Court ruled prayer in public schools unconstitutional, public schools all over the country were still allowing prayer and Bible readings. What explains this?
   (A) The Supreme Court's decision was vague, and schools were not sure how to implement it.
   (B) The courts have no police force or army; hence, they have no enforcement powers.
   (C) School districts could still legally engage in school prayer because they continued to file appeals.
   (D) Both President George H. W. Bush and President Clinton supported school prayer, so they ordered the executive branch not to enforce the Court's decision.
   (E) The areas where school prayer was still being held were all Christian, so no one challenged the practice.

7. What is the role of judicial review in the system of checks and balances?
   (A) It undermines the Constitution by making the Supreme Court the final arbiter of the law.
   (B) It enhances the power of Congress by overturning decisions of the president.
   (C) It enhances the power of the president by overturning decisions of Congress.
   (D) It makes the courts a co-equal branch with the president and Congress.
   (E) It enhances the power of the states by overturning national laws.

8. Which of the following statements best describes the jurisdiction of the Supreme Court?
   (A) The Court is exclusively a court of appellate jurisdiction.
   (B) The Court's jurisdiction is mostly appellate, but it has original jurisdiction in a few specified types of cases.
   (C) The Court is exclusively a court of original jurisdiction.
   (D) The Court can choose which cases of original jurisdiction to take.
   (E) Most of the Court's cases come directly from trial courts.

9. What is required for the Supreme Court to grant a petition for a writ of certiorari?
   (A) The majority of the justices must vote to hear the case.
   (B) The justices from the majority party on the Court must agree to hear the case.
   (C) A circuit court of appeals must recommend that the justices hear the case.
   (D) The Constitution requires that four of the nine justices vote to hear a case.
   (E) The unwritten "rule of four" means at least four justices must agree to hear a case.

10. Several churches filed briefs in *Roe v. Wade*, the landmark Supreme Court decision about abortion. Which term best describes these briefs?
    (A) solicitor general's brief
    (B) interest group brief
    (C) plaintiff's brief
    (D) defendant's brief
    (E) *amicus curiae* brief

11. On which of the following courts do judges have a lifetime term?
    (A) Supreme Court
    (B) Court of Appeals for the Federal Circuit

(C) Tax Court

(D) Claims Court

(E) Court of Veterans Appeals

12. All of the following are checks on judicial power EXCEPT:

(A) statutory amendment

(B) impeachment

(C) lack of enforcement power

(D) removal by the president

(E) constitutional amendment

13. What is senatorial courtesy?

(A) The ability of a senator to "veto" a judicial nomination.

(B) The requirement that the Supreme Court obtain preclearance from the Senate before exercising judicial review.

(C) The Senate's ability to review and invalidate Supreme Court decisions.

(D) The ability of the Senate's Judiciary Committee to remove a justice after 10 years in office.

(E) The ability of members of the Senate Judiciary Committee to participate in the writing of opinions from district courts in their states.

14. What is the court of original jurisdiction for the vast majority of federal cases?

(A) Supreme Court

(B) Circuit Court

(C) District Court

(D) Superior Court

(E) Court of First Instance

15. Approximately how many cases does the Supreme Court accept for review?

(A) 50

(B) 100

(C) 500

(D) 1000

(E) 1500

Free Response Questions

1. The federal courts have played a larger role in our government over time. The role of the federal government changed as a result of court decisions involving the following issues: slavery, the economy, civil liberties, and federalism.

(a) Pick one issue from the list above and explain how the Supreme Court changed the role of the federal government, giving an example.

(b) Pick another issue from the list above, and explain how the Supreme Court changed the role of the federal government, giving an example.

2. (a) Define "checks and balances" as it is used in relation to the US Constitution.

(b) Select two of the following checks on the judiciary:

• Constitutional Amendment

• Appointment

• Statutory Amendment

For each selection explain how it checks judicial power. Additionally, explain the limits of the check's effectiveness.

Answers
Multiple Choice Answers

1. (E) Judicial review allows the Supreme Court to determine the meaning and application of the Constitution and overturn a law or regulation that violates the Constitution. Because amendments are part of the Constitution, they are, by definition, constitutional, and the Supreme Court may not overturn them (*American Government*, 14th ed., pages **409–410**).

2. (A) Justice Thomas is a strict constructionist who believes the Constitution should be interpreted directly by the language of the Constitution (*American Government*, 14th ed., pages **409–410**).

3. (E) The federal courts do not have jurisdiction to hear criminal cases involving violations of state law unless there is an alleged violation of the defendant's constitutional rights (*American Government*, 14th ed., pages **420–423**).

4. (E) Over time, the Supreme Court has expanded the power of the federal government by allowing the creation of a national bank, upholding railroad regulations, permitting the use of federal injunctions in labor disputes, and validating wage and hour regulations (*American Government*, 14th ed., pages **411, 413**).

5. (E) The Supreme Court chooses the cases it accepts by issuing a writ of *certiorari*. Although it is expensive and time consuming to take a case to the Supreme Court, the government provides lawyers for people who are *in forma pauperis* (*American Government*, 14th ed., pages **421, 423**).

6. (B) The courts have no enforcement power. Unless the failure to comply is easily detected

and brought to the Court's attention, it is difficult to ensure compliance with decisions (*American Government*, 14th ed., pages **411, 431**).

7. (D) Judicial review gives the Supreme Court the power to check the president and Congress by overturning laws that are unconstitutional. This makes the Court a co-equal branch of government (*American Government*, 14th ed., page **409**).

8. (B) Most of the Court's jurisdiction is appellate. The Court has original jurisdiction over cases involving ambassadors and other public ministers and cases in which a state is a party (*American Government*, 14th ed., pages **411, 420**).

9. (E) At least four justices must agree to hear a case. This is the unwritten "rule of four" (*American Government*, 14th ed., page **421**).

10. (E) An amicus curiae brief is filed by an individual or group that is not a party to a legal action but has an interest in the case. Amicus curiae briefs are filed to persuade the court to reach the decision desired by the group (*American Government*, 14th ed., page **426**).

11. (A) The Supreme Court is an Article III court. Its judges have lifetime tenure (*American Government*, 14th ed., page **435**).

12. (D) The president does not have the ability to remove federal judges that he or she has appointed. Even judges with fixed terms cannot be removed by the president, although he may refuse to reappoint them when their terms expire (*American Government*, 14th ed., page **417**).

13. (A) While the Constitution specifies that the President appoints judges with the advice and consent of the Senate, custom gives the senior senator from a state a "veto" over nominations to federal district courts in his or her state. (*American Government*, 14th ed., page **419**).

14. (C) District court is the court of original jurisdiction for virtually all federal cases. The (*American Government*, 14th ed., page **420**).

15. (B) The Supreme Court grants *certiorari* to approximately 100 cases per year (*American Government*, 14th ed., page **422**).

Free Response Answers

1. (a) By dealing with the issue of slavery, the Supreme Court played a large role in setting the stage for the Civil War. In the *Dred Scott* case, the court tackled the issue of whether a slave must be given his freedom once he was taken into a free state. The Court ruled that, under the Constitution, African Americans could never be citizens. This meant that there would be no dividing line between slave states and free states.

Because slaves were considered property, they could be taken north, thus expanding slavery and preventing its prohibition. In rendering this decision, the court played a major role in exacerbating the tensions between the North and the South that would lead to the Civil War (*American Government*, 14th ed., page **411**).

(b) The federal courts have expanded the government's role in the economy. They have upheld railroad regulations, anti-child-labor laws, and regulations setting minimum wages and maximum hours. In addition, they have upheld wage and price controls. Until the late 19th century, this level of government regulation of the economy was unheard of, but because of court decisions, the government now regulates (but does not control) the economy (American Government, 14th ed., pages **411, 413**). (*Alternate answer*): Judicial activism, particularly by the Warren Court, has enlarged the scope of government in protecting civil rights and civil liberties. For example, in *Brown v. Board of Education*, the Supreme Court held that school segregation is unconstitutional. Later, when Central High School, in Little Rock, Arkansas, refused to desegregate, President Eisenhower called in federal troops. This expanded the scope of government—all as a result of the *Brown* decision. When the Court held that indigent defendants must be provided with counsel, this also expanded the scope of government through the creation of public defenders offices (*Alternate answer*): Beginning in the early 1990s, the Supreme Court began restoring some rights of the states relative to the federal government. For example, the Court held that bringing a gun to school was not interstate commerce. Therefore, Congress's attempt to ban guns in schools was invalid. The Court also struck down a congressional attempt to allow Indian tribes to sue states. Furthermore, it held that certain provisions of the Brady handgun law were unconstitutional because they infringed on the powers of state and local officials. These cases lessened the power of the national government and strengthened states' power (*American Government*, 14th ed., pages **415, 424**).

2. (a) Checks and balances refers to the system set forth in the U.S. Constitution that allows one branch of government to counteract or "check" the others (*American Government*, 14th ed., page **409**).

(b) Any two of the following:

Constitutional Amendment – If the Court interprets the Constitution in a manner that Congress does not like, the Congress can propose, by a two-thirds vote, a constitutional amendment. The amendment is ratified if three-fourths of the states agree. This seldom occurs, because it is incredibly difficult to garner two-thirds of the Congress to support an amendment.

Appointment – Presidents attempt to change the ideological direction of the court through the appointment process.

This check is limited because once on the court, there is nothing to prevent a justice from change his or her ideology (*American Government*, 14th ed., page **431**).

Statutory Amendment – If the Court interprets a law in a manner that Congress does not like, Congress can change the law through the legislative process. While not as difficult a proposing an amendment, changing existing law is no small feat. As such, this check is limited in effectiveness as well (*American Government*, 14th ed., page **427**).

Unit XV: Policy Making in the Federal System

Correlates to Chapters 1 & 17 in *American Government, 14th Edition*

Policy making at the federal level is rarely accomplished consistently and routinely. An issue must first find its way to the political agenda, and then decisions must be made about how to address the issue. Coalitions are formed that struggle over the issue, and the policy that results depends on who gains, who loses, and the perceptions, beliefs, and values of key political actors.

Key Terms

client politics
costs and benefits
entrepreneurial politics
interest group politics
legitimacy
log-rolling
majoritarian politics
policy entrepreneurs
political agenda
pork-barrel legislation

Key Concepts

- The political agenda determines which issues will receive consideration in formulating new policy.

- Costs and benefits determine who supports a policy, who opposes it, and the coalitions that form to compete over a policy.

- Business regulation is an excellent case study of the different types of policies and policy making.

- Perceptions, beliefs, interests, and values all play a critical role in the policy-making process.

For a full discussion of policy making in the federal system, see *American Government*, 14th ed., Chapters 1 & 17.

AP Tip

The political agenda consists of the issues that people believe require government action. The political agenda involves virtually all of the participants in the policy-making process, and the term may appear on the AP exam.

Multiple Choice Questions

1. The political agenda is affected by all of the following EXCEPT

    (A) a crisis, such as the terrorist attacks of September 11, 2001

    (B) pressures by interest groups, such as organized labor, to address certain issues, such as working conditions

    (C) pressures by institutions, such as the Supreme Court, to change practices, such as segregation

    (D) pressures by unfriendly foreign nations to change U.S. foreign policy

    (E) the use of the media to publicize matters, such as automobile safety

2. Which of the following events or literature did NOT prompt the corresponding attention to policy:

    (A) Upton Sinclair's *The Jungle* shed light on the conditions of the meat-packing industry and the Meat Inspection Act of 1906.

    (B) The stock market collapse of 1929 helped develop support for the Securities and Exchange Act.

    (C) Oil spilled on the beaches of Santa Barbara, California, drew attention to problems addressed by the Water Quality Improvement Act of 1970.

    (D) Ralph Nader's 1965 book *Unsafe at Any Speed: The Designed-In Dangers of the American Automobile* had criticized the safety of certain GM cars and drew Congress's attention to auto safety.

    (E) Rachel Carson's 1962 book *Silent Spring* shed light on starvation of the homeless on American soil.

3. Almost everyone has to pay Social Security taxes, and almost everyone will receive Social Security benefits when they retire. This is an example of

    (A) interest group politics, in which a single group benefits most from the policy-making process

    (B) majoritarian politics, in which the policy-making process benefits large numbers of people who also bear the costs

(C) client politics, in which small identifiable groups will receive most of the benefits from the policy-making process

(D) entrepreneurial politics, in which a large number of people benefit from a policy that imposes costs on a small group

(E) pork-barrel politics, in which pet projects benefit the constituents of a member of Congress

4. Which of the following policies were adopted because a policy entrepreneur dramatized the issue, galvanized public opinion, and mobilized congressional support?

I. automobile safety legislation

II. legislation regulating food safety

III. legislation cutting highway funding for states that did not raise the drinking age

IV. the creation of the Department of Homeland Defense

(A) I and II

(B) I, II, and III

(C) II and III

(D) II, III, and IV

(E) I, II, and IV

5. According to Figure 17.1 below, all of the following are true EXCEPT:

(A) With client politics, a few people, or some particular community or organization benefits, but most people pay for what they get.

(B) In majoritarian politics, all or most people benefit, and all or most people pay.

(C) With interest-group politics, almost all people, communities, or organizations benefit, and most people, communities, or organizations pay.

(D) In entrepreneurial politics, almost everybody benefits, but only a few people, communities, or organizations pay the costs.

(E) Widely distributed benefits and widely distributed costs best describes majoritarian politics.

6. Which of the following is a distinctive feature in environmental policy making in America that differentiates it from most European nations?

I. U.S. policy making is far more adversarial.

II. In the United States, policy making depends heavily on the states.

III. Separation of powers guarantees mutual influence over the policy-making opportunity.

(A) I

(B) I and II

(C) I and III

(D) II and III

(E) I, II and III

7. Sometimes policies not demanded by the public nevertheless become items on the political agenda. What explains this?

(A) Key people in government, the political elites, become interested in certain problems and try to solve them.

(B) Policy makers rather than the public set the agenda, so the public has little impact on the political agenda.

(C) The public does not pay much attention to the policy agenda.

(D) Members of Congress are more interested in helping their districts than in making policy for the nation.

(E) The policy-making process is so complicated that it is difficult to determine what the public wants.

FIGURE 17.1 **A Way of Classifying and Explaining the Politics of Different Policy Issues**

PERCEIVED COSTS

Distributed | Concentrated

PERCEIVED BENEFITS

Distributed: **Majoritarian Politics** | **Entrepreneurial Politics**

Concentrated: **Client Politics** | **Interest Group Politics**

© Cengage Learning

8. Why has the Senate become a major source of political change?

    (A) The one-party South collapsed, leading to the rise of activist Senators on both sides of the aisle.

    (B) Senators have more time to deliberate than members of the House of Representatives have, so they are more able to introduce policies.

    (C) Senators "fly under the radar" more than the president; as a result, they have become policy innovators.

    (D) The Senate has stricter party discipline than the House; as a result, more policies can be enacted.

    (E) Senators are held more accountable to their constituents than representatives are.

9. Every policy-making decision involves balancing what competing interests?

    (A) the balance between who will write the laws and who will implement them

    (B) the balance between the legislative branch and the executive branch

    (C) the balance between judicial activism and judicial restraint

    (D) the balance between who will benefit and who will bear the costs

    (E) the balance between the powers of the state and federal government

10. What kinds of projects typically are "log-rolled" (exchanging votes on bills)?

    (A) bills that will create new nationwide social programs

    (B) bills involving controversial issues, such as abortion

    (C) bills for funding the military and defense

    (D) bills funding "pork-barrel" projects

    (E) bills regulating the environment

11. All of the following are true in regard to food stamps EXCEPT

    (A) Food Stamp recipients increased from about 28 million in 2008 to about 47 million in 2012.

    (B) During the 2012 presidential campaign, a debate began over the estimated 2 million or so "able-bodied" Food Stamp recipients that did not meet all the usual program eligibility criteria.

    (C) About 40 percent of all Food Stamps beneficiaries are children.

    (D) About 30 percent of all Food Stamps beneficiaries are senior citizens.

    (E) Food Stamps are now a part of the Supplemental Nutrition Assistance Program, SNAP.

12. Three Iowa legislators placed $196,000 in the federal budget for research on reducing swine and poultry odors. Which of the following terms might describe this provision?

    I.   earmarking

    II. pork-barrel

    III. client politics

    IV. entrepreneural politics

    (A) I and II

    (B) II and III

    (C) I, II, and III

    (D) I, II, and IV

    (E) II and IV

13. Activists in or out of government who pull together a political majority on behalf of unorganized interests are called

    (A) policy entrepreneurs

    (B) clients

    (C) majoritarians

    (D) labor union organizers

    (E) deregulators

14. In 2009, following the financial crisis, President Obama proposed centralizing financial regulatory power in a few federal agencies. This is most similar to which of the following?

    (A) creation of the Department of Homeland Security following the September 11 attacks

    (B) deregulation of the airline industry

    (C) breaking up AT&T, forcing it to compete with other long- distance service providers

    (D) the Clinton Administration's anti-trust lawsuit against Microsoft

    (E) the creation of both the Food and Drug Administration and the Consumer Product Safety Commission

15. The National Labor Relations Board was created to hear complaints of unfair labor practices. Later, the Taft-Hartley Act made certain union practices illegal. This is an example of

    (A) entrepreneurial politics, where a small group pays for the benefits of others

    (B) interest group politics, where organized groups struggle to receive favorable policy

(C) majoritarian politics, where laws are passed that represent the views of most voters

(D) client politics, where a small group benefits

(E) regulation, followed by a cycle of deregulation

Free Response Questions

1. Sometimes policies are adopted that provide benefits to most of society and impose substantial costs on a small group.

   (a) Identify an environmental policy that has been adopted, and describe who benefits and who bears the costs.

   (b) Identify at least three of the five reasons why the consumer and environmental protection agencies may not be as vulnerable to capture as some critics contend.

2. Interest groups compete for favorable policies. Even after policies are passed, interest groups continue to compete as they are enforced.

   (a) Define the National Labor Relations Board (NLRB).

   (b) Identify the major interest groups that influence policy implementation by the NLRB.

   (c) Define the Occupational Safety and Health Administration (OSHA).

   (d) Identify the major interest groups that influence policy implementation by OSHA.

Answers

Multiple Choice Answers

1. (D) Interest groups, institutions, and the media all impact the policy agenda. In addition, the agenda changes when there is a crisis (*American Government*, 14ᵗʰ ed., pages **10–11**).

2. (E) When Rachel Carson published *Silent Spring* in 1962, she set off a public outcry about the harm to wildlife caused by the indiscriminate use of DDT, a common pesticide. In 1972, the EPA banned the use of DDT (*American Government*, 14ᵗʰ ed., page **457**).

3. (B) Most people pay for Social Security, and most people will receive its benefits. This is an example of majoritarian politics (*American Government*, 14ᵗʰ ed., page **441**).

4. (B) Policy entrepreneurs pursued legislation affecting automobile safety, the meatpacking industry, and highway safety (*American Government*, 14ᵗʰ ed., pages **441, 449**).

5. (C) Narrowly concentrated benefits and narrowly concentrated costs, or interest-group politics. A few people, communities, or organizations benefit, and a few people, communities, or organizations pay (*American Government*, 14ᵗʰ ed., page **441**).

6. (E) U.S. policymaking is far more adversarial than in European countries, it depends heavily on the states, and is influenced by separation of powers. (*American Government*, 14ᵗʰ ed., pages **462–463**).

7. (A) A policy not demanded by the public can be addressed if someone in government is interested in it (*American Government*, 14ᵗʰ ed., pages **458–461**).

8. (A) The Senate moved slowly when it was controlled by the one-party South. Today senators on both sides of the aisle want to be policy innovators on attention-grabbing issues (*American Government*, 14ᵗʰ ed., pages **45–460**).

9. (D) Under cost-benefit analysis, every policy involves a group that will be helped and a group that will bear the expense. The interests of both groups are considered as part of the policy-making process (*American Government*, 14ᵗʰ ed., pages **13–14**).

10. (D) Log-rolling occurs when members of Congress agree to vote for one another's bills. These bills usually contain several projects to benefit specific district and are known as "pork-barrel" legislation (*American Government*, 14ᵗʰ ed., page **16**).

11. (D) About 8% of Food Stamp recipients are senior citizens (*American Government*, 14ᵗʰ ed., page **453**).

12. (C) An appropriation that benefits a particular group is an example of pork-barrel spending. Such provisions are known as earmarks. Client politics benefit a particular group (*American Government*, 14ᵗʰ ed., pages **14–16**).

13. (A) Those who are activists in or out of government who pull together a political majority on behalf of unorganized interests are called policy entrepreneurs. (*American Government*, 14ᵗʰ ed., pages **16–17**).

14. (A) A consolidated agency to oversee financial markets is similar to the Department of Homeland Security, which consolidated several intelligence-gathering and other security agencies under a single department.

15. (B) In interest group politics, groups like management and labor compete for policies that will benefit them. As illustrated by the Wagner Act, which benefited unions, and the Taft Hartley Act, which favored management, different groups benefit at different times (*American Government*, 14ᵗʰ ed., pages **456–457**).

Free Response Answers

1. (a) Environmental regulations provide widespread benefits for the public and impose substantial costs on a relatively small group—those who pollute the environment. The Environmental Protection Agency was created to identify those sites and develop clean-up plans. Owners of toxic waste dumps who do not comply with clean-up programs can be fined. There are also heavy penalties for the illegal dumping of toxic waste.

    (b) First, these agencies often enforce laws that impose specific standards in accordance with strict timetables, and so they have relatively little discretion. Second, the newer agencies usually regulate many different industries and so do not confront a single, unified opponent like the Occupational Safety and Health Administration. Third, the very existence of these agencies has helped strengthen the hand of the "public-interest" lobbies that initially demanded their creation. Fourth, these lobbies can now call upon many sympathetic allies in the media who will attack agencies thought to have a pro-business bias. Finally, it has become easier for groups to use the federal courts to put pressure on the regulatory agencies (*American Government*, 14th ed., pages **458–461**).

2. (a) The National Labor Relations Board adjudicates disputes between management and labor unions. The president appoints its members.

    (b) One of the ways management and labor compete is by trying to get their representatives on the NLRB board. Management and labor interpret NRLB decisions differently, and when either side receives an unfavorable ruling, it may decide to take the issue to the courts, where the issue is fought out again.

    (c) The Occupational Safety and Health Administration sets standards for workplace safety. For example, there are limits to how much a worker may be exposed to chemicals. OSHA inspects thousands of workplaces.

    (d) Companies have criticized the agency for detailed regulations that increase the costs of doing business and result in unnecessary red tape. One struggle between management and labor concerned who would supervise OSHA. Supervisory duties ended up falling to the Department of Labor, as workers had hoped. However, industry pressured the Reagan administration, and during his presidency, OHSA issued fewer citations (*American Government*, 14th ed., pages **456–457**).

Unit XVI: Economic Policy and the Budget

Correlates to Chapter 18 in *American Government, 14ᵗʰ Edition*

Although the federal government has run deficits for most years since 1969, Americans have never liked the idea of the government spending more money than it receives. Deficits occur when the government spends more than it takes in during a given year. The national debt is the accumulation of deficits over the years. The public is split over two broad philosophies of economic management: manipulating supply or controlling demand. Policy makers face two big issues: the tax burden, which includes deficits and debt, and economic health.

Key Terms

budget
budget resolution
deficit
discretionary spending
economic planning
entitlements
fiscal policy
fiscal year
globalization
gross domestic product
Keynesianism
monetarism
monetary policy
national debt
sequester
supply-side theory

Key Concepts

- Deficit is the shortfall in the budget when revenue is lower than spending. National Debt is the total amount of money the United States owes. Gross domestic product is the total of all goods and services produced in an economy.

- Taxing and spending policies are difficult to enact because most people want both lower taxes on themselves and more spending on programs that benefit them.

- The federal government spends about 80 percent of its money on Social Security, Medicare and Medicaid, national defense and nondefense programs

- The ability of the federal government to manage the economy is divided among many political actors including the President, the Congress, and the Federal Reserve.

- Deficits are the result of the inability of politicians to agree whether to cut spending (on which programs) and or to raise taxes (on whom).

For a full discussion of economic policy and the budget, see *American Government*, 14ᵗʰ ed., Chapter 18.

AP Tip

Keynesianism, supply-side economics, and monetarism are ways of managing the economy and may appear on the AP exam.

Multiple Choice Questions

1. What is the relationship between voting behavior and economic conditions?

    (A) People who are unemployed are less likely to vote for an incumbent, but voting behavior and economic conditions are not correlated for those who have jobs.

    (B) There is a strong correlation between economic conditions and voting behavior, with people less likely to vote for incumbents in poor economic times.

    (C) Most voters do not believe that the president has much impact on economic conditions, so there is little correlation between voting behavior and the economy.

    (D) Most voters blame Congress when the economy is poor, so incumbent congressmen are more likely than an incumbent president to lose their jobs.

    (E) In poor economic times, incumbents are more likely to be re-elected because the public is hesitant to change leadership in hard times.

FIGURE 18.1 Federal Budget Deficit (or Surplus), FY1960–2013 in Billions of Constant FY 2005 Dollars (President's Proposals)

Source: Office of Management and Budget, *Historical Tables*.

2. When does a surplus occur?

 (A) when revenues in a given year exceed expenditures

 (B) when expenditures in a given year exceed revenues

 (C) when income tax revenues exceed the revenues from excise taxes

 (D) when the government has excess funds because the national debt has been eliminated

 (E) when payments have reduced the national debt to a level at which the government can give money to the states in the form of revenue sharing

3. The figure above supports which of the following conclusions?

 (A) There were budget deficits every year from 1961 until 2013.

 (B) The budget deficit grew at a steady rate from 1975 until 1996.

 (C) President Clinton's economic policies resulted in budget surpluses in 1997 and 1998.

 (D) There were budget surpluses for four years in the late 1990s and early 2000s.

 (E) The deficit doubled under George W. Bush's presidency from 2004 to 2005.

4. Which of the following statements best reflects the traditional budget ideology of Democrats and Republicans?

 (A) Democrats are more worried about inflation, and Republicans are more worried about unemployment.

 (B) Democrats are more worried about interest rates, and Republicans are more concerned with the money supply.

 (C) Democrats are more worried about unemployment, and Republicans are more worried about inflation.

 (D) Both Democrats and Republicans are more worried about inflation than unemployment.

 (E) It is difficult to determine a particular budget ideology for the political parties because these beliefs change with changing economic conditions.

5. An economist believes that inflation is caused when there is too much money chasing too few goods. This theory can best be described as

 (A) Keynesianism

 (B) supply-side economics

 (C) Reaganomics

 (D) monetarism

 (E) fiscal conservatism

FIGURE 18.2   Federal Revenues in 2012

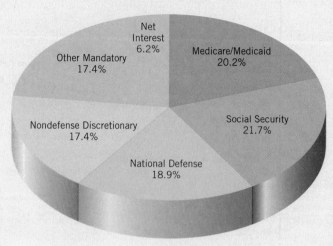

Source: Adapted from Office of Management and Budget, *Historical Tables.*

6. The figure above supports which of the following statements?

   (A) corporate tax rates are higher than individual tax rates

   (B) individual and Social Security taxes made up more than 80 percent of federal revenue in 2012

   (C) Social Security taxes make up the largest percentage of federal revenue

   (D) raising the corporate tax rate would reduce the deficit

   (E) excise taxes are a significant form of federal revenue

7. All of the following are responsibilities of the Federal Reserve Board EXCEPT

   (A) buying and selling federal government securities

   (B) regulating the amount of money a member bank must keep on hand as reserve

   (C) reviewing the federal budget and making recommendations to prevent deficits

   (D) changing the interest rates charged to banks that borrow from the Fed

   (E) setting monetary policy and making predictions about the economy

8. Which of the following best describes the federal budget?

   (A) It is a document that announces how much the government expects to collect in taxes and how expenditures will be allocated on various programs.

   (B) It is a document that just predicts a bottom line, including the dollar amount of a projected surplus or deficit.

   (C) It is a document that describes the federal debt and proposes a payment plan.

   (D) It is a document that changes over the course of a year, as revenue and expenditures change with the times.

   (E) It is a general policy statement outlining the economic goals of the federal government for the upcoming year.

9. Which of the following statements best describes the tax system in the United States?

   (A) It changes very little from year to year.

   (B) It is complicated because it includes differing tax rates and a complex system of exemptions and deductions.

   (C) It is based on a flat tax, where every citizen pays the same rate on income.

   (D) It penalizes the poor, who have few deductions.

   (E) It penalizes the wealthy, who have fewer deductions than the poor.

10. All of the following federal programs are aimed at stimulating the economy EXCEPT

    (A) buying shares in troubled banks and insurance companies

    (B) making loans to American car manufacturers

    (C) the Federal Reserve Board decreasing the amount of money in circulation

(D) grants to the states for highway and school construction

(E) tax cuts for people earning less than $75,000

11. Which economic theory holds that the key to stimulating the economy is pumping more money into it
    (A) Monetarism
    (B) Keynesianism
    (C) Supply-side economics
    (D) Mercantilism
    (E) Communism

12. Which of the following is responsible for developing estimates of budget needs of for federal agencies?
    (A) Budget Committees
    (B) Appropriations Committees
    (C) Congressional Budget Office
    (D) Treasury Department
    (E) Office of Management and Budget

13. Which of the following political actors is primarily responsible for monetary policy?
    (A) The Treasury Department
    (B) The President
    (C) The Congress
    (D) The Office of Management and Budget
    (E) The Federal Reserve

14. Taxing and spending policy is the definition of which of the following terms?
    (A) monetary policy
    (B) budget policy
    (C) economic policy
    (D) fiscal policy
    (E) financial policy

15. Which of the following is NOT a tool with which the Federal Reserve makes policy
    (A) Increasing the interest rate
    (B) Increased spending
    (C) buying government securities
    (D) selling government securities
    (E) decreasing the reserve rate

Free Response Questions

1. Despite its use of monetary and fiscal policy, it is often difficult for the government to control the economy.

(a) Identify and explain one reason why it is difficult for the government to control the economy.

(b) Identify and explain another reason why it is difficult for the government to control the economy.

2. Many economists agree that increasing the amount of money in circulation can stimulate the economy. This can be done through both fiscal and monetary policy:

(a) Identify who is responsible for setting fiscal policy.

(b) Identify and explain one way to increase the amount of money in circulation.

(c) Identify who is responsible for setting monetary policy.

(d) Identify and explain one way to increase the amount of money in circulation.

Answers
Multiple Choice Answers

1. (B) Incumbents are less likely to be re-elected in hard times (*American Government*, 14ᵗʰ ed., page **473**).
2. (A) A surplus occurs when revenues exceed expenditures in a given year (*American Government*, 14ᵗʰ ed., page **471**).
3. (D) In the late 1990s and early 2000s, there were budget surpluses for four years. Although these may be partly a result of President Clinton's policies, other factors also played a part (*American Government*, 14ᵗʰ ed., pages **471–472**).
4. (C) Republicans concentrate more on keeping inflation low. Democrats concentrate on lowering unemployment (*American Government*, 14ᵗʰ ed., page **473**).
5. (D) Monetarists believe that the government should have a steady and predictable increase in the money supply that is equal to the rate of economic growth (*American Government*, 14ᵗʰ ed., page **475**).
6. (B) Individual and Social Security taxes accounted for more than 81 percent of federal revenue in 2012 (*American Government*, 14ᵗʰ ed., page **482**).
7. (C) The Federal Reserve Board makes economic forecasts and sets monetary policy. This includes establishing the amount of money a bank must keep on reserve and setting the interest rates charged to banks that borrow from the Fed (*American Government*, 14ᵗʰ ed., pages **477–478**).
8. (A) The budget is a document announcing proposed revenue collections and explaining how the money will be spent (*American Government*, 14ᵗʰ ed., pages **480–481**).

9. (B) The tax system is complicated by differing rates depending on income. Furthermore, there are hundreds of special exemptions and deductions (*American Government*, 14th ed., pages **482–483**).

10. (C) In order to stimulate the economy, the Federal Reserve Board increased the amount of money in circulation (*American Government*, 14th ed., page **474**).

11. (B) Keynesianism suggests that to stimulate the economy it is necessary to "prime the pump" by injecting money into the economy (*American Government*, 14th ed., page **485**).

12. (E) OMB develops budget estimates for the various federal agencies that reflect the president's priorities (*American Government*, 14th ed., page **475**).

13. (E) The Federal Reserve or "Fed" is responsible for monetary policy. It is an independent regulatory agency (*American Government*, 14th ed., pages **477–478**).

14. (D) Fiscal policy is the taxing and spending policy of the United States. It is set by the interplay between the president and Congress (*American Government*, 14th ed., pages **478–479**).

15. (B) The Federal Reserve does not appropriate money. That is the function of Congress (*American Government*, 14th ed., pages **478–479**).

Free Response Answers

1. (a) One reason it is difficult for the government to control economic outcomes is foreign competition. In many countries labor costs are less than they are in the United States. As a consequence, goods made in those countries are less expensive to produce than goods made here. One result of this is that American companies may move their plants overseas, reducing the number of industrial jobs available in the United States and raising unemployment levels. The government can try to control this through our trade policies, but industries that sell goods abroad want free trade. Thus it is difficult for the government to control international trade (*American Government*, 14th ed., page **479**).

   (b) Another reason it is difficult for the government to control the economy is that some decisions affect the economy in both positive and negative ways. For example, decisions

to reduce inflation can require the government to raise interest rates. It becomes more expensive for new businesses to get start-up loans. It is also more expensive for ongoing businesses to borrow the money they need to expand their productivity. The result might be a slower economy. (*Alternate answer*): Unexpected events, such as terrorist attacks, can make it difficult for the government to control the economy. After the attacks of September 11, 2001, the airline industry lost passengers and revenues because some people were afraid to fly. The wars in Afghanistan and Iraq that followed the attacks were expensive, and the government had not budgeted for them. The result was a deficit that the government had not anticipated just a year earlier (*American Government*, 14th ed., page **473**).

2. (a) Fiscal policy is set through the interaction between the president and Congress.

   (b) One of the following:

   Cutting taxes – By cutting taxes, taxpayers will have more money to spend. This has the effect of increasing the amount of money in circulation.

   Increasing spending – By increasing government spending more money will be injected into the economy by the additional goods and services that the government purchases.

   (c) The Federal Reserve is responsible for setting monetary policy.

   (d) One of the following:

   Lowering interest rates – Lowered interest rates will spur borrowing, thus increasing money in circulation.

   Lowering reserve requirements – Reducing the portion of deposits the bank are required to keep on hand allows the banks to lend money. This increases the amount of money in circulation.

   Buying government securities – The Federal Reserve can purchase securities issued by the government. These securities are effectively IOUs that the federal government has issued to people who have lent it money. By purchasing these securities from lenders the Federal Reserve is injecting money into the economy (*American Government*, 14th ed., pages **477–479**).

Unit XVII: Domestic Policy: Social Welfare and the Environment

Correlates to Chapters 17 in *American Government, 14th Edition*

The politics of social welfare and the environment are controversial, largely because they often create winners and losers.

Key Terms

assistance program
charitable choice
client politics
entrepreneurial politics
environmental impact statement
insurance program
interest group politics
majoritarian politics
means test

Key Concepts

- Four types of politics matter, each based on how most people perceive the distribution of monetary and other costs and benefits associated with the policy or program: majoritarian (everybody benefits, everybody pays), interest group (one small group pays, another small group benefits), client (almost everybody pays, one small group benefits), and entrepreneurial (almost everybody benefits, one small group pays).

- America's social welfare policies and programs differ from those of many other modern democracies in four main ways. First, Americans have taken a more restrictive view of who is entitled to or "deserves" to benefit from government assistance. Second, America was slower to embrace the need for "the welfare state," and, in turn, slower to adopt and enact relevant policies and programs. Third, state governments have played a large role in administering or co-funding many "national" social welfare measures (like, for example, Medicaid). Fourth, nongovernmental organizations, both for-profit firms and nonprofit groups (secular as well as religious) have played a large role in administering Washington's social welfare initiatives.

- Some social welfare policies and programs are politically protected while others are politically imperiled. This relates mainly to who benefits directly, or who is perceived to benefit directly, from given social welfare policies and programs. For example, Social Security and Medicare benefit almost all people who have reached a certain age, while the Food Stamps program, like the old AFDC program's successor, TANF, benefits only people with low incomes. The first type of social welfare program has no means test (they are available to everyone without regard to income), while the second type is means-tested (only people who fall below a certain income level are eligible). The first type represents majoritarian politics and is almost always politically protected; the second type represents client politics and is often politically imperiled. Medicaid, the federal–state health program, is means-tested, but it has as beneficiaries not only low-income persons but also the aged and the disabled. It mixes majoritarian and client politics, making it less politically sacrosanct than Social Security or Medicare, but more so than the Food Stamps program, TANF, and other means-tested programs.

- There is no political consensus about how to address the solvency challenges facing major social welfare programs, not unless one counts as the "political consensus" on these issues the persistent public majority opposed to making either major or minor cuts to each program. Even the ostensibly far-reaching, bipartisan plans offered in recent sessions of Congress have been predicated on preserving (or expanding) all extant benefits to all present-day and near-term beneficiaries without raising taxes and without reducing services. For good or for ill, their majoritarian politics forbid any truly far-reaching reforms.

- Government regulations on certain big businesses have been imposed over the objections of those industries because of entrepreneurial politics. Big oil companies, auto manufacturing companies, drug companies, pesticides producers, and other corporations that once had, or were perceived to have, cozy relationships with government were challenged by consumer advocates or environmental activists. A half-century or so ago, policy entrepreneurs outside government like Ralph Nader and Rachel Carson dramatized how existing public policies and programs helped the companies to profit but hurt most people in the pocketbook, jeopardized public health and safety, or both. By the 1970s and 1980s, policy entrepreneurs inside government, like those at the Environmental Protection Agency (founded in 1970), began regulating the businesses even more closely than they had in the past. Although business regulation policy still generates much controversy and many debates over its cost-effectiveness, most people now favor diverse regulations on big oil companies and other large-scale businesses.

- Environmental policies are designed and enforced differently in America than in other industrialized nations because the adversarial nature of American politics, as well as the system of federalism, complicates policy making in America, as illustrated by efforts to pass and enforce legislation on automobile emissions, clean air and water, and other environmental issues.

- While entrepreneurial politics figure prominently in environmental policy dynamics, including on an issue like protecting endangered species, there are environmental issues in each "box," like pollution from automobiles (majoritarian), acid rain (interest group), and agricultural pesticides (client politics). The same can be said for social welfare, business regulation, and other domestic policies and programs.

For a full discussion of domestic policy as it pertains to social welfare and the environment, see *American Government,* 14th ed., Chapter 17.

AP Tip

Social Security and Medicare are expensive and controversial policies. Raising the age of eligibility or reducing benefits are two possible ways to increase funds for these programs, but these changes may be difficult to enact. The problems of funding Medicare and Social Security cut across several aspects of the policy-making process and may appear on the AP exam.

Multiple Choice Questions

1. All of the following statements about America's social welfare policy-making are true EXCEPT

    (A) Americans would prefer that the needy be given services rather than money

    (B) Americans believe in help for the "deserving poor"

    (C) the United States did not provide social welfare benefits until relatively late, in comparison with much of Europe

    (D) Americans support redistribution of wealth to provide everyone with a fair share

    (E) Americans are uncomfortable giving money to people who are already working or could work if they wanted to

2. Which of the following are major social welfare programs?

    I. Medicare and Medicaid

    II. Social Security

    III. tuition subsidies

    IV. unemployment insurance

    (A) I and II

    (B) I, II, and III

    (C) II and III

    (D) III and IV

    (E) I, II, and IV

3. Why did Social Security meet popular demands and fit within the framework of American beliefs about social welfare?

    (A) because it was viewed as an insurance program that would be available to all Americans who contributed, whether rich or poor

    (B) because it was an insurance program that would be available to all Americans on a voluntary basis

    (C) because it would be available to middle-class and poor Americans as a kind of retirement savings account

    (D) because it was a means-tested program to help those who could not afford retirement

    (E) because it was a means of redistributing wealth, and that philosophy had great popular appeal during the Great Depression

4. All of the following solutions have been proposed to make sure there is enough Social Security when future generations retire EXCEPT

    (A) raise the retirement age

    (B) freeze the level of retirement benefits

    (C) end the program entirely by the year 2040

    (D) privatize Social Security so that people could invest those funds in the stock market

    (E) permit citizens to invest some of their Social Security taxes in carefully chosen mutual funds

5. In 1996 Aid to Families with Dependent Children (AFDC) was abolished. Why did support for AFDC weaken?

   (A) Many recipients were unwed mothers who had been on the program for more than eight years.

   (B) Many recipients were children in families in which both parents were working.

   (C) Many recipients were widows who did not obtain employment upon the death of their husbands.

   (D) Many recipients were disabled and were unable to work full-time.

   (E) Support for the program did not weaken, but the government was unable to continue the program in the face of a weak economy.

6. What is the impact of filing an environmental impact statement (EIS)?

   (A) None. It is merely a statement and does not require any specific action.

   (B) The statement notifies federal authorities of the potential environmental damage caused by a project, and the government may file an injunction to block the project.

   (C) Opponents have used the EIS as a way of blocking, changing, or delaying projects.

   (D) The EIS notifies the public of the impact of a project and outlines specific steps the builder will take to prevent environmental damage.

   (E) The EIS must show that environmental damage will be minimal, or the federal government will not approve the project.

7. Much of the antitrust legislation passed in this country, including the Sherman Act (1890) and parts of the Federal Trade Commission Act (1914) and the Clayton Act (1914), has been the result of

   (A) majoritarian politics

   (B) interest group politics

   (C) client politics

   (D) entrepreneurial politics

   (E) environmental policy

8. When is a pesticide most likely to be taken off the market?

   (A) when independent scientists determine that it harms the environment

   (B) when the National Institute of Health finds that it might cause cancer

   (C) when there has been an incident that caused heavy media coverage

   (D) when a manufacturer voluntarily decides to remove it because of the research of the company's scientists

   (E) when farmers protest the use of the pesticide

9. Which of the following is an example of how America's social welfare policies and programs differ from those of many other modern democracies?

   (A) Nongovernmental organizations, both for-profit firms and nonprofit groups (secular as well as religious) have played a large role in administering Washington's social welfare initiatives.

   (B) Americans have taken a more restrictive view of who is entitled to or "deserves" to benefit from government assistance.

   (C) America was slower to embrace the need for "the welfare state," and, in turn, slower to adopt enact relevant policies and programs.

   (D) State governments have played a large role in administering or co-funding many "national" social welfare measures (like, for example, Medicaid).

   (E) All of the above.

10. What type of politics is based on the idea that a small group pays and another small group benefits?

    (A) majoritarian

    (B) interest group

    (C) client

    (D) entrepreneurial

    (E) environmental

11. Which of the following increased the growth of the welfare state in America?

    I.   the New Deal

    II. the Reagan era

    III. the War on Poverty

    IV. the Medicare drug plan

    (A) I and III

    (B) II and IV

    (C) I, II, and III

    (D) I, III, and IV

    (E) I, II, III, and IV

12. What is the major difference between Medicare and Medicaid?

   (A) Medicare is needs-based, and Medicaid is available to all Americans over age 65.

   (B) Medicaid acts as a supplement to private insurance.

   (C) Medicare is available only to retired Americans.

   (D) Medicaid provides coverage to all children in the United States, while Medicare provides coverage for the elderly.

   (E) Medicare is available to all Americans over age sixty-five while Medicaid is needs-based.

13. Which of the following is NOT a provision to the Patient Protection and Affordable Care Act of 2010?

   (A) extends health care insurance to some 32 million uninsured Americans

   (B) imposes a "tax" penalty on people who do not buy health insurance

   (C) the elimination of Medicaid

   (D) levies fees and taxes on medical devices, drugs, high-cost health insurance plans, health insurers

   (E) provides federal subsidies to people who have trouble paying

14. Charitable Choice programs illustrate what unique feature of American welfare policy?

   (A) American welfare policies are often administered by state-supported churches.

   (B) American welfare policies are administered by the states, rather than the federal government.

   (C) Americans can choose whether to spend their tax dollars on religious organizations.

   (D) Much of American welfare policy is administered through grants and contracts with nongovernmental agencies.

   (E) Americans believe that welfare recipients should be carefully screened before receiving aid.

15. Which of the following environmental issue is CORRECTLY paired with a type of politics?

   (A) Agricultural Pesticides: Entrepreneurial Politics

   (B) Acid Rain: Entrepreneurial Politics

   (C) Endangered Species: Majoritarian Politics

   (D) Acid Rain: Majoritarian Politics

   (E) Agricultural Pesticides: Client Politics

Free Response Questions

1. Social Security and Medicare are badly in need of reform if they are to continue for future generations.

   (a) For Social Security, identify the problem it is facing and explain one possible solution to that problem.

   (b) For Medicare, identify the problem it is facing and explain one possible solution to that problem.

2. The policy-making process often balances competing interests. This is especially true of environmental policies, which include the following problems:

   • endangered species
   • acid rain
   • automobile emissions

   (a) Pick one of the problems listed above. Identify two competing interests related to the problem and explain how the policy-making process has addressed the problem.

   (b) Pick another of the problems listed above. Identify two competing interests related to the problem and explain how the policy-making process has addressed the problem.

Answers
Multiple Choice Answers

1. (D) American social welfare policies were created long after those in most European countries. Americans believe that welfare should be given to the deserving poor and favor giving services rather than money (*American Government*, 14th ed., pages **450–452**).

2. (E) Major social welfare programs include Medicare, Medicaid, Social Security, and unemployment insurance. Although federal student loan money is available and veterans receive tuition assistance, the vast majority of college tuition is not subsidized (*American Government*, 14th ed., pages **450–452**).

3. (A) Social Security is available to all Americans, rich or poor, who contribute. It was viewed as an insurance program (although it has become more of an inter-generational contract) (*American Government*, 14th ed., pages **442–443**).

4. (C) There are several proposals to save Social Security, including raising the retirement age, freezing benefits, and privatizing all or part of the system (*American Government*, 14ᵗʰ ed., pages **448–450**).

5. (A) Support for AFDC weakened because the public became less sympathetic to the recipients. Many were unwed mothers who had been receiving assistance for more than eight years (*American Government*, 14ᵗʰ ed., page **446**).

6. (C) The EIS is a statement of the probable impact of a project on the environment. Environmental interest groups can then mobilize to block, change, or delay the project (*American Government*, 14ᵗʰ ed., page **465**).

7. (A) Antitrust legislation is a result of majoritarian politics. From time to time, laws are passed that reflect the views of a majority of voters that is neither imposing its will on a hostile business community nor acceding to the desires of a privileged industry (*American Government*, 14ᵗʰ ed., pages **455–456**).

8. (C) A pesticide is most likely to be taken off the market when there is well-publicized environmental harm, such as the impact of DDT on birds (*American Government*, 14ᵗʰ ed., page **456**).

9. (E) They differ in four main ways. First, Americans have taken a more restrictive view of who is entitled to or "deserves" to benefit from government assistance. Second, America was slower to embrace the need for "the welfare state," and, in turn, slower to adopt enact relevant policies and programs. Third, state governments have played a large role in administering or co-funding many "national" social welfare measures (like, for example, Medicaid). Fourth, nongovernmental organizations, both for-profit firms and nonprofit groups (secular as well as religious) have played a large role in administering Washington's social welfare initiatives (*American Government*, 14ᵗʰ ed., pages **450–452**).

10. (B) With interest group politics, one small group pays, another small group benefits (*American Government*, 14ᵗʰ ed., page **441**).

11. (D) The New Deal, the War on Poverty, and Medicare prescription drug benefits expanded the welfare state. During the Reagan administration, the growth of the welfare state slowed (*American Government*, 14ᵗʰ ed., pages **442–444**).

12. (E) All Americans over the age of 65 qualify for Medicare. Medicaid is needs-based (*American Government*, 14ᵗʰ ed., page **444**).

13. (C) The Patient Protection and Affordable Care Act of 2010 added more people to Medicaid (*American Government*, 14ᵗʰ ed., page **445**).

14. (D) Charitable choice programs administered by faith-based organizations are an example of federal contracts and grants given to nongovernmental organizations. This is a unique feature of the American welfare system (*American Government*, 14ᵗʰ ed., page **452**).

15. (E) Some client groups have so far escaped the Agricultural Pesticide momentum. One such group is organized farmers, who have more or less successfully resisted efforts to restrict, sharply, the use of pesticides or to control the runoff of pesticides from farmlands. (*American Government*, 14ᵗʰ ed., page **467**).

Free Response Answers

1. (a) Social Security is facing a crisis. Rather than being an individual retirement fund, as was originally envisioned, it is now an intergenerational contract. The problem is that soon there will not be enough people working to support the people who have retired. This is because new groups, such as the disabled, have been added to the program. In addition, the retirement of the baby boomers will add millions of new recipients. Furthermore, the amounts contributed to the system are not enough to make ends meet, due, in part, to inflation. One proposal to alleviate this problem is to allow people to invest their Social Security funds in the stock market. The market usually performs better than mutual funds or savings accounts in the long run. However, there is the risk that people will lose their retirement funds in unsafe investments.

   (b) Medicare pays for the health care costs of those who qualify for Social Security benefits. With an aging population and expensive life-saving technologies, the costs of medical care have skyrocketed. Because people can go to the doctor whenever they want, sometimes they visit the doctor when it is not necessary. Although the vast majority of doctors are honest, some have overcharged Medicare patients because the government is picking up the tab. One possible solution would be to nationalize health care, although Clinton's plan to provide national health care coverage failed in Congress. Another potential solution would be for the government to provide Medicare money that could be used to purchase private health insurance (*American Government*, 14ᵗʰ ed., pages **447–450**).

2. (a) The Endangered Species Act forbids any action that would harm a plant or animal on the endangered list. This list consists of species whose population has diminished so much that they need special protection.

The two competing interests involved in making this policy are developers and environmentalists. The Endangered Species Act has prevented the building of dams, industrial buildings, and residential housing, and altered farming. Developers complain that their property interests are being sacrificed. Sometimes the species being protected—for example, the snail darter—are obscure. The public as a whole, however, supports protecting endangered species.

(b) Acid rain is created when the runoff from factories is turned into precipitation that contains sulfur and other acidic compounds. Steel mills and electric power plants, large sources of acid rain, have an interest in keeping their plants running. Acid rain has spoiled lakes and killed trees in New England and Canada. The residents of these areas, along with the fishing and logging industries, are affected. The first solution involved the addition of scrubbers to clean the air, but they didn't work very well. The 1990 Clean Air Act contained provisions that gave something to each of the interest groups. Power plants are required to reduce sulfur emissions. Coal miners who were laid off as a result of their employers' compliance with the new limits were provided with some compensation. (*Alternate answer*): The Clean Air Act regulates automobile emissions. People who drive cars, as well as automobile manufacturers, have an interest in both car prices and gas prices. Everyone has an interest in breathing clean air. Automobile engines were designed to pollute less and be more fuel efficient, but they were more expensive. States had to design programs, including rapid transit, to reduce air pollution. The deadlines of the Clean Air Act were hard to meet for both states and automobile manufacturers, and they were extended several times. States like California and Colorado continue to work on plans to reduce smog (*American Government*, 14th ed., pages **462–465**).

Unit XVIII: Foreign and Military Policy

Correlates to Chapter 19 in *American Government, 14ᵗʰ Edition*

The terrorist attacks of September 11, 2001, created a new focus and a new set of problems for American foreign policymakers. Yet dealing with foreign terrorists still involves many traditional questions: How great are the powers of the president? What role should Congress play? How important is public opinion?

Key Terms

bipolar world
containment
cost overruns
disengagement
gold plating
human rights
isolationism
military-industrial complex
polarization
unipolar world
worldviews

Key Concepts

- American foreign policy is impacted by both public opinion and the views of the elite.

- While only Congress has the power to "declare war," the president has the ability to send troops into combat without a declaration of war. Congress has attempted to limit this ability with the passage of the War Powers Act in 1973.

- There is conflict in Congress as to the degree to which the United States' concern for human rights should impact military policy.

For a full discussion of foreign and military policy, see *American Government,* 14ᵗʰ ed., Chapter 19.

AP Tip

The War Powers Act represents the ongoing struggle between the president and Congress for control of foreign policy and may appear on the AP exam.

Multiple Choice Questions

1. All of the following are struggles over foreign policy between the president and Congress EXCEPT
    (A) the president is commander-in-chief, but Congress must authorize funding for the armed forces
    (B) the president appoints ambassadors, but the Senate must confirm them
    (C) the president negotiates treaties, but the Senate must ratify them with a two-thirds vote
    (D) the president declares war, but Congress must authorize troop deployments
    (E) the president appoints ambassadors, but the Senate must confirm them

2. Which of the following statements best describes the "imperial presidency"?
    (A) The president can overstep his constitutional powers by making unilateral foreign policy decisions that create an "empire" in foreign affairs.
    (B) Presidents have used their powers in foreign policy to create empires overseas.
    (C) Presidents must rely on Congress for funding and troops, so they cannot act unilaterally.
    (D) Presidents have only those powers specifically given to them in the Constitution, yet they are still able to influence foreign policy in significant ways.
    (E) Presidents are given more power over domestic affairs, allowing them to create an empire at home.

3. What position has the Supreme Court generally taken regarding foreign affairs?
    (A) The Court has intervened to prevent the president from committing troops without congressional approval.

FIGURE 19.1 Public's View of America as World Leader

Public's View of America's Role as World Leader

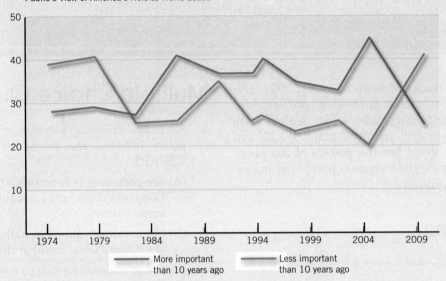

Source: Pew Research Center for the People & the Press, "U.S. Seen As Less Important, China as More Powerful: Isolationist Sentiment Surges to Four-Decade High," 3 December 2009.

(B) The Court has been reluctant to intervene in disputes over the conduct of foreign affairs.

(C) The Court has made decisions to protect civil rights, especially during wartime.

(D) The Court has supported the decisions of Congress but has overturned executive orders.

(E) The Court has rarely deferred to presidential power for fear of upsetting the balance of powers.

4. What has been the presidential response to the War Powers Act?

(A) The War Powers Act has had little impact on presidents' decisions regarding military actions.

(B) Because of the War Powers Act, Congress has consistently refused to appropriate funds for troops once they have been deployed.

(C) The War Powers Act has been used successfully by Congress to prevent troop commitments.

(D) The War Powers Act has encouraged every president since Nixon to consult with Congress before taking military action.

(E) The War Powers Act was challenged in court by President Nixon and found to be unconstitutional.

5. What is the role of Congress with regard to intelligence gathering?

(A) Committees have an oversight function and can block proposed actions by the intelligence community.

(B) Committees are informed of proposed covert activities, but they do not have the authority to prevent action by the intelligence services.

(C) Committees are informed of covert activities after they take place.

(D) The Congress as a whole is informed of proposed covert activities during a special session.

(E) Congress has no role regarding the gathering of intelligence; this is an executive function.

6. The figure above supports which of the following conclusions?

(A) 41 percent of the public believes that today the United States plays less of a role as a world leader in comparison to 10 years ago.

(B) The percentage of people who believe the United States is playing more of a role as world leader is steadily climbing.

(C) 25 percent of the public believes the United States plays a more important role in world affairs today than it did 10 years ago.

(D) In 2004, the public believed the United States hit an all-time low as an influential world leader.

(E) Both A and C.

7. The military paid $435 for hammers that could have been purchased at any local hardware store. This is blamed on
   (A) the military-industrial complex
   (B) inaccuracies in estimating budgetary expenditures
   (C) the expenses associated with conflicting regulations
   (D) the failure of the military to communicate effectively with defense contractors
   (E) the ability of defense contractors to overcharge the military without any oversight

8. Why would a member of Congress, even one who strongly believes that military spending should be reduced, fight to keep a military base open?
   (A) Most Americans strongly oppose closing military bases.
   (B) Bases are needed, even when defense spending is cut, to keep the country prepared for war.
   (C) Bases provide important training for both the military and civilian work forces.
   (D) Members fight to keep bases open in their districts because a base benefits their communities and helps with re-election.
   (E) A member of Congress who strongly believes that military spending should be reduced would not fight to keep bases open.

9. Which committee is made up of the uniformed heads of each branch of the military service and plays a key role in defense planning?
   (A) the Defense Department
   (B) the Joint Chiefs of Staff
   (C) the State Department
   (D) the Pentagon
   (E) the National Security Council

10. Which of the following best illustrates the concept of polarization?
    (A) World War I
    (B) World War II
    (C) the war in Iraq
    (D) the containment policy
    (E) the Persian Gulf War

11. Which of the following may be potentially used by the president to circumvent Senate ratification of a treaty?
    (A) Executive Privilege
    (B) Presidential Decree
    (C) Executive Agreement
    (D) Commander-in-Chief Clause
    (E) Executive Order

12. All of the following are provisions of the War Powers Act of 1973 EXCEPT
    (A) Notification within 48 hours
    (B) 60 day operational time limit
    (C) Congressional review of presidential action
    (D) Review by the Supreme Court
    (E) 30 day withdrawal time period

13. Which of the following describes the process by which a treaty is proposed and approved?
    (A) Negotiation by the Senate, approval by the president
    (B) Negotiation by the Senate Foreign Relations committee, approval by the Congress
    (C) Negotiation by the Speaker of the House, approval by the Senate
    (D) Negotiation by the president, approval by both houses of Congress
    (E) Negotiation by the president, approval by the Senate

14. Upon a sudden attack on the United States, the president would most likely look to whom for advice and counsel?
    (A) Cabinet
    (B) National Security Council
    (C) House and Senate Armed Services Committees
    (D) Senate Foreign Relations Committee
    (E) Senate President and House Speaker

15. If the War Powers Act (1973) is found to be unconstitutional, what could be done to stop an undeclared war waged by the president?
    (A) Judicial review
    (B) Cabinet veto
    (C) Elimination of funding
    (D) Congressional declaration of peace
    (E) Withdrawal of Senatorial "Advice and Consent"

FIGURE 19.2   **Trends in Military Spending (outlays in constant dollars)**

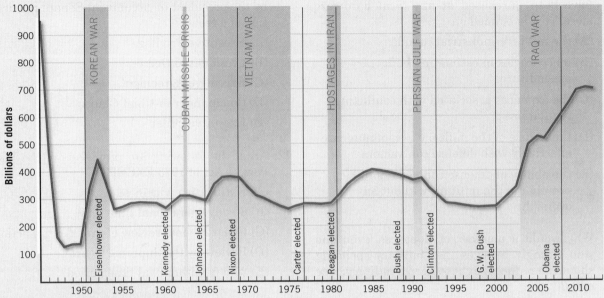

Source: Office of the Under Secretary of Defense (Comptroller), National Defense Budget Annual Estimates and Reports."

Free Response Questions

1. Using the chart above, complete the following tasks:
    (a) identify two trends in military spending.
    (b) identify one event that increased military spending and explain why.
    (c) identify one event that decreased military spending and explain why.

2. Under the Constitution, control over military and foreign policy is shared between the president and the Congress. This creates a tension between the two institutions.
    (a) Explain how each of the following can be used by Congress to check the power of the president over military and foreign policy.
    - appropriations
    - treaties
    - confirmation
    (b) Explain how each of the following can be used by the president to circumvent checks imposed by Congress.
    - commander-in-chief
    - executive agreements

Answers

Multiple Choice Answers

1. (D) Congress has the power to declare war, although the War Powers Act allows the president to commit troops for 60 days (*American Government*, 14th ed., pages **493–494**).

2. (A) Arthur Schlesinger, Jr. used the term "imperial presidency" to criticize presidents who, in his opinion, overstepped their constitutional authority by acting unilaterally in foreign affairs (*American Government*, 14th ed., page **492**).

3. (B) The Supreme Court is reluctant to make decisions involving foreign affairs (*American Government*, 14th ed., page **492**).

4. (A) Many presidents believe that the War Powers Act is an unconstitutional infringement on their powers as commander in chief. As a result, it has had little impact (*American Government*, 14th ed., page **494**).

5. (B) Both the House and Senate have intelligence committees, which are informed of proposed covert actions, but they do not have the authority to block those actions (*American Government*, 14th ed., page **494**).

6. (E) Both statistics are right: 41 percent of the public believe that the United States plays less of a role in 2009 as a world leader while 25 percent believe the United States plays a more important role (*American Government*, 14th ed., page **115**).

7. (A) The military-industrial complex is the cozy relationship that has developed between defense contractors and the military. Costs are higher because military equipment must meet tougher standards, because it operates under extreme conditions. Another reason for higher costs is strict standards, and manufacturers often have a say in drafting those standards. This benefits big corporations and the members of Congress whose districts benefit from defense projects (*American Government*, 14th ed., pages **503–504**).

8. (D) Even those members of Congress who fought to reduce military spending during the

1990s wanted to keep bases in their districts open. This is because bases are important to an area's economy, and keeping bases open helps the member at election time (*American Government*, 14th ed., pages **503–504**).

9. (B) The Joint Chiefs of Staff includes the heads of each branch of the military, plus a chairman and a vice chairman, who are also military officers. The chairman of the Joint Chiefs of Staff is the president's principal military advisor (*American Government*, 14th ed., pages **509–510**).

10. (C) Polarization means a deep and wide conflict, usually along party lines. While Republican voters strongly supported the invasion of Iraq, Democratic voters opposed it (*American Government*, 14th ed., page **502**).

11. (C) Executive Agreements are agreements between the leaders of different countries. They function somewhat like treaties but do not require ratification (*American Government*, 14th ed., page **490**).

12. (D) The Supreme Court does not play a role under the War Powers Act of 1973 (*American Government*, 14th ed., pages **493–494**).

13. (E) The Constitution gives the president the power to make treaties "by and with the advice and consent of the Senate." Effectively this means that treaties are negotiated by the president and approved by the Senate with a two-thirds vote (*American Government*, 14th ed., page **490**).

14. (B) The NSC can be used to coordinate the activities of the various agencies and military branches involved in military and foreign policy. The president relies upon it during times of crises (*American Government*, 14th ed., page **495**).

15. (C) One the principal powers of Congress is the "power of the purse." This power to control money can be used by Congress to end a conflict (*American Government*, 14th ed., page **493**).

Free Response Answers

1. (a) One trend is that prior to the election of 2004, military spending remained stable at about $300 billion during election years. Another trend is that military spending increases during wartime.

(b) One event that increased military spending was the election of Ronald Reagan. President Reagan believed in increasing military spending to invest in new defensive technology. Congress approved his proposals, and as a result, military spending increased from $300 billion in 1980 to about $700 billion in 2012.

(c) One event that resulted in a decrease in military spending was the end of the Cold War. In 1991, the Soviet Union (USSR) broke up. Until that point the USSR was considered one of the major threats to the United States, and much of our military spending was geared toward dealing with that threat. After the end of the Cold War, there was a period of lessened tensions, which resulted in a "peace dividend." As a result military spending declined (*American Government*, 14th ed., pages **504–506**).

2. (a) Appropriations – Congress can use the power of the purse to cut off funding for any military action that it dislikes. This was the case in the Vietnam War.

Treaties –The Constitution gives the president the power to make treaties. However, for a treaty to be binding on the United States, the Senate must approve it with a two-thirds vote. Confirmation – the President has the power under the Constitution to appoint the civilian leadership of the Defense Department (Secretary of Defense, Assistant Secretary of the Navy, etc.) the Secretary of State and ambassadors, as well as the power to commission all officers of the military. These appointments and commissions are subject to review and confirmation by the Senate.

(b) Commander-in-Chief – The president is commander-in-chief of the military. Presidents have interpreted this to mean that they, on occasion, can deploy the military into combat without congressional authorization. Politically, it is almost impossible for Congress to prevent this. Executive Agreements - The President can avoid conflict with the Senate by use of an executive agreement. An executive agreement functions much like a treaty. However, it does not require Senate approval (*American Government*, 14th ed., pages **490, 493**).

Unit XIX: Civil Rights

Correlates to Chapter 6 in *American Government, 14ᵗʰ Edition*

Civil rights issues involve discrimination against a group. The government has the authority to treat different people differently—but only if the differences in treatment are reasonable in the view of the courts.

Key Terms

affirmative action
civil disobedience
civil rights
de facto segregation
de jure segregation
equality of opportunity
equality of results
police powers
reverse discrimination
separate-but-equal doctrine
strict scrutiny
suspect classifications

Key Concepts

- While sex and race have both been the basis discrimination, the courts treat them differently. Laws related to race are subjected to strict scrutiny, and laws related to sex subjected to intermediate scrutiny.

- The courts use three main tests relating to discriminatory treatment. Strict scrutiny is most stringent, with intermediate scrutiny next, and rational basis the least stringent.

- Sexual harassment can occur as a result of the demand for sexual favors or the existence of hostile work environment.

- Many groups have been subjected to discrimination. Congress has chosen to focus on some groups while ignoring others. This is due to the political nature of Congress.

- After the Supreme Court ordered the desegregation of schools, it was up the president and Congress to implement the decision.

- Men and women can be treated differently if the distinction is fair, reasonable, and not arbitrary.

- There has been growing acceptance of homosexuality by the public and the Supreme Court.

For a full discussion of the topic of civil rights, see *American Government,* 14th ed., Chapter 6.

AP Tip

Brown v. Board of Education is one of the most important decisions ever rendered by the Supreme Court and may appear on the AP exam.

Multiple Choice Questions

1. Which of the following cases most likely involves a violation of civil rights?
   (A) classifying people into brackets on the basis on income and taxing them at different rates
   (B) conducting a search without a warrant or probable cause
   (C) classifying people using any system that treats one group of people differently from another
   (D) classifying people and treating them differently on the basis of race or gender
   (E) giving adults more rights, such as voting and drinking alcohol, than the rights possessed by minors

2. All of the following made it difficult for African Americans to gain equality EXCEPT
   (A) blacks were in the minority population in the states with the most discrimination
   (B) lower-income whites were worried that gains by blacks would be at their expense
   (C) because blacks could not vote, they had little influence in policy making
   (D) racism by whites blocked blacks' efforts to gain equality
   (E) until the early 1960s, most citizens of the North did little to help blacks in the South gain equality

3. In the 1960s, Denver, Colorado, had several racially distinct neighborhoods. Denver public schools developed a neighborhood schools plan in which students would attend the school closest to home. On what grounds was this plan challenged?
   (A) that it was *de jure* segregation
   (B) that it was *de facto* segregation

(C) that the plan did not allow students the freedom to travel to a school of their choice

(D) that the plan would not allow black students to attend schools with whites

(E) there was no valid legal basis for challenging this plan

4. As a result of desegregation plans that required students to be bused in central-city schools, many whites moved to the suburbs. How did the courts respond to this "white flight"?

(A) The Supreme Court held that white flight was de facto segregation and ordered busing across district lines.

(B) The Supreme Court ordered central-city schools to develop magnet programs to prevent white flight.

(C) The Supreme Court ruled that intercity busing could be ordered only if both districts practiced school segregation.

(D) The Supreme Court refused to take the case on grounds of federalism because school district boundaries are set by the states.

(E) The Supreme Court refused to order cross-district busing because most of the public opposed it.

5. After many delays, all of the following events enabled the passage of the Civil Rights Act of 1964 EXCEPT

(A) public opinion was changing, and more whites supported civil rights

(B) the media, making the public aware of the discrimination faced by blacks, showed violence by white segregationists

(C) President Kennedy, who was a proponent of civil rights, was assassinated

(D) most southern whites favored desegregation once public schools became integrated

(E) the government was united, with Democrats controlling the presidency, House, and Senate

6. Why is the all-male draft constitutional even though it is gender discrimination?

(A) because it meets the standard of strict scrutiny—men are much more effective in combat than women

(B) because it meets mid-level scrutiny—on average, women have less upper body strength than men

(C) because there is a rational basis for the law—the nation has never needed so many troops that it required women in combat

(D) because discrimination against men is legal—they are not in a protected class

(E) the all-male draft has not been challenged in the Supreme Court because the Court avoids what it considers political questions

7. What is the overall impact of the Supreme Court's rulings on abortion?

(A) Abortion is a social, moral, and family issue and is left to the discretion of the states.

(B) Abortion is prohibited except in cases of rape or incest.

(C) Abortion may not be prohibited or regulated during the first two trimesters.

(D) Abortion may not be prohibited during the first two trimesters, but it can be regulated as long as there is no undue burden.

(E) There is a broad right to abortion throughout pregnancy.

8. Which of the following statements best describes the Supreme Court's position on affirmative action?

(A) Quotas can be used in college admissions to achieve a racially balanced student body.

(B) Laws should be color-blind and race neutral.

(C) Quotas can be used in construction contracts, but not in hiring or in college admissions.

(D) Affirmative action programs are not legal, because they are reverse discrimination.

(E) Quotas are viewed with strict scrutiny, but preferences are acceptable for the purpose of achieving diversity.

9. What was the Court's decision in *Roe v. Wade* (1971)?

(A) A woman has an unrestricted right to abortion throughout her pregnancy.

(B) States may restrict abortions throughout pregnancy to protect the woman's health.

(C) States may prohibit abortion during the second and third trimesters.

(D) The right of abortion is unlimited during the first trimester, but states may regulate abortions to protect the woman's health in the second trimester.

(E) Abortion was outlawed, except in cases of rape or incest, or where the woman's health would be seriously compromised.

10. Different standards are used to determine whether or not unconstitutional discrimination has occurred. What standard is used in claims of race discrimination?

    (A) The discrimination must be "substantially related to an important government interest."

    (B) The discriminating practice must be "narrowly tailored" to attain a "compelling government interest."

    (C) The policy must use a reasonable means test to achieve a legitimate government goal.

    (D) The policy will be considered on a case-by-case basis, depending on the parties involved.

    (E) Trick question! Race discrimination is always unconstitutional.

11. Which of the following protects people from *private* (nongovernmental) acts of discrimination?

    (A) Due Process Clause of the Fourteenth Amendment

    (B) Equal Protection Clause of the Fourteenth Amendment

    (C) Equal Rights Amendment

    (D) Civil Rights Act of 1964

    (E) the precedent in *Brown v. Board of Education*

12. What was the significance of the case *Reed v. Reed*?

    (A) overturned restrictions on abortion

    (B) outlawed the use of the "rational basis test"

    (C) required equal funding for male and female athletics

    (D) declared that sex discrimination violates the Equal Protection Clause

    (E) prohibited the male-only military draft

13. Based upon the information in Table 6.1, which of the following is true?

    (A) The number of black elected members of Congress and state legislatures decreased between 1970 and 2010.

    (B) There was a greater increase in black judges and sheriffs between 1991 and 2010 than between 1970 and 1991.

    (C) The number of black members of Boards of Education remained almost constant between 1970 and 2010.

    (D) The total number of black elected officials in 1970 was greater than the number of black members of Boards of Education.

    (E) The greatest increase in black elected officials was in city and county offices.

TABLE 6.1 Increase in Number of Black Elected Officials

	1970	2010
Federal Office	10	43
State Office	169	642
Local Office	1,290	9,800

Source: Statistical Abstract of the United States, 2003, table 417; Joint Center for Political and Economic Studies, *Roster of Black Elected Officials*, November 2011; "A Time to Reflect: Charting the Quality of Life for Black Americans: Politics," *USA Today*, February 21, 2011.

14. Information in the above table is most likely the product of

    (A) the Civil Rights Act of 1964

    (B) the Fourteenth Amendment

    (C) the Voting Rights Act of 1965

    (D) the precedent created in *Brown v. Board of Education*

    (E) the precedent created in *Swann v. Charlotte-Mecklenburg Board of Education*

15. In cases involving differential treatment of women, the Court would most likely use which standard?

    (A) rational basis

    (B) strict scrutiny

    (C) intermediate scrutiny

    (D) basic scrutiny

    (E) constitutional scrutiny

Free Response Questions

1. The Supreme Court has decided a number of cases involving civil rights. These issues include
   abortion
   affirmative action
   homosexual rights

    (a) For one of the topics listed above, identify the legal issue involved and summarize the Court's decisions on the issue.

    (b) For another of the topics listed above, identify the legal issue involved and summarize the Court's decisions on the issue.

2. The second half of the 20th century chronicled the struggle for civil rights. In the 1950s and the 1960s, this struggle was primarily concerned with racial equality. The 1970s saw the emergence of the modern feminist movement and the struggle for gender equality.

    (a) The following cases relate to racial equality. For each case describe the holding of the Court in the case and its significance in U.S. politics.

Brown v. Board of Education (1954)
University of California v. Bakke (1978)

(b) The following case relates to gender equality. Describe the holding of the court in the case and its significance in U. S. politics. *Craig v. Boren* (1976)

Answers

Multiple Choice Answers

1. (D) Civil rights laws protect people from being discriminated against if they are in a protected class, such as race or gender (*American Government*, 14ᵗʰ ed., page **129**).

2. (A) Although blacks were in a majority in many places in the Deep South, it was difficult for them to gain equality because of fear, racism, and the lack of Northern support (*American Government*, 14ᵗʰ ed., pages **122–124**).

3. (B) The neighborhood schools plan was challenged as *de facto* segregation because it resulted in racially separate schools (*American Government*, 14ᵗʰ ed., pages **129–130**).

4. (C) The Supreme Court has refused to order busing across school district lines unless there is a history of segregation by both the city and the suburban school districts (*American Government*, 14ᵗʰ ed., page **130**).

5. (D) The Civil Rights Act of 1964 was finally passed because of increasing white support and reactions by the public to the violence against civil rights advocates as shown by the media. President Kennedy's assassination led many to support civil rights in his honor, and under the erroneous theory that the right wing was responsible for his death. The law was passed by a Democratic Congress and signed by President Johnson (*American Government*, 14ᵗʰ ed., pages **132–133**).

6. (B) The all-male draft meets the standard of mid-level scrutiny required for gender discrimination cases. In general, men are physically stronger than women (*American Government*, 14ᵗʰ ed., pages **137–138**).

7. (D) Abortion may not be outlawed during the first two trimesters of pregnancy, although it may be regulated, as long as those regulations do not create an undue burden on the pregnant woman (*American Government*, 14ᵗʰ ed., pages **138–139**).

8. (E) The Supreme Court has upheld affirmative action programs but dislikes quotas. Preferences are acceptable to reach a goal of increased diversity (*American Government*, 14ᵗʰ ed., pages **139–144**).

9. (D) In *Roe v. Wade*, the Supreme Court ruled that women have a right of privacy that encompasses the decision to have an abortion. Abortion is unrestricted during the first trimester. During the second trimester, states may impose regulations but only to protect the woman's health (*American Government*, 14ᵗʰ ed., page **140**).

10. (B) The Court uses "strict scrutiny" in race discrimination cases. This means that there must be a compelling reason for the practice, and the practice must be the least restrictive way to reach the goal. This is a very high standard (*American Government*, 14ᵗʰ ed., page **129**).

11. (D) The Civil Right Act of 1964 protects individuals from nongovernmental discrimination. The Equal Protection Clause has only been interpreted to prohibit discriminatory practices of state and local governments, not businesses (*American Government*, 14ᵗʰ ed., pages **125–126**).

12. (D) *Reed v. Reed* (1971) was the first time that the U. S. Supreme Court held that sex discrimination violates the Equal Protection Clause of the Fourteenth Amendment. It is followed by the case of *Craig v. Boren* (1976) where that Court held that sex discrimination is subject to intermediate scrutiny (*American Government*, 14ᵗʰ ed., page **137**).

13. (E) The table indicates that the greatest increase in black elected officials was in city and county offices (*American Government*, 14th ed., page **121** of this volume).

14. (C) The increase in black elected officials indicated in the table is directly attributed to the passage and enforcement of the Voting Rights Act of 1965 (*American Government*, 14ᵗʰ ed., page **134**).

15. (C) The Court would most likely invoke intermediate scrutiny. In cases involving racial discrimination, the Court would use strict scrutiny. In all other cases not involving a suspect class, the Court would use rational basis (*American Government*, 14ᵗʰ ed., page **136**).

Free Response Answers

1. (a) Abortion is one of the most contentious issues in the United States today. Until the Supreme Court's decision in *Roe v. Wade*, abortion was regulated by the states. Some states allowed unrestricted access to abortion, while other states prohibited it. In the *Roe* case, the Court held that the Fourth and Fourteenth Amendments protect a right of privacy that includes abortion. In that decision, the Court said that there was an unrestricted right of abortion during the first trimester. States could regulate abortion in the second trimester and could prohibit it in the third. Subsequent Court decisions have allowed regulations

on abortion as long as they do not create an undue burden. For example, parental notification and short waiting periods have been upheld. On the other hand, a spousal consent law was overturned.

(b) Affirmative action programs use preferential practices in hiring and college admissions. The goals of these programs are to foster more diversity and to make up for past and present discrimination. These programs were challenged in *Bakke v. University of California*, when a white medical school applicant with good grades and test scores was not admitted because of a quota system. The Court upheld affirmative action plans in general, but it overturned the quota system. The quota system was found to be race discrimination under the equal protection clause of the Fourteenth Amendment. In a similar case involving the Seattle public school system, the Supreme Court held that race cannot be used to decide which students may attend the system's most well regarded schools. The Court is more willing to accept programs when there has been a history of past discrimination or when the federal government is involved.

(c) Conflicts over homosexuality continue. Sexual conduct has usually been regulated by the states. However, state laws banning certain sexual practices have been overturned by the Supreme Court because of the privacy interests protected by the Fourth and Fourteenth Amendments. When Colorado passed a law banning special protections for gays, the Supreme Court overturned it as a violation of the Equal Protection Clause. However, the Court upheld a rule by the Boy Scouts excluding gays. The Court held that private organizations could choose their own members. Some states allow gay marriages, while other states provide that marriage must be between one man and one woman. Thus the status of gay rights is not clear (*American Government*, 14th ed., pages **138–146**).

2. (a) *Brown v. Board of Education*. The Court held that "separate is inherently unequal." Separate schools for blacks and whites violate the Equal Protection Clause of the Fourteenth Amendment. The significance of the case is that it became unconstitutional for state and local governments to discriminate based upon race. It set the stage for the continuation of the civil rights movement, culminating in the passage of the Civil Rights Act of 1964 and the Voting Rights Act of 1965. *University of California v. Bakke*. The Court held that the racial quotas in the admissions policy at UC Davis medical school were unconstitutional. The court also held that while racial quotas were unconstitutional, affirmative action itself was not unconstitutional. The significance of the case is that it allowed affirmative action to continue. As a result of affirmative action, the number of persons of color attending institutions of higher education increased dramatically.

(b) *Craig v. Boren*. The Court held that the different legal drinking ages mandated by the State of Oklahoma were unconstitutional. The Court applied the test of intermediate scrutiny. The significance was that from this time forward the government would be required to show "important governmental interest" when drawing distinctions based on sex. Few laws can pass this test (*American Government*, 14th ed., pages **138–146**).

Unit XX: Civil Liberties

Correlates to Chapter 5 in *American Government, 14th Edition*

Civil liberties are the constitutional protections an individual has against government. In order to understand the nature of civil liberties, it is necessary to understand why the liberties stated in the Bill of Rights are important, how they came to apply to the states, and why they have grown in scope and meaning.

Key Terms

clear-and-present danger test
Due Process Clause
equal protection of the law
Establishment Clause
exclusionary rule
freedom of expression
freedom of religion
free-exercise clause
good-faith exception
inevitable discovery
libel
prior restraint
probable cause
public safety exception
search warrant
selective incorporation
symbolic speech
wall of separation

Key Concepts

- The courts play a large role in deciding the extent of civil liberties because they are somewhat insulated from the political process. Civil liberties are not subject to majority rule. Because of this, the precise meaning and extent of civil liberties should not be determined by the "political branches" —the president and the Congress.

- With a few exceptions, the rights protected in the Bill of Rights are now applicable to the states. This happened through a process called selective incorporation. The constitutional language that makes this possible is the Due Process Clause of the Fourteenth Amendment.

- There are several types of expression that are not constitutionally protected. Among these are libel, "fighting words," and obscenity. Also not protected are certain forms of symbolic speech.

- Almost all political advertising is constitutionally protected: including, beginning in 2010, political advertising by corporations, unions, and nonprofit organizations.

- The national government cannot establish an official religion because of the Establishment Clause. However, prior to the Fourteenth Amendment, states were free to do so. Many states had established churches well into the 19th century. Furthermore, many democratic counties still have established religions.

- There are many constitutional protections for the accused. These protections include the exclusionary rule, requirements for a search warrant, and the Miranda warning. The Supreme Court has ruled that terrorist detainees and enemy combatants must have access to a neutral court to determine if they have been placed in custody legally.

For a full discussion of civil liberties, see *American Government*, 14th ed., Chapter 5.

AP Tip

Selective incorporation is basic to an understanding of civil liberties and has appeared several times on the AP exam.

Multiple Choice Questions

1. All of the following situations involve civil liberties EXCEPT
   (A) an angry protestor burns an American flag
   (B) a burglary suspect is read her rights before questioning
   (C) homosexuals challenge a ban on gay marriage in court
   (D) a group sacrifices a goat as part of a religious ceremony
   (E) a state provides funds to increase salaries of teachers in religious schools

2. The Supreme Court has upheld which of the following limits on free speech?
   I. laws against libel
   II. laws against speech that presents a clear and present danger
   III. laws against flag burning
   IV. laws against obscenity

(A) I and II

(B) I, II, and III

(C) II and IV

(D) I, II, and IV

(E) I and IV

3. What is "selective incorporation"?

(A) the idea that corporations cannot be held liable for violations of civil liberties because they are nongovernmental entities

(B) the interpretation of the Due Process Clause of the Fourteenth Amendment to apply the fundamental rights in the Bill of Rights to protect people from state action

(C) the interpretation of the Due Process Clause of the Fourteenth Amendment to apply all of the Bill of Rights to protect people from state action

(D) the concept that rights must be balanced with liberties and that the rights of the majority generally prevail

(E) the idea that each state must include the Bill of Rights in its constitution

4. Members of a church protest at military funerals, displaying signs that say, "Thank God for dead soldiers." Many people view the signs as hateful and offensive. Would the courts protect this form of speech?

(A) Yes. The First Amendment protects hate speech.

(B) No. The First Amendment does not protect hate speech because it is intimidating.

(C) No. The First Amendment does not protect speech that is designed to hinder the operation of the military.

(D) Yes. The First Amendment protects hate speech, unless a community decides to ban it.

(E) No. The First Amendment does not protect hate speech.

5. Colorado passed a law requiring that all schoolchildren say the Pledge of Allegiance every morning. The law was challenged as a violation of which civil liberties?

I. free-exercise clause

II. right to petition

III. freedom of speech

IV. freedom of assembly

(A) I and III

(B) I, II, and III

(C) II and III

(D) II, III, and IV

(E) I, III, and IV

6. A house is searched without a valid search warrant, and a dead body is found. What would be the most likely outcome?

(A) The discovery of the body could be used in court because it is the best evidence that a murder occurred.

(B) The discovery of the body could not be used as evidence because it was discovered without a warrant, but hair samples on the body could be used in DNA testing.

(C) The case could not be prosecuted because the exclusionary rule would prevent any evidence of the murder from being presented in court.

(D) The case could be prosecuted with independent evidence, but the discovery of the body could not be used under the exclusionary rule.

(E) This case would be decided under state law because many states have passed laws eliminating the exclusionary rule.

7. What is the result of the Supreme Court's ruling in *Miranda v. Arizona*?

(A) Police officers must read a suspect his or her rights upon arrest; otherwise, the case against the defendant must be dismissed.

(B) If a police officer fails to read a suspect his or her rights upon arrest, the suspect's confession cannot be used in court.

(C) This case established the exclusionary rule that any illegally obtained evidence cannot be used in court.

(D) If a defendant is not read his or her rights upon arrest, a confession cannot be used in court unless it is given voluntarily.

(E) The confession of a defendant who has not been read his or her rights upon arrest may be used in court, but the defendant may bring a civil suit against the arresting officer.

8. Which of the following types of speech is not protected by the First Amendment?

(A) symbolic speech that conveys a political message

(B) student's political opinions, expressed at school

(C) indecent material sent over the internet

(D) restrictions on campaign contributions to candidates and political parties

(E) speech that creates a "clear and present danger" in times of war

9. May a state ban the private possession of firearms?

(A) No, the Supreme Court ruled that states cannot prohibit individual gun ownership.

(B) No, the Court ruled that the Second Amendment provides an unrestricted right to gun ownership.

(C) Yes, because the right to regulate firearms is a moral, social, and family issue left to the states.

(D) Yes, the Supreme Court ruled that state governments may ban guns in the interest of public safety.

(E) Yes, according to the Supreme Court, states may ban guns if citizens have a right to apply for a waiver.

10. May a state government provide funding for math books in both public and private, religious schools?

(A) No, because tax dollars cannot be used to support religious institutions.

(B) Yes, because math books have a secular purpose.

(C) No, because private schools are funded by tuition.

(D) No, because this would violate the Establishment Clause.

(E) Yes, because states have a duty to provide equal funding to both public and private schools.

11. What has been the impact of *Gitlow v. New York* (1925) and *Palco v. Connecticut* (1937) on the United States political system?

(A) Expands the power of state governments to regulate aberrant behavior.

(B) Expands the power of the national government to regulate "symbolic speech."

(C) Allows for national security exceptions to search and seizure protections found in the Fourth Amendment.

(D) Prohibits the national government from establishing a national religion.

(E) Sets the stage for selective incorporation.

12. What is the significance of *Gideon v. Wainwright*?

(A) States must provide attorneys for persons accused of felonies even if they cannot afford it.

(B) States cannot require students to pray before the beginning of class each day.

(C) Schools cannot prohibit students' "symbolic speech."

(D) Suspects must be informed of their constitutional rights at the time of arrest.

(E) Government aid to religious schools is NOT necessarily a violation of the Constitution.

13. Which of the following is true about the Bill of Rights in relationship to the states?

(A) The Bill of Rights has always been applicable against the states.

(B) The Bill of Rights is NOT applicable against the states. States are restricted only by their own bills of rights.

(C) Portions of the Bill of Rights are applicable against the states.

(D) Only the First Amendment is enforceable against the states.

(E) The entire Bill of Rights is applicable against the states.

14. With regard to free speech, which of the following is true?

(A) Citizens have an absolute, unqualified right to free speech.

(B) Only the national government can restrict free speech.

(C) States can prohibit "symbolic speech."

(D) The U. S. Supreme Court will tolerate very few restrictions of free speech.

(E) Freedom of speech is subject to "contemporary community standards."

15. The major function of the First Amendment's Establishment Clause is:

(A) Allows the creation of a national religion subject to majority vote of Congress.

(B) Prohibits states from accommodating religious beliefs of citizens.

(C) Requires a strict separation of church and state.

(D) Prohibits the establishment of a national church.

(E) Restricts citizens in the practice of their religious faiths.

Free Response Questions

1. Civil liberties include the right of criminal defendants to be treated fairly during investigation, arrest, and trial. Rules against illegal search and seizure and self-incrimination protect a defendant's right to due process.

(a) Identify one rule regarding illegal search and seizure, and explain how that rule operates to protect a defendant's right to due process.

(b) Identify one rule regarding self-incrimination, and explain how that rule operates to protect a defendant's right to due process.

2. According to many observers, The First Amendment protects people's most important rights, in particular freedom of religion.

   (a) Identify and explain the two clauses of the United States Bill of Rights that deal with religion.

   (b) Describe a way that the Supreme Court has permitted government to restrict the practice of a person's religious faith.

Answers

Multiple Choice Answers

1. (C) Civil liberties are protections individuals have from the government. These include free speech, religious freedom, separation of church and state, and defendants' rights. Civil rights include protections for groups, such as homosexuals (*American Government*, 14th ed., pages **96–97**).

2. (D) Although the First Amendment protects freedom of speech, this right is not absolute. The Court has upheld laws against libel, obscenity, and speech that present a clear and present danger (*American Government*, 14th ed., pages **103, 107**).

3. (B) In *Gitlow v. New York* the Supreme Court held that the Due Process Clause of the Fourteenth Amendment protects individuals from state action that violates fundamental rights. Not all of the Bill of Rights has been incorporated (*American Government*, 14th ed., page **100**).

4. (A) The First Amendment protects unpopular and offensive speech, whether verbal or symbolic, such as burning a cross. In *Snyder v. Phelps* (2010), the Supreme Court held that protesting at military funerals is protected speech (*American Government*, 14th ed., page **97**).

5. (A) A law requiring the Pledge of Allegiance was challenged as a violation of the Free-Exercise Clause, which protects a person's right to practice—or not to practice—religion. It was also challenged as a violation of the First Amendment, which protects the right to speak—or not to speak. The Colorado law was replaced with a statute making the Pledge of Allegiance voluntary.

6. (D) With some exceptions, the exclusionary rule prohibits evidence from an invalid search from being used in court. It also excludes evidence that is "fruit of the poisonous tree"— evidence that stems from an illegal search. However, the case could still be prosecuted with other evidence (*American Government*, 14th ed., page **112**).

7. (B) Under *Miranda*, if a suspect is not read his or her rights upon arrest, his or her confession cannot be used in court even if that confession was given voluntarily (*American Government*, 14th ed., pages **114–115**).

8. (E) In *Schenck v. United States* (1919), the Supreme Court ruled that speech that creates a "clear and present danger," like yelling "fire" in a crowded theater, is not protected by the First Amendment (*American Government*, 14th ed., pages **101–102**).

9. (C) In *District of Columbia v. Heller* (2008), the Supreme Court ruled that the federal government could not outlaw the private possession of weapons in Washington, D.C. Based on other cases, it will still be possible for the federal and state governments to place some regulations on gun purchases (*American Government*, 14th ed., page **100**).

10. (B) Some state funding for religious schools is acceptable, as long as it has a secular purpose, does not advance or inhibit religion, and does not result in excessive entanglement between government and religion. Math textbooks would meet these standards (*American Government*, 14th ed., pages **110–111**).

11. (E) Both cases set the stage for selective incorporation. Selective incorporation is the process of applying parts of the U.S. Bill of Rights to the States on a case-by-case basis over time. Originally, the U.S. Bill of Rights only applied to the national government (*American Government*, 14th ed., page **100**).

12. (A) *Gideon v. Wainwright* requires that states pay for the services of an attorney for any person, accused of a felony, who cannot afford one. Prior to this case, individuals were only entitled to a state paid attorney in cases with "special circumstances" (*American Government*, 14th ed., pages **101, 118**).

13. (C) Originally, the Bill of Rights only applied to the national government. Through the process of selective incorporation most, but not all, of the protections of the Bill of Rights are now applicable to states as well (*American Government*, 14th ed., pages **100–101**).

14. (D) Some restrictions on free speech are permitted. However, the Supreme Court views as suspect any restriction on free speech. The court upholds very few restrictions on free speech (*American Government*, 14th ed., page **105**).

15. (D) The Establishment Clause prohibits the national government, and through selective incorporation the states, from recognizing or giving official sanction to any religion (*American Government*, 14th ed., pages **100–101, 108**).

Free Response Answers

1. (a) One rule that protects a defendant's right to due process is the exclusionary rule. This rule prevents illegally obtained evidence from being used against a defendant at trial. The Supreme Court established the exclusionary rule in *Mapp v. Ohio*. The defendant was suspected of possessing illegal drugs. When police broke into her home, they did not find drugs, but they found obscene pictures. The Court ruled that the pornography could not be used as evidence in court because the police did not obtain a search warrant, even though they had time to do so. The exclusionary rule protects due process, because it encourages authorities to obtain search warrants and discourages illegal searches.

    (b) Miranda warnings also protect defendants' due-process rights. In *Miranda v. Arizona,* a rape suspect, Ernesto Miranda, gave a confession after hours of questioning. He had not been read his rights. The Supreme Court held that the confession was inadmissible because Miranda did not know that he had the right to remain silent or to have an attorney present during questioning. Now when police take suspects into custody, they read from a "Miranda card." Miranda warnings protect defendants' rights to due process by ensuring that they understand their legal rights. This prevents uninformed self-incrimination (*American Government*, 14th ed., pages **101, 112–115**).

2. (a) Establishment Clause – The government cannot create a religion or give sanction to any particular religion.

3. Free Exercise Clause – The government cannot unduly interfere in the practice of a person's religious faith.

    (a) The court has permitted restrictions on the practice of religious faith if those restrictions are equally binding on other citizens and do not work as an undue hardship on the members of the faith. For example, members of certain Native American tribes desire to use the drug peyote in the practice of their religious ceremonies. This can be prohibited by state and local laws that ban the use of drugs (*American Government*, 14th ed., page **108**).

Practice Test 1

UNITED STATES GOVERNMENT AND POLITICS

Section I

Time: 45 minutes 60 Questions

Directions The questions or incomplete statements below are each followed by five suggested answers. Select the best answer.

Multiple-Choice Questions

1. What was the result of the Court's ruling in *Miranda v. Arizona*?

   (A) It established the exclusionary rule.

   (B) It established the good-faith exception to the exclusionary rule.

   (C) If a suspect has not been informed of his rights, his confession cannot be used as evidence.

   (D) If a suspect has not been informed of his rights, the charges against him must be dropped.

   (E) The state must provide an attorney if a defendant cannot afford one.

2. The president has all of the following expressed powers under the Constitution EXCEPT

   (A) to grant reprieves and pardons for federal offenses

   (B) to convene Congress in special sessions

   (C) to exercise the line-item veto

   (D) to appoint ambassadors, subject to Senate confirmation

   (E) to commission officers in the armed forces

3. All of the following statements about voter turnout are true EXCEPT

   (A) voter turnout in presidential elections was at its highest point in the late 1800s

   (B) people ages 18–21 have the lowest voter turnout rates

   (C) voter turnout has dropped in every presidential election since 1960

   (D) voter turnout is higher in federal elections than in state and local elections

   (E) voter turnout is greater in presidential elections than in midterm congressional elections

4. What encourages a two-party system in the United States?

   (A) the inclusion of ballot initiatives and referendums

   (B) the selection of candidates through primaries

   (C) the selection of candidates through caucuses

   (D) ticket-splitting by voters between the Republican and Democratic parties

   (E) the fact that elections are for single-member districts, winner-take-all

5. Which of the following serves as a check by Congress over the executive?

   (A) Congress can change the number and jurisdiction of the lower courts.

   (B) Congress can refuse to confirm a person nominated to be a judge.

   (C) All revenue bills must originate in the House of Representatives.

   (D) Congress can override a presidential veto by a majority vote of both houses.

   (E) Congress can remove cabinet secretaries.

6. What role does political party affiliation play in the selection of federal judges?

   (A) Presidents usually appoint members of their political party, and these people are generally qualified.

   (B) None. Federal judges are appointed based upon their qualifications rather than their party affiliation.

   (C) Some. Federal judges are appointed based upon their qualifications, but equally qualified candidates are judged based upon party affiliation.

   (D) Party affiliation is much more important than qualifications. Many unqualified judges are appointed because they are party faithful.

   (E) Under the merit rules for civil service, presidents are barred from considering party affiliation in appointing federal judges.

7. Beginning in 2010, it was difficult for President Obama to get his domestic program passed. What is the best explanation for this?

   (A) His approval ratings suffered a steady decline.

   (B) The government was divided.

   (C) The poor economy made it difficult for Congress to fund new programs.

   (D) The impeachment process took up the last six years of his presidency.

   (E) He concentrated on foreign affairs and did not put forth a domestic agenda.

8. What is the basis of James Madison's argument in the *Federalist Paper* No. 10?

   (A) Factions are dangerous and must be destroyed.

   (B) The government can eliminate the causes of faction.

   (C) Political parties should be encouraged to form so that all viewpoints are represented.

   (D) A balanced government can control factions and prevent one faction from gaining too much power.

   (E) State government will prevent factions from forming.

9. Why does environment regulation cause friction between the state and federal governments?

   (A) because environmental policy creates an underfunded or unfunded mandate

   (B) because the federal government does not provide any funding for compliance with the law

   (C) because states did not agree with the goal of providing a clean environment

   (D) because most states already had tough environmental protection

   (E) because environmental protection is a state, rather than federal, issue

10. One criticism of the media is that it does not cover candidates' speeches in depth. This is best illustrated in which of the following?

    (A) the rise of the internet

    (B) horse-race journalism

    (C) the shrinking sound bite

    (D) the liberal bias in the media

    (E) sensationalism

FIGURE 18.3   Social Security and Medicare Cost as a Percentage of GDP

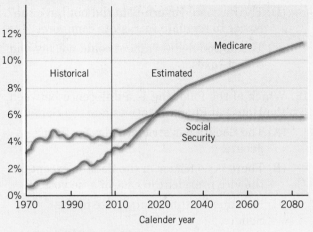

Source: Trustees' Report, 2009.

11. The graph above best supports which of the following conclusions?

    (A) Medicare is an uncontrollable expenditure.

    (B) Social Security is an uncontrollable expenditure.

    (C) The number of Social Security recipients will continue to rise, due to retiring baby boomers.

    (D) The mandatory retirement age will have to be raised in order to balance the budget.

    (E) Medicare expenses, as a percentage of GDP, are expected to rise through 2080.

12. What is the primary source of political socialization?

    (A) family

    (B) peer groups

    (C) television

    (D) the internet

    (E) public schools

13. The Supreme Court has upheld all of the following restrictions on abortion EXCEPT

    (A) a twenty-four-hour waiting period

    (B) parental consent

    (C) prohibition of abortion after the fetus is viable

    (D) spousal consent

    (E) required pamphlets with information about alternatives

14. What was the biggest problem with the Articles of Confederation?

    (A) The national government imposed heavy taxes on the wealthy.

    (B) The states did not have enough power.

(C) Individual states could not control their economies.

(D) The national government did not have the power to regulate intrastate commerce.

(E) The national government could not lay and collect taxes.

15. Which of the following is a difference between the House of Representatives and the Senate?

(A) The Senate has stricter rules for floor debate.

(B) There is no leader in the Senate, except for the vice president in case of a tie vote.

(C) Revenue bills must originate in the Senate.

(D) Floor rules and debate are more casual in the Senate than in the House.

(E) The Senate has standing committees, but the House uses only select committees.

16. All of the following statements about filibusters are true EXCEPT

(A) either political party may use the filibuster

(B) senators who vote for cloture risk having their own filibusters ended the same way

(C) filibusters have been used to block judicial appointments

(D) cloture votes are rare, because they require seventy-five votes

(E) both filibusters and cloture votes are becoming more common

17. What are political action committees?

(A) registered organizations that donate money to campaigns and causes

(B) committees that work as part of an iron triangle to change bureaucratic regulations

(C) interest groups that have raised more than $200,000 in a single fiscal year

(D) groups of people who are interested in a cause and lobby on its behalf

(E) organizations whose primary purpose is to lobby Congress

18. How does an executive order differ from legislation?

(A) Executive orders are submitted by the president to Congress for approval; bills are submitted by the Congress to the president for approval.

(B) Executive orders have the force of law but do not have to be approved by Congress.

(C) Executive orders expire after five years.

(D) Executive orders require ratification by the Senate but not the House.

(E) The Supreme Court cannot rule on the constitutionality of an executive order.

19. Compared to citizens of other nations,

(A) Americans place more value on maintaining good relations with colleagues.

(B) Americans are more willing to respect authority.

(C) Americans place more value on individualism and competition.

(D) Americans are more sensitive to the personal needs of others.

(E) Americans are more likely to defer to experts and specialists in decision making.

20. What is judicial review?

(A) the review of judicial appointments by members of the Senate, who have the power to confirm nominees

(B) the ability of the Supreme Court to overturn rulings by federal district court judges

(C) the power of the Supreme Court to overturn rulings by federal appeals court judges

(D) the power of the chief justice of the Supreme Court to preside over impeachment hearings

(E) the power of the Supreme Court to declare acts of Congress or the states unconstitutional

21. Some evidence suggests that in the 1980 election, voters did not vote for Ronald Reagan as much as they voted against Jimmy Carter. What best describes this kind of voting behavior?

(A) prospective voting

(B) ideological voting

(C) retrospective voting

(D) group-benefits voting

(E) no-issue-content voting

22. What advantage does Congress have by sending bills to the president more than ten days before the end of a congressional session?

(A) The president will not have much time to write a veto message.

(B) The bill cannot be pocket vetoed.

(C) The president cannot use a line-item veto.

(D) Congress has time to rewrite the bill if the president does not like it.

(E) Congress will have the time to call a special session if necessary.

23. Which of the following statements best describes the accuracy of public opinion polls?

(A) Even in a close election, most public opinion polls accurately predict the winner.

(B) The bigger the sample, the more room there is for sampling error.

(C) Different polling organizations often have different results, even when they ask the same question.

(D) The sampling error is usually plus or minus 3 percent.

(E) Public opinion polls cannot predict elections with any degree of accuracy.

24. All of the following are necessary for an accurate public opinion poll EXCEPT

(A) the question must be asked in an unbiased manner

(B) the persons interviewed must be selected based on a random sample

(C) the questions must be understandable

(D) the answer categories must offer people a choice between different responses

(E) the number of people sampled must be at least 10 percent of the population

25. Which constitutional provision gives states most of their powers?

(A) the Ninth Amendment

(B) the Tenth Amendment

(C) the Commerce Clause

(D) the Necessary and Proper Clause

(E) the Full Faith and Credit Clause

26. What is the main reason for the shift from dual to cooperative federalism?

(A) court decisions that required the states and federal government to coordinate policies

(B) inconsistent welfare policies at the state level, which required national coordination

(C) the increase in federal grants-in-aid to the states

(D) the global economy and the importance of improving the trained work force

(E) revenue sharing, which occurred during budgetary surpluses

27. What is the role of the federal courts of appeal?

(A) to send cases to the Supreme Court when there is a constitutional issue involved

(B) to hear appeals from the federal district courts

(C) to hear new testimony in cases being retried

(D) to hear appeals from state supreme courts when there is a constitutional issue involved

(E) to review acts of Congress before they are sent to the Supreme Court for final judicial review

28. A state, which is not Maine or Nebraska, has eight members in the House of Representatives. In a presidential election, that state's population votes 40 percent for the Democratic candidate and 60 percent for the Republican candidate. How are that state's electoral votes allocated?

(A) Eight electoral votes are pledged to the Republican candidate.

(B) Ten electoral votes are pledged to the Republican candidate.

(C) Four votes are pledged to the Democrat, and six votes are pledged to the Republican.

(D) Six votes are pledged to the Democrat and four votes are pledged to the Republican.

(E) It is impossible to determine the number of electoral college votes from the facts given.

29. All of the following are likely to vote for a candidate from the Democratic Party EXCEPT

(A) African Americans

(B) non-Cuban Hispanics

(C) union members

(D) women

(E) small business owners

30. What is the term for a sharp, lasting shift that occurs in the popular coalitions supporting one or both parties?

(A) readjustment

(B) deviating election

(C) electoral shift

(D) critical realignment

(E) party reorganization

FIGURE 16.2 Female and Minority Judicial Appointments, 1963–2013

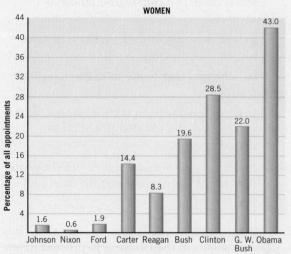

WOMEN

Johnson 1.6, Nixon 0.6, Ford 1.9, Carter 14.4, Reagan 8.3, Bush 19.6, Clinton 28.5, G. W. Bush 22.0, Obama 43.0

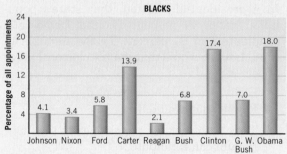

BLACKS

Johnson 4.1, Nixon 3.4, Ford 5.8, Carter 13.9, Reagan 2.1, Bush 6.8, Clinton 17.4, G. W. Bush 7.0, Obama 18.0

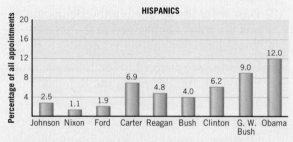

HISPANICS

Johnson 2.5, Nixon 1.1, Ford 1.9, Carter 6.9, Reagan 4.8, Bush 4.0, Clinton 6.2, G. W. Bush 9.0, Obama 12.0

Source: Updated from Harold W. Stanley and Richard G. Niemi, *Vital Statistics on American Politics, 2005–2006* (Washington, D.C. : Congressional Quarterly, 2006), Table 7.5.

31. Figure 16.2 best supports which of the following conclusions?

(A) From 1963 until 2000, Democratic presidents appointed more blacks to the judiciary than Republican presidents did.

(B) Blacks being appointed to the judiciary are appointed to the district court level, rather than to the appellate courts.

(C) Twenty percent of the judges appointed by Clinton were black.

(D) President George H. W. Bush appointed more black judges than President Johnson did.

(E) The percentage of black judges appointed by President Carter mirrored the percentage of blacks in the population.

32. Figure 9.1 below best supports which of the following statements?

(A) In 2000 there were more Republicans than Democrats.

(B) The biggest gap between strong Republicans and strong Democrats occurred in 1984.

(C) The number of independent voters was the highest in 2000 and 2008.

(D) Since 1980 there has been steady increase in the number of voters who identify themselves as Republican.

(E) The number of weak Republicans has outnumbered strong Republicans since 1976.

FIGURE 9.1 Decline in Party Identification, 1952–2012

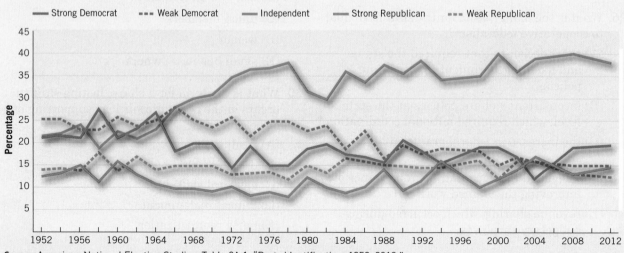

—— Strong Democrat   ■■■ Weak Democrat   —— Independent   —— Strong Republican   ■■■ Weak Republican

Source: American National Election Studies, Table 2A.1, "Party Identification, 1952–2012."

33. What is the typical method for becoming a member of the White House staff?

(A) be a longtime associate of the president who has served on his campaign staff

(B) be a longtime member of Congress with substantial experience in policy making

(C) serve on the staff of the president's predecessor if the former president was a member of the president's political party

(D) have experience in business and industry and apply for the job based upon qualifications

(E) have experience in academia, preferably as a professor at an Ivy League college

34. How do delegates to national conventions differ ideologically from most party members?

(A) They are more moderate because they represent the interests of an entire state.

(B) The Republicans are more right wing, and the Democrats are more moderate.

(C) The Democrats are more left wing, and the Republicans are more moderate.

(D) The Democrats are more left wing, and the Republicans are more right wing.

(E) There is no significant difference in ideology between the ideology of the delegates and that of party members.

35. All of the following are advantages of incumbency for members of Congress EXCEPT

(A) the recognition they receive by sitting on oversight committees

(B) the use of franking privileges to let members of their districts know what they have been doing

(C) the ability to provide casework

(D) the ability to bring pork-barrel projects to their states

(E) name recognition

36. All of the following arguments have been made about the electoral college EXCEPT

(A) it benefits small states because they receive a disproportionate share of votes

(B) it benefits large states because they receive a disproportionate share of attention from the candidates

(C) it benefits third parties because they can control entire regions of the country

(D) it is undemocratic because the winner of the popular vote may not win in the electoral college

(E) states with large urban populations get more attention from the candidates

37. What is gerrymandering?

(A) an intentional overcount in a census to inflate a state's population total

(B) drawing legislative boundaries to favor a political party

(C) when a bureaucratic agency submits an inflated budget

(D) when the president is from one political party and one or both houses of Congress are controlled by the opposing party

(E) when a senator takes the floor to "talk a bill to death"

38. Those who attempt to influence governmental decisions, especially legislation, often on behalf of interest groups, are best described as

(A) PACs
(B) influence peddlers
(C) social movements
(D) lobbyists
(E) campaign strategists

39. Which of the following policies would a conservative voter most likely support?

(A) maintaining a pro-choice policy on abortion
(B) reducing government regulations on business
(C) increasing taxes to balance the budget
(D) expanding the civil liberties of criminal defendants
(E) increasing social programs during periods of recession

40. In the following scenario, the Senate has fifty Republicans and fifty Democrats and the president is Republican. What would be the result if one Republican senator changed his affiliation to become an independent?

(A) No major changes would occur in the conduct of the Senate.

(B) The Senate would have a Democratic majority, and it would become impossible for the president to enact his program.

(C) The Republican whip would be used to make sure the independent senator voted with the Republicans.

(D) The Republican committee heads would be replaced with Democrats.

(E) The vice president would no longer be the president of the Senate.

41. In which of the following situations would presidential power be the greatest?

(A) During times of divided government.

(B) At the beginning of a war

(C) After several years of war

(D) During an economic recession

(E) Midway through his second term

42. In which of the following ways can the Congress check the power of the judiciary?

(A) Veto a decision of the Supreme Court by a two-thirds majority

(B) Issue a declaration of nullification

(C) Restrict the jurisdiction of the Supreme Court

(D) Restrict the president's power to appoint judges

(E) Raise the educational requirements for judges

43. Which of the following types of grants carries the least amount of restrictions for states and local governments?

(A) Block grants

(B) Categorical grants

(C) Assistance grants

(D) General governmental grant

(E) Omnibus grant

44. What is the practice of "Senatorial Courtesy"?

(A) The requirement that the House of Representatives pre-clear legislation with the Senate.

(B) The deference show the Senate by the president when picking a vice president

(C) The unofficial power individual senators to pick federal judges who serve in their states.

(D) The respect one member of the Senate shows another member

(E) The power of the Senate's judiciary committee to appoint federal prosecutors

45. Which of the following best explains why presidents might focus on foreign policy during their second terms?

(A) The fact that most presidents have achieved almost all of their domestic agenda by this time.

(B) The desire of Congress to help a president achieve his foreign policy goals

(C) Competition from the vice president in the area of domestic policy

(D) Increasing conflicts with the judiciary

(E) Declining popularity

46. Why might a president threatened to veto a bill before it is passed rather than wait for the bill to be a passed and then veto it?

(A) It is easy for Congress to override the veto.

(B) A threatened veto often forces Congress to negotiate.

(C) Vetoing a bill prohibits Congress from future action on the same issue.

(D) Supreme Court decisions have made the veto power difficult to exercise.

(E) Vetoing a bill typically results in a decline in presidential approval rating.

47. All of the following are required under the War Powers Resolution of 1973 EXCEPT

(A) Congressional authorization prior to military operations

(B) 60 day operation period

(C) 30 day withdrawal period

(D) Congressional notification within 48 hours

(E) Option for Congressional extension of the 60 operation period

48. What was the Court's decision in *Citizens United v. Federal Election Commission*?

(A) Restrictions on spending by political parties are unconstitutional.

(B) Special interest groups must coordinate with a candidate.

(C) Restrictions on individual contributions are unconstitutional.

(D) Labor unions and corporation have a right to free speech.

(E) Governmental funding of candidates is unconstitutional.

49. Which of the following provisions of the Fourteenth Amendment has made possible selective incorporation?

(A) Supremacy Clause

(B) Citizenship Clause

(C) Privileges and Immunities Clause

(D) Equal Protection Clause

(E) Due Process Clause

50. A judges who use their role to interpret the constitution based upon their own views rather than its historic meaning are said to be engaged in

(A) strict construction

(B) judicial restraint

(C) federal expansion

(D) judicial activism

(E) judicial evolution

51. What is significant about the presidential contests in Iowa and New Hampshire?

 (A) They are the last contests in the presidential nomination process.

 (B) They are the location of the national conventions of both parties.

 (C) They are the states that award the greatest amount of delegates.

 (D) They are the midpoint of the presidential nomination process.

 (E) They are the first contests in the presidential nomination process.

52. Voting *for* a candidate based upon the candidate's views and qualification rather *against* the candidate's opponent is an example of

 (A) retrospective voting

 (B) straight ticket voting

 (C) absentee voting

 (D) prospective voting

 (E) protest voting

53. All of the following have been used to expand the power of the national government EXCEPT

 (A) Commerce Clause

 (B) Fourteenth Amendment

 (C) Tenth Amendment

 (D) Supremacy Clause

 (E) Elastic Clause

54. Special interest groups attempting to influence judicial decision making in cases where they have no standing will use which of the following

 (A) *writs of mandamus*

 (B) *amicus curiae* briefs

 (C) *habeas corpus*

 (D) *stare decisis*

 (E) *ex post facto* laws

55. What is the function of a conference committee?

 (A) set the legislative agenda

 (B) determine the rules under which a bill will be considered

 (C) conduct investigations

 (D) select the leadership of the House and Senate

 (E) reconcile the House and Senate versions of a bill

56. Which of the following is most closely tied to the national government's ability to regulate business activity?

 (A) Necessary and Proper Clause

 (B) Business Clause

 (C) Commerce Clause

 (D) Supremacy Clause

 (E) Interstate Clause

57. In which of the following cases the Court rule that flag burning is constitutionally protected speech?

 (A) *Texas v. Johnson*

 (B) *Marbury v. Madison*

 (C) *Gibbons v. Ogden*

 (D) *Miranda v. Arizona*

 (E) *Gideon v. Wainwright*

58. What is the primary function of the census?

 (A) determine the level of taxation for a given state

 (B) scientific demographic research

 (C) Set the number of Senators for each state

 (D) allocate federal grants

 (E) apportion representatives

59. In a federal system, where is political power vested?

 (A) In the national government

 (B) In the regional governments

 (C) Power is divided between the national government and regional governments with the regional governments being supreme

 (D) Power is divided between the national government and regional governments with the national government being supreme

 (E) Power is shared equally between national, regional, and local government.

60. In American politics what was the function of the literacy test with the grandfather clause exception?

 (A) ensure an informed electorate

 (B) provide for representation for older citizens

 (C) disenfranchise African Americans

 (D) disenfranchise young Americans

 (E) ensure the candidates for public office were educated

STOP

END OF SECTION I

IF YOU FINISH BEFORE TIME IS CALLED, YOU MAY CHECK YOUR WORK ON THIS SECTION. DO NOT GO ON TO SECTION II UNTIL YOU ARE TOLD TO DO SO.

UNITED STATES GOVERNMENT AND POLITICS

Section II

Time—100 minutes

Directions You have 100 minutes to answer all four of the following questions. Unless the directions indicate otherwise, respond to all parts of each question. It is recommended that you take a few minutes to plan and outline each answer. Spend approximately 25 minutes on each question. Support your essay with specific examples where appropriate. Be sure to number each of your answers.

1. The federal government cannot control the economy, but it can take measures to improve the health of the American economy.

   a. Identify and explain one way that the government uses monetary policy to influence the economy.

   b. Identify and explain one way that the government uses the budget to influence the economy.

   c. Identify and explain one way Congress can influence the economy.

   d. Identify and explain one way the president can influence the economy.

2. Using the data in Figure 13.1 below and your knowledge of United States politics, perform the following tasks:

   a. Identify one trend shown in the graph as it relates to members of the House of Representatives, and explain one reason for this trend.

   b. Identify one trend shown in the graph as it relates to senators, and explain one reason for this trend.

   c. Identify one trend that relates to the differences in the graph between members of the House of Representatives and senators, and explain one reason for this trend.

3. Federalism is political system by which power is divided between a national governments and regional governments. Federalism in the United States is dynamic force. Deference in power between the national government and the states changes over time.

   (A) Define devolution.

   (B) Identify and explain two ways in which devolution has occurred in the United States

FIGURE 13.1   Re-election Rates for House and Senate Incumbents, 1964–2012

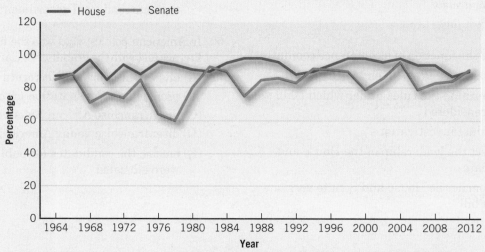

Sources: For 1964–2008 data, The Center for Responsive Politics; 2010 data compiled by author; and 2012 data drawn from The Center for Responsive Politics, OpenSecrets.org, accessed by Jesse Crosson, May 28, 2013.

4. The Bill of Rights protects freedom of religion is very specific ways.
   (A) Identify the two clauses the in First Amendment that deal with religion.
   (B) Explain how the court and applied these clauses to the states
   (C) Explain the court's ruling in *Engel v. Vitale*. In your explanation correctly identify which clause from the first amendment the court used.

END OF EXAMINATION

Answer Key for Multiple-Choice Questions

1.	C	19.	C
2.	C	20.	E
3.	C	21.	C
4.	E	22.	B
5.	B	23.	D
6.	A	24.	E
7.	B	25.	B
8.	D	26.	C
9.	A	27.	B
10.	C	28.	B
11.	E	29.	E
12.	A	30.	D
13.	D	31.	D
14.	E	32.	C
15.	D	33.	A
16.	D	34.	D
17.	A	35.	A
18.	B	36.	C

37.	B	49.	E
38.	D	50.	D
39.	B	51.	E
40.	D	52.	D
41.	B	53.	C
42.	C	54.	B
43.	A	55.	E
44.	C	56.	C
45.	E	57.	A
46.	B	58.	E
47.	A	59.	D
48.	D	60.	C

Answers to Multiple-Choice Questions

1. ANSWER: (C) In *Miranda v. Arizona*, the court held that suspects must be read their rights. Otherwise, their confessions are not admissible in court (*American Government*, 14th ed., pages 114–118).
2. ANSWER: (C) While the president may veto a bill in its entirety, he cannot veto a portion of a bill (*American Government*, 14th ed., page 357).
3. ANSWER: (C) While turnout in 1996 was slightly above 49 percent, turnout in the 2008 election was 62 percent (*American Government*, 14th ed., pages 173, 179).
4. ANSWER: (E) Single-member districts with winner-take-all elections favor two parties and make it difficult for third parties to compete (*American Government*, 14th ed., page 206).
5. ANSWER: (B) Congress can refuse to confirm a judge nominated by the president. This is a check on both the executive and judicial branches (*American Government*, 14th ed., pages 409, 419, 431).
6. ANSWER: (A) Presidents usually appoint judges from the ranks of their political party. These candidates are also chosen based upon

their qualifications (*American Government*, 14th ed., pages 417–420).

7. ANSWER: (B) Beginning in 2010, Obama faced divided government, in which the party opposing the president holds one or both houses of Congress. The Republican Party controlled the House of Representatives. This makes it difficult for a president to get programs passed (*American Government*, 14th ed., pages 341–343).

8. ANSWER: (D) Madison believed that a balanced government (including separation of powers, checks and balances, and federalism) could eliminate "the mischiefs of faction" (*American Government*, 14th ed., pages 35–36).

9. ANSWER: (A) Environment protection laws caused friction between the state and federal governments because the number of federal mandates is high and the funding received from the national government is inadequate (*American Government*, 14th ed., page 68).

10. ANSWER: (C) The sound bite dropped from about 42 seconds in 1968 to 7.3 seconds in 2000. As a result, candidates' speeches are not covered in depth (*American Government*, 14th ed., page 281).

11. ANSWER: (E) Medicare expenses as a percent of GDP are expected to rise from under 4 percent in 2010 to over 11 percent in 2080 (*American Government*, 14th ed., page 482).

12. ANSWER: (A) Families have the most influence in political socialization (*American Government*, 14th ed., pages 156–158).

13. ANSWER: (D) Abortion may be banned during the third trimester. The court has upheld parental consent laws, a twenty-four-hour waiting period, and a requirement that women be given information about alternatives. The Court struck down a spousal consent requirement (*American Government*, 14th ed., pages 138–139).

14. ANSWER: (E) Under the Articles of Confederation, the national government did not have the power to tax (*American Government*, 14th ed., page 27).

15. ANSWER: (D) Because the House is larger than the Senate, it is more difficult to control. The House is more formal and has more rules in the conduct of its business (*American Government*, 14th ed., page 319).

16. ANSWER: (D) Sixty votes are required to end a filibuster by cloture (*American Government*, 14th ed., page 311).

17. ANSWER: (A) PACs are committees set up to raise and spend campaign contributions on behalf of one or more candidates or causes (*American Government*, 14th ed., page 252).

18. ANSWER: (B) Executive orders are presidential directives that have the force of law but do not need to be approved by Congress (*American Government*, 14th ed., page 370).

19. ANSWER: (C) In many other countries cooperation is highly valued. In contrast, Americans are individualists who tend to value competition more than collaboration (*American Government*, 14th ed., page 83).

20. ANSWER: (E) Judicial review was established in *Marbury v. Madison*. It is the power of the Supreme Court to declare state or federal laws unconstitutional (*American Government*, 14th ed., pages 33, 409–410).

21. ANSWER: (C) Retrospective voting means looking at how things have gone in the recent past. Voters were not happy with the track record of the Carter administration, and he lost the 1980 election (*American Government*, 14th ed., pages 243–244).

22. ANSWER: (B) A pocket veto occurs when a president does not sign a bill within ten days and Congress has adjourned. A pocket veto cannot occur if Congress sends the president a bill more than ten days prior to adjournment (*American Government*, 14th ed., page 357).

23. ANSWER: (D) Normal sampling error is plus or minus 3 percent. This makes it difficult to predict the winner in a close election (*American Government*, 14th ed., page 155).

24. ANSWER: (E) For any population over 500,000, at least 1,065 people need to be polled to achieve a sampling error of plus or minus 3 percent, 95 percent of the time (*American Government*, 14th ed., page 155).

25. ANSWER: (B) The Tenth Amendment reserves powers not delegated to the national government, nor prohibited to the states, to the states and the people. It is the main basis for state power (*American Government*, 14th ed., pages 38, 53–54).

26. ANSWER: (C) Federal grants-in-aid often come with strings attached. This was a major reason for the move from dual to cooperative federalism (*American Government*, 14th ed., pages 57–58).

27. ANSWER: (B) The federal courts of appeals hear appeals from the federal district courts.

If a litigant is unhappy with an appeals court decision, the final level of appeal is the Supreme Court, which may or may not grant a writ of certiorari to decide the case (*American Government*, 14th ed., pages 420–421).

28. ANSWER: (B) In all states except Maine and Nebraska, a winner-take-all system is used. The state will have ten electoral college votes (eight for its members in the House of Representatives and two for its senators), all of which will be pledged to the Republican candidate (*American Government*, 14th ed., pages 350–351).

29. ANSWER: (E) African Americans, Jews, and union members tend to vote for Democrats. In addition, there is a gender gap, with women favoring the Democrats and men favoring the Republicans (*American Government*, 14th ed., pages 160–164).

30. ANSWER: (D) A critical or realigning period occurs when there is a major and permanent shift in the groups supporting the political parties (*American Government*, 14th ed., page 195).

31. ANSWER: (D) Blacks accounted for 6.5 percent of President George H. W. Bush's appointments. This is greater than the 4.1 percent appointed by President Johnson (*American Government*, 14th ed., page 418).

32. ANSWER: (C) In 2000 and 2008, about 40 percent of the electorate identified themselves as independent. This is the highest percentage shown on the table (*American Government*, 14th ed., page 190).

33. ANSWER: (A) Senior White House staff members are typically drawn from the ranks of the president's campaign staff and are long-time associates of the president ((*American Government*, 14th ed., page 363).

34. ANSWER: (D) Delegates are more extreme in their ideology than average party members are. This means that Republican delegates are more right wing, and Democratic delegates are more left wing (*American Government*, 14th ed., page 212).

35. ANSWER: (A) Incumbent members of Congress benefit from name recognition, the use of franking privileges, casework, and by bringing pork-barrel projects to their states. Sitting on oversight committees usually does not bring much attention (*American Government*, 14th ed., pages 222, 314).

36. ANSWER: (C) The electoral college hurts third parties because it is difficult for them to get a majority in any state. It is difficult for third parties to get any electoral college votes (*American Government*, 14th ed., page 206).

37. ANSWER: (B) Gerrymandering is drawing the boundaries of legislative districts, often in strange shapes, to favor a political party (*American Government*, 14th ed., pages 224–225).

38. ANSWER: (D) Lobbyists, often working for interest groups, attempt to influence legislation (*American Government*, 14th ed., page 252).

39. ANSWER: (B) Conservatives favor the free market and want to reduce the number of government regulations on business (*American Government*, 14th ed., pages 164–166).

40. ANSWER: (D) The majority party in the Senate appoints committee heads. Under the scenario, the Democrats would have a majority and would appoint committee chairs (*American Government*, 14th ed., page 322).

41. ANSWER: (B) Presidents usually get a bump in their popularity and approval ratings at the beginning of a conflict or during times of crises. This decreases with time. Popularity and approval ratings are highly correlated with power and influence (*American Government*, 14th ed., pages 354–355).

42. ANSWER: (C) The Congress, under Article III section 2 of the Constitution, can restrict the jurisdiction of federal courts (*American Government*, 14th ed., page 414).

43. ANSWER: (A) Block grants have the fewest restrictions for state and local government. This is contrasted with categorical grants which have many restrictions and mandates for state and local government (*American Government*, 14th ed., pages 66–67).

44. ANSWER: (C) The Constitution gives the president the power to appoint federal judges with the advice and consent of the Senate. In practice this power is exercised by individual senators with regard to federal district court judges (*American Government*, 14th ed., pages 418–419).

45. ANSWER: (E) Presidential popularity is typically in decline during a second term. Power and popularity are correlated. As presidential power declines Congress begins to assert itself. President can take refuge in foreign policy where a cooperative Congress is less important than it is in the area of domestic policy (*American Government*, 14th ed., page 356).

46. ANSWER: (B) Presidents can threaten to veto a bill and thus bring Congress to the negotiation table. This allows the president a greater hand in the content of the bill than a simple use of the veto after the bill is passed.

47. ANSWER: (A) Under the War Powers Resolution of 1973, the President is not required to get the approval of Congress prior to the start of the military operations (*American Government*, 14th ed., pages 493–494).

48. ANSWER: (D) In the decision, the Court held the labor unions and corporations have a right to free speech. Therefore restrictions on political advertisements made by those organizations are unconstitutional as long as there is no coordination with a candidate (*American Government*, 14th ed., page 268).

49. ANSWER: (E) The Court has used the Due Process Clause of the Fourteenth Amendment to apply most of the protection of the Bill of Rights to the states through a process known as selective incorporation (*American Government*, 14th ed., pages 100–101).

50. ANSWER: (D) Judicial activism is when a judges interpret the Constitution consistent with their own views rather than its historic context. These judges are more likely to disregard precedent (*American Government*, 14th ed., pages 413, 429).

51. ANSWER: (E) These contests are the first test of a candidate's strength. Candidates who finish poorly in Iowa and New Hampshire have a difficult time recovering. (*American Government*, 14th ed., page 227).

52. ANSWER: (D) A prospective voter is influenced more by a candidate's views and qualifications than the dislike of his opponent (*American Government*, 14th ed., page 243).

53. ANSWER: (C) The Tenth Amendment protects state's reserved powers. It has been used to stop the expansion of national power (*American Government*, 14th ed., page 34).

54. ANSWER: (B) An amicus curiae brief, "friend of the court," is filed by special interest groups and other interested parties in an attempt to influence the decision in cases where they are not directly involved. While they may not be directly involved, special interests may concerned about the outcome because of the precedent that might be created (*American Government*, 14th ed., page 426).

55. ANSWER: (E) Conference committees reconcile the House and Senate versions of legislation. As such they write the final version of the bill that will be voted on by both houses (*American Government*, 14th ed., page 322).

56. ANSWER: (C) The Commerce Clause gives the national government the power to regulate businesses that are engaged in interstate commerce. By judicial interpretation virtually all business activities today fall under the classification of interstate commerce. As such, this has led to a dramatic increase in the power of the national government. (*American Government*, 14th ed., page 57).

57. ANSWER: (A) In *Texas v. Johnson* the Court ruled that flag burning is a form of constitutionally protected symbolic speech under the First Amendment (*American Government*, 14th ed., page 107).

58. ANSWER: (E) The primary purpose for the census is to determine the number of people in each state so that the House of Representatives can be apportioned based on population as required by the Constitution (*American Government*, 14th ed., pages 225–226).

59. ANSWER: (D) In a federal government, power is divided between the national and regional "state" government. The national government is superior to the states. Local governments derived their powers from the regional governments (*American Government*, 14th ed., page 51).

60. ANSWER: (C) The literacy test was used to keep African Americans from voting. Illiterate whites were allowed to vote because of the grandfather clause (*American Government*, 14th ed., page 177).

Answers to Free-Response Questions

QUESTION 1

Part (a): One way that monetary policy is used to influence the economy is by changing interest rates. The Federal Reserve Board sets the interest rates it charges banks to borrow from the federal government. This is called the discount rate. If the Fed raises the discount rate, banks pay more to borrow money, and they pass these higher interest rates on to their customers. This makes money more expensive to borrow and slows the rate of inflation.

Part (b): One way the budget is used to influence the economy is through spending policies. Based on Keynesian economics, the Obama administration wanted to stimulate economic growth through government spending. Under this theory, money is pumped into the economy to ease the recession and assist troubled businesses. For example, under the Troubled Asset Relief Program (TARP), billions were invested to buy shares in troubled financial institutions, loans were given to American car manufacturers, and lenders received funds to help mortgage holders.

Part (c): One way Congress can influence the economy comes from its role in approving all taxes and almost all expenditures. Appropriations committees in both houses must approve all spending. Budget committees, assisted by the Congressional Budget Office, make recommendations about the budget submitted by the president.

Part (d): The president has some influence over the economy because he appoints the members of the Federal Reserve Board (subject to Senate confirmation). This board sets monetary policy, and the president appoints candidates who share his philosophy about regulating the money supply. Members serve for a nonrenewable term of fourteen years, and this gives them significant influence over the economy (*American Government*, 14th ed., pages 472–484).

Scoring

This essay is worth 5 points. Part (a) is worth 2 points—1 point for identifying a monetary tool (interest rates), and 1 point for explaining how this tool influences the economy (higher interest rates control inflation). Points would be awarded for other identifications and explanations, such as changing the amount of reserves a bank must keep on hand. Part (b) is worth 1 point—1/2 point for identifying a budgetary tool (taxation), and 1/2 point for explaining how this tool influences the economy (lower taxes may stimulate growth). Points would be awarded for identifying and explaining other budgetary tools, such as using government spending to stimulate the economy.

Part (c) is worth 1 points—1/2 point for identifying a way Congress influences the economy (by approving taxing and spending) and 1/2 point for the explanation (Congress can influence the budget by proposing its own plan with the assistance of the CBO). Points would be awarded for identifying other ways Congress influences the economy, such as Senate confirmation of members of the Federal Reserve Board.

Part (d) is worth 1 points—1/2 point for identifying a way the president influences the economy (by appointing members of the Federal Reserve Board), and 1/2 point for the explanation (members are appointed for long terms and share the president's monetary philosophy). Points would be awarded for identifying other ways the president can influence the economy, such as by proposing an annual budget.

QUESTION 2

Part (a): One trend is that members of the House of Representatives are reelected at high rates. Most years, the rate is reelection is around 90 percent, and it has never fallen below 80 percent. In 2008, the reelection rate was about 95 percent for representatives and 80 percent for senators. One reason for this trend is that most members of the House of Representatives do not represent an entire state but represent a district. They can do casework for constituents in their districts, and satisfied constituents will vote for their reelection.

Part (b): One trend shown is that the reelection rate for senators drops during periods of instability. For example, during the period from 1964 to 1968, the Vietnam War caused national discontent. The reelection rate for senators dropped. During the early 1970s in the period following Watergate, the reelection rate for senators also dropped. The reason for this is that senators are visible and represent an entire state. They are held accountable for the performance of the federal government.

Part (c): One trend shown is that members of the House of Representatives are elected at higher rates than senators are. This is because House members are elected every two years and are therefore constantly campaigning. Also, House members represent smaller constituencies than most senators do, and it is easier for them to stay in touch with their constituents. Furthermore, many representatives live in "safe districts" where their political party dominates (*American Government*, 14th ed., page 313).

Scoring

This essay is worth 6 points. Part (a) is worth 2 points—1 point for identifying a trend (incumbents in the House are elected at high rates), and 1 point for the explanation (casework encourages voters to reelect them). Points would be awarded for identifying other trends, such as a fairly stable reelection rate over time, and for other explanations, such as the use of franking privileges or bringing in pork barrel projects.

Part (b) is worth 2 points—1 point for identifying a trend (fewer incumbent senators are reelected during periods of instability), and 1 point for giving an explanation (senators represent larger areas that are harder to please). Points would be awarded for identifying other trends, such as relatively big differences in reelection rates from election to election, and for other explanations, such as the diversity of interests within a state.

Part (c) is worth 2 points—1 point for identifying a trend (more House incumbents are reelected), and 1 point for an explanation (House members are accountable to fewer people). Points would be awarded for identifying other trends, such are more volatility in the Senate, and for other explanations, such as the shorter term of office for the House.

QUESTION 3

Sample answer for part (A) Devolution is the process by which power has been returned from the national government to the states.

Sample answer for part (B) Judicial decisions - According the many commentators the Supreme Court rediscovered the Tenth Amendment in the 1990s. Through a series of decisions, including *United States v. Morrison*, and *United States v. Lopez*, the Court has signaled that it will be increasingly suspect of increases in national power at the expense of the states. In particular the Court is applying greater scrutiny when Congress uses the commerce clause as a justification for policy.

Grants - Over the last few decades the Congress has begun the process of combining categorical grants into block grants. Block grants allow state and local governments' greater flexibility. This flexibility increases the discretion of state and local governments (*American Government*, 14th ed., pages 70–72).

Scoring

This essay is worth 5 points. One point is earned for the correct definition of devolution in part A. Four points are earned in part B. One point each for the correct identifications of Judicial Decisions and Grants. One each is earned for correctly explaining how those identifications returned power to the states.

QUESTION 4

Sample answer Part (A) The First Amendment protects freedom of religion with two specific clauses, the Establishment Clause and the Free Exercise Clause. The Establishment Clause prohibits the creation of an officially sanctioned religion. The Free Exercise Clause prohibits undue governmental interference with religious practice.

Sample answer Part (B) The Court has applied these clauses to the states using the Fourteenth Amendment's Due Process Clause through a process known as selective incorporation. The overall thrust of these rulings is that government must remain neutral in the realm of religion.

Sample answer Part (C) The Court, in the case of *Engel v. Vitale*, prohibited teacher led, school prayer. It stated that this constituted a violation of Establishment Clause. It reasoned that utilizing a government employee, the teacher, to lead students amounted to a government endorsement of religion (*American Government*, 14th ed., pages 108–111).

Scoring

This essay is worth 5 points. Part A: One point each is earned for two correct identifications of the religion clauses in the First amendment. Part B: One point is earned for correctly describing the process of selective incorporation. Part C One point is earned for a correct explanation of the Court's reasoning. One is earned for correctly identifying the correct clause.

Calculating your score on the AP Exam

SECTION 1: MULTIPLE-CHOICE QUESTIONS

Total number answered correctly _____

SECTION II: FREE-RESPONSE QUESTIONS

Question 1 ____ × 3 equals _____

    Out of 5   do not round

Question 2 ____ × 2.5 equals _____

    Out of 6   do not round

Question 3 ___ × 3.0 equals _____

    Out of 5   do not round

Question 4 ___ × 3 equals _____

    Out of 5   do not round

TOTAL FOR SECTION II ___

COMPOSITE SCORE:

_____ + _____ = _____

Section I   Section II   Composite Score

    Student scores are weighted differently each year to determine the final AP score. The conversion chart below is according to the weighting on the 2009 exam:

COMPOSITE SCORE RANGE	AP GRADE
93–120	5
82–92	4
66–81	3
48–65	2
0–47	1

Practice Test 2

UNITED STATES GOVERNMENT AND POLITICS

Section I

Time—45 minutes 60 Questions
Directions The questions or incomplete statements below are each followed by five suggested answers. Select the best answer.

Multiple-Choice Questions

1. How can the executive branch check the judicial branch?

   (A) by approving the nomination of federal judges

   (B) by nominating federal judges, subject to senate approval

   (C) by issuing an executive order overturning a court's decision

   (D) by firing a federal judge for cause

   (E) by reducing the number of federal courts

2. A conservative is likely to support all of the following EXCEPT

   (A) increased military spending

   (B) tax cuts

   (C) prayer in schools

   (D) affirmative action

   (E) restrictions on abortion

3. Which statement best describes the importance of the vice president?

   (A) He checks on the health of the president daily and attends the funerals of Third World dictators.

   (B) He has an important role as the president of the Senate.

   (C) His importance depends on his relationship with the president and the duties the president asks him to assume.

   (D) He is a lightning rod for criticism that would be otherwise directed at the president.

   (E) He does not have an important role; his function is largely ceremonial.

4. Which of the following candidates would most likely receive the most money from a PAC?

   (A) an incumbent who has consistently supported the PAC's positions

   (B) a challenger whose viewpoints are unknown

   (C) a challenger whose viewpoints are opposed to the PAC's

   (D) an incumbent who has not voted consistently to support the PAC's positions in the past

   (E) any candidate who is likely to win

5. Which of the following best describes supply-side economics?

   (A) the theory that tax cuts should be offset by reductions in military spending

   (B) the belief that private investment should be replaced with investment in government bonds

   (C) the belief that the government should take an active role in stimulating demand

   (D) the belief that the largest tax cuts should go to the poorest Americans

   (E) the belief that tax cuts and fewer regulations will stimulate the economy

6. Why was the election of 2000 significant?

   (A) because there was no winner in the electoral college, and the election was decided by a majority vote in the House of Representatives

   (B) because there was no winner in the electoral college, and the election was decided by one vote per state in the House of Representatives

   (C) because for the first time in more than a century, the winner in the electoral college lost the popular vote

   (D) because a third party, the Green party, won electoral college votes in three states

   (E) because the Supreme Court overturned the electoral college's decision

7. What is the best rationale for allowing Supreme Court justices to serve for life terms?

(A) It takes time for a justice to gain experience in decision making, so they serve for life to make sure the judiciary is experienced.

(B) They protect the rights of the minority, and the protection of life tenure allows them to make legally correct, but unpopular, decisions.

(C) Congress should not be able to remove them, because the average member of Congress does not have a legal background.

(D) Their salaries are so low that it is difficult to attract good candidates; job security makes their positions more attractive.

(E) They serve for life terms so that they may develop a body of consistent and understandable law over time.

8. Which of the following falls under the original jurisdiction of the Supreme Court?

(A) cases involving a state law that is alleged to violate the United States Constitution

(B) cases involving a federal law that is alleged to violate the United States Constitution

(C) controversies between two or more states

(D) cases where the amount in controversy exceeds $50,000

(E) conflicts between the president and Congress

9. The president can influence legislation in all of the following ways EXCEPT

(A) by having his staff write a legislative program that is then introduced by a member of his party in Congress

(B) by asking the public to call Congress and express support for his legislative agenda

(C) by threatening to veto a bill when there is not enough likely support in Congress to override the veto

(D) by personally contacting members of Congress and asking for their support

(E) by rewriting a portion of a bill and then signing the amended bill into law

10. What do the decisions of the Court led by Chief Justice Earl Warren illustrate about the relationship between the Court and the presidency?

(A) Supreme Court justices closely follow the views of the presidents who appointed them, and try to use those views in making decisions.

(B) Supreme Court justices stay in close contact with the presidents who nominate them, and they often become close friends.

(C) Supreme Court justices are independent. You can never predict with certainty what they will do once in office.

(D) Supreme Court justices are more likely to consider the opinions of the public if the president supports those beliefs.

(E) Supreme Court justices are hesitant to lose the political support of the party that nominated them.

11. What has been the impact of the War Powers Act on American military actions?

(A) Presidents have carefully followed the law and have asked Congress for permission before committing troops.

(B) Presidents have committed troops and then asked for Congress to continue the troop commitments beyond sixty days.

(C) Presidents have generally ignored the law because they believe it violates their powers as commander-in-chief.

(D) Congress has used the law to call troops home once they have been committed for more than sixty days.

(E) None. The Supreme Court ruled the War Powers Act unconstitutional under the political questions doctrine.

12. The Civil Rights Act of 1964 did all of the following EXCEPT

(A) barred race discrimination in public accommodations

(B) banned discrimination in housing

(C) outlawed race discrimination in hiring and firing

(D) barred race discrimination in movie theaters, stadiums, and arenas

(E) authorized the attorney general to bring suit to enforce school desegregation

13. What is the incorporation doctrine, first established in *Gitlow v. New York?*

    (A) The Bill of Rights protects individuals from the federal government but not from state government.

    (B) The Fourteenth Amendment protects individuals from state violations of all of the rights in the Bill of Rights.

    (C) The Fourteenth Amendment protects individuals from state violations of all of the rights in the Bill of Rights plus other fundamental rights.

    (D) The First Amendment protects individuals from state violations of free speech rights.

    (E) The Fourteenth Amendment protects individuals from state violations of fundamental personal rights.

14. What case established that the Necessary and Proper Clause could be used to extend the national government's power beyond its expressed authority?

    (A) *McCulloch v. Maryland*

    (B) *Marbury v. Madison*

    (C) *Gitlow v. New York*

    (D) *Gibbons v. Ogden*

    (E) *Barron v. Baltimore*

15. Which of the following most accurately describes the origins of political attitudes (political socialization)?

    (A) The media has the biggest influence on the political attitudes of people ages eighteen to twenty-one.

    (B) Teenagers aged eighteen to twenty-one tend to vote opposite of their parents because they want to rebel against their parents.

    (C) The family usually plays the largest role in political socialization, and people tend to vote the same way as their parents vote.

    (D) Schools play a large role in socialization, and high school students tend to follow the ideology of their social studies teachers.

    (E) There are so many influences on political socialization that no single factor determines ideology.

16. Which statement describes the "swing voter," who often decides elections?

    (A) prospective

    (B) no issue content

    (C) group benefits

    (D) retrospective

    (E) ideological

17. Which of the following accurately describes the outcome of impeachment in United States history?

    (A) President Nixon was impeached, but he resigned before he was removed from office.

    (B) Nixon and Clinton are the only presidents who have faced impeachment.

    (C) Articles of impeachment were approved against President Clinton, but he was not impeached.

    (D) Bill Clinton and Andrew Johnson were impeached but not convicted or removed from office.

    (E) Andrew Johnson is the only president to have been impeached and removed from office.

18. Iron triangles have weakened, and some have been replaced by groups of people in interest groups, on congressional staffs, in universities, from the media, and in other interested organizations who debate policies. These are known as

    (A) policy entrepreneurs

    (B) policy allies

    (C) issue networks

    (D) PACs

    (E) social movements

19. The Supreme Court is most likely to issue a writ of certiorari in which of the following cases?

    (A) a conflict between two circuits that have issued opposite rulings about the constitutionality of a federal law

    (B) a conflict between the president and Congress over the War Powers Act

    (C) a criminal case from a state court in which the defendant proclaims his innocence

    (D) a conflict between a federal agency and a state government

    (E) a conflict over the meaning of an unclear regulation issued by an administrative agency

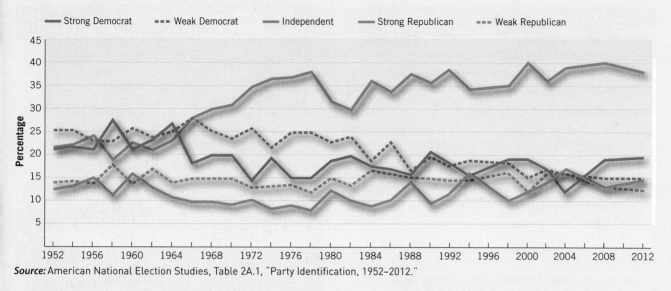

FIGURE 9.1 **Decline in Party Identification, 1952–2012**

Legend: —— Strong Democrat   ---- Weak Democrat   —— Independent   —— Strong Republican   ---- Weak Republican

Source: American National Election Studies, Table 2A.1, "Party Identification, 1952–2012."

20. The above graph supports which of the following conclusions?

   (A) The Republican Party is consistently more popular than the Democratic Party.

   (B) There are consistently more weak Republicans than strong Democrats.

   (C) As of 2008, most Americans were dissatisfied with both major political parties.

   (D) Support for Democrats increases during hard economic times.

   (E) The percentage of independent voters has increased from 1952 to 2012.

21. There are 538 total votes in the electoral college. The Democrat receives 265, the Republican receives 255, and an Independent candidate receives 18. How will the election be decided?

   (A) The Democrat will win because he received the most electoral college votes.

   (B) The Democrat will win because no candidate received the majority of the electoral votes and the Democrat won the popular vote.

   (C) There will be a runoff election between the Democrat and the Republican.

   (D) The House of Representatives will decide, with each representative casting one vote.

   (E) The House of Representatives will decide, with each state casting one vote.

22. Which statement best describes the media's coverage of presidential campaigns?

   (A) The media focus primarily on the issues and platforms.

   (B) The media focus primarily on the differences between the candidates.

   (C) The media focus primarily on the horse-race aspects of the campaign.

   (D) Sensational or unusual aspects of the campaigns are the focus of most reports.

   (E) Each candidate is given significant free media time to address the issues.

23. What has been the impact of the Twenty-sixth Amendment?

   (A) People between eighteen and twenty-one years of age are now an important demographic group that significantly influences national policy.

   (B) Voters between eighteen and twenty-one years of age are leading a campaign to lower the drinking age to eighteen.

   (C) Young voters are important at election time, and as a result of their efforts, the move to reinstate the military draft was defeated.

   (D) Voters between eighteen and twenty-one years of age have the lowest turnout rate of any age category.

   (E) More people in this age group are running for office.

24. Which of the following constitutional provisions has been used to strengthen state powers?

   (A) Tenth Amendment

   (B) Full Faith and Credit Clause

   (C) Necessary and Proper Clause

   (D) Privilege and Immunities Clause

   (E) Commerce Clause

TABLE 8.4   Political Participation Here and Abroad

Percent of People Who ...	USA	Rank among 20 Democracies	Outranked by ...
Tried to persuade others to vote for a candidate	44%	2nd	Canada
Supported party by attending meeting, putting up poster	30%	2nd	Canada
Donated money to political group	21%	1st	None
Were contacted by party or candidate	47%	3rd	Canada, Ireland

Source: Professor Martin Wattenberg, University of California, Irvine, using data from the *Comparative Study of Electoral Systems.*

25. All of the following were problems under the Articles of Confederation EXCEPT

   (A) Shays's Rebellion
   (B) state constitutions did not contain bills of rights
   (C) the national government was in debt
   (D) inflation
   (E) states fought over western lands

26. Which of the following is an advantage of a federal system?

   (A) Local governments are more likely to be dominated by factions.
   (B) It is easy to determine which level of government is responsible for a particular problem.
   (C) States can experiment with programs, and the successful ones can be adopted on the national level.
   (D) A federal system is less expensive than a unitary system because there are fewer national government entities.
   (E) States have traditionally protected the rights of minority groups more than the national government has.

27. Table 8.4 above supports which of the following statements?

   (A) Political participation is higher in Canada than it is in the United States.
   (B) Americans give more money to political campaigns than citizens of any other country.
   (C) More than half of all Americans donate money to campaigns.
   (D) Trying to persuade others is the least frequent form of participation for Americans.
   (E) Less than half of all Americans were contacted by a candidate or a party.

JP Laffront/Sygma/Corbis

28. The above picture best illustrates which of the following?

   (A) members of an interest group protesting to put pressure on Congress
   (B) how the rapidly growing aging population will strain Social Security and Medicare
   (C) the increased use of violent protest
   (D) the power of PACs in influencing legislation to provide prescription drug benefits
   (E) the growing social movement in support of health care reform.

29. How do political parties choose their presidential nominee?

   (A) by a majority vote in the primaries
   (B) by a majority vote in the caucuses
   (C) through a majority vote of delegates at the national convention
   (D) through a vote of party leaders at the national convention
   (E) through a primary runoff election between the top two candidates

30. Which statement best describes how presidential power has changed over time since ratification of the Constitution?

(A) Presidential power over foreign affairs has increased, but power over the bureaucracy has decreased over time.

(B) Presidential power over foreign affairs has decreased because the War Powers Act requires presidents to consult with Congress.

(C) Presidential power over legislation has decreased because of negative press coverage of presidential proposals.

(D) Presidential power over foreign affairs has increased, along with power over the bureaucracy.

(E) Presidential power has not changed significantly since the Constitution was ratified.

31. All of the following are ways that Congress oversees the bureaucracy EXCEPT

(A) it can fire agency heads

(B) the Senate confirms the appointment of cabinet heads

(C) Congress can submit legislation to the president that cuts an agency's budget

(D) congressional committees can hold oversight hearings

(E) Congress can write legislation to clarify agency regulations and procedures

32. All of the following features of elections in the United States favor a two-party system EXCEPT

(A) winner-take-all in the electoral college

(B) single-member districts

(C) a plurality vote determines the winner

(D) one member of Congress is elected from each district

(E) proportional representation

33. The House of Representatives and Senate pass different versions of a bill. What happens next?

(A) The bill is sent to a conference committee, then back to both houses for final approval, and then to the president.

(B) The bill is sent to a conference committee, then back to its original committees for approval, and then to the president.

(C) The bill is sent to a conference committee, and if the changes are not significant, it is sent directly to the president.

(D) Both versions of the bill are sent to the president, who signs the version that he prefers.

(E) The bill is sent to the Speaker of the House and the president pro tempore of the Senate, who agree on common language and then send the bill to the president for signature.

34. Which of the following is the best example of constituent casework?

(A) A senator places an earmark in a bill.

(B) A congressional staff member responds directly to a resident of his district, solving a problem.

(C) A representative returns to his district to attend a town hall meeting.

(D) A senator meets with a lobbyist to discuss an environmental bill.

(E) A law clerk for the Supreme Court writes a draft of an opinion.

35. The Food and Drug Administration decides whether new drugs should be put on the market. Which of the following presents the potential for undue influence?

(A) Pharmaceutical companies are asked to write the new legislation, subject to agency approval.

(B) Pharmaceutical PACs contribute to the campaigns of members of Congress who support their industry with favorable legislation.

(C) If a new drug is approved, leaders within the FDA might be offered lucrative positions with a pharmaceutical company.

(D) An issue network may form to advocate for the availability of prescription drugs from Canada.

(E) The FDA may ask for more funding from Congress to keep up with its increased workload.

36. Which of the following represent attempts by Congress to regain power in comparison to the president?

I. the Budget Reform Act (Impoundment and Control Act) of 1974

II. the Patriot Act

III. creation of the Office of Independent Counsel

IV. the War Powers Act

(A) I and II

(B) I, III, and III

(C) II and IV

(D) II, III, and IV

(E) I, III, and IV

TABLE 10.3 Changes in State Representation in the House of Representatives

States	Number of Seats After 1990 Census	After 2000 Census	After 2010 Census	Change
Gained/Maintained Seats				
Arizona	6	8	9	+3
California	52	53	53	+1
Florida	23	25	27	+4
Georgia	11	13	14	+3
North Carolina	12	13	13	+1
Texas	30	32	36	+6
Lost Seats				
Illinois	20	19	18	−2
Michigan	16	15	14	−2
New York	31	29	27	−4
Ohio	19	18	16	−3
Pennsylvania	21	19	18	−3

Source: U.S. Bureau of the Census

37. Which of the following statements best describes the term "lame duck" when referring to the president?

(A) Presidents are expected to work, even when they are sick or injured.

(B) After dealing with Congress, presidents often feel battered.

(C) A politician's power may diminish when he or she is about to leave office.

(D) Presidents are expected to juggle many issues at once.

(E) Presidents are often an easy target for the media.

38. Sometimes members of Congress form groups based upon their characteristics or interests. Which term best describes these groups?

(A) interest groups

(B) committees

(C) PACs

(D) caucuses

(E) issue networks

39. The table above best supports which of the following statements?

(A) Most states that lost representatives after the 1990 census regained some of those seats in the 2010 census.

(B) The states that are gaining in population are the "sunbelt" states in the South and West.

(C) The states that are losing representatives do not have big cities.

(D) The states that are gaining in populations all have coastlines.

(E) There is no geographical pattern to explain why some states are growing in population and other states are decreasing.

40. If voting patterns among African Americans and non-Cuban Hispanics continue, what is the likely implication of having a minority-majority?

(A) More Republicans will be elected.

(B) More Independents will be elected.

(C) Voter turnout will decrease.

(D) More Democrats will be elected.

(E) There are so many minorities that having a minority-majority is unlikely to affect elections.

41. Which of the following is way that the Judiciary can check the power of the executive?

(A) Provide preclearance of administrative orders before they go into effect

(B) Approve the appointment of the Attorney General

(C) Issue binding advisory opinions to the president when requested to do so

(D) Review presidential nominations to the position of United States Attorneys

(E) Declare acts of the president unconstitutional

42. What is the function of primary election?

    (A) determine the initial level of support for a candidate

    (B) determine who has the right to vote

    (C) determine who wins the office

    (D) select a party's nominees for office

    (E) select a candidate's running mate.

43. What type of committee will typically determine the details of legislation?

    (A) Select Committee

    (B) Standing Committee

    (C) Rules Committee

    (D) Legal Committee

    (E) Special Committee

44. Which of the following is a power that Senate has the House does not have?

    (A) introduce money bills

    (B) introduce commerce bills

    (C) confirm ambassadors

    (D) declare war

    (E) impeachment

45. All of the following have been used to expand Civil Rights and Civil Liberties EXCEPT:

    (A) Due Process Clause

    (B) Equal Protection Clause

    (C) Commerce Clause

    (D) Exceptions Clause

    (E) Supremacy Clause

46. Which of the following is the constitutional basis for the Courts decision in *Tinker v. Des Moines School Iowa*?

    (A) Free Speech

    (B) Equal Protection

    (C) Full Faith and Credit

    (D) Double Jeopardy

    (E) Self-Incrimination

47. Why is the rules committee the most powerful committee in the House of Representatives?

    (A) Writes the rules under which the judiciary operates

    (B) Determines the rules and regulations for interstate commerce

    (C) Assigns bills to committees

    (D) Selects the Speaker of the House

    (E) Sets the conditions for debate and amendments

48. What is the significance of *Gibbons v. Ogden*?

    (A) It was the first time that the Court ruled a law unconstitutional.

    (B) It restricted the power of Congress to regulate interstate commerce

    (C) It applied the exclusionary rule to the states.

    (D) It established a loose interpretation of the Elastic Clause

    (E) It established that the Constitution gave the national government the exclusive right to regulate interstate commerce

49. Which of the following is used to end a filibuster?

    (A) cloture

    (B) a majority vote of the Senate

    (C) a ruling issued by the Majority Leader

    (D) ex post facto

    (E) executive order

50. Which of the following correctly describes the impeachment process?

    (A) accusation in the House of Representatives and trial in the Senate

    (B) accusation by a grand jury and trial in the Senate

    (C) accusation in the House of Representative and trial by the Chief Justice

    (D) accusation by the Senate and trail in the House of Representative

    (E) accusation by the Speaker and trial by the Chief Justice

51. All of the following have been used to expand the power of the national government EXCEPT

    (A) Commerce Clause

    (B) Elastic clause

    (C) Due Process Clause

    (D) Tenth Amendment

    (E) power to tax and spend

52. Which of the following sets of political actors would be considered agenda setters?

    (A) president and the Supreme Court

    (B) Supreme Court and House majority whip

    (C) president and the media

    (D) House majority whip and vice president

    (E) media and Supreme Court

53. What has been the impact of the growth of broadcast media on presidential power?
   (A) generally increased
   (B) mostly increased during economic prosperity only
   (C) no effect
   (D) mostly decreased during short wars
   (E) generally decreased

54. What is the significance of *Mapp v. Ohio*?
   (A) required law enforcement officials to inform suspects of their constitutional rights
   (B) applied the exclusionary rule to the states
   (C) prohibited double jeopardy
   (D) expanded freedom of expression
   (E) prohibited organized, teacher-led prayer in schools

55. Which of the following is an example of discretionary spending?
   (A) military
   (B) interest on the national debt
   (C) Social Security
   (D) Medicare
   (E) Medicaid

56. Who is generally responsible for drawing Congressional district boundaries?
   (A) the United State House of Representatives
   (B) the president
   (C) state legislatures
   (D) the Census Bureau
   (E) the Supreme Court

57. What is critical or realigning election?
   (A) an election where the incumbent president loses
   (B) an election during wartime
   (C) an election where the constituent groups for each party change
   (D) an election where the outcome is determined by the Supreme Court
   (E) an election that ends divided government.

58. All of the following contribute to incumbency advantage EXCEPT
   (A) pork barrel legislation
   (B) casework
   (C) paid staff
   (D) name recognition
   (E) automatic renomination

59. Which of the following requires that public acts, records, and judicial proceedings of one state be valid in other states?
   (A) due process
   (B) reciprocity
   (C) Full Faith and Credit Clause
   (D) Equal Protection Clause
   (E) Establishment Clause

60. What is the function of the Ninth Amendment?
   (A) expand the powers of the state
   (B) restrict civil liberties
   (C) expand the powers of the executive branch
   (D) protect rights not listed in the Bill of Rights
   (E) protect the right to trial by jury

STOP
END OF SECTION I

IF YOU FINISH BEFORE TIME IS CALLED, YOU MAY CHECK YOUR WORK ON THIS SECTION. DO NOT GO ON TO SECTION II UNTIL YOU ARE TOLD TO DO SO.

UNITED STATES GOVERNMENT AND POLITICS
Section II

Time—100 minutes

Directions You have 100 minutes to answer all four of the following questions. Unless the directions indicate otherwise, respond to all parts of each question. It is recommended that you take a few minutes to plan and outline each answer. Spend approximately 25 minutes on each question. Support your essay with specific examples where appropriate. Be sure to number each of your answers.

1. Since 1960, there have been significant changes in the way the media covers government and politics.
   a. Explain one way in which the media's coverage of United States government and politics has changed since 1960, giving a specific example.

FIGURE 9.2 **Split-Ticket Voting for President/House, 1952–2008**

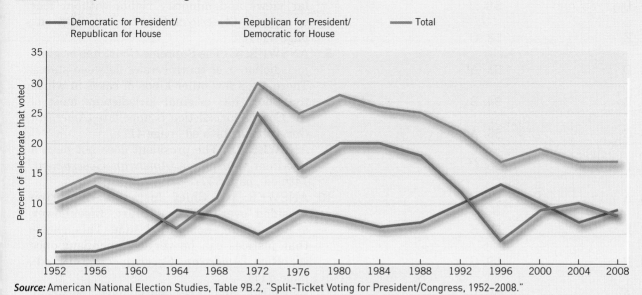

Source: American National Election Studies, Table 9B.2, "Split-Ticket Voting for President/Congress, 1952–2008."

b. Explain another way in which the media's coverage of United States government and politics has changed since 1960, giving a specific example.

2. Using the information from Figure 9.2 and your knowledge of United States government and politics, complete the following tasks:
   a. Define split-ticket voting.
   b. Identify and explain one trend in split-ticket voting.
   c. Identify and explain one reason for split-ticket voting.

3. Identify the three parts of Iron Triangle. For each part explain a connection to another part.

4. Congress is the legislative branch of the national government. However, its powers extend beyond the mere passage of legislation.
   (A) Define Legislative oversight.
   (B) Identify and explain 2 tools of legislative oversight.

END OF EXAMINATION

Answer Key for Multiple-Choice Questions

1. B	3. C
2. D	4. A

5. E	22. C
6. C	23. D
7. B	24. A
8. C	25. B
9. E	26. C
10. C	27. E
11. C	28. A
12. B	29. C
13. E	30. D
14. A	31. A
15. C	32. E
16. D	33. A
17. D	34. B
18. C	35. C
19. A	36. E
20. E	37. C
21. E	38. D

39. B	50. A
40. D	51. D
41. E	52. C
42. D	53. A
43. B	54. B
44. C	55. A
45. D	56. C
46. A	57. C
47. E	58. E
48. B	59. C
49. A	60. D

Answers to Multiple-Choice Questions

1. ANSWER: (B) The executive has a check on the judiciary by nominating federal judges, subject to Senate confirmation (*American Government*, 14th ed., page 32).

2. ANSWER: (D) Conservatives tend to support tax cuts, increased military spending, and prayer in schools. They oppose abortion and affirmative action (*American Government*, 14th ed., pages 164–165).

3. ANSWER: (C) Vice presidents have varied in their duties and importance, depending on their relationship with the president and the duties the president wants them to assume (*American Government*, 14th ed., page 372).

4. ANSWER: (A) Most PAC money goes to incumbents because they are more likely to win. Money goes to candidates who support a PAC's position (*American Government*, 14th ed., pages 265–269).

5. ANSWER: (E) Supply-side economists believe that lowering taxes and reducing government regulations will stimulate economic growth (*American Government*, 14th ed., pages 475–476).

6. ANSWER: (C) In the 2000 presidential election, for the first time since 1888, the winner of the popular vote lost the election because of the electoral college vote (*American Government*, 14th ed., pages 350–351).

7. ANSWER: (B) Supreme Court justices serve for life to enable them to protect unpopular views and minority rights without fear of reprisal (*American Government*, 14th ed., page 417).

8. ANSWER: (C) The Supreme Court has original jurisdiction over controversies between states. There are a few other kinds of cases in which the Court has original jurisdiction; most of the Court's jurisdiction is appellate (*American Government*, 14th ed., page 412).

9. ANSWER: (E) The president does not have a line-item veto power (*American Government*, 14th ed., page 357).

10. ANSWER: (C) Chief Justice Earl Warren presided over a liberal court. Eisenhower, a Republican, nominated him. This shows that justices can be very independent once in office (*American Government*, 14th ed., page 417).

11. ANSWER: (C) Presidents have generally ignored the War Powers Act and committed troops for more than sixty days without congressional approval (*American Government*, 14th ed., page 494).

12. ANSWER: (B) The Civil Rights Act of 1964 banned discrimination in public places and employment. It authorized the attorney general to bring suits to desegregate schools. A similar law passed in 1968 banned racial discrimination in housing (*American Government*, 14th ed., page 124).

13. ANSWER: (E) Under the incorporation doctrine, the Fourteenth Amendment protects individuals from state violations of "fundamental personal rights" (*American Government*, 14th ed., pages 100–102).

14. ANSWER: (A) In *McCulloch v. Maryland*, the Supreme Court held that the necessary and proper clause enabled the federal government to establish a bank because such a power was implied in the power to regulate the currency (*American Government*, 14th ed., pages 55–56).

15. ANSWER: (C) The family plays the largest role in political socialization (*American Government*, 14th ed., pages 156–157).

16. ANSWER: (D) Retrospective voters vote based upon how things have gone in the recent past (*American Government*, 14th ed., pages 243–244).

17. ANSWER: (D) Presidents Johnson and Clinton were impeached. Impeachment is a process in which a president is charged by the House and tried by the Senate. Neither president was

convicted or removed (*American Government*, 14th ed., pages 373–374).

18. ANSWER: (C) Issue networks are groups of people from interest groups, congressional staffs, universities, and the media who debate specific issues, like health care (*American Government*, 14th ed., page 397).

19. ANSWER: (A) The Supreme Court is most likely to take a case when two different circuit courts make opposite rulings over the constitutionality of a federal law. The Court would take the case to clarify the meaning of the Constitution (*American Government*, 14th ed., page 421).

20. ANSWER: (E) The number of independent voters has risen from slightly over 20 percent in 1952 to nearly 40 percent in 2012 (*American Government*, 14th ed., page 190).

21. ANSWER: (E) If no candidate receives a majority vote (270 votes) in the electoral college, the House of Representative decides, with each state casting one vote (*American Government*, 14th ed., pages 350–351).

22. ANSWER: (C) The media focuses primarily on the horse race—who is winning in the polls and by how much (*American Government*, 14th ed., page 287).

23. ANSWER: (D) Voters ages eighteen to twenty-one have the lowest turnout of any age group (*American Government*, 14th ed., page 175).

24. ANSWER: (A) The Tenth Amendment reserves for the states and the people those powers that are not expressly given to the national government or prohibited to the states (*American Government*, 14th ed., page 34).

25. ANSWER: (B) Under the Articles of Confederation, there was inflation, the nation was in debt, and states fought over western lands. Shays's Rebellion illustrated the weaknesses of the national government. Most state constitutions contained bills of rights (*American Government*, 14th ed., pages 27–28).

26. ANSWER: (C) Under federalism, states can become laboratories for experimental programs and policies (*American Government*, 14th ed., page 72).

27. ANSWER: (E) Only 47 percent of Americans were contacted by a candidate or campaign. While Canadians are politically active, the graph does not measure voting—an important form of political participation. America leads the world in the percentage of citizens who donate to campaigns, but the chart does not indicate how much is donated (*American Government*, 14th ed., page 183).

28. ANSWER: (A) Farmers used to have more influence in Congress. Today they often use mass protests to call attention to their demands (*American Government*, 14th ed., page 262).

29. ANSWER: (C) Delegates are pledged to candidates during state primaries and caucuses. The candidate is formally selected by a vote of the delegates at the national convention (*American Government*, 14th ed., page 201).

30. ANSWER: (D) Presidential power over foreign affairs has increased along with military technology and sophisticated weaponry. In addition, the bureaucracy has increased to fifteen cabinet departments from the three originally established (*American Government*, 14th ed., page 345, 381).

31. ANSWER: (A) Congress can rewrite agency regulations, propose cuts in their budgets, and hold oversight hearings. The Senate confirms the appointments of cabinet secretaries (*American Government*, 14th ed., pages 397–400).

32. ANSWER: (E) The winner-take-all, single-member district, and plurality vote favor a two-party system. In proportional systems used in some European countries and elsewhere, smaller parties benefit by being allocated a proportional amount of seats in the legislature (*American Government*, 14th ed., page 206).

33. ANSWER: (A) When the House and Senate pass different versions of a bill, it is sent to a conference committee to work out the language. Both houses must approve it before the bill is sent to the president (*American Government*, 14th ed., page 322).

34. ANSWER: (B) Casework is when a member of Congress or her staff works to help a constituent solve a particular problem (*American Government*, 14th ed., page 324).

35. ANSWER: (C) Private industry often recruits people from the agencies that once regulated them. This enables them to lobby the agency more effectively (*American Government*, 14th ed., page 269).

36. ANSWER: (E) The War Powers Act, Office of Independent Counsel, and Budget Control Act are all attempts by Congress to reassert power over the presidency (*American Government*, 14th ed., page 359, 493–494).

37. ANSWER: (C) Presidents who have been term limited or voted out of office are called "lame

ducks." They often have difficulty in getting their policies passed (*American Government*, 14th ed., pages 354–6).

38. ANSWER: (D) A congressional caucus is a group formed by members of Congress who share characteristics (for example, women's caucuses) or interests (for example, mushrooms) ((*American Government*, 14th ed., pages 321–322).

39. ANSWER: (B) States that gained in population and representation between 1990 and 2010 are in the sunbelt in the South and West (*American Government*, 14th ed., pages 225–226).

40. ANSWER: (D) African Americans and non-Cuban Hispanics are the largest ethnic groups. They tend to vote for the Democratic Party. The most likely outcome of having a minority-majority is that more Democrats will be elected (*American Government*, 14th ed., pages 161–162).

41. ANSWER: (E) Actions of the executive branch, such as executive orders and administrative regulations are subject to judicial review as are laws issued by Congress (*American Government*, 14th ed., pages 409–410).

42. ANSWER: (D) Primary elections are contests inside of a party to determine who will advance to the general election (*American Government*, 14th ed., pages 230–231).

43. ANSWER: (B) Details of legislation are worked out in standing committees. Standing committees are the first stop for a bill in congress (*American Government*, 14th ed., pages 322–324).

44. ANSWER: (C) The Senate has the sole power to confirm ambassadors and other officials. The other powers listed are either shared with the House or possessed only by the House. (*American Government*, 14th ed., page 328).

45. ANSWER: (D) The exceptions (Article III, Section 2) clause gives Congress the ability to restrict the jurisdiction of the Judiciary (*American Government*, 14th ed., page 414).

46. ANSWER: (A) *Tinker* deal with high school student wearing black armbands to school to protest the Vietnam War. The held that the students had right symbolic speech of the First Amendment (*American Government*, 14th ed., page 107).

47. ANSWER: (E) The Rules Committee writes a rule for each bill that determines how long the bill will be debated and if amendments are allowed. Further, the Rules Committee controls the flow of legislation from the committees to the full House (*American Government*, 14th ed., page 327).

48. ANSWER: (B) It was the first significant case that dealt with interstate commerce. It established that the national government has the exclusive right to regulate interstate commerce. This contributes to the growth of national power. (*American Government*, 14th ed., page 59).

49. ANSWER: (A) A filibuster is ended when cloture is invoked. Cloture requires three fifths to pass. (*American Government*, 14th ed., page 328).

50. ANSWER: (A) Articles of impeachment are passed by the House of Representatives. This is an accusation of official misconduct. At this point in time the persona has been impeached. A trial is then held in the Senate. Two thirds of the Senate is required to convict on impeachment (*American Government*, 14th ed., pages 373–374).

51. ANSWER: (D) The Tenth Amendment protects the reserved powers of the states. (*American Government*, 14th ed., page 34).

52. ANSWER: (C) Agenda setting is the process by which the issues are selected and elevated to be discussed by the public. In American political two of the main agenda setters are the media and the president. (*American Government*, 14th ed., pages 10–13).

53. ANSWER: (A) The media has generally increased the power and influence of the president. This is because the broadcast media allows the president to speak directly to the American people (*American Government*, 14th ed., page 281).

54. ANSWER: (B) *Mapp* applied the exclusionary rule to the states. The exclusionary rule prohibits the use of illegally obtained evidence (*American Government*, 14th ed., pages 112–113).

55. ANSWER: (A) Discretionary spending that requires yearly authorization from Congress is the Military (*American Government*, 14th ed., page 481).

56. ANSWER: (C) In most states the state legislature is responsible for the drawing of congressional district boundaries. (*American Government*, 14th ed., pages 224–225).

57. ANSWER: (C) A critical election is an election where traditions patterns of alignment change. During this time groups that had

previously voted for one party begin to vote for the other. (*American Government*, 14th ed., page 249).

58. ANSWER: (E) Neither political party provides to automatic renomination of its candidates. (*American Government*, 14th ed., pages 312–313).

59. ANSWER: (C) All of these deal with relations between states. Full Faith and Credit deals specifically with publics acts, records, and judicial proceedings (*American Government*, 14th ed., page 56).

60. ANSWER: (D) The Ninth Amendment protects "non-enumerated rights" That is rights that are not listed in the text of the Bill of Rights. Under the judicial interpretation, there is a constitutionally protected right to privacy under the penumbra of the Ninth Amendment (*American Government*, 14th ed., page 38).

Answers to Free-Response Questions

QUESTION 1

Part (a): One change in the way the media report issues is that press coverage of the government is more adversarial. Following the Vietnam War and revelations that the government was not honest with the press about the war's progress, the relationship between the media and the government became more mistrustful. Because of this mistrust, and because scandalous stories sell papers, reporters now investigate potential government wrongdoing and report on it. The best example of this is the Watergate scandal. Two reporters from the *Washington Post* investigated a burglary at Democratic party headquarters and discovered that the Nixon administration tried to cover up the break-in.

Part (b): Another change in the media's coverage of government and politics is increased sensationalism. The major news networks are now competing with cable stations for viewers. Furthermore, fewer people are watching news programs. This gives networks a big financial incentive to rely on sensationalized news stories involving violence, sex, and intrigue. An example of this is the scandal involving President Clinton and his relationship with a White House intern, Monica Lewinsky (*American Government*, 14th ed., pages 279–282).

Scoring

This essay is worth 6 points—1 point is awarded for identifying each change in the media's coverage of government and politics (a more adversarial relationship between the media and the government, and increased sensationalism), 1 point for explaining each change (reporters investigate the government looking for wrongdoing, and networks have an incentive to produce scandalous stories), and 1 point for each specific example (Watergate and the Lewinsky scandal). Points would be awarded for identifying other changes, such as the increasing use of sound bites; for identifying other changes, such as the increasing use of sound bites; and for citing other examples, such as the Whitewater scandal.

QUESTION 2

Part (a): Split-ticket voting occurs when a person votes for a president from one political party and votes for a member of either house of Congress from the opposing political party. The result of split-ticket voting is divided government.

Part (b): One trend in split-ticket voting is that it decreased in frequency from 1972, when 30 percent of voters split their tickets, until 2004, when about 17 percent of voters did so. An explanation for the decrease in split-ticket voting over time is that America's two party system remains strong. In most elections, voters who are registered to a party are loyal and vote along party lines.

Part (c): One explanation for ticket splitting is that more people consider themselves to be independent. Because these voters do not have an allegiance to a party, they are more likely to vote based upon the individual candidates, without regard to party affiliation. The result is more ticket splitting (*American Government*, 14th ed., page 197).

Scoring

This essay is worth 5 points.

Part (a) is worth 1 point for defining ticket splitting (voting for a president of one party and a member of Congress from a different party).

Part (b) is worth 2 points—1 point for identifying a trend (decrease in ticket splitting since 1972) and 1 point for an explanation (America still has a strong two-party system). Points would be awarded for identifying other trends, such as an increase in ticket splitting from 1952 to 1972.

Part (c) is worth 2 points—1 point for identifying a reason for ticket splitting (more independent voters) and 1 point for an explanation (independent voters have no party allegiance and vote for the candidate instead of the party). Points would be awarded for other reasons for ticket splitting, such as southern Democrats who voted for Reagan while voting for Democratic members of Congress.

QUESTION 3

The three parts of the Iron Triangle are Special Interest Groups, Congressional Committees and Bureaucratic Agencies

There are numerous connections between the three parts. Examples are:

Special Interest Groups are connected to congressional Committees because they provide campaign funding, through PACs, to committee members. The will also provide expert information to the committee. Special Interest Groups are also connected to bureaucratic agencies because they will also expert information. Further they will provide political support for the agency when dealing with Congress.

Congressional Committees are connected to bureaucratic agencies in that they provide funding and political support to the agency. Congressional committees are also connected to special interest groups because they will write law in the manner that will be beneficial to the special interest group.

Bureaucratic Agencies are connected to them, along with special interest groups, and provide information to the committee. Bureaucratic Agencies are also connected to Special Interest Groups because they make administrative regulations that benefit the special interest group. Further they will enforce laws in a manner that will benefit the special interest group (*American Government*, 14th ed., page 396).

Scoring

This essay is worth 6 points. One point each for correctly identifying the parts of the iron triangle for a maximum of three points. One point each for correctly explaining the connections between the parts for a maximum of three points.

QUESTION 4

(A) Legislative oversight is the prerogative of Congress to supervise the implementation of public policy by the bureaucracy.

(B) There are many tools of legislative oversight. Any three of the following IDs and explanations are acceptable.

Specialized Agencies - Congress has created specialized agencies who work only for it. The Governmental Accountability Office and the Congressional Budget Office are two such examples. These agencies provide Congress with independent information about executive branch performance.

Budget - Congress controls each agency's budget. By altering the budget Congress has effective control over the actions of that agency. Congress has the ability to "defund" those actions that they do not approve of.

Confirmation - High-ranking executives appointed by the president typically require Senatorial confirmation. By confirming or rejecting these appointments the Senate exercise a degree of control over the bureaucracy.

Structure or Organization - Congress sets up the structure of the executive branch and can reorganize it. Congress has the power restructure the bureaucracy by moving agencies from one department to another. Further, it can alter each agencies jurisdiction (*American Government*, 14th ed., pages 398–400).

Scoring

This essay is worth 5 points. In part (A) one point is earned for correctly defining legislative oversight. In part (B) one point is earned for each of the two correct identifications of the tools of legislative oversight for a maximum of two points. One point is earned for each of two correct explanations of how those tools enable Congress to oversee the bureaucracy for a maximum of two points.

Calculating your score on the AP Exam

SECTION 1: MULTIPLE-CHOICE QUESTIONS

Total number answered correctly _____

SECTION II: FREE-RESPONSE QUESTIONS

Question 1 _____ × 2.5 equals _____

Out of 6   do not round

Question 2 ____ × 3 equals _____

    Out of 5   do not round

Question 3 ____ × 2.5 equals _____

    Out of 6   do not round

Question 4 ____ × 3.0 equals _____

    Out of 5   do not round

TOTAL FOR SECTION II ___

COMPOSITE SCORE:

_____ + _____ = _____

Section I   Section II   Composite Score

Student scores are weighted differently each year to determine the final AP score. The conversion chart below is according to the weighting on the 2009 exam:

COMPOSITE SCORE RANGE	AP GRADE
93–120	5
82–92	4
66–81	3
48–65	2
0–47	1

The Declaration of Independence

In Congress, July 4, 1776

The Unanimous Declaration of the Thirteen United States of America

When, in the course of human events, it becomes necessary for one people to dissolve the political bands which have connected them with another, and to assume, among the powers of the earth, the separate and equal station to which the laws of nature and of nature's God entitle them, a decent respect to the opinions of mankind requires that they should declare the causes which impel them to the separation.

We hold these truths to be self-evident: That all men are created equal; that they are endowed by their Creator with certain unalienable rights; that among these are life, liberty, and the pursuit of happiness; that, to secure these rights, governments are instituted among men, deriving their just powers from the consent of the governed; that whenever any form of government becomes destructive of these ends, it is the right of the people to alter or to abolish it, and to institute new government, laying its foundation on such principles, and organizing its power in such form, as to them shall seem most likely to effect their safety and happiness. Prudence, indeed, will dictate that governments long established should not be changed for light and transient causes; and accordingly all experience hath shown that mankind are more disposed to suffer, while evils are sufferable, than to right themselves by abolishing the forms to which they are accustomed. But when a long train of abuses and usurpations, pursuing invariably the same object, evinces a design to reduce them under absolute despotism, it is their right, it is their duty, to throw off such government, and to provide new guards for their future security. Such has been the patient sufferance of these colonies; and such is now the necessity which constrains them to alter their former systems of government. The history of the present King of Great Britain is a history of repeated injuries and usurpations, all having in direct object the establishment of an absolute tyranny over these states. To prove this, let facts be submitted to a candid world.

He has refused to assent to laws, the most wholesome and necessary for the public good.

He has forbidden his governors to pass laws of immediate and pressing importance, unless suspended in their operation till his assent should be obtained; and, when so suspended, he has utterly neglected to attend to them.

He has refused to pass other laws for the accommodation of large districts of people, unless those people would relinquish the right of representation in the legislature, a right inestimable to them, and formidable to tyrants only.

He has called together legislative bodies at places unusual, uncomfortable, and distant from the depository of their public records, for the sole purpose of fatiguing them into compliance with his measures.

He has dissolved representative houses repeatedly, for opposing, with manly firmness, his invasions on the rights of the people.

He has refused for a long time, after such dissolutions, to cause others to be elected; whereby the legislative powers, incapable of annihilation, have returned to the people at large for their exercise; the state remaining, in the mean time, exposed to all dangers of invasions from without and convulsions within.

He has endeavored to prevent the population of these states; for that purpose obstructing the laws for naturalization of foreigners; refusing to pass others to encourage their migration hither, and raising the conditions of new appropriations of lands.

He has obstructed the administration of justice, by refusing his assent to laws for establishing judiciary powers.

He has made judges dependent on his will alone, for the tenure of their offices, and the amount and payment of their salaries.

He has erected a multitude of new offices, and sent hither swarms of officers to harass our people, and eat out their substance.

He has kept among us, in times of peace, standing armies, without the consent of our legislatures.

He has affected to render the military independent of, and superior to, the civil power.

He has combined with others to subject us to a jurisdiction foreign to our constitution, and unacknowledged by our laws, giving his assent to their acts of pretended legislation:

For quartering large bodies of armed troops among us:

For protecting them, by a mock trial, from punishment for any murders which they should commit on the inhabitants of these states;

For cutting off our trade with all parts of the world;

For imposing taxes on us without our consent;

For depriving us, in many cases, of the benefits of trial by jury;

For transporting us beyond seas, to be tried for pretended offenses;

For abolishing the free system of English laws in a neighboring province, establishing therein an arbitrary government, and enlarging its boundaries, so as to render it at once an example and fit instrument for introducing the same absolute rule into these colonies;

For taking away our charters, abolishing our most valuable laws, and altering fundamentally the forms of our governments;

For suspending our own legislatures, and declaring themselves invested with power to legislate for us in all cases whatsoever.

He has abdicated government here, by declaring us out of his protection and waging war against us.

He has plundered our seas, ravaged our coasts, burned our towns, and destroyed the lives of our people.

He is at this time transporting large armies of foreign mercenaries to complete the works of death, desolation, and tyranny already begun with circumstances of cruelty and perfidy scarcely paralleled in the most barbarous ages, and totally unworthy the head of a civilized nation.

He has constrained our fellow-citizens, taken captive on the high seas, to bear arms against their country, to become the executioners of their friends and brethren, or to fall themselves by their hands.

He has excited domestic insurrection among us, and has endeavored to bring on the inhabitants of our frontiers the merciless Indian savages, whose known rule of warfare is an undistinguished destruction of all ages, sexes, and conditions.

In every stage of these oppressions we have petitioned for redress in the most humble terms; our repeated petitions have been answered only by repeated injury. A prince, whose character is thus marked by every act which may define a tyrant, is unfit to be the ruler of a free people.

Nor have we been wanting in our attentions to our British brethren. We have warned them, from time to time, of attempts by their Legislature to extend an unwarrantable jurisdiction over us. We have reminded them of the circumstances of our emigration and settlement here. We have appealed to their native justice and magnanimity; and we have conjured them, by the ties of our common kindred, to disavow these usurpations, which would inevitably interrupt our connections and correspondence. They, too, have been deaf to the voice of justice and of consanguinity. We must, therefore, acquiesce in the necessity which denounces our separation, and hold them, as we hold the rest of mankind, enemies in war, in peace friends.

We, therefore, the representatives of the United States of America, in General Congress assembled, appealing to the Supreme Judge of the world for the rectitude of our intentions, do, in the name and by the authority of the good people of these colonies, solemnly publish and declare, that these United Colonies are, and of right ought to be, FREE AND INDEPENDENT STATES; that they are absolved from all allegiance to the British crown, and that all political connection between them and the state of Great Britain is, and ought to be, totally dissolved; and that, as free and independent states, they have full power to levy war, conclude peace, contract alliances, establish commerce, and do all other acts and things which independent states may of right do. And for the support of this declaration, with a firm reliance on the protection of Divine Providence, we mutually pledge to each other our lives, our fortunes, and our sacred honor.

JOHN HANCOCK [*President*]
[*and fifty-five others*]

The Constitution of the United States

Preamble

We the People of the United States, in Order to form a more perfect Union, establish Justice, insure domestic Tranquility, provide for the common defence, promote the general Welfare, and secure the Blessings of Liberty to ourselves and our Posterity, do ordain and establish this Constitution for the United States of America.

Article I.

Bicameral Congress

Section 1. All legislative Powers herein granted shall be vested in a Congress of the United States, which shall consist of a Senate and House of Representatives.

Membership of the House

Section 2. The House of Representatives shall be composed of Members chosen every second Year by the People of the several States, and the Electors in each State shall have the Qualifications requisite for Electors of the most numerous Branch of the State Legislature.

No person shall be a Representative who shall not have attained to the age of twenty five Years, and been seven Years a Citizen of the United States, and who shall not, when elected, be an Inhabitant of that State in which he shall be chosen.

Representatives and direct Taxes shall be apportioned among the several States which may be included within this Union, according to their respective Numbers, which shall be determined by adding to the whole Number of free Persons, including those bound to Service for a Term of Years, and excluding Indians not taxed, three fifths of all other Persons.[1] The actual Enumeration shall be made within three Years after the first Meeting of the Congress of the United States, and within every subsequent Term of ten Years, in such Manner as they shall by Law direct. The Number of Representatives shall not exceed one for every thirty Thousand, but each State shall have at Least one Representative; and until such enumeration shall be made, the State of New Hampshire shall be entitled to chuse three, Massachusetts eight, Rhode-Island and Providence Plantations one, Connecticut five, New-York six, New Jersey four, Pennsylvania eight, Delaware one, Maryland six, Virginia ten, North Carolina five, South Carolina five, and Georgia three.

When vacancies happen in the Representation from any State, the Executive Authority thereof shall issue Writs of Election to fill such Vacancies.

Power to impeach

The House of Representatives shall chuse their Speaker and other Officers; and shall have the sole Power of Impeachment.

Membership of the Senate

Section 3. The Senate of the United States shall be composed of two Senators from each State, *chosen by the Legislature thereof,*[2] for six Years; and each Senator shall have one Vote.

Immediately after they shall be assembled in Consequence of the first Election, they shall be divided as equally as may be into three Classes. The Seats of the Senators of the first class shall be vacated at the Expiration of the second Year, of the second Class at the Expiration of the fourth Year, and of the third Class at the Expiration of the sixth Year, so that one third may be chosen every second Year; *and if Vacancies happen by Resignation, or otherwise, during the Recess of the Legislature of any State, the Executive thereof*

NOTE: The topical headings are not part of the original Constitution. Excluding the Preamble and Closing, those portions set in italic type have been superseded or changed by later amendments.
1. Changed by the Fourteenth Amendment, section 2.
2. Changed by the Seventeenth Amendment.

may make temporary Appointments until the next Meeting of the Legislature, which shall then fill such Vacancies.[3]

No Person shall be a Senator who shall not have attained to the Age of thirty Years, and been nine Years a Citizen of the United States, and who shall not, when elected, be an Inhabitant of that State for which he shall be chosen.

The Vice President of the United States shall be President of the Senate, but shall have no Vote, unless they be equally divided.

Power to try impeachments

The Senate shall chuse their other Officers, and also a President pro tempore, in the Absence of the Vice President, or when he shall exercise the Office of President of the United States.

The Senate shall have the sole Power to try all Impeachments. When sitting for that Purpose, they shall be on Oath or Affirmation. When the President of the United States is tried the Chief Justice shall preside: And no Person shall be convicted without the Concurrence of two thirds of the Members present.

Judgment in Cases of Impeachment shall not extend further than to removal from Office, and disqualification to hold and enjoy any Office of honor, Trust or Profit under the United States: but the Party convicted shall nevertheless be liable and subject to Indictment, Trial, Judgment and Punishment, according to Law.

Laws governing elections

Section 4. The Times, Places and Manner of holding Elections for Senators and Representatives, shall be prescribed in each State by the Legislature thereof; but the Congress may at any time by Law make or alter such Regulations, except as to the Places of chusing Senators.

The Congress shall assemble at least once in every Year, and such Meeting shall be on the *first Monday in December, unless they shall by Law appoint a different Day.*[4]

Rules of Congress

Section 5. Each House shall be the Judge of the Elections, Returns and Qualifications of its own Members, and a Majority of each shall constitute a Quorum to do Business; but a smaller number may adjourn from day to day, and may be authorized to compel the Attendance of absent Members, in such Manner, and under such Penalties as each House may provide.

Each House may determine the Rules of its Proceedings, punish its Members for disorderly Behaviour, and, with the Concurrence of two thirds, expel a Member.

Each House shall keep a Journal of its Proceedings, and from time to time publish the same, excepting such Parts as may in their Judgment require Secrecy; and the Yeas and Nays of the Members of either House on any question shall, at the Desire of one fifth of those Present, be entered on the Journal.

Neither House, during the Session of Congress, shall, without the Consent of the other, adjourn for more than three days, nor to any other Place than that in which the two Houses shall be sitting.

Salaries and immunities of members

Section 6. The Senators and Representatives shall receive a Compensation for their Services, to be ascertained by Law, and paid out of the Treasury of the United States. They shall in all Cases, except Treason, Felony and Breach of the Peace, be privileged from Arrest during their Attendance at the Session of their respective Houses, and in going to and returning from the same; and for any Speech or Debate in either House, they shall not be questioned in any other Place.

---

3. *Changed by the Seventeenth Amendment.*
4. *Changed by the Twentieth Amendment, section 2.*

Bar on members of Congress holding federal appointive office

No Senator or Representative shall, during the Time for which he was elected, be appointed to any civil Office under the Authority of the United States, which shall have been created, or the Emoluments whereof shall have been encreased during such time; and no Person holding any Office under the United States, shall be a Member of either House during his Continuance in Office.

Money bills originate in House

Section 7. All Bills for raising Revenue shall originate in the House of Representatives; but the Senate may propose or concur with Amendments as on other Bills.

Procedure for enacting laws; veto power

Every Bill which shall have passed the House of Representatives and the Senate, shall, before it become a Law, be presented to the President of the United States; If he approve he shall sign it, but if not he shall return it, with Objections to that House in which it shall have originated, who shall enter the Objections at large on their Journal, and proceed to reconsider it. If after such Reconsideration two thirds of that House shall agree to pass the Bill, it shall be sent, together with the Objections, to the other House, by which it shall likewise be reconsidered, and if approved by two thirds of that House, it shall become a Law. But in all such Cases the Votes of both Houses shall be determined by yeas and Nays, and the Names of the Persons voting for and against the Bill shall be entered on the Journal of each House respectively. If any Bill shall not be returned by the President within ten Days (Sundays excepted) after it shall have been presented to him, the Same shall be a Law, in like Manner, as if he had signed it, unless the Congress by their Adjournment prevent its Return, in which Case it shall not be a Law.

Every Order, Resolution, or Vote to which the Concurrence of the Senate and House of Representatives may be necessary (except on a question of Adjournment) shall be presented to the President of the United States; and before the Same shall take Effect, shall be approved by him, or being disapproved by him, shall be repassed by two thirds of the Senate and House of Representatives, according to the Rules and Limitations prescribed in the Case of a Bill.

Powers of Congress—taxes

Section 8. The Congress shall have Power To lay and Collect Taxes, Duties, Imposts and Excises, to pay the Debts and provide for the common Defence and general Welfare of the United States; but all Duties, Imposts and Excises shall be uniform throughout the United States.

—borrowing

To borrow Money on the credit of the United States;

—regulation of commerce

To regulate Commerce with foreign Nations, and among the several States, and with the Indian Tribes;

naturalization and bankruptcy

To establish an uniform Rule of Naturalization, and uniform Laws on the subject of Bankruptcies throughout the United States;

—money

To coin Money, regulate the Value thereof, and of foreign Coin, and fix the Standard of Weights and Measures;

—counterfeiting

To provide for the Punishment of counterfeiting the Securities and current Coin of the United States;

—post office

To establish Post Offices and post Roads;

—patents and copyrights

To promote the Progress of Science and useful Arts, by securing for limited Times to Authors and Inventors the exclusive Right to their respective Writings and Discoveries;

—create courts

To constitute Tribunals inferior to the Supreme Court;

—punish piracies

To define and punish Piracies and Felonies committed on the high Seas, and Offences against the Law of Nations;

—declare war

To declare War, grant Letters of Marque and Reprisal, and make Rules concerning Captures on Land and Water;

—create army and navy

To raise and support Armies, but no Appropriation of Money to that Use shall be for a longer Term than two Years;

To provide and maintain a Navy;

To make Rules for the Government and Regulation of the land and naval Forces;

—call the militia

To provide for calling forth the Militia to execute the Laws of the Union, suppress Insurrections and repel Invasions;

To provide for organizing, arming, and disciplining, the Militia, and for governing such Part of them as may be employed in the Service of the United States, reserving to the States respectively, the Appointment of the Officers, and the Authority of training the Militia according to the discipline prescribed by Congress;

— govern District of Columbia

To exercise exclusive Legislation in all Cases whatsoever, over such District (not exceeding ten Miles square) as may, by Cession of Particular States, and the Acceptance of Congress, become the Seat of the Government of the United States, and to exercise like Authority over all Places purchased by the Consent of the Legislature of the State in which the Same shall be, for the Erection of Forts, Magazines, Arsenals, dock-Yards and other needful Buildings;—And

— "necessary-and-proper" clause

To make all Laws which shall be necessary and proper for carrying into Execution the foregoing Powers, and all other Powers vested by this Constitution in the Government of the United States, or in any Department or Officer thereof.

Restrictions on powers of Congress
—slave trade

Section 9. The Migration or Importation of such Persons as any of the States now existing shall think proper to admit, shall not be prohibited by the Congress prior to the Year one thousand eight hundred and eight, but a Tax or duty may be imposed on such Importation, not exceeding ten dollars for each Person.

—habeas corpus

The Privilege of the Writ of Habeas Corpus shall not be suspended, unless when in Cases of Rebellion or Invasion the public Safety may require it.

— no bill of attainder or ex post facto law

No bill of Attainder or ex post facto Law shall be passed.

No Capitation, or other direct, Tax shall be laid, *unless in Proportion to the Census or Enumeration herein before directed to be taken.*[5]

—no interstate tariffs
— no preferential treatment for some states

No Tax or Duty shall be laid on Articles exported from any State.

No Preference shall be given by any Regulation of Commerce or Revenue to the Ports of one State over those of another; nor shall Vessels bound to, or from, one State, be obliged to enter, clear or pay Duties in another.

—appropriations

No Money shall be drawn from the Treasury, but in Consequence of Appropriations made by Law; and a regular Statement and Account of the Receipts and Expenditures of all public Money shall be published from time to time.

—no titles of nobility

No Title of Nobility shall be granted by the United States: And no Person holding any Office of Profit or Trust under them, shall, without the Consent of the Congress, accept of any present, Emolument, Office, or Title, of any kind whatever, from any King, Prince, or foreign State.

Restrictions on powers of states

Section 10. No State shall enter into any Treaty, Alliance, or Confederation; grant Letters of Marque and Reprisal; coin Money; emit Bills of Credit; make any Thing but gold and silver Coin a Tender in Payment of Debts; pass any Bill of Attainder, ex post facto Law, or Law impairing the Obligation of Contracts, or grant any Title of Nobility.

No State shall, without the Consent of Congress, lay any Imposts or Duties on Imports or Exports, except what may be absolutely necessary for executing its inspection Laws; and the net Produce of all Duties and Imposts, laid by any State on Imports or Exports, shall be for the Use of the Treasury of the United States; and all such Laws shall be subject to the Revision and Controul of the Congress.

No State shall, without the Consent of Congress, lay any Duty of Tonnage, keep Troops, or Ships of War in time of Peace, enter into any Agreement or Compact with another State, or with a foreign Power, or engage in War, unless actually invaded, or in such imminent Danger as will not admit of delay.

5. *Changed by the Sixteenth Amendment.*

Article II.

Office of president

Section 1. The executive Power shall be vested in a President of the United States of America. He shall hold his Office during the Term of four Years, and, together with the Vice President, chosen for the same Term, be elected, as follows:

Election of president

Each State shall appoint, in such Manner as the Legislature thereof may direct, a Number of Electors, equal to the whole Number of Senators and Representatives to which the State may be entitled in the Congress: but no Senator or Representative, or Person holding an Office of Trust or Profit under the United States, shall be appointed an Elector.

The Electors shall meet in their respective States, and vote by Ballot for two Persons, of whom one at least shall not be an Inhabitant of the same State with themselves. And they shall make a List of all the Persons voted for, and of the Number of Votes for each; which List they shall sign and certify, and transmit sealed to the Seat of the Government of the United States, directed to the President of the Senate. The President of the Senate shall, in the Presence of the Senate and House of Representatives, open all the Certificates, and the Votes shall then be counted. The Person having the greatest Number of Votes shall be the President, if such Number be a Majority of the whole Number of Electors appointed; and if there be more than one who have such Majority, and have an equal Number of Votes, then the House of Representatives shall immediately chuse by Ballot one of them for President; and if no Person have a Majority, then from the five highest on the List said House shall in like Manner chuse the President. But in chusing the President, the Votes shall be taken by States, the Representation from each State having one Vote; a quorum for this Purpose shall consist of a Member or Members from two thirds of the States, and a Majority of all the States shall be necessary to a Choice. In every Case, after the Choice of the President, the Person having the greatest Number of Votes of the Electors shall be the Vice President. But if there should remain two or more who have equal Votes, the Senate shall chuse from them by Ballot the Vice President.[6]

The Congress may determine the Time of chusing the Electors, and the Day on which they shall give their Votes, which Day shall be the same throughout the United States.

Requirements to be president

No Person except a natural born Citizen, or a Citizen of the United States, at the time of the Adoption of this Constitution, shall be eligible to the Office of President; neither shall any person be eligible to that Office who shall not have attained to the Age of thirty five Years, and been fourteen Years a Resident within the United States.

In Case of the Removal of the President from Office, or of his Death, Resignation, or Inability to discharge the Powers and Duties of the said Office, the Same shall devolve on the Vice President, and the Congress may by Law provide for the Case of Removal, Death, Resignation or Inability, both of the President and Vice President, declaring what Officer shall then act as President, and such Officer shall act accordingly, until the Disability be removed, or a President shall be elected.[7]

Pay of president

The President shall, at stated Times, receive for his Services, a Compensation, which shall neither be increased nor diminished during the Period for which he shall have been elected, and he shall not receive within that Period any other Emolument from the United States, or any of them.

Before he enter on the Execution of his Office, he shall take the following Oath or Affirmation:—"I do solemnly swear (or affirm) that I will faithfully execute the Office of President of the United States, and will to the best of my Ability preserve, protect and defend the Constitution of the United States."

Powers of president
—commander in chief

Section 2. The President shall be Commander in Chief of the Army and Navy of the United States, and of the Militia of the several States, when called into

---

6. *Superseded by the Twelfth Amendment.*
7. *Modified by the Twenty-fifth Amendment.*

—*pardons*

the actual Service of the United States; he may require the Opinion, in writing, of the principal Officer in each of the executive Departments, upon any Subject relating to the Duties of their respective Offices, and he shall have Power to grant Reprieves and Pardons for Offences against the United States, except in Cases of Impeachment.

—*treaties and appointments*

He shall have Power, by and with the Advice and Consent of the Senate, to make Treaties, provided two thirds of the Senators present concur; and he shall nominate, and by and with the Advice and Consent of the Senate, shall appoint Ambassadors, other public Ministers and Consuls, Judges of the supreme Court, and all other Officers of the United States, whose Appointments are not herein otherwise provided for, and which shall be established by Law: but the Congress may by Law vest the Appointment of such inferior Officers, as they think proper, in the President alone, in the Courts of Law, or in the Heads of Departments.

The President shall have Power to fill up all Vacancies that may happen during the Recess of the Senate, by granting Commissions which shall expire at the End of their next Session.

Relations of president with Congress

Section 3. He shall from time to time give to the Congress Information of the State of the Union, and recommend to their Consideration such Measures as he shall judge necessary and expedient; he may, on extraordinary Occasions, convene both Houses, or either of them, and in Case of Disagreement between them, with Respect to the Time of Adjournment, he may adjourn them to such Time as he shall think proper; he shall receive Ambassadors and other public Ministers; he shall take Care that the Laws be faithfully executed, and shall Commission all the Officers of the United States.

Impeachment

Section 4. The President, Vice President and all civil Officers of the United States, shall be removed from Office on Impeachment for, and Conviction of, Treason, Bribery, or other high Crimes and Misdemeanors.

Article III.

Federal courts

Section 1. The judicial Power of the United States, shall be vested in one supreme Court, and in such inferior Courts as the Congress may from time to time ordain and establish. The Judges, both of the supreme and inferior Courts, shall hold their Offices during good Behaviour, and shall, at stated Times, receive for their Services, a Compensation, which shall not be diminished during their Continuance in Office.

Jurisdiction of courts

Section 2. The judicial Power shall extend to all Cases, in Law and Equity, arising under this Constitution, the Laws of the United States, and Treaties made, or which shall be made, under their Authority;—to all Cases affecting Ambassadors, other public Ministers and Consuls;—to all Cases of admiralty and maritime Jurisdiction;—to Controversies to which the United States shall be a Party;—to Controversies between two or more States;—*between a State and Citizens of another State*;[8] —between Citizens of different States;—between Citizens of the same State claiming Lands under Grants of different States, and between a State, or the Citizens thereof, and foreign States, Citizens or Subjects.

—*original*

In all Cases affecting Ambassadors, other public Ministers and Consuls, and those in which a State shall be Party, the supreme Court shall have original Jurisdiction. In all the other Cases before mentioned, the supreme Court shall have appellate Jurisdiction, both as to Law and Fact, with such Exceptions, and under such Regulations as the Congress shall make.

—*appellate*

The Trial of all Crimes, except in Cases of Impeachment, shall be by Jury; and such Trial shall be held in the State where the said Crimes shall have

---

8. *Modified by the Eleventh Amendment.*

been committed; but when not committed within any State, the Trial shall be at such Place or Places as the Congress may by Law have directed.

Treason

Section 3. Treason against the United States, shall consist only in levying War against them, or in adhering to their Enemies, giving them Aid and Comfort. No Person shall be convicted of Treason unless on the Testimony of two Witnesses to the same overt Act, or on Confession in open Court.

The Congress shall have Power to declare the Punishment of Treason, but no Attainder of Treason shall work Corruption of Blood, or Forfeiture except during the Life of the Person attainted.

Article IV.

Full faith and credit

Section 1. Full Faith and Credit shall be given in each State to the public Acts, Records, and judicial Proceedings of every other State. And the Congress may by general Laws prescribe the Manner in which such Acts, Records and Proceedings shall be proved, and the Effect thereof.

Privileges and immunities

Section 2. The Citizens of each State shall be entitled to all Privileges and Immunities of Citizens in the several States.

Extradition

A person charged in any State with Treason, Felony, or other Crime, who shall flee from Justice, and be found in another State, shall on Demand of the executive Authority of the State from which he fled, be delivered up, to be removed to the State having Jurisdiction of the Crime.

No Person held to Service or Labour in one State, under the Laws thereof, escaping into another, shall, in Consequence of any Law or Regulation therein, be discharged from such Service or Labour, but shall be delivered up on Claim of the Party to whom such Service or Labour may be due.[9]

Creation of new states

Section 3. New States may be admitted by the Congress into this Union; but no new State shall be formed or erected within the Jurisdiction of any other State; nor any State be formed by the Junction of two or more States, or Parts of States, without the Consent of the Legislatures of the States concerned as well as of the Congress.

Governing territories

The Congress shall have Power to dispose of and make all needful Rules and Regulations respecting the Territory or other Property belonging to the United States; and nothing in this Constitution shall be so construed as to Prejudice any Claims of the United States, or of any particular State.

Protection of states

Section 4. The United States shall guarantee to every State in this Union a Republican Form of Government, and shall protect each of them against Invasion; and on Application of the Legislature, or of the Executive (when the Legislature cannot be convened) against domestic Violence.

Article V.

Amending the Constitution

The Congress, whenever two thirds of both Houses shall deem it necessary, shall propose Amendments to this Constitution, or, on the Application of the Legislatures of two thirds of the several States, shall call a Convention for proposing Amendments, which, in either Case, shall be valid to all Intents and Purposes, as Part of this Constitution, when ratified by the Legislatures of three fourths of the several States, or by Conventions in three fourths thereof, as the one or the other Mode of Ratification may be proposed by the Congress; Provided that no Amendment which may be made prior to the Year One thousand eight hundred and eight shall in any Manner alter the first and fourth Clauses in the Ninth Section of the first Article; and that no State, without its Consent, shall be deprived of its equal Suffrage in the Senate.

---

9. *Changed by the Thirteenth Amendment.*

Article VI.

Assumption of debts of Confederation

All Debts contracted and Engagements entered into, before the Adoption of this Constitution, shall be as valid against the United States under this Constitution, as under the Confederation.

Supremacy of federal laws and treaties

This Constitution, and the Laws of the United States which shall be made in Pursuance thereof; and all Treaties made, or which shall be made, under the Authority of the United States, shall be the Supreme Law of the Land; and the Judges in every State shall be bound thereby, any Thing in the Constitution or Laws of any State to the Contrary notwithstanding.

No religious test

The Senators and Representatives before mentioned, and the Members of the several State Legislatures, and all executive and judicial Officers, both of the United States and of the several States, shall be bound by Oath or Affirmation, to support this Constitution; but no religious Test shall ever be required as a Qualification to any Office or public Trust under the United States.

Article VII.

Ratification procedure

The Ratification of the Conventions of nine States, shall be sufficient for the Establishment of this Constitution between the States so ratifying the Same.

Done in Convention by the Unanimous Consent of the States present the Seventeenth Day of September in the Year of our Lord one thousand seven hundred and Eighty seven and of the Independence of the United States of America the Twelfth In witness whereof We have hereunto subscribed our Names,

G°. WASHINGTON—*Presid^t.*
and deputy from Virginia

New Hampshire
- JOHN LANGDON
- NICHOLAS GILMAN

Maryland
- JAMES M^cHENRY
- DAN OF S^T THO.^S JENIFER
- DAN^L CARROLL

Massachusetts
- NATHANIEL GORHAM
- RUFUS KING

Virginia
- JOHN BLAIR—
- JAMES MADISON JR.

New Jersey
- WIL: LIVINGSTON
- DAVID BREARLEY
- W..^MPATERSON
- JONA: DAYTON

North Carolina
- W^MBLOUNT
- RICH.^D DOBBS SPAIGHT
- HU WILLIAMSON

Pennsylvania
- B FRANKLIN
- THOMAS MIFFLIN
- ROB.^T MORRIS
- GEO. CLYMER
- THO.^S FITZSIMONS
- JARED INGERSOLL
- JAMES WILSON
- GOUV MORRIS

South Carolina
- J. RUTLEDGE
- CHARLES COTESWORTH PINCKNEY
- CHARLES PINCKNEY
- PIERCE BUTLER

Connecticut {	W.ᴹSAM.ᴸ JOHNSON ROGER SHERMAN	*Delaware* {	GEO: READ GUNNING BEDFORD JUN JOHN DICKINSON RICHARD BASSETT JACO: BROOM
New York {	ALEXANDER HAMILTION	*Georgia* {	WILLIAM FEW ABR BALDWIN

[The first ten amendments, known as the "Bill of Rights," were ratified in 1791.]

AMENDMENT I.

Freedom of religion, speech, press, assembly

Congress shall make no law respecting an establishment of religion, or prohibiting the free exercise thereof, or abridging the freedom of speech, or of the press; or the right of the people peaceably to assemble, and to petition the Government for a redress of grievances.

AMENDMENT II.

Right to bear arms

A well regulated Militia, being necessary to the security of a free State, the right of the people to keep and bear Arms, shall not be infringed.

AMENDMENT III.

Quartering troops in private homes

No Soldier shall, in time of peace be quartered in any house without the consent of the Owner, nor in time of war, but in a manner to be prescribed by law.

AMENDMENT IV.

Prohibition against unreasonable searches and seizures

The right of the people to be secure in their persons, houses, papers, and effects, against unreasonable searches and seizures, shall not be violated, and no Warrants shall issue, but upon probable cause, supported by Oath or affirmation, and particularly describing the place to be searched, and the persons or things to be seized.

AMENDMENT V.

Right when accused; "due-process" clause

No person shall be held to answer for a capital, or otherwise infamous crime, unless on a presentment or indictment of a Grand Jury, except in cases arising in the land or naval forces, or in the Militia, when in actual service in time of War or public danger; nor shall any person be subject for the same offence to be twice put in jeopardy of life or limb; nor shall be compelled in any criminal case to be a witness against himself, nor be deprived of life, liberty, or property, without due process of law, nor shall private property be taken for public use, without just compensation.

AMENDMENT VI.

Rights when on trial

In all criminal prosecutions, the accused shall enjoy the right to a speedy and public trial, by an impartial jury of the State and district wherein the crime shall have been committed, which district shall have been previously ascertained by law, and to be informed of the nature and cause of the accusation; to be confronted with the witnesses against him; to have compulsory process for obtaining witnesses in his favor, and to have the Assistance of Counsel for his defence.

AMENDMENT VII.

Common-law suits

In Suits at common law, where the value in controversy shall exceed twenty dollars, the right of trial by jury shall be preserved, and no fact tried by a jury, shall be otherwise reexamined in any Court of the United States, than according to the rules of the common law.

AMENDMENT VIII.

Bail; no "cruel and unusual" punishments

Excessive bail shall not be required, nor excessive fines imposed, nor cruel and unusual punishments inflicted.

AMENDMENT IX.

Unenumerated rights protected

The enumeration in the Constitution, of certain rights, shall not be construed to deny or disparage others retained by the people.

AMENDMENT X.

Powers reserved for states

The powers not delegated to the United States by the Constitution, nor prohibited by it to the States, are reserved to the States respectively, or to the people.

AMENDMENT XI.
[Ratified in 1795.]

Limits on suits against states

The Judicial power of the United States shall not be construed to extend to any suit in law or equity, commenced or prosecuted against one of the United States by Citizens of another state, or by Citizens or Subjects of any Foreign State.

AMENDMENT XII.
[Ratified in 1804.]

Revision of electoral-college procedure

The Electors shall meet in their respective states and vote by ballot for President and Vice President, one of whom, at least, shall not be an inhabitant of the same state with themselves; they shall name in their ballots the person voted for as President, and in distinct ballots the person voted for as Vice President, and they shall make distinct lists of all persons voted for as President, and of all persons voted for as Vice President, and of the number of votes for each, which lists they shall sign and certify, and transmit sealed to the seat of government of the United States, directed to the President of the Senate;—The President of the Senate shall, in the presence of the Senate and House of Representatives, open all the certificates and the votes shall then be counted;—The person having the greatest number of votes for President, shall be the President, if such number be a majority of the whole number of Electors appointed; and if no person have such majority, then from the persons having the highest numbers not exceeding three on the list of those voted for as President, the House of Representatives shall choose immediately, by ballot, the President. But in choosing the President, the votes shall be taken by states, the representation from each state having one vote; a quorum for this purpose shall consist of a member or members from two-thirds of the states, and a majority of all the states shall be necessary to a choice. *And if the House of Representatives shall not choose a President whenever the right of choice shall devolve upon them, before the fourth day of March next following, then the Vice President shall act as President, as in the case of the death or other constitutional disability of the President.*—[10] The person having the greatest number of votes as Vice President, shall be the Vice President, if such number be a majority of the whole number of Electors appointed, and if no person have a majority, then from the two highest numbers on the list, the Senate shall choose the Vice President; a quorum for the purpose shall consist of two-thirds of the whole number of Senators, and a majority of the whole number shall be necessary to a choice. But no person constitutionally ineligible to the office of President shall be eligible to that of Vice President of the United States.

AMENDMENT XIII.
[Ratified in 1865.]

Slavery prohibited

Section 1. Neither slavery nor involuntary servitude, except as a punishment for crime whereof the party shall have been duly convicted, shall exist within the United States, or any place subject to their jurisdiction.

Section 2. Congress shall have power to enforce this article by appropriate legislation.

AMENDMENT XIV.
[Ratified in 1868.]

Ex-slaves made citizens

Section 1. All persons born or naturalized in the United States and subject to the jurisdiction thereof, are citizens of the United States and of the State wherein they reside. No State shall make or enforce any law which shall abridge the privileges or immunities of citizens of the United States; nor shall any State deprive any person of life, liberty, or property, without due process of law; nor deny to any person within its jurisdiction the equal protection of the laws.

"Due-process" clause applied to states
"Equal-protection" clause

Reduction in congressional representation
for states denying adult males the right to vote

Section 2. Representatives shall be apportioned among the several States according to their respective numbers, counting the whole number of persons in each State, excluding Indians not taxed. But when the right to vote at any election for the choice of electors for President and Vice President of the United States, Representatives in Congress, the Executive and Judicial officers of a State, or the members of the Legislature thereof, is denied to any of the male inhabitants of such State, being *twenty-one*[11] years of age and citizens of the United States, or in any way abridged, except for participation in rebellion, or other crime, the basis of representation therein shall be reduced in the proportion which the number of such male citizens shall bear to the whole number of male citizens twenty-one years of age in such State.

Southern rebels denied federal office

Section 3. No person shall be a Senator or Representative in Congress, or elector of President and Vice President, or hold any office, civil or military, under the United States, or under any State, who, having previously taken an oath, as a member of Congress, or as an officer of the United States, or as a member of any State legislature, or as an executive or judicial officer of any State, to support the Constitution of the United States, shall have engaged in insurrection or rebellion against the same, or given aid or comfort to the

---

10. *Changed by the Twentieth Amendment, section 3.*
11. *Changed by the Twenty-sixth Amendment.*

enemies thereof. But Congress may by a vote of two-thirds of each House, remove such disability.

Rebel debts repudiated

Section 4. The validity of the public debt of the United States, authorized by law, including debts incurred for payment of pensions and bounties for services in suppressing insurrection or rebellion, shall not be questioned. But neither the United3nor any State shall assume or pay any debt or obligation incurred in aid of insurrection or rebellion against the United States, or any claim for the loss or emancipation of any slave; but all such debts, obligations and claims shall be held illegal and void.

Section 5. The Congress shall have power to enforce, by appropriate legislation, the provisions of this article.

AMENDMENT XV.
[Ratified in 1870.]

Blacks given right to vote

Section 1. The right of citizens of the United States to vote shall not be denied or abridged by the United States or by any State on account of race, color, or previous condition of servitude.

Section 2. The Congress shall have power to enforce this article by appropriate legislation.

AMENDMENT XVI.
[Ratified in 1913.]

Authorizes federal income tax

The Congress shall have power to lay and collect taxes on incomes, from whatever source derived, without apportionment among the several States, and without regard to any census or enumeration.

AMENDMENT XVII.
[Ratified in 1913.]

Requires popular election of senators

The Senate of the United States shall be composed of two Senators from each State, elected by the people thereof, for six years; and each Senator shall have one vote. The electors in each State shall have the qualifications requisite for electors of the most numerous branch of the State legislatures.

When vacancies happen in the representation of any State in the Senate, the executive authority of such State shall issue writs of election to fill such vacancies: Provided, That the legislature of any State may empower the executive thereof to make temporary appointments until the people fill the vacancies by election as the legislature may direct.

This amendment shall not be so construed as to affect the election or term of any Senator chosen before it becomes valid as part of the Constitution.

AMENDMENT XVIII.
[Ratified in 1919.]

Prohibits manufacture and sale of liquor

Section 1. *After one year from the ratification of this article the manufacture, sale, or transportation of intoxicating liquors within, the importation there-of into, or the exportation thereof from the United States and all territory subject to the jurisdiction thereof for beverage purposes is hereby prohibited.*

Section 2. *The Congress and the several States shall have concurrent power to enforce this article by appropriate legislation.*

Section 3. *This article shall be inoperative unless it shall have been ratified as an amendment to the Constitution by the legislatures of the several States,* *as provided in the Constitution, within seven years from the date of the submission hereof to the States by the Congress.*[12]

AMENDMENT XIX.

[Ratified in 1920.]

Right to vote for women

The right of citizens of the United States to vote shall not be denied or abridged by the United States or by any State on account of sex.

Congress shall have power to enforce this article by appropriate legislation.

AMENDMENT XX.

[Ratified in 1933.]

Federal terms of office to begin in January

Section 1. The terms of the President and Vice President shall end at noon on the 20th day of January, and the terms of Senators and Representatives at noon on the 3d day of January, of the years in which such terms would have ended if this article had not been ratified; and the terms of their successors shall then begin.

Section 2. The Congress shall assemble at least once in every year, and such meeting shall begin at noon on the 3d day of January, unless they shall by law appoint a different day.

Emergency presidential succession

Section 3. If, at the time fixed for the beginning of the term of the President, the President elect shall have died, the Vice President elect shall become President. If a President shall not have been chosen before the time fixed for the beginning of his term, or if the President elect shall have failed to qualify, then the Vice President elect shall act as President until a President shall have qualified; and the Congress may by law provide for the case wherein neither a President elect nor a Vice President elect shall have qualified, declaring who shall then act as President, or the manner in which one who is to act shall be selected, and such person shall act accordingly until a President or Vice President shall have qualified.

Section 4. The Congress may by law provide for the case of the death of any of the persons from whom the House of Representatives may choose a President whenever the right of choice shall have devolved upon them, and for the case of the death of any of the persons from whom the Senate may choose a Vice President whenever the right of choice shall have devolved upon them.

Section 5. Sections 1 and 2 shall take effect on the 15th day of October following the ratification of this article.

Section 6. This article shall be inoperative unless it shall have been ratified as an amendment to the Constitution by the legislatures of three-fourths of the several States within seven years from the date of its submission.

AMENDMENT XXI.

[Ratified in 1933.]

Repeals Prohibition

Section 1. The eighteenth article of amendment to the Constitution of the United States is hereby repealed.

Section 2. The transportation or importation into any State, Territory, or possession of the United States for delivery or use therein of intoxicating liquors, in violation of the laws thereof, is hereby prohibited.

---

12. Repealed by the Twenty-first Amendment.

Section 3. This article shall be inoperative unless it shall have been ratified as an amendment to the Constitution by conventions in the several States, as provided in the Constitution, within seven years from the date of submission hereof to the States by the Congress.

AMENDMENT XXII.

[Ratified in 1951.]

Two-term limit for president

Section 1. No person shall be elected to the office of the President more than twice, and no person who has held the office of President, or acted as President, for more than two years of a term to which some other person was elected President shall be elected to the office of President more than once. But this Article shall not apply to any person holding the office of President when this Article was proposed by the Congress, and shall not prevent any person who may be holding the office of President, or acting as President, during the term within which this Article becomes operative from holding the office of President or acting as President during the remainder of such term.

Section 2. This Article shall be inoperative unless it shall have been ratified as an amendment to the Constitution by the legislatures of three-fourths of the several States within seven years from the date of its submission to the States by the Congress.

AMENDMENT XXIII.

[Ratified in 1961.]

Right to vote for president in District of Columbia

Section 1. The District constituting the seat of Government of the United States shall appoint in such manner as the Congress may direct:

A number of electors of President and Vice President equal to the whole number of Senators and Representatives in Congress to which the District would be entitled if it were a State, but in no event more than the least populous State; they shall be in addition to those appointed by the States, but they shall be considered, for the purposes of the election of President and Vice President, to be electors appointed by a State; and they shall meet in the District and perform such duties as provided by the twelfth article of amendment.

Section 2. The Congress shall have power to enforce this article by appropriate legislation.

AMENDMENT XXIV.

[Ratified in 1964.]

Prohibits poll taxes in federal elections

Section 1. The right of citizens of the United States to vote in any primary or other election for President or Vice President, for electors for President or Vice President, or for Senator or Representative in Congress, shall not be denied or abridged by the United States or any State by reason of failure to pay any poll tax or other tax.

Section 2. The Congress shall have the power to enforce this article by appropriate legislation.

AMENDMENT XXV.

[Ratified in 1967.]

Presidential disability and succession

Section 1. In case of the removal of the President from office or of his death or resignation, the Vice President shall become President.

Section 2. Whenever there is a vacancy in the office of the Vice President, the President shall nominate a Vice President who shall take office upon confirmation by a majority vote of both Houses of Congress.

Section 3. Whenever the President transmits to the President pro tempore of the Senate and the Speaker of the House of Representatives his written declaration that he is unable to discharge the powers and duties of his office, and until he transmits to them a written declaration to the contrary, such powers and duties shall be discharged by the Vice President as Acting President.

Section 4. Whenever the Vice President and a majority of either the principal officers of the executive departments or of such other body as Congress may by law provide, transmit to the President pro tempore of the Senate and the Speaker of the House of Representatives their written declaration that the President is unable to discharge the powers and duties of his office, the Vice President shall immediately assume the powers and duties of the office as Acting President.

Thereafter, when the President transmits to the President pro tempore of the Senate and the Speaker of the House of Representatives his written declaration that no inability exists, he shall resume the powers and duties of his office unless the Vice President and a majority of either the principal officers of the executive department[s] or of such other body as Congress may by law provide, transmit within four days to the President pro tempore of the Senate and the Speaker of the House of Representatives their written declaration that the President is unable to discharge the powers and duties of his office. Thereupon Congress shall decide the issue, assembling within forty-eight hours for that purpose if not in session. If the Congress, within twenty-one days after receipt of the latter written declaration, or, if Congress is not in session, within twenty-one days after Congress is required to assemble, determines by two-thirds vote of both Houses that the President is unable to discharge the powers and duties of his office, the Vice President shall continue to discharge the same as Acting President; otherwise, the President shall resume the powers and duties of his office.

AMENDMENT XXVI.

[Ratified in 1971.]

Voting age lowered to eighteen

Section 1. The right of citizens of the United States, who are eighteen years of age or older, to vote shall not be denied or abridged by the United States or by any State on account of age.

Section 2. The Congress shall have power to enforce this article by appropriate legislation.

AMENDMENT XXVII.

[Ratified in 1992.]

Congressional pay raises

No law varying the compensation for the services of the Senators and Representatives shall take effect, until an election of Representatives shall have intervened.

A Brief Guide To Reading The Federalist Papers

In 1787, to help win ratification of the new Constitution in the New York state convention, Alexander Hamilton decided to publish a series of articles defending and explaining the document in the New York City newspapers. He recruited John Jay and James Madison to help him, and the three of them, under the pen name "Publius," wrote 85 articles that appeared from late 1787 through 1788. The identity of the authors was kept secret at the time, but we now know that Hamilton wrote 51 of them, Madison 26, and Jay five, and that Hamilton and Madison jointly authored three.

The *Federalist* papers probably played only a small role in securing ratification. Like most legislative battles, this one was not decisively influenced by philosophical writings. But these essays have had a lasting value as an authoritative and profound explanation of the Constitution. Though written for political purposes, the *Federalist* has become the single most important piece of American political philosophy ever produced. Ironically, Hamilton and Madison were later to become political enemies; even at the Philadelphia convention they had different views of the kind of government that should be created. But in 1787–1788, they were united in the belief that the new constitution was the best that could have been obtained under the circumstances.

Although Hamilton wrote most of the *Federalist* papers, Madison wrote the two most famous articles—Nos. 10 and 51, reprinted here in the Appendix. On your first reading of the papers, you may find Madison's language difficult to understand and his ideas overly complex. The following pointers will help you decipher his meaning.

In *Federalist* No. 10, Madison begins by stating that "a well constructed Union" can "break and control the violence of faction." He goes on to define a *faction* as any group of citizens who attempt to advance their ideas or economic interests at the expense of other citizens, or in ways that conflict with "the permanent and aggregate interests of the community" or "public good." Thus what Madison terms "factions" are what we today call "special interests."

One way to defeat factions, according to Madison, is to remove whatever causes them to arise in the first place. This can be attempted in two ways. First, government can deprive people of the liberty they need to organize: "Liberty is to faction what air is to fire." But that is surely a cure "worse than the disease." Second, measures can be taken to make all citizens share the same ideas, feelings, and economic interests. However, as Madison observes, some people are smarter or more hard-working than others, and this "diversity in the faculties" of citizens is bound to result in different economic interests as some people acquire more property than others. Consequently, protecting property rights, not equalizing property ownership, "is the first object of government." Even if everyone shared the same basic economic interests, they would still find reasons "to vex and oppress each other" rather than cooperate "for their common good." Religious differences, loyalties to different leaders, even "frivolous and fanciful distinctions" (not liking how other people dress or their taste in music) can be fertile soil for factions. In Madison's view, people are factious by nature; the "causes of faction" are "sown" into their very being.

Madison thus proposes a second and, he thinks, more practical and desirable way of defeating faction. The way to cure "the mischiefs of faction" is not by removing its causes but by "controlling its effects." Factions will always exist, so the trick is to establish a form of government that is likely to serve the public good through the even-handed "regulation of these various and interfering interests." Wise and public-spirited leaders can "adjust these clashing interests and -render them all subservient to the public good," but, he cautions, "enlightened statesmen will not always be at the helm." (Madison implies that "enlightened statesmen"—such as himself, Washington, and Jefferson—were at the "helm" of government in 1787.)

Madison's proposed cure for the evils of factions is in fact nothing other than a republican form of government. Use the following questions to guide your own analysis of Madison's ideas. Why does Madison think the problem of a "minority" faction is easy to handle? Conversely, why is he so troubled by the potential of a majority faction? How does he distinguish direct democracy from republican government? What is he getting at when he terms elected representatives "proper guardians of the public weal," and why does he think that "extensive republics" are more likely to produce such representatives than small ones?

When you are finished with *Federalist* No. 10, try your hand at *Federalist* No. 51. You will find that the ideas in the former paper anticipate many of those in the latter. And you will find many points on which you may or may not agree with Madison. For example, do you agree with his assumption that people—even your best friends or college roommates—are factious by nature? Likewise, do you agree with his view that government is "the greatest of all reflections on human nature"?

By attempting to meet the mind of James Madison, you can sharpen your own mind and deepen your understanding of American government.

The Federalist No. 10

November 22, 1787

James Madison

TO THE PEOPLE OF THE STATE OF NEW YORK.

Among the numerous advantages promised by a well constructed Union, none deserves to be more accurately developed than its tendency to break and control the violence of faction. The friend of popular governments, never finds himself so much alarmed for their character and fate, as when he contemplates their propensity to this dangerous vice. He will not fail therefore to set a due value on any plan which, without violating the principles to which he is attached, provides a proper cure for it. The instability, injustice and confusion introduced into the public councils, have in truth been the mortal diseases under which popular governments have every where perished; as they continue to be the favorite and fruitful topics from which the adversaries to liberty derive their most specious declamations. The valuable improvements made by the American Constitutions on the popular models, both ancient and modern, cannot certainly be too much admired; but it would be an unwarrantable partiality, to contend that they have as effectually obviated the danger on this side as was wished and expected. Complaints are everywhere heard from our most considerate and virtuous citizens, equally the friends of public and private faith, and of public and personal liberty; that our governments are too unstable; that the public good is disregarded in the conflicts of rival parties; and that measures are too often decided, not according to the rules of justice, and the rights of the minor party; but by the superior force of an interested and over-bearing majority. However anxiously we may wish that these complaints had no foundation, the evidence of known facts will not permit us to deny that they are in some degree true. It will be found indeed, on a candid review of our situation, that some of the distresses under which we labor, have been erroneously charged on the operation of our governments; but it will be found, at the same time, that other causes will not alone account for many of our heaviest misfortunes; and particularly, for that prevailing and increasing distrust of public engagements, and alarm for private rights, which are echoed from one end of the continent to the other. These must be chiefly, if not wholly, effects of the unsteadiness and injustice, with which a factious spirit has tainted our public administrations.

By a faction I understand a number of citizens, whether amounting to a majority or minority of the whole, who are united and actuated by some common impulse of passion, or of interest, adverse to the rights of other citizens, or to the permanent and aggregate interests of the community.

There are two methods of curing the mischiefs of faction: the one, by removing its causes; the other, by controlling its effects.

There are again two methods of removing the causes of faction: the one by destroying the liberty which is essential to its existence; the other, by giving to every citizen the same opinions, the same passions, and the same interests.

It could never be more truly said than of the first remedy, that it is worse than the disease. Liberty is to faction, what air is to fire, an aliment without which it instantly expires. But it could not be a less folly to abolish liberty, which is essential to political life, because it nourishes faction, than it would be to wish the annihilation of air, which is essential to animal life, because it imparts to fire its destructive agency.

The second expedient is as impracticable, as the first would be unwise. As long as the reason of man continues fallible, and he is at liberty to exercise it, different opinions will be formed. As long as the connection subsists between his reason and his self-love, his opinions and his passions will have a reciprocal influence on each other; and the former will be objects to which the latter will attach themselves. The diversity in the faculties of men from which the rights of property originate, is not less an insuperable obstacle to a uniformity of interests. The protection of these faculties is the first object of Government. From the protection of different and unequal faculties of acquiring property, the possession of different degrees and kinds of property immediately results: and from the influence of these on the sentiments and views of the respective proprietors, ensues a division of the society into different interests and parties.

The latent causes of faction are thus sown in the nature of man; and we see them every where brought into different degrees of activity, according to the different circumstances of civil society. A zeal for different opinions concerning religion, concerning Government and many other points, as well of speculation as of practice; an attachment to different leaders ambitiously contending for pre-eminence and power; or to persons of other descriptions whose fortunes have been interesting to the human passions, have in turn divided mankind into parties, inflamed them with mutual animosity, and rendered them much more disposed to vex and oppress each other, than to cooperate for their common good. So strong is this propensity of mankind to fall into mutual animosities, that where no substantial occasion presents itself, the most frivolous and fanciful distinctions have been sufficient to kindle their unfriendly passions, and excite their most violent conflicts. But the most common and durable source of factions, has been the various and unequal distribution of property. Those who hold, and those who are without property, have ever formed distinct interests in society. Those who are creditors, and those who are debtors, fall under a like discrimination. A landed interest, a manufacturing interest, a mercantile interest, a monied interest, with many lesser interests, grow up of necessity in civilized nations, and divide them into different classes, actuated by different sentiments and views. The regulation of these various and interfering interests forms the principal task of modern Legislation, and involves the spirit of party and faction in the necessary and ordinary operations of Government.

No man is allowed to be judge in his own cause; because his interest would certainly bias his judgment, and, not improbably, corrupt his integrity. With equal, nay with greater reason, a body of men, are unfit to be judges and parties, at the same time; yet, what are many of the most important acts of legislation, but so many judicial determinations, not indeed concerning the rights of single persons, but concerning the rights of large bodies of citizens, and what are the different classes of legislators, but advocates and parties to the causes which they determine? Is a law proposed concerning private debts? It is a question to which the creditors are parties on one side, and the debtors on the other. Justice ought to hold the balance between them. Yet the parties are and must be themselves the judges; and the most numerous party, or, in other words, the most powerful faction must be expected to prevail. Shall domestic manufactures be encouraged, and in what degree, by restrictions on foreign manufactures? are questions which would be differently decided by the landed and the manufacturing classes; and probably by neither, with a sole regard to justice and the public good. The apportionment of taxes on the various descriptions of property, is an act which seems to require the most exact impartiality; yet, there is perhaps no legislative act in which greater opportunity and temptation are given to a predominant party, to trample on the rules of justice. Every shilling with which they over-burden the inferior number, is a shilling saved to their own pockets.

It is in vain to say, that enlightened statesmen will be able to adjust these clashing interests, and render them all subservient to the public good. Enlightened statesmen will not always be at the helm: Nor, in many cases, can such an adjustment be made at all, without taking into view indirect and remote considerations, which will rarely prevail over the immediate interest which one party may find in disregarding the rights of another, or the good of the whole.

The inference to which we are brought, is, that the *causes* of faction cannot be removed; and that relief is only to be sought in the means of controlling its *effects*.

If a faction consists of less than a majority, relief is supplied by the republican principle, which enables the majority to defeat its sinister views by regular vote: It may clog the administration, it may convulse the society; but it will be unable to execute and mask its violence under the forms of the Constitution. When a majority is included in a faction, the form of popular government on the other hand enables it to sacrifice to its ruling passion or interest, both the public good and the rights of other citizens. To secure the public good, and private rights, against the danger of such a faction, and at the same time to preserve the spirit and the form of popular government, is then the great object to which our inquiries are directed: Let me add that it is the great desideratum, by which alone this form of government can be rescued from the opprobrium under which it has so long labored, and be recommended to the esteem and adoption of mankind.

By what means is this object attainable? Evidently by one of two only. Either the existence of the same passion or interest in a majority at the same time, must be prevented; or the majority, having such co-existent passion or interest, must be rendered, by their number and local situation, unable to concert and carry into effect schemes of oppression. If the impulse and the opportunity be suffered to coincide, we well know that neither moral nor religious motives can be relied on as an adequate control. They are not found to be such on the injustice and violence of individuals, and lose their efficacy in proportion to the number combined together; that is, in proportion as their efficacy becomes needful.

From this view of the subject, it may be concluded, that a pure Democracy, by which I mean, a Society, consisting of a small number of citizens, who assemble and administer the Government in person, can admit of no cure for the mischiefs of faction. A common passion or interest will, in almost every case, be felt by a majority of the whole; a communication and concert results from the form of Government itself; and there is nothing to check the inducements to sacrifice the weaker party, or an obnoxious individual. Hence it is, that such Democracies have ever been spectacles of turbulence and contention; have ever been found incompatible with personal security, or the rights of property; and have in general been as short in their lives, as they have been violent in their deaths. Theoretic politicians, who have patronized this species of Government, have erroneously supposed, that by reducing mankind to a perfect equality in their political rights, they would, at the same time, be perfectly equalized and assimilated in their possessions, their opinions, and their passions.

A republic, by which I mean a government in which the scheme of representation takes place, opens a different prospect, and promises the cure for which we are seeking. Let us examine the points in which it varies from pure democracy, and we shall comprehend both the nature of the cure and the efficacy which it must derive from the union.

The two great points of difference, between a democracy and a republic, are, first, the delegation of the government, in the latter, to a small number of citizens, elected by the rest; secondly, the greater number of citizens, and greater sphere of country, over which the latter may be extended.

The effect of the first difference is, on the one hand, to refine and enlarge the public views, by passing them through the medium of a chosen body of citizens, whose wisdom may best discern the true interest of their country, and whose patriotism and love of justice, will be least likely to sacrifice it to temporary or partial considerations. Under such a regulation, it may well happen, that the public voice, pronounced by the representatives of the people, will be more consonant to the public good, than if pronounced by the people themselves, convened for the purpose. On the other hand the effect may be inverted. Men of factious tempers, of local prejudices, or of sinister designs, may by intrigue, by corruption, or by other means, first obtain the suffrages, and then betray the interest of the people. The question resulting is, whether small or extensive republics are most favorable to the election of proper guardians of the public weal, and it is clearly decided in favor of the latter by two obvious considerations.

In the first place, it is to be remarked that, however small the republic may be, the representatives must be raised to a certain number, in order to guard against the cabals of a few; and that however large it may be, they must be limited to a certain number, in order to guard against the confusion of a multitude. Hence, the number of representatives in the two cases not being in proportion to that of the constituents, and being proportionally greatest in the small republic, it follows, that if the proportion of fit characters be not less in the large than in the small republic, the former will present a greater option, and consequently a greater probability of a fit choice.

In the next place, as each Representative will be chosen by a greater number of citizens in the large than in the small Republic, it will be more difficult for unworthy candidates to practise with success the vicious arts, by which elections are too often carried; and the suffrages of the people being more free, will be more likely to center on men who possess the most attractive merit, and the most diffusive and established characters.

It must be confessed, that in this, as in most other cases, there is a mean, on both sides of which inconveniences will be found to lie. By enlarging too much the number of electors, you render the representatives too little acquainted with all their local circumstances and lesser interests; as by reducing it too much, you render him unduly attached to these, and too little fit to comprehend and pursue great and national objects. The Federal Constitution forms a happy combination in this respect; the great and aggregate interests being referred to the national, the local and particular, to the state legislatures.

The other point of difference is, the greater number of citizens and extent of territory which may be brought within the compass of Republican, than of Democratic Government; and it is this circumstance principally which renders factious combinations less to be dreaded in the former, than in the latter. The smaller the society, the fewer probably will be the distinct parties and interests composing it; the fewer the distinct parties and interests, the more frequently will a majority be found of the same party; and the smaller the number of individuals composing a majority, and the smaller the compass within which they are placed, the more easily they will concert and execute their plans of oppression. Extend the sphere, and you take in a greater variety of parties and interests; you make it less probable that a majority of the whole will have a common motive to invade the rights of other citizens; or if such a common motive exists, it will be more difficult for all who feel it to discover their own strength, and to act in unison with each other. Besides other impediments, it may be remarked, that where there is a consciousness of unjust or dishonorable purposes, communication is always checked by distrust, in proportion to the number whose concurrence is necessary.

Hence it clearly appears, that the same advantage, which a Republic has over a Democracy, in controlling the effects of factions, is enjoyed by a large over a small Republic—is enjoyed by the Union over the States composing it. Does this advantage consist in the substitution of Representatives, whose enlightened views and virtuous sentiments render them superior to local prejudices, and to schemes of injustice? It will not be denied, that the

Representation of the Union will be most likely to possess these requisite endowments. Does it consist in the greater security afforded by a greater variety of parties, against the event of any one party being able to outnumber and oppress the rest? In an equal degree does the increase variety of parties, comprised within the Union, increase this security? Does it, in fine, consist in the greater obstacles opposed to the concert and accomplishment of the secret wishes of an unjust and interested majority? Here, again, the extent of the Union gives it the most palpable advantage.

The influence of factious leaders may kindle a flame within their particular States, but will be unable to spread a general conflagration through the other States: a religious sect, may degenerate into a political faction in a part of the Confederacy but the variety of sects dispersed over the entire face of it, must secure the national Councils against any danger from that source: a rage for paper money, for an abolition of debts, for an equal division of property, or for any other improper or wicked project, will be less apt to pervade the whole body of the Union, than a particular member of it; in the same proportion as such a malady is more likely to taint a particular county or district, than an entire State.

In the extent and proper structure of the Union, therefore, we behold a Republican remedy for the diseases most incident to Republican Government. And according to the degree of pleasure and pride, we feel in being Republicans, ought to be our zeal in cherishing the spirit, and supporting the character of Federalists.

PUBLIUS

The Federalist No. 51

February 6, 1788

James Madison

TO THE PEOPLE OF THE STATE OF NEW YORK.

To what expedient then shall we finally resort for maintaining in practice the necessary partition of power among the several departments, as laid down in the constitution? The only answer that can be given is, that as all these exterior provisions are found to be inadequate, the defect must be supplied, by so contriving the interior structure of the government, as that its several constituent parts may, by their mutual relations, be the means of keeping each other in their proper places. Without presuming to undertake a full development of this important idea, I will hazard a few general observations, which may perhaps place it in a clearer light, and enable us to form a more correct judgment of the principles and structure of the government planned by the convention.

In order to lay a due foundation for that separate and distinct exercise of the different powers of government, which to a certain extent, is admitted on all hands to be essential to the preservation of liberty, it is evident that each department should have a will of its own; and consequently should be so constituted, that the members of each should have as little agency as possible in the appointment of the members of the others. Were this principle rigorously adhered to, it would require that all the appointments for the supreme executive, legislative, and judiciary magistracies, should be drawn from the same fountain of authority, the people, through channels, having no communication whatever with one another. Perhaps such a plan of constructing the several departments would be less difficult in practice than in it may in contemplation appear. Some difficulties however, and some additional expense, would attend the execution of it. Some deviations therefore from the principle must be admitted. In the constitution of the judiciary department in particular, it might be inexpedient to insist rigorously on the principle; first, because peculiar qualifications being essential in the members, the primary consideration ought to be to select that mode of choice, which best secures these qualifications; secondly, because the permanent tenure by which the appointments are held in that department, must soon destroy all sense of dependence on the authority conferring them.

It is equally evident that the members of each department should be as little dependent as possible on those of the others, for the emoluments annexed to their offices. Were the executive magistrate, or the judges, not independent of the legislature in this particular, their independence in every other would be merely nominal.

But the great security against a gradual concentration of the several powers in the same department, consists in giving to those who administer each department, the necessary constitutional means, and personal motives, to resist encroachments of the others. The provision for defense must in this, as in all other cases, be made commensurate to the danger of attack. Ambition must be made to counteract ambition. The interest of the man must be connected with the constitutional right of the place. It may be a reflection on human nature, that such devices should be necessary to control the abuses of government. But what is government itself but the greatest of all reflections on human nature? If men were angels, no government would be necessary. If angels were to govern men, neither external nor internal controls on government would be necessary. In framing a government which is to be administered by men over men, the great difficulty lies in this: You must first enable the government to control the governed; and in the next place, oblige it to control itself. A dependence on the people is no doubt the primary control on the government; but experience has taught mankind the necessity of auxiliary precautions.

This policy of supplying by opposite and rival interests, the defect of better motives, might be traced through the whole system of human affairs, private as well as public. We see it particularly displayed in all the subordinate distributions of power; where the constant aim is to divide and arrange the several offices in such a manner as that each may be a check on the other; that the private interest of every individual, may be a sentinel over the public rights. These inventions of prudence cannot be less requisite in the distribution of the supreme powers of the state.

But it is not possible to give each department an equal power of self defense. In republican government the legislative authority, necessarily, predominates. The remedy for this inconvenience is, to divide the legislative into different branches; and to render them by different modes of election, and different principles of action, as little connected with each other, as the nature of their common functions, and their common dependence on the society, will admit. It may even be necessary to guard against dangerous encroachments by still further precautions. As the weight of the legislative authority requires that it should be thus divided, the weakness of the executive may require, on the other hand, that it should be fortified. An absolute negative, on the legislature, appears at first view to be the natural defense with which the executive magistrate should be armed. But perhaps it would be neither altogether safe, nor alone sufficient. On ordinary occasions, it might not be exerted with the requisite firmness, and on extraordinary occasions, it might be prefidiously abused. May not this defect of an absolute negative be supplied, by some qualified connection between this weaker department, and the weaker branch of the stronger department, by which the latter may be led to support the constitutional rights of the former, without being too much detached from the rights of its own department?

If the principles on which these observations are founded be just, as I persuade myself they are, and they be applied as a criterion, to the several state constitutions, and to the federal constitution, it will be found, that if the latter does not perfectly correspond with them, the former are infinitely less able to bear such a test.

There are moreover two considerations particularly applicable to the federal system of America, which place the system in a very interesting point of view.

First. In a single republic, all the power surrendered by the people, is submitted to the administration of a single government; and usurpations are guarded against by a division of the government into distinct and separate departments. In the compound republic of America, the power surrendered by the people, is first divided between two distinct governments, and then the portion allotted to each, subdivided among distinct and separate departments. Hence a double security arises to the rights of the people. The different governments will control each other; at the same time that each will be controlled by itself.

Second. It is of great importance in a republic, not only to guard the society against the oppression of its rulers; but to guard one part of the society against the injustice of the other part. Different interests necessarily exist in different classes of citizens. If a majority be united by a common interest, the rights of the minority will be insecure. There are but two methods of providing against this evil: The one by creating a will in the community independent of the majority, that is, of the society itself, the other by comprehending in the society so many separate descriptions of citizens, as will render an unjust combination of a majority of the whole, very improbable, if not impracticable. The first method prevails in all governments possessing an hereditary or self appointed authority. This at best is but a precarious security; because a power independent of the society may as well espouse the unjust views of the major, as the rightful interests, of the minor party, and may possibly be turned against both parties. The second method will be exemplified in the federal republic of the United States. While all authority in it will be derived from and dependent on the society, the society itself will be broken into so many parts, interests and classes of citizens, that the rights of individuals or of the minority, will be in little danger from interested combinations of the majority. In a free government, the security for civil rights must be the same as for religious rights. It consists in the one case in the multiplicity of interests, and in the other, in the multiplicity of sects. The degree of security in both cases will depend on the number of interests and sects; and this may be presumed to depend on the extent of country and number of people comprehended under the same government. This view of the subject must particularly recommend a proper federal system to all the sincere and considerate friends of republican government: Since it shows that in exact proportion as the territory of the union may be formed into more circumscribed confederacies or states, oppressive combinations of a majority will be facilitated, the best security under the republican form, for the rights of every class of citizens, will be diminished; and consequently, the stability and independence of some member of the government, the only other security, must be proportionally increased. Justice is the end of government. It is the end of civil society. It ever has been, and ever will be pursued, until it be obtained, or until liberty be lost in the pursuit. In a society under the forms of which the stronger faction can readily unite and oppress the weaker, anarchy may as truly be said to reign, as in a state of nature where the weaker individual is not secured against the violence of the stronger: And as in the latter state even the stronger individuals are prompted by the uncertainty of their condition, to submit to a government which may protect the weak as well as themselves: So in the former state, will the more powerful factions or parties be gradually induced by a like motive, to wish for a government which will protect all parties, the weaker as well as the more powerful. It can be little doubted, that if the state of Rhode Island was separated from the confederacy, and left to itself, the insecurity of rights under the popular form of government within such narrow limits, would be displayed by such reiterated oppressions of factious majorities, that some power altogether independent of the people would soon be called for by the voice of the very factions whose misrule had proved the necessity of it. In the extended republic of the United States, and among the great variety of interests, parties and sects which it embraces, a coalition of a majority of the whole society could seldom take place on any other principles than those of justice and the general good; and there being thus less danger to a minor from the will of the major party, there must be less pretext also, to provide for the security of the former, by introducing into the government a will not dependent on the latter; or in other words, a will independent of the society itself. It is no less certain than it is important, notwithstanding the contrary opinions which have been entertained, that the larger the society, provided it lie within a practicable sphere, the more duly capable it will be of self government. And happily for the *republican cause*, the practicable sphere may be carried to a very great extent, by a judicious modification and mixture of the *federal principle*.

PUBLIUS

Rev. Dr. Martin Luther King, Jr.'s Speech:"I Have a Dream"
Aug. 28, 1963

I am happy to join with you today in what will go down in history as the greatest demonstration for freedom in the history of our nation.

Five score years ago a great American in whose symbolic shadow we stand today signed the Emancipation Proclamation. This momentous decree came as a great beacon light of hope to millions of Negro slaves who had been seared in the flames of withering injustice. It came as a joyous daybreak to end the long night of their captivity. But one hundred years later, the Negro still is not free. One hundred years later, the life of the Negro is still sadly crippled by the manacles of segregation and the chains of discrimination. One hundred years later, the Negro lives on a lonely island of poverty in the midst of a vast ocean of material prosperity. One hundred years later, the Negro is still languished in the corners of American society and finds himself an exile in his own land. So we've come here today to dramatize a shameful condition.

In a sense we've come to our nation's capital to cash a check. When the architects of our republic wrote the magnificent words of the Constitution and the Declaration of Independence, they were signing a promissory note to which every American was to fall heir. This note was a promise that all men—yes, black men as well as white men—would be guaranteed the unalienable rights of life, liberty, and the pursuit of happiness. It is obvious today that America has defaulted on this promissory note insofar as her citizens of color are concerned. Instead of honoring this sacred obligation, America has given the Negro people a bad check, a check which has come back marked "insufficient funds."

But we refuse to believe that the bank of justice is bankrupt. We refuse to believe that there are insufficient funds in the great vaults of opportunity of this nation. So we have come to cash this check, a check that will give us upon demand the riches of freedom and the security of justice.

We have also come to this hallowed spot to remind America of the fierce urgency of now. This is no time to engage in the luxury of cooling off or to take the tranquilizing drug of gradualism. Now is the time to make real the promises of democracy. Now is the time to rise from the dark and desolate valley of segregation to the sunlit path of racial justice. Now is the time to lift our nation from the quicksands of racial injustice to the solid rock of brotherhood.

Now is the time to make justice a reality for all of God's children. It would be fatal for the nation to overlook the urgency of the moment. This sweltering summer of the Negro's legitimate discontent will not pass until there is an invigorating autumn of freedom and equality. 1963 is not an end, but a beginning. Those who hope that the Negro needed to blow off steam and will now be content will have a rude awakening if the nation returns to business as usual.

There will be neither rest nor tranquility in America until the Negro is granted his citizenship rights. The whirlwinds of revolt will continue to shake the foundations of our nation until the bright day of justice emerges. But there is something that I must say to my people who stand on the warm threshold which leads into the palace of justice. In the process of gaining our rightful place we must not be guilty of wrongful deeds. Let us not seek to satisfy our thirst for freedom by drinking from the cup of bitterness and hatred.

We must forever conduct our struggle on the high plane of dignity and discipline. We must not allow our creative protest to degenerate into physical violence. Again and again we must rise to the majestic heights of meeting physical force with soul force. The marvelous new militancy which has engulfed the Negro community must not lead us to distrust of all white people, for many of our white brothers, as evidenced by their presence here today, have come to realize that their destiny is tied up with our destiny.

And they have come to realize that their freedom is inextricably bound to our freedom. We cannot walk alone. And as we walk, we must make the pledge that we shall always march ahead. We cannot turn back. There are those who are asking the devotees of civil rights, "When will you be satisfied?" We can never be satisfied as long as the Negro is the victim of the unspeakable horrors of police brutality.

We can never be satisfied as long as our bodies, heavy with the fatigue of travel, cannot gain lodging in the motels of the highways and the hotels of the cities.

We cannot be satisfied as long as the Negro's basic mobility is from a smaller ghetto to a larger one. We can never be satisfied as long as our children are stripped of their selfhood and robbed of their dignity by signs stating "For Whites Only."

We cannot be satisfied as long as a Negro in Mississippi cannot vote and a Negro in New York believes he has nothing for which to vote.

No, no, we are not satisfied, and we will not be satisfied until justice rolls down like waters and righteousness like a mighty stream.

I am not unmindful that some of you have come here out of great trials and tribulations. Some of you have come fresh from narrow jail cells. Some of you have come from areas where your quest for freedom left you battered by the storms of persecution and staggered by the winds of police brutality. You have been the veterans of creative suffering.

Continue to work with the faith that unearned suffering is redemptive. Go back to Mississippi, go back to Alabama, go back to South Carolina, go back to Georgia, go back to Louisiana, go back to the slums and ghettos of our northern cities, knowing that somehow this situation can and will be changed. Let us not wallow in the valley of despair.

I say to you today, my friends, though, even though we face the difficulties of today and tomorrow, I still have a dream. It is a dream deeply rooted in the American dream. I have a dream that one day this nation will rise up and live out the true meaning of its creed: "We hold these truths to be self-evident, that all men are created equal."

I have a dream that one day on the red hills of Georgia the sons of former slaves and the sons of former slave owners will be able to sit down together at a table of brotherhood. I have a dream that one day even the state of Mississippi, a state sweltering with the heat of injustice, sweltering with the heat of oppression, will be transformed into an oasis of freedom and justice.

I have a dream that my four little children will one day live in a nation where they will not be judged by the color of their skin but by the content of their character. I have a dream today. I have a dream that one day down in Alabama, with its vicious racists, with its governor having his lips dripping with the words of interposition and nullification, one day right there in Alabama little black boys and black girls will be able to join hands with little white boys and white girls as sisters and brothers.

I have a dream today.

I have a dream that one day every valley shall be exalted, every hill and mountain shall be made low. The rough places will be made plain, and the crooked places will be made straight. And the glory of the Lord shall be revealed, and all flesh shall see it together. This is our hope. This is the faith that I go back to the South with. With this faith we will be able to hew out of the mountain of despair a stone of hope. With this faith we will be able to transform the jangling discords of our nation into a beautiful symphony of brotherhood. With this faith we will be able to work together, to pray together, to struggle together, to go to jail together, to stand up for freedom together, knowing that we will be free one day.

This will be the day when all of God's children will be able to sing with new meaning, "My country, 'tis of thee, sweet land of liberty, of thee I sing. Land where my fathers died, land of the pilgrim's pride, from every mountainside, let freedom ring." And if America is to be a great nation, this must become true. So let freedom ring from the prodigious hilltops of New Hampshire. Let freedom ring from the mighty mountains of New York. Let freedom ring from the heightening Alleghenies of Pennsylvania. Let freedom ring from the snowcapped Rockies of Colorado. Let freedom ring from the curvaceous slopes of California.

But not only that. Let freedom ring from Stone Mountain of Georgia. Let freedom ring from Lookout Mountain of Tennessee. Let freedom ring from every hill and molehill of Mississippi. From every mountainside, let freedom ring…

And when this happens, when we allow freedom to ring—when we let it ring from every village and every hamlet, from every state and every city, we will be able to speed up that day when all of God's children, black men and white men, Jews and Gentiles, Protestants and Catholics, will be able to join hands and sing in the words of the old Negro spiritual, "Free at last! Free at last! Thank God Almighty, we are free at last!"

Presidents and Congresses, 1789–2009

Year	President and Vice President	Party of President	Congress	House		Senate	
				Majority Party	Minority Party	Majority Party	Minority Party
1789–1797	**George Washington**	None	1st	38 Admin	26 Opp	17 Admin	9 Opp
	John Adams		2d	37 Fed	33 Dem-Rep	16 Fed	13 Dem-Rep
			3d	57 Dem-Rep	48 Fed	17 Fed	13 Dem-Rep
			4th	54 Fed	52 Dem-Rep	19 Fed	13 Dem-Rep
1797–1801	**John Adams**	Federalist	5th	58 Fed	48 Dem-Rep	20 Fed	12 Dem-Rep
	Thomas Jefferson		6th	64 Fed	42 Dem-Rep	19 Fed	13 Dem-Rep
1801–1809	**Thomas Jefferson**	Dem-Rep	7th	69 Dem-Rep	36 Fed	18 Dem-Rep	13 Fed
	Aaron Burr (to 1805)		8th	102 Dem-Rep	39 Fed	25 Dem-Rep	9 Fed
	George Clinton (to 1809)		9th	116 Dem-Rep	25 Fed	27 Dem-Rep	7 Fed
			10th	118 Dem-Rep	24 Fed	28 Dem-Rep	6 Fed
1809–1817	**James Madison**	Dem-Rep	11th	94 Dem-Rep	48 Fed	28 Dem-Rep	6 Fed
	George Clinton (to 1813)		12th	108 Dem-Rep	36 Fed	30 Dem-Rep	6 Fed
	Elbridge Gerry (to 1817)		13th	112 Dem-Rep	68 Fed	27 Dem-Rep	9 Fed
			14th	117 Dem-Rep	65 Fed	25 Dem-Rep	11 Fed
1817–1825	**James Monroe**	Dem-Rep	15th	141 Dem-Rep	42 Fed	34 Dem-Rep	10 Fed
	Daniel D. Tompkins		16th	156 Dem-Rep	27 Fed	35 Dem-Rep	7 Fed
			17th	158 Dem-Rep	25 Fed	44 Dem-Rep	4 Fed
			18th	187 Dem-Rep	26 Fed	44 Dem-Rep	4 Fed
1825–1829	**John Quincy Adams**	Nat-Rep	19th	105 Admin	97 Jack	26 Admin	20 Jack
	John C. Calhoun		20th	119 Jack	94 Admin	28 Jack	20 Admin
1829–1837	**Andrew Jackson**	Democrat	21st	139 Dem	74 Nat Rep	26 Dem	22 Nat Rep
	John C. Calhoun (to 1833)		22d	141 Dem	58 Nat Rep	25 Dem	21 Nat Rep
	Martin Van Buren (to 1837)		23d	147 Dem	53 AntiMas	20 Dem	20 Nat Rep
			24th	145 Dem	98 Whig	27 Dem	25 Whig
1837–1841	**Martin Van Buren**	Democrat	25th	108 Dem	107 Whig	30 Dem	18 Whig
	Richard M. Johnson		26th	124 Dem	118 Whig	28 Dem	22 Whig
1841	**William H. Harrison***	Whig					
	John Tyler						

NOTES: Only members of two major parties in Congress are shown; omitted are independents, members of minor parties, and vacancies. Party balance as of beginning of Congress.

Congresses in which one or both houses are controlled by party other than that of the president are shown in color.

During administration of George Washington and (in part) John Quincy Adams, Congress was not organized by formal parties; the split shown is between supporters and opponents of the administration.

ABBREVIATIONS: **Admin** = Administration supporters; **AntiMas** = Anti-Masonic; **Dem** = Democratic; **Dem-Rep** = Democratic-Republican; **Fed** = Federalist; **Jack** = Jacksonian Democrats; **Nat Rep** = National Republican; **Opp** = Opponents of administration; **Rep** = Republican; **Union** = Unionist; **Whig** = Whig.

*Died in office.

Year	President and Vice President	Party of President	Congress	House Majority Party	House Minority Party	Senate Majority Party	Senate Minority Party
1841–1845	**John Tyler**	Whig	27th	133 Whig	102 Dem	28 Whig	22 Dem
	(VP vacant)		28th	142 Dem	79 Whig	28 Whig	25 Dem
1845–1849	**James K. Polk**	Democrat	29th	143 Dem	77 Whig	31 Dem	25 Whig
	George M. Dallas		30th	115 Whig	108 Dem	36 Dem	21 Whig
1849–1850	**Zachary Taylor***	Whig	31st	112 Dem	109 Whig	35 Dem	25 Whig
	Millard Fillmore						
1850–1853	**Millard Fillmore**	Whig	32d	140 Dem	88 Whig	35 Dem	24 Whig
	(VP vacant)						
1853–1857	**Franklin Pierce**	Democrat	33d	159 Dem	71 Whig	38 Dem	22 Whig
	William R. King		34th	108 Rep	83 Dem	40 Dem	15 Rep
1857–1861	**James Buchanan**	Democrat	35th	118 Dem	92 Rep	36 Dem	20 Rep
	John C. Breckinridge		36th	114 Rep	92 Dem	36 Dem	26 Rep
1861–1865	**Abraham Lincoln***	Republican	37th	105 Rep	43 Dem	31 Rep	10 Dem
	Hannibal Hamlin (to 1865)		38th	102 Rep	75 Dem	36 Rep	9 Dem
	Andrew Johnson (1865)						
1865–1869	**Andrew Johnson**	Republican	39th	149 Union	42 Dem	42 Union	10 Dem
	(VP vacant)		40th	143 Rep	49 Dem	42 Rep	11 Dem
1869–1877	**Ulysses S. Grant**	Republican	41st	149 Rep	63 Dem	56 Rep	11 Dem
	Schuyler Colfax (to 1873)		42d	134 Rep	104 Dem	52 Rep	17 Dem
	Henry Wilson (to 1877)		43d	194 Rep	92 Dem	49 Rep	19 Dem
			44th	169 Dem	109 Rep	45 Rep	29 Dem
1877–1881	**Rutherford B. Hayes**	Republican	45th	153 Dem	140 Rep	39 Rep	36 Dem
	William A. Wheeler		46th	149 Dem	130 Rep	42 Dem	33 Rep
1881	**James A. Garfield***	Republican	47th	147 Rep	135 Dem	37 Rep	37 Dem
	Chester A. Arthur						
1881–1885	**Chester A. Arthur**	Republican	48th	197 Dem	118 Rep	38 Rep	36 Rep
	(VP vacant)						
1885–1889	**Grover Cleveland**	Democrat	49th	183 Dem	140 Rep	43 Rep	34 Dem
	Thomas A. Hendricks		50th	169 Dem	152 Rep	39 Rep	37 Dem
1889–1893	**Benjamin Harrison**	Republican	51st	166 Rep	159 Dem	39 Rep	37 Dem
	Levi P. Morton		52d	235 Dem	88 Rep	47 Rep	39 Dem
1893–1897	**Grover Cleveland**	Democrat	53d	218 Dem	127 Rep	44 Dem	38 Rep
	Adlai E. Stevenson		54th	244 Rep	105 Dem	43 Rep	39 Dem
1897–1901	**William McKinley***	Republican	55th	204 Rep	113 Rep	47 Rep	34 Dem

*Died in office.

Year	President and Vice President	Party of President	Congress	House		Senate	
				Majority Party	Minority Party	Majority Party	Minority Party
	Garret A. Hobart (to 1901)		56th	185 Rep	163 Rep	53 Rep	26 Dem
	Theodore Roosevelt (1901)						
1901–1909	**Theodore Roosevelt**	Republican	57th	197 Rep	151 Dem	55 Rep	31 Dem
	(VP vacant, 1901–1905)		58th	208 Rep	178 Dem	57 Rep	33 Dem
	Charles W. Fairbanks		59th	250 Rep	136 Dem	57 Rep	33 Dem
	(1905–1909)		60th	222 Rep	164 Dem	61 Rep	31 Dem
1909–1913	**William Howard Taft**	Republican	61st	219 Rep	172 Dem	61 Rep	32 Dem
	James S. Sherman		62d	228 Dem	161 Rep	51 Rep	41 Dem
1913–1921	**Woodrow Wilson**	Democrat	63d	291 Dem	127 Rep	51 Dem	44 Rep
	Thomas R. Marshall		64th	230 Dem	196 Rep	56 Dem	40 Rep
			65th	216 Dem	210 Rep	53 Dem	42 Rep
			66th	240 Rep	190 Dem	49 Rep	47 Dem
1921–1923	**Warren G. Harding***	Republican	67th	301 Rep	131 Dem	59 Rep	37 Dem
	Calvin Coolidge						
1923–1929	**Calvin Coolidge**	Republican	68th	225 Rep	205 Dem	51 Rep	43 Dem
	(VP vacant, 1923–1925)		69th	247 Rep	183 Dem	56 Rep	39 Dem
	Charles G. Dawes (1925–1929)		70th	237 Rep	195 Dem	49 Rep	46 Dem
1929–1933	**Herbert Hoover**	Republican	71st	267 Rep	167 Dem	56 Rep	39 Dem
	Charles Curtis		72d	220 Dem	214 Rep	48 Rep	47 Dem
1933–1945	**Franklin D. Roosevelt***	Democrat	73d	310 Dem	117 Rep	60 Dem	35 Rep
	John N. Garner		74th	319 Dem	103 Rep	69 Dem	25 Rep
	(1933–1941)		75th	331 Dem	89 Rep	76 Dem	16 Rep
	Henry A. Wallace		76th	261 Dem	164 Rep	69 Dem	23 Rep
	(1941–1945)		77th	268 Dem	162 Rep	66 Dem	28 Rep
	Harry S. Truman (1945)		78th	218 Dem	208 Rep	58 Dem	37 Rep
1945–1953	**Harry S. Truman**	Democrat	79th	242 Dem	190 Rep	56 Dem	38 Rep
	VP vacant, 1945–1949		80th	245 Rep	188 Dem	51 Rep	45 Dem
	Alben W. Barkley		81st	263 Dem	171 Rep	54 Dem	42 Rep
	(1949–1953)		82d	234 Dem	199 Rep	49 Dem	47 Rep
1953–1961	**Dwight D. Eisenhower**	Republican	83d	221 Rep	211 Dem	48 Rep	47 Dem
	Richard M. Nixon		84th	232 Dem	203 Rep	48 Dem	47 Rep

*Died in office.

Year	President and Vice President	Party of President	Congress	House		Senate	
				Majority Party	Minority Party	Majority Party	Minority Party
			85th	233 Dem	200 Rep	49 Dem	47 Rep
			86th	283 Dem	153 Rep	64 Dem	34 Rep
1961–1963	**John F. Kennedy***	Democrat	87th	263 Dem	174 Rep	65 Dem	35 Rep
	Lyndon B. Johnson						
1963–1969	**Lyndon B. Johnson**	Democrat	88th	258 Dem	177 Rep	67 Dem	33 Rep
	(VP vacant, 1963–1965)		89th	295 Dem	140 Rep	68 Dem	32 Rep
	Hubert H. Humphrey		90th	247 Dem	187 Rep	64 Dem	36 Rep
	(1965–1969)						
1969–1974	**Richard M. Nixon**†	Republican	91st	243 Dem	192 Rep	57 Dem	43 Rep
	Spiro T. Agnew††		92d	254 Dem	180 Rep	54 Dem	44 Rep
	Gerald R. Ford§						
1974–1977	**Gerald R. Ford**	Republican	93d	239 Dem	192 Rep	56 Dem	42 Rep
	Nelson A. Rockefeller§		94th	291 Dem	144 Rep	60 Dem	37 Rep
1977–1981	**Jimmy Carter**	Democrat	95th	292 Dem	143 Rep	61 Dem	38 Rep
	Walter Mondale		96th	276 Dem	157 Rep	58 Dem	41 Rep
1981–1989	**Ronald Reagan**	Republican	97th	243 Dem	192 Rep	53 Rep	46 Dem
	George Bush		98th	269 Dem	165 Rep	54 Rep	46 Dem
			99th	253 Dem	182 Rep	53 Rep	47 Dem
			100th	257 Dem	178 Rep	54 Dem	46 Rep
1989–1993	**George Bush**	Republican	101st	262 Dem	173 Rep	55 Dem	45 Rep
	Dan Quayle		102d	267 Dem	167 Rep	56 Dem	44 Rep
1993–2000	**Bill Clinton**	Democrat	103d	258 Dem	176 Rep	57 Dem	43 Rep
	Albert Gore, Jr.		104th	230 Rep	204 Dem	53 Rep	47 Dem
			105th	228 Rep	206 Dem	55 Rep	45 Dem
			106th	223 Rep	211 Dem	54 Rep	46 Dem
2000–2009	**George W. Bush**	Republican	107th	220 Rep	215 Dem	50 Rep	50 Dem
	Dick Cheney		108th	229 Rep	204 Dem	51 Rep	48 Dem
			109th	233 Rep	206 Dem	55 Rep	44 Dem
			110th	229 Dem	196 Rep	51 Dem	49 Rep
2009–2012	**Barack Obama**	Democrat	111th	256 Dem	179 Rep	60 Dem	40 Rep
	Joe Biden		112th	193 Dem	242 Rep	51 Dem	47 Rep
			113th**	200 Dem	233 Rep	53 Dem	45 Rep

*Died in office. †Resigned from the presidency. ††Resigned from the vice presidency. §Appointed vice president. **At the start of the 113th Congress, there were 2 vacancies in the House. There were also 2 Independents in the Senate that caucused with Democrats.

Glossary

527 organizations Organizations operating under section 527 of the Internal Revenue Code that raise and spend money to advance political causes.

Activists People who tend to participate in all forms of politics.

Activist approach The view that judges should discern the general principles underlying laws or the Constitution and apply them to modern circumstances.

Ad hoc structure Several subordinates, cabinet officers, and committees report directly to the president on different matters.

Adversarial press The tendency of the national media to be suspicious of officials and eager to reveal unflattering stories about them.

Affirmative action Laws or administrative regulations that require a business firm, government agency, labor union, school, college, or other organization to take positive steps to increase the number of African Americans, other minorities, or women in its membership.

Amendments A new provision in the Constitution that has been ratified by the states.

Amicus curiae A brief submitted by a "friend of the court."

Antifederalists Those who favor a weaker national government.

Appropriation A legislative grant of money to finance a government program or agency.

Articles of Confederation A weak constitution that governed America during the Revolutionary War.

Assistance program A government program financed by general income taxes that provide benefits to poor citizens without requiring contribution from them.

Australian ballot Adopted by many states around 1890 to reduce voting fraud associated with party-printed ballots, a government-printed ballot of uniform dimensions to be cast in secret.

Authority The right to use power.

Authorization legislation Legislative permission to begin or continue a government program or agency.

Background A public official's statement to a reporter given on condition that the official not be named.

Benefit A satisfaction that people believe they will enjoy if a policy is adopted.

Bicameral legislature A lawmaking body made up of two chambers or parts.

Bill of attainder A law that declares a person, without a trial, to be guilty of a crime.

Bill of Rights First ten amendments to the Constitution.

Bipolar world A political landscape with two superpowers.

Blanket primary A primary election in which each voter may vote for candidates from both parties.

Blog A series, or log, of discussion items on a page of the World Wide Web.

Brief A written statement by an attorney that summarizes a case and the laws and rulings that support it.

Budget A document that states tax collections, spending levels, and the allocation of spending among purposes.

Budget resolution A congressional decision that states the maximum amount of money the government should spend.

Bully pulpit The president's use of his prestige and visibility to guide or enthuse the American public.

Bureaucracy A large, complex organization composed of appointed officials.

Bureaucratic view View that the government is dominated by appointed officials.

Cabinet The heads of the 15 executive branch departments of the federal government.

Categorical grants Federal grants for specific purposes, such as building an airport.

Caucus A meeting of party members to select delegates backing one or another primary candidate. An association of congressional members created to advance a political ideology or a regional, ethnic, or economic interest.

Charitable choice Name given to four federal laws passed in the late 1990s specifying the conditions under which nonprofit religious organizations could compete to administer certain social service delivery and welfare programs.

Checks and balances Authority shared by three branches of government.

Circular structure Several of the president's assistants report directly to him.

Civic competence A belief that one can affect government policies.

Civic duty A belief that one has an obligation to participate in civic and political affairs.

Civil disobedience Opposing a law one considers unjust by peacefully disobeying it and accepting the resultant punishment.

Civil liberties Rights—chiefly, rights to be free of government interference—accorded to an individual by the Constitution: free speech, free press, and so on.

Civil rights The rights of people to be treated without unreasonable or unconstitutional differences.

Civil society Voluntary action that makes cooperation easier.

Class-action suit A case brought by someone to help both himself or herself and all others who are similarly situated.

Class-consciousness A belief that one is a member of an economic group whose interests are opposed to people in other such groups.

Class view View that the government is dominated by capitalists.

Clear-and-present danger test Law should not punish speech unless there was a clear and present danger of producing harmful actions.

Client politics A policy in which one small group benefits and almost everybody pays.

Closed primary A primary election in which voting is limited to already registered party members.

Closed rule An order from the House Rules Committee that sets a time limit on debate; forbids a bill from being amended on the floor.

Clothespin vote The vote cast by a person who does not like either candidate and so votes for the less objectionable of the two, putting a clothespin over his or her nose to keep out the unpleasant stench.

Cloture rule A rule used by the Senate to end or limit debate.

Coalition An alliance of groups.

Coattails The alleged tendency of candidates to win more votes in an election because of the presence at the top of the ticket of a better-known candidate, such as the president.

Committee clearance The ability of a congressional committee to review and approve certain agency decisions in advance and without passing a law.

Competitive service The government offices to which people are appointed on the basis of merit, as ascertained by a written exam or by applying certain selection criteria.

Concurrent powers Powers shared by the national and state governments.

Concurrent resolution An expression of opinion without the force of law that requires the approval of both the House and the Senate, but not the president.

Concurring opinion A signed opinion in which one or more members agree with the majority view but for different reasons.

Conditions of aid Terms set by the national government that states must meet if they are to receive certain federal funds.

Conference committee Joint committees appointed to resolve differences in the Senate and House versions of the same bill.

Congressional campaign committee A party committee in Congress that provides funds to members and would-be members.

Conservative coalition An alliance between republican and conservative democrats.

Constitutional Convention A meeting in Philadelphia in 1787 that produced a new constitution.

Constitutional court A federal court authorized by Article III of the Constitution that keeps judges in office during good behavior and prevents their salaries from being reduced. They are the Supreme Court (created by the Constitution) and appellate and district courts created by Congress.

Containment The belief that the United States should resist the expansion of aggressive nations, especially the former Soviet Union.

Cost A burden that people believe they must bear if a policy is adopted.

Cost overruns When the money actually paid to military suppliers exceeds the estimated costs.

Courts of appeals Federal courts that hear appeals from district courts; no trials.

Creedal passion view View that morally impassioned elites drive important political changes.

Critical or **realignment periods** A period when a major, lasting shift occurs in the popular coalition supporting one or both parties.

De facto segregation Racial segregation that occurs in schools, not as a result of the law, but as a result of patterns of residential settlement.

Deficit The result of when the government in one year spends more money than it takes in from taxes.

De jure segregation Racial segregation that is required by law.

Democracy The rule of the many.

Direct or participatory democracy A government in which all or most citizens participate directly.

Discharge petition A device by which any member of the House, after a committee has had the bill for 30 days, may petition to have it brought to the floor.

Discretionary authority The extent to which appointed bureaucrats can choose courses of action and make policies not spelled out in advance by laws.

Discretionary spending Spending that is not required to pay for contracts, interest on the national debt, or entitlement programs such as Social Security.

Disengagement The belief that the United States was harmed by its war in Vietnam and so should avoid supposedly similar events.

Dissenting opinion A signed opinion in which one or more justices disagree with the majority view.

District courts The lowest federal courts; federal trials can be held only here.

Diversity cases Cases involving citizens of different states who can bring suit in federal courts.

Divided government One party controls the White House and another party controls one or both houses of Congress.

Division vote A congressional voting procedure in which members stand and are counted.

Double tracking A procedure to keep the Senate going during a filibuster in which the disputed bill is shelved temporarily so that the Senate can get on with other business.

Dual federalism Doctrine holding that the national government is supreme in its sphere, the states are supreme in theirs, and the two spheres should be kept separate.

Due process of law Denies the government the right, without due process, to deprive people of life, liberty, and property.

Earmark A "hidden" provision in a law that provides a direct benefit to a client (funding for specific projects or tax or fee exemptions for specific persons or groups) without the benefit having been reviewed on the merits by all of Congress.

Economic planning The belief that government plans, such as wage and price controls or the direction of investment, can improve the economy.

Electoral College The people chosen to cast each state's votes in a presidential election. Each state can cast one electoral vote for each senator and representative it has. The District of Columbia has three electoral votes, even though it cannot elect a representative or a senator.

Elite Persons who possess a disproportionate share of some valued resource, such as money, prestige, or expertise.

Entitlements A claim for government funds that cannot be changed without violating the rights of the claimant.

Entrepreneurial politics A policy in which almost everybody benefits and a small group pays.

Enumerated powers Powers given to the national government alone.

Environmental impact statement A report required by federal law that assesses the possible effect of a project on the environment if the project is subsidized in whole or part by federal funds.

Equality of opportunity Giving people an equal chance to succeed.

Equality of results Making certain that people achieve the same result.

Equal protection of the laws A standard of equal treatment that must be observed by the government.

Equal time rule An FCC rule that if a broadcaster sells time to one candidate, it must sell equal time to other candidates.

Establishment clause First Amendment ban on laws "respecting an establishment of religion."

Exclusionary rule Improperly gathered evidence may not be introduced in a criminal trial.

Exit polls Polls based on interviews conducted on Election Day with randomly selected voters.

Ex post facto law A law that makes an act criminal although the act was legal when it was committed.

Faction A group with a distinct political interest.

Feature stories Media stories about events that, though public, are not regularly covered by reporters.

Federalism Government authority shared by national and local governments.

Federalists Those who favor a stronger national government.

Federal-question cases Cases concerning the Constitution, federal laws, or treaties.

Fee shifting A rule that allows a plaintiff to recover costs from the defendant if the plaintiff wins.

Filibuster An attempt to defeat a bill in the Senate by talking indefinitely, thus preventing the Senate from taking action on the bill.

Fiscal policy Managing the economy by the use of tax and spending laws.

Fiscal year For the federal government, October 1 through the following September 30.

Franking privilege The ability of members to mail letters to their constituents free of charge by substituting their facsimile signature for postage.

Freedom of expression Right of people to speak, publish, and assemble.

Freedom of religion People shall be free to exercise their religion, and government may not establish a religion.

Free-exercise clause First Amendment requirement that law cannot prevent free exercise of religion.

General election An election held to choose which candidate will hold office.

Gerrymandering Drawing the boundaries of legislative districts in bizarre or unusual shapes to favor one party.

Globalization The growing integration of the economies and societies of the world.

Gold plating The tendency of Pentagon officials to ask weapons contractors to meet excessively high requirements.

Good faith exception An error in gathering evidence sufficiently minor that it may be used in a trial.

Government by proxy Washington pays state and local governments and private groups to staff and administer federal programs.

Grandfather clause A clause in registration laws allowing people who do not meet registration requirements to vote if they or their ancestors had voted before 1867.

Grants-in-aid Money given by the national government to the states.

Great Compromise Plan to have a popularly elected House based on state population and a state-selected Senate, with two members for each state.

Gridlock The inability of the government to act because rival parties control different parts of the government.

Gross domestic product The total of all goods and services produced in the economy during a given year.

Habeas corpus An order to produce an arrested person before a judge.

Horse-race journalism News coverage that focuses on who is ahead rather than on the issues.

Human rights The view that we should try to improve the lives of people in other countries.

Ideological interest groups Political organizations that attract members by appealing to their political convictions or principles.

Ideological party A party that values principled stands on issues above all else.

Impeachment Charges against a president approved by a majority of the House of Representatives.

Incentive Something of value one cannot get without joining an organization.

Incumbent The person already holding an elective office.

Independent expenditures Spending by political action committees, corporations, or labor unions to help a party or candidate but done independently of them.

Inevitable discovery The police can use evidence if it would inevitably have been discovered.

In forma pauperis A method whereby a poor person can have his or her case heard in federal court without charge.

Initiative Process that permits voters to put legislative measures directly on the ballot.

Insider stories Media stories about events that are not usually made public.

Insurance program A self-financing government program based on contributions that provide benefits to unemployed or retired persons.

Interest group An organization of people sharing a common interest or goal that seeks to influence public policy.

Interest group politics A policy in which one small group benefits and another small group pays.

Iron triangle A close relationship between an agency, a congressional committee, and an Interest group.

Isolationism The opinion that the United States should withdraw from world affairs.

Issue A conflict, real or apparent, between the interests, ideas, or beliefs of different citizens.

Issue network A network of people in Washington, D.C., that is based interest groups, on congressional staffs, in universities and think tanks, and in the mass media, who regularly discuss and advocate public policies.

Joint committees Committees on which both senators and representatives serve.

Joint resolution A formal expression of congressional opinion that must be approved by both houses of Congress and by the president; constitutional amendments need not be signed by the president.

Judicial restraint approach The view that judges should decide cases strictly on the basis of the language of the laws and the Constitution.

Judicial review The power of courts to declare laws unconstitutional.

Keynesianism The belief the government must manage the economy by spending more money when in a recession and cutting spending when there is inflation.

Laissez-faire An economic theory that government should not regulate or interfere with commerce.

Legislative courts Courts created by Congress for specialized purposes whose judges do not enjoy the protections of Article III of the Constitution.

Legislative veto The authority of Congress to block a presidential action after it has taken place. The Supreme Court has held that Congress does not have this power.

Legitimacy Political authority conferred by law or by a state or national constitution.

Libel Writing that falsely injures another person.

Line-item veto An executive's ability to block a particular provision in a bill passed by the legislature.

Literacy test A requirement that citizens show that they can read before registering to vote.

Litmus test An examination of the political ideology of a nominated judge.

Loaded language Words that imply a value judgment, used to persuade a reader without having made a serious argument.

Lobbyist A person who tries to influence legislation on behalf of an interest group.

Log-rolling A legislator supports a proposal favored by another in return for support of his or hers.

Majoritarian politics A policy in which almost everybody benefits and almost everybody pays.

Majority leader The legislative leader elected by party members holding the majority of seats in the House or the Senate.

Malapportionment Drawing the boundaries of legislative districts so that they are unequal in population.

Mandates Terms set by the national government that states must meet whether or not they accept federal grants.

Marginal districts Political districts in which candidates elected to the House of Representatives win in close elections, typically by less than 55 percent of the vote.

Material incentives Money or things valued in monetary terms.

Means test An income qualification program that determines whether one is eligible for benefits under government programs reserved for lower-income groups.

Military-industrial complex An alleged alliance between military leaders and corporate leaders.

Minority leader The legislative leader elected by party members holding a minority of seats in the House or the Senate.

Monetarism The belief that inflation occurs when too much money is chasing too few goods.

Monetary policy Managing the economy by altering the supply of money and interest rates.

Mugwumps or **progressives** Republican Party faction of the 1890s to the 1910s, composed of reformers who opposed patronage.

Name-request job A job filled by a person whom an agency has already identified.

National chair Day-to-day party manager elected by the national committee.

National committee Delegates who run party affairs between national conventions.

National convention A meeting of party delegates held every four years.

National debt The total deficit from the first presidency down to the present.

"Necessary and proper" clause Section of the Constitution allowing Congress to pass all laws "necessary and proper" to its duties, and which has permitted Congress to exercise powers not specifically given to it (enumerated) by the Constitution.

New Jersey Plan Proposal to create a weak national government.

Norm A standard of right or proper conduct.

Nullification The doctrine that a state can declare null and void a federal law that, in the state's opinion, violates the Constitution.

Office-bloc ballot A ballot listing all candidates of a given office under the name of that office; also called a "Massachusetts" ballot.

Open primary A primary election in which voters may choose in which party to vote as they enter the polling place.

Open rule An order from the House Rules Committee that permits a bill to be amended on the floor.

Opinion of the court A signed opinion of a majority of the Supreme Court.

Orthodox A belief that morality and religion ought to be of decisive importance.

Partisan polarization A vote in which a majority of democratic legislators oppose a majority of republican legislators.

Party-column ballot A ballot listing all candidates of a given party together under the name of that party; also called an "Indiana" ballot.

Party vote There are two measures of such voting. By the stricter measure, a party vote occurs when 90 percent or more of the Democrats in either house of Congress vote together against 90 percent or more of the Republicans. A looser measure counts as a party vote any case where at least 50 percent of the Democrats vote together against at least 50 percent of the Republicans.

Per curiam opinion A brief, unsigned court opinion.

Personal following The political support provided to a candidate on the basis of personal popularity and networks.

Plaintiff The party that initiates a lawsuit.

Pluralist view View that competition among all affected interests shapes public policy.

Plurality system An electoral system in which the winner is the person who gets the most votes, even if he or she does not receive a majority; used in almost all American elections.

Pocket veto A bill fails to become law because the president did not sign it within 10 days before Congress adjourns.

Polarization A deep and wide conflict over some government policy.

Police powers State power to enact laws promoting health, safety, and morals.

Policy entrepreneurs Activists in or out of government who pull together a political majority on behalf of unorganized interests.

Political Action Committee (PAC) A committee set up by a corporation, labor union, or interest group that raises and spends campaign money from voluntary donations.

Political agenda Issues that people believe require governmental action.

Political cue A signal telling a legislator what values are at stake in a vote, and how that issue fits into his or her own political views on party agenda.

Political culture A patterned and sustained way of thinking about how political and economic life ought to be carried out.

Political elites Persons with a disproportionate share of political power.

Political ideology A more or less consistent set of beliefs about what policies government ought to pursue.

Political machine A party organization that recruits members by dispensing patronage.

Political participation The many different ways that people take part in politics and government.

Political party A group that seeks to elect candidates to public office.

Political question An issue the Supreme Court will allow the executive and legislative branches to decide.

Political socialization Process by which background traits influence one's political views.

Politics The activity by which an issue is agitated or settled.

Poll A survey of public opinion.

Poll tax A requirement that citizens pay a tax in order to register to vote.

Pork-barrel legislation Legislation that gives tangible benefits to constituents in several districts or states in the hope of winning their votes in return.

Position issue An issue about which the public is divided and rival candidates or political parties adopt different policy positions.

Power The ability of one person to get another person to act in accordance with the first person's intentions.

Power elite view View that the government is dominated by a few top leaders, most of whom are outside of government.

Primary election An election held to choose candidates for office.

Prior restraint Censorship of a publication.

Probable cause Reasonable cause for issuing a search warrant or making an arrest; more than mere suspicion.

Progressive A belief that personal freedom and solving social problems are more important than religion.

Prospective voting Voting for a candidate because you favor his or her ideas for handling issues.

Public-interest lobby A political organization whose goals will principally benefit nonmembers.

Public opinion How people think or feel about particular things.

Public safety exception The police can question an un-mirandized suspect if there is an urgent concern for public safety.

Purposive incentive A benefit that comes from serving a cause or principle.

Pyramid structure A president's subordinates report to him through a clear chain of command headed by a chief of staff.

Quorum The minimum number of members who must be present for business to be conducted in Congress.

Random sample Method of selecting from a population in which each person has an equal probability of being selected.

Ratings Assessments of a representative's voting record on issues important to an interest group.

Recall Procedure whereby voters can remove an elected official from office.

Red tape Complex bureaucratic rules and procedures that must be followed to get something done.

Referendum Procedure enabling voters to reject a measure passed by the legislature.

Registered voters People who are registered to vote.

Remedy A judicial order enforcing a right or redressing a wrong.

Representative democracy A government in which leaders make decisions by winning a competitive struggle for the popular vote.

Republic A government in which elected representatives make the decisions.

Reserved powers Powers given to the state government alone.

Restrictive An order from the House Rules Committee that permits certain kinds of amendments but not others to be made into a bill on the floor.

Retrospective voting Voting for a candidate because you like his or her past actions in office.

Reverse discrimination Using race or sex to give preferential treatment to some people.

Riders Amendments on matters unrelated to a bill that are added to an important bill so that they will "ride" to passage through the congress. When a bill has many riders, it is called a "Christmas-tree" bill.

Roll-call vote A congressional voting procedure that consists of members answering "yea" or "nay" to their names.

Routine stories Media stories about events regularly covered by reporters.

Runoff primary A second primary election held when no candidate wins a majority of the votes in the first primary.

Safe districts Districts in which incumbents win by margins of 55 percent or more.

Sampling error The difference between the results of random samples taken at the same time.

Search warrant A judge's order authorizing a search.

Select committees Congressional committees appointed for a limited time and purpose.

Selective attention Paying attention only to those news stories with which one already agrees.

Selective incorporation The process whereby the court has applied most, but not all, parts of the Bill of Rights to the states.

Separate-but-equal doctrine The doctrine established in *Plessy v. Ferguson* (1896) that African Americans could constitutionally be kept in separate but equal facilities.

Separation of powers Constitutional authority is shared by three different branches of government.

Sequester Automatic spending cuts.

Shays's Rebellion A 1787 rebellion in which ex–Revolutionary War soldiers attempted to prevent foreclosures of farms as a result of high interest rates and taxes.

Simple resolution An expression of opinion either in the House or Senate to settle procedural matters in either body.

Social movement A widely shared demand for change in some aspect of the social or political order.

Soft money Funds obtained by political parties that are spent on party activities, such as get-out-the-vote drives, but not on behalf of a specific candidate.

Solidary incentives The social rewards (sense of pleasure, status, or companionship) that lead people to join political organizations.

Sophomore surge An increase in the votes congressional candidates usually get when they first run for re-election.

Sound bite A radio or video clip of someone speaking.

Sovereign immunity The rule that a citizen cannot sue the government without the government's consent.

Speaker The presiding officer of the House of Representatives and the leader of his or her party in the House.

Split ticket Voting for candidates of different parties for various offices in the same election.

Sponsored party A local or state political party largely supported by another organization in the community.

Standing A legal rule stating who is authorized to start a lawsuit.

Standing committees Permanently established legislative committees that consider and are responsible for legislation within a certain subject area.

Stare decisis "Let the decision stand," or allowing prior rulings to control the current case.

Straight ticket Voting for candidates of the same party.

Strict scrutiny The standard by which "suspect classifications" are judged. To be upheld, such a classification must be related to a "compelling government interest," be "narrowly tailored" to achieve that interest, and use the "least restrictive means" available.

Superdelegates Party leaders and elected officials who become delegates to the national convention without having to run in primaries or caucuses.

Supply-side theory The belief that lower taxes and fewer regulations will stimulate the economy.

Suspect classification Classifications of people based on their race or ethnicity; laws so classifying people are subject to "strict scrutiny."

Symbolic speech An act that conveys a political message.

Teller vote A congressional voting procedure in which members pass between two tellers, the "yeas" first and the "nays" second.

Trial balloon Information leaked to the media to test public reaction to a possible policy.

Trust funds Funds for government programs collected and spent outside the regular government budget.

Two-party system An electoral system with two dominant parties that compete in national elections.

Unalienable A human right based on nature or God.

Unified government The same party controls the white house and both houses of congress.

Unipolar world A political landscape with one superpower.

Valence issue An issue about which the public is united and rival candidates or political parties adopt similar positions in hopes that each will be thought to best represent those widely shared beliefs.

Veto Literally, "I forbid": it refers to the power of a president to disapprove a bill; it may be overridden by a two-thirds vote of each house of Congress.

Virginia Plan Proposal to create a strong national government.

Voice vote A congressional voting procedure in which members shout "yea" in approval or "nay" in disapproval, permitting members to vote quickly or anonymously on bills.

Voting-age population (VAP) Citizens who are eligible to vote after reaching the minimum age requirement.

Voting-eligible population (VEP) Citizens who have reached the minimum age to be eligible to vote, excluding those who are not legally permitted to cast a ballot.

Waiver A decision by an administrative agency granting some other part permission to violate a law or rule that would otherwise apply to it.

Wall of separation Court ruling that government cannot be involved with religion.

Whip A senator or representative who helps the party leader stay informed about what party members are thinking.

White primary The practice of keeping blacks from voting in the southern states' primaries through arbitrary use of registration requirements and intimidation.

Worldviews A comprehensive opinion of how the United States should respond to world problems.

Writ of certiorari An order by a higher court directing a lower court to send up a case for review.

Notes

Chapter 1

The Study of American Government

1. *Federalist*, No. 45.
2. Patrick Henry, Virginia Convention, June 12, 1788, in Bernard Bailyn, ed., *The Debate on the Constitution*, Part Two (New York: The Library of America, 1993), p. 683.
3. Rockefeller Institute of Government and Pew Center on the States, *States' Revenue Estimating: Cracks in the Crystal Ball*, March 2011.
4. Martin Meyerson and Edward C. Banfield, *Politics, Planning, and the Public Interest* (New York: Free Press, 1955), p. 304.
5. Ibid.
6. Henry Milner, *The Internet Generation: Engaged Citizens or Political Dropouts* (Medford, MA: Tufts University Press, 2010).
7. Jane Eisner, *Taking Back the Vote: Getting American Youth Involved in Our Democracy* (Boston, MA: Beacon Press, 2004).
8. Martin P. Wattenberg, *Is Voting for Young People?* 3ᵈ ed. (Boston, MA: Pearson, 2012), which prescribes compulsory voting.
9. David E. Campbell, *Why We Vote: How Schools and Communities Shape Our Civic Life* (Princeton, NJ: Princeton University Press, 2006), which prescribes enhanced civic education in high schools.
10. Aristotle, *Politics*, iv.4.
11. Joseph A. Schumpeter, *Capitalism, Socialism, and Democracy*, 3ᵈ ed. (New York: Harper Torchbooks, 1950), p. 269. First published in 1942.
12. Samuel P. Huntington, *The Third Wave: Democratization in the Late Twentieth Century* (Norman, OK: University of Oklahoma Press, 1993), p. 7.
13. Ibid.
14. Ibid., pp. 12–13.
15. Karl Marx and Friedrich Engels, "The Manifesto of the Communist Party," in *The Marx-Engels Reader*, 2ᵈ ed. Robert C. Tucker (New York: Norton, 1978), pp. 469–500.
16. C. Wright Mills, *The Power Elite* (New York: Oxford University Press, 1956).
17. H. H. Gerth and C. Wright Mills, eds. *From Max Weber: Essays in Sociology* (London: Routledge and Kegan Paul, 1948), pp. 232–235.
18. David B. Truman, *The Governmental Process: Political Interests and Public Opinion* (New York: Knopf, 1951).
19. Samuel P. Huntington, *American Politics: The Promise of Disharmony* (Cambridge, MA: Harvard University Press, 1981).
20. David O. Sears and J. B. McConahay, *The Politics of Violence* (Boston: Houghton Mifflin, 1973).
21. Daniel Patrick Moynihan, *Maximum Feasible Misunderstanding* (New York: Free Press, 1969), ch. 2.
22. Nelson W. Polsby, "Goodbye to the Senate's Inner Club," in Congress: *Change in Change: Evolution and Reform*, ed. Norman J. Ornstein (New York: Praeger, 1975), pp. 208–215.
23. Jack L. Walker, "Setting the Agenda in the U.S. Senate: A Theory of Problem Selection," *British Journal of Political Science* 7 (1977): pp. 434, 439, 441.
24. James Q. Wilson, *Political Organizations* (New York: Basic Books, 1973), Chapter 16, and *The Politics of Regulation* (Basic Books, 1980), pp. 367–372. There are other ways of classifying public policies, notably that of Theodore J. Lowi, "American Business, Public Policy, Case Studies, and Theory," *World Politics* 16 (July 1964).
25. Donald F. Kettl, *Sharing Power: Public Governance and Private Markets* (Washington, D.C.: Brookings Institution, 1993); Lawrence J. Hajna, "Superfund: Costly Program Under Fire," *Courier-Post* (February 13, 1994), p. 6A.
26. Aristotle, *The Niomachean Ethics*, I.3.

Chapter 2

The Constitution

1. Quoted in Bernard Bailyn, *The Ideological Origins of the American Revolution* (Cambridge: Harvard University Press, 1967), p. 61, n. 6.
2. Quoted in Bailyn, ibid., pp. 135–137.
3. Quoted in Bailyn, ibid., p. 77.
4. Quoted in Bailyn, ibid., p. 160.
5. *Federalist* No. 37.
6. Gordon S. Wood, *The Creation of the American Republic* (Chapel Hill: University of North Carolina Press, 1969). See also *Federalist* No. 49.
7. Letter of George Washington to Henry Lee (October 31, 1787), in *Writings of George Washington*, vol. 29, ed. John C. Fitzpatrick (Washington, D.C.: Government Printing Office, 1939), p. 34.
8. Letters of Thomas Jefferson to James Madison (January 30, 1787) and to Colonel William S. Smith (November 13, 1787), in *Jefferson Himself*, ed. Bernard Mayo (Boston: Houghton Mifflin, 1942), p. 145.
9. Thomas Hobbes, *Leviathan* (Oxford: Basil Blackwell, 1957). First published in 1651; John Locke, *Second Treatise of Civil Government* (New York: Hafner Publishing Co., 1956). First published in 1690.
10. *Federalist* No. 51.
11. *Federalist* No. 48.
12. *Federalist* No. 51.
13. Ibid.
14. Ibid.
15. "The Address and Reasons of Dissent of the Minority of the State of Pennsylvania to Their Constituents," in *The Anti-Federalist*, ed. Cecelia Kenyon (Indianapolis: Bobbs-Merrill, 1966), p. 39.
16. Max Farrand, *The Framing of the Constitution of the United States* (New Haven, CT: Yale University Press, 1913), p. 185.
17. See, for example, John Hope Franklin, *Racial Equality in America* (Chicago: University of Chicago Press, 1976), ch. 1, esp. pp. 12–20.
18. Max Farrand, *The Records of the Federal Convention of 1787*, 4 vols. (New Haven, CT: Yale University Press), pp. 1911–1937.
19. Theodore J. Lowi, *American Government: Incomplete Conquest* (Hinsdale, IL: Dryden Press, 1976), p. 97.
20. Article I, section 2, para. 3.
21. Gary Wills, *"Negro President": Jefferson and the Slave Power* (Boston: Houghton Mifflin, 2003).
22. Article I, section 9, para. 1.
23. Article IV, section 2, para. 3
24. Charles A. Beard, *An Economic Interpretation of the Constitution* (New York: Macmillan, 1913), esp. pp. 26–51, 149–151, 324–325.
25. Forrest McDonald, *We the People* (Chicago: University of Chicago Press, 1958); Robert E. Brown,

Charles Beard and the Constitution (Princeton: Princeton University Press, 1956).

26. Robert A. McGuire, "Constitution Making: A Rational Choice Model of the Federal Convention of 1787," *American Journal of Political Science* 32 (May 1988): pp. 483–522. See also Forrest McDonald, *Novus Ordo Seclorum* (Lawrence: University of Kansas Press, 1985), p. 221.

27. McDonald, *Novus Ordo Seclorum*, pp. 202–221.

28. Robert A. McGuire and Robert L. Ohsfeldt, "Economic Interests and the American Constitution: A Quantitative Rehabilitation of Charles A. Beard," *Journal of Economic History* 44 (June 1984): pp. 509–519.

29. Lloyd N. Cutler, "To Form a Government," *Foreign Affairs* (Fall 1980): pp. 126–143.

Chapter 3

Federalism

1. Woodrow Wilson, *Constitutional Government in the United States* (New York: Columbia University Press, 1961), p. 173. First published in 1908.

2. Martin Diamond, "The Federalists' View of Federalism," in *Essays in Federalism*, ed. George C. S. Benson (Claremont, Calif.: Institute for Studies in Federalism, 1961), pp. 21–64; Samuel H. Beer, "Federalism, Nationalism, and Democracy in America," *American Political Science Review* 72 (March 1978): pp. 9–21.

3. *United States v. Sprague*, 282 U.S. 716 (1931).

4. *Garcia v. San Antonio Metropolitan Transit Authority*, 105 S. Ct. 1005 (1985), overruling *National League of Cities v. Usery*, 426 U.S. 833 (1976).

5. *McCulloch v. Maryland*, 4 Wheat. 316 (1819).

6. *Pollock v. Farmers' Loan & Trust Co.*, 157 U.S. 429 (1895); *South Carolina v. Baker*, No. 94 (1988).

7. *Texas v. White*, 7 Wall. 700 (1869).

8. *Champion v. Ames*, 188 U.S. 321 (1903).

9. *Hoke v. United States*, 227 U.S. 308 (1913).

10. *Clark Distilling Co. v. W. Md. Ry.*, 242 U.S. 311 (1917).

11. *Hipolite Egg Co. v. United States*, 220 U.S. 45 (1911).

12. *United States v. E. C. Knight Co.*, 156 U.S. 1 (1895).

13. *Paul v. Virginia*, 8 Wall. 168 (1869).

14. *Veazie Bank v. Fenno*, 8 Wall. 533 (1869).

15. *Brown v. Maryland*, 12 Wheat. 419 (1827).

16. *Wickard v. Filburn*, 317 U.S. 111 (1942); *NLRB v. Jones & Laughlin Steel Corp.*, 301 U.S. 58 (1937).

17. *Kirschbaum Co. v. Walling*, 316 U.S. 517 (1942).

18. *Goldfarb v. Virginia State Bar*, 421 U.S. 773 (1975); *Flood v. Kuhn*, 407 U.S. 258 (1972); *Gonzales v. Raich*, No. 03-1454 (2005).

19. David B. Truman, "Federalism and the Party System," in *Federalism: Mature and Emergent*, ed. Arthur McMahon (Garden City, N.Y.: Doubleday, 1955), p. 123.

20. Harold J. Laski, "The Obsolescence of Federalism," *New Republic* (May 3, 1939): pp. 367–369.

21. William H. Riker, *Federalism: Origin, Operation, Significance* (Boston: Little Brown, 1964), p. 154.

22. Daniel J. Elazar, *American Federalism: A View from the States* (New York: Crowell, 1966), p. 216.

23. Martha Derthick, *Keeping the Compound Republic: Essays on American Federalism* (Washington, D.C.: Brookings Institution, 2001), p. 140.

24. Donald F. Kettl, ed., *The Department of Homeland Security's First Year: A Report Card* (New York: Century Foundation Report, 2004), pp. 18, 102.

25. Samuel H. Beer, "The Modernization of American Federalism," *Publius* 3 (Fall 1973): esp. pp. 74–79; and Beer, "Federalism," pp. 18–19.

26. Congressional Budget Office, *Federal Constraints on State and Local Government Actions* (Washington, D.C.: Government Printing Office, 1979).

27. William T. Gormley, Jr., "Money and Mandates: The Politics of Intergovernmental Conflict," *Publius: The Journal of Federalism* 36(4): p. 527.

28. Ibid., pp. 535–537.

29. U.S. Advisory Commission on Intergovernmental Relations, *Federally Induced Costs Affecting State and Local Governments*, September 1994.

30. This is according to a study by a George Mason University researcher—see http://mercatus. org/publication/rapid-expansion-federal-spending-household.

31. Information taken from http:// www.usgovernmentrevenue.com/ downchart_gr.php?year=1900_2010 &units=p&title=Revenue%20as% 20percent%20of%20GDP.

32. Paul Teske, *Regulation in the States* (Washington, D.C.: Brookings Institution, 2004).

33. Stephen V. Monsma, *Putting Faith in Partnerships: Welfare-to-Work in Four Cities.* (Ann Arbor: University of Michigan Press, 2004).

34. Baylor University Institute for Studies of Religion, *Ohio Governor's Office of Faith-Based and Community Initiatives: A Case Study*, January 2007.

35. United States Governmental Accountability Office, "Opportunities to Reduce Potential Duplication in Government Programs, Save Tax Dollars, and Enhance Revenue," March 2011. Available at http://www.gao.gov/ new.items/d11318sp.pdf.

Chapter 4

American Political Culture

1. Alexis de Tocqueville, *Democracy in America*, vol. 1, ed. Phillips Bradley (New York: Knopf, 1951), vol. 1, "Principal Causes Which Tend to Maintain the Democratic Republic in the United States" chapter. First published in 1835.

2. *The Public Perspective* (November/ December 1991): 5, 7, reporting survey data from the Roper Center for Public Opinion Research.

3. Fred I. Greenstein, "The Benevolent Leader Revisited: Children's Images of Political Leaders in Three Democracies," *American Political Science Review* 69 (December 1975): 1387.

4. Alexis de Tocqueville, *Democracy in America*, vol. 1, 288.

5. Donald J. Devine, *The Political Culture of the United States* (Boston: Little, Brown, 1972), 185; Herbert McClosky and John Zaller, *The American Ethos: Public Attitudes Toward Capitalism and Democracy* (Cambridge: Harvard University Press, *1984*), ch. 3, *esp.* 74–75.

6. *McClosky and Zaller, The American Ethos*, 74–77.

7. Ibid., 66.

8. Gunnar Myrdal, *An American Dilemma: The Negro Problem in Modern Democracy* (New York: Harper, 1944), intro. and ch. 1.

9. Frank R. Westie, "The American Dilemma: An Empirical Test,"

American Sociological Review 30 (August 1965): 536–537.

10. Samuel P. Huntington, *American Politics* (Cambridge, MA: Harvard University Press, 1983), 202.

11. Eric L. McKitrick, "Party Politics and the Union and Confederate War Efforts," in *The American Party Systems*, 2d ed., ed. William Nisbet Chambers and Walter Dean Burnham (New York: Oxford University Press, 1975), 117–121.

12. Russell J. Dalton, *The Good Citizen* (Washington, D.C.: CQ Press, 2008), 38, 71, 168–171.

13. McClosky and Zaller, *The American Ethos*, 174.

14. Sidney Verba and Gary R. Orren, *Equality in America: The View from the Top* (Cambridge: Harvard University Press, 1985), 146–147.

15. McClosky and Zaller, *The American Ethos*, 82–84, 93, 95.

16. Verba and Orren, *Equality in America*, 72, 254.

17. Donald Kinder and David Sears, "Symbolic Racism Versus Racial Threats to the Good Life," *Journal of Personality and Social Psychology* 40 (1981): 414–431.

18. Paul M. Sniderman and Michael Gray Hagen, *Race and Inequality: A Study in American Values* (Chatham, NJ: Chatham House, 1985), 111.

19. Ibid., 37–38.

20. Theodore Caplow and Howard M. Bahr, "Half a Century of Change in Adolescent Attitudes: A Replication of a Middletown Survey by the Lynds," *Public Opinion Quarterly* 43 (1979): 1–17, table 1.

21. Thomas J. Anton, "Policy-Making and Political Culture in Sweden," *Scandinavian Political Studies* 4 (1969): 88–100; M. Donald Hancock, *Sweden: The Politics of Post-Industrial Change* (Hinsdale, IL: Dryden Press, 1972); Sten Johansson, "Liberal-Democratic Theory and Political Processes," in *Readings in the Swedish Class Structure*, ed. Richard Scarse (New York: Pergamon Press, 1976); Steven J. Kelman, *Regulating America, Regulating Sweden: A Comparative Study of Occupational Safety and Health Policy* (Cambridge, MA: MIT Press, 1981), 118–123.

22. Lewis Austin, *Saints and Samurai: The Political Culture of American and Japanese Elites* (New Haven, CT: Yale University Press, 1975).

23. Gabriel Almond and Sidney Verba, *The Civic Culture* (Princeton, NJ: Princeton University Press, 1963), 169, 185. See also Gabriel Almond and Sidney Verba, eds., *The Civic Culture Revisited* (Boston: Little, Brown, 1980).

24. Sidney Verba, et al., *Voice and Equality: Civic Voluntarism in American Politics* (Cambridge: Harvard University Press, 1995), 69, 70.

25. Kenneth Newton and Pipa Norris, "Confidence in Public Institutions: Faith, Culture or Performance?" Paper presented at the Annual Meeting of the American Political Science Association, Atlanta, GA, September 1999, tables 8.1 and 8.3.

26. Paul M. Sniderman, *A Question of Loyalty* (Berkeley: University of California Press, 1981).

27. Verba and Orren, *Equality in America*, 255.

28. Pippa Norris and Ronald Ingelhart, *Sacred and Secular: Religion and Politics Worldwide* (Cambridge: Cambridge University Press, 2004); George Gallup, Jr., and Thomas Jones, *The Next American Spirituality* (Colorado Springs, CO: Cook, 2000).

29. Arthur C. Brooks, *Who Really Cares? America's Charity Divide* (New York: Basic Books, 2006), ch. 2; Ram A. Cnaan, *The Other Philadelphia Story: How Local Congregations Support Quality of Life in Urban America* (Philadelphia: University of Pennsylvania Press, 2006).

30. Max Weber, *The Protestant Ethic and the Spirit of Capitalism*, trans. Talcott Parsons (New York: Scribner's, 1930). First published in 1904.

31. Erik H. Erikson, *Childhood and Society* (New York: Norton, 1950), ch. 8.

32. James Davison Hunter, *Culture Wars: The Struggle to Define America* (New York: Basic Books, 1991), and Hunter, *Before the Shooting Begins* (New York: Macmillan, 1994).

33. Morris P. Fiorina, *Culture War? The Myth of a Polarized America*, rev. ed. (New York: Pearson Longman, 2006); and Fiorina and Matthew S. Levendusky, "Disconnected: The Political Class Versus the People," in Pietro S. Nivola and David W. Brady, eds., *Red and Blue Nation?* (Washington, D.C.: Brookings Institution, 2006), 49–71.

34. Alan I. Abramovitz, "Comment," in Nivola and Brady, op. cit., 72–85, 111–114; Gary C. Jacobson, "Comment," in Nivola and Brady, op. cit., 85–95.

35. Philip D. Zelikow and David C. King, eds., *Why People Don't Trust Government* (Cambridge, MA: Harvard University Press, 1997).

36. Marc J. Hetherington, *Why Trust Matters* (Princeton, NJ: Princeton University Press, 2005).

37. Robert D. Putnam, *Bowling Alone: The Collapse and Revival of American Community* (New York: Simon & Schuster, 2000); and Putnam, et al., *Better Together: Report of the Saguaro Seminar* (Cambridge, MA: Kennedy School of Government, Harvard University), 2001.

38. James Q. Wilson, "Bowling with Others," *Commentary* (October 2007), 30–33.

39. James W. Prothro and Charles M. Grigg, "Fundamental Principles of Democracy: Bases of Agreement and Disagreement," *Journal of Politics* 22 (Spring 1960): 275–294.

40. General Social Survey of the National Opinion Research Center, University of Chicago.

41. Gallup Poll data compiled by Professor John Zaller, Department of Political Science, UCLA.

42. *The American Enterprise* (January/February 1999): 37, reporting data from various polls.

43. John L. Sullivan, James Piereson, and George F. Marcus, *Political Tolerance and American Democracy* (Chicago: University of Chicago Press, 1982), 194–202.

Chapter 5

Civil Liberties

1. P. Ford, ed., *Works of Thomas Jefferson*, 1905, vol. 9, p. 449.

2. *Zamora v. Pomeroy*, 639 F.2d 662 (1981); *Goss v. Lopez*, 419 U.S. 565 (1975); *Tinker v. Des Moines Community School District*, 393 U.S. 503 (1969); *Smith v. Goguen*, 415 U.S. 566 (1974); *New Jersey v. T.L.O.*, 469 U.S. 325 (1985); *Morse v. Frederick*, No. 06-278 (2007).

3. *Snyder v. Phelps*, 131 S. Ct. 1207 (2011); *New York Times Co. v. United States*, 403 U.S. 713 (1971); *Kunz v. New York*, 340 U.S. 290 (1951).

4. *Barron v. Baltimore*, 7 Pet. 243 (1833).

5. *Chicago, Burlington, and Quincy Railroad Co. v. Chicago*, 166 U.S. 226 (1987); *Gitlow v. New York*,

268 U.S. 652 (1925); *Palko v. Connecticut*, 302 U.S. 319 (1937).

6. *District of Columbia v. Heller*, 554 U.S. 570 (2008); *McDonald v. Chicago*, 130 S. Ct. 3020 (2010).

7. William Blackstone, *Commentaries*, vol. 4 (1765), pp. 151–152.

8. Jefferson's remarks are from a letter to Abigail Adams (quoted in Walter Berns, *The First Amendment and the Future of American Democracy*, New York: Basic Books, 1976, p. 82), and from a letter to Thomas McKean, governor of Pennsylvania, February 19, 1803 (Paul L. Ford, ed., *The Writings of Thomas Jefferson: 1801–1806*, vol. 8, New York: Putnam, 1897, p. 218).

9. *Schenck v. United States*, 249 U.S. 47 (1919), p. 52.

10. *Gitlow v. New York*, 268 U.S. 652 (1925), p. 666.

11. *Fiske v. Kansas*, 274 U.S. 380 (1927); *Stromberg v. California*, 283 U.S. 359 (1931); *Near v. Minnesota*, 283 U.S. 697 (1931); *De Jonge v. Oregon*, 299 U.S. 353 (1937).

12. *Dennis v. United States*, 341 U.S. 494 (1951), 510ff. The test was first formulated by Judge Learned Hand of the court of appeals: see *Dennis v. United States*, 183 F.2d 201 (1950), p. 212.

13. *Yates v. United States*, 354 U.S. 298 (1957).

14. *Brandenburg v. Ohio*, 395 U.S. 444 (1969).

15. *Village of Skokie v. National Socialist Party*, 432 U.S. 43 (1977); 366 N.E.2d 349 (1977); and 373 N.E.2d 21 (1978).

16. *R.A.V. v. City of St. Paul*, 112 S. Ct. 2538 (1992).

17. *Wisconsin v. Mitchell*, No. 92–515 (1993).

18. C. Herman Pritchett, *Constitutional Civil Liberties* (Englewood Cliffs, NJ: Prentice-Hall, 1984), p. 100.

19. *New York Times v. Sullivan*, 376 U.S. 254 (1964); but compare *Time, Inc. v. Firestone*, 424 U.S. 448 (1976).

20. Henry J. Abraham, *Freedom and the Court*, 4th ed. (New York: Oxford University Press, 1982), 193, fn 189.

21. Justice Stewart's famous remark was made in his concurring opinion in *Jacobellis v. Ohio*, 378 U.S. 184 (1964), p. 197.

22. *Miller v. California*, 413 U.S. 15 (1973).

23. *Jenkins v. Georgia*, 418 U.S. 153 (1974).

24. *Schad v. Borough of Mt. Ephraim*, 452 U.S. 61 (1981).

25. *Barnes v. Glen Theatre*, 111 S. Ct. 2456 (1991).

26. *American Booksellers Association v. Hudnut*, 771 F.2d 323 (1985), affirmed at 475 U.S. 1001 (1986).

27. *Renton v. Playtime Theatres*, 475 U.S. 41 (1986). See also *Young v. American Mini-Theatres, Inc.*, 427 U.S. 50 (1976).

28. *Reno v. American Civil Liberties Union*, 521 U.S. 844 (1997); *Ashcroft v. Free Speech Coalition*, 122 S. Ct. 1389 (2002).

29. *United States v. O'Brien*, 391 U.S. 367 (1968).

30. *Texas v. Johnson*, 109 S. Ct. 2533 (1989).

31. *United States v. Eichman*, 496 U.S. 310 (1990).

32. *First National Bank of Boston v. Bellotti*, 435 U.S. 765 (1978); *Federal Election Commission v. Massachusetts Citizens for Life, Inc.*, 479 U.S. 238 (1986).

33. *44 Liquormart v. Rhode Island*, 517 U.S. 484 (1996); *Greater New Orleans Broadcasting Association v. United States*, 527 U.S. 173 (1999).

34. *Pacific Gas and Electric Co. v. Public Utilities Commission*, 475 U.S. 1 (1986). Some limitations on corporate speech have been upheld, including a state law prohibiting a firm from spending money on candidates for elective office. *Austin v. Michigan Chamber of Commerce*, 100 S. Ct. 1391 (1990).

35. *Board of Trustees of the State University of New York v. Fox*, 492 U.S. 469 (1989).

36. *Bates v. State Bar of Arizona*, 433 U.S. 350 (1977); *Edenfield v. Bane*, 113 S. Ct. 1792 (1993).

37. *McConnell v. Federal Election Commission*, 124 S. Ct. 619 (2003); *Federal Election Commission v. Wisconsin Right to Life*, No. 06-969 (2007).

38. *Hazelwood School District v. Kuhlmeier et al.*, 484 U.S. 260 (1988).

39. *Murdock v. Pennsylvania*, 319 U.S. 105 (1943).

40. *Church of the Lukumi Babalu Aye v. City of Hialeah*, 508 U.S. 520 (1993).

41. *Reynolds v. United States*, 98 U.S. 145 (1878).

42. *Jacobson v. Massachusetts*, 197 U.S. 11 (1905).

43. *Employment Division, Department of Human Resources of Oregon v. Smith*, 110 S. Ct. 1595 (1990).

44. *Society for Krishna Consciousness v. Lee*, 112 S. Ct. 2701 (1992).

45. *Welsh v. United States*, 398 U.S. 333 (1970); Pritchett, *Constitutional Civil Liberties*, pp. 140–141.

46. *Sherbert v. Verner*, 374 U.S. 398 (1963); *Wisconsin v. Yoder*, 406 U.S. 205 (1972); *Hobbie v. Unemployment Appeals Commission of Florida*, 480 U.S. 136 (1987); *Estate of Thornton v. Caldor, Inc.*, 472 U.S. 703 (1985).

47. Berns, *The First Amendment*.

48. Pritchett, *Constitutional Civil Liberties*, pp. 145–147.

49. *Everson v. Board of Education*, 330 U.S. 1 (1947).

50. *Engel v. Vitale*, 370 U.S. 421 (1962).

51. *Lubbock Independent School District v. Lubbock Civil Liberties Union*, 669 F.2d 1038.

52. *School District of Abington Township v. Schempp*, 374 U.S. 203 (1963).

53. *Lee v. Weisman*, 112 S. Ct. 2649 (1992); *Santa Fe Independent School District v. Jane Doe*, 530 U.S. 290 (2000).

54. *Epperson v. Arkansas*, 393 U.S. 97 (1968); *McLean v. Arkansas Board of Education*, 529 F. Supp. 1255 (1982).

55. *McCollum v. Board of Education*, 333 U.S. 203 (1948); *Zorach v. Clauson*, 343 U.S. 306 (1952).

56. *Tilton v. Richardson*, 403 U.S. 672 (1971).

57. *Board of Education v. Allen*, 392 U.S. 236 (1968).

58. *Walz v. Tax Commission*, 397 U.S. 664 (1970).

59. *Mueller v. Allen*, 463 U.S. 388 (1983).

60. *Zobrest v. Catalina Foothills School District*, 509 U.S. 1 (1993); *Mitchell v. Helms*, 2000 Lexis 4485.

61. *Lemon v. Kurtzman*, 403 U.S. 602 (1971).

62. *Committee for Public Education v. Nyquist*, 413 U.S. 756 (1973).

63. *Meek v. Pittenger*, 421 U.S. 349 (1975); *Wolman v. Walter*, 433 U.S. 229 (1977).

64. *Edwards v. Aguillard*, 482 U.S. 578 (1987); *Board of Education of Kiryas Joel Village School v. Louis Grumet*, 114 S. Ct. 2481 (1994).

65. *Agostini v. Felton*, 521 U.S. 203 (1997), overruled *Aguilar v. Felton*, 473 U.S. 402 (1985).

66. *Zelman v. Simmons-Harris*, 536 U.S. 639 (2002).

67. *Lemon v. Kurtzman*, 403 U.S. 602 (1971).

68. *Lynch v. Donelly*, 465 U.S. 668 (1984); *Allegheny v. ACLU*, 109 S. Ct. 3086 (1989); *McCreary County, Kentucky,*

v. ACLU, 125 S. Ct. 2722 (2005); *Van Orden v. Perry*, 125 S. Ct. 2854 (2005).

69. *Marsh v. Chambers*, 492 U.S. 573 (1983).
70. Yale Kamisar, "Does (Did) (Should) the Exclusionary Rule Rest on a 'Principled Basis' Rather Than an 'Empirical Proposition'?" *Creighton Law Review* 16 (1982–1983): pp. 565–667.
71. *Wolf v. Colorado*, 338 U.S. 25 (1949).
72. *Mapp v. Ohio*, 367 U.S. 643 (1961).
73. *Chimel v. California*, 395 U.S. 752 (1969).
74. *Washington v. Chrisman*, 455 U.S. 1 (1982).
75. *Oliver v. United States*, 466 U.S. 170 (1984).
76. *Arkansas v. Sanders*, 442 U.S. 753 (1979); *Robbins v. California*, 453 U.S. 420 (1981).
77. *United States v. Ross*, 456 U.S. 798 (1982); *Maryland v. Dyson*, 199 S. Ct. 2013 (1999); *Wyoming v. Houghton*, 119 S. Ct. 1297 (1999); *Whren v. United States*, 517 U.S. 806 (1996).
78. *Winston v. Lee*, 470 U.S. 753 (1985).
79. *South Dakota v. Neville*, 459 U.S. 553 (1983); *Schmerber v. California*, 384 U.S. 757 (1966).
80. *United States v. Dunn*, 480 U.S. 294 (1987); *California v. Ciraolo*, 476 U.S. 207 (1986); *California v. Carney*, 471 U.S. 386 (1985).
81. *O'Connor v. Ortega*, 480 U.S. 709 (1987).
82. *Escobedo v. Illinois*, 378 U.S. 478 (1964); *Miranda v. Arizona*, 384 U.S. 436 (1966).
83. *Malloy v. Hogan*, 378 U.S. 1 (1964).
84. *Miranda v. Arizona*, 384 U.S. 436 (1966).
85. *Gilbert v. California*, 388 U.S. 263 (1967); *Kirby v. Illinois*, 406 U.S. 682 (1972).
86. *Estelle v. Smith*, 451 U.S. 454 (1981).
87. *Brewer v. Williams*, 430 U.S. 387 (1977).
88. *Illinois v. Perkins*, 496 U.S. 292 (1990).
89. *Missouri v. Seibert*, 542 U.S. 600 (2004).
90. *Dickerson v. United States*, 530 U.S. 428 (2000).
91. *Fare v. Michael C.*, 442 U.S. 707 (1979).
92. *United States v. Leon*, 468 U.S. 897 (1984); *Massachusetts v. Sheppard*, 468 U.S. 981 (1984); *Herring v. United States*, No. 07–513 (2008).
93. *New York v. Quarles*, 467 U.S. 649 (1984); *Arizona v. Fulminante*, 499

U.S. 279 (1991); *Kentucky v. King*, No. 09-1272 (2011).
94. *Nix v. Williams*, 467 U.S. 431 (1984).
95. *Ex parte Quirin*, 317 U.S. 1 (1942).
96. *Rasul v. Bush*, 542 U.S. 466 (2004).
97. *Hamdi v. Rumsfeld*, 542 U.S. 507 (2004).
98. Military Commissions Act, Public Law 109-366 (2006).
99. Public Law 109-13 (2005).
100. *In re Sealed Case*, Foreign Intelligence Review Court, No. 02-001 (2001).

Chapter 6
Civil Rights

1. *United States v. Carolene Products Co.*, 304 U.S. 144 (1938); *San Antonio Independent School District v. Rodriguez*, 411 U.S. 1 (1973).
2. Gunnar Myrdal, *An American Dilemma* (New York: Harper, 1944), ch. 27.
3. Richard Kluger, *Simple Justice* (New York: Random House/Vintage Books, 1977), pp. 89–90.
4. Paul B. Sheatsley, "White Attitudes Toward the Negro," in *The Negro American*, ed. Talcott Parsons and Kenneth B. Clark (Boston: Houghton Mifflin, 1966), pp. 305, 308, 317.
5. *Strauder v. West Virginia*, 100 U.S. 303 (1880).
6. *Civil Rights Cases*, 109 U.S. 3 (1883).
7. *Plessy v. Ferguson*, 163 U.S. 537 (1896).
8. *Cumming v. Richmond County Board of Education*, 175 U.S. 528 (1899).
9. *Missouri ex rel. Gaines v. Canada*, 305 U.S. 337 (1938).
10. *Sipuel v. Board of Regents of the University of Oklahoma*, 332 U.S. 631 (1948).
11. *Sweatt v. Painter*, 339 U.S. 629 (1950); *McLaurin v. Oklahoma State Regents for Higher Education*, 339 U.S. 637 (1950).
12. *Brown v. Board of Education of Topeka*, 347 U.S. 483 (1954).
13. *Brown v. Board of Education of Topeka*, 349 U.S. 294 (1955). This case is often referred to as "Brown II."
14. Frederick S. Mosteller and Daniel P. Moynihan, eds., *On Equality of Educational Opportunity* (New York: Random House, 1972), pp. 60–62.
15. *Brown v. Board of Education of Topeka*, 347 U.S. 483 (1954).
16. C. Herman Pritchett, *Constitutional Civil Liberties* (Englewood

Cliffs, NJ: Prentice-Hall, 1984), pp. 250–251, 261.
17. *Green et al. v. County School Board of New Kent County*, 391 U.S. 430 (1968).
18. *Swann v. Charlotte-Mecklenburg Board of Education*, 402 U.S. 1 (1971).
19. Busing *within* the central city was upheld in *Armour v. Nix*, 446 U.S. 930 (1980); *Keyes v. School District No. 1*, Denver, 413 U.S. 189 (1973); *Milliken v. Bradley*, 418 U.S. 717 (1974); *Board of School Commissioners of Indianapolis v. Buckley*, 429 U.S. 1068 (1977); and *School Board of Richmond v. State Board of Education*, 412 U.S. 92 (1972). Busing *across* city lines was upheld in *Evans v. Buchanan*, 423 U.S. 963 (1975), and *Board of Education v. Newburg Area Council*, 421 U.S. 931 (1975).
20. *Pasadena City Board of Education v. Spangler*, 427 U.S. 424 (1976).
21. See, for example, Herbert McClosky and John Zaller, *The American Ethos* (Cambridge: Harvard University Press, 1984), pp. 92, 100; and data reported in Chapter 5 of this text.
22. NES, *1952–1990 Cumulative Data File, 1992 NES Pre/Post Election Study* (1992).
23. *Freeman v. Pitts*, 112 S. Ct. 1430 (1992); *Parents v. Seattle School District*, No. 05-908 (2007).
24. Robert S. Erikson and Norman R. Luttbeg, *American Public Opinion* (New York: Wiley, 1973), 49; Hazel Erskine, "The Polls: Demonstrations and Race Riots," *Public Opinion Quarterly* 31 (Winter 1967–1968): pp. 654–677.
25. Howard Schuman, Charlotte Steeh, and Lawrence Bobo, *Racial Attitudes in America* (Cambridge: Harvard University Press, 1985), pp. 69, 78–79.
26. Ibid., pp. 102, 110, 127–135.
27. *Grove City College v. Bell*, 465 U.S. 555 (1984).
28. *Mueller v. Oregon*, 208 U.S. 412 (1908).
29. Equal Pay Act of 1963; Civil Rights Act of 1964, Title VII, and 1978 amendments thereto; Education Amendments of 1972, Title IX.
30. *Reed v. Reed*, 404 U.S. 71 (1971).
31. *Frontiero v. Richardson*, 411 U.S. 677 (1973).
32. *Stanton v. Stanton*, 421 U.S. 7 (1975).
33. *Craig v. Boren*, 429 U.S. 190 (1976).

34. *Dothard v. Rawlinson*, 433 U.S. 321 (1977).

35. *Cleveland Board of Education v. LaFleur*, 414 U.S. 632 (1974).

36. *Fortin v. Darlington Little League*, 514 F.2d 344 (1975).

37. *Roberts v. United States Jaycees*, 468 U.S. 609 (1984); *Board of Directors Rotary International v. Rotary Club of Duarte*, 481 U.S. 537 (1987).

38. *Arizona Governing Committee for Tax Deferred Annuity and Deferred Compensation Plans v. Norris*, 463 U.S. 1073 (1983).

39. *EEOC v. Madison Community Unit School District No. 12*, 818 F.2d 577 (1987).

40. *Michael M. v. Superior Court*, 450 U.S. 464 (1981).

41. *Vorchheimer v. School District of Philadelphia*, 430 U.S. 703 (1977).

42. *Kahn v. Shevin*, 416 U.S. 351 (1974).

43. *Schlesinger v. Ballard*, 419 U.S. 498 (1975).

44. *Bennett v. Dyer's Chop House*, 350 F. Supp. 153 (1972); *Morris v. Michigan State Board of Education*, 472 F.2d 1207 (1973); *Fitzgerald v. Porter Memorial Hospital*, 523 F.2d 716 (1975); *Kruzel v. Podell*, 226 N.W.2d 458 (1975).

45. *United States v. Virginia*, 116 S. Ct. 2264 (1996).

46. *Rostker v. Goldberg*, 453 U.S. 57 (1981).

47. *Gebser v. Lago Vista School District*, 118 S. Ct. 1989 (1998); *Faragher v. Boca Raton*, 118 S. Ct. 2275 (1998); *Burlington Industries v. Ellerth*, 118 S. Ct. 2257 (1998).

48. *Griswold v. Connecticut*, 381 U.S. 479 (1965).

49. *Roe v. Wade*, 410 U.S. 113 (1973).

50. Though the constitutionality of the Hyde Amendment was upheld in *Harris v. McRae*, 448 U.S. 297 (1980), other limitations on access to abortions were struck down in *Planned Parenthood Federation of Central Missouri v. Danforth*, 428 U.S. 52 (1976); *Akron v. Akron Center for Reproductive Health*, 462 U.S. 416 (1983); and *Thornburgh v. American College of Obstetricians and Gynecologists*, 476 U.S. 747 (1986).

51. *Planned Parenthood v. Casey*, 112 S. Ct. 2791 (1992).

52. *Gonzales v. Carhart*, No. 05-380 (2007).

53. For an argument in support of a color-blind Constitution, see Andrew Kull, *The Color-Blind Constitution* (Cambridge: Harvard University Press, 1992).

54. *Regents of the University of California v. Bakke*, 438 U.S. 265 (1978).

55. *Fullilove v. Klutznick*, 448 U.S. 448 (1980).

56. *City of Richmond v. J.A. Croson Co.*, 488 U.S. 469 (1989).

57. *Metro Broadcasting v. FCC*, 497 U.S. 547 (1990).

58. *Northeastern Florida Contractors v. Jacksonville*, 508 U.S. 656 (1993).

59. *Firefighters Local Union No. 1784 v. Stotts*, 467 U.S. 561 (1984); *Wygant v. Jackson Board of Education*, 476 U.S. 267 (1986); *City of Richmond v. J.A. Croson Co.*, 488 U.S. 469 (1989).

60. *Local No. 28 of the Sheet Metal Workers' International Association v. Equal Employment Opportunity Commission*, 478 U.S. 421 (1986); *Wards Cove Packing Co. v. Atonio*, 490 U.S. 642 (1989); *Price Waterhouse v. Hopkins*, 490 U.S. 228 (1989). (Note: *Wards Cove* and *Price* were both superseded in part by the Civil Rights Act of 1991.)

61. *Fullilove v. Klutznick*, 448 U.S. 448 (1980); *Metro Broadcasting v. FCC*, 497 U.S. 547 (1990).

62. *United Steelworkers of America v. Weber*, 443 U.S. 193 (1979); *Johnson v. Santa Clara County Transportation Agency*, 480 U.S. 616 (1987).

63. *Wygant v. Jackson Board of Education*, 476 U.S. 267 (1986); *United States v. Paradise*, 480 U.S. 149 (1987).

64. Seymour Martin Lipset and William Schneider, "An Emerging National Consensus," *The New Republic* (October 15, 1977): pp. 8–9.

65. John R. Bunzel, "Affirmative Re-Actions," *Public Opinion* (February/March 1986): pp. 45–49; *The New York Times* (December 14, 1997).

66. *Adarand Constructors v. Pena*, 515 U.S. 200 (1995).

67. *Hopwood v. Texas*, 78 F.3d 932 (1996).

68. *Gratz v. Bollinger*, 539 U.S. 244 (2003).

69. *Grutter v. Bollinger*, 539 U.S. 306 (2003).

70. *Bowers v. Hardwick*, 478 U.S. 186 (1986).

71. *Romer v. Evans*, 517 U.S. 620 (1996).

72. *Lawrence v. Texas*, 539 U.S. 558 (2003).

73. *Goodridge v. Department of Public Health*, 440 Mass. 309 (2003) and 440 Mass. 1201 (2004).

74. *Boy Scouts of America v. Dale*, 530 U.S. 640 (2000).

Chapter 7
Public Opinion

1. *Federalist* No. 50.

2. *Federalist* No. 63.

3. George W. Bishop, Alfred J. Tuchfarber, and Robert W. Oldendick, "1984: How Much Can We Manipulate and Control People's Answers to Public Opinion Surveys?" Paper delivered at the 1984 annual meeting of the American Political Science Association; Howard Schuman and S. Presser, *Questions and Answers in Attitude Surveys* (New York: Academic Press, 1981), ch. 5.

4. For example, see Bernard Berelson, et al., *Voting: A Study of Opinion Formation in a Presidential Campaign* (Chicago: University of Chicago Press, 1954), and Phillip E. Converse, "The Nature of Belief Systems in Mass Publics," in *Ideology and Discontent*, ed. David E. Apter (New York: Free Press, 1964).

5. For example, see V. O. Key, *The Responsible Electorate* (Cambridge: Harvard University Press, 1966); Samuel Popkin, *The Reasoning Voter: Communication and Persuasion in Presidential Campaigns* (Chicago: University of Chicago Press, 1991); Benjamin I. Page and Robert Y. Shapiro, *The Rational Public: Fifty Years of Trends in Americans' Policy Preferences* (Chicago: University of Chicago Press, 1991).

6. Terry M. Moe, *Schools, Vouchers, and the American Public* (Washington, D.C.: Brookings Institution, 2001), p. 253.

7. James Q. Wilson, "The Press at War," *City Journal* (Autumn 2006): pp. 54–63.

8. M. Kent Jennings and Richard G. Niemi, "The Transmission of Political Values from Parent to Child," *American Political Science Review* 62 (March 1968): 173; Robert D. Hess and Judith V. Tomey, *The Development of Political Attitudes in Children* (Chicago: Aldine, 1967), p. 90.

9. John R. Alford, Carolyn L. Funk, and John R. Hibbing, "Are Political Orientations Genetically Transmitted?" *American Political Science Review*, 99 (May 2005): pp. 153–167; James Q. Wilson, "The DNA of Politics," *City Journal* (Winter 2009): pp. 83–87; Thomas J. Bouchard, et al., "Evidence

for the Construct Validity and Heritability of the Wilson-Patterson Conservatism Scale," *Personality and Individual Differences*, 24 (2003): pp. 959–969.

10. Several studies of child-parent agreement on party preference are summarized in David O. Sears, "Political Behavior," in *The Handbook of Social Psychology*, 2d ed., ed. Gardner Lindzey and Elliot Aronson (Reading, MA: Addison-Wesley, 1969), vol. 5, p. 376.

11. Norman H. Nie, Sidney Verba, and John R. Petrocik, *The Changing American Voter* (Cambridge: Harvard University Press, 1976), ch. 4.

12. Richard Niemi and M. Kent Jennings, "Issues and Inheritance in the Formation of Party Identification," *American Journal of Political Science* (November 1991): pp. 970–988.

13. Pew Forum on Religion and Public Life, "Support for Same-Sex Marriage Edges Upward," October 6, 2010.

14. Elizabeth Humel, et. al., "Younger Voters," *Public Perspective* (May/June 2003): p. 11.

15. Pew Forum on Religion and Public Life, *Survey: More Americans Question Religion's Role in Politics*, August 21, 2008.

16. Pew Forum on Religion and Public Life, *Survey: Religious Groups Agree—Fixing the Nation's Economy Is Job One*, March 4, 2009.

17. V. O. Key, Jr., *Public Opinion and American Democracy* (New York: Knopf, 1961), pp. 122–138.

18. Richard E. Dawson, *Public Opinion and Contemporary Disarray* (New York: Harper & Row, 1973), ch. 4.

19. David Bositis, *Public Opinion 1998: Political Attitudes* (Washington, D.C.: Joint Center for Political and Economic Studies, 1998), table 18A.

20. "The Black and White of Public Opinion," Pew Research Center for the People & the Press (October 31, 2005).

21. Ibid.

22. Lisa J. Montoya, et al., "Latina Politics: Gender, Participation, and Leadership," *PS: Political Science and Politics* 33 (September 2000): p. 557.

23. Bruce Cain and Roderick Kiewit, "California's Coming Minority Majority," *Public Opinion* (February/March 1986): pp. 50–52.

24. Ibid.

25. Pew Hispanic Center, *Survey of Latino Attitudes on the War in Iraq*, Pew Research Center, February 7, 2005.

26. Richard Frey, et al., *Hispanics and the Social Security Debate*, Pew Research Center, March 16, 2005.

27. Ibid.

28. Nie, Verba, and Petrocik, *The Changing American Voter*, pp. 247–250.

29. Lydia Saad, "Conservatives Maintain Edge as Top Ideological Group," Gallup Organization, October 26, 2009.

30. Adam J. Berinsky, *Silent Voices: Public Opinion and Political Participation in America* (Princeton, NJ: Princeton University Press, 2004); Berinsky, "Two Faces of Public Opinion," *American Journal of Political Science* (October 1999): pp. 1209–1230.

31. Ibid.

32. John Zaller, *The Nature and Origins of Mass Opinion* (Cambridge: Cambridge University Press, 1992).

33. Ibid.

34. Lawrence R. Jacobs and Robert Y. Shapiro, "Debunking the Myth of the Pandering Politician," *Public Perspective* (April/May 1997): pp. 3–5.

Chapter 8

Political Participation

1. Michael McDonald and Samuel L. Popkin, "The Myth of the Vanishing Voter," *American Political Science Review* 95 (December 2001).

2. U.S. Bureau of the Census, *Current Population Survey*, "Reasons for Not Voting," June 2008, table 6.

3. Matthew R. Knee and Donald P. Green, "The Effects of Registration Laws on Voter Turnout: An Updated Assessment," in Paul M. Sniderman and Benjamin Highton, eds., *Facing the Challenges of Democracy* (Princeton, NJ: Princeton University Press, 2011): p. 326; and John P. DiIulio, "The Liberalization of Absentee and Mail-In Voting, 1996-2008," unpublished paper, November 2008.

4. Raymond E. Wolfinger and Jonathan Hoffman, "Registering and Voting with Motor Voter," *PS: Political Science and Politics* 34 (March 2001): p. 90.

5. Donald P. Green and Alan S. Gerber, *Get Out the Vote: How to Increase Voter Turnout* (Washington, D.C. :

The Brookings Institution Press, 2008).

6. Alan S. Gerber, et al., "Social Pressure and Voter Turnout: Evidence from a Large-Scale Field Experiment," *American Political Science Review* 102 (February 2008).

7. Morton Keller, *Affairs of State* (Cambridge, MA: Harvard University Press, 1977), p. 523.

8. *United States v. Reese*, 92 U.S. 214 (1876); *United States v. Cruikshank*, 92 U.S. 556 (1876); and *Ex Parte Yarbrough*, 110 U.S. 651 (1884).

9. *Guinn and Beall v.* United States, 238 U.S. 347 (1915).

10. *Smith v. Allright*, 321 U.S. 649 (1944).

11. *Schnell v. Davis*, 336 U.S. 993 (1949).

12. *Historical Statistics of the United States: Colonial Times to 1970*, part 2, pp. 1071–1072.

13. Walter Dean Burnham, "The Changing Shape of the American Political Universe," *American Political Science Review* 59 (March 1965): p. 11; and William H. Flanigan and Nancy H. Zingale, *Political Behavior of the American Electorate*, 3d ed. (Boston, MA: Allyn and Bacon, 1975), p. 15.

14. Burnham, "The Changing Shape;" and E. E. Schattschneider, *The Semi-Sovereign People* (New York: Holt, Rinehart & Winston, 1960), chs. 5, 6.

15. Philip E. Converse, "Change in the American Electorate," in *The Human Meaning of Social Change*, ed. Angus Campbell and Philip E. Converse (New York: Russell Sage Foundation, 1972), pp. 263–338.

16. Raymond Wolfinger and Benjamen Highton, "What If They Gave an Election and Everyone Came?," Public Affairs Report, University of California at Berkeley, June 1999, pp. 11–13; Stephen Ansolabehere and Eitan Hersh, "Who *Really* Votes?," in Sniderman and Highton, *Facing the Challenge of Democracy*, op. cit.: p. 290.

17. Sidney Verba and Norman H. Nie, *Participation in America (*New York: Harper and Row, 1972), p. 30.

18. Sidney Verba, et al., *Voice and Equality: Civic Voluntarism in American Politics* (Cambridge, MA: Harvard University Press, 1998), p. 79.

19. Ibid., p. 77.

20. Verba and Nie, *Participation in America*, ch. 6.

21. Catherine E. Wilson, *The Politics of Latino Faith: Religion, Identity and Urban Community* (New York: New York University Press, 2008).

Chapter 9
Political Parties

1. Leon D. Epstein, "Political Parties," in *Handbook of Political Science*, ed. Fred I. Greenstein and Nelson W. Polsby (Reading, MA: Addison-Wesley, 1975), vol. 4, p. 230.
2. Quoted in Henry Adams, *History of the United States of America during the Administrations of Jefferson and Madison*, ed. Ernest Samuels, abridged ed. (Chicago: University of Chicago Press, 1967), p. 147.
3. Walter Dean Burnham, *Critical Elections and the Mainsprings of American Politics* (New York: Norton, 1970), p. 10.
4. James L. Sundquist, *Dynamics of the Party System* (Washington, D.C.: Brookings Institution, 1973), ch. 7.
5. Edward G. Carmines and James A. Stimson, "Issue Evolution, Population Replacement, and Normal Partisan Change," *American Political Science Review* 75 (March 1981): pp. 107–118; and Gregory Markus, "Political Attitudes in an Election Year," *American Political Science Review* 76 (September 1982): pp. 538–560.
6. Ray Wolfinger and Michael G. Hagen, "Republican Prospects: Southern Comfort," *Public Opinion* (October/November 1985): pp. 8–13. But compare Richard Scammon and James A. Barnes, "Republican Prospects: Southern Discomfort," *Public Opinion* (October/November 1985): pp. 14–17.
7. Jerold G. Rusk, "The Effect of the Australian Ballot Reform on Split-Ticket Voting: 1876–1908," *American Political Science Review* 64 (December 1970): pp. 1220–1238.
8. Morton Keller, *Affairs of State* (Cambridge: Harvard University Press, 1977), p. 239.
9. Quoted in Keller, ibid., p. 256.
10. Martin Shefter, "Parties, Bureaucracy, and Political Change in the United States," in *The Development of Political Parties*, Sage Electoral Studies Yearbook, vol. 4, ed. Louis Maisel and Joseph Cooper (Beverly Hills, CA: Sage, 1978).
11. James Q. Wilson, *The Amateur Democrat: Club Politics in Three Cities* (Chicago: University of Chicago Press, 1962).

12. Samuel J. Eldersveld, *Political Parties: A Behavioral Analysis* (Chicago: Rand McNally, 1964), pp. 278, 287.
13. Robert H. Salisbury, "The Urban Party Organization Member," *Public Opinion Quarterly* 29 (Winter 1965–1966): pp. 550–564.
14. Ibid., pp. 557, 559
15. Eldersveld, *Political Parties*; and J. David Greenstone, *Labor in American Politics* (New York: Knopf, 1969), p. 187.
16. David R. Mayhew, *Placing Parties in American Politics* (Princeton, NJ: Princeton University Press, 1986), chs. 2, 3.
17. *Boston Globe* (July 9, 1984): p. 1.
18. Congressional Quarterly. "Browse by Party System." Political Handbook of the World. Last modified 2012. Accessed May 31, 2013.
19. American National Election Studies, August 5, 2010, table 2B.4; reporting data for the period 1952–2008.
20. For example, see *The Public Perspective* (April/May 1998).
21. American National Election Survey, November 27, 2005, table 2B.3; reporting data for the period 1972–2000.
22. *Williams v. Rhodes*, 393 U.S. 23 (1968).
23. James Q. Wilson, *Political Organizations* (New York: Basic Books, 1973), ch. 12; and Samuel Stouffer, *Communism, Conformity, and Civil Liberties* (Garden City, NY: Doubleday, 1955).
24. Updated from Jeane Kirkpatrick, *The New Presidential Elite* (New York: Russell Sage Foundation and Twentieth Century Fund, 1976), pp. 297–315.
25. Nelson W. Polsby, *Consequences of Party Reform* (New York: Oxford University Press, 1983), pp. 9–11, 64.
26. Ibid., 158. But compare John G. Geer, "Voting in Presidential Primaries," paper delivered to the 1984 annual meeting of the American Political Science Association.
27. Center for the Study of the American Electorate, April 2000.
28. Michael J. Malbin, "Democratic Party Rules Are Made to Be Broken," *National Journal* (August 23, 1980): p. 1388.

Chapter 10
Elections and Campaigns

1. The Center for Public Integrity, *Campaign Consultants*, Georgetown University,

Washington, D.C., September 26, 2006, p. 1.
2. Ted Bader, *Campaigning for Hearts and Minds: How Emotional Appeals Work in Political Ads* (Chicago: University of Chicago Press, 2006).
3. Ibid., pp. 140–143.
4. Steven Levy, "Every Voter a 'Microtarget,'" *The Washington Post*, April 23, 2008, D1.
5. Joe Klein, *Politics Lost: How American Democracy Was Trivialized by People Who Think You're Stupid* (New York: Doubleday, 2006), p. 54.
6. Ibid., pp. 14–16; and Bader, op. cit., pp. 19–20.
7. Bader, op. cit., ch. 2, endnote 5, reporting data from AAPC, 220.
8. *Wesberry v. Sanders*, 376 U.S. 1 (1964).
9. Richard F. Fenno, Jr., "U.S. House Members and Their Constituencies: An Exploration," *American Political Science Review* 71 (September 1977): pp. 883–917, esp. 914.
10. John A. Ferejohn, *Pork Barrel Politics* (Stanford, CA: Stanford University Press, 1974).
11. Douglas Arnold, *Congress and the Bureaucracy* (New Haven, CT: Yale University Press, 1979).
12. Arthur H. Miller, et al., "A Majority Party in Disarray: Policy Polarization in the 1972 Election," *American Political Science Review* 70 (1976): p. 757.
13. Donald E. Stokes and John J. DiIulio, Jr., "Valence Politics in Modern Elections," in *The 1992 Elections*, ed. Michael J. Nelson (Washington, D.C.: Congressional Quarterly Press, 1993), ch. 1.
14. Michael Kelley, "The Making of a First Family: A Blueprint," *The New York Times* (November 14, 1992): pp. 1, 9.
15. Ibid.
16. Thomas E. Patterson and Robert D. McClure, *The Unseeing Eye: The Myth of Television Power in National Politics* (New York: Putnam, 1976); and Xandra Kayden, *Campaign Organization* (Lexington, MA: D. C. Heath, 1978), ch. 6.
17. Gerald M. Pomper, et al., *The Election of 1980* (Chatham, NJ: Chatham House, 1981), pp. 75, 105–107.
18. Gary C. Jacobson, *The Politics of Congressional Elections*, 2d ed. (Boston: Little, Brown, 1987), p. 49.
19. Donald Philip Green and Jonathan S. Krasno, "Salvation

for the Spendthrift Incumbent: Reestimating the Effects of Campaign Spending in House Elections," *American Journal of Political Science* 32 (1988): pp. 884–960; Stephen Ansolabehre, "Winning Is Easy But It Sure Ain't Cheap," Working Paper pp. 90–91, Center for American Politics and Public Policy, UCLA, 1990; Robert S. Erickson and Thomas R. Palfrey, "The Puzzle of Incumbent Spending in Congressional Elections," Social Science Working Paper 806, California Institute of Technology, August 1992.

20. Angus Campbell, Philip E. Converse, Warren E. Miller, and Donald E. Stokes, *The American Voter* (New York: Wiley, 1960), ch. 8.

21. V. O. Key, Jr., *The Responsible Electorate* (Cambridge: Harvard University Press, 1966).

22. Morris P. Fiorina, *Retrospective Voting in American National Elections* (New Haven, CT: Yale University Press, 1981).

23. Jay P. Greene, "Forewarned before Forecast: Presidential Election Forecasting Models and the 1992 Election," *P.S.: Political Science and Politics* (March 1993): p. 20.

24. Paul Freedman and Ken Goldstein, "Measuring Media Exposure and the Effects of Negative Campaign Ads," *American Journal of Political Science* 43 (October 1999): pp. 1189–1208.

25. Robert Axelrod, "Where the Votes Come From: An Analysis of Electoral Coalitions, 1952–1968," *American Political Science Review* 66 (1972): pp. 11–20; and Axelrod, "Communication," *American Political Science Review* 68 (1974): pp. 718–719.

26. Gerald M. Pomper, *Elections in America* (New York: Dodd, Mead, 1971), p. 178.

27. Benjamin Ginsberg, "Elections and Public Policy," *American Political Science Review* 70 (March 1976): pp. 41–49.

Chapter 11

Interest Groups

1. Lee Jared Drutman, *The Business of America Is Lobbying: The Expansion of Corporate Activity and the Future of American Pluralism*, Ph.D. Dissertation, University of California, Berkeley, Fall 2010; Kay Lehrman Schlozman, et al., "Who Sings in the Heavenly Chorus? The Shape of Organized Interest Group Activity," paper presented at the annual meeting of the American Political Science Association, Boston, MA, August 2008.

2. Ibid.

3. The use of injunctions in labor disputes was restricted by the Norris-LaGuardia Act of 1932; the rights to collective bargaining and to the union shop were guaranteed by the Wagner Act of 1935.

4. *Historical Abstract of the United States, Colonial Times to 1970*, vol. 1, p. 386.

5. Dana Priest and William M. Arkin, "A Hidden World, Growing Beyond Control" and "National Security Inc.," *The Washington Post*, July 19–21, 2010.

6. Timothy P. Carney, "The TSA and the Full-Body Scanner Lobby," *The Washington Examiner*, December 29, 2009; Kimberly Kindy, "Ex-Homeland Security Chief Head Said to Abuse Public Trust by Touting Body Scanners," *The Washington Post*, January 1, 2010.

7. The distinction is drawn from Kay Lehman Schlozman and John T. Tierney, *Organized Interests and American Democracy* (New York: Harper and Row, 1985).

8. Center for Responsive Politics, "Lobbying: Top Spenders," data available by year at opensecrets.org.

9. Gabriel A. Almond and Sidney Verba, *The Civic Culture* (Princeton, NJ: Princeton University Press, 1963), p. 194.

10. Robert D. Putnam, *Bowling Alone: The Collapse and Revival of American Community* (New York: Simon and Shuster, 2001); and Robert D. Putnam and David Campbell, *American Grace: How Religion Unites and Divides Us* (New York: Simon and Shuster, 2010).

11. Mancur Olson, Jr., *The Logic of Collective Action* (Cambridge: Harvard University Press, 1965), pp. 153–157.

12. Derek C. Bok and John T. Dunlop, *Labor and the American Community* (New York: Simon and Shuster, 1970), p. 134.

13. J. Scott Applewhite, "What Is the 'Tea Party' and How Is It Shaking Up American Politics?" *Christian Science Monitor*, September 15, 2010.

14. Walter A. Rosenbaum, *Environmental Politics and Policy*, 8th ed. (Washington, D.C.: Congressional Quarterly College Press, 2010).

15. Jane Mansbridge, *Why We Lost the ERA* (Chicago: University of Chicago Press, 1986), ch. 10.

16. Ibid.

17. Drutman, *The Business of America*, p. 5.

18. Robert Kaiser, *So Damn Much Money* (New York: Knopf, 2009).

19. Federal Election Commission data compiled on Center for Responsive Politics website, opensecrets.org.

20. Kindy, "Ex-Homeland Security Chief."

21. Robert O'Harrow and Scott Higham, "Report Finds DHS Lax on Contracting Procedures," *The Washington Post*, November 22, 2006.

22. Susan Weaver, *Decision to Prosecute* (Cambridge, MA: MIT Press, 1977): pp. 154–163.

23. *United States v. Harris*, 347 U.S. 612 (1954).

24. *United States Code*, Title 26, section 501(c)(3).

Chapter 12

The Media

1. See "The Watergate Story," *The Washington Post*, available at http://www.washingtonpost.com/wp-srv/politics/special/watergate/.

2. Coverage of the Iran-Contra affair by selected news networks is available through the Vanderbilt University Television News Archive.

3. Mayhill Fowler, "Obama: No Surprise That Hard-Pressed Pennsylvanians Turn Bitter," *Huffington Post*, 11 April 2008.

4. Pew Research Center for the People & the Press, "In Changing News Landscape, Even Television Is Vulnerable," September 27, 2012. Available at http://www.people-press.org/2012/09/27/in-changing-news-landscape-even-television-is-vulnerable/.

5. David E. Butler, "Why America's Political Reporting Is Better than England's," *Harper's* (May 1963): pp. 15–25.

6. Gerard Alexander, "Illiberal Europe," *Weekly Standard*, April 10, 2006.

7. Quoted in F. L. Mort, *American Journalism, 1690–1960*, 3rd ed. (New York: Macmillan, 1962), p. 529.

8. Center for Media and Public Affairs, "The Incredible Shrinking Sound Bite," press release, Washington, D.C., September 28, 2000.

9. Pew Internet & American Life Project, "The Internet and Campaign 2010," March 2011.

10. Updated from Times Mirror Center for the People and the Press, June 28, 1990.

11. Edward J. Epstein, *News from Nowhere: Television and the News* (New York: Random House, 1973), p. 37.

12. *Near v. Minnesota*, 283 U.S. 697 (1931).

13. *New York Times v. United States*, 403 U.S. 713 (1971).

14. *New York Times v. Sullivan*, 376 U.S. 254 (1964).

15. *Miami Herald Publishing Co. v. Tornillo*, 418 U.S. 241 (1974).

16. *Yates v. United States*, 354 U.S. 298 (1957).

17. *Branzburg v. Hayes*, 408 U.S. 665 (1972).

18. *Zurcher v. Stanford Daily*, 436 U.S. 547 (1978), overturned by the Privacy Protection Act of 1980 (P.L. 96–440).

19. S. Robert Lichter, Stanley Rothman, and Linda S. Lichter, *The Media Elite* (Bethesda, MD: Adler and Adler, 1986); Stanley Rothman and Amy Black, "Elites Revisited: American Social and Political Leadership in the 1990s," *International Journal of Public Opinion Research* 11 (1999): pp. 169–195; William Schneider and I. A. Lewis, "Views on the News," *Public Opinion* (August/September 1985): p. 7.

20. Rothman and Black, "Elites Revisited," p. 182.

21. Ibid., 177; Jeffrey A. Dvorkin, "Pew Study: Journalists and Liberal Bias," *National Public Radio*, June 2, 2004.

22. Gallup Poll, February 2003; Pew Research Center for the People and the Press poll, July 2003; Pew Research Center for the People & the Press, "Most Voters Say News Media Wants Obama to Win," October 22, 2008.

23. William G. Mayer, "Why Talk Radio Is Conservative," *The Public Interest* (Summer 2004): pp. 86–103.

24. David W. Brady and Jonathan Ma, "Spot the Difference," *The Wall Street Journal* (November 12, 2003).

25. Lichter, Rothman, and Lichter, *Media Elite*.

26. John R. Lott, Jr., and Kevin A. Hassett, "Is Newspaper Coverage of Economic Events Politically Biased?" unpublished paper, American Enterprise Institute (September 1, 2004). See also

Tim Groseclose and Jeff Milyo, "A Measure of Media Bias," *Quarterly Journal of Economics*, 120 (November 2005): pp. 1191–1237.

27. Matthew Gentzkow and Jesse M. Shapiro, "What Drives Media Slant?" NBER paper 1207 (Cambridge, MA: National Bureau of Economic Research, 2006).

28. David O. Sears and Richard E. Whitney, "Political Persuasion," in Pool, *Handbook of Communication*, pp. 253–289.

29. Robert S. Erickson, "The Influence of Newspaper Endorsements in Presidential Elections: The Case of 1964," *American Journal of Political Science* 20 (May 1976): pp. 207–233.

30. Kim Fridkin Kahn and Patrick J. Kenney, "The Slant of the News: How Editorial Endorsements Influence Campaign Coverage and Citizens' Views of Candidates," *American Political Science Review* 96 (2002): pp. 381–394; James N. Druckman and Michael Parkin, "The Impact of Media Bias," *Journal of Politics* 67 (2005): pp. 1030–1049.

31. Stefano Della Vigna and Ethan Kaplan, "The Fox News Effect: Media Bias and Voting," Working paper 12160 (Cambridge, MA: National Bureau of Economic Research, 2006).

32. Alan Gerber, Dean Karlan, and Daniel Bergan, "Does the Media Matter? A Field Experiment," Unpub. paper, Department of Political Science, Yale University, January 2006. See also Gerber, et al., "How Large and How Long-lasting Are the Persuasive Effects of Televised Ads?" *American Political Science Review* 105 (2011): pp. 135–150.

33. Maxwell E. McCombs and Donald R. Shaw, "The Agenda Setting Function of the Mass Media," *Public Opinion Quarterly* 36 (Summer 1972): pp. 176–187; Shanto Iyengar and Donald R. Kinder, *News That Matters* (Chicago: University of Chicago Press, 1987).

34. G. Ray Funkhouser, "The Issues of the Sixties," *Public Opinion Quarterly* 37 (Spring 1973): pp. 62–75.

35. Benjamin I. Page, Robert Y. Shapiro, and Glenn R. Dempsey, "What Moves Public Opinion?" *American Political Science Review* 81 (March 1987): pp. 23–43; Benjamin I. Page, "The Media as Political Actors," *PS: Political Science and Politics* (March 1996): p. 21.

36. Pew Research Center for the People and the Press, "Media Seen as Fair, But Tilting to Gore," press release, Washington, D.C., October 15, 2000.

37. Center for Media and Public Affairs, "Public to Press: Keep in Touch!," press release, Washington, D.C., 1996.

38. Pew Center for the People and the Press, "Terror Coverage Boost News Media's Images," press release, November 28, 2001.

39. Will Lester, "Poll: Interest in News Stabilizes," *The Macon Telegraph* (June 9, 2002).

Chapter 13
Congress

1. Thomas E. Mann and Norman J. Ornstein, *The Broken Branch: How Congress Is Failing America and How to Get It Back on Track*, 2nd ed. (New York: Oxford University Press, 2008). Also see Richard F. Fenno, "If as Ralph Nader Says Congress Is the 'Broken Branch,' How Come We Love Our Congressmen So Much More than Our Congress?" in *Congress in Change: Evolution and Reform*, ed. Norman J. Ornstein (New York: Praeger Publishers, 1975).

2. Fenno, "If as Ralph Nader Says," p. 286.

3. Norman J. Ornstein and Thomas E. Mann, *Vital Statistics on Congress, 1995–1996* (Washington, D.C.: Congressional Quarterly Press, 1996), pp. 199–200.

4. "A Polarized Congress," *National Journal* (January 21, 2006): p. 21, reporting data compiled by David Rhode and John Aldrich.

5. Ibid.

6. "Vicious or Virtuous? America's Political System May Have Become Too Polarized to Produce Compromise," *The Economist* (April 16, 2011): p. 38.

7. Tim Alberts, "The Cabal that Quietly Took Over the House," *National Journal*, May 26, 2013.

8. Alan I. Abramowitz, *The Disappearing Center: Engaged Citizens, Polarization, and American Democracy* (New Haven and London: Yale University Press, 2010).

9. Morris P. Fiorina, *Disconnect: The Breakdown of Representation in American Politics* (Oklahoma: Oklahoma University Press, 2009).

10. *Federalist* No. 10.

11. Ibid.

12. H. Douglas Price, "Careers and Committees in the American Congress," in *The History of Parliamentary Behavior*, ed. William O. Aydelotte (Princeton: Princeton University Press, 1977); John F. Bibby, et al., *Vital Statistics on Congress, 1980* (Washington, D.C.: American Enterprise Institute, 1980), pp. 53–54.

13. David Mayhew, *Congress: The Electoral Connection* (New Haven: Yale University Press, 1974).

14. Harold W. Stanley and Richard G. Niemi, *Vital Statistics on American Politics, 1999–2000* (Washington, D.C.: Congressional Quarterly Press, 2000), table 1-18, and post-2000 data updated by Marc Siegel.

15. Mayhew, *Congress*; Morris P. Fiorina, *Congress: Keystone of the Washington Establishment* (New Haven: Yale University Press, 1977).

16. Rhodes Cook, "House Republicans Scored a Quiet Victory in '92," *Congressional Quarterly* (April 17, 1993): p. 966.

17. Bruce E. Cain and David Butler, "Redrawing District Lines: What's Going On and What's At Stake," *The American Enterprise* (July/August 1991): p. 37.

18. "Redistricting Rows: Not So Easy," *The Economist* (May 7, 2011): p. 27.

19. Abramowitz, *The Disappearing Center*.

20. Ibid.

21. Ibid.

22. Ibid.

23. Matthew Levendusky, *The Partisan Sort: How Liberals Became Democrats and Conservatives Became Republicans* (Chicago: University of Chicago Press, 2009); Fiorina, *Disconnect*; and Abramowitz, *The Disappearing Center*.

24. Fiorina, *Disconnect*; Morris P. Fiorina and Matthew Levendusky, "Disconnected: The Political Class and the People," in *Red and Blue Nation?* vol. I, eds. Pietro Nivola and David Brady (Washington, D.C., and Stanford: Brookings Institution and Hoover Institution, 2006).

25. Fiorina, *Disconnect*, Ibid.

26. Ibid.

27. Keith T. Poole and Howard Rosenthal, *A Political Economic History of Roll Call Voting* (New York: Oxford University Press, 1997), p. 8.

28. Nolan McCarty, et al., "The Hunt for Party Discipline in Congress," *American Political Science Review* 95, no. 3 (September 2001): p. 66.

29. Richard F. Fenno, *Congressmen in Committees* (Boston: Little, Brown, 1973).

30. Bibby, et al., *Vital Statistics*, pp. 65–74.

31. Fiorina, *Congress*.

32. Bibby, et al., *Vital Statistics*, p. 60.

33. Michael J. Malbin, "Delegation, Deliberation, and the New Role of Congressional Staff," in *The New Congress*, eds. Thomas E. Mann and Norman J. Ornstein (Washington, D.C.: American Enterprise Institute, 1981), pp. 134–177, esp. 170–171.

34. Malcolm E. Jewell and Samuel C. Patterson, *The Legislative Process in the United States*, 3rd ed. (New York: Random House, 1977), p. 349.

35. Mann and Ornstein, *Broken Branch*; Joshua D. Clinton and John S. Lapinski, "Measuring Legislative Accomplishment," *American Journal of Political Science* 56 (2006): pp. 232–249; J. Tobin Grant and Nathan J. Kelly, "Legislative Productivity of the U.S. Congress," *Political Analysis* 16 (2008): pp. 303–323.

36. Mann and Ornstein, *Broken Branch*.

37. David Mayhew, *Divided We Govern: Party Control, Lawmaking, and Investigations* (New Haven: Yale University Press, 1991); Grant and Kelly, "Legislative Productivity."

38. Tom Coburn, "The Spending Process Is Broken," *Extensions: Journal of the Carl Albert Research and Studies Center* (Spring 2007): p. 16, reporting data from the Congressional Research Service and the Congressional Budget Office.

39. Continuity of Government Commission, *Preserving Our Institutions: The Continuity of Congress—First Report*, Washington, D.C. (June 3, 2003): pp. 3–4.

40. *The 9/11 Commission Report: Final Report of the National Commission on Terrorist Attacks upon the United States* (New York and London: W.W. Norton & Company, 2004).

41. Diana Evans, "Appropriations in the Republican Era," *Extensions: Journal of the Carl Albert Congressional Research and Studies Center* (Spring 2007): p. 13.

Chapter 14

The Presidency

1. Nicholas Confessore and Jo Craven McGinty, "Obama, Romney, and Their Parties on Track to Raise $2 Billion," *The New York Times*, 25 October 2012.

2. Jean Blondel, *An Introduction to Comparative Government* (New York: Praeger, 1969), as cited in Nelson W. Polsby, "Legislatures," in *Handbook of Political Science*, ed. Fred I. Greenstein and Nelson W. Polsby (Reading, MA: Addison-Wesley, 1975), vol. 5, p. 275.

3. Donald F. Kettl, *Deficit Politics: Public Budgeting in Its Institutional and Historical Context* (New York: Macmillan, 1992), p. 13.

4. Morris P. Fiorina, *Divided Government* (New York: Macmillan, 1992), pp. 86–111.

5. David Mayhew, *Divided We Govern: Party Control, Lawmaking, and Investigations, 1946–1990* (New Haven, CT: Yale University Press, 1991), p. 76.

6. Woodrow Wilson, *Congressional Government* (New York: Meridian Books, 1956), pp. 167–168, 170. First published in 1885.

7. Mark A. Peterson, *Legislating Together: The White House and Congress from Eisenhower to Reagan* (Cambridge: Harvard University Press, 1990).

8. Richard E. Cohen, *Washington at Work: Back Rooms and Clean Air* (New York: Macmillan, 1992), pp. 154–155.

9. Ibid., p. 169.

10. Kettl, *Deficit Politics*, p. 138.

11. Richard E. Neustadt, *Presidential Power and the Modern Presidents: The Politics of Leadership from Roosevelt to Reagan* (New York: The Free Press, 1990), ch. 4.

12. Walter D. Burnham, "Insulation and Responsiveness in Congressional Elections," *Political Science Quarterly* 90 (Fall 1975): pp. 412–413; George C. Edwards III, *Presidential Influence in Congress* (San Francisco: Freeman, 1980), pp. 70–78; Warren E. Miller, "Presidential Coattails: A Study in Political Myth and Methodology," *Public Opinion Quarterly* 19 (Winter 1955–1956): p. 368; and Miller, "The Motivational Basis for Straight and Split Ticket Voting," *American Political Science Review* 51 (June 1957): pp. 293–312.

13. *Clinton v. City of New York*, 118 S. Ct. 2091 (1998).

14. *Marbury v. Madison*, 1 Cranch 137 (1803).

15. *United States v. Nixon*, 418 U.S. 683 (1974).

16. *Clinton v. Jones,* 520 U.S. 681 (1997); *In re Grand Jury Subpoena Duces Tecum,* 112 F.3d 910 (1997); *In re Sealed Case,* 121 F.3d 729 (1997).

17. Christopher S. Kelley, "A Comparative Look at the Constitutional Signing Statement," paper presented at the Midwest Political Science Association meeting, April 2003; Kelley, "To Be (Unitarian) or Not to Be (Unitarian): Presidential Power in the George W. Bush Administration," *White House Studies* 10, no. 2 (2010): pp. 115–129.

18. Data available through the University of California, Santa Barbara, American Presidency Project at http://www.presidency.ucsb.edu/.

19. Walter Dellinger, "Memorandum for Bernard N. Nussbaum, Counsel to the President," Office of Legal Counsel, U.S. Department of Justice, November 3, 1993.

20. *Chevron v. NRDC,* 467 U.S. 837 (1984).

21. Edwin S. Corwin, *The Presidency: Office and Powers* (New York: New York University Press, 1957), p. 171.

22. Stephen Hess, *Organizing the Presidency* (Washington, D.C.: Brookings Institution, 1976), p. 3; R. W. Apple, "Clinton's Refocusing," *The New York Times,* May 6, 1993, A22; Michael K. Frisby, "Power Switch," *The Wall Street Journal,* March 26, 1993, A1, A7.

23. U.S. Department of Health and Human Services, "Fiscal Year 2014 Budget in Brief." Available at http://www.hhs.gov/budget/fy2014/fy-2014-budget-in-brief.pdf.

24. David T. Stanley, et al., *Men Who Govern* (Washington, D.C.: Brookings Institution, 1967), pp. 41–42, 50.

25. Daniel J. Elazar, "Which Road to the Presidency?" in *The Presidency,* ed. Aaron Wildavsky (Boston: Little, Brown, 1969), p. 340.

26. Marcus Cunliffe, *American Presidents and the Presidency* (New York: American Heritage Press/McGraw-Hill, 1972), pp. 63, 65.

27. Ibid., 214.

28. Adapted from Paul C. Light, *The President's Agenda* (Baltimore, MD: Johns Hopkins University Press, 1982), pp. 217–225.

Chapter 15

The Bureaucracy

1. Charles E. Lindblom, *Politics and Markets* (New York: Basic Books, 1977), p. 114.

2. Donald F. Kettl, *Government by Proxy: (Mis?) Managing Federal Programs* (Washington, D.C.: Congressional Quarterly Press, 1988); John J. DiIulio, Jr., "Government by Proxy: A Faithful Overview," *Harvard Law Review* (March 2003): pp. 1272–1284.

3. Mark Hemmingway, "Warriors for Hire," *Weekly Standard,* December 18, 2006, p. 25.

4. Ibid., p. 26.

5. Martha Derthick, *Keeping the Compound Republic: Essays on American Federalism* (Washington, D.C.: Brookings Institution, 2001), p. 63.

6. Donald F. Kettl, *The Next Government of the United States: Why Our Institutions Fail Us and How to Fix Them* (New York: W.W. Norton, 2008), pp. 1–14.

7. Article II, section 2, para. 2.

8. Article II, section 3.

9. Calculated from data in *Historical Statistics of the United States: Colonial Times to 1970* (Washington, D.C.: Government Printing Office, 1975), vol. 2, pp. 1102–1103.

10. *Panama Refining Co. v. Ryan,* 293 U.S. 388 (1935).

11. *Hampton Jr. & Co. v. United States,* 276 U.S. 394 (1928).

12. Edward S. Corwin, *The Constitution and What It Means Today,* 13th ed. (Princeton, NJ: Princeton University Press, 1973), p. 151.

13. Bruce D. Porter, "Parkinson's Law Revisited: War and the Growth of American Government," *Public Interest* (Summer 1980): pp. 50–68.

14. See the cases cited in Corwin, *The Constitution,* p. 8.

15. *U.S. Statutes,* vol. 84, sec. 799 (1970).

16. *Historical Statistics of the United States,* vol. 2, p. 1107.

17. Department of Homeland Security, Hearings Before the Subcommittee on Oversight and Management Efficiency, Committee on Homeland Security, U.S. House of Representatives, 113th, 1st Sess. (2013); U.S. Government Accountability Office, *Key Issues: DHS Implementation and Transformation,* 2013; also see Kettl, *The Next Government,* op. cit., p. 52.

18. Donald F. Kettl, et al., *Civil Service Reform: Building a Government That Works* (Washington, D.C.: Brookings Institution, 1996), p. 15.

19. Hugh Heclo, "Issue Networks and the Executive Establishment," in *The New American Political System,* ed. Anthony King (Washington, D.C.: American Enterprise Institute, 1978), pp. 87–124.

20. Quoted in Hugh Heclo, *A Government of Strangers* (Washington, D.C.: Brookings Institution, 1977), p. 225.

21. Alexis Simendinger, "Of the People, for the People," *National Journal* (April 18, 1998): pp. 852–855. Data from the Pew Charitable Trusts Research Center for the People and the Press.

22. Kenneth Meier and Lloyd Nigro, "Representative Bureaucracy and Policy References: A Study of the Attitudes of Federal Executives," *Public Administration Review* 36 (July/August 1976): pp. 458–467; Bernard Mennis, *American Foreign Policy Officials* (Columbus: Ohio State University Press, 1971).

23. David Stockman, *The Triumph of Politics* (New York: Harper and Row, 1986).

24. James Q. Wilson, *Bureaucracy* (New York: Basic Books, 1989), ch. 6.

25. Heclo, "Issue Networks and the Executive Establishment," pp. 87–124.

26. David H. Rosenbloom, "Reevaluating Executive-Centered Public Administrative Theory," in *The Oxford Handbook of American Bureaucracy,* ed. Robert F. Durant. Oxford University Press, 2010, p. 114.

27. Ibid., pp. 121–122.

28. Richard F. Fenno, Jr., *The Power of the Purse* (Boston: Little, Brown, 1966), pp. 450, 597.

29. John E. Schwartz and L. Earl Shaw, *The United States Congress in Comparative Perspective* (Hinsdale, IL.: Dryden Press, 1976), 262–263; *National Journal* (July 4, 1981): pp. 1211–1214.

30. *Immigration and Naturalization Service v. Chadha,* 462 U.S. 919 (1983); *Maine v. Thiboutot,* 448 U.S. 1 (1980).

31. See cases cited in Corwin, *The Constitution,* 22.

32. William Safire, *Safire's Political Dictionary* (Random House, 1978).

33. Steven Kelman, "The Grace Commission: How Much Waste in Government?" *Public Interest* (Winter 1985): pp. 62–87.

34. Daniel Katz, et al., *Bureaucratic Encounters* (Ann Arbor: Survey

Research Center, University of Michigan, 1975), pp. 63–69, 118–120, 184–188.

35. U.S. Government Accountability Office, *Government Performance Lessons Learned*, GAO Report, July 24, 2008, as cited in Kettl, *The Next Government*, op. cit., 173, p. 255.

36. Ibid.

Chapter 16

The Judiciary

1. Russell Wheeler, *Judicial Nominations and Confirmations in Obama's First Term*, Governance Studies, Brookings Institution, December 13, 2012, p.1.

2. Ibid.

3. Ibid.

4. Henry J. Abraham, *The Judicial Process*, 3d ed. (New York: Oxford University Press, 1975), pp. 279–280.

5. Robert G. McCloskey, *The American Supreme Court* (Chicago: University of Chicago Press, 1960), p. 27.

6. *Marbury v. Madison*, 5 U.S. 137 (1803); and *McCulloch v. Maryland*, 17 U.S. 316 (1819).

7. *Martin v. Hunter's Lessee*, 14 U.S. 304 (1816) and *Cohens v. Virginia*, 19 U.S. (1821).

8. *Gibbons v. Ogden*, 22 U.S. (1824).

9. Quoted in Albert J. Beveridge, *The Life of John Marshall* (Boston: Houghton Mifflin, 1919), vol. 4, p. 551.

10. *Dred Scott v. Sandford*, 60 U.S. 393 (1857).

11. Abraham, *The Judicial Process*, p. 286.

12. *In re Debs*, 158 U.S. 564 (1895).

13. *Pollock v. Farmers' Loan & Trust Co.*, 157 U.S. 429 (1895).

14. *United States v. Knight*, 156 U.S. 1 (1895).

15. *Cincinnati, N.O. & T.P. Railway Co. v. Interstate Commerce Commission*, 162 U.S. 184 (1896).

16. *Hammer v. Dagenhart*, 247 U.S. 251 (1918).

17. *Lochner v. New York*, 198 U.S. 45 (1905).

18. McCloskey, *The American Supreme Court*, p. 151.

19. *Munn v. Illinois*, 94 U.S. 113 (1877).

20. *Dayton-Goose Creek Railway Co. v. United States*, 263 U.S. 456 (1924).

21. *Atchison, Topeka, and Santa Fe Railroad Co. v. Matthews*, 174 U.S. 96 (1899).

22. *Mugler v. Kansas*, 123 U.S. 623 (1887).

23. *St. Louis Consolidated Coal Co. v. Illinois*, 185 U.S. 203 (1902).

24. *New York Central Railroad Co. v. White*, 243 U.S. 188 (1917).

25. *German Alliance Insurance Co. v. Lewis*, 233 U.S. 389 (1914).

26. Morton Keller, *Affairs of State* (Cambridge: Harvard University Press, 1977), p. 369. See also Mary Cornelia Porter, "That Commerce Shall Be Free: A New Look at the Old Laissez-Faire Court," in *The Supreme Court Review*, ed. Philip B. Kurland (Chicago: University of Chicago Press, 1976), pp. 135–159.

27. *Chief of Capitol Police v. Jeannette Rankin Brigade*, 409 U.S. 972 (1972).

28. *Aptheker v. Secretary of State*, 378 U.S. 500 (1964).

29. *Trop v. Dulles*, 356 U.S. 86 (1958); *Afroyim v. Rusk*, 387 U.S. 253 (1967); and *Schneider v. Rusk*, 377 U.S. 163 (1964).

30. *Lamont v. Postmaster General*, 381 U.S. 301 (1965); and *Blount v. Rizzi*, 400 U.S. 410 (1971).

31. *Richardson v. Davis*, 409 U.S. 1069 (1972); *U.S. Department of Agriculture v. Murry*, 413 U.S. 508 (1973); *Jimenez v. Weinberger*, 417 U.S. 628 (1974); and *Washington v. Legrant*, 394 U.S. 618 (1969).

32. *United States v. Lopez*, 514 U.S. 549 (1995).

33. *Seminole Tribe of Florida v. Florida*, 517 U.S. 44 (1996); *Alden v. Maine*, 527 U.S. 706 (1999); *Florida v. College Savings Bank*, 527 U.S. 627 (1999).

34. Daniel R. Pinello, "Linking Party to Judicial Ideology in American Courts: A Meta-Analysis," *Justice System Journal* 20 (1999): pp. 219–254.

35. An opinion survey of federal judges shows how party affects ideology: see Althea K. Nagai, Stanley Rothman, and S. Robert Lichter, "The Verdict of Federal Judges," *Public Opinion* (November/December 1987): pp. 52–56.

36. *United States v. Lanza*, 260 U.S. 377 (1922). Cf. *Abbate v. United States*, 359 U.S. 187 (1959), and *Bartkus v. Illinois*, 359 U.S. 121 (1989).

37. *Gideon v. Wainwright*, 372 U.S. 335 (1963). The story is told in Anthony Lewis, *Gideon's Trumpet* (New York: Random House, 1964).

38. Erwin Griswold, "Rationing Justice: The Supreme Court's Case Load and What the Court Does Not Do," *Cornell Law Review* 60 (1975): pp. 335–354.

39. Joseph Weis, Jr., "Disconnecting the Overloaded Circuits—A Plan for a Unified Court of Appeals," *St. Louis University Law Journal* 39 (1995): p. 455.

40. *Alyeska Pipeline Service Co. v. Wilderness Society*, 421 U.S. 240 (1975).

41. *Flast v. Cohen*, 392 U.S. 83 (1968), which modified the earlier *Frothingham v. Mellon*, 262 U.S. 447 (1923); *United States v. Richardson*, 418 U.S. 166 (1947).

42. *Brown v. Board of Education of Topeka*, 347 U.S. 483 (1954).

43. *Baker v. Carr*, 369 U.S. 186 (1962).

44. See Louise Weinberg, "A New Judicial Federalism?" *Daedalus* (Winter 1978): pp. 129–141.

45. Quoted in Abraham, *The Judicial Process*, p. 330.

46. Carolyn D. Richmond, "The Rehnquist Court: What Is in Store for Constitutional Precedent?" *New York Law Review* 39 (1994): p. 511.

47. *Colegrove v. Green*, 328 U.S. 549 (1946).

48. The Court abandoned the "political question" doctrine in *Baker v. Carr*, 369 U.S. 186 (1962), and began to change congressional-district apportionment in *Wesberry v. Sanders*, 376 U.S. 1 (1964).

49. Donald L. Horowitz, *The Courts and Social Policy* (Washington, D.C.: Brookings Institution, 1977), p. 6.

50. *Gates v. Collier*, 349 F. Supp. 881 (1972).

51. *Lau v. Nichols*, 414 U.S. 563 (1974).

52. Jane Burnbaum, "Guilty! Too Many Lawyers and Too Much Litigation," *Business Week* (April 13, 1992): pp. 60–61.

53. Joel B. Grossman and Austin Sarat, "Litigation in the Federal Courts: A Comparative Perspective," *Law and Society Review* 9 (Winter 1975): pp. 321–346.

54. Administrative Office of the U.S. Courts, *Annual Report, 1988*, p. 109.

55. Jack W. Peltason, *Fifty-Eight Lonely Men: Southern Federal Judges and School Desegregation* (New York: Harcourt Brace, 1961).

56. Anthony Partridge and William B. Eldridge, *The Second Circuit Sentencing Study* (Washington, D.C.: Federal Judicial Center, 1974).

57. *Abington School District v. Schempp*, 374 U.S. 203 (1963).

58. Robert H. Birkby, "The Supreme Court and the Bible Belt," *Midwest Journal of Political Science* (1966): p. 3.

59. Cass R. Sunstein, "Impeaching the President," *University of Pennsylvania Law Review* 147 (1998): p. 279.

60. *United States v. Butler*, 297 U.S. (1936).

61. *Ex parte McCardle*, 74 U.S. 506 (1869)

62. Walter F. Murphy, *Congress and the Court* (Chicago: University of Chicago Press, 1962); and C. Herman Pritchett, *Congress Versus the Supreme Court* (Minneapolis: University of Minnesota Press,1961).

63. Gregory A. Caldeira, "Neither the Purse nor the Sword: Dynamics of Public Confidence in the U.S. Supreme Court," *American Political Science Review* 80 (1986): pp. 1209–1226. See also Joseph T. Tannenhaus and Walter F. Murphy, "Patterns of Public Support for the Supreme Court: A Panel Study," *Journal of Politics* 43 (1981): pp. 24–39.

Chapter 17
Public Policy and American Democracy

1. Barack Obama, speech at Jefferson-Jackson dinner, Des Moines, Iowa, November 10, 2007, available at www.washingtonpost.com/wp-dyn/content/article/2008/12/17/AR2008121703661.html; John McCain, speech at Republican National Convention, Minneapolis, Minnesota, September 4, 2008, available at http://elections.nytimes.com/2008/president/conventions/videos/20080904_MCCAIN_SPEECH.html.

2. Lydia Saad, "More Americans Still Prioritize Economy Over Environment," Princeton, NJ, Gallup, April 3, 2013.

3. Environment: Gallup Historical Trends, available at www.gallup,com/poll/1615/Environment/aspx

4. Edwin E. Witte, *The Development of the Social Security Act* (Madison: University of Wisconsin Press, 1962); Martha Derthick, *Policymaking for Social Security* (Washington, D.C.: Brookings Institution Press, 1979).

5. Theodore Marmor, "Doctors, Politics, and Health Insurance for the Aged: The Enactment of Medicare," in *Cases in Contemporary American Government*, ed. Allan Sindler (Boston: Little, Brown, 1969).

6. Washington Post Staff, *Landmark: The Inside Story of America's New Health Care Law and What It Means for All of Us (*New York: Public Affairs, 2010).

7. *National Federation of Independent Business Et Al v. Sebelius, Secretary of Health and Human Services, Et Al.*, 576 U.S. (2012).

8. Richard P. Nathan, "America's Health Care Cost Crisis and What to Do About It," Rockefeller Institute, March 2013, available at www.rockinst.org.

9. Sarah Kliff and Dan Keating, "One Hospital Charges $8,000—Another $38,000," *The Washington Post*, May 8, 2013.

10. Ibid.

11. Ibid.

12. *2012 Annual Report of the Boards of Trustees of the Federal Hospital Insurance and Federal Supplementary Medical Insurance Trust Funds*: 28, available at www.cms.gov.

13. Charles E. Gilbert, "Welfare Policy," in *Handbook of Political Science*, ed. Fred I. Greenstein and Nelson W. Polsby (Reading, MA: Addison-Wesley, 1975) vol. 6, ch. 4; Lawrence M. Mead, *From Prophecy to Charity: How to Help the Poor* (Washington, D.C.: American Enterprise Institute, 2011): pp. 14–18.

14. *Congress and the Nation,1945–1964* (Washington, D.C.: Congressional Quarterly Service, 1965): p. 1225.

15. Harold E. Raynes, *Social Security in Britain: A History* (London: Pitman, 1960), ch. 18; Hugh Heclo, *Modern Social Politics in Britain and Sweden* (New Haven, CT: Yale Journal of Law and Economics University Press, 1974).

16. *The Values We Live By: What Americans Want from Welfare Reform* (New York: Public Agenda Foundation, 1996): p. 42.

17. Edward S. Greenberg, *Serving the Few: Corporate Capitalism and the Bias of Government Policy* (New York: Wiley, 1974).

18. Charles E. Lindblom, *Politics and Markets* (New York: Basic Books, 1977).

19. Joseph Schumpeter, *Capitalism, Socialism, and Democracy* (New York: Harper and Row, 1950).

20. Louis Galambos, *The Public Image of Big Business in America, 1880–1940* (Baltimore: Johns Hopkins University Press, 1975).

21. Suzanne Weaver, *Decision to Prosecute: Organization and Public Policy in the Antitrust Division*

(Cambridge, MA: MIT Press, 1977); Robert H. Bork, *The Antitrust Paradox* (New York: Basic Books, 1977).

22. Richard A. Posner, *Antitrust Law: An Economic Perspective* (Chicago: University of Chicago Press, 1976): p. 25.

23. Alan L. Seltzer, "Woodrow Wilson as 'Corporate-Liberal': Toward a Reconsideration of Left Revisionist Historiography," *Western Political Quarterly* 30 (June 1977): pp. 183–212.

24. Weaver, Decision to Prosecute; Robert A. Katzmann, *Regulatory Bureaucracy: The Federal Trade Commission and Antitrust Policy* (Cambridge, MA: MIT Press, 1980).

25. Charles R. Plott, "Occupational Self-Regulation: A Case Study of the Oklahoma City Dry Cleaners," *Journal of Law and Economics* 8 (October 1965): pp. 195–222.

26. Paul H. MacAvoy, ed. *Federal Milk Marketing Orders and Price Supports* (Washington, D.C.: American Enterprise Institute, 1977).

27. Ibid.

28. *Congressional Quarterly Weekly Report* (April 21, 1990): pp. 1184–1188.

29. Will Allen, *The Good Food Revolution: Growing Healthy Food, People, and Communities* (New York: Gotham, 2012).

30. Pietro Nivola, "The New York Pork Barrel," *Brookings Review* (Winter 1998): pp. 6–13.

31. The list would include the following laws: The 1962 amendments to the Pure Food and Drug Act; the Motor Vehicle Air Pollution Control Act of 1965; the National Traffic and Motor Vehicle Safety Act of 1966; the Wholesome Poultry Act of 1968; the Children's Protection and Toy Safety Act of 1969; the Clean Air Act of 1970; and the Toxic Substances Control Act of 1976.

32. Upton Sinclair, *The Jungle* (New York: Doubleday and Company, 1906).

33. Ralph Nader, *Unsafe at Any Speed: The Designed-In Dangers of the American Automobile* (New York: Grossman Publishers, 1965).

34. Mark V. Nadel, *The Politics of Consumer Protection* (Indianapolis, IN: Boobs-Merill, 1971): pp. 143–144.

35. Alfred A. Marcus, *Promise and Performance: Choosing and Implementing and Environmental*

Policy (Westport, CT: Greenwood Press, 1980).

36. Nadel, *Politics*: pp. 66–68.

37. Ryan Lizza, "As the World Burns," *New Yorker*, October 22, 2010.

38. David Vogel, *National Styles of Regulation* (Ithaca, NY: Cornell University Press, 1986): pp. 19–30.

39. R. Shep Melnick, *Regulation and the Courts: The Case of the Clean Air Act* (Washington, D.C.: Brookings Institution Press, 1983), ch. 9.

40. Pietro S. Nivola, *The Politics of Energy Conservation* (Washington, D.C.: Brookings Institution Press, 1986): pp. 11–12, 244–247.

41. Robert W. Crandall, "Pollution, Environmentalists, and the Coal Lobby," in *The Political Economy of Deregulation*, ed. Roger G. Noll and Bruce M. Own (Washington, D.C.: American Enterprise Institute, 1983): pp. 83–84; Crandall, *Controlling Industrial Pollution* (Washington, D.C.: American Enterprise Institute, 1983).

42. Bruce A. Ackerman and William T. Hassler, *Clear Coal/Dirty Air* (New Haven, CT: Yale University Press, 1981).

43. Bill Chalmeides, "U.S. Acid Rain Regulations: Did They Work?," Huffington Post, May 5, 2012, available at http://www.huffingtonpost.com/bill-chameides/us-acid-rain-regulations_b_1507392.html

44. Rachel Carson, *Silent Spring* (New York: Houghton Mifflin, 1962).

45. Robert Dorfman, "Lessons from Pesticide Regulation," in *Reform of Environmental Regulation*, ed. Wesley A. Magat (Cambridge, MA: Ballinger, 1982): pp. 13–30.

46. Arthur Grube et al, *Pesticide Industry Sales and Usage 2006 and 2007: Market Estimates* (Washington, D.C.: U.S. Environmental Protection Agency, February 2011).

Chapter 18

Economic Policy

1. Edward R. Tufte, *Political Control of the Economy* (Princeton, NJ: Princeton University Press, 1978): p. 84; Douglas A. Hibbs, Jr., "The Mass Public and Macroeconomic Performance: The Dynamics of Public Opinion Toward Unemployment and Inflation," *American Journal of Political Science* 23 (1979): pp. 705–731.

2. D. Roderick Kiewiet, *Macroeconomics and Micropolitics: The Electoral Effect of Economic Issues* (Chicago: University of Chicago Press, 1983); Morris P. Fiorina, "Economic Retrospective Voting in American National Elections: A Micro-Analysis," *American Journal of Political Science* 22 (1978): pp. 426–443; Donald R. Kinder and D. Roderick Kiewiet, "Sociotropic Politics: The American Case," *British Journal of Political Science* 11 (1981): pp. 129–161.

3. *The New York Times*/CBS News poll cited in Douglas A. Hibbs, Jr., "President Reagan's Mandate from the 1980 Elections: A Shift to the Right?" *American Politics Quarterly* 10 (1982): pp. 387–420.

4. Hibbs, "The Mass Public."

5. Ibid.

6. Kiewiet, *Macroeconomics and Micropolitics*.

7. Michael S. Lewis-Beck, "Comparative Economic Voting: Britain, France, Germany, Italy," *American Journal of Political Science* 30 (1986): pp. 315–346.

8. Douglas A. Hibbs, Jr., "Political Parties and Macroeconomic Policy," *American Political Science Review* 71 (1977): pp. 1467–1487.

9. Kiewiet, *Macroeconomics and Micropolitics*, p. 69.

10. *Pollock v. Farmers' Loan & Trust Co.*, 157 U.S. 429, affirmed at 158 U.S. 601 (1895).

11. NBC News/*The Wall Street Journal* poll, as reported in *National Journal* (July 12, 1986): p. 1741.

Chapter 19

Foreign and Military Policy

1. Alexis de Tocqueville, *Democracy in America, vol. 1*, ed. Phillips Bradley (New York: Knopf, 1951), p. 235.

2. See Victor Davis Hanson, *Carnage and Culture* (New York: Anchor Books, 2002); and Hanson, *The Soul of Battle* (New York: Free Press, 1999).

3. Richard Lau, Thad A. Brown, and David O. Sears, "Self-Interest and Civilians' Attitudes Toward the Vietnam War," *Public Opinion Quarterly* 42 (1978): pp. 464–481.

4. Edward S. Corwin, *The President: Office and Powers* (New York: New York University Press, 1940), p. 200.

5. Louis W. Koenig, *The Chief Executive*, 6th ed. (Fort Worth, TX: Harcourt Brace, 1992), p. 216.

6. Louis Fisher, *President and Congress* (New York: Free Press, 1972), p. 45; *United States v. Belmont*, 301 U.S. 324 (1937).

7. Aaron Wildavsky, "The Two Presidencies," in *The Presidency*, ed. Wildavsky (Boston: Little, Brown, 1969), p. 231.

8. Loch Johnson and James M. McCormick, "The Making of International Agreements: A Reappraisal of Congressional Involvement," *Journal of Politics*, 40 (1978): pp. 468–478.

9. Bernard E. Brown, "The Decision to End the Algerian War," in *Cases in Comparative Politics*, ed. James B. Christoph (Boston: Little, Brown, 1965), pp. 154–180; Roy C. Macridis, "De Gaulle and NATO," in *Modern European Governments*, ed. Macridis (Englewood Cliffs, NJ: Prentice-Hall, 1968), pp. 92–115; and John E. Schwartz and L. Earl Shaw, *The United States Congress in Comparative Perspective* (Hinsdale, IL: Dryden Press, 1976), pp. 235–236.

10. Peter G. Richards, *Parliament and Foreign Affairs* (London: George Allen and Unwin, 1967), pp. 37–38; Schwartz and Shaw, *The United States Congress in Comparative Perspective*, p. 235.

11. Arthur M. Schlesinger, Jr., *A Thousand Days: John F. Kennedy in the White House* (Boston: Houghton Mifflin, 1965), chs. 30, 31. Schlesinger, at p. 841, described Kennedy's actions as a "brilliantly controlled," "matchlessly calibrated" combination of "nerve and wisdom." His view of Nixon's actions was a good deal less charitable in *The Imperial Presidency* (Boston: Houghton Mifflin, 1974), ch. 7.

12. *United States v. Curtiss-Wright Export Co.*, 299 U.S. 304 (1936).

13. *Mitchell v. Laird*, 488 F.2d 611 (1973).

14. *Prize Cases*, 67 U.S. 635 (1863); *Mora v. McNamara*, 389 U.S. 934 (1964); *Massachusetts v. Laird*, 400 U.S. 886 (1970).

15. *Dames and Moore v. Regan*, 435 U.S. 654 (1981).

16. *Korematsu v. United States*, 323 U.S. 214 (1944).

17. *Youngstown Sheet & Tube Co. v. Sawyer*, 343 U.S. 579 (1952).

18. *Immigration and Naturalization Service v. Chadha*, 103 S. Ct. 2764 (1983).

19. Robert S. Erikson and Norman R. Luttbeg, *American Public Opinion* (New York: Wiley, 1973), pp. 50–51.

20. William R. Caspary, "The 'Mood Theory': A Study of Public Opinion

and Foreign Policy," *American Political Science Review* 64 (June 1970): pp. 536–547.

21. Erikson and Luttbeg, *American Public Opinion*, p. 52.

22. John E. Mueller, *War, Presidents, and Public Opinion* (New York: Wiley, 1973), p. 110.

23. Ibid., p. 112.

24. Milton J. Rosenberg, Sidney Verba, and Philip E. Converse, *Vietnam and the Silent Majority* (New York: Harper and Row, 1970), pp. 26–27.

25. Erikson and Luttbeg, *American Public Opinion*, p. 155.

26. John R. Oneal and Brad Lian, "Presidents, the Use of Military Force, and Public Opinion," Working Papers in International Security I–92–8, Hoover Institution, Stanford, CA (July 1992).

27. Benjamin C. Schwarz, *Casualities, Public Opinion, and U.S. Military Intervention* (Santa Monica, CA: RAND, 1994).

28. Mueller, *War, Presidents, and Public Opinion,* 45–47, p. 169.

29. James Q. Wilson and Karlyn Bowman, "Defining the Peace Party," *The Public Interest* (Fall 2003): p. 69–78.

30. Jones, Jeffrey M. "Americans Approve of Military Action Against Libya, 47% to 37%." *Gallup Politics.* Last modified March 22, 2011.

31. Everett Carll Ladd, "Since World War II, Americans Have Persistently Looked Outward," *The Public Perspective* (August/September 1997): pp. 5–34.

32. Howard Schuman, "Two Sources of Antiwar Sentiment in America," *American Journal of Sociology* 78 (1973): pp. 513–536.

33. Philip E. Converse, Warren E. Miller, Jerrold G. Rusk, and Arthur C. Wolfe, "Continuity and Change in American Politics," *American Political Science Review* 63 (December 1969):

pp. 1083–1105; John P. Robinson, "Public Reaction to Political Protest: Chicago, 1968," *Public Opinion Quarterly* 34 (Spring 1970): pp. 1–9.

34. James D. Wright, "Life, Time, and the Fortunes of War," *Transaction* 9 (January 1972).

35. John E. Rielly, *American Public Opinion and U.S. Foreign Policy, 1999* (Chicago: Chicago Council on Foreign Relations, 1999).

36. X, "The Sources of Soviet Conduct," *Foreign Affairs* 25 (July 1947): p. 566.

37. Walter Lippmann, *The Cold War* (New York: Harper Brothers, 1947).

38. Erikson and Luttbeg, *American Public Opinion*, p. 52.

39. Mueller, *War, Presidents, and Public Opinion*, p. 40.

40. Michael Roskin, "From Pearl Harbor to Vietnam: Shifting Generational Paradigms and Foreign Policy," *Political Science Quarterly* 89 (Fall 1974): p. 567.

41. Frank L. Klingberg, "The Historical Alternation of Moods in American Foreign Policy," *World Politics* 4 (1952): pp. 239–273.

42. Roskin, "From Pearl Harbor," p. 567.

43. *American Public Opinion and U.S. Foreign Policy, 1987* (Chicago: Chicago Council on Foreign Relations, 1987), p. 33.

44. Carl M. Cannon, "Comment," in Pietro S. Nivola and David W. Brady, eds., *Red and Blue Nation?* (Washington, D.C.: Brookings Institution, 2006), p. 168; and Cannon, "Administration: A New Era of Partisan War," *National Journal*, March 18, 2006.

45. For a lively debate over the extent of political polarization, see Morris Fiorina and Matthew S. Levendusky, "Disconnected: The Political Class Versus the People"; Alan I. Abramowitz, "Comment"; and Gary C. Jacobson, "Comment,"—all in Nivola and Brady, op. cit.

46. Commission on the Intelligence Capabilities of the United States Regarding Weapons of Mass Destruction, *Report to the President* (Washington, D.C.: Government Printing Office, 2005), pp. 243–249.

47. Quoted in Robert J. Art, *The TFX Decision* (Boston: Little, Brown, 1968), p. 126.

48. *The National Security Strategy of the United States of America*, September 2002, cover letter and p. 6.

49. The vote on the Persian Gulf War as reported in *Congress and the Nation*, vol. 8 (Washington, D.C.: Congressional Quarterly Press, 1993), p. 310; the vote on the war in Iraq as reported in *The New York Times*, October 12, 2002, A11.

50. There were no congressional votes on our military efforts in Bosnia and Kosovo, but speeches supporting them were made by (among others) Democratic Senators Barbara Boxer, Carl Levin, and Paul Wellstone and Representative David Bonior; speeches opposing them were made by (among others) Republican Senators Don Nickles and John Warner and by Representatives Robert Barr and Dan Burton. In the vote on the invasion of Iraq, each group took the opposite position.

51. James Dobbins, et al., *America's Role in Nation Building* (Santa Monica, CA: RAND, 2003).

Chapter 20

American Democracy, Then and Now

1. Donald F. Kettl, "Heading for Disaster, "*Government Executive*, February 1, 2009.

2. Ibid.

3. Alexis de Tocqueville, *Democracy in America*, vol. 2, ed. Phillips Bradley (New York: Knopf, 1951), book 2, ch. 1.

Index

AMERICAN GOVERNMENT: INSTITUTIONS

The American System

The Federalist Papers
http://thomas.loc.gov/home/histdox/fedpapers.html

The Library of Congress's website, named after Thomas Jefferson, includes the full text of all 85 Federalist Papers, published by James Madison, Alexander Hamilton, and John Jay under the pseudonym Publius in New York City newspapers in 1787-88 to rally public support for the Constitution.

The Anti-Federalist Papers
http://www.constitution.org/afp/afp.htm

Selected Anti-Federalist Papers, written by several authors, also under pseudonyms, who opposed ratification of the Constitution, are reprinted by a private, non-profit organization, the Constitution Society.

Documents pertaining to the American Constitution
http://avalon.law.yale.edu/subject_menus/constpap.asp
http://avalon.law.yale.edu/default.asp

The Avalon Project of Yale Law School is an online database of document collections, including one on the American Constitution that includes colonial state charters, constitutional convention records, and ratification statements. The website also contains links to presidential papers, the State Department's Foreign Relations of the United States series, and numerous other sites pertaining to American politics and diplomacy.

Opinions, Interests, and Organizations

Current news sources
http://www.realclearpolitics.com

This website provides a daily compilation of news articles, commentary, public opinion polls, and other information about current issues in American politics.

Public opinion polls
http://www.pollster.com/

This website compiles polling data for state and national elections, and also includes commentary by website contributors.

http://www.pollingreport.com/

This website compiles public opinion polling data on key issues in American politics.

Major political parties
http://www.democrats.org/

This is the website of the Democratic National Committee.

http://www.rnc.org/splashpage/index.aspx

This is the website of the Republican National Committee.